The Popular Incumbent with the Multimedia Advantage

American Government, Roots and Reform, Second Edition

by **Karen O'Connor**, Emory University
and **Larry Sabato**, University of Virginia

C-SPAN Video: The Clean Air Act Amendments of 1990

NEW — CNN VIDEO

NEW — LASER DISK

NEW — CD ROM with lecture enhancement modules.

NEW — AUDIO TAPE of Supreme Court Decisions

NEW — AMERICA ONLINE

Written by two distinguished political scientists and award-winning instructors

IS-i

Now available from ALLYN & BACON

KAREN O'CONNOR

is Professor of Political Science and Adjunct Professor of Law at Emory University. Her areas of specialty include public law, the Constitution, the judiciary, political institutions, and women in politics. She has served as President of the Women's Caucus for Political Science, and regularly appears on local Atlanta television news programs as a Supreme Court Analyst. Dr. O'Connor has written seven books and Monographs.

In 1991, Dr. O'Connor was honored with the Emory Williams Distinguished Teaching Award. She regularly teaches American Government.

LARRY J. SABATO

is an election analyst and Professor of Government and Foreign Affairs at the University of Virginia. His areas of specialty include campaigns, elections, parties, interest groups, and the media. A former Rhodes Scholar and Danforth Fellow, he regularly appears as a political analyst on major national network news programs. Dr. Sabato has written twelve books and monographs.

In 1985, Dr. Sabato was honored with the University of Virginia's Outstanding Young Teacher Award. He regularly teaches American Government.

the Multimedia Advantage

ROOTS: Understanding government as it exists TODAY

In order to understand the workings of present-day government, authors O'Connor and Sabato show your students how it was designed in the Constitution and how to build an appreciation for how government has reached its current state. This dynamic and accessible approach helps students understand current political behavior and its effects. Toward this goal, the authors approach each chapter's topic with a combination of perspectives.

REFORM: Examining the EVOLUTION of government

The Second Edition of the remarkably successful *American Government: Roots and Reform* gives your students the most complete and up-to-date understanding of American government. Examining how America is governed, this new edition looks not just at present behavior — including 1994 election results — but also at the Constitutional Framers' intentions and how they have been implemented over the years. Your students will gain a critical understanding of the Framers' fears of factionalism, their fear of a too powerful central government as well as the evolution of political parties.

The Popular Incumbent with

HISTORICAL PERSPECTIVES show how institutions and processes have evolved to their present state.

In each chapter a historical perspective explores issues the Framers could never have envisioned, and shows how the basic institutions of our government have responded to these new demands.

THEN AND NOW
The Second Amendment and the Right of the People to Keep and Bear Arms

During colonial times, the English tradition of distrust of standing armies was evident: all white men in whole sections of the colonies were deputized to defend their settlements against Indians and other European powers. Most colonies required all white men to keep and bear arms. These local militias were viewed as the best way to keep order and liberty.

The Second Amendment was added to the Constitution to ensure that Congress could not pass laws to disarm state militias. It also appeased Anti-Federalists who feared that the new Constitution would cause them to lose the right to keep and bear arms. And it recognized an unstated right—the right to revolt against governmental tyranny.

Through the 1930s, few state statutes regulating firearms were passed (generally these few laws dated from the pre-Civil War era and dealt with the possession of firearms by slaves). And the Supreme Court's decision in *Barron v. Baltimore* (1833), limiting the application of the Bill of Rights to actions of Congress alone, prevented federal review of those state laws. Moreover, in *Dred Scott v. Sanford* (1857; see Chapter 3), Chief Justice Taney listed the right to own and carry arms as a basic right of citizenship.

In 1934, Congress passed the National Firearms Act in response to the increase in organized crime that occurred in the 1920s and 1930s. The Act imposed taxes...

remains a particularly hot topic in American politics. In the aftermath of the assassination attempt on President Ronald Reagan in 1981, many lawmakers called for passage of gun control legislation. At the forefront of that effort was Sarah Brady, the wife of James Brady, the presidential press secretary who was badly wounded and left partially disabled by John Hinkley, Jr. Her efforts led to passage of the "Brady Bill" in 1993, which imposed a federal five-day waiting period on the purchase of handguns.

In 1994, in spite of extensive lobbying by the National Rifle Association, Congress passed the Violent Crime Control and Law Enforcement Act. In addition to providing money to the states for additional police officers and prisons, the Act banned the manufacture, transport, sale, or possession of nineteen semi-automatic assault weapons. Because owners may keep guns purchased before the effective date of the law, most gun shop owners reported a tremendous increase in business.

...and Sarah Brady being applauded for their efforts to ...ongressional approval of the Brady Bill after it was ...d into law by President Clinton.

---

344 ❖ Chapter 8 The Bureaucracy

4. **Insufficient Funding.** Congress often fails to fund some programs fully, making their success unlikely. Head Start and the Food Stamps program, for example, are never sufficiently funded to allow all who are eligible to receive the benefits of those programs. Domestic social welfare programs (see Chapter 16) are perennially the target of presidential and congressional budget cutters who seek political gains from attacking the "bloated bureaucracy" while seriously attempting to get the national deficit in check.

Toward Reform

Historically, politicians and presidents have called for reform of the bureaucracy. Thomas Jefferson was the first. He attempted to cut the waste and bring about a "wise and frugal government." But it wasn't until the Progressive Era (1890–1920) that calls for reform began to be taken seriously. Later, Calvin Coolidge urged spending cuts and other reforms. His Two Percent Club was created to cut staff, as its name implies, by 2

Re-Re-Re-Re-Re-Reinventing Government

U.S. leaders before Bill Clinton and Al Gore Jr. have had high hopes for domestic *perestroika*

President	Name Of Plan	Comment
Johnson	Programming, Planning, And Budgeting Systems	"[This is] a very revolutionary system...so that through the tools of modern management the full promise of a finer life can be brought to every American at the lowest possible cost."
Nixon	Management By Objectives	"The time has come...to organize the government by conscious, comprehensive design to meet the new needs of a new era."
Carter	Zero-Based Budgeting	"It's simple and it works...It will make sure that the money that is allocated...goes further."
Reagan	President's Private Sector Survey On Cost Control (Grace Commission)	"[The commission] will work like tireless bloodhounds, leaving no stone unturned in their search to root out inefficiency and waste of taxpayer dollars."
Bush	Right-Sizing Government	"I honestly believe that this is the only way to get the size and spending of government under control."
Clinton/Gore	Reinventing Government (National Performance Review)	"It's about whether we can restore the trust of the American people in their government"

Source: From: "Re-Re-Re-Re-Re-Reinventing Government, *Time*, September 13, 1993.Copyright ©1993 Time, Inc. Reprinted by permission. Clinton/Gore information provided by authors.

EXPANDED Toward Reform sections

A *Toward Reform* section at the end of each chapter offers students insight on the continuing changes of government, and how those challenges are being met.

IS-v

the Multimedia Advantage

VISION: Exploring issues the Framers could have never envisioned

In addition to examining perennial questions raised by the Framers, this text explores issues they could never have envisioned and how the basic institutions of government have responded to these new demands. Your students will see how these new demands have periodically forced governmental adaptation to new circumstances.

The Second Edition helps students understand the dynamics of changes such as

★ Election campaigns in an age of television and electronic databases

★ The media's pressure on our government to respond to international incidents

★ The complexity of crafting foreign policy in the Post Cold War Era

★ Environmental policy

★ Health care intervention

★ On-going civil rights issues

The Popular Incumbent with

MEANINGFUL ILLUSTRATIONS

Integrated examples of the Clean Air Act Amendments of 1990

This real-world example is referred to in appropriate chapters in the text and supplemented with the C-SPAN video and optional *Washington At Work, Second Edition* by Richard Cohen.

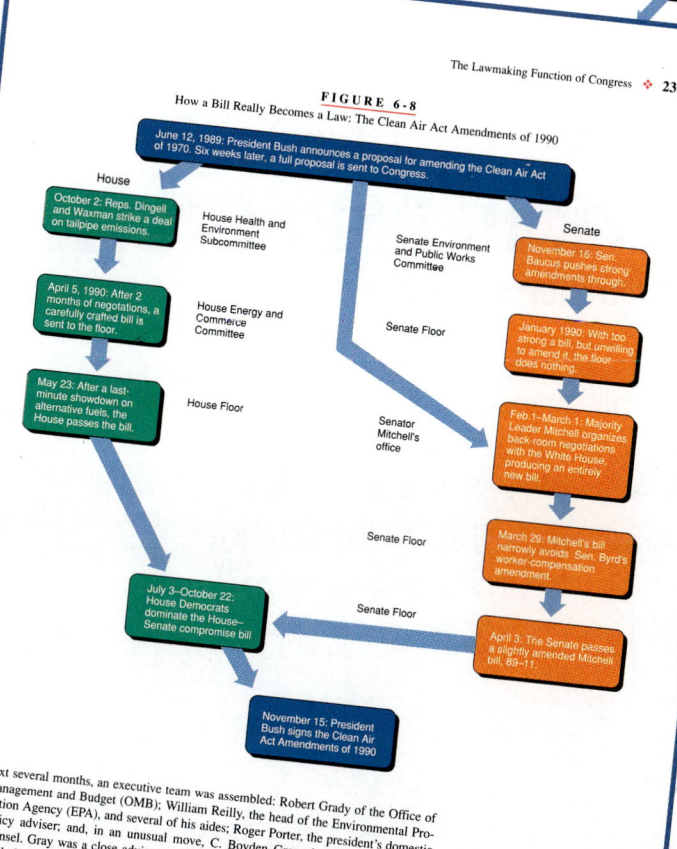

This integrated example shows students the twists and turns of government at work and helps them understand the perennial subject of how a bill becomes a law.

the Multimedia Advantage

PHILOSOPHICAL PERSPECTIVES
Government born amidst the burning issues of representation and power.

At the beginning of every chapter you'll find a few sentences from the *Federalist Papers* (Ch. 4 begins with an Anti-Federalist quotation). The context and meaning of these passages are explained in captions and used as references at relevant points in the chapter, giving students a flavor of the Framer's debates — showing students that the issues of representation and power surrounding the design of the Constitution still smolder today.

COMPARATIVE PERSPECTIVES
Presidential versus parliamentary democracies

Changes in governments around the world such as in the former Soviet Union, South Africa, the Middle East, Eastern Europe, Latin America, and Asia remind us of the preeminence of democracy in theory if not always in fact. As new democratic experiments spring up around the globe, the *Second Edition* helps your students understand the rudiments of these presidential versus parliamentary governments, and multiparty systems versus two party systems.

The Popular Incumbent with

AMERICA AND GREAT BRITAIN —
Integrated comparisons throughout the text

This text puts American government in perspective by using Great Britain as a point of comparison. By comparing the two governments, students learn the basic differences between presidential and parliamentary democracies.

---

12 ❖ Chapter 1 American Government: Roots and Reform

Table 1.1 ❖ Types of Government

TYPES	EXAMPLE	HOW MANY ARE INVOLVED IN THE GOVERNING PROCESS
Monarchy	Eighteenth-century Great Britain	One
Oligarchy	El Salvador, 1960s; Brazil, 1970s	Small number
Aristocracy	Seventeenth-century Poland; Haiti, 1980s	Small number
Indirect Democracy	United States today	Many
Direct Democracy	Ancient Athens	Nearly all (free males)

The Theory of Democratic Government

As evidenced by the early creation of the Virginia House of Burgesses in 1619, and its objections to "taxation without representation," the colonists were quick to create participatory forms of government in which most men (subject to some landowning requirements) were allowed to participate. The New England town meeting (see "Then and Now," p. 13), where all citizens gather to discuss and decide issues facing the town, today stands as a surviving example of a **direct democracy**, such as was used in ancient Greece when all free, male citizens came together periodically to pass laws and "elect" leaders by lot.

Direct democracies, however, soon proved unworkable in the colonies. Although Rousseau argued that true democracy is impossible unless *all* citizens participate in governmental decision-making, as more and more settlers came to the New World, many town meetings were replaced by a system called **indirect** or **representative democracy**. Ironically, this system of government, in which representatives of the people are chosen by ballot, was considered undemocratic by ancient Greeks, who believed that all citizens must have a direct say in their governance.

Representative or indirect democracies, which call for the election of representatives to a governmental decision-making body, were formed first in the colonies and then in [...]ns were uncomfortable with the term "democracy" and [...]oid any confusion between the system adopted and direct [...]resentative democracies are more commonly called "re-[...]ocracy" and "republic" often are used interchangeably. [...]lic" implied a system of government in which the interests [...]ed by more educated or wealthier citizens. In the early [...], only those who owned land could vote. But today, those

[Charac]teristics of American Democracy?

[...]rect democracy with several distinguishing characteris-[...]ced on the individual. All individuals are deemed ratio-[...]as Thomas Jefferson proclaimed in the Declaration of

---

The Members of Congress ❖ 219

Race Matters: Senator Carolyn Moseley-Braun and the Confederate Flag
❖ ❖ ❖

For years, the U.S. Senate has routinely extended the design patent of the Daughters of the Confederacy that included the Confederate flag. That was before the first African-American woman became a member of the Senate.

Since her election in 1992, Carol Moseley-Braun (D.-Ill.), the only African American in the Senate, has tried to sensitize her colleagues about issues of race. In 1993, Senator Jesse Helms (R.-N.C.), for example, sought to amend the national service bill in such a way as to preserve the design patent held by the United Daughters of the Confederacy that included the Confederate flag. Most senators had no idea what they were voting on, and the amendment to the bill passed on a vote of fifty-two to forty-eight. Then, Senator Moseley-Braun took to the floor to express her outrage at Helms's support of a symbol of slavery: "On this issue there can be no consensus. It is an outrage. It is an insult."* Although Helms angrily insisted that slavery and race were not at issue, the Senate killed the Helms amendment on a vote of seventy-five to twenty-five, as twenty-seven senators changed their votes. Said Senator Barbara Boxer (D.-Calif.), "If there ever was proof of the value of diversity, we have it here today."**

** Ibid.

*Adam Clymer, "Daughter of Slavery Hushes Senate," *New York Times* (July 23, 1993):B-6.

Senator Carol Moseley-Braun (D.-Ill.) speaks out angrily on the floor of the Senate.

How a representative views his or her role—as a trustee, delegate, or politico—may still not answer the question of whether it makes a difference if a representative or senator is male or female; African American, Hispanic, Native American, or white; young or old; gay or straight. Can a man, for example, represent the interests of women as well as a woman? Can a rich woman represent the interests of the poor? The combinations are endless.

Senator Edward M. Kennedy (D.-Mass.), for example, is one of the wealthiest members of the Senate, yet he has been an effective champion of the poor, of women, and of other minorities throughout his six terms in the Senate. But during the Clarence Thomas hearings (see p. 379) many commentators noted that Kennedy's well-chronicled problems in his personal life precluded him from effectively questioning Thomas and contributed to his uncharacteristic silence during those hearings. Female representatives in the House were outraged by the glaring absence of any women on the Senate Judiciary Committee that grilled Anita Hill concerning her charges that Thomas had sexually harassed her while he was her supervisor at the Equal Employment Opportunity Commission. Presumably in response, to this com-

---

the Multimedia Advantage

People of the Past boxes in every chapter present a biographical passage highlighting an interesting personality form America's political past.

Then and Now boxes in each chapter contrast an institution, process or arena from the past with its present incarnation. Some examples include
- ★ Native Americans and Land Rights (Chapter 5)
- ★ The Equal Employment Opportunity Commission (Chapter 8)
- ★ The Character Issue from Grover Cleveland to Bill Clinton (Chapter 14)

NEW — A focus on the role of women and minorities in government.

NEW — 3 policy chapters in Part IV have been completely revised and expanded. James Anderson, Texas A&M, is co-author for Chapters 16 & 17

NEW — A Table of Cases that offers a handy index to all the cases referred to in the text.

UPDATED THROUGHOUT — to reflect the most current events including results of the November 1994 elections and demonstrating the relevance of topics.

NEW — Detailed Chapter Summaries are now included to help students review concepts and issues.

Toward Reform sections

Plus numerous general content boxes that present interesting histotical and current people, issues, and events.

IS-x

The Popular Incumbent with

A Strong emphasis on Minorities and their roles in government.

Present students with a better understanding of the roles and influence of African Americans, Hispanics, and Asian Americans in the development of the American government.

---

220 ❖ Chapter 6 Congress

Ben Nighthorse Campbell (D.-Col.)

plaint two women—Diane Feinstein (D.-Cal.) and Carol Moseley-Braun (D.-Ill.) were added to the Committee in 1993.

Female representatives historically have played prominent roles in efforts to expand women's rights. It was Representative Martha Griffiths (D.-Mich.) who successfully added "sex" to the list of discriminatory qualifications prohibited by the Civil Rights Act of 1964 and Representative Bella Abzug (D.-N.Y.) who led the fight for congressional passage of the Equal Rights Amendment.

Studies reveal that female legislators are more likely than their male counterparts to sponsor legislation of concern to women.[14] In the 101st Congress, for example, two bills supported by most women in Congress were passed: an extension of Medicare to cover mammograms for women over sixty-five and the establishment of a $30-million screening program for breast and cervical cancer for poor women, who die of these diseases at higher rates than does the rest of the population. Representative Mary Rose Oakar (D.-Ohio), who co-sponsored these bills, noted that she made progress by seeking help from male representatives whose wives had breast cancer. "There are at least ten of them, and when it hits you in the family, boy, do attitudes change."[15] Without a push from women, however, it is unlikely that even those male representatives would have acted.

Actions of the one Native American and one African American in the Senate underscore the representative function that can be played in Congress. Ben Nighthorse Campbell (D.-Col.), for example, sits on the Senate Committee on Indian Affairs. As a member of the House, he led the fight to change the name of Custer Battlefield Monument in Montana to Little Bighorn Battlefield National Monument to honor the Indians who died in battle. He also fought successfully for legislation to establish the National Museum of the American Indian within the Smithsonian Institution. But his biggest fight on behalf on Native Americans has been to block congressional approval of a $200-million stadium for the Washington Redskins unless the football team changes its name. Campbell told a House panel that the word "redskin" is a racial slur.

How Congress Is Organized

Every two years, a new Congress is seated. After determining qualifications of new ...nizes its business for the coming session: it elects leaders, ...ents for the two-year period, and sets its agenda. Each ...introduce up to 10,000 bills and pass between 700 and ...s and organization is, therefore, critical to Congressional ...tes the leadership structure of each house. The Democrats ...oth houses during the 103rd Congress. Figure 6-6 shows ...o houses in the Capitol building.

...islate (New York: Oxford University Press, 1994).
...ealth Act to End Discrimination in Health Issues, Mikulski Says,"
...27, 1991) NEXIS.

Devising a National Government ❖ 13

THEN AND NOW

Direct Democracy

The town meeting, which is still the form of government of some municipalities in New England, is an example of direct democracy. Starting in colonial times, the men of the town would congregate at the local meeting hall to discuss issues ranging from public drunkenness to education.

Today some people suggest that electronic voting provides a means to return to direct democracy. This idea received particular attention during the 1992 presidential campaign when candidate Ross Perot called for electronic town meetings in which officials would offer three possible solutions to a public problem and viewers would electronically vote for their choice.*

Different plans—including voting by telephone, interactive TV, computer bulletin boards and on-line information services—have been proposed as possible means of conducting electronic voting. USA VOTE, a nonpartisan, nonprofit group located in Arlington, Virginia, has launched an interactive public affairs television show that consists of a 30-minute debate on a specific issue followed by an opportunity for viewers to call a toll-free number and express their opinions.

Interactive Network, Inc., a California-based company, offers another method of electronic political interaction. Consumers who purchase this firm's control units at retail stores (at a cost of $199) gain interactive access to various news programs, sports events and information services. San Franciscans had the opportunity to utilize this network after each televised presidential debate of 1992. A viewer subscribing to the service was able to vote on issues raised in the debate by pushing buttons on the control unit. Computers then compiled results and displayed them on the control unit's screen.

However, practical and philosophical problems exist with all methods. When CBS asked viewers to call in questions after George Bush's 1992 State of the Union Address, only 315,000 of 25 million calls got through. Other problems include: deciding who controls the agenda, ensuring that the meetings have a representative sample of the population, providing electronic access for poor citizens, and preventing ballot box stuffing. Political scientist Theodore Becker supports a multilayer web of decentralized electronic meetings run by an independent, private commission and not by the White House or any government agency" to overcome some of these problems. Still, it is unlikely that a return to a pure direct democracy will occur in the near future.

*Much of this discussion is adapted from Mitch Betts, "Electronic Town Meeting. A Safe Vote?," Computerworld (October 26, 1992): 25; and Katherine McCarron, "Lobbying Congress from Your La-Z-Boy," The National Journal (November 21, 1992): 2688.

An interactive TV unit

IS-xi

the Multimedia Advantage

Expanded MULTIMEDIA Supplements help students envision text concepts.

C-SPAN Video: The Clean Air Act Amendments of 1990
Brings the intrigue of executive lobbying, committees, and floor voting right into your classroom

This colorful presentation shows students how a bill becomes a law. As an example of the complexity of modern legislation, this video mirrors discussions of the Clean Air Act in chapters 6 and 17, as students learn how to analyze public policy.

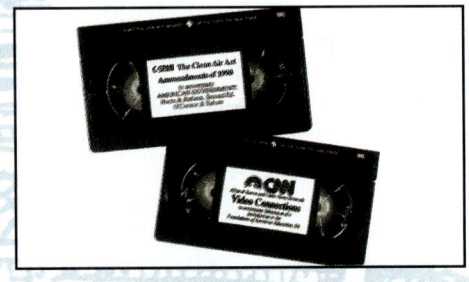

NEW — CNN Video

Through an exclusive agreement with Cable News Network, Allyn & Bacon offers specially edited video segments from CNN's news reports on timely issues that illustrate concepts discussed in each chapter.

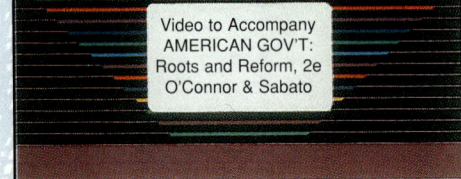

NEW — LASER DISK

Provides the same specially edited CNN video footage in a laser disk format.

IS-xii

The Popular Incumbent with

NEW — CD ROM with lecture enhancement modules.

A combination of text, CNN video, audio, and 4-color graphics help your lectures with information on topics such as how a bill passes through Congress, campaign financing, and media and politics.

NEW — AUDIO TAPE of Supreme Court Decisions

Selected recordings of oral arguments presented before the Supreme Court on key cases. Selected and edited by Karen O'Connor.

Allyn & Bacon Video Library

A full set of videos on every major course topic, including Congress, the presidency, the courts, and elections. Now available through ALLYN & BACON. Collection curated by Joe Losco and Ralph Baker of Ball State University.

America Online — Connect to a Whole New World of Teaching and Learning!

We'll help you get started. Adopt this textbook and we'll waive the America Online membership fee for the first two months! Use this introductory membership to access a wide range of interactive services and educational information including a fast and easy gateway to the Internet. You'll gain a whole new means of communication when you start to experience AMERICA ONLINE. Its award-winning interface makes navigating easy. Just point and click to download any of thousands of programs; attend real-time, online conferences and forums; keep in touch through electronic mail; and get the latest news and information from leading magazines and news wires. All you need is a computer and a modem. We'll make it easy for your students to get started too! What's more, Simon & Schuster Higher Education Group will be developing *COLLEGE Online*, an online services specifically for college and university faculty and student use!

Ask your local Allyn & Bacon representative for details on America Online. Or, if you have already selected this textbook for your course adoption, please call **1-800-827-6364**, ext. 4314 and we'll send your free America Online starter kit.

the Multimedia Advantage

Additional Supplements

Instructor's Manual
This manual includes lecture ideas, discussion questions, and classroom activities, as well as lecture suggestions for using the Video Library.

Test Bank
The Test Bank provides questions for the text and the Video Library, allowing instructors to integrate all student materials easily. It contains more than 1,500 multiple-choice, true/false, and essay questions, as well as midterm and final exams.

Computerized Test Bank
A computerized version of the above Test Bank is available in IBM and Macintosh formats.

Transparencies
A full set of color transparencies including U.S. and world maps is available to complement classroom lectures.

Study Guide
Includes multiple-choice, matching, and true/false questions, as well as study outlines.

Computerized Study Guide
A computerized version of the above Study Guide.

IS-xiv

The Popular Incumbent with

NEW — AMERICAN GOVERNMENT: Readings and Cases, by Karen O'Connor

This up-to-date reader combines the best of classic and contemporary readings along with critical thinking questions that ask students to think about and discuss politics relative to the era when the Constitution was written.

WASHINGTON AT WORK: Back Rooms and Clean Air, Second Edition, by Richard Cohen

This dramatic text covers the twists and turns of The Clean Air Act Amendments of 1990 in detail. The new *Second Edition* provides several changes including a new final chapter discussiing events that have teaken place since the enactment of the law.

NEW — The Washington Post JIT customized reader

Through Allyn & Bacon's innovative Just-In-Time Publishing program you can created your own reader and choose from a database of over 300 current articles from The Washington Post.

the Multimedia Advantage

American Government

American Government

ROOTS AND REFORM

Second Edition

Karen O'Connor
*Professor of Political Science
Emory University*

Larry J. Sabato
*Robert Kent Gooch Professor of
Government and Foreign Affairs
University of Virginia*

Allyn and Bacon

Boston ◆ London ◆ Toronto ◆ Sydney ◆ Tokyo ◆ Singapore

Copyright ©1995 by Allyn & Bacon
Needham Heights, Massachusetts 02194

A Simon & Schuster Company

Copyright ©1993 by Macmillan Publishing Company,
A division of Macmillan, Inc.

All rights reserved. No part of the material protected by this copyright notice may be reproduced or utilized in any form or by any means, electronic or mechanical, including photocopying, recording, or by any information storage and retrieval system, without the written permission of the copyright owner.

Senior Editor: Stephen Hull
Vice President: Joseph Opiela
Marketing Manager: Lisa Kimball
Development Editor: Jane Tufts
Production Administrator: Marjorie Payne
Editorial Assistant: Brenda Conaway
Cover Administrator: Linda Knowles
Cover Designer: Studio Nine
Composition/Prepress Buyer: Linda Cox
Manufacturing Buyer: Louise Richardson
Photo Researcher: Yvonne Gerin
Text and Art Designer: Deborah Schneck, Schneck-DePippo Graphics

Library of Congress Cataloging-in-Publication Data

O'Connor, Karen, 1952–
    American government: roots and reform / Karen O'Connor, Larry J. Sabato. — 2nd ed.
       p. cm.
    Includes bibliographical references and index.
    ISBN 0-02-388904-7
    1. United States—Politics and Government. I. Sabato, Larry.
II. Title.
JK274.026 1995
320.473—dc20   94-27939
                                                CIP

Review copy ISBN: 0-205-16930-9

Photo credits are found on the last two pages of the book, which should be considered extensions of the copyright page.

Printed in the United States of America
10 9 8 7 6 5 4 3 2 1   99 98 97 96 95 94

To Meghan, always the trouper
    Karen O'Connor

―――――◆◆◆―――――

*To my Government 101 students
over the years, who all know
that "politics is a good thing"*
    Larry Sabato

BRIEF CONTENTS

Part One ♦ Foundations of Government

1. American Government: Roots and Reform   3
2. The Constitution   25
3. Federalism   69
4. Civil Liberties   105
5. Civil Rights   151

Part Two ♦ Institutions of Government   201

6. Congress   203
7. The Presidency   257
8. The Bureauocracy   305
9. The Judiciary   349

Part Three ♦ Political Behavior   403

10. Public Opinion   405
11. Political Parties   443
12. Voting and Elections   497
13. The Campaign Process   543
14. The News Media   577
15. Interest Groups   613

Part Four ♦ Public Policy   657

16. Social Welfare Policy   659
17. Economic Policy   703
18. Foreign and Military Policy   749

Appendices

I   The Declaration of Independence   A1
II The Constitution of the United States of America   A4
III Presidents, Congresses, and Chief Justices: 1789–1992   A14

Case Glossary   C1
Glossary   G1
Index   I1

CONTENTS

Preface xvii

Part One ♦ Foundations of Government

1
AMERICAN GOVERNMENT: ROOTS AND REFORM 3

Where Did Our Ideas of Government Come From? 7
- From Aristotle to the Enlightenment 7
- A Growing Idea: Popular Consent 7
- *People of the Past* ♦ Hobbes; Locke 10

Devising a National Government 11
- The Theory of Democratic Government 12
- What Are the Characteristics of American Democracy 12
- *Then and Now* ♦ Direct Democracy 13
- Who Makes Decisions in America? 15

Why a Capitalist System? 17

Understanding Our Democratic System 20

2
THE CONSTITUTION 25

The Origins of a New Nation 28
- Trade and Taxation 29
- *People of the Past* ♦ Samuel Adams 30
- First Steps Toward Independence 31
- The First Continental Congress 32
- The Second Continental Congress 33

The Declaration of Independence 34
- Social Contract Theory 34

The First Attempt at Government: The Articles of Confederation 36
- Problems Under the Articles of Confederation 37

The Miracle at Philadelphia: Writing a Constitution 39
- The Framers 40
- The Virginia Plan 40
- The New Jersey Plan 42
- The Great Compromise 42
- Compromise on the Presidency 44
- Selecting a President: The Electoral College 44
- Removing a President 45

The U.S. Constitution 45
- The Basic Principles of the Constitution 46
- The Articles of the Constitution 49

The Drive for Ratification 52
- Federalists versus Anti-Federalists 54

Amending the Constitution 57
- *Then and Now* ♦ The Constitution and the Right to Vote 60
- Informal Methods of Amending the Constitution 64

Toward Reform 65

3
FEDERALISM 69

The Roots of the Federal System 71
- The Powers of Government in the Federal System 71

The Evolution and Development of Federalism 75
- The Supreme Court 75
- *People of the Past* ♦ Dred Scott 79
- The Transformation of Dual Federalism 80

ix

The New Deal and a Rapidly Changing Balance of Power 82

The Changing Nature of Federalism 85
Federal Grants 86

Then and Now ♦ The Sheppard-Towner Maternity Act of 1923 87

Reagan's New Federalism 89
Controlling the States through Preemption and Mandates 90
Rethinking Federalism 93
Clinton's New Federalism 93

The Intergovernmental Lobby 93

Federalism and the Supreme Court 96

Toward Reform 100

4
CIVIL LIBERTIES 105

The First Constitutional Amendments: The Bill of Rights 107

First Amendment Guarantees: Freedom of Religion 109
The Establishment Clause 110
The Free Exercise Clause 112

First Amendment Guarantees: Freedom of Speech and Press 114
The Alien and Sedition Acts 116
Slavery, the Civil War, and Rights Curtailments 116
New Restrictions/New Tests 117

People of the Past ♦ Eugene V. Debs 118

The First Amendment Applied to the States: The Incorporation Doctrine 119
Symbolic Speech 122

Then and Now ♦ The Second Amendment and the Right of the People to Keep and Bear Arms 123

Prior Restraint 124
"Politically Correct" Speech 124
Libel and Slander 127
Obscenity and Pornography 127

The Rights of Criminal Defendants 129
The Fourth Amendment and Searches and Seizures 131
The Fifth Amendment and Self-Incrimination 134
The Exclusionary Rule 135
The Sixth Amendment and the Right to Counsel 136
The Sixth Amendment and Jury Trials 138
The Eighth Amendment and Cruel and Unusual Punishment 139

The Right to Privacy 141
Birth Control 142
Abortion 142
Homosexuality 145

Toward Reform 146

5
CIVIL RIGHTS 151

Slavery, Abolition, and Winning the Right to Vote, 1800–1890 153
Slavery and Congress 153
The Abolitionist Movement: The First Civil Rights Movement 155

People of the Past ♦ Frederick Douglass 155

The Civil War and Its Aftermath: Civil Rights Laws and Constitutional Amendments 157
Civil Rights and the Supreme Court 160

The Push for Equality, 1889–1954 163
The Founding of the National Association for the Advancement of Colored People 164
Key Women's Groups 165
Litigating for Equality 167

The Civil Rights Movement 172
School Desegregation After *Brown* 172
A New Move for African-American Rights 174
The Civil Rights Act of 1964 176
The Effect of the Civil Rights Act of 1964 178
The Equal Protection Clause and Constitutional Standards of Review 183

Other Groups Mobilize for Rights 187
Native Americans 187

Then and Now ♦ Native Americans and Land Rights   190

Hispanic Americans   190
Homosexuals   192
Disabled Americans   193

The Politics of Civil Rights   194

Affirmative Action   195
The Legislative Response   196

Toward Reform   197

Part Two ♦ Institutions of Government

6
CONGRESS   203

The Roots of the Legislative Branch   204

The Constitution and the Legislative Branch of Government   205

Apportionment and Redistricting   206
Constitutional Powers of Congress   209

The Members of Congress   212

Formal Requirements   213
Informal Requirements   213
What Does Congress Look Like?   216
The Representational Function of Members of Congress   217

How Congress Is Organized   220

The House of Representatives   222

People of the Past ♦ Henry Clay   223

The Senate   225

Then and Now ♦ Life on the Floor and in the Halls of Congress   226

The Role of Political Parties in Congress   227
The Committee System   228

The Lawmaking Function of Congress   235

How a Bill Becomes a Law: The Textbook Way   236
How a Bill Really Becomes a Law: The Clean Air Act Amendments of 1990   238

How Members Make Decisions   241

Political Parties   242
Colleagues and Caucuses   242
Staff   244
Interest Groups   246
Constituents   247

Congress and the President   248

Oversight of the Executive Branch   249
Confirmation of Presidential Appointments   251

Toward Reform   252

Reform from Within   252
Citizen Efforts   252

7
THE PRESIDENCY   257

The Roots of the Office of President of the United States   258

The Framers and the Creation of the Presidency   259

Qualifications for Office   260
Term of Office   260
Removal   260
Succession   261
The Vice President   262

The Constitutional Powers of the President   267

The Appointment Power   267
The Power to Convene Congress   269
The Power to Make Treaties   269
Veto Power   271
Commander-in-Chief of the Military   273
The Pardoning Power   273

The Development of Presidential Power   274

People of the Past ♦ George Washington   276

The First Three Presidents   277
Congressional Triumph: 1804–1933   278
The Growth of the Modern Presidency   279
The Role of the President in the Legislative Process   282
Presidential Style   285

The Presidential Establishment   293

The Cabinet   294

Then and Now ♦ First Ladies   294
   The Executive Office of the President   297
   White House Staff   298

Toward Reform   300
   The Two-Term Limitation   302
   The Line-Item Veto   302

8
THE BUREAUCRACY   305

Then and Now ♦ The Equal Opportunity Commission and Sex Discrimination   307

The Development of the Federal Bureaucracy   308
   The Civil War and Big Government   309
   Becoming a Bureaucrat: From Spoils to Merit   310

People of the Past ♦ William Henry Harrison and Office Seekers   312

   National Efforts to Regulate the Economy   312

The Modern Bureaucracy   316
   Who Are Bureaucrats?   317
   Formal Organization   321

Policy Making   327
   Rule Making   328
   Administrative Adjudication   331

Making Agencies Accountable   332
   Executive Control   333
   Congressional Control   336
   Judicial Control   338

Problems with the Modern Bureaucracy   338
   Iron Triangles and Issue Networks   338
   Accountability   340

Toward Reform   344

9
THE JUDICIARY   349

The Creation of the Judicial Branch   351
   The Judiciary Act of 1789 and the Creation of the Federal Judicial System   352
   The Marshall Court (1801–1835)   355
   Judicial Review   355

People of the Past ♦ John Marshall   356

The Legal System   357
   Jurisdiction   358
   Criminal and Civil Law   359

The Federal Court System   360
   District Courts   360
   The Courts of Appeal   362
   The Supreme Court   364

Then and Now ♦ Law Clerks   366

How Federal Judges Are Selected   368
   Appointments to the U.S. Supreme Court   371
   Nomination Criteria   372
   The Supreme Court Confirmation Process   376

The Supreme Court Today   380
   Deciding to Hear a Case   380
   Jurisdiction   381
   The Rule of Four   382
   Characteristics of a Supreme Court Case   383
   Starting the Case   385
   Oral Arguments by Attorneys   387
   The Conference and Vote   389
   Writing the Opinions of the Court   389

How the Justices Vote   391
   Legal Factors   391
   Extra-Legal Factors   393

Judicial Policy Making and Implementation   396
   Implementing Court Decisions   397

Toward Reform   399

Part Three ♦ Political Behavior

10
PUBLIC OPINION   405

What Is Public Opinion?   406

Early Efforts to Influence Public Opinion   408

Early Attempts to Gauge Public Opinion   410

Then and Now ♦ Straw Polls   412

Political Socialization: The First Step Toward Forming Opinions 413

People of the Past ♦ George Gallup 414

The Family 414
School 415
Peers 416
The Impact of Events 417
Social Groups 417

Political Ideology 423

How We Form Political Opinions 427

Personal Benefits 427
Political Knowledge 427
Cues from Leaders 429

How We Measure Public Opinion 429

Determining the Content and Phrasing the Questions 430
Selecting the Sample 430
Kinds of Polls 432
Shortcomings of Polling 436

How Polling and Public Opinion Affect Politicians, Politics, and Policy 437

Toward Reform 440

11
POLITICAL PARTIES 443

What Is a Political Party? 444

The Evolution of American Party Democracy 445

The Early Parties Fade 448
Democrats and Republicans: The Golden Age 450
The Modern Era versus the Golden Age 450
Is the Party Over? 451
The Parties Endure 451

The Roles of the American Parties 453

Mobilizing Support and Gathering Power 453
A Force for Stability 453
Unity, Linkage, Accountability 453
The Electioneering Function 454

People of the Past ♦ Plunkitt of Tammany Hall 455

Party as a Voting and Issue Cue 456
Policy Formulation and Promotion 456

One-Partyism and Third-Partyism 458

Minor Parties 459
Explanations 459

The Basic Structure of American Political Parties 463

National Committees 463
Leadership 464
National Conventions 465
States and Localities 466

Then and Now ♦ The Political Machines 466

Informal Groups 468

The Party in Government 469

The Congressional Party 469
The Presidential Party 473
The Parties and the Judiciary 478
The Parties and State Governments 479

The Modern Transformation of Party Organization 480

Republican Strengths 480
Results 483
Democratic Party Gains 483

The Party-in-the-Electorate 485

Party Identification 485
Declining Loyalty 487
Group Affiliations 488

Toward Reform 491

12
VOTING AND ELECTIONS 497

The Purposes Served by Elections 498

Different Kinds of Elections 500

Primary Elections 500
General Elections 501
Initiative, Referendum, and Recall 502

Presidential Elections 502

Primaries versus Caucuses 503
The Party Conventions 506

Then and Now ♦ Dark Horses versus Worn-out Horses 510

The Electoral College: How Presidents Are Elected 515

xiv ❖ Contents

People of the Past ♦ How Rutherford B. Hayes Was Elected President in 1876   520

Superdelegates   522

Patterns of Presidential Elections   523

Congressional Elections   528

The Incumbency Advantage   528
Redistricting, Scandals, and Coattails   528
Off-Year Elections   530

Voting Behavior   532

Why Is Voter Turnout So Low?   534
A New Voting Pattern: Ticket-Splitting   536

Toward Reform   538

13
THE CAMPAIGN PROCESS   543

At the Starting Block: Ambition and Strategy   544

The Structure of a Campaign   544

The Nomination Campaign   546
The General Election Campaign   546
The Personal Campaign   547
The Organizational Campaign   549
The Media Campaign   550

People of the Past ♦ William Henry Harrison and the Media Campaign of 1840   551

The Candidate or the Campaign: Which Do We Vote For?   552

Modern Campaign Challenges   553

The News Media   553
Raising the Money   556
Are PACs a Good or Bad Part of the Process?   560
A Summary of Contributions and Expenses   563

Bringing It Together: The 1992 Presidential Campaign and Election   564

The Party Nomination Battle   564

Then and Now ♦ The Television Advertising Campaigns of 1952 and 1992   564

The Third Force: Ross Perot   567
The Party Conventions   568
The Fall Campaign and General Election Results   569

Toward Reform   572

14
THE NEWS MEDIA   577

The American Press of Yesteryear   578

A Less Partisan Press   579

The Contemporary Media Scene   581

Media That Matter   586

People of the Past ♦ Pioneers of the Broadcasting Industry   586

How the Media Cover Politicians and Government   588

Covering the Presidency   588
Covering Congress   589
Covering the Courts   592
Watergate and the Era of Investigative Journalism   592

The Post-Watergate Era   594

The Character Issue in Media Coverage of Politicians   594

Then and Now ♦ The Character Issue from Grover Cleveland to Bill Clinton   596

The Question of Bias   597

The Media's Influence on the Public   602

How Politicians Use the Media   602

Government Regulation of the Electronic Media   604

Content Regulation   605
Confidentiality of Sources   606
Censorship   607

Toward Reform   608

15
INTEREST GROUPS   613

What Are Interest Groups?   614

Types of Interest Groups   615

The Roots of American Interest Groups   618

The Early Years: The Colonial Period to 1830   620
National Groups Emerge (1830–1880)   621
National Groups Increase (1890–1920)   623

People of the Past ♦ Florence Kelley   626

The Modern Era of Interest-Group Activity (1960 to the present)   628

Then and Now ♦ Lobbying   630

What Do Interest Groups Do?   635
Election Activities   645

What Makes an Interest Group Successful?   650
The Role of Leaders   652
Group Structure   652
Funding   653
Membership   653

Toward Reform   655

Part Four ♦ Public Policy

16
SOCIAL WELFARE POLICY   659

The Policy-Making Process   661
Problem Definition   662
Agenda Setting   664

People of the Past ♦ Rachel Carson   667

Policy Formulation   668
Policy Adoption   669
Budgeting   670
Policy Implementation   670
Policy Evaluation   672

Social Welfare Policies   673

Public Education   674
Federal Aid to Education   675
Inequality in Spending Among School Districts   678

Income Security   678
Roots of Income Security Programs   680
Social Insurance   681
Means-Tested Programs   686
The Effectiveness of Income Security Programs   689

Medical Care   689
The Roots of National Health Insurance   690

Then and Now ♦ From the '60s to Now: Medicaid's Legal Activists   694

The Costs of Health Care   695

Toward Reform   696

17
ECONOMIC POLICY   703

Roots of Government Intervention in the Economy   704
The Nineteenth Century   704
The Progressive Era 1901–1917   707
The Great Depression and the New Deal   708

Then and Now ♦ Regulation of Financial Markets and the Fed   712

The Post-World War II Era   714
The Social Regulation Era   716
Deregulation   718

Stabilizing the Economy   720
Monetary Policy   721
Fiscal Policy   725

People of the Past ♦ Walter Heller   726

The Budgetary Process   727
The Deficit and the Debt   731

The Economics of Regulating Environmental Pollution   736
Environmental Policy Making   737
The Environmental Protection Agency   739

Toward Reform   745

18
FOREIGN AND MILITARY POLICY   749

The Roots of U.S. Foreign and Military Policy   750
The Pre-Constitutional Era   750
The Constitution   752

The Early History of Foreign and Military Policy   752

People of the Past ♦ John Jay   754

Early Trade and Aid Policy   757

The Monroe Doctrine   758
The United States as an Emerging Power   759
Foreign Trade and Aid Policy at the Turn of the Century   760
World War I   761

The Great Shift   764
The Origins of the Cold War   765
The Marshall Plan, NATO, and Containment   766
The Cold War Era   768

The Machinery of Modern Foreign Policy Making   773
The Information Gap   775

Then and Now ♦ Communication Technology and Foreign Policy   776

Challenges to Presidential Power   777
Congress   777
The Bureaucracy   782
The News Media   783
The Public   784

Toward Reform   787
The Lack of Consensus   788
Finding the United States' Place in the World   789

APPENDICES

I   The Declaration of Independence   A1
II The Constitution of the United States of America   A4
III The Presidents, Congresses, and Chief Justices: 1789–1995   A14

Case Glossary   C1

Glossary   G1

Index   I1

PREFACE

Teaching introductory American government presents special challenges and rewards. It is a challenge to introduce a new discipline to beginning students. It is a challenge to jump from topic to topic each week. Above all, it is a challenge to motivate large and disparate groups of students to master new material. The rewards offered by success, however, can accumulate in students who pay more attention to their government, who participate in its workings as more informed citizens, and who better understand the workings of democracy as practiced in the United States.

We have witnessed some of these rewards from the lecture podium. With this book, we hope to offer our experiences in written form. Students need perspective and motivation; they also need to be exposed to information that will withstand the test of time. Our goal with this text is to transmit just this sort of information.

This Second Edition of our popular *American Government: Roots and Reform* is not simply an update of the earlier edition of this book. Some chapters have been completely revised, old features such as "People of the Past" and "Then and Now" sections have been kept, but, in many chapters they have been replaced with new examples of the role that history plays in what happens today in American politics. User and reviewer suggestions prompted us to expand our popular "Toward Reform," and to add more detailed and expanded chapter summaries keyed to major headings in each chapter. Moreover, all of the Public Policy chapters have been completely rewritten. We've also added maps of the United States and the world on the inside of the front and back covers of this edition. And, the Glossary has been expanded and a new Case Glossary added.

Approach

We believe that we cannot fully understand the actions, issues, and policy decisions facing the U.S. government, its constituent states, or "the people" unless these issues are examined from the perspective of how they have evolved over time. Consequently, the title of this book is *American Government: Roots and Reform*. In its pages we try to examine how the United States is governed today by looking not just at present behavior but also at the Framers' intentions and how they have been implemented over the years. For example, we believe that it is critical to an understanding of the role of political parties in the United States to understand the Framers' fears of factionalism, how parties evolved, and when and why realignments in party identification occurred. In turn, a comprehension of these processes will help us to understand the kinds of officials we have elected over the years.

In addition to perennial questions raised by the Framers, we explore issues that the Framers could never have envisioned, and how the basic institutions of government have responded to these new demands. For instance, no one more than two centuries ago could have forseen election campaigns in an age when nearly all American homes contained television sets, and the airwaves abounded with political discussion on "talk radio." Moreover, new demands have periodically forced governmental reforms, so understanding the dynamics of change is essential for introductory students.

Our overriding concern is that students understand their government as it exists *today*. In order to do so, they must understand how it was designed in the Constitution. They must appreciate a little of how it reached its effects. Each chapter, therefore, approaches its topic with a combination of perspectives that we believe will best facilitate this approach.

In writing this book, we chose to put the Institutions of Government (Part Two) before Political Behavior (Part Three). Both sections, however, were written independently, making them easy to switch for those who prefer to teach about the actors in government and elections *before* discussing the institutions of government. To test the book, we have each taught from it in both orders with no pedagogical problems.

Features

Philosophical Perspective. Every chapter begins with a few sentences from *The Federalist Papers* (with the exception of Chapters 4 and 17 which begin with Anti-Federalist quotations). These passages are explained in captions and then used as references at relevant points in the chapter. From them, students learn that government was born amidst burning issues of representation and power, issues that continue to smolder today.

Historical Perspective. Every chapter uses history to serve two purposes: first, to show how institutions and processes have evolved to their present states, and second, to provide some of the color that makes information memorable. A richer historical texture helps to explain the present; it also helps to free the course from the time-bound nature of newspaper headlines.

Comparative Perspective. Changes in Eastern Europe, the former Soviet Union, Latin and Central America, and Asia reminds us of the preeminence of democracy, in theory if not always in fact. As new democratic experiments spring up around the globe, it becomes increasingly important for students to understand the rudiments of presidential *versus* parliamentary government, of multiparty *versus* two-party systems, and so on. In order to put American government in perspective, therefore (while avoiding the enormous complexities of huge transnational comparisons), we have used the model of Great Britain as a comparison. Throughout our chapter discussions, comparisons are drawn to Great Britain wherever appropriate points arise. By comparing the two governments, students learn the basic differences between presidential and parliamentary democracies.

In this new edition we have added diagrams to better illustrate these points.

The Ancillary Package

The ancillary package for *American Government: Roots and Reform,* Second Edition, reflects the pedagogical goals of the text: to provide information in a useful context and with colorful examples. We have tried especially hard to provide materials that are useful for instructors and interesting and helpful to students.

Special Features

We are particularly pleased to present a unique blend of text, video, and supplementary reading on the perennial subject of how a bill becomes a law. In Chapter 6, we use the Clean Air Act Amendments of 1990 as an example of the complexity of modern legislation, and we refer to it again in Chapter 17, "Economic Policy," as we illustrate how to analyze public policy. Instructors can supplement this coverage with a video showing highlights of C-SPAN's coverage of the bill. It is available from Allyn & Bacon. After reading about executive lobbying, committees, and floor voting, students will greatly enjoy the chance to see the twists and turns of the Clean Air Act Amendments on video. Furthermore, students can buy at special reduced price a package from Allyn & Bacon combining this text with a copy of *National Journal* reporter Richard Cohen's *Washington at Work: Back Rooms and Clean Air,* Second Edition, covering the amendments in detail. By this means instructors can combine text, video, and a colorful case study in the tradition of *The Dance of Legislation.*

Also Available

To further extend the application of multimedia learning enhancements to the teaching of American Government, the following supplements are available for use in conjunction with *American Government: Roots and Reform:*

CNN Video. Through an exclusive arrangement with CNN, adopters of the book will receive a specially edited compilation of recent CNN News stories for classroom use. News footage is organized chapter by chapter, and keyed to topics in the text. Ask your Allyn & Bacon representative for details.

Video Library. A full set of videos on every major course topic is available to adopters of the text. Again, your Allyn & Bacon representative has details.

Laserdisc. The same specially edited CNN programming is available in a laser disc format for easy search and retrieval.

CD-ROM. Organized as a set of discrete, lecture-enhancement modules for both faculty and student use, the CD-ROM combines text, graphics, photographs, audio and full-motion video to provide students with a greater understanding of key concepts and processes. These include how a bill becomes law, media coverage of campaigns, Supreme Court nomination and ratification procedures, and more. Ask your Allyn & Bacon representative for details.

Audio Tape of Supreme Court Arguments. This unique new supplement presents selected recordings of oral arguments presented before the Supreme Court on key constitutional and civil liberties cases. These cases have been selected and edited by Karen O'Connor.

America Online. Connect the teaching of American Government to the world of the fastest-growing on-line service with College OnLine from Allyn & Bacon. A wealth of services and products, updated frequently, keep faculty and students in step with the latest data, pedagogy, and public opinion, all linked to American Government. Adopters of this text receive a two-months free subcription to America OnLine; students receive one free month. Ask your Allyn & Bacon representative for details.

***The Washington Post* Just-In-Time Custom Reader.** By exclusive arrangement with *The Washington Post,* the Allyn & Bacon JIT reader in American Government allows faculty to assemble their own collection of articles to suit individual course demands. Faculty can choose from a frequently updated database of over 300 articles on topics ranging across the spectrum of American Government. Ask your Allyn & Bacon representative for details.

American Government: Readings and Cases. This separate, full-scale reader in American Goverment by Karen O'Connor may be packaged along with the text at a reduced price to students. This reader combines classic articles, including extensive selections from *The Federalist,* with some of the best current political science and a strong component of key and landmark cases. Thoughtful pedagogy includes chapter introductions and end of chapter questions to foster students' critical thinking.

Study Guide. Includes chapter synopses, outlines, key terms, multiple choice, matching and true/false questions with answers for student self-tests. A new **Computerized Study Guide** gives students the same advantage on disc.

Instructor's Manual. Includes lecture ideas, discussion questions, classroom activities, and a guide to video and other resources.

Test Bank. Completely revised and expanded, the test bank provides over 1,500 multiple-choice, true/false, and essay questions, ranked in order of difficulty. A **Computer Test Bank** in IBM or Macintosh formats is also available.

Transparencies. A full set of over 40 color transparencies, including U. S and world maps, is available for classroom use.

Acknowledgments

Karen O'Connor thanks the thousand-plus students in her National Government courses who, over the years, have pushed her to learn more about American government and to have fun in the process. She especially thanks some of her Emory colleagues—Alan Abramowitz, Courtney Brown, and Cornell Hooten—who were always willing to share books, ideas, suggestions, and newspaper clippings. She also thanks Dean Howard Hunter of the Emory Law School for providing access to LEXIS and NEXIS, which allowed this book to be as current as possible. Thanks also to former students John R. Hermann, Sue Davis, Kaenan Hertz, Jenny Jacob and Paul Fabrizio for their research assistance at various phases of the first edition. Kimberley Beakley, now at Duke University and Bernadette Nye at Emory University helped in innumerable ways in our preparation of this second edition. And, Gregg Ivers at American University and Nancy E. McGlen at Niagara University have always been there to offer suggestions, friendship, and encouragement.

While we were writing the first edition, Laura Van Assendelft provided the assistance and fresh perspective that only a graduate student studying for her Ph.D. comprehensive exam in American Government could offer. Laura worked tirelessly on the book and even brought homemade cookies as a reward for completed chapters. Her familiarity with the book proved invaluable as later when, as an assistant professor at Mary Baldwin College, she compiled the Test Bank for this new edition.

Larry Sabato wishes to thank his University of Virginia colleagues and staff, including Clifton McCleskey, Chairman of the Department of Government and Foreign Affairs; graduate students Bruce Larson and Dan Kritenbrink; and technical assistant Nancy Rae.

Particular thanks from both of us go to James Anderson at Texas A & M who co-authored Chapters 16 and 17, the Domestic Policy and Economic Policy chapters and to Richard Cupitt at the Center for East-West Trade at the University of Georgia who co-authored Chapter 18, Foreign and Military Policy. We also thank Jeffrey Anderson of Brown University, who helped provide comparisons between the American and British systems of government.

No project such as this can ever be completed on time without tremendous support from the publisher. As we began the first edition of this book, in Bruce Nichols we have had the rare fortune to work with the best editor in all of political science. He guided this project every step of the way and acted as a cheerleader, friend, stern taskmaster, and even as pushy editor. Although he left as we neared production of the first edition, his influence and impact on this project is a constant. One of the nicest aspects of this project was the opportunity to become good friends with Bruce and with Jane Tufts, our development editor. Jane's years of experience and her decision to freelance benefitted the book tremendously. Although at times we cringed to see the arrival of a Federal Express package from Jane or a FAX from Bruce, they made us write a better book, even if, at times, it must have seemed to them that it was in spite of ourselves. We would also like to thank Robert Miller who "inherited" us and this project from Bruce. Robert, along with David Chodoff, saw us through the final production and promotion of the first edition, the launching of the brief edition of this text, and the initial work on this edition. As Macmillan Publishing Company was sold, we were "acquired" by Allyn and Bacon and adopted by our third new editor, Steve Hull. Under Steve's tutalage we hope we have created yet a better book profitting not only from Steve's new ideas and experience but also others at Allyn and Bacon, including Marjorie Payne and Lisa Kimball as well as the numerous reviewers and friends who offered comments, criticisms, and suggestions.

Finally, many of our peers reviewed various stages of the manuscript and earned our gratitude in the process: Martin Wiseman, Mississippi State University; Mark Silverstein, Boston University; Steve Mazurana, University of Northern Colorado; Shirley Anne Warshaw, Gettysburg College; Jon Bond, Texas A&M University; Doris Graber, University of Illinois at Chicago; Bruce Oppenheimer, Vanderbilt University; Cary Covington, University of Iowa; Marjorie Hershey, Indiana University; Ruth Bamberger, Drury College; Greg Caldeira, Ohio State University; David Cingranelli, SUNY at Binghamton; Mark Landis, Hofstra University; Charles Hadley, University of New Orleans; Danny Adkison, Oklahoma State University; Kenneth Kennedy, College of San Mateo; and Evelyn Fink, University of Nebraska.

Other individuals at Macmillan and Allyn and Bacon deserve special thanks. David Chodoff assisted with text development and oversaw the development of the line art program. Deborah Schneck of Schneck-DePippo rendered it beautifully. Nick Sklitsis and John Sollami spent many long hours keeping us on schedule. Yvonne Gerin and Chris Migdol worked hard to find many excellent photographs. AGT and Deborah Schneck produced a stunning design. Marjorie Payne, our production administrator at Allyn and Bacon, worked prodigiously to coordinate a complicated manuscript and kept it flowing smoothly on a very tight schedule. Finally, Fred Hamden and Scott Rubin combined to create one of the most impressive marketing campaigns we could ever have imagined.

This Second Edition greatly profited from the painstaking reviews and comments of

James Anderson	Texas A&M University
Judith Baer	Texas A&M University
Christine Barbour	Indiana University
Stephen A. Borrelli	University of Alabama
Ann Bowman	University of South Carolina
Steve Chan	University of Colorado
Clarke E. Cochran	Texas Tech University
Anne N. Costain	University of Colorado
John Domino	Sam Houston State University
Alan S. Engel	Miami University
Stacia L. Haynie	Louisiana State University
Marjorie Hershey	Indiana University
Cornell Hooton	Emory University
Dennis Judd	University of Missouri-St.Louis
Donald F. Kettl	University of Wisconsin
Nancy Kucinski	University of North Texas
John Kincaid	University of North Texas
Valerie Martinez	University of North Texas

Clifton McCleskey	University of Virginia
Joseph Nogee	University of Houston
Mary Alice Nye	University of North Texas
Richard Pacelle	University of Missouri-St. Louis
Marian Lief Palley	University of Delaware
Leroy N. Rieselbach	Indiana University
David Robertson	Public Policy Research Centers, University of Missouri-St.Louis
Frank Rourke	Johns Hopkins University
Frank J. Sorauf	University of Minnesota

American Government

Part One

Foundations of Government

The accumulation of all powers, legislative, executive, and judiciary, in the same hands . . . may justly be pronounced the very definition of tyranny.

James Madison
Federalist No. 47

The creation of the American system of government, as this quotation from The Federalist Papers *indicates, was motivated above all by the need to break away from the English model of government and its arbitrary concentration and use of power. The colonists wanted a representative government in which their elected officials would consider their needs and opinions when forming policies that affected their lives.*

CHAPTER 1

American Government: Roots and Reform

WHERE DID OUR IDEAS OF GOVERNMENT COME FROM?
DEVISING A NATIONAL GOVERNMENT
WHY A CAPITALIST SYSTEM?
UNDERSTANDING OUR DEMOCRATIC SYSTEM

*I*t is not only Americans who have wrestled with the problems of creating a government to meet their needs. In 1789, cries of "Liberty, Equality, and Fraternity" rang out in France as members of the working class, inspired by the American Revolution, rose up against King Louis XVI. The king, members of his family, and many French aristocrats were executed. Civil unrest continued and mobs controlled Paris until order was restored through the creation of a provisional government.

In the early 1900s in Russia, the radical Bolshevik Party mobilized citizens who were demoralized by war and who were without jobs or food, to overthrow and ultimately execute Czar Nicholas II and his family. The Bolshevik Revolution was followed by a period of civil war, and the Union of Soviet Socialist Republics was created from the ruins of the Russian Empire. Inspired by the Bolshevik model, Chinese communists similarly established a communist government in the late 1940s after a prolonged period of civil war.

More recently, these once revolutionary communist governments have themselves been faced with revolutionary discontent. In 1989, Chinese students demonstrated for democracy in Tienanmen Square, but to little avail. The communist rulers responded with a massive and bloody show of force that left many dead or injured. These events caused little political change in China. The early 1990s, however, saw the breakup of the Soviet Union. Most of this breakup was spurred by citizen demands, particularly in Eastern Europe, for democratization. In one new Eastern European state after another, citizens have gone to the polls to elect new leaders. Some of the changes have occurred with relatively little violence; others, such as the carving out of Bosnia-Herzogovenia from the former Yugoslavia, have produced all-out war and tremendous personal tragedy.

One of the hallmarks of the American system of government, the peaceful transition of power from one administration to the next, stands in marked contrast to such power shifts under other systems. Russians and the entire world watched in horror as the Russian parliament building burned in the chaos and violence that accompanied the break-up of the Soviet Union.

In each of these situations, whether peaceful or not, men and women have attempted to create new political systems to resolve the classic, age-old question of politics: Who gets what, when, and how?

Even in the short time between when you get up in the morning and when you leave for classes or work, this question pervades your life. The national or state government, for example, sets the standards for whether you wake up on Eastern, Central, or Western Time. The national government regulates the airwaves and licenses the radio or television broadcasts you might tune in to as you eat and get dressed. States, also, regulate and tax telecommunications. Whether the water you use as you brush your teeth contains fluoride is a state or local governmental issue. The federal Food and Drug Administration inspects your breakfast meat and sets standards for the advertising on your cereal box, orange juice carton, and other food packaging. And states set standards for food labelling. Are the elements of your breakfast really "lite," "high in fiber," or "fresh squeezed"? Usually, one or more levels of government is authorized to decide these matters.

How governments get their powers, and what rights their citizens or subjects retain, is a major focus of this book. All governments—whether democracies, such as the United States, Great Britain, and France, or authoritarian regimes such as Iraq under Saddam Hussein—exercise some kind of authority over the daily lives of their people. To understand how the U. S. government and our political system work today, it is critical to understand the philosophies that guided the American colonists as they created a system of governance different from those then in existence. It is also necessary to know how that system evolved and changed in order to understand better how government affects you and the world around you. And, just as important, a thorough understanding of the workings of government will allow you to question and think about the system—the good parts and the bad—and decide for yourself the advantages and disadvantages of possible reforms.

The question of who exercises power, and how and why they acquired it, is important to understanding a political system. As we will see, there is no simple answer to that question. For example, do elected representatives actually represent the people who elect them, or do they respond to other interests? High school civics classes often

Spring Forward, Fall Back

❖ ❖ ❖

Daylight Saving Time was introduced during World War I as a measure to save coal, which was used to produce electricity for lighting. In order to provide more natural light at the end of the working day, clocks are advanced one hour. In the United States, Daylight Saving Time begins on the first Sunday in April (clocks are moved ahead one hour) and ends on the last Sunday in October (clocks are moved back one hour). Any state may decide to remain on Standard Time during this period, as do Arizona and Hawaii; Indiana even allows *counties* to decide whether to switch.

Source: USA *Today,* April 2–4, 1991: p. 1-A.

American Government: Roots and Reform   5

The break-up of the Soviet Union was not met with universal support within the populace. Here, a Russian man poignantly clings to the old Soviet flag and the symbol of the Soviet communism.

teach that elected representatives, working through legitimate channels, produce policies and govern. Yet simple explanations such as this one do not hold together. How, for example, could the savings and loan crisis, involving massive failures of numerous savings and loan banks, have occurred? Despite numerous national and state banking laws designed to prevent banks from going under, precisely that happened, often taking the savings of many Americans along with them. Laws were broken, many who were involved got very rich, and few went to jail. Yet, the final "bill" to the American taxpayer was over one hundred and fifty billion dollars.

The public, political parties, interest groups, the bureaucracy, and congressional committees are just part of the answer to the question of who has power, and why and how it is used. Consider, for example, the tobacco industry in the United States. A 1991 draft report from the Environmental Protection Agency concluded that *secondhand* cigarette smoke kills 53,000 nonsmokers annually. The U. S. Surgeon General requires strong warnings on tobacco products concerning the link between tobacco use and cancer. Nevertheless, not only does the government permit smoking, but it also provides *billions* of dollars a year in subsidies to tobacco farmers. At the same time, however, the national, state, and even some local governments tax cigarettes. In 1993 the federal excise tax on cigarettes was 24 cents a pack, and state excise taxes ranged from 2.5 cents in Virginia (a major tobacco-growing state) to 51 cents in Massachusetts. But in spite of the health threat, taxes on cigarettes are lower in the United States than in virtually any other industrialized nation.

In the case of cigarettes, the powerful tobacco lobby, in conjunction with equally powerful senators and representatives from tobacco-growing states, has been instrumental in seeing that the tobacco industry is allowed to flourish. In contrast, red dye number 2, used to add color to certain food products, was banned in the mid-1970s when it, like tobacco, was found to contain cancer-causing agents. Unlike tobacco, it had few supporters (lobbyists) to argue for its continued use in the food industry.

Although all governments have problems, it is important to stress the good they can do in their attempts to decide who gets what, when, and how. In the aftermath of the Great Depression in the United States, for example, the government created the Social Security program, which dramatically decreased poverty among the elderly. Our contract laws and judicial system provide an efficient framework for business, assuring people that they have a recourse in the courts should someone fail to deliver goods or services as promised. And even something seemingly as mundane as our uniform bankruptcy laws help protect both a business enterprise and its creditors if the business collapses.

Just as it is important to recognize that governments serve many important purposes, it is also important to recognize that government and **politics,** the process by which policy decisions are made, are not static. They are part of a never-ending dynamic process of action and interaction. Governmental actions do not occur in isolation. The United States and its people, for example, are actors in a world order that from this nation's beginning has affected and continues to affect our laws, policies, and actions. Undoubtedly, the Framers at the Constitutional Convention in Philadelphia were reacting to what they viewed as the tyrannical rule of King George when they drafted Article II of the Constitution, creating a president of the United States. Similarly, the actions of President George Bush and the U. S. Congress in the Persian Gulf War of 1991 were the product of a series of events and reactions to them. So too were President Bill Clinton's approach to the crisis in Bosnia-Herzogovenia. The unpopular and unsuccessful Vietnam War, the United States need for oil, Iraq's invasion of Kuwait, reelection concerns, and probably even George Bush's desire to be viewed as a strong leader—all contributed to some extent to the final decision to deploy troops and then to commence Operation Desert Storm. Similarly, Bill Clinton's decision not to send

Women in combat: Operation Desert Storm. In August 1990, Iraq invaded the oil-rich country of Kuwait. In response, President Bush sent tens of thousands of U.S. troops to contain Iraq's army. For the first time in U.S. history, Americans were faced with the reality of women in the armed services. Here, a young mother displays a photo of her infant left at home as she fights in the Gulf.

ground troops into Eastern Europe, in spite of numerous urgings to do so, was also the product of his perception of the crisis and past events. Thus, many major national and international policy decisions have their roots in the politics and policies of the past. The lessons of history are often in the mind of policy makers as they seek to lead the nation on a sure course.

Where Did Our Ideas of Government Come From?

The current American political system did not spring into being overnight. It is the result of an intellectual tradition, as well as trial and error, and even luck. To understand how we came to have the form of government we have today, we must first understand the theories of government that influenced the Framers.

From Aristotle to the Enlightenment

Aristotle (384–322 B.C.) and the Greeks were the first to articulate the notion of **natural law,** the doctrine that human affairs should be governed by certain ethical principles. Being nothing more nor less than the nature of things, these principles can be understood by reason. In the thirteenth century, the Italian priest and philosopher Thomas Aquinas (1225–1274) gave the idea of natural law a new, Christian framework, arguing that natural law and Christianity were compatible because God created the natural law that established individual rights to life and liberty. In contradiction to this view, throughout Europe, kings continued to rule as absolute monarchs by divine right from God. Thus, citizens were bound by the government under which they found themselves, regardless of whether they had a say in its workings: If government reflected God's will, who could argue with it?

In the early sixteenth century, a religious movement to reform the doctrine and institutions of Roman Catholicism began to sweep through Europe. In many cases, these efforts at reform resulted in the founding of Protestant churches separate from their Catholic source. This Reformation and the resultant growth in the Protestant faith, which promoted the belief that people could talk directly to God without the intervention of a priest, altered the nature of government as people began to believe they could also have a say in their own governance. So did the ideas of philosophers and scientists such as Isaac Newton (1642–1727) during the period called the Enlightenment. Newton and others argued that the world could be improved through the use of human reason, science, and religious toleration. He and other theorists directly challenged earlier notions that fate alone controlled an individual's destiny and that kings ruled by divine right. Together the intellectual and religious developments of the Reformation and Enlightenment periods encouraged people to seek alternatives to absolute monarchy and to ponder new methods of governing.

A Growing Idea: Popular Consent

In England, when one faction called "separatists" split from the Anglican church, they did so believing that the ability to speak directly to God gave them the power to par-

The Mayflower Compact. While on the Mayflower, English colonists drew up a compact declaring their intention to form a "Civil Body Politick," or government, to preserve order and peace.

ticipate directly in the governing of their own local congregations. In establishing self-governing congregations, the separatists were responsible for the first widespread appearance of self-government in the form of social compacts. The separatists who moved to the English colonies in America brought their beliefs about self-governance with them. The Mayflower Compact, written while that ship was still at sea, reflects this tradition. Although it addressed itself to secular government, the Pilgrims called it a "covenant" (its form was akin to other common religious "covenants"; note the use of this word in the reproduction of the Mayflower Compact above) adopted by Congregationalists, Presbyterians, and Baptists.[1]

Two English theorists of the seventeenth century, Thomas Hobbes (1588–1679) and John Locke (1632–1704), built on conventional notions in proposing a social contract theory of government (see "People of the Past," p. 10). In contrast to Aquinas and the theorists of God-ordained government, they argued that even before the creation of governments, all individuals were free and equal by natural right. This freedom, in turn, required that all men give their consent to be governed.[2]

Hobbes and Locke. In his now-classic political treatise *Leviathan* (1651), Hobbes argued pessimistically that man's natural state was war. In his attempt to make sense

---

[1] The English and Scots often signed covenants with their churches in a pledge to defend and further their religion. In the Bible, covenants were solemn promises made to humanity by God. In the colonial context, then, covenants were formal agreements sworn to a new government to abide by its terms.

[2] The term *men* is used here because only males were considered fit to vote.

The title page from Thomas Hobbes's *Leviathan*, 1651

of King Charles's restoration to the throne, he theorized that life without government was a "state of nature," where, without written, enforceable rules, people would live like animals—foraging for food, stealing, and killing when necessary. To escape the horrors of the natural state, Hobbes argued, men must, in order to protect their lives, give up to government certain rights. Without government, Hobbes warned, life would basically be "solitary, poor, nasty, brutish, and short"—a constant struggle to survive against the evil of others. For this reason, governments had to intrude on people's rights and liberties in order to better control society and provide the proper safeguards for property.

People of the Past

Hobbes

Thomas Hobbes was born in 1588 in Gloucestershire (Glouster), England and began his formal education at the age of four. By age six he was learning Latin and Greek, and by nineteen he had obtained his bachelor's degree from Oxford University. In 1608, Hobbes accepted a position as a family tutor with the Earl of Devonshire, a post he retained for the rest of his life.

Hobbes was greatly influenced by the chaos of the English Civil War of the mid-seventeenth century. Its impact is evident in his most famous work, *Leviathan* (1651), a treatise on governmental theory that states his views on Man and Citizen. *Leviathan* is commonly described as a book about politics, but it also deals with religion and moral philosophy. Hobbes characterized humans as selfishly individualistic and constantly at war with one another. Without an effective government, argued Hobbes, life would be "solitary, poor, nasty, brutish, and short." People, he claimed, surrendered themselves to rulers in exchange for protection from their neighbors.

Hobbes was quite an energetic man, and at the age of eighty-four he wrote his autobiography in Latin verse. He died at the age of ninety-one.

Locke

John Locke, born in England in 1632, was admitted to an outstanding public school at the age of fifteen. It was there that he began to question his upbringing in the Puritan faith. At twenty he went on to study at Oxford, where he became a lecturer in Aristotelian philosophy. Soon, however, he found a new interest in medicine and experimental science.

In 1666, Locke met Anthony Ashley Cooper, the first Earl of Shaftesbury, a liberal politician. It was through Cooper that Locke discovered his own talent for philosophy. In 1689, Locke published his most famous work, *Second Treatise on Civil Government,* in which he set forth a theory of natural rights. He used the concept of natural rights to support his "social contract [theory]—the view that the consent of the people is the only true basis of any sovereign's right to rule." Governments exist, he argued, because individuals agree through a contract to form one to protect their rights under natural law. They agree to abide by decisions made by majority vote in the resolution of disputes. Locke died on October 28, 1704 at the age of seventy-two.

Hobbes argued strongly for a single ruler, no matter how evil, to guarantee the rights of the weak against the strong. Leviathan, a biblical sea monster, was his characterization of an all-powerful government. Strict adherence to Leviathan's laws, however encompassing or intrusive on liberty, was but a small price to pay for living in a civilized society, or even for life itself.

In contrast, John Locke—like many other political philosophers of the era—took the basic survival of humanity for granted and argued that government's major responsibility was the preservation of private property, an idea that ultimately found its way into the Constitution of the United States. In two of his works (*Essay Concerning Hu-*

man Understanding [1690] and *Second Treatise on Civil Government* [1689]), Locke responded to King James II's abuses of power directed at the Anglican church and Parliament. Locke denied the divine right of kings to govern. More important, he argued that men were born equal and with equal rights in nature that no king had the power to void. Under what Locke termed **social contract theory,** the consent of the people is the only true basis of any sovereign's right to rule. According to Locke, men form governments largely to preserve life, liberty, and property, and to assure justice. If governments act improperly, they break their "contract" with the people and therefore no longer enjoy the consent of the governed. Because he believed that true justice comes from laws, Locke argued that the branch of government that makes laws—as opposed to the one that enforces or interprets laws—should be the most powerful.

Locke believed that a chief executive to administer laws was important, but that he should necessarily be limited by law or by the "social contract" with the governed. Locke's writings influenced many American colonists, especially Thomas Jefferson, whose original draft of the Declaration of Independence noted the rights to "life, liberty, and property" as key reasons to split from England.[3]

Devising a National Government

Although social contract theorists agreed on the need for government, they did not necessarily agree on the form that a government should take. Thomas Hobbes argued for a single leader; John Locke and Jean-Jacques Rousseau, a French philosopher (1712–1778) saw the need for less centralized power.

As depicted in Table 1.1, the colonists rejected a system with a strong ruler, like the British **monarchy,** as soon as they had declared their independence. Most European monarchical systems gave hereditary rulers absolute power over all forms of activity. Many of the colonists had fled from Great Britain to avoid religious persecution and other harsh manifestations of power wielded by George II, whom they viewed as a malevolent despot. They naturally were reluctant to put themselves in the same position in their new nation.

While some colonies such as Massachusetts originally established theocracies in which religious leaders eventually ruled claiming divine guidance, they later looked to more secular forms of governance. Colonists also did not want to create an **oligarchy,** or "rule by the few," in which the right to participate is conditioned on the possession of wealth or property. Aristotle defined this form of government as a perversion of an **aristocracy,** or "rule of the highest." Again, the colonists were fearful of replicating the landed and titled system of the British aristocracy and viewed the formation of a representative form of government as far more in keeping with the ideas of social contract theorists. But the **democracy** in which we live, as settled on by the Framers, is difficult to define. Nowhere is the word mentioned in the Declaration of Independence or the U. S. Constitution. Like many of our ideas about government, however, the term comes from two Greek words: *demos* (the people) and *kratia* (power or authority). Thus, democracy can be interpreted as a form of government that gives power to the people. The question, then, is how and to which people is this power given?

---

[3] Jefferson ultimately and without explanation changed these words to "Life, Liberty, and the pursuit of Happiness," although most of the signers were far more concerned with property.

Table 1.1 ♦ Types of Government

TYPES	EXAMPLE	HOW MANY ARE INVOLVED IN THE GOVERNING PROCESS
Monarchy	Eighteenth-century Great Britain	One
Oligarchy	El Salvador, 1960s Brazil, 1970s	Small number
Aristocracy	Seventeenth-century Poland Haiti, 1980s	Small number
Indirect Democracy	United States today	Many
Direct Democracy	Ancient Athens	Nearly all (free males)

The Theory of Democratic Government

As evidenced by the early creation of the Virginia House of Burgesses in 1619, and its objections to "taxation without representation," the colonists were quick to create participatory forms of government in which most men (subject to some landowning requirements) were allowed to participate. The New England town meeting (see "Then and Now," p. 13), where all citizens gather to discuss and decide issues facing the town, today stands as a surviving example of a **direct democracy**, such as was used in ancient Greece when all free, male citizens came together periodically to pass laws and "elect" leaders by lot.

Direct democracies, however, soon proved unworkable in the colonies. Although Rousseau argued that true democracy is impossible unless *all* citizens participate in governmental decision-making, as more and more settlers came to the New World, many town meetings were replaced by a system called **indirect** or **representative democracy.** Ironically, this system of government, in which representatives of the people are chosen by ballot, was considered undemocratic by ancient Greeks, who believed that all citizens must have a direct say in their governance.

Representative or indirect democracies, which call for the election of representatives to a governmental decision-making body, were formed first in the colonies and then in the new Union. Many citizens were uncomfortable with the term "democracy" and used the term **republic** to avoid any confusion between the system adopted and direct democracy. Even today, representative democracies are more commonly called "republics" and the words "democracy" and "republic" often are used interchangeably. Historically, the term "republic" implied a system of government in which the interests of the people were represented by more educated or wealthier citizens. In the early days of America, for example, only those who owned land could vote. But today, those barriers no longer exist.

What Are the Characteristics of American Democracy?

The United States is an indirect democracy with several distinguishing characteristics. Tremendous value is placed on the individual. All individuals are deemed rational and fair, and endowed, as Thomas Jefferson proclaimed in the Declaration of

Over the years, the electorate has expanded as more and more diverse groups have been able to exercise the franchise. Political equality implies that all citizens have an equal opportunity to cast their ballot on election day free from discriminatory laws or practices designed to prevent their exercise of that basic right.

Then and Now

Direct Democracy

The town meeting, which is still the form of government of some municipalities in New England, is an example of direct democracy. Starting in colonial times, the men of the town would congregate at the local meeting hall to discuss issues ranging from public drunkenness to education.

Today some people suggest that electronic voting provides a means to return to direct democracy. This idea received particular attention during the 1992 presidential campaign when candidate Ross Perot called for electronic town meetings in which officials would offer three possible solutions to a public problem and viewers would electronically vote for their choice.*

Different plans—including voting by telephone, interactive TV, computer bulletin boards and on-line information services—have been proposed as possible means of conducting electronic voting. USA VOTE, a nonpartisan, nonprofit group located in Arlington, Virginia, has launched an interactive public affairs television show that consists of a 30-minute debate on a specific issue followed by an opportunity for viewers to call a toll-free number and express their opinions.

Interactive Network, Inc., a California-based company, offers another method of electronic political interaction. Consumers who purchase this firm's control units at retail stores (at a cost of $199) gain interactive access to various news programs, sports events and information services. San Franciscans had the opportunity to utilize this network after each televised presidential debate of 1992. A viewer subscribing to the service was able to vote on issues raised in the debate by pushing buttons on the control unit. Computers then compiled results and displayed them on the control unit's screen.

However, practical and philosophical problems exist with all methods. When CBS asked viewers to call in questions after George Bush's 1992 State of the Union Address, only 315,000 of 25 million calls got through. Other problems include deciding who controls the agenda, ensuring that the meetings have a representative sample of the population, providing electronic access for poor citizens, and preventing ballot-box stuffing. Political scientist Theodore Becker supports a "multilayer web of decentralized electronic meetings run by an independent, private commission and not by the White House or any government agency" to overcome some of these problems. Still, it is unlikely that a return to a pure direct democracy will occur in the near future.

An interactive TV unit

---

*Much of this discussion is adapted from Mitch Betts, "Electronic Town Meeting, A Safe Vote?," *Computerworld* (October 26, 1992): 25; and Katherine McCarron, "Lobbying Congress from Your La-Z-Boy," *The National Journal* (November 21, 1992): 2688.

14 ❖ Chapter 1 American Government: Roots and Reform

Lani Guinier waits on the steps of the University of Pennsylvania Law School to be interviewed on the air. Guinier told reporters that President Clinton's withdrawal of her nomination to head the Civil Rights Division in the Department of Justice was "fundamentally unfair."

Independence "with certain unalienable rights." And the individual is deemed more important than the state.

Another key characteristic of our democracy is the American emphasis on political equality, the definition of which has varied considerably over time (as discussed in Chapter 5). The importance of political equality is another reflection of American stress on the importance of the individual. Although some individuals clearly wield more political clout than others, the adage "one man, one vote" implies a sense of political equality for all.

Popular consent, the idea that governments must draw their powers from the consent of the governed, is another distinguishing characteristic of American democracy. Derived from social contract theory, the notion of popular consent was central to the Declaration of Independence and its underlying assumption that governments *must* derive their powers from the consent of the governed. A citizen's willingness to vote is thus an essential premise of democracy.

Majority rule and the preservation of minority rights are two additional facets of American democracy. Majority rule implies that only policies supported by most of the population will be made into law. This right of the majority to govern themselves is summed up by the term **popular sovereignty.** This term, however, did not come into wide usage until pre-Civil War debates over slavery. At that time, supporters of popular sovereignty argued that the citizens of new states seeking admission to the Union should be able to decide whether or not their states would allow slavery within their borders.

Today, emphasis on majority rule also usually stresses concern with minority rights, although tension between the two concepts still exists. One example of that tension is illustrated by the issues and controversy generated over President Bill Clinton's nomination of his long-time friend and former law school classmate Lani Guinier, a University of Pennsylvania Law School professor, to head the Civil Rights Division of the U. S. Justice Department. When her position on the respective roles of the majority and the minority became public, the controversy was such that Clinton was forced to withdraw her nomination. In a 1991 *Michigan Law Review* article, Guinier attacked a "hostile permanent (white) majority" often unwilling to give minorities in legislatures their share of power. Thus Guinier proposed, among other things, a "minority veto" to allow black legislators the ability to veto measures passed by majorities in cases where minority legislators were unable to make inroads. Once he read her work, even Clinton was unwilling to accept Guinier's ideas or defend them, noting, "I cannot fight a battle . . . if I do not believe in the ground of the battle."[4]

Personal liberty is perhaps the single most important characteristic of American democracy. The Constitution itself was written to assure "life" and "liberty." Over the years, our concepts of liberty have changed. Liberty was first considered to be freedom "from." Thus, Americans were to be free from governmental infringements on freedom of religion and speech, from unreasonable search and seizure, and so on (see Chapter 4). The addition to the Constitution of the Fourteenth Amendment and its emphasis on equal protection of the laws and subsequent passage of laws guaranteeing civil rights, however, expanded Americans' concept of liberty to include demands for "freedom to" be free from discrimination. Debates over how much the government should do to guarantee these rights or liberties illustrate the conflicts that continue to occur in our democratic system.

---

[4] Margaret Carlson, "Where Is 'My Center'?" *Time* (June 14, 1993): 22.

Hillary Rodham Clinton became only the third First Lady (the other two were Eleanor Roosevelt and Rosalyn Carter) to address a congressional committee. Rodham Clinton, in fact, appeared before five congressional committees to explain and lobby on behalf of the administration's health care plan. Health care is yet another example of how Americans' view of the proper role of government has changed over time.

Who Makes Decisions in America?

How conflicts are resolved, and how much emphasis is placed on any of these characteristics of American democracy, is often determined by how the government is operated, and by whom. Over the years, several theorists have posited widely different points of view in their attempts to answer this important question. No one view completely explains "who gets what, when, and how," although most political scientists of today probably subscribe to the pluralist view (see p. 16).[5] Nevertheless, a knowledge of these divergent perspectives will make it possible for you to analyze political questions from more than one vantage point.

Elite Theory. In *The Power Elite* (1956), American sociologist C. Wright Mills argued that important policies are set by a loose coalition of three groups with some overlap among them. According to his **elite theory,** these three major influencers of policy—corporate leaders, military leaders, and a small group of key governmental leaders—are the true "power elite" in America. (Other elite theorists have argued that the news media should be included as a fourth element in the United States.) These elite theorists believe that government has become increasingly alienated from the people and is rarely responsive to their wishes.

---

[5] Harold D. Lasswell, *Politics: Who Gets What, When, and How* (New York: McGraw-Hill, 1938).

Bureaucratic Theory. Max Weber (1864–1920), the founder of modern sociology, argued that *all* institutions, governmental and nongovernmental, have fallen under the control of a large and ever-growing bureaucracy. This view is called **bureaucratic theory.** Because all institutions have grown more complex, Weber concluded that the expertise and competence of bureaucrats allows them to wrest power from others, especially elected officials. As we will see in Chapter 8, there is no doubt that in certain policy areas bureaucrats carry increasing amounts of power. Politicians come and go, yet most bureaucrats stay on in their positions for a good part of their working lives.

Interest Group Theory. Political scientist David B. Truman postulated what is termed the **interest group theory** of democracy in *The Governmental Process* (1951). According to Truman, interest groups—not elites, sets of elites, or bureaucrats—control the governmental process.[6]

Truman believes there are so many potential pressure points in the executive, legislative, and judicial branches of the federal government—as well as at the state level—that groups can step in on any number of competing sides, and that government becomes the equilibrium point in the system.

Pluralist Theory. Another, more widely accepted theory about the nature of power is held by those who follow the *pluralist* school of thought. According to political scientists such as Robert Dahl, the structure of our democratic government allows only for a pluralist model of democracy. Borrowing from Truman's work, Dahl argued that resources are scattered so widely in our diverse democracy that no single elite group can ever have a monopoly over any substantial area of policy. In *Who Governs?* (1961), for example, Dahl concluded that political competition and elections coupled with the growing ethnic and socioeconomic diversity of New Haven, Connecticut, led to a situation in which a single elite could never take and hold power legally. James Madison had argued in *Federalist No. 10* that a large number of interests and "factions" clashing in the public arena serve to enhance compromise. Dahl observed this need for compromise in New Haven in the areas of public education, urban renewal, and political nomination.[7]

Adding to this debate, political scientist Theodore J. Lowi has coined the term "interest group liberalism" to describe how political decision-making occurs today. According to Lowi, participants in every political controversy get something; thus, each has some impact on how political decisions are made. Lowi also states that governments rarely say no to any well-organized interests. Thus, all interests ultimately receive some benefits or rewards. Lowi bemoans the fact that the public interest (what is good for the public at large) often tends to lose in this system.[8]

All these theories provide interesting ways to begin to view how policy decisions are made, whether at local, state, or national levels. It could be, as Dahl has argued, that no single group or interest can ever have a monopoly over any issue, let alone over

---

[6] David B. Truman, *The Governmental Process* (New York: Knopf, 1951).

[7] See also Robert Dahl, *Dilemmas of Pluralist Democracy: Autonomy vs. Control* (New Haven, CT: Yale University Press, 1982) and Iris Marion Young, *Justice and the Politics of Difference* (Princeton, NJ: Princeton University Press, 1990).

[8] Theodore S. Lowi, *The End of Liberalism* (New York: Norton, 1979), Chapter 3.

larger policy programs. It also stands to reason that the patterns we discover in the United States may apply to a certain extent in other parts of the world.

Why a Capitalist System?

In addition to fashioning a democratic form of government, the colonists were also confronted with the dilemma of what kind of role the government should play in the economy. Concerns with liberty, both personal and economic, were always at the forefront of their actions and decisions in creating a new government. They were well aware of the need for a well-functioning economy, and saw that government had a key role in maintaining this. What constitutes a malfunction in the economy, however, and what steps the government should take to remedy it, were questions that dogged the Framers and continue to puzzle politicians and theorists today (see Chapter 17).

The private ownership of property and a **free market economy** are key tenets of the American system called **capitalism.** In contrast to **socialism,** in which the working class owns and controls all means of production and distribution, capitalism favors private control of business and minimal governmental regulation of private industry.

Capitalism. Capitalism is a mode of economic production characterized by private ownership by individuals or groups of land, factories, raw materials, and other instruments of production. It is the economic system found in the United States, Great Britain, and most nations of Western Europe. In capitalist systems, the laws of supply and demand in the marketplace and free trade set prices of goods and drive production.

In 1776, the same year as the signing of the Declaration of Independence, Adam Smith (1723–1790) published *An Inquiry into the Nature and Causes of the Wealth of Nations* (generally known as *The Wealth of Nations*). Smith's book marked the beginning of the modern capitalist era. He argued that free trade would result in full production and economic health. These ideas were greeted with great enthusiasm in the colonies as independence was proclaimed. Colonists no longer wanted to participate in the mercantile system of Great Britain and other Western European nations. These systems bound trade and its administration to national goals and not those of the individual. Smith and his supporters saw free trade as "the invisible hand" that produced the wealth of nations. This wealth, in turn, became the inspiration and justification for capitalism.

Under capitalism, sales occur for the profit of the individual. Capitalists believe that both national and individual production is greatest when individuals are free to do as they wish with their property and goods. The government, however, plays an indispensable role in creating and enforcing the rules of the game. One such rule is the "contract clause" in the U.S. Constitution, which prevents states from extending the time in which debtors can meet their payments or get out of contractual obligations.

From the mid- to late eighteenth century through the mid-1930s in the United States and in much of the Western world, the idea of *laissez-faire* economics (from the French, to let do) enjoyed considerable popularity. While most states regulated and intervened heavily in their economies well into the nineteenth century, the national governments routinely followed a "hands off" economic policy. By the late 1800s, however (as discussed in Chapters 8, 16, and 17) the U. S. government felt increasing pressure to regulate some aspects of the nation's economy. This pressure often arose

> ## Understanding the "ISMs"
> ♦ ♦ ♦
>
> These humorous definitions of political systems of the world appeared in an FDR-era farm journal:
>
> **Socialism:** You have two cows. The government takes one and gives it to your neighbor because he doesn't have a cow.
>
> **Communism:** You have two cows. The government takes both and gives you the milk.
>
> **Nazism:** You have two cows. The government takes both and shoots you.
>
> **New Dealism:** You have two cows. The government takes both and shoots one, milks the other and throws the milk away.
>
> **Capitalism:** You have two cows. You sell one and buy a bull.
>
> *Atlanta Journal-Constitution,* June 20, 1993: A2.

from the difficulties states faced in regulating large multistate industries such as the railroads, and big industry's desire to override the patchwork of regulations produced by the states. Thus, true capitalism ceased to exist.[9] The extent of this trend, however, varied by country and over time. In post–World War II Britain, for example, the extent of government economic regulation in industrial policy and social welfare was much greater than that attempted by American policy makers in the same period.

Socialism. Reaction to the overwhelming wealth of millionaire industrialists and a corresponding exploitation of workers in France, England, and ultimately the United States, led to the development of socialism, a philosophy that advocates collective ownership and control of the means of economic production. Karl Marx (1818–1883), the German socialist and founder of communism, once stated that socialism was a transitional phase between capitalism and communism.

In direct opposition to the ideas of capitalism favored by the Framers, socialists (and communists) call for governmental—rather than private—ownership of all land, property, and industry and, in turn, an equitable distribution of the income from those holdings. In Marx's words, "From each according to his ability, to each according to his needs."[10]

It is important to note that some socialists actually tolerate capitalism as long as the government maintains some kind of control over the economy. Others, including communists, reject capitalism outright and insist on the abolition of all private enterprise. Thus, all communists are socialists, but not all socialists are communists.

Over the years, socialists have been united in their view of concern for all men and women, but have not agreed about the means by which to reach a socialist ideal.

Karl Marx

---

[9] Modern disciples of *laissez-faire* are called libertarians. Libertarians adamantly oppose all forms of government regulation and action unless it is critical to the protection of life, liberty, or property. They argue that while governments are at best an evil necessity, governments are best when they govern least.

[10] Karl Marx, "Critique of the Gotha Program," in *Marx Selections,* ed. Allen W. Wood (New York: Macmillan, 1988), p. 190.

Some, especially in Western Europe, have argued that socialism can evolve through democratic processes. Thus, in nations like Great Britain, certain critical industries or services such as health care or the coal industry have been *nationalized,* or taken over by the state to provide for more efficient supervision and to avoid the major concentrations of wealth that occur when individuals own key industries.

Communism. Karl Marx grew up in Germany as the socialist movement developed there and in many other parts of Western Europe. Its influence on him was profound. He came to argue that government was simply a manifestation of underlying economic forces and could be understood according to types of economic production.

According to Marx, all societies went through five stages:

(1) primitive communalism, (2) slavery, (3) feudalism, (4) capitalism, and (5) socialism. He believed that history brought with it an evolving economic and political system in which a class struggle between workers and property owners was inevitable. The clash of the interests of these two classes led to the development of the state or government. In turn, governments were used by rich capitalists, called by the French term *bourgeoisie,* to protect their property in much the same way that, according to Charles Beard, the Framers of the U. S. Constitution were motivated by their personal economic concerns when they drafted the Constitution (see p. 59). In *Das Kapital* (1867), Marx argued that capitalist states would inevitably be replaced by socialist states in which the working class would own the means of production and distribution and would be able to redistribute the wealth to meet its needs.

Ultimately, Marx advocated **communism,** a scheme more radical than socialism. Through communism Marx sought to abolish all class differences and to create a system of common ownership of the means of sustenance and production. In essence, Marx viewed communism as the sixth stage of history, beyond socialism. To achieve communism, Marx believed that capitalist systems would have to be overthrown, no matter how violent the means. The communism espoused by Marx, however, continues to be a theory. It was never fully implemented even in the former Soviet Union. In most countries that still profess communism, such as China, economic and political control are held by a single, frequently authoritarian political party. Moreover, economic growth and planning are overseen by some sort of central authority.

Totalitarianism. Whereas socialist and communist systems spread the wealth and control of publicly owned industries and other means of production to all members of society, in a **totalitarian** system governments retain unlimited powers for the benefit of elite rulers. In contrast to systems based on democratic beliefs, totalitarian governments have total authority over their people and their economies. George Orwell's novel *1984* is perhaps the best depiction of what a pure totalitarian regime would be like. The reign of the Ayatollah Ruhollah Khomeini in Iran from 1979 until his death, and that of President Saddam Hussein in Iraq, come close to the "total" control of forms of production, the airwaves, education, the arts, and even sports implied by totalitarianism. Some communist systems also approach totalitarianism.

Because total control by a single ruler or elite requires technological innovations and weapons of mass destruction that only modern science can provide, totalitarianism, even in partial form, did not present itself to the world until well into the 1900s.[11]

---

[11] Hannah Arendt, *The Origins of Totalitarianism* (Cambridge, MA: Harvard University Press, 1958).

Even Adolf Hitler's Germany, perhaps the most totalitarian government that has appeared so far, probably lacked the resources to assert complete control over every aspect of life for all citizens.

Understanding Our Democratic System

One key to understanding our democratic system is a recognition of the role that history and its lessons have played in the development of the American political system. The lessons of history provide a context in which to understand not only policies of the past but also policies today. Changes in ideas and public expectations about government lead to reform no less than do crisis situations.

Changes in Ideas and Public Expectations. Americans' ideas about and expectations of their government have changed and grown tremendously since colonial times. As ideas about social compacts were adopted and transmitted to the New World, colonists' ideas of government were altered. Once the Declaration of Independence and Constitution were drafted, expectations about the role of government evolved and continue to evolve.

Expectations about the "proper" role of government are often tempered by an individual's (or government's) ideological approach. As discussed in Chapter 10, whether one is "liberal" (by today's definition, generally favoring social and political reform and governmental solutions) or "conservative" (favoring the existing order with less governmental intervention in business or society), may also affect expectations. Although many continue to debate government's proper role, public opinion polls reveal that most Americans have come to expect "big government," and to want the government—especially the national government—to tackle economic and social problems. Thus, while a small percent of Americans are libertarians, those who stress that government should not involve itself in the plight of the people or attempt to remedy any social ills, most Americans today look to government for support in many areas, including education, medical research, and relief from poverty.

In the 1980s, for example, more than 175,000 people became infected with the HIV virus, and 109,000 of them died. Although AIDS was first viewed as a rare disease primarily afflicting homosexual men in California and New York, its demographics have changed, and now AIDS is the most common cause of non-accidental death among large segments of the population, including, for example, women in certain age groups. As more people from all groups and of all ages fall victim to AIDS, pressure on the national government to find a solution to this problem increases. Victims or those in high-risk groups are fighting for federal budget increases for AIDS research in addition to antidiscrimination legislation. Others argue for better screening of the blood supply and for compulsory testing of those in the medical profession. Governmental response was urged by C. Everett Koop, U. S. Surgeon General during Ronald Reagan's presidency, who played a major role in the decision to increase the federal government's effort for AIDS education over the protest of some conservative groups. Thus, as new problems occur, the public increasingly has looked to the government for help and solutions.

The Lessons of History. As historians are fond of noting, history often repeats itself. Clear cycles can be seen in the evolution of our democratic system. For example,

Mary Fisher, the wealthy, socialite daughter of the honorary chair of the Bush/Quayle Finance Committee, addresses the Republican National Convention in 1992. Fisher, who is HIV positive and the founder of the Family Aids Network, urged Republicans to recognize that government AIDS efforts were inadequate.

in the mid-1800s, many women's rights activists sought the right to vote on a state-by-state basis and rejected suggestions to seek a constitutional amendment. The same state-by-state approach was used later in the suffrage movement (1890–1920) by a new generation of women who sought the right to vote, but again it proved unworkable as efforts in individual states were costly and often unsuccessful. Women finally decided that an amendment to the U. S. Constitution would be the most expeditious way to secure voting rights.

In the 1980s, after a series of decisions indicated an increased willingness on the part of the U. S. Supreme Court to restrict abortion rights, pro-choice forces initially sought to fight for the right to an abortion on a state-by-state basis. But by mid-1991, the National Abortion Rights Action League (NARAL) had admitted that it had lost far more than it had won with this strategy as state after state passed increasingly restrictive laws. In an effort reminiscent of that adopted by women suffragists in the 1910s, NARAL decided to throw all its efforts behind passage of the national *Freedom of Choice Act* to guarantee a woman's right to an abortion free from any state restrictions. Thus, an understanding of the difficulty women have encountered historically helps us to understand the effectiveness (and even the adoption) of some political strategies today.

The Role of Crises and Reform. As government at all levels continues to grow, we cannot ignore the role that crises have played. The development of the power of the national government as well as realignments in the powers of the various institutions have also been affected by crises, as will be discussed in succeeding chapters. Crises do not affect only the American state; democracies like Britain have witnessed the shaping of their politics, institutions, and conflicts by unforeseen domestic and international emergencies. The two world wars, for example, placed many new issues on the national agenda—for example, nationalization of industry, social welfare, and economic planning.

Although the U. S. Civil War and other national crises, such as the Great Depression and even the Watergate scandal (see pp. 264–265), created major turmoil, they demonstrated that our system can survive and even change in the face of enormous political, societal, and even institutional crisis. Often, these crises have produced considerable reforms. The Civil War led to the dismantling of the slavery system and to the passage of the Thirteenth, Fourteenth, and Fifteenth Amendments (see Chapter 5), which led to the seeds of recognition of African Americans as American citizens. The Great Depression led to the New Deal and the creation of a government more actively involved in economic and social regulation. More recently, the Watergate scandal resulted in stricter ethics laws that have led to the resignation or removal of many elected officials.

In this text we present you with the tools to understand the political system in which you live. We hope that you will approach the study of American politics with an open mind. When you read a daily newspaper or watch a television news program, you are actually engaged in the study of politics. Your study of the processes of government should help you become a better citizen as you become more informed about your government and its operations. We hope that you learn to ask questions. Know who gets "what, when, and how." Learn to understand why a particular law was enacted. Ask, how was it implemented? And make sure your vote counts.

Summary

To understand how our current system of government works, it is important to understand choices that were made many years ago. To that end, in this chapter we have made the following points:

1. The American political system was based on several notions that have their roots in classical Greek ideas, including natural law, the doctrine that human affairs should be governed by certain ethical principles that can be understood by reason. Also heavily influencing our ideas of how government should work were the ideas of the Reformation, the period when people began to believe that they could talk directly to God without the intermediary of a priest; the Enlightenment, the movement in Western Europe in the 1700s that espoused human reason, science, and religious toleration; and the ideas of social contract theorists John Locke and Thomas Hobbes, who held the belief that people are free and equal by God-given right. In turn, this freedom requires that all men give their consent to be governed.

2. In devising a new national government and a democratic system, the colonists opted for an indirect democracy, or republic, in which citizens may vote for representatives to work on their behalf. Key ideals of this indirect democracy are the value of the individual, political equality, popular consent, majority rule and the preservation of minority rights, and personal liberty.

   Several different theories have been offered to explain how decisions are made in an indirect democracy. They include elite theory, the idea that important policies are set by three loose coalitions of groups including the military, corporate leaders, and a small set of government officials; bureaucratic theory, the belief that all governmental and nongovernmental institutions are, in effect, controlled by an all-powerful bureaucracy; interest group theory, the belief that interest groups—not elites, sets of elites, or bureaucrats—control the governmental process; and pluralist theory, in which resources are seen as so widely scattered in our diverse democracy that no single elite group can ever have a monopoly over any substantial area of policy.

3. The system set up by the Framers was capitalism, which advocates private ownership of property and a free market economy. Other nations have opted for socialism, which advocates public ownership and control of the means of economic production, or communism, in which government is seen simply as a manifestation of underlying economic forces, understood according to types of economic production.

4. Three factors are key to understanding our democratic system and its development: (1) changes in ideas and public expectations, (2) the lessons of history, and (3) the role of crisis and reform.

Key Terms

politics	indirect (representative) democracy	pluralist theory
natural law	republic	free market economy
social contract theory	popular consent	capitalism
monarchy	majority rule	socialism
oligarchy	popular sovereignty	*laissez-faire*
aristocracy	elite theory	communism
democracy	bureaucratic theory	totalitarian
direct democracy	interest group theory	

Suggested Readings

Bentley, Arthur. *The Process of Government.* Chicago: University of Chicago Press, 1908.

Dahl, Robert. *Polyarchy: Participation and Opposition.* New Haven, CT: Yale University Press, 1971.

———*Who Governs?* New Haven, CT: Yale University Press, 1961.

Hobbes, Thomas. *Leviathan.* New York: Everyman (Library Edition), 1914.

Locke, John. *Two Treatises of Government,* ed. Peter Lasleti. New York: Mentor, 1960.

Marx, Karl. *Das Kapital.* Chicago: Regnery, 1970.

Mills, C. Wright. *The Power Elite.* New York: Oxford University Press, 1956.

Schumpeter, Joseph A. *Capitalism, Socialism, and Democracy.* New York: Harper, 1942.

Schlesinger, Arthur M. *The Age of Jackson.* Boston: Little, Brown, 1945.

Truman, David. B. *The Governmental Process.* New York: Knopf, 1951.

Weber, Max. *From Max Weber: Essays in Sociology,* trans. and ed. H. H. Gerth and C. Wright Mills. London: Routledge & Kegan Paul, 1948.

Every view we may take of the subject, as candid inquirers after truth, will serve to convince us, that it is both unwise and dangerous to deny the federal government an unconfined authority.

James Madison
Federalist No. 23

According to the Federalists, the major triumph of the new Constitution was its expansive grant of authority to the new national government over, and "unconfined" by, the states.

CHAPTER 2

The Constitution

THE ORIGINS OF A NEW NATION

THE DECLARATION OF INDEPENDENCE

THE FIRST ATTEMPT AT GOVERNMENT:
THE ARTICLES OF CONFEDERATION

THE MIRACLE AT PHILADELPHIA: WRITING A CONSTITUTION

THE U.S. CONSTITUTION

THE DRIVE FOR RATIFICATION

AMENDING THE CONSTITUTION

TOWARD REFORM

*I*n *Federalist No. 23,* James Madison walked a tight line. He fervently wanted the citizenry to adopt the proposed constitution, which conferred considerable powers on the national government at the expense of the states, yet he realized that some citizens (and states) might object. He and the Framers were nonetheless willing to confront these objections. Madison and other Federalists were convinced that a new form of government, one with a written constitution defining its scope, was key to the continued survival of the states.

Today, Americans take their Constitution for granted. And although it is continually being reinterpreted, it has never been seriously questioned as the supreme law of the land. We might amend it occasionally, and we might change our minds over what it allows or does not allow, but we always rely on it. It is probably rare for more than a day or two to go by without your hearing about some action, policy, or practice being challenged as unconstitutional. Are laws or practices that favor one race over another constitutional? Are abortion restrictions unconstitutional? Moreover, as members of Congress deliberate potential legislation, the constitutionality of that legislation is often questioned.

In 1993, for example, some charged that Congress lacked the constitutional authority to enact a national Freedom of Choice Act ensuring the basic principles of the U.S. Supreme Court's decision in *Roe* v. *Wade* (1973) guaranteeing a woman's right to an abortion.

While today we take these kinds of questions in stride, in 1789 the Constitution was not adopted without question. Great Britain did not then have a written constitution,

The Constitution of the United States

nor does it today. Instead, Great Britain had a king, who was guided by a House of Lords to represent the nobility, and by a House of Commons to represent all others. Moreover, England and English courts were guided by principles of **common law**, the body of law in England that arose from judge-made decisions.

Since these "laws" were not written, common law underwent many changes as it was broadened by local custom and judicial interpretation. In addition to common law, there is an unwritten British "constitution," composed of statutory law and conventions—rules of behavior that have been followed for so long that they are regarded as binding, even though they lack the force of law. This "unwritten law" was quite different from the Constitution suggested by the Framers, which carefully created three branches of government and *expressly* gave certain powers to each branch.[1]

The authors of *The Federalist Papers*, Alexander Hamilton, James Madison, and John Jay, had to convince the electorate not only that the particular wording of the

---

[1] Sir William Blackstone attempted to codify the common laws' most widely accepted principles. His multi-volume *Commentaries on the Law of England* remain the single best source of English law.

Constitution proposed in 1789 was the best, but also that the new nation needed a written document at all. Moreover, they had to explain why they made the choices they did, and how and why the new system would be better than the existing government. Their task was made more difficult by the fact that their proposed constitution took away from the state governments many rights that they had acquired after breaking with Great Britain in 1776. Fortunately, because all thirteen states had drafted written constitutions after independence was declared, most colonists agreed on the need for a written plan of government. Looking outside the continent, however, they saw few models to imitate.

The idea of a written code of laws can be traced to ancient times. But by the seventeenth and eighteenth centuries, most European legal and governmental systems were rooted in the notion of the common law and in systems in which a monarch ruled through divine right (see Chapter 1). Since 1215, the British monarch's power had been limited somewhat by the Magna Carta, a charter signed by King John guaranteeing the people certain liberties, including landowners' and tenants' rights, the right to trial by jury, restrictions against unreasonable punishment, and some measure of religious freedom. In contrast, most other European monarchies had no written guarantees of rights.

In the New World, however, Massachusetts Bay colonists successfully lived according to a minimal set of rules contained in the Mayflower Compact of 1620 (as dis-

James Madison (left), Alexander Hamilton (center), and John Jay (right) were important early Federalist leaders. Jay wrote five of *The Federalist Papers,* and Madison and Hamilton wrote the rest. Madison served in the House of Representatives (1789–1797) and as Secretary of State in the Jefferson administration (1801–1808). In 1808 he was elected fourth president of the United States and served two terms (1809–1817). Hamilton became the first Secretary of the Treasury (1789–1795) at the age of thirty-four. He was killed in 1804 in a duel with vice-president Aaron Burr, who was angered by Hamilton's negative comments about his character. Jay became the first Chief Justice of the Supreme Court (1789–1795) and negotiated the Jay Treaty with Great Britain in 1794. He then served as governor of New York from 1795 to 1801.

cussed in Chapter 1). And later, in 1781, as discussed in this chapter, the thirteen colonies formally came together to form a union under the *written* **Articles of Confederation**, which established the basic framework for the national government that had directed the conduct of the Revolutionary War.

For the most part, the Framers charted new territory when writing the Constitution in 1789. Their achievement has survived for more than 200 years, and constitutional democracy has spread to many other countries. How did they do it? What issues did they face? What logic did they use? How can we understand their results? This chapter answers these questions by first examining the historical environment from which the Constitution emerged. We then analyze the document itself and turn to a discussion of how the Constitution has changed over time, through both formal and informal methods. We conclude with a review of proposals that have been made to change the Constitution to eliminate some problems unforeseen by the Founders.

The Origins of a New Nation

Starting in the early seventeenth century, colonists came to the New World for a variety of reasons. Often it was to escape religious persecution. Others came seeking a new start on a continent where land was plentiful. The independence and diversity of the settlers in the New World made the question of how best to rule the new colonies a tricky one. Although the king ruled by decree at home, the Crown's new and distant American possessions were hard to understand, hard to reach, and hard to communicate with. More than merely an ocean separated the two; the colonists were an independent sort, and it soon became clear that the Crown could not govern the colonies with the same close rein used at home. King James I thus allowed some local participation in decision making through arrangements such as the first elected colonial assembly, the Virginia House of Burgesses, and the elected General Court that governed the Massachusetts Bay Company and that colony after 1629. Almost all the colonists agreed that the king ruled by divine right; but English monarchs allowed the colonists significant liberties in terms of self-government, religious practices, and economic organization. For 140 years, this system worked fairly well.[2]

By the early 1760s, however, a century and a half of physical separation, colonial development, and the relative self-governance of the colonies had led to weakening ties with—and loyalties to—the Crown. By this time, each of the thirteen colonies had drafted its own written constitution, which provided the fundamental rules or laws for each colony. Moreover, many of the most oppressive British traditions—feudalism, a rigid class system, and the absolute authority of church and king—were absent in the New World. Land was abundant. The restrictive guild and craft systems that severely limited entry into many skilled professions in England did not exist in the colonies. Although the role of religion was central to the lives of most colonists, there was no single state church, and the British practice of compulsory tithing (giving a fixed percentage of one's earnings to the state-sanctioned and -supported church) was nonexistent.

---

[2] For an account of the early development of the colonies, see D.W. Meining, *The Shaping of America*, Vol. 1: *Atlantic America, 1492–1800* (New Haven, CT: Yale University Press, 1986).

Trade and Taxation

Mercantilism, an economic theory based on the belief that a nation's wealth is measured by the amount of gold and silver in its treasury, justified Britain's maintenance of strict import/export controls on the colonies. After 1650, for example, Parliament passed a series of navigation acts to prevent its chief rival, Holland, from trading with the English colonies. From 1650 until well into the 1700s, England tried to regulate colonial imports and exports, believing that it was critical to export more goods than it imported as a way of increasing gold and silver in its treasury. These policies, however, were difficult to enforce, and were widely ignored by the colonists, who saw little benefit for themselves in them. Thus for years an unwritten agreement existed: The colonists relinquished to the Crown and the British Parliament the authority to regulate trade and conduct international affairs, but they retained the right to levy their own taxes.

This fragile agreement was soon put to the test. The French and Indian War, fought from 1755 to 1760 on the "western frontier" of the colonies and in Canada, was part of a global war initiated by the British. The American phase of the Seven Years' War was fought between England and France with its Indian allies. In North America its immediate cause was the rival claims of those two European nations for the lands between the Allegheny Mountains and the Mississippi River, as depicted in Figure 2-1. The Treaty of Paris (signed in 1763) signaled the end of the war. The colonists expected

FIGURE 2-1
North America Before and After the Seven Years' War

 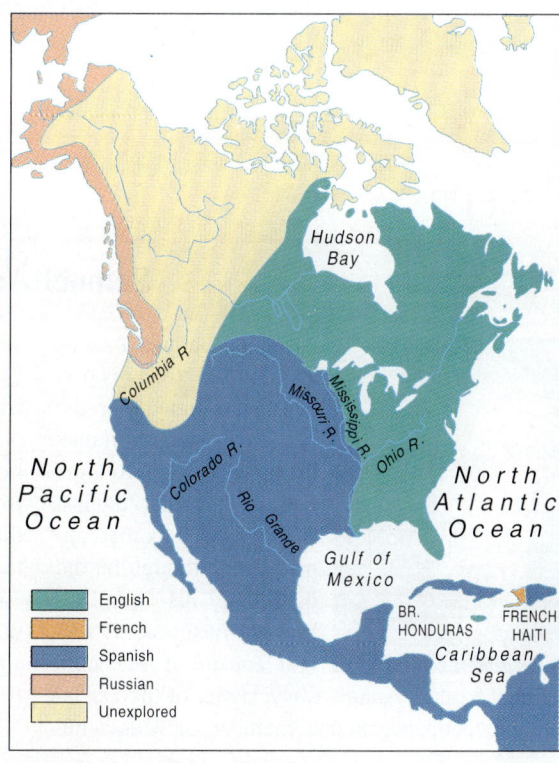

In 1754, before the Seven Years' War   After the Treaty of Paris in 1763

that with the "Indian problem" on the western frontier now "under control," westward migration and settlement could begin in earnest. They were shocked when the Crown decreed in 1763 that there was to be no further westward movement by British subjects. Parliament believed that expansion into Native American territory would lead to new expenditures for the defense of the settlers, draining the British treasury, which had yet to recover from the high cost of waging the war.

To raise money to pay for the war as well as the expenses of administering the colonies, Parliament enacted the Sugar Act in 1764, which placed taxes on sugar, wine, coffee, and other products commonly exported to the colonies. A postwar colonial depression heightened resentment of the tax. Around the colonies the political cry "No taxation without representation" was heard. Major protest, however, failed to materialize until imposition of the Stamp Act in 1765, a law passed by the British Parliament that required the purchase of stamps for all documents, including newspapers, magazines, and commercial papers. To add insult to injury, in 1765 Parliament passed the Mutiny or Quartering Act, which required the colonists to furnish barracks or provide living quarters within their own homes for British troops.

Most colonists, especially those in New England, where these acts hit hardest, were outraged. Men throughout the colonies organized the Sons of Liberty, under the leadership of Samuel Adams (see "People of the Past," below) and Patrick Henry. Whereas the Sugar Act was a tax on trade—still viewed as being within the legitimate authority of the Crown—the Stamp Act was a direct tax on many items not traditionally under the control of the king, and protests against it were violent and loud. Riots, often led by the Sons of Liberty, broke out. They were especially violent in Boston, where the colonial governor's home was burned by an angry mob, and British stamp agents charged with collecting the tax were threatened. A boycott of goods needing the stamps as well as British imports was also organized.

PEOPLE OF THE PAST

Samuel Adams

Although Samuel Adams (1722–1803) today is perhaps best known for the beer that bears his name, his original claim to fame was as a leader against British and Loyalist oppressors (although he did bankrupt his family's brewery business). A second cousin of President John Adams, Samuel Adams was a signer of the Declaration of Independence and a member of Massachusetts's constitutional convention that ratified the U.S. Constitution. He served as governor of Massachusetts from 1794 to 1797.

Adams was heavily influenced by John Locke's belief in man's natural right to be self-governing and free from taxation without representation. As a member of the Massachusetts legislature, he advocated defiance of the Stamp Act. With the passage of the Townshend Acts of 1767, he organized a letter-writing campaign urging other colonies to join in resistance. Later, in 1772, he founded the Committees of Correspondence to unite the colonies.

First Steps Toward Independence

In 1765, the colonists called for the **Stamp Act Congress**, the first official meeting of the colonies and the first step toward a unified nation. Nine of the thirteen colonies sent representatives to a meeting in New York City, where a detailed list of Crown violations of their fundamental rights was drawn up. Attendees defined what they thought to be the proper relationship between the various colonial governments and the British Parliament; they ardently believed that Parliament had no authority to tax them without colonial representation in the British Parliament. In contrast, the British believed that direct representation of the colonists was impractical and that members of Parliament represented the best interests of all the English, including the colonists.

The Stamp Act Congress and its petitions to the Crown did little to stop the onslaught of taxing measures. Parliament did, however, repeal the Stamp Act and revise the Sugar Act in 1766, largely because of the uproar made by British merchants who were losing large sums of money as a result of the boycotts. Rather than appeasing the colonists, however, these actions emboldened them to increase their resistance. In 1767, when Parliament enacted the Townshend Acts, which imposed duties on all kinds of colonial imports, including tea, response from the Sons of Liberty was immediate. Another boycott was announced, and almost all colonists gave up their favorite drink in a united show of resistance to the tax and British authority.[3]

Tensions continued to run high, especially after the British sent 4,000 troops to Boston. On March 5, 1770, English troops opened fire on a mob that included disgruntled dock workers, whose jobs had been taken by British soldiers, and members of the Sons of Liberty who were taunting the soldiers in front of the Boston Customs House. Five colonists were killed in what became known as the "Boston Massacre." Following this confrontation, all duties except those on tea were lifted. The tea tax, however, continued to be a symbolic irritant. In 1772, at the suggestion of Samuel Adams, Boston and other towns around Massachusetts set up **Committees of Correspondence** to articulate ideas and keep communications open around the colony. By 1774, twelve colonies had formed committees to maintain a flow of information among like-minded colonists.

Meanwhile, despite dissent in England over the treatment of the colonies, Parliament passed another tea tax designed to shore up the sagging sales of the East India Company. The colonists' boycott had left that British trading house with more than 18 million pounds of tea in its warehouses. To rescue British merchants from disaster, in 1773 Parliament passed the Tea Act, granting a monopoly to the financially strapped East India Company to sell the tea imported from Britain. The company was allowed to funnel business to American merchants loyal to the Crown, thereby undercutting colonial merchants, who could sell only tea imported from other nations. The effect was to drive down the price of tea and hurt colonial merchants, who were forced to buy tea at the higher prices from other sources.

When the next shipment of tea arrived in Boston from Great Britain, the colonists responded by throwing the Boston Tea Party. In the night of December 18, 1773, after a militant town meeting presided over by Samuel Adams, about 150 colonists dressed as Indians or made up as blacks stole their way onto three British ships in Boston Harbor. As a large crowd watched from the docks, they proceeded to open and then dump

---

[3] For an excellent chronology of the events leading up to the writing of the Declaration of Independence and the colonists' break with Great Britain, see Calvin D. Linton, ed., *The Bicentennial Almanac* (Nashville, TN: Thomas Nelson, 1975).

nearly 350 chests of tea into the waters below. Similar "tea parties" were held in other colonies. When the news of these actions reached King George, he flew into a rage against the actions of his disloyal subjects. "The die is now cast," the king told his prime minister. "The colonies must either submit or triumph."

His first act was to persuade Parliament to pass the Coercive Acts in 1774. Known in the colonies as the Intolerable Acts, they contained a key provision calling for a total blockade of Boston Harbor until restitution was made for the tea. Another provision reinforced the Quartering Act, giving royal governors the authority to quarter in the homes of private citizens the additional 4,000 British soldiers sent to patrol Boston.

The First Continental Congress

The British could never have guessed how the cumulative impact of these actions would unite the colonists. Samuel Adams's Committees of Correspondence spread the word, and food and money were sent to the people of Boston from all over the thirteen

Paul Revere's engraving of the Boston Massacre was a potent piece of political propaganda. Five men were killed, not seven, as the legend states, and the rioters in front of the State House (left) were scarcely as docile as Revere shows them.

colonies. The tax itself was no longer the key issue; now, the extent of British authority over the colonies was the far more important question. At the request of the colonial assemblies of Massachusetts and Virginia, all but one colonial assembly agreed to select a group of delegates to attend a continental congress authorized to communicate with the king on behalf of the now united colonies.

The **First Continental Congress** met in Philadelphia from September 5 to October 26, 1774. It was made up of fifty-six delegates from every colony except Georgia. The colonists had yet to think of breaking with Great Britain; at this point, they simply wanted to iron out their differences with the king. By October they had agreed upon a series of resolutions to oppose the Coercive Acts and establish a formal organization to boycott British goods. The Congress also drafted a Declaration of Rights and Resolves, portions of which later found their way into the Declaration of Independence and the U.S. Constitution.

The Declaration of Rights and Resolves called for colonial rights of petition and assembly, trial by peers, freedom from a standing army, and the selection of representative councils to levy taxes. The attendees further agreed to meet again in Philadelphia in May 1775 unless the king capitulated to their demands.

The Second Continental Congress

King George refused to yield, tensions continued to rise, and a **Second Continental Congress** was called. Before it could meet, fighting broke out early in the morning of April 19, 1775 at Lexington and Concord, Massachusetts, with what Ralph Waldo Emerson called "the shot heard round the world." Eight colonial Minutemen were killed, and 16,000 British troops besieged Boston.

When the Second Continental Congress convened in Philadelphia on May 10, 1775, delegates were united by their increased hostility to Great Britain. The bloodshed at Lexington left no other course but war. To solidify colonial support, a Southerner was selected as the commander of the new Continental Army, since up to that date, British oppression had been felt most keenly in the Northeast. On June 15, 1775, George Washington of Virginia, who had fought in the French and Indian War, strongly hinted at his desire to head the army by being the only delegate to appear in a military uniform. He was named commander-in-chief, with the authority to enlist soldiers. The Congress sent envoys to France to ask for assistance. In a final attempt to avert conflict, the Second Continental Congress adopted the Olive Branch Petition on July 5, 1775, asking the king to end hostilities. King George rejected the petition and sent an additional 20,000 troops to quell the rebellion. The stage was set for war.

Although the colonists had not gone into the Second Continental Congress expecting to be a free and independent nation, the king's actions seemed to leave them no other choice than to declare independence. In 1774, Thomas Paine (1737–1809), whose radical political views had gotten him into considerable trouble in his native Great Britain, came to the colonies with the help of Benjamin Franklin, who saw Paine's potential use to the budding independence movement. Franklin, sensing the need for sentiment to unite the colonies, urged Paine to pen a document to fuel colonial sentiments. In January 1776, Paine issued (at first anonymously) *Common Sense,* a pamphlet forcefully arguing for independence from Great Britain. In frank, easy-to-understand language, Paine denounced the corrupt British monarchy and offered reasons for breaking with Great Britain. Concerning the English monarchy, Paine wrote, "Ye that dare oppose not only tyranny but the tyrant, Stand forth!" Moreover, "Every-

After the success of *Common Sense,* Thomas Paine wrote a series of essays collectively entitled *The Crisis* to arouse colonists' support for the Revolutionary War. The first *Crisis* papers contain the famous words "These are the times that try men's souls."

thing that is right," Paine argued, ". . . pleads for separation. The blood of the slain, the weeping voice of nature cries 'Tis Time to Part.'"

Common Sense, widely read throughout the colonies, was instrumental in changing minds in a very short time. In its first three months of publication, the 47-page *Common Sense* sold 120,000 copies, the equivalent of approximately 18.75 million books today (given the U.S. population in 1995). One copy of *Common Sense* was in distribution for every thirteen people in the colonies, a truly astonishing number given the low literacy rate.

The Declaration of Independence

The impact of *Common Sense* on the mood of the nation cannot be underscored too strongly. It galvanized the American public, and ridiculed all arguments for reconciliation with England. As the mood in the colonies changed, so did that of the Second Continental Congress. On May 15, 1776, Virginia became the first colony to call for independence, instructing one of its delegates to the Second Continental Congress to introduce a resolution to that effect. On June 7, 1776, Richard Henry Lee of Virginia rose to move "that these United Colonies are, and of right ought to be, free and independent States, and that all connection between them and the State of Great Britain is, and ought to be, dissolved." His three-part resolution—which called for independence, the formation of foreign alliances, and preparation of a plan of confederation—triggered hot debate. A proclamation of independence from Great Britain was treason, a crime punishable by death. Although six of the thirteen colonies had already instructed their delegates to vote for independence, the Second Continental Congress was suspended to allow its delegates to return home to their respective colonial legislatures for final instructions. Independence was not a move to be taken lightly.

At the same time, committees were set up to consider each point of Lee's proposal. A committee of five was selected to begin work on a **Declaration of Independence**. The Congress selected Benjamin Franklin, John Adams, Robert Livingston, and Roger Sherman as members. Adams lobbied hard for a Southerner to add balance. Thus, owing to his Southern origin as well as his "peculiar felicity of expression," Thomas Jefferson was selected as chair.

On July 2, twelve of the thirteen colonies (with New York abstaining) voted for independence. Two days later, the Second Continental Congress voted to adopt the Declaration of Independence penned by Thomas Jefferson. On July 9, the Declaration, now with the approval of New York, was read aloud in Philadelphia.[4]

Social Contract Theory

In simple but eloquent language, Jefferson set out the reasons for the colonies' separation from Great Britain. Most of his stirring rhetoric drew heavily on the works of seventeenth- and eighteenth-century political philosophers, particularly the great John Locke of England (see "People of the Past," p. 10), who actually wrote South Car-

---

[4] See Garry Wills, *Inventing America: Jefferson's Declaration of Independence* (New York: Random House, 1978). Wills argues that the Declaration was signed solely to secure foreign aid in the ongoing war effort.

Landmark Events Leading to the Declaration of Independence	
1620 ♦	Mayflower Compact; settlement in Massachusetts
1754 ♦	Colonies settled and developed
1760 ♦	French and Indian War
1763 ♦	Crown decrees no more westward movement
1764 ♦	Sugar Act
1765 ♦	Stamp Act—Sons of Liberty organized; Stamp Act Congress convened
1766 ♦	Stamp Act repealed; Sugar Act revised
1767 ♦	Townshend Acts—colonists boycott tea
1770 ♦	Boston Massacre
1772 ♦	Committees of Correspondence set up
1773 ♦	Tea Act; Boston Tea Party
1774 ♦	Coercive or Intolerable Acts; First Continental Congress convened
1775 ♦	Fighting breaks out at Lexington and Concord; Second Continental Congress convened
1776 ♦	Declaration of Independence

olina's first constitution as a colonial charter when it was formed by the king and mercantile houses in England.

The colonists agreed with Locke's argument that people have certain natural, or God-given, inalienable rights that cannot be taken away by any government.[5] They had come to cherish, among other things, the right to property. In colonial times "property" did not mean just land; Locke's notion of property rights included life, liberty, and material possessions.

According to Locke and his adherents, government existed by the consent of the governed. Under this brand of social contract theory, individuals free and equal by natural right agree to set up a government for certain defined purposes. These individuals have the right to resist or remove rulers who deviate from those purposes. Essentially, under social contract theory, government exists for the good of its subjects and not for the benefit of those who govern. Locke argued, furthermore, that rebellion was the ultimate sanction against a government that abused its power.

---

[5] For John Locke's influence on the Declaration of Independence, see Carl L. Becker, *The Declaration of Independence: A Study in the History of Political Ideas* (New York: Random House, 1942).

It is easy to see the colonists' debt to John Locke. In ringing language the Declaration of Independence proclaims:

> We hold these truths to be self-evident, that all men are created equal, that they are endowed by their Creator with certain unalienable Rights, that among these are Life, Liberty and the pursuit of Happiness.

Jefferson and others in attendance at the Second Continental Congress wanted to have a document that would stand for all time, justifying their break with the Crown and clarifying their notions of the proper form of government. So, Jefferson continued:

> That to secure these rights, Governments are instituted among Men, deriving their just powers from the consent of the governed. That whenever any Form of Government becomes destructive of these ends, it is the Right of the People to alter or abolish it, and to institute new Government, laying its foundation on such Principles and organizing its Powers in such form, as to them shall seem most likely to effect their Safety and Happiness.

After this stirring preamble, the Declaration went on to enumerate the wrongs that the colonists had suffered under British rule. All pertained to the denial of personal rights and liberties, many of which would later be guaranteed by the U.S. Constitution via the Bill of Rights.

After the Declaration was signed and transmitted to the king, the Revolutionary War was fought with a greater vengeance. At a September 1776 peace conference on Staten Island (New York), British General William Howe demanded revocation of the Declaration of Independence. The Americans refused, and the war raged on while the Congress attempted to fashion a new united government.

The First Attempt at Government: The Articles of Confederation

As noted earlier, the British had no written constitution. Now the colonists in the Second Continental Congress were attempting to codify arrangements that had never before been put into legal terminology. To make things more complicated, the delegates had to arrive at these decisions in a wartime atmosphere. Nevertheless, in late 1779 the Articles of Confederation, creating a loose "league of friendship" between the sovereign or independent states, were passed by the Congress and presented to the states for their ratification.

The Articles created a type of government called a **confederation**, in which the national government derives its powers from the states it comprises, as depicted in Figure 2-2. Although the authority of the states rested on powers derived directly from the people, the national government held only the powers that the states were willing to give it. Key provisions in the Articles included:

- A national government with a Congress empowered to make peace, coin money, appoint officers for an army, control the post office, and negotiate with Indian tribes.
- Each state's retention of its independence and sovereignty, or ultimate authority to govern within its territories.

- One vote in the Continental Congress for each state, regardless of size.
- The vote of nine states to pass any measure (a unanimous vote for any amendment).
- The selection and payment of delegates to the Congress by their respective state legislatures.

Thus, the Articles—finally ratified by all thirteen states in 1781—fashioned a government well reflective of the political philosophy of the times.[6]

Although it had its flaws, the government under the Articles of Confederation saw the nation through the Revolutionary War. However, once the British surrendered in 1782 and the new nation found itself no longer united by the war effort, the government quickly fell into chaos.

Problems Under the Articles of Confederation

By 1784, just one year after the Revolutionary army was disbanded, governing the new nation under the Articles of Confederation proved unworkable.[7] Congress could rarely assemble the required quorum of nine states to conduct business. Even when it could, there was little agreement among them. To raise revenue to pay off war debts and run the government, various land, poll, and liquor taxes were proposed. But since Congress had no specific power to tax, all these proposals were rejected. At one point, Congress was even driven out of Philadelphia (then the capital) by its own unpaid army. And, although the national government could coin money, it had no resources to back up the value of its currency. Continental dollars were worth little, and trade between states became chaotic as some states began to coin their own money. Another weakness of the Articles was their failure to allow Congress to regulate commerce among the states and with foreign nations. As a result, individual states attempted to enter into agreements with other countries, and foreign nations were suspicious of trade agreements made with the United States. In 1785, for example, Massachusetts banned the export of goods in British ships, and Pennsylvania levied heavy duties on ships of nations that did not have a treaty with the U.S. government.

Fearful of a chief executive who would rule tyrannically, moreover, the draftees of the Articles had made no provision for an executive branch of government that would be responsible for executing, or implementing, laws passed by the legislative branch. Instead, the "president" was merely the presiding officer at meetings. John Hanson, a former member of the Maryland House of Delegates and of the first Continental Congress, was the first person to preside over the Congress of the Confederation, as the new government under the Articles was called. Therefore, he is often referred to as the first President of the United States.

In addition, the Articles of Confederation had no provision for a judicial system to handle the growing number of economic conflicts and boundary disputes among the individual states. Several states claimed the same lands to the west; Pennsylvania and Virginia went to war with each other; Vermont threatened to annex itself to Canada.

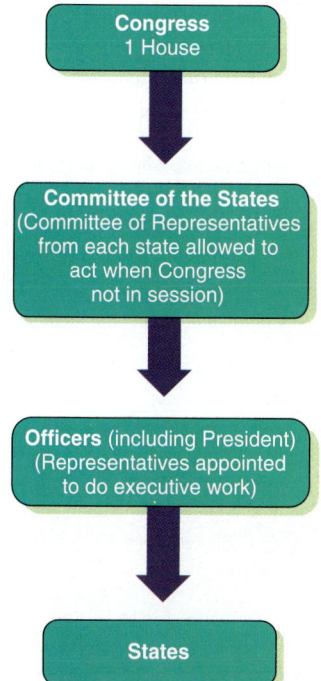

FIGURE 2-2

The Structure of Government Under the Articles of Confederation

Five Major Failures of the Articles

❖❖❖

1. No power to tax
2. No authority to regulate commerce
3. No executive to administer the government
4. No judicial system to resolve disputes among the states
5. No strong central government

---

[6] See Gordon Wood, *The Creation of the American Republic, 1776–1787* (Chapel Hill: University of North Carolina Press, 1969).

[7] For more about the Articles of Confederation, see Merrill Jensen, *The Articles of Confederation* (Madison: University of Wisconsin Press, 1940).

During the Revolutionary War and under the Articles of Confederation, the national government printed so much currency that its worth plummeted, giving rise to the expression "not worth a continental." Each state also coined and printed its own money, further compounding financial confusion and leading to economic chaos. Shown here is a facsimile reproduction of currency issued in Rhode Island.

The Articles' greatest weakness, however, was their lack of creation of a strong central government. While states had operated independently before the war, during the war they acceded to the national government's authority to wage armed conflict. Once the war was over, however, each state resumed its sovereign status, and was unwilling to give up rights, such as the power to tax, to an untested national government. Consequently, the government was unable to force the states to abide by the provisions of the Treaty of Paris, signed in 1783, which had officially ended the war. For example, states passed laws to stay the bills of debtors who owed money to Great Britain and failed to restore property to many who had remained loyal to Britain during the war, both of which actions were in violation of the Treaty.

The crumbling economy and a series of bad harvests that failed to produce cash crops, making it difficult for farmers to get out of debt quickly, took their toll on the new nation. George Washington and Alexander Hamilton, both interested in the questions of trade and frontier expansion, soon saw the need for a stronger national government with the authority to act to solve some of these problems. They were not alone. In 1785 and 1786 some state governments began to discuss ways to strengthen the national government. Finally, several states joined together to call for a convention in Philadelphia in 1787.

Before that meeting could take place, however, new unrest broke out in America. In 1780, Massachusetts adopted a state constitution that appeared to favor the interests of the wealthy. Property-owning requirements barred the lower and middle classes from voting and office holding. And, as the economy of Massachusetts worsened, banks foreclosed on farms to pay off debts to Massachusetts Continental Army veterans who were waiting for promised bonuses. The last straw came in 1786 when the Massachusetts legislature enacted a new law requiring the payment of all debts in cash. Frustration and outrage at the new law caused Daniel Shays, a former Revolutionary War army captain, and 1,500 armed, disgruntled, and angry farmers to march to Springfield. This group forcibly restrained the state court from foreclosing on mortgages on their farms.

The Congress immediately authorized the Secretary of War to call for a new national militia. A $530,000 appropriation was made for this purpose, but every state ex-

With Daniel Shays in the lead, a group of farmers and Revolutionary War veterans marched on the courthouse in Springfield, Massachusetts, to prevent foreclosure on their mortgages.

cept Virginia refused the Congress's request for money. The governor of Massachusetts then tried to raise a state militia, but because of the poor economy, funds were unavailable in the state treasury. Frantic attempts at private support were made, and a militia was finally assembled. By February 4, 1787, this privately paid force put a stop to what was called **Shays's Rebellion**. The failure of the Congress to muster an army to put down the rebellion was yet another example of the weaknesses inherent in the Articles of Confederation.

The Miracle at Philadelphia: Writing a Constitution

In the throes of economic turmoil and with domestic tranquility gone haywire, on February 21, 1787, the Congress passed an official resolution that called for a Constitutional Convention in Philadelphia for "the sole and express purpose of revising the Articles of Confederation." All states but Rhode Island sent delegates. (Rhode Island was a strong supporter of the government under the Articles and had as its state motto Thomas Paine's words "Government is best which governs least." Its absence from the meeting led some present to suggest that its name be changed to "Rogue Island" or that it be dropped from the Union altogether.)

When twenty-nine individuals met in sweltering Philadelphia on May 14, they had much on their minds. While many of them at that initial meeting were intellectuals, others were shrewd farmers or businessmen, and others were astute politicians. All recognized that what they were doing could be considered treasonous. Revising the Articles of Confederation was one thing; to call for an entirely new government, as suggested by the Virginia delegation, was another. So they took their work quite seriously, even to the point of adopting a pledge of secrecy. George Washington, who was unanimously elected the convention's presiding officer, warned:

> Nothing spoken or written can be revealed to anyone—not even your family—until we have adjourned permanently. Gossip or misunderstanding can easily ruin all the hard work we shall have to do this summer.[8]

So concerned about leaks were those in attendance that the delegates agreed to accompany Benjamin Franklin to all of his meals, fearing that the normally gregarious gentleman might get carried away with the mood or by liquor and inadvertently let news of the proceedings slip from his tongue.

The Framers

Fifty-five out of the seventy-four delegates ultimately chosen by their state legislatures to attend the Constitutional Convention labored long and hard that hot summer behind closed doors in Philadelphia. They are often referred to as the "Founding Fathers." Most of them were quite young; many were in their twenties and thirties, and only one—Benjamin Franklin, at eighty-one—was very old. Here we generally refer to those delegates as Framers because their work provided the framework for our new government. The Framers brought with them a vast amount of political, educational, legal, and business experience. Eight had signed the Declaration of Independence, thirty-nine had attended at least one Continental Congress, and seven were former governors. One-third were college graduates, and thirty-four were lawyers. Notably absent were individuals like Patrick Henry, who had proclaimed in the Virginia House of Burgesses, "Give me liberty or give me death!" Now he stayed away because he "smelt a rat," fearing that the states could lose their powers. Also missing were Thomas Jefferson, author of the Declaration of Independence, and John Adams. Both were on ambassadorial stays in Europe. Although some scholarly debate continues concerning the motives of the Framers for shaping the new national government (see "Motives of the Framers," p. 53), it is clear that they were an exceptional lot who ultimately produced a brilliant document reflecting the best efforts of all present.

The Virginia Plan

Soon after George Washington called the meeting to order, Edmund Randolph of Virginia rose to present a framework of government that James Madison had prepared prior to the meeting. The preamble of what is commonly referred to as the **Virginia Plan** proposed that "a *national* government ought to be established, consisting of a *supreme* Legislative, Executive and Judiciary" (emphasis added). Those in attendance unanimously agreed to debate that idea, and the remainder of Madison's plan was introduced for discussion.

---

[8] Quoted in Selma R. Williams, *Fifty-Five Fathers: The Story of the Constitutional Convention* (New York: Dodd, Mead, 1970), p. 10.

Once the Framers had voted to consider Madison's proposals, the die was cast. The purpose of the convention was changed from revision of the Articles to the creation of an entirely new form of government.[9]

The Virginia Plan contained several key elements that shaped the new government and its final structure. It called for:

1. A national government with three separate branches of government: a legislative branch to make laws, an executive branch to enforce them, and a judicial branch to interpret them.
2. The creation of a national legislature or lawmaking body with two parts, or houses. One house was to be elected directly by the people; the other house was to be chosen from among persons nominated by the state legislatures. Total representation in the legislature would be in proportion to taxes paid to the federal or national government, corresponding to the population of free people within each state.
3. A single "national Executive" to be chosen by the national legislature for a single term.
4. A Council of Revision, consisting of the national executive and several federal judges, that would have the authority to approve or veto acts of the legislature. Vetoes could be overridden by a vote of both houses of the legislature.
5. A federal judiciary headed by a Supreme Court appointed for life by the legislature.
6. A national government with the power to override state laws. Since the government was to derive its powers from the people and the states, the plan argued that the national government should have the ability to operate on both.

During the first few weeks of the convention, discussion of this plan, which created a far stronger national government than had existed under the Articles of Confederation, dominated the proceedings. After only six days of debate, Virginia's proposal to create a new national government was voted on by the convention. By the narrowest of margins, the Virginia Plan won its first crucial test and gave momentum to those forces favoring a strong central government.

The delegates then debated other sections of the Virginia Plan. The first structural aspect of the new government that the Framers agreed on was a **bicameral legislature**, that is, one with two distinct bodies. When Thomas Jefferson returned from Paris, he asked Washington why the delegates had agreed to a two-house legislature. "Why do you pour coffee into your saucer?" asked Washington. "To cool it," responded Jefferson. "So," responded Washington, "we pour legislation into the senatorial saucer to cool it."[10]

Delegates initially appeared far from agreement over how members of each house of Congress were to be selected. Many of them appeared set against direct election of members of one house. Many who held to that view feared the idea of democracy. Their elitist views led them to believe that not "all the people" were fit to make decisions concerning the government. They feared the kinds of uprisings that Daniel Shays's actions had typified.

On the other side, Madison and other supporters of a strong central government, while still fearful of a "mobocracy," continued to insist on direct election of some rep-

---

[9] See Samuel Beer, "Federalism, Nationalism and Democracy in America," *American Political Science Review*, 72 (March 1978): 9–21.

[10] Quoted in Doris Faber and Harold Faber, *We the People* (New York: Charles Scribner's Sons, 1987), p. 25.

resentatives. They reasoned that without the confidence of the people, government could not long exist.

The Virginia Plan called for a national system with a powerful central government. It was based heavily on the European nation–state model, wherein the national government derives its powers from the people and not from the member states. In contrast, proponents of what was *at that time* termed a federal system favored a looser confederation of states in which powers could be shared between the national and state governments. Basically comfortable with the arrangements under the Articles of Confederation, they offered another model of government, the New Jersey Plan.

The New Jersey Plan

As supporters of a strong national government continued to debate various aspects of the Virginia Plan, representatives from the smaller states took advantage of a rule that allowed reconsideration of any proposal that had previously been adopted. Under the direction of William Paterson of New Jersey, the smaller states offered their own plan after about two weeks of deliberation on the Virginia Plan. The **New Jersey Plan** suggested that the Articles, instead of being replaced, only be strengthened. Its key features included:

1. A one-house legislature with one vote for each state. Representatives to the Congress were to be chosen by state legislatures. The Congress would have the power to raise revenue from duties and a post office. All other funds had to be requested from the states.
2. A multi-person "executive" to be chosen by Congress with powers similar to those in the Virginia Plan, except that the executive would not have the authority to veto acts of Congress.
3. The establishment of the acts of Congress as the "supreme law" of the land, and authorization of the federal executive to use force to compel obedience.
4. A supreme judiciary with very limited authority (although there was no provision for a system of national courts).

Not surprisingly, the New Jersey Plan was defeated, but its consideration showed that the smaller states had sufficient concerns and political clout to force some changes in the Virginia Plan.

The Great Compromise

The most serious disagreement between the Virginia and New Jersey Plans concerned representation in the two chambers of Congress. When a deadlock on this point loomed, Connecticut offered its own compromise. Each state would have an equal vote in the Senate. Again, there was a stalemate. As Benjamin Franklin put it,

> The diversity of opinions turns on two points. If a proportional representation takes place, the small states contend that their liberties will be in danger. If an equality of votes is to be put in its place, large states say that their money will be in danger.

He continued:

> When a broad table is to be made and the edges of a plank do not fit, the artist takes a little from both sides and makes a good joint. In like manner, both sides

must part with some of their demands, in order that they both join in some accommodating position.[11]

A committee was appointed to see if some sort of agreement could be worked out over the Fourth of July weekend. That committee reported back what became known as the **Great Compromise**. Taking ideas from both the Virginia and New Jersey Plans, it recommended:

1. In one house of the legislature (later called the House of Representatives), there should be 56 representatives—one representative for every 40,000 inhabitants.
2. That house should have the power to originate all bills for raising and spending money.
3. In the second house of the legislature (later called the Senate), each state should have an equal vote, and representatives would be selected by the state legislatures.[12]

An additional compromise, however, was necessary before state populations could be determined. After considerable dissension, it was decided that representation in the House of Representatives was to be based on population, calculated by adding the "whole Number of Free Persons" to "three fifths of all other Persons." "All other Persons" was the delegates' "tactful" way of referring to slaves. Known as the **Three-Fifths Compromise**, this formula was based on the prevailing assumption that slaves were only three-fifths as productive as white men.[13]

Since the slave population in the Southern states was so large, these states sought to have slaves counted as part of the population for the purpose of representation. Yet they never considered the possibility of allowing these same slaves to cast ballots for representatives. In fact, throughout most of the colonies, suffrage, or the right to vote, was not universal. Instead, it was generally limited to white male property owners.

The Great Compromise ultimately met with the approval of all states in attendance. The smaller states were pleased because they got equal representation in the Senate; the larger states were satisfied with the proportional representation in the House of Representatives. The small states then would dominate the Senate while the large states, such as Virginia and New York, would control the House. But because both houses had to pass any legislation, neither body could dominate the other.

With passage of the Great Compromise, and after ten weeks of hard work, agreement was reached on most of its basic principles. On August 6, 1787, a draft of a constitution—seven pages long, with broad margins for notations—was submitted to the delegates. It contained twenty-three articles subdivided into forty-one separate sections. Still to be included, however, were provisions for an executive branch and a president.

In 1787, Virginia's population was twice that of New York, four times that of New Jersey, and ten times that of Delaware.

---

[11] Ibid., p. 31.
[12] For more on the political nature of compromise at the Convention, see Calvin C. Jillson, *Constitution Making: Conflict and Consensus in the Federal Constitution of 1787* (New York: Agathon, 1988).
[13] This kind of assumption about slaves was never specifically spelled out in the Constitution. In fact, slavery is nowhere specifically mentioned in that document. Although many of the Framers were morally opposed to slavery, they recognized that if the convention attempted to abolish or seriously restrict it in the short term, the Southern states would walk away from the new Union (as they eventually did, resulting in the Civil War).

DOONESBURY copyright G. B. Trudeau. Reprinted with permission of UNIVERSAL PRESS SYNDICATE. All rights reserved.

Compromise on the Presidency

By August, the Framers had agreed on the idea of a one-person executive, but they could not settle on the length of the term of office, nor on how the chief executive should be selected. With Shays's Rebellion still fresh in their minds, the delegates feared putting too much power into the hands of the lower classes. At the same time, representatives from the smaller states feared that the selection of the chief executive by the legislature would put additional power into the hands of the large states.

Amid these fears, the Committee on Unfinished Portions, whose sole responsibility was to iron out problems and disagreements concerning the office of chief executive, conducted its work. The Committee recommended that the presidential term of office be fixed at four years instead of seven, as had earlier been proposed. By choosing not to mention a time-span within which the chief executive would be eligible for reelection, they made it possible for a president to serve more than one term. The president was to be chosen by electors. And, for the first time, the post of vice president was mentioned.

Selecting a President: The Electoral College

In setting up a system for electing the president, the Framers put in place an electoral college (see Chapter 12). The electoral college system gave individual states a key role, because each state would select electors equal to the number of representatives it had in the House *and* Senate. It was a vague compromise that removed election of the president and vice president from both the Congress and the people and put it in the hands of electors whose method of selection would be left to the states.

The delegates were quite happy with this compromise and believed that it would be acceptable to all sides. The smaller states believed they would have an equal voice should the election be forced into the House of Representatives, and the larger states believed they had a good opportunity to elect a president before this contingency would occur.

Removing a President

One more matter concerning the president remained, however. Still fearful of a leader who might turn out to resemble a British monarch, the Framers were careful to include a provision for removal of the chief executive. They proposed that both the legislative and the judicial branches be involved in the impeachment process. The House of Representatives was given the sole responsibility of investigating and charging a president or vice president with "Treason, Bribery, or other high Crimes and Misdemeanors." A majority vote would then result in the issuing of Articles of Impeachment against the president. In turn, the Senate was given sole responsibility to try the chief executive on the charges issued by the House. A two-thirds vote of the Senate was required to convict and remove the president from office. The Chief Justice of the United States was to preside over the Senate proceedings in place of the vice president (that body's usual leader) in order to prevent any appearance of impropriety on the vice president's part.

The U.S. Constitution

After the compromise on the presidency, work proceeded quickly on the remaining resolutions of the Constitution. A committee of five members was chosen to formalize all that had been accomplished in Philadelphia. The final document was largely written by Gouverneur Morris of Pennsylvania, a friend of Washington's, and treasurer of the Continental Congress. The committee submitted its work, which included some new proposals as well as changes in matters previously accepted, to the delegates on August 6, 1787.

The Preamble to the Constitution, the last section to be drafted, contains exceptionally powerful language that formed the bedrock of American political tradition. The

A ticket for entry to the Senate's impeachment trial of Andrew Johnson, the only time in U.S. history when the full impeachment machinery created in the U.S. Constitution was used.

"Remember, gentlemen, we aren't here just to draft a constitution. We're here to draft the best damned constitution in the world."

Drawing by Steiner, © 1982 The New Yorker Magazine, Inc.

Preamble is directly attributable to Morris, who had a true gift for simplifying complex language. Its opening line, "We the People of the United States," boldly proclaimed that a loose confederation of independent states no longer existed; instead, there was but one American people and nation. The original version of the Preamble opened with:

> We the people of the States of New Hampshire, Massachusetts, Rhode Island and the Providence Plantations, Connecticut, New Jersey, New York, Pennsylvania, Delaware, Maryland, Virginia, North Carolina, South Carolina and Georgia, do ordain, declare and establish the following Constitution for the government of ourselves and our Posterity.

Note how different the phrases ended up under Morris's pen. The simple phrase "We the people" ended at least for the time being the question of whence the government derived its power—it came directly from the people, not from the states.

The next phrase of the Constitution explained the need for the new outline of government. "[I]n Order to form a more perfect Union" indirectly acknowledged the weaknesses of the Articles of Confederation in governing a growing nation. Next, the optimistic goals of the Framers for the new nation were set out: to "establish Justice, insure domestic Tranquility, provide for the common defense, promote the general Welfare, and secure the Blessings of Liberty to ourselves and our Posterity"; followed by the formal creation of a new government: "do ordain and establish this Constitution for the United States of America."

In *The Miracle at Philadelphia* (1966) Catherine Drinker Bowen wrote, "The seven verbs flowed out—to form, establish, insure, provide, promote, secure, ordain. . . . One might challenge the centuries to better these verbs."[14] These powerful words fanned the flames of a new nation. On September 17, 1787, the Constitution was finally approved by the delegates from all twelve states in attendance (Rhode Island had not sent any representatives.) While the completed document did not satisfy all the delegates, of the forty-one in attendance, thirty-nine ultimately signed. The sentiments uttered by Benjamin Franklin probably well reflected those of many others: "Thus, I consent, Sir, to this Constitution because I expect no better, and because I am not sure that it is not the best."[15]

The Basic Principles of the Constitution

The ideas of political philosophers, especially the French Baron de la Brède et de Montesquieu (1689–1755) and the English John Locke (see "People of the Past," p. 10), heavily influenced the shape and nature of the government proposed by the Framers. Montesquieu, who actually drew many of his ideas about government from the works of the Greek political philosopher Aristotle, was heavily quoted during the Constitutional Convention. Acknowledging the Framers' debt to Montesquieu, James Madison noted in *Federalist No. 47,* "if he be not the author of this invaluable precept [separation of powers] in the science of politics, he has the merit of at least displaying and recommending it most effectually to the attention of mankind."

---

[14] Quoted in Faber and Faber, *We the People,* p. 43. (See n. 9.)
[15] Quoted in Richard N. Current, T. Harry Williams, Frank Freidel, and Alan Brinkley, *American History: A Survey,* 6th ed. (New York: McGraw-Hill, 1983), p. 168.

The proposed structure of the new national government also owed much to the writings of Montesquieu, who advocated distinct functions for each branch of government, with a system of checks and balances between them. And the Constitution's concern with the distribution of power between states and the national government also reveals the heavy influence of political philosophers, as well as the colonists' experience under the Articles of Confederation.[16]

Federalism. Under the Articles of Confederation, only a loose "league of friendship" existed among the states. Given the nation's experiences under the Articles, the Framers believed that a strong national government was necessary for the new nation's survival. However, they were reluctant to create a powerful government on the model of Britain, the country from which they had just won their independence. Its **unitary government**, in which all major powers resided at the national level, was not even considered by the colonists. Instead, they fashioned a system now known as **federal system,** which divides the power of government between a strong national government and the individual states. Opponents of this system feared that a strong national government would infringe on their liberty, but James Madison argued that a strong national government with distinct state governments could, if properly directed by constitutional arrangements, actually be a source of expanded liberties and national unity. The Framers viewed the division of governmental authority between the national government and the states as a means of checking power with power, and providing the people with "double security" against governmental tyranny. Later, the passage of the Tenth Amendment, which stated that powers not given to the national government were reserved by the states or the people, further clarified the federal structure (see Chapter 3).

Separation of Powers. Madison and many of the Framers clearly feared putting too much power into the hands of any one individual or branch of government. His famous words, "Ambition must be made to counteract ambition," were widely believed at the Philadelphia convention.

Separation of powers is simply a way of parceling out power among the three branches of government. It has three key features:

1. Three distinct branches of government: the legislative, the executive, and the judicial.
2. Three separately staffed branches of government to exercise these functions.
3. Constitutional equality and independence of each branch.

Thus, as illustrated in Figure 2-3, the Framers were careful to create a system in which lawmaking, law-enforcing, and law-interpreting functions were assigned to independent branches of government. On the national level (and in most states), only the legislature has the authority to make laws; the chief executive enforces and the judiciary interprets them. Moreover, members of the House of Representatives, members of the Senate, the President, and members of the federal courts are selected by and are therefore responsible to different constituencies. Madison believed that the scheme devised by the Framers would divide the offices of the new government and their methods of selection among many individuals, providing each office holder with the "necessary means and personal motives to resist encroachment" on his power.

---

[16] Bernard Bailyn, *The Ideological Origins of the American Revolution* (Cambridge, MA: Harvard University Press, 1967).

FIGURE 2-3

Separation of Powers: The American and British Systems Compared

The Framers could not have foreseen the intermingling of governmental functions that has since evolved. Locke, in fact, cautioned against giving a legislature the ability to delegate its powers. In Article I of the Constitution, the legislative power is vested in the Congress, but the president is also given legislative powers via his ability to veto legislation, although his veto can be overridden by a two-thirds vote in Congress. Judicial interpretation then helps to clarify the implementation of legislation enacted through this process.

So instead of a pure system of separation of powers, a symbiotic, or interdependent, relationship among the three branches of government has existed from the beginning. Or as one scholar has explained, there are "separated institutions sharing powers."[17] While Congress is still entrusted with making the laws, most proposals for legislation originate with the president. And although the Supreme Court's major function is to interpret the law, its involvement in areas such as criminal procedure, abortion, and other fields has led many to charge that it has surpassed its constitutional authority and become a law-making body.

In this regard, the blurring of the separation of powers has moved the American system a little closer to Britain's parliamentary democracy (see Figure 2-3). There, too, a symbiotic relationship between the legislature and executive exists, since the prime minister and the cabinet come from the lower house of the legislature. Members of the executive branch in a parliamentary system usually retain their seats in the legislature, and thus wear two hats: one as a representative of the people and the other as an executive officer. And some members of the House of Lords also serve as justices.

Checks and Balances. The principle of **checks and balances** also guided the Framers as they designed the new government.[18] As illustrated in Table 2.1, power is checked and balanced because the legislative, executive, and judicial branches of government share some authority, and no branch has exclusive domain over any activity. The creation of this system of checks and balances allowed the Framers to minimize the threat of tyranny from any one branch. Thus, for almost every power granted to one branch, an equal control was established in the other two branches. The Congress could "check" the power of the president, the Supreme Court, and so on, carefully creating "balance" among the three branches.

The Articles of the Constitution

The document finally signed by the Framers condensed numerous resolutions into a Preamble and seven separate articles. The first three articles established the three branches of government, defined their internal operations, and clarified their relationships with one another. All branches of government were technically considered equal, yet some initially appeared more "equal" than others. It is likely that the order in which the articles appear, and especially the relative amount of detail in the first three articles, reflects the Framers' concern that the branches of the government might abuse their powers. The four remaining articles define the relationships among the states, declare national law to be supreme, and set out methods of amending the Constitution.

Article I: The Legislative Branch. Article I vests all legislative powers in the Congress and establishes a bicameral legislature, the Senate and the House of Representatives. It also sets out the qualifications for holding office in each house, the terms of office, methods of selection of representatives and senators, and apportionment among the states of membership in the House of Representatives. Operating procedures and the officers for each house are also briefly outlined and described.

---

[17] Richard E. Neustadt, *Presidential Power: The Politics of Leadership from FDR to Carter* (New York: Macmillan, 1980), p. 26.

[18] See E.P. Panagopoulos, *Essays on the History and Meaning of Checks and Balances* (Landham, MD: University Press of America, 1985).

Table 2.1 ♦ Separation of Powers and Checks and Balances Outlined

POWERS OF CONGRESS

Passes all federal laws

Establishes lower federal courts and the number of judges

Can impeach the president

Can override the president's veto by a two-thirds vote

Passes the federal budget, which finances the executive branch

Approves treaties and presidential appointments, including those to the federal courts

CHECKS ON CONGRESSIONAL POWERS

President can veto legislation

Supreme Court can rule laws unconstitutional

Both houses of Congress must vote to enact a law, thereby checking power within the legislature

POWERS OF THE CHIEF EXECUTIVE

Can approve or veto acts of Congress

Is responsible for carrying out the laws passed by Congress

Can call Congress into special session

Can submit legislation to Congress

Makes foreign treaties

Nominates Supreme Court justices and federal judges

Can pardon people convicted in federal court

Is responsible for execution of court orders

Is commander-in-chief of armed forces

CHECKS ON EXECUTIVE POWERS

Congress can override vetoes of legislation by a two-thirds vote

Senate can refuse to confirm nominees or ratify treaties

Congress can impeach and remove president (with Chief Justice of the Supreme Court presiding)

Congress can declare war

Supreme Court can declare presidential acts unconstitutional

POWERS OF THE JUDICIARY

Can invalidate, on grounds of unconstitutionality, laws passed by Congress

Can invalidate executive branch orders or actions on grounds of unconstitutionality or absence of authorizing legislation

CHECKS ON JUDICIAL POWERS

Congress can change jurisdiction (authority to hear cases) of the Supreme Court

Congress can impeach and remove federal judges

President appoints federal judges (who must be confirmed by the Senate)

Congress can propose amendments to override Supreme Court decisions

Perhaps the most important section of Article I is Section 8. It carefully lists the powers the Framers wished the new Congress to possess. These **enumerated**—or specified—**powers** contain many key provisions that had been denied to the Continental Congress under the Articles of Confederation. For example, one of the major weaknesses of the Articles was Congress's lack of authority to deal with trade wars. The Constitution remedied this problem by authorizing Congress to "regulate Commerce with foreign Nations, and among the several States."

After careful enumeration of seventeen powers of Congress, a key clause authorizing Congress to "make all Laws which shall be necessary and proper for carrying into Execution the foregoing Powers" was added to Article I. Often referred to as the **elastic clause**, the "necessary and proper" clause has been the source of tremendous congressional activity never anticipated by the Framers, as definitions of "necessary" and "proper" have been stretched to accommodate changing needs and times. The Supreme Court, for example, has coupled Congress's authority to regulate commerce with the "necessary and proper" clause to allow Congress to ban prostitution (where travel across state lines is involved), regulate trains and planes, establish uniform federal minimum wage and maximum hour laws, and mandate drug testing for certain workers (see Chapter 6).

Article II: The Executive Branch. Article II vests the executive power, that is, the authority to execute the laws of the nation, in a president of the United States. Section 1 sets the president's term of office at four years and explains the electoral college. It also states qualifications for office and describes a mechanism to replace the president in case of death, disability, or removal.

The powers and duties of the president are set out in Section 3. Among the most important of these are the president's role as commander-in-chief of the armed forces, the authority to make treaties with the consent of the Senate, and the authority to "appoint Ambassadors, other public Ministers and Consuls, the Judges of the supreme Court,

President Clinton giving his State of the Union Address on January 25, 1994. While the Constitution requires only that the president report to Congress from time to time on the state of the union, over the years an annual State of the Union message has become a regular event, attended with much pomp and circumstance. Clinton's address in January 1993 was not technically a "State of the Union" address because he had only recently assumed office.

and all other Officers of the United States." Other sections of Article II instruct the president to report directly to Congress "from time to time," in what has come to be known as the "State of the Union Address," and to "take Care that the Laws be faithfully executed." Section 4 provides the mechanism for removal of the president, vice president, and other officers of the United States for "Treason, Bribery, or other high Crimes and Misdemeanors" (see Chapter 7).

Article III: The Judicial Branch. Article III establishes a Supreme Court and defines its jurisdiction. During the Philadelphia meeting, the small and large states differed significantly as to the desirability of an independent judiciary, and on the role of state courts in the national court system. The smaller states feared that a strong unelected judiciary would trample on their liberties. In compromise, Congress was permitted, but not required, to establish lower national courts. Thus, state courts and the national court system would exist side by side with distinct areas of authority. Federal courts were given authority to decide cases arising under federal law. The Supreme Court was also given the power to settle disputes between states, or between a state and the national government.

Although some delegates to the convention had urged that the president be allowed to remove federal judges, ultimately judges were given appointments for life, presuming "good behavior." And, like the president's, their salaries cannot be lowered while they hold office. This provision was adopted to ensure that the legislature did not attempt to punish the Supreme Court or any other judges for unpopular decisions.

Perhaps the most important power of the Supreme Court is that of **judicial review** (the authority of a court to determine the constitutional validity of acts of the legislature), although it is not mentioned in the Constitution. That power would later be assumed by the Court after Chief Justice John Marshall, writing for a unanimous Supreme Court in *Marbury* v. *Madison* (1803), concluded that the power was "implied" in the Constitution (see Chapter 9).

Articles IV through VII. Article IV deals with relations between the state and national governments, and includes the mechanisms for admitting new states to the Union. Article V specifies how amendments can be added to the Constitution. Article VI emphatically announces that the Constitution "shall be the supreme Law of the Land" and requires that all state and national members of the legislature, chief executives, and judicial officers shall swear an oath to support the Constitution. Mindful of the potential problems that could occur if church and state were too enmeshed, this article specifies that no religious test shall be required for holding any office. The seventh and final article of the Constitution concerns the procedures for ratification of the new Constitution: Nine of the thirteen states would have to agree to, or ratify, its new provisions.

The Drive for Ratification

While delegates to the Constitutional Convention labored in Philadelphia, the Second Continental Congress continued to govern the former colonies under the Articles of Confederation. The day after the Constitution was signed, William Jackson, the secretary of the Constitutional Convention, left for New York City, then the nation's capital, to deliver the official copy of the document to the Congress. He also took with him a

The Motives of the Framers

Debate about the Framers' motives filled the air during the ratification struggle and has provided grist for the mill of historians and political scientists over the years. Anti-Federalists, who opposed the new Constitution, charged that Federalist supporters of the Constitution were a self-serving, landed, and propertied elite with a vested interest in the capitalistic system that had evolved in the colonies. Federalists countered that they were simply trying to preserve the nation.

In his *Economic Interpretation of the Constitution of the United States* (1913), the highly respected political scientist and historian Charles A. Beard argued that the 1780s were a "critical period" (as the time under governance by the Articles of Confederation had come to be known) not for the nation as a whole, but rather for businessmen. These men feared that a weak, decentralized government could harm their economic interests. Beard argued that the merchants wanted a strong national government to promote industry and trade, protect private property, and most importantly, ensure payment of the public debt—much of which was owed to them. Therefore, according to Beard, the Constitution represents "an economic document drawn with superb skill by men whose property interests were immediately at stake."*

By the 1950s this view had fallen into disfavor when other historians were unable to find direct links between wealth and the Framers' motives for establishing the Constitution. In the 1960s, however, another group of historians began to argue that social and economic factors were, in fact, important motives for supporting the Constitution. In *The Anti-Federalists* (1961), Jackson Turner Main posited that while the Constitution's supporters might not have been the united group of creditors suggested by Beard, they were wealthier, came from high social strata, and had greater concern for maintaining the prevailing social order than the general public.

In 1969, Gordon Wood's *The Creation of the American Republic* resurrected this debate. Wood deemphasized economics to argue that major social divisions explained different groups' support for (or opposition to) the new Constitution. He concluded that the Framers were representatives of a class that favored order and stability over some of the more radical ideas that had inspired the Revolution.

* Quoted in Richard N. Current, et al., *American History: A Survey,* 6th ed. (N.Y.: Knopf, 1983), p. 170.

---

resolution of the delegates calling upon each of the states to vote on the new Constitution. Anticipating resistance from the representatives in the state legislatures, however, the Framers required the states to call special ratifying conventions to consider the proposed Constitution.

Jackson carried a letter from General George Washington with the proposed Constitution. In a few eloquent words, Washington summed up the sentiments of the Framers and the spirit of compromise that had permeated the long weeks in Philadelphia:

That it will meet the full and entire approbation of every state is not perhaps to be expected, but each [state] will doubtless consider, that had her interest alone been consulted, the consequences might have been particularly disagreeable or injurious to others; that it is liable to as few exceptions as could reasonably have been expected, we hope and believe; that it may promote lasting welfare of that country so dear to us all, and secure her freedom and happiness is our ardent wish.[19]

---

[19] Quoted in Faber and Faber, *We the People,* pp. 51–52. (See n. 9.)

The Second Continental Congress immediately accepted the work of the convention and forwarded the proposed constitution to the states for their vote. It was by no means certain, however, that the new constitution would be adopted.

From the fall of 1787 to the summer of 1788, the proposed constitution was debated hotly around the nation. State politicians understandably feared a strong central government. Farmers and other working class people were fearful of a distant national government. And those who had accrued substantial debts during the economic chaos following the Revolutionary War feared that a new government with a new financial policy would plunge them into even greater debt. The public in general was very leery of taxes—these were the same people who had revolted against the king's taxes. At the heart of many of their concerns was an underlying fear of the massive changes that would be brought about by a new system.

Favoring the Constitution were wealthy merchants, lawyers, bankers, and those who believed that the new nation could not continue to exist under the Articles of Confederation. For them, it all boiled down to one simple question offered by Madison: "Whether or not the Union shall or shall not be continued."

Federalists versus Anti-Federalists

Almost as soon as the ink was dry on the last signature to the Constitution, those who favored the new strong national government chose to call themselves **Federalists**. They were well aware that many still generally opposed the notion of a strong national government. Thus they did not want to risk being labeled "nationalists," so they tried to get the upper hand in the debate by nicknaming their opponents **Anti-Federalists**. Those put in the latter category insisted that they were instead "Federal Republicans" who believed in a federal system. As noted in Table 2.2, Anti-Federalists argued that they simply wanted to protect state governments from the tyranny of a too powerful national government.[20]

Federalists and Anti-Federalists participated in the mass meetings that were held in state legislatures to discuss the pros and cons of the new plan. Tempers ran high at public meetings where differences between the opposing groups were highlighted. Fervent debates were published in newspapers. Indeed, newspapers played a powerful role in the adoption process. The entire Constitution, in fact, was printed in the *Pennsylvania Packet* just two days after the convention's end. Other major papers quickly followed suit. Soon, articles on both sides of the adoption issue began to appear around the nation, often written under pseudonyms such as "Caesar" or "Constant Reader," as was the custom of the day.

One name stood out from all the rest: "Publius" (Latin for "the people"). Between October 1787 and May 1788, eighty-five articles written under that pen name routinely appeared in newspapers in New York, a state where ratification was in doubt. Most were written by Alexander Hamilton and James Madison. Hamilton, a young, fiery New Yorker born in the British West Indies, wrote fifty-one, Madison wrote twenty-six, and jointly they penned another three. John Jay, also of New York, and later the first Chief Justice of the United States, wrote five of the pieces. These eighty-five essays became known as **The Federalist Papers**.[21]

---

[20] Federal Republicans favored a republican or representative form of government (do not confuse this term with the modern Republican Party, which came into being in 1854; see Chapter 11). Ultimately the word *federal* came to mean the form of government embodied in the new Constitution, just as *confederation* meant the "league of states" under the Articles, and later came to mean the "Confederacy" of 1861–1865.

[21] Numerous editions of *The Federalist Papers* exist. The one most commonly used is: Clinton Rossiter, ed., *The Federalist* (New York: New American Library, 1961)

Table 2.2 ♦ Federalists and Anti-Federalists Compared

	FEDERALISTS	ANTI-FEDERALISTS
Who were they?	Property owners, landed rich, merchants of Northeast and Middle Atlantic states	Small farmers, shopkeepers, laborers
Political philosophy	Elitist: saw themselves and those of their class as most fit to govern (others were to *be* governed)	Believed in decency of common man and in participatory democracy; viewed elites as corrupt; sought greater protection of individual rights
Type of government favored	Powerful central government; two-house legislature; upper house (six-year term) further removed from the people, whom they did not trust	Wanted stronger state governments (closer to the people) at the expense of the powers of the national government. Sought smaller electoral districts, frequent elections, referendum and recall, large unicameral legislature to provide for greater class and occupational representation
Alliances	Pro-British Anti-French	Anti-British Pro-French

Today, *The Federalist Papers* are considered masterful explanations of the Framers' intentions as they drafted the new Constitution. At the time, although they were reprinted widely, they were far too theoretical to have much impact on those who would ultimately vote on the proposed Constitution. Dry and scholarly, they lacked the fervor of much of the political rhetoric that was then in use. *The Federalist Papers* did, however, highlight the reasons for the structure of the new government and its benefits. According to *Federalist No. 10,* for example, the new Constitution was called "a republican remedy for the disease incident to republican government." Moreover, these musings of Madison, Hamilton, and Jay continue to be the best single source of the political theories and philosophies at the heart of our Constitution.

Forced on the defensive, the Anti-Federalists responded with their own series of "letters" written under the pen names of "Brutus" and "Cato," two ancient Romans famous for their intolerance of tyranny. These "letters" (actually essays) undertook a line-by-line critique of the Constitution and were designed to counteract *The Federalist Papers*.

Anti-Federalists argued that a strong central government would render the states powerless.[22] They stressed the strengths the government had been granted under the Articles, and argued that these Articles, not the proposed Constitution, created a true federal system. Moreover, they argued that the strong national government would tax

---

[22] See Ralph Ketcham, ed., *The Anti-Federalist Papers and the Constitutional Debates* (New York: New American Library, 1986).

heavily, that the Supreme Court would overwhelm the states by invalidating state laws, and that the president eventually would have too much power, as commander-in-chief of a large and powerful army.

In particular, the Anti-Federalists feared the power of the national government to run roughshod over the liberties of the people. They proposed that the taxing power of Congress be limited, that the executive be curbed by a council, that the military consist of state militias rather than a national force, and that the jurisdiction of the Supreme Court be limited to prevent it from reviewing and potentially overturning the decisions of state courts. But their most effective argument concerned the absence of a bill of rights in the Constitution.

James Madison answered these criticisms in *Federalists Nos. 10* and *51*. In *Federalist No. 10,* he pointed out that the voters would not always succeed in electing "enlightened statesmen" as their representatives. The greatest threat to individual liberties would therefore come from factions within the government, who might place narrow interests above broader national interests and the rights of citizens. While recognizing that no form of government could protect the country from unscrupulous politicians, Madison argued that the organization of the new government would minimize the effects of political factions. The great advantage of a federal system, Madison maintained, was that it created the "happy combination" of a national government too large to be controlled by any single faction, and several state governments that would be smaller and more responsive to local needs. Moreover, he argued in *Federalist No. 51* that the proposed federal government's separation of powers would prohibit any one branch from either dominating the national government or violating the rights of citizens.

Debate continued in the thirteen states as votes were taken from December 1787 to June 1788, in accordance with the ratifying process laid out in Article VII of the proposed Constitution. As shown in Figure 2-4, three states acted quickly to ratify the new Constitution. Two small states, Delaware and New Jersey, voted to ratify before the large states could rethink the notion of equal representation of the states in the Senate. Pennsylvania, where Federalists were well organized, was one of the first three states to ratify. Massachusetts assented to the new government but tempered its support by calling for an immediate addition of amendments including one protecting personal rights. New Hampshire became the crucial ninth state to ratify on June 21, 1788. This action completed the ratification process outlined in Article VII of the Constitution and marked the beginning of a new nation. But because New York and Virginia (which between them accounted for more than 40 percent of the new nation's population) had not yet ratified the Constitution, the practical future of the new nation remained in doubt.

Hamilton in New York and Madison in Virginia worked feverishly to convince delegates to their state conventions to vote for the new government. In New York, sentiment against it was high. In Albany, New York, fighting broke out over the proposed Constitution, resulting in injuries and death. While *The Federalist Papers* undoubtedly had some impact on the delegates, the support of prestigious backers such as Benjamin Franklin and George Washington also helped the ratification effort. Washington, in fact, was widely reported to say, "There is more wickedness than ignorance in Anti-Federalism." When news of Virginia's acceptance of the Constitution reached the New York convention, Hamilton was finally able to convince a majority of those present to follow suit by a narrow margin (thirty to twenty-seven). Both states also recommended the addition of a series of structural amendments, and a bill of rights.

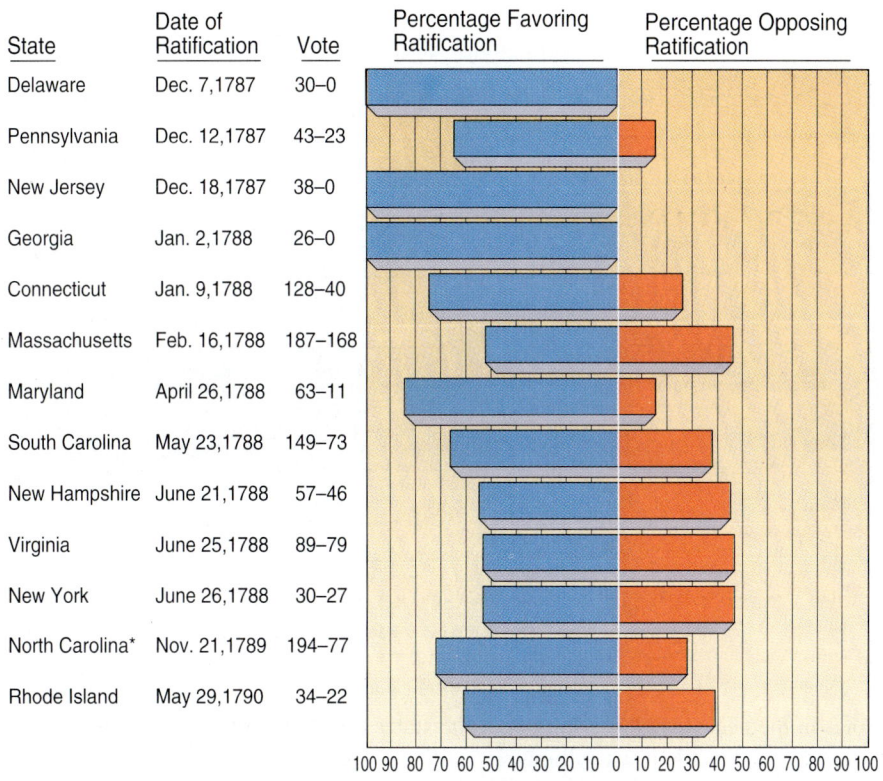

FIGURE 2-4

Ratification of the Constitution, by State

*Ratification originally defeated in August, 1788.

Two of the original states—North Carolina and Rhode Island—continued to hold out against ratification. Both had recently printed new currencies and feared that values would plummet in a federal system where the Congress was authorized to coin money. On August 2, 1788, North Carolina became the first state to reject the Constitution on the ground that no Anti-Federalist amendments were included. Soon after Congress submitted a Bill of Rights in September 1789, North Carolina ratified the Constitution by a vote of 194 to 77. Rhode Island, the only state that had not sent representatives to Philadelphia, remained out of the Union until 1790. Finally, under threats from its largest cities to secede from the state, the legislature called a convention that ratified the Constitution by a very narrow vote (34 to 32) one year after George Washington became the first president of the United States.

Amending the Constitution

Once the Constitution was ratified, elections were held. When Congress convened, it immediately sent a set of amendments to the states for their ratification. An amendment authorizing the enlargement of the House of Representatives and another to prevent members of the House from raising their own salaries failed to garner favorable

With the Constitution ratified in eleven states and only North Carolina and Rhode Island still uncommitted, cartoonists celebrated certain victory.

votes in the necessary three-fourths of the states (see "The Twenty-Seventh [Madison] Amendment," p. 61; it was ultimately ratified more than 200 years after it was sent to the states). The remaining ten amendments, known as the **Bill of Rights**, were ratified by 1791 in accordance with the procedures set out in the Constitution (see Table 2.3). Sought by Anti-Federalists as a protection for individual liberties, they offered numerous specific limitations on the national government's ability to interfere with a wide variety of personal liberties, some of which were already guaranteed by many state constitutions (see Chapters 4 and 5).

The Bill of Rights includes numerous specific protections of personal rights. Freedom of expression, speech, press, religion, and assembly are guaranteed by the First Amendment. The Bill of Rights also contains numerous safeguards for those accused of crimes.

In addition to guaranteeing these important rights, two of the amendments of the Bill of Rights were reactions to British rule—the right to bear arms (Second Amendment) and the right not to have soldiers quartered in private homes (Third Amendment). More general rights are also included in the Bill of Rights. The Ninth Amendment notes that these enumerated rights are *not* inclusive, meaning they are not the only rights to be enjoyed by the people, and the Tenth Amendment states that powers not given to the national government are reserved by the states or the people.

Article V of the Constitution creates a two-stage amendment process: proposal and ratification.[23] The Constitution specifies two ways to accomplish each stage. As illustrated in Figure 2-5, amendments to the Constitution can be proposed by:

1. A vote of two-thirds of the members in both houses of Congress, or
2. A vote of two-thirds of the state legislatures specifically requesting Congress to call a national convention to propose amendments.

[23] See Alan P. Grimes, *Democracy and the Amendments to the Constitution* (Lexington, MA: Lexington Books, 1978).

Table 2.3 ♦ The Bill of Rights*

First Amendment	Freedom of religion, speech, press, and assembly
Second Amendment	The right to bear arms
Third Amendment	Prohibition against quartering of troops in private homes
Fourth Amendment	Prohibition against unreasonable searches and seizures
Fifth Amendment	Rights guaranteed to the accused: requirement for grand jury indictment; protections against double jeopardy, self-incrimination; guarantee due process
Sixth Amendment	Right to a speedy and public trial before an impartial jury, to cross-examine witnesses, and to have counsel
Seventh Amendment	Right to a trial by jury in civil suits
Eighth Amendment	Prohibition against excessive bail and fines, and cruel and unusual punishment
Ninth Amendment	Rights not listed in the Constitution retained by the people
Tenth Amendment	States or people reserve those powers not denied to them by the Constitution or delegated to the national government

*For full text of the Bill of Rights, see Appendix II, page A4.

The second method has never been used. Historically, it has served as a fairly effective threat, forcing Congress to consider amendments that might otherwise never have been debated. In the 1980s, for example, several states called on Congress to enact a balanced-budget amendment. To forestall the need for a special constitutional convention, Congress began to debate the merits of just such an amendment and ultimately enacted the Gramm-Rudman-Hollings Act, which called for a balanced budget.

Of the thousands of amendments that have been introduced on one or both floors of the Congress, only thirty-three have mustered the two-thirds vote required for them to be sent to the states for debate and ratification. Only six proposed amendments sent to the states have failed to achieve ratification.

FIGURE 2-5

Methods of Amending the Constitution

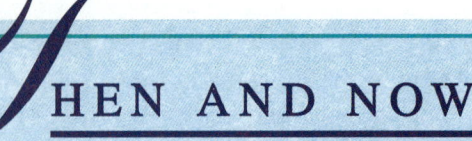

THEN AND NOW

The Constitution and the Right to Vote

On March 31, 1776 Abigail Adams wrote to her husband, John, in attendance at the Continental Congress, urging him to "Remember the Ladies" in any "new Code of Laws" that was to be written. She urged him and other delegates to "be more generous . . . to them than [their] ancestors." And, she warned, ultimately women would not consider themselves "bound by any Laws in which [they had] no voice, or Representation."* In spite of Abigail Adams's admonitions, neither the Articles of Confederation nor the Constitution mention women.

While the Constitution begins with the ringing words "We the People," at the time the Constitution was ratified, *no* state allowed women to vote in their state elections (Article I specifies that each state could set qualifications for voters in national elections). Nor could women hold state or national elective office. Moreover, the Constitution makes frequent use of the masculine pronouns "him" and "he."

* Quoted in H. L. Butterfield, et al., eds. *The Book of Abigail and John* (Cambridge, MA: Harvard University Press, 1975), p. 21.

It was not only women who were denied participation in ratification of the Constitution. Most states had stringent land-owning or property requirements. Thus, few poor men could vote, either.

Over the years, states eliminated most of the restrictions on voter eligibility. After the Civil War, in spite of the complaints of many women, the Fourteenth Amendment was added to the Constitution. For the first time the term *male* was specifically introduced into that document. Adding insult to injury, passage of the Fifteenth Amendment guaranteeing the right to vote to newly freed male slaves soon followed, without a provision to guarantee women the same right. Women did not secure the right to vote until the 1920 passage of the Nineteenth Amendment.

In 1971, fifty-one years after passage of the Nineteenth Amendment, the Constitution was again altered to expand the electorate. In 1971, the Twenty-Sixth Amendment, guaranteeing the right to vote to all U.S. citizens "eighteen years of age or older" was formally adopted. Today, no constitutional bans exist on voting, yet many citizens choose not to exercise this right so hard fought for by many groups.

The ratification process is fairly straightforward. When Congress votes to propose an amendment, the Constitution specifies that the ratification process must occur in one of two ways:

1. A favorable vote in three-fourths of the state legislatures, or
2. A favorable vote in specially called ratifying conventions in three-fourths of the states.

The Constitution itself, however, was to be ratified by specifically called ratifying conventions. The Framers feared that the power of special interests in state legislatures would prevent a positive vote on the new Constitution. Since ratification of the Constitution, however, only one ratifying convention has been called. The Eighteenth Amendment, which caused the "Prohibition Era" by outlawing the sale of alcoholic beverages, was ratified by the first method—a vote in state legislatures. Millions broke the law, others died from drinking homemade liquor, and others made their fortunes

The Twenty-Seventh (Madison) Amendment

On June 8, 1789, in a speech before the House of Representatives, James Madison stated,

> [T]here is seeming impropriety in leaving any set of men without controul [sic] to put their hand into the public coffers, to take out money to put into their pockets. . . . I have gone therefore so far as to fix it, that no law, varying the compensation, shall operate until there is a change in the legislation.

When Madison spoke these words about his proposal, now known as the Twenty-Seventh Amendment, he had no way of knowing that more than two centuries would pass before it would become an official part of the Constitution. In fact, Madison deemed it worthy of addition only because the conventions of three states (Virginia, New York, and North Carolina) had demanded that it be included.

By 1791, when the Bill of Rights (see Table 2.3, page 59) was added to the Constitution, only six states had ratified Madison's amendment, and it seemed destined to fade into obscurity. In 1982, however, George Watson, a sophomore majoring in economics at the University of Texas-Austin, discovered the unratified compensation amendment while looking for a paper topic for an American government class. Intrigued, Watson wrote a paper arguing that the proposed amendment was still viable because it had no internal time limit and, therefore, should be adopted. Watson received a "C" on the paper.

Despite his grade, Watson began a ten-year, $6,000 self-financed crusade to renew interest in the compensation amendment. Watson and his allies reasoned that the amendment should be revived because of the public's growing anger with the fact that members of Con-

Gregory Watson with a document that contains the first ten amendments to the constitution, as well as the compensation amendment ("Article the second: No law varying the compensation for the services of the Senators and Representatives shall take effect until an election of Representatives shall have intervened") that was finally ratified as the Twenty-Seventh Amendment in 1992.

gress had sought to raise their salaries without going on the record as having done so. Watson's perseverance paid off, and on May 7, 1992, the amendment was ratified. On May 18, the United States Archivist certified that the amendment was part of the Constitution, a decision that was overwhelmingly confirmed by the House of Representatives on May 19 and by the Senate on May 20.

At the same time that the Senate approved the Twenty-Seventh Amendment, it also took action to ensure that a similar situation never occurred by declaring "dead" four other amendments that did not have internal deadlines.

Source: Fordham Law Review, December 1992, pp. 497–539, and Anne Marie Kilday, "Amendment Expert Agrees with Congressional Pay Ruling." *The Dallas Morning News*, February 14, 1993: p. 13A.

---

selling bootleg or illegal liquor. After a decade of these problems, Congress decided to act. An additional amendment—the Twenty-first—was proposed to repeal the Eighteenth Amendment. It was sent to the states for ratification, but with a call for ratifying conventions, *not* a vote in the state legislatures.[24] Members of Congress correctly pre-

---

[24] David E. Kyvig, *Repealing National Prohibition* (Chicago: University of Chicago Press, 1978).

> ### Amendments That Have Failed State Ratification
>
> 1. A provision allowing Congress to regulate the number of members of the House once the proportions went beyond 100,000 persons per Representative. Proposed: 1789.
> 2. A provision stripping U.S. citizenship from any individual who "shall accept, claim, receive or retain any title of nobility or honour, or shall without consent of Congress, accept and retain any present pension, office or emolument of any kind whatever, from any emperor, king, prince or foreign power." Proposed: 1811.
> 3. A provision barring the federal government from interfering with or abolishing slavery. Proposed: 1861.
> 4. A provision banning child labor. Proposed: 1924.
> 5. A provision stating that "equality of rights shall not be denied or abridged by the United States or by any State on account of sex." Proposed: 1972.
> 6. A provision giving the District of Columbia representation in Congress. Proposed: 1978.

dicted that the move to repeal the Eighteenth Amendment would encounter opposition in the statehouses, which were largely controlled by conservative rural interests. Thus, Congress's decision to use the convention method led to quick approval of the Twenty-first Amendment.

The intensity of efforts to amend the Constitution has varied considerably depending on the nature of the change proposed. Whereas the Twenty-First Amendment took only ten months to ratify, an equal rights amendment (ERA) was introduced in every session of Congress from 1923 until 1972, when Congress finally voted favorably on it.

Even then, years of lobbying by women's groups were insufficient to garner necessary state support. By 1982, the congressionally mandated date for ratification, only thirty-five states—three short of the number required—had voted favorably on the amendment.[25]

As illustrated in Table 2.4, amendments passed after the Bill of Rights can be organized into four categories: (1) those effecting a structural change in government, (2) those affecting public policy, (3) those expanding rights, and (4) those overruling a U.S. Supreme Court decision.

Most amendments that change the structure or mechanics of government have been ratified quite easily in response to some sort of "emergency." In the wake of President John F. Kennedy's assassination in 1963, which left the nation without a vice president when Lyndon B. Johnson became president, the Twenty-Fifth Amendment was added to the Constitution to allow the president to fill, subject to the approval of Congress, a vacancy in the office of vice president. For the most part, the public has accepted the structural changes as a natural working out of the kinks in the Constitution.

Amendments expanding rights, especially those concerned with enlarging the electorate, make up the next significant group of amendments. Generally, once these amendments secure congressional favor, state ratification follows quickly. For exam-

---

[25] See Jane J. Mansbridge, *Why We Lost the ERA* (Chicago: University of Chicago Press, 1986).

Table 2.4 ♦ Types of Constitutional Amendments

EFFECTING STRUCTURAL CHANGE

12th	Electors required to vote separately for president and vice president (1804)
17th	Direct vote of U.S. senators (1913)
20th	Date of presidential inauguration changed (1933)
22nd	Presidents limited to two terms (1951)
25th	Presidential and vice-presidential succession (1967)
27th	Salaries of members of Congress (1992)

AFFECTING PUBLIC POLICY

18th	Liquor sales prohibited (1919)
21st	18th Amendment repealed (1933)

EXPANDING RIGHTS

1st–10th	The Bill of Rights (1791)
13th	Slavery banned (1865)
14th	Equal protection and due process guaranteed (1868)
15th	Suffrage extended to black males (1870)
19th	Suffrage extended to women (1920)
23rd	Residents of District of Columbia given right to vote in presidential elections (1961)
24th	Poll taxes abolished (1964)
26th	Suffrage extended to 18-year-olds (1971)

OVERRULING SUPREME COURT DECISIONS*

11th	Individuals prohibited from suing a state without its permission (1798)
16th	Congress given power to tax personal income (1913)

*The Fourteenth and Twenty-sixth Amendments also effectively overruled Supreme Court decisions.

ple, women tried for decades to secure a constitutional amendment guaranteeing their right to vote, yet once Congress voted favorably on the Nineteenth Amendment, ratification by the states took less than two years.[26]

Amendments designed to affect existing public policies form a third category of constitutional amendments. Many constitutional scholars regard these amendments as troublesome. They argue that the Constitution should be a basic outline of principles, and not a list of desired outcomes. Critics today, for example, fear that efforts to amend the Constitution to prohibit flag burning, allow prayer in schools, or ban abortions would be foolhardy and unnecessary interference with the basic nature of the Constitution. The first two are regarded as particularly risky because they would alter the First Amendment, which to this day has never been modified.

---

[26] Eleanor Flexner, *Century of Struggle: The Woman's Rights Movement in the United States* (New York: Atheneum, 1974).

A final category of amendments consists of those enacted to overrule specific Supreme Court decisions. As discussed in greater detail in Chapter 9, the Supreme Court is the final authority on the Constitution. Once the Court construes a provision of the Constitution, only the Court itself or a constitutional amendment can change that interpretation. Only two of the Supreme Court's decisions have been overruled by constitutional amendments.

Informal Methods of Amending the Constitution

The formal amendment process is not the only way that the Constitution has been changed over time. Judicial interpretation, cultural change, and technological change also have had a major impact on the way the Constitution has evolved.

Judicial Interpretation. As early as 1803, under the brilliant leadership of Chief Justice John Marshall, the Supreme Court declared that the federal courts had the power to nullify acts of the nation's government when they were found to be in conflict with the Constitution. Over the years this check on the other branches of government and on the states has increased the authority of the Court and has significantly altered the meaning of various provisions of the Constitution, a fact that prompted Woodrow Wilson to call the Supreme Court "a constitutional convention in continuous session."

When the Framers authorized Congress to regulate commerce among the states, they could not have imagined the controversial course that interpretation of that authorizing clause would take. In *Gibbons* v. *Ogden* (1824), Chief Justice Marshall proclaimed that commerce was "any intercourse between states," including navigation. This interpretation allowed Congress to increase its regulatory activity. Later, in the 1930s, a pro-business Court interpreted the commerce clause very narrowly as it repeatedly ruled unconstitutional legislation backed by President Franklin D. Roosevelt, designed to bring the country out of the economic chaos of the Depression. It was not until 1937—in the face of strong public pressure and the threat of congressional attacks—that the Court reinterpreted the commerce clause to find constitutional justification for such sweeping congressional power. Since that time, most congressional efforts to regulate any form of business or employment practice have been held to be within the scope of Congress's power under the commerce clause.

Today, some argue that the original intent of the Framers, as evidenced in *The Federalist Papers* as well as in private notes taken by James Madison at the Constitutional Convention, should govern judicial interpretation of the Constitution.[27] Others argue that the Framers knew that a changing society needed an elastic, flexible document that could conform to the ages.[28] In all likelihood, the vagueness of the document was purposeful. Those in attendance in Philadelphia recognized that they could not agree on everything and that it was wiser to leave interpretation to those who would follow them.

Social and Cultural Change. Even the most far-sighted of those in attendance at the constitutional convention could not have anticipated the vast changes that have occurred in the United States. For example, although many were uncomfortable with the Three-Fifths Compromise and others hoped for the abolition of slavery, none could

---

[27] Speech by Attorney General Edwin Meese III before the American Bar Association, July 9, 1985, Washington, DC.

[28] Speech by William J. Brennan Jr. at Georgetown University, Text and Teaching Symposium, October 10, 1985, Washington, DC.

have imagined the status of African Americans today, or that Colin Powell could serve as Chairman of the Joint Chiefs of Staff and be frequently mentioned as a viable candidate for president or vice president in 1992 and 1996. Likewise, few of the Framers could have anticipated the diverse roles that women would come to play in American society. The Constitution has often been bent to accommodate such social and cultural changes. Thus, although there is no specific amendment guaranteeing women equal protection of the law, the federal courts have interpreted the Constitution to prohibit many forms of gender discrimination, thereby recognizing cultural and societal change.

Technological Change. Technological innovation has also contributed to a changing Constitution. The Framers could not have envisioned the need for an air traffic control system or for regulation of the airwaves. In 1993, for example, instantaneous forms of communication allowed many Americans to watch in horror as the Branch Davidian compound in Waco, Texas was enveloped in flames, killing at least eighty-five cult members, and to watch the wreckage caused by the bombing of New York City's World Trade Center. Moreover, as computers and other technological advances have allowed the government and, in particular, the bureaucracy (see Chapter 8) to grow, our expectations of the role of government have also changed. It is unlikely that the Framers could have envisioned a Social Security system that has the capacity to mail more than 35 million checks per month to retirees and the disabled.

Advances in technology have required new interpretations of the Bill of Rights. Wiretapping and other forms of electronic surveillance, for example, are now regulated by the First and Fourth Amendments. Similarly, HIV testing and drug screening, which involve scientifically advanced tests, must be juxtaposed against constitutional protections.

Toward Reform

When asked in a May 1987 CBS News/New York Times poll, "Do you think it is too easy or too hard to amend the Constitution, or is the process about right?" 11 percent of those polled responded, "Too easy"; 20 percent responded, "Too hard"; and 60 percent responded, "About right." A Gallup poll conducted the same year found that 72 percent of those questioned believed that a modern constitutional convention might make things worse, but 44 percent expressed their belief that the "Constitution needs basic changes." (Some of these respondents may have been ardent supporters of the ERA or a Right to Life Amendment, who continue to believe that the Constitution should be amended.)

When the Framers met in Philadelphia in 1787, they sought to fashion a constitution that would provide the basic framework for running the nation not only in 1787 but also well into the future. Since ratification of the Bill of Rights in 1791, only seventeen amendments have been added, and only fifteen continue to be functional (the Twenty-First Amendment repealed the Eighteenth Amendment). The basic framework of government, although "reformed" considerably over time through informal means, remains vital today. Emotionally charged calls for change often have occurred in the wake of highly unpopular Supreme Court decisions such as *Texas* v. *Johnson* (1989), in which the justices ruled that flag burning was a form of political speech protected by the First Amendment. Politicians, veterans' groups, and members of the general public all immediately clamored for passage of a constitutional amendment to limit the reach of the First Amendment and expressly to prohibit flag burning. But, as time passed, cooler heads prevailed, and this move to amend the Constitution failed to make headway.

As early as 1889, James Bryce argued that the Constitution had two major defects—too much power was divided between the president and Congress to allow for prompt and effective action, and the system of checks and balances caused excessive friction between these two branches.[29] Many of these problems continue to the present day. The Committee on the Constitutional System (CCS), an influential non-partisan group of more than 200 former members of Congress, former Cabinet officials, and political scientists, has made several serious proposals to stop this "gridlock."[30] Political scientist and CCS member James L. Sundquist, for example, has written extensively about the negative effects of "divided government;" that is, the situation that results when Congress and the President come from different political parties.[31] Since the Framers did not envision the role of political parties in the system, the separation of powers and checks and balances schemes that unify the national government can become gridlocked when different political parties control the legislative and executive branches of government. Although he admits that it would be politically and practically infeasible, Sundquist has suggested altering the electoral system to prohibit split ticket voting (i.e., voting for a Democrat for Congress and a Republican for President in national elections).

Prohibitions against split ticket voting could take several forms, such as allowing voters to select from political "teams" of candidates composed of a single party's candidates for president, vice president, Senate and House,[32] or requiring a party's congressional candidates to be its candidates for electors in the electoral college. Other proposed reforms include making the American system operate more like the British: whenever divided government became gridlocked, either the president or the majority of both Houses of Congress could dissolve the government and call for new elections.[33]

While these suggestions for reform provide food for thought, the CCS admits that these ideas would not be greeted with open arms in the Congress, where under normal constitutional amendment procedures, such changes would have to be initiated. Thus, major constitutional reform is unlikely to occur. Relatively simple changes have often sparked tremendous controversy. Just imagine what serious calls for a total overhaul of the government could bring.

[29] James Bryce. *The American Commonwealth*, vol. I, (New York: Macmillan, 1889), pp. 293–295.

[30] For a full critique of these proposals see Mark P. Petracca with Lance Bailey and Pamela Smith, "Proposals for Constitutional Reform: An Evaluation of the Committee on the Constitutional System," *Presidential Studies Quarterly*, 20 (Summer 1990): 503–532.

[31] James L. Sundquist, "Needed: A Political Theory for the New Era of Coalition Governments in the United States," *Political Science Quarterly*, 103 (1988): 613–635.

[32] Ibid. 631.

[33] Hedrick Smith, "The Politics of Blame," *The New York Times*, October 7, 1984: 36.

Summary

The U.S. Constitution has proven to be a remarkably enduring document. In explaining how and why the Constitution came into being, this chapter has covered the following points:

1. While settlers came to the New World for a variety of reasons, most remained loyal to Great Britain and considered themselves subjects of the king. Over the years, those ties weakened as new generations of Americans were born on colonial soil. A series of taxes levied by the Crown ultimately led the colonists to convene a Continental Congress and to declare their independence.

2. The Declaration of Independence (1776), which drew heavily on the writings of John Locke, carefully enu-

merated the wrongs of the Crown and galvanized public resentment and willingness to take up arms against Great Britain in the Revolutionary War (1775–1782).
3. The Articles of Confederation (1781) created a loose league of friendship between the new national government and the states. Numerous weaknesses in the new government became apparent by 1784. Among the major flaws were Congress's inability to tax or regulate commerce, the absence of an executive to administer the government, and a weak central government.
4. When the weaknesses under the Articles of Confederation became apparent, the states called for a meeting to reform them. The Constitutional Convention (1787) quickly threw out the Articles of Confederation and fashioned a new, more workable form of government. The Constitution was the result of a series of compromises, including those over representation questions involving large and small states, and over how to determine population. Compromises were also made about how members of each branch of government were to be selected. The electoral college was created to give states a key role in the selection of the president.
5. The proposed U.S. Constitution created a federal system that drew heavily on Montesquieu's ideas about separation of powers; that is, a way of parcelling out power among the three branches of government, and checks and balances to prevent any one branch from having too much power.
6. The drive for ratification became a fierce fight between Federalists and Anti-Federalists. Federalists lobbied for the strong national government created by the Constitution; Anti-Federalists favored greater state power.
7. The Framers created a formal two-stage amendment process to include the Congress and the states. Amendments could be proposed by a two-thirds vote in Congress or of state legislatures, requesting that Congress call a national convention to propose amendments. Amendments could be ratified by a positive vote of three-fourths of the state legislatures or specially called state ratifying conventions. Judicial interpretation and cultural and technological changes have also caused constitutional change.

Key Terms

common law
Articles of Confederation
Stamp Act Congress
Committees of Correspondence
First Continental Congress
Second Continental Congress
Declaration of Independence
confederation
Shays's Rebellion

Virginia Plan
bicameral legislature
New Jersey Plan
Great Compromise
Three-Fifths Compromise
unitary government
federal system
separation of powers

checks and balances
enumerated powers
elastic clause
judicial review
Federalists
Anti-Federalists
The Federalist Papers
Bill of Rights

Suggested Readings

Bailyn, Bernard. *The Ideological Origins of the American Revolution*. Cambridge, MA: Harvard University Press, 1967.

Beard, Charles. *An Economic Interpretation of the Constitution of the United States*. New York: Macmillan, 1913.

Bernstein, Richard B. and Jerome Agel. *Amending America*. New York: Random House, 1992.

Bowen, Catherine Drinker. *Miracle at Philadelphia*. Boston: Little-Brown, 1966.

Hamilton, Alexander, James Madison, and John Jay. *The Federalist Papers*, ed. Isaac Kramnick. New York: Penguin, 1987 (first published in 1788).

Ketchman, Ralph. *The Anti-Federalist Papers and the Constitutional Convention Debated*. New York: New American Library, 1986.

Levy, Leonard W., ed. *Essays on the Making of the Constitution*. New York: Oxford University Press, 1969.

McDonald, Forest. *The Formation of the American Republic*. New York: Penguin, 1967.

Main, Jackson Turner. *The Social Structure of Revolutionary America*. Princeton, NJ: Princeton University Press, 1965.

Rossiter, Clinton. *1787: Grand Convention*. New York: Macmillan, 1966.

Wood, Gordon S. *The Creation of the American Republic*. Chapel Hill: University of North Carolina Press, 1969.

The power surrendered by the people is first divided between two distinct governments, and then . . . subdivided among distinct and separate departments. Hence, a double security arises to the rights of the people.

James Madison
FEDERALIST NO. 51

The Framers, fearing tyranny, divided powers between the state and the national governments. At each level, moreover, powers were divided among executive, legislative, and judicial branches.

CHAPTER 3

Federalism

THE ROOTS OF THE FEDERAL SYSTEM
THE EVOLUTION AND DEVELOPMENT OF FEDERALISM
THE NEW DEAL AND A RAPIDLY CHANGING BALANCE OF POWER
THE CHANGING NATURE OF FEDERALISM
THE INTERGOVERNMENTAL LOBBY
FEDERALISM AND THE SUPREME COURT
TOWARD REFORM

From its very beginning, the challenge for the United States of America was to preserve the traditional independence and rights of the states while establishing an effective national government. In *Federalist No. 51,* James Madison highlighted the unique structure of governmental powers created by the Framers.

Although most of the delegates to the Constitutional Convention favored a strong federal government, they knew that some compromise about the distribution of powers would be necessary. Some of the Framers wanted to continue with the confederate form of government defined in the Articles of Confederation; others wanted a more centralized system like that of Great Britain. Their solution was to create the world's first **federal system**, in which the thirteen sovereign or independent states were bound together under one national government. The result was a system of government that was "neither wholly *national* nor wholly *federal*," as Madison explained in *The Federalist Papers.*

The nature of the federal relationship between the national government and the states, including their respective duties, obligations, and powers, is outlined in the U.S. Constitution, although the word *federal* does not appear in that document. Throughout history, however, this system and the rules that guide it have been continually stretched, reshaped and reinterpreted by crises, historical evolution, public expectations, and judicial interpretation. All these forces have had tremendous influence on who makes policy decisions and how these decisions get made.

Issues involving the distribution of power between the national government and the states affect you on a daily basis. You do not, for example, need a passport to go from Texas to Oklahoma. There is one national currency and a national minimum wage. But many differences exist among the laws of the various states. The age at which you may marry is a state issue, as are laws governing divorce, child custody, and the purchase of guns. As revealed in Figure 3-1, even before congressional passage of the Brady Bill requiring a five-day waiting period for the purchase of handguns, two-thirds of the states already required some sort of waiting period.

While some policies or programs are under the authority of the state or local government, others, such as air traffic regulation, are solely within the province of the national government.[1] In many areas, however, the national and state governments work together cooperatively. For example, you may receive national as well as state loans, grants, or other forms of assistance to finance your education. Similarly, many of the poor receive help from the national, state, and local governments. At times the national government cooperates or supports programs only if the states meet certain conditions. In order to receive federal funds for the construction and maintenance of highways, for example, states must follow federal rules about the kinds of roads they build.

In this chapter, we look at the nature of the government created by the Framers, and at their attempt to divide the power and the functions of government between one na-

---

[1] In *City of Burbank* v. *Lockheed*, 411 U.S. 624 (1973), the U.S. Supreme Court ruled that the city could not impose curfews on plane takeoff or landing times. The Court said that one uniform *national* standard was critical for safety and the national interest.

FIGURE 3-1

States with Waiting Periods for Handgun Purchases Before the 1993 Passage of the Brady Bill

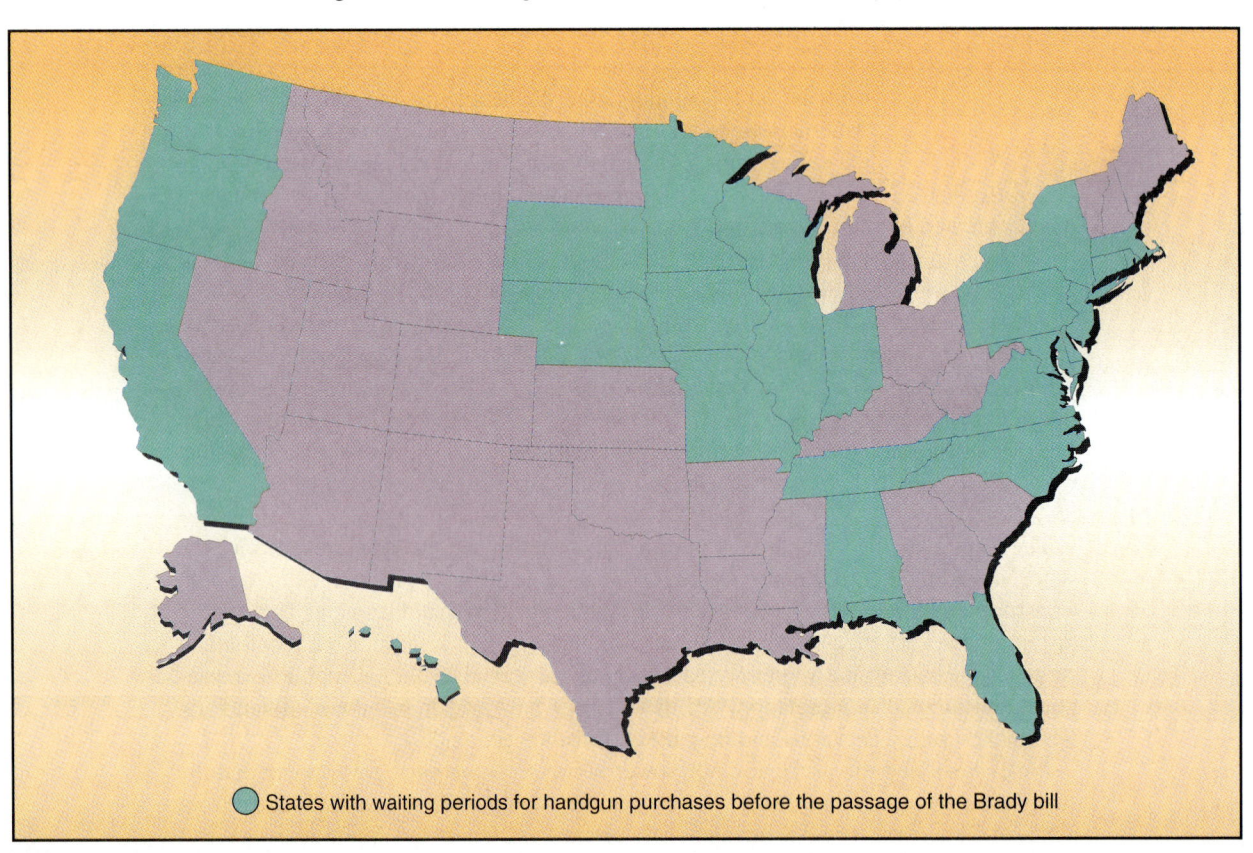

○ States with waiting periods for handgun purchases before the passage of the Brady bill

Source: USA Today, November 26–28, 1993: p. A1.

tional and several state governments. We also explore the reasons why a federal system was adopted, and analyze how the relationship and allocation of powers between the national and state governments have changed over time. Crises, public expectations, political ideology, and decisions of the Supreme Court have played especially important roles in the development of what political scientists today mean by federalism. As you read this chapter, keep in mind the arguments made by the Framers in support of the system they created. How close to or far from the original intentions of the Founders is the federalism of the twentieth century?

The Roots of the Federal System

The Framers worked to create a form of government familiar to Americans, but one that would remedy many of the problems experienced under the Articles of Confederation. The relationship between and the intertwined powers of the national and state governments are the heart of **federalism**, which has its origins in the Latin *foedus*, or "covenant." Thus, federalism can be envisioned as the philosophy that defines the allocation of power between the national government and the states. Ironically, as discussed in Chapter 2, those who supported the government under the Articles of Confederation argued for what *they* called a federal system. But the fear of being labeled "nationalists" prompted supporters of the new Constitution to call themselves "Federalists," thus co-opting this popular term of the day. Like other Federalist supporters of the new Constitution, Alexander Hamilton articulated three major arguments for federalism: (1) the prevention of tyranny; (2) the provision for increased participation in politics; and (3) the use of the states as testing grounds or "laboratories" for new policies and programs.

The national government created by the Framers draws its powers directly from the people, so that both national *and* state governments are ultimately directly accountable to the public. Each government also has the ability to tax, and has its own set of public officials. The Framers envisioned each government to be supreme in some spheres, as depicted in Figure 3-2. In *Federalist No. 51,* James Madison explained what he perceived to be the beauty of this system: The shifting support of the electorate between the two governments would serve to keep each in balance.

In fashioning the new federal system of government, the Framers recognized that they could not define precisely how all the relations between the national government and the individual states would work. But the Constitution makes it clear that separate spheres of government were to be at the very core of the federal system, with some allowances made for concurrent powers.

The Powers of Government in the Federal System

The distribution of powers in the federal system is often described as two overlapping circles, as illustrated in Figure 3-2. On the left are powers specifically granted to Congress in Article I. Chief among the exclusive powers delegated to the national government are the authorities to coin money, conduct foreign relations, provide for an army and navy, declare war, and establish a national court system. All of these powers set out in Article I, Section 8 of the Constitution are called **enumerated powers**.

Article I, Section 8 also contains the **necessary and proper clause**, giving Congress the authority to enact any laws "necessary and proper" for carrying out any of its enu-

FIGURE 3-2
The Distribution of Governmental Power in the Federal System

National Powers
- Coin money
- Conduct foreign relations
- Regulate commerce with foreign nations and among states
- Provide an army and a navy
- Declare war
- Establish courts inferior to the Supreme Court
- Make laws necessary and proper to carry out the foregoing powers

Concurrent Powers
- Tax
- Borrow money
- Establish courts
- Make and enforce laws
- Charter banks and corporations
- Spend money for the general welfare
- Take private property for public purposes, with just compensation

State Powers
- Set time, place and manner of electors
- Ratify amendments to the federal Constitution
- Take measures for public health, safety, and morals
- Exert powers the Constitution does not delegate to the national government or prohibit the states from using
- Establish local governments
- Regulate commerce within a state

---

merated powers. Thus, for example, Congress's power to charter a national bank (see pp. 76–77) has been held to be an **implied power** derived from its enumerated power to tax and spend.[2]

The Constitution does not specifically delegate or enumerate many specific powers to the states. Because states had all the power at the time the Constitution was written, the Framers felt no need, as they did for the new national government, to list and restate the powers of the states. Article I, however, allows states to set the "Times, Places and Manner, for holding elections for senators and representatives," and Article II requires that each state appoint electors to vote for president. States were also given the power to ratify amendments to the U.S. Constitution. Nevertheless, the enumeration of so many specific powers to the national government and so few to the states is a clear indication of the Federalist leanings of the Framers. It was not until the addition of the Bill of Rights and the Tenth Amendment that the states' powers were better described: "The powers not delegated to the United States by the Constitution, nor prohibited by it to the States, are reserved to the States respectively, or to the people." These powers, often called the states' reserve or police powers, include the ability to legislate for the public health, safety and morals of their citizens.

As revealed in Figure 3-2, national and state powers also overlap. The area where the circles overlap represents **concurrent powers**—powers shared by the national and state governments. States already had the power to tax; the Constitution extended this power to the national government as well. Other important concurrent powers include the right to borrow money, establish courts, and enact and enforce laws necessary to carry out these powers.

---

[2] *McCulloch* v. *Maryland*, 4 Wheat. 316 (1819).

Denied Powers. Article I also *denies* certain powers to the national and state governments. In keeping with the Framers' desire to forge a national economy, states are prohibited from entering treaties, coining money, or impairing obligation of contracts.

States are also prohibited from entering into "compacts" with other states without express congressional approval. In a similar vein, Congress is barred from favoring one state over another in regulating commerce, nor can it lay duties on items exported from any state.

Both the national and state governments are denied the authority to take arbitrary actions affecting constitutional rights and liberties. Neither national nor state governments may pass a **bill of attainder**, a law declaring an act illegal without a judicial trial. The Constitution also bars either from passing **ex post facto** laws, laws that make an act punishable as a crime if the action was legal at the time it was committed.

Guarantees to the States. In return for giving up some of their powers, the states received several guarantees in the Constitution. Among them:

- Article I guarantees each state two members in the U.S. Senate and guarantees that Congress would not limit slavery before 1808.
- Article IV guarantees the citizens of each state the privileges and immunities of citizens of all other states, guarantees each state a "Republican Form of Government," meaning one that represents the citizens of the state, and guarantees that the national government will protect the states against foreign attacks and domestic rebellion.

Relations Among the States. The Constitution was designed to improve relations among the squabbling states. To that end, it provides that disputes between states are to be settled directly by the U.S. Supreme Court under its original jurisdiction to avoid any sense of favoritism (see Chapter 9). Moreover, Article IV requires that each state give "Full Faith and Credit . . . to the public Acts, Records and judicial Proceedings of every other State." This clause ensures that judicial decrees and contracts made in one

The Port Authority jointly operated by New York and New Jersey is just one example of cooperative ventures of the states approved by Congress. States are encouraged to enter into these kinds of compacts by the nature of our federal system. Before adoption of the U.S. Constitution, the states were not encouraged to share their powers and commerce often suffered.

> **Landmark Periods in the Evolution of the Federal System**
>
> 1789–1834 ♦ **Nationalization:** The Marshall Court broadly interprets the Constitution to expand and consolidate national power.
>
> 1835–1860 ♦ **Dual Federalism:** Phase 1—Power of national government limited to enumerated powers; states consider themselves sovereign; governments in state of tension over scope of their respective authorities.
>
> 1861–1933 ♦ **Dual Federalism:** Phase 2—Dual characteristics continue, but national government gains power; land-grant era.
>
> 1934–1960 ♦ **Cooperative Federalism:** Dramatic increase in grants-in-aid; federal, state, and local sharing of responsibilities; increased regulation by national government.
>
> 1960–1968 ♦ **Creative Federalism:** Hallmark of Johnson era; increased grants to state and local governments and direct aid to individuals.
>
> 1968–1993 ♦ **New Federalism:** Emphasis on the return of power to the states; later characterized by the significant reduction in federal aid to the states.

state will be binding and enforceable in another, thereby facilitating trade and other commercial relationships.

In a similar vein, the Constitution requires states to extradite, or return, criminals to states where they have been convicted or are to stand trial. Moreover, Article IV, Section 2 specifies that escaped slaves must be returned to their owners.[3] For example, Willis Lago, a free black man living in Ohio, was accused of helping a female slave from Kentucky escape to Ohio, a free state. In 1861, the Supreme Court ruled that although the governor of Ohio had a *legal* obligation to return Lago to Kentucky for prosecution for his crime, the federal government lacked the power to force the governor to comply, in spite of Article IV.[4] In 1987, however, the Supreme Court ruled that this decision under Article IV must be interpreted in light of the fact that it was made during the Civil War, when the federal government's power over the states was at its lowest ebb. Thus, when the governor of Iowa refused to honor Puerto Rico's request to extradite a man charged with first degree murder, the Court ruled that the extradition clause is binding on the states and is *not* discretionary. Iowa's governor had argued that the charges against the accused were unreasonable, and because the defendant was white, he would be unlikely to receive a fair trial in Puerto Rico.[5] Nevertheless, because the federal government today has the authority to enforce the extradition law, the Court found that Iowa was bound by the Constitution.

---

[3] The Constitution does not specifically mention slaves. It does, however, contain the mandate that "No Person held to Service or Labour in one State . . . escaping into another, shall . . . be discharged from such service . . . but shall be delivered up."

[4] *Kentucky* v. *Dennison*, 65 U.S. 66 (1861).

[5] *Puerto Rico* v. *Branstad*, 483 U.S. 219 (1987).

National Supremacy. Even during the Constitutional Convention, the Framers were aware that conflict and friction between the national government and the states was inevitable. Article VI, Section 2 was added to the Constitution to provide a way to resolve these conflicts. It declares that the U.S. Constitution, the Laws of the United States, and its treaties are to be "the supreme Law of the Land; and the Judges in every State shall be bound thereby . . ."

In spite of this explicit language, the meaning of what is called the "**supremacy clause**" has been subject to continuous judicial interpretation and reinterpretation. In *Missouri* v. *Holland* (1920),[6] for example, Missouri sought to prevent a U.S. game warden from enforcing the Migratory Bird Treaty Act of 1918, which prohibited the killing or capturing of many species of birds as they made their annual migration across the international border from Canada to parts of the United States. Missouri argued that the Tenth Amendment, which reserved a state's powers to legislate for the general welfare of its citizens, allowed Missouri to regulate hunting. But the Court ruled that since the treaty was legal, it was the supreme law of the land. Thus, when national law and state law come into conflict, national law (including treaties) is supreme. (See also *McCulloch* v. *Maryland* [1819], pp. 76–77.)

The Evolution and Development of Federalism

The victory of the Federalists—those who supported a strong national government—had long-lasting consequences on the future of the nation. Over the course of our nation's history, the nature of federalism and its allocation of power between the national government and the states have changed dramatically. And because the distribution of power between the national and state governments is not clearly delineated in the Constitution, over the years the U.S. Supreme Court has played a major role in defining the nature of the federal system.

The Supreme Court

From the beginning, the courts were involved in developing the structure and mechanics of the federal system. At the head of the federal judiciary sat John Marshall (1801–1835), an ardent Federalist. In a series of important decisions, Chief Justice Marshall and the Supreme Court reaffirmed the Federalists' beliefs in a strong national government. Federalist sentiments could be seen especially clearly in the Court's broad interpretations of the Constitution's supremacy clause and the commerce clause, both of which were used to expand and consolidate the power of the national government.

It is important to remember, however, that during the period the Marshall Court was nationalizing the federal system, the national government itself was small, with limited activities and minimal spending. In contrast, the state governments' role in everyday life was far more pervasive than it is today. States exercised tremendous powers over the electoral process (including who voted and how congressional districts were drawn) and were the center of party organizations. States also controlled labor conditions, race relations, education, property rights, criminal and family law, and, in the South, slavery.

---

[6] 252 U.S. 416 (1920).

***McCulloch v. Maryland* (1819).** *McCulloch* was the first major decision of the Marshall Court to define the relationship between the national and state governments. In 1816 Congress chartered the Second Bank of the United States. (The charter of the First Bank had been allowed to expire.) The Second Bank was never popular and had detractors on several fronts. As was true since the time of Daniel Shays's march on the courthouse in Massachusetts, farmers and the poor had a strong suspicion and hatred of banks. So did many Jeffersonian Democratic-Republicans (see Chapter 11) who believed that the national government lacked the authority to establish a bank. They believed that because the power to issue corporate charters was not granted to Congress by the Constitution, the Bank of the United States was unconstitutional. States also disliked the national bank; it was the largest corporation in the United States and provided stiff competition for state-chartered banks.

In 1818, the Democratic-Republican–controlled Maryland assembly levied a tax requiring all banks not chartered by Maryland (that is, the Second Bank of the United States) to (1) buy stamped paper from the state on which the Second Bank's notes were to be issued, (2) pay the state $15,000 a year, or (3) go out of business. Maryland was not the only state to attempt to tax the U.S. bank out of business. Tennessee, Georgia, Ohio, and North Carolina, for example, enacted laws requiring each branch of the national bank to pay $50,000 to their respective state treasuries to stay in business. Illinois and Indiana, which had no branches of the national bank, passed laws prohibiting their establishment.

James McCulloch, the head cashier of the Baltimore branch of the Bank of the United States, refused to pay the tax, and Maryland brought suit against him. After losing in a Maryland court, McCulloch appealed his conviction to the U.S. Supreme Court by order of the U.S. Secretary of the Treasury. Arguing on behalf of the federal government and for the constitutionality of the Bank was Daniel Webster, a former Federalist member of Congress and one of the best lawyers in the nation. Maryland was represented by Luther Martin, who had been an active opponent of the new Constitution at the Philadelphia Convention. There he had railed against the chains being forged for "his country"—Maryland—and its subjugation to new national power.[7]

Although Chief Justice John Marshall still presided over the Court, only he and one other Federalist justice remained. The other five justices were Democratic-Republicans appointed by Presidents Jefferson and Madison. Nevertheless, in a unanimous opinion, the Court answered the two central questions that had been put to it: First, did Congress have the authority to charter a bank, and, second, if it did, could a state tax it?

As to the first question—whether Congress had the right to establish a bank or another type of corporation, given that the Constitution does not explicitly mention such a power—Chief Justice Marshall's answer continues to stand as the classic exposition of the doctrine of implied powers, and as a reaffirmation of the propriety of a strong national government. Therefore, although the word *bank* cannot be found in the Constitution, the Constitution enumerates powers that give Congress the authority to levy and collect taxes, issue a currency, and borrow funds. From these enumerated powers, Marshall found, it was reasonable to imply that Congress had the power to charter a bank, which could be considered "necessary and proper" to the exercise of its enumerated powers.

---

[7] John A. Garraty, ed., *Quarrels That Have Shaped the Constitution* (New York: Harper & Row, 1987), Chapter 3.

In some of the most famous language from the case, Marshall carefully set out an expansive interpretation of the necessary and proper clause of Article I, Section 8, and the possible scope of implied powers, proclaiming:

> Let the end be legitimate, let it be within the scope of the Constitution, and all means which are appropriate, which are plainly adapted to that end, which are not prohibited, but consistent with the letter and spirit of the Constitution, are constitutional.[8]

Marshall next addressed the question of whether a federal bank could be taxed by any state government. To Marshall, this was not a difficult question. The national government was dependent on the people, not the states, for its powers. In addition, Marshall noted, the Constitution specifically calls for the national law to be supreme. Thus, the national government and its "instrumentalities" such as the Bank had to be immune from state interference. "The power to tax involves the power to destroy," wrote Marshall. Thus, the state tax violated the supremacy clause, since states cannot interfere with the operations of the national government, whose laws are supreme.

Gibbons* v. *Ogden*. Shortly after *McCulloch*, the Marshall Court had another opportunity to rule in favor of a broad interpretation of the scope of national power. *Gibbons* involved a dispute that arose after the New York state legislature granted to Robert Fulton the exclusive right to operate steamboats on the Hudson River. Simultaneously, Congress licensed a ship to sail on the same waters. By the time the case reached the Supreme Court, it was complicated both factually and procedurally. Suffice it to say that both New York and New Jersey wanted to control shipping on the lower Hudson River. But, *Gibbons* actually addressed one simple, very important question: What was the scope of Congress's authority under the commerce clause? The states argued that "commerce," as mentioned in Article I, should be interpreted narrowly to include only direct dealings in products. Thus, regulation of shipping on inland waterways would be beyond the scope of Congress's authority to regulate. In *Gibbons,* however, Chief Justice Marshall ruled that Congress's power to regulate interstate commerce included

---

[8] *McCulloch* v. *Maryland*, 4 Wheat. 316 (1819).

The *Gibbons* v. *Ogden* decision opened the waters to free competition; this is the New York waterfront in 1839.
New York Public Library, Stokes Collection.

Daniel Webster's 1821 handwritten note to Cornelius Vanderbilt acknowledging receipt of a $500 retainer to represent Thomas Gibbons in the case of *Gibbons* v. *Ogden*.

the power to regulate commercial activity as well, and that the commerce power had no limits *except* those specifically found in the Constitution. Thus, New York had no constitutional authority to grant a monopoly to a single steamboat operator, thereby interfering with interstate commerce.[9]

The Taney Court. In spite of the nationalist Marshall Court decisions, strong debate continued in the United States over national versus state power. It was under the leadership of Chief Justice Marshall's successor, Roger B. Taney (1835–1863), that the Supreme Court articulated the notions of concurrent power, the belief that separate and equally powerful levels of government is the best arrangement, and **dual federalism,** which holds that the national government should not exceed its enumerated powers expressly set out in the Constitution.

In a series of cases involving the scope of Congress's power under the commerce clause, the Taney Court further developed doctrines first enunciated by Marshall, but put greater stress on a concurrent national/state relationship that allowed state involvement in commerce, so long as it did not interfere with federal law. The Taney Court attempted to allow new businesses to flourish, broadened the sphere of *laissez-faire*, and allowed the states greater involvement in corporate affairs. In spite of Taney's major contributions defining the economic and commercial roles of the national and state governments in the federal system, his Court is best remembered for its unfortunate handling of the slavery issue, which threatened the federal system itself.

Federalism and Slavery. During the Taney era, the comfortable role of the Court as the arbiter of competing national and state interests became troublesome when the Court found itself called upon to deal with the highly political issue of slavery. In cases such as *Dred Scott* v. *Sandford* (1857) and others, the Court tried to manage the slavery issue by resolving questions of ownership, the status of fugitive slaves, and slavery in the new territories.[10] These cases generally were settled in favor of slavery and states' rights within the framework of dual federalism. In its treatment of slavery (see "People of the Past," p. 79), the Taney Court erred grievously and thereby contributed to the coming of the Civil War, since its decision seemed to rule out any political (legislative) solution by the national government.

---

[9] *Gibbons* v. *Ogden*, 22 U.S. 1 (1824).
[10] 19 How. 393 (1857).

People of the Past

Dred Scott

Dred Scott was born into slavery in Virginia around 1795. In 1833 he was sold by his original owners, the Blow family, to an army surgeon named Dr. Emerson, who lived in St. Louis. In 1834 he was taken by the doctor to Illinois and later to the Wisconsin Territory, returning to St. Louis in 1838.

When Emerson died in 1843, Scott tried to buy his freedom. Before he could, however, he was transferred to Emerson's widow, who moved to New York state, leaving Scott in the custody of his first owners, the Blows. Some of the Blows (Henry Blow later founded the anti-slavery Free Soil Party) and other abolitionists gave money to support a test case seeking Scott's freedom on the ground that since he had resided in Illinois and in the Wisconsin Territory, both of which prohibited slavery, he became free by virtue of his residence there. His return to a slave state could not invalidate this change in his condition, and even in Missouri, he was a free man.

After many delays, in 1857 the U.S. Supreme Court ruled seven to two that Scott was not a citizen and that slaves "were never thought of or spoken of except as property."

At the urging of President James Buchanan, Justice Roger B. Taney tried to fashion a broad ruling that would settle the slavery question. He ruled that the Congress of the United States lacked the constitutional authority to bar slavery in the territories, thus narrowing the scope of national power while enhancing that of the states. Moreover, for the first time since *Marbury* v. *Madison* (1803), the Court found an act of Congress—the Missouri Compromise—unconstitutional.

Source: Excerpts from *Quarrels That Have Shaped the Constitution*, by John A. Garraty (ed.). Copyright © 1963 by Harper & Row Publishers, Inc. Reprinted by permission of HarperCollins Publishers.

While the Court was carving out the appropriate role of each level of government in the federal system, the political debate over states' rights (especially where slavery was concerned) continued to swirl in large part over the **nullification doctrine**, the purported right of a state to nullify a federal law. As early as 1798, Congress approved the very unpopular Alien and Sedition Acts to prevent criticism of the national government (see Chapter 4). Men like Thomas Jefferson and James Madison who opposed the Acts suggested that the states had the right to nullify any federal law that *in the opinion of the states* violated the Constitution.

The question of nullification came up again in 1828 when the national government enacted a tariff act, commonly referred to as the "Tariff of Abominations," which raised duties on raw materials (iron, hemp, and flax) and reduced protections against imported woolen goods. John C. Calhoun, who served as vice president from 1825 to 1832 under President Andrew Jackson, broke with Jackson over the tariff act because it badly affected his home state of South Carolina. Not only did South Carolinians have to pay more for raw materials because of the new tariff law; it was also becoming more and more difficult for them to sell their dwindling crops abroad for a profit. Calhoun thus used the nullification doctrine to justify South Carolina's refusal to abide by the federal tariff law. Later, he used the same doctrine to justify the Southern states' resistance to national actions to limit slavery.

Calhoun theorized that the federal government was but the agent of the states (the people and the individual state governments) and that the Constitution was simply a compact that provided instructions about how the agent was to act. Calhoun thus reasoned that the U.S. Supreme Court was not competent to pass on the constitutional validity of acts of Congress. Like Congress, the Court was only a branch of a government created by and answerable to the states. Calhoun posited that if the people of any individual state did not like an act of Congress, they could hold a convention to declare that act null and void. In the state contesting the act, the law would have no force until three-fourths of all of the states ratified an amendment expressly giving Congress that power. If the nullifying state still did not wish to be bound by the new provision, it could secede (withdraw) from the Union. In their fight (begun in the 1850s) to keep slavery, the Southern states relied heavily on Calhoun's theories to justify their secession from the Union, ultimately leading to the Civil War.

The Transformation of Dual Federalism

The Civil War forever changed the nature of federalism, but the Supreme Court continued to adhere to its belief in the concept of dual federalism. Thus, the importance and powers of the states were not diminished in spite of the addition of the Thirteenth, Fourteenth, and Fifteenth Amendments to the Constitution (see Chapter 5), or by Abraham Lincoln's appointment of the first Republican Chief Justice, Salmon Chase (1864–1873). In *The Slaughterhouse Cases* (1873), for example, the Court interpreted the Civil War Amendments very narrowly.[11] Other cases also indicated the Court's reluctance to allow Congress to expand its authority further, whether by amendment or by statute.

Between 1865 (the end of the Civil War) and 1933 (when the next major change in the federal system occurred) the Court generally continued to support dual federalism along several lines. State courts, for example, were considered to have the final say on the construction of laws affecting local affairs.[12] Generally, the Court upheld any laws passed under the states' police powers, which allow states to pass laws to protect the general welfare of their citizens. These laws included those affecting commerce, labor relations, and manufacturing. After the Court's decision in *Plessy* v. *Ferguson* (1896)[13] (see pp. 163–164), in which the Court ruled that state maintenance of "separate but equal" facilities for blacks and whites was constitutional, most civil rights and voting cases also became state matters, in spite of the Civil War Amendments.

The Court also developed legal doctrine in a series of cases that reinforced the national government's ability to regulate commerce. By the 1930s, these two somewhat contradictory approaches led to confusion: states, for example, could not tax gasoline used by federal vehicles,[14] and the national government could not tax the sale of mo-

---

[11] 16 Wall. 36 (1873); see Chapter 5.
[12] *Lane County* v. *Oregon*, 74 U.S. 71 (1869).
[13] 163 U.S. 537 (1896).
[14] *Panhandle Oil Co.* v. *Knox*, 277 U.S. 218 (1928).

This famous cartoon by noted political cartoonist Thomas Nast pokes fun at the myriad trusts that led to congressional passage of the Sherman Anti-Trust Act.

torcycles to the city police department.[15] In this period the Court did recognize the need for national control over new technological developments, such as the telegraph.[16] And beginning in the 1880s, the Court allowed Congress to regulate many aspects of economic relationships such as outlawing monopolies, a type of regulation or power formerly thought to be in the exclusive realm of the states. Passage of laws such as the Interstate Commerce Act in 1887 and the Sherman Anti-Trust Act in 1890 allowed Congress to establish itself as an important player in the growing national economy.

Despite finding that most of these laws were constitutional, the Supreme Court did not consistently enlarge the scope of national power. In 1895, for example, the United States filed suit against four sugar refiners, alleging that their sale would give their buyer control of 98 percent of the U.S. sugar-refining business. The Supreme Court ruled that congressional efforts to control monopolies (through passage of the Sherman Anti-Trust Act) did not give Congress the authority to prevent the sale of these sugar-refining businesses, because manufacturing was not commerce. Therefore, the companies and their actions were beyond the scope of Congress's authority to regulate.

---

[15] *Indian Motorcycle Co. v. United States*, 238 U.S. 570 (1931).
[16] *Pensacola Telegraph v. Western Union*, 96 U.S. 1 (1877).

The New Deal and a Rapidly Changing Balance of Power

The era of dual federalism came to an abrupt end in the 1930s. Its demise began in a series of economic events that ended in the cataclysm of the Great Depression:

- In 1921, the nation experienced a severe slump in agricultural prices.
- In 1926, the construction industry went into decline.
- In the summer of 1929, inventories of consumer goods and automobiles were at an all-time high.
- Throughout the 1920s, bank failures had become common.
- On October 29, 1929, stock prices, which had risen steadily since 1926, crashed, taking with them the entire national economy.

Rampant unemployment (historians estimate it was as high as 40 to 50 percent) was the hallmark of the Great Depression. To combat this unemployment and a host of other problems facing the nation, newly elected President Franklin D. Roosevelt (FDR) proposed in 1933 a variety of innovative programs under the rubric "the New Deal." Just as historical circumstances propelled the writings of Hobbes and Locke discussed in Chapter 1, the economic chaos of the period inspired the New Deal and ushered in a new era in American politics. FDR used the full power of the office of president as well as his highly effective communication skills to sell the American public and Congress on a whole new ideology of government. Not only were the scope and role of national government remarkably altered, but so was the relationship between each state and the national government. (See "Landmark Periods," p. 74.)

The New Deal period (1933 to 1939) was characterized by intense government activity on the national level. It was clear to most politicians that to find national solutions to the Depression, which was affecting the citizens of every state in the Union, the national government would have to exercise tremendous authority.

In the first few weeks of the legislative session after FDR's inauguration, Congress and the president acted quickly to bolster confidence in the national government. Soon after, Congress passed a series of acts creating programs proposed by the president. These new agencies, often known by their initials, created what many termed an "alphabetocracy" (see "New Deal Legislation and the Alphabetocracy," p. 84). Among the more significant programs were the Federal Housing Administration (FHA), which provided federal financing for new home construction; the Civilian Conservation Corps (CCC), a work relief program for farmers and homeowners; and the Agricultural Adjustment Administration (AAA) and the National Recovery Administration (NRA), which imposed restrictions on production in agriculture and many industries.

These programs tremendously enlarged the scope of the national government. Those who feared this unprecedented use of national power quickly challenged the constitutionality of New Deal programs in court.[17] And at least initially, the Supreme Court often agreed with them.

Through the mid-1930s, the Supreme Court continued to rule that certain aspects of the New Deal went beyond the authority of Congress to regulate commerce. In fact, many believe that the Court considered the Depression to be no more than the sum of

---

[17] Lee Epstein, *Conservatives in Court* (Knoxville: University of Tennessee Press, 1985).

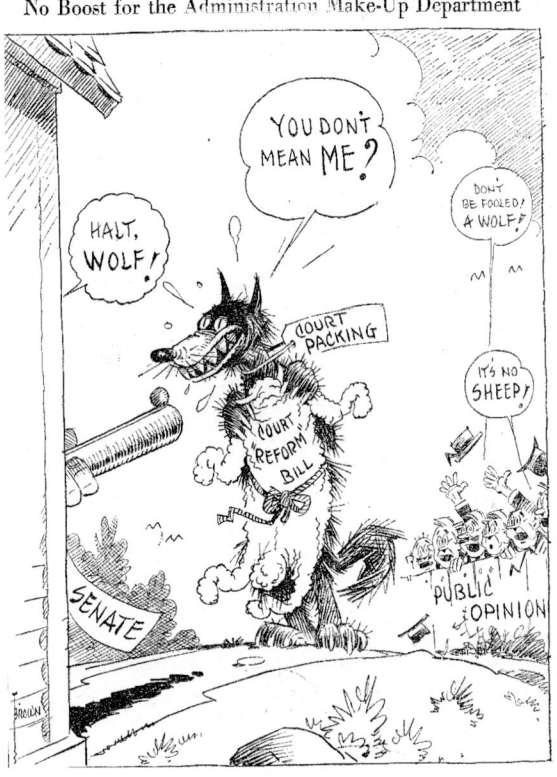

This *New York Tribune* cartoon reflects the Senate and the public's overwhelming negative reaction to FDR's efforts to enlarge the size of the Supreme Court, which were really not a "reform" plan; instead, the Court packing plan was simply a way for him to ensure judicial acceptance of New Deal programs.

the economic woes of the individual states and that it was a problem most appropriately handled by the states. The Court's *laissez-faire* or "hands-off" attitude toward the economy was reflected in a series of decisions ruling various aspects of New Deal programs unconstitutional.

FDR and the Congress were outraged. FDR's frustration with the *laissez-faire* attitude of the Court prompted him to suggest what was ultimately nicknamed his "Court-packing plan." Knowing that there was little he could do to change the minds of those already on the Court, FDR suggested enlarging its size from nine to thirteen justices, which would have given him the opportunity to "pack" the Court with a majority predisposed to the constitutional validity of the New Deal.

Even though Roosevelt was popular, the Court-packing plan was not. Congress and the public were outraged that he even suggested tampering with an institution of government. Nevertheless, the Court appeared to respond to this threat. In 1937, it reversed its series of anti-New Deal decisions, concluding that Congress (and therefore the national government) had the authority to legislate in areas that only *affected* commerce. Congress then used this newly recognized power to legislate in a wide array of areas, including maximum hour and minimum wage laws, and regulation of child labor. Moreover, the Court also upheld the constitutionality of the bulk of the massive New Deal relief programs, such as the National Labor Relations Act of 1935, which authorized collective bargaining between unions and employees,[18] the Fair Labor

---

[18] *NLRB* v. *Jones & Laughlin Steel Co.*, 301 U.S. 1 (1937).

New Deal Legislation and the Alphabetocracy

AGRICULTURE

- The Agricultural Adjustment Act (1938) attempted to stabilize farm prices, reduce crop surpluses, and restore farmers' purchasing power; it succeeded the Soil Conservation and Domestic Allotment Act (1936) and created the Agricultural Adjustment Administration (AAA).
- The Farm Credit Administration (FCA) (1933), created by the Farm Credit Act, took over all federal agricultural credit programs including the Federal Farm Mortgage Corporation (FFMC) (1934).
- The Rural Electrification Administration (REA) (1935) was created to bring electricity to isolated areas without private utility service.

BUSINESS AND INDUSTRY

- The National Industrial Recovery Act (NIRA) (1933) established the National Recovery Administration (NRA) and the Public Works Administration (PWA) to increase employment, establish fair trade regulation, and revive business.
- The Securities and Exchange Commission (SEC) (1934) was established by the Securities Exchange Act (1934) to regulate securities transactions.
- The Federal Communications Commission (FCC) (1934) was established by the Federal Communications Act to regulate interstate and international telegraph, radio, and cable communications.

CONSERVATION AND THE ENVIRONMENT

- The Tennessee Valley Authority (TVA) (1933) was created to harness the energy potential of the Tennessee River and to aid the area's economic and social welfare.
- The Civilian Conservation Corps (CCC) (1933) was created to provide employment on soil, road, and reforestation projects to males between the ages of eighteen and twenty-five.

LABOR AND SOCIAL WELFARE

- The National Labor Relations Board (NLRB) was created by the National Labor Relations Act (1935) to supervise labor/management relations.
- The Social Security Act (1935) created the Social Security Administration and established programs for retirement pensions, unemployment insurance, and other social welfare services.
- The Federal Housing Administration (FHA) (1934) was established by the National Housing Act (1934) to provide home financing and to revive home construction.

RELIEF

- The Federal Emergency Relief Act (FERA) (1933) authorized grants to states in proportion to amounts spent on relief by the states.
- The Works Progress Administration (WPA) (1935), a national relief program to use unemployed on public projects, was called the Works Projects Administration from 1939.

Standards Act of 1938, which prohibited the interstate shipment of goods made by employees earning less than the federally mandated minimum wage,[19] and the Agriculture Adjustment Act of 1938, which provided crop subsidies to farmers.[20]

The New Deal programs forced all levels of government to work cooperatively with one another. Indeed, local governments—mainly big cities—became a third partner in the federal system, as FDR relied on big city Democratic political machines to turn out voters to support his programs. For the first time in U.S. history, in essence, cities were embraced as equal partners in an intergovernmental system and became players in the national political arena.

---

[19] *United States v. Darby*, 312 U.S. 100 (1941).
[20] *Wickard v. Filburn*, 317 U.S. 111 (1942).

One of the hallmarks of the New Deal and FDR's presidency was the national government's new involvement of cities in the federal system. Here, New York City mayor Fiorello La Guardia is commissioned as Director of Civil Defense by FDR.

The Changing Nature of Federalism

Prior to the Depression and the New Deal, most political scientists likened the federal system to a layer cake; each level or layer of government—national, state and local—had clearly defined powers and responsibilities. After the New Deal, however, the nature of the federal system changed:

> The federal system is not accurately symbolized by a neat layer cake of three distinct and separate planes. A far more realistic symbol is that of the marble cake. Wherever you slice through it you reveal an inseparable mixture of differently colored ingredients.... Vertical and diagonal lines almost obliterate the horizontal ones, and in some places there are unexpected whirls and an imperceptible merging of colors, so that it is difficult to tell where one ends and the other begins. So it is with federal, state, and local responsibilities in the chaotic marble cake of American government.[21]

This kind of "marble cake" federalism is often called **cooperative federalism**, a term used to characterize the relationship between the national and state governments that began with the New Deal. The New Deal created a stronger, more influential national government, and federalism again experienced a change. States began to take a

---

[21] Morton Grodzins, "Centralization and Decentralization in the American Federal System," *A Nation of States*, ed. Robert A. Goldwin (Chicago: Rand McNally, 1963), pp. 3–4.

secondary, albeit important, "cooperative" role in the scheme of governance. Nowhere is this shift in power more clear than in the growth of federal grant programs that began in earnest during the New Deal. The tremendous growth in these programs and in federal government spending in general, as illustrated in Table 3.1, changed the nature and discussion of federalism from "How much power should the national government have?" to "How much say in the policies of the states can the national government buy?"

Federal Grants

As early as 1790, Congress appropriated funds for the states to pay debts incurred during the Revolutionary War. But it wasn't until the Civil War that Congress enacted its first true federal grant program, in which federal funds were allocated to the states for a specific purpose.

Most view the start of this redistribution of funds with the Morrill Land Grant Act of 1862, which gave each state 30,000 acres of public land for each representative in Congress. Income from the sale of these lands was to be earmarked for the establishment and support of agricultural and mechanical arts colleges. Sixty-nine land-grant colleges—including Texas A&M University, Purdue University, and Michigan State University—were founded, making this grant program the single most important piece of education legislation passed in the United States up to that time.

Franklin Roosevelt's New Deal program included massive federal dollars for a variety of programs such as road construction and other public works. These grants made the imposition of national goals on the states easier, and as the federal grant idea began to flourish, it often appeared that there would be no stopping it.

Table 3.1 ♦ Federal Grants-in-Aid, 1950–1993

Year	Total (in billions of dollars)	Grants-in-Aid as a Percentage of Federal outlays	Grants-in-Aid as a Percentage of State and local outlays
1950	$ 2.3	5.3	—
1955	3.2	4.7	—
1960	7.0	7.6	15.0
1965	10.9	9.2	16.0
1970	24.1	12.3	20.0
1975	49.8	15.0	24.0
1980	91.5	15.5	28.0
1985	105.9	11.2	23.0
1990	135.4	10.8	20.0
1992	178.1	12.8	22.0
1996 *est.*	262.8	16.2	23.0

Source: 1950–1991: Office of Management and Budget, *Budget Baselines, Historical Data, and Alternatives for the Future* (Washington, DC: U.S. Government Printing Office, 1993), p. 428; *Budget of the United States Government, Fiscal Year 1994* (Washington, DC: U.S. Government Printing Office, 1993), pp. 6, 22, 77, 79.

THEN AND NOW

The Sheppard–Towner Maternity Act of 1923

The Sheppard–Towner Maternity Act (STMA) was enacted by Congress at the urging of women's rights groups who were still flushed with the success of their efforts to win the right to vote. The Act called for Congress to make money available to the states for pre- and postnatal care for mothers and infants. The program was passed largely due to findings that the United States had the highest infant mortality rate in the Western world. Those who had opposed suffrage challenged this first grant-in-aid program in court, arguing that Congress had surpassed its authority under the commerce clause. In *Frothingham* v. *Mellon* (1923), the Supreme Court ruled that federal taxpayers lacked standing to challenge the constitutional validity of these kinds of programs, because their interest in the program *as taxpayers* was too remote to give them a sufficient stake in the outcome of the case. Thus, to this day, most congressionally enacted aid programs remain out of the reach of taxpayer challenge. Congress allowed the Act to expire in 1929.

In the boom times of World War II, new programs were introduced, and by the 1950s and 1960s, federal grant-in-aid programs were well entrenched. They often defined federal/state relationships and made the national government a major player in domestic policy.

Until the 1960s, most federal grants programs were constructed in cooperation with the states and were designed to assist the states in furthering their traditional responsibilities to protect the health, welfare, and safety of their citizens. Most of these programs were **categorical grants**, ones for which Congress appropriates funds for a specific purpose. Funds are allocated by a precise formula and are subject to detailed conditions imposed by the national government, often on a matching basis; that is, states must contribute money to match federal funds, although the national government may pay as much as 90 percent of the total.

By the early 1960s, however, as concern about the poor and minorities rose, and as states (especially in the South) were blamed for perpetuating discrimination,[22] those in power in the national government saw grants as a way to force states to behave in ways desired by the national government: if the states would not cooperate with the national government to further its goals, it would withhold funds.

In 1964, the Democratic administration of President Lyndon B. Johnson (1963–1969) launched its renowned War on Poverty, a broad attempt to combat poverty and discrimination. In a frenzy of activity in Washington not seen since the New Deal, federal funds were channeled to states, to local governments, and even directly to citizen action groups in an effort to alleviate social ills that the states had been unable or unwilling to remedy. The move to fund local groups directly was made by the most liberal members of Congress in order to bypass not only conservative state legislatures but also conservative mayors and councils in cities like Chicago.

---

[22] Alice M. Rivlin, *Reviving the American Dream*, (Washington, DC, Brookings Institution, 1992), p. 92.

These new grants altered the fragile federal/state balance of power that had been at the core of most older federal grant programs. During the Johnson administration, the national government began to use federal grants as a way to further what federal (and not state) officials perceived to be national needs. Thus, grants based on what states wanted or believed they needed began to decline, while grants based on what the national government wanted states to do in order to foster national goals increased dramatically. Soon, states routinely asked Washington for help: "pollution, transportation, recreation, economic development, law enforcement and even rat control evoked the same response from politicians: create a federal grant."[23] As shown in Table 3.1, by 1970 federal aid accounted for 20 percent of all state and local government spending; this amount of money made the states ever more dependent on the national government.

As Congress increased the number of programs for which cities were eligible, many critics argued that the federal grants system was out of hand. By 1971, there were more than 500 different types of grants available, in contrast to only 51 in 1964.[24] Each program had its own complicated set of rules and formulas for matching and distributing the money, and had bureaucracies and recipients with a vested interest in enlarging the program.

Between 1965 and 1980, federal aid to cities and states tripled. One political scientist ventured that in the world of bake-shop metaphors, a "new special" was in the offing: "fruitcake federalism." Not only was it formless, but it also offered (political) plums to all.[25]

Negative reaction to this far-reaching federalism was not long in coming. States simply wanted more control. Many believed that the grant situation had produced ridiculous consequences as states and local governments found themselves applying for federal money they did not particularly need. These "federal-aid junkies," as one commentator called them, could not resist the lure of federal funds, no matter what the nature of the grant.[26] As states and localities tailored their budgets to maximize their share of federal dollars, they often neglected basic services. Said New York City Mayor Edward I. Koch,

> Left unnoticed in the cities' rush to reallocate their budgets so as to draw down maximum . . . aid were the basic service-delivery programs. . . . New roads, bridges, and subway routes were an exciting commitment to the future, but they were launched at the expense of routine maintenance to the unglamorous, but essential, infrastructure of the existing systems.[27]

Revenue Sharing. In 1964, the Chair of President Johnson's Council of Economic Advisors proposed a new program, a form of revenue sharing that would channel federal dollars back to the states without the strings that went with categorical grants. Johnson rejected the proposal and favored continued federal control of grant programs. President Richard M. Nixon, however, found the idea attractive. He believed that states

---

[23] Ibid., p. 98.

[24] Advisory Commission on Intergovernmental Relations, "The Federal Role in the Federal System: The Dynamics of Growth" (Washington, DC: 1980), pp. 120–121.

[25] Aaron Wildavsky, "Birthday Cake Federalism," in Robert E. Hawkins, ed. *American Federalism: A New Partnership for the Republic* (New Brunswick, NJ: Transaction Press, 1982), p. 182.

[26] Samuel H. Beer, "The Modernization of American Federalism," *Publius* 3 (Fall 1973): 74–79.

[27] Edward I. Koch, "The Mandate Millstone," *The Public Interest* 61 (Fall 1980): 43.

and local governments needed federal assistance but should have greater freedom to spend it. Under his **revenue-sharing** program, money was given to state and local governments to spend where they believed the money was most needed, with no "strings attached."

Revenue sharing was popular with states, which in 1972 were in fiscal crisis. But during the second Reagan administration, when the budget deficit soared, there were few funds to share. Thus, Congress terminated the program over which it had little control. By 1987 it had been phased out completely.

The growth of government spending revealed in Table 3.1 was one reason that Jimmy Carter, a former governor of Georgia, was able to run successfully for president in 1976 as an "outsider" opposed to big government and federal grants mandating state policies. The reforms Carter introduced were insufficient to override the rest of his political woes, however, and in 1980 Ronald Reagan was elected, in part by pledging a "New Federalism."

Reagan's New Federalism

President Reagan's New Federalism had many facets. The "Reagan Revolution" had at its heart strong views about the role of states in the federal system. Shortly after taking office, he proposed massive cuts in domestic programs and drastic income tax cuts. The Reagan administration's budget and its policies dramatically altered the relationships among the federal, state, and local governments. For the first time in thirty years, federal aid to state and local governments declined.[28]

President Reagan, picking up on Richard M. Nixon's revenue-sharing plan, persuaded Congress to consolidate many categorical grants (for specific programs that often require matching funds) into far fewer, less restrictive **block grants**. Block grants are broad grants to states for specified activities such as secondary education or health services, with few strings attached. Seventy-seven categorical grants covering a range of broad programs—including health care, child welfare, and crime prevention—were collapsed into nine block grants. Initially, the states were happy with this action—until they learned that the administration also proposed to cut back on the financing of these programs by 25 percent. These cuts fell heaviest on cities. In 1980, federal funds made up 26 percent of state expenditures and 17.7 percent of city and county budgets. By 1990, however, federal dollars were 18 percent of state and 6.4 percent of city and county budgets, respectively. Moreover, as indicated in Figure 3-3, the proportion of federal income security aid to individuals in the forms of assistance programs such as Medicaid, Social Security, and Aid to Families with Dependent Children (AFDC) rose significantly at the same time that the proportion of moneys to the state and local governments for general purposes fell by half.

Many programs cut by the Reagan administration involved those in aid of the "have nots" of society, and the poor and working poor were hard hit. Though even more people were poorer and technically qualified for benefits, the rate of spending growth for programs declined. By 1992 most federal grants fell into four areas: (1) health; (2) income security; (3) education; and (4) transportation. Health costs went from 3 percent of the federal aid dollars to states in 1960 to a whopping 37 percent in 1992. (In fact,

---

[28] Richard P. Nathan et al. *Reagan and the States* (Princeton, NJ: Princeton University Press, 1987), p. 4.

Types of Grants-in-Aid
♦ ♦ ♦

Categorical Grants: U.S. government gives money for more specific purposes and has more control. There are two types:

a. Formula Grants: Generally designated to apply to certain geographical areas within states; local governments must compete for dollars.

b. Project Grants: Government units and agencies apply for projects that federal agencies have announced. Generally reflect agency agendas; very competitive.

Block Grants: U.S. government gives money to the states for a general purpose, such as education. No strings attached. Preferred by states.

FIGURE 3-3
The Changing Allocation of Federal Grants-in-Aid to the States.

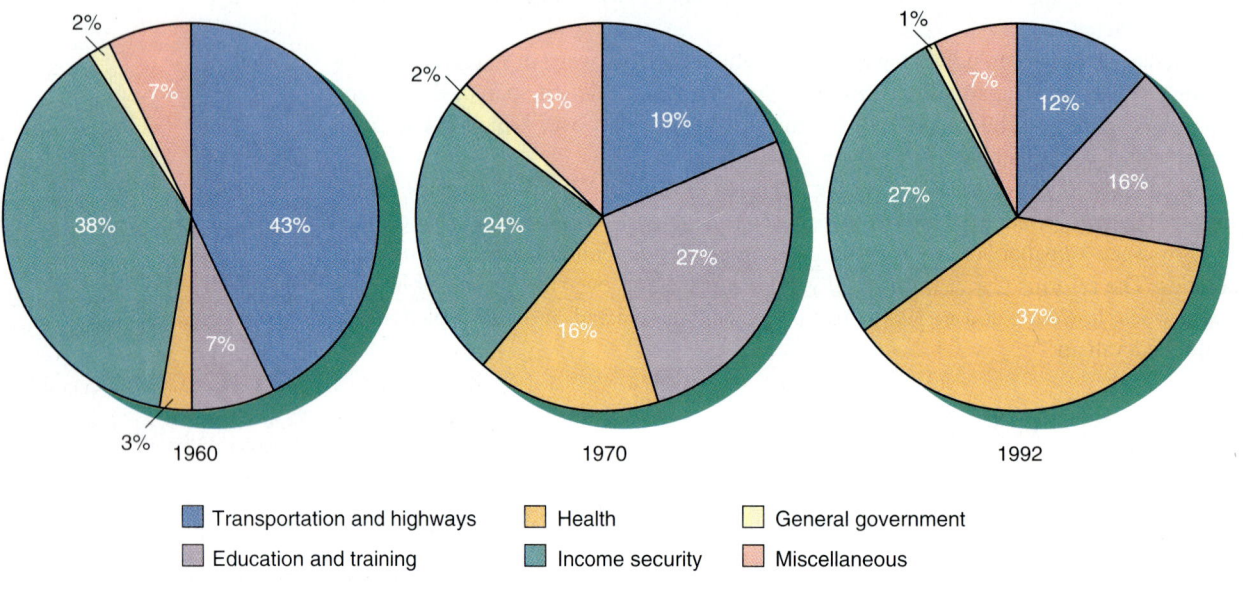

Source: United States Budget, Fiscal Year 1992, Table C–3

the high cost of health-related programs such as Medicaid is one reason the Clinton administration is seeking reform of the health care system.)

Controlling the States through Preemption and Mandates

In *Federalist No. 17,* Alexander Hamilton noted that "it will always be far more easy for the State government to encroach upon the national authorities than for the national government to encroach upon the State authorities." How wrong he was. In fact, today some argue that the federal/state relationship has moved from "cooperation to coercion."[29] Even though the actual value of grants-in-aid to the states declined in the 1980s (when controlled for inflation), the national government continued to "direct" state policy through statutes preempting traditional state functions and federal mandates. Fewer federal dollars have not led to fewer federal controls.

Preemption.[30] One method through which the federal government has cut into the authority of the states to set their own policy preferences derives from the Constitution's supremacy clause. This practice, known as **preemption**, allows the national government to override, or preempt, state or local actions in certain areas. As discussed earlier, the Tenth Amendment expressly reserved to the states and the people all powers not delegated to the national government. The phenomenal growth of preemption

---

[29] John Kincaid, "From Cooperation to Coercion in American Federalism: Housing, Fragmentation, and Preemption, 1789–1992," *Journal of Law and Politics* 9 (Winter 1993): 333–430.

[30] This discussion of preemption relies heavily on Joseph F. Zimmerman, *Contemporary American Federalism: The Growth of National Power* (New York: Praeger, 1992), pp. 55–81.

statutes, laws that Congress has passed to allow the federal government to assume partial and/or full responsibility for traditional state and local governmental functions, began in 1965 during the Johnson administration. Since then, Congress has routinely used its authority under the commerce clause to preempt state laws. The Clean Air Act Amendments of 1990, the Hazardous and Solid Waste Amendments of 1984, the Safe Drinking Water Act Amendments of 1986, and the Water Quality Act of 1987 are examples of federal preemption at work. These statutes not only take authority away from states, they often impose significant costs on them in the form of mandates.

When thousands of city officials met in Orlando, Florida, in late 1993, one of the most popular accessories was this "Stop Unfunded Mandates" button, which was distributed by the National League of Cities.

Mandates. From the beginning, most categorical grants were matching grants that came with a variety of strings attached. As categorical grants have declined, the national government continues to exercise a significant role in state policy priorities through **mandates**—laws that direct states or local governments to comply with federal rules or regulations (such as clean air or water standards) under threat of civil or criminal penalties, or as a condition of receipt of any federal grants (a city might not get federal transportation funds, for example, unless the disabled have access to particular means of transportation).

The federal government requires the states to shoulder the financial burden of programs it does not fund. Today, unfunded mandates often make up as much as 30 percent of a local government's annual operating budget. Between 1983 and 1990, it is estimated that the cumulative cost of unfunded mandates to the states and local governments was between 8.9 and 12.7 billion dollars.[31]

As shown in Figure 3-4, the enactment of federal regulations requiring state and local spending has increased tremendously. During the 1980s, twenty-seven new programs were added, not including many expensive unfunded provisions that were attached to existing grant-in-aid programs. For example, costly new requirements were

---

[31] Timothy J. Conlan and David R. Beam, "Federal Mandates: The Record of Reform and Future Prospects," *Intergovernmental Perspective* (Fall, 1992). 9.

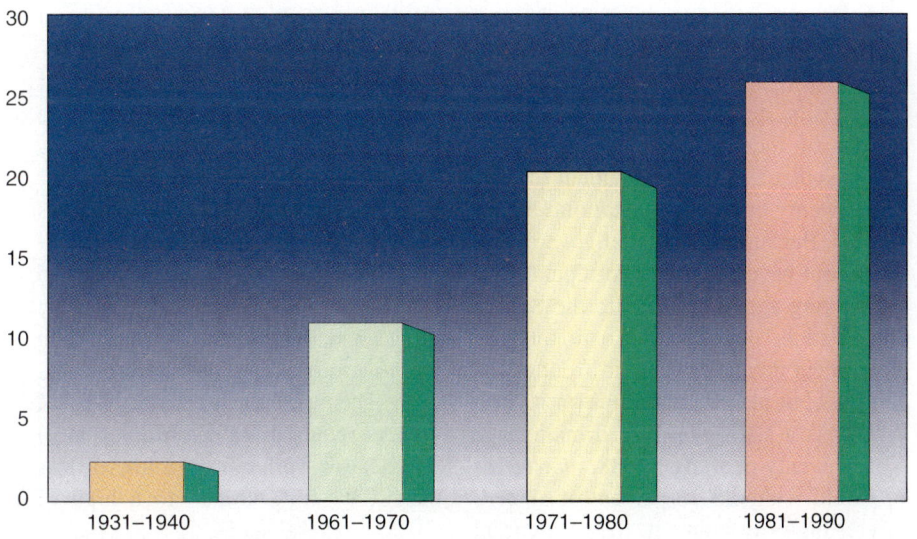

FIGURE 3-4

The Growth of Regulatory Federalism: Enactments Added per Decade, 1931–1990 (includes new programs and major amendments)

Source: ACIR, *Regulatory Federalism,* Appendix Table 1. Reprinted in Timothy J. Conlan and David R. Beam, "Federal Mandates: The Record of Reform and Future Prospects," *Intergovernmental Perspective* (Fall 1992): 9.

tacked on to the Medicaid program, workfare conditions were added to the Aid to Families with Dependent Children program as a welfare reform measure, and local contributions to mandated federal water projects were added.[32] Columbus, Ohio, for example, with 633,000 residents, is faced with a one-billion dollar bill to comply with the federal Clean Water Act and the Safe Drinking Water Act at an estimated cost of $685 a year per household. Likewise, New York City faces a $1.3 billion bill with no federal financial support to refit elevators in subways to accommodate the disabled.[33] Compliance with the National Literacy Act will cost states an estimated $27 million. And since most states, unlike the national government, are required to have balanced budgets, mandates increasingly mean more taxes and more trouble for state and local legislators.

In 1993, costs like these led two states, Alabama and South Dakota, to pass laws summoning their senators and representatives home to explain to their state legislatures why laws are passed imposing costly regulations on states without providing funds to implement them.[34] Similar "mandate consultation acts" are being considered by other states where lawmakers are challenging Congress's authority to force states to achieve national goals.

---

[32] Ibid.

[33] William Claiborne, "States Demand an Explanation; Federal Lawmakers Summoned to Justify Unfunded Mandates," *Washington Post,* July 5, 1993: A17.

[34] When senators were directly elected by state legislatures, senators were much more responsive to state legislators than they are today. In fact, these summonses have no legal force. But it is unlikely they can be ignored without a high political cost.

Forcing a National Policy: The Twenty-One-Year-Old Drinking Age

In 1984, only sixteen U.S. senators voted "Nay" on an amendment to the Surface Transportation Act of 1982, a provision designed to withhold 5 percent of federal highway funds from states that allowed those under the age of twenty-one to buy alcoholic beverages. Because the national government did not have the power to regulate the drinking age, it resorted to the "carrot and stick," whereby the national government dangles money in front of the states but places conditions on its use. Unless a state raised its drinking age to twenty-one by 1988, Congress would withhold 10 percent of all federal highway grants to the recalcitrant states. In other words, no raised drinking age, no federal dollars. Even most conservative Republican senators—those most attached to the notion of states' rights—supported the provision in spite of the fact that it imposed a national ideal on the states. And after congressional action, the bill was signed into law by Ronald Reagan, another conservative long concerned with the national government's trampling on state power. States still retain the power to define intoxication, however. The presumptive blood alcohol content required for determining legal intoxication varies from a low of less than .05% in Colorado to a high of .10% in several states.

Rethinking Federalism

Federal grants-in-aid have forced the states to rethink their position in the federal system. Today, many Republicans, who generally favor a more limited role for the national government, attack grants-in-aid as a way for the national government to exercise powers reserved to the states under the Tenth Amendment. Senator Paul Coverdell (R-Ga.), for example, introduced a Federal Mandate Relief Act, which would require approval of two-thirds of the Congress, instead of a simple majority, to pass any federal program that mandates state or local funding.

Some argue that the original reason for federal grants—perceived overrepresentation of rural interests in state legislatures, for example—has been removed as the Supreme Court has ordered redistricting to ensure better representation of urban and suburban interests. Moreover, state legislatures have become more professional, state and local bureaucracies more responsive, and the delivery of services better. In fact, the greatest growth in government hiring has been in the state and local sectors.

While many argue that grants-in-aid are an effective way to raise the level of services provided to the poor, others attack them as imposing national priorities on the states. Policy decisions are largely made at the national level, and the states, always in search of funds, are forced to follow the priorities of the national government. States find it very hard to resist the lure of grants, even though many are contingent upon some sort of state investment of matching or proportional funds.

Clinton's New Federalism

As a former governor, President Clinton is keenly aware of the impact of the national government's actions on the states. Many of his ideas build on those of former President Reagan. He advocates continued shifting of responsibilities and burdens from the national government to the states—with a twist. Clinton wants to redirect responsibilities to the states to avoid costly duplication of programs, but also to accompany those shifts with more funding from the national government. He also wants to reduce the burden that federal requirements impose on some state and local programs. Vice President Gore, for example, has described the "hodgepodge of categorical mandates that are uncoordinated, costly, and cumbersome" and advocates the "transfer of the power and authority to the grass roots level."[35]

The Intergovernmental Lobby

Increasing federal regulations, mandates, and conditions of aid have all contributed to the need for state and local governments to hire lobbyists to advance their interests in Washington. School districts, school systems, cities, states, police chiefs, hospital administrators, and many more groups form part of the **intergovernmental lobby**. Many of these groups have either banded with others or set up individual offices in Washington to lobby for funds. Others hire full-time or part-time lobbyists to work solely on their behalf to keep abreast of funding opportunities, or to lobby for programs. Today, searches for scarcer federal dollars can be nearly as futile as Ponce de León's search for the Fountain of Youth. (See Figure 3-5.)

---

[35] "Vice President Al Gore Calls for New Federalism to Meet Concerns, Goals," *Government Employee Relations Report*, 31 (August 23, 1993): 1119.

FIGURE 3-5

How Well Did Your State Do in the Scramble for Federal Dollars?

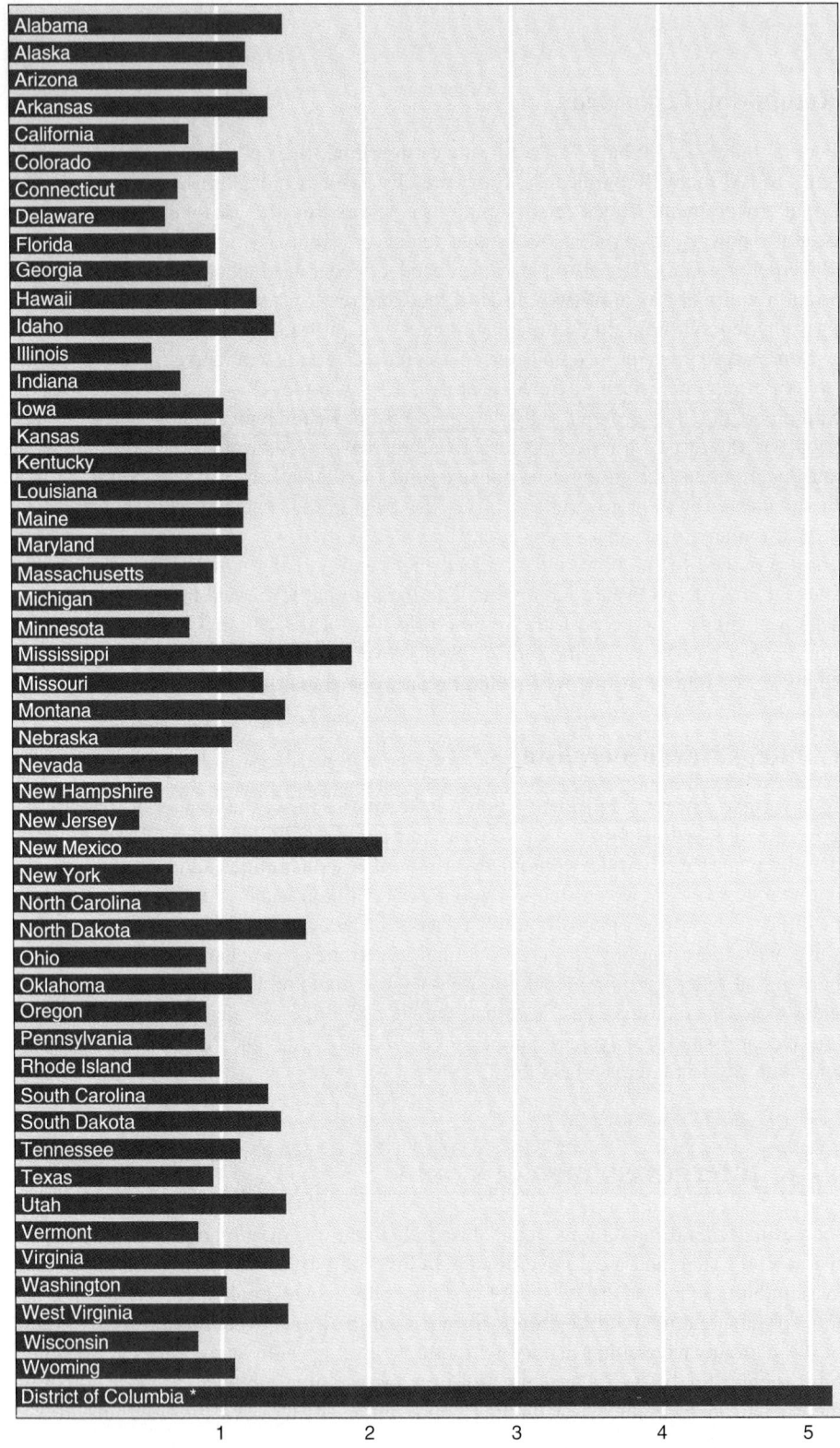

* Figures for the District of Columbia are so high because it is not a state and therefore depends heavily on Congress for support.

Source: From Harold W. Stanley and Richard G. Niemi, "Vital Statistics on American Politics," CQ Press, 1993, Table 10-4, pp. 321-322.

Table 3.2 ♦ Number of Governments in the U.S. in 1987

U.S. government	1
State governments	50
Local governments	
County	3,042
Municipal (city)	19,200
Township and town	16,691
School district	14,721
Special district	29,532
TOTAL	83,237

Source: U.S. Bureau of the Census, *Statistical Abstract of the U.S.: 1990,* 110th ed. (Washington, DC: 1990).

Literally thousands of governments exist in the United States, and most have a Washington presence. Table 3.2 reveals that, in 1990, there were over 83,000 governmental units in the United States. Many of these units—even within a single state—find themselves in competition with one another as the "New Federalism" has changed the nature of state politics. Caught by revenue shortfalls caused by the recession of the early 1990s, legal requirements mandating balanced budgets, and growing demands for new social services and the replacement of some formerly provided by the federal government, governors around the nation are in trouble as they slash services and ask for tax increases. "A governor with over a 50 percent approval is more the exception than the rule now, and that just wasn't true three or four years ago," noted one pollster in 1991.[36]

---

[36] Quoted in David E. Anderson, "Conservative Think Tanks Go Local," *UPI* (June 10, 1991), BC Cycle.

As federal money to the states dried up in the late 1980s and into the 1990s, many governors felt the pinch and the wrath of voters as they struggled to balance their states' budgets. New Jersey Governor James Florio, shown here debating his Republican opponent Christine Todd Whitman, was one of the casualties of the 1993 election.

96 ❖ Chapter 3 Federalism

A former governor, President Clinton addresses the National Governors' Conference.

The public's blaming of governors for the effects of New Federalism first became evident in the fall of 1990 when an unprecedented ten incumbent governors chose not to seek reelection, and an additional six were defeated. In contrast, only one incumbent senator was ousted. In 1993, in New Jersey, Governor James Florio was ousted by voters who were angered by tax increases. Similarly, incumbent mayors and county executives were turned out of office by voters angered by property tax increases which were often required to fund federally mandated programs.

Thus, the fiscal policies of New Federalism have essentially altered the economic relationship between the national government and the states. Ironically, the national government's plan to return power to the states has actually left the states in a weaker position, at least for the time being. In 1991, for example, legislators in forty-six of the fifty states narrowly avoided missing deadlines for new budget authorizations.

Federalism and the Supreme Court

Funds from the national government have not been the only factor that has altered the nature of the federal system. The Supreme Court also has played an important role in the configuration of power between the national government and the states. From the days of Marshall's Federalist opinions to *laissez-faire* to the New Deal, the Supreme Court has periodically interjected itself into areas (most notably education and the electoral process) that the Framers intended to leave within the authority of the states.

Education. Congress has long tried to encourage the states to develop their university and educational systems through grants-in-aid programs like the Morrill Land Grant Act of 1862, through the 1950s. Still, education was usually considered a function of the states under their police powers, which allow them to provide for public health and welfare. That tradition was shattered when the Supreme Court ruled in *Brown* v. *Board of Education of Topeka* (1954) that state-mandated segregation has no place in the public schools (see Chapter 5). *Brown* forced states to dismantle their segregated school systems and ultimately led the federal courts to play an important role in monitoring the efforts of state and local governments to tear down the vestiges of segregation.

The Electoral Process. A decade after *Brown*, the Supreme Court again involved itself in one of the most sacred areas of state regulation in the federal system—the conduct of elections. Convention attendees in Philadelphia had, as a trade-off for giving the national government more powers, allowed the states control over voter qualifications in national elections, as well as over how elections were to be conducted. But in 1964, the Court began to limit the states' ability to control the process of congressional redistricting. In 1966, for example, the Supreme Court invalidated the poll tax, a state-imposed tax of from one to five dollars imposed on those who wished to vote. The poll tax was widely used in the Southern states as an effective barrier to the poor, who often were black.[37] Most Southern legislators assailed the Court's decision, viewing it as illegal interference with their powers to regulate elections under the Constitution, and as a violation of state sovereignty.

On other fronts, however, states' power has been upheld by the U.S. Supreme Court. In 1991, for example, Missouri's policy of mandatory retirement at age seventy was ruled constitutional, because a state's power to determine qualifications of its key government officials lies "at the heart of representative government." According to the U.S. Supreme Court, the federal Age Discrimination Act could not be applied to state court judges. If a state wants to impose a mandatory retirement age on its state court judges, it can.[38]

The Performance of State Functions. In 1974, Congress extended the provisions of the Fair Labor Standards Act (FLSA), which regulated minimum wages and maximum hours for most workers, to cover state and local employees. The National League of Cities, a clearinghouse association of the National Governors' Conference, and several individual states and cities challenged the new measures, arguing that Congress had no authority to regulate the wages of state employees. In *National League of Cities* v. *Usury* (1976), a closely divided Court (five to four), decided that Congress had overstepped its authority. In 1941, the Supreme Court had upheld the constitutionality of the FLSA and of Congress's authority to set minimum wages for employees in the private sector. The 1974 amendment (which covered state and local employees), said the Court, had gone too far: "Congress has sought to wield its power in a fashion that would impair the States' ability to function effectively in a federal system,"[39] concluded the majority. The case was viewed as especially important because it was the first major instance of the Court's establishing any limits on national authority over the states since before the New Deal era. States' rights advocates believed that this brake on federalism was long overdue. Conservatives hailed the decision as the dawn of a "New Federalism."

Ironically, *National League of Cities* was reversed by an equally divided Court just nine years later in *Garcia* v. *San Antonio Metropolitan Transit Authority* (1985).[40] This

---

[37] *Harper* v. *Virginia Board of Elections*, 383 U.S. 663 (1966).
[38] *Gregory* v. *Ashcroft*, 111 S.Ct. 2395 (1991).
[39] 426 U.S. 833 (1976).
[40] 469 U.S. 528 (1985).

case also involved the constitutionality of applying federally imposed minimum wage and maximum hour provisions to state governments. In *Garcia*, the Court ruled that Congress has broad power to impose its will on state and local governments, even in areas that traditionally have been left to their discretion. The Court ruled that the "political process ensures that laws that unduly burden the states will not be promulgated" and that it should not be up to an "unelected" judiciary to preserve state powers. Furthermore, the majority of the Court concluded that the Tenth Amendment, which ensured that any powers not given to the national government be reserved for the states, was, at least for the time being, essentially meaningless! But by 1992, there were indications that the Court may eventually return to the *National League of Cities* standard. In a case involving the Low-Level Radioactive Waste Policy Amendments Act of 1985, the Court concluded that although Congress had substantial constitutional power to encourage states to provide for the disposal of radioactive waste within their own borders, the Constitution did "not confer upon Congress the ability simply to compel the states to do so."[41] Thus, the question of state authority in the federal system remains open.

Federalism and the Reagan–Bush Court. When Ronald Reagan left Washington to return to California at the end of his second term of office in January 1989, he left a lasting legacy. While president, he had the opportunity to appoint not only the Chief Justice, William Rehnquist, but also Associate Justices Sandra Day O'Connor, Antonin Scalia, and Anthony Kennedy. All were staunch conservatives, but O'Connor in particular, as a former state legislator and then state court judge, held a strong belief that the national government had intruded far too many times on the powers of the states. The Bush appointments of David Souter, a former state attorney general and state court judge, and Clarence Thomas, a leading African-American conservative, solidified the new, conservative, states'-rights–oriented majority.

Mario M. Cuomo, the liberal Democratic New York governor, has referred to the decisions of the Reagan–Bush Court as creating "a kind of new judicial federalism." (See "The New Judicial Federalism," on p. 99.) According to Cuomo, this new federalism can be characterized by the Court's withdrawal of "rights and emphases previously thought to be national."[42] Perhaps most illustrative of this trend were the Supreme Court's decisions in *Webster* v. *Reproductive Health Services* (1989)[43] and *Casey* v. *Planned Parenthood of Southeastern Pennsylvania* (1992).[44] In *Webster*, the Court first gave new latitude—and even encouragement—to the states to fashion more restrictive abortion laws. Since *Webster*, as illustrated in Figure 3-6, numerous states have enacted or are considering new restrictions. In 1991 alone, more than 200 bills restricting abortion were introduced in forty-five state legislatures.[45] Moreover, the Court has consistently upheld the authority of the individual states to limit a minor's access to abortion through imposition of parental consent or notification laws. And it has consistently declined to review other restrictions, including twenty-four–hour waiting requirements.

---

[41] *New York* v. *United States*, 112 S.Ct. 2408 (1992).

[42] Marianne Arneberg, "Cuomo Assails Judicial Hodgepodge," *Newsday,* August 15, 1990, p. 15.

[43] 492 U.S. 490 (1989).

[44] 112 S.Ct. 931 (1992).

[45] Maralee Schwartz, "Louisiana Lawmakers Override Abortion Bill Veto," *Washington Post,* June 19, 1991: A4.

The New Judicial Federalism

THE STATES' LEAD IN RIGHTS PROTECTION

Claus von Bulow, whose trial was popularized in the film *Reversal of Fortune*, might not be a free man today but for the protection afforded individual rights in Rhode Island's Constitution.

Incriminating evidence in his wife's death was thrown out by the state court under the state's exclusionary rule. That decision hinged on the state high court's interpretation of search-and-seizure provisions in Rhode Island's Constitution. The U.S. Supreme Court later declined to review the state ruling because the decision was based on independent and adequate state grounds.

Rhode Island is not alone in going farther than the U.S. Supreme Court in protecting individual rights. The emergence since 1970 of many state high courts as assertive protectors of individual rights comes as a surprise to many people. The fact that state courts are expanding protections beyond those guaranteed by the Bill of Rights is even more surprising. This development, called the new judicial federalism, has seen the federal government eclipsed by the states in every field.

The new judicial federalism generally refers to the authority of a state court to interpret its state constitution so as to provide broader rights protections than those recognized by U.S. Supreme Court interpretations of the federal Constitution. As in the von Bulow case, such state decisions are immune from Supreme Court review when they are based on "independent and adequate" state constitutional grounds.

In a 1970 decision, for instance, the Alaska Supreme Court wrote:

> While we must enforce the minimum constitutional standards imposed upon us by the United States Supreme Court's interpretation of the Fourteenth Amendment, we are free, and we are under a duty to develop additional constitutional rights and privileges under our Alaska Constitution. . . . We need not stand by idly and passively, waiting for constitutional direction from the highest court of the land.

The new judicial federalism revives some basic questions about rights. If rights are universal, should they not apply equally everywhere? If not, what rights are universal, and what rights can vary among states? Just as women once crossed state lines to obtain abortions, will ambulances carry people across borders to states with more liberal right-to-die laws? Will some ambulances go in the opposite direction, carrying patients away from relatives eager to "pull the plug" under liberal state rules?

Although universal rights may seem to be the natural order, independent state constitutions offer opportunities to entrench certain rights, at least in some places, when the nation or its highest court cannot agree on applying these rights. We have already seen signs of this with regard to privacy, victims' rights, women's rights and environmental rights provisions in some state constitutions. In this way, states can also serve as laboratories for rights experimentation.

The new judicial federalism may have implications for emerging democracies worldwide, as well. Often, ethnic, religious and linguistic hostilities preclude consensus on common rights. However, entrenching even a few common rights in the national constitution is a step in the right direction that can foster the trust needed to break down barriers to the recognition of more universal rights.

Source: Copyright © 1992. John Kincaid, the Council of State Governments. Reprinted with permission from *Spectrum: The Journal of State Governments.*

For the most part, decisions of the Reagan–Bush Court support Cuomo's characterization of the role of the national government in the newest federalism. But in spite of its conservative, pro-states' rights leanings, the Court has surprised observers. Even before Justice Souter was added to the Court, for example, it upheld the authority of a federal district court judge who had imposed a local tax increase to finance a school

100 ❖ Chapter 3 Federalism

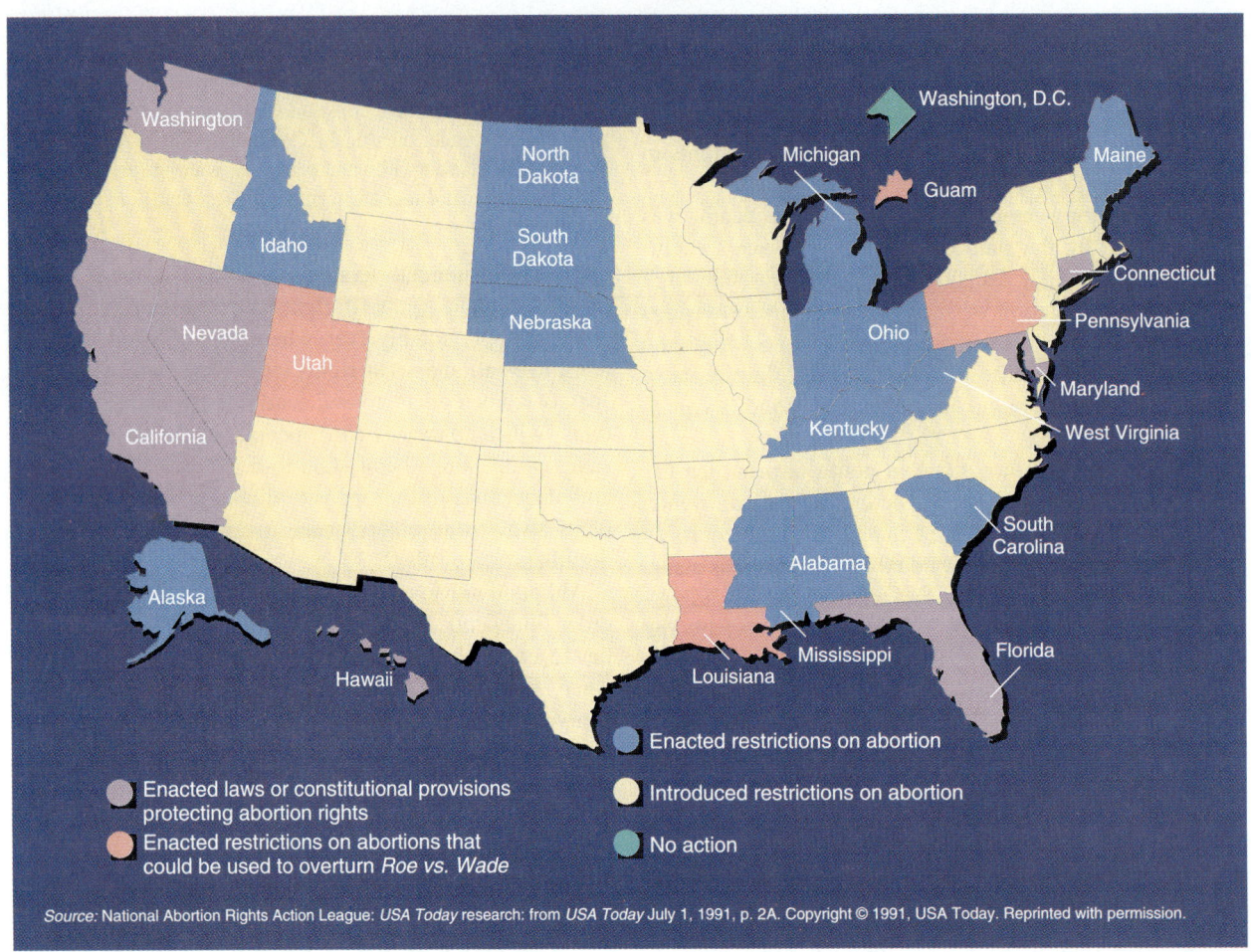

FIGURE 3-6

State-by-State Abortion Restrictions

Source: National Abortion Rights Action League: *USA Today* research: from *USA Today* July 1, 1991, p. 2A. Copyright © 1991, USA Today. Reprinted with permission.

desegregation order.[46] National authority also received a boost when the Court ruled that a federal law limiting the authority of state governors to withhold consent for state National Guards' active duty does not violate the militia clauses of the U.S. Constitution. Several governors had argued that the Constitution reserved to the states the power to train militia.[47]

Toward Reform

As the power of the national government has risen at the expense of the states, a variety of calls for reform of the federal system have been made by politicians and politi-

---

[46] *Missouri* v. *Jenkins*, 495 U.S. 33 (1990).
[47] *Perpich* v. *Department of Defense*, 110 S. Ct. 2418 (1990).

In the wake of the Supreme Court's decision in *Webster* v. *Reproductive Health Services* (1989), individual state governments have taken a more active role in setting guidelines (which may be restrictions) for abortion access. Here, Wichita residents rally for greater restrictions.

cal scientists. Moreover, inconsistent Court decisions—on the one hand returning costly national programs to the states while on the other hand continuing to order expensive educational and penal programs—have prompted fifteen state legislatures to approve resolutions calling for an amendment to the Constitution giving the states more authority in relation to the federal government. With the strong support of the Bush administration, those states proposed two avenues of change, largely in response to recent Court decisions. One seeks to allow the states to initiate amendments without calling a constitutional convention. The other would change the Tenth Amendment to direct the state courts to determine whether the Supreme Court had overstepped its boundaries with respect to the states. Neither proposal stands much chance of success.

Not only Republicans have called for change. In 1993, the Progressive Policy Institute, a project of the Democratic Leadership Council (see Chapter 11), called on the Clinton administration to "transform the federal government's entire approach to state and local grant programs."[48] Among its recommendations were:

1. Establishment of a commission to create a new federal compact to draft legislation eliminating 100 categorical grants and to consolidate 400 others in performance-based block grants renamed "Challenge Grants."

---

[48] David Osborne, "A New Federal Compact: Sorting Out Washington's Proper Role," in Will Marshall and Martin Schram, *Mandate for Change* (New York: Berkeley Books, 1993), p. 239.

2. Development of proposals to increase the numbers of waivers of federal regulations to states and local governments. Waivers allow state and local governments to act with greater flexibility to meet local needs. Yet, waivers in areas such as education (historically a state function) are virtually impossible to obtain.
3. Presidential appointment of a Cabinet-level federalism "czar" to move these recommendations through Congress.

In the wake of the Clinton administration's proposals to reinvent government, the Progressive Policy Institute's suggestion to increase the number of waivers, in particular, was greeted with enthusiasm. Clinton believes that these waivers will enhance state and local government flexibility. Waivers, however, do raise serious questions about rules of law, in that they allow for selective exemption from the coverage of certain statutes.

Summary

The inadequacies of the confederate form of government created by the Articles of Confederation led the Framers to create an entirely new, federal system of government. From the summer of 1776 until today, the tension between the national and state governments has been at the core of our federal system. In describing the origins of that tension and its results, we have made the following points:

1. The Framers created a federal system to replace the confederate form of government that had existed under the Articles of Confederation. The national government has both enumerated and implied powers, and also exercises concurrent powers with the states. Certain powers are denied to both the state and national governments. Certain guarantees concerning representation in Congress and protection against foreign attacks and domestic rebellion were made to the states in return for giving up some of their powers in the new federal system. Despite limitations, the national government is ultimately supreme.
2. Over the years, the powers of the national government have increased tremendously at the expense of the states. The Supreme Court, in particular, has played a key role in defining the relationship and powers of the national government through its broad interpretations of the supremacy and commerce clauses. For many years, however, it adhered to the notion of dual federalism, which tended to limit the national government's authority in areas such as slavery and, after the Civil War, civil rights. This notion of a limited role for the national government in some spheres ultimately fell by the wayside after the Great Depression.
3. The rapid creation of New Deal programs to alleviate many problems caused by the Depression led to a tremendous expansion of the federal government through the growth of federal services and grant-in-aid programs. This growth escalated during the Johnson administration and in the mid- to late 1970s. After his election in 1980, Ronald Reagan, upset by the growth of federal services, tried to reverse the tide through what he termed "New Federalism." He built on earlier efforts by Richard Nixon to consolidate categorical grants into fewer block grant programs, and to give state and local governments greater control over programs. In spite of these efforts, however, mandates and national preemption of state laws continue to influence state policies and budgets.
4. The intergovernmental lobby exists to help states and local governments resist federal mandates, learn more about conditions of aid, and advance their interests in Washington.
5. The Supreme Court has been a major player in recent trends in the federal–state relationship. Its decisions in the areas of education, civil rights, voting rights, and the performance of state functions have given the federal government a wider role in the day-to-day functioning of the states, and have limited the scope of the states' police powers. During the Reagan–Bush era, however, the Supreme Court, especially in the area of abortion, was willing to return some powers to the states.

Key Terms

federal system
federalism
enumerated powers
necessary and proper clause
implied power
concurrent powers
bill of attainder
ex post facto
supremacy clause
dual federalism
nullification doctrine
cooperative federalism
categorical grants
revenue sharing
block grants
preemption
mandates
intergovernmental lobby

Suggested Readings

Bowman, Ann O'M., and Richard Kearney. *The Resurgence of the States*. Englewood Cliffs, NJ: Prentice Hall, 1986.

Derthick, Martha. *The Influence of Federal Grants*. Cambridge, MA: Harvard University Press, 1970.

Elazar, Daniel. *American Federalism: A View from the States*. New York: Harper & Row, 1984.

Grodzins, Morton. *The American System*. Chicago: Rand McNally, 1966.

Hamilton, Christopher, and Donald T. Wells. *Federalism, Power, and Political Economy: A New Theory of Federalism's Impact on American Life*. Englewood Cliffs, NJ: Prentice Hall, 1990.

Daphne A. Kenyon and John Kincaid, eds. *Competition among States and Local Governments*. Washington, DC: The Urban Institute Press, 1991.

Phillips, Kevin. *The Politics of Rich and Poor: Wealth and the American Electorate in the Reagan Aftermath*. New York: HarperCollins, 1990.

Riker, William H. *Federalism: Origin, Operation, Significance*. Boston: Little, Brown, 1964.

Rivlin, Alice M. *Reviving the American Dream: The Economy, the States, and the Federal Government*. Washington, DC: The Brookings Institution, 1993.

Zimmerman, Joseph F. *Contemporary American Federalism: The Growth of National Power*. New York: Praeger, 1992.

> The constitution of this commonwealth . . . provides *that people have a right to* FREEDOM OF SPEECH. . . . How long those rights will appertain to you, you yourselves are called upon to say. . . .
>
> *Samuel Bryan*
> *"CENTINEL" NO. 1*

The Constitution of Pennsylvania included guarantees of free speech. Bryan, an Anti-Federalist, warned Philadelphians against the U.S. Constitution, saying that since it did not include such guarantees, they risked losing those hard-won freedoms.

CHAPTER 4

Civil Liberties

THE FIRST CONSTITUTIONAL AMENDMENTS: THE BILL OF RIGHTS
FIRST AMENDMENT GUARANTEES: FREEDOM OF RELIGION
FIRST AMENDMENT GUARANTEES: FREEDOM OF SPEECH AND PRESS
THE RIGHTS OF CRIMINAL DEFENDANTS
THE RIGHT TO PRIVACY
TOWARD REFORM

When Samuel Bryan penned the words opening this chapter on October 5, 1787, he voiced the fears not only of other Anti-Federalists but also of some supporters of the proposed Constitution. Although the Federalists—Alexander Hamilton and James Madison in particular—argued that the checks and balances proposed in the Constitution prevented the national government from usurping the civil liberties of Americans, many others were not so certain. In 1787, most state constitutions explicitly protected a variety of personal liberties: speech, religion, freedom from unreasonable searches and seizures, trial by jury, and more. It was clear that the new Constitution would redistribute power in the new federal system between the national government and the states. Without the guarantee of specific civil liberties, could the national government be trusted to uphold the freedoms already granted to citizens by their states?

Recognition of the increased power that would be held by the new national government led Anti-Federalists to stress the need for a bill of rights. Note that the Bill of Rights—as drafted by the Framers—applies only to the national government. It was not until much later that the Supreme Court interpreted the Bill of Rights as applying to the states (see pp. 119–122). In 1790, however, it was the power of the national government, not that of the states, that the people feared. Anti-Federalists and many others were confident that they could control the actions of their own state legislators, and most state constitutions already included bills of rights guaranteeing various civil liberties.

Although the debate over the Bill of Rights and its ratification may seem far removed from or even irrelevant to your life today, the liberties contained in it are central to many of today's most controversial issues. Can prayer be a part of a public high school graduation? Can a student be expelled from college for shouting racial slurs at other students? Can a state prohibit a physician from performing an abortion not nec-

106 ❖ Chapter 4 Civil Liberties

In spite of the First Amendment's general ban on state entanglement with religion, prayer is still common at many public ceremonies. Here, the President of the United States is shown praying at the 1993 graduation at West Point, a public institution.

essary to save the life of the mother? Why aren't hand guns banned by the national government? Why is there a death penalty in some states and not in others? Many of these questions involve issues never envisioned by the authors of the Bill of Rights. Nevertheless, each of these issues has found its way into the courts where the Constitution, the Bill of Rights, and the civil liberties it contains have been subject to interpretation and reinterpretation over the course of our nation's history.

Civil liberties are the personal rights and freedoms that the federal government cannot abridge, either by law, constitution, or judicial interpretation. Civil liberties place limitations on the power of the government to restrain or dictate how individuals act. Thus, when we discuss civil liberties such as those found in the Bill of Rights, we are concerned with limits on what governments can and cannot do. In contrast, when we discuss **civil rights,** the subject of Chapter 5, we are concerned with political and social rights—to be free from governmental discrimination based on race or gender, for example—that the government must provide its citizens. As discussed in Chapter 5, the term *civil rights* implies that the government is expected to play a positive role in ensuring all citizens equal protection under the laws and equal opportunity to participate in all aspects of national life. Clearly, the concepts of liberty and equality often overlap and interact.

Long ago, political observers learned that even though many Americans say they strongly support the Bill of Rights in principle, they are sharply divided when it comes to evaluating how the federal courts actually interpret its guarantees in specific cases.[1] Although we believe in free speech, for example, we may not want Ku Klux Klan (KKK) members or Nazis parading down our streets, or a pornography shop opening on our corner. Similarly, we may believe that Americans should be free from unreasonable searches and seizures, but many complain when criminals are released because the results of an illegal search cannot be used as evidence in their trials. The

---

[1] James M. Prothro and Charles M. Grigg, "Fundamental Principles of Democracy: Bases of Agreement and Disagreement," *Journal of Politics* 22 (1960): 276–294.

courts are repeatedly called upon to address what can be perceived as conflicting liberties. Does one group's right not to be harassed by the KKK outweigh the rights of KKK members to parade or speak their minds? Is a woman's right to enter an abortion clinic outweighed by the rights of others to blockade the clinic? Are the personal freedoms of victims of violent crime outweighed by the constitutional protections guaranteed to their attackers? Questions like these come continually before the courts and legislatures. The way these two branches of government resolve these issues as they interpret the Bill of Rights reflects a delicate balance of many forces, including historical events, cultural and technological changes, and personnel changes on the U.S. Supreme Court.

In this chapter, we trace the origins of the Bill of Rights and then examine many of its key guarantees in detail. Just as the meaning of the U.S. Constitution has been altered over time by judicial interpretation and by cultural and technological change, so has our concept of civil liberties and the proper role of the government in protecting them. Each guarantee in the Bill of Rights could be (and indeed is) the subject of several books. Here we hope to give you a greater appreciation of the historical development of the liberties Americans enjoy today, an understanding of the conflicts and crises these liberties often cause, and the key role the Supreme Court has played in this debate.

The First Constitutional Amendments: The Bill of Rights

As we saw in Chapter 2, most of the Framers originally opposed even the idea of a bill of rights. When George Mason of Virginia proposed that such a bill be added to the preface of the proposed constitution, for example, his resolution was defeated unanimously.[2] In the subsequent ratification debates, Federalists advanced three main arguments in opposition to the Bill of Rights:

1. A bill of rights was unnecessary. Most state constitutions already contained bills of rights. Alexander Hamilton asked, "Why declare that things shall not be done which there is no power to do?"[3]
2. A bill of rights would be dangerous.
3. A national bill of rights would be impractical. Enforcement would depend largely on public opinion and the spirit of the people and government.

Some Federalists, however, supported the idea. After the Philadelphia Convention, for example, James Madison conducted a lively correspondence about the need for a national bill of rights with Thomas Jefferson. Jefferson was far quicker to support such guarantees than was Madison, who continued to doubt their utility. Politics soon intervened, however, when Madison found himself in a close race against James Monroe for a seat in the House of Representatives in the First Congress. The district was

---

[2] The absence of a bill of rights led Mason to refuse to sign the proposed Constitution, noting that he "would sooner chop off his right hand than put it to the constitution as it now stands." (Quoted in Eric Black, *Our Constitution: The Myth That Binds Us* [Boulder, CO: Westview Press, 1988], p. 75.)

[3] Alexander Hamilton, *Federalist No. 84*.

Table 4.1 ♦ Civil Liberties Specified in the Bill of Rights

Amendment 1	Freedom of religion, speech, press and assembly. The right to petition the government.
Amendment 2	Right to keep and bear arms.
Amendment 3	Right not to have troops quartered in homes in peacetime.
Amendment 4	Freedom from unreasonable searches or seizures.
Amendment 5	Requirement of a grand jury indictment to prosecute a person for a serious crime. Prohibition of "double jeopardy" (being tried twice for the same offense); forcing a person to testify against himself or herself prohibited; loss of life, liberty, or property without due process.
Amendment 6	Right to a speedy, public, impartial trial with defense counsel and right to cross-examine witnesses.
Amendment 7	Right to jury trials in civil lawsuits involving amounts in excess of $20.
Amendment 8	Prohibition of excessive bail or fines, no cruel and unusual punishments.
Amendment 9	Possibility of existence of unlisted rights.
Amendment 10	Reservation to the states of powers not delegated to the United States or denied to states.

largely Anti-Federalist. So to garner support, Madison, in an act of political expediency, issued a series of public letters vowing support for a bill of rights.

Once elected, he made good on that promise. He became the prime mover and author of the Bill of Rights, although he considered the Congress to have far more important matters to handle and viewed his labors on the Bill of Rights "a nauseous project."[4] The insistence of Anti-Federalists on a bill of rights, the fact that some states conditioned their ratification of the Constitution on addition of these guarantees, and the disagreement among Federalists about such a bill led to prompt congressional action to put an end to further controversy, since this was a time when national stability and support for the new government were particularly needed. In 1789, the proposed Bill of Rights was sent to the states by Congress for ratification; this was finally achieved in 1791.

As enumerated in Table 4.1, the Bill of Rights contains numerous specific guarantees, including those of free speech, press, and religion (see Appendix II for the full text). The Ninth and Tenth Amendments, moreover, highlight Anti-Federalist fears of too powerful a national government. The Ninth Amendment makes it clear that this special listing of rights does not mean that others don't exist. It simply reiterated that powers not delegated to the national government are reserved to the states or the people.

---

[4] Quoted in Jack N. Rakove, "Madison Won Passage of the Bill of Rights But Remained a Skeptic," *Public Affairs Report* (March 1991), p. 6.

First Amendment Guarantees: Freedom of Religion

A democracy depends on a free exchange of ideas, and the First Amendment shows that the Framers were well aware of this. Despite the fact that many colonists had fled Europe primarily to escape religious persecution, most colonies actively persecuted those who did not belong to their predominant religious groups. Pennsylvania, for example, was a "Quaker" colony. The Congregationalist Church of Massachusetts, a "Puritan" colony, taxed and harassed those who held other religious beliefs. Nevertheless, the colonists were uniformly outraged in 1774 when the British Parliament passed a law establishing Anglicanism and Roman Catholicism as official religions in the colonies. The First Continental Congress immediately sent a letter of protest announcing its "astonishment that a British Parliament should ever consent to establish . . . a religion [Catholicism] that has deluged [England] in blood and dispersed bigotry, persecution, murder and rebellion through every part of the world."[5]

This distaste for a national church or religion was reflected in the Constitution. Article VI of the Constitution, for example, provides that "no religious Test shall ever be required as a Qualification to any Office or Public Trust under the United States." This simple sentiment, however, did not reassure those who feared the new Constitution would curtail individual liberty. Thus, the First Amendment to the Constitution was ultimately ratified to lay those fears to rest.

The First Amendment to the Constitution begins, "Congress shall make no law respecting an establishment of religion, or prohibiting the free exercise thereof." This statement sets the boundaries of governmental action. The **establishment clause** ("Congress shall make no law respecting an establishment of religion") directs the na-

---

[5] Continental Congress to the People of Great Britain, October 21, 1774, in Philip Kurland and Ralph Lerner, eds., *The Founders' Constitution*, Vol. 5 (Chicago: University of Chicago Press, 1987), p. 61.

The Absolutist Approach

The First Amendment opens with the words "Congress shall make no law...," and a question that has over the years troubled the Supreme Court and public commentators is whether those words should be interpreted *absolutely*; that is, whether any leeway can be granted to the clause. Supreme Court Justice Hugo Black, who served from 1937 to 1971, was the most ardent supporter of the absolutist approach. To him "no law" meant no law whatsoever. Most other justices, however, have taken less drastic approaches, especially when First Amendment rights appear to be in conflict. So, for example, the Court has allowed states to restrict some forms of speech and to regulate some religious practices considered harmful.

The separation of church and state advocated by Thomas Jefferson has not always been clearly defined. In *Lynch* v. *Donnelly* (1984) the Supreme Court upheld the constitutionality of a city-sponsored nativity scene as part of a larger Christmas display in a park. In response to this decision, many municipalities began to erect nativity scenes that were not part of a larger seasonal display. For example, in 1987 the city of Chicago erected, removed, and then re-erected a creche when faced with lawsuits from various groups protesting what they viewed as an unconstitutional intermingling of church and state. At first the city asked local churches to raise a $100,000 bond for protection against litigation. The money was not forthcoming, and the city dismantled the scene. A federal judge then ruled that the city had not violated the First Amendment, and the scene returned.

tional government not to involve itself in religion. It creates, in Thomas Jefferson's immortal words, a "wall of separation" between church and state. The **free exercise clause** ("or prohibiting the free exercise thereof") guarantees citizens that the national government will not interfere with their practice of religion. These guarantees, however, are not absolute. In *Cantwell* v. *Connecticut* (1940), the Supreme Court observed that the First Amendment "embraces two concepts—freedom to believe and freedom to act. The first is absolute, but in the nature of things, the second cannot be. Conduct remains subject to regulation of society."[6] In the mid-1800s, for example, Mormons traditionally practiced and preached polygamy, the taking of multiple wives. In 1879, when it was first called on to interpret the free exercise clause, the Supreme Court upheld the conviction of a Mormon under a federal law barring polygamy. The Court reasoned that to do otherwise would provide constitutional protections to a full range of religious beliefs, including those as extreme as human sacrifice. "Laws are made for the government of actions," noted the Court, "and while they cannot interfere with mere religious belief and opinions, they may with practices."[7]

The Establishment Clause

Over the years, the Court has been divided over how to interpret the establishment clause. Does this clause erect a total wall between church and state, or is some governmental accommodation of religion allowed?

In 1947, for example, the Court split five to four in upholding the constitutionality of a New Jersey town's practice of reimbursing parents for the costs of transporting

---

[6] 310 U.S. 296 (1940).

[7] *Reynolds* v. *U.S.*, 98 U.S. 145 (1879).

their children to Roman Catholic schools. In *Everson v. Board of Education of Ewing Township* (1947),[8] the majority made it clear that the monies were not spent in furtherance of a religion, but were a subsidy to parents, not to churches. Writing for the narrow majority, Justice Hugo L. Black suggested, moreover, that a strict separation of church and state required only that a state be neutral in its relationships with religious groups and nonbelievers.

Over the years, state subsidies that could be considered to aid children or certain other identifiable recipients have been held not to violate the Constitution. This analysis has allowed the Court to permit "dismissed time" (allowing parochial school children to leave school early to attend religious instruction off public school grounds),[9] federal aid for the construction of buildings on religiously affiliated college campuses,[10] state-loaned textbooks for parochial school children,[11] and state laws giving parents tax deductions for parochial school tuitions.[12] And, again in a five-to-four decision, the Rehnquist Court ruled in 1993 that public funding to provide sign language interpreters for deaf students in religious schools did not violate the constitutionally required separation of church and state.[13]

While it has upheld the constitutionality of these kinds of church/state entanglements, the Court has held fast to the rule of strict separation between church and state when issues of prayer in school are involved. In *Engel v. Vitale* (1962),[14] the Court ruled that the recitation in public school classrooms of a twenty-two-word nondenominational prayer drafted by the New Hyde Park, New York, school board was unconstitutional.

The Court has gone back and forth in its effort to come up with a workable way to deal with church/state questions. In *Lemon v. Kurtzman* (1971),[15] the Court heard a case that challenged direct state aid to parochial schools, including the use of state funds to pay salaries of teachers at these schools. In its decision, the Court tried—as it often does—to carve out a new "test" by which to measure the constitutionality of these types of laws. To be constitutional, a challenged law or practice must:

1. Have a secular purpose;
2. Have a primary effect that neither advances nor inhibits religion; and
3. Not foster an excessive government entanglement with religion.

State funding of parochial school teachers' salaries was found to fail this test and was therefore prohibited by the Constitution, said the Court in *Lemon*.[16] In 1980, the *Lemon* test was interpreted to invalidate a Kentucky law that required the posting of the Ten Commandments in public school classrooms. The Court ruled the posting had no secular purpose.[17] And later, in *Wallace v. Jaffree* (1985),[18] an Alabama law re-

---

[8] 330 U.S. 1 (1947).
[9] *McCollum v. Board of Education*, 333 U.S. 203 (1948).
[10] *Tilton v. Richardson*, 403 U.S. 672 (1971).
[11] *Board of Education v. Allen*, 392 U.S. 236 (1968).
[12] *Mueller v. Allen*, 463 U.S. 388 (1983).
[13] *Zobrest v. Catalina Foothills School District*, 1993 U.S. LEXIS 4211.
[14] 370 U.S. 421 (1962).
[15] 403 U.S. 602 (1971).
[16] Ibid.
[17] *Stone v. Graham*, 449 U.S. 39 (1980).
[18] 472 U.S. 38 (1985).

quiring a daily minute of silence for meditation or voluntary prayer was also ruled unconstitutional.

Even the more conservative Rehnquist Court has been for the most part unwilling to lower the wall of separation when it comes to religious influences in the public schools. In *Edwards* v. *Aguillard* (1987),[19] for example, the Court found that a Louisiana statute requiring that creationism be taught as a balance to evolution also violated the establishment clause. And in *Lee* v. *Weisman* (1992),[20] the Court continued its unwillingness to allow prayer in public schools by finding unconstitutional the saying of prayer at a middle school graduation.

After 1980, however, the Court has appeared more willing to ignore the *Lemon* test and lower the wall between church and state so long as school prayer is not involved. In 1981, for example, the Court ruled unconstitutional a Missouri law prohibiting the use of state university buildings and grounds for "purposes of religious worship," that had been used to ban religious groups from using school facilities. With only one dissent, the Court ruled that "University students are . . . less impressionable than younger students and should be able to appreciate that the university's policy is one of neutrality towards religion."[21]

This decision was taken by many members of Congress as a sign that this principle could be extended to secondary and even primary schools. In 1984, Congress passed the Equal Access Act, which bars public schools from discriminating against groups of students on the basis of "religious, political, philosophical or other content of the speech at such meetings." The constitutionality of this law was upheld in *Board of Education* v. *Mergens* (1990),[22] when the Court ruled that a school board's refusal to allow a Christian Bible club to meet in a public high school classroom during a twice weekly "activity period" violated the Act. According to Justice Sandra Day O'Connor, writing for the majority, the primary effect of the Act was neither to advance religion nor to excessively entangle government and religion—in spite of the fact that religious meetings would be held on school grounds with a faculty sponsor. The important factor seemed to be that the students had complete choice in their selection of activities with numerous non-religious options. In 1993, the Court also ruled that religious groups must be allowed to use public schools after hours if that access is also given to other community groups.[23] The 1993 replacement of Justice White by Ruth Bader Ginsburg, a former attorney for the American Civil Liberties Union (see "The American Civil Liberties Union," p. 126) could halt this trend toward lowering the wall between church and state.

The Free Exercise Clause

The free exercise clause of the First Amendment proclaims that "Congress shall make no law . . . prohibiting the free exercise [of religion]." As in the case of the establishment clause, the Supreme Court has been continually forced to interpret this clause, often trying to balance the sometimes conflicting implications of the two clauses. Is it,

Members of the Church of God, a faith-healing sect, revived snake-handling ceremonies in the 1950s despite a 1940 Kentury statute that expressly prohibited using poisonous snakes in religious rites. Although banned by law, snake-handling practices as part of religious services continue today in many parts of the South.

[19] 482 U.S. 578 (1987).
[20] 112 S. Ct. 2649 (1992).
[21] *Widmar* v. *Vincent*, 454 U.S. 263 (1981).
[22] 110 S. Ct. 2356 (1990).
[23] *Lamb's Chapel* v. *Center Moriches Union Free School District*, 113 S. Ct. 2141 (1993).

for example, permissible for a state to ban the use of snakes during religious services, although some fundamentalist Christians view snake handling as an important part of their religious services? Is it reasonable to force some men into combat if their religious beliefs ban them from participating? In the latter example, if exemptions (called "conscientious objector deferments") are given to some men and not to others, is the government favoring one religion over another?

Although the free exercise clause of the First Amendment guarantees individuals the right to be free from governmental interference in the exercise of their religion, this guarantee, like other First Amendment freedoms, is not absolute. When secular law comes into conflict with religious law, the right to exercise one's religious beliefs is often denied—especially if the religious beliefs in question are held by a minority, or by an unpopular or "suspicious" religious group. State statutes barring the use of certain illegal drugs, snake handling, and polygamy—all practices of particular religious sects—have been upheld as constitutional. Similarly, states can require some businesses to close on Sundays although some major religious groups observe Saturday as their day of worship. Nonetheless, the Court has made it clear that the free exercise clause requires that a state or the national government remain neutral toward religion.

Many critics of rigid enforcement of such neutrality argue that the government should do what it can to accommodate the religious diversity in our nation. In the early 1960s, for example, a South Carolina textile mill shifted to a six-day work week, requiring that all employees work on Saturday. When an employee, a Seventh-Day Adventist whose Sabbath was Saturday, said she could not work on Saturdays, she was fired. She sought to receive unemployment compensation and her claim was denied. She then sued to obtain her benefits. The Supreme Court ordered South Carolina to extend benefits to the woman in spite of its law that *required* an employee to be available for work on all days but Sundays. The Court ruled that the state law was an unconstitutional violation of the free exercise clause because it failed to accommodate the worker's religious beliefs.[24]

This accommodationist approach was further advanced in *Wisconsin* v. *Yoder* (1972),[25] a challenge to the constitutionality of a Wisconsin law requiring all students to stay in school through the age of sixteen. Yoder and several other members of the Old Order Amish religion were convicted of violating the Wisconsin law when they refused to send their children to school after they had completed the eighth grade. The Amish believed that high school attendance would expose their children to secular influences and "worldly views," thus endangering their way of life. Citing the long, peaceful history of the Amish and their traditional ways, the Court concluded that the statute violated the free exercise clause and interfered with the Amish's practice of their religion. In another case, however, the Court did rule that it was permissible for Minnesota to compel the Amish to comply with highway safety laws.[26]

In the same vein, the Court has interpreted the Constitution to mean that governmental interests can outweigh free exercise rights: in 1986, for example, it ruled that it was reasonable for the military to ban the wearing of yarmulkes by Orthodox Jewish officers.[27] In 1988, the Court upheld the U.S. Forest Service's right to permit road con-

The ways of the Amish often stand in sharp contrast to those of their neighbors. Often, they coexist with no problems. In *Wisconsin* v. *Yoder* the Supreme Court ruled that Amish children did not have to attend public school past the eighth grade although state law required all other children to attend school until age 16. The Amish, however, have been required to have lanterns on their buggies at night as a public safety measure, First Amendment considerations notwithstanding.

---

[24] *Sherbert* v. *Verner*, 374 U.S. 398 (1963).
[25] 406 U.S. 208 (1972).
[26] *Minnesota* v. *Hershberger*, 110 S. Ct. 1918 (1990).
[27] *Goldman* v. *Weinberger*, 475 U.S. 503 (1986).

struction and tree harvesting in areas of the national forest traditionally used for religious purposes by American Indian tribes.[28] Later, in *Oregon* v. *Smith* (1990), the Supreme Court ruled that the free exercise clause allowed Oregon to ban the use of sacramental peyote (an illegal hallucinogenic drug) in some American Indian tribes' traditional religious services. The Court upheld the state's right to deny unemployment compensation to two workers who had been fired by a private drug rehabilitation clinic because they had ingested an illegal substance.[29] (In 1994 the Religious Freedom Restoration Act was passed and signed into law to overturn this decision.) In contrast, in 1993 the Supreme Court ruled that members of the Santería Church, an Afro-Cuban religion, had the right to sacrifice animals during religious services. In upholding that practice, the Court ruled that a city ordinance banning such practices was unconstitutionally aimed at the group, thereby denying its members the right to free exercise of their religion.[30]

Although conflicts between religious beliefs and the government are often difficult to settle, the Court has attempted to walk the fine line between the free exercise and establishment clauses. Moreover, in the area of free exercise, the Court often has had to confront questions of "What is a god?" and "What is a religious faith?"—questions that theologians have grappled with for centuries. In *U.S.* v. *Seeger* (1965),[31] for example, a case involving three men who had been denied conscientious objector deferments during the Vietnam War because they did not subscribe to "traditional" organized religions, the Court ruled unanimously that the men were entitled to the deferments because their belief in a supreme being placed their views parallel to those who practiced traditional religions. In contrast, despite the Court's having ruled that Catholic, Protestant, Jewish, and Buddhist prison inmates must be allowed to hold religious services,[32] in 1987 it held that Islamic prisoners could be denied the same right for security reasons.[33]

First Amendment Guarantees: Freedom of Speech and Press

Historically, one of the most volatile areas of constitutional interpretation has been in the interpretation of the First Amendment's mandate that "Congress shall make no law . . . abridging the freedom of speech, or of the press." Like the establishment and free exercise clauses of the First Amendment, the speech and press clauses have not been interpreted as absolute bans against government regulation. In fact, over the years the Court has used a hierarchical approach, with some items getting greater protection than others. Generally, thoughts have received the greatest protection, and actions or deeds the least. Words have come somewhere in the middle, depending on their content and purpose.

---

[28] *Lyng* v. *Northwest Indian Cemetery Protective Association*, 485 U.S. 439 (1988).
[29] 494 U.S. 872 (1990).
[30] *Church of the Lukumi Babalu Aye* v. *Hialeah*, 113 S. Ct. 2217 (1993).
[31] 380 U.S. 163 (1965).
[32] *Cruz* v. *Beto*, 405 U.S. 319 (1972).
[33] *O'Lone* v. *Shabazz*, 482 U.S. 342 (1987).

In the United States, with few exceptions, thoughts are considered beyond the scope of governmental regulation. Although people may experience a negative reaction for revealing their thoughts, the government has no legal right to punish or sanction Americans for what they think. Words, or speech, which stand between thoughts and deeds, are subject to some forms of restraint. Speech that is obscene, libelous (false, or causing someone disrepute), or seditious (advocating violent overthrow of the government), or that amounts to "fighting words" that could incite or cause injury to those to whom they are addressed, has been interpreted as not protected by the First Amendment. Often, however, these exceptions to constitutional protection have troubled the Court. What is considered obscene in rural Mississippi, for example, may not offend someone in another part of the nation.

Actions, or deeds, are given the least constitutional protection. Thus, actions are subject to the most governmental restrictions. You may have a right to shoot a pistol in your back yard, but you can't do it on a city street. Over the years these competing rights have been balanced by the now classic observation that your "right to swing your arm ends at the tip of my nose."[34]

When the First Amendment was ratified in 1791, it was considered to protect only against **prior restraint**; that is, the government could not prohibit speech or publication before the fact. As was the case in Great Britain concerning free speech (see

---

[34] See, for example, the opinion in *Boissonneault* v. *Flint City Council*, 392 Mich. 685 (1974).

Freedom of Speech and the Common-Law Tradition

♦ ♦ ♦

In Great Britain, government censorship of the press and speech had its origins in a 1275 pronouncement from the Crown. Later, in the sixteenth and seventeenth centuries, the King's Council, which sat in what was fearfully called the "Star Chamber" by British subjects, harshly meted out cruel sentences for seditious libel, that is, language tending to incite rebellion against the state. In one of the Star Chamber's most infamous cases, the Trial of William Prynn (1632), Prynn was sentenced to life imprisonment, branded on the forehead, had his nose split, his ears cut off, and was fined £10,000 for publishing a book that criticized actors and actresses. The book was viewed as seditious libel against the queen, because she had recently appeared in a play!

The Star Chamber was abolished in 1641, but its precedents were often relied upon by common-law courts. Criminal liability for slander (unlawful, untrue speech) remained a question of law, not of fact, to be decided by juries. Moreover, partisan publications were discouraged by law. In sum, the British experience concerning speech laws focused largely on issues of prior restraint and not on the protection of speech per se.

Source: From *Constitutional Law and Politics, Volume Two. Civil Rights and Civil Liberties,* by David M. O'Brien, by permission of the author and W. W. Norton & Company, Inc. Copyright © 1991 by David M. O'Brien.

"Freedom of Speech and the Common Law Tradition," p. 115), the First Amendment was not considered to provide absolute immunity from governmental sanction for what speakers or publishers might say or print. Thus, over the years, the meaning of this amendment's mandate has been subject to thousands of cases seeking judicial interpretation of its meaning.

The Alien and Sedition Acts

Soon after passage of the Bill of Rights, a constitutional crisis arose in 1798 when the Federalist Congress enacted the Alien and Sedition Acts. Designed to ban any political criticism by the growing numbers of Jeffersonian Democratic-Republicans, these Acts made publication of "any false, scandalous writing against the government of the United States" a criminal offense. Overtly partisan Federalist judges imposed fines and even jail terms on at least ten Democratic-Republican newspaper editors for allegedly violating the Acts. The Acts became a major issue in the 1800 presidential election campaign, which led to the election of Thomas Jefferson, a vocal opponent of the Acts. He quickly pardoned all who had been convicted under their provisions, and the new Democratic-Republican Congress allowed the Acts to expire before the Supreme Court had an opportunity to rule on the constitutionality of these serious infringements of the First Amendment.

Slavery, the Civil War, and Rights Curtailments

After the public outcry over the Alien and Sedition Acts, the national government largely got out of the business of regulating speech, but in its place the states began to prosecute those who published articles critical of governmental policies. In the 1830s, at the urgings of abolitionists, the publication or dissemination of any positive information about slavery became a punishable offense in the North. In the opposite vein, in the South, supporters of the "peculiar institution" of slavery enacted laws to prohibit publication of any anti-slavery sentiments. Southern postmasters refused to deliver Northern abolitionist papers throughout the South, which amounted to censorship of the mails.

During the Civil War, President Abraham Lincoln effectively suspended the free press provision of the First Amendment (as well as many other sections of the Constitution) and even went so far as to order the arrest of the editors of two New York papers that were critical of him. Far from protesting against these blatant violations of the First Amendment, Congress acceded to them. Right after the war, for example, Congress actually prevented the Supreme Court from issuing a judgment on a case, *Ex parte McCardle* (1869),[35] because members feared its decision would be critical of the powers Lincoln had taken on during the war. William McCardle, a Mississippi newspaper editor, had sought to arouse sentiment against Lincoln and the Union occupation. Even though he was a civilian, McCardle was jailed by a military court without having any charges brought against him. He appealed to the U.S. Supreme Court, arguing that he was being held unlawfully. Congress, fearing that a victory for McCardle would prompt other Confederate newspaper editors to follow his lead, enacted a law barring the Supreme Court from hearing appeals of cases involving convictions for

---

[35] 7 Wall. 506 (1869).

publishing statements critical of the Union. Because Article III of the Constitution gives Congress the power to determine the jurisdiction of the Court, the Court was forced to conclude that it had no authority to rule in the matter.

After the Civil War, states also began to prosecute individuals for seditious speech when they uttered or printed statements critical of the government. Between 1890 and 1900, for example, there were more than 100 state prosecutions for sedition in state courts.[36] Moreover, by the dawn of the twentieth century, public opinion in the United States had become exceedingly hostile to the preachings of such groups as socialists and communists (see "People of the Past: Eugene Debs," p. 118) who attempted to appeal to the thousands of new and disheartened immigrants. Groups espousing socialism and communism became the targets of state laws curtailing speech and the written word. By the end of World War I, over thirty states had passed laws (often known as criminal syndicalism statutes) to punish seditious speech, and more than 1,900 individuals and over 100 newspapers were prosecuted for violations.[37]

New Restrictions/New Tests

The first major federal law restricting freedom of speech and the press since the Alien and Sedition Acts was the Espionage Act of 1917. Nearly 2,000 Americans were convicted of violating its various provisions, especially those making it illegal to urge resistance to the draft, and prohibiting the distribution of anti-war leaflets.

In 1919, the Supreme Court decided several important cases calling for interpretation of the First Amendment. Charles T. Schenck, a secretary of the Socialist Party, was tried and convicted for printing, distributing, and mailing anti-war leaflets to men eligible for the draft. In *Schenck* v. *United States* (1919),[38] his conviction for urging others to resist military induction was upheld in an opinion written by Justice Oliver Wendell Holmes. The Court interpreted the First Amendment to allow Congress to restrict speech that was "of such a nature as to create a clear and present danger that will bring about the substantive evils that Congress has a right to prevent." Holmes relied on the **bad tendency test**, which had been used in earlier cases. He reasoned that in times of war, Schenck's leaflets could obstruct recruitment into the military because their "tendency" and "intent" were the same. During the same term, in another case involving the bad tendencies of anti-war speech, Holmes concluded for a unanimous Court that the leaflets in question constituted a danger. He explained that even the U.S. Constitution does not protect an individual from "falsely shouting fire in a theater and causing a panic."[39]

Under the **clear and present danger test**, which allowed Congress to ban speech that could cause a clear and present danger to society, the circumstances surrounding the incident counts, according to the Court. Whereas the leaflets might have been permissible in peacetime, they posed too much of a danger in wartime to be allowed. The clear and present danger test used by the Court attempted to draw a line between protected and unprotected speech in this new area of constitutional interpretation. Holmes appeared to use the clear and present danger and bad tendency tests interchangeably.

---

[36] David M. O'Brien, *Constitutional Law and Politics, Vol. Two* (New York: Norton, 1991), p. 345.

[37] See Frederick Siebert, *The Rights and Privileges of the Press* (New York: D. Appleton-Century, 1934), pp. 886, 931–940.

[38] 249 U.S. 47 (1919).

[39] *Frohwerk* v. *United States*, 249 U.S. 204 (1919).

For example, in *Debs* v. *United States* (1919), Holmes concluded for the Court that Eugene Debs's anti-war speeches "had as their natural tendency and reasonably probable effect to obstruct the recruitment" of men into the armed services, and that his conviction was thus constitutional.[40]

---

[40] 249 U.S. 211 (1919).

PEOPLE OF THE PAST

Eugene V. Debs

Eugene Victor Debs was a prominent American socialist and a central figure in challenging the free speech restrictions of the Espionage Act of 1917. He was born in Terre Haute, Indiana in 1855. Debs went to work on the railroads in 1870, and in 1875 he helped form a lodge of the Brotherhood of Locomotive Firemen, an early union, and later served as its national secretary and treasurer, and editor of its magazine. In 1893 he helped form the American Railway Union and was made its president.

As part of the Cleveland administration's attempts to crush the 1894 Pullman strike in Chicago, Debs was held in contempt of court for violating a federal injunction against striking and was sentenced to six months in jail. While in jail, he read widely on the philosophy of socialism, and in 1897 he transformed the remains of the American Railway Union into the Social Democratic Party of America, later called the Socialist Party of America.

Debs ran for president of the United States on the Socialist ticket in 1900, 1904, 1908, and 1912. In 1918, as one of the most visible critics of Woodrow Wilson's decision to enter World War I, he again found himself in court, this time charged with violating the Espionage Act of 1917.

Debs was tried and sentenced to ten years in prison for a speech he delivered in Canton, Ohio at a socialist anti-war rally. In his speech, Debs praised other imprisoned leaders of his party who had been jailed for aiding draft resistors. He accused the U.S. government of using false testimony to convict another anti-war activist and labeled the war a plot by "the predator capitalists in the United States" against the working class "who furnish the corpses. . . . You need to know," he told his listeners, that "you are fit for something better than slavery and cannon fodder."

By the time the appeal of his conviction reached the Supreme Court, a post-war "red scare" had spread through the country. Without even a reference to the "clear and present danger" test enunciated just a week earlier in *Schenck* v. *United States*, a unanimous Court affirmed his conviction. Although in *Debs* v. *United States* (1919) Justice Oliver Wendell Holmes conceded that "the main theme" of Debs's speech was the growth and eventual triumph of socialism, he argued that "if a part of the manifest intent of the more general utterance was to encourage those present to obstruct recruiting . . . the immunity of the general theme may not be enough to protect the speech."

Although he was in prison, Debs again ran for president in 1920 and received more than 900,000 votes. President Wilson, still bitter about Debs's opposition to the war, refused to pardon him. Wilson's successor, Warren G. Harding, showed more compassion and pardoned him in 1921. Debs devoted much of his remaining life to campaigning for improved prison conditions. He died in 1926.

In that same year, however, division among the members of the Court concerning the clear and present danger test became apparent. In *Abrams* v. *United States* (1919),[41] a majority of the Court upheld Abrams's conviction for distributing leaflets critical of President Wilson's decision to send American soldiers to Russia. In dissent, however, Holmes rejected the majority's reliance on the clear and present danger test. He concluded that the activities of six anarchists who had been convicted for writing a "silly leaflet by an unknown man" protesting the U.S. government's attempts to overthrow Russia's newly formed Bolshevik government posed no imminent danger to the United States. The majority, however, remained unconvinced by Holmes's arguments. From 1919 to 1927, the convictions of defendants in five other cases brought under the Espionage Act were upheld by the Court.

For decades, the Supreme Court continued to wrestle with what constituted a "danger." Finally, fifty years after the Abrams decision, in *Brandenburg* v. *Ohio* (1969),[42] the Court fashioned a new test: the **direct incitement test**. Now the government could punish the advocacy of illegal action only if "such advocacy is directed to inciting or producing imminent lawless action and is likely to incite or produce such action." Brandenburg was convicted under an Ohio law after he advocated racial strife during a televised KKK hearing. A trial court concluded that his speech, in context, produced no imminent danger. Thus, the statute, in its interpretation, and his conviction were unconstitutional. The requirement of "imminent harm" makes it more difficult for the government to punish speech and is consistent with the Framer's notion of the special role played by speech in a democratic society.

The First Amendment Applied to the States: The Incorporation Doctrine

As discussed in Chapter 2, the Bill of Rights was intended to limit the powers of the *national* government to infringe upon the rights and liberties of the citizenry. And in *Barron* v. *Baltimore* (1833),[43] the Supreme Court ruled that the federal Bill of Rights limited only the U.S. government and *not* the states. In 1868, however, the Fourteenth Amendment was added to the U.S. Constitution. Its language suggested the possibility that some or even all of the protections guaranteed in the Bill of Rights might be interpreted to prevent *state* infringement of those rights. Section 1 of the Fourteenth Amendment reads: "No State shall . . . deprive any person of life, liberty, or property, without due process of law."

Until 1925, the Supreme Court steadfastly rejected numerous arguments urging it to interpret the **due process clause** as making various provisions contained in the Bill of Rights applicable to the states. As a consequence, states were free throughout this period to pass sedition laws, knowing that the Supreme Court would uphold their constitutional validity. Then, in 1925, all of this changed dramatically. Benjamin Gitlow, a member of the Left Wing Section of the Socialist Party, was convicted of violating a New York law which, in language very similar to that of the federal Espionage Act, prohibited the advocacy of the violent overthrow of the government. Gitlow had printed 16,000 copies of a manifesto in which he urged workers to rise up to overthrow the U.S. government. Although Gitlow's conviction was upheld, in *Gitlow* v. *New York*

---

[41] 250 U.S. 616 (1919).
[42] 395 U.S. 444 (1969).
[43] 7 Pet. 243 (1833).

Until *Gitlow* v. *New York* (1925) involving Benjamin Gitlow, the Executive Secretary of the Socialist Party, it was generally thought that the Fourteenth Amendment did not apply the protections of the Bill of Rights to the states. Here Gitlow is shown testifying before the Dees Committee, which was investigating un-American activities.

(1925) the Supreme Court noted that the states were not completely free to limit forms of political expression:

> For present purposes we may and do assume that freedom of speech and of the press—which are protected by the First Amendment from abridgement by Congress—are among the *fundamental personal rights and "liberties"* protected by the due process clause of the Fourteenth Amendment from impairment by the states (emphasis added).[44]

Gitlow, with its finding that states could not abridge free speech protections, was the first step in the slow process of the judicial development of the **incorporation doctrine**. After *Gitlow*, it took the Court six more years to "incorporate" another First Amendment freedom—that of the press. *Near* v. *Minnesota* (1931)[45] was the first case in which the Supreme Court found that a state law violated freedom of the press as protected by the First Amendment. Jay Near, the publisher of a weekly Minneapolis newspaper, regularly attacked a variety of groups—blacks, Catholics, Jews, and labor union leaders. Few escaped his hatred. Near's paper was closed under the authority of a state criminal libel law banning "malicious, scandalous, or defamatory" publications. Near appealed the closing of his paper, and the Supreme Court ruled that "The fact that the liberty of the press may be abused by miscreant purveyors of scandal does not make any the less necessary the immunity of the press from previous restraint."[46]

As revealed in Table 4.2, not all the guarantees in the Bill of Rights have been made applicable to the states through the due process clause of the Fourteenth Amendment. Instead, the Court has selectively chosen to limit the rights of states by protecting the rights it considers most fundamental. This process is referred to as selective incorporation.

Selective Incorporation and Fundamental Freedoms. The rationale for **selective incorporation**, the judicial application to the states of only some of the rights enumerated by the Bill of Rights, was set out in *Palko* v. *Connecticut* (1937).[47] Frank Palko was charged with first-degree murder for killing two police officers, found guilty of a lesser charge of second-degree murder, and sentenced to life imprisonment. Connecticut appealed, Palko was retried, found guilty of first-degree murder, and re-sentenced to death.

Palko then appealed his second conviction on the grounds that it violated the Fifth Amendment's prohibition against double jeopardy, because the Fifth Amendment had been made applicable to the states by the due process clause of the Fourteenth Amendment.

The Supreme Court upheld Palko's second conviction and the death sentence, thereby choosing not to bind states to the Fifth Amendment's double jeopardy clause. Writing for the majority, Justice Benjamin Cardozo set forth principles that were to guide the Court's interpretation of the incorporation doctrine for the next several decades. Some protections found in the Bill of Rights were absorbed into the concept of due process only because they are so fundamental to our notions of liberty and jus-

---

[44] *Gitlow* v. *New York*, 268 U.S. 652 (1925).
[45] 283 U.S. 697 (1931).
[46] For more about *Near*, see Fred W. Friendly, *Minnesota Rag* (New York: Random House, 1981).
[47] 302 U.S. 319 (1937).

Table 4.2 ♦ Selective Incorporation and the Bill of Rights

AMENDMENT	RIGHT	DATE	CASE
I.	Speech	1925	*Gitlow* v. *New York*
	Press	1931	*Near* v. *Minnesota*
	Assembly	1937	*DeJonge* v. *Oregon*
	Religion	1940	*Cantwell* v. *Connecticut*
II.	Right to bear arms		*not incorporated* (Generally, the Supreme Court has upheld reasonable regulations of the right of private citizens to bear arms. Should a tough gun-control law be adopted by a state or local government and a challenge to it be made, a test of incorporation might be presented to the Court in the future.)
III.	No quartering of soldiers		*not incorporated* (The quartering problem has not recurred since colonial times.)
IV.	Unreasonable searches and seizures	1949	*Wolf* v. *Colorado*
	The exclusionary rule	1961	*Mapp* v. *Ohio*
V.	Just compensation	1897	*Chicago, B&O RR. Co.* v. *Chicago*
	Self-incrimination	1964	*Malloy* v. *Hogan*
	Double jeopardy	1969	*Benton* v. *Maryland*
	Grand jury indictment		*not incorporated* (The trend in state criminal cases is away from grand juries and toward reliance upon the sworn written accusation of the prosecuting attorney.)
VI.	Public trial	1948	*In re Oliver*
	Right to counsel	1963	*Gideon* v. *Wainright*
	Confrontation of witnesses	1965	*Pointer* v. *Texas*
	Impartial trial	1966	*Parker* v. *Gladden*
	Speedy trial	1967	*Klopfer* v. *North Carolina*
	Compulsory process	1967	*Washington* v. *Texas*
	Jury trial	1968	*Duncan* v. *Louisiana*
VII.	Right to jury trial in civil cases		*not incorporated* (While Warren Burger was Chief Justice he conducted a campaign to abolish jury trials in civil cases to save time and money, and for other reasons.)
VIII.	Freedom from cruel and unusual punishment	1962	*Robinson* v. *California*
	Freedom from excessive fines or bail		*not incorporated*

Source: Adapted from: William C. Louthan, *The United States Supreme Court.* Englewood Cliffs: Prentice Hall, 1991, pp. 205–206.

tice that they cannot be denied by the states. "Neither liberty nor justice would exist if [fundamental rights] are sacrificed," wrote Cardozo. Because the Court concluded that the protection against double jeopardy was not a fundamental right, Palko died in Connecticut's gas chamber one year later. Cardozo's argument that those rights were necessary to a "fair and enlightened system of justice" was nonetheless gradually expanded by the Court in later years to include most guarantees contained in the Bill of Rights and were especially critical in the development of criminal law (see Table 4.2, "Selective Incorporation and the Bill of Rights," p. 121).

Symbolic Speech

In addition to the general protection accorded pure speech, the Supreme Court has extended the reach of the First Amendment to other means of expression often called **symbolic speech**—symbols, signs, and the like—as well as to activities like picketing, sit-ins, and demonstrations. In the words of Justice John Marshall Harlan, these kinds of "speech" are part of the "free trade in ideas."[48]

The Supreme Court first acknowledged that symbolic speech was entitled to First Amendment protection in *Stromberg* v. *California* (1931).[49] There, the Court overturned the conviction of the director of a communist youth camp under a state statute prohibiting the display of a red flag, a symbol of opposition to the U.S. government. Later, in 1943, the Supreme Court struck down a state law requiring students to salute the American flag, thus reaffirming the notion that nonverbal expressions are also entitled to First Amendment protection.[50] In a similar vein, the right of high school students to wear black armbands to protest the Vietnam War was upheld in *Tinker* v. *Des Moines Independent Community School District* (1969).[51]

---

[48] *Abrams* v. *United States*, 250 U.S. 616 (1919).
[49] 283 U.S. 359 (1931).
[50] *West Virginia State Board of Education* v. *Barnette*, 319 U.S. 503 (1943).
[51] 393 U.S. 503 (1969).

By Dana Summers © 1990, Washington Post Writers Group. Reprinted with permission.

Then and Now

The Second Amendment and the Right of the People to Keep and Bear Arms

During colonial times, the English tradition of distrust of standing armies was evident: all white men in whole sections of the colonies were deputized to defend their settlements against Indians and other European powers. Most colonies required all white men to keep and bear arms. These local militias were viewed as the best way to keep order and liberty.

The Second Amendment was added to the Constitution to ensure that Congress could not pass laws to disarm state militias. It also appeased Anti-Federalists who feared that the new Constitution would cause them to lose the right to keep and bear arms. And it recognized an unstated right—the right to revolt against governmental tyranny.

Through the 1930s, few state statutes regulating firearms were passed (generally these few laws dated from the pre-Civil War era and dealt with the possession of firearms by slaves). And the Supreme Court's decision in *Barron* v. *Baltimore* (1833), limiting the application of the Bill of Rights to actions of Congress alone, prevented federal review of those state laws. Moreover, in *Dred Scott* v. *Sanford* (1857; see Chapter 3), Chief Justice Taney listed the right to own and carry arms as a basic right of citizenship.

In 1934, Congress passed the National Firearms Act in response to the increase in organized crime that occurred in the 1920s and 1930s. The Act imposed taxes on automatic weapons (such as machine guns) and sawed-off shotguns. In *United States* v. *Miller* (1939) a unanimous Court upheld the constitutionality of the Act by finding that the Second Amendment was intended to protect a citizen's right to own ordinary militia weapons, and not unregistered sawed-off shotguns, which were at issue in the *Miller* case. *Miller* was the last time the Supreme Court directly addressed the Second Amendment. In *Quilici* v. *Village of Morton Grove* (1983), the Supreme Court refused to review a lower court's ruling that had upheld the constitutionality of a local ordinance banning handguns.

In the 1980s through the 1990s, as crime and violence increased, the issue of gun control became and remains a particularly hot topic in American politics. In the aftermath of the assassination attempt on President Ronald Reagan in 1981, many lawmakers called for passage of gun control legislation. At the forefront of that effort was Sarah Brady, the wife of James Brady, the presidential press secretary who was badly wounded and left partially disabled by John Hinkley, Jr. Her efforts led to passage of the "Brady Bill" in 1993, which imposed a federal five-day waiting period on the purchase of handguns.

In 1994, in spite of extensive lobbying by the National Rifle Association, Congress passed the Violent Crime Control and Law Enforcement Act. In addition to providing money to the states for additional police officers and prisons, the Act banned the manufacture, transport, sale, or possession of nineteen semi-automatic assault weapons. Because owners may keep guns purchased before the effective date of the law, most gun shop owners reported a tremendous increase in business.

James and Sarah Brady being applauded for their efforts to win congressional approval of the Brady Bill after it was signed into law by President Clinton.

The Pledge of Allegiance

❖ ❖ ❖

The flag and even the Pledge of Allegiance have long inspired controversy. The Pledge of Allegiance was written in 1892 as a way for schoolchildren to celebrate the new national holiday, Columbus Day. The pledge was officially recognized by Congress in 1945, although in 1945 the Supreme Court ruled that no person could be required to recite it. In 1954, when the Cold War spread fear of communism and "godlessness," President Eisenhower signed a law to add "under God" after "one nation" to its text.

Burning the American flag has also been held to be a form of protected symbolic speech. In 1989, a sharply divided Supreme Court (five to four) reversed the conviction of Gregory Johnson, who had been found guilty of setting fire to an American flag during the 1984 Republican national convention in Dallas.[52] A major public outcry against the Court went up, and President George Bush and numerous members of Congress called for a constitutional amendment to ban flag burning. Others, including Justice William J. Brennan, Jr., noted that if it had not been for acts like that of Johnson, the United States would never have been created, nor would a First Amendment guaranteeing a right to political protest exist.

Instead of a constitutional amendment, Congress passed the Federal Flag Protection Act of 1989, which authorized federal prosecution of anyone who intentionally desecrated a national flag. Those who originally had been arrested burned another flag and were convicted; their conviction was again overturned by the Supreme Court. As they had in *Johnson*, the justices divided five to four in holding that this federal law "suffered from the same fundamental flaw" as had the earlier state law that was declared in violation of the First Amendment.[53] After that decision by the Court, additional efforts were made to pass a constitutional amendment so that congressional attempts to ban flag burning would not be subject to "interpretation." Those efforts, however, fell thirty-four votes short of passage in the House of Representatives and nine votes short in the Senate.

Prior Restraint

In *Near* v. *Minnesota* (1931), the Court made it clear that individuals could be punished by the state *after the fact* for libelous statements. But, with only a few exceptions, the Court made it clear that it would not tolerate **prior restraint** of speech or expression; that is, prohibition of speech or publication before the fact. Later, for example, in *New York Times Co.* v. *United States* (1971)[54] (also called the "Pentagon Papers" case), the Supreme Court ruled that the U.S. government could not block the publication of secret Defense Department documents illegally furnished to the *Times* by anti-war activists. In *Nebraska Press Association* v. *Stuart* (1976), the Supreme Court went even further, noting that any attempt by the government to prevent expression carried "a 'heavy presumption' against its constitutionality."[55] In *Nebraska*, a trial court had issued a "gag order" barring the press from reporting the lurid details of a crime. In balancing the defendant's constitutional right to a fair trial against the press's right to cover a story, the trial judge concluded that the defendant's right carried greater weight. The Supreme Court disagreed, holding the press's right to cover the trial paramount.

"Politically Correct" Speech

A particularly thorny First Amendment area has emerged as universities have attempted to ban what they view as offensive speech. Since 1989, more than 200 colleges and universities have banned racial slurs directed at minority groups. The

---

[52] *Texas* v. *Johnson*, 491 U.S. 397 (1989).
[53] *U.S.* v. *Eichman*, 496 U.S. 310 (1990).
[54] 403 U.S. 713 (1971).
[55] 427 U.S. 539 (1976).

University of Connecticut, for example, banned "inappropriately directed laughter" and "conspicuous exclusion of students from conversations."

While easy to poke fun at, the "PC movement," as it is known, has a serious side. At Dartmouth, a student was expelled for shouting anti-Semitic, anti-black, and anti-homosexual obscenities at students in their dorm rooms at 2:00 A.M. At the University of Michigan in 1990, a student was accused of violating the university's regulation banning speech that stigmatizes individuals for their sexual orientation, when he said during a classroom discussion that he considered homosexuality to be a disease treatable with therapy. The university's code was challenged by the American Civil Liberties Union and found unconstitutional by a federal district court.

In 1993 some began to question if the PC Movement had gone too far. In January 1993, Eden Jacobowitz, an Israeli student at the University of Pennsylvania, was charged with violating the school's speech policy and threatened with expulsion when he called five African-American women "water buffaloes." The black students were noisily participating in a sorority rite below the Israeli student's dorm room late at night. Frustrated by his inability to study, Jacobowitz yelled, "Shut up, you water buffaloes. If you're looking for a party there's a zoo a mile from here."[56] A national debate

---

[56] "Penn Students Drop Racism Charge," *Facts on File, World News Digest* (June 10, 1993): 427, A1.

From THATCH by Jeff Shesol
Copyright © 1991 by Jeff Shesol. Reprinted by permission of Random House, Inc.

In this debut installment of a controversial cartoon strip that runs in the Brown University school paper, the PC movement is targeted for sometimes taking to excess its insistence on language free of sexism.

The American Civil Liberties Union

The American Civil Liberties Union (ACLU) was created in 1920 by a group that had defended the civil liberties of conscientious objectors to World War I. As the nation's oldest, largest, and premier nonpartisan civil liberties organization, the ACLU works in three major areas of the law: freedom of speech and religion, due process, and equality before the law. The ACLU lobbies for legislation affecting these areas and conducts extensive public education campaigns to familiarize Americans with the guarantees granted in the Bill of Rights. Its main energies historically have been devoted to litigation to maintain these rights and liberties.

The ACLU has been involved in most speech and religion cases heard by the U.S. Supreme Court. In its own words, it "has been a zealous advocate of the First Amendment and has steadfastly opposed government efforts to regulate either free speech or free thought, no matter how well-intentioned those efforts might be."* It also has specialized projects. The National Prison Project, for example, monitors prison conditions to ensure that prisoner rights are not violated. Its Women's Rights Project, originally headed by Ruth Bader Ginsburg, has been at the fore of advancing women's rights through litigation. Similarly, its Reproductive Freedom Project is one of the most active litigators on behalf of pro-choice activists. It regularly sponsors challenges to restrictive state abortion laws and files "friend of the court" briefs in cases in which it is not lead counsel. Among the major cases in which the ACLU has participated since the 1960s are:

First Amendment Rights:

The *Scopes Case* (1945): challenged a Tennessee law making the teaching of evolution a crime

Tinker v. *Des Moines Independent School Board* (1969): upheld the right of students to wear black armbands in protest of the Vietnam War

Lynch v. *Donnelly* (1984): in a defeat for the ACLU, the court held that a city's inclusion of a creche in its annual Christmas display in a private park did not violate the establishment clause

Criminal Defendants' Rights:

Mapp v. *Ohio* (1961): established that illegally obtained evidence cannot be used at trial

Gideon v. *Wainwright* (1963): granted indigents the right to counsel

Miranda v. *Arizona* (1966): guaranteed all suspects a right to counsel

Privacy Rights:

Roe v. *Wade* and *Doe* v. *Bolton* (1973): established a woman's right to an abortion

Bowers v. *Hardwick* (1986): unsuccessfully challenged Georgia's sodomy law

Planned Parenthood v. *Casey* (1992): unsuccessfully challenged Pennsylvania's restrictive abortion regulations

Although the positions taken by the ACLU on these cases generally have been extremely popular with its members, an outcry arose in 1977 when it decided to represent members of the National Socialist Party who had been denied a parade permit to march in Nazi uniforms through Skokie, Illinois, home to many Nazi concentration camp survivors. The ACLU lost more than 60,000 members who protested its involvement in the case, but it stayed true to its purpose—upholding the First Amendment, no matter how offensive the speech or actions in question. Its 1993 membership was approximately 300,000.

Recognition of the growing conservative nature of the Supreme Court has caused the ACLU to rethink its litigation strategies. In fact, from 1987 to 1993 the ACLU's policy was to stay as far away from the Supreme Court as possible, a major shift in tactics. Previously, the ACLU had appeared before the Court more than any organization except the Justice Department. "We're going to be looking for appropriate ways to bring cases in state courts and to insulate them from Supreme Court review,"** said one ACLU official in 1987. Recognizing also that "Civil liberties are not something people intuitively grasp,"† the ACLU is undertaking a campaign to gain more attention for its cause. But, with its former legal counsel, Ruth Bader Ginsburg, now on the Supreme Court and with a Democrat in the White House, it may rethink its strategies.

---

* Brief Amicus Curiae, *Wisconsin* v. *Mitchell,* October Term, 1992, LEXIS.

** Quoted in Tony Mauro, "Supreme Court v. Civil Liberties; the ACLU's New Strategy of Avoidance," *Legal Times* (June 1, 1987): 13.

† Ibid.

ensued, and much was made of the fact that the Israeli student maintained that "water buffalo" was a loose translation of a mild Hebrew epithet referring to a rude person. The African-American students ultimately dropped their racial harassment charge, but the ACLU, which had represented Jacobowitz, vowed to continue seeking the repeal of the university's speech code, which it argues violates the First Amendment.

Libel and Slander

False or libelous statements are not restrained by the courts, yet the Supreme Court has consistently ruled that individuals or the press can be sued after the fact for untrue or libelous statements. **Libel** is a written statement that defames the character of a person. If the statement is spoken, it is **slander.** In many nations—such as Great Britain, for example—it is relatively easy to sue someone for libel. In the United States, however, the standards of proof are much more difficult. A person who believes that he or she has been a victim of libel, for example, must show that the statements made were untrue. Truth is an absolute defense against the charge of libel, no matter how painful or embarrassing the revelations.

It is often more difficult for individuals the Supreme Court considers to be "public persons or public officials" to sue for libel or slander. *New York Times Co.* v. *Sullivan* (1964),[57] was the first major libel case considered by the Supreme Court. An Alabama state court had found the *Times* guilty of libel for printing a full-page advertisement accusing Alabama officials of physically abusing blacks during various civil rights protests (the ad was paid for by civil rights activists, including former First Lady Eleanor Roosevelt). The Supreme Court ruled that a finding of libel against a public official could stand only if there were a showing of "actual malice." Proof that the statements were false or negligent was not sufficient to prove "actual malice."

The concept of actual malice can be difficult and confusing. In 1991, the Court directed lower courts to use the phrases "knowledge of falsity" and "reckless disregard of the truth" when giving instructions to juries in libel cases.[58] Given the high degree of proof required, few public officials or public persons have been able to win libel cases.

Obscenity and Pornography[59]

Although the Supreme Court has allowed few governmental bans on most types of speech, some forms of expression are not protected. In *Chaplinsky* v. *New Hampshire* (1942), the Supreme Court set out the rationale by which it would distinguish between protected and unprotected speech. According to the Court, obscenity, lewdness, libel, and fighting words are not protected by the First Amendment because "such expressions are no essential part of any exposition of ideas, and are of such slight social

---

[57] 376 U.S. 254 (1964).

[58] *Masson* v. *New Yorker Magazine*, 111 S. Ct. 2419 (1991).

[59] Technically, obscenity refers to those things considered "disgusting, foul or morally unhealthy." Pornography, in contrast, is often broader in meaning and generally refers to "depictions of sexual lewdness or erotic behavior." While distasteful to many, pornography is not necessarily obscene. See Donald Downs, "Obscenity and Pornography," in Kermit Hall, ed. *The Oxford Companion to the Supreme Court of the United States* (New York: Oxford University Press, 1992), pp. 602-604.

value as a step to truth that any benefit that may be derived from them is clearly outweighed by the social interest in order and morality."[60]

U.S. courts have often based their decisions of what was obscene on an English common-law test that had been set out in *Regina* v. *Hicklin* (1868): "whether the tendency of the matter charged as obscenity is to deprive and corrupt those whose minds are open to such immoral influences and into whose hands a publication of this sort might fall."[61] Under a test this broad, many materials—especially those that could fall into the hands of children—could be considered obscene. The Supreme Court's use of this test prompted Justice Felix Frankfurter to note, "The incidence of this standard is to reduce the adult population of [the United States] to reading what is fit for children."[62]

The Court did not abandon use of the *Hicklin* test until 1957. In *Roth* v. *United States* (1957), the Court held that to be considered obscene, the material in question must be "utterly without redeeming social importance," and articulated a new test for obscenity: "whether to the average person, applying contemporary community standards, the dominant theme of the material taken as a whole appeals to the prurient interests."[63] In many ways, the *Roth* test brought with it as many problems as it attempted to solve. Throughout the 1950s and 1960s, "prurient" remained hard to define, as the Court struggled to find a standard by which to judge actions or words. In general, only "hardcore" pornography was found obscene by the liberal Warren Court, prompting some to argue that the Court fostered the increase in the number of sexually oriented publications designed to appeal to those living amidst what many called the "sexual revolution." Nevertheless, in 1968, the Court upheld the conviction of Ralph Ginzburg for "pandering" by selectively mailing his magazine *Eros* from such cities as Middlesex, New Jersey; Blue Balls, Montana; and Intercourse, Pennsylvania. Ginzburg's sense of humor was clearly lost on the Court, which decided that he had chosen to exploit the sexual nature of his publication by selective use of provocative postmarks.[64]

Richard M. Nixon made the growth in pornography a major issue when he ran for president in 1968, and he pledged to appoint to federal judgeships only those who would uphold "law and order." Once elected president, Nixon made several appointments to the Court including Chief Justice Warren Burger, and Associate Justices Harry A. Blackmun, William H. Rehnquist, and Lewis F. Powell, Jr. In *Miller* v. *California* (1973),[65] the Burger Court began to formulate rules designed to return to communities a greater role in determining what is obscene, based on local standards.

In *Miller* v. *California* the Court set out a test that redefined obscenity. To determine whether or not material in question was obscene, the Justices instructed that a court must ask "whether the work depicts or describes, in a patently offensive way, sexual conduct specifically defined by state law." Moreover, courts were to determine "whether the work, taken as a whole, lacks serious literary, artistic, political or scientific value." And in place of the contemporary community standards gauge used in earlier cases, the Court defined community standards to mean local, and not national,

---

[60] 315 U.S. 568 (1942).
[61] L.R. 2 Q.B. 360 (1868).
[62] *Butler* v. *Michigan*, 352 U.S. 380 (1957).
[63] 354 U.S. 476 (1957).
[64] *Ginzburg* v. *United States*, 383 U.S. 463 (1968).
[65] 413 U.S. 15 (1973).

standards under the rationale that what is acceptable in Times Square in New York City might not be tolerated in Peoria, Illinois.

Until recently, however, community standards could not be the sole criterion of obscenity. In 1974, for example, the Court overturned a decision of a Georgia state court that found *Carnal Knowledge* (a movie starring Jack Nicholson, Ann-Margret, and Art Garfunkel, that included scenes of a partially nude woman) obscene. The Court concluded that the scenes were neither "patently offensive" nor designed to appeal to "prurient interest."[66] As Justice Potter Stewart had once announced, he couldn't define obscenity, but "I know it when I see it."[67] He did not see it in *Carnal Knowledge*.

Time and contexts clearly have altered the Court's and indeed, much of America's perceptions of what is obscene. *Carnal Knowledge* is now often shown on television on Saturday afternoons with only minor editing. But through the early 1990s, the Rehnquist Court (William H. Rehnquist became Chief Justice in 1986; see Chapter 9) allowed communities greater leeway in drafting statutes to deal with obscenity, and even more important, forms of non-obscene expression. In 1991, for example, the Supreme Court voted five to four to allow Indiana to ban totally nude erotic dancing, concluding that its statute did not violate the First Amendment's guarantee of freedom of expression.[68] Justice Antonin Scalia, concurring in the opinion, went so far as to state that the law should be upheld on the ground that moral opposition to nudity is a sufficient reason for the state to ban it altogether.

The Rights of Criminal Defendants

The Fourth, Fifth, Sixth, and Eighth Amendments provide a variety of procedural guarantees (often called **due process rights**) for those accused of crimes. As Table 4.3 shows, particular amendments, as well as other portions of the Constitution, specifically provide procedural guarantees to protect individuals accused of crimes at all stages of the criminal justice process. And as is the case with the First Amendment, many of these rights have been seen as applying to the states (see Table 4.2).

In interpreting the amendments dealing with what are frequently termed "criminal rights," the courts have to grapple not only with the meaning of the amendments, but also with how their protections are to be implemented. The Eighth Amendment, for example, prohibits "cruel and unusual punishments." The question of what is cruel and unusual, however, has vexed the Supreme Court for years. In 1972, for example, the Supreme Court interpreted the Eighth Amendment to mean that the death penalty was cruel and unusual. But as crime increased and public opinion toward the death penalty changed, so did the Court's interpretation of the Eighth Amendment.

Today the Court routinely allows executions to be carried out. Perhaps even more than in the area of First Amendment guarantees, prevailing thoughts about the rights of criminal defendants are changing quickly and dramatically as the Supreme Court moves away from what some view as the "excesses" of the Warren Court (1953–1969).

---

[66] *Jenkins v. Georgia*, 418 U.S. 153 (1974).
[67] *Jacobellis v. Ohio*, 378 U.S. 184 (1964).
[68] *Barnes v. Glen Theater*, 111 S. Ct. 2456 (1991).

Table 4.3 ♦ The Constitution, the Bill of Rights, and the Procedural Protections Guaranteed Throughout the Criminal Justice Process

STAGE	PROTECTIONS
Before a Trial	
1. Investigation process	The Fourth Amendment prohibits "unreasonable searches and seizures."
	The Fifth Amendment guarantees that "no person shall be held to answer for a capital, or otherwise infamous crime," without a Grand Jury indictment.
2. Arrest made	The Fifth Amendment prohibits the government from forcing the accused to incriminate him or herself.
	The Sixth Amendment guarantees the right to the "Assistance of Counsel."
3. Interrogation held	The Eighth Amendment forbids "excessive bail."
At the Trial	Article III guarantees a trial by jury.
	The Fifth Amendment bars "double jeopardy" (being tried twice for the same crime).
	The Sixth Amendment guarantees a "speedy and public trial, by an impartial jury."
	The Sixth Amendment guarantees defendants the right to confront witnesses and to call defense witnesses.
Punishment	The Eight Amendment bans "excessive fines" and "cruel and unusual punishments."

Over the years, many individuals have criticized the liberal Warren Court's rulings, arguing that they gave criminals more "rights" than their victims. As detailed in "Landmark Dates in the Incorporation of the Bill of Rights," from 1961 to 1969 the Warren Court made several provisions of the Bill of Rights dealing with the rights of criminal defendants applicable to the states through the Fourteenth Amendment. It is important to remember that most procedural guarantees apply to individuals charged with crimes, that is, *before* they have been tried. These rights were designed to protect those wrongfully accused, although, of course, they often have helped the guilty. But as Justice William O. Douglas once noted, "respecting the dignity even of the least worthy citizen . . . raises the stature of all of us."[69] Many continue to argue, however, that only the guilty are helped by the American system and that criminals should not go unpunished because of simple police error. The dilemma of balancing the rights of the individual against those of society permeates the entire debate, and often even judicial interpretations of the rights of criminal defendants.

---

[69] *Stein* v. *N.Y.*, 346 U.S. 156 (1953).

Landmark Dates in the Incorporation of the Bill of Rights		
1897 ♦ Amendment V	Just compensation
1925 ♦ Amendment I	Speech
1931 ♦ Amendment I	Press
1937 ♦ Amendment I	Assembly
1940 ♦ Amendment I	Religion
1948 ♦ Amendment VI	Public trial
1949 ♦ Amendment IV	Freedom from unreasonable searches and seizures
1961 ♦ Amendment IV	Exclusionary rule
1962 ♦ Amendment VIII	Freedom from cruel and unusual punishments
1963 ♦ Amendment VI	Right to counsel
1964 ♦ Amendment V	Prohibition against self-incrimination
1965 ♦ Amendment VI	Confrontation of witnesses
1966 ♦ Amendment VI	Impartial trial
1967 ♦ Amendment VI	Speedy trial; compulsory process
1968 ♦ Amendment VI	Jury trial
1969 ♦ Amendment V	Double jeopardy

The Fourth Amendment and Searches and Seizures

The Fourth Amendment to the Constitution declares:

> The right of the people to be secure in their persons, houses, papers, and effects, against unreasonable searches and seizures, shall not be violated, and no Warrants shall issue, but upon probable cause, supported by Oath or affirmation, and particularly describing the place to be searched, and the persons or things to be seized.

This amendment's purpose was to deny the national government the authority to make general searches. The English Parliament had often issued general "writs of assistance" that allowed such searches. These general warrants were also used against religious and political dissenters, a practice the Framers wanted banned in the new nation. But still, the language that they chose left numerous questions to be answered, including, what is an "unreasonable" search? Over the years, in a number of decisions, the Supreme Court has interpreted the Fourth Amendment to allow the police to search:

1. The person arrested;
2. Things in plain view of the accused person; and,
3. Places or things that the arrested person could touch or reach or are otherwise in the arrestee's "immediate control."

Surveillance can include indoor as well as outdoor activities. This photo was taken after state and federal narcotics agents raided this sophisticated indoor marijuana farming operation in east Texas.

Warrantless searches often occur "incident to an arrest," meaning simultaneously with it. In such cases, the police may generally seize only potential evidence in "plain view" or in the "immediate control" of the person detained. In 1993, the Court unanimously ruled that police could seize contraband discovered through what it termed a "plain feel" based on an officer's sense of touch.[70] Police may also search if they are in "hot pursuit" of a suspect, or if they believe evidence will be destroyed.

If police suspect that someone is committing or is about to commit a crime, they may "stop and frisk" the individual under suspicion. Whereas the liberal Warren Court limited those searches to "outer clothing . . . in an attempt to discover weapons which might be used to assault [a police officer],"[71] the Burger and Rehnquist Courts have expanded that limitation. In 1989, the Court upheld a drug-enforcement officer's search of a suspected drug courier at an airport. Chief Justice Rehnquist ruled that there need be only a "reasonable suspicion" for stopping a suspect—a much lower standard than "probable cause."[72]

Searches can also be made without a warrant if consent is obtained, and the Court has ruled that consent can be given by a variety of persons. It has ruled, for example, that police can search a bedroom occupied by two persons as long as they have the consent of one of them.[73]

In situations where no arrest occurs, police must obtain search warrants from a "neutral and detached magistrate" prior to conducting more extensive searches of houses, cars, offices, or any other place where an individual would reasonably have some expectation of privacy.[74] Police can't get search warrants, for example, to require you to undergo surgery to remove a bullet that might be used to incriminate you since your expectation of bodily privacy outweighs the need for evidence.[75] But courts don't require search warrants in possible drunk driving situations. Thus, the police can require you to take a Breathalyzer test to determine whether you have been drinking in excess of legal limits.[76]

Homes, too, are presumed to be private. Firefighters can enter your home to fight a fire without a warrant. But if they decide to investigate the cause of the fire, they must obtain a warrant before their reentry.[77] In contrast, under the "open fields doctrine" first articulated by the Supreme Court in 1924,[78] if you own a field, and even if you post "No Trespassing" signs, the police can search your field without a warrant to see if you are illegally growing marijuana, because you cannot reasonably expect privacy in an open field.[79] In a series of five-to-four decisions, the Rehnquist Court expanded the open fields doctrine to allow other kinds of warrantless searches, including aerial observations of a fenced-in back yard by police looking for marijuana,[80] aerial pho-

---

[70] *Minnesota* v. *Dickerson*, 113 S. Ct. 2130 (1993).
[71] *Terry* v. *Ohio*, 392 U.S. 1 (1968).
[72] *U.S.* v. *Sokolov*, 490 U.S. 1 (1989).
[73] *U.S.* v. *Matlock*, 415 U.S. 164 (1974).
[74] *Johnson* v. *U.S.*, 333 U.S. 10 (1948).
[75] *Winston* v. *Lee*, 470 U.S. 753 (1985).
[76] *South Dakota* v. *Neville*, 459 U.S. 553 (1983).
[77] *Michigan* v. *Tyler*, 436 U.S. 499 (1978).
[78] *Hester* v. *U.S.*, 265 U.S. 57 (1924).
[79] *Oliver* v. *U.S.*, 466 U.S. 170 (1984).
[80] *California* v. *Ciraolo*, 476 U.S. 207 (1986).

tography of a Dow Chemical site to inspect for pollution violations,[81] and a nighttime search of a barn in a field.[82]

Cars have proven problematic for police and the courts because of their mobile nature. As noted by Chief Justice William Howard Taft as early as 1925, "the vehicle can quickly be moved out of the locality or jurisdiction in which the warrant must be sought."[83] Over the years the Court has become increasingly lenient about the scope of automobile searches. In 1991, for example, the Court upheld a warrantless search of a container found in a car, even though the police lacked probable cause to search the car itself.[84]

Testing for Drugs and HIV. Testing for drugs and HIV has become an especially thorny search-and-seizure issue. If the government can require you to take a Breathalyzer test, can it require you to be tested for drugs? For HIV? In the wake of growing public concern over drug use, in 1986 President Ronald Reagan signed an executive order requiring many federal employees to undergo drug tests. While many private employers and professional athletic organizations routinely require drug tests upon application or as a condition of employment, *governmental* requirements present constitutional questions of the scope of permissible searches and seizures. Initially, the federal courts adopted the view that mandatory testing of those in certain occupations such as the police and firefighting forces was unconstitutional unless there was suspicion that the employee had been using drugs. In 1989, however, the Supreme Court ruled that mandatory drug and alcohol testing of employees involved in accidents was

---

[81] *Dow Chemical Company* v. *U.S.*, 476 U.S. 227 (1986).
[82] *U.S.* v. *Dunn*, 480 U.S. 294 (1987).
[83] *Carroll* v. *U.S.*, 267 U.S. 132 (1925).
[84] *California* v. *Acevedo*, 111 S. Ct. 1982 (1991).

Kimberly Bergalis, who claimed that she contracted HIV from her dentist, appears with her parents before a House subcommittee to advocate mandated HIV testing of all health care workers.

constitutional.[85] And in the same year, the Court upheld the constitutionality of a compulsory drug-testing program for U.S. Customs Service employees.[86]

Testing for the human immunodeficiency virus (HIV), which causes AIDS, has also produced questions of unreasonable searches and seizures, especially since those with the virus generally experience discrimination in many walks of life. In July 1991, the Centers for Disease Control (CDC) recommended that all health-care professionals who perform surgery undergo voluntary testing to determine if they are infected with HIV. If they are, the CDC suggested that they disclose the condition to patients and refrain from practicing unless they are cleared to do so by a local medical review panel. In the absence of federal legislation, however, many medical organizations have refused to comply with the CDC's recommendations.

The Fifth Amendment and Self-Incrimination

The Fifth Amendment provides that "No person shall be . . . compelled in any criminal case to be a witness against himself." The Supreme Court has interpreted this guarantee to be "as broad as the mischief against which it seeks to guard,"[87] finding that criminal defendants do not have to take the stand at trial to answer questions, nor can a judge make mention of their failure to do so as evidence of guilt. Moreover, lawyers cannot imply that a defendant who refuses to take the stand must be guilty or have something to hide. This right not to testify extends to defendants in grand jury proceedings and legislative investigations, and even to witnesses in judicial proceedings, if the information they give could result in their own prosecution. "Taking the Fifth" is shorthand for exercising one's constitutional right not to self-incriminate.

This right also means that prosecutors cannot use as evidence in a trial any of a defendant's statements or confessions that were not "voluntary." As is the case in many areas of the law, however, judicial interpretation of the term *voluntary* has changed over time. Police often used to beat defendants to obtain their confessions. In 1936, however, the Supreme Court ruled convictions for murder based solely on confessions given after physical beatings unconstitutional.[88] Police then began to resort to other measures to force confessions. Defendants, for example, were "given the third degree"— questioned for hours on end with no sleep or food, or threatened with physical violence until they were mentally "beaten" into a confession. In other situations family members were threatened. In one case a young mother was told that her welfare benefits would be terminated and her children taken away from her if she failed to talk.[89]

Miranda v. *Arizona* (1966) was the Supreme Court's response to these creative efforts to obtain confessions that were not truly voluntary.[90] On March 3, 1963, an eighteen-year-old girl was kidnapped and raped on the outskirts of Phoenix, Arizona. Ten days later, police arrested Ernesto Miranda, a poor, mentally disturbed man with a ninth-grade education. In a police-station lineup, the victim identified Miranda as her

---

[85] *Skinner* v. *Railway Labor Executives' Association*, 489 U.S. 602 (1989).
[86] *National Treasury Employees Union* v. *Von Raab*, 489 U.S. 656 (1989).
[87] *Counselman* v. *Hitchcock*, 142 U.S. 547 (1892).
[88] *Brown* v. *Mississippi*, 297 U.S. 278 (1936).
[89] *Lynumn* v. *Illinois*, 372 U.S. 528 (1963).
[90] 384 U.S. 436 (1966).

attacker. Police then took Miranda to a separate room and questioned him for two hours. At first he denied guilt. Eventually, however, he confessed to the crime and wrote and signed a brief statement describing the crime and admitting his guilt. At no time was he told that he did not have to answer any questions or that he could be represented by an attorney.

After Miranda's conviction, his case was appealed on the grounds that his Fifth Amendment right not to incriminate himself had been violated, because his confession had been coerced. Writing for the Court, Chief Justice Earl Warren, himself a former district attorney and California State Attorney General, noted that because police have a tremendous advantage in any interrogation situation, criminal suspects must be given greater protection. A confession obtained in the manner of Miranda's was not truly voluntary; thus, it was inadmissible at trial.

To provide guidelines for police to implement *Miranda*, the Court mandated that:

> Prior to any questioning, the person must be warned that he has a right to remain silent, that any statements he does make may be used as evidence against him, and that he has a right to the presence of an attorney, either retained or appointed.

In response, police routinely began to read suspects their **Miranda rights**, a practice you undoubtedly have seen repeated over and over in movies or on TV police dramas.

Although the Burger Court did not enforce the reading of Miranda rights as vehemently as had the Warren Court, Chief Justice Burger, Warren's successor, acknowledged that they had become an integral part of established police procedures.[91] The Rehnquist Court, however, has been more tolerant of the use of coerced confessions and has employed a much more flexible standard to allow their admissibility. In 1991, for example, it ruled that the use of a coerced confession in a criminal trial does not automatically invalidate a conviction.[92]

The Exclusionary Rule

In *Weeks* v. *United States* (1914),[93] the U.S. Supreme Court adopted the **exclusionary rule**, barring the use of illegally seized evidence at trial. Thus, although the Fourth and Fifth Amendments do not bar the use of evidence obtained in violation of their provisions, the exclusionary rule is a judicially created remedy to deter constitutional violations. In *Weeks*, for example, the Court reasoned that allowing police and prosecutors to use the "fruits of a poisonous tree" (a tainted search) would only encourage that activity. Later, in *Mapp* v. *Ohio* (1961),[94] where a questionable search of a house was at issue, the Court ruled that the exclusionary rule applied to the states via the Fourteenth Amendment.

The Warren Court resolved the dilemma of balancing the goal of deterring police misconduct against the likelihood that a guilty individual would go free in favor of deterrence. In contrast, the Burger and Rehnquist Courts have gradually chipped away at the exclusionary rule. In 1976, for example, the Burger Court dramatically reduced the opportunities for defendants to appeal their convictions based on tainted evidence in

Even though Ernesto Miranda's confession was not admitted as evidence at his retrial, his ex-girlfriend's testimony and that of the victim were enough to convince the jury of his guilt. He served nine years in prison before he was released on parole. After his release, he routinely sold autographed cards inscribed with the Miranda rights now read to all suspects. In 1976, four years after his release, Miranda was stabbed to death in Phoenix in a bar fight during a card game. Two Miranda cards were found on his body, and the person who killed him was read his Miranda rights upon his arrest.

---

[91] *Rhode Island* v. *Innis,* 446 U.S. 291 (1980).
[92] *Arizona* v. *Fulminante,* 111 S. Ct. 2067 (1991).
[93] 232 U.S. 383 (1914).
[94] 367 U.S. 643 (1961).

violation of the Fourth Amendment.[95] If objections to the evidence have already been raised in state court, convicted defendants cannot seek a rehearing of the issue in federal court. The Court noted that the exclusionary rule "deflects the truth-finding process and often frees the guilty." Since then, the Court has carved out a variety of what it terms "good faith exceptions" to the exclusionary rule, allowing the use of "tainted" evidence in a variety of situations, especially when police thought that they were acting within the Fourth Amendment's mandates.

The Sixth Amendment and the Right to Counsel

The Sixth Amendment guarantees to an accused person "the Assistance of Counsel in his defense." In the past, this provision meant only that an individual could hire an attorney to represent him or her in court. Since most criminal defendants are impoverished, this provision was of little assistance to many who found themselves on trial. Recognizing this, Congress required federal courts to provide an attorney for defendants too poor to afford one. This was first required in capital cases (where the death penalty is a possibility); eventually attorneys were provided to the poor in all federal criminal cases.[96] In 1932, the Supreme Court directed states to furnish lawyers to defendants in capital cases.[97] It also began to expand the right to counsel to other state offenses, but did so in a piecemeal fashion that gave the states little direction. Given the high cost of providing legal counsel, this ambiguity often made it cost-effective for the states not to provide counsel at all.

These ambiguities came to an end with the Court's decision in *Gideon* v. *Wainwright* (1963).[98] As depicted in Anthony Lewis's book *Gideon's Trumpet* and in the made-for-television movie of the same name, Clarence Earl Gideon, a fifty-one–year-old drifter, was charged with breaking into a Panama City, Florida, pool hall and stealing beer, wine, and some change from a vending machine. At his trial he asked the judge to appoint a lawyer for him because he was too poor to hire one himself. The judge refused, and Gideon was convicted and given a five-year prison term for petty larceny. The case against Gideon had not been strong, but as a layperson unfamiliar with the law and with trial practice and procedure, he was unable to point out its weaknesses.

The apparent inequities in the system that had resulted in Gideon's conviction continued to bother him. Eventually he borrowed some paper from a prison guard and, after consulting the prison library, drafted and mailed to the U.S. Supreme Court a petition asking it to overrule his conviction.

In a unanimous decision, the U.S. Supreme Court agreed with Gideon and his court-appointed lawyer, Abe Fortas, a future associate justice of the Supreme Court. Writing for the Court, Justice Hugo Black explained that "lawyers in criminal courts are necessities, not luxuries." Therefore, the Court concluded, the state *must* provide an attorney to poor defendants in felony cases. Underscoring the Court's point, Gideon was acquitted when he was retried with a lawyer to argue his case.

---

[95] *Stone* v. *Powell*, 428 U.S. 465 (1976).
[96] *Johnson* v. *Zerbst*, 304 U.S. 458 (1938).
[97] *Powell* v. *Alabama*, 287 U.S. 45 (1932).
[98] 372 U.S. 335 (1963).

When Clarence Earl Gideon wrote out his petition for a writ of *certiorari* to the Supreme Court (asking the Court, in its discretion, to hear his case) he had no way of knowing that his case would lead to the lankmark ruling on the right to counsel, *Gideon* v. *Wainwright.* Nor did he know that Chief Justice Earl Warren had actually instructed his law clerks to be on the lookout for a *habeas corpus* petition (literally "you have the body," which argues that the person in jail is there in violation of some statutory or constitutional right) that could be used to guarantee the assistance of counsel for defendants in criminal cases.

In 1972, the Burger Court expanded the *Gideon* rule, holding that "even in prosecutions for offenses less serious than felonies, a fair trial may require the presence of a lawyer."[99] Seven years later, the Court clarified its decision by holding that defendants charged with offenses where imprisonment is authorized but not actually imposed do not have a Sixth Amendment right to counsel.[100]

---

[99] *Argersinger* v. *Hamlin*, 407 U.S. 25 (1972).
[100] *Scott* v. *Illinois*, 440 U.S. 367 (1979).

The Sixth Amendment and Jury Trials

The Sixth Amendment (and to a lesser extent, Article III of the Constitution) provides that a person accused of a crime shall enjoy the right to a speedy and public trial by an impartial jury—that is, a trial in which a group of the accused's peers act as a fact-finding, deliberative body to determine guilt or innocence. The Supreme Court has held that jury trials must be available if a prison sentence of six or more months is possible.

"Impartiality" is a requirement of jury trials that has undergone significant change, with the method of selecting jurors being the most frequently challenged part of the process. For example, whereas potential individual jurors who have prejudged a case are not eligible to serve, no groups can be systematically excluded from serving. In 1880, for example, the Supreme Court ruled that African Americans could not be excluded from state jury pools (lists of those eligible to serve).[101] And in 1975, the Court ruled that to bar women from jury service violated the mandate that juries be a "fair cross section" of the community.[102]

In the 1980s, the Court expanded the requirement that juries reflect the community by invalidating various indirect means of excluding African Americans. For example, when James Batson, a black man, was tried for second-degree burglary, the state prosecutor used all his peremptory challenges to the jury to eliminate all four potential black jurors, leaving an all-white jury.[103] The state court judge overruled the contention of Batson's lawyer that the exclusion of African Americans violated Batson's constitutional rights, and Batson was found guilty. The Supreme Court, however, overturned his conviction. While noting that lawyers historically used peremptory challenges to select juries they believed most favorable to the outcome they desired, the Court held that the use of peremptory challenges specifically to exclude African-American jurors violated the equal protection clause of the Fourteenth Amendment.[104]

In 1994, the Supreme Court answered the major remaining unanswered question about jury selection—can lawyers exclude women from juries through their use of peremptory challenges? This question came up frequently because in rape trials and sex discrimination cases, one side or another often finds it advantageous to select jurors on the basis of their sex. At issue in *J.E.B.* v. *Alabama* ex rel *T.B.* (1994)[105] was Alabama's use of peremptory challenge to exclude nine men from a group of potential jurors in a case brought by the state to establish that James Bowman, Sr. had fathered a child and was responsible for child support payments. Bowman was declared to be the father by a jury of twelve women. The Supreme Court ruled that the equal protection clause prohibits discrimination in jury selection on the basis of gender. Thus, striking all potential male jurors based on the belief that males might be more sympathetic to the arguments of a man charged in a paternity suit, is unconstitutional.

---

[101] *Strauder* v. *West Virginia,* 100 U.S. 303 (1880).

[102] *Taylor* v. *Louisiana,* 419 U.S. 522 (1975).

[103] Peremptory challenges are discretionary challenges. A lawyer representing an abortion clinic protestor, for example, could use peremptory challenges to rid the jury of pro-choice advocates. "For cause" challenges, by contrast, are based on legal reasoning and not on an educated guess about the best persons to serve on the jury. In a capital case, for example, persons morally opposed to the death penalty could be removed "for cause."

[104] *Batson* v. *Kentucky,* 476 U.S. 79 (1986).

[105] 114 S. Ct. 1419 (1994).

The Eighth Amendment and Cruel and Unusual Punishment

The Eighth Amendment prohibits "cruel and unusual punishments," a concept rooted in the English common-law tradition. In the 1500s, religious heretics and those critical of the Crown were subjected to torture to extract confessions, and then were condemned to an equally hideous death by the rack, disembowelment, or other barbarous means. The English Bill of Rights and its safeguard against "cruel and unusual punishments" was a result of public outrage against those practices. The same language found its way into the U.S. Bill of Rights. Prior to the 1960s, however, little judicial attention was paid to the meaning of that phrase, especially in the context of the death penalty.

The death penalty was in use in all the colonies at the time the Constitution was adopted, and its constitutionality went unquestioned. In fact, in two separate cases in the late 1800s, the Supreme Court ruled that deaths by public shooting[106] and electrocution were not "cruel and unusual" forms of punishment in the same category as "punishments which inflict torture, such as the rack, the thumbscrew, the iron boot, the stretching of limbs and the like. . . ."[107]

In the 1960s, the National Association for the Advancement of Colored People (NAACP) Legal Defense Fund, believing that the death penalty was applied more frequently to African Americans than to members of other groups, orchestrated a carefully designed legal attack on its constitutionality.[108]

---

[106] *Hallinger* v. *Davis*, 146 U.S. 314 (1892).
[107] *O'Neil* v. *Vermont*, 144 U.S. 323 (1892).
[108] See Michael Meltsner, *Cruel and Unusual: The Supreme Court and Capital Punishment* (New York: Random House, 1973).

"Cruel and unusual punishment" has meant different things to different societies. In colonial America, the dunking stool was a common form of punishment that few would advocate today.

Warren McCleskey and the Death Penalty

When forty-six–year-old Warren McCleskey, a former aerospace company worker, was executed in Georgia's electric chair on September 26, 1991, his death marked a new era in criminal law. McCleskey's path to immortality began on a dark night in 1978 when an off-duty Atlanta police officer was shot and killed as he investigated a break-in at an Atlanta furniture store. There was never any question that McCleskey was there; the question was whether he killed the officer. McCleskey maintained his innocence to the end.

In McCleskey's first appeal, decided in 1987, the Supreme Court rejected his claim that death penalty laws are unconstitutional even if statistics indicate that racial discrimination affect the way the death sentence is imposed. In his second appeal, decided in 1991 in a six-to-three ruling, the Court rebuffed McCleskey's appeal in a decision that severely restricts the ability of state prisoners to seek more than one *habeas corpus* review (a "writ of *habeas corpus*" allows prisoners who have exhausted their state-level appeals to bring constitutional challenges—in separate appeals with no time limit—to the federal courts). Experts anticipate that the decision will shorten the average time between commission of a crime and execution—currently nine years—to six or seven years.

Writing for the majority of the Court, Justice Anthony Kennedy said that death row inmates may bring additional appeals only when they can show that some external factor, such as improper suppression of evidence, prevented them from raising the claim in the first appeal. In addition, a prisoner must show that the new evidence would have had a substantial effect on the conviction or sentence.

In his second appeal, McCleskey had argued that his Sixth Amendment right to counsel was violated by the state when a cellmate—whom the police had placed with McCleskey to gather incriminating evidence in exchange for reducing the charges against him—coerced McCleskey to confess to the murder, and then testified against him at trial. Although another court had ruled that this government action was illegal because the jury was not told that the witness was an informant, the Supreme Court said McCleskey's lawyers should have raised the issue earlier. Even a last-minute attempt by his attorneys, who filed affidavits from two of McCleskey's original jurors saying they would *not* have voted for the death sentence had they been told an informant had been planted in the cell, was not enough to convince the Court to stop the execution.

Public opinion polls revealed that in 1971, on the eve of the NAACP's first major death sentence case to reach the Supreme Court, support for the death penalty had fallen to below 50 percent of the American public. With the timing just right, in *Furman* v. *Georgia* (1972), the Supreme Court upheld the NAACP's position and effectively put an end to capital punishment, at least in the short run.[109] The Court ruled that because the death penalty was often imposed in an arbitrary manner, it constituted cruel and unusual punishment in violation of the Eighth and Fourteenth Amendments.

Following *Furman*, several state legislatures enacted new laws designed to meet the Court's objections to the arbitrary nature of the sentence. In *Gregg* v. *Georgia* (1976), Georgia's rewritten death penalty statute was ruled constitutional by the Supreme Court in a seven-to-two decision.[110] Troy Gregg had murdered two hitchhikers and was awaiting execution on Georgia's death row. Although his lawyers argued that to

---

[109] 408 U.S. 238 (1972).
[110] 428 U.S. 153 (1976).

put him to death would constitute cruel and unusual punishment, the Court concluded that the death penalty "is an expression of society's outrage at particularly offensive conduct. . . . [I]t is an extreme action, suitable to the most extreme of crimes." Before he could be executed, however, Gregg escaped from death row using a hand-crafted hacksaw and a homemade prison guard uniform. He and three other inmates escaped to North Carolina, where Gregg was beaten to death before he could be recaptured by authorities.

Unless minors are involved, the Supreme Court is currently unwilling to intervene to overrule state courts' imposition of the death penalty. In *McCleskey* v. *Kemp* (1987),[111] a five-to-four Court ruled that imposition of the death penalty—even when it appeared to discriminate against blacks—did not violate the equal protection clause. Despite the testimony of social scientists and evidence that the state was eleven times more likely to seek the death penalty against a black defendant, the Court upheld Warren McCleskey's death sentence (see "Warren McCleskey and the Death Penalty," p. 140). It noted that even if statistics clearly show discrimination, "racial bias is an inevitable part of our criminal justice system." Within hours of that defeat, McCleskey's lawyers filed a new appeal, arguing that the informant who gave the only testimony against McCleskey at trial had been placed in McCleskey's cell illegally. Four years later, McCleskey's death sentence challenge again produced an equally, if not more important ruling on the death penalty and criminal procedure from the U.S. Supreme Court. In the second *McCleskey* case, *McCleskey* v. *Zant* (1991), the Court found that the issue of the informant should have been raised during the first appeal, in spite of the fact that McCleskey's lawyers were initially told by the state that the witness was *not* an informer. *McCleskey* v. *Zant* produced new standards designed to make it much more difficult for death-row inmates to file repeated appeals, a practice frequently decried by many of the justices.[112] Ironically, the informant against McCleskey was freed the night before McCleskey was electrocuted.

The Right to Privacy

There is no mention of a right to privacy in either the main body of the Constitution or the Bill of Rights. Nevertheless, as Justice William O. Douglas noted in 1965, the notion of privacy is "older than the Bill of Rights." It is questionable, however, whether the Framers would ever have considered birth control, surrogate motherhood, or *in vitro* fertilization, all defended under "right to privacy" claims, proper subjects of constitutional protection.

Although the Constitution is silent about the right to privacy, the Bill of Rights contains many indications that the Framers expected that some areas of life were "off limits" to governmental regulation. The right to freedom of religion guaranteed in the First Amendment implies the right to exercise private, personal beliefs. The guarantee against unreasonable searches and seizures contained in the Fourth Amendment similarly implies that persons are to be secure in their homes and should not fear that po-

---

[111] 481 U.S. 279 (1987).
[112] 111 S. Ct. 2841 (1991).

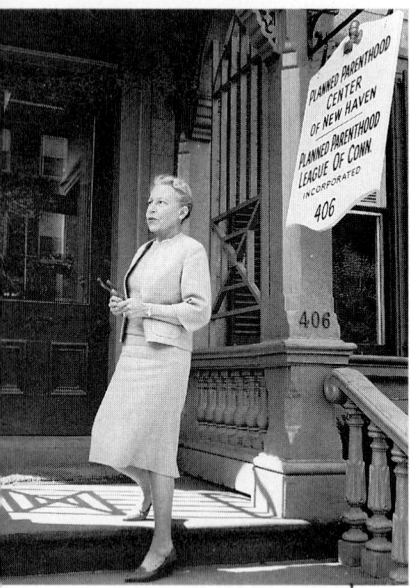

In order to challenge the constitutionality of a Connecticut law that barred physicians and clinics from prescribing contraceptives, Estelle Griswold, the director of Planned Parenthood, opened a clinic for the express purpose of being arrested. Her appeal of her conviction resulted in the Supreme Court ruling that the state law was unconstitutional in *Griswold* v. *Connecticut* (1965).

lice will show up at their doorsteps without cause. As early as 1928, Justice Louis Brandeis hailed **privacy** as "the right to be left alone—the most comprehensive of rights and the right most valued by civilized men."[113] It was not until 1965, however, that the Court attempted to explain the origins of this right.

Birth Control

Griswold v. *Connecticut* (1965)[114] involved a challenge to the constitutionality of an 1879 Connecticut law prohibiting the dissemination of information about and/or the sale of contraceptives. In 1943 and again in 1961, groups seeking legislative repeal of the law had challenged its constitutionality. In 1961, the Supreme Court, however, with four justices dissenting, refused to address the merits of the case. The majority concluded that a doctor who had not been charged with violating the statute had no standing (legal right) to bring the lawsuit.[115] But because the majority opinion had stressed the fact that the law had long gone unenforced, Planned Parenthood officials decided that they would need to create a test case. So Estelle Griswold, the executive director of Planned Parenthood League of Connecticut, and Dr. C. Lee Buxton opened a birth-control clinic, and were arrested ten days later. Now Planned Parenthood had parties actually charged with violating the law, a prerequisite to a challenge of its constitutionality. After Griswold and Buxton's conviction in the state courts, they appealed to the U.S. Supreme Court. In *Griswold*, seven justices decided that various portions of the Bill of Rights, including the First, Third, Fourth, Fifth, and Fourteenth Amendments, cast "penumbras" (unstated liberties on the fringes or in the shadow of more explicitly stated rights), thereby creating zones of privacy, including a married couple's right to plan a family. Thus, the Connecticut statute was ruled unconstitutional as a violation of marital privacy, a right the Court concluded could be read into the U.S. Constitution.

Later, the Court expanded the right of privacy to include the right of unmarried individuals to have access to contraceptives. "If the right of privacy means anything," wrote Justice William J. Brennan, "it is the right of the individual, married or single, to be free from unwarranted governmental intrusion into matters so fundamentally affecting a person as the decision to bear or beget a child."[116]

Abortion

In the early 1960s, a worldwide panic arose after the birth of babies with congenital defects to pregnant women who had been given the drug thalidomide, and a nationwide measles epidemic resulting in the birth of more babies with other severe problems. Simultaneously, the increasing medical safety of abortions, and the growing women's rights movement combined with these tragedies to put pressure on the legal and medical establishments to institute laws that would guarantee a woman's access to

---

[113] *Olmstead* v. *United States*, 277 U.S. 438 (1928).
[114] 381 U.S. 481 (1965).
[115] *Poe* v. *Ullman*, 367 U.S. 497 (1961).
[116] *Eisenstadt* v. *Baird*, 410 U.S. 113 (1972).

Operation Rescue staged large-scale protests in Buffalo, New York in front of several abortion clinics in 1992. Protesters were welcomed to the city by the pro-life mayor, an act that angered pro-choice activists who viewed the clinic blockades as illegal and costly (in terms of overtime pay for police officers, etc.).

In 1994, in response to these kinds of demonstrations and violence, Congress passed an abortion clinic access act providing prison terms and fines for those convicted of blocking access to clinics or threatening patients or employees of clinics.

safe and legal abortion. By the late 1960s, fourteen states had voted to liberalize their abortion policies, and four states decriminalized abortion in the early stages of pregnancy. But many women's rights activists wanted more. They argued that the decision to carry a pregnancy to term was a woman's fundamental constitutional right. In 1973, in one of the most controversial decisions ever handed down, seven members of the Court agreed with this position.

The woman whose case became the catalyst for pro-choice and anti-abortion groups was an itinerant circus worker. Norma McCoevey was the mother of one toddler she was unable to care for; she could not leave another child in her mother's care. So she decided to terminate her second pregnancy. Unable to secure a legal abortion and frightened by the conditions she found when she sought an illegal, back-alley abortion, McCoevey turned to two young Texas lawyers who were looking for a plaintiff to bring a lawsuit to challenge Texas's restrictive statute, which allowed abortions only when they were necessary to save the life of the mother. Although McCoevey was unable to obtain a legal abortion and later gave birth and put the baby up for adoption, she allowed her lawyers to proceed with the case using her, under the pseudonym Jane Roe, to challenge the Texas law as enforced by Henry Wade, the district attorney for Dallas County, Texas.

When the case finally came before the Supreme Court, Justice Harry A. Blackmun, a former lawyer at the Mayo Clinic, relied heavily on medical evidence to rule that the Texas law violated a woman's constitutionally guaranteed right to privacy, which he argued included her decision to terminate a pregnancy. Writing for the majority in *Roe v. Wade*, Blackmun divided pregnancy into three stages. In the first trimester, a woman's right to privacy gave her an absolute right (in consultation with her physician), free from state interference, to terminate her pregnancy. In the second trimester, the state's interest in the health of the mother gave it the right to regulate abortions—but only to protect the woman's health. Only in the third trimester—when the fetus became potentially viable—did the Court find that the state's interest in potential life outweighed the woman's privacy interests. Even in the third trimester, however, abortions to save the life or health of the mother were to be legal.[117]

Roe v. *Wade* unleashed a torrent of political controversy. Anti-abortion groups, caught off guard, scrambled to recoup their losses in Congress. Representative Henry Hyde (R.-Ill.) persuaded Congress to ban the use of Medicaid funds for abortions for poor women, and the constitutionality of the Hyde Amendment was upheld by the Supreme Court in 1977 and again in 1980.[118]

From the 1970s through the present, the right to an abortion and its constitutional underpinnings in the right to privacy have been under attack by well-organized anti-abortion groups. The Reagan and Bush administrations were strong advocates of the anti-abortion position, regularly urging the Court to overrule *Roe*. They came close to victory in *Webster* v. *Reproductive Health Services* (1989).[119] In *Webster*, the Court upheld state-required fetal viability tests in the second trimester, even though these tests would increase the cost of an abortion considerably. The Court also upheld Missouri's refusal to allow abortions to be performed in state-supported hospitals or by state-funded doctors or nurses. Perhaps most noteworthy, however, were the facts that four justices seemed willing to overrule *Roe* v. *Wade*, and that Justice Antonin Scalia publicly rebuked his colleague Sandra Day O'Connor, then the only woman on the Court, for failing to provide the critical fifth vote to overrule *Roe*.

After *Webster*, states began to enact more restrictive legislation (see map on p. 100). In the most important abortion case since *Roe*, *Planned Parenthood of Southeastern Pennsylvania* v. *Casey* (1992), Justice O'Connor, in an opinion supported by Justices Kennedy and Souter, wrote that Pennsylvania could limit abortions as long as its regulations did not pose "an undue burden" on pregnant women.[120]

The narrowly supported decision, which upheld a twenty-four-hour waiting period and parental consent requirements, did not overrule *Roe*, but clearly limited its scope by abolishing its trimester approach and substituting the "undue burden" standard. Since *Casey*, the Court has, for example, refused to find unconstitutional Mississippi's mandatory twenty-four-hour waiting period before an abortion. Mississippi has only three abortion clinics—all in Jackson. With this required waiting period, many women have to take time off work to drive over 100 miles, and then pay for a hotel. The number of abortions dropped 40 percent, and the clinics unsuccessfully argued that the waiting period posed an "undue burden." The U.S. Supreme Court refused to hear the appeal.[121] Moreover, in 1993, the Court ruled that judges cannot use federal civil rights laws to stop those who block access to abortion clinics, narrowing federal protections for women seeking abortions.[122]

---

[117] 410 U.S. 113 (1973).
[118] *Beal* v. *Doe*, 432 U.S. 438 (1977) and *Harris* v. *McRae*, 448 U.S. 297 (1980).
[119] 492 U.S. 490 (1989).
[120] 112 S. Ct. 931 (1992).
[121] *Barnes* v. *Moore*, 113 S. Ct. 656 (1992).
[122] *Bray* v. *Alexandria Women's Health Clinic*, 113 S. Ct. 753 (1993).

Given these decisions, pro-choice activists concluded that the Supreme Court was not the place to seek protection of what they see as basic privacy rights. In the wake of the 1992 elections, they decided to press Congress to pass a Freedom of Choice Act and looked to President Clinton, who ran on a pro-choice platform, for support. On the twentieth anniversary of *Roe*, Clinton ended bans on fetal tissue research, abortions at military hospitals, and federal financing for overseas population control programs, and lifted the "gag" rule, a federal regulation barring public health clinics receiving federal dollars from discussing abortion, which had been upheld by the Supreme Court in *Rust v. Sullivan* (1991).[123] He also ordered a review of the ban of RU-486, the French abortion pill. President Clinton used the occasion of his first appointment to the U.S. Supreme Court to select a longtime supporter of abortion rights to the Supreme Court, Ruth Bader Ginsburg, to replace Justice Byron White, one of the original dissenters in *Roe*. Most commentators believe that this was an important first step in shifting the Court away from any further curtailment of abortion rights as was the later appointment of Justice Stephen Breyer in 1994.

Homosexuality

Although the Supreme Court has ruled that the right to privacy includes the right to decide whether "to bear or beget a child," it has declined to interpret the right of privacy to include the right to engage in homosexual acts. In 1985, the Court, in a four-to-four decision (Justice Lewis F. Powell was ill), upheld a lower court decision that found un-

---

[123] 111 S. Ct. 1759 (1991).

In April 1993 gay rights activists and their supporters staged one of the largest marches ever to take place in Washington, D.C. to draw attention to their numbers and discriminatory laws and treatment.

constitutional an Oklahoma law allowing the dismissal of teachers who advocate homosexual relations.[124] So the next year, when another case involving homosexual rights (*Bowers* v. *Hardwick* [1986][125]) was argued before the Court, Lawrence Tribe, the lawyer representing Michael Hardwick, pitched his arguments toward Justice Powell, who he believed would be the crucial swing vote in this controversial area. Tribe, a professor at the Harvard Law School, argued against the constitutionality of a Georgia law prohibiting consensual heterosexual and homosexual oral or anal sex.

In August 1982, in Atlanta, Georgia, Michael Hardwick was arrested in his bedroom by a police officer who was there to serve an arrest warrant on Hardwick for his failure to appear in court on another charge. One of his roommates let the officer in and directed him to Hardwick's room. After Hardwick's arrest on a sodomy charge, the local prosecutor decided not to prosecute. Nonetheless, Hardwick, a local gay activist, joined forces with the American Civil Liberties Union to challenge the constitutionality of the law under which he had been arrested. In a five-to-four decision, the Supreme Court upheld the law. At conference, Justice Powell reportedly seemed torn by the case. He believed that the twenty-year sentence that came with conviction was excessive but was troubled by the fact that Hardwick hadn't actually been tried and convicted. Although he originally voted with the majority to overturn the law, he was bothered by the broadness of Justice Blackmun's original draft of the majority opinion. Thus, he changed his mind and voted with the minority view to uphold the law, making it the new majority.[126]

The Court's refusal to expand the right to privacy to invalidate state laws criminalizing some aspects of homosexual behavior is not that surprising. As discussed in Chapter 5, the controversy over allowing gays to join or remain in the military revealed how distasteful the gay lifestyle is to many, including, as *Hardwick* indicated, several members of the Court.

Toward Reform

The addition of the Bill of Rights to the Constitution was one of the first acts of the First Congress. Since that time, no amendments have been added to the Constitution to alter the basic liberties guaranteed by the Bill of Rights. In the aftermath of the flag-burning controversy in the 1980s, many called for the enactment of an amendment to ban flag burning. But reluctance to alter the First Amendment's far-reaching protections in any way ultimately led to the defeat of such proposals. Opponents argued fervently that this nation was built upon political protest and that free expression should be constitutionally protected at all costs, no matter how repugnant to the majority.

Congress has occasionally acted to restrict various guarantees contained in the Bill of Rights but the Court has often ruled those acts unconstitutional, as was the case

---

[124] *Board of Education of City of Oklahoma City* v. *National Gay Task Force*, 53 U.S.L.W. 4408 (1985).
[125] 478 U.S. 186 (1986).
[126] Reported in David M. O'Brien, *Constitutional Law and Politics,* Vol. 1 (New York: Norton, 1991), p. 1223.

with the flag desecration statute. In 1993, in the wake of stepped-up violence against abortion clinics and providers, a new drive was launched to make it a federal crime to threaten, commit violence, or to blockade clinics, and to give the U.S. Justice Department the power to obtain court orders to break up the blockaders. The need for this kind of law was lessened, however, after the U.S. Supreme Court ruled that the Pro-Life Action Network and groups such as Operation Rescue could be prosecuted under a federal criminal law for engaging in a national conspiracy to shut down abortion clinics "through threatened or actual force, violence or fear." Pro-life activists claimed that the ruling violated their First Amendment rights, arguing that it interfered with their rights to freedom of speech and assembly.[127] In spite of that ruling, however, in 1994 Congress passed legislation making it a crime to block access to women's reproductive health clinics or to threaten patients or employees of those clinics.

In response to the continued vitality of some liberal Warren Court decisions regarding criminal rights, several "crime bills" were introduced in Congress. President George Bush, for example, sponsored a crime bill package that died in the Senate. In 1993 and again in 1994, President Clinton proposed a crime bill package very similar to Bush's. As passed by Congress in 1994, the Violent Crime Control and Law Enforcement Act extended the death penalty to more than 50 federal crimes, including treason and carjacking resulting in death. It also provided funds for DNA testing and research (Currently the accuracy of DNA is controversial as evidenced by the O. J. Simpson proceedings.) and to fight violence against women.

---

[127] *National Organization for Women* v. *Scheidler*, 114 S. Ct. 798 (1994).

Summary

The Bill of Rights is a fundamental part of the American tradition. Within its provisions are the heart of Americans' protections from the excesses of government the Framers sought to avoid. Disputes over the scope of its provisions are common, and over the years all three branches of government—especially the legislative and the judicial—have played key roles in defining them.

In this chapter, we have made the following points:

1. Most of the Framers originally opposed the Bill of Rights. Anti-Federalists, however, continued to stress the need for a Bill of Rights during the drive for ratification of the Constitution, and some states tried to make their ratification contingent on the addition of a Bill of Rights. Thus, during its first session, Congress sent the first ten amendments to the Constitution, the Bill of Rights, to the states for their ratification.

2. The First Amendment guarantees freedom of religion. The establishment clause, which prohibits the national government from establishing a religion, does not, according to Supreme Court interpretation, create an absolute wall between church and state. While the national and state governments may generally not give direct aid to religious groups, many forms of aid, especially many that benefit children, have been held to be constitutionally permissible. In contrast, the Court has generally barred prayer in public schools. Moreover, the Court generally has adopted an accommodationist approach when interpreting the free exercise clause by allowing some governmental regulation of religious practices.

3. The First Amendment also guarantees freedom of speech and of the press. The Alien and Sedition Acts

in 1798 were the first national effort to curtail free speech, but they were never reviewed by the U.S. Supreme Court.

Some forms of speech were punished during the Civil War, and the Supreme Court refused to address their constitutionality directly. By the twentieth century, several states, and later the national government, passed laws restricting freedoms of speech and of the press. These curtailments were upheld by the Court, using the clear and present danger test. Later, the Court used the more liberal, direct incitement test, which required a stronger showing of imminent danger before speech could be restricted.

The First Amendment and most others were made applicable to the states by the Fourteenth Amendment and the incorporation doctrine.

Symbolic speech has been afforded the same protection as other forms of speech. Historically, the Supreme Court has disfavored any attempts at prior restraint of speech or press; thus, "politically correct speech" requirements have come under constitutional challenge.

Libel, slander and obscenity (as well as some forms of pornography) are not protected by the First Amendment.

4. The Fourth, Fifth, Sixth, and Eighth Amendments provide a variety of procedural guarantees to persons accused of crimes. In particular, the Fourth Amendment prohibits unreasonable searches and seizures, and the Court has generally refused to allow evidence seized in violation of this safeguard to be used at trial.

Among other rights, the Fifth Amendment guarantees that "no person shall be compelled to be a witness against himself." The Supreme Court has interpreted this provision to require that the government inform the accused of his or her right to remain silent. This provision has also been interpreted to require that illegally obtained confessions must be excluded at trial.

The Sixth Amendment's guarantee of "assistance of counsel" has been interpreted by the Supreme Court to require that the government provide counsel to defendants unable to pay for it in cases where prison sentences may be imposed. The Sixth Amendment also requires an "impartial" jury, although the meaning of "impartial" continues to evolve through judicial interpretation.

The Eighth Amendment's ban against "cruel and unusual punishments" has been held not to bar imposition of the death penalty.

5. The right to privacy is a judicially created right carved from several amendments including the First, Third, Fourth, Fifth, and Fourteenth Amendments. Statutes limiting access to birth control and abortion rights have been ruled unconstitutional violations of the right to privacy. In contrast, the Supreme Court has not expanded the right to privacy to invalidate state statutes criminalizing homosexual acts.

6. Few efforts have been made to alter the basic guarantees contained in the Bill of Rights. Periodically, however, Congress has enacted legislation to "clarify" certain provisions or to restrict rights in times of emergency.

Key Terms

civil liberties
civil rights
establishment clause
free exercise clause
prior restraint
bad tendency test

clear and present danger test
direct incitement test
due process clause
incorporation doctrine
selective incorporation
symbolic speech

libel
slander
due process rights
Miranda rights
exclusionary rule
privacy

Suggested Readings

Chafe, Zachariah, Jr. *Free Speech in the United States*. Cambridge, MA: Harvard University Press, 1948.

Clor, Harry M. *Obscenity and Public Morality*. Chicago: University of Chicago Press, 1967.

Craig, Barbara Hinkson, and David M. O'Brien. *Abortion and American Politics*. Chatham, NJ: Chatham House Publishers, 1993.

Friendly, Fred. W. *Minnesota Rag: The Dramatic Story of the Landmark Case That Gave New Meaning to Freedom of the Press*. New York: Random House, 1981.

Ivers, Gregg. *Redefining the First Freedom: The Supreme Court and the Consolidation of State Power*. New Brunswick, NJ: Transaction Press, 1993.

Leonard, Levy, et al. *The First Amendment*. New York: Macmillan, 1986.

Lewis, Anthony. *Make No Law: The Sullivan Case and the First Amendment*. New York: Random House, 1991.

Manwaring, David R. *Render unto Caesar: The Flag Salute Controversy*. Chicago: University of Chicago Press, 1962.

O'Brien, David M. *Constitutional Law and Politics, Vol. 2: Civil Rights and Civil Liberties*. New York: Norton and Co., 1991.

Weddington, Sarah. *A Question of Choice*. New York: Grosset/Putnam, 1993.

It were doubtless to be wished that the power of Prohibiting the transportation of slaves had not been postponed.... It ought to be considered as a great point gained in favor of humanity ... that [it] may terminate forever.

James Madison
Federalist No. 42

Madison considered slavery a blight on the nation and wanted the importation of slaves to be banned altogether. Yet it would take some of the country's most tumultuous times—including the Civil War and the civil rights movement of the 1960s—to begin to rectify the evils of slavery and its legacy.

CHAPTER 5

Civil Rights

SLAVERY, ABOLITION, AND WINNING THE RIGHT TO VOTE, 1800–1890
THE PUSH FOR EQUALITY, 1889–1954
THE CIVIL RIGHTS MOVEMENT
OTHER GROUPS MOBILIZE FOR RIGHTS
THE POLITICS OF CIVIL RIGHTS
TOWARD REFORM

While the Declaration of Independence boldly proclaims, "We hold these truths to be self-evident, that all men are created equal, that they are endowed by their Creator with certain inalienable rights," the Constitution is silent on the concept of equality. And only through constitutional amendment and Supreme Court definition and redefinition of the rights contained in that document have Americans come close to attaining equal rights.

Those at the Constitutional Convention—in spite of pleas such as those of Abigail Adams to her husband, John, to "remember the ladies" in the new code of laws—generally gave little thought to what we call today **civil rights**—the powers or privileges guaranteed to individuals and protected by law from arbitrary infringement by the government or any individual. Today, gay and lesbian rights activists press for many rights, especially the right to serve in the military. Similarly, individuals with disabilities lobby for the enforcement of existing legislation, such as the Americans with Disabilities Act of 1990, and for greater constitutional protections against abridgements of their civil rights. But in the late 1700s, the Framers were more concerned with rights we take for granted, such as the Sixth Amendment's guarantee of the right to a trial by jury. In the 1990s, when we think of civil rights, we usually think of those policies that explicitly and specifically extend basic rights to women and minority groups including African Americans, Hispanic Americans, the elderly, and other groups whose members have historically faced discrimination and differential treatment. One could say that civil liberties place limitations on the power of the state to restrain or dictate how individuals act; civil rights concern rights that the government must provide to its citizens.

Some civil rights issues were considered by the Framers, but, as James Madison's reflections in *Federalist No. 42* indicate, slaves were treated in the new Constitution more like property than like persons. Whereas earlier the Declaration of Independence had so eloquently proclaimed that "all men are created equal," the delegates to the Constitutional Convention put political expediency before the immorality of slavery. In fact, the Constitution specifically stated that the importation of slaves could not be prohibited for twenty years. Through the Three-Fifths Compromise, slaves were considered three-fifths of a person for the purpose of calculating state populations upon which representation in the House of Representatives was to be based (see p. 43). Why three-fifths? A committee of twelve members, one representing each state at the Constitutional Convention, concluded that a slave was, on average, "three-fifths" as productive as a white man. Thus, slaves could not vote, but they counted, at least fractionally.

There was never any question that white women would be considered full citizens for purposes of determining state population. But voting qualifications were left to the states and none allowed women to vote at the time the Constitution was ratified.

In general, the idea of voting rights or any other civil rights did not concern the Framers. Since the 1700s, however, concepts of civil rights have changed dramatically. The addition of the Fourteenth Amendment, one of three amendments passed after the Civil War, introduced the notion of equality into the Constitution by specifying that states could not deny their citizens "equal protection of the laws."

Since its addition to the Constitution, the Fourteenth Amendment has generated more litigation to determine and specify its meaning than any other provision of the Constitution. Within a few years of its ratification, women—and later, African Americans and other minorities and disadvantaged groups—took to the courts to seek expanded civil rights in all walks of life. But the struggle to augment rights was not limited to the courts. Public protest, civil disobedience, legislative lobbying, and appeals to public opinion have all been part of the arsenal of those seeking equality.

As we will see, the Constitution has been interpreted to protect African Americans and women from discrimination or any other unequal treatment that violates their civil rights. The Supreme Court, however, has chosen not to interpret the **equal protection clause** of the Fourteenth Amendment to prohibit discrimination against a variety of other groups, including the poor, the disabled, the elderly, and people with HIV/AIDS. Congress, however, *has* acted to extend rights to many of those groups by passage of various anti-discrimination laws.

Since passage of the Civil War Amendments (1865–1870), there has been a fairly consistent pattern of the expansion of civil rights to more and more groups. To better understand how notions of equality and civil rights have changed in this country, we examine the evolution of African-American rights and women's rights in tandem. Until recently, African-Americans' struggle for rights and women's efforts to achieve greater rights have been closely intertwined. To appreciate how each group has drawn ideas, support, and success from the other, we discuss their parallel developments. In addition, as African Americans and women have gained fuller equality, their actions have become the model for other groups that consider themselves disadvantaged in the political system—Native Americans, Hispanics, homosexuals, and the disabled, for example.

Full equality still remains a dream for many groups, but major improvements and progress have been made. As was the case in the development of civil liberties, the Supreme Court has played a major role in the development and even our conception of civil rights through its interpretation of the U.S. Constitution and federal civil rights laws. A Democratic administration and the addition of new, more liberal justices to replace conservatives who retire from the Court are likely to change this direction. How far the tide will turn is yet to be seen.

> *Immediately after the Revolutionary War, women had voted in some parts of Virginia and New Jersey, but those rights were terminated by the adoption of state constitutions limiting suffrage to white, property-owning males.*

Confederate President Jefferson Davis's slaves are shown here anxiously awaiting announcement of their fate in a photograph taken after the fall of Vicksburg, which ended the Civil War.

Slavery, Abolition, and Winning the Right to Vote, 1800–1890

The period from 1800 to 1890 was one of tremendous change and upheaval in America. The Civil War was fought and slaves were freed, yet the promise of equality guaranteed to African Americans by the Civil War Amendments failed to become a reality. And, while women's rights activists also began to make claims for equality, often using the arguments enunciated for the abolition of slavery, they too fell far short of their goals.

Slavery and Congress

Congress banned slave trade in 1808 (after the expiration of the twenty-year period specified by the Constitution). In 1820, blacks made up 25 percent of the population. By 1840, that figure had fallen to 20 percent. As the South became even more dependent on agriculture after the invention of the cotton gin (a machine invented in 1793 that separated seeds from cotton very quickly), technological advances turned the Northern states into an increasingly industrialized region. The growing industrialization of the North intensified the cultural and political differences and animosity between the two regions.

Slavery presented the national government with a divisive political issue. Conflicts between Northern and Southern states over the admission of new states to the Union with "free" or "slave" status emerged as the nation grew westward. The first major sectional crisis occurred in 1820, when the territory of Missouri applied for admission to the Union as a "slave state"—that is, one in which slavery would be legal. Missouri's admission would have weighted the Senate in favor of slavery and was therefore opposed by Northern senators. Tne resultant Missouri Compromise of 1820 allowed the admission of Missouri as a slave state, along with the admission of Maine

Landmark Events in the Quest for Civil Rights: From the Nineteenth Century to *Brown v. Board of Education of Topeka*

1833	American Anti-Slavery Society founded by William Lloyd Garrison
1840	International Anti-Slavery Society meeting in London
1848	Seneca Falls Convention
1851	*Uncle Tom's Cabin* published
1857	*Dred Scott* v. *Sanford*
1861–1865	Civil War
1863	Emancipation Proclamation
1865	Thirteenth Amendment ratified Lincoln assassinated
1865–1876	Reconstruction
1868	Fourteenth Amendment ratified
1869	American Woman Suffrage Association created National Woman Suffrage Association created
1870	Fifteenth Amendment ratified
1873	Women's Christian Temperance Union founded *Bradwell* v. *Illinois*
1875	*Minor* v. *Happersett*
1889–1920	The Progressive Era
1890	National American Woman Suffrage Association founded
1896	*Plessy* v. *Ferguson*
1908	*Muller* v. *Oregon*
1909	NAACP founded
1914–1918	World War I
1920	Nineteenth Amendment ratified
1939	Legal Defense and Educational Fund of the NAACP created
1941–1945	World War II
1947	Commission on Civil Rights created by Harry S Truman
1954	*Brown* v. *Board of Education of Topeka*

(formed out of the territory of Massachusetts with the permission of Congress and Massachusetts) as a free state. Other compromises concerning slavery were eventually necessitated as the nation continued to grow and new states were added to the Union.

The Abolitionist Movement: The First Civil Rights Movement

The controversy that occurred over the Compromise of 1820, while solidifying the South in its determination to keep slavery legal, fueled the fervor of those who opposed slavery. In the early 1800s, some private charities purchased slaves and transported them to the west coast of Africa, where, in the 1820s, eighty-eight former slaves formed the independent nation of Liberia.[1] But this solution to the slavery problem was not all that practical. Few owners were willing to free their slaves, and the trip to Africa and conditions there were dangerous. The abolitionist movement might have fizzled had it not been for William Lloyd Garrison, a white New Englander who became active in the movement in the early 1830s. Garrison founded the American Anti-

---

[1] By 1831, only 1,420 former slaves had returned to Liberia.

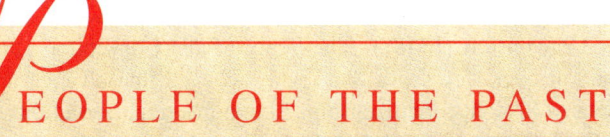

PEOPLE OF THE PAST

Frederick Douglass

Frederick Douglass (1817–1895), a leading advocate of civil rights for both blacks and women, was the son of a slave and an unidentified white man. Although born into slavery, Douglass learned how to read and write. Once he escaped to the North (where 250,000 free blacks lived), he became a well-known orator and journalist. He spoke to abolitionist groups about his experiences as a slave and included these experiences in his autobiography, *Narrative of the Life of Frederick Douglass*. His life was also romanticized in song.

In 1847 he started a newspaper, *The North Star*, in Rochester, New York, and it quickly became a powerful voice against slavery. Douglass was a strong abolitionist, who urged President Abraham Lincoln to emancipate the slaves and helped recruit black soldiers for the Union forces in the Civil War. His home in Rochester, New York, was a station along the Underground Railroad. Douglass was also a firm believer in women's suffrage, and he attended the Seneca Falls Convention in 1848. He was a close friend of John Brown, whose raid at Harpers Ferry was a pivotal moment in the anti-slavery movement. Douglass was appointed to several minor federal posts, including that of minister to Haiti from 1889 to 1891. He was considered the greatest black leader of his time. When he died in 1895, five states adopted resolutions of regret, and two U.S. senators and one Supreme Court justice were among his honorary pallbearers.

Source: New York Public Library.

Slavery Society in 1833; by 1838 it had more than 250,000 members. To put this number in perspective, that would be equivalent to the National Association for the Advancement of Colored People's (NAACP) having 3.8 million members in the United States today. (In 1994, it actually had 500,000 members.)

The Women's Rights Tie-in. Slavery was not the only inequality that people began to question in the decades following adoption of the Constitution. In 1840, for example, Garrison and even Frederick Douglass (see "People of the Past," p. 155) parted from the Anti-Slavery Society when it refused to accept their demand that women be allowed to participate equally in all its activities. At that time, custom dictated that women not speak out in public, and most laws made women second-class citizens. In most states, for example, women could not divorce their husbands or keep their own wages and inheritances. And, of course, they could not vote.

Also in 1840, Elizabeth Cady Stanton and Lucretia Mott, two women who were to found the woman's movement, attended the 1840 meeting of the International Anti-Slavery Society in London with their husbands. They were not allowed to participate because they were women. As they sat in the balcony apart from the male delegates, they paused to compare their status to that of the slaves they sought to free. Believing that women were not much better off than slaves, they resolved to call a meeting to address these issues. In 1848 they sent out a call for the first women's rights convention. Three hundred women and men, including Frederick Douglass, traveled to the sleepy little town of Seneca Falls, New York, to attend the first meeting for women's rights.

The Seneca Falls Convention (1848). The Seneca Falls Convention attracted women and men from all over New York State who believed that all men and women should be able to enjoy all rights of citizenship. At that meeting, resolutions calling for the abolition of legal, economic, and social discrimination against women were passed. All the documents reflected the attendees' dissatisfaction with contemporary moral codes, divorce and criminal laws, and the limited opportunities for women in education, the church, and careers in medicine, law, and politics. Only the call for an expanded franchise—the legal right of women to vote—failed to win unanimous approval. Most who attended the Seneca Falls meeting continued to press for women's rights along with the abolition of slavery.

The 1850s: The Calm Before the Storm. By 1850, much was changing in America—the Gold Rush had spurred westward migration, cities grew as people were lured from their farms, railroads and the telegraph increased mobility and communication, and immigrants flooded into the United States. Reformers called for change, the women's movement gained momentum, and slavery continued to tear the nation apart. Harriet Beecher Stowe's *Uncle Tom's Cabin*, which showed the evils of slavery by depicting a slave family torn apart, further inflamed the country. *Uncle Tom's Cabin* sold more than 300,000 copies in a single year, 1852.

The tremendous national reaction to Stowe's work, which later prompted Abraham Lincoln to call Stowe "the little woman who started the big war," had not yet faded when a new controversy over the 1820 Missouri Compromise became the lightning rod of the first major civil rights case to be addressed by the U.S. Supreme Court. As discussed in Chapter 3, in *Dred Scott* v. *Sandford* (1857),[2] the Supreme Court bluntly

Uncle Tom's Cabin, by Harriet Beecher Stowe.

---

[2] 60 U.S. 393 (1857).

ruled unconstitutional the 1820 Missouri Compromise, which prohibited slavery north of the 36° 30′ line. Furthermore, the Court found that slaves were not U.S. citizens and therefore could not bring suits in federal court. Moreover, the justices concluded that "the Negro might justly and lawfully be reduced to slavery for his benefit." Ironically, after the case was decided, Scott's owner freed him.

The Civil War and Its Aftermath: Civil Rights Laws and Constitutional Amendments

The Civil War had many causes, including (1) the political conflict between the North and the South over the doctrines of nullification and secession, (2) the Northern states' increasing political strength in Congress, (3) Southern agrarianism versus Northern industrialization, and (4) the clash of conservative Southern culture with more progressive Northern ideas. Slavery, however, was clearly the key issue.

During the war (1861–1865), abolitionists kept their activities alive and were rewarded in 1863 when President Abraham Lincoln issued the Emancipation Proclamation, which provided that all slaves in states still in active rebellion against the United States would automatically be freed on January 1, 1863. Designed as a measure to gain favor for the war in the North, the Emancipation Proclamation did not free all slaves—it freed only those who lived in the Confederacy. Complete abolition of slavery did not occur until congressional passage and ultimate ratification of the Thirteenth Amendment.

The Civil War Amendments. Enacted in 1865, the **Thirteenth Amendment** was the first of the three so-called Civil War Amendments. It banned all forms of "slavery [and] involuntary servitude." Although Southern states were required to ratify the Thirteenth Amendment as a condition of their readmission to the Union after the war,

The 1848 Seneca Falls Convention was viewed with contempt by many leading political cartoonists.

Students who took their school district to court to challenge compulsory "volunteerism."

> ### "The Thirteenth Amendment Revisited"
>
> Since the 1860s, the Thirteenth Amendment, which bans "slavery or involuntary servitude," has not been an issue in American courts. But in the 1990s, as more and more school districts made community service work a requirement for high school graduation, some students have questioned the legality of those programs in federal court. "People should volunteer because they want to, not because of a government threat," says Lynn Steirer, one of 175 seniors who may not graduate because they failed to perform the sixty hours of public service required by their high school. She and another student, with the help of the Institute for Justice, a Washington, D.C.-based libertarian group, took their school district to court arguing that the policy violates the Thirteenth Amendment's ban against slavery. Two lower courts upheld the requirements.*
>
> And, in 1993, the United States Supreme Court refused to review the case, thus letting the decision of the lower courts stand.
>
> *Steirer v. Bethlehem Area School District, 987 F. 2nd 989 (1992).

most quickly passed laws that were designed to restrict opportunities for newly freed slaves dramatically. These **Black Codes** prohibited African Americans from voting, sitting on juries, or even appearing in public places. Although Black Codes differed from state to state, all empowered local law-enforcement officials to arrest unemployed blacks, fine them for vagrancy, and hire them out to employers to satisfy their fines. Some state codes went so far as to require African Americans to work on plantations or to be domestics. The Black Codes laid the groundwork for Jim Crow laws, which would later institute segregation in all walks of life (see "Who Was Jim Crow?" p. 162).

The outraged Reconstructionist Congress (see "Reconstruction," p. 159), enacted the Civil Rights Act of 1866 to invalidate some of the Black Codes. President Andrew Johnson vetoed the legislation, but for the first time in history Congress overrode a presidential veto. The Civil Rights Act formally made African Americans citizens of the United States and gave the Congress and the courts the power to intervene when states attempted to restrict male, African-American citizenship rights in matters such as voting. Congress reasoned that African Americans were unlikely to fare well if they had to file discrimination complaints in state courts where judges were elected. Passage of a federal law allowed African Americans to challenge discriminatory state practices in the federal courts, where judges were appointed.

Because controversy remained over the constitutionality of the Act (since the Constitution gives states the right to determine qualifications of voters), the **Fourteenth Amendment** was proposed simultaneously with the Civil Rights Act to guarantee, among other things, citizenship to all freed slaves. Other key provisions of the Fourteenth Amendment barred states from abridging "the privileges and immunities of citizenship" or depriving "any person of life, liberty, or property without due process of law."

Reconstruction

♦ ♦ ♦

In the aftermath of the Civil War, the national government was faced with the problem of bringing the Southern states back into the Union. Its efforts to do so are referred to as *Reconstruction*. Aside from measures of political integration, Reconstruction encompassed physical and financial rehabilitation. The Radical Republicans in Congress found Presidents Lincoln and Johnson too conciliatory toward the South. The U.S. Congress declared the Southern state governments illegal and divided the region into five military districts, each governed by a major-general. New state governments were formed, run by coalitions of "scalawags" (white Southerners who agreed with the Radical Republicans), "carpetbaggers" (immigrants from the North who took their name from the cloth baggage they used), and African Americans. Because these governments were imposed on Southerners from the outside, they were weak and could be maintained only through the use of military force. The "carpetbag regimes" were corrupt, and conditions in the South worsened under the Reconstruction policies of the Radical Republicans. The closeness of the 1876 presidential campaign between Republican Rutherford B. Hayes and Democrat Samuel J. Tilden brought promises from Hayes to improve conditions in the South. Hayes won the election, and Reconstruction ended.

Thomas Nast, the most famous political cartoonist of the day, drew this rendition of a "carpetbagger" headed South with a bag on his back. The bag contains the faults of his own he never sees, while he so easily sees the faults of Southerners.

Unlike the Thirteenth Amendment, which had near-unanimous support in the North, the Fourteenth Amendment was opposed by many women. During the Civil War, women's rights activists, including Elizabeth Cady Stanton and Susan B. Anthony, put aside their claims for expanded rights for women, most notably the right to vote, and threw their energies into the war effort. They were convinced that once slaves were freed and blacks were given the right to vote, women similarly would be rewarded with the franchise. They were wrong.

After ratification of the Fourteenth Amendment (which specifically added the word "male" to the Constitution for the first time), women's rights activists met in Washington, D.C. in early 1869 for the first National Woman's Suffrage convention. There, activists argued against passage of any new amendment that would extend suffrage to black males and not to women. The convention resolved that "a *man's* government is worse than a *white* man's government, because, in proportion as you increase the tyrants, you make the condition of the disenfranchised class more hopeless and degraded."

In spite of these arguments, the **Fifteenth Amendment** was passed by Congress in February, 1869. It guaranteed the "right of citizens" to vote regardless of their "race, color or previous condition of servitude."

Women's rights activists were shocked when Congress failed to include a provision to enfranchise females. Abolitionists' continued support of the Fifteenth Amendment prompted many women's rights supporters to leave that movement to work solely for the cause of women's rights. Twice burned, Anthony and Stanton decided to form their own National Woman Suffrage Association (NWSA) to achieve that goal.[3] In spite of the NWSA's opposition, however, the Fifteenth Amendment was ratified by the states in 1870.

Civil Rights and the Supreme Court

While the Congress was clear in its wishes that the rights of African Americans be expanded and that the Black Codes be rendered illegal, the Supreme Court was not nearly so protective of those rights under the Civil War Amendments. In the first two tests of the scope of the Fourteenth Amendment, the Supreme Court ruled that the citizenship rights guaranteed by the amendment applied only to rights of national citizenship and not to state citizenship. Ironically, neither case involved African Americans. In *The Slaughterhouse Cases* (1873),[4] the Court upheld Louisiana's right to create a monopoly in the operation of slaughterhouses, despite the Butcher's Benevolent Association's claim that this action deprived its members of their livelihood and thus the privileges and immunities of citizenship guaranteed by the Amendment. Similarly, in *Bradwell* v. *Illinois* (1873),[5] when Myra Bradwell asked the U.S. Supreme Court to find that Illinois's refusal to allow her to practice law (although she had passed the bar examination) violated her citizenship rights guaranteed by the privileges and immunities clause of the Fourteenth Amendment, her arguments fell on deaf ears. In *Bradwell*, the Court went even further than it had in *The Slaughterhouse Cases*, ruling that it was reasonable for the state to bar women from the practice of law because "the natural and proper timidity and delicacy which belongs to the female sex evidently unfits it for many of the occupations of civil life." The combined message of these two cases was that state and national citizenship were separate and distinct. In essence, the Supreme Court ruled that neither African Americans nor any others could be protected from discriminatory state action, because the Fourteenth Amendment did not enlarge the limited rights guaranteed by U.S. citizenship.

Claims for expanded rights, and requests for a clear definition of U.S. citizenship rights continued to fall on deaf ears in the halls of the Supreme Court. In 1875, for example, the Court heard *Minor* v. *Happersett*,[6] the culmination of a series of test cases

---

[3] See Ellen Carol DuBois, *Feminism and Suffrage* (Ithaca, New York: Cornell University Press, 1980).
[4] 83 U.S. (16 Wall.) 36 (1873).
[5] 83 U.S. (16 Wall.) 130 (1873).
[6] 88 U.S. (21 Wall.) 162 (1875).

launched by women's rights activists.[7] Virginia Minor, after planning with Anthony and other NWSA members, attempted to register to vote in her hometown of St. Louis, Missouri. When the registrar refused to record her name on the list of eligible voters, Minor sued, arguing that the state's refusal to let her vote violated the privileges and immunities clause of the Fourteenth Amendment. Rejecting her claim, the justices ruled unanimously that voting was not a privilege of citizenship.

In the same year, Southern resistance to African-American equality led Congress to pass the Civil Rights Act of 1875, designed to grant equal access to public accommodations such as theaters, restaurants, and transportation. The Act also prohibited the exclusion of African Americans from jury service. After 1877, however, as Reconstruction was dismantled, national interest in the legal condition of African Americans waned. Most white Southerners had never believed in equality for "freedmen," as former slaves were called. Any rights freedmen received had been contingent upon federal enforcement. Once federal troops were no longer available to guard polls and prevent whites from excluding black voters, Southern states moved to limit African Americans' access to the ballot. Other forms of discrimination were also allowed by judicial decisions upholding **Jim Crow laws**, which required segregation in public schools and facilities including railroads, restaurants, and theaters (see "Who Was Jim Crow?" p. 162). Many also barred interracial marriage. All these laws, at first glance, appeared to conflict with the Civil Rights Act of 1875. In 1883, however, a series of cases decided by the Supreme Court severely damaged the vitality of the 1875 Act. In the **Civil Rights Cases** (1883)[8] (five separate cases involving the convictions of pri-

---

[7] See Karen O'Connor, *Women's Organizations' Use of the Courts* (Lexington, MA: Lexington Books, 1980).
[8] 109 U.S. 3 (1883).

Throughout the South, examples of Jim Crow laws abounded. One such law required separate public drinking fountains, shown here. Notice the obvious difference in quality.

vate individuals found to have violated the Civil Rights Act by refusing to extend accommodations to African Americans in theaters, a hotel, and a railroad), the Supreme Court ruled that Congress could prohibit only state or governmental action, and not private acts of discrimination. The Court thus seriously limited the scope of the Fourteenth Amendment by concluding that Congress had no authority to prohibit private discrimination in public accommodations.

The Court's opinion in the *Civil Rights Cases* provided a moral reinforcement for the Jim Crow system. Southern states viewed the Court's ruling as an invitation to gut the Thirteenth, Fourteenth, and Fifteenth Amendments.

In devising ways to make certain that African Americans did not vote, Southerners had to avoid the *intent* of the Fifteenth Amendment. This amendment did not guarantee suffrage; it simply said that states could not deny anyone the right to vote on account of race or color. So to exclude African Americans in a seemingly racially neutral way, Southern states used two devices before the 1890s: (1) poll taxes (small taxes on the right to vote that often came due when poor African-American sharecroppers had the least amount of money on hand) or some form of property-owning qualifications, and (2) "literacy" or "understanding" tests, which allowed local registrars to administer difficult reading-comprehension tests to potential voters whom they did not know.

These voting restrictions had an immediate impact. By the late 1890s, black voting fell by 62 percent from the Reconstruction period, while white voting fell by only 26

Who Was Jim Crow?
♦ ♦ ♦

The term "Jim Crow" symbolized the continued discrimination of African Americans in the South through state-enacted "separate but equal" laws following *Plessy* v. *Ferguson* (1896). African Americans could be denied the use of public facilities if separate but equal facilities existed for them. The name "Jim Crow" came from a song-and-dance routine first performed in the 1830s, by Thomas Dartmouth Rice in which, having blackened his face with a burnt cork, he sang:

> Weel a-bout and turn a-bout
> And do just so
> Every time I weel about
> I jump Jim Crow

This act is an early example of the popular minstrel show, wherein whites made fun of black songs and speech. Jim Crow was "a comic, jumping, stupid rag doll of a man." The term "Jim Crow" quickly became a synonym for "Negro."* The actual identity of Jim Crow, however, is unknown. Historians suggest that he may have been a soldier whom Rice had met in Kentucky or Ohio, a slave, or "old man Crow", a legendary slaveholder.

The Jim Crow laws created separate facilities for African Americans in public places including railroad cars, restaurants, and schools. The last was perhaps the most damaging, because black schools were not given the same funding or teachers of the same quality as white schools. It was not until 1954, in *Brown* v. *Board of Education of Topeka*, that racial segregation was ruled unconstitutional.

* Davis, Kenneth C. *Don't Know Much About History* (New York: Crown, 1990), p. 215.

percent. To make certain that these laws didn't further reduce the numbers of poor or uneducated white voters, many Southern states added **grandfather clauses** to their voting qualification provisions, granting voting privileges to those who failed to pass a wealth or literacy test only if their grandfathers had voted before Reconstruction. Grandfather clauses effectively denied the descendants of slaves the right to vote.

While African Americans continued to face wide-ranging racism on all fronts, women, too, confronted discrimination. During this period, married women, by law, could not be recognized as legal entities. Women often were treated in the same category as juveniles and "imbeciles," and in many states were not entitled to wages, inheritances, or custody of their children.

The Push for Equality, 1889–1954

The Progressive Era (1889–1920) was characterized by a concerted effort to reform political, economic, and social affairs. Evils like child labor, the concentration of economic power in the hands of a few industrialists, limited suffrage, political corruption, business monopolies, and prejudice against African Americans were all targets of progressive reform efforts. Distress over the legal inferiority of African Americans was aggravated by the U.S. Supreme Court's decision in *Plessy* v. *Ferguson* (1896), a case that some commentators point to as the Court's darkest hour.

Plessy v. Ferguson: "Separate But Equal." In 1892, a group of African Americans in Louisiana decided to test the constitutionality of a Louisiana law mandating racial segregation on all public trains. They found an "ideal" individual to test the law. Homer Adolph Plessy, with blond hair and blue eyes, was widely known in the community to have had an African-American great-grandmother. His coloring made him an excellent subject for a potential test case of the Louisiana law. Plessy boarded a train in New Orleans and proceeded to the "whites only" car. He was arrested when he refused to leave his seat and take one in the car reserved for African Americans. Plessy sued the railroad company, arguing that segregation was illegal under the provisions of the Fourteenth Amendment.[9]

The Supreme Court disagreed. After analyzing the history of African Americans in the United States, the majority concluded that the Louisiana law was constitutional. The justices based the decision on their belief that separate facilities for blacks and whites provided equal protection of the laws. After all, they reasoned, African Americans were not prevented from riding the train; the Louisiana statute required only that the races travel separately. Justice John Marshall Harlan (1877–1911), the lone dissenter on the Court, criticized the majority and argued that it was senseless to hold constitutional a law "which, practically, puts the badge of servitude and degradation upon a large class of our fellow citizens."

Not surprisingly, the separate-but-equal doctrine enunciated in *Plessy* v. *Ferguson* soon came to mean only "separate," as new legal avenues for states to discriminate against African Americans opened up. The Jim Crow system soon became a way of life in the American South. In 1898, the Court upheld the constitutionality of literacy tests[10] and indicated its apparent willingness to allow the Southern states to define

---

[9] 163 U.S. 537 (1896).
[10] *Williams* v. *Mississippi*, 170 U.S. 213 (1898).

their own suffrage standards, whether or not they disproportionately affected African Americans. One year later, the Supreme Court chose to ignore the fact that educational opportunities for African-American children were far inferior to those of whites. In *Cumming* v. *County Board of Education* (1899),[11] black parents who were also taxpayers challenged their tax assessments because the money was used to support a "whites only" high school. The Board of Education had originally supported a black public high school, but when funds got tight, it was closed to free up funds for the black elementary school. The Supreme Court unanimously upheld the constitutionality of this disparate treatment. The justices appeared concerned that the relief requested could have impaired the functioning of the white high school or required that it be closed altogether.

By 1900, then, equality for African Americans was far from the promise first offered by the passage of the Civil War Amendments. Again and again the Supreme Court nullified the intent of the amendments and sanctioned racial segregation while the states avidly followed its lead. While discrimination was widely practiced in many parts of the North, Southern states passed laws legally imposing segregation in education, housing, public accommodations, employment, and most other spheres of life. Miscegenation laws, for example, prohibited blacks and whites from marrying.

Laws alone were not the only practices designed to keep African Americans in a secondary position. Jim Crow established a way of life with strong social as well as legal codes. Journalist Juan Williams notes in *Eyes on the Prize*:

> There were Jim Crow schools, Jim Crow restaurants, Jim Crow water fountains, and Jim Crow customs—blacks were expected to tip their hats when they walked past whites, but whites did not have to remove their hats even when they entered a black family's home. Whites were to be called "sir" and "ma'am" by blacks, who in turn were called by their first names by whites. People with white skin were to be given a wide berth on the sidewalk; blacks were expected to step aside meekly.[12]

Notwithstanding these degrading practices, by the early 1900s, a small cadre of African Americans (largely from the North) had been able to attain some formal education and were ready to push for additional rights. They found some progressive citizens and politicians amenable to their cause.

The Founding of the National Association for the Advancement of Colored People

In 1909, a handful of individuals active in a variety of progressive causes—including women's suffrage and better working conditions for women and children—met to discuss the idea of a group devoted to the problems of "the Negro." Major race riots had recently occurred in several American cities, and progressive reformers who sought change in political, economic, and social relations were concerned about these outbreaks of violence and the possibility of others. Oswald Garrison Villard, the influential publisher of the New York *Evening Post*—and grandson of William Lloyd Garrison—called a conference to discuss the problem. This group soon evolved into the National Association for the Advancement of Colored People (NAACP). Among

William E. DuBois (second from the right in the second row, facing left) is pictured with the original leaders of the Niagara Movement in this 1905 photo taken on the Canadian side of Niagara Falls.

---

[11] 175 U.S. 528 (1899).

[12] Juan Williams, *Eyes on the Prize: America's Civil Rights Years, 1954–1965* (New York: Penguin, 1987), p. 10.

its first leaders were Villard; Jane Addams of Hull House, vice president of the National American Woman Suffrage Association; Moorfield Storey, a past president of the American Bar Association; and W.E.B. DuBois, a founder of the Niagara Movement, a group of educated African Americans who took their name from their first meeting place, Niagara Falls, in Ontario, Canada. (The Niagara reformers met in Canada because no hotel on the American side of the Falls would accommodate them.)

Key Women's Groups

The NAACP was not the only group getting off the ground. The struggle for women's rights was revitalized by the formation of the National American Woman Suffrage Association (NAWSA) in 1890, when the National and American Woman Suffrage Associations merged, with Susan B. Anthony as its president. Unlike the National Woman Suffrage Association, which had sought a wide variety of expanded rights for women, this new association was devoted largely to securing women's suffrage. Its task was greatly facilitated by the proliferation of women's groups that emerged during the Progressive Era. In addition to the rapidly growing temperance movement, which sought to ban the sale of alcohol, which many women blamed for many social ills, women's groups were created to seek protective legislation in the form of maximum hour or minimum wage laws for women and to work for improved sanitation, public morals, education, and the like. Other organizations that were part of what was called the "club movement" were created to provide increased cultural and literary experiences for middle-class women. With increased industrialization, some women found for the first time that they had the opportunity to pursue activities other than those centered on the home.

One of the most active groups lobbying on behalf of women during this period was the National Consumers' League (NCL). After it successfully lobbied for Oregon leg-

Suffragettes demonstrating for the franchise. Parades like this one took place in cities all over the United States.

In 1908, the U.S. Supreme Court ruled that Oregon's law barring women from working more than 10 hours a day in laundries was constitutional. Thus, the conviction of Curt Muller (with arms folded) for violating the statute was upheld.

islation limiting women to ten hours of work a day, it insisted that its legislative effort be properly defended before the U.S. Supreme Court when its constitutionality was challenged. Curt Muller had been convicted of employing women more than ten hours a day in his small laundry. When the U.S. Supreme Court agreed to hear his appeal, the NCL sought permission from the state to conduct the defense of the statute.

At the urging of NCL attorney and future U.S. Supreme Court Justice Louis Brandeis, NCL members amassed an impressive array of sociological and medical data that were incorporated into what became known as "The Brandeis brief." This contained only three pages of legal argument, while more than 100 were devoted to nonlegal data. Sociological and other data were used to convince the Court that Oregon's statute was constitutional—a position not supported by other legal precedents. And, in finding

The *Muller* Opinion

According to the Court in *Muller* (1908):

That woman's physical structure and the performance of maternal functions place her at a disadvantage in the struggle for subsistence is obvious. . . . As healthy mothers are essential to vigorous offspring, the physical well-being of women becomes an object of public interest and care in order to preserve the strength and vigor of the race. . . . As minors though not to the same extent, she has been looked upon in the courts as needing especial care that her rights may be preserved.

the law constitutional in *Muller* v. *Oregon* (1908),[13] the Court relied heavily on these data to document women's unique status as mothers to justify their differential treatment.

Women seeking the vote used reasoning reflecting the Court's opinion in *Muller*. Discarding earlier notions of full equality, NAWSA based its claim to the right to vote largely on the fact that women, as mothers, should be enfranchised. Furthermore, although many members of the suffrage movement were NAACP members, the new women's movement—called the **suffrage movement** because of its focus on the vote alone and not on broader issues of women's rights—took on racist overtones as women argued that if undereducated African Americans could vote, why couldn't women? Some NAWSA members even argued that "the enfranchisement of women would ensure immediate and durable white supremacy."[14]

Diverse attitudes were clearly present in the growing suffrage movement, which often tried to be all things to all people. Its roots in the Progressive Era gave it an exceptionally broad base that transformed NAWSA from a small organization of just over 10,000 members in the early 1890s to a true social movement of more than 2 million members in 1917. By 1920, this coalition was able to secure ratification of the Nineteenth, or Susan B. Anthony, Amendment to the Constitution. And, unlike the provision first passed in Great Britain in 1918 that gave only women over the age of thirty the right to vote, this Amendment guaranteed *all* women the right to vote, albeit fifty-five years after African-American males had been enfranchised by the Fifteenth Amendment.[15]

After passage of the suffrage amendment in 1920, the fragile alliance of diverse women's groups that had come together to fight for the vote quickly disintegrated. Women returned to their "home" groups, such as the NCL, the Women's Christian Temperance Union, or a book club, to pursue their goals of protective legislation, prohibition of alcohol, or self-improvement. In fact, after the tumult of the suffrage movement, widespread, organized activity on behalf of women's rights did not reemerge until the 1960s. In the meantime, however, the NAACP continued to fight racism. In fact, its activities and those of others in the civil rights movement would later give impetus to a new women's movement.

Litigating for Equality

During the 1930s, leaders of the NAACP began to sense that the time was right to launch a full-scale challenge in the federal courts to the constitutionality of *Plessy*'s separate-but-equal doctrine. The NAACP mapped out a long-range strategy that would first target segregation in professional and graduate education. Clearly, the separate-but-equal doctrine and the proliferation of Jim Crow laws were a bar to any hope of full equality for African Americans. Traditional legislative channels were unlikely to work, given blacks' limited or nonexistent political power. Thus, the federal courts and a long-range litigation strategy were the NAACP's only hope. And it often relied on Brandeis-type briefs, so-called because they relied heavily on sociological data. In fact, the NAACP eventually hired a statistician to help its lawyers amass data to help present evidence of discrimination to the courts.

---

[13] 208 U.S. 412 (1908).

[14] Quoted in Judith Papachristou, *Women Together* (New York: Knopf, 1976), p. 144.

[15] See Eleanor Flexner, *Century of Struggle* (New York: Atheneum, 1971).

Test Cases. The NAACP opted first to challenge the constitutionality of Jim Crow law schools. In 1935, all Southern states maintained fully segregated elementary and secondary schools. Colleges and universities were also segregated, but most states did not provide for postgraduate education for African Americans. NAACP lawyers chose to target law schools because they were institutions that judges could well understand, and integration there could prove less threatening to most whites.

Lloyd Gaines, a graduate of Missouri's all-black Lincoln University, sought admission to the all-white University of Missouri Law School in 1936. He was immediately rejected, but the state offered to build a law school at Lincoln (although no funds were allocated for the project) or, if he didn't want to wait, to pay his tuition at an out-of-state law school. Gaines lost his appeal of this rejection in the lower court, and the case was appealed to the U.S. Supreme Court.[16]

Gaines's case was filed at an auspicious time. As you may recall from Chapter 3, a "constitutional revolution" occurred in 1937. Prior to 1937, the Court was most receptive to and interested in the protection of economic liberties. In 1937, however, the Court reversed itself in a series of cases and began to place individual freedoms and personal liberties on a more protected footing. Thus, in 1938, it was to a far more sympathetic Supreme Court that Gaines's lawyers finally pleaded his appeal. NAACP attorneys argued that the creation of a separate law school of any less caliber than that of the University of Missouri would not and could not afford Gaines an *equal* education. The justices agreed with the NAACP's contention and ruled that Missouri had failed to meet the separate-but-equal requirements of *Plessy*, and the Court ordered Missouri to admit Gaines to the school.

Recognizing the importance of the Court's ruling, in 1939 the NAACP created a separate, tax-exempt, legal defense fund to devise a strategy to build on *Gaines* to

---

[16] *Missouri* ex rel. *Gaines* v. *Canada*, 305 U.S. 337 (1938).

Lloyd Gaines was the subject of the major test case, *Missouri* ex rel. *Gaines* v. *Canada,* which contested the principle of segregated schools. Gaines chose to attend the University of Michigan, from which he strangely disappeared, never to be heard from again.

bring about equal educational opportunities for all African-American children. The first head of the NAACP Legal Defense and Educational Fund (LDF), as it was called, was Thurgood Marshall, who later became the first African American to serve on the U.S. Supreme Court (1967–1991). Sensing that the Court would be more amenable to the NAACP's broader goals if it was first forced to address a variety of less threatening claims to educational opportunity, Marshall and the LDF brought a series of carefully crafted test cases to the Court.

The first case involved a forty-six-year-old African-American mail carrier, Herman Sweatt, who in 1946 applied for admission to the all-white University of Texas Law School. Rejected on racial grounds, Sweatt sued and the judge gave the state six months to establish a law school or to admit him to the University of Texas. The university then rented a few rooms in downtown Houston and hired two local African-American attorneys to be part-time faculty members. (At that time there was only one full-time African-American law school professor in the United States.) The state legislature, seeing the handwriting on the wall, authorized $3 million for the creation of the Texas State University for Negroes. One hundred thousand dollars of that money was to be for a new law school in Austin across the street from the state capitol. It consisted of three small basement rooms, a library of more than 10,000 books and access to the state law library, and three part-time first-year instructors as the "faculty." Sweatt declined the opportunity to obtain an education there and instead chose to continue his legal challenge.

While working on *Sweatt*, the NAACP LDF and Marshall also decided to pursue another case. Thurgood Marshall chose to use the case of George W. McLaurin, a retired university professor who had been denied admission to the doctoral education program at the University of Oklahoma. Marshall reasoned that McLaurin, at sixty-eight years of age, would be immune from the charges that African Americans wanted integration in order to intermarry. After a lower court ordered McLaurin's admission, the university reserved a dingy alcove in the cafeteria for him to eat in during off hours, and he was given his own table in the library behind a shelf of newspapers. And, in what surely "was Oklahoma's most inventive contribution to legalized bigotry since the adoption of the 'grandfather clause,'"[17] McLaurin was forced to sit outside classrooms while lectures were given and seminars were held.

The Supreme Court handled these two cases—*Sweatt* v. *Painter*[18] and *McLaurin* v. *Oklahoma State Regents for Higher Education*[19]—as companion cases. The eleven Southern states filed an *amicus curiae* (friend of the court) brief, in which they argued that *Plessy* should govern both cases. The NAACP LDF received assistance, however, from an unexpected source—the U.S. government. In a dramatic departure from the past, the administration of Harry S Truman filed a friend of the court brief urging the Court to overrule *Plessy*. Since the late 1870s, the U.S. government had never sided against the Southern states in a civil rights matter and had never submitted an *amicus* brief supporting the rights of African-American citizens. President Truman believed that because many African Americans had fought and died for their country in World War II, this kind of executive action was proper. The Court traditionally gives great weight to briefs from the U.S. government. The Court, however, again did not overrule *Plessy*, but the justices found that the measures taken by the states in each case failed

---

[17] Richard Kluger, *Simple Justice* (New York: Vintage, 1975), p. 268.
[18] 339 U.S. 629 (1950).
[19] 339 U.S. 637 (1950).

to live up to the strictures of the separate-but-equal doctrine. The Court unanimously ruled that the "remedies" to each situation were inadequate to afford a sound education. In the *Sweatt* case, for example, the Court declared that the "qualities which are incapable of objective measurement but which make for greatness in a law school . . . includ(ing) the reputation of the faculty, experience of the administration, position and influence of the alumni, standing in the community, traditions and prestige" made it impossible for the state to provide an equal education in a segregated setting.

After these decisions were handed down in 1950, the NAACP LDF concluded that the time had come to launch a full-scale attack on the separate-but-equal doctrine. The decisions of the Court were encouraging, and the position of the U.S. government and the population in general appeared to be more receptive to an outright overruling of *Plessy*.

***Brown v. Board of Education of Topeka, Kansas* (1954).**[20] As discussed in "Why It's Called *Brown* v. *Board of Education of Topeka*" (see p. 171), *Brown* was actually four cases brought from different areas of the South, the border states, and others involving public elementary or high school systems that mandated separate schools for blacks and whites.

In *Brown*, NAACP lawyers, again headed by Thurgood Marshall, argued that *Plessy*'s separate-but-equal doctrine was unconstitutional under the equal protection clause of the Fourteenth Amendment, and that if the Court was still reluctant to overrule *Plessy*, the only way to equalize the schools was to integrate them. A major component of the NAACP's strategy was to prove that the intellectual, psychological, and financial damage that befell African Americans as a result of segregation precluded any court from finding that equality was served by the separate-but-equal policy.

In *Brown*, the NAACP LDF presented the Supreme Court with evidence of the harmful consequences of state-imposed racial discrimination. To buttress its claims the NAACP introduced the now-famous "doll study," conducted by Kenneth Clark, a prominent African-American sociologist who had long studied the negative effects of segregation on African-American children. His research revealed that black children not only preferred white dolls when shown black and white dolls, but that most liked the white doll better, many adding that the black doll looked "bad." This information was used to illustrate the negative impact of racial segregation and bias on an African-American child's self-image.

The NAACP's legal briefs were supported by important *amicus curiae* briefs submitted by the U.S. government and major civil rights groups, labor unions, and religious groups decrying racial segregation. On May 17, 1954, Chief Justice Earl Warren delivered the fourth opinion of the day, *Brown* v. *Board of Education of Topeka*. Writing for the Court, Warren stated:

> To separate [some school children] from others . . . solely because of their race generates a feeling of inferiority as to their status in the community that may affect their hearts and minds in a way very unlikely ever to be undone.
>
> We conclude, unanimously, that in the field of public education the doctrine of "separate but equal" has no place.[21]

There can be no doubt that *Brown* was the most important civil rights case decided in the twentieth century. It immediately evoked an uproar that shook the nation. Some

---

[20] 347 U.S. 483 (1954).
[21] 347 U.S. at 495 (1954).

Why It's Called *Brown v. Board of Education of Topeka*

Seven-year-old Linda Brown of Topeka, Kansas, lived close to a good public school, but it was reserved for whites. So every day she had to cross railroad tracks to catch a run-down school bus that took her across town to a school for black students. Her father, Oliver Brown, concerned for her safety and the quality of her education, became increasingly frustrated with his daughter's having to travel far from home to get an education.

"The issue came up, and it was decided that Reverend Brown's daughter would be the goat, so to speak," recalled a member of the Topeka NAACP. "He put forth his daughter to test the validity of the [law], and we had to raise the money."*

The NAACP continued to gather plaintiffs and test cases from around the nation. The Supreme Court first agreed to hear *Brown* and *Briggs* v. *Elliott* (South Carolina) in 1952. Two days before they were to be heard, the Court issued a postponement and added *Davis* v. *Prince Edward County* (Virginia) to its docket. A few weeks later, the Court added *Bolling* v. *Sharpe* (District of Columbia) and *Gebhart* v. *Belton* (Delaware). According to U.S. Supreme Court Justice Tom Clark of Texas, the Court "consolidated them and made *Brown* the first so that the whole question would not smack of being purely a Southern one."** Thus, the case became known as *Brown* v. *Board of Education of Topeka*.

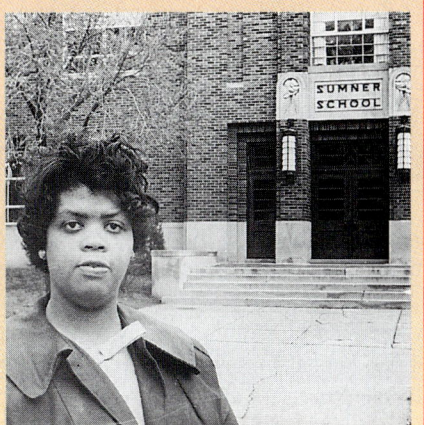

Ten years after the Court's decision in *Brown* v. *Board of Education*, Linda Brown Smith stood in front of the school whose refusal to admit her ultimately led to the Court's 1954 ruling, *Brown* v. *Board of Education,* named after her. The decision came too late for her, but her two younger sisters were able to attend integrated schools.

* Quoted in Juan Williams, *Eyes on the Prize: America's Civil Rights Years, 1954–1965* (New York: Penguin, 1987), p. 21.

** Ibid., p. 31.

---

called the day the decision was handed down "Black Monday." The governor of South Carolina decried the decision, saying, "Ending segregation would mark the beginning of the end of civilization in the South as we know it."[22] The NAACP LDF lawyers who had argued these cases and those leading to *Brown,* however, were jubilant.

[22] Quoted in Juan Williams, *Eyes on the Prize: America's Civil Rights Years, 1954–1965* (New York: Penguin Books, 1987), p. 34.

Since 1890, remarkable changes had occurred in the civil rights of Americans. Women had won the right to vote, and after a long and arduous trail of litigation in the federal courts, the Supreme Court had finally overturned the most racist case of the era, *Plessy* v. *Ferguson*. The Court boldly proclaimed that separate but equal (at least in education) would no longer pass constitutional muster. The question then became how *Brown* would be interpreted and implemented. Could it be used to invalidate other Jim Crow laws and practices? Would African Americans be truly equal under law?

The Civil Rights Movement

Since 1954, profound changes have occurred in our notion of civil rights. First African Americans and then women have built upon existing organizations to forge successful movements for increased rights. *Brown* served as a catalyst for change, sparking the development of the modern civil rights movement. Women's work in that movement and the student protest movement that arose in reaction to the U.S. government's involvement in Vietnam gave women the experience needed to form their own organizations to press for full equality.[23] As African Americans and women became more and more successful, they served as the model for others who sought equality—Native Americans, Hispanic Americans, homosexuals, the disabled, and others.

School Desegregation After *Brown*

One year after *Brown I*, in what is referred to as *Brown II*,[24] the Court ruled that racially segregated systems must be dismantled "with all deliberate speed." To facilitate implementation, the Court placed enforcement of *Brown* in the hands of non-elected federal district court judges, who were considered more immune to local political pressures than were regularly elected state court judges.

The NAACP and its Legal Defense Fund continued to resort to the courts to see that *Brown* was implemented, while the South entered into a near-conspiracy to avoid the mandates of *Brown II*. In Arkansas, for example, Governor Orval Faubus, facing a re-election bid, announced that he would not "be a party to any attempt to force acceptance of change to which people are overwhelmingly opposed."[25] The day before school was to begin, Faubus announced that he would surround Little Rock's Central High School with National Guardsmen to prevent African-American students from entering. While the federal courts in Arkansas continued to order the admission of African-American children, the governor remained adamant. Finally, President Dwight D. Eisenhower sent federal troops to Little Rock to protect the rights of the nine students who had attempted to attend Central High.

In reaction to the governor's outrageous conduct, in *Cooper* v. *Aaron* (1958),[26] each justice individually signed the unanimous opinion, underscoring each one's personal support of the statement that "no state legislator or executive or judicial officer can war

---

[23] Nancy E. McGlen and Karen O'Connor, *Women, Politics and American Society* (New York: Prentice Hall, 1995).

[24] *Brown* v. *Board of Education of Topeka II*, 349 U.S. 294 (1955).

[25] Quoted in Williams, *Eyes on the Prize*, p. 37.

[26] 358 U.S. 1 (1958).

Landmark Events in the Quest for Civil Rights: From 1954 to 1982

1954 ♦ *Brown v. Board of Education of Topeka I*

1955 ♦ *Brown v. Board of Education of Topeka II*
Rosa Parks arrested
Montgomery Bus Boycott begins

1960 ♦ First sit-ins

1961 ♦ Freedom sit-ins

1963 ♦ John F. Kennedy assassinated
March on Washington, D.C.
Martin Luther King, Jr. leads March on Birmingham
Betty Friedan's *The Feminine Mystique* published

1964 ♦ Martin Luther King, Jr. wins Nobel Peace Prize
Summer riots in Northern ghettos
Civil Rights Act of 1964
Twenty-fourth Amendment banning poll taxes ratified

1965 ♦ Voting Rights Act

1966 ♦ National Organization for Women formed
Black ghetto riots

1968 ♦ Martin Luther King, Jr. assassinated

1971 ♦ *Reed v. Reed*

1972 ♦ Equal Rights Amendment sent to states for ratification

1982 ♦ Equal Rights Amendment fails to be ratified

against the Constitution without violating his undertaking to support it." (Unanimous opinions are usually written and signed by a single justice.) The state's actions, thus, were ruled unconstitutional and its "evasive schemes" illegal.

The saga of Little Rock is telling and illustrative of the massive resistance to *Brown* and the NAACP throughout the South. It is hard to imagine these kinds of confrontations occurring today—a governor calling a press conference to announce that he would defy a federal order, a president sending in federal troops to protect the rights of African-American citizens against the state militia, and legislation requiring the NAACP to identify its members. All of this, including the violence that greeted the new students, was duly recorded in the press and on television in vivid detail. And it added fuel to the fire of opponents of racism throughout the South and elsewhere.

A New Move for African-American Rights

In 1955, soon after *Brown II*, in Montgomery, Alabama, the local NAACP's Youth Council advisor, Rosa Parks, wanted to challenge the constitutionality of the segregated bus system. So Parks and other NAACP officials began to raise money for litigation and made speeches around town to garner public support. On December 1, 1955, Rosa Parks made history when she refused to leave her seat on a bus to move to the back and make room for a white male passenger. Parks was arrested for violating an Alabama law banning integration of public facilities, including buses. After being freed on bond, Parks and the NAACP decided to enlist city clergy to help her cause. At the same time, 35,000 handbills calling for African Americans to boycott the Montgomery bus system on the day of Parks's trial were distributed. Black ministers used Sunday services to urge their members to support the boycott. That Monday, African Americans walked, carpooled, or used black-owned taxicabs. That night, local ministers decided that the boycott should be continued. A twenty-six-year-old minister, Martin Luther King, Jr., was selected to lead the newly formed "Montgomery Improvement Association." King was new to town, and church leaders had been looking for a way to get him more involved in civil rights work.

After a ruling from the U.S. Supreme Court that banned segregation on public buses operated by the city of Montgomery, Alabama, Rosa Parks, whose refusal to give up her seat on the bus sparked the Montgomery Bus Boycott, takes a seat on an integrated bus.

As the boycott dragged on, Montgomery officials and local business owners began to harass the city's African-American citizens. But King urged Montgomery's African-American citizens to continue their protest. The residents held out, despite suffering personal hardship for their actions, ranging from harassment to bankruptcy to job loss. In 1956, a federal court ruled that the segregated bus system violated the equal protection clause of the Fourteenth Amendment.[27] After a year of walking, African Americans ended their protest as the buses were ordered to integrate. The first effort at nonviolent protest had been successful.

Formation of New Groups. The recognition and respect that King earned within the African-American community helped him to launch the Southern Christian Leadership Conference (SCLC) in 1957, soon after the end of the Montgomery bus boycott. Unlike the NAACP, which had Northern origins and had come to rely largely on litigation as a means of achieving expanded equality, the SCLC had a Southern base and was rooted more closely in black religious culture. The SCLC's philosophy was reflective of King's growing belief in the importance of nonviolent protest.

On February 1, 1960, students at the all-black North Carolina Agricultural and Technical College participated in the first "sit-in." Angered by their inability to be served at local lunch counters and heartened by the success of the Montgomery bus boycott, African-American students marched to the local Woolworth's and ordered a cup of coffee. They were refused service. So they sat at the counter until police came and carted them off to jail. Soon thereafter, African-American college students around the South joined together to challenge the Jim Crow laws in the region. These mass actions immediately brought extensive attention from the national news media.

With the assistance of an $800 grant from the SCLC, over spring break 1960, 200 student delegates—black *and* white—met at Shaw University in North Carolina to consider recent sit-in actions and to plan for the future. Later that year, two more meetings were held in Atlanta, Georgia, and the Student Nonviolent Coordinating Committee (SNCC) was formed.

---

[27] *Browder v. Gayle*, 142 F. Supp. 707 (1956).

Among SNCC's first leaders were Marion Barry, who was to serve as mayor of Washington, D.C. (1978–1990); John Lewis, who at this writing is a member of Congress serving as the Deputy House Majority Whip; and Marian Wright Edelman (a close friend of Bill and Hillary Rodham Clinton), who became first an NAACP lawyer and later the founder and head of the Children's Defense Fund. While the SCLC generally worked with church leaders in a community, SNCC was much more of a grassroots organization. Always perceived as more radical than the SCLC, SNCC tended to focus its organizing activities on the young, both black and white.

In addition to joining the sit-in bandwagon, SNCC also came to lead what were called "freedom rides," designed to focus attention on segregated public accommodations. Bands of college students and other civil rights activists traveled throughout the South by bus in an effort to force bus stations to desegregate. These protesters were frequently met with brutal violence as local police chose not to defend protesters' basic constitutional rights to free speech and peaceful assembly against angry mobs of segregationists. Not only African Americans participated in these freedom rides; increasingly, white college students from the North began to play an important role in SNCC.

While SNCC continued to sponsor sit-ins and freedom rides, in 1963 Martin Luther King, Jr. launched a series of massive nonviolent demonstrations in Birmingham, Alabama, long considered a major stronghold of segregation. Thousands of blacks and whites marched to Birmingham in a show of solidarity. Peaceful marchers were met there by Birmingham Police Commissioner Eugene "Bull" Conner, who ordered his officers to use dogs, clubs, fire hoses, and other tactics on the marchers, whose ranks included small children. All the marchers, including the children, suffered at the hands of local police. Americans across the nation watched in horror as they witnessed the brutality and abuse heaped on the protestors. As the marchers hoped, these shocking scenes helped convince President John F. Kennedy to propose important civil rights legislation.

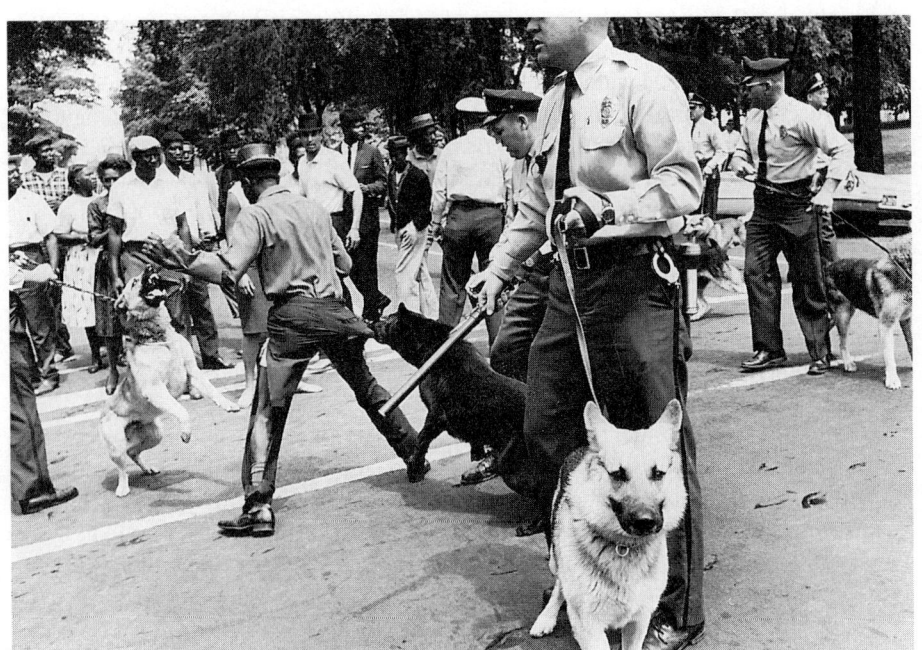

A prime objective of the protesters in Birmingham was to focus national attention on their cause. For the first time in American history, a majority of the public owned television sets and could see the horrors of police brutality. But the print media continued to be a powerful tool. This picture was reprinted over and over again and even frequently mentioned on the floor of Congress during debates on the Civil Rights Act of 1964.

The Civil Rights Act of 1964

At this historic gathering in March, 1963, on the Mall in Washington D.C., Martin Luther King, Jr. delivered his famous "I Have a Dream" speech.

The older faction of the civil rights movement, as represented by the SCLC, and the younger branch, represented by SNCC, both sought a similar goal: implementation of Supreme Court decisions and an end to racial segregation and discrimination. The cumulative effect of collective actions such as sit-ins, boycotts, marches, and freedom rides—as well as the tragic bombings and deaths inflicted in retaliation—led to congressional passage of the first major piece of civil rights legislation since the post-Civil War era.

In 1963, President Kennedy requested that Congress pass a law banning discrimination in public accommodations. Seizing the moment and recognizing the potency of a show of massive support, Martin Luther King, Jr. called for a monumental march on Washington, D.C., to demonstrate widespread support for legislation to ban discrimination in *all* aspects of life, not just public accommodations. Held only four months after the Birmingham demonstrations, the "March on Washington for Jobs and Freedom" was attended by more than 250,000 people, who heard King's immortal "I Have a Dream" speech, delivered from the Lincoln Memorial. Before Congress had the opportunity to vote on any legislation, however, Kennedy was assassinated in Dallas, Texas.

It was clear that national laws outlawing discrimination were the only answer, because Southern legislators would never vote to repeal Jim Crow laws. It was much more feasible for African Americans to seek national laws and then their implementation from the federal judiciary. But through the 1960s, African Americans lacked sufficient political power or the force of public opinion to sway enough congressional leaders. Their task was further stymied by loud and strong opposition from Southern members of Congress, many of whom, because of the Democratic Party's total control of the South, had been in office far longer than most, and therefore held powerful committee chairmanships that were awarded on seniority. The Senate Judiciary Committee was controlled by a coalition of Southern Democrats and conservative Republicans, and the House Rules Committee was chaired by a Virginian who was opposed to any civil rights legislation and who, by virtue of his position, could block such legislation in committee.

When Vice President Lyndon B. Johnson, a Southern-born former Senate majority leader, succeeded John F. Kennedy as president, he put civil rights reform at the top of his legislative priority list, and civil rights activists gained a critical ally. Thus, through the 1960s, the movement subtly changed in focus from peaceful protest and litigation to legislative lobbying. Now its focus had broadened from integration of school and public facilities and voting rights to issues of housing, jobs, and equal opportunity.

The push for civil rights legislation in the halls of Congress was also helped by changes in public opinion. As illustrated in Figure 5-1, between 1959 and 1965, Southern attitudes toward integrated schools had changed enormously as the proportion of Southerners who responded that they would not mind their child's attendance at a half-black school doubled.

In spite of strong presidential support and the sway of public opinion, however, the Civil Rights Act of 1964 did not sail through Congress easily. Southern senators, led by South Carolina's Strom Thurmond, a Democrat who later switched to the Republican Party, conducted the longest filibuster in the history of the Senate. For eight weeks they held up voting on the bill until cloture (see Chapter 6) was invoked and the filibuster was brought to an end. Once passed, the **Civil Rights Act of 1964:**

FIGURE 5-1

Attitudes of Whites to Integrated Education, North and South

Reprinted by permission of the publishers from, *Racial Attitudes in America; Trends and Interpretations* by Howard Schuman, Charlotte Steeh, and Lawrence Bobo, Cambridge, Mass: Harvard University Press, copyright © 1985 by the President and Fellows of Harvard College.

- Barred discrimination based on race, color, religion, or national origin in the "full and equal enjoyment" of goods and services in any public accommodation.
- Authorized the Attorney General to initiate lawsuits to force desegregation of public schools on behalf of private individuals.
- Made illegal the use of literacy tests or other administrative devices or tests designed to impede minority voting.
- Barred discrimination in any program or activity receiving federal assistance.
- Prohibited discrimination in employment on grounds of race, color, religion, national origin, or sex.
- Created the Equal Employment Opportunity Commission (EEOC) to monitor and enforce the bans on employment discrimination.

While these changes were occurring in the law, other changes were sweeping the nation. Violence began to rock the country as ghetto riots broke out in the Northeast. Although Northern African Americans were not subject to Jim Crow laws, many lived in poverty and faced pervasive daily discrimination and its resultant frustration. Some, including Malcolm X, even argued that to survive, African Americans must separate themselves in every way from white culture. Thus, given a growing "black power" movement and increased racial tensions, it is not surprising that from 1964 to 1968, many Northern African Americans took to the streets, burning and looting to vent their rage.

Violence also marred the continued activities of civil rights workers in the South. During the summer of 1964 three civil rights workers—one black, two white—were killed in Neshoba County, Mississippi. In 1965, King again led his supporters on a massive march, this time from Selma to the Alabama state capital in Montgomery, in support of additional voting rights protections. Again, Southern officials unleashed a reign of terror in Selma as they used whips, dogs, cattle prods, clubs, and tear gas to deter the protestors. One marcher was killed. Again, Americans watched in horror as

Controversial Black Muslim leader, Malcolm X.

they witnessed this brutality on their television screens. This march and the public's reaction to it led to quick passage of the Voting Rights Act of 1965, which suspended the use of literacy tests and authorized the federal government to monitor all elections in areas where discrimination was found to be practiced or where less than 50 percent of the voting-age public was registered to vote in the 1964 election. (For more on the effect of the Voting Rights Act, see Chapter 12).

The Effect of the Civil Rights Act of 1964

Many Southerners were adamant in their belief that the 1964 and 1965 Acts were unconstitutional because they went beyond the scope of Congress's authority to legislate under the Constitution.

Public Accommodations. The Supreme Court heard the first challenge to the Civil Rights Act of 1964 on an expedited review (which bypasses the intermediate courts). In *Heart of Atlanta Motel* v. *United States* (1964),[28] the operator of a hotel that refused African-American guests asked the Court to rule Section 2 of the Act, barring discrimination in public accommodations, unconstitutional. Hotel attorneys argued that the Act exceeded congressional authority granted by the commerce clause to "regulate interstate commerce." The Court disagreed and found that Congress was acting within the scope of its authority when it acted to prohibit discrimination in any commercial enterprises engaged in interstate commerce.

Education. One of the key provisions of the Civil Rights Act of 1964, Title VI, authorized the U.S. Justice Department to bring actions against school districts that had not complied with *Brown* v. *Board of Education*. In 1964, a full decade after *Brown*, fewer than 1 percent of African-American children in the South attended integrated schools.[29]

In 1968, the Supreme Court ruled that a "freedom of choice plan" under which pupils could choose which school they attended was unconstitutional when it resulted in schools with an overwhelming majority of either black or white students.[30] And in 1969, the Supreme Court ruled unanimously that state-sanctioned dual school systems must cease immediately.[31]

Just two years later, in *Swann* v. *Charlotte-Mecklenburg School District* (1971),[32] the Supreme Court ruled that lower federal courts could order busing as an appropriate remedy to end dual, segregated school systems. After *Brown*, the school board assigned students to schools closest to their homes without regard to race, leaving over half of African-American students attending schools at least 99 percent black. In interpreting Title VI's provisions, the Court ruled that because the school district formerly had engaged in intentional, statutory discrimination (***de jure***, or *by law*, **discrimination**), the continued presence of so many all black or white schools created a legal presumption that the school board intended to discriminate.

---

[28] 379 U.S. 241 (1964).
[29] Paul Brest and Sanford Levinson, *Processes of Constitutional Decision-making*, 2nd ed. (Boston: Little, Brown, 1983), pp. 471-480.
[30] *Green* v. *County School Board*, 391 U.S. 430 (1968).
[31] *Alexander* v. *Holmes County Board of Education*, 396 U.S. 19 (1969).
[32] 402 U.S. 1 (1971).

The Supreme Court ruled that busing was an appropriate remedy only when the discrimination was a result of *de jure* discrimination. In *Swann*, the Court was careful to distinguish *de jure* from **de facto discrimination**, unintentional discrimination often attributable to housing patterns and/or private acts. The Court was careful to note its approval of busing as a remedy for intentional, governmental-imposed or -sanctioned discrimination. The Court did not, however, address the question of where busing was an appropriate remedy if it was the result of *de facto* discrimination.

Swann actually signalled the end of an era. In the South, *Brown I* and *Brown II* had been stunningly successful. By 1971, 44 percent of the black students in the South attended majority white schools; only 28 percent in the North and West did.[33] The distinction between *de jure* and *de facto* discrimination became critical as the Justice Department and the NAACP LDF turned their attention to segregated school systems north of the Mason-Dixon line. In *Keyes* v. *School District No. 1, Denver, Colorado* (1973),[34] the Court ruled that the school board's maintenance of segregated schools through racially gerrymandered (see Chapter 6) school district attendance zones was *de jure* discrimination. Thus, a rash of lawsuits was filed around the North and West by African-American parents seeking an end to segregated schools. One federal district court after another ordered busing or other forms of remedial action, including the creation of magnet schools to draw white students into black neighborhoods.

Busing, however, soon became a highly emotional issue. Few parents want to see their child bused, and most Americans argue that it is better for children to attend schools close to their homes. In fact, the relative quality of local school districts is often the reason why many families move to particular neighborhoods or localities. When busing was ordered in urban school districts, many whites fled to the suburbs. And the Supreme Court found that federal courts lacked the authority to impose interdistrict remedies for school segregation without a showing of an interdistrict violation of the law.[35] A suburban majority white school district, for example, could not be ordered to merge with a city school district where intentional discrimination was present, making truly integrated schools more difficult to achieve. For example, in the late 1970s, the public elementary school population of Atlanta, Georgia, was approximately 90 percent black, whereas the student population in school districts in the areas that ringed the city ranged from 5 to 30 percent black. Clearly, it would be useless to order busing within Atlanta alone. So, the NAACP and the American Civil Liberties Union asked the federal courts to require busing between the surrounding areas and the city. The Supreme Court rejected this plea because there was no showing of intentional discrimination on the part of the outlying school districts.[36]

Over the years, forced, judicially imposed busing has found less and less favor with the Supreme Court, even in situations where *de jure* discrimination had earlier been proven. In 1992, the U.S. Supreme Court even ruled that in situations where all-black schools still existed after having been under a court order since 1969 to dismantle the *de jure* system, a showing that the persistent segregation was not a result of the board's actions was sufficient to remove the district from court supervision.[37]

---

[33] See Remarks of Sen. John Stennis, 18 *Cong. Record*, sec. 564, January 20, 1972.
[34] 413 U.S. 189 (1973).
[35] *Milliken* v. *Bradley*, 418 U.S. 717 (1974).
[36] *Armour* v. *Nix*, 448 U.S. 908 (1980).
[37] *Freeman* v. *Pitts*, 112 S. Ct. 1430 (1992).

Employment. Title VII of the Civil Rights Act of 1964 prohibits employers from discriminating against employees for a variety of reasons, including race, sex, age, and national origin. (In 1978 the Act was amended to prohibit discrimination based on pregnancy.)

In one of the first major cases decided under the Act, the Supreme Court found that employers could be found liable for discrimination if the *effect* of their employment practices was to exclude African Americans from certain positions. So in *Griggs* v. *Duke Power Company* (1971),[38] African-American employees were allowed to use statistical evidence to show that they had been excluded from all but one department of Duke Power Company. Blacks were effectively kept out of all but low-paying, manual labor positions because the company instituted a high-school education requirement, or passing of a special test in order to be eligible for promotion. Many of the African-American applicants had been deeply affected by the inferior education provided by North Carolina segregated school systems and either had no high school diploma or scored badly on the test.

The Supreme Court ruled that although the tests did not *appear* to discriminate against African Americans, their effects—that there were no African-American employees in any other departments—were sufficient to shift the burden of proving lack of discrimination on the employer. Thus, the Duke Power Company would have to prove that the tests were "a business necessity" that had a "demonstrable relationship to successful performance" (of a particular job).

The notion of "business necessity" as set out in the Civil Rights Act of 1964 and interpreted by the federal courts was especially important for women. For years, women had been kept out of many occupations as employers argued that their customers preferred to deal with male personnel. Conversely, males were barred from flight-attendant positions because the airlines believed that passengers preferred to be served by women. The airlines justified their "females only" employment policy by noting that flyers often became nervous, and many male passengers would feel uneasy if they had to seek comfort from another male. Similarly, many large factories, manufacturing establishments, and police and fire departments refused outright to hire women by using arbitrary height and weight requirements. These height and weight requirements also often disproportionately affected Hispanics. Like the tests in *Griggs*, these requirements often could not be shown to be related to job performance and were eventually ruled illegal by the federal courts.

As noted earlier, one of the key provisions of the Civil Rights Act allowed the Justice Department and/or the **Equal Employment Opportunity Commission (EEOC)** to enforce key provisions of the Act. Employment discrimination litigation is very expensive and beyond the means of most salaried workers. Thus, if the EEOC chooses to enforce the law vigorously and bring cases on behalf of individuals, an employee's chances of proving discrimination increase tremendously, especially since the courts generally look with favor on claims brought by the U.S. government. In fact, the failure of the EEOC to investigate claims of sex discrimination contributed to the rise of the modern women's rights movement.

The Women's Rights Movement. Just as women had been involved in the abolitionist movement in the 1800s, women from all walks of life also participated in the civil rights movement. Women were important members of both SNCC and more tra-

---

[38] 401 U.S. 424 (1971).

ditional groups like the NAACP and the SCLC.[39] Yet they often found themselves treated as second-class citizens. At one point, Stokely Carmichael, chair of SNCC, openly proclaimed: "The only position for women in SNCC is prone."[40] Statements and attitudes like these led some women to found early women's liberation groups that were generally quite radical, small in membership, and not intended to use more conventional political tactics.

As discussed earlier, initial efforts to convince the Supreme Court to declare women enfranchised under the Fourteenth Amendment were uniformly unsuccessful. The paternalistic attitude of the Supreme Court, and perhaps society as well, continued well into the 1970s. As late as 1961, Florida required women who wished to serve on juries to travel to the county courthouse and register for that duty. In contrast, all men who were registered voters were automatically eligible to serve. When Gwendolyn Hoyt was convicted of bludgeoning her adulterous husband to death with a baseball bat, she appealed her conviction, claiming that the exclusion of women from juries prejudiced her case. She believed that female jurors—her peers—would have been more sympathetic to her and the emotional turmoil that led to her attack on her husband and her claim of "temporary insanity." She therefore argued that her trial by an all-male jury violated her rights as guaranteed by the Fourteenth Amendment. In rejecting her contention, Justice John Harlan (the grandson of the lone dissenting justice in *Plessy*) wrote in *Hoyt* v. *Florida* (1961):

> Despite the enlightened emancipation of women from the restrictions and protections of bygone years, and their entry into many parts of community life formerly considered to be reserved to men, a woman is still regarded as the center of home and family life.[41]

These kinds of attitudes and decisions were not sufficient to forge a new movement for women's rights. Shortly after *Hoyt*, however, three events occurred to move women to action. In 1961, soon after his election, President John Kennedy had created a President's Commission on the Status of Women. The Commission's report, *American Women*, released in 1963, documented pervasive discrimination against women in all walks of life. In addition, the civil rights movement and publication of Betty Friedan's *The Feminine Mystique* (1963),[42] which led some women to question their lives and status in society, added to their dawning recognition that something was wrong. Soon after, the Civil Rights Act of 1964 prohibited discrimination based not only on race, but also on sex. Ironically, that provision had been added to Title VII of the Civil Rights Act by Southern Democrats. These senators saw a prohibition against sex discrimination in employment as a joke, and viewed its addition as a means to discredit the entire Act and ensure its defeat. Thus it was added at the last minute, and female members of Congress seized the opportunity to garner support for the measure.

In 1966, after the Equal Employment Opportunity Commission failed to enforce Title VII as it applied to sex discrimination, women activists formed the National Organization for Women (NOW). From its inception, NOW was closely modeled on the NAACP. Women in NOW were quite similar to the founders of the NAACP; they wanted to work within the system to prevent discrimination. Initially, most of this

---

[39] Mary King, *Freedom Song* (New York: Morrow, 1987).
[40] Quoted in Jo Freeman, *The Politics of Women's Liberation* (New York: Longman, 1975), p. 57.
[41] 368 U.S. 57 (1960).
[42] New York: Dell, 1963.

Sargent © Austin-American Statesman. Reprinted with permission of Universal Syndicate. All rights reserved.

activity was geared toward two goals: achievement of equality through passage of an equal rights amendment to the Constitution, or by judicial decision. But because the Supreme Court failed to extend constitutional protections to women, the only recourse that remained was an amendment.

The Equal Rights Amendment (ERA). Not all women agreed with the notion of full equality for women. Members of the National Consumers' League, for example, feared that an ERA would invalidate protective legislation of the kind specifically ruled constitutional in *Muller* v. *Oregon* (1908). Nevertheless, from 1923 to 1972, a proposal for an equal rights amendment was made in every session of every Congress. Every president since Harry S Truman backed it, and by 1972, public opinion favored its ratification.

Finally, in 1972, in response to NOW, the National Women's Political Caucus, and a wide variety of other women's groups, Congress passed the Equal Rights Amendment by overwhelming majorities (84–8 in the Senate; 354–24 in the House).

The amendment provided that:

- Equality of rights under the law shall not be denied or abridged by the United States or by any state on account of sex.
- The Congress shall have the power to enforce, by appropriate legislation, the provisions of this article.

Within a year, twenty-two states had ratified the amendment, most by overwhelming margins. In *Roe* v. *Wade* (1973),[43] however, the Supreme Court decided that women had a constitutionally protected right to privacy that included the right to terminate a pregnancy. Almost overnight *Roe* gave the ERA's opponents political fuel. Although privacy rights and the ERA have nothing to do with each other, opponents effectively

---

[43] 410 U.S. 113 (1973).

persuaded many persons in states that had yet to ratify the Amendment that the two were linked. If abortion was legal, why not marriages between and adoptions by homosexuals? They also claimed that the ERA would force women out of their homes and into the workforce, as husbands would no longer be responsible for their wives' support.[44]

These arguments and the amendment's potential to make women eligible for the military draft brought the ratification effort to a near standstill. In 1974–1975, the amendment only squeaked through the Montana and North Dakota legislatures, and two states—Nebraska and Tennessee—voted to rescind their earlier ratifications.[45]

By 1978, one year before the deadline for ratification was to expire, thirty-five states—three short of the three-fourths necessary for ratification—had voted for the Amendment. Efforts in key states such as Illinois and Florida failed as opposition to the Amendment intensified.

Faced with the prospect of defeat, ERA supporters heavily lobbied Congress to extend the deadline. Congress extended the time period for ratification by three years, but to no avail. No additional states ratified the Amendment, but three more rescinded their votes.[46]

Thus, what began as a simple correction to the Constitution turned into a highly controversial proposed change. In spite of the fact that large numbers of the public favored the ERA, opponents needed to stall ratification in only thirteen states while supporters had to convince legislators in thirty-eight. Hurting the effort was the success that women's rights activists were having in the courts. When women first sought the ERA in the late 1960s, the Supreme Court had yet to rule that women were protected by the Fourteenth Amendment from any kind of discrimination, thus clearly showing the need for an amendment. But as the Court widened its interpretation of the Constitution to protect women from some sorts of discrimination, in the eyes of many the need for a new amendment became less urgent.

Litigation for Equal Rights. While several women's groups worked toward passage of the ERA, NOW and several other groups, including the Women's Rights Project of the American Civil Liberties Union (ACLU), formed litigating arms to pressure the courts. An immediate roadblock that women faced was the Supreme Court's interpretation of the equal protection clause of the Fourteenth Amendment.

The Equal Protection Clause and Constitutional Standards of Review

The Fourteenth Amendment protects all U.S. citizens from state action that violates equal protection of the laws. But early on, the Supreme Court decided that certain rights were entitled to a heightened standard of review. As early as 1937,[47] the Supreme Court recognized that certain rights were so fundamental that a very heavy burden would be placed on any government that sought to restrict those rights. When fundamental rights such as First Amendment freedoms or **suspect classifications** such

---

[44] Rex E. Lee, *A Lawyer Looks at the ERA* (Provo, UT: Brigham Young University Press, 1980).

[45] The U.S. Constitution is silent on the effect of a state's recision of its earlier ratification while an amendment is pending.

[46] See Jane J. Mansbridge, *Why We Lost the ERA* (Chicago: University of Chicago Press, 1986).

[47] *Palko* v. *Connecticut*, 302 U.S. 319 (1937).

as race are involved, the Court uses a heightened standard of review called **strict scrutiny** to determine the constitutional validity of the challenged practices, as detailed in Table 5.1. Beginning with *Brown* v. *Board of Education* (1954), the Supreme Court viewed race-based distinctions with strict scrutiny. In legal terms, this means that if a statute or governmental practice makes a classification based on race, the statute is presumed to be unconstitutional unless the state can provide "compelling affirmative justifications"—that is, unless the state can prove the law in question is necessary to accomplish a permissible goal. During the 1960s and into the 1970s, the Court routinely stuck down as unconstitutional practices and statutes that discriminated on the basis of race. "Whites only" public parks and recreational facilities, tax-exempt status for private schools that discriminated, and statutes prohibiting racial intermarriage were declared unconstitutional. In contrast, the Court refused even to consider the fact that the equal protection clause might apply to discrimination against women. Finally, in a case brought in 1971 by Ruth Bader Ginsburg as Director of the Women's Rights Project of the ACLU (see "The American Civil Liberties Union," p. 126), the Supreme Court ruled that an Idaho law granting male parents automatic preference over female parents as the administrator of their deceased children's estates violated the equal protection clause of the Fourteenth Amendment.

Table 5.1 ♦ The Equal Protection Clause and Standards of Review Used by the Supreme Court to Determine If It Has Been Violated

TYPES OF CLASSIFICATION	STANDARD OF REVIEW	TEST	EXAMPLE
What kind of statutory classification is an issue?	What standard of review will be used?	What does the court ask?	How does the court apply the test?
Fundamental freedoms: Religion, assembly, press, privacy, "suspect" classifications (including race)	Strict scrutiny or heightened standard	Is classification *necessary* to the accomplishment of a permissible state goal?	*Brown* v. *Board of Education* (1954) Racial segregation not necessary to accomplish the state goal of educating its students
Gender	Intermediate standard	Does it serve an important governmental objective, and is it substantially related to those ends?	*Craig* v. *Boren* (1976) Keeping drunk drivers off the roads may be an important governmental objective, but allowing eighteen- to twenty-one-year-old women to drink alcoholic beverages while prohibiting men of the same age from drinking is not substantially related to that goal.
Others (including age, wealth, and sexual preference)	Minimum rationality standard	Is there any rational foundation for the discrimination?	*Bowers* v. *Hardwick* (1986) It is rational for Georgia to prohibit consensual sodomy because of traditional taboos against homosexual behavior.

Reed v. *Reed* (1971),[48] the Idaho case, turned the tide in terms of constitutional litigation. While the Court did not rule that sex was a suspect classification, it concluded that the equal protection clause of the Fourteenth Amendment prohibited unreasonable classifications based on sex. And in 1976, the Court ruled that sex-discrimination complaints would be judged by a new, judicially created intermediate standard of review a step below strict scrutiny. In *Craig* v. *Boren* (1976),[49] the owner of the Honk 'n' Holler Restaurant in Stillwater, Oklahoma, and Craig, a male under twenty-one, challenged the constitutionality of a state law prohibiting the sale of 3.2 percent beer to males under the age of twenty-one and to females under the age of eighteen. The state introduced a considerable amount of evidence in support of the statute, including:

- Eighteen- to twenty-year–old males were more likely to be arrested for driving under the influence than were females of the same age.
- Youths aged seventeen to twenty-one were the group most likely to be injured or to die in alcohol-related traffic accidents, with males exceeding females.
- Young men were more inclined to drink and drive than females.

The Supreme Court found that this information was "too tenuous" to support the legislation. In coming to this conclusion, the Court carved out a new "test" to be used in examining claims of sex discrimination. According to the Court, "[T]o withstand constitutional challenge, . . . classifications by gender must serve important governmental objectives and must be substantially related to achievement of those objectives." As *Craig* demonstrates, men, too, can use the Fourteenth Amendment to fight gender-based discrimination. Since 1976, the Court has applied that intermediate standard to most claims that it has heard involving gender. Thus, the following kinds of practices have been found to violate the Fourteenth Amendment:

- Single-sex public nursing schools.
- Laws that consider males adults at twenty-one years but females at eighteen years.
- Laws that allow women but not men to receive alimony.
- State prosecutors' use of pre-emptory challenges to reject men or women to create more sympathetic juries.

In contrast, the Court has upheld the following governmental practices and laws:

- Draft registration provisions for males only.
- Statutory rape laws that apply only to female victims.

The level of review used by the Court is crucial. Clearly, a statute excluding African Americans from draft registration would be unconstitutional. But, because gender is not subject to the same higher standard of review that is used in racial discrimination cases, the exclusion of women from the requirements of the Military Selective Service Act was ruled permissible because the government policy was considered to serve "important governmental objectives."[50]

---

[48] 404 U.S. 71 (1971).
[49] 429 U.S. 190 (1976).
[50] *Rostker* v. *Goldberg*, 453 U.S. 57 (1981).

Cartoonists around the nation poked fun at the all-male Senate Judiciary Committee's insensitive treatment of Anita Hill during Clarence Thomas's nomination hearings to the U.S. Supreme Court.

Don Wright, *The Palm Beach Post.*

This history has perhaps clarified why women's rights activists continue to argue that until the passage of an equal rights amendment, women will never enjoy the same rights as men. An amendment would automatically raise the level of scrutiny that the Court applies to gender-based claims.

Statutory Remedies for Sex Discrimination. In part because of the limits of the intermediate standard of review and the fact that the equal protection clause applies only to *governmental* discrimination, women's rights activists began to bombard the courts with sex-discrimination cases. These cases have been filed under Title VII of the Civil Rights Act, which prohibits discrimination by private (and, after 1972, public) employers, or Title IX of the Education Amendments of 1972, which bars educational institutions receiving federal funds from discriminating against female students. Key victories under Title VII include:

- Consideration of sexual harassment as discrimination.
- Inclusion of law firms, which many argued were *private* partnerships, in the coverage of the Act.
- A broad definition of what can be considered sexual harassment.
- Allowance of voluntary affirmative action programs to redress historical discrimination against women.

Title IX, which parallels Title VII, has also greatly expanded the opportunities for women in elementary, secondary, and post-secondary institutions. Since women's groups, like the NAACP before them, saw eradication of educational discrimination as key to improving other facets of women's lives, they lobbied for it heavily.[51] Most of today's college students did not go through school being excluded from home economics or shop classes on account of their sex. Nor, probably, did many attend schools that had no team sports for females. Yet, this was commonly the case in the United States prior to passage of Title IX.

---

[51] Joyce Gelb and Marian Lief Palley, "Women and Interest Group Politics: A Case Study of the Equal Credit Opportunity Act," *American Politics Quarterly* (July 1977): 336.

Other Groups Mobilize for Rights

African Americans and women are not the only groups that have suffered unequal treatment under the law. Denial of civil rights has led many other disadvantaged groups to mobilize to achieve greater civil rights. And their efforts to achieve those rights have many parallels to the efforts made by African Americans and women. In the wake of the successes of those two groups in achieving greater rights, and sometimes even before, other traditionally disenfranchised groups have organized to gain fuller equality. Many of them have also recognized that litigation and the use of test-case strategies would be key to further civil rights gains. The Ford Foundation, which had heavily funded the NAACP LDF and some women's rights litigation, also helped interested Mexican-Americans to found the Mexican American Legal Defense and Education Fund (MALDEF). Established in 1968, and modeled after the NAACP LDF, MALDEF has played and continues to play a major role in expanding civil rights for Hispanics. The Ford Foundation also facilitated the 1970 creation of the Native American Rights Fund to litigate for Indian rights.

Native Americans

Native Americans are the first "true" Americans, and their status under U.S. law is unique. Under the U.S. Constitution, "Indian tribes" are considered distinct governments, which has affected Native Americans' treatment by the Supreme Court in contrast to other groups of ethnic minorities. And "minority" is truly a term that accurately describes American Indians. It is estimated that there were as many as 10 million Indians in the New World at the time it was discovered with 3 to 4 million living in what is today the United States. By 1900, the number in the continental United States had plummeted to less than 2 million, as shown in Figure 5-2.

Many commentators would agree that for years the Congress and the courts manipulated Indian law to promote the westward expansion of the United States. The Northwest Ordinance of 1787, passed by the Continental Congress, specified that "the good faith should always be observed toward the Indians; their lands and property shall never be taken from them without their consent, and their property rights, and liberty, they shall never be invaded or disturbed, unless in just and lawful wars authorized by Congress" . . .[52] This is not what happened. Instead, over the years "American Indian policy has been described as 'genocide-at-law' promoting both land acquisition and cultural extermination."[53] At first, during the eighteenth and nineteenth centuries, the U.S. government isolated Indians on reservations as it confiscated their lands and denied them basic political rights. Indian reservations were administered by the federal government and Native Americans often lived in squalid conditions.

With passage of the Dawes Act in 1887, however, the government switched policies to promote assimilation over separation. Each Indian family was given land within the reservation; the rest was sold to whites, thus reducing Indian lands from about 140 million acres to about 47 million. Moreover, to encourage Native Americans' "assimilation," Indian children were sent to boarding schools off the reservation, and native

---

[52] U.S. Senate, Subcommittee on Indian Education, *Indian Education: A National Tragedy—A National Challenge*, 91st Congress, 1st Session, (1969), p. 9.

[53] Rennard J. Strickland, "Native Americans," in Kermit L. Hall, ed., *The Oxford Companion to the Supreme Court of the United States* (New York: Oxford University Press, 1992), p. 557.

188 ❖ Chapter 5 Civil Rights

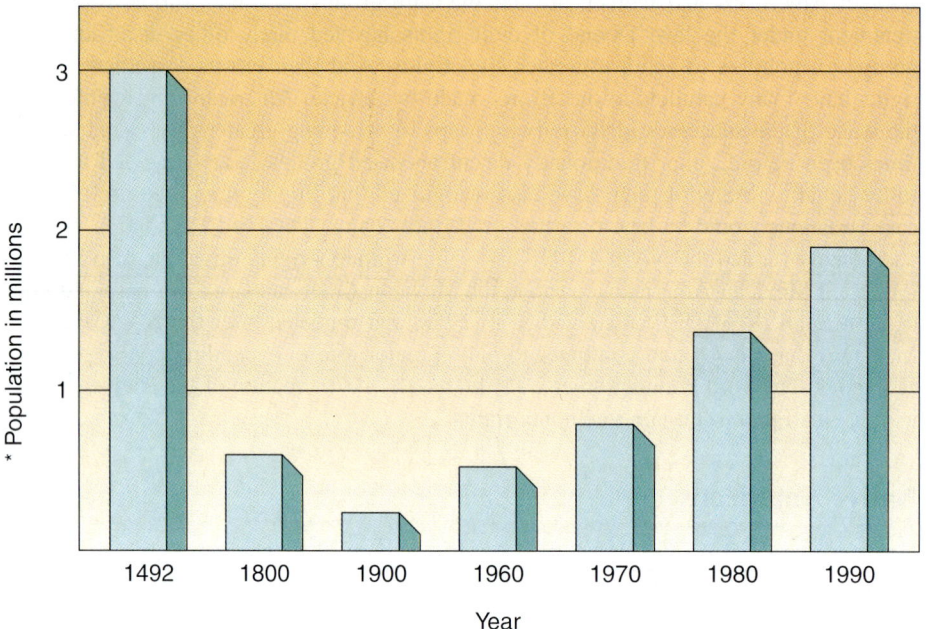

FIGURE 5-2
Native Americans in the United States*

* Numbers before 1900 based on historical estimates and Bureau of Indian Affairs data. Other data from U.S. Census Bureau reports.

languages and rituals were banned. In 1924, Native Americans were made U.S. citizens and given the right to vote.

At least in part because tribes were small and scattered (and the number of Indians declining), no protest movement was formed in reaction to these drastic policy changes. It was not until the 1960s, at the same time that women were beginning to mobilize for greater civil rights, that Indians too began to mobilize to act. And, like the civil rights and women's rights movements, it had a radical as well as a more traditional branch. In the late 1960s, for example, a small band of Indians occupied Alcatraz Island, claiming it as part of their ancestral lands. In 1972, several hundred Indians marched to Washington, D.C. to "sit in" at the Bureau of Indian Affairs to draw attention to government mistreatment. And in 1973, national attention was drawn to the plight of Indians when members of the radical American Indian Movement took over Wounded Knee, South Dakota, the site of the massacre of 150 Indians by the U.S. government army in 1890. Just two years before the protest, the treatment of Indians had been highlighted in the best-selling *Bury My Heart at Wounded Knee*,[54] which in many ways served to mobilize public opinion against the oppression of Native Americans the same way *Uncle Tom's Cabin* had against slavery.

---

[54] Dee Brown, *Bury My Heart at Wounded Knee* (New York: Holt, Rinehart and Winston, 1971).

Native Americans in Washington, D.C. protest the name of the Washington Redskins football team. Similar demonstrations took place in other cities with team names offensive to Native Americans and at least one newspaper has refused to refer to offending teams by any name other than their city.

At the same time, just as the growing number of women in the legal profession contributed to the push to secure greater rights for women through litigation, Indians, many attracted by the American Indian Law Center at the University of New Mexico, began to file hundreds of test cases in the federal courts involving tribal fishing rights, tribal land claims, and the taxation of tribal profits. Soon, the Native American Rights Fund (NARF), founded in 1970, became the NAACP LDF of the Indian rights movement as the "courts became the forum of choice for Indian tribes and their members."[55]

Native Americans have won some very important victories concerning hunting, fishing, and land rights (as discussed in "Then and Now," p. 190). Native American tribes all over America have begun to sue to reclaim lands they say were stolen from them by the U.S., often more than 200 years ago. Communities all over the U.S. have been entering into agreements to settle these suits, which cloud the titles to all properties in issue.

Native Americans have not fared nearly so well in areas such as religious freedom, especially where tribal practices come into conflict with state law. As noted in Chapter 4, the Supreme Court has limited their use of peyote in religious ceremonies and their access to religious sites during timber harvesting, but Congress has acted to restore some of those rights.

Given the uncertain and uneven treatment of Indians by the U.S Supreme Court, in the 1990s Congress has replaced the courts as the preferred forum of Native Americans. The 1992 election of Ben Nighthorse Campbell (D-Colo.) as the only Native

---

[55] Strickland, "Native Americans," p. 579.

THEN AND NOW

Native Americans and Land Rights

When Americans first began colonizing what is now the United States, Indians populated the land from Maine to Florida, and from the Carolinas to the west coast. Of the nearly 2 billion acres controlled by Indians 500 years ago, by 1900 they had but 140 million acres. Today, less than 50 million acres are controlled by Indian tribes as tribe after tribe was forced off its lands. "Land is the basis of all things Indian," concluded a Citizens Advisory Report in 1969. Moreover, an integral part of many tribes' beliefs is that most land is sacred. The relationship of a tribe to its land defines the tribe. In 1993, only 287 federal Indian reservations existed in the United States. It is not surprising, then, that since the 1970s, Native Americans have been litigating against the United States over two major questions in the land area: (1) In the eastern states, are the treaties ceding lands to white settlers valid? and (2) In the west, where most Indians were forced to live on reservations, were the treaties violated, and if so, how should tribes be compensated? This litigation has produced some strange allies and some surprising victories.

One of the largest Indian land claims lawsuits was filed in 1972 on behalf of the Passamaquoddie and the Penobscot tribes, who were seeking return of 12.5 million acres in Maine—about two-thirds of the entire state—and 25 billion dollars in damages. The suit was filed by the Native American Rights Fund and the Indian Service Unit of a legal services office that was funded by the U.S. Office of Economic Opportunity. It took intervention from the White House before a settlement was reached in 1980, giving each tribe over 40 million dollars.

Native Americans are also litigating to gain access to their sacred places. All over the nation they have filed lawsuits to stop the building of roads and new construction on ancient burial grounds or other sacred spots. "We are in a battle for the survival of our very way of life," said one tribal leader. "The land is gone. All we've got left is our religion."*

* Hugh Dellios, "Rites by Law: Indians Seek Sacred Lands," *Chicago Tribune* (July 4, 1993): C-1.

American in the U.S. Senate should heighten legislative sensitivity to these issues. Campbell, for example, introduced a bill to prevent the U.S. government from transferring property to facilitate building a new football stadium for the Washington Redskins unless the team's owner changes the name, which Campbell considers derogatory to Native Americans.

Hispanic Americans

Like women's efforts to garner expanded political rights, Hispanic Americans, too, can date their first real push for equal rights to 1965–1975. This civil rights movement included many tactics drawn from the African-American civil rights movement, including sit-ins, boycotts, marches, and other activities designed to attract publicity to their cause.[56] Like blacks, women, and Native Americans, Hispanic Americans have some

[56] F. Chris Garcia, *Latinos and the Political System* (Notre Dame: University of Notre Dame Press, 1988), p. 1.

radical militant groups, but have been dominated by more conventional organizations. The more conventional groups have pressed for Chicano and Latino studies programs and have built up ties with existing, powerful mainstream associations, including unions and the Roman Catholic church.

They have also relied heavily on litigation to secure greater rights. Key groups are the Mexican American Legal Defense and Educational Fund (MALDEF) and the Puerto Rican Legal Defense and Educational Fund.

MALDEF was founded in 1968 after members of the League of United Latin American Citizens (LULAC), the nation's largest and oldest Hispanic organization, met with NAACP LDF leaders and, with their assistance, secured a $2.2 million start-up grant from the Ford Foundation. Not only was MALDEF helped into being by the NAACP LDF, but like women's groups that were beginning to litigate for expanded civil rights, it was modeled after the older organization. It was created to bring test cases to force school districts to allocate more funds to schools with predominantly low-income minority populations, to implement bilingual education programs, to force employers to hire Chicanos, and to challenge election rules and apportionment plans that undercount or dilute Hispanic voting power.[57] Just as Native American and women's rights groups had depended on the legal expertise of their own constituents, MALDEF quickly drew on the talent of Hispanic attorneys to staff offices in San Antonio and Los Angeles. It also started a scholarship fund to train more Hispanic attorneys, and established a New Mexico branch office in conjunction with the New Mexico Law School.

MALDEF lawyers quickly moved to bring major test cases to the U.S. Supreme Court, both to enhance the visibility of their cause and to win cases. MALDEF has been quite successful in its efforts to expand voting rights and opportunities to Hispanic-Americans. In 1973, for example, it won a major victory when the Supreme Court ruled that multi-member electoral districts (in which more than one person represents a single district) in Texas discriminated against African Americans and Hispanic Americans.[58] In multi-member systems, legislatures generally add members to larger districts instead of drawing smaller districts in which a minority candidate could get a majority of the votes necessary to win.

MALDEF, LULAC, and other civil rights groups have successfully challenged election plans that make it more difficult for Hispanics to win elective office. LULAC has played a key role in legislative redistricting and has joined with MALDEF when court action is necessary. In 1990, for example, a U.S. Court of Appeals ruled that Los Angeles County's governing body intentionally diluted Hispanic voting strength (Hispanics made up one-third of the county's population) when it redrew county election districts after the 1980 census. Nine candidates—eight of them Hispanic—ran in the new district the county was forced to create.

While enjoying greater access to elective office (see Chapter 12), Hispanics still suffer discrimination. Language barriers and substandard educational opportunities continue to plague their progress. In 1973, for example, the U.S. Supreme Court refused to find that a Texas law under which the state appropriated a set dollar amount to each school district per pupil, while allowing wealthier districts to enrich educational pro-

School boards have been taken to court to compel them to provide education to the children of illegal aliens.

---

[57] See Karen O'Connor and Lee Epstein, "A Legal Voice for the Chicano Community: The Activities of the Mexican-American Legal Defense and Educational Fund, 1968–1982," *Social Science Quarterly* 65 (June 1984): 245–256.

[58] *White* v. *Regester*, 412 U.S. 755 (1973).

grams from other funds, violated the equal protection clause of the Fourteenth Amendment.[59] The lower courts had found that wealth was a suspect classification (see Table 5.1) entitled to strict scrutiny. Using that test, the court had found the Texas plan discriminatory. In contrast, a divided Supreme Court concluded that education was not a fundamental right (see Chapter 4), and that a charge of discrimination based on wealth would be examined only under a minimal standard of review (the rational basis test).

Throughout the 1970s and 1980s, inter-school-district inequalities continued, and often had their greatest impact on poor Hispanic children, who often had inferior educational opportunities. Recognizing that the increasingly conservative federal courts (see Chapter 9) offered no recourse, in 1984 MALDEF filed suit in *state* court alleging that the Texas school finance policy violated the Texas constitution. In 1989, it won a case in which a state district judge elected by the voters of only a single county declared the state's entire method of financing public schools to be unconstitutional under the state constitution.[60]

Homosexuals

Homosexuals have had an even harder time than African Americans, women, Native Americans, or Hispanics in achieving fuller rights. Gays do, however, have on average far higher household incomes and educational levels than do these other groups. And they are beginning to convert these advantages into political clout at the ballot box. As discussed in Chapter 4 (pp. 145–146), the cause of gay and lesbian rights, like that of African Americans and women early in their quest for greater civil rights, did not fare well in the Supreme Court. In the late 1970s, the Lambda Legal Defense and Education Fund, the Lesbian Rights Project, and Gay and Lesbian Advocates and Defenders were founded by gay and lesbian activists dedicated to ending legal restrictions on the civil rights of homosexuals. Although these groups have won important legal victories concerning HIV/AIDS discrimination, insurance policy survivor benefits, and even some employment issues, they generally have not been as successful as other disadvantaged groups.

In *Bowers* v. *Hardwick* (1986),[61] for example, the Supreme Court ruled that a Georgia law that made private acts of consensual sodomy illegal (whether practiced by homosexuals or by heterosexual married adults) was constitutional. Gay and lesbian rights groups had argued that a constitutional right to privacy included the right to engage in consensual sex within one's home, but the Court disagreed. Although privacy rights may attach to relations of "family, marriage, or procreation," those rights did not extend to homosexuals, wrote Justice Byron White for the Court. In a concurring opinion—his last written on the Court—Chief Justice Warren Burger called sodomy "the infamous crime against nature."

The public's and Congress's discomfort with gay and lesbian rights can be seen most clearly in the controversy that occurred after Bill Clinton attempted to lift the ban on gays in the armed services. Clinton tried to get an absolute ban on discrimination against homosexuals, who were subject to immediate discharge if their sexual orientation was discovered. Military leaders and Senator Sam Nunn (D-Ga.), head of the Senate Armed Services Committee, led the effort against Clinton's proposal. Eventually,

---

[59] *San Antonio Independent School District* v. *Rodriguez,* 411 U.S. 1 (1973).
[60] *Edgewood Independent School District* v. *Kirby,* 777 S. W. 2d 391 (1989).
[61] 478 U.S. 186 (1986).

In May 1993 members of ADAPT protested and marched in Washington, D.C. to draw attention to the need for full implementation of the Americans with Disabilities Act.

Clinton and the Senate leaders compromised on what was called the "don't ask, don't tell" policy. It stipulated that gays and lesbians would no longer be asked if they were homosexual, but barred them from revealing their sexual orientation (under threat of discharge from the service). But when the Senate finally voted on the "compromise," its version of the new policy labelled homosexuality "an unacceptable risk" to morale. In spite of gay and lesbian groups' labeling the new policy "lie and hide," the Clinton administration chose to back off on the issue, correctly sensing only minimal support in Congress.[62]

The Supreme Court's unwillingness to expand privacy rights or special constitutional protections to homosexuals, and Congress's failure to end discrimination in the military, has led many gay and lesbian rights groups to other, potentially more responsive, political forums: state and local governments. Around the nation, such groups have lobbied for anti-discrimination legislation with mixed success. In 1992 in Colorado, for example, voters passed a state constitutional amendment that rescinded several local gay and lesbian rights ordinances and prevents the adoption of any such measures. (It was, however, declared unconstitutional the following year by a federal district court.) Generally, gay and lesbian groups have been most successful in gaining anti-discrimination ordinances in cities like San Francisco and Atlanta, which have large gay populations although many city ordinances have faced constitutional challenge.

Disabled Americans

Disabled Americans also have lobbied hard for anti-discrimination legislation. In the aftermath of World War II, many veterans returned to a nation unequipped to handle

---

[62] Paul Quinn-Judge, "Senate OKs Tougher Version of Policy on Gays in Military," *The Boston Globe* (September 10, 1993): 6.

their disabilities. The Korean and especially the Vietnam Wars made the problems of disabled veterans all the more clear. These disabled veterans saw the successes of African Americans, women, and other minorities, and they too began to lobby for greater protection against discrimination. In 1990, in coalition with other disabled persons, veterans were finally able to convince Congress to pass the Americans with Disabilities Act. The statute defines a disabled person as someone with a physical or mental impairment that limits one or more "life activities," or who has a record of such impairment. It thus extends the protections of the Civil Rights Act of 1964 to all of those with physical or mental disabilities, including persons with AIDS. It guarantees access to public facilities, employment, and communication services. It also requires employers to acquire or modify work equipment, adjust work schedules, and make existing facilities accessible. Thus, buildings must be accessible to those in wheelchairs, and telecommunications devices provided for deaf employees, for example.

Changing laws alone, however, while often important first steps in achieving civil rights, is not the end of the process. Attitudes must also change. And, as history has shown, that can be a very long process. Stereotypes often are hard to eliminate.

The Politics of Civil Rights

The Civil Rights Act of 1964 was passed by a Democratic Congress at the urgings of a Democratic president, Lyndon B. Johnson. The Republican Nixon and Ford administrations were not avid supporters of some of the more sweeping provisions of the Act—especially those that were disfavored by employers, who often supported the Republican Party. But many perceived the Reagan and Bush administrations as particularly hostile to civil rights laws. In the 1980s, for example, the effectiveness of civil rights legislation was put in jeopardy.

In the late 1970s, the Democratic Carter administration moved to terminate all student loan moneys to students at Grove City College, a small religious school in Pennsylvania that accepted no direct federal funds. It refused public funds largely to assure its independence from federal rules and regulations. Many students in attendance, however, were eligible for federal student loans. When the university refused to sign a letter stating that it was in full compliance with Title IX, the Carter administration's Justice Department moved to terminate funds to the students at Grove City College. Students at the college sued. By the time the case reached the Supreme Court, Ronald Reagan had been elected president.

The Reagan administration abandoned the position taken by the Carter Justice Department and urged the Court to find that institutions receiving federal funds were not required to comply with the ever-widening net of anti-discrimination statutes that covered race, sex, age, disabilities, and national origin. Instead, the Court was asked to find that only those programs *directly* affected by the federal funding were bound by federal anti-discrimination provisions.

In a decision widely hailed by conservatives and bemoaned by civil rights activists, the Court agreed with the Reagan administration and limited the coverage of anti-discrimination statutes to the particular university programs directly receiving federal funds and not to the entire institution. In one fell swoop, the Court eviscerated one of the most potent weapons in the civil rights movement's arsenal—the potential withdrawal of thousands, and even millions, of dollars as penalties for noncompliance.

The Reagan administration's victory in *Grove City College* v. *Bell* (1984),[63] however, was short-lived. An angry Democratic House of Representatives quickly acted to pass the Civil Rights Restoration Act to overrule the decision. But, at the urging of the Reagan administration, the Republican-controlled Senate of the 98th and 99th Congresses failed to pass the Act. After the Democrats regained control of the Senate in the 1986 elections, in 1988 the Democratic 100th Congress passed the Civil Rights Restoration Act over the veto of President Reagan.

But a conservative Supreme Court continued to interpret civil rights statutes very narrowly, and even overruled several earlier landmark discrimination rulings. A particularly troublesome area of civil rights law was the concept of affirmative action.

Affirmative Action

The civil rights debate has often centered on the question of equality of opportunity versus equality of results. Most civil rights and women's rights organizations argue that the lingering and pervasive burdens of racism and sexism can be overcome only by taking race or gender into account in fashioning remedies for discrimination. They argue that the Constitution is not and should not be color- or sex-blind. Therefore, busing should be used to integrate schools, and women should be given child-care assistance to allow them to compete equally in the marketplace.

The counter-argument holds that if it was once wrong to use labels to discriminate against a group, it should be wrong to use those same labels to help a group. Laws should be neutral or color-blind. According to this view, quotas and other forms of **affirmative action**, policies designed to give special attention or compensatory treatment to members of a previously disadvantaged group, should be illegal. As early as 1871, Frederick Douglass ridiculed the idea of racial quotas, arguing that they would promote "an image of blacks as privileged wards of the state." They were "absurd as a matter of practice" because some could use them to argue that blacks "should constitute one-eighth of the poets, statesmen, scholars, authors and philosophers."

The debate over affirmative action and equality of opportunity became particularly intense during the Reagan years in the wake of two court cases that were generally decided in favor of affirmative action shortly before Reagan's election.

In 1978, the Supreme Court for the first time fully addressed the issue of affirmative action. Allen Bakke, a thirty-one–year-old paramedic, sought admission to several medical schools and was rejected because of his age. The next year, he applied to the University of California at Davis and was placed on its waiting list. The Davis Medical School maintained two separate admissions committees—one for white students and another for minority students. Bakke was not admitted to the school, although his grades and standardized test scores were higher than those of all of the African-American students admitted to the school. In *Regents of the University of California* v. *Bakke* (1978),[64] a sharply divided Court concluded that Bakke's rejection had been illegal because the use of strict quotas was inappropriate. The medical school, however, was free to "take race into account."

Bakke was quickly followed in 1979 by another case in which the Court ruled that a factory and a union could voluntarily adopt a quota system in selecting black workers over more senior white workers for a training program.[65]

Alan Bakke, whose initial rejection from law school led to an important Supreme Court ruling on affirmative action, was ultimately admitted to the medical school he sued. Here, he is shown at his 1982 medical school graduation. He did well enough in medical school to be selected to intern at the prestigious Mayo Clinic.

---

[63] 465 U.S. 555 (1984).
[64] 438 U.S. 265 (1978).
[65] *United Steelworkers of America* v. *Weber*, 443 U.S. 197 (1979).

For a while, the Court continued to uphold affirmative action plans, especially when there was clear-cut evidence of prior discrimination, although it was by five-to-four votes. And in 1987, in *Johnson* v. *Transportation Agency, Santa Clara County* (1987),[66] the Court for the first time ruled that a public employer could use a voluntary plan to promote women even if there was no judicial finding of prior discrimination.

In all these cases, the Reagan administration strongly urged the Court to invalidate the plans in question, but to no avail. With changes on the Court, however, including the 1986 elevation to Chief Justice of William Rehnquist, a strong opponent of affirmative action, the continued efforts of the Reagan administration finally began to pay off as the Court heard a new series of cases signaling an end to the advances in civil rights law. In a three-month period in 1989, the Supreme Court handed down five civil rights decisions limiting affirmative action programs and making it harder to prove employment discrimination.

The Legislative Response

In February 1990, congressional and civil rights leaders unveiled legislation designed to make it easier for minorities and women to fight job bias through the courts. In introducing the legislation, Senator Edward M. Kennedy (D.-Mass.) noted that the act was necessary to overrule the Court's rulings, which "were an abrupt and unfortunate departure from its historic vigilance in protecting"[67] the rights of minorities. The bill sought to blunt the effort of recent Court rulings by:

- Barring harassment or firing of employees based on racial bias. (The Court had ruled that the 1866 Civil Rights Act, used by a North Carolina credit union worker to press her racial-bias claim, barred only hiring discrimination, not on-the-job harassment.)
- Forcing employers to show that any practice with proven discriminatory impact was prompted by business necessity. (The Court had ruled that the burden of proof belongs with workers who allege they are the victims of discrimination.)
- Making it clear that it is always illegal to use race, ethnicity, gender, or religion as the criterion for employment decisions. (The Court had ruled that the burden of proof belongs to employers if accused of discriminating illegally in personnel decisions; however, the ruling was vague enough to confuse lower courts.)
- Making permanent the court-approved affirmative action plans designed to remedy discrimination. (The Court had made it easier for white men to challenge such plans years after they were put into effect.)
- Easing the deadlines for workers who sue over allegedly biased seniority systems. (The Court had ruled that the time frame for filing such lawsuits is determined by when a seniority plan is adopted, not when an individual worker is affected.)
- Assuring victims of intentional discrimination the right to sue for monetary damages.

The bill passed both houses of Congress but was vetoed by President Reagan's successor, George Bush, and Congress failed to override the veto. In late 1991, however, Congress and the White House reached a compromise on a weaker version of the civil rights bill, which was passed by overwhelming majorities in both the House (381–31) and Senate (93–5). The Civil Rights Act of 1991 overruled the Supreme Court rulings noted above, but specifically prohibited the use of quotas. And in the wake of the

---

[66] 480 U.S. 616 (1987).
[67] Ruth Marcus, "Hill Coalition Aims to Counter Court in Job Bias," *Washington Post* (February 8, 1990): A10.

Clarence Thomas hearings and their focus on sexual harassment, victims of sexual harassment were given the explicit right to sue for intentional discrimination. The new Act also made it easier for victims of discrimination to recover damages, which should encourage more victims of discrimination to sue.

Toward Reform

In March 1990, civil rights activists met in Selma, Alabama, to recreate the famous march from Selma to Birmingham on its twenty-fifth anniversary. Clearly, tremendous progress has been made in the years since so much blood was shed in Alabama. All around the nation, individuals who played major roles in the civil rights movement are in important positions of power. A new generation of African-American and female leaders is emerging as additional barriers continue to fall.

Women, too, are reaping the rewards of legislation and judicial interpretation. They are being elected or appointed to policy-making positions where they can be expected to continue to urge civil rights reform.

The civil rights movement has had international effects as well. In the late 1960s and 1970s, the leaders of racial minority communities in Britain consciously patterned their organizations on American models. Moreover, the urban riots that rocked Liverpool, Birmingham, and London during the 1980s evoked the image of those in the United States during the hot summers of the 1960s. The emerging British feminist movement also looked to the United States for both positive and negative lessons.

In this country, the political environment for minorities is changing as some begin to be assimilated, and more groups press for rights. The 1980s was not a good decade for most who advocated expanded civil rights. Presidents Reagan and Bush were not particularly receptive to the expansion of civil rights. Both men appointed conservatives to fill vacancies on the U.S. Supreme Court. George Bush's replacement for Thurgood Marshall, Clarence Thomas, the African-American former head of the EEOC, publicly stated his opposition to affirmative action and quotas prior to his appointment.

Not surprisingly, the election of President Bill Clinton in 1992 was met with elation by most civil rights activists. Clinton quickly moved to appoint more women and minorities to high-level positions than had any other president in history. He also appointed a longtime advocate of women's rights, Ruth Bader Ginsburg, to the Supreme Court.

But his withdrawal of Lani Guinier's nomination to head the Civil Rights Division in the Justice Department angered many as did the fact that it took him nearly two years to fill that position and to appoint someone to chair the Equal Employment Opportunity Commission. And in spite of his campaign promise to end the ban on gays in the military, he ultimately backed down, to the dismay of many of his supporters.

At this point in history, while some legislation to ensure fuller rights is still necessary for some groups (Native Americans and gays, in particular), enforcement is key. President Clinton and his Attorney General pledged to enforce civil rights laws to the fullest extent of the law. This position is in sharp contrast to that of earlier Republican administrations, which left many laws unenforced.

But for groups like gays, for whom there are few statutory or constitutional protections, the achievement of full civil rights may be more difficult. Although they have taken some steps toward reform at the local level, conservative Christian groups are mobilizing to run local candidates who actively oppose any expansion of homosexual rights. In 1992, for example, the liberal People for the American Way estimated that conservative fundamentalist Christians ran in about 500 local races and won 40 percent of those offices. Thus, reform, especially at the local level, could become more difficult for liberals to achieve in the wake of growing local conservative opposition, despite a generally sympathetic Democratic national administration.

At the same time, there is growing opposition to the goals of some civil rights groups. African Americans and women in particular may be hampered by their very successes. Leaders have found it increasingly difficult to mobilize followers, since the most blatant discriminatory practices have ended, and disagreement exists on how to achieve remaining goals. For example, although African Americans still agree on the need for improved educational opportunities, they disagree on how best to achieve that goal. At a time when 40 percent of the African-American men in the United States are functionally illiterate and many cities are overwhelmingly African American, busing is no longer as major an issue as it was in the past. For some, the trend in the 1990s should be toward reinstating all-black schools with a focus on black pride. In 1990 and 1991, several big cities, including Detroit and Milwaukee, set up all-male black elementary and high schools designed to provide young African-American males from female-headed households with positive black male role models and a better education. The constitutionality of these schools, however, was challenged in court by women's rights groups who argue that gender-segregated schools—black, white, or racially mixed—are unconstitutional.

To some extent, the civil rights movement has come full circle. Opportunities for African Americans and women have improved, lessening (in the eyes of some) the need for further reform. Equality of opportunity enjoys more support than equality of results. Much of the American public no longer believes that African Americans, women, or other minorities need additional help from the government, and most believe that the quality of life for African Americans has improved. But, as the rioting in Los Angeles reveals, equal rights for all is still a dream.

Summary

While the Framers and other Americans basked in the glory of the newly adopted Constitution and Bill of Rights, their protections did not extend to all Americans. In this chapter we have shown how rights have been expanded to ever-increasing segments of the population. To that end, we have made the following points:

1. When the Framers tried to "compromise" on the issue of slavery, they only postponed dealing with a volatile question that was later to rip the nation apart. Ultimately, the Civil War was fought to end slavery. Among its results were the triumph of the abolitionist position and adoption of the Thirteenth, Fourteenth, and Fifteenth Amendments. During this period, women also sought expanded rights, especially the right to vote, but to no avail.
2. Although the Civil War Amendments were added to the Constitution, the Supreme Court limited their application. As Jim Crow laws were passed around the South, the NAACP was founded in the early 1900s to press for equal rights for African Americans. Women's groups were also active during this period as they successfully lobbied for passage of the Nineteenth Amendment assuring them the right to vote.

    First, women's groups such as the National Consumers' League, and then others, including the NAACP, began to view litigation as a means to their ends. The NCL was forced to court to argue for the constitutionality of legislation protecting women workers; in contrast, the NAACP sought the Court's help in securing equality under the Constitution.
3. In 1954, the U.S. Supreme Court ruled in *Brown v. Board of Education* that state segregated school systems were unconstitutional. This victory empowered African Americans as they sought an end to other forms of pervasive discrimination. Bus boycotts and sit-ins were common tactics.

    As new groups were formed, freedom rides, pressure for voting rights, and massive non-violent demonstrations became common "lobbying" tactics. This activity culminated in passage of the Civil Rights Act of 1964 and the Voting Rights Act of 1965. These acts gave African-American and women's rights groups two potential weapons in their legal arsenals: They could attack private discrimination under the Civil Rights Act, or state-sanctioned discrimination under the Equal Protection Clause of the Fourteenth Amendment. And over the years, the Supreme Court developed different tests to determine the constitutionality of various forms of discrimination. In general, strict scrutiny, the most stringent standard, was applied to race-based claims. An intermediate standard of review was developed to assess the constitutionality of sex discrimination claims.

4. Building on the successes of African Americans and women, other groups, including Native Americans, Hispanic Americans, homosexuals, and the disabled have organized to litigate for expanded civil rights as well as to lobby for anti-discrimination laws.

5. Although 1960s civil rights legislation was at first widely acclaimed in most sections of the country, lax enforcement soon plagued many of its provisions. Affirmative action programs came under particular attack from the Reagan administration. Soon, a conservative Supreme Court overruled earlier liberal interpretations of anti-discrimination laws, forcing Congress to enact new civil rights legislation in 1986 and 1991 to reverse these decisions.

Key Terms

civil rights
equal protection clause
Thirteenth Amendment
Black Codes
Fourteenth Amendment
Fifteenth Amendment
Jim Crow laws

Civil Rights Cases
grandfather clauses
suffrage movement
Brown v. *Board of Education of Topeka*
Civil Rights Act of 1964
de jure discrimination

de facto discrimination
Equal Employment Opportunity Commission
suspect classifications
strict scrutiny
affirmative action

Suggested Readings

Browning, Rufus P., Dale Rogers Marshall, and David H. Tabb. *Protest Is Not Enough*. Berkeley: University of California Press, 1984.

Bullock, Charles III, and Charles Lamb, eds. *Implementation of Civil Rights Policy*. Monterey, CA: Brooks/Cole, 1984.

Flexner, Eleanor. *Century of Struggle*. New York: Atheneum, 1971.

Freeman, Jo. *The Politics of Women's Liberation*. New York: Longman, 1975.

King, Mary. *Freedom Song*. New York: Morrow, 1987.

Kluger, Richard. *Simple Justice*. New York: Vintage, 1975.

McGlen, Nancy E., and Karen O'Connor. *Women, Politics and American Society*. Englewood Cliffs, NJ: Prentice Hall, 1995.

Mansbridge, Jane J. *Why We Lost the ERA*. Chicago: University of Chicago Press, 1986.

Sindler, Allan P. *Bakke, DeFunis, and Minority Admissions*. New York: Longman, 1978.

Verba, Sidney, and Gary R. Orren. *Equality in America: The View from the Top*. Cambridge, MA: Harvard University Press, 1985.

Vose, Clement E. *Constitutional Change: Amendment Politics and Supreme Court Litigation Since 1900*. Lexington, MA: Heath, 1972.

Williams, Juan. *Eyes on the Prize: America's Civil Rights Years, 1954—1965*. New York: Penguin, 1987.

Woodward, C. Vann. *The Strange Career of Jim Crow*. New York: Oxford University Press, 1957.

Institutions of Government

In republican government, the legislative authority naturally predominates. The remedy for this inconvenience is to divide the legislature into different branches....

James Madison
Federalist No. 51

The Framers believed that a legislature would dominate the national government. By dividing Congress into two houses—the Senate and the House of Representatives—they thought they could diffuse its power to prevent the tyranny of the legislative branch of government over the other two branches.

CHAPTER 6

Congress

THE ROOTS OF THE LEGISLATIVE BRANCH
THE CONSTITUTION AND THE LEGISLATIVE BRANCH OF GOVERNMENT
THE MEMBERS OF CONGRESS
HOW CONGRESS IS ORGANIZED
THE LAWMAKING FUNCTION OF CONGRESS
HOW MEMBERS MAKE DECISIONS
CONGRESS AND THE PRESIDENT
TOWARD REFORM

As indicated by James Madison in *Federalist No. 51*, the Framers quickly opted for a two-house legislature, as was the practice in England. But the nature of the powers vested in Congress as a whole and in each house individually caused a considerable amount of debate at the Philadelphia convention. Moreover, the Framers also had to consider whose interests were to be represented in each legislative body. Was it to be "We the People," or the states, or special interests? In the centuries since the writing of the Constitution and the creation of the Congress, Congress has evolved in size, shape, and power. And despite the difficulties that sometimes seem to occur in the legislative process, there is no doubt that Congress has overwhelming powers *and* that most Americans believe that it should—to an extent.

The relationship between Americans and the Congress is full of contradictions. For example, in 1993, in the wake of hearings on Clarence Thomas' nomination to the U.S. Supreme Court and the House check-cashing scandal, only 12 percent of the American people had confidence in Congress, and criticism of it, its members, and its rules and procedures abounded.[1] In 1994, the public's confidence in Congress fell to 8 percent. This general disapproval of Congress as a whole stands in stark contrast to the public's generally high level of support for their *individual* representatives. One 1994 poll, for example, found that 59 percent of those polled believed that their *own* repre-

---

[1] Humphrey Taylor, "Louis Harris Poll: Confidence in Leaders Down," Gannett News Service, March 6, 1994, NEXIS.

203

Rep. Marjorie Margolies-Mezvinsky here defends her vote in support of the Clinton budget plan at an angry town meeting in her district. She, like many other first-time Democrats, was defeated in the 1994 midterm elections after having been targeted by angry Republicans.

sentatives deserved another term.[2] Part of this seeming public schizophrenia may stem from the dual roles that Congress plays—its members must combine representation functions with law- and policy-making functions—a combination that often produces role conflicts for individual legislators.

In the 103rd Congress, for example, many Democratic members were often torn between party, the president, and their constituents. Tremendous pressure was placed on Democratic representatives and senators to support the president's budget reform bill, and many voted for it in spite of anticipated wrath of the voters back home. Shortly after the budget bill's passage, however, the Democratic House leadership split evenly on the North American Free Trade Agreement (NAFTA), which was widely supported by Republicans and the Democratic president.

In the sections that follow, we analyze the powers of Congress and the competing roles members of Congress play as they represent the interests of their constituents, make laws, and oversee the actions of the other two branches of government. We also see that as these functions have changed throughout U.S. history, so has Congress itself.

The Roots of the Legislative Branch

As discussed in Chapter 2, Congress's powers evolved from Americans' experiences in the colonies and under the Articles of Confederation. When the colonists came to the New World, their general approval of Britain's parliamentary system led them to adopt similar two-house legislative bodies in the individual colonies. One house was directly elected by the people; the other was a Crown-appointed council that worked under the authority of the colonial government.

While originally established as advisory bodies to the royal governors appointed by the king, the colonial assemblies gradually assumed more power and authority in each

---

[2] Richard Benedetto, "Congress Knows It's 'Show-Me Time' to Voters," *USA Today*, March 7, 1994:11A.

colony, particularly over taxation and spending. The assemblies also legislated on religious issues and established quality standards for such colonial goods as flour, rice, tobacco, and rum. Prior to the American Revolution, colonists turned to their colonial legislatures (the only bodies elected directly by the "people") to represent and defend their interests against British infringement.

The first truly national legislature in the colonies, the First Continental Congress, met in Philadelphia in 1774 to develop a common colonial response to the Coercive Acts. All the colonies except Georgia sent a representative. Even though this Congress had no power to force compliance, it advised each colony to establish a militia and organized an economic boycott of British goods, among other things (see Chapter 2).

By the time the Second Continental Congress met in Philadelphia in May 1775, fighting had broken out at Lexington and Concord. The Congress quickly helped the now-united colonies gear up for war, raise an army, and officially adopt the Declaration of Independence. During the next five years, the Congress directed the war effort and administered a central government. But it did so with little money or stability as the Revolutionary War necessitated that it move from city to city.

Although the Articles of Confederation were drafted and adopted by the Second Continental Congress in 1777, the states did not ratify them until 1781. Still, throughout the Revolutionary War, the Congress exercised the authorities the Articles granted it: to declare war, raise an army, make treaties with foreign nations, and coin money. As described in Chapter 2, however, the Congress had no independent sources of income; it had to depend on the states for money and supplies. After the war, the states began acting once again as if they were separate nations rather than parts of one nation, despite the national government created under the Articles of Confederation. The "national" government, moreover, was insufficient to establish the new nation securely and to serve its needs. Discontent with the Articles grew and led eventually to the Constitutional Convention in Philadelphia in 1787.

The Constitution and the Legislative Branch of Government

Article I of the Constitution created the legislative branch of government we know today. Any two-house legislature, such as the one created by the Framers, is called a bicameral legislature. All states except Nebraska, which has a one-house or unicameral legislature, follow this model. As discussed in Chapter 2, the Great Compromise resulted in the creation of an upper house, the Senate, and a lower house, the House of Representatives. Each state is represented in the Senate by two senators, regardless of the state's population. The number of representatives each state sends to the House of Representatives, in contrast, is determined by that state's population.

Members of each body were to be elected differently and would thus represent different interests and constituencies. Senators were to be elected to six-year terms by state legislatures, and one-third of them would be up for reelection every two years. Senators were to be closely tied to their state legislatures and were expected to represent those interests in the Senate. State legislators lost this influence with ratification of the Seventeenth Amendment in 1913, which provides for the direct election of senators by the voters.

In contrast to senators' six-year terms, members of the House of Representatives were to be elected to two-year terms by a vote of the eligible voters in each congressional district. It was expected that the House would be the more "democratic" branch

This oil painting by an unknown artist depicts the Capitol from Pennsylvania Avenue around 1827. Note the dirt road leading to the building.

of government because its members would be more responsible to the people. Not only were they directly elected by the people, but they also were up for reelection every two years.

Apportionment and Redistricting

The U.S. Constitution requires that a census, which entails the counting of all Americans, be conducted every ten years. Until the first census could be taken, the Constitution fixed the number of representatives at sixty-five. In 1790, then, one member represented 37,000 people. As the population of the new nation grew and states were added to the Union, the House became larger and larger. In 1910 it expanded to 435 members, and in 1929 its size was fixed at that number by statute.

Because the Constitution requires that representation in the House be based on state population, congressional districts must be redrawn by state legislatures to reflect population shifts so that each member in Congress will represent approximately the same number of residents. When shifts occur in the national population, states gain or lose congressional seats. For example, in the 1990 census (as in most censuses since 1960), many Northeastern states showed a population decline and lost congressional seats, whereas states in the South, Southwest, and West (the sunbelt) showed great population growth and gained seats. New York lost five congressional seats after the 1980 census and an additional three in 1990. Conversely, Florida picked up four seats after the 1980 census and an additional four after the 1990 census. And, California picked up seven seats in 1990 for a total of fifty-two seats. In contrast, Alaska, Delaware, Montana, North Dakota, South Dakota, Vermont, and Wyoming, the least populous states, have only one representative each.

Through the process of **redistricting**, or the redrawing of congressional districts to reflect increases or decreases in seats allotted to the states as well as population shifts within a state, the majority party in each statehouse tries to assure that the maximum number of representatives from its political party can be elected to Congress. This redistricting process, which has gone on since the first census in 1790, is often called

The Size of Congress

When the first House convened in 1789, it had sixty-five members from thirteen states, with each member representing 30,000 people. In the 1890s, each member represented 173,901 people, and in 1910 the number of representatives in the House was increased to 435, with each member representing approximately 210,583 constituents. In 1929, the size of the House was fixed by statute at 435 members. In 1990, there was one representative for every 573,394 people. In 1991, in the wake of the 1990 census, the state of Montana filed a lawsuit after it appeared that its two congressional districts would be combined into one statewide district of more than 800,000 people, which would be the nation's largest. State officials argued that Montana residents would be underrepresented in the House, but a federal district court disagreed. In 1992, the Supreme Court ruled unanimously that the reapportionment plan used by Congress was constitutional.

Senate size, of course, has increased as states were added to the Union. The Senate had only twenty-six members in 1790 and grew to sixty-two by 1850 and ninety-two by 1910. It reached its current size of one hundred members after Alaska was admitted to the Union in 1958 and Hawaii in 1959.

gerrymandering. The term was first coined in 1812, when the powerful Republican governor of Massachusetts, Elbridge Gerry, persuaded the state legislature to create the oddly shaped district reproduced in Figure 6-1 in order to favor the election of a fellow Republican. The story goes that upon seeing how the district was drawn, one critic observed, "Why, that looks like a salamander!" to which another retorted, "That's not a salamander, that's a gerrymander."

The two most common forms of gerrymandering are "packing" and "cracking." Packing involves drawing a district so that it has a large number of supporters from a particular political party, thus making it a "safe" district. Cracking means dividing up supporters of the opposition party so that they become minorities in a number of districts, thus weakening their influence. Whether cracking or packing is used, the resulting districts often take unusual shapes.

Creative redistricting and the actions of state legislators have often created problems that have ended up in litigation. The Supreme Court faced the question of **apportionment**—the determination and assignment of representation in a legislature—in *Baker v. Carr* (1962).[3] The Court found that the Tennessee legislature's apportionment plan, which failed to alter district lines despite large shifts in population, was unconstitutional because it violated the constitutional principle of equal protection of the law. Furthermore, the Court ruled that the equitable apportionment of voters among districts was a legal question of constitutional rights and *not a political question*, thereby allowing the courts to direct states to correct malapportionment. Two years later, in *Reynolds v. Sims* (1964),[4] the Supreme Court ruled that congressional as well as state

---

[3] 369 U.S. 186 (1962).
[4] 377 U.S. 533 (1964).

FIGURE 6-1
Gerrymandering

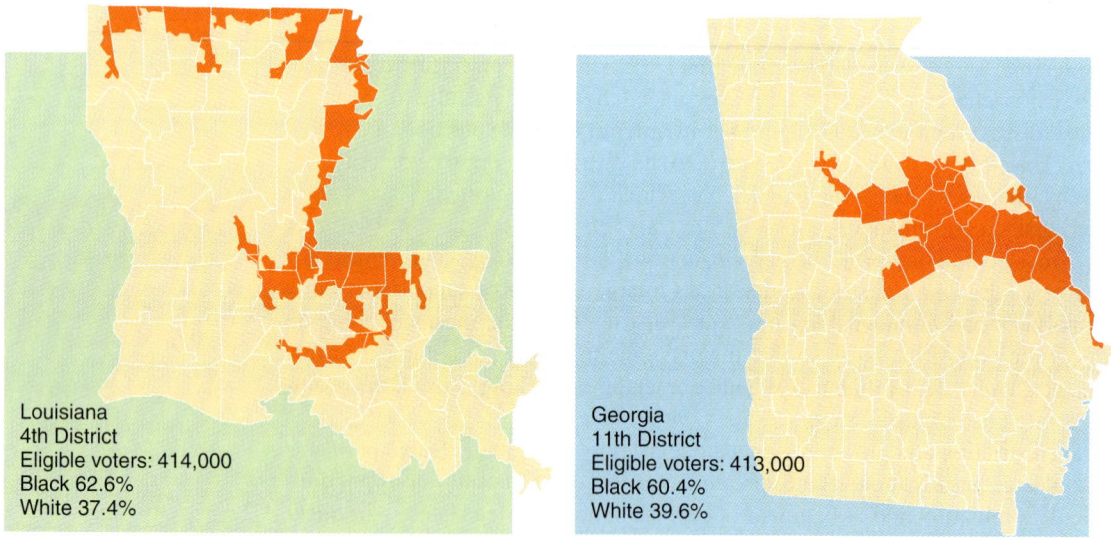

Source: From David Van Biema, "Snakes or Ladders?" Time, July 12, 1993, p. 30. Copyright 1993 Time, Inc. Reprinted by permission.

legislative districts must have "substantially equal" populations and enunciated the principle of "one man, one vote."

In 1986, the Supreme Court ruled that any gerrymandering of a congressional district that purposely dilutes minority strength—a common reason for gerrymandering in the past—was illegal under the 1965 Voting Rights Act.[5] Most observers interpreted the ruling to mean that the drawing of districts to enhance party strength was permissible, but redistricting to dilute African-American or Hispanic political clout was not. Just how far a state can go to "create" congressional districts to facilitate the election of minority representatives continues to be questioned.

After the 1990 census, for example, North Carolina proposed to create one African-American majority congressional district; the Bush administration Justice Department demanded two districts to more accurately reflect the racial composition of the state. (African Americans made up 22 percent of North Carolina's population; the state had twelve congressional districts.) To create the second district, the Democratic majority in the statehouse created the serpentine district shown in Figure 6-1 on page 208. It basically connected small black population centers by winding down I-85 like a 160-mile-long ribbon. In finding this kind of gerrymander in violation of the Voting Rights Act of 1965, Justice Sandra Day O'Connor called the district "bizarre" and even quoted one legislator's joke about the district: "If you drove down the interstate with both car doors open, you'd kill most of the people in the district." This kind of redrawing of districts for obvious racial purposes was unconstitutional, concluded a majority of the Court, because it denies the constitutional rights of white citizens.[6]

After that decision, state legislators and the U.S. Justice Department were left in a quandary about how future congressional districts were to be drawn. It appears that states will no longer be given the kind of latitude they were in the 1980s to fashion districts ensuring minority representation in Congress. Indeed, the constitutionality of many of these minority districts (which resulted in the election of more African Americans to Congress in 1992) has been called into question in many lawsuits.

Constitutional Powers of Congress

The Constitution specifically gives to Congress its most important power—the authority to make laws. This law-making power is shared by both houses. No bill (proposed law) can become a law without the consent of both houses. Examples of other powers shared by both houses include the power to declare war, raise an army and navy, coin money, regulate commerce, establish the federal courts and their jurisdiction, establish rules of immigration and naturalization, and to "make all Laws which shall be necessary and proper for carrying into Execution the foregoing Powers."

The powers of Congress, enumerated on page 210, provide it with far-reaching authority to make not only individual laws but also broader public policy. As interpreted by the Supreme Court, the necessary and proper clause, when coupled with one or more of the specific powers enumerated in Article I, section 8, has allowed Congress to increase the scope of its authority, often at the expense of the states and into areas not necessarily envisioned by the Framers.

Reflecting the different constituencies and size of each house of Congress (as well as the Framer's intentions), Article I also gives special, exclusive powers to each house. As noted in Table 6.1, for example, the Constitution specifies that all revenue bills must originate in the House of Representatives. Over the years, however, this mandate has been blurred, and it is not unusual to see budget bills being considered si-

---

[5] *Thornburg v. Gingles*, 478 U.S. 30 (1986). The Act was amended in 1982.
[6] *Shaw v. Reno*, 113 S. Ct. 2816 (1993).

> ## The Powers of Congress
>
> Article I, section 8, of the Constitution gives Congress the power to undertake the following actions:
>
> - Lay and collect taxes and duties.
> - Borrow money.
> - Regulate commerce with foreign nations and among the states.
> - Establish rules for naturalization (that is, the process of becoming a citizen) and bankruptcy.
> - Coin money, set its value, and fix the standard of weights and measures.
> - Punish counterfeiting.
> - Establish a post office and post roads.
> - Issue patents and copyrights.
> - Define and punish piracies, felonies on the high seas, and crimes against the law of nations.
> - Create courts inferior to (that is, below) the Supreme Court.
> - Declare war.
> - Raise and support an army and navy and make rules for their governance.
> - Provide for a militia (reserving to the states the right to appoint militia officers and to train the militia under congressional rules).
> - Exercise legislative powers over the seat of government (the District of Columbia) and over places purchased to be federal facilities (forts, arsenals, dockyards, and "other needful buildings").
> - "Make all Laws which shall be necessary and proper for carrying into Execution the foregoing Powers, and all other Powers vested by this Constitution in the Government of the United States." (Note: This "necessary and proper," or "elastic," clause has been expansively interpreted by the Supreme Court, as explained in Chapter 2.)

multaneously in both houses, especially since each must approve all bills in the end, whether or not they involve revenues. In 1993, for example, President Clinton submitted a budget deficit-reduction plan to Congress, and both houses deliberated his and similar proposals simultaneously.

The House also has the power of **impeachment**, the authority to charge the president, vice president, or other "civil officers," including federal judges, with "Treason, Bribery or other high Crimes and Misdemeanors." Only the Senate is authorized to conduct trials of impeachment, and a two-thirds vote is necessary before a federal official can be removed from office.

Only one president, Andrew Johnson, has been impeached by the House, but he was acquitted by the full Senate by a one-vote margin. More recently, as we discuss in greater detail in Chapter 7, President Richard M. Nixon resigned from office in 1974 after the House Judiciary Committee voted to impeach him for his role in the Watergate scandal. In 1986, for the first time in fifty years, the House voted to impeach a federal judge. Judge Harry R. Claiborne was impeached after he had been convicted in federal court of income-tax evasion but had refused to resign from the bench. Following a trial in the Senate, he was removed from the bench after being convicted on three of the four articles of impeachment that the House had brought against him.

In 1988, in the most unusual case to date, the process was repeated: Florida's first black federal judge, Alcee Hastings, was impeached and removed from the bench even

Table 6.1 ♦ Key Differences Between the House and Senate

CONSTITUTIONAL DIFFERENCES

House	Senate
Initiates all revenue bills	Offers "advice and consent" on many major presidential appointments.
Initiates impeachment procedures and passes articles of impeachment	Tries impeached officials
Two-year terms	Six-year terms ($1/3$ up for reelection every two years)
Comprises 435 members (apportioned by population)	Comprises 100 members (2 from each state)
	Approves treaties

DIFFERENCES IN OPERATION

House	Senate
More centralized, more formal; stronger leadership	Less centralized, less formal; weaker leadership
Rules Committee fairly powerful in controlling time and rules of debate (in conjunction with the majority leader)	No Rules Committee; limits on debate come through unanimous consent or cloture of filibuster
More impersonal	More personal
Power less evenly distributed	Power more evenly distributed
Members are highly specialized	Members are generalists
Emphasizes tax and revenue policy	Emphasizes foreign policy
Seniority important in determining power	Seniority less important in determining power

CHANGES IN THE INSTITUTION

House	Senate
Power formerly centralized in the hands of key committees and the leadership; breaking down	Senate workload increasing and informality breaking down
House procedures are becoming more efficient, with less debate and fewer amendments	Members are becoming more specialized; debate and deliberations less frequent
Turnover is low	Turnover is moderate

though he had been acquitted of bribery charges in a U.S. federal district court. In 1992, twelve years after the original charges were filed, Hastings was elected to the House of Representatives, the body that had originally initiated the impeachment proceedings against him.

While the House and Senate share in the impeachment process, the Senate has the sole authority to approve major presidential appointments, including those of federal judges, ambassadors, and Cabinet and sub-Cabinet-level positions. The Senate, too, must approve by a two-thirds vote all treaties entered into by the president. Failure by the president to court the Senate can be costly. For example, at the end of World War I, President Woodrow Wilson worked long and hard to convince other nations to accept the Treaty of Versailles, which contained the charter of the proposed League of

Rep. Alcee Hastings is shown here before his impeachment from the federal bench, which inspired him to run for Congress.

Nations. He overestimated his support in the Senate, which refused to ratify the treaty, dealing Wilson and his international stature a severe setback.

The Members of Congress

For most, being a member of Congress is a glamorous and exciting job. Rep. Newt Gingrich (R.-Ga.) once gleefully remarked, "There are very few games as fun as being a congressman."[7] It is also a difficult job that requires one continually to seek reelection, expend enormous sums of money, and work very long hours, often for much less pay than could be earned in the private sector (although as the box below indicates, a variety of perks go with the job). According to one study, the average member of the House of Representatives spends 11.18 hours a day working on congressional-related

[7] Hedrick Smith, *The Power Game* (New York: Ballantine Books, 1989), p. 97.

The Perks of Office
♦ ♦ ♦

The bonuses or perquisites (often called "perks") that go with being a member of Congress include the following:

- An annual salary of $133,600 (the Speaker earns $171,500, the same as the vice president and Chief Justice).
- Free life insurance and a generous retirement plan.
- Free office space in Washington and in the home district.
- A staff allowance of $752,400 for each House member and from $400,000 to $2.4 million (depending on the population of his or her state and its distance from the Capitol) for each senator, plus more for committee aides.
- An expense account for telephone, stationery, and other office costs.
- Thirty-two fully reimbursed round trips home a year.
- Travel allowances and free travel to foreign lands on congressional inquiries (often called "junkets" by critics).
- Nearly unlimited franking (free mailing) privileges ($60 million in fiscal 1994).
- Access to free congressionally owned and operated video and film studios to record messages for constituents.
- Discounts in Capitol Hill tax-free shops and restaurants (the bean soup at $1.40 a cup in the Senate Dining Room is famous).
- $10 haircuts at the congressional barbershop.
- Free reserved parking at Washington National Airport.
- Use of the House gym or the Senate "baths" for $100 a year (women members were not allowed to use the House gym until 1985).
- Free fresh-cut flowers from the Botanic Garden.
- Free assistance in the preparation of income taxes.

activities. Hedrick Smith, a Pulitzer Prize-winning reporter for the *New York Times*, notes that:

> Days are a kaleidoscopic jumble: breakfast with reporters, morning staff meetings, simultaneous committee hearings to juggle, back-to-back sessions with lobbyists and constituents, phone calls, briefings, constant buzzers interrupting office work to make quorum calls and votes on the run, afternoon speeches, evening meetings, receptions, fund-raisers, all crammed into four days so they can race home for a weekend gauntlet of campaigning. It's a rat race. . . .[8]

In spite of the long hours and hard work, thousands of people aspire to the job every year. Yet a total of only 535 men and women get to vote in the U.S. Congress. (The District of Columbia's members are not allowed to vote.)

Formal Requirements

The U.S. Constitution sets out the legal requirements for membership in the House and Senate. House members must be at least twenty-five years old; Senators, thirty. Members of the House must have resided in the United States for at least seven years; those elected to the Senate, nine. In addition to being U.S. citizens, representatives and senators must be legal residents of the states from which they are elected.

Informal Requirements

These formal requirements, however, are only part of the picture. There also are several informal requirements, for example, membership in one of the two major political parties is almost always the norm. Election laws in various states often discriminate against independents (those without party affiliation) and minor-party candidates.

Money is another informal requirement. As discussed in Chapter 13, money is the mother's milk of politics. And often key to any member's victory is his or her ability to raise money (see Chapter 13).

Incumbency is another informal factor. Being in office helps you stay in office. This "incumbency factor" weighs against non-incumbents in a variety of ways, including fund raising. As illustrated in Figure 6-2, which compares the way poll respondents feel about Congress overall to the way they feel about their own representatives. Most Americans approve of their own members of Congress. Thus, while people may criticize the Congress as a whole, they rarely reject their own incumbent representatives at the polls (see Figure 6-3). From 1980 to 1990, in fact, an average of 95 percent of those who ran actually won their primary and general election races.[9] One study concluded that unless a member of Congress was involved in a serious scandal, his or her chances of defeat were minimal.[10] The incumbency factor has facilitated the growth in what some term "congressional careerists," that is, individuals who make a career for themselves in the nation's capital.

The incumbency factor diminished in 1992, when fifty-two House members and eight Senators chose not to seek re-election and thirteen other House incumbents opted

As House Minority Leader in the 103rd Congress, Newt Gingrich was the second most powerful Republican in the House and a continual thorn in the side of House leaders. And he wasn't too popular back home—at least with the Democratic majority that controlled the Georgia legislature. As a result of the 1990 census, Georgia was given an additional congressional district. An outraged Gingrich complained that Democratic legislators had carved his congressional district into four pieces "in an effort to destroy me." His home was then thrown into the overwhelmingly Democratic district of John Lewis, the Deputy House Whip, which forced Gingrich to run in a new district in 1992. He handily won reelection in 1994 and was elected Speaker of the House when his party trounced Democrats in the midterm elections.

---

[8] Ibid. p. 108.
[9] Marjorie Randon Hershey, "The Congressional Elections," in Gerald M. Pomper et al., eds. *The Election of 1992: Reports and Interpretations* (Chatham, NJ: Chatham House, 1993), p. 159.
[10] Alan I. Abramowitz, "Incumbency, Congressional Spending, and the Decline of Competition in House Elections," 53 *Journal of Politics*, (February 1991): 34–56.

FIGURE 6-2

Approval of Congress

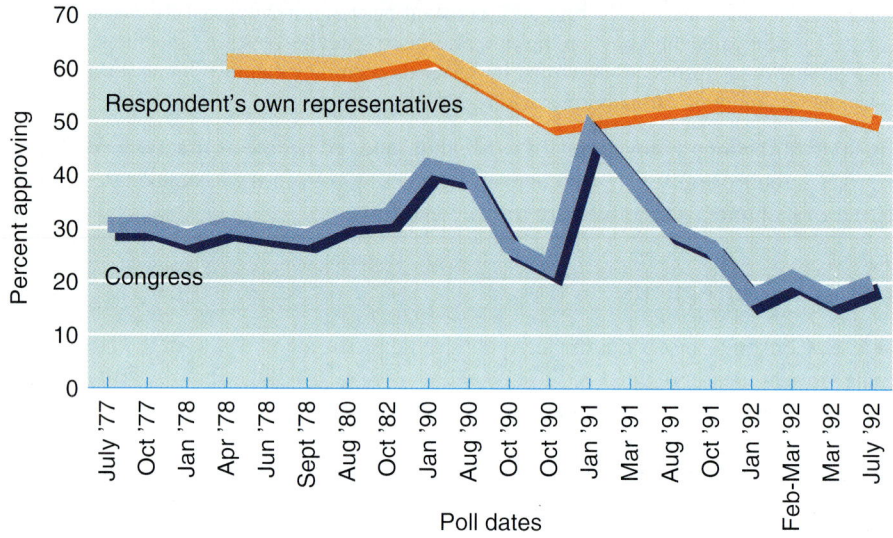

Source: Marjorie Randon Hershey, "Congressional Elections," in *The Election of 1992* by Gerald M. Pomper et al. (1993) Reprinted by permission of Chatham House Publishers.

to run for other political offices.[11] Their decisions not to run were the result of several factors, including redistricting, an unpopular series of congressional pay raises, the savings and loan scandal, mismanagement of the House Post Office and House "bank," Congress's seeming inability to solve the budget crisis, and a loophole in federal election law that allowed members of Congress leaving by 1992 to keep any leftover campaign monies for their personal use.

For many House members, the decision not to seek reelection was a wise move. In the 1992 primaries, more House members lost their primary bids than at any other time since World War II.[12] Political scientist Marjorie Randon Hershey concludes that most of those who lost were involved in the House bank scandal; "the biggest overdrafters were themselves bounced."[13] Nonetheless, in the 1992 November general elections, after the scandal had faded somewhat, nearly 90 percent of the incumbents who sought reelection were returned to office, as shown in Figure 6-3.

Similarly, during the 1994 congressional elections, the decision of many incumbents not to run left a sizable number of seats open. These open seats, coupled with a public that was fueled by an anti-incumbency, anti-Washington, anti-Clinton mood led to what one political scientist called "a revolution that happened without any bullets." Although in the 1994 midterm elections incumbency showed no ill effects on Republicans—all Republican Senators, Representatives, and even governors who sought reelection won—for Democrats, incumbency proved to be a decided negative even if they had only recently been elected. In fact, the fifteen Democrats elected in 1992 who lost in 1994 made up one-half of all of the Democratic incumbents who lost their

[11] Hershey, "The Congressional Elections," p. 166. (See n. 9.)
[12] Ibid.
[13] Ibid., p. 175.

FIGURE 6-3

The Percentage of Incumbents in the House and Senate Successfully Seeking Reelection, 1946–1992

Source: Marjorie Randon Hershey, "Congressional Elections," in *The Election of 1992* by Gerald M. Pomper et al. (1993) Reprinted by permission of Chatham House Publishers.

House races. Women elected for the first time in 1992 when an unprecedented 24 new women were added to the U.S. House of Representatives fared especially badly; seven of them, or 30 percent, lost in their effort to seek a second term.

Voters were clearly turned off by the present Congress. As revealed in Figure 6–2, since the 103rd Congress took office, Congress has rarely enjoyed better than a 20 percent approval rating. Seeking to take advantage of voter frustration, House Minority Whip Newt Gingrich persuaded 350 Republican candidates to come to Washington D.C., to sign what he called a "Contract with America." By signing this contract, Republican candidates pledged to pass a balanced budget amendment, enact a line item veto, pass meaningful welfare reform, cut taxes, raise national defense spending, roll back government regulations, reform the legal system to prevent excessive claims, and enact congressional term limits. If Republicans cannot make good on these pledges as the party in power, incumbency may serve no better purpose than it did the Democrats in 1994.

House Minority Whip Newt Gingrich of Georgia addresses Republican Congressional candidates on Capitol Hill Tuesday, Sept. 27, 1994 during a rally in which they pledged a "Contract with America."

216 ❖ Chapter 6 Congress

Senator Bob Packwood (R-Oregon) ran afoul of a different sort of scandal in 1993. Long a supporter of women's rights issues, Packwood was accused of sexual harrassment by several female former staff and campaign workers. While still under investigation by the Ethics Committee, Packwood assumed the chairmanship of the powerful Senate Finance Committee when control of the Senate reverted to the Republicans in 1994.

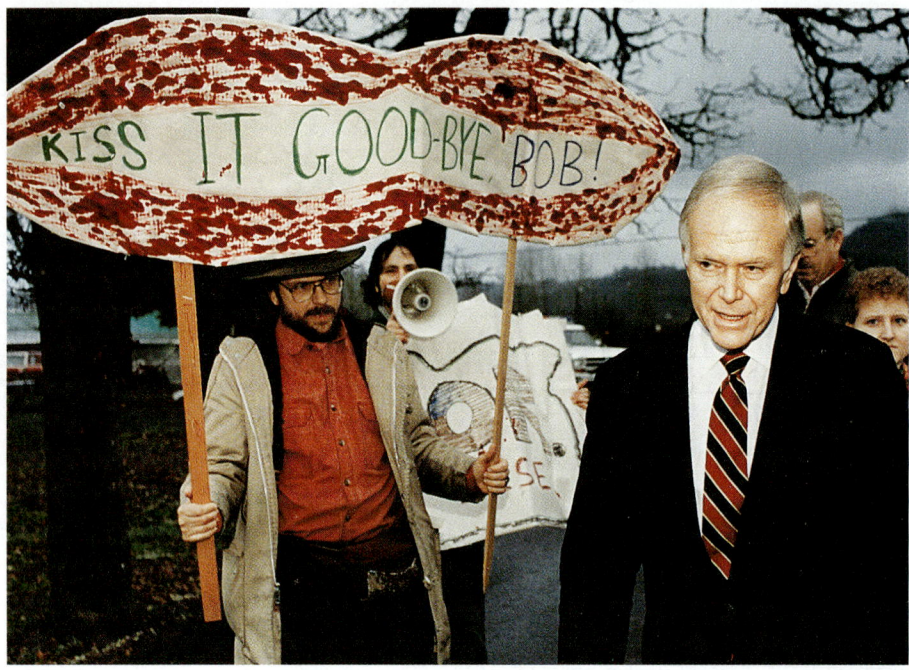

What Does Congress Look Like?

When Bill Clinton was elected president in 1992, he said that he wanted to appoint an administration that "looked like America." Historically, Congress has never looked like America—it is richer, older, better educated, more white, and more male. Most members of Congress are well-off if not wealthy (the Senate has often been called the "Millionaires' Club"). In the 104th Congress (1995–1997) nearly half the Senators are millionaires and many have a net worth of more than $2 million. Many, in fact, criticized the millions spent—much of it personal wealth—in Senate races as Republicans and Democrats alike called for campaign finance reform. In the House, which has historically had a more "common man" orientation than the Senate, fewer than 10 percent of the members are multi-millionaires.

The Congress, especially the Senate, still has the "look" of a private club, although, since the 1992 election, both bodies are more diverse than ever before. In the 104th Congress, the average age of Senators is 58 years, 57 percent are lawyers, and 89 percent are white males.

Change is occurring, however. Over the years, more and more women and minorities have been running for office and winning (see Figure 6-4). In the 103rd Congress, for example, twenty-nine new women were elected, and a record fifty-five women served; the number of women in the Senate rose from two to seven—a 350 percent increase! Both senators elected from California were women.

The 103rd Congress also saw the election of the largest class of new African-American legislators since Reconstruction (see Figure 6-4) and the election of the first African-American woman, Carol Moseley-Braun (D.-Ill.), to the Senate (she is also the only African American in the Senate).

Table 6.2 ♦ Some Characteristics of the 104th Congress

	HOUSE	SENATE
Total Membership	435	100
Party affiliation		
Democrats	204	47
Republicans	230	53
Independents	1	0
New Members*	83	11
Race		
African American	38	1
Hispanic	17	0
Asian American	4	2
Native American	0	1
% With law degree	35	57
Average age	51	58
% Baby boomers	41	14
Average length of service	8 yrs	11 yrs

*As of press date.

The 1992 elections were also a banner year for other minority groups. The number of Hispanic Americans in the House rose from thirteen to seventeen (see Figure 6-4). Moreover, the first Korean American was elected to the House of Representatives (Jay Kim, R.-Cal.), and Ben Nighthorse Campbell (D.-Col.) became the first Native American to serve in the U.S. Senate in more than sixty years.

The 1994 midterm elections were disappointing for women and minorities. After their record gains in 1992, 1994 was more of a holding action. Women appear to have gained no new seats in the House in spite of the fact that a record number of women sought seats. Only one additional woman was added to the Senate, former House member Olympia Snowe (R.-Me.). Similarly, although 23 Republican African-Americans sought election to the House, only two won, and the total number of African-Americans in both houses remained the same. The same held true for other minority groups.

The Representational Function of Members of Congress

Does it make a difference if members of Congress actually come from or are members of a particular group? The answer to this question may depend on your view of the representative function of legislators.

In Great Britain, although members of Parliament are elected from specific districts, they are expected to represent the *entire* nation. This is called virtual representation. Because members are the "virtual" or actual representatives of all English people, in colonial times it followed that they could legislate for all British subjects—even those living in America. Colonists, in contrast, argued for a system of "actual representation," in which members represent only those voters who elect them.

FIGURE 6-4
Numbers of Women and Minorities in Congress

Source: From Harold W. Stanley and Richard G. Niemi, "Vital Statistics on American Politics", 4/e, *Congressional Quarterly*, 1994, p.203.

Six female House members attempted to gain entrance to a meeting of Senate Democrats in 1991 to demand that allegations of sexual harassment receive a full hearing before the Senate vote to confirm Clarence Thomas to the Supreme Court.

Questions of who should be represented and how this representation should be achieved are critical in a republic. Over the years, political theorists have enunciated various ideas about how constituents' interests are best represented in any legislative body. One famous political theorist, Edmund Burke (1729–1797), who also served as a member of the British House of Commons in the late 1700s, argued that once elected, a representative need not vote the way his constituents would expect him to. According to Burke, representatives should be "trustees" who listen to the opinions of their constituents and then use their own best judgment to make final decisions.

A second theory of representation holds that representatives are "delegates." A delegate representative votes according to constituents' opinions regardless of whether those opinions coincide with those of the representative.

Members of Congress and other legislative bodies generally don't fall neatly into either category. It is often unclear how constituents feel about a particular issue, or conflicting opinions may abound within a single constituency. With these difficulties in mind, a third theory of representation holds that "politicos" alternately don the hats of trustee or delegate, depending on the issue. On an issue of great concern to voters in their districts, representatives will most likely vote as delegates; on other issues, perhaps on issues that are less visible, representatives will act as trustees and use their own best judgment as they cast their votes.

Race Matters: Senator Carolyn Moseley-Braun and the Confederate Flag

For years, the U.S. Senate has routinely extended the design patent of the Daughters of the Confederacy that included the Confederate flag. That was before the first African-American woman became a member of the Senate.

Since her election in 1992, Carol Moseley-Braun (D.-Ill.), the only African American in the Senate, has tried to sensitize her colleagues about issues of race. In 1993, Senator Jesse Helms (R.-N.C.), for example, sought to amend the national service bill in such a way as to preserve the design patent held by the United Daughters of the Confederacy that included the Confederate flag. Most senators had no idea what they were voting on, and the amendment to the bill passed on a vote of fifty-two to forty-eight. Then, Senator Moseley-Braun took to the floor to express her outrage at Helms's support of a symbol of slavery: "On this issue there can be no consensus. It is an outrage. It is an insult."[*] Although Helms angrily insisted that slavery and race were not at issue, the Senate killed the Helms amendment on a vote of seventy-five to twenty-five, as twenty-seven senators changed their votes. Said Senator Barbara Boxer (D.-Calif.), "If there ever was proof of the value of diversity, we have it here today."[**]

[**] Ibid.

[*] Adam Clymer, "Daughter of Slavery Hushes Senate," *New York Times* (July 23, 1993):B–6.

Senator Carol Moseley-Braun (D.-Ill.) speaks out angrily on the floor of the Senate.

How a representative views his or her role—as a trustee, delegate, or politico—may still not answer the question of whether it makes a difference if a representative or senator is male or female; African American, Hispanic, Native American, or white; young or old; gay or straight. Can a man, for example, represent the interests of women as well as a woman? Can a rich woman represent the interests of the poor? The combinations are endless.

Senator Edward M. Kennedy (D.-Mass.), for example, is one of the wealthiest members of the Senate, yet he has been an effective champion of the poor, of women, and of other minorities throughout his six terms in the Senate. But during the Clarence Thomas hearings (see p. 379) many commentators noted that Kennedy's well-chronicled problems in his personal life precluded him from effectively questioning Thomas and contributed to his uncharacteristic silence during those hearings. Female representatives in the House were outraged by the glaring absence of any women on the Senate Judiciary Committee that grilled Anita Hill concerning her charges that Thomas had sexually harassed her while he was her supervisor at the Equal Employment Opportunity Commission. Presumably in response, to this com-

Ben Nighthorse Campbell (D.-Col.)

plaint two women—Diane Feinstein (D.-Cal.) and Carol Moseley-Braun (D.-Ill.) were added to the Committee in 1993.

Female representatives historically have played prominent roles in efforts to expand women's rights. It was Representative Martha Griffiths (D.-Mich.) who successfully added "sex" to the list of discriminatory qualifications prohibited by the Civil Rights Act of 1964 and Representative Bella Abzug (D.-N.Y.) who led the fight for congressional passage of the Equal Rights Amendment.

Studies reveal that female legislators are more likely than their male counterparts to sponsor legislation of concern to women.[14] In the 101st Congress, for example, two bills supported by most women in Congress were passed: an extension of Medicare to cover mammograms for women over sixty-five and the establishment of a $30-million screening program for breast and cervical cancer for poor women, who die of these diseases at higher rates than does the rest of the population. Representative Mary Rose Oakar (D.-Ohio), who co-sponsored these bills, noted that she made progress by seeking help from male representatives whose wives had breast cancer. "There are at least ten of them, and when it hits you in the family, boy, do attitudes change."[15] Without a push from women, however, it is unlikely that even those male representatives would have acted.

Actions of the one Native American and one African American in the Senate underscore the representative function that can be played in Congress. Ben Nighthorse Campbell (D.-Col.), for example, sits on the Senate Committee on Indian Affairs. As a member of the House, he led the fight to change the name of Custer Battlefield Monument in Montana to Little Bighorn Battlefield National Monument to honor the Indians who died in battle. He also fought successfully for legislation to establish the National Museum of the American Indian within the Smithsonian Institution. But his biggest fight on behalf on Native Americans has been to block congressional approval of a $200-million stadium for the Washington Redskins unless the football team changes its name. Campbell told a House panel that the word "redskin" is a racial slur.

How Congress Is Organized

Every two years, a new Congress is seated. After determining qualifications of new members, the Congress organizes its business for the coming session: it elects leaders, chooses committee assignments for the two-year period, and sets its agenda. Each year, members of Congress introduce up to 10,000 bills and pass between 700 and 2,000 into law. Having rules and organization is, therefore, critical to Congressional operation. Figure 6-5 illustrates the leadership structure of each house. The Democrats were the majority party in both houses during the 103rd Congress. Figure 6-6 shows the physical layout of the two houses in the Capitol building.

---

[14] Sue Thomas, *How Women Legislate* (New York: Oxford University Press, 1994).

[15] Quoted in Stacey Edwards, "Health Act to End Discrimination in Health Issues, Mikulski Says," *States News Service* (February 27, 1991) NEXIS.

FIGURE 6-5

Organizational Structure of the House of Representatives and the Senate during the 104th Congress (1995–1997)

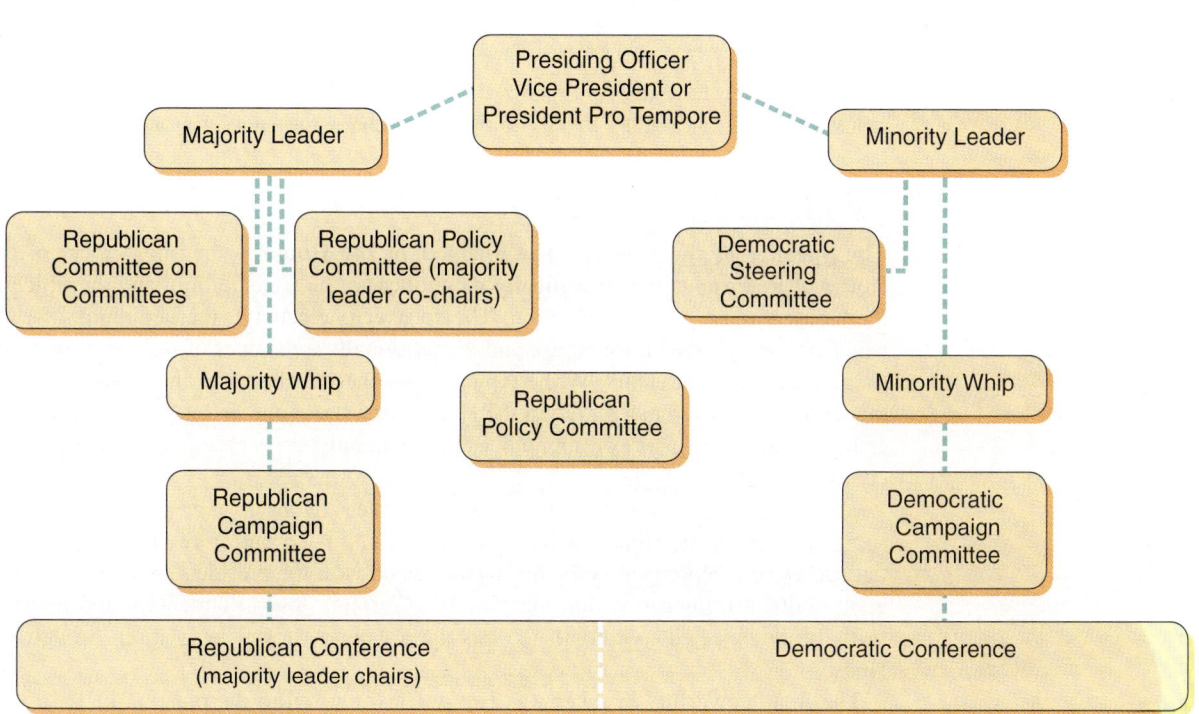

FIGURE 6-6
Floor Plan of the Capitol Building

House of Representatives
1. Speaker's Office Suite
2. Committee on Ways and Means
3. Cloakrooms
4. Members' Retiring Room and Lobby
5. House Chamber
6. Committee on Appropriations
7. Minority Whip
8. House Reception Room
9. House Conference Room
10. Committee Meeting Room
11. Representatives' Offices
12. Minority Leader

Central Area
13. Statuary Hall
14. Rotunda
15. Senate Rotunda
16. Old Senate Chamber

Senate
17. Senators' Offices
18. Senate Conference Room
19. Minority Leader
20. Majority Leader
21. Office of the Vice President
22. Senators' Reception Room
23. Cloakrooms
24. Senate Chamber
25. President's Room

The House of Representatives

Even in the First Congress in 1789, the House of Representatives was almost three times larger than the Senate. It is not surprising, then, that from the beginning, the House has been more tightly organized, more elaborately structured, and governed by stricter rules. Traditionally, loyalty to the party leadership and voting along party lines have been more common in the House than in the Senate. House leaders also play a key role in moving along the business of the House.

The Speaker of the House. The **Speaker of the House** is the only officer of the House of Representatives specifically mentioned in the Constitution, and the office is the House's most powerful position. The speaker is elected at the beginning of each new Congress by the entire House and is traditionally a member of the majority party, as are all committee chairs. While typically not the member with the longest service, the speaker generally has served in the House for a long time and in other House leadership positions as a sort of apprenticeship. Generally, a speaker is reelected until he chooses to retire.

The Speaker presides over the House, oversees House business, is the official spokesperson for the House of Representatives, and is second in the line of presidential succession. Moreover, he is the House liaison with the president and generally has great political influence within the chamber. Through his parliamentary and political skills he is expected to smooth the passage of party-backed legislation through the House.

The first "powerful" Speaker was Henry Clay, elected to the position in 1810 (see "People of the Past: Henry Clay," p. 223). Clay dominated the Democratic-Republican

PEOPLE OF THE PAST

Henry Clay

Henry Clay (1777–1852) was a congressional giant of his time, playing an active role in national politics for more than forty years. He served as Speaker of the House as a Democratic-Republican for six terms (longer than anyone else in the nineteenth century) and later was a leader of the new Whig Party. He was five times an unsuccessful presidential candidate, and he served as Secretary of State under John Quincy Adams.

Clay's personality and skill in oratory won him authority in Washington. As Speaker of the House of Representatives, in 1812 Clay became the leader of the "War Hawks," urging President James Madison to declare war on Great Britain in order to prevent British control of the seas, which Madison did on June 1, 1812.

As a presidential candidate, Clay developed his "American System," calling for national defense, construction of roads and canals using federal aid, protection of home industry through duties on foreign imports, and establishment of a second Bank of the United States. Clay wanted federal land in the West to be sold rather than given away to homesteaders so that the proceeds could be used to build schools and roads. The American System became the major plank in the platform of Clay's Whig Party.

Clay is remembered as the Great Compromiser. As a Southerner and a slaveholder on the one hand, and a friend to Northern industry on the other, Clay mediated between North and South over the question of slavery. Clay played a major role in three landmark compromises: the Missouri Compromise of 1820, the Tariff Compromise of 1850, and the Compromise of 1850. Clay hoped that the last of these compromises would prevent a civil war.

Although Clay's actions were not able to prevent the Civil War and his Whig Party disappeared shortly after his death, many features of his American System were later put into operation by the Republican Party.

Party in the House and kept party members in line by the use of his power to appoint committee members and committee chairs. Clay used not only the **party caucus** (a formal gathering of all party members), which he controlled, to decide which issues were to be addressed on the House floor, but also his power as Speaker to appoint his "hawk" allies to key positions on the Military and Foreign Affairs Committees in anticipation of the War of 1812.

Modern speakers do not enjoy the formal powers of their predecessors who served before 1910. Nevertheless, they have substantial powers based largely on their personal ability to persuade. The 103rd Congress was presided over by a Democrat, Thomas Foley (D.-Wash.), because Democrats held a majority of House seats—256 Democrats and 178 Republicans. In the Republican landslide midterm elections of 1994, however, not only did Republicans take control of the House (and Senate, too), Speaker Foley

224 ❖ Chapter 6 Congress

In the Republican sweep of the 1994 midterm election, Thomas Foley (D.-Wash.) became the first Speaker of the House to be voted out of office since 1860. Robert Dole (R.-Kans.) became Senate Majority Leader.

was defeated. Foley's defeat made him the first Speaker since Abraham Lincoln's time not to be reelected to his House seat.

Foley was a prominent lawyer in his native state of Washington prior to his election to the 89th Congress in the Democratic landslide of 1964. He moved through the ranks of the House leadership, serving first as the Democratic whip and then as the majority leader. He became the forty-ninth Speaker in June 1989. His replacement, the fiftieth Speaker, Newt Gingrich (R.-GA.), also served as whip before being elected to preside over the House.

As illustrated in Table 6.3, the Speaker enjoys both formal and informal powers. Speaker Foley used those powers rarely, but in 1993 he chose to take advantage of new House rules that gave the Speaker increased power over committee chairs, including the power to remove them from Senate-House Conference Committees. He removed Representative Dave McCurdy (D.-Okla.) as Chair of the House Intelligence Committee because he believed that McCurdy tried to undercut other Democrats in his unsuccessful bid to become the Secretary of Defense. That position ultimately went to Les

Table 6.3 ♦ Formal and Informal Powers of the Speaker of the House

FORMAL	INFORMAL
Presides over House when in session	Tries to build support for the president's programs when they are from the same party
Plays a major role in committee assignments (appoints 12 of 33 members of the Democratic Steering Committee, which functions as the "Committee on Committees" to select committee members)	Acts as national party leader when president is from different party
Appoints or plays a major role in the selection of other party leaders	Sets the public agenda through ability to attract media attention
Exercises considerable control over assignment of bills to particular committees	Helps other members with fund raising by making appearances at events in their districts

Aspin, Chairman of the House Armed Services Committee (Aspin resigned from that position in late 1993 to become Secretary of Defense). McCurdy was a vocal critic of Foley during the House banking scandal; he frequently accused Foley of inadequate leadership and even suggested publicly that Foley be replaced. Instead, Foley opted to replace McCurdy.

Other House Leaders. After the Speaker, the most powerful people in the House are the majority and minority leaders, who are elected in their individual party caucuses. The majority leader is the second most important person in the House; his counterpart on the other side of the aisle (the House is organized so that Democrats sit on the left side and Republicans on the right side of the center aisle) is the minority leader. The majority and minority leaders work closely with Speaker Newt Gingrich, and the majority leader helps the Speaker schedule proposed legislation for debate on the House floor.

The Speaker and majority and minority leaders are assisted in their leadership efforts by the majority and minority whips. The concept of whips originated in the British House of Commons, where they were named after the "whipper in," the rider who keeps the hounds together in a fox hunt. Party whips, who were first designated in the House in 1899 and in the Senate in 1913, do, as their name suggests, try to "whip" fellow Democrats or Republicans into line on partisan issues. They try to maintain close contact with all party members on important votes, prepare summaries of content and implications of bills, get "nose counts" during debates and votes, and in general get members to toe the party line. For example, when John Conyers, Jr. (D.-Mich.), became upset that no one consulted him in drafting the crime bill in 1993, he voted against the budget package out of irritation. "House Democratic whips swarmed over him like bees to honey," and he soon fell in line after being told he would become a major player.[16]

Whips and assistant whips are elected by party members in caucuses. When Republicans took control of both houses of Congress in 1994, Newt Gingrich, the House Republican whip, became the Speaker, and new majority and minority whips as well as assistant whips were elected by the party caucuses. (The Republican minority leader did not seek re-election in 1994).

The Senate

The Constitution specifies that the presiding officer of the Senate is the president of the Senate (see Figure 6-5). The vice president of the United States fills this job. Because he is not a member of the Senate, he votes only in the case of a tie. Vice President Al Gore Jr., for example, cast the tie-breaking vote in the Senate on the Budget Deficit Reduction bill in 1993.

The official chair of the Senate is the president pro tempore, who is selected by the majority party and presides over the Senate in the absence of the vice president. The position of president pro tempore is today primarily an honorary office that generally goes to the most senior senator of the majority party. Once elected, the pro tem, as he is called, stays in that office until there is a change in the majority party in the Senate. Because presiding over the Senate is a rather dull duty, neither the vice president nor the president pro tempore performs the task often. Instead, the duty of presiding over the Senate rotates among junior members of the chamber.

---

[16] Clifford Krauss, "The Budget Struggle: The House; Whips Use Soft Touch to Succeed," *New York Times* (August 7, 1993): A7.

THEN AND NOW

Life on the Floor and in the Halls of Congress

Throughout Congress's first several decades, partisan, sectional, and state tensions of the day often found their way onto the floors of the U.S. House and Senate. Many members were armed, and during one House debate thirty members brandished their weapons. In 1826, for example, Senator John Randolph of Virginia insulted Secretary of State Henry Clay from the floor of the Senate, referring to Clay as "this being, so brilliant yet so corrupt, which, like a rotten mackerel by moonlight, shined and stunk." Clay immediately challenged Randolph to a duel on the Virginia side of the Potomac River. Both missed, although Randolph's coat fell victim to a bullet hole. Reacting to public opinion, however, in 1839 Congress passed a law prohibiting dueling in the District of Columbia.

Nevertheless, dueling continued. A debate in 1851 between representatives from Alabama and North Carolina ended in a duel, but no one was hurt. In 1856, Representative Preston Brooks of South Carolina, defending the honor of his region and family, assaulted Senator Charles Sumner of Massachusetts on the floor of the Senate. Sumner was disabled and unable to resume his Congressional duties for several years. Guns and knives were abundantly evident on the floor of both House and Senate, along with a wide variety of alcoholic beverages.

Today the House and the Senate are usually much more sedate. In 1984, however, a group of newly elected Republican representatives began taking over the House floor every day after the end of normal hours to berate their Democratic colleagues. The chamber was usually empty but, like all other action on the floor, those speeches were broadcast live on C-SPAN and often used by the members for distribution to local television stations back home. During a particularly strong attack on several Democrats' views on Central America, Representative Newt Gingrich (R.-Ga.) paused suggestively in mid-speech, as though waiting for an objection or daring the Democrats to respond. No other House members were on the floor at the time, but since C-SPAN cameras focused only on the speaker, viewers were unaware of that fact.

Speaker Thomas P. O'Neill angrily reacted by ordering C-SPAN cameras to span the empty chamber to expose the tactics of Gingrich and other Republicans, but he failed to inform the Republicans of the change. O'Neill later apologized to the House Minority Leader, Robert Michel (R.-Ill.), but what Republicans labeled "CAMSCAM" ignited a firestorm on the floor. Incensed by remarks made by Gingrich, O'Neill dropped his gavel, left his spot on the dais, and took to the floor, roaring at Gingrich, "You challenged their [House Democrats'] patriotism, and it is the lowest thing that I have ever seen in my thirty-two years in Congress!" Trent Lott (R.-Miss.) then demanded that the Speaker be "taken down," the House term to call someone to order for violating House rules prohibiting personal attacks. The House Parliamentarian looked in the dictionary to see if the word "lowest" was a slur. As a hush fell on the House, the presiding officer told O'Neill that he had violated House rules. Bristled O'Neill, "I was expressing my views very mildly because I think much worse than I said."

O'Neill's penalty? The rarely invoked enforced silence for the remainder of the day's debate. So uncomfortable with that action was the House Minority Leader that he asked Lott to make a motion exempting O'Neill from the penalty, to which Lott agreed. No other House Speaker has ever been so reprimanded.*

---

* Alexander Stanley, "Tip Topped: O'Neill Tangles with Some Republican Turks over Camera Angles," *Nation* (May 28, 1984): 36.

The true leader of the Senate is the majority leader, elected by Senators of the majority party. Although not as powerful as the Speaker of the House, as the leader of the majority party, he sets the Senate agenda, refers legislation to committees, and assigns members to committees. George Mitchell (D.-Me.), served in this position from 1988 to 1994, when he resigned from the Senate. When Republicans won control of the Senate in the 1994 midterm elections, the Senate Republican minority leader, Robert Dole (R.-Kans.), became the majority leader. (Dole served as the majority leader during the Republicans' control of the Senate from 1981 to 1987.) The majority and minority whips round out the leadership positions in the Senate; they perform functions similar to those of their House counterparts.

The organization of both houses of Congress is closely tied to political parties. The parties also play a key role in the committee system, an organizational feature of Congress that facilitates its law-making and oversight functions.

The Role of Political Parties in Congress

When the first Congress met in 1789 in New York City, the nation's temporary capital, it consisted of only twenty-six senators and sixty-five representatives. These men faced the enormous task of creating much of the machinery of government as well as drafting a bill of rights, for which the Anti-Federalists had argued so vehemently. During their debates, the political differences that had divided Americans during the early years of the union were renewed. When Alexander Hamilton, the first Secretary of the Treasury and a staunch Federalist, proposed to fund the national debt and create a national bank, for example, he aroused the ire of those who feared vesting the national government with too much power. This conflict led Hamilton's opponents to create the Democratic-Republican Party to counter the Federalists, creating a two-party system in Congress. Control of the political parties quickly gave Congress many more powers. The Democratic-Republican Party caucus nominated Thomas Jefferson (1804), James Madison (1808 and 1812), and James Monroe (1816) for president, all of whom were elected.

At the beginning of each new Congress—the 104th Congress sits in two sessions, one in 1995 and one in 1996—the members of each party gather in caucus or conference. Historically, these caucuses have enjoyed varied powers, but today the party caucuses—called "caucus" by House Democrats and "conference" by House and Senate Republicans and Senate Democrats—are used by party members to select leaders and make decisions on pending issues.

The **majority party** in each house is the party with the greatest number of members. Being in the majority party allows members of that party to choose the major officers of Congress and thereby control debate on the floor, hold all committee chairmanships, and have a majority on all committees. In parliamentary systems like Britain's, the majority party in the House of Commons is entitled to form the government.

The Democratic Party in the House of Representatives also includes a Steering and Policy Committee, a small committee that consists of members appointed by the Speaker and representatives of each of the regional caucuses. It assigns Democratic representatives to House committees. The Republicans have a Committee on Committees that performs this function. Each party also has a Congressional Campaign Committee to assist members in their reelection bids. In the Senate, the twenty-five-person Democratic Steering Committee makes Democratic committee assignments. Republican assignments are made by its smaller, five-member Committee on Committees.

Loyalty to party is an important concept in both houses. Senate and House leaders and whips try to keep members of their respective parties in line, although this is often a very difficult task. During the 1993 vote on the North American Free Trade Agreement (NAFTA), for example, the House Democratic Majority Leader and an assistant whip opposed NAFTA, while the Speaker of the House and the House Whip supported it. In general, however, party loyalty is more common in the House. There, members rely more on the party for reelection help. And, because of its larger size, members also rely on the party for rewards of committee assignments.

The Committee System

"Congress in session is Congress on exhibition, whilst Congress in its committee rooms is Congress at work."[17] This statement is even more true today than when Woodrow Wilson wrote it in 1883. A quick look at the floor of the House or the Senate would lead most observers to conclude that not much goes on up on "the Hill" (as the Capitol is often called). Unless a vote is in progress, few members are on the floor. Instead, they are attending committee or subcommittee meetings. It is in these "little legislatures" that the most important legislative action takes place: Bills are drafted and discussed, and substantive and technical amendments are debated.[18] In essence, committees are the first and last places that all bills go. (When different versions of a bill are passed in the House and Senate, a conference committee with members of both houses meets to iron out the differences.) And it is usually committee members who play key roles in floor debate in the full House or Senate about the merits of the proposed bill.

Committees allow members of Congress to specialize and become experts in a small number of areas instead of attempting to be "jacks-of-all-trades, masters of none." The establishment of subcommittees further subdivides issues and allows for even greater specialization. In addition, some committee assignments allow members to act on behalf of the specific interests of their constituents. Western representatives, for example, favor an assignment to the Interior and Insular Affairs Committee because of that committee's jurisdiction over all Western lands. And in the Senate, committee assignments and chairs often determine the policy orientation of the committee, and thus the kind of proposed legislation that comes out of the committee.

Committees are not mentioned in the Constitution. Originally, they were created on an ad hoc (as necessary) basis, but they had historical precedents in the British Parliament and in the colonial legislatures. These ad hoc committees were dissolved as soon as their specific tasks were accomplished. By the Second Congress, 350 such committees had been formed, and soon the increasing scope of congressional activities made the establishment, dissolution, and reestablishment of ad hoc committees increasingly time-consuming and inconvenient.

Over the years, as issues became more complex, some specialization became an absolute necessity. An institutionalized committee system was created in 1816, and com-

---

[17] Woodrow Wilson, *Congressional Government: A Study in American Government* (New York: Meridian Books, 1956, originally published in 1885), p. 79.

[18] Richard L. Hall, "Participation, Abdication, and Representation in Congressional Committees," in Lawrence C. Dodd and Bruce I. Oppenheimer, *Congress Reconsidered*, 5th ed. (Washington, DC: CQ Press, 1993), p. 162.

mittees have been added over time. Committees are especially important in the House of Representatives because its size makes organization and specialization especially key, as noted in Table 6.4.

Types of Committees. There are four types of congressional committees: standing, ad hoc or select, joint, and conference.

1. *Standing committees* are the committees to which proposed bills are referred for consideration. Fewer than 10 percent of the more than 10,000 measures sent to them are ever reported out of the standing committees. These committees are called "standing" because they continue from one Congress to the next; therefore, they are generally viewed as the permanent workshops of congressional lawmaking.
2. *Ad hoc* or *select committees* are temporary committees appointed for specific purposes with fairly limited mandates, generally to conduct special investigations or studies and to report back to the chamber that established them. Unlike standing committees, select committees do not ordinarily draft and report legislation.

Table 6.4 ♦ House–Senate Committee Comparisons

CATEGORY	HOUSE	SENATE
Number of standing committees	22	17
Total committee assignments per member	About 7	About 11
Power or prestige committees	Appropriations, Budget, Rules, Ways and Means	Appropriations, Armed Services, Finance, Foreign Relations; almost every senator assigned to one of these four
Treaties and nominations submitted by the president	No authority	Committees review
Floor debate	Representatives' activity is somewhat confined to the bills reported from the panels on which they serve	Senators can choose to influence any policy area regardless of their committee assignments
Subcommittee government	The norm on many committees	Notable on some but not most committees
Committee consideration of legislation	More difficult to bypass	Easier to bypass (for example, by allowing "riders"—unrelated policy proposals—to measures pending on the floor)
Committee chairmen	Subject to party and House rules that limit their discretionary authority over committee operations	Freer reign to manage and organize their committees
Committee staff	Less assertive in advocating ideas and proposals	More aggressive in shaping the legislative agenda
Eligibility for subcommittee chairmanships	Representatives of the major party usually must wait at least 1 term	A majority-party senator, regardless of seniority, usually chairs a subcommittee

Source: From Roger H. Davidson and Walter J. Oleszek, *Congress and Its Members,* 3rd ed. (Congressional Quarterly Press, 1994), p. 216.

3. *Joint committees* are formed with members from both houses of Congress, generally to coordinate investigations or special studies. In practice, they are set up to expedite business between the houses and to help focus public attention on major matters such as the economy, taxation, or scandals. A joint committee, for example, was formed to investigate the Iran-Contra scandal.
4. *Conference committees* are a special kind of joint committee with the explicit function of reconciling differences in bills passed by the House and Senate. The conference committee is made up of members from the House and Senate committees that originally considered the bill. Because the Constitution mandates that all bills pass both houses in the same form, compromises are often needed on the versions that pass each house of Congress. Once the committee comes up with a satisfactory compromise bill, it is presented to both houses of Congress for their approval. At this point, they can only accept or decline the compromise legislation; they cannot change or amend it in any way.

The House and Senate **standing committees** listed in Table 6.5 were created by statute. The House has 22 standing committees (and a total of 127 subcommittees) each with an average of about thirty-five members. The standing committees collectively act as the eyes, ears, and hands of the House. They consider issues roughly parallel to those of the departments represented in the president's cabinet. For example, there are committees on agriculture, the judiciary, veterans' affairs, transportation, and labor.

Standing committees have tremendous power. They can defeat bills, delay them, amend them so that they are radically changed, or hurry them through the process. A committee reports out to the full House or Senate only a small fraction of the bills first assigned to it. Bills can be "forced" out of a House committee by a **discharge petition** signed by a majority (218) of the House membership, but legislators are reluctant to take this drastic measure. Discharge petitions were begun in 1924 to give a majority in the House the ability to bring a matter to the floor in the face of committee inaction. Since World War II, fewer than five bills have been enacted into law through this procedure. In 1971, for example, a discharge petition was used to force the proposed equal rights amendment out of the Judiciary Committee, where it had been stalled by the committee's powerful chair, Emanuel Celler (D.-N.Y.). It later went on to be passed by the full House on a vote of 350 to 15.

Discharge petitions, in spite of a House rule that keeps the names of the signees secret, are under attack in the House. In late 1993, the system was targeted by House Republicans; they charged that the secrecy surrounding discharge petitions allows some members to claim that they support legislation bottled up in committee even though they have done nothing to advance it (such as sign a discharge petition to allow a vote). The secrecy rule assures that there is no way for constituents to learn if their legislators have tried to force a stalled bill out of committee. A proposed bill would force a change in the sixty-three-year-old House tradition and make public the names of those signing a discharge petition.

The Senate has seventeen standing committees that range in size from sixteen to twenty-nine members. It also has more than eighty-five subcommittees, allowing nearly all senators the opportunity to chair one. As illustrated in Table 6.5, the Senate Judiciary Committee, for example, has seven subcommittees. The plethora of subcommittees in the Senate, in fact, has been the subject of much debate in the Senate, and numerous calls have been made to reduce that number.

Table 6.5 ♦ Committees of the House and Senate (with a Subcommittee Example)

STANDING COMMITTEES

House

Agriculture
Appropriations
Armed Services
Banking, Finance, and Urban Affairs
Budget
Education and Labor
District of Columbia
Energy and Commerce
Foreign Affairs
Government Operations
House Administration
Interior and Insular Affairs
Judiciary
Merchant Marine and Fisheries
Post Office and Civil Service
Public Works and Transportation
Rules
Science, Space, and Technology
Small Business
Standards of Official Conduct (Ethics)
Veterans' Affairs
Ways and Means

Senate

Agriculture, Nutrition, and Forestry
Appropriations
Armed Services
Banking, Housing, and Urban Affairs
Budget
Commerce, Science, and Transportation
Energy and Natural Resources
Environment and Public Works
Finance
Foreign Relations
Governmental Affairs
Judiciary   *Judiciary Subcommittees:*
    Antitrust, Monopolies, and Business Rights
    Constitution
    Courts and Administrative Practice
    Immigration and Refugee Affairs
    Patents, Copyrights, and Trademarks
    Technology and the Law
    Juvenile Justice
Labor and Human Resources
Rules and Administration
Small Business
Veterans' Affairs
Ways and Means

SELECT COMMITTEES

House

Aging
Hunger
Intelligence
Narcotics Abuse and Control

Senate

Aging
Ethics
Indian Affairs
Intelligence

JOINT COMMITTEES

Joint Economic Committee
Joint Committee on Taxation
Joint Committee on Printing
Joint Committee on the Library

In contrast to the House, whose members hold few committee assignments (an average of two standing and four subcommittees), senators are spread more thinly, with each serving on an average of three to four committees and seven subcommittees. Whereas the committee system allows House members to become policy or issue specialists, Senate members are often generalists (see Table 6.5). Senator Nancy Kassebaum (R.-Kans.) is typical; she sits on the Foreign Relations, Labor and Human Resources, and Indian Affairs standing committees in addition to the Joint Committee on the Organization of Congress. Paul Simon (D.-Ill.) sits on the Budget, Foreign Relations, Judiciary, and Labor and Human Resources committees; he also chairs three subcommittees while serving on five others.

Senate committees enjoy the same power over framing legislation as do House committees, but the Senate is more likely to force bills out of committee by the use of discharge petitions. During the 1960s, in particular, the Senate was regularly forced to use discharge petitions to bypass the Judiciary Committee in order to get full consideration of civil rights laws. The Judiciary Committee as chaired by Senator James Eastland (D.-Miss.) became known as the "graveyard of civil rights legislation." (From 1953 to 1963 only 1 of 121 civil rights bills emerged from Eastland's fiefdom.)

Committee Membership. To gain a seat on a committee, one must be associated with either of the two major political parties. This becomes important on the rare occasions when an independent or third-party candidate is elected to one of the chambers. In 1990, for example, when Socialist Bernard Sanders of Vermont was elected to the House of Representatives, he had to choose a party affiliation for the purposes of committee placement. (He chose the Democratic Party.)

New members and those seeking changes in their assignments inform their party's selection committee of their preferences. Generally, preferences can be filled because junior members do not request more influential or prestigious committees, such as Ways and Means in the House or Armed Services in the Senate. Instead, they request assignments based on their own interests or expertise or on a particular committee's ability to help their prospects for reelection. Political scientist Kenneth A. Shepsle has noted that committee assignments are to members what stocks are to investors—they seek to acquire those that will add to the value of their portfolio.[19] For example, in his first term in the Senate, Robert Kerrey (D.-Nebr.) was assigned to the Agriculture Committee, where he could advance his state's farm industry.

Representatives also seek committee assignments that have access to what is known as the **pork barrel**. Pork barrel legislation allows representatives to "bring home the bacon" to their districts in the form of public works programs, military bases, or other programs designed to benefit their districts directly. Until the recent end of the Cold War, a seat on the Armed Services Committee, for example, was particularly attractive. It could allow members to bring lucrative defense contracts back to their districts, encourage the building of bases, or discourage their closing within their districts or states, thus pleasing constituents.

The House Public Works and Transportation Committee also is a plum assignment for some representatives. For example, if all of the money allotted for local transportation projects were divided evenly among all 435 congressional districts, each district would get approximately $14.5 million. However, in 1991, the district of the chairman of that committee, Robert Roe (D.-N.J.), was slated to receive $225 million to finish

---

[19] Kenneth A. Shepsle, *The Giant Jigsaw Puzzle: Democratic Committee Assignments in the Modern House* (Chicago: University of Chicago Press, 1978).

a highway and $14.2 million to elevate fourteen bridges in his district. The second-ranking minority member's district, Bud Schuster (R.-Pa.) was set to get $287 million in new public works projects. Other committee members' districts received from $75 to $411 million.

Legislators who bring this kind of pork barrel back to their districts are hard to beat at the polls. In 1984, Jesse Helms (R.-N.C.), for example, turned down the chairmanship of the Senate Committee on Foreign Relations to stay on as Chairman of the less prestigious Committee on Agriculture, Nutrition, and Forestry, where he could better ensure continued support for the tobacco industry so vital to his home state's economy.

There always are members, however, who end up with "bad" committee assignments. After her 1968 election, Representative Shirley Chisholm (D.-N.Y.), the first African-American woman elected to Congress, was assigned to the House Agriculture Committee. "Apparently all they know here in Washington about Brooklyn is that a tree grows there," complained Chisholm. "I think it would be hard to imagine an assignment that is less relevant to my background or to the needs of the predominantly black and Puerto Rican people who elected me," she protested. In spite of the fact that some urban Democrats welcome serving on the committee that oversees the food stamp program, Chisholm fought for a different assignment and ultimately landed one on the Veterans Affairs Committee. "There are a lot more veterans in my district than there are trees," she later explained.[20]

In both the House and the Senate, committee membership generally reflects the party distribution within that chamber. For example, if the Democrats are the majority party and hold two-thirds of the seats, they control the chairmanship of and usually hold two-thirds of the seats on a committee, with the Republicans making up the other one-third. This distribution is based on tradition, not rules. Moreover, some committees have traditions of either partisanship or bipartisanship. For instance, the House Armed Services Committee has a tradition of strong bipartisanship and therefore has a large number of **minority party** members. In contrast, the House Rules Committee has tended to be more partisan and thus has a higher number of majority party members. In the 103rd Congress, for example, it had nine Democrats and only four Republicans.

Although most committees in one house parallel those in the other, one committee unique to the House of Representatives plays a key role in the lawmaking process: the House Rules Committee. This committee reviews most bills after they come from a committee and before they go to the full chamber for consideration. Performing a "traffic cop" function, the House Rules Committee gives each bill what is called a rule, which contains the date the bill will come up for debate, the amount of time that will be allotted for discussion, and often even specifications concerning what kinds of amendments can be offered. Majority party members of this committee are directly appointed by the Speaker.

The Power of Committee Chairs. The position of committee chair is one of tremendous power and prestige. When House speakers were strong, they personally selected all committee chairs on the basis of friendships and loyalty. After what is termed the "revolution of 1910," when members revolted against the powerful speaker Joseph Cannon, committee chairs were chosen by **seniority**—the person of the majority party with the longest continuous service on that committee was automatically made chair.

Robert C. Byrd, President Pro Tem and Prince of Pork

❖ ❖ ❖

As Chairman of the powerful Senate Appropriations Committee, Robert C. Byrd (D.-W.Va.) has made his home state his number one priority. When he took control of the committee in 1989 he pledged to bring $1 billion to West Virginia within the next five years. It took him less than two and earned him the nickname "King of Pork." It could be "a lot worse," says Byrd. "Besides, it represents a job well done in the interest of the infrastructure, in the interest of my people, and in the interest of the country."* His biggest coup was the moving of the FBI's $185-million fingerprinting center with 2,600 jobs from Washington, D.C., to his home state.

* Leslie Phillips, "In the Senate, Buck Stops (and Goes) with Byrd," *USA Today* (June 21, 1993): 8–A.

---

[20] Reported in *Woman's Almanac* (New York: Newspaper Enterprises Association, 1977), p. 200.

In 1971 and again in 1973, moderate and liberal Democrats pushed through a series of changes in the House designed to break the hold that conservative committee chairs from the South had long enjoyed because of the seniority system. In 1971, House Democrats voted to elect committee chairs by secret ballot in the party caucus at the beginning of the session, and seniority was no longer the sole criterion for becoming a House chair. (In the Senate there was little change, because seniority is not nearly so important there; however, if one-fifth of the party caucus requests it, a secret ballot may be used to elect committee chairs.)

In 1975, in the wake of these reforms—and with the election in 1974 of a bumper crop of "Young Turks," seventy-five new liberal House Democrats—three long-entrenched House chairs who were considered dictatorial, on the conservative fringes of the party, or both, were removed from their positions. Later, in 1985, eighty-year-old Melvin Price was voted out as chair of the Armed Services Committee, in spite of his promise to resign at the end of the term and passionate pleas from Speaker Thomas P. O'Neill to retain Price in this position.

Although their power was reduced by these reforms, committee chairs still establish the agenda for the committee in conjunction with the ranking minority member and may sit as nonvoting members on all subcommittees. Moreover, committee chairs call meetings, strategize, recommend majority members to sit on conference committees, and direct the committee staff. The chair may choose not to schedule a hearing on a bill so that the bill can die, may convene meetings when opponents are absent, and may adjourn meetings when things are going badly. Personal skill, influence, and expertise are a chair's best allies.

In 1994, proposals to limit full committee chairs from chairing any subcommittees in the House and only one subcommittee in the Senate were introduced. Despite the large influx of new legislators, few give these proposals chances to succeed.

The Rise of Subcommittees. Another reform that occurred in the early 1970s was the adoption of "the subcommittee bill of rights," which decentralized committee power enormously. It took power away from the committee chairs of the 22 House standing committees and divided it among 127 subcommittees whose chairs now control their own budgets and staffs. Previously, subcommittee chairs were appointed by the committee chair. House Democrats now require that committee Democrats bid for subcommittee chairs and that their choices be accepted by a vote of party members on that committee. Seniority is generally used, but this new method does give majority party members the right to reject a subcommittee chair.[21]

Before the rule changes, committee chairs often chose to head important subcommittees themselves or appointed their close friends to those positions. As the power and number of subcommittees have increased, House Democrats have abolished the practice of multiple subcommittee chairships, allowing each member to chair only one. This practice allowed so many House members to become subcommittee chairs and have their own base of power that former Representative Morris K. Udall (D.-Ariz.) once joked that if he passed a young colleague in the hall and didn't remember his name, he'd simply greet him with "good morning, Mr. Chairman," knowing he'd be right about half the time.[22] In the 103rd Congress, for example, nearly half of all Democrats in the House chaired some committee or subcommittee.

---

[21] Steven S. Smith and Christopher J. Deering, *Committees in Congress*, 2nd ed. (Washington, DC: CQ Press, 1990), p. 126.

[22] Ibid.

As the workload of Congress has increased, so has the importance of subcommittees, leading to the rise of what some term "subcommittee government." On some committees it has become the norm for committee members simply to defer to the judgment of the subcommittee and its specialists in order to speed up the legislative process.

The Lawmaking Function of Congress

Chief among the responsibilities of Congress is its lawmaking function, which is greatly facilitated by the committee system. Proposals for legislation can come from the president, executive agencies, committee staffs, interest groups, or even private individuals, but only members of the House or Senate can formally submit a bill for congressional consideration. Once a bill is proposed, it usually reaches a dead end. Of the more than 6,000 bills introduced each year in Congress, fewer than 25 percent are enacted, or made into law.

It is probably useful to think of Congress as a system of multiple vetoes, which was what the Framers desired. They wanted to disperse power, and as Congress has evolved it has come closer and closer to the Framers' intentions. As a bill goes through Congress, a dispersion of power occurs as roadblocks to passage must be surmounted at numerous steps in the process. In addition to realistic roadblocks, caution signs and other opportunities for delay abound. A member who sponsors a bill must get through *every* obstacle; in contrast, successful opposition means "winning" at only one of many stages, including (1) the House subcommittee, (2) the House full committee, (3) the House Rules Committee, (4) the House, (5) the Senate subcommittee, (6) the full Senate committee, (7) the Senate, (8) floor leaders in both Houses, (9) the House–Senate Conference Committee, and (10) the president.

In Britain, the daily rhythm of parliamentary activity contrasts sharply with that in the U.S. Congress. The emphasis in Parliament is overwhelmingly on formal debate, in which government and opposition teams clash regularly and in an animated fashion. For an individual Member of Parliament (MP), the fastest route to prestige and influence is to shine in debate and thus come to the attention of the party leadership. Consequently, there are few incentives for members to spend a lot of time in committee, since committee work takes the MP off the debate floor and encourages cross-party cooperation. The combination of strong parliamentary parties and a neglected committee system leads to a situation where Parliament, though a spirited forum, is a relatively weak institution in the overall governmental scheme. Virtually all bills emanate from the executive (Prime Minister), and the scope for an individual MP's influence on the legislative process is minimal. The British parliament is, to employ the conventional distinction, a debating parliament, not a working parliament (like the U.S. Congress or the German Bundestag).

In the United States, the story of how a bill becomes a law can be told in two ways. The first is the "textbook" method—you may have seen a flowchart on a television show or in a news magazine that tracks the course of a bill from inception through subcommittee and committee action and finally to presidential approval or veto. The textbook method provides a greatly simplified road map of the process to make it easier to understand. A second method looks at an actual example of how a particular bill became a law and shows the true complexities of the process.

How a Bill Becomes a Law: The Textbook Way

A bill must survive three stages before it becomes a law. Because it may be killed during any of these stages, it is much easier to defeat a bill than it is to get one passed. The House and Senate have parallel processes, and often the same bill is introduced in each chamber at the same time.

Although a bill must be introduced by a member of Congress, it is often sponsored by a whole list of other members in an early effort to show support for it. Once introduced, the bill is sent to the clerk of the chamber, who gives it a number (for example, HR 1, or S 1—indicating House or Senate bill number one for the session). The bill is then printed, distributed, and sent to the appropriate committee for consideration.

The first stage of action takes place within the committee. The committee usually refers the bill to one of its subcommittees, which researches the bill and decides whether to hold hearings on it. The subcommittee hearings provide the opportunity for people on both sides of the issue to voice their opinions. Most of these hearings are now open to the public because of 1970s "sunshine" laws, which require open sessions. After the hearings, the bill is revised, and the subcommittee votes to approve or defeat the bill. If the subcommittee votes in favor of the bill, it is returned to the full committee, which then either rejects the bill or sends it to the House or Senate floor (see Figure 6-7).

The second stage of action takes place on the House or Senate floor. Before the bill may be debated on the floor, it must be sent to the Rules Committee to be given a rule and a place on the calendar, or schedule. The rule given to the bill determines the limits on the floor debate and specifies what types of amendments, if any, may be attached. (Budget bills do not go to the Rules Committee.) Once the Rules Committee considers the bill, it is put on the calendar.

When the day arrives for floor debate, the House may choose to form a "Committee of the Whole," which allows the House to deliberate with the presence of only one hundred members, to expedite consideration of the bill. On the House floor, the bill is debated, amendments are offered, and a vote is taken by the full House. If the bill survives, it is sent to the other chamber of Congress for consideration if it has not been considered there simultaneously.

Unlike the House, where debate is necessarily limited given the size of the body, in the Senate bills may be held up by **holds** or **filibusters**. A hold is a tactic by which a senator asks to be informed before a particular bill is brought to the floor. This request signals the Senate leadership and the sponsors of the bill that a colleague may have objections to the bill and should be consulted.

The hold system has recently come under attack by some Senate members. "It's gotten out of control," says Senator Bennett Johnston (D.-La.).[23] In the first session of the 102nd Congress, for example, holds were placed on more than two-thirds of the 250 bills reported out of committee in the Senate. In the 103rd Congress, holds were used to delay several presidential appointments.

Filibusters, which allow for unlimited debate on a bill, grew out of the absence of rules to limit speech in the Senate and are often used to "talk a bill to death" (see page 238). In contrast to a hold, a filibuster is a more formal way of halting action on a bill

---

[23] Quoted in "Senate 'Holds' System Developing as Sophisticated Tactic for Leverage, Delay," 1991 *Daily Reports for Executives* (August 26, 1991, No. 165): C–1.

The Lawmaking Function of Congress ❖ 237

FIGURE 6-7

How a Bill Becomes a Law: The Textbook Way

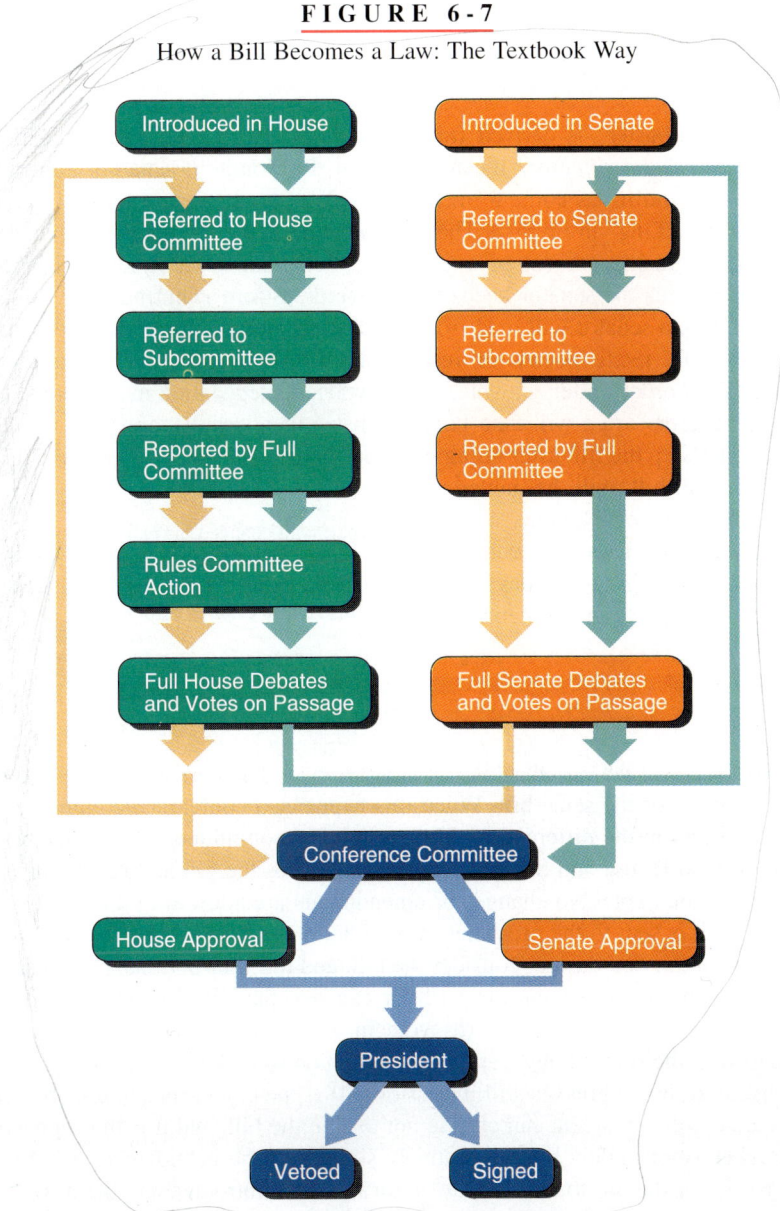

by means of long speeches or unlimited debate in the Senate. The filibuster became an increasingly common feature of Senate life during the slavery debates. In 1917, after eleven senators waged a filibuster against an important foreign policy matter supported by President Woodrow Wilson, the Senate adopted a rule to avoid the potential disaster of tying the president's hands during World War I. To end a filibuster, cloture must be invoked. To cut off debate, sixteen senators must first sign a motion for cloture. Then, a roll-call vote is taken. Two-thirds of the senators—subsequent changes now require only sixty instead of sixty-six—must vote to end the filibuster. Each member of the Senate can then speak for one hour before debate is closed and the legislation on the floor is brought to a vote.

Filibusters

The term "filibuster" is derived from the Dutch word *vrijbuiter*, meaning "freebooter," and it has come to mean "continuous talking" in English. There are no rules on the content of a filibuster as long as the senator keeps on talking. Often a senator will read from a phone book, recite poetry, or read cookbooks in order to delay a vote. A team of senators often will take turns speaking to keep the filibuster going in hopes that a bill will be tabled or killed. In 1964, for example, a group of Northern liberal senators continued a filibuster for eighty-two days in an effort to prevent amendments that would weaken a civil rights bill. It has been the Southern senators, however, who have made the most use of the filibuster in their efforts to circumvent or at least delay civil rights legislation. Senator Strom Thurmond (D.-S.C.) holds the record for the longest one-man filibuster; in 1957 he opposed civil rights legislation in a personal filibuster that lasted more than twenty-four hours.*

* Thurmond changed his party affiliation from Democrat to Republican on September 16, 1964, shortly after passage of the Civil Rights Act of 1964.

The third stage of action takes place when the two chambers of Congress approve different versions of the same bill. When this happens, a conference committee is established to iron out the differences. The conference committee, whose members are from the original House and Senate committees, revises the bill and returns it to each chamber for a final vote. No changes or amendments are allowed at this stage. If the bill is passed, it is sent to the president, who either signs it or vetoes it.

The president has ten days to consider the bill, and has four options. (1) He can sign the bill, at which point it becomes law. (2) He can veto the bill. Congress may override the president's veto with a two-thirds vote in each chamber, a very difficult task. (3) He can wait the full ten days, at the end of which time the bill becomes law without his signature if Congress is still in session. (4) If the Congress adjourns before the ten days are up, the president can choose not to sign the bill, and it is thus "pocket vetoed." **Pocket vetoes** allow bills figuratively stashed in the president's pocket to die. The only way for the bill to become law is for it to be reintroduced in the next session and go through the process again. Because Congress sets its own date of adjournment, technically the session could be continued the few extra days necessary to prevent a pocket veto. Extensions are unlikely, however, as sessions are scheduled to adjourn close to the November elections or the Christmas holidays.

How a Bill Really Becomes a Law: The Clean Air Act Amendments of 1990

Passage of the Clean Air Act Amendments of 1990, while following the general steps outlined above, was much more complex and interesting (see Figure 6-8). Like most major modern legislation, this act officially began with the White House. After campaigning for president in 1988 as an environmentalist, George Bush promised, in his inaugural address, to send Congress a major clean air legislative package. Over the

The Lawmaking Function of Congress ❖ 239

FIGURE 6-8

How a Bill Really Becomes a Law: The Clean Air Act Amendments of 1990

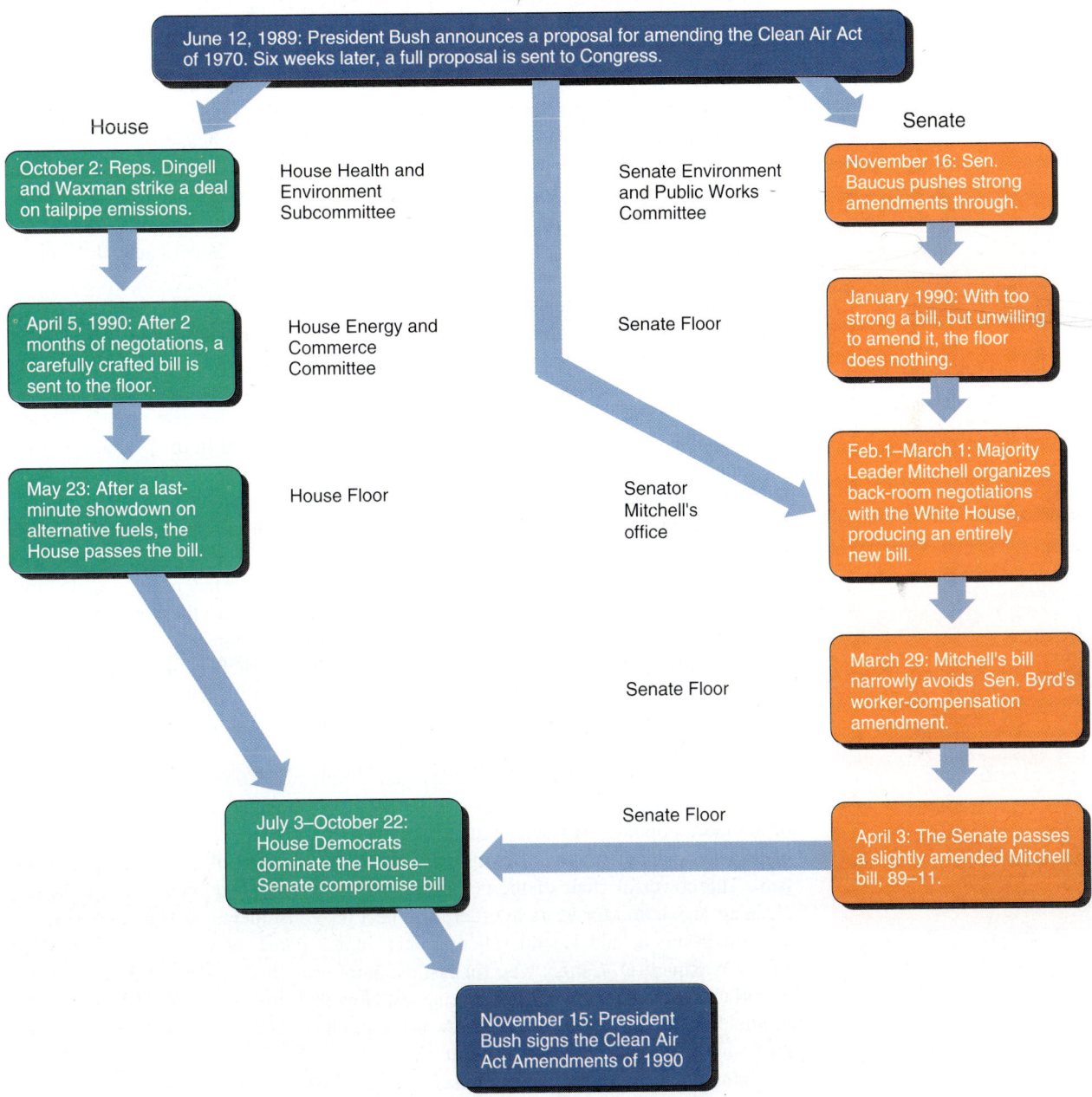

next several months, an executive team was assembled: Robert Grady of the Office of Management and Budget (OMB); William Reilly, the head of the Environmental Protection Agency (EPA), and several of his aides; Roger Porter, the president's domestic policy adviser; and, in an unusual move, C. Boyden Gray, the White House chief counsel. Gray was a close adviser to the president and considered by many to be the "real clean air nut" in the administration. Notably excluded were members of the Department of Energy.

After considerable discussion, study, and interviewing of academics and other people, this team hammered together a vast proposal in Bush's name. Fully 140 representatives and 25 senators, led by Representative John Dingell (D.-Mich.) and Senator John Chafee (R.-R.I.), introduced it as a bill in each house.

In the Senate, the bill was assigned to the Environment and Public Works Committee, which is so pro-environmentalist that it is out of sync with the rest of the Senate. When its version of the bill was reported back to the floor, the committee had stretched the bill's provisions so much that the package was unacceptable to the full Senate. Automobile tailpipe emission standards, for example, were far too strict. Instead of igniting a flurry of amendments and arguments, individual senators ignored the extreme bill entirely because they didn't want to touch it. Supporters knew that calling a vote would bring defeat, but they couldn't figure out how to amend the bill to make it acceptable to the majority.

George Mitchell, then the Senate majority leader, took over in a typical modern party leadership maneuver. He called a series of closed-door negotiations that included representatives of the administration, Robert Dole, the minority leader, and other key senators who were called in on points in which they had a vested interest. After six long weeks of hard negotiating, this process produced an agreement among Democrats, Republicans, and the administration on every single point in the package, including tailpipe emissions and air-quality standards. As a group, the participants agreed to fight off every amendment that might be proposed from the floor, with the stipulation that any amendment successfully passed would free up any party to walk away from the deal.

This process, though extraordinary by historical standards, has become quite common on major bills as political parties have strengthened and the committees have proven unsuccessful at managing a more unruly Senate or House floor. When the bill was brought to the floor, the powerful team led by Mitchell, Dole, and the White House succeeded in fending off all major amendments—only a few minor adjustments were allowed to pass—and the Senate proceeded to pass the resultant package by an overwhelming margin.

In the House, meanwhile, the Energy and Commerce Committee had much more say, partly because of the typically greater expertise in technical issues that members of the more populous House can afford to attain. First, a rule was assigned to the bill so that no amendment could be offered without the approval of key committee members. The powerful chair of the committee, John Dingell, had been trying to scuttle clean air legislation for years in order to protect his constituents, Detroit auto workers. The Environment and Health subcommittee of his panel, however, was chaired by Henry Waxman (D.-Calif.), who for just as many years had championed clean air for his smog-ridden constituents in Los Angeles. Now that Bush had broken the legislative deadlock with a proposal, Dingell knew he would have to deal with Waxman and have the committee report out some kind of bill.

Taking a cue from the Senate, these two pulled back behind closed doors in informal negotiations that only indirectly involved other members of the committee. When they reached a deal on tailpipe emissions, their biggest sticking point, the official committee proceedings got back on track. Unlike what had transpired in the Senate, however, none of these behind-the-scenes or committee negotiations involved the White House. This was because House Republicans had become so ineffectual after so many years of Democratic control that the Democrats, in effect, could ignore them and their party leader in the White House. Dingell, Waxman, Speaker Thomas Foley, and their colleagues were much more willing to slam the door on those on the other side of the aisle than their counterparts in the Senate had been.

Once both houses passed versions of the bill, the conference committee phase commenced. Because of House members' greater knowledge and expertise, they controlled the course of deliberations, making the bill stronger than the one originally proposed by the White House. President Bush was in no position to veto the stronger bill, however, because he had taken part (through his teammates) in the Senate's side of the deal making and had campaigned so loudly on the environment. In the end, therefore, the House crafters like Waxman who wanted a strong bill were able to carry the day.

Any kind of legislation is more difficult to pass when the president and Congress are of different political parties. For years, Republican presidents blamed the Democrats, who controlled the Congress, for gridlock, as fewer and fewer important pieces of legislation could be agreed on by both parties. If Reagan or Bush wanted passage of certain legislation, the Democratic Congress often rejected their proposals. Conversely, if Congress passed a particular bill, President Bush, in particular, often vetoed it and the Democrats repeatedly failed to muster enough votes to override his veto.

In 1993, however, for the first time since 1968, both Houses of Congress and the presidency were controlled by the same political party. Most major presidential programs were passed, and several bills previously passed by Congress but vetoed by George Bush became law. "Gridlock is gone," declared House Majority Leader Richard Gephardt (D.-Mo.) after the end of the first session of the 103rd Congress, which was one of the most productive sessions in recent years. In 1993 Bill Clinton enjoyed an exceptionally high success rate as Congress supported 86.4 percent of legislation he supported including the budget bill, NAFTA, the Family and Medical Leave Act, and the Brady Bill. In 1994, however, his fortunes were reversed as crime and health care reform proved to be divisive issues in Congress. Health care, welfare reform and lobbying, and campaign finance bills—along with further budget reductions—are likely to produce little harmony in Congress.

How Members Make Decisions

As a bill wends its way through the labyrinth of the lawmaking process described above, members are confronted with this question: How should I vote? Although most legislation pertains to fairly mundane matters, members nonetheless fear that they will "miss" something in a bill and vote the "wrong" way, alienating voters at home. Unless a bill is controversial, this could be easy to do. In the 102nd Congress, for example, 9,601 bills were introduced and 603 were passed. Yet, these 603 bills amounted to more than 7,000 pages of new laws.

Of course, members often listen to their own personal beliefs on the matter. But those views can often be moderated by other considerations. In an effort to avoid making any voting mistakes, members look to a variety of sources for "cues." Major cue givers include political parties, colleagues, caucuses, interest groups, staff members, the president, and, of course, constituents. And frequently, how a member ultimately decides or votes on any particular measure will vary according to the issues involved and in the context in which they are presented.[24]

---

[24] Aage R. Clausen, *How Congressmen Decide: A Policy Focus* (New York: St. Martin's Press, 1973).

Political Parties

Not all issues voted on in Congress divide members along party lines. In fact, only one-third to one-half of the votes in Congress are considered to be party votes (that is, when a majority in one party opposes a majority in the other). However, on these party votes members vote with their party between 70 and 80 percent of the time. In the first session of the 103rd Congress, that figure was even higher. Democrats voted with other Democrats 90 percent of the time. For Republicans, the figure was 88 percent. Interestingly, freshman Democrats of both parties supported their party even more frequently—93 percent for Democrats and 90 percent for Republicans. Political parties clearly have an interest in increasing their representation in Congress and in maintaining party unity on votes in Congress. Toward that end, party officials have several sources of influence.

Members of Congress elected on a partisan ticket feel a degree of obligation to their party and also to the president if he is of the same party. Although the national political parties have little say in who gets a party's nomination for the U.S. Senate or the House, once a candidate has emerged successfully from a primary contest (see Chapter 12), both houses have committees that provide campaign assistance since it is to each party's advantage to win as many seats as possible in each house. Once a member is elected, especially if he or she was the recipient of financial support or campaign visits from popular members, party leaders expect some degree of loyalty in return.

Each party in Congress also has a whip system used to disseminate information, keep track of who is voting with the party and who is not, and influence and pressure the undecided. Generally, this pressure is subtle; in some instances, however, party leaders turn on the heat. For example, when in 1987 Senate Democratic leaders wanted to override a veto by President Ronald Reagan, they adopted a "baby-sitting" strategy in which wavering Democrats were accompanied at all times by two other Democrats with the "right" views. Obviously, the party cue can be strong at times, and going along on legislation of importance to the party leadership can have its rewards. Although it is rare to see a vote along straight party lines, in recent years there has been a general trend toward party unity on floor votes, especially in the House.

In Britain, virtually all votes (called *divisions*) taken in the House of Commons divide Members of Parliament along party lines; indeed, in this sense we speak of British parliamentary parties as "disciplined," as they are able to marshal the support of their members on questions before the legislature.

Because each political party includes a wide spectrum of members, special-interest groups or caucuses exist within each party. Liberal Democrats belong to the Democratic Study Group, conservative Republicans to the Arms Control Caucus. In the early 1980s, conservative Southern Democrats—called "boll weevils" because, like their namesake, they bore from within the cotton boll—created the Conservative Democratic Forum.

Colleagues and Caucuses

Special-interest caucuses, including such disparate groups as farmers, footwear manufacturers, and first-term members of Congress, allow members from either party to cross party lines in order to band together with their colleagues who have a common interest. More than one hundred such caucuses exist, including the Black Caucus, the Congressional Caucus for Women's Issues, and caucuses formed to promote certain industries, such as textiles, tourism, wine, coal, steel, mushrooms, and cranberries; or to advance particular views or interests. Many of these caucuses lie low unless their interests are threatened. In the 1970s, when an influx of mushrooms from China and Taiwan threatened the sale of U.S. mushrooms, the sixty-member Mushroom Caucus sprang into action to defend its product.

African-American legislators formed their own caucus in 1971, and lobbyists from major women's rights groups urged the women in Congress to do likewise. But senior female House members were opposed to the idea, and other members feared being associated with the liberal agenda of Bella Abzug (D.-N.Y.). Thus, the Congresswoman's Caucus was not formed until 1977, with fifteen of the eighteen women in the House joining. The Caucus soon changed its name to the Congressional Women's Caucus, but it was hurt by the refusal of several Republican women to join after their election in 1980.

The Caucus reorganized in 1981, changed its name to the Congressional Caucus for Women's Issues, and opened its doors to men. Now, one of the largest caucuses in the House, it has more than 150 members, most of whom are men. (It is more formal than many caucuses; women pay $1,500 a year, men $650, to support its staff.) This Caucus has been instrumental in garnering support for increased research on women's health issues and for the Family and Medical Leave Act, among other items. In 1991, it outlined the Women's Health Equity Act, a package of twenty-two bills designed to improve women's health through new initiatives in research, services, and prevention. In 1993, the Caucus, bolstered by the addition of 24 new women, had its most successful year ever. "Issues of concern to women and families truly came of age . . . and, largely, it was the congresswomen who set the agenda," said Representative Patricia Schroeder (D.-Colo.), co-chair of the Caucus.[25] She claimed that Congress passed more legislation of importance to U.S. women in 1993 than in any other year since the Caucus began keeping track a decade ago. Among its victories: the Family and Medical Leave Act, several laws increasing federal research on women's health issues, and the Violence Against Women Act.

Women in Congress were so successful in 1993 that African-American women began discussing whether they should form their own caucus. During a heated debate on the Hyde Amendment, dealing with federal funding of abortions for poor women, Representative Henry Hyde (R.-Ill.) was surrounded by several angry African-American female lawmakers. "It is intimidating to have five or six women all glaring at you," said Hyde. "it was like lighting a firecracker."[26] Says Cynthia McKinney (D.-Ga.), leader of the informal group and one of the ten African-American women who served in the 103rd Congress, "We're shaking up the place," as they focus on issues that combine the concerns of women, children, and youth. And, when the day is over, says McKinney, they often reconvene off the floor for post-mortems.[27]

Members also strongly identify by their class—that is, the year in which they were elected. For example, until 1993, the largest "new" class in years was the class of 1974, when the Watergate scandal and the resignation of President Richard M. Nixon resulted in a Democratic landslide that produced seventy-five new House Democrats. In 1978, thirty-six new Republicans arrived in the House, followed by fifty-two more in 1980. Members of the same class share information with one another and form networks that often solidify as the members' tenure in the House increases.

> ### Caucus for Every Interest
> ❖ ❖ ❖
>
> Among the 100-plus caucuses in Congress are:
>
> - The Arms Control and Foreign Policy Caucus
> - The Arts Caucus
> - The Caucus on Biomedical Research
> - The Caucus on Ethiopian Jewry
> - The Caucus on Unfunded Mandates
> - The Congressional Competitiveness Caucus
> - The Congressional Fire Services Caucus
> - The Congressional Populist Caucus
> - The Hispanic Caucus
> - The Human Rights Caucus
> - The Senate Rural Health Caucus
> - The Sunbelt Caucus
> - The Travel and Tourism Caucus
> - The Urban Caucus

[25] Lynn Marek, "Schroeder Hails Women's Gains," *The Plain Dealer* (December 28, 1993): 1–C.
[26] Kevin Merida, " 'Sisterhood' of the Hill 'Shaking Up the Place'; Black Female Lawmakers Have Early Impact," *The Washington Post* (August 2, 1993):A 1.
[27] Ibid.

State and regional caucuses are two other important sources of information exchange among members and across party lines. Large state delegations, such as those of California, New York, and Texas, often work together, regardless of party lines, to bring the bacon home to their states. Some state caucuses hold weekly meetings to assure that their interests are adequately represented on important committees and to keep abreast of pending legislation that might affect their states.

Regional caucuses cut across not only state lines but both houses of Congress as well. In the early years of the nation, members of Congress even roomed in boarding houses organized around the regions from which they came. These "boarding-house networks" enforced discipline through the threat of social ostracism. While these kinds of strictures no longer exist, informal frostbelt and sunbelt caucuses advance sectional interests.[28]

Because members, especially those in the House, tend to specialize, they often look to certain of their colleagues for what Donald R. Matthews and James A. Stimson call "cues."[29] Each member has a different set of cue givers, depending on the issue involved. A cue giver may be a respected member of a particular caucus, the state delegation, or a committee chair or subcommittee chair whom a member particularly admires or who has a reputation for exceptional expertise. In the Senate, for example, the highly respected Senator Sam Nunn (D.-Ga.) presently heads the Armed Services Committee, and many members often take cues from him as to how to vote on arms appropriations bills. Other cue-givers can be friends who tend to think the same way as the representative does.

Members also trade votes with friends or even foes in a practice called logrolling. For example, vote trading often takes place on specialized bills designed to bring home the bacon to certain areas. A yea vote by an unaffected member often is given in exchange for the promise of a future yea vote on a similar piece of legislation affecting his or her district.

Other appeals are of a more personal nature. During the Democrats' last-minute efforts to secure passage of the Omnibus Budget Reconciliation Act in 1993, President Clinton and many of his aides did all they could to convince Senator Bob Kerrey (D.-Neb.) to cast his critical vote for the Act. At the request of Majority Leader Senator George Mitchell, the chair of the Senate Finance Committee, Senator Daniel Patrick Moynihan (D.-N.Y.), talked to Kerrey and even brought Kerrey to his home to talk to Moynihan's wife. The next day, after Kerrey had been courted again by the president at a White House breakfast, Moynihan went to Kerrey's office and told him: "I need you on this one. If you give me this one, I promise I'll never ask you for anything else."[30] Sometimes a personal plea from a close colleague can ultimately win a vote. (In this case, without Kerrey's vote, Clinton's budget plan would have failed.)

Staff

Because of the amount of work members have, they tend to rely heavily on members of their staff for information on pending legislation. Generally, staff members prepare summaries of bills and brief the representative or senator based on their research. If

---

[28] James Sterling Young, *The Washington Community, 1800–1820* (New York: Columbia University Press, 1966), pp. 98–105.

[29] Donald R. Matthews and James A. Stimson, *Yeas and Neas* (Chapel Hill: University of North Carolina Press, 1975).

[30] Howard Fineman et al., "Whew!" *Newsweek* (August 16, 1993): 19.

the bill is non-ideological or one on which the member has no real position, staff members can be very influential. Staff members also do research on and even draft bills that a member wishes to introduce.

Staff aides are especially crucial in the Senate. Because senators have so many committee assignments and are often spread quite thin, they frequently rely heavily on aides. The next time you see a televised Senate hearing, notice how each senator has at least one aide sitting behind him or her, ready with information and often even with questions for the senator to ask. Some critics believe that staff members have become too important, too powerful, and that their bosses are too dependent on them. Said Senator Lloyd Bentsen (D.-Tx.) (who resigned to become Secretary of the Treasury), "I get so damned tired of members who can't go any place without staff. They don't know the issues themselves."[31]

Congress actually employs more than 30,000 workers (approximately 19,000 in its offices on Capitol Hill) to assist its members as personal aides or to staff committees or work in a congressional support agency (discussed on page 246). In 1991, there were about 12,500 staff members for the House and 7,200 for the Senate. The average size of a House member's personal staff in Washington is 18; the average senator has twice that number. Senators from more populous states get proportionately more staff. House staff sizes are generally similar, given that House district sizes are comparable. In 1993, each House member received $752,000 to hire his or her staff members. By way of comparison, each British member of Parliament was given the equivalent of approximately $80,000 in 1992.

From the 1950s until the late 1970s, the size of congressional staffs grew, as did the kinds of problems staffers were called on to address. Problems with a constituent's mail delivery, lost Social Security checks, information for students doing school term papers, and constituents' tickets for Washington tourist attractions are only some of the congressional duties that come under the label of **constituency service**. While members routinely service their constituents by bringing federal grants and projects to cities, businesses, colleges, and other groups in their districts, they also help through casework. In this form of service, staffers help constituents cut through the maze of bureaucratic red tape in order to get government assistance to which they believe they are entitled.

As aides were hired and the scope of Congress's activities increased, especially its oversight function discussed below, Congress has been forced to build new office buildings for itself as well as to convert nearby hotels, apartments, and federal buildings into offices to house its aides and support agencies. And more and more frequently, members of Congress use their staff allowances to maintain offices back home in the district in order to help with constituent problems, to keep themselves apprised of home-district concerns, and to keep themselves aware of how the voters in the district feel on particular issues. In fact, about one-third of House staffers and one-quarter of Senate staffers do not work in Washington. Congress also has added to the size of its staff in an effort to reassert itself in the lawmaking process. It has hired additional staff to help members with their committee duties and to work for the committees themselves. In essence, Congress has created a mini-bureaucracy with many parallels to the executive bureaucracy discussed in Chapter 8.

Congress is the only legislature in the world with such a vast staff. The British Parliament, for example, has a negligible number of staffers to assist its members, and in-

---

[31] Quoted in Martin Tolchin, "19,000 Congressional Aides Discover Power but Little Glory on Capitol Hill," *New York Times* (November 12, 1991): A–22.

dividual members are rarely in a financial position to hire more than one or two full-time staffers to assist them both in London and in their home districts. In fact, the British parliamentary internship programs, so popular with American university students, not only provide participants with an unforgettable experience, but also help in a small way to fill a chronic institutional gap in staffing requirements.

Support Agencies. Congress has developed four support agencies—the Congressional Research Service, the General Accounting Office, the Office of Technology Assessment, and the Congressional Budget Office—in order to provide the specialized knowledge necessary for members of Congress to make informed decisions on complex issues.

Congressional Research Service (CRS). Created in 1914 as the Legislative Research Service (LRS), the CRS is administered by the Library of Congress and responds to more than a quarter of a million congressional requests for information each year. The CRS is staffed with almost 900 employees, many of whom have advanced academic training. The service provides nonpartisan studies of public issues, compiling facts on many sides of each issue, and conducts major research projects for committees at the request of members. The CRS also prepares summaries of all bills introduced and tracks the progress of major bills. All this information is available via computer terminals in Senate and House offices.

General Accounting Office (GAO). The GAO was established in 1921 as an independent regulatory agency for the purpose of auditing the financial expenditures of the executive branch and federal agencies. Today, staffed with more than 5,000 employees, the GAO has expanded to perform four additional functions: It sets government standards for accounting, provides a variety of legal opinions, settles claims against the government, and conducts studies on congressional request. Through its investigation of the efficiency and effectiveness of agencies, the GAO has acted as a watchdog of military funds in particular, often making headlines by reporting when products are bought at prices far above market value.

Office of Technology Assessment (OTA). The OTA, an agency of about one hundred employees, was created in 1972 to study and evaluate the long-range effects of new and existing technology. The OTA has dealt with such issues as the impact of computers on privacy rights and the effect of the chemical Agent Orange on Vietnam veterans and their children.

Congressional Budget Office (CBO). The CBO was created in 1974 in order to evaluate the economic effect of different spending programs and to provide information on the cost of proposed policies. The CBO employs more than 200 people on its staff and is responsible for analyzing the president's budget and economic projections, thereby providing Congress and individual members with a valuable second opinion for use in budget debates.

Interest Groups

The primary function of most interest-group lobbyists is to provide information to supportive or potentially supportive legislators and their staffs. It's likely, for example, that a representative knows the position of the National Rifle Association (NRA) on gun control legislation. What the legislator needs to get from the NRA are information and substantial research on the feasibility and impact of such legislation. How could the states implement such legislation? Is it constitutional? Will it really have an impact on violent crime or crime in schools? It is in presenting this kind of information that an interest group can solidify a member's support or influence a member leaning in its direction. Pressure groups often urge their members in a particular state or district to call or write their senator or representative. Lobbyists can't vote, but voters back home can. Thus, an interest group can attempt to influence how a member votes by drawing his or her attention to the issue, providing information, and urging voters to contact their representatives.

As technology has improved, so has the force of interest groups. When Congress proposed to reduce the deductibilty of business meals from 80 to 50 percent, the National Restaurant Association fought back. It launched a well-done television ad featuring a waitress discussing how she might lose her job and her ability to support her three sons. The punch line? "Call 1–800–999–8945 now, and you'll be connected to your Senator."[32] Banks of operators were on hand to patch irate constituents through to their representatives' offices. (Ultimately, however, the 50-percent deduction was passed.) These kinds of measures are designed to alert legislators as quickly as possible to concerns back home.

Constituents

Constituents—the people who live and vote in a member's district or state—are always in mind when a member casts a vote. It is rare for a legislator to vote against the wishes of his or her constituency regularly, particularly on issues of welfare rights or domestic policy or on other highly salient issues such as affirmative action, abortion, or war. Most constituents often have strong convictions on one or more of these issues. For example, during the 1960s, representatives from Southern states could not hope to keep their seats for long if they voted in favor of proposed civil rights legislation. But gauging how voters feel about any particular issue is often not easy. Because it is virtually impossible to know how the folks back home feel on all issues, a representative's perception of their preferences is important.

Political scientist Richard F. Fenno Jr. concludes that members perceive their constituencies to consist of four groups, as illustrated in Figure 6-9. Members initially describe their "geographical constituency"—the location and size of the district—and its internal makeup, or socioeconomic and political characteristics, and the proportion of people who are "blue collar," Jewish, Democratic, or elderly, for example. Within the geographical constituency, members define a second group, the "reelection constituency," consisting of the people who the member thinks vote for him or her. This is the member's perceived political base; to disagree with the reelection constituency could cost the member his or her seat. Within the reelection constituency is a third, smaller group consisting of the member's strongest supporters, the "primary constituency." These loyalists vote for the member and provide campaign assistance and financial support. The fourth and final constituency is made up of the people closest to the member—his or her "personal constituency"—including friends and advisers.

Thus, a member of Congress may perceive his district in a variety of ways, and sometimes the four constituencies may be in conflict. The typical voter in the district may have quite different views from those of the member's strongest supporters. Although most of the member's constituency will usually be unaware of the member's

FIGURE 6-9

How Members View Their Districts

---

[32] Ann Reilly Dowd, "How To Get Things Done in Washington," *Fortune* (August 9, 1993): 60.

voting decisions, it would be foolish for a representative or senator to ignore an overwhelming majority of his or her constituents' views on an issue of salience.

Congress and the President

Over the years, especially since the presidency of Franklin D. Roosevelt, Congress has allowed the president to play an ever-growing role in the legislative process. Today, for example, Congress often finds itself responding to executive branch proposals, as it did in the case of the Clean Air Act Amendments of 1990 discussed earlier in this chapter. Critics of Congress point to its slow, unwieldy process and the complexity of national problems as reasons why Congress often seems not to act on its own.

Individual members, especially if the president is popular with voters, often find themselves voting in favor of legislation supported by the White House. Legislators "on the fence" often are targeted by the White House or inundated with invitations to state dinners. Lyndon B. Johnson was a master of this strategy. One widely recounted story tells how Lyndon Johnson called Senator Harry Byrd (D.-Va.) over to the White House because he was resisting passage of the civil rights bill. According to Senator Dale Bumpers (D.-Ark.), Johnson said, " 'You know, Harry, [Defense Secretary Robert] McNamara says we got to close that Norfolk naval base down there, and I don't much want to do it.' And Harry Byrd couldn't wait to get back over to the Senate to vote for the civil rights bill."[33]

President Clinton's efforts at "persuasion" are also being hailed by some people. During his efforts to convince Congress to pass his budget deficit-reduction plan and NAFTA, he courted and cajoled numerous legislators and punished those who didn't go along. After Representative Richard Shelly (D.-Ala.) criticized Clinton's tax plan, the White House retaliated by moving ninety federal jobs out of the Marshall Space Flight Center in Alabama and even denied Shelly an extra ticket to a White House South Lawn ceremony honoring his alma mater's championship football team.[34] It doesn't take many episodes like these to convince some legislators how to vote.

Although the president, especially a popular one, undoubtedly can have an impact on how a member votes, political scientist John W. Kingdon found that overall, colleagues and constituents have the greatest impact of the many factors discussed here.[35]

Over the years, the balance of power between Congress and the executive branch has seesawed. The post–Civil War Congress attempted to regain control of the vast executive powers that President Abraham Lincoln, recently slain, had taken from them. Angered at the refusal of Lincoln's successor, Andrew Johnson, to go along with its radical "reforms" of the South, Congress passed the Tenure of Office Act, which prevented the president, under the threat of civil penalty, from removing any cabinet-level appointments of the previous administration. Johnson accepted the challenge and suspended Lincoln's Secretary of War, Edwin M. Stanton, who many believed guilty of heinous war crimes. The House voted to impeach Johnson, but only the desertion of a handful of Republican senators prevented him from being removed from office. (The impeachment effort fell short by one vote.) Nonetheless, the president's power had

---

[33] Lloyd Grove, "White House Declares War on Upstart Senator," *Atlanta Constitution* (April 6, 1993): A–15.

[34] Ibid.

[35] John W. Kingdon, *Congressmen's Voting Decisions*, 3rd ed. (Ann Arbor: University of Michigan Press, 1989).

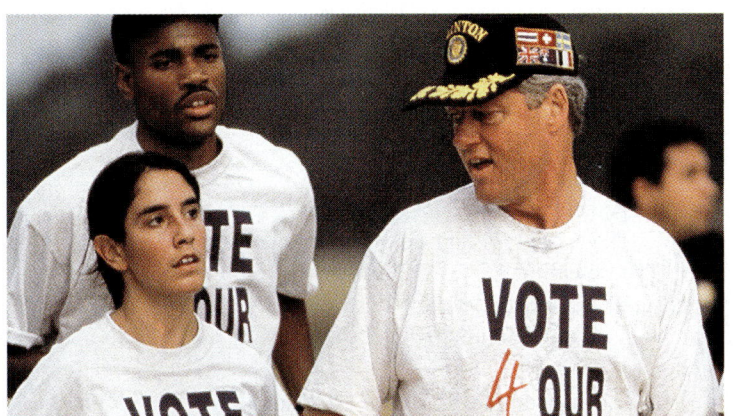

President Bill Clinton uses every possible opportunity to generate support for his favorite programs.

been greatly weakened, and the Congress again became the center of power and authority in the federal government.

Beginning in the early 1900s, however, a series of strong presidents acted at the expense of congressional power. Theodore Roosevelt, Franklin D. Roosevelt, and Lyndon B. Johnson, especially, all viewed the presidency as carrying with it enormous powers. Although these presidents facilitated an expansion of the role of the federal government, over time the perception grew that presidents were abusing their power, particularly after the events of the Vietnam War and Watergate. By the 1970s, then, scholars were discussing the "imperial presidency,"[36] and Congress made efforts to reassert itself by exercising its oversight function zealously.

Oversight of the Executive Branch

According to political scientist Joel D. Aberbach, since 1961 there has been a substantial increase in the oversight activity of Congress.[37] Key to Congress's performance of its oversight function is its ability to question members of the administration and the bureaucracy to see if they are enforcing and interpreting the laws passed by Congress as its members intended. Oversight occurs on both the domestic and foreign policy fronts.

Domestic Oversight. The greatest increases in domestic oversight occurred in the 1970s, when mushrooming budget deficits, fiscal shortfalls, and public suspicion about any forms of new (or old, for that matter) spending discouraged lawmakers from supporting expensive new programs.[38] In 1974, Congress passed the Budget and Im-

---

[36] Arthur Schlesinger, *The Imperial Presidency* (New York: Houghton Mifflin, 1973).
[37] Joel D. Aberbach, *Keeping a Watchful Eye: The Politics of Congressional Oversight* (Washington, DC: The Brookings Institution, 1990).
[38] Morris S. Ogul and Bert A. Rockman, "Overseeing Oversight: New Departures and Old Problems," *Legislative Studies Quarterly*, 25 (1990): 548–574.

poundment Control Act in response to President Nixon's refusal to spend money on certain programs authorized by Congress. The act also created budget committees in the House and in the Senate and the Congressional Budget Office (CBO) to analyze budget proposals and their potential impact on the economy. The 1974 Act requires Congress to consider and thoroughly study the president's fiscal policy goals and to set specific spending, tax, and deficit limits for each fiscal year. Prior to 1974, the Office of Management and Budget (OMB) in the executive branch controlled the budget process, and Congress had no way of systematically evaluating budgets or their impact. "The creation of the CBO began to redress the balance of power," said Stuart Eisenstadt, the Carter White House domestic policy chief.[39] It ended the president's monopoly on information and gave Congress a powerful weapon to oversee the budget process.

In 1977, for example, Joseph A. Califano, then the Secretary of Health, Education and Welfare, proposed some changes in welfare programs, estimating their cost at $5 billion in 1978. The newspaper headline the day after read "CBO to Carter: Welfare Reform $17 Billion." The Carter White House knew immediately that the reform would be killed. Eisenstadt said, "Our program's over. There's no way Congress is going to pass what they think is a $17 billion welfare reform proposal."[40]

Believing it could not trust the executive branch to provide it with accurate information, Congress also expanded the staffs of members and committees in both houses. It also added to the research service of the Library of Congress, and other support services were expanded.

All these developments have helped Congress improve its oversight of the executive branch. Hearings and investigations are common ways for members of Congress to make sure that laws are routinely and properly administered by the executive branch. Authorizations and frequent reviews of agency performance and appropriations are probably the most effective types of oversight. Since money is the lifeblood of any agency, threatening funding can often assure compliance with congressional wishes.

Legislative vetoes, a procedure by which one or both houses of Congress could disallow an act of an executive agency by a simple majority vote, also help Congress perform its oversight function. Provisions for so-called legislative vetoes were first added to statutes in 1932 but were not used frequently until the 1970s. They were usually included in laws that delegated congressional powers to the executive branch while retaining the power of Congress to restrict their use. By 1981, more than 200 statutes contained legislative veto provisions.

In *Immigration and Naturalization Service* v. *Chadha* (1983), however, the U.S. Supreme Court ruled that the legislative veto as used in many circumstances was unconstitutional.[41] The Court concluded that although the Constitution gave Congress the power to make laws, the Framers were clear in their intent that Congress should separate itself from executing or enforcing the laws. In spite of *Chadha*, however, the legislative veto continues to play an important role in executive–legislative relations.

Foreign Affairs Oversight. The Constitution divides foreign policy powers between the executive and the legislative branches. The president has the power to wage war and negotiate treaties, whereas the Congress has the power to declare war and the Sen-

---

[39] Quoted in Smith and Deering, *Committees in Congress*, p. 23. (See n. 21.)
[40] Ibid.
[41] 462 U.S. 919 (1983).

ate has the power to ratify treaties. Throughout the twentieth century, the executive branch has become preeminent in foreign affairs despite the constitutional division of powers. This is partly due to the series of crises and the development of nuclear weapons in this century; both have necessitated quick decision making and secrecy, which are much easier to manage in the executive branch. Congress, with its 535 members, has a more difficult time reaching a consensus and keeping secrets.

After years of playing second fiddle to a series of presidents from Theodore Roosevelt to Richard M. Nixon, a "snoozing Congress" was "aroused"[42] and seized for itself the authority and expertise necessary to go head-to-head with the chief executive. In a delayed response to Lyndon B. Johnson's 1964–1969 conduct of the Vietnam War, Congress passed in 1973 the **War Powers Act** over President Nixon's veto. This Act requires any president to obtain congressional approval before committing U.S. forces to a combat zone and to notify Congress within forty-eight hours of committing troops to foreign soil. In addition, the president must withdraw troops within sixty days unless Congress votes to declare war. The president is also required to consult with Congress, if at all possible, prior to committing troops.

The War Powers Act has been of limited effectiveness in claiming a larger congressional role in international crisis situations. Presidents Ford, Carter, and Reagan never consulted Congress in advance of committing troops, citing the need for secrecy and swift movement, although each president did notify Congress shortly after the incidents. They contended that the War Powers Act was probably unconstitutional—although it has been upheld by the Supreme Court—because it limits presidential prerogatives as commander-in-chief.

President Bush, however, after months of refusing to acknowledge that Congress had a role, consulted with Congress before and after committing troops in the Persian Gulf in 1990–1991 and even requested a congressional resolution for the conduct of the war. On January 12, 1991, a solemn and sharply divided Congress voted to authorize the president to go to war against Iraq if Iraq did not end its occupation of Kuwait. Along Republican Party lines, with the support of a few Democrats, the Senate voted fifty-two to forty-seven for the Authorization for Use of Military Force Against Iraq Resolution. Minutes later, the House voted 250 to 183. With these votes, Congress had acted after months of indecision about its role in the conflict that had begun when Iraq invaded Kuwait on August 2, 1990. Much of the debate over the resolution underscored the fact that the Democratic-controlled Congress had acted too late to do anything but support the president. Even Democratic House Majority Leader Richard Gephardt (D.-Mo.) underscored the need for a united national front before the vote, noting, "Whatever our decision, we will leave this room one again and whole again."[43]

Confirmation of Presidential Appointments

The Senate's ability to confirm key members of the executive branch as well as presidential appointments to the federal courts gives it a special oversight function. As discussed in Chapters 8 and 9, although the Senate confirms most presidential nominees, it does not always do so. And a wise president will consider senatorial reaction before

---

[42] *The Wall Street Journal* (April 13, 1973): 10.

[43] Quoted in "Bush Is Given Authorization to Use Force Against Iraq," *Congressional Quarterly Weekly Report* (January 12, 1991): 65.

nominating potentially controversial individuals to his administration or the federal courts. Furthermore, thanks to a policy called **senatorial courtesy**, presidents often defer to senators of their own party to suggest nominees for district court vacancies in the senators' states, giving them considerable influence over the nomination of district court judges.

Toward Reform

In the aftermath of the 1992 congressional elections, in which questions about perks, campaign finances, the honesty of individual members, and the integrity and usefulness of the Congress itself seemed to be at issue, Speaker of the House Thomas Foley opened the 103rd Congress heralding a "year of reform." The public was angry, and Foley and the rest of the members of Congress knew it. Still, little change or "reform" has come about as yet.

Reform from Within

Although the 103rd Congress spent a significant amount of time dealing with the issue of reform, members had a hard time agreeing on any concrete results. The House bank was closed in the aftermath of the overdraft scandal (see p. 215), and the Speaker did take some other actions to limit the perks enjoyed by members. Parking ticket fixing—a long-standing practice for lawmakers "on official business"—was ended, and, in exchange for a salary increase, members of Congress gave up their right to accept money for making speeches. But other efforts fell short. For example,

1. Attempts at meaningful campaign finance reform produced no significant results (see Chapter 13).
2. Although Congress has debated lobbying and gift-disclosure laws, lawmakers continue to be able to accept controversial trips and gifts from lobbyists, so long as they disclose them.
3. After nearly a year of work and six months of hearings, the bipartisan Joint Committee on the Organization of Congress suggested that Congress move to a two-year budget cycle to facilitate planning, eliminate several committees and subcommittees, reduce staff bureaucracy, and improve deliberation and accountability. Some members of the committee also recommended that Congress extend coverage of workplace safety and anti-discrimination laws to itself. (Congress has chosen to exempt itself from many laws that govern the private workplace.) But, by the end of 1994, few changes had occurred.

Citizen Efforts

As attempts by Congress to reform itself have come to little, private citizens and some interest groups have taken up the call for reform. The Committee on the Constitutional System, for example, has called on the Senate to change its rules to limit use of the filibuster. In the last five years, there has been an average of 17.5 filibuster attempts each year, a dramatic increase. The Committee notes that filibusters and holds stymie legislative efforts and should be limited in order for the Senate to function more efficiently. It also suggests realigning the jurisdiction of congressional committees to avoid duplication and overlap.[44]

Term Limits. Frustrated by apparent inaction, gridlock, and ethics problems in Congress, in the late 1980s a term-limits movement began sweeping the nation as citizens and citizens groups lobbied their statehouses for laws to limit the number of elected terms of not only their state representatives but also members of Congress. Given the power of incumbency, proponents of term limits argued that election to Congress, in essence, equaled life tenure. The concept of term limits is a simple one that has appealed to many people who oppose the notion of career representatives. As it generally applies to Congress, it allows members of the Houses to serve three two-year terms; Senators can serve two six-year terms. By 1994, fifteen states had enacted some form of term-limit laws and action was pending in eight more.

Most members of Congress and many interest groups who profit from long-term relationships with some members of Congress oppose term limits and argue that they are unconstitutional. Opponents of term limits, led by the League of Women Voters, argue that career politicians increase the expertise of Congress and are initiating court challenges to those provisions already enacted. And on the other side, US Term Limits, a lobby group, is pressing the cause in state legislatures around the nation.

The idea of term limits isn't new. In 1787, the Framers considered, but rejected, the Virginia Plan, which restricted members of the House to one term. Moreover, many of the Founders believed in the regular rotation of offices among worthy citizens, and for the most part this was the practice in the early years of the republic. There is also a precedent for term limitation in the office of governor. From the very first, Americans were suspicious of executive power and have preferred to restrict their governors to a fixed number of terms in the statehouse, and even today, the two-term limit (with each term four years in length) is the gubernatorial norm. And, of course, the president of the United States has been limited to two full four-year terms since the Twenty-second Amendment was ratified after the death of four-term President Franklin D. Roosevelt.

Contemporary advocates of term limits for members of Congress argue that incumbents have too many advantages in running for office and that limits are the only sure way to build in more competition and ensure turnover. They believe that many good people now hesitant to start a lengthy second career in politics would be willing to serve for a short period of time, just as some of the Founders had envisioned. Many Republicans are especially strong supporters of term limits, seeing this reform as an opportunity to eliminate entrenched Democratic incumbents who constitute a majority of both houses of Congress and most state legislatures. Republicans believe they will gain under a term-limits scheme because many Democrats will be forced out of office and the resulting "open seats" with no incumbent will be more vulnerable to Republican takeover. Also, the business-based, private enterprise-centered Republican Party has more difficulty than the government-service-oriented Democrats in recruiting candidates for full-time, semi-permanent political careers. With limited tenure requiring less long-term commitment to government service (and its relatively low salaries, compared with private enterprise), Republicans think they can convince more of their qualified activists to run.

---

[44] James L. Sundquist, ed. *Beyond Gridlock? Prospects for Governance in the Clinton Years—and After* (Washington, DC: The Brookings Institution, 1993).

254 ❖ Chapter 6 Congress

OLIPHANT copyright 1990 UNIVERSAL PRESS SYNDICATE. Reprinted with permission. All rights reserved.

STILL THE BEST CONGRESSIONAL TERM-LIMITING DEVICE.

Term-limit opponents have a very different view of this reform. They note that the people already have the power to limit terms—and to do so more severely than the reformers' proposals advocate. If the electorate so desires, for example, it could replace the entire U.S. House of Representatives every two years. This does not happen, because many voters are pleased with the representation provided by their legislators. Yet term limits deny these constituents their right to retain a good member of Congress in office if they so desire; under term limitation, good and bad legislators are ousted equally and without distinction.

Term-limit opponents also note that the loss of senior, experienced legislators means the diminishing of an important check on other actors in the legislative process who would *not* be limited by term, such as lobbyists, legislative staff, and executive department bureaucrats. Few Americans are any more fond of these groups than they are of legislators. This last problem with term limits is an example of the *unintended consequences* of reform. The U.S. system of government is so complex that each new action can produce somewhat unpredictable reactions, and wise reformers must be alert to the "ripple effects" of their proposals.

In June 1994, the U.S. Supreme Court agreed to hear a challenge to an Arkansas term limit provision. While upholding portions of the state law that set term limits for state legislators, the Arkansas Supreme Court ruled that state-imposed term limits for members of the U.S. House and Senate were unconstitutional.

Where do *you* stand?

Summary

The size, scope, and demands on Congress have increased tremendously over the years. In presenting the important role that Congress plays in U.S. politics, we have made the following points:

1. The experiences of Great Britain, colonial assemblies, and the Articles of Confederation all contributed in a variety of ways to the powers granted to the new Congress.

2. The Constitution created a bicameral legislature, with members of each body to be elected, and thus to represent, different constituencies. The Constitution also requires that seats in the House of Representatives be apportioned by population. Thus, after every census,

district lines must be redrawn to reflect population shifts. The Constitution also provides a vast array of enumerated and implied powers to Congress. Some, such as lawmaking and oversight, are shared by both houses of Congress; others are not.

3. Members of Congress must meet formal, constitutional requirements before they can take office. They also must generally conform to several informal requirements, including membership in a major political party, and must have the ability to attract campaign contributions. Once elected, the incumbency factor helps to keep them in office, as do some of the perks of the job. Most members are wealthy, well educated, older, and male. This shared perspective may have important consequences on how members vote, or on how they view their representational function.

4. Each house of Congress has a hierarchical leadership structure in which political party and the seniority system play major roles, especially in the committee system, which facilitates the workings and organization of Congress. Because committees and subcommittees are where most of the work of Congress gets done, committee chairs are very powerful actors in the legislative process.

5. The chief power of Congress is making laws. Numerous formal rules exist to facilitate the passage of legislation. Yet in spite of these formal guideposts, most bills do not pass in a "textbook" fashion.

6. Members of Congress rely on a variety of sources to help them make up their minds on how to vote. These sources include political parties, colleagues, informal caucuses, staff (including support agencies), interest groups, and constituents. The president, if he is of the same political party, can also be a factor.

7. The president and the Congress enjoy a peculiar, symbiotic relationship. Today, the president plays an increasingly important role in the legislative process, yet without congressional approval, he can do little. To reassert itself in the legislative process, Congress has stepped up its oversight role in both domestic and foreign affairs arenas. And the Senate has always played a significant oversight function through its ability to ratify treaties and confirm presidential appointments.

Key Terms

redistricting
gerrymandering
apportionment
impeachment
Speaker of the House
party caucus
majority party

standing committees
discharge petition
pork barrel
minority party
seniority
hold

filibuster
pocket veto
special-interest caucuses
constituency service
War Powers Act
senatorial courtesy

Suggested Readings

Aberbach, Joel D. *Keeping a Watchful Eye: The Politics of Congressional Oversight*. Washington, DC: The Brookings Institution, 1990.

Cain, Bruce, John Ferejohn, and Morris P. Fiorina. *The Personal Vote*. Cambridge, MA: Harvard University Press, 1987.

Dodd, Lawrence C., and Bruce I. Oppenheimer. *Congress Reconsidered*, 4th ed. Washington, DC: CQ Press, 1985.

Fenno, Richard F., Jr. *Congressmen in Committees*. Boston: Little, Brown, 1973.

———*Home Style: House Members in Their Districts*. Boston: Little, Brown, 1978.

Fox, Harrison W., and Susan Webb Hammond. *Congressional Staffs: The Invisible Force in American Lawmaking*. New York: Free Press, 1977.

Hinckley, Barbara. *Coalitions and Politics*. San Diego: Harcourt Brace Jovanovich, 1981.

Jones, Rochelle, and Peter Woll. *The Private World of Congress*. New York: Free Press, 1979.

Loomis, Burdett A. *The American Politician*. New York: Basic Books, 1988.

Mayhew, David R. *Congress: The Electoral Connection*. New Haven, CT: Yale University Press, 1974.

Sabato, Larry J. *PAC Power*. New York: Norton, 1984.

Sinclair, Barbara, *The Transformation of the U.S. Senate*. Baltimore: Johns Hopkins University Press, 1989.

Smith, Hedrick. *The Power Game*. New York: Ballantine Books, 1989.

> Energy in the Executive is a leading character in the definition of good government. It is essential to the protection of the community against foreign attacks; it is not less essential to the steady administration of the laws.
>
> *Alexander Hamilton*
> *Federalist No. 70*

Hamilton and other Federalists believed that a chief executive was critical to the proper functioning of a strong national government. While aware of the excesses of those who "aspired to tyranny," Hamilton argued that the Constitution protected against excess while recognizing the importance of a vigorous president.

CHAPTER 7

The Presidency

THE ROOTS OF THE OFFICE OF PRESIDENT OF THE UNITED STATES

THE FRAMERS AND THE CREATION OF THE PRESIDENCY

THE CONSTITUTIONAL POWERS OF THE PRESIDENT

THE DEVELOPMENT OF PRESIDENTIAL POWER

THE PRESIDENTIAL ESTABLISHMENT

TOWARD REFORM

*I*n 1787, when Alexander Hamilton penned *Federalist No. 70,* he was expressing the views of the majority of the Framers who saw a need for a chief executive, but feared putting significant powers into the hands of any one individual. Under the Articles of Confederation, there had been no executive branch of government, and the eighteen men who served as the "president" of the Continental Congress of the United States of America were president in name only—they had no actual authority or power in the new nation. Yet, since the Framers were sure that George Washington, who had led the new nation as its general during the Revolutionary War, would become the first president of the new nation, many of their deepest fears were calmed. They agreed upon the necessity of having one individual speak on behalf of the new nation, and they all agreed that that one individual should be George Washington.

Though the Framers agreed nearly unanimously about the need for a strong central government and a greatly empowered Congress, they did not agree about the proper role of the president or the sweep of his authority. In contrast to Article I's laundry list of provisions for authority of the legislative branch, Article II details few presidential powers. Distrust of a powerful chief executive led to the Constitution's intentionally vague prescriptions for the presidency.

It is highly unlikely that the Framers—even Alexander Hamilton, probably the greatest supporter of a strong chief executive—ever envisioned the growth in executive power that has occurred over the years. Just think of the differences in governance faced by two Georges—Washington and Bush. George Washington supervised the nation from a temporary headquarters with a staff of but one aide—his nephew, paid out of Washington's own funds—and only four Cabinet members. In contrast, when George Bush left office in 1993, he had presided over a White House staff of 461, a Cabinet of fourteen members, and an executive branch of government that employed

Presidents Clinton, Bush, Reagan, Carter and Ford stand with their wives in order of their presidencies at the grave side ceremony of Richard Nixon in 1994.

more than 3 million people. Both presidents faced staggering federal budget deficits, but what was considered staggering in Washington's day pales in comparison with the national deficit of nearly $3 trillion the year George Bush left office.

The changes in the size of government and in public expectations about government, especially about the role of the president in our political system, were not foreseen by the Framers. In fact, as the president has been brought closer to the people through democratization, expansion of the electorate, and technological change—from Franklin D. Roosevelt's "Fireside Chats" to Bill Clinton's unprecedented use of Town Hall meetings to bring his programs (and himself) directly to the public—the president's formal powers have often been inadequate to allow him to deliver on his promises.

The tension between public expectations and formal powers of the president permeate our discussion of how the presidency has evolved from its humble origins in Article II of the Constitution to its current stature. In particular, we focus on the "modern presidency," which began with the election of Franklin D. Roosevelt in 1932. The term "modern presidency" refers not only to the change in expectations about the role of the president in national affairs, but also to the growth of what some term the presidential establishment. This includes a large staff, Cabinet positions, and an executive bureaucracy that has grown to help the president meet expectations about his role in the policy process.

The Roots of the Office of President of the United States

The earliest form of executive power in the colonies was the position of royal governor. A royal governor was appointed by the king of England to govern a colony and was normally entrusted with the "powers of appointment, military command, expenditure, and—within limitations—pardon, as well as with large powers in connection with the powers of law making."[1] Royal governors often found themselves at odds with the colonists and especially with the elected colonial legislatures. As representatives of the Crown, the governors were distrusted and disdained by the people, many of whom had fled from Great Britain to escape royal domination, and others who, after generations removed from England, no longer felt strong ties to the King.

When the colonists declared their independence from England in 1776, their distrust of a strong chief executive remained. Most state constitutions reduced the office of governor to a symbolic post, whose holder was elected annually by the legislature. Governors were stripped of most rights we assume essential today, including the rights to call the legislature into session and to veto its acts. The constitution adopted by Virginia in 1776 illustrates prevailing colonial sentiment. It cautioned that "the executive powers of government" were to be exercised "according to the laws" of the state, and that no powers could be claimed by the governor on the basis of "any law, statute, or custom of England."[2]

Although most of the states opted for a more "symbolic" governor, some states did entrust wider powers to their chief executives. The governor of New York, for example, was elected directly by the people. And, perhaps *because* he was directly accountable to the people, he was given the power to pardon, the duty to execute the law faithfully to the best of his ability, and to act as commander-in-chief of the state militia.

The Framers and the Creation of the Presidency

As we saw in Chapter 2, the delegates to the Philadelphia Convention quickly decided to dispense with the Articles of Confederation and fashion a new government composed of three branches—the legislative (to make the laws), the executive (to execute, or implement, the laws), and the judicial (to interpret the laws).

The Framers had little difficulty in agreeing that executive authority should be vested in one person, although some delegates suggested multiple executives to diffuse the power of the executive branch. The Framers also had no problem in agreeing on a title for the new office. Borrowing from the constitutions of Pennsylvania, Delaware, New Jersey, and New Hampshire, the Framers called the new chief executive the "president." How and by whom the president was to be chosen was a major stumbling block. The Virginia delegation proposed a "Virginia Plan" which called for a single national executive, elected by the national legislature, who would be ineligible for a second term. Reflecting the limited powers given to the Virginia governor by the state constitution, Virginia's delegates proposed an executive strictly accountable to the legislature.

In contrast, James Wilson of Philadelphia suggested a single, more powerful president who would be elected by the people and would be "independent of the legislature." Wilson also suggested giving the executive an absolute veto over the acts of

---

[1] Edward S. Corwin, *The President: Office and Powers, 1787–1957*, 4th ed. (New York: New York University Press, 1957), p. 5.

[2] F.N. Thorpe, ed., *American Charters, Constitutions, Etc.*, VIII (Washington, 1909), pp. 3816–3817.

At the 1968 Democratic National Convention, Julian Bond of Georgia's name was placed in nomination for the vice presidency. Bond was forced to decline the honor because he was only twenty-eight; the Constitution requires that the vice president be at least thirty-five years of age.

Congress. "Without such a defense," he wrote, "the legislature can at any moment sink it [the executive] into non-existence."[3]

The manner of the president's election haunted the Framers, and their solution to the dilemma is described in detail in Chapter 12. We leave that issue aside for now and turn instead to details of the issues the Framers resolved quickly.

Qualifications for Office

The Constitution requires that the president (and the vice president, whose major function is to succeed the president in the event of his death or disability) be a natural-born citizen of the United States, at least thirty-five years old, and a resident of the United States for at least fourteen years. In the 1700s it was not uncommon for those engaged in international diplomacy to be out of the country for substantial periods of time. Thus, the Framers wanted to make sure that prospective presidents spent some time in this country before running for its highest elective office.

Term of Office

Initially, the length of the executive's term of office was the subject of considerable controversy. Four-, seven-, and eleven-year terms with no eligibility for reelection were suggested by various delegates to the Constitutional Convention. Alexander Hamilton suggested that a president serve during "good behavior." Not surprisingly, the issue of term length quickly became associated with eligibility to seek reelection. From the beginning, it was clear that if the delegates agreed to allow the *state* legislatures to choose the president, then shorter terms with the possibility of reelection would be favored. If they agreed to allow the national legislature to select the president, there would be no possibility for reelection. After the Framers of the Constitution reached agreement on the selection process (see Chapter 12), the delegates in favor of a reelection option prevailed, and a four-year term with eligibility for reelection was added to the proposed Article II of the Constitution.

The first president, George Washington (1789–1797), sought reelection only once, and a two-term limit for presidents became traditional. Although Ulysses S. Grant unsuccessfully sought a third term, the two terms established by Washington remained the standard for 150 years, avoiding the Framers' much-feared "constitutional monarch," a perpetually reelected tyrant. In the 1930s and 1940s, however, Franklin D. Roosevelt ran successfully in four elections as Americans fought first the Great Depression and then World War II. Despite Roosevelt's popularity, negative reaction to his long tenure in office ultimately led to passage (and ratification in 1951) of the Twenty-Second Amendment, which limits presidents to two four-year terms or a total of ten years in office, should a vice president assume a portion of a president's remaining term.

Removal

During the Constitutional Convention, Benjamin Franklin, a staunch supporter of impeachment, a process for removing an official from office, noted that "historically, the

---

[3] Quoted in Corwin, *The President*, p. 11.

Not everyone was enthusiastic about FDR's unprecedented attempt for a third term.

lack of power to impeach had necessitated recourse to assassination."[4] Not surprisingly, he urged the rest of the delegates to formulate a legal mechanism for removing the president and vice president.

Just as the presidential veto power was a check on Congress, the impeachment provision ultimately included in Article II was adopted as a check on the power of the president (as well as the judiciary). Each house of Congress was given a role to play to assure that the chief executive could be removed only for "Treason, Bribery, or other high Crimes and Misdemeanors."

The Constitution gives the House of Representatives the power to conduct a thorough investigation to determine (in a manner similar to a grand jury proceeding) whether the president had engaged in any impeachable offenses (see Chapter 4). If the finding is affirmative, the House is empowered to vote to impeach the president by a simple majority. The precise charges against the president are called **articles of impeachment**, which are similar to a grand jury indictment. The Senate then acts as a court of law and tries the president for the charged offenses. The Chief Justice of the United States Supreme Court presides over the vote on the articles and the Senate hearing. A two-thirds majority vote in the Senate on any count contained in the articles of impeachment is necessary to remove the president from office. As noted in Chapter 6, only one president, Andrew Johnson in 1868, has ever been impeached, but the Senate vote fell one vote short of forcing his removal.

Succession

Through 1994, eight presidents have died in office, through illness or assassination. William Henry Harrison was the first president to die in office—he caught a cold at his

---

[4] Winston Solberg, *The Federal Convention and the Formation of the Union of the American States* (Indianapolis: Bobbs-Merrill, 1958), p. 235.

inauguration in 1841 and died one month later. John Tyler thus became the first vice president to succeed to the presidency. In 1865, Abraham Lincoln became the first president to be assassinated. And in 1974, Richard M. Nixon, facing impeachment and likely conviction, became the first president to resign from office.

Whether the president has died or resigned, the vice president has always taken over the reins of office. The Constitution directs Congress to select a successor if the office of vice president is vacant. To clarify this provision, Congress passed the Presidential Succession Act of 1947, which lists in order those in line (after the vice president) to succeed the president:

1. Speaker of the House of Representatives
2. President pro tempore of the Senate
3. Secretaries of State, Treasury, and Defense, and other Cabinet heads in order of the creation of their department (see page 296)

The Succession Act has never been used because there has always been a vice president to take over. The Twenty-Fifth Amendment, in fact, was added to the Constitution in 1967 to assure that this will continue to be the case. Should a vacancy occur in the office of vice president, the Twenty-Fifth Amendment directs the president to appoint a new vice president, subject to the approval (by a simple majority) of both houses of Congress. (See also "What Happens If a President Can't Do His Job?," p. 263.)

The Twenty-Fifth Amendment has been used twice in its relatively short history. In 1973, President Richard M. Nixon selected the House Minority Leader, Gerald R. Ford, to replace Vice President Spiro T. Agnew, after Agnew resigned in the wake of charges that he had accepted bribes while a local public official in Maryland and while vice president. Less than a year later, when Vice President Ford became the thirty-eighth president after Nixon's resignation after the **Watergate** scandal (see "Watergate and its Effect on the Presidency," pp. 264–265), he appointed (and the Senate approved) former four-term New York State Governor Nelson A. Rockefeller to the vice presidency. This set up, for the first time in U.S. history, a situation in which neither the president nor the vice president had been elected to those positions.

Formal procedures for succession, removal, and impeachment have no parallels in the British parliamentary system. When the prime minister resigns, dies in office, or loses the confidence of the majority party in Parliament, one of two things can happen: (1) either a new prime minister is named out of the sitting Parliament, again from the majority party, or (2) Parliament is "dissolved" and new elections are held, with a new prime minister emerging from the new Parliament.

The Vice President

The Framers gave little attention to the office of vice president beyond the need to have an immediate official "stand in" for the president. Initially, the vice president's only function was to assume the office of president in the case of the death of the president or some other emergency. After further debate, the delegates made the vice president the presiding officer of the Senate (except in cases of presidential impeachment). They feared that if the Senate's presiding officer were chosen from the Senate itself, one state would be short a representative. The vice president was given the authority to vote only in the event of a tie, however.

With so little authority, the office of vice president was considered until recently a sure place for a public official to disappear into obscurity. When John Adams wrote to

What Happens If a President Can't Do His Job?

When the twentieth president, James A. Garfield, was wounded by an assassin's bullet in July 1881, he lingered until mid-September. In 1919, President Woodrow Wilson had what many believed to be a nervous collapse in the summer and a debilitating stroke in the fall that incapacitated him for several months. His wife, Edith Bolling Galt Wilson, refused to admit his advisers to his sickroom, and rumors flew about "the First Lady President," as many suspected it was his wife and not Wilson who was issuing written orders.

A section of the Twenty-Fifth Amendment allows the vice president and a majority of the Cabinet (or some other body determined by Congress) to deem a president unable to fulfill his duties. It sets up a procedure to allow the vice president to become "acting president" if the president is incapacitated. The president can also voluntarily relinquish his power. Following the spirit of the amendment, before he underwent surgery for cancer of the colon in 1985, President Ronald Reagan sent his vice president, George Bush, a letter that made him acting president for eight hours.

Woodrow Wilson with his wife Edith

his wife, Abigail, about his position as America's first vice president, he said it was "the most insignificant office that was the invention of man . . . or his imagination conceived."[5] A similar sentiment is evident in a story told by Thomas R. Marshall, Woodrow Wilson's little-remembered vice president: "Once there were two brothers. One ran away to sea. The other was elected vice president, and nothing was heard of either of them again."[6] Franklin D. Roosevelt's first vice president, John Nance Garner, more bluntly observed that his job was not worth "a pitcher of warm spit."

Power and fame generally come only to those vice presidents who become president. Just "one heartbeat away" from the presidency, the vice president serves as a constant reminder of the president's mortality. In part, this situation has given rise to a trend of uneasy relationships between presidents and vice presidents, beginning as

---

[5] Alfred Steinberg, *The First Ten: The Founding Presidents and Their Administrations* (New York: Doubleday, 1967), p. 59.

[6] As a presiding officer in the Senate, Marshall helped break the monotony of a lengthy speech on "What This Country Needs" by quipping his oft-repeated words: "What this country needs is a really good five-cent cigar." All comments noted in Carol Haas, *In the World of Politics* (Hauppauge, NY: Barron's Educational Services, 1991), p. 223.

Watergate and Its Effect on the Presidency

Richard M. Nixon, in a recorded conversation from the Oval Office:

> I don't give a —— what happens, I want you to stonewall it, let them plead the Fifth Amendment, cover up or anything else, if it'll save the plan.

Nixon's plan was to get reelected to the presidency by any means necessary. What Nixon did not anticipate was getting caught. On June 17, 1972, five men were arrested during a break-in at the Democratic National Committee's (DNC) headquarters in the Watergate office complex in Washington, D.C. The men were caught with burglary tools, bugging devices, and a stack of $100 bills; their mission was to install listening devices in the phones of the DNC to learn of campaign strategies and information that could be used against the Democratic presidential nominee, who was to be selected the next month at the 1972 Democratic National Convention. Among the burglars was James W. McCord Jr., the security director of the Committee to Re-Elect the President (CREEP). Later, two former White House aides also working on the re-election campaign were arrested for their role in planning the break-in. Immediately after the arrests, the White House and CREEP shredded all documents in their possession that might link the burglars to the White House. Meanwhile, Nixon assured the press that there was no connection between him or his staffers and the burglary.

In 1973, after pleading guilty, McCord wrote to Judge John J. Sirica, who had accepted his plea of guilty, explaining that he and the other Watergate defendants had been pressured to remain silent and that other highly placed public officials were involved, including John N. Mitchell, a close friend of Richard Nixon's, who had resigned from his position as U.S. Attorney General to head CREEP.

Soon thereafter, the director of the FBI resigned after admitting he had destroyed evidence connected to the Watergate case. Ten days later Attorney General Richard Kleindienst and two top presidential aides resigned, and Nixon fired the presidential counselor, John Dean.

In June, Dean testified before the specially impaneled Senate Watergate Committee that Nixon had participated in an attempt to cover up the Watergate affair, that the break-in was part of a larger program of political espionage, and that the president was a party to an attempt to cover that up too. In July, a former White House aide disclosed that the president had secretly tape-recorded all conversations that took place in the Oval Office. The Committee immediately demanded the tapes, but the president refused to turn them over, citing "executive privilege," and continuing to maintain his innocence. The Committee then obtained subpoenas for several of the taped conversations. The White House special prosecutor, Archibald Cox, who had been appointed by Nixon to "investigate" the break-in, also requested the tapes, and refused to accept a White House compromise that would have provided him with a "synopsis" of their content. When Cox refused to back down, the president ordered that he be fired. Both the Attorney General and his deputy refused to carry out the president's order. Cox was finally fired by Solicitor General Robert H. Bork.

Three days later, the House Judiciary Committee announced that it would begin hearing impeachment charges against Nixon. Finally, on October 30, Nixon reluctantly turned over the requested tapes, but two were "missing." Moreover, one contained a "mysterious" 18 1/2-minute gap that the White House claimed was erased accidentally by Nixon's secretary, Rose Mary Woods. (Later analysis of the tape determined that the erasure had been deliberate.) By January 1974, Nixon was still refusing to surrender the additional 500 tapes and documents subpoenaed by the Senate Watergate Committee. As Nixon steadfastly refused to turn over the tapes, the Supreme Court, acknowledging the gravity of the matter, agreed to hear the case immediately.

On July 24, 1974, a unanimous Court ruled in *United States* v. *Nixon* that there was no absolute "executive privilege" that could justify Nixon's refusal to comply with a court order to produce information. Nixon was ordered to turn over the tapes, and within hours the White House agreed to comply. One of the three tapes released revealed that the president had ordered not only a halt to the FBI's investigation of the

Continued

Watergate break-in, but also a subsequent coverup to prevent the discovery that his campaign was involved. This was the "smoking gun" for which congressional investigators had been looking. On July 27, 1974, the House Judiciary Committee approved the first of three articles of impeachment against Nixon. On August 9, Nixon resigned.

One month later, President Gerald R. Ford pardoned Nixon, arguing that this action was necessary to prevent the spectacle of a former president on trial, and that it was time for the nation to turn its attention elsewhere.

Watergate made a lasting impact on the presidency. It proved that the system created by the Framers worked: Under threat of certain impeachment and conviction, a president was succeeded in an orderly, nonviolent fashion. Watergate also facilitated the 1976 election of Jimmy Carter, who ran as an "outsider" in opposition to the corrupting influences of Washington. It also spurred many reforms. Ethics laws were tightened up, stricter campaign finance laws were enacted, and a special prosecutor law, allowing for independent investigation of the executive branch, was enacted.

Rosemary Woods, Richard Nixon's secretary, in her office.

early as Adams and Jefferson. As historian Arthur M. Schlesinger, Jr., once noted, "The Vice President has only one serious thing to do: that is, to wait around for the President to die. This is hardly the basis for a cordial and enduring friendship."[7]

In the past, presidents chose their vice presidents largely to "balance"—politically, geographically, or otherwise—the presidential ticket, with little thought given to the possibility of the vice president becoming president. Franklin D. Roosevelt, for example, a liberal New Yorker, selected Garner, a conservative Texan, to be his running mate in 1932. After serving two terms, Garner—who openly disagreed with Roosevelt over many policies, including Roosevelt's Court-packing plan (see Chapter 9) and his decision to seek a third term—unsuccessfully sought the 1940 presidential nomination himself.

In general, presidential candidates since Eisenhower have selected running mates of such a caliber that they might eventually take over the reins of the nation's highest office. Since Jimmy Carter, recent presidents have given their vice presidents more and

---

[7] "Is the Vice Presidency Necessary?" *Atlantic* 233 (May 1974): 37.

Gore's Top Ten

♦ ♦ ♦

In an appearance on David Letterman's show in September, 1993, Vice President Al Gore Jr. listed the top ten best things about being vice president:

10. Police escort gets you to the movies faster.
9. You know that game tetherball? I played tetherball with the inventor of tetherball.
8. After they sign a bill, there's lots of free pens.
7. If you close your left eye, the seal on the podium reads "President of the United States."
6. I get intellectual property rights to my speeches.
5. Dan Quayle and Gerald Ford are pretty easy to beat during Vice-President's Week on Jeopardy!
4. You don't have to be funny to get invited on the Letterman show.
3. You get to eat all the french fries the president can't get to.
2. You don't have to be a good speller to get the job.
1. Secret Service code name "Buttafuoco."

The usually formal Vice President Gore really loosened up with David Letterman, going so far as to introduce his own "Top Ten" list.

Source: World Wide Pants, Incorporated.

President Jimmy Carter confers with Walter F. Mondale, his vice president.

more responsibility as well as access to information vital to the country's national security. Thus, the office of vice president has begun to come into its own after years of ridicule and insignificance. Today, it is viewed as a jumping-off point for higher office, and not as a dead-end position, as more and more vice presidents have become president. Since 1952, the only elected vice president* who has not received his party's nod to run for president was Alben W. Barkley, who served under President Truman. Of the six vice presidents who have run for president since 1960, three have been elected: Lyndon B. Johnson, Richard M. Nixon, and George Bush. Hubert Humphrey, Gerald R. Ford, and Walter F. Mondale ran but lost. Dan Quayle is considered to be a possible candidate for the Republican nomination for president in 1996. Vice President Al Gore Jr. too, is likely to be a presidential candidate in the future, since he sought his party's nomination (unsuccessfully) in 1988.[8]

How much power a vice president has, however, depends upon how much the president is willing to give him. Although Jimmy Carter, a Southerner, chose Walter F. Mondale, a Northerner, as his running mate in 1976 to balance the ticket, he was also the first president to give his vice president more than ceremonial duties. Mondale—a former senator from Minnesota with Washington connections—became an important adviser to President Carter, who had run for office as a Washington "outsider." Whereas previous vice presidents had tried to make numerous trivial tasks appear significant, Mondale did his best to carve out a new role as an adviser to the president, an activity encouraged by Carter.

---

* Spiro Agnew was forced to resign from office.

[8] See Jules Whitcover, *Crapshoot: Rolling the Dice on the Vice Presidency* (New York: Crown, 1992).

The "Mondale model" of an active vice president set the expectations for what the influence, powers, and limitations of modern vice presidents should be. President Ronald Reagan's vice president, George Bush, a former director of the Central Intelligence Agency (CIA), was given the unprecedented responsibility of heading the National Security Crisis Management team. Following the assassination attempt on President Reagan in March 1981, Vice President Bush worked closely with the recuperating president to keep the government in order. George Bush also made good use of Vice President Dan Quayle. Quayle was a key player in keeping conservatives happy, and he also chaired the Council on Competitiveness, an executive council created by Bush to review all federal regulations that could have an adverse effect on business.

President Clinton has expanded on the "Mondale model." Gore and Clinton forged a close working (and apparently personal) relationship when they traveled the country campaigning by bus in 1992. With many more personal characteristics in common than many president/vice president teams (they are both Southerners, young, religious, fathers of teenage girls, and married to strong, independent women, for example), Clinton made sure Gore was at his side when key appointments were made, and the two consult on a daily basis.

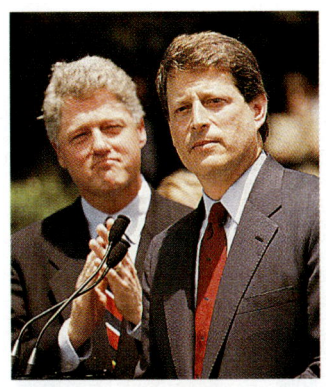

In keeping with and even expanding upon the "Mondale model," President Clinton has attempted to involve Vice President Al Gore Jr. in all aspects of decision making. Gore was at Clinton's side in Little Rock, Arkansas, as Cabinet selections were made and is playing a key role in policy making, especially concerning the environment and bureaucratic waste.

The Constitutional Powers of the President

Despite the Framers' faith in George Washington as their intended first president, it took considerable compromise to overcome their continued fear of a king. The specific powers of the executive branch that the Framers agreed upon are enumerated in Article II of the Constitution. Perhaps the most important section of Article II is its first sentence. It provides that "The executive Power shall be vested in a President of the United States of America." Just what the Framers meant by "executive power" was left intentionally vague.

Over the years, the expected limits of these constitutional powers have changed as individual presidents asserted themselves in the political process. Some presidents are powerful and effective; others just limp along in office. Much of the president's authority stems from his position as the symbolic leader of the nation and his ability to wield power. When the president speaks—especially in the area of foreign affairs—he speaks for the whole nation. But the base of all presidential authority is Article II, which outlines only a limited policy-making role for the president. Thus, as administrative head of the executive branch, the president is charged with taking "Care that the Laws be faithfully executed," but he has no actual power to make Congress enact legislation he supports.

The Appointment Power

To help him enforce the laws passed by Congress, the Constitution authorizes the president to appoint, with the advice and consent of the Senate,

> Ambassadors, other public Ministers and Consuls, judges of the supreme Court, and all other Officers of the United States, whose Appointments are not herein otherwise provided for, and which shall be established by Law. . . .

Joycelyn Elders' appointment as U.S. Surgeon General was controversial from the start, and conservatives continue to pressure the President for her removal.

Today, with the growth of the Executive Office of the President—as well as of the Cabinet, executive agencies, and commissions discussed in Chapter 8—the president has accumulated the authority to make more than 3,000 appointments to his administration (technically more than 75,000, if military officers are included). Although only about half of these appointments are to policy-making positions, this power gives a president considerable influence over policy making. In the context of his ability to make appointments to the federal courts, especially, his influence can be felt far past his term of office. The British prime minister enjoys a similarly broad power of appointment; however, the prime minister does not have to seek the approval of either chamber of the legislature for executive and bureaucratic appointments. This ability to select an executive team without the formal participation of Parliament is one of the many sources of the prime minister's power.

Selecting the "right" people is often one of a president's most important tasks. Presidents must look for a blend of loyalty, competence and integrity. Identifying these qualities in people is a major challenge that every new president faces. And, as every president has learned, appointees who lack any of those characteristics endanger the success of their administration, and many presidents have paid dearly for appointment mistakes.

Once a president sends appointments to the Senate, they are traditionally given great respect—especially those for the Cabinet. Although Senator Nancy Kassebaum (R.-Kan.) has commented, "I firmly believe that our founding fathers did not intend for the United States Senate to be a rubber stamp,"[9] it is rare for the Senate to reject a presidential appointment. President Dwight D. Eisenhower's nomination of Lewis L. Strauss to be Secretary of Commerce was rejected by a forty-nine to forty-six vote because of a combination of policy differences and lingering questions about Strauss's integrity. After Eisenhower, it was thirty years before the next Cabinet nominee was rejected. In fact, the Senate's rejection of President Bush's nominee for Secretary of Defense, former Senator John G. Tower (R.-Tex.), marked only the eighth time in history that a president's choice for a Cabinet post has been rejected. Tower's nomination was rejected on a vote of fifty-three to forty-seven, because of charges of a potential conflict of interest with defense contractors (for whom he had worked since retiring from the Senate), excessive drinking, and womanizing.

Certain kinds of nominees receive more congressional scrutiny than others. Regulatory commission members, discussed in detail in Chapter 8, are located in the world of politics somewhere between the legislative and executive branches, yet they are appointed by the president. Supreme Court appointees also lie outside the executive branch of government and are increasingly subject to greater senatorial review and public, televised grilling.

In general, however, few presidential appointments are turned down. This is not to say that all appointments sail through, however. President Clinton's nomination of openly lesbian Roberta Actenberg to be Assistant Secretary for Fair Housing and Equal Opportunity in the Department of Housing and Urban Development faced strong opposition in the Senate when many conservative senators protested her appointment. Similarly, his nomination of Joycelyn Elders to the post of U.S. Surgeon General was delayed for several months because many senators had misgivings about her controversial views about passing out condoms in schools and her support of mar-

---

[9] "Senate Votes to Reject Tower; Bush Nominates Rep. Cheney," *The National Bureau of National Affairs, Inc. Federal Contracts Report*, Vol. 51, No. 11 (March 13, 1989): 465.

ijuana for medical purposes, as well as questions about her ethics while on a bank board in Arkansas. Ultimately, her confirmation was approved in a sixty-five to thirty-four vote. Generally, when a nominee appears to be "in trouble," presidents often withdraw the nomination or hint that it would be wise for the nominee to do so. For example, after Robert Gates was nominated by President Reagan in 1987 to succeed CIA Director William J. Casey, Gates withdrew his name amid questions of the agency's involvement in the Iran–Contra affair. Later, however, he was renominated to the position by President Bush and after 138 days of questioning by the Senate Select Committee on Intelligence, he was confirmed.

Senatorial courtesy, the tradition requiring that a president consult members of the Senate about nominees from their home states, often grants senators of the president's party a virtual veto over appointments to posts in their states. Although this limits the president's discretion in filling state-specific jobs, especially federal district court vacancies, "national" positions provide the opportunity for the president to shape the direction and image of his administration. There are, of course, some traditions—such as the nomination of a Westerner to be Secretary of the Interior—but these are not requirements.

The quality of presidential appointments directly reflects upon the president. Presidents Ulysses S. Grant, Warren G. Harding, and Richard M. Nixon, for example, were hurt by the low quality of some of their appointments. Likewise, President Ronald Reagan's reputation suffered when the behavior of several of his appointees led to numerous resignations and/or federal prosecutions of high-ranking appointees. And President Bill Clinton was widely criticized about the way some of his appointments were handled and for the fact that it took him so long to fill key positions. The Constitution is silent on the president's authority to remove those subject to senatorial appointment, but the Supreme Court has interpreted the Constitution to allow the president to remove most appointees at will.

The Power to Convene Congress

The Constitution requires the president to inform the Congress periodically on "the State of the Union," and authorizes the president to convene either or both houses of Congress on "extraordinary Occasions." In *Federalist No. 77*, Hamilton justified the latter by noting that because the Senate and the chief executive enjoy concurrent powers to make treaties, "it might often be necessary to call it together with a view to this object, when it would be unnecessary and improper to convene the House of Representatives."

The British prime minister possesses one power relative to the legislature that the President does not: the power to dissolve Parliament and call new elections. While a Parliament has a maximum life of five years, technically speaking, the prime minister can call an election at any time, which gives the party in power a significant advantage in terms of picking the optimal time—politically and economically—to go to the people. This power contributes to an executive branch that is ascendant over its legislature.

Because Thomas Jefferson spoke with a lisp, he sent a written message to Congress, establishing a tradition that lasted 113 years, until 1913, when Woodrow Wilson became the first president since John Adams to deliver his State of the Union message to Congress in person.

The Power to Make Treaties

The president's power to make treaties with foreign nations is checked by the Constitution's stipulation that all treaties must be approved by at least two-thirds of the members of the Senate. The chief executive can also "receive ambassadors," wording that

President Clinton meeting with his national security team to discuss the situation in Bosnia.

has been interpreted to allow the president to recognize the very existence of other nations.

Historically, the Senate ratifies about 70 percent of the treaties submitted to it by the president.[10] Only sixteen that have been put to a vote have been rejected, often under highly partisan circumstances. Perhaps the most notable example of the Senate's refusal to ratify a treaty was its defeat of the Treaty of Versailles submitted by President Woodrow Wilson. The Treaty was an agreement among the major nations to end World War I, and it called for, at Wilson's insistence, the creation of a League of Nations—a precursor of the United Nations—to foster continued peace and international disarmament. In struggling to gain international acceptance for the League, Wilson had taken American support for granted. This was a dramatic miscalculation. Isolationists, led by Senator William Jennings Bryan (D.-Neb.), opposed U.S. participation in the League on the grounds that the League would place the United States in the center of every major international conflict. Proponents countered that, League or no League, the United States had emerged from World War I as a world power, and that membership in the League would enhance its new role. The vote for ratification was very close, but the isolationists prevailed—the United States stayed out of the League, and Wilson was devastated.

The Senate may also require substantial amendment of a treaty prior to granting its consent. When President Carter proposed the controversial Panama Canal Treaties in

---

[10] Benjamin I. Page and Mark P. Petracca, *The American Presidency* (New York: McGraw-Hill, 1983), p. 268.

1977, for example, the Senate required that several conditions be ironed out between the Carter and Torrijos administrations before its approval was forthcoming.

Presidents often try to get around the "advise and consent" requirement of treaties by entering into an **executive agreement**, which allows the president to enter into secret and highly sensitive arrangements with foreign nations without congressional approval. Presidents have used these agreements since the days of George Washington, and their use has been upheld by the courts. Although executive agreements are not binding on subsequent administrations, since 1900 they have been used far more frequently than treaties, further cementing the role of the president in foreign affairs.

Veto Power

Another way presidents can affect the policy process is through **veto** power, the authority to reject any congressional legislation. Proponents of a strong executive at the Constitutional Convention argued that the president should have an absolute and final veto over acts of Congress. Opponents of this idea, including Benjamin Franklin, countered that in their home states the executive veto "was constantly made use of to extort money" from the legislature. James Madison made the most compelling argument for a compromise on the issue:

> Experience has proven a tendency in our governments to throw all power into the legislative vortex. The Executives of the States are in general little more than Ciphers, the legislatures omnipotent. If no effectual check be devised for restraining the instability and encroachments of the latter, a revolution of some kind or other would be inevitable.[11]

In keeping with the system of checks and balances, then, the president was given veto power but only as a "qualified negative." Although the president was given the authority to veto any act of Congress (with the exception of joint resolutions that propose constitutional amendments), Congress was given the authority to override an executive veto by a two-thirds vote in each House. The veto is a powerful policy tool because Congress cannot usually muster enough votes to override it. Thus, in over 200 years there have been approximately 2,500 presidential vetoes and only 100-odd have been overridden (see Figure 7-1).

President Bush was never reluctant to use his veto power and only one of his vetoes was overridden. Moreover, he often vetoed bills that enjoyed wide popular support, including bills authorizing parental leave from work after the birth of a baby, and several versions of a civil rights bill. In 1991, for example, although a $6.5 billion bill providing twenty additional weeks of unemployment compensation was passed by 300 to 118 in the House and 65 to 35 in the Senate, the Congress was not able to override Bush's subsequent veto. Congress passed a similar version of the bill in 1991, which President Bush signed when Senate Democrats used his threatened veto to argue that he was insensitive to the plight of the jobless. In October 1992, however, his impressive use of the veto to stop legislation he did not favor ended when both houses of Congress voted overwhelmingly to override his veto of a bill re-regulating the cable television industry. During Bill Clinton's first year in office, he became the first president since James A. Garfield (1881) not to veto any act of Congress.

---

[11] Quoted in Solberg, *The Federal Convention and the Formation of the Union of American States*, p. 91. (See n. 4.)

FIGURE 7-1

Presidential Vetoes, 1789–1993

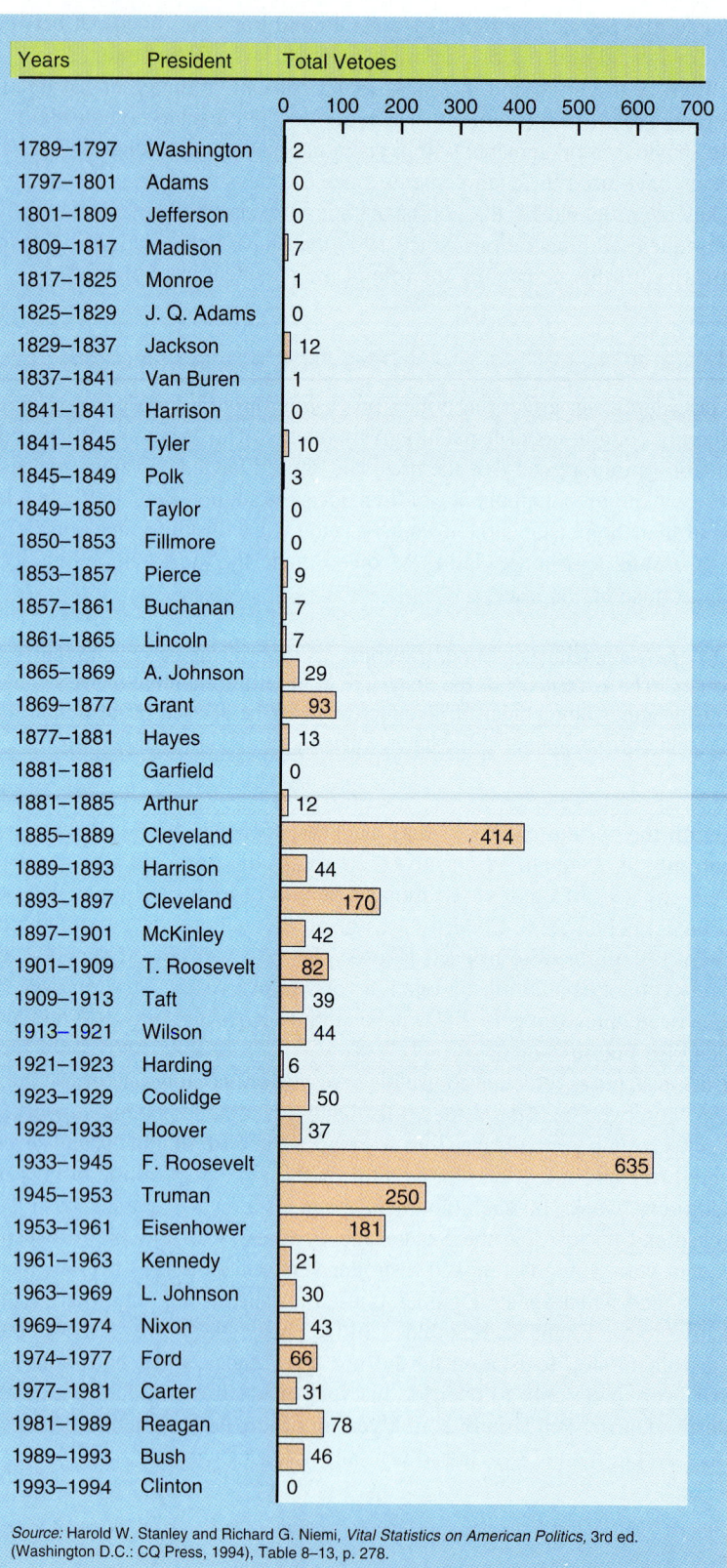

Years	President	Total Vetoes
1789–1797	Washington	2
1797–1801	Adams	0
1801–1809	Jefferson	0
1809–1817	Madison	7
1817–1825	Monroe	1
1825–1829	J. Q. Adams	0
1829–1837	Jackson	12
1837–1841	Van Buren	1
1841–1841	Harrison	0
1841–1845	Tyler	10
1845–1849	Polk	3
1849–1850	Taylor	0
1850–1853	Fillmore	0
1853–1857	Pierce	9
1857–1861	Buchanan	7
1861–1865	Lincoln	7
1865–1869	A. Johnson	29
1869–1877	Grant	93
1877–1881	Hayes	13
1881–1881	Garfield	0
1881–1885	Arthur	12
1885–1889	Cleveland	414
1889–1893	Harrison	44
1893–1897	Cleveland	170
1897–1901	McKinley	42
1901–1909	T. Roosevelt	82
1909–1913	Taft	39
1913–1921	Wilson	44
1921–1923	Harding	6
1923–1929	Coolidge	50
1929–1933	Hoover	37
1933–1945	F. Roosevelt	635
1945–1953	Truman	250
1953–1961	Eisenhower	181
1961–1963	Kennedy	21
1963–1969	L. Johnson	30
1969–1974	Nixon	43
1974–1977	Ford	66
1977–1981	Carter	31
1981–1989	Reagan	78
1989–1993	Bush	46
1993–1994	Clinton	0

Source: Harold W. Stanley and Richard G. Niemi, *Vital Statistics on American Politics*, 3rd ed. (Washington D.C.: CQ Press, 1994), Table 8–13, p. 278.

Commander-in-Chief of the Military

One of the most important executive powers is the president's authority over the military. Article II states that the president is "Commander-in-Chief of the Army and Navy of the United States." The Framers saw this power as consistent with state practices, and since the eighteenth century it has proven to be wide-ranging. While the Constitution specifically grants Congress the authority to declare war, presidents since Abraham Lincoln have used the commander-in-chief clause in conjunction with the chief executive's duty to "take Care that the Laws be faithfully executed" to wage war (and to broaden various powers).

Modern presidents continually clash with Congress over who has the power to commence hostilities. The Vietnam War, in which 58,000 American soldiers were killed and 300,000 wounded, was conducted (at a cost of $150 billion) without a congressional declaration of war. In fact, acknowledging President Johnson's claim to war-making authority, in 1964 Congress passed, with only two dissenting votes, the Gulf of Tonkin Resolution which authorized a massive commitment of U.S. forces in South Vietnam.

During that highly controversial war, Presidents Johnson and Nixon routinely assured members of Congress that victory was near. In 1971, however, publication of the Pentagon Papers revealed what many had suspected all along—Lyndon Johnson had systematically altered casualty figures and distorted key facts to place the conduct of the war in a more positive light. In 1973, Congress passed the War Powers Act, limiting the president's authority to introduce American troops into foreign nations without congressional approval (as noted in Chapter 6). President Nixon's veto of the Act was overridden by a two-thirds majority in both houses of Congress.

President Bill Clinton, already the object of derision from many members of the military because of the questions surrounding his failure to fight in the Vietnam War, faced a strong test of his commander-in-chief abilities when he proposed that discrimination against gays in the military be ended.

George Washington enjoyed dressing in full military regalia as commander-in-chief.

The Pardoning Power

Presidents can exercise a check on judicial power through their constitutional authority to grant reprieves or pardons. A **pardon,** which restores all rights and privileges of citizenship, is usually granted to a specific individual convicted of a crime. In 1974, President Gerald R. Ford granted the most famous presidential pardon, to former President Richard M. Nixon, who had not been formally charged with any crime, "for any offenses against the United States, which he, Richard M. Nixon, has committed or may have committed while in office." (See "Watergate and Its Effects on the Presidency," pp. 264–265.) This unilateral pardon unleashed a torrent of public criticism that many blame for Ford's ultimate defeat in his 1976 bid for the presidency.

In the waning days of his term, George Bush was showered with a torrent of criticism when he pardoned former Secretary of Defense Caspar Weinberger and five other administration officials on Christmas Eve, 1993 for their conduct related to the Iran–Contra affair. Bush tried to place his pardons in the context of the historic use of the pardoning power to "put bitterness behind us and to look to the future." Said Bush:

> This healing tradition reaches at least from James Madison's pardon of Lafitte's pirates after the War of 1812, to Andrew Johnson's pardon of soldiers who had

fought for the Confederacy, to Harry Truman's and Jimmy Carter's pardons of those who violated the Selective Service laws in World War II and Vietnam.[12]

In spite of Bush's claims about the propriety of the pardons, Independent Counsel Lawrence E. Walsh, who had prosecuted all six men pardoned by Bush, claimed that Bush pardoned them to lead prosecutors away from himself. Walsh claimed that Bush was guilty of "misconduct" and may have "illegally withheld" documents from investigators.[13]

Even though pardons are usually directed toward specific individuals, presidents historically have used their pardoning power to offer general amnesties. Presidents Washington, John Adams, Madison, Lincoln, Andrew Johnson, Theodore Roosevelt, and Carter all used general pardons to grant amnesty to large groups of individuals for illegal acts. Carter, for example, incurred the wrath of many veterans' groups when he made an offer of unconditional amnesty to approximately 10,000 men who had fled the United States or gone into hiding to avoid being drafted to serve in the Vietnam War.

The Development of Presidential Power

Each of the forty-one men who has served as president of the United States has brought with him some expectation of presidential authority.

Said John F. Kennedy in his Inaugural Address:

> The President . . . is rightly described as a man of extraordinary powers, yet it is also true that he must wield these powers under extraordinary limitations. . . . Every president must endure a gap between what he would like and what is possible.[14]

Less optimistically, after serving two terms, Harry S Truman mused about what surprises awaited his successor, Dwight D. Eisenhower, a former general: "He'll sit here and he'll say, 'Do this! Do that!' *And nothing will happen.* Poor Ike—it won't be a bit like the army. He'll find it very frustrating."[15] Like Truman, political scientist Richard E. Neustadt notes that presidents have been limited in their ability to turn the formal powers of the presidency into effective policy making. The tension that limitation produces puts them in a position that Neustadt likens to that of "a cat on a hot tin roof."

A president's personal expectation of authority (and the public's expectations of him) are limited by the formal powers bestowed on the president by the Constitution and by the Supreme Court's interpretation of those constitutional provisions. These formal checks on presidential power are also affected by the times in which the president serves, and by the president's personality. The postwar era of good feelings and economic prosperity presided over in the 1950s by the grandfatherly war hero Dwight Eisenhower, for instance, called for a very different kind of leader from that needed by the Civil War-torn nation governed by Abraham Lincoln.

---

[12] "Text of Bush's Pardon of Weinberger, 5 Others in Iran–Contra Probe," *Los Angeles Times* (December 25, 1992): A20.

[13] Walter Pincus, "Bush Pardons Weinberger in Iran–Contra Affair; 5 Others Also Cleared; Angry Walsh Indicates a Focus on President," *The Washington Post* (December 25, 1992): A1.

[14] Elizabeth Frost, ed. *The Bully Pulpit: Quotations from America's Presidents* (New York: Facts on File Publications, 1988), p. 187.

[15] Quoted in Richard E. Neustadt, *Presidential Power: The Politics of Power from FDR to Carter* (New York: Wiley, 1980), p. 9.

The Development of Presidential Power ❖ 275

Chief law enforcer: National Guard troops sent by President Eisenhower enforce federal court decisions ordering the integration of public schools in Little Rock, Arkansas.

Commander-in-chief: President Bush and his wife Barbara with troops in the Persian Gulf.

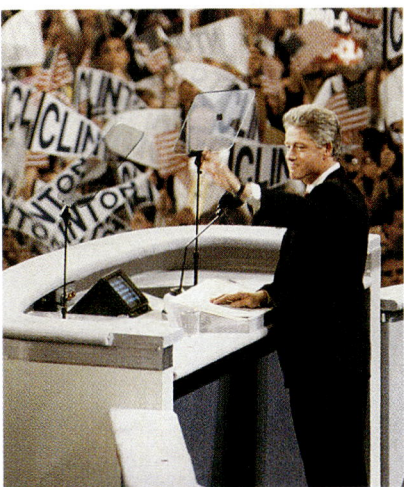

Leader of the party: Presidential candidate Bill Clinton accepts the Democratic Party's nomination for president at the party's 1992 convention.

The President's Many Hats

Key player in the legislative process: Clinton confers with Republican leaders to promote bipartisanship.

Shaper of domestic policy: President Lyndon B. Johnson conferring with the Reverend Martin Luther King, Jr. and other black leaders about Johnson's War on Poverty.

Chief of State: President Kennedy and his wife, Jacqueline, are greeted by the President of France and his wife during the Kennedys' widely publicized 1961 trip to that nation.

The presidency that we see today is quite different from the office assumed by George Washington in 1789. According to Benjamin I. Page and Mark P. Petracca, two main trends are responsible for the office's evolution:[16]

1. Democratization of the office, which has brought the president closer to the people. As the presidency has been brought closer to the people, however, people have expected more of their presidents, so presidential actions often fall short of public expectations. These expectations have contributed to the second trend, namely:
2. The phenomenal growth in presidential responsibilities and the need for the president to delegate authority. And, because modern presidents often realize how difficult it is to deliver on their promises, many have responded by trying to centralize authority and responsibility in the White House, where their control is greatest.[17]

[16] Page and Petracca, *The American Presidency*, p. 40. (See n. 10.)
[17] See also Terry Moe, "The Politicized Presidency" in John E. Chubb and Paul Petersen, *New Directions in American Politics* (Washington, DC: Brookings Institution, 1985).

PEOPLE OF THE PAST

George Washington

On April 30, 1789, thirteen guns sounded in New York City to signal the inaugural day of the first president of the United States, George Washington. Around noon, a delegation from Congress arrived to escort Washington, who greeted them in powdered hair, a brown suit, and silk stockings. They went in a carriage drawn by four horses amidst a cheering crowd to the steps of Federal Hall in New York City. After his swearing in, Washington went to church to offer up a prayer, and then went home for dinner.

George Washington's heritage is a part of our daily lives. His name is that of the nation's capital and its forty-second state, and his portrait appears on the nation's basic unit of currency, the dollar bill.

Unlike some presidents to follow him, Washington reveled in the dignity of the office. He rode in a carriage drawn by six cream-colored horses, or alone on a white steed with a saddle trimmed in gold. His house had fourteen white servants and seven slaves to help with elaborate dinners. And his birthday was a day of celebration in many towns across the new nation as it had been since the Revolutionary War. "Even Cincinnatus received no adulations of this kind," the *National Gazette* observed. "Surely the office [the President] enjoys is a sufficient testimony of the people's favor, without worshipping him likewise."

Washington's appreciation of regality was also evident in his tours through the new nation. From October to November 1789, he traveled through New England in a hired coach, accompanied by his aide, his private secretary, six servants, nine horses, and a luggage wagon.

During Washington's administration, a string of measures was pushed through Congress to make the new nation stronger. A national currency was instituted, the Bank of the United States was established, manufacturing and trade were fostered by tariffs and bounties, and inventions were protected by patent and copyright laws. While the United States reorganized the armed forces and built new fortifications in the East and West, national security was preserved by a neutrality proclamation in regard to an ever-widening European war between France and Great Britain. In fact, in his Farewell Address, Washington warned against any entangling alliances, noting that it should be "our true policy to steer clear of permanent alliances with any portion of the foreign world."

The First Three Presidents

Each of the first three presidents—George Washington, John Adams, and Thomas Jefferson—contributed significantly to the development of the office of chief executive, although in different ways. When George Washington was sworn in as the first president of the United States, he took over an office and government that were really yet to be created. Eventually a few hundred postal workers were hired, and Washington appointed a small group of Cabinet advisers and clerks. During Washington's two terms, the entire federal budget was only about $40 million, or approximately $10 for every citizen. In contrast, in fiscal 1995 the federal budget was about $1.5 trillion, or about $6,000 for every man, woman, and child.

As the first president, Washington set several important precedents for future presidents:

- He took every opportunity to establish the primacy of the national government. For example, when John Hancock, the governor of Massachusetts, came to New York City, Washington insisted that Hancock call upon *him* rather than the other way around. For two days, Washington played an uncomfortable waiting game, but his patience and insistence paid off when the governor finally came to pay his respects. In 1794, Washington's use of the militia of four states to put down the Whiskey Rebellion, an uprising of 3,000 Western Pennsylvania farmers opposed to the payment of federal excise tax on liquor, also helped establish the idea of federal supremacy and the authority of the executive branch to collect the taxes levied by Congress. (Leading the 1,500 troops of the militias was Alexander Hamilton, Secretary of the Treasury, whose duty it was to collect federal taxes.)

- Washington began the practice of regular meetings with his advisers (called the Cabinet), thus establishing the Cabinet system, the popular name for the meeting of the executive departments.

- He asserted the prominence of the role of the chief executive in the conduct of foreign affairs. He sent envoys to negotiate the Jay Treaty with Great Britain. Then, over senatorial objection, he continued to assert his authority to negotiate treaties first, and then simply submit them to the Senate for its approval. Washington made it clear that the Senate's function was limited to approval of treaties and did *not* include negotiation with foreign powers.

- He claimed the **inherent power** of the presidency as the basis for proclaiming a policy of strict neutrality when the British and French were at war. Although the Constitution is silent about a president's authority to declare neutrality, Washington's supporters argued that the Constitution granted the president inherent powers, that is, powers that can be derived or inferred from what is formally described in the Constitution. Thus, they argued that the president's power to conduct diplomatic relations could be inferred from the Constitution. And since neither Congress nor the Supreme Court disagreed, this power was added to the list of presidential powers that other presidents consider to be theirs.

The next two presidents, John Adams and Thomas Jefferson, also acted in ways critical to the development of the office of the chief executive, especially the president's role in the political system. Adams's poor leadership skills, for example, heightened the divisions between Federalists and Anti-Federalists, and probably quickened the development of political parties (see Chapter 11). Soon thereafter, Jefferson used the party system to cement strong ties with the Congress and thereby expand the role of the president in the legislative process.

Congressional Triumph: 1804–1933

The first three presidents made enormous contributions to the office of the chief executive and established important precedents to guide the conduct of those who came after them. But the very nature of the way government had to function in its formative years caused the balance of power to be heavily weighted in favor of a strong Congress. Americans routinely had intimate contacts with their representatives in Congress, while to most, the president seemed a remote figure.

By the end of Jefferson's first term, it seemed clear that the Framers' initial fear of an all-powerful, monarchical president was unfounded. The strong Congress and the relatively weak presidents who came after Jefferson allowed Congress quickly to assert itself as the most powerful branch of government. In fact, with but two exceptions—Andrew Jackson and Abraham Lincoln—most presidents from Jefferson to Franklin D. Roosevelt failed to exercise the powers of the presidency in any significant manner.

Exception to the Rule, No. 1: Jackson. Andrew Jackson was the first president truly to act as a strong *national* leader. By the time Jackson ran for president in 1828, eleven new states had been added to the Union, and the number of white males eligible to vote had increased dramatically as property requirements for voting were removed by nearly all states. When Jackson, a Tennessean, was elected the seventh president, it signalled the end of an era; he was the first president not to be either a Virginian or an Adams. His election launched "Jacksonian democracy," a label that embodied the Western, frontier, egalitarian spirit personified by Jackson, the first "common man" to be elected president. The masses loved him, and legends were built

Andrew Jackson, widely hailed as the "People's President," threw open the White House to celebrate his inauguration. In 1993, the Clintons followed his lead.

around his down-to-earth image. Jackson, for example, once was asked to give a postmastership to a soldier who had lost his leg on the battlefield and needed the job to support his family. Although he was also told that the man hadn't voted for him, Jackson responded: "If he lost his leg fighting for his country, that is vote enough for me."[18]

Jackson used his image and personal power to buttress the developing party system. For example, he rewarded loyal followers of his Democratic Party with presidential appointments. And, frequently finding himself at odds with Congress, Jackson also made extensive use of the veto power. His vetoes of twelve bills surpassed the combined total of nine vetoes used by his six predecessors. Jackson also reasserted the supremacy of the national government (and the presidency) by facing down South Carolina's nullification of a federal tariff law.

Exception to the Rule, No. 2: Lincoln. Abraham Lincoln's approach to the presidency was similar to Jackson's. Moreover, the unprecedented emergency of the Civil War allowed Lincoln to assume powers that no president before him had claimed. Lincoln believed that he needed to move quickly for the very survival of the Union. Thus, he frequently acted without first obtaining the approval of Congress. Among many of Lincoln's "questionable" acts were:

- The suspension of the writ of *habeas corpus* (which allows those in prison to petition to be released), citing the need to jail persons even suspected of disloyal practices (see Chapter 4).
- The expansion of the size of the U.S. army above congressionally mandated ceilings.
- The institution of a blockade of Southern ports, in effect initiating a war without the approval of Congress.
- Closing the mails to treasonable correspondence.

Lincoln argued that the inherent powers of his office allowed him to circumvent the Constitution in a time of war or national crisis. Since the Constitution conferred upon the president the duty to make sure that the laws of the United States are faithfully executed, reasoned Lincoln, the acts enumerated above were constitutional. He simply refused to allow the nation to crumble because of what he viewed as technical requirements of the Constitution. Noting the secession of the Southern states and their threat to the sanctity of the Union, Lincoln queried, "Are all of the laws *but one* to go unexecuted, and the Government itself go to pieces lest that one be violated?"[19]

Few presidents other than Jackson and Lincoln subscribed to a broad and expansive interpretation of executive power prior to the administration of Franklin D. Roosevelt (1933–1945). Neither Jackson nor Lincoln was succeeded by strong presidents; the nation was possibly just not ready to submit to a series of powerful leaders.

The Growth Of The Modern Presidency

Before the days of instantaneous communication, the nation could afford to allow the relatively slow deliberative processes of Congress to make most decisions. And it was

---

[18] Quoted in Paul F. Boller, Jr., *Presidential Anecdotes* (New York: Penguin Books, 1981), p. 78.
[19] Abraham Lincoln, "Special Session Message," July 4, 1861, in *Borzoi Reader in American Politics*, Edward Keynes and David Adamany, eds. (New York: Knopf, 1973), p. 539.

Congress, not the president, that was closest to the people. But as times and especially technology have changed, the public now personalizes the presidency and has high expectations of anyone who holds that office. Moreover, as the times have changed, and national and international events are reported with breakneck speed by the electronic media such as the Cable News Network (CNN), the need for one individual to act quickly and decisively on behalf of the entire nation seems clear. Congress is often just too slow to respond to the fast-changing pace of events—especially in foreign affairs.

The need to act quickly appears especially vital in times of crisis, which long have played a key role in the development of presidential authority. Lincoln, for example, one of the most powerful presidents, and as noted in "The Best and the Worst Presidents" on page 289, generally ranked as the "best" president, governed during the peculiar circumstances of a national civil war. Times of danger to the union required that a strong leader take up the reins of government. In the twentieth century, especially, presidential—as opposed to congressional—decision making has become more and more important. And much of this growth can be traced to the four-term presidency of Franklin D. Roosevelt (FDR), which included several crises, including World War II.

FDR and the Modern Presidency. FDR took office in 1933 in the midst of a major crisis, the Great Depression. Noting the sorry state of the national economy in his inaugural address, he concluded, "This nation asks for action and action now." To jump-start the American economy, FDR asked Congress for "broad executive powers to wage a war against the emergency, as great as the power that would be given to me if we were in fact invaded by a foreign foe."[20]

Just as Lincoln had taken bold steps upon his inauguration, Roosevelt also acted quickly. He immediately fashioned a plan for national recovery called the "New Deal."

---

[20] Quoted in Page and Petracca, *The American Presidency*, p. 57. (See n. 10.)

Chicago Historical Society

The New Deal was a package of bold and controversial programs designed to invigorate the failing American economy. As part of that plan, Roosevelt

- Declared a bank holiday to end public runs on the depleted resources of many banks.
- Persuaded Congress to pass broad pieces of legislation providing for emergency relief, public works jobs, regulation of farm production, and improved terms and conditions of work for thousands of workers in a variety of industries.
- Regularized the practice of sending legislative programs from the executive branch to Congress for its approval, instead of merely reacting to congressional proposals.
- Increased the size of the federal bureaucracy from fewer than 600,000 to more than 1 million workers.

Throughout Roosevelt's unprecedented twelve years in office (he was elected to four terms but died shortly after beginning the last one), which saw the nation go from the economic "war" of the Great Depression to the real international conflict of World War II, the institution of the presidency changed profoundly and permanently. All kinds of federal agencies were created to implement New Deal programs, and the executive branch became more and more involved in a wide variety of programs.

Not only did FDR create a new bureaucracy by which to implement his pet programs, he also established a new relationship between the presidency and the people. In his radio addresses—or "fireside chats," as he liked to call them—he spoke directly to the public in a relaxed and informal manner, yet he discussed serious issues. He opened his radio addresses with "My friends . . . ," making it seem as though he were speaking directly to each listener. In response to these chats, Roosevelt began to receive about 4,000 letters per day, in contrast to the 40 per day received by his predecessor, Herbert Hoover. The head of the White House correspondence section remembered that "the mail started coming in by the truckload. They couldn't even get the envelopes open."[21] One letter that found its way to the White House was simply addressed "My Friend, Washington, D.C." Roosevelt "personalized" the presidency—his style was successful, and his innovations became the routine and the expected. To his successors FDR left the "modern presidency," including a burgeoning (many would say bloated) federal bureaucracy (see Chapter 8), an active and usually leading role in foreign policy, and a nationalized executive office, as technology—first radio and then television—brought the president closer to the public than ever before.

The rhetorical and personalized styles of post-FDR presidents are very different from those of their predecessors. George Washington believed that the purpose of public appearances was to "see and be seen," not to discuss policy issues. Today, presidents use every opportunity to sell their programs. Whereas the rhetoric of early presidents was written, formal, and addressed principally to Congress, today oral speeches addressed to the public at large are the norm. Abraham Lincoln was applauded for refusing to speak about the impending Civil War. In contrast, Ronald Reagan was hailed as "the Great Communicator." And Bill Clinton has truly taken the personalized presidency to new levels. Beginning during his campaign, Clinton often appeared on "Larry King LIVE ON CNN." Even after becoming president, Clinton continued to take his case directly to the people. He launched his health care reform proposals, for example, on a prime time edition of Nightline hosted by Ted Koppel.

---

[21] Merlin Gustafson, "The President's Mail," *Presidential Studies Quarterly* 8 (1978): 36.

For an hour-and-a-half, the president took audience questions about his health plan, impressing even the plan's opponents with his grasp of details.

Clinton is keenly aware of the importance of maintaining his connection with the public. At a black-tie dinner honoring radio and television correspondents, Clinton responded to criticisms levied against him for not holding traditional press conferences by pointing out how clever he was to ignore the traditional press. "You know why I can stiff you on the press conferences? Because Larry King liberated me from you by giving me to the American people directly," quipped Clinton.[22]

The Role of the President in the Legislative Process

When FDR sent his first legislative package to Congress, he broke the traditional model of law making. Said FDR of this new relationship, "It is the duty of the President to propose and it is the privilege of the Congress to dispose."[23] Since FDR, the public has looked to the president to formulate concrete legislative plans to propose to Congress.

Although the public looks to the president to set the agenda, "merely placing a program before Congress is not enough," declared President Lyndon B. Johnson. "Without constant attention from the administration, most legislation moves through the congressional process at the speed of a glacier."[24] The president's most important power (and often the source of his greatest frustration) is his ability to construct coalitions to work for passage of his legislation. Frequently, presidents must "deal" with legislators and have "goodies" to trade for votes. Ronald Reagan's first budget director, David Stockman, once stated that "the last 10 or 20 percent of the votes needed for a majority of both houses [on the 1981 tax cut bill] had to be bought, period." Concessions took the form of real estate tax shelters, special breaks for oil lease holders, and loopholes in the corporate income tax. "The hogs were really feeding," said Stockman. "The greed level, the level of opportunism, just got out of control."[25] When asked by the administration if his vote could be bought, one representative from Louisiana retorted, "No, but it can be rented." With votes bought and rented, Reagan ultimately was able to get what he wanted from Congress.

FDR and Lyndon B. Johnson (LBJ) were among the best presidents at "working" Congress, but they, like Bill Clinton, were helped by Democratic majorities in both houses of Congress.[26] On the whole, presidents, especially when they preside over what is called a "divided government" (when the presidency and Congress are controlled by different political parties), have a hard time getting Congress to pass their programs. Figure 7-2, "Congressional Support for the President," reveals that throughout their terms presidents experience declining support for policies they favor. That's why it is so important for a president to propose key plans early in his administration. Figure 7-2, however, reflects congressional support only for legislation about which the president made his support known to Congress. Presidents have an even harder

---

[22] Dan Balz, "Changing the Capital, More So the Man," *The Washington Post* (January 17, 1994): A1.

[23] Franklin Delano Roosevelt, Press Conference, July 23, 1937.

[24] Lyndon B. Johnson, *The Vantage Point* (New York: Holt, Rinehart and Winston, 1971), p. 448.

[25] David Stockman, *The Triumph of Politics* (New York: Harper and Row, 1986), p. 251.

[26] Morris P. Fiorina, *Divided Government* (New York: Macmillan Publishing Co., 1992).

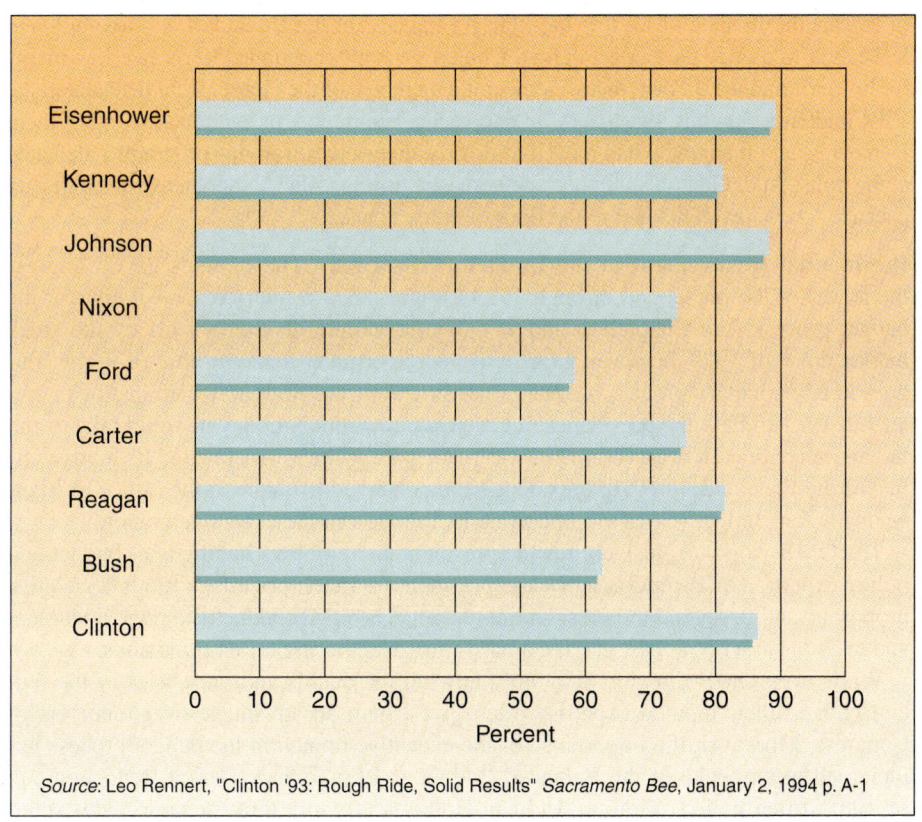

FIGURE 7-2
Congressional Support for the President

Source: Leo Rennert, "Clinton '93: Rough Ride, Solid Results" *Sacramento Bee*, January 2, 1994 p. A-1

time getting legislation advancing their own agenda passed. In Nixon's first term, only 35 percent of his publicly requested programs were enacted. Kennedy had fared little better. Even LBJ, who was able to get about 57 percent of his programs through Congress, noted: "You've got to give it all you can, that first year . . . before they start worrying about themselves. . . . You can't put anything through when half the Congress is thinking how to beat you."[27]

President Clinton faced several tests of his ability to make good on his campaign promises when his proposals came to Congress in 1993. Although Clinton campaigned against the gridlock that occurred in Washington when the Democratic Congress and the Republican president failed to agree on many programs, Clinton's programs did not find smooth sailing in Congress either—even though Democrats controlled both houses of Congress. One of Clinton's first victories occurred with passage of the National Service Education Plan, a cornerstone of his campaign platform, that revitalizes national service and helps students pay for their education. But he won passage of his

---

[27] Quoted in Thomas E. Cronin, *The State of the Presidency,* 2nd ed. (Boston: Little, Brown, 1980), p. 169.

budget deficit reduction plan by only one vote: the Senate was tied, and Vice President Gore cast the decisive vote. As revealed in Figure 7-2, high congressional support of many presidential programs eventually allowed Clinton to secure passage of many priority pieces of legislation. In spite of leading the fight for passage of the Brady bill, a crime bill, and legislation to reduce the budget deficit, Clinton generally continued to receive low marks for his performance. In fact, many Democratic members of the House were defeated in the 1994 midterm elections, which saw an unprecedented number of incumbents—all of them Democrats and many who had moved to divorce themselves from his programs—defeated at the polls. And, Clinton's number one domestic priority—his comprehensive health care package—never even made it to the floor of either House.

Presidential Involvement in the Budgetary Process. The Framers gave Congress the power of the purse, and through 1930 Congress had primary responsibility for the budget process (see Chapters 6 and 17). The economic disaster set off by the stock market crash of 1929, however, gave FDR the opportunity to assert himself in the congressional budgetary process. In 1939, the Bureau of the Budget, which had been created in 1921 to help the president tell Congress how much money it would take to run the executive branch of government, was made part of the newly created Executive Office of the President. In 1970, President Nixon changed its name to the Office of Management and Budget (OMB) to underline its function in the executive branch.

The OMB works exclusively for the president and employs hundreds of budget and policy experts. OMB reports allow the president to attach price tags to his legislative proposals, and to defend the presidential budget. The OMB budget is a huge document and even those who prepare it have a hard time deciphering all its provisions.

While even OMB directors may not know all the details and intricacies of the federal budget, their reputed expertise often gives them an advantage over members of Congress. Moreover, the importance of the executive branch in the budget process has increased in the wake of the Balanced Budget and Emergency Deficit Reduction Act of 1985 (often called "Gramm-Rudman-Hollings" for the three senators who sponsored it). This Act outlined debt ceilings and targeted a balanced budget for 1991. To meet that goal, the act required that the president reduce or even eliminate cost-of-living increases and similar automatic spending programs found in programs such as Social Security. It also gave tremendous power to the president's Director of the Office of Management and Budget, who was made responsible for keeping all appropriations in line with congressional understanding and presidential goals.

In 1990, Congress, recognizing that its goal of a balanced budget would not be met, gave the OMB the authority to access each appropriations bill. Although this action gutted Gramm-Rudman, it "had the effect of involving [OMB] even more directly than it already is in congressional law-making."[28]

Faced with a continued budget deficit crisis, President Clinton played a critical role in passage of the 1993 Budget Deficit Reduction Act. Growing public (and even congressional) concern over the deficit (see Chapter 17) has thus contributed to the president's increasing role in the budget process. As a single actor, the president may be able to do more to harness the deficit and impose order on the federal budget and its myriad programs than can the 535 members of Congress, who are torn by several different loyalties.

Winning Support. According to political scientist Thomas E. Cronin, a president has three ways to improve his role as a legislative lobbyist to get his favored programs passed. He can use **patronage** (jobs, grants, or other special favors given to friends

[28] *Congressional Quarterly Weekly Report* (December 1, 1990), 4034.

and political allies as rewards for support) and personal rewards to win supporters. Invitations to the White House and campaign visits to members of Congress running for office are two such ways to curry favor with legislators. Inattention to key members can prove deadly to a president's legislative program. House Speaker Thomas P. ("Tip") O'Neill reportedly was quite irritated when the Carter team refused his request for extra tickets to Carter's inaugural, getting the president off to a poor start with the powerful Speaker. In contrast, President Reagan was famous for giving out gift cufflinks and theater tickets along with plugs for legislation he favored. Bill Clinton made extensive use of the "rewards" system to curry support for his budget bill. Freshman Rep. Marjorie Margolies-Mezvinsky (D.-PA), for example, originally failed to support Clinton's 1993 budget bill, fearing that voters in her district would hold her accountable for aspects they disliked. In return for her vote, Clinton promised to hold an economic summit in her district. Similarly, during the period before the NAFTA vote, so many presidential favors were doled out that NAFTA opponent Ross Perot charged Bill Clinton with "buying the votes with American tax dollars. . . . [H]e's opened up the vaults in the Treasury."[29] "It's NAFTA Claus time at the White House," complained Democratic Whip David Bonior (D.-Mich.), who led the opposition to NAFTA.[30] Yet Clinton's efforts to persuade particular legislators proved highly effective. In spite of early indications that NAFTA would fail, it passed by a vote of 234 to 200 in the House and 61 to 38 in the Senate.

A second way a president can bolster support for his legislative package is to call on his party. As the informal leader of his political party, he should be able to use that position to his advantage in Congress, where party loyalty is very important. This strategy works best when the president has carried members of his party into office on his coattails, as was the case in the Johnson and Reagan landslides of 1964 and 1984.

Party support for the executive's proposals in the legislature is much less problematic in parliamentary systems. For example, since the British prime minister holds office precisely because he or she enjoys the support of the majority party in Parliament, many of the roadblocks that plague legislative–executive relations in the United States do not exist in Britain. But if the president is unpopular, even members of his own party may not jump to his support. After all, if you are a member of the House seeking re-election, the last visitor you want coming to your district is an unpopular president. Thus, a president popular with the folks back home is most likely to get support from a member of Congress, regardless of party affiliation.

The third way a president can influence Congress is through close contact with the American people. By going directly to the public on a particular issue, the president can bring constituent pressures on key members of Congress. This is just what Bill Clinton did to gain support of his health care reform program, for example. The quality and effectiveness of a president's success in the policy making process are often dependent on what is termed "**presidential style**."

Presidential Style

A president's ability to get things done depends on many factors, including his character, his approach to the office, others' perceptions of his ability to lead, and his ability to mobilize public opinion to support his actions. The forty-one men who have held

---

[29] Gaylord Shaw, "Clinton's Free Trade: Capital Deals," *Newsday* (November 18, 1993): 23.
[30] Ibid.

the nation's highest office are a diverse lot. (Bill Clinton is considered the forty-second president because Grover Cleveland served as the twenty-second and twenty-fourth presidents, having been elected to nonconsecutive terms in 1884 and 1892.) Some have been quite unassuming in their approach to the office. James Madison, for example, wore out-of-date knee breeches, silk stockings, and a sword. He met visitors in ink-spotted clothing and worn-down shoes, often looking more like an unkempt clerk than president of the United States.[31] Jimmy Carter also adopted an unassuming approach to the presidency. During the energy crunch of the 1970s he ordered White House thermostats set to a chill 65 degrees and suggested that his advisers wear sweaters to work. Carter often appeared before the nation in cardigan sweaters instead of suits. He tried to build his "common man" image by carrying his own luggage and prohibiting the Marine band from playing the traditional fanfare "Hail to the Chief" to signify his arrival on official occasions.

In contrast, other presidents have been much more attuned to the trappings of office. Many believe that the Kennedys did it best. During their thousand days in the White House, it became a royal palace—"Camelot." John F. Kennedy (JFK) and his family had looks, youth, and wealth, and JFK was a gifted speaker. When the young, beautiful, and popular Jacqueline Kennedy filled the White House with expensive antiques, she was praised; when Nancy Reagan bought new china for the White House she was widely attacked and lampooned as "Queen Nancy."

Presidential Character. How one approaches the job of president often reflects long-held behaviors. Political scientist James David Barber has suggested that patterns of behavior, many ingrained during childhood, can help explain presidential behavior.[32] Barber believes that there are four **presidential character** types, based on

---

[31] Boller, *Presidential Anecdotes,* p. 50. (See n. 18.)

[32] James David Barber, *The Presidential Character: Predicting Performance in the White House*, 3rd ed. (Englewood Cliffs, NJ: Prentice Hall, 1985).

President Bush, one of the most physically active presidents in recent history, was an avid fisherman who tired even his younger Secret Service detail with his frenetic schedule.

(1) energy level (whether the president is active or passive), and (2) the degree of enjoyment a president finds in his job (whether the president has a positive or negative attitude about what he does). Barber believes that active and positive presidents are more successful than passive and negative presidents. Active-positive presidents generally enjoyed warm and supportive childhood environments and are basically happy individuals open to new life experiences. They approach the presidency with a zest for life and have a drive to lead and succeed. In contrast, passive presidents find themselves reacting to circumstances, and are likely to take direction from others, thus failing to make full use of the enormous resources of the executive office. Table 7.1 classifies presidents from Taft through Bush according to Barber's categories. Where would you place Bill Clinton?

A classic example of an active-positive president is Franklin D. Roosevelt. Reared in tremendous wealth, Roosevelt enjoyed a considerable amount of self-confidence in spite of his severe health problems (he was paralyzed from the waist down by polio). Roosevelt simply loved the game of politics. When he suffered setbacks—such as the Supreme Court's rulings that portions of his New Deal legislative program were unconstitutional—he repeatedly sought new ways to achieve his policy objectives. Other active-positives such as John F. Kennedy and George Bush enjoyed similar stable family relationships and relished the idea of being president. Even during the dark days of the Iraqi occupation of Kuwait in 1990, President Bush kept to his vacation schedule of water sports, running, and golf while handling the crisis from Kennebunkport, his Maine vacation home. Although his anguish and concern about the situation were clear, he did not appear to experience the dark bouts of gloom that pervaded the presidencies of Lyndon B. Johnson, Richard M. Nixon, and even Abraham Lincoln, whom Barber considers active-negative presidents.

Although an active-positive president, George Bush was often criticized for sharing one active-negative feature with LBJ: a tendency to surround himself with "yes-men." LBJ's press secretary, George E. Reedy, once noted: "[the president] moves through

Younger than any recent president since John F. Kennedy, President Clinton is often kidded as a "fast food junkie" whose work schedule allows little time for rest. His taste for McDonald's, however, has enhanced his image of being in touch with the public.

Table 7.1 ♦ Barber's Presidential Personalities

	ACTIVE	PASSIVE
Positive	F. D. Roosevelt Truman Kennedy Ford Carter* Bush	Taft Harding Reagan
Negative	Wilson Hoover L. B. Johnson Nixon	Coolidge Eisenhower

*Some scholars think that Carter better fits the active-negative typology.

his days surrounded by literally hundreds of people whose relationship to him is that of a doting mother to a spoiled child."[33] Like LBJ, "Bush wants twins around him, and that can be dangerous," concludes Barber, speaking of Bush's tendency to surround himself with like-minded individuals.[34]

Although Barber's typology can be an amusing way to discuss the men who have served as president, some disagree with his approach and its ability to predict presidential success. Journalist Garry Wills, for example, describes Barber's work as an example of the "games academics play."[35]

The Power to Persuade. A president is many things to many people: a symbol of the nation, a political organizer, a moral teacher. But to do his job, according to George E. Reedy, a president must be able to accomplish two things: first, resolve policy questions that will not yield to quantitative, empirical analyses; and second, persuade enough of the country that his actions are right that he can carry them out without national strife.[36] Exercising the constitutional powers of the chief executive is not enough; a president's personality and ability to persuade others are key to amassing greater power and authority.

Frequently, the difference between great and mediocre presidents centers on their ability to grasp this fact of political life. Truly "great" presidents, such as Lincoln and Franklin D. Roosevelt, understood that the White House was a seat of power from which decisions could flow to shape the national destiny. They recognized that their day-to-day activities should be designed to bolster support for their policies, and to secure backing that could translate their intuitive judgment into meaningful action. Mediocre presidents, on the other hand, have tended to regard the White House as "a stage for the presentation of performances to the public" or a fitting honor to cap a career.[37]

Presidential character and political skills often determine how effectively a president can exercise the broad powers of the modern presidency. Political scientist Richard E. Neustadt has developed a theory of how presidents win, lose, or maintain their personal power and influence. According to Neustadt, "Presidential power is the *power to persuade*,"[38] and the power to persuade comes largely from an individual's ability to bargain. And, according to Neustadt, persuasion is key because constitutional powers alone do not provide modern presidents with the authority to meet rising public expectations.

When Neustadt's *Presidential Power* was first published in 1960, it was widely hailed as a guidebook for those interested in wielding power. Both Presidents Kennedy and Johnson studied it intensively, and Kennedy even hired Neustadt as a staff consultant. Throughout his book, Neustadt argued that there were nine steps to achieving a

---

[33] George E. Reedy, *The Twilight of the Presidency* (New York: New American Library, 1970), p. 38.

[34] Quoted in Larry Berman and Bruce W. Jentleson, "Bush and the Post-Cold-War World: New Challenges for American Leadership," in Colin Campbell, S. J. and Bert A. Rockman, *The Bush Presidency: First Appraisals* (Chatham, NJ: Chatham House, 1991), p. 103.

[35] Gary Wills, *The Kennedy Imprisonment* (Boston: Little, Brown, 1982), p. 186.

[36] Reedy, *Twilight of the President*, p. 33.

[37] Ibid., pp. 38–39.

[38] Neustadt, *Presidential Power: The Politics of Leadership from FDR to Carter*, p. 10. (See n. 15.)

The Best and the Worst Presidents

Who was the best president and who was the worst? Many surveys of scholars have been taken over the years to answer this question, and virtually all have ranked Abraham Lincoln the best and Warren G. Harding the worst. A 1982 Chicago Tribune poll,* for example, came up with these results:

TEN BEST PRESIDENTS	TEN WORST PRESIDENTS
1. Lincoln (best)	1. Harding (worst)
2. Washington	2. Nixon
3. F. Roosevelt	3. Buchanan
4. T. Roosevelt	4. Pierce
5. Jefferson	5. Grant
6. Wilson	6. Fillmore
7. Jackson	7. A. Johnson
8. Truman	8. Coolidge
9. Eisenhower	9. Tyler
10. Polk (10th best)	10. Carter (10th worst)

Lincoln broke all kinds of laws and violated the Constitution to keep the nation together in its darkest hour—the Civil War. Had he not succeeded he would undoubtedly be ranked with Harding at the bottom of the heap.

And just who was Harding? In 1923, he said, "This is a hell of a job! I have no trouble with my enemies. I can take care of my enemies all right. But my damn friends, my God-damned friends...! [T]hey're the ones who keep me walking the floor nights." Indeed, it *was* Harding's friends who got him into trouble. He was elected in a landslide victory in 1920 not so much because of his popularity, but because of public backlash against World War I and Woodrow Wilson's League of Nations fiasco. When he came to Washington, he brought with him "friends" bent more on enriching themselves than on public service. They found abundant opportunities for corruption, including the sale of property owned by aliens in the aftermath of World War I, the sale of U.S. ships, the enforcement of Prohibition after 1921, outlays for the care of veterans, and the management of oil-rich lands. Eventually, numerous scandals surfaced during Harding's administration. The head of the Veterans' Bureau was forced to resign and was ultimately jailed for corruption. Other scandals were emerging when Harding suddenly died in office in 1923.

*From Arthur Murphy, "Evaluating the Presidents of the United States," *Presidential Studies Quarterly* 14 (1984): 117–126.

---

successful presidency (notice how closely related many of his points are to key elements of Barber's typology of successful presidents):

1. To be a successful leader, a president must have a will for power.
2. The ability of a president to win over others is key to getting other institutions of government to act. He must be the agenda setter for the national government.
3. Introverts cannot be successful presidents. Instead, a president must be receptive and sensitive to the thoughts and ideas of others in order to come to effective compromises and solutions to national problems.
4. Because members of Congress are motivated by the prospect of reelection, the president must persuade members of Congress to see that his way is also in their best interest.
5. A president must be able to ride out events and crises.
6. A strong, effective president must be his own intelligence officer and not rely on others to assess the political and power stakes involved in particular actions. A successful president cannot delegate the job of chief politician.

7. A president must always act as an expert even if he is not. The public expects the president to know a lot about all important issues.
8. Popularity and prestige are pluses for any president. Conversely, public disapproval encourages the resistance of the Washington community to his programs.
9. Because presidential power is so difficult to attain, a president must always remain mindful of the need for multiple channels of information, the importance of persuasion in bargaining situations, and the art of the deal. Confrontational demands should be avoided at all costs.

Truly effective presidents have the ability and power to persuade not only what Neustadt calls "Washingtonians"[39]—members of Congress, interest-group leaders, and media moguls—but also the general public.

FDR and LBJ both had excellent reputations among lawmakers for being able to get their legislative packages through Congress. Presidents Kennedy and Carter had more mixed successes, whereas Richard M. Nixon believed (wrongly) that the power of his office was enough to get recalcitrant legislators to support his programs. He failed to grasp the importance of the need to persuade members of Congress personally of the soundness of legislation he sought.

Public Opinion and the President. Recognition of the need to persuade the public and the ability to do so are also key elements of a successful presidency. Even before the days of FDR's personal presidency, others reached out to gain public support for their programs. Theodore Roosevelt (1901–1909) referred to the presidency as a "bully pulpit" that he used to try to garner support for progressive programs. Woodrow Wilson took a whistle-stop train tour around the country to try (in vain) to build support for the League of Nations. Not until the development of commercial air travel and television were presidents able to communicate directly with large numbers of people.

Harry S Truman was the first president to address the nation on television, although neither he nor Eisenhower, his successor, used that medium very often. By the 1960s, television and jet transportation were no longer novel. John F. Kennedy, the first real "media darling," made even his press conferences media events as he used his good looks and quick sense of humor to his advantage to drum up public support for his programs.

Political scientist Sam Kernell refers to these kinds of direct, presidential appeals to the electorate as "going public."[40] Going public, in essence, means that a president goes over the heads of members of Congress to gain support from the people, who, in turn, can place pressure on their elected officials in Washington.

Presidents Carter and Reagan—both Washington outsiders—used direct appeals to the public with widely differing degrees of success. Jimmy Carter often went on TV to gain support for his policies, but his low-key, "toned down," and "de-pomped styles" failed to stir television audiences.[41] His efforts were less successful than those of Ronald Reagan, who earned the nickname that says it all: "the Great Communicator." Reagan, a former film and television actor, understood the use of television as a medium from the beginning. In a 1981 television address explaining and drumming up support for his proposed tax cuts, he exhorted the public "to put aside any feeling of

---

[39] Neustadt, *Presidential Power,* p. 44. (See n. 15.)
[40] Sam Kernell, *Going Public: New Strategies of Presidential Leadership* (Washington, DC: CQ Press, 1986).
[41] Neustadt, *Presidential Power,* p. 235.

frustration . . . about our political institutions . . . [and] contact your senators and congressmen."[42] According to Kernell, the public's reaction was "swift and overwhelming."[43] Democrats, especially those from the South, joined with Republicans to enact the tax cuts.

Most presidents do all they can to woo public opinion because of its impact on their ability to govern. Nevertheless, "cycles" of popularity have occurred since 1938, when pollsters first began to track presidential popularity. As revealed in Figure 7-3, until the presidency of George Bush, the general trend has been toward increasingly lower rates of support for presidents. Many credit this trend to events such as Vietnam, Watergate, the Iran hostage crisis, and the Iran–Contra scandal, which have made the public increasingly skeptical of presidential performance. The sole exception to this pattern is George Bush, the first president in a long time to reclaim a "pride in America" sentiment, which occurred in the aftermath of the major and, perhaps more important, quick victory in the 1991 Persian Gulf war. Even Bush's popularity, however, plummeted as the good feelings from the Gulf war faded and Americans began to feel the pinch of recession.

Bill Clinton used the "town hall meeting" format as an effective tool during his campaign and later as president to mobilize support for his programs.

[42] Quoted in Kernell, *Going Public,* p. 120.
[43] Ibid.

FIGURE 7-3

Presidential Approval Since 1938

Presidential popularity generally follows a cyclical pattern.

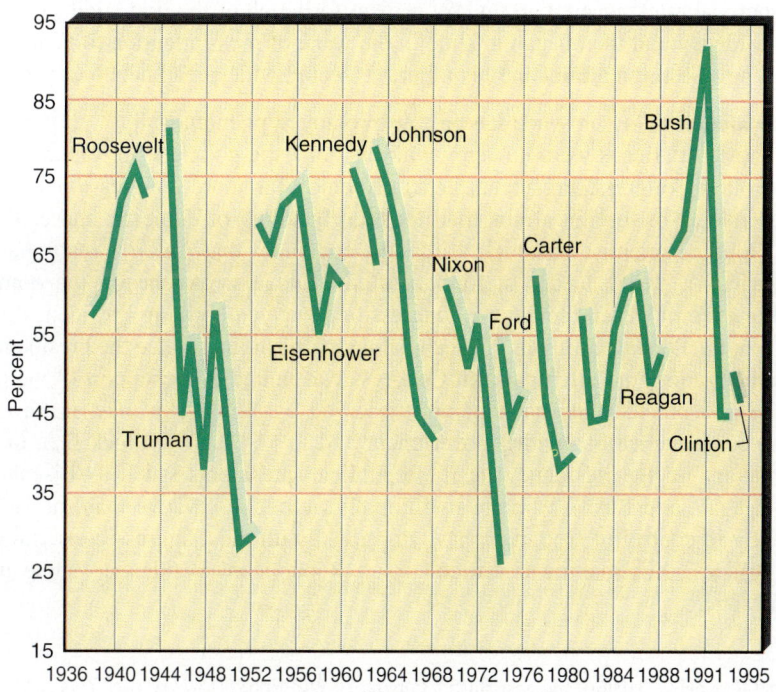

Source: Harold W. Stanley and Richard G. Niemi, *Vital Statistics on American Politics,* 4th ed. (Washington D.C.: CQ Press, 1994), Figure 8–1, p. 279, from Gallup Poll data, 1938–1991. 1991–September 1994 data based on USA Today/CNN/Gallup Poll data.

Presidential popularity generally follows a cyclical pattern. Typically, presidents enjoy their highest level of popularity at the beginning of their terms. Presidents try to take advantage of this "honeymoon" period and work hard to get their programs passed by Congress as soon as possible. Each action a president takes, however, is divisive—some people will approve, and others will disapprove. And disapproval tends to have a cumulative effect. Inevitably the honeymoon ends about midway through the term.

Although surges caused by major international events do occur, they generally don't last long. As revealed in Table 7.2, each of the last ten presidents experienced at least one "rallying" point based on a foreign event. Rallies lasted an average of ten weeks, with the longest being seven months.[44]

A president's overall approval rating may allow him to make some unpopular policy decisions. George Bush's unprecedented sustained popularity until mid-1991 occurred in spite of the fact that voters gave him low marks for his handling of the economy, education, and health care. No other presidents, however, have been so lucky. Even Ronald Reagan, whom many called the "Teflon president" because criticisms seemed not to stick to him, suffered a beating in public opinion polls as unemployment rates rose in his first term and the Iran–Contra hearings proceeded in his second. Bill Clinton's presidency, which began with the support of only 41.9 percent of the electorate, got off to a rocky start in the wake of several public relations disasters. He was forced to withdraw the names of several nominees for Cabinet positions, interest groups criticized his initial failure to appoint more women and minorities to Cabinet-level positions, he was forced to back down on his pledge to remove the ban on gays in the military, and his economic stimulus package died in the Senate when Republicans filibustered it. His approval ratings took a similar drubbing, as revealed in Figure 7-3. Unlike most presidents, Clinton failed to enjoy much of a honeymoon period. Instead, his public approval rates hovered around 50 percent for much of the first eighteen months of his presidency and then began to slide in the wake of press attention to Whitewater, his handling of foreign affairs and his failure to secure widespread health care reform.

Two Presidencies. Even when George Bush enjoyed phenomenally high popularity ratings, most Americans were unhappy with his domestic policies. So was the Democrat-controlled Congress. Presidents generally enjoy far more congressional support for their conduct of foreign affairs than for their handling of domestic and economic matters. Political scientist Aaron B. Wildavsky concludes that America really has **two presidencies**—a strong leader in foreign affairs, and a weak one on the domestic side.[45] For example, even though the congressional vote authorizing President Bush to use force in the Persian Gulf was close and along partisan lines, once the president was given authorization, the often partisan Congress was united in its support of the president. The two presidencies phenomenon observed by Wildavsky may, however, be more the consequence of divided government and its resultant gridlock than of anything inherent in the presidency itself. Republican presidents (such as Eisenhower, Nixon, Reagan, and Bush), who are traditionally more conservative than the Democrats usually in control of Congress, have disagreed with the Congress concerning domestic policies, thus making it difficult for a Republican president to shine in the domestic sphere.

---

[44] Michael R. Kagay, "History Suggest Bush's Popularity Will Ebb," *The New York Times* (May 22, 1991): A10.

[45] Aaron B. Wildavsky, "The Two Presidencies," *Transaction* (December, 1966): 7–14.

Table 7.2 ♦ Temporary Rises in Presidential Popularity

Gallup poll measurements of the size and duration of the largest increase in each president's approval rating before and after dramatic international events.

PRESIDENT/EVENT	PERCENTAGE POINT INCREASE IN PUBLIC APPROVAL	DURATION OF THE INCREASE IN WEEKS
Franklin D. Roosevelt		
Pearl Harbor	12	30
Harry S Truman		
Truman Doctrine	12	N.A.[a]
South Korea invaded	9	10
Dwight D. Eisenhower		
Bermuda Conference/Atoms for Peace speech	10	20
John F. Kennedy		
Cuban Missile Crisis	13	31
Lyndon B. Johnson		
Speech halting bombing of North Vietnam and withdrawing from 1968 campaign	14	19
Richard M. Nixon		
Vietnam peace agreement	16	15
Gerald R. Ford		
Mayaquez incident	11	25
Jimmy Carter		
Hostages seized in Iran	19	30
Ronald Reagan		
Beirut bombing/Grenada invasion	8	N.A.[b]
First summit with Gorbachev	7	4
George Bush		
Iraqi invasion of Kuwait	14	9
Gulf War begins	18	30

[a] No polls conducted
[b] Overlapping events

Source: The Gallup Poll Monthly, #309 (June 1991), pp. 15–27; *The New York Times* (May 22, 1991): p. A-10. Copyright 1991 by The New York Times Company. Reprinted by permission.

The Presidential Establishment

As the responsibilities and scope of presidential authority have grown over the years, so has the executive branch of government and the number of people working directly for the president in the White House itself. No longer does the executive branch consist of the small group of men who gathered around George Washington's dining room table to discuss affairs of state. Today a president is surrounded by policy advisers of all types—from the Attorney General, who advises him on legal issues, to the Surgeon General, who advises him on health matters. His personal staff, the vice president, and the Cabinet all help him fulfill his duties as chief executive.

The Cabinet

Although the Framers had discussed the idea of some form of national executive council, they did not include a provision for one in the Constitution. They did, however, recognize the need for departments of government and departmental heads. Consequently, although there is no provision for a cabinet in the Constitution per se, Article II, Section 2, notes that the president "may require the Opinion, in writing, of the Prin-

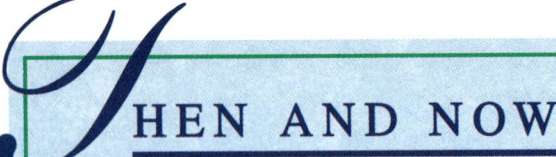

Then and Now

First Ladies

From Martha Washington to Hillary Rodham Clinton, First Ladies (a term coined during the Civil War) have made significant contributions to American society. Until recently, the only formal national recognition given to that role was an exhibit of inaugural ball gowns at the Smithsonian Institution. Not any more. Heightened interest—doubtless at least partially attributable to the highly visible role Hillary Rodham Clinton plays in the Clinton administration—has led the Smithsonian to launch an exhibit highlighting the personal accomplishments of First Ladies since Martha Washington. The new exhibit is built around three themes: the political role of the First Ladies, including how they have been portrayed in the media and perceived by the public; their contributions to society, especially their personal causes; and, of course, a display of their gowns.

Although every action and even haircut of Hillary Rodham Clinton is chronicled by the media, she is not the first First Lady to work for or with her husband. Martha Washington followed George to his winter camps. At Valley Forge she helped feed the troops and nursed the wounded.

Abigail Adams was a constant sounding board for her husband, and an early feminist. As early as 1776 she cautioned him to "Remember the Ladies" in any new code of laws.

Edith Bolling Galt Wilson was probably the most powerful First Lady. When Woodrow Wilson collapsed and was left partly paralyzed in 1919, Mrs. Wilson became his surrogate as she decided whom and what the stricken president saw. Her detractors dubbed her "Acting First Man."

Eleanor Roosevelt, too, played a powerful and much criticized role in national affairs. Not only did she write a nationally syndicated daily newspaper column, she also traveled and lectured widely. She worked tirelessly on thankless Democratic Party chores while raising six children. After FDR's death she shone in her own right as U.S. delegate to the United Nations, where she headed the commission that drafted the covenant on human rights. Later she headed John F. Kennedy's Commission on the Status of Women until her death.

Rosalyn Carter also took an activist role. Not only did she help with Cabinet chores, she also attended Cabinet meetings (as did Helen Taft).

When Hillary Rodham Clinton is viewed in the light of some strong First Ladies who came before her, her prominent role in the administration is not that surprising. Her role is not so much a radical break with tradition as a logical evolution in a society where women's role is no longer simply that of homemaker. As a former law professor and nationally prominent lawyer and activist, she is continuing much of the work she did as First Lady of Arkansas.

> ### The British Cabinet
>
> Although it bears the same name, the British Cabinet is quite distinct from its American counterpart. There are some similarities: for example, Cabinet officials in both countries are appointed by their respective chief executives and provide political guidance to the bureaucracy. However, British Cabinet ministers hail exclusively from the legislature (indeed, they retain their seats in Parliament while they serve as executive officers), and they participate in a collective executive decision-making body—the Cabinet—for which there is no counterpart in the United States. As a result, although the prime minister is clearly "first among equals" in the Cabinet, the decisions of the British government are issued formally in the name of the Cabinet, not the prime minister.

cipal Officer in each of the executive Departments, upon any Subject relating to the Duties of their respective Offices...."

Just prior to and immediately after Washington's inauguration on April 30, 1789, he consulted with Hamilton, Madison, and others concerning their views of the powers and duties of the president. Collectively they adopted the position that department heads should be assistants to the president, rather than to Congress. These sentiments led Washington to ask Congress to create three executive departments—one for foreign affairs (State), one for military affairs (War, which was incorporated into the Defense Department in 1947), and one for fiscal matters (Treasury). These three departments closely reflected what these men saw as the major role of the new national government—the conduct of foreign affairs and regulation of a national economy. Washington viewed his advisers as a council of sorts, and frequently called them together. He also established the tradition that Cabinet members' loyalties must be to the president. After his Secretary of State publicly disagreed with Washington's support of the Jay Treaty, for example, he fired him.

Over the years, the Cabinet has grown as departments have been added to accommodate new pressures on the president to act in more and more areas not initially considered within the national government's scope of concern. As interest groups, in particular, pressured Congress and the president to recognize their demands for services and governmental action, they often were rewarded with the creation of an executive department. And since each was headed by a secretary who automatically became a member of the president's Cabinet, powerful groups including farmers (Agriculture), business persons (Commerce), workers (Labor), and teachers (Education) saw creation of a department as increasing their access to the president.

Under President Clinton, the Cabinet is composed of thirteen secretaries, the Attorney General, the Vice President, and the U.S. Ambassador to the United Nations. The departments and their responsibilities are detailed in Table 7.3.

From the beginning, Cabinet secretaries have found themselves in the uncomfortable position of having two masters. They serve the president, but must also report to Congress on the activities of their respective departments. The inevitable clash between these two roles first surfaced in 1833. Disliking the National Bank, Andrew Jackson ordered his Secretary of the Treasury to transfer federal funds to another bank.

Table 7.3 ♦ The U.S. Cabinet

DEPARTMENT	DATE OF CREATION	RESPONSIBILITIES
Department of State	1789	Responsible for making foreign policy, including treaty negotiation
Department of the Treasury	1789	Responsible for government funding and regulation of alcohol, firearms and tobacco
Department of Defense	1789; 1947	Responsible for national defense; created by consolidating the former departments of War, the Army, the Navy, and the Air Force
Department of Justice	1870 (Attorney General's position created in 1789)	Represents U.S. government in all federal courts, investigates and prosecutes violations of federal law
Department of the Interior	1849	Manages the nation's natural resources, including wildlife and public lands
Department of Agriculture	Created in 1862; elevated to Cabinet status in 1889	Assists nation's farmers, oversees food quality programs, administers food stamp and school lunch programs
Department of Commerce	1903	Aids businesses and conducts the U.S. census (originally the Department of Commerce and Labor)
Department of Labor	1913	Runs manpower programs, keeps labor statistics, aids labor through enforcement of laws
Department of Health and Human Services	1953	Runs health, welfare, and Social Security programs; created as the Department of Health, Education, and Welfare (lost its education function in 1979)
Department of Housing and Urban Development	1965	Responsible for urban and housing programs
Department of Transportation	1966	Responsible for mass transportation and highway programs
Department of Energy	1977	Responsible for energy policy and research, including atomic energy
Department of Education	1979	Responsible for the federal government's education programs
Department of Veterans' Affairs	1989	Responsible for programs aiding veterans

The secretary believed the National Bank to be sound, and Congress had recently voiced its support of the bank in a resolution to that effect. When the secretary refused to comply with Jackson's direct order, he was fired.

Instances like this are not uncommon. Although some members of the Cabinet may be very close to the president—John F. Kennedy's Attorney General was his brother Robert, and George Bush's Secretary of State, James Baker, was a long-time friend—some Cabinet members are chosen to appease various presidential constituencies, and may not have the president's ear. Kennedy, for example, was almost openly scornful of his Cabinet. During the Cuban Missile Crisis, he virtually ignored the Cabinet (rarely holding meetings) while enlarging the National Security Council (see Chapter 18) and directing policy through an ad hoc "executive" committee made up of officials in

President Clinton's first Secretary of Housing and Urban Development Henry Cisneros inspects damage done by the Los Angeles earthquake.

whom he had special confidence.[46] Distrust of his Cabinet and of the agendas of several of its members led President Carter to fire four of his Cabinet secretaries on the advice of his White House staffers. And White House staffers' chagrin with foreign policy mismanagement led, at least in part, to the resignation of President Clinton's first Secretary of Defense, Les Aspin.

The Executive Office of the President

The **Executive Office of the President** (EOP) is actually several offices, a "mini-bureaucracy" located in the ornate Executive Office Building next to the White House on Pennsylvania Avenue. FDR established the EOP in 1939 because he needed someone to oversee his New Deal programs. The EOP has expanded over time to include eight advisory and policy-making agencies responsible to the executive branch. These expert staff units play key roles in advancing the president's policy preferences. Three of the most important agencies are the National Security Council, the Council of Economic Advisors, and the Office of Management and Budget.

The National Security Council (NSC) was established in 1947 to advise the president on American military and foreign policies. The NSC is composed of the president, the vice president, and the Secretaries of State and Defense. The president's national security adviser runs the staff of the NSC, coordinates information and options, and advises the president (see Chapter 19).

The Council of Economic Advisors (CEA) consists of three economic experts appointed by the president, subject to Senate confirmation, plus a small staff evenly divided between support personnel and professional economists. The CEA prepares the *Annual Report of the Council of Economic Advisors* and advises the president on eco-

---

[46] Reedy, *The Twilight of the Presidency,* p. 77. (See n. 33.)

nomic policy. Through constant analysis of the economy and economic trends, the CEA attempts to anticipate rather than react to economic events.

As we mentioned earlier, the Office of Management and Budget (OMB) was created in 1970 as a replacement for the Bureau of the Budget (created in 1921). While the CEA's major concern is with controlling the business cycle and achieving national economic growth, the OMB's major focus is on preparing the president's annual budget proposal, designing the president's program, and reviewing the progress, budget, and program proposals of the executive department agencies. It also supplies economic forecasts to the president and conducts detailed analyses of proposed bills and agency rules.

Although the president appoints the members of these bodies, they must still perform their tasks in accordance with congressional legislation. Thus, like the Cabinet, depending on who serves in key positions, these mini-agencies may not be truly responsible to the president.

White House Staff

George Washington's closest confidants were Alexander Hamilton and Thomas Jefferson—both Cabinet secretaries—but this has often not been the case with modern presidents. As the size and complexity of the government grew, Cabinet secretaries had to preside over their own ever-burgeoning staffs, and presidents increasingly looked to a different inner circle of informal advisers. By the 1830s, Andrew Jackson had chosen to rely on his own inner circle, nicknamed his "Kitchen Cabinet," instead of his department heads, to advise him. So too, FDR surrounded himself with New York political operatives and his more intellectual "brain trust;" Jimmy Carter brought several Georgians to the White House with him; and Ronald Reagan initially surrounded himself with fellow Californians—Edwin Meese III, William French Smith (the Attorney General), and Michael Deaver. Bill Clinton initially followed suit by appointing two of his best friends—Thomas "Mack" McLarty and Vincent Foster[47]—to important White House positions. Several other White House advisers, including George Stephanopoulos, played key roles in Clinton's campaign.

Loyalty is often the strong suit of presidential aides. Richard M. Nixon's first chief of staff, H.R. Haldeman, for example, believed it was his role to "take the heat" for any presidential gaffes. According to him, "Every president needs a son of a bitch and I'm Nixon's. I get what he wants done and I take the heat instead of him."[48] This loyalty led President Nixon to consider Haldeman his alter ego.

Although each president organizes his staff in different ways, presidents typically have a chief of staff. John Sununu, the former governor of New Hampshire whom George Bush credited with his key primary victory there in 1988, was his first chief of staff. A series of public relations disasters forced Sununu to resign in 1991. His successor, former Transportation Secretary Samuel Skinner, fared little better, and he was replaced with Bush's close friend, James Baker. Perhaps learning from Bush's experiences, Bill Clinton selected childhood friend Thomas "Mack" McLarty, an Arkansas businessman, to be his first chief of staff.

Reaching back into Ronald Reagan's successful playbook, after a shaky start using the single head of staff model, Clinton installed a "troika" command system at the

---

[47] Foster committed suicide in July 1993, leaving behind a note indicating the stresses of the job led him to that action.

[48] Quoted in Page and Petracca, *The American Presidency*, p. 169. (See n. 10.)

D.C.—Still a Man's Town—But Changing

♦ ♦ ♦

Washington, D.C. is still considered a man's town, and the White House is generally no exception. George Bush filled fewer than 20 percent of his full-time presidential appointments with women. And as with his predecessors, the women he appointed generally filled traditionally female positions.

President Clinton has attempted to fulfill his campaign pledges to women by appointing more women to important policy-making and Cabinet-level positions. By the end of his first year in office, over one-third of his appointees and 27% of his Cabinet-level appointments were female. In perhaps the most important sign of change, however, Hillary Rodham Clinton, whom the president has acknowledged to be his closest policy adviser, moved her office from the traditional space reserved for the First Lady in the White House's East Wing to the West Wing, where the Oval Office is located. In White House politics, proximity to the president equals power.

White House. Chief of Staff McLarty, presidential confidant George Stephanopoulos, and David Gergen, the presidential counselor for communications and policy, were brought together to help the president and smooth out White House operations. Although Clinton initially started out using the single-chief model favored by Bush, McLarty, often called "Mack the Nice," and Clinton quickly recognized after a string of public relations and White House staff disasters that the troika model would work better. But his tapping of David Gergen, a former aide to Republican Presidents Nixon and Ford and communications director for Reagan, surprised many. So, too, did his move in June of 1994, when he again reorganized his top command system by replacing McLarty with former Office of Management and Budget head Leon Panetta, and moved Gergen—at least temporarily—to the State Department to better coordinate Clinton's oft-criticized foreign policy decision making.

Other key White House aides include those who help plan domestic policy, maintain relations with Congress and interest groups, deal with the media, provide economic expertise, and execute political strategies. Presidents also typically have a national security adviser (who runs the NSC) who provides them with daily briefings on international affairs. During the Persian Gulf war, for example, National Security Adviser Brent Scowcroft played an important role in advising President Bush. Too many advisers, however, can lead to confusion over policies. When several American soldiers, for example, were killed in Somalia in late 1993, initial press reports noted that the Secretaries of State and Defense, and National Security Adviser Anthony Lake all appeared unclear about who was running the show.

As presidents have tried to consolidate power in the White House and as demands on the president have grown, so has the size of the White House staff—from 51 in 1943, to 247 in 1953, to a high of 583 in 1972. Since that time, staffs have been trimmed, generally running in the 400-person range. During his campaign for the presidency, Bill Clinton promised to cut the size of the White House staff and the Executive Office. As revealed in Table 7.4, he reduced the size of his staff by approximately 25 percent.

Bill Clinton hugs his childhood friend, Thomas "Mack" McLarty, at a Little Rock, Arkansas news conference announcing McLarty as White House Chief of Staff.

Table 7.4 ♦ Comparisons of Bush and Clinton Staffs

	BUSH STAFF	CLINTON STAFF
Office of the President	461	419
Executive Residence	95	89
Office of the Vice President	49	35
National Security Council	179	147
Policy Development	58	*
National Economic Council	*	28
Domestic Policy	*	21
Office of National Drug Control Policy	146	25
CEQ**/Environmental Policy	31	10
Science, Technology and Space Policy	95	46
Council of Economic Advisors	42	35
National Critical Material Council	2	0
Office of Administration	236	189
TOTAL	1,394	1,044

*Reflects Clinton's resructuring of Policy Development Office
**Council on Environmental Quality

Source: The White House, Office of Personnel Management.

White House office space is limited, so many staffers are relegated to the old Executive Office Building next door. In spite of small offices, most prefer to be located in the White House (see Figure 7-4). In Washington, the size of the office is not the measure of power it often is in corporations. Instead, power in the White House goes to those who have the president's ear and the offices closest to the Oval Office.

Toward Reform

The presidency is a peculiar institution. Only forty-one men have held the position, and each has been different in style and temperament. Some have been brilliant; others have not. Some have appeared to thrive in office; others have labored under the strain. Several have broken laws for different reasons and to very different fates: Lincoln earned a place in history as one of the greats; Richard M. Nixon resigned to avoid impeachment.

Over the years, various reforms have been proposed to "improve" the presidency, but the consensus appears to be that as an institution it works fairly well. Most serious calls for reform have not been concerned with the Framers' chief fear—a too-powerful president. Instead they have centered on giving the president greater power.

Toward Reform ❖ 301

FIGURE 7-4

Office Space at the White House, 1994

West Wing Second Floor

This floor includes the offices of First Lady Hillary Rodham Clinton; the president's domestic policy adviser; legal counsel; senior economic policy adviser; political director; public liaison director; Cabinet secretary; and congressional lobbyist.

West Wing Basement

This floor houses the top-secret "Situation Room," where national security officials monitor foreign crises; the White House lunchroom reserved for senior officials; administrative offices; official photographers; and the copying room.

West Wing Third Floor Offices

Old Executive Office Building

The Old Executive Office Building houses some other members of the president's staff, which totals more than 1,800. Among those next door at the Old EOB are the budget director; chairman of the Council of Economic Advisers; director of the Office of National Service; many of Hillary Rodham Clinton's aids and the staff of the health care task force, and Vice President Gore's second office suite.

The Two-Term Limitation

Ever since passage of the Twenty-Second Amendment, some have argued against the two-term limit, believing it, too, to be "undemocratic." After all, if a president is enjoying the support of the people and doing a good job, why shouldn't he be allowed to seek a third or fourth term? Early in the second terms of Richard Nixon and Ronald Reagan, some of their supporters launched trial balloons concerning third terms, but to little avail.

Although it is likely that calls for change in the office, election procedures, and term of office will continue, change is highly unlikely as long as the system continues to work with some degree of effectiveness.

The Line-Item Veto

As early as 1873 in his State of the Union message, President Ulysses S. Grant proposed a constitutional amendment to give the president a **line-item veto**, the power enjoyed by many governors to veto individual items within a spending bill without invalidating the bill in its entirety. Since then, over 150 resolutions calling for a line-item veto have been introduced in Congress, and FDR, Eisenhower, Ford, Carter, Reagan, Bush, and Clinton have supported the concept.

George Bush was a particularly vocal proponent of the line-item veto although only one of his vetoes was overridden. Said Bush during his 1992 State of the Union message, "the press has a field day making fun of outrageous examples [of pork barrel appropriations]: A Lawrence Welk museum, research grants for Belgian endive.... Maybe you need someone to help you say no. I know how to say it, and I know what I need to make it stick. Give me the same thing 43 governors have: the line-item veto."[49] Many agree with Bush that the line-item veto could result in considerable savings, since it would allow a president to do away with more outrageous examples of "pork," or what a president might see as needless fat in the budget.

Thus, picking up on calls made earlier by President Ronald Reagan, Bush supporters in the Senate introduced legislation that would give the president the authority to kill spending measures he dislikes. Senator Robert C. Byrd (D.-W. Va.), often called the "King of Pork," however, made an eight-hour impassioned speech likening the Republican's line-item veto proposal to "quack medicine better regarded as snake oil."[50]

In June, 1994, the Senate began hearings on the line item veto. The head of the Department of Justice's Office of Legal Counsel agreed with Senate members that the president has no constitutional authority for this kind of veto. Thus, a Constitutional amendment would be necessary.

---

[49] "Address Before a Joint Session of the Congress of the Union, January 28, 1992," *Weekly Compilation of Presidential Documents*, 28 (February 3, 1992): 175.

[50] "Senate Rejects Giving Bush Line-Item Veto," *The New York Times* (February 28, 1992): A6.

Summary

Because the Framers feared a tyrannical monarch, they gave considerable thought to the office of the chief executive. Since ratification of the Constitution, the office has changed considerably—more through practice and need than from changes in the Constitution. In chronicling these changes, we have made the following points:

1. Distrust of a too-powerful leader led the Framers to create an executive office with limited powers. They mandated that a president be thirty-five years old and opted not to limit the president's term of office. To further guard against tyranny, they also made provisions for the removal of the president and created an office of vice president to provide for an orderly transfer of power.
2. The Framers gave the president a variety of specific constitutional powers in Article II, including the powers to make appointments, to convene Congress, to make treaties, and to veto. The president also derives considerable power from being Commander-in-Chief of the military. The Constitution also grants the president the power to grant pardons.
3. The development of presidential power has been highly dependent on the force of those who have held the office. George Washington, in particular, took several actions to establish the primacy of the president in national affairs and as true chief executive of a strong national government. But, with the exceptions of Andrew Jackson and Abraham Lincoln, subsequent presidents often let Congress dominate in national affairs. The election of FDR, however, forever changed all that as a new era of the modern presidency began. A hallmark of the modern presidency is the close relationship between the American people and their chief executive.
4. Since FDR, the public has looked to the president to propose legislation to Congress. The modern president also plays a major role in the budgetary process. To gain support of his programs or proposed budget, the president can use patronage, personal rewards, and party connections, and can go directly to the public. How the president goes about winning support is reflected in his style, affected by his character and his ability to persuade, and, in general, his ability to maintain high ratings in public opinion polls.
5. As the responsibilities of and expectations about the president have grown, so has the executive branch of government. The Cabinet has expanded, and FDR established the Executive Office of the President to help him govern. Perhaps the most key policy advisers are those closest to the president—the White House staff.
6. Ending term limits and the line-item veto are often discussed as possible ways to reform the presidency.

Key Terms

articles of impeachment
Watergate
executive agreement
veto
pardon
inherent power
patronage
presidential style
presidential character
two presidencies
Executive Office of the President
line-item veto

Suggested Readings

Campbell, Colin, S.J., and Bert A. Rockman. *The Bush Presidency: First Appraisals*. Chatham, NJ: Chatham House, 1991.

Corwin, Edwin S. *The Presidential Office and Powers, 1787–1957*, 4th ed. New York: New York University Press, 1957.

Cronin, Thomas E. *The State of the Presidency*, 2nd ed. Boston: Little, Brown, 1980.

Edwards, George C., III. *At the Margins*. New Haven, CT: Yale University Press, 1989.

Edwards, George, C. III. et al., eds. *Researching the Presidency: Vital Questions, New Approaches*. Pittsburgh: University of Pittsburgh Press, 1993.

George, Alexander L. *Presidential Decisionmaking in Foreign Policy*. Boulder, CO: Westview Press, 1980.

Kellerman, Barbara. *The Political Presidency*. New York: Oxford University Press, 1984.

Neustadt, Richard E. *Presidential Power: The Politics of Power from FDR to Carter*. New York: Wiley, 1980.

Reedy, George E. *The Twilight of the Presidency*. New York: New American Library, 1970.

Skowrorek, Stephen. *The Politics Presidents Make: Leadership from John Adams to George Bush*. Cambridge: Harvard University Press, 1993.

Tulis, Jeffrey K. *The Rhetorical Presidency*. Princeton, NJ: Princeton University Press, 1987.

Watson, Richard A., and Norman C. Thomas. *The Politics of the Presidency*, 2nd ed. Washington, DC: CQ Press, 1988.

The true test of a good government is its aptitude and tendency to produce a good administration.... It is not easy to conceive a plan better calculated than this to produce a judicious choice of men for filling the offices of the Union.

Alexander Hamilton
Federalist No. 76

Hamilton believed that the separation of powers to appoint and confirm (appointment by the president, confirmation by the Senate) key members of the bureaucracy would assure the appointment of only those well qualified for the job.

CHAPTER 8

The Bureaucracy

THE DEVELOPMENT OF THE FEDERAL BUREAUCRACY
THE MODERN BUREAUCRACY
POLICY MAKING
MAKING AGENCIES ACCOUNTABLE
PROBLEMS WITH THE MODERN BUREAUCRACY
TOWARD REFORM

Alexander Hamilton could not have envisioned that the power of the president to appoint "a good administration" would ultimately result in an executive branch that numbered over 2.9 million civilian non-postal federal employees in 1993. This federal **bureaucracy**, a set of complex hierarchical departments, agencies, commissions, and their staffs, exists to help the president carry out his constitutionally mandated charge to enforce the laws of the nation. As the bureaucracy has grown to help the president, it has become so large that it is often called the "fourth branch" of government. Without the bureaucracy, government as we know it would come to a grinding halt. The military could not function, social service programs would cease, and all air traffic would be grounded.

Harold D. Lasswell once defined political science as the "study of who gets what, when, and how."[1] It is by studying the bureaucracy that those questions can perhaps best be answered.

The term *bureaucracy* is used to refer to any large, complex organization in which employees have specified responsibilities and work within a hierarchy of authority. Corporations, companies, states, and the federal government have bureaucracies. Without them, these organizations could not function.

The employees who work in bureaucracies are called **bureaucrats**. While the term is often used derisively today, the term *bureau* originally referred to the cloth covering of desks and writing tables used by seventeenth-century French government officials. In the eighteenth century, the word was coupled with the suffix *-cracy*, signifying rule of government (as in *aristocracy*, *democracy*, and *theocracy*).[2]

---

[1] Harold D. Lasswell, *Politics: Who Gets What, When, and How* (New York: McGraw-Hill, 1938).
[2] In Britain, the bureaucracy is commonly referred to as the *civil service* or *Whitehall*, the name of the building in London that houses many government ministries.

The American bureaucracy is distinctive in many ways. For example, political authority over the bureaucracy is not in a single set of hands, but is shared by many institutions. Although the president can remove officials from their positions in the executive branch, it has never been clear exactly how much authority the chief executive actually exercises in this regard. Because of the system of checks and balances created by the Framers of the Constitution, Congress can authorize the creation of departments, fund them, and pass the laws that the agencies are expected to implement. Therefore, it is often unclear to whom bureaucratic loyalty lies.

The bureaucracy can be thought of as that part of the government that links together the three branches of the national government and the federal system. Although Congress makes the laws, it must rely on the executive branch and the bureaucracy to enforce those laws. For example, when Congress enacted the Civil Rights Act of 1964 to eliminate discrimination in employment, it created the Equal Employment Opportunity Commission (EEOC) to enforce the provisions of the act. (See "Then and Now: The Equal Employment and Opportunity Commission and Sex Discrimination," p. 307.) The head of the EEOC is appointed by the president with the advice and consent of the Senate; thus, the EEOC often reflects the political views of the chief executive. During the Lyndon B. Johnson presidency, for instance, the EEOC was generally given high marks for its handling of racial discrimination claims. In contrast, the Reagan and Bush administrations were often accused of lax enforcement of rules geared toward preventing or discouraging discrimination.

Commissions like the EEOC have the power not only to make rules but also to settle disputes between parties concerning the enforcement and implementation of those rules. More often than not, however, agency determinations end up being challenged in the courts. Almost every type of agency decision is likely to end up in court. However, because most administrative agencies that make up part of the bureaucracy enjoy reputations for special expertise in clearly defined policy areas, the federal judiciary routinely defers to administrative decision makers.

We study the federal bureaucracy because of the key role it plays in the democratic process and in facilitating interactions within the federal system. Although many bureaucratic agencies interact directly with the public—the Internal Revenue Service collects your taxes, and the Postal Service delivers your mail—other bureaucratic agencies routinely interact with only state and local governments, and act as key players in the continuing definition and redefinition of federalism. For example, federal grants-in-aid for programs dealing with poverty and disability are supervised by the Social Security Administration (SSA). The SSA is a division of the Department of Health and Human Services, which sets up guidelines for eligibility, distributes money to the states, and oversees the implementation of the various state programs.

Even though the bureaucracy performs many valuable tasks we have come to take for granted, attacking the bureaucracy often appears to be a national pastime. Americans dislike the bureaucracy for a variety of reasons. Conservatives charge that it is too liberal and that its functions constitute unnecessary government meddling in our lives. They argue that the bureaucracy is too large, too powerful, and too unaccountable to the people or to elected officials. In contrast, liberals view it as too slow, too unimaginative to solve America's problems, and too zealous a guardian of the status quo. Whether conservative, liberal, or moderate, most Americans think that the bureaucracy works poorly and is wasteful. Tales of bureaucratic agency payments for $640 toilet seats and $7,622 coffee makers (no matter how these costs are justified) do not help the public's image of the bureaucracy.

Then and Now

The Equal Employment Opportunity Commission and Sex Discrimination

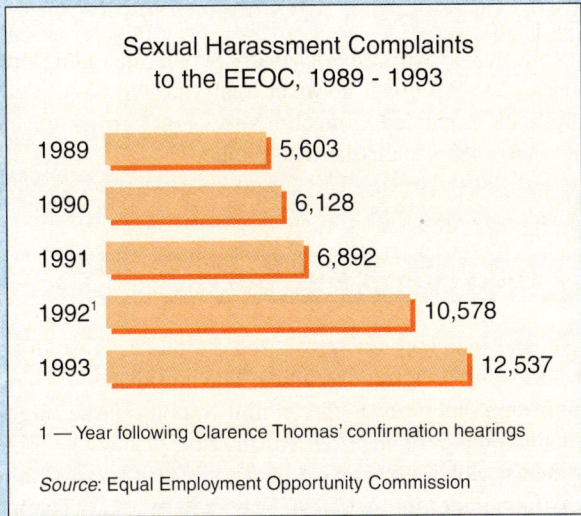

Sexual Harassment Complaints Before and After the Thomas Hearings

The EEOC was created in 1965 to implement the antidiscrimination provisions of the Civil Rights Act of 1964. It prohibited discrimination by private employers on the basis of race, creed, color, religion, national origin, or sex. In spite of that broad mandate, the EEOC initially failed to investigate complaints of sex discrimination. In fact, the National Organization for Women was founded by women who saw the need to create an advocacy group to pressure the EEOC to treat claims of sex discrimination seriously and enforce the law.*

Over the years, in spite of pressure on the EEOC from numerous women's rights groups, many continued to fault its handling of sex discrimination.

Women's rights groups were particularly irritated by the EEOC's apparent foot dragging on developing regulations to define sexual harassment as a form of sex discrimination illegal under the Civil Rights Act of 1964. Once regulations were finally issued in 1985 defining sexual harassment as employment discrimination if it involved conduct that "has the purpose or effect of unreasonably interfering with an individual's work performance or creating an intimidating, hostile or offensive working environment," women began to file complaints. Still, the EEOC, under the direction of Clarence Thomas from 1982 to 1990, often failed to treat those complaints with the same seriousness as other grievances. As the accompanying figure shows, in 1989, just before Thomas was appointed to the U.S. Circuit Court of Appeals, 5,603 complaints involving sexual harassment were filed with the EEOC. By 1991, that number had increased by nearly 20 percent.

Ironically, when Clarence Thomas was nominated by George Bush to be the 106th Justice of the U.S. Supreme Court, sexual harassment quickly became the major issue when a former employee of Thomas's charged he had harassed her while he headed that agency. In the wake of nationally televised hearings into the allegations, public awareness of the problem increased. In the year following Thomas's appointment, complaints of sexual harassment in the workplace were up 35 percent. Then, in late 1993, a unanimous U.S. Supreme Court ruled that a woman did not have to show severe psychological damage to prove that illegal sexual harassment occurred.** This decision was expected to open the flood gates to the filing of more complaints with the agency.

*Jo Freeman, *The Politics of Women's Liberation* (New York: Longman, 1975).

** *Harris* v. *Forklift Systems*, 1993 LEXIS 7155.

Candidates for public office, presidents, and Congress constantly criticize the bureaucracy and speak about it as though it were a foreign power to be conquered. Members of Congress joke that there is a game called "Bureaucracy" in which "There is only one rule. The first one to move loses." Even *Roget's Thesaurus* equates the term "bureaucracy" with officialism and red tape.

In spite of the criticisms, the bureaucracy is here to stay. This chapter traces the growth of the bureaucracy and examines how it is organized, how it interacts with the three branches of government, how it implements policy, and what role it plays in our national system of government.

As you read the pages that follow, you will see why many people, including presidents, have criticized the bureaucracy. We hope, however, that you will also see that the bureaucracy has in many respects expanded to meet the needs of a growing nation and the rising expectations and demands of the American public.

The Development of the Federal Bureaucracy

Just as the legislative, executive, and judicial branches started out modestly, so did the bureaucracy (or federal service, as some preferred to call it). The presidency of George Washington was quite uncomplicated, and so was the administration that he hired to assist him. As noted in the timeline on p. 309, in 1789, Washington's executive branch consisted of only three departments, which had existed under the Articles of Confederation: State (called Foreign Affairs under the Articles), War, and Treasury. The head of each department was called its *secretary*. Since the president often needed legal advice, the Congress created the office of Attorney General. The original status of the Attorney General, however, was unclear; i.e., was he a member of the judicial or executive branch? That confusion was remedied in 1870 with the creation of the Justice Department as part of the executive branch, with the Attorney General as its head. From the beginning, individuals appointed as Cabinet secretaries (as well as the Attorney General) were subject to approval by the U.S. Senate, but were "removable by the president" alone. Even the first Congress realized how important it was for a president to be surrounded by those in whom he had complete confidence and trust.

Differing views of the role of the national government in general, and of the executive branch in particular, were apparent right away in the differing styles of the first Cabinet secretaries. The State Department, headed by Thomas Jefferson, had but nine employees. Jefferson, always an opponent of big national government, saw no need for additional staff members. In contrast, Secretary of the Treasury Alexander Hamilton perceived himself as head of the most critical new department: the Treasury Department was charged with collecting taxes, issuing money, and printing postage stamps—responsibilities crucial to the survival of the new nation. Therefore, Hamilton presided over a much larger staff.

From 1816 to 1861, the size of the federal bureaucracy grew as increased demands were made on existing departments. For example, the Post Office, which Congress was constitutionally authorized to create in Article I, was forced to expand to meet the needs of a growing and westward-expanding population. In 1892, the Post Office was removed from the jurisdiction of the Treasury Department by Andrew Jackson. Recognizing the tremendous potential increases in demands on the Post Office, Jackson promoted the Postmaster General to Cabinet rank, thereby giving him greater control over the office and its immense number of employees.

Landmark Events in the Development of the Bureaucracy

1789	♦ First three departments created
1861–1865	♦ Civil War
1883	♦ Civil Service Reform Act (Pendleton Act)
1887	♦ Interstate Commerce Commission created
1903	♦ Department of Commerce and Labor established
1921	♦ General Accounting Office and Bureau of Budget created
1933–1937	♦ New Deal "alphabetocracy" established
1939	♦ Hatch Act
1964–1966	♦ New social welfare agencies created; EEOC, Departments of Housing and Urban Development and Transportation created
1978	♦ Civil Service Reform Act
1993	♦ Federal Employees Political Activities Act

The Post Office Department was not the only department created during this period. On his last day in office, President James K. Polk (1845–1849) signed into law a bill creating the Department of the Interior. He and Congress recognized the need not only for a department to be in charge of the millions of new acres the United States had acquired, but also for a government agency to deal with the Native Americans who lived on this land. The new department was given responsibility for supervising the use of natural resources on those lands, issuing patents on new inventions, and conducting the census every ten years (a task performed initially by the Treasury Department and later by the Department of Commerce).

The Civil War and Big Government

The Civil War (1861–1865) permanently changed the nature of the federal bureaucracy. As the nation geared up for war, thousands of additional employees were added to existing departments. The Civil War also spawned the need for new government agencies. A series of poor harvests and marketing problems led President Abraham Lincoln (who understood that one needs food in order to conduct a war) to create the Department of Agriculture in 1862, although it was not given full Cabinet-level status until 1889.

After the Civil War, the need for big government continued unabated. In 1866, the Pension Office was established to pay benefits to the thousands of northern veterans

More than two hundred years after its founding, the Post Office employs more civilians than any other segment of the federal government.

who had fought in the war (more than 127,000 veterans were initially eligible for benefits). Justice was made a department in 1870 and other departments were added through 1900. Agriculture became a full-fledged department and began to play an important role in informing farmers about the latest developments in soil conservation, livestock breeding, and planting techniques. The increase in the types and nature of government services resulted in a parallel rise in the number of federal jobs, as illustrated in Figure 8-1. Many of the new jobs were used by the president or leaders of the president's political party for **patronage**; that is, jobs, grants, or other special favors given as rewards to friends and political allies for their support.

Becoming a Bureaucrat: From Spoils to Merit

In 1831, describing a "rotation in office" policy for bureaucrats supported by President Andrew Jackson, Senator William Learned Marcy of New York commented, "To the victor belong the spoils." From his statement derives the phrase **spoils system** to describe the firing of public-office holders of the defeated political party and their re-

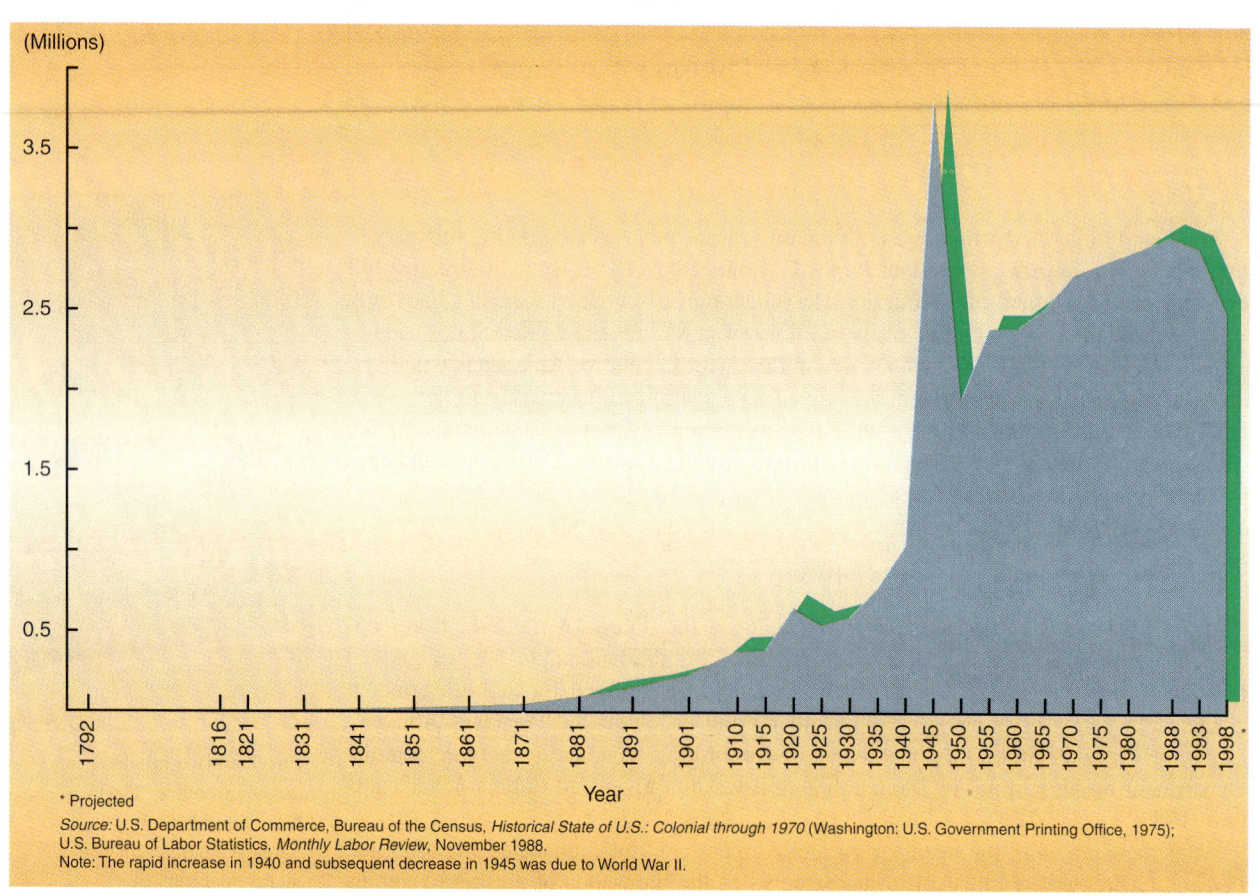

FIGURE 8-1
Number of Federal Employees, 1792–2000

* Projected
Source: U.S. Department of Commerce, Bureau of the Census, *Historical State of U.S.: Colonial through 1970* (Washington: U.S. Government Printing Office, 1975); U.S. Bureau of Labor Statistics, *Monthly Labor Review*, November 1988.
Note: The rapid increase in 1940 and subsequent decrease in 1945 was due to World War II.

An artist's representation of President Garfield's assassination. He was killed by an unhappy office seeker.

placement with loyalists of the new administration. Jackson, in particular, faced severe criticism for populating the federal government with his political cronies. But many presidents, including Jackson, argued that in order to implement their policies, they had to be able to appoint those who subscribed to their political views.

By the time James A. Garfield, a former distinguished Civil War officer, was elected president in 1880, many reformers were calling publicly for changes in the **civil service system**, by which appointments to the federal bureaucracy are made. Upon his election to office, Garfield, like many presidents before him, was besieged by office seekers. Washington, D.C., had not seen such a demand for political jobs since the election of Abraham Lincoln as the first president of the Republican Party. Garfield's immediate predecessor, Rutherford B. Hayes, had favored the idea of the replacement of the spoils system with a merit system based on test scores and ability. Congress, however, failed to pass the legislation he proposed. Possibly because potential job seekers wanted to secure positions before Congress had the opportunity to act on an overhauled civil service system, thousands pressed Garfield for positions. This siege prompted Garfield to record in his diary: "My day is frittered away with the personal seeking of people when it ought to be given to the great problems which concern the whole country."[3] And although he resolved to reform the civil service, Garfield's life was cut short by the bullets of an assassin who, ironically, was a frustrated job seeker.

Public reaction to Garfield's death prompted Congress to pass the Civil Service Reform Act in 1883, more commonly known as the **Pendleton Act**, to reduce patronage. It created a bipartisan three-member Civil Service Commission, which operated until 1978. Under the Act's provisions, about 15 percent of the positions in the federal civil service were classified into grades or levels to which appointments would be made on

---

[3] Quoted in Robert G. Caldwell, *James A. Garfield* (Hamden, CT: Archon Books, 1965).

People of the Past

William Henry Harrison and Office Seekers

Nominated by the Whig Party in 1839, William Henry Harrison was the "log cabin, hard cider" candidate in the presidential campaign of 1840. Although Harrison was the son of a wealthy Virginia planter, the Whig Party developed an image of Harrison as one who had risen to distinction through his own efforts while retaining the tastes of the ordinary citizen. Harrison went to college and then enlisted in the army, where he was promoted to major general. Harrison was a hero in the Battle of Tippecanoe, thus earning the nickname "Tippecanoe," which led to the catchy campaign slogan "Tippecanoe and Tyler too" when Harrison selected his running mate, John Tyler.

Harrison ran his campaign without a platform. The advice given to him by Whig leaders was to say nothing about principles or creed. Many silly campaign songs were composed and noisy conventions and rallies were held everywhere, but no campaign promises were made.

At his inaugural address on March 4, Harrison droned on for close to two hours, producing the longest inaugural speech on record. He paid dearly for it. It was a cold and wintry day and Harrison did not wear gloves or an overcoat. Not surprisingly, he developed pneumonia later that month and died on April 4, serving the shortest term of any president.

Repeatedly dunned by supporters seeking patronage jobs, Harrison's last words were: "I can't stand it.... Don't trouble me.... These applications, will they never cease...?" Even on Harrison's deathbed, the problems of a growing bureaucracy continued to hound him.

---

the basis of performance on competitive examinations. This was called the **merit system**. The Pendleton Act also made it illegal to fire a civil servant for failure to contribute to a political party or campaign.

National Efforts to Regulate the Economy

Soon after passage of the Pendleton Act, Congress took other actions that served to spur the growth of the bureaucracy. In the wake of the tremendous growth of big business (especially railroads), widespread price fixing, and other unfair business practices, in 1887 Congress created the Interstate Commerce Commission (ICC), the first independent **regulatory commission** (an agency of the executive branch that generally is concerned with a particular aspect of the economy). The creation of the ICC also marked a shift in the focus of the bureaucracy from service to regulation. In the case of the ICC, Congress was reacting to public outcries over the exorbitant rates charged by railroad companies for hauling freight. Independent regulatory commissions such as the ICC are created by Congress to be independent of direct presidential authority. Com-

As this cartoon depicts, the ICC was created by Congress to help regulate the monopolistic practices of the gigantic railroad industry. Here, ICC commissioners are shown trying to tame the unruly railroads.

mission members, although appointed by the president, hold their jobs for fixed terms and are not removable by the president unless they fail to uphold their oaths of office.

The 1900 election of Theodore Roosevelt, a progressive Republican, strengthened the movement toward regulation and further increased the size of the bureaucracy when Roosevelt asked Congress to establish a Department of Commerce and Labor in 1903 to oversee employer/employee relations. Roosevelt was motivated by the existence of intolerable labor practices, including low wages, long hours, substandard working conditions, the refusal of employers to recognize the rights of workers to join a union, and the fact that many businesses had grown so large and powerful that they could force workers to accept substandard conditions.

In 1913, President Woodrow Wilson created a separate Department of Labor when it became clear that one agency could not well represent the interests of both employers and employees, factions with greatly differing perspectives. The creation of this department reflected the economic and societal changes that occurred as immigration increased and the economy became increasingly industrialized. One year later, in 1914, Congress created the Federal Trade Commission (FTC). Its function was to protect small businesses and the public from unfair competition, especially from big business.

Also affecting the size of government and the possibilities for growth was the ratification of the Sixteenth Amendment to the Constitution in 1913. It gave Congress the authority to implement a federal income tax to supplement the national treasury, which provided an infusion of funds to support new federal agencies, services, and governmental programs.

Laissez-Faire **Attitudes.** During the early 1900s, while Progressives raised the public cry for regulation of business, many Americans, especially members of the business community, continued to resist such moves. They believed that any federal government regulation was wrong. Instead they favored governmental facilitation of

President Franklin D. Roosevelt urges the Court to work with the executive and legislative branches in a cooperative effort to end the Great Depression.

the national economy through a commitment to *laissez-faire*, a French term literally meaning *to allow to do; to leave alone*. In America, the term was used to describe a governmental hands-off policy concerning the economy. And the courts, especially the U.S. Supreme Court, were at the forefront of the philosophical debate over how much power the national government had to regulate the private sector. In a series of key decisions made through 1937, the Supreme Court repeatedly invalidated key provisions in congressional legislation designed to regulate various aspects of the economy. The Court and others who subscribed to *laissez-faire* principles of a free enterprise system argued that natural economic laws at work in the marketplace control the buying and selling of goods. Thus, it was believed, the government had no right to regulate business in any way.

The New Deal and Bigger Government. In the wake of the high unemployment and weak financial markets of the Great Depression, Franklin Roosevelt's plan to revitalize the economy included the creation of hundreds of new government agencies to regulate business practices and various aspects of the economy. Although the *laissez-faire*-minded Supreme Court stood adamantly opposed to increased regulation and bureaucratization, Roosevelt proposed and the Congress enacted far-ranging economic legislation. The desperate mood of the nation supported these moves as most Americans began to change their ideas about the proper role of government and the provision of governmental services. Formerly, Americans had believed in a hands-off approach; they now considered it the government's job to get the economy going and get Americans back to work.

Within the first 100 days of Roosevelt's administration, Congress approved every new regulatory measure proposed by the president. Among others, Congress approved the National Industrial Recovery Act (NIRA), an unprecedented attempt to regulate industry; and the Agricultural Adjustment Act (AAA), to provide government support for farm prices and to regulate farm production to ensure market-competitive prices. Congress also created the Federal Deposit Insurance Corporation (FDIC) to insure bank deposits and passed the Federal Securities Act, which gave the Federal Trade Commission the authority to supervise and regulate the issuance, buying, and selling of stocks and bonds.

Until 1937, however, the Supreme Court refused to allow Congress or the president to delegate to the executive branch or the bureaucracy such far-ranging authority to regulate the economy. *Laissez-faire* was alive and well at the Court, and attempts to end the economic slump through greater governmental involvement were repeatedly stymied by the justices. In 1937, however, FDR, frustrated by the Court, proposed his famous Court-packing plea (see Chapter 9), which would have allowed him to add his own appointees to the Court. In the wake of that institution-threatening proposal, the Court quickly fell into sync with public opinion. In a series of cases discussed in Chapter 9, the Supreme Court reversed a number of its earlier decisions and upheld what some have termed the "alphabetocracy" (see Chapter 3). For example, the Court upheld the constitutionality of the National Labor Relations Act of 1935 (NLRA), which allowed recognition of unions and established formal arbitration procedures for employers and employees.[4] Subsequent decisions upheld the validity of the Fair Labor Standards Act (FLSA) and the Agricultural Adjustment Act (AAA).[5]

---

[4] *NLRB* v. *Jones & Laughlin Steel Corp.*, 301 U.S. 1 (1937).

[5] *U.S.* v. *Darby Lumber Co.* 312 U.S. 100 (1941) and *Wickwood* v. *Filburn*, 317 U.S. 111 (1942).

Poor working conditions in the early 1900s: a sweatshop in New York.

Once these new programs were declared constitutional, the bureaucracy needed to expand yet again in order to monitor the numerous programs created by the new laws. And with the growth in the bureaucracy came more calls for reform of the system.

The Hatch Act. As an increasing proportion of the American workforce came to work for the U.S. government as a result of the New Deal recovery programs, many began to fear that the members of the civil service would play major roles not only in implementing public policy but also in electing members of Congress and even the president. Consequently, in 1939, Congress enacted what is commonly known as the **Hatch Act**, which was designed to prohibit the use of federal employees to affect elections. In effect, the Hatch Act was intended to neutralize the civil service politically by prohibiting civil servants from taking activist roles in partisan campaigns; under its provisions, federal employees could not run for public office, campaign for or against candidates, make speeches, raise funds for candidates, organize political rallies, circulate petitions, or participate in registration drives that seek voters for one party only.

Although presidents as far back as Thomas Jefferson had advocated efforts to limit the opportunities for federal civil servants to influence the votes of others, many criticized the Hatch Act as too extreme. Critics argued that it denied millions of federal employees the First Amendment guarantees of freedom of speech and association, and discouraged political participation among a group of people who might otherwise be strong political activists. Critics also argued that civil servants *should* become more involved in campaigns, particularly at the state and local level, in order to understand better the needs of the citizens they serve.

The Federal Employees Political Activities Act. In response to these criticisms and at the urgings of President Bill Clinton, Congress enacted the **Federal Employees Political Activities Act**. This liberalization of the Hatch Act allows employees to run for

> ## The Liberalized Hatch Act
>
> Here are some examples of permissible and prohibited activities for federal employees under the Hatch Act, as modified by the Federal Employees Political Activities Act of 1993.
>
> - **May** be candidates for public office in nonpartisan elections
> - **May** assist in voter registration drives
> - **May** express opinions about candidates and issues
> - **May** contribute money to political organizations
> - **May** attend political fundraising functions
> - **May** attend and be active at political rallies and meetings
> - **May** join and be an active member of a political party or club
> - **May** sign nominating petitions
> - **May** campaign for or against referendum questions, constitutional amendments, municipal ordinances
> - **May** campaign for or against candidates in partisan elections
> - **May** make campaign speeches for candidates in partisan elections
> - **May** distribute campaign literature in partisan elections
> - **May** hold office in political clubs or parties
>
> - **May not** use their official authority or influence to interfere with an election
> - **May not** collect political contributions unless both individuals are members of the same federal labor organization or employee organization and the one solicited is not a subordinate employee
> - **May not** knowingly solicit or discourage the political activity of any person who has business before the agency
> - **May not** engage in political activity while on duty
> - **May not** engage in political activity in any government office
> - **May not** engage in political activity while wearing an official uniform
> - **May not** engage in political activity while using a government vehicle
> - **May not** solicit political contributions from the general public
> - **May not** be candidates for public office in partisan elections
>
> *Source:* U.S. Special Counsel's Office.

public office in non-partisan elections, contribute money to political organizations, and campaign for or against candidates in partisan elections. During the signing ceremony, Clinton said the law will "mean more responsive, more satisfied, happier, and more productive federal employees."[6]

The Modern Bureaucracy

One of the most difficult tasks facing those who study the bureaucracy is determining to whom bureaucracies are responsible. Is it the president? Congress? the citizenry? We often think of bureaucrats as "them." But they are actually quite like "us." To understand the modern bureaucracy, it is essential to understand who bureaucrats are, how the bureaucracy is organized, and how it works.

---

[6] "Federal News: Hatch Act," *Inc., Government Employee Relations Report* (October 11, 1993): 1317.

Who Are Bureaucrats?

Federal bureaucrats are career government employees who work in the executive branch, in the fourteen Cabinet-level departments and the more than 60 independent agencies that comprise more than 2,000 bureaus, divisions, branches, offices, services, and other sub-units of the federal government. There are approximately 2.9 million federal bureaucrats (in contrast to only 800,000 in Great Britain) who come from all walks of life—they vary in race, religion, ethnicity, level of education, and income. Because the representation of women and minorities at higher levels is still low (see Figure 8-2 on page 318), Congress has ordered federal agencies to make special efforts in their recruitment of minority and other disadvantaged workers. And overall, women and minorities are better represented as a proportion of the workforce in the bureaucracy than in the nation as a whole, as revealed in Figure 8-2.

World War II and Its Aftermath

During World War II, as revealed in Figure 8-2, the federal government grew tremendously to meet the needs of a nation at war. Tax rates were increased to support the war, and they never again fell to prewar levels. After the war, this infusion of new monies and veterans' demands for services led to a variety of new programs and much bigger government. The G.I. Bill, for example, provided college loans for returning veterans and reduced mortgage rates to allow them to buy homes. Again, Americans became accustomed to the increasingly important role that the national government was playing in entirely new areas, such as middle-class housing. And, the national government was involved not only in more service programs that affected more people, but in more regulation as well. Homes bought with Veterans' Housing Authority loans, for example, had to meet certain specifications.

After World War II, the civil rights movement and President Lyndon B. Johnson's War on Poverty (see Chapter 3) produced additional growth in the bureaucracy. As discussed earlier, the Equal Employment Opportunity Commission (EEOC) was created in 1964; the Department of Housing and Urban Development and the Department of Transportation in 1966. These expansions of the bureaucracy corresponded to increases in the president's power and his ability to persuade Congress that new agencies would be an effective way to solve pressing problems. Remember that most major expansions in the power of the presidency have occurred during times of war or economic emergency. Most of the important changes in the size of the bureaucracy through the 1970s also occurred in response to war, economic chaos, or civil unrest.

This pattern is not unique to the United States. In Britain, the two world wars left the country with a vastly expanded bureaucracy capable, among other things, of economic planning, and delivering a wide variety of social services.

FIGURE 8-2

Characteristics and Rank Distributions of Federal Civilian Employees, 1991

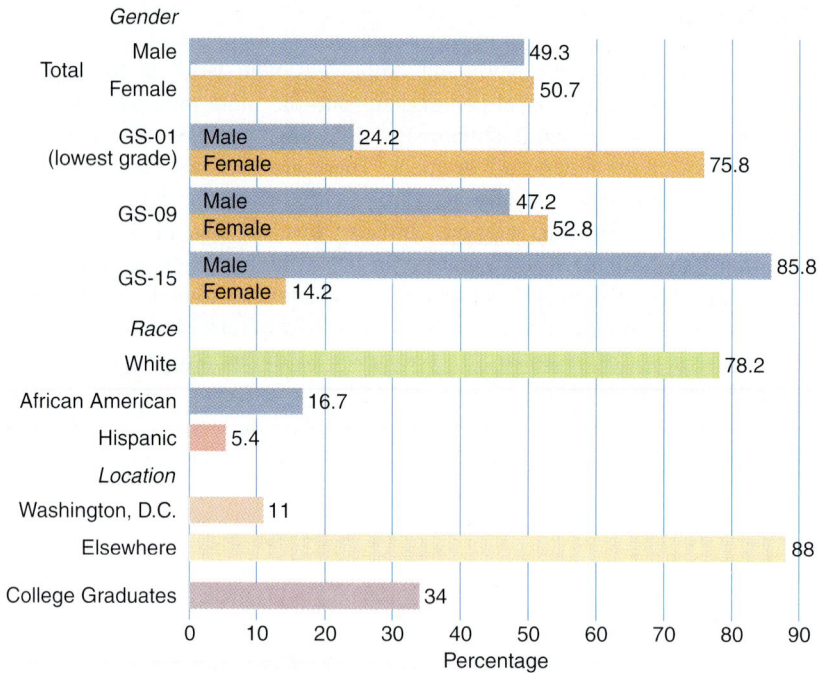

Sources: *Statistical Abstract of the United States, 1990* (Washington: U.S. Government Printing Office, 1990), pp. 323–326. Office of Personnel Management, *Federal Civilian Workforce Statistics, Employment and Trends as of November 1988* (Washington: U.S. Government Printing Office, 1989), pp. 70. Harold W. Stanley and Richard G. Niemi, *Vital Statistics on American Politics*, 4th ed. (Washington, D.C.: Congressional Quarterly Press, 1994), p. 406.

As a result of reforms made during the Truman administration, most civilian federal governmental employees are selected by merit standards, which include tests (such as civil service or foreign service exams) and educational criteria. Merit systems protect federal employees from being fired for political reasons. Positions in the politically neutral civil service in Britain are also filled on the basis of competitive examinations; nevertheless, most entrants continue to come from either Oxford University or Cambridge University, which has given the English bureaucracy, unlike its American counterpart, an elitist image.

At one time, federal employees were underpaid in comparison with their civilian counterparts, but now salaries are largely competitive except at the senior ranks. Most federal employees have a GS (Graded Service) job rank; these range from GS-1 to GS-18. Rankings are determined by position and employee qualifications.

A Senior Executive Service (SES) was created in 1978 at the urging of President Jimmy Carter.[7] It represents a compromise between two traditions: a president-led bureaucracy and one composed of experts. The SES contains approximately 8,000 top-level career employees (spread throughout the various agencies) who receive higher salaries than GS employees, but who can be moved or transferred by the order of the president. Unlike regular presidential appointees, however, they cannot be fired by the president at will.

---

[7] See Mark W. Huddleston, "The Carter Civil Service Reforms," *Political Science Quarterly* (Winter 1981–82): 607–622.

While the stereotypical image of a bureaucrat is that of the "paper pusher," more than 15,000 job skills are represented in the federal government, and its workers are perhaps the best trained and most skilled and efficient in the world. Working for the government are forest rangers, FBI agents, foreign service officers, computer programmers, security guards, librarians, administrators, engineers, plumbers, lawyers, doctors, postal carriers, and zoologists, among others. And the diversity of government jobs mirrors the diversity of jobs in the private sector.

Another myth is the perception that most bureaucrats work in Washington. In reality, only about 11 percent of the nearly 3 million federal bureaucrats work in the nation's capital; the rest are located in regional, state, and local offices scattered throughout the country. The decentralization of the bureaucracy facilitates accessibility. The Social Security Administration, for example, has numerous offices so that its clients may have a place nearby to take their paperwork, questions, and problems. Decentralization also helps distribute jobs and incomes across the country. Although the Centers for Disease Control and Prevention might easily have been situated in Washington, it is instead located in Atlanta, Georgia. Likewise, the headquarters for the National Aeronautics and Space Administration (NASA) is located in Houston, Texas.

Many Americans also believe that the federal bureaucracy is growing bigger each year. Although it is true that the number of federal government employees has been increasing until lately, most growth has taken place at the state and local levels, as revealed in Figure 8-3.

The stability of a federal agency and the expansion or reduction in the number of its employees are the responsibility of Congress; legislators have the power to abolish existing agencies or to create new ones as they see fit. But as one study conducted several years ago reveals, not only do old government agencies never die, but they hardly ever fade away. Of 175 agencies in selected areas operating in 1923, all but twenty-seven were alive and well fifty years later.[8]

Moreover, as each president has entered office, most have pledged to eliminate an agency or two or, at the very least, combine some. But as President Ronald Reagan soon learned after he campaigned in part on a pledge to eliminate the Department of Education, abolishing an agency is easier said than done. (Reagan, in fact, ended up elevating the Veterans Administration to the Department of Veterans Affairs by an act of Congress in 1988.) More typical are President Carter's actions. In 1978, he proposed reforms in the civil service system: The Civil Service Commission was split into two agencies, the Office of Personnel Management (OPM) and the Merit Systems Protection Board. OPM, in charge of hiring most civil service workers, has elaborate rules for hiring, promotion, and firing. Until the 1978 reforms, it was virtually impossible to fire a federal worker. Reforms urged by President Carter gave OPM more latitude, but because of the strength of federal employee unions and the regulations that protect federal workers, it is virtually impossible to remove an employee whose performance is substandard (see "How to Fire a Federal Bureaucrat," p. 321).

Even the U.S. Supreme Court has gotten involved with the government's right to terminate protected workers. In 1974, the Court ruled that federal jobs were private property, just like a house or a car. According to the Supreme Court, the due process clause of the Fifth Amendment protects federal employees who have been fired and re-

---

[8] Herbert Kaufman, *Are Government Organizations Immortal?* (Washington: Brookings Institution, 1976).

FIGURE 8-3

Number of Federal, State, and Local Government Employees, 1929–1991

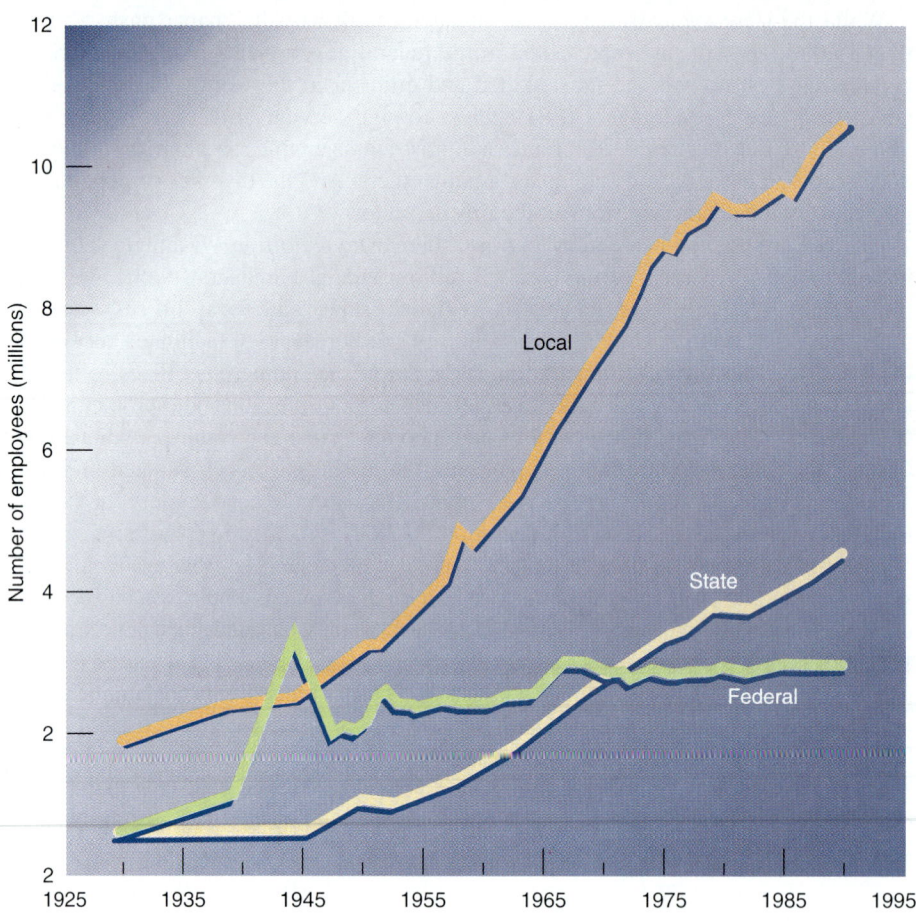

Source: Harold W. Stanley and Richard G. Niemi, *Vital Statistics on American Politics*, 4th ed. (Washington: CQ Press, 1994), p. 315. 1929–1944, 1949, 1954, 1959, 1964, 1969–1988: U.S. Advisory Commission on Intergovernmental Relations, *Significant Features of Fiscal Federalism, 1990*, vol. 2 (Washington: U.S. Advisory Commission on Intergovernmental Relations, 1990), p. 177; other years: Bureau of the Census, *Historical Statistics of the United States*, Series Y189–198 (Washington: U.S. Government Printing Office, 1975), p. 1100.

quires the government to provide an appeals procedure before termination.[9] And in 1990, the U.S. Supreme Court virtually eliminated the use of political patronage in the hiring and firing of most public employees.[10]

The courts and Congress have also attempted to uphold the rights of **whistle blowers**, federal employees who publicly disclose waste or mismanagement in their agencies. In the past, whistle blowers were sometimes punished or transferred to undesirable positions. During the Nixon administration, for example, when a top Pentagon employee testified before Congress about huge cost overruns on the C-5A troop transport plane, President Nixon was so angered that he ordered Defense Department officials to "get rid of that [expletive deleted]." Recently, however, whistle blowers have been honored and awarded for serving the public interest. In 1989, Congress,

---

[9] *Arnett v. Kennedy*, 416 U.S. 134 (1974).

[10] *Rutan v. Republican Party of Illinois*, 110 S. Ct. 2729 (1990).

> ### How to Fire a Federal Bureaucrat
> ♦ ♦ ♦
>
> Firing a bureaucrat can be very difficult. To fire a member of the competitive civil service, explicit procedures must be followed:
>
> 1. At least thirty days' written notice must be given to an employee in advance of firing or demotion for incompetence or misconduct.
> 2. The written notification must contain a statement of reasons for the action and specific examples of unacceptable performance.
> 3. The employee has the right to reply both orally and in written form to the charges, and has the right to an attorney.
> 4. Appeals from any adverse action against the employee can be made to the three-person Merit Systems Protection Board (MSPB), a bipartisan body appointed by the president and confirmed by the Senate.
> 5. All employees have the right to a hearing and to an attorney in front of the MSPB.
> 6. All decisions of the MSPB may be appealed by the employee to the U.S. Court of Appeals.
>
> This process has resulted in very few terminations. Of the 2.2 million federal employees in 1992, only 293 were fired for incompetence!

with the support of President George Bush, passed legislation to ensure protection for whistle blowers. The legislation grants relief to federal employees who can link a demotion or firing to whistle blowing, and allows them to appeal their cases in the federal courts. In some instances, federal law even provides financial rewards for whistle blowers.

Formal Organization

While even experts can't agree on the exact number of separate agencies that make up the bureaucracy,[11] there are probably more than 400. A distinctive feature of the bureaucracy is its division into areas of specialization: One agency handles occupational safety, for example, another specializes in education, another in foreign affairs, another in employment discrimination, another in the environment, and so on. Because each concentrates on a particular issue area, no two agencies are identical, but they do fall into four general types: (1) departments, (2) government corporations, (3) independent agencies, and (4) regulatory commissions.

Departments. As depicted in Figure 8-4, the largest units of the federal bureaucracy are the fourteen executive branch departments headed by Cabinet members called secretaries (except the Justice Department, which is headed by the Attorney General). The secretaries are responsible for establishing their department's general policy and overseeing its operations. As discussed in Chapter 7, Cabinet secretaries are directly responsible to the president, although they are often viewed as having two masters—the

---

[11] On the difficulty of counting the exact number of government agencies, see David Nachmias and David H. Rosenbloom, *Bureaucratic Government: U.S.A.* (New York: St. Martin's Press, 1980).

322 ❖ Chapter 8 The Bureaucracy

FIGURE 8-4
Departments of the Executive Branch

Source: *United States Government Manual 1990–91* (Washington: Government Printing Office).

president and those affected by their department. Cabinet secretaries are also tied to Congress, from which they get their appropriations and discretion to implement legislation and make rules.

Although departments vary considerably in size, prestige, and power, they share certain features. Each department covers a broad area of responsibility generally reflected by its name. Each secretary is assisted by a deputy or undersecretary to take part of the administrative burden off the secretary's shoulders, as well as by several assistant secretaries, who direct major programs within the department. In addition, each secretary, like the president, has numerous assistants who help with planning, budgeting, personnel, legal services, public relations, and other key staff functions. All departments are subdivided into smaller agencies, bureaus, offices, and services, and it is at this level that the real work of each agency is done. Most departments are subdivided along function lines, but the basis for division may be geography, work processes (for example, the Economic Research Service in the Department of Agriculture), or clientele (such as the Bureau of Indian Affairs in the Department of Interior).

In addition to national offices in Washington, D.C., or its immediate suburbs, each executive department has regional offices to serve all parts of the United States. The Department of Health and Human Services (HHS) follows a typical departmental organization (see Figure 8-5). The Secretary of HHS presides over a variety of smaller agencies, centers, and programs. The Centers for Disease Control and Prevention, a division of the Public Health Service that has played an important role in conducting research on the AIDS virus, is under her jurisdiction. So, too, are programs that provide assistance to poor pregnant women, and the Social Security Administration, a major bureaucracy in its own right. In mid-1991, HHS was reorganized to consolidate its many programs and divisions that deal with families and children. The new Administration for Children and Families in one agency combines Head Start (which provides preschool education to poor children); job opportunities and basic skills programs; Aid to Families with Dependent Children; child-support enforcement; Adoption Assistance; foster care; anti-child abuse programs; and two block grant programs. This new division alone has an annual budget of more than $25 billion and a staff of more than 2,000.

FIGURE 8-5

Organization of the Department of Health and Human Services

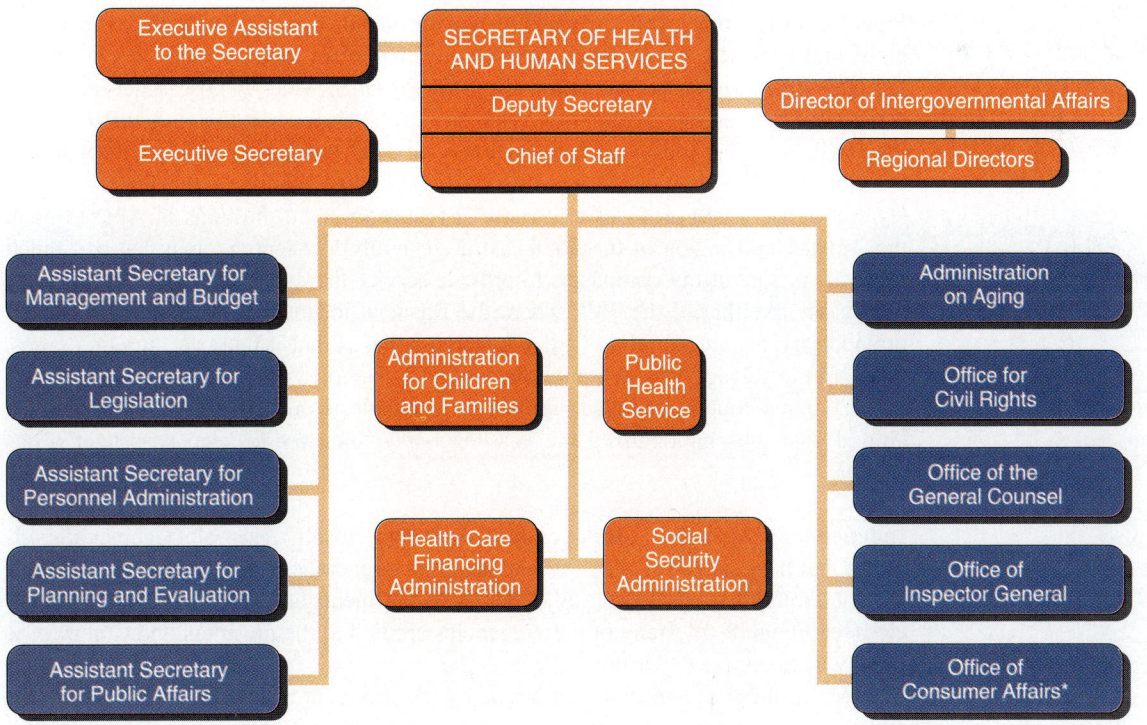

*Located administratively in HHS, but reports to the president

Some departments are directed by law to foster and promote the interests of a given clientele—that is, a specific segment or group in the U.S. population. Such departments are called **clientele agencies**. Some of the best known are listed below:

- Department of Agriculture
- Department of Commerce
- Department of Education
- Department of Energy
- Department of the Interior
- Department of Labor
- Department of Veterans Affairs

Because many of these agencies were created at the urgings of well organized interests to advance their particular objectives, it is not surprising that clientele groups are powerful lobbies with their respective agencies in Washington. The clientele agencies and groups are also active at the regional level, where the agencies devote a substantial part of their resources to program implementation. One of the most obvious examples of regional "outreach" is the Extension Service of the Department of Agriculture. Agricultural extension agents are scattered throughout the farm belt and routinely work with farmers on farm productivity and other problems. Career bureaucrats in the Agriculture Department know that farm interests will be dependable allies year in and year out. Congress and/or the president are not nearly so reliable because they must balance the interests of farmers with those of other segments of society.

Government Corporations. **Government corporations** are businesses set up and created by Congress to perform functions that could be provided by private businesses. Figure 8-6 lists some of the better-known government corporations. Unlike other governmental agencies, government corporations charge for their services. For example, the largest government corporation, the U.S. Postal Service—whose functions could be handled by a private corporation, such as Federal Express or the United Parcel Service (UPS)—exists today to ensure delivery of mail throughout the United States at cheaper rates than those a private business might charge. Similarly, the Tennessee Valley Authority (TVA) provides electricity at reduced rates to millions of Americans in the Appalachian region of the Southeast, a generally low-income area that had failed to attract private utility companies to provide service there.

In cases like that of the TVA where the financial incentives for private industry to provide services are minimal, Congress often believes that it must act. In other cases, it steps in to salvage valuable public assets. For example, when passenger rail service in the United States no longer remained profitable, Congress stepped in to create Amtrak and thus nationalized the passenger-train industry to keep passenger trains running.

Independent Agencies. **Independent agencies** closely resemble Cabinet departments, but have narrower areas of responsibility. Generally speaking, all agencies that are not corporations or do not fall under the departments are called independent agencies (see Figure 8-6). Many of these agencies are tied to the president and Congress as closely as executive departments.

Heads of these agencies are appointed by the president and serve, like Cabinet secretaries, at his pleasure. Among the largest independent agencies are:

FIGURE 8-6

Corporations, Independent Agencies, and Regulatory Commissions

Some Government Corporations

Amtrak
Export-Import Bank
Federal Deposit Insurance Corporation
Government National Mortgage Association
Resolution Trust Corporation
Pennsylvania Avenue Development Corporation
Pension Benefit Guaranty Corporation
U.S. Postal Service
Tennessee Valley Authority

Some Independent Agencies

ACTION
Central Intelligence Agency
Federal Emergency Management Agency
General Services Administration
National Aeronautics and Space Administration
National Archives and Records Administration
Peace Corps
Selective Service System
Small Business Administration
U.S. Information Agency

Some Regulatory Agencies or Commissions

Consumer Product Safety Commission
Commodity Futures Trading Commission
Equal Employment Opportunity Commission
Federal Communications Commission
Federal Election Commission
Federal Housing Finance Board
Federal Trade Commission
Interstate Commerce Commission
National Labor Relations Board
Nuclear Regulatory Commission
Securities and Exchange Commission

- The General Services Administration, which functions as the landlord of the federal government and oversees buildings, supplies, purchasing, and rents.
- The National Science Foundation, which supports academic and scientific research.
- The Central Intelligence Agency, which coordinates intelligence activities at different levels of government as a means of strengthening national security.

Independent agencies most frequently exist apart from executive departments for practical or symbolic reasons. The National Aeronautics and Space Administration (NASA), for example, could have been placed within the Department of Defense. That kind of placement, however, could have conjured up thoughts of a space program dedicated solely to military purposes, rather than for civilian satellite communication or scientific exploration.

Regulatory Boards or Commissions. Another type of independent agency is the independent regulatory board or commission, such as the National Labor Relations Board, the Federal Reserve Board, and the Securities and Exchange Commission (SEC) (see Figure 8-6).[12] Congress started setting up regulatory commissions as early as 1887, recognizing the need for close and continuous guardianship of particular economic activities. Once the Supreme Court decided to allow Congress to begin regulating aspects of the economy, the number of independent regulatory agencies—now over sixty—grew. Older boards and commissions, such as the Interstate Commerce Commission (ICC), the Securities and Exchange Commission, and the Federal Reserve Board, are generally charged with overseeing a certain industry. Regulatory agencies created since the 1960s are more concerned with how the business sector relates to public health and safety. The Occupational Safety and Health Administration (OSHA), for example, promotes job safety, and the Environmental Protection Agency (EPA) regulates industrial pollution. (In 1994, the Senate voted to elevate the EPA to Cabinet-level status, but action was stalled in the House.)

Most of the older independent agencies were specifically created to be relatively free from immediate (partisan) political pressure. They are headed by a board composed of several members (always an odd number to avoid ties) who are selected by the president and confirmed by Congress. (Commissioners are appointed for fixed, staggered terms to increase the chances of a bipartisan board.) Unlike executive department heads, they cannot be easily removed by the president. In 1935, the U.S. Supreme Court ruled that in creating independent commissions, the Congress had intended that they be independent panels of experts as far removed as possible from immediate political pressures.[13]

Newer regulatory boards lack this kind of autonomy and freedom from political pressures; they are generally headed by a single administrator who can be removed by the president. These boards and commissions, such as the EEOC, are therefore far more susceptible to political pressure and political wishes.

Presidential appointments have a clear impact on these commissions. When Jimmy Carter was president, he appointed Michael Pertschuk, a public-interest law activist, to head the Federal Trade Commission (FTC), which became a staunchly pro-consumer organization. President Reagan's choice to replace Pertschuk was economist James Miller III, who was known for his anti-regulationist, free market beliefs. Miller's appointment gave Reagan supporters a majority on the five-member commission. Under Miller's leadership, the FTC abandoned its practice of policing the industry for false advertising, and instead adopted a policy of undertaking investigations only in response to specific complaints filed with the Commission. American business generally hailed Miller's actions, but consumer activists were outraged because the change in

---

[12] The classic work on regulatory commissions is Marver Bernstein, *Regulating Business by Independent Commission* (Princeton, NJ: Princeton University Press, 1955).

[13] *Humphrey's Executor* v. *U.S.*, 295 U.S. 602 (1935).

policy meant that the FTC would be less aggressive. In this case, a change in presidents clearly led to a change in policy. Bill Clinton opted not to replace FTC head Janet Steiger, a Republican holdover on the Commission, in spite of urgings from consumer advocacy groups who had hoped that under the new administration the FTC's mission would be redirected toward greater concern with consumer issues.

Policy Making

When Congress creates any kind of department, agency, or commission, it is actually delegating some of its powers listed in Article I, Section 8, of the U.S. Constitution. Therefore, the laws creating agencies carefully describe their purpose and give them the authority to make numerous policy decisions, which have the effect of law. Congress recognizes that it does not have the time, expertise, or ability to involve itself in every detail of every program; therefore, it sets general guidelines for agency action and leaves it to the agency to work out the details. How agencies execute congressional wishes is called **implementation**, the process by which a law or policy is put into operation (see Chapter 16). Essentially, bureaucrats make as well as implement policy. They take the laws and policies made by Congress, the president, and the courts, and develop rules and procedures for making sure they are carried out. Most implementation involves what is called **administrative discretion**, the ability to make choices concerning the best way to implement congressional intentions. If Congress does not like an agency's actions, it can pass laws that invalidate specific rules or procedures. Members of Congress, however, are not always able to agree on how policies are to be implemented. More often than not, then, when Congress is unable to decide upon clear-cut guidelines, it passes the political hot potato to an agency for resolution.

A good example of how Congress often passes the buck is the Occupational Safety and Health Act of 1970. It provided only a rough expression of the desired end results of ensuring a safe and healthy workplace for every man and woman in the nation. The legislation, however, was silent on how two competing interests were to be balanced: the rights of workers injured, killed, or exposed to hazards on the job and the interests of employers who, in order to minimize risks, would have to expend large sums of money to comply with OSHA mandates. Congress left it to the Occupational Safety and Health Administration (OSHA) to determine how to implement the Act.

The same problem apparently occurred with passage of the Clean Air Act Amendments of 1990. After much political wrangling, the Amendments were sent to the Environmental Protection Agency to be used in drafting regulations for a law that, according to one representative of the utility industry, contained all sorts of "discontinuities and contradictions."[14]

Policy making takes place on informal and formal levels. Practically, many decisions are left to individual government employees on a day-to-day basis. Justice Department lawyers, for example, make daily decisions about whether or not to prosecute someone. Similarly, Internal Revenue Service agents make many decisions during personal audits. Other forms of bureaucratic policy making are more formal.

---

[14] Stacey Evers, "Politics Pollute Clean Air Act" (States News Service), December 22, 1991.

Rule Making

Administrative discretion is also exercised through two formal administrative procedures: rule making and adjudication. **Rule making** is the administrative process that results in regulations. **Regulations** are the rules that govern the operation of all government programs and have the force of law. In essence, then, bureaucratic rule makers often act as lawmakers as well as law enforcers when they make rules or draft regulations to implement various congressional statutes. Thus, rule making is called a quasi-legislative process.

As we discuss both rule making and administrative adjudication below, it is important to remember that a great deal of bureaucratic policy making occurs through informal channels, rather than through these formal processes. How bureaucrats interpret or apply (or choose not to apply) various policies are equally important parts of the policy-making process. Thus, what is sometimes called administrative discretion allows decision makers (whether they are in a Cabinet-level position or at the lowest GS levels) a tremendous amount of leeway.

In the case of OSHA, for example, although all the various groups and legislators that pressed for its passage agreed that industrial hazards (such as breathing asbestos-filled air) were potentially more harmful to a worker's health than were safety hazards (such as dangerously heavy machinery), OSHA chose first to address safety rather than health concerns. Not surprisingly, regulation writers found it easier to address safety concerns—they are easier to describe, assess, and control. If a worker falls from a platform, for example, the cause is clear—no railing or restraint system. Moreover, the results—a broken arm, leg, or neck (or all three)—are easier to quantify than the lingering effects of some chemicals and their possible long-term relationship to cancer.

But regulation writers got carried away in an effort to bring about quick compliance with the Act. The first set of regulations took up nearly 250 pages in the *Federal Register*, a daily publication of the federal government that contains all proposed and final regulations of all federal agencies (see Figure 8-7). Some regulations were intricately detailed, such as ones requiring toilets to have hinged, open-front seats.[15]

Because regulations often involve political conflict, the 1946 Administrative Procedure Act established rule-making procedures to give everyone the chance to participate in the process. The Act requires that (1) public notice of the time, place, and nature of the rule-making proceedings be provided in the *Federal Register*, (2) interested parties be given the opportunity to submit written arguments and facts relevant to the rule, and (3) the statutory purpose and basis of the rule be stated. Once rules have been written, thirty days must elapse before they take effect.

Sometimes an agency is required by law to conduct a formal hearing before issuing rules. Evidence is gathered, and witnesses testify and are cross-examined by opposing interests. The process can take weeks, months, or even years, at the end of which agency administrators must review the entire record and then justify the rules. Although cumbersome, the process has reduced criticism of the rules and bolstered the deference given by the courts to agency decisions.

---

[15] Dennis J. Palumbo, *Public Policy in America* (New York: Harcourt Brace Jovanovich, 1988), p. 196.

Policy Making ❖ 329

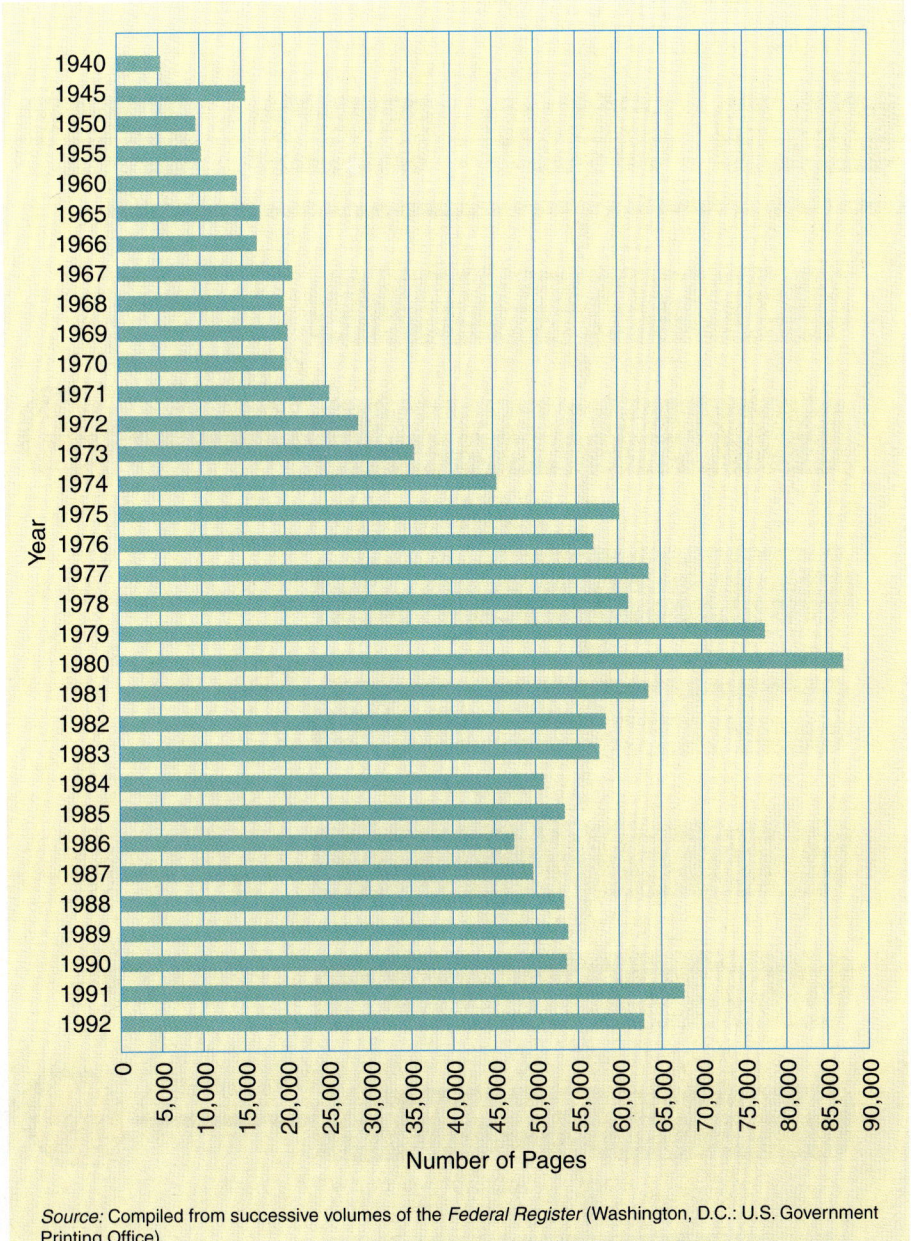

FIGURE 8-7

Number of Pages in the Federal Register, 1940–1992

Source: Compiled from successive volumes of the *Federal Register* (Washington, D.C.: U.S. Government Printing Office).

Even when groups have had the opportunity to testify, they may be unhappy about the outcome of regulations. In spite of the drafting process depicted in Figure 8-8, critics of OSHA complained that its regulations were ridiculous and not cost-effective. After the rules had been in effect for only a year, members of Congress were besieged with complaints prompting efforts to amend and even repeal the Act. Even President

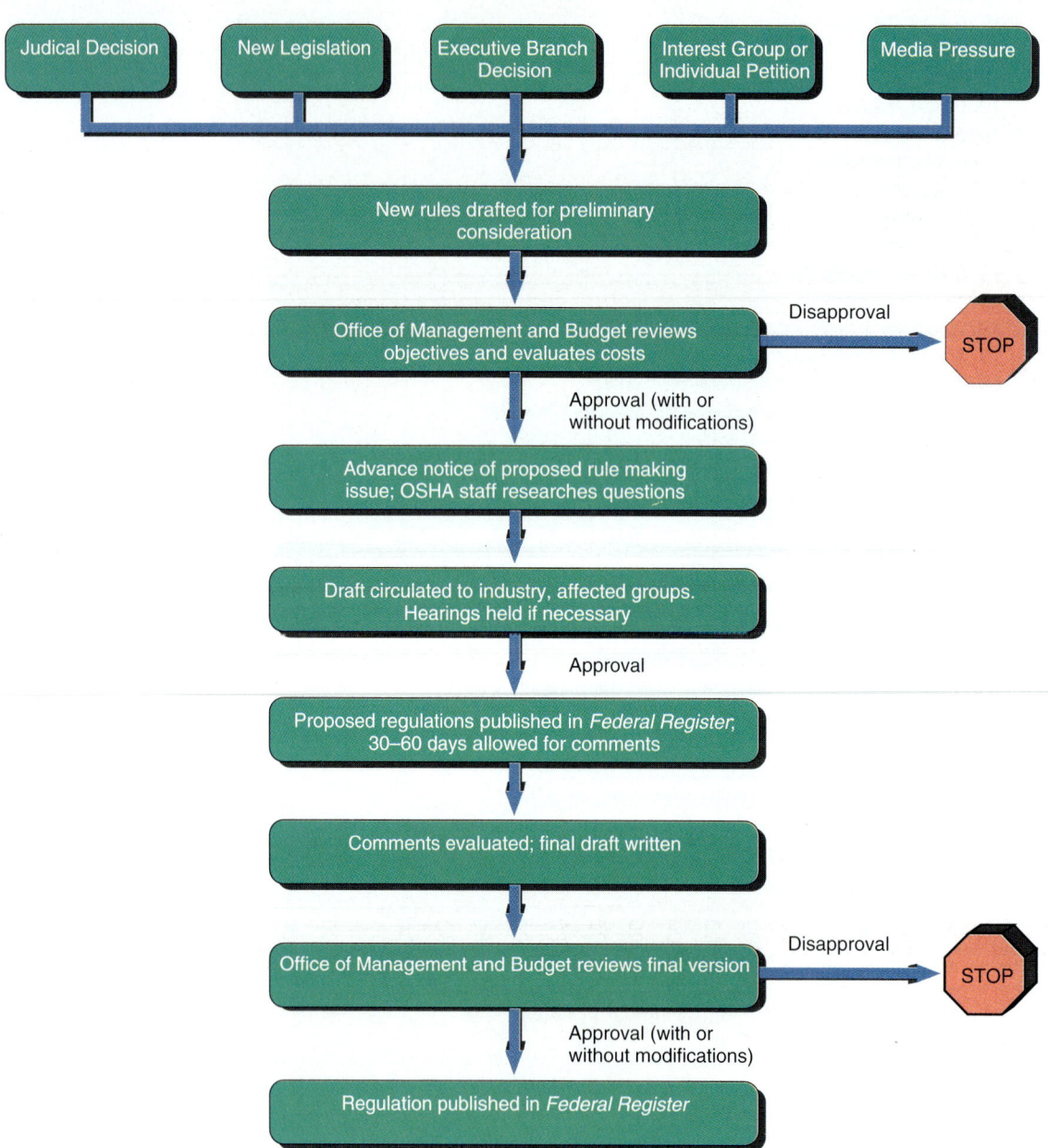

FIGURE 8-8
How a Regulation Is Made: The Case of OSHA

Gerald Ford spoke out against the "overzealous" and "nitpicking" regulations being issued by OSHA.[16] By 1977, OSHA had revoked 1,100 of its safety regulations.

Similar problems have occurred more recently in the case of the EPA and the Clean Air Act Amendments. The process was complicated by the White House's industry-

---

[16] James Q. Wilson, *Bureaucracy: What Government Agencies Do and Why They Do It* (New York: Basic Books, 1989), p. 198.

Every year, thousands upon thousands of pages of regulations are created, modified, replaced by still more of the same, and published in the *Federal Register.*

oriented Council on Competitiveness. Headed by Vice President Dan Quayle, the Council forcibly weakened more than 100 EPA rules. The president, as head of the executive branch, made the Council responsible for reviewing all new federal regulations that could place undue burdens on industry. Thus, the Council directed the EPA in ways that Congress specifically had rejected, a move that drew the ire of members of the House Health and Environment Subcommittee. According to its chair, Representative Henry Waxman (D.-Cal.), by November 15, 1991 (one year after passage of the Act), the EPA had failed to take any of the sixteen important actions required by statute. The subcommittee was particularly chagrined by Vice President Quayle's refusal to answer questions about the Council and its role in the rule-making process.[17] Environmental interest groups charged that the Bush administration was trying to "gain through regulation what it lost in legislation."[18] Bill Clinton abolished the Council soon after he took office.

Administrative Adjudication

Administrative adjudication is a quasi-judicial process in which a bureaucratic agency settles disputes between two parties in a manner similar to the way courts resolve disputes. Administrative adjudication, like rule making, is referred to as "quasi" (meaning "almost") judicial, because law making by any body other than Congress, or

---

[17] Federal News Service, Hearing of the Health and Environment Subcommittee, November 14, 1991, NEXIS.
[18] Ibid.

A worker from the Environmental Protection Agency disposing of toxic waste.

adjudication by any body other than the judiciary would be a violation of the constitutional principle of separation of powers.

Agencies regularly find that persons or businesses are not in compliance with the federal laws the agencies are charged with enforcing, or that they are in violation of an agency rule or regulation. To force compliance, some agencies resort to administrative adjudication, which is generally less formal than a trial. Several agencies and boards employ administrative law judges to conduct the hearings. Although these judges are employed by the agency, they are strictly independent and cannot be removed except for gross misconduct. OSHA, for example, is charged with trying to settle disputes between employers and employees who allege violations of the Act. It also fines employers for infractions of its safety regulations; in 1991 it levied $180 million in fines and through closer oversight hopes to raise that amount to $1.5 billion by 1995. In virtually every case adjudicated by an agency, appeals to the federal courts are guaranteed by statute, although most federal judges give great weight to the expertise of the agencies and regularly defer to their judgements.

OSHA is also empowered to refer cases to the Department of Justice for possible criminal prosecution if employers willfully violate OSHA standards and the death of an employee results. Some lawmakers have not been happy with its enforcement efforts. The Clinton administration, for example, was criticized in late 1993 for its and OSHA's slow pace and lack of attention to safety and health issues.

Making Agencies Accountable

The question of to whom bureaucrats should be responsible is one that continually comes up in any debate about governmental accountability. Should the bureaucracy be answerable to itself? to organized interest groups? to its clientele? to the president? to Congress? or to some combination of all of these? While many would argue that bureaucrats should be responsive to the public interest, the public interest is difficult to define. As it turns out, several factors work to control the power of the bureaucracy and, to some degree, the same kinds of checks and balances that operate among the three branches of government serve to check the bureaucracy (see the box on p. 334).

Many argue that the president should be in charge of the bureaucracy because it is up to him to see that popular ideas and expectations are translated into administrative action. But under our constitutional system, the president is not the only actor in the policy process. Congress creates the agencies, funds them, and establishes the broad rules of their operation. Moreover, Congress continually reviews the various agencies through oversight committee investigations, hearings, and its power of the purse.

The question of bureaucratic accountability is even more acute in Britain. The oversight function provided by Parliament, though improved in the 1980s, has generally been inadequate. Because political appointees constitute no more than the top two or three layers of Britain's bureaucracy, the vast majority of civil servants are shielded from national election results and therefore, some would argue, from executive control. The perception is of a small set of relatively inexperienced ministers set against a large, permanent, expert civil service. It is no wonder, critics argue, that elections produce so little change in Britain's governmental policies. Although often exaggerated, these concerns have sparked numerous attempts to reform the British civil service.

> ## Making Agencies Accountable
>
> The president has the authority to:
>
> - Appoint and remove agency heads and a few additional top bureaucrats.
> - Reorganize the bureaucracy (with congressional approval).
> - Make changes in an agency's annual budget proposals.
> - Ignore legislative initiatives originating within the bureaucracy.
> - Initiate or adjust policies that would, if enacted by Congress, alter the bureaucracy's activities.
> - Issue executive orders.
>
> Congress has the authority to:
>
> - Reduce an agency's annual budget.
> - Pass legislation that alters the bureaucracy's activities.
> - Abolish existing programs.
> - Investigate bureaucratic activities and force bureaucrats to testify about them.
> - Influence presidential appointments of agency heads and other top bureaucratic officials.
> - Write legislation to limit the bureaucracy's discretion.
>
> The courts have the authority to:
>
> - Rule on whether bureaucrats have acted within the law and require policy changes to comply with the law.
> - Force the bureaucracy to respect the rights of individuals through hearings and other proceedings.

Executive Control

As the size and scope of the American national government in general, and of the executive branch and the bureaucracy in particular, have grown, presidents have delegated more and more power to bureaucrats. Recognizing this, each chief executive tries to appoint the best possible persons to carry out his wishes and policy preferences. Presidents may make thousands of appointments to the executive branch; in doing so, they have the opportunity to appoint individuals who share their views on a range of policies. And although presidential appointments make up less than 1 percent of all federal jobs, presidents usually fill most top policy-making positions.

While some spots go to party loyalists, campaign workers, or close friends, others go to "experts," although generally carefully screened ones who share the president's basic approach to government and political beliefs. President Reagan, in particular, looked for agency heads who shared his political philosophies. He appointed James Watt, the former head of a conservative public-interest law firm (the Mountain States Legal Foundation), to head the Department of the Interior. While at the Mountain States Legal Foundation, Watt had headed a successful litigation program that had challenged many key public-lands regulatory programs run by the Department of the Interior.[19]

---

[19] Karen O'Connor and Lee Epstein, "Rebalancing the Scales of Justice," *Harvard Journal of Law and Public Policy* (Fall 1984): 483–506.

Health Care Reform: A Bureaucracy within a Bureaucracy?

For anyone with a horror of big government, President Clinton's health care reform plan could be a nightmare.

Clinton's Health Security Act calls for creating a powerful national health board that would set the rules by which the new system plays; for the creation of dozens of new committees and the unlimited hiring of staff to help the board do its work; and for at least $9.6 billion in start-up costs.

Once the board is in place, it will decide—among other things—how many fledgling doctors will be allowed to become specialists; what experimental treatments will be covered; whether the care you receive is any good.

"It's unbelievable, the power it's conferred with. It's like the Supreme Court of health care," said Ed Gillespie, policy and communications director for the House Republican Conference.

Besides the national board, each state will be asked to start its own set of advisory boards and regional alliances (which sell health plans to consumers).

"I see a structure long on government bureaucracy and short on the ability to maneuver," said Rep. Cliff Stearns (R.-Fla.) at a recent House subcommittee hearing. "It sounds to me like the ones doing all the choosing are the new bureaucracies created under this plan."

Administration officials say the heavy government involvement is necessary at the beginning to make sure that market forces do the job right in the long run. In no way is their system run by the government, they say.

"What it is, is a system in which the government sets the rules," says Judith Feder, one of the president's top health advisors. "When you do that, it takes a significant amount of pages (of legislation).

But once the rules are in place, the government gets out of the way."

Republicans and other critics doubt that.

The national health board also had the power to hire all the staff it needs, and to contract out any work it wants. Yet the government historically has a poor track record in controlling the costs of contractors.

Case in point: The Department of Energy, which relies heavily on contractors to clean up its contaminated nuclear weapons plants. A federal audit last years found that DOE cleanup costs had been inflated by hundreds of millions because of overestimates by contractors.

But both the president and First Lady Hillary Rodham Clinton regularly discount complaints that the new system is too complicated, bureaucratic, intrusive.

"I ask that it be compared against what we have now, because none of us could devise a system more complex, more burdensome, more administratively costly than the one we have now," Clinton said in sending Congress his plan last month.

Feder said that the states would regulate the alliances and health plans, but questions of authority still trouble the National Governors' Association, which largely supports the Clinton Plan.

"Within the text of the legislation, there seems to be a fair amount of regulatory authority and regulation," said Carl Volpe, director of health policy and legislation for the NGA. "We're concerned about the ambiguity of authority."

Source: Elizabeth Neus, "Analysis: Health Care Reform Would Create New Bureaucracy," Gannett News Service, November 6, 1993. Copyright 1993, *USA Today.* Reprinted with permission.

Many presidents have expressed dismay over their inability to oversee the day-to-day workings of the bureaucracy. John F. Kennedy claimed that to give anyone at the State Department an instruction was comparable to putting it in a dead-letter box.[20] George Bush faced similar problems. In December 1990, for example, the Assistant Secretary for Civil Rights in the Department of Education announced that it was illegal

---

[20] Arthur Schlesinger, Jr., *A Thousand Days* (Greenwich, CT: Fawcett Books, 1967), p. 377.

> ## Whom to Call?
>
> As part of the Clinton administration's efforts to assert executive control of "waste, fraud, and abuse," Vice President Al Gore Jr. was put in charge of a program to make government "less expensive and more efficient." In announcing the program, the President released toll-free telephone numbers for twenty-one federal agencies, and invited all Americans to call them with complaints, or to write to him or the vice president at 1600 Pennsylvania Avenue, Washington, D.C. 20006.
>
> Here are the numbers:
>
> - Commerce
>   1-800-424-5197
> - Commission on Civil Rights
>   1-800-552-6843
> - Defense
>   1-800-424-9098
> - Education
>   1-800-647-8733
> - Energy
>   1-800-541-1625
> - Environmental Protection Agency
>   1-800-424-4000
> - Health and Human Services
>   1-800-368-5779
> - Housing and Urban Development
>   1-800-347-3735
> - Justice
>   1-800-869-4499
> - Labor
>   1-800-347-3756
> - Nuclear Regulatory Commission
>   1-800-233-3497
> - Treasury
>   1-800-359-3898
> - Veterans Affairs
>   1-800-488-8244

for colleges and universities supported by federal monies to give scholarships designated solely for minority students. Although the White House strongly opposed quotas, the ruling deeply embarrassed Bush, who learned of it only after it was reported in the press. Still smarting from the wide criticisms he received over his vetoing of a civil rights bill, Bush ordered his aides to come up with a way to reverse the policy.[21]

Presidents can issue **executive orders** to provide direction to bureaucrats. Executive orders are presidential directives to an agency that provide the basis for carrying out laws or for establishing new policies. Even before Congress acted to protect women from discrimination by the federal government, for example, the National Organization for Women convinced President Lyndon B. Johnson to sign Executive Order 11375 in 1967. This amended an earlier order prohibiting the federal government from discriminating on the basis of race, color, religion, or national origin in the awarding of federal contracts, by adding to it the category of "gender." Nevertheless, although the president signed the Order, the Office of Federal Contract Compliance, the executive agency charged with implementing the Order, failed to draft appropriate guidelines for implementation of the Order until several years later.[22] A president can direct an agency to act, but it may take some time for his orders to be carried out. Given the

---

[21] Andrew Rosenthal, "White House Retreats on Ruling That Curbs Minority Scholarships," *The New York Times* (December 18, 1990): A1.

[22] Irene Murphy, *Public Policy on the Status of Women* (Lexington, MA: Lexington Books, 1974).

many "jobs" of any president, few can ensure that all their orders will be carried out, or, as was the case with minority scholarships, that they will like all the rules that are made.

Historically, presidents have tried to control the bureaucracy by reorganizing it, but in general these efforts have not been particularly successful.[23] All recent presidents have tried to streamline the bureaucracy, a persistent goal of government reform, to make it more accountable. President Nixon, for example, proposed a plan to combine fifty domestic agencies and seven different departments into four large "super departments." This proposal would have given Nixon tighter control of domestic programs, but it was fought tooth and nail by the agencies to be consolidated and their clientele groups. It was also opposed by several members of Congress. They feared that centralization would reduce their power as the Congressional committee structure would have to be changed to better monitor the proposed new agencies. In the end, with the exception of the creation of the Office of Management and Budget to replace the old Bureau of the Budget and the establishment of the Domestic Council within the Executive Office of the President, none of Nixon's plan got through Congress. (President Clinton's reform package is discussed in the "Toward Reform" section at the end of the chapter.)

Because sweeping changes are seldom adopted, most presidents try only to tinker with the bureaucracy. Minor changes, however, don't appear to be of much real consequence, and the same problems of control generally reemerge elsewhere.[24] According to political scientists Benjamin I. Page and Mark P. Petracca, "In any case, reorganization is only an ultimate weapon—of last resort—in a continuing widespread struggle between presidents and the bureaucracy."[25]

Congressional Control

Congress, too, plays an important role in checking the power of the bureaucracy. Congress exercises considerable oversight over the bureaucracy in three main areas: its investigatory powers, its "powers of the purse," and its law-making power.

1. Investigatory powers. It is not at all unusual for a congressional committee or subcommittee to hold hearings on a particular problem, and then to direct the relevant agency to study the problem or find ways to remedy it. Representatives of the agencies also appear before these committees on a regular basis to inform members about agency activities, ongoing investigations, and so on.

2. Power of the purse. To control the bureaucracy, Congress dangles its ability to fund or not fund an agency's activities like the sword of Damocles over the heads of various agency officials.[26] The House Appropriations Committee routinely holds hear-

In 1993 President Clinton made history when he appointed Dade County, Florida, prosecutor Janet Reno as the first female U.S. Attorney General.

[23] Peter Woll, *American Bureaucracy*, 2nd ed. (New York: Norton, 1977), p. 244.
[24] James G. March and Johan P. Olson, "Organizing Political Life: What Administrative Reorganization Tells Us About Government," *American Political Science Review* 77 (June 1983): 281–296.
[25] Benjamin I. Page and Mark P. Petracca, *The American Presidency* (New York: McGraw-Hill, 1983), p. 224.
[26] According to Greek legend, Damocles was a courtier and constant flatterer of Dionysus, King of Syracuse. Damocles coveted the happiness and glory of kings until Dionysus gave a banquet in his honor. Damocles enjoyed the banquet immensely until he looked up and saw a sword over his head, hung by a single thread. The sword was meant to teach him of the constant danger faced by the kings he so envied.

Adding Agencies: The Politics of Accountability

Presidents have generally been much more successful in creating new agencies, generally under the guise of making the bureaucracy more efficient and accountable. In 1965, for example, Lyndon B. Johnson convinced Congress that the nation's decaying cities needed federal help. The result was the creation of the Department of Housing and Urban Development, whose function was to implement Johnson's ideas for urban development and renewal. Similarly, Jimmy Carter, reacting to the energy crisis, asked Congress to establish a Department of Energy to plan conservation policies for industry and private citizens. Presidents of late have called for the creation of new agencies stressing words like *development* to make new agencies politically palatable and economically justifiable. In the case of HUD, for example, the new agency was not called the Department of Urban Problems. "Developers" are one of the largest lobbies in Washington. Their support and the way the new department was packaged made its creation easier.

This tendency to create new agencies has increased the president's ability to control and coordinate bureaucratic functions. And, although George Bush called for elevation of the Environmental Protection Agency (EPA) to Cabinet-level department status as did Bill Clinton, action on his proposal remained stalled in Congress through 1994.

---

ings to allow agency heads to justify their budget requests. Authorization legislation originates in the various legislative committees that oversee particular agencies (such as Agriculture, Veterans Affairs, Education, and Labor) and sets the maximum amounts that agencies can spend on particular programs. While some authorizations, such as Social Security, are permanent, others, including the State Department and Defense Department procurements, are watched closely and are subject to annual authorizations.

Once funds are authorized, they must be appropriated before they can be spent. Appropriations originate with the House Appropriations Committee, not the specialized legislative committees. Often, the Appropriations Committee allocates sums smaller than those authorized by the legislative committee. Thus, the Appropriations Committee, a budget cutter, has an additional oversight function.

3. Law Making. Congress can also pass new legislation to clarify policies or overturn regulations or rules. If Congress, for example, does not approve of agency regulations written to enforce existing statutes, it can redraft legislation to make its wishes clearer.

Congress's oversight of the bureaucracy is difficult, has few political rewards unless the problems addressed are of interest to a member's district or otherwise worthy of publicity, and requires professional accounting expertise. Recognizing that the bureaucracy's financial affairs were big and important enough to be professionally handled, in 1921 Congress created the General Accounting Office (GAO; see p. 246) at the same time that the Office of the Budget was created in the executive branch. And with the establishment of the GAO, the Congressional Research Service, and later, the Congressional Budget Office, Congress essentially created its own bureaucracy to keep an eye on what the executive branch and its bureaucracy were doing.

Today the GAO not only tracks how money is spent in the bureaucracy, but also monitors how policies are implemented. The Congressional Budget Office also conducts oversight studies. If it or the GAO uncovers problems with an agency's work, Congress is notified immediately.

Judicial Control

The judiciary's oversight function is less direct than that of the other two branches of government. Although injured parties can bring suit against agencies for their failure to enforce the law, or even challenge agency interpretations of the law, in general the courts give great weight to the opinions of bureaucrats and usually defer to their expertise.

The courts have, however, ruled that agencies must give all affected individuals their due process rights guaranteed by the U.S. Constitution. A Social Security recipient's checks cannot be stopped, for example, unless that individual is provided with reasonable notice and an opportunity for a hearing.

Problems with the Modern Bureaucracy

As the modern bureaucracy has grown, so have its problems. Not only do the executive branch and Congress have difficulty in overseeing the actions of the numerous bureaus, agencies, and commissions, but often the right hand of any agency does not know what its left hand is doing. This confusion is complicated by the presence of interagency committees, which have been established to coordinate the implementation of various public policies that require interdepartmental cooperation. Other factors that contribute to problems with the bureaucracy include red tape, waste, conflict, and duplication.

Iron Triangles and Issue Networks

While Congress and the president continually criticize the bureaucracy and, indeed, often take steps to control it, the strong ties that agencies enjoy with interest groups on the one hand and congressional committees and subcommittees on the other help to explain the uphill battle to "control" the bureaucracy.

Iron Triangles. For many years, political scientists observed the relatively stable relationships and patterns of interaction that occur among an agency, interest groups, and congressional committees or subcommittees, and dubbed these relationships **iron triangles**, or subgovernments (see Figure 8-9).

Policy-making subgovernments are "iron" because they are virtually impenetrable to outsiders and are largely autonomous. Even presidents have difficulty piercing the workings of these subgovernments, which have endured over time. Examples of iron triangles abound. Senior citizens' groups (especially the American Association of Retired Persons), the Social Security Administration, and the House Subcommittee on Aging all are likely to agree on the need for increased Social Security benefits. Simi-

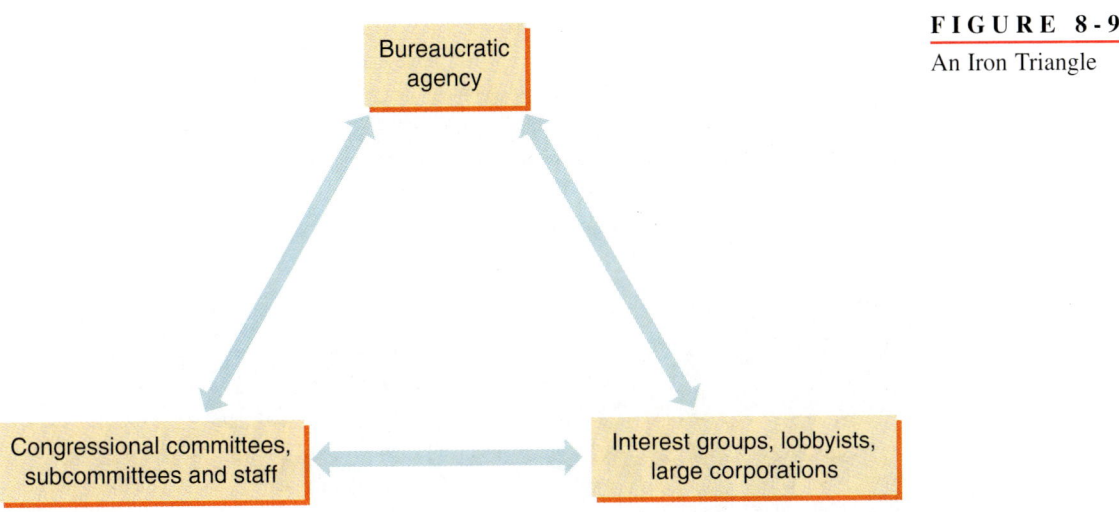

FIGURE 8-9

An Iron Triangle

larly, the Department of Veterans Affairs, the House Committee on Veterans Affairs, and the American Legion and Veterans of Foreign Wars—the two largest organizations representing veterans—are usually in agreement on the need for expanded programs for veterans.

The policy decisions made within these iron triangles often foster the interests of a clientele group and have little to do with the advancement of national policy goals. In part, subgovernmental decisions often conflict with other governmental policies and tend to tie the hands of larger institutions such as Congress and the president. The White House is often too busy dealing with international affairs or crises to deal with smaller issues like veterans' benefits. Likewise, Congress defers to its committees and subcommittees. Thus, these subgovernments decentralize policy making and make it more difficult to control.[27]

One precondition for an iron triangle is a strong legislature. In Britain, for example, where Parliament is quite weak, iron triangles are a rarity. The term "iron bars" more appropriately describes the situation in Britain where close relationships between interest groups and the bureaucracy have evolved in numerous policy areas.

Issue Networks. Today, iron triangles no longer dominate most policy processes for three main reasons: an increasingly complex society, issues that cut across several policy areas, and the phenomenal increase in number of Washington, D.C.-based interest groups. As these three changes have occurred, many iron triangles have become rusty, and new terms have been coined to describe the policy-making process and the bureaucracy's role in it. Hugh Heclo argues that this system of separate subgovernments is overlaid with an amorphous system of **issue networks**;[28] that is, the fuzzy set of relationships among a large number of actors in broad policy areas. In general, like iron triangles, issue networks are made up of agency officials, members of Congress (and

---

[27] For more on iron triangles, see Randall Ripley and Grace Franklin, *Congress, Bureaucracy and Public Policy*, 4th ed. (Homewood, IL: Dorsey Press, 1984).

[28] "Issue Networks and the Executive Establishment," in Anthony King, ed., *The New American Political System* (Washington, DC: American Enterprise Institute, 1978), pp. 87–124.

The Department of Veteran Affairs helps veterans' groups, such as the Veterans of Foreign Wars, work with the House and Senate Veterans Affairs Committees to lobby for increased funds for veterans' hospitals.

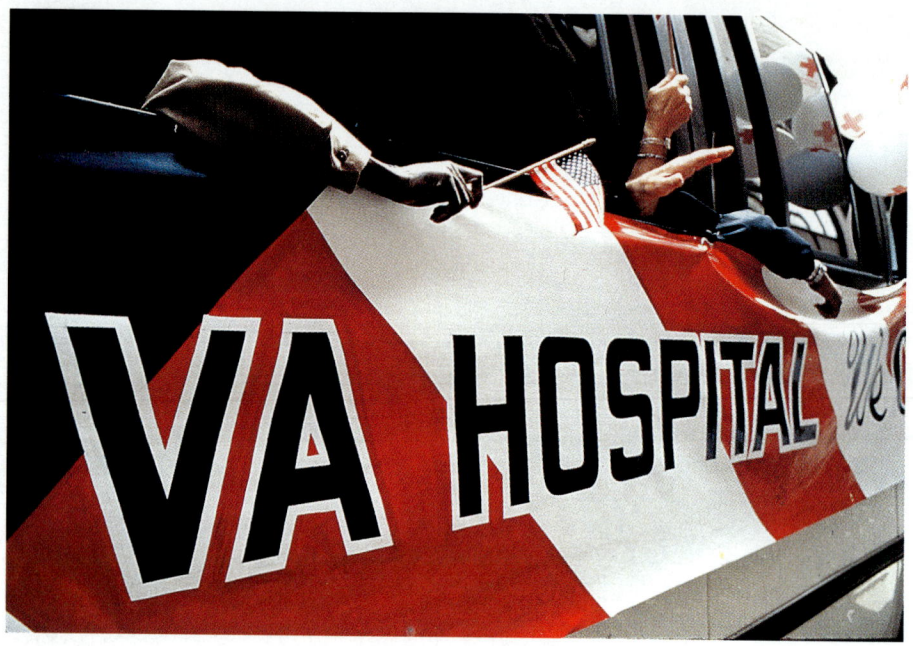

committee staffers), and interest-group lobbyists. But they also often include lawyers, consultants, academics, public relations specialists, and sometimes even the courts.[29] Unlike iron triangles, issue networks are constantly changing as members with technical expertise become involved in various issues.

Issue networks reflect the complexity of the issues that lawmakers and policy makers face. As an example, let's look at the plight of many American children. Lawmakers routinely call for new programs to make children's lives better, and the Clinton administration is sympathetic. First Lady Hillary Rodham Clinton, in fact, at one time chaired the board of the Children's Defense Fund, a national child advocacy group. But the plight of children isn't an easy problem to solve. All kinds of complex and interrelated issues are involved. It is, for example, a health issue, because many children don't have access to medical care; an education issue because many can't read, go to poor schools, or are dropouts; a labor issue because many have no job skills; and a drug and crime issue because many of these children live in drug-infested neighborhoods and often ultimately turn to crime, ending up in jail as a result. But given the segmented nature of policy making, how can the nation expect one coherent and encompassing policy to better the lives of American children from the Departments of Health and Human Services, Education, Labor, and Justice—*plus* all their associated House and Senate subcommittees, interest groups, and experts? And most of these agencies have to make do in the face of growing budget cutbacks.

Accountability

Accountability, that is, holding members of the bureaucracy responsible for how they implement laws and presidential directives, is one of the greatest issues in bureaucratic

---

[29] Martin Shapiro, "The Presidency and the Federal Courts," in Arnold Meltsner, ed. *Politics and the Oval Office*, (San Francisco: Institute for Contemporary Studies, 1981), Chapter 8.

politics. Because the way bureaucracies are designed affects the way they operate, most presidents have tried to change the structure and design of many agencies to make them function better and to facilitate oversight. This would make bureaucrats more accountable to both the president and Congress for their decisions. Making bureaucrats more accountable is problematic for two main reasons: the sheer size of the bureaucracy and shortcomings inherent in the bureaucratic system itself.

Size Problems. The bureaucracy's size has led to a system that encourages some bureaucrats to believe that they, and not elected officials, actually make laws and policy:

1. Red Tape. As rules and regulations established by the huge bureaucracy become increasingly complex, policy goals are often lost in a mass of red tape, complex rules, and procedures that must be followed before anything can get done. The paperwork and maze of regulations that one must get through, to obtain, say, Social Security disability benefits or veteran's benefits are so overwhelming that many people are discouraged from ever applying for what is rightfully theirs.

2. Waste. Duplication of services and faulty coordination are also problems in an ever-mushrooming bureaucracy. As discussed earlier, in 1991 the Department of Health and Human Services underwent a massive reorganization to streamline programs, because so many existed to deal with the problems faced by unmarried women with small children. Streamlining is the exception rather than the rule, however. It is far more likely to see a situation where programs abound not just in a single agency but in a variety of agencies, making duplication and even turf wars inevitable. Within the executive branch, for example, economic policy is split among the Office of Management and Budget, the Departments of Treasury and Commerce, the Council of Economic Advisors, and the Federal Reserve Board. Lack of coordination among these bodies helps explain the problems inherent in economic policy making described in Chapter 17. Interagency problems also affect performance when the right hand

President Clinton and Vice President Gore stand in front of a forklift loaded with tons of government regulations to dramatize their plan to cut and reshape government in an effort to trim over $100 billion from the national budget.

doesn't know what the left hand is doing. For example, during the botched siege and subsequent fire at the Branch Davidian compound in Waco, Texas that killed more than eighty cult members, Attorney General Janet Reno did not get involved until after the Bureau of Alcohol, Tobacco and Firearms—part of the Treasury Department—failed in its original mission to arrest cult leader David Koresh. But reports reveal that a local U.S. Attorney was involved in early stages of the case, drafting search warrants, etc. And once Reno became involved, some questioned whether she had less contact with the White House about Waco than other members of her staff.[30]

System Problems. While red tape and waste result from the size of the bureaucracy, other problems arise from the way the bureaucratic system is set up.

1. Inadequate Mechanisms for Evaluation. Often, the success of a program may be difficult to gauge, because there are no precise standards of evaluation. EPA air cleanup targets in the 1970s, for example, were not based on scientific analysis. And if information concerning success is not available or cannot be measured with any precision, it becomes difficult for policy makers to know what to do with the program. Should it be continued, changed, or eliminated?

One of the most interesting examples of the difficulty of measuring success can be seen in the Head Start program. One of the Great Society programs initiated by Congress and Lyndon B. Johnson in the 1960s, Head Start was designed to help some low-income and minority students do better in school. Head Start programs provided preschool enrichment classes for these youngsters on the theory that this "head start" would allow poorer children to compete in school on a more equal footing with those from more privileged backgrounds. Initially, the results were disappointing, when it appeared that children enrolled in Head Start did no better in school than those who

---

[30] "Siege Debriefing," *National Law Journal* (May 10, 1993): 23.

The Head Start program identifies deserving preschool children and provides much needed education, nutrition, and socializing.

did not participate in the program. In spite of these discouraging results, the program was continued, although critics were quick to point to early lack of results. Later, however, long-term studies of the effectiveness of the program revealed that the Head Start program did have a positive effect on later school performance.[31] And, perhaps just as important, the Head Start Program has always enjoyed a great deal of public approval. How could giving poor children a "head start" in school be a bad thing? In fact, it was one of the few domestic programs targeted for an increase in the budget proposed by President Clinton in 1994.

2. Decentralized Authority. The basic structure of a central agency in Washington, D.C. and regional offices makes coordination difficult, as does the structure of the federal system itself. While an agency in Washington, D.C., may have clear ideas concerning how a particular program should work, state and local officials may have very different ideas and different ways of implementing them.

3. Vague Objectives. Vague instructions are yet another problem that haunts bureaucrats. Congress often states only broad policy goals in its legislation and leaves the specifics of how to achieve these goals up to bureaucrats. In this way Congress cannot be blamed for any particularly unpopular interpretations.

One particularly controversial policy was at the heart of Title IX of the Education Amendments of 1972, which mandated that

> No person in the United States shall, on the basis of sex, be excluded from participation in, be denied the benefits of, or be subjected to discrimination under any education program or activity receiving federal financial assistance.

The law further instructed the Secretary of Health, Education, and Welfare (it now applies to the Secretary of Education) to "prepare and publish proposed regulations . . . which shall include with respect to intercollegiate athletic activities reasonable provisions considering the nature of particular sports" to implement the amendments. Supporters of women's athletics in colleges and universities went around and around with HEW officials over the intent of Congress. Supporters of women's sports argued that discrimination against women in all sports was prohibited. Others said that revenue-producing sports such as basketball and football were exempt.

Finally, in December, 1978—six years after passage of the amendments—the Office for Civil Rights in HEW released a "policy interpretation" of the law dealing largely with the section that concerned intercollegiate athletics.[32] More than thirty pages of text were devoted to dealing with 100 or so words from the statute. Football was recognized as unique, so it could be inferred that male-dominated football programs could continue to outspend women's athletic programs. The more than sixty women's groups that had lobbied for equality of spending were outraged, and turned their efforts toward seeking more favorable rulings on the construction of the statute from the courts.

We can probably expect similar litigation over the Clean Air Act. Vague directives from Congress often result in more confusion and make policy implementation extremely difficult.

Title IX guidelines have led to dramatic changes in most schools' athletic programs. Today, even middle schools and high schools maintain teams for players of both sexes, in stark contrast to earlier times.

---

[31] Fred M. Hechinger, "Blacks Found to Benefit from Preschooling," *The New York Times* (September 11, 1984): C4.

[32] See Joyce Gelb and Marian Lief Palley, *Women and Public Policies* (Princeton, NJ: Princeton University Press, 1982), Chapter 5.

4. **Insufficient Funding.** Congress often fails to fund some programs fully, making their success unlikely. Head Start and the Food Stamps program, for example, are never sufficiently funded to allow all who are eligible to receive the benefits of those programs. Domestic social welfare programs (see Chapter 16) are perennially the target of presidential and congressional budget cutters who seek political gains from attacking the "bloated bureaucracy" while seriously attempting to get the national deficit in check.

Toward Reform

Historically, politicians and presidents have called for reform of the bureaucracy. Thomas Jefferson was the first. He attempted to cut the waste and bring about a "wise and frugal government." But it wasn't until the Progressive Era (1890–1920) that calls for reform began to be taken seriously. Later, Calvin Coolidge urged spending cuts and other reforms. His Two Percent Club was created to cut staff, as its name implies, by 2

Re-Re-Re-Re-Re-Reinventing Government
♦ ♦ ♦

U.S. leaders before Bill Clinton and Al Gore Jr. have had high hopes for domestic *perestroika*

President	Name Of Plan	Comment
Johnson	Programming, Planning, And Budgeting Systems	"[This is] a very revolutionary system...so that through the tools of modern management the full promise of a finer life can be brought to every American at the lowest possible cost."
Nixon	Management By Objectives	"The time has come...to organize the government by conscious, comprehensive design to meet the new needs of a new era."
Carter	Zero-Based Budgeting	"It's simple and it works...It will make sure that the money that is allocated...goes further."
Reagan	President's Private Sector Survey On Cost Control (Grace Commission)	"[The commission] will work like tireless bloodhounds, leaving no stone unturned in their search to root out inefficiency and waste of taxpayer dollars."
Bush	Right-Sizing Government	"I honestly believe that this is the only way to get the size and spending of government under control."
Clinton/Gore	Reinventing Government (National Performance Review)	"It's about whether we can restore the trust of the American people in their government"

Source: From: "Re-Re-Re-Re-Re-Reinventing Government, *Time,* September 13, 1993. Copyright ©1993 Time, Inc. Reprinted by permission. Clinton/Gore information provided by authors.

percent each year; his Correspondence Club was designed to reduce bureaucratic letter writing by thirty percent.[33] And as the box on page 344 illustrates, all recent presidents have had a plan to streamline government. Some plans, like those of Presidents Johnson and Carter, have involved budget systems; others, like Nixon's, have been more programmatic. As discussed earlier in this chapter, Nixon suggested that all executive departments be combined into four "super" departments organized by function. But according to his former aide John Erlichman, this plan to "disrupt iron triangles" was dead on arrival. "Why? Because such a reorganization would have broken up the hoary congressional committee organization that corresponded to the existing departments and agencies." More specifically,

> A subcommittee chairman with oversight of the Agriculture Department would lose power, perks and status if we were authorized to fold Agriculture into a new Department of Natural Resources. The powerful farm lobbies were equally hostile to the idea.[34]

President Bill Clinton also offered a reform plan. As part of his "reinventing government campaign" Clinton signed executive orders early in 1993 to:

- cut the size of the federal work force by 252,000 people within five years.
- cut in half the growing number of federal regulations within three years.
- set customer service standards to direct agencies to put the people they serve first.

Heading the President's Task Force on Reinventing Government is Vice President Gore. His task force report, the 200-page *National Performance Review*, made over 800 recommendations, citing problems and offering solutions. As noted on page 344, most of the solutions were geared toward making the bureaucracy more accountable and cost-effective. While some of these reforms may be fairly easy to implement, if we are to learn anything from the lessons of history, major change is unlikely.

Over the years, however, some reform of the system has occurred. Perhaps most notable are **sunshine** and **sunset laws.**

Sunshine Laws. One of the most successful first steps in reforming the bureaucracy and making it more accountable was congressional passage in 1976 of the Government in the Sunshine Act. For the first time, it required that about fifty multi-headed federal agencies hold their meetings in sessions open to the public. The Act defined *meetings* very broadly. Included in the open meetings requirement were almost any formal or informal meeting of agency members—including conference calls. The Act exempted some meetings, including those dealing with personnel matters or judicial proceedings, but it went a long way toward opening up the process. Many states also require that their agency meetings be held in the open.

Sunset Laws. Over the years, the bureaucracy has grown because Congress and the president have agreed on the need for new agencies to assist them in lawmaking and

---

[33] Thomas V. DiBacco, "Veep Gore Reinventing Government—Again!" *USA Today* (September 9, 1993): 13A.

[34] John Erlichman, "Government Reform: Will Al Gore's Package of Changes Succeed Where Others Failed? Washington's 'Iron Triangles'," *Atlanta Journal and Constitution* (September 16, 1993): A15.

346 ❖ Chapter 8 The Bureaucracy

law-enforcing. Wars, national emergencies, and changes in demographics, technology, and public expectations are just some of the reasons for that growth. Of the bureaucracy, President Gerald R. Ford once wrote,

> One of the enduring truths of the nation's capital is that bureaucrats survive. Agencies don't fold their tents and quietly fade away after their work is done. They find Something New to Do. Invariably, that Something New involves more people with more power and more paperwork—all involving more expenditures.[35]

One proposal to limit the size and scope of government and the problems noted by Ford are **sunset laws**, which provide that agencies or programs be abolished automatically after a fixed period of years unless Congress extends their life. The theory behind this reform is that new agencies or programs will not have the opportunity to be "captured" by special interests and will perform their duties more free of outside influences and more in accord with the public interest.

Sunset legislation was first suggested by Franklin D. Roosevelt when he proposed such a large number of new agencies as part of the New Deal. He thought that each agency charter should contain a sunset provision abolishing it after ten years unless specifically reauthorized by Congress. Obviously, Congress chose not to incorporate that suggestion when it created the myriad agencies that were part of the New Deal (see page 314). In fact, it was not until 1976 that a state legislature (Colorado) adopted a sunset law for state regulatory commissions giving them a life of six years. Today, a majority of the states have some type of sunset legislation, but Congress has yet to act similarly.

---

[35] Gerald R. Ford, *A Time to Heal: The Autobiography of Gerald R. Ford* (New York: Harper and Row, 1979), p. 272.

Author Karen Berger holds a silicone gel breast implant at a press conference in November, 1991. Berger testified at a Food and Drug Administration hearing considering banning the implants due to health fears. In 1992, the FDA took those implants off the market. Manufacturers failed to prove the implants were safe.

Summary

The bureaucracy plays a major role in America as a shaper of public policy, earning it the nickname the "fourth branch" of government. To explain the evolution and scope of bureaucratic power, in this chapter we have made the following points:

1. The federal bureaucracy started off quite small. George Washington, for example, presided over an executive branch that had only three departments—State, War, and Treasury. It was not until the Civil War that significant gains occurred in the size of the federal bureaucracy as the government geared up to conduct a war. As employment opportunities within the federal government increased, concurrent reforms in the civil service system assured that more and more jobs were filled according to merit and not by patronage. By the late 1800s, reform efforts led to further increases in the size of the bureaucracy, as independent regulatory commissions were created. And in the wake of the Depression, many new agencies were created to get the national economy back on course as part of FDR's New Deal.
2. The modern bureaucracy is composed of nearly 3 million civilian workers from all walks of life. Most hold merit appointments and are very hard to discharge. In general, bureaucratic agencies fall into four general types: departments, government corporations, independent agencies, and regulatory boards or commissions.
3. Bureaucrats not only make, but implement public policy. Administrative discretion allows bureaucrats to decide how to implement congressional and presidential directives. Administrative discretion can be exercised on an informal basis, or more formally through rule making and administrative adjudication.
4. While agencies enjoy considerable discretion, they are subjected to many formal controls. The president, Congress, and the judiciary all exercise various degrees of control over the bureaucracy.
5. In spite of all of the direct and indirect checks and balances on the bureaucracy, it is still difficult to control. Iron triangles and issue networks make control more difficult. Accountability is made almost impossible by the vast size of the bureaucracy and several systems problems, including inadequate mechanisms for evaluation, decentralized authority, vague objectives and insufficient funding.
6. Presidents since Jefferson have called for reforms in the bureaucracy to cut waste and to make it more efficient. Few have succeeded.

Key Terms

bureaucracy
bureaucrats
patronage
spoils system
civil service system
Pendleton Act (Civil Service Reform Act of 1883)
merit system
regulatory commission
Hatch Act
Federal Employees Political Activities Act
whistle blowers
clientele agencies
government corporations
independent agencies
implementation
administrative discretion
rule making
regulations
administrative adjudication
executive orders
iron triangles
issue networks
sunshine laws
sunset laws

Suggested Readings

Derthick, Martha, and Paul J. Quirk. *The Politics of Deregulation*. Washington: Brookings Institution, 1985.

Dodd, Lawrence, and Richard Schott. *Congress and the Administrative State*. New York: Wiley, 1979.

Gormley, William T. Jr. *Taming the Bureaucracy: Muscles, Prayers and Other Strategies*. Princeton, NJ: Princeton University Press, 1989.

Knott, Jack H., and Gary J. Miller. *Reforming Bureaucracy: The Politics of Institutional Choice*. Englewood Cliffs, NJ: Prentice Hall, 1987.

Rourke, Francis E. *Bureaucracy, Politics and Public Policy*. Boston: Little, Brown, 1984.

Seidman, Harold, and Robert Gilmour. *Politics, Position, and Power*, 4th ed. New York: Oxford University Press, 1986.

Stillman, Richard J. *The American Bureaucracy*. New York: Nelson Hall, 1987.

Weiss, Carol H., and Allen H. Barton., ed. *Making Bureaucracies Work*. Beverly Hills: Sage Publications, 1980.

Wilson, James Q. *Bureaucracy: What Government Agencies Do and Why They Do It*. New York: Basic Books, 1989.

The judiciary, from the nature of its functions, will always be the least dangerous to the political rights of the Constitution; because it will be least in a capacity to annoy or injure them.

Alexander Hamilton
Federalist No. 78

The Framers worried about the tyranny of taxation, military despotism, a too-powerful presidency, and the balance of power between national and state governments. Because the judiciary cannot normally make policy in these areas, Hamilton feared the courts far less than he feared Congress or the president.

CHAPTER 9

The Judiciary

❖

THE CREATION OF THE JUDICIAL BRANCH
THE LEGAL SYSTEM
THE FEDERAL COURT SYSTEM
HOW FEDERAL COURT JUDGES ARE SELECTED
THE SUPREME COURT TODAY
HOW THE JUSTICES VOTE
JUDICIAL POLICY MAKING AND IMPLEMENTATION
TOWARD REFORM

❖

When Alexander Hamilton wrote under the pen name of "Publius" to urge support of the U.S. Constitution in 1787, he firmly believed that the judiciary was the weakest of the three departments of government. And in its formative years, the judiciary was, in Hamilton's terms, "the least dangerous" branch. So seemingly inconsequential was the judicial branch that when the national government made its move to the District of Columbia, Congress forgot to include any space to house the justices of the Supreme Court! Last-minute conferences with the Capitol architects led to the allocation of a small area in the basement of the Senate wing of the Capitol Building for a courtroom. No other space was allowed for the justices, however. Noted one commentator, "A stranger might traverse the darkest avenues of the Capitol for a week, without finding the remote corner in which justice is served in the American Republic."[1]

Today, the role of the courts, particularly the U.S. Supreme Court, is significantly different from that envisioned in 1788, the year the national government came into being. The "least dangerous branch" is now perceived by many as having too much power. During different periods of the judiciary's history, the role and power of the federal courts have varied tremendously. They have often played a key role in creating a strong national government and have boldly led the nation in social reform. Yet at other times, the federal courts, especially the U.S. Supreme Court, have stubbornly stood as a major obstacle to important social and economic change.

[1] Bernard Schwartz, *The Law in America*, (New York: American Heritage Publishing Co., 1974), p. 48.

The Supreme Court does not operate in a vacuum. Here, protesters line up in front of the Court to comment on issues ranging from privacy to coerced confessions.

In this chapter we explore the development of the national judiciary. The Framers could never have envisioned that the authority of the Supreme Court and other federal courts would grow to include issues as diverse as the right of married couples to use birth control, the right of parents to withdraw life-support systems from their children, and the question of whether a pregnant woman could be forced to undergo a caesarean section prior to going into natural labor. As some recent battles over nominations to the Supreme Court reveal, a growing segment of the public views the Court as the final word on many important, controversial issues.

We pay special attention to the political nature of the courts and examine how the power of the courts, especially that of the Supreme Court, has expanded over time. Many Americans have been raised to think of the Supreme Court as far above the fray of politics. That is simply not the case. *Elected* presidents nominate justices to the Supreme Court, often to advance their personal politics, and *elected* Senators ultimately confirm (or decline to confirm) presidential nominees. Not only is the selection process political, but the process by which cases ultimately get heard by the Supreme Court is often political, too. Interest groups routinely seek out good test cases to advance their policy positions. Even the U.S. government, generally through the Justice Department and the U.S. Solicitor General (another political appointee), seeks to advance its version of the public interest in court. Interest groups then often line up on opposing sides, each in the form of an **amicus curiae** (friend of the court), and file briefs advancing their positions much in the same way that lobbyists do in Congress.

Moreover, as we will discuss, the justices of the Supreme Court don't make decisions in a vacuum. Not only do they read legal briefs and hear oral arguments, but they also read newspapers, watch television, and have some knowledge of public opinion—especially on controversial issues. In 1989, for example, pro-choice and right-to-life forces not only marched on Washington to highlight their respective causes, they also jammed the Court's phones and inundated the justices with mail. Similarly, in 1993, the Court's switchboard lit up like the national Christmas tree with calls about Baby Jessica, the two-year-old who was returned to her birth parents after they spent two years in legal wrangling with her custodial parents. Operators reported that some callers sobbed, others yelled, and others wanted to know how to impeach the Chief Justice. While actions like these probably have little impact on a particular justice's view of a particular case, they do make the Court aware of the intensity of public opinion on some issues.

A note on terminology before we start: When we refer to the Supreme Court, the Court, or high court here, we mean the U.S. Supreme Court, which sits at the pinnacle of the federal and state court systems. The Supreme Court is referred to by the name of the Chief Justice who presided over it during a particular period (e.g., the Marshall Court is the Court presided over by John Marshall from 1801 to 1835). When we use the term "courts," we refer to all federal or state courts unless otherwise noted.

The Creation of the Judicial Branch

At the Philadelphia Convention, James Madison took detailed notes that were released after his death. His notes make it clear that the Framers devoted little time to the writing or the content of Article III, which created the judicial branch of government. The Framers believed that it posed little of the threat of tyranny that they feared from the other two branches. One scholar has even suggested that for at least some delegates to the Constitutional Convention,

> provision for a national judiciary was a matter of theoretical necessity . . . more in deference to the maxim of separation [of powers] than in response to clearly formulated ideas about the role of a national judicial system and its indispensability.[2]

Anti-Federalists, however, did not agree about the need for a supreme court, in particular, or a federal judiciary, in general. They particularly objected to a judiciary whose members had life tenure and the ability to interpret what was to be "the supreme law of the land," a phrase that Anti-Federalists feared would give the Supreme Court too much power.

The Framers also debated the need for any federal courts below the level of the Supreme Court. Some argued in favor of deciding all cases in state courts, with only appeals going before the Supreme Court. Others argued for a system of federal courts. A compromise left the final choice to Congress, and Article III began simply by vesting "The judicial Power of the United States . . . in one supreme Court, and in such inferior Courts as the Congress may from time to time ordain and establish." Although there was some debate over whether the Court should have the power of **judicial review** (which allows the judiciary to review acts of the other branches of government and the states) the question was left unsettled in Article III (and not finally resolved until *Marbury* v. *Madison* [1803], discussed on p. 357). This vagueness was not all that unusual, given the numerous compromises that took place in Philadelphia.

Had the Supreme Court been viewed as the potential policy maker it is today, it is highly unlikely that the Founders would have provided for life tenure with "good behavior" for federal judges in Article III. This feature was agreed upon because the Framers did not want the justices (or any federal judges) subject to the whims of politics, the public, or politicians. Moreover, Alexander Hamilton argued in *Federalist*

---

[2] Julius Goebel Jr., *History of the Supreme Court of the United States*, Vol. 1: *Antecedents and Beginnings to 1801* (New York: Macmillan, 1971), p. 206.

The old chambers of the Supreme Court located in the basement of the U.S. Senate. Cases were heard there until 1935.

No. 78 that the "independence of judges" was needed "to guard the Constitution and the rights of individuals." Because the Framers viewed the Court as quite powerless, Hamilton stressed the need to place federal judges above the fray of politics. Yet although there is no denying that judges are political animals and carry the same prejudices and preferences to the bench that others do to the statehouse, Congress, or the White House, the provision of life tenure for "good behavior" has functioned well.

Some checks on the power of the judiciary were nonetheless included in the Constitution. Congress can alter the Court's jurisdiction (its ability to hear certain kinds of cases). Congress can also propose constitutional amendments that, if ratified, can effectively reverse judicial decisions, and it can impeach and remove federal judges. In one further check, it is the president who (with the "advice and consent" of the Senate) appoints all federal judges.

The Judiciary Act of 1789 and the Creation of the Federal Judicial System

In spite of the Framers' intentions, the pervasive role of politics in the judicial branch quickly became evident with the passage of the Judiciary Act of 1789. Congress spent nearly the entire second half of its first session deliberating the various provisions of the Act needed to give form and substance to the federal judiciary. As one early observer noted, "The convention has only crayoned in the outlines. It left it to Congress to fill up and colour the canvas."[3]

The Judiciary Act was drafted largely by U.S. Senator Oliver Ellsworth, a former member of the Constitutional Convention from Connecticut who later served on the

---

[3] Quoted in Ibid., p. 280.

Supreme Court as its second Chief Justice, from 1796 to 1800. The Act established the basic three-tiered structure of the federal court system. At the bottom were the federal district courts—one in each state (except Massachusetts and Virginia, with two apiece)—each staffed by a federal judge. Appeals from the district courts were to be made to one of the three circuit courts. Each circuit court was composed of one district court judge and two itinerant Supreme Court justices who joined them in twice-yearly meetings. Although the Constitution mentions "the supreme Court," it was silent on its size. In the Judiciary Act of 1789, Congress set the size of the Supreme Court at six—the Chief Justice plus five associate justices.

When the justices met in their first public session in New York City in 1790, they were magnificently garbed in black and scarlet robes in the English fashion, but they had discarded what Thomas Jefferson termed "the monstrous wig which makes English judges look like rats peeping through bunches of oakum!"[4] The elegance of their attire, however, could not make up for the relatively ineffective status of the Court. Its first session even had to be adjourned when not enough justices showed up. And the Jay Court only decided one really important case—*Chisholm* v. *Georgia* (1793), discussed on page 355. Moreover, in an indication of its status, one associate justice left the Court to become Chief Justice of the South Carolina Supreme Court. (Although such a move would be considered a step down today, keep in mind that in the early years of the United States, many viewed the states as more important than the new national government.)

---

[4] Schwartz, *The Law in America*, p. 11.

Left: The Supreme Court held its first two sessions in this building, called the Exchange, in New York City. Right: The minutes from the first session of the Supreme Court of the United States, held on February 1, 1790. Not much went on—the session had to be adjourned when too few justices showed up.

> ### Burdens of the Early Court
>
> We really, sir, find the burdens laid upon us so excessive that we cannot forbear representing them in strong and explicit terms. That the task of holding twenty-seven Circuit Courts a year, in the different States, from New Hampshire to Georgia, besides two sessions of the Supreme Court at Philadelphia, in the two most severe seasons of the year, is a task which, considering the extent of the United States and the small number of Judges, is too burdensome. That to require of the Judges to pass the greater part of their days on the road, and at inns, at a distance from their families, is a requisition which in their opinion, should not be made unless in cases of necessity.
>
> *Source:* Letter to the president of the United States, August 19, 1792, signed by all the justices. Quoted in Charles Warren, *The Supreme Court in United States History*, Vol. I (Boston: Little, Brown, 1926), pp. 88–89.

John Jay (1745–1829), one of the authors of *The Federalist Papers,* was the first Chief Justice of the U.S. Supreme Court, a position he held from 1789 to 1795. While serving as Chief Justice, he left the country for a year to lead a diplomatic mission to Great Britain which resulted in an agreement that bears his name—the Jay Treaty. Jay was one of the architects of New York's first state constitution, and while still Chief Justice, he ran unsuccessfully for governor of that state. He was elected as governor in 1794 while in England. Jay resigned as Chief Justice in 1795 to assume the New York governorship.

Hampered by frequent changes in personnel, limited space for its operations, no clerical support, and no system of reporting its decisions, the Court and its meager activities did not impress many people. From the beginning, the circuit court duties of the Supreme Court justices presented problems for the prestige of the Court. Few good lawyers were willing to accept nominations to the high court because its circuit court duties entailed a substantial amount of travel—most of it on horseback over poorly maintained roads in frequently inclement weather. Southern justices often tallied up as much as 10,000 miles a year on horseback. George Washington tried to prevail upon several friends and supporters to fill vacancies on the Court as they appeared, but most refused the "honor." John Adams, the second president of the United States, ran into similar problems. When he asked John Jay, the first Chief Justice, to resume the position after he resigned to become governor of New York, Jay declined the offer. Jay had once remarked of the Court that it had lacked "energy, weight and dignity" as well as "public confidence and respect." Given Jay's view of the Court and its performance statistics, his refusal was not surprising.

In spite of all its problems, in its first decade the Court took several actions to help mold the new nation. First, by declining to render advisory opinions, the justices attempted to establish the Supreme Court as an independent, nonpolitical branch of government. Although John Jay frequently gave the president advice in private, the Court refused to answer questions Washington posed to it concerning the construction of international laws and treaties. The justices wanted to avoid the appearance of prejudging an issue that could later arise before them.

The early Court also tried to advance principles of nationalism and to maintain the supremacy of the national government over the states. As circuit court jurists, the justices rendered numerous decisions on such matters as national suppression of the Whiskey Rebellion and the constitutionality of the Alien and Sedition Acts, which made it a crime to criticize national governmental officials or their actions (see Chapter 4).

During the ratification debates, Anti-Federalists had warned that Article III extended federal judicial power to controversies "between a State and Citizens of another

State," meaning that a citizen of one state could sue any other state in federal court, a prospect unthinkable to defenders of state sovereignty. Although Federalists, including Hamilton and Madison, had scoffed at the idea, the nationalist Supreme Court quickly proved them wrong in *Chisholm* v. *Georgia* (1793).[5] In *Chisholm*, the justices interpreted the Court's jurisdiction under Article III, Section 2, to include the right to hear suits brought by a citizen of one state against another state. Writing in *Chisholm*, Justice James Wilson, for example, denounced the "haughty notions of state independence, state sovereignty, and state independence." The states' reaction to this perceived attack on their authority led to speedy passage and ratification (in 1798) of the Eleventh Amendment, which specifically limited judicial power by stipulating that the federal courts' authority could not "extend to any suit . . . commenced or prosecuted against one of the United States by citizens of another State."

Finally, in a series of circuit and Supreme Court decisions, the justices paved the way for announcement of the doctrine of judicial review by the third Chief Justice, John Marshall. (Oliver Ellsworth served from 1796 to 1800.) Justices "riding circuit" frequently held state laws unconstitutional because they violated the U.S. Constitution. And in *Hylton* v. *United States* (1796),[6] the Court evaluated for the first time the constitutionality of an act of Congress. In *Hylton*, the Court ruled that a congressional excise tax on carriages was not a direct tax and was therefore valid even though it was not apportioned evenly among the states (as called for in the Constitution).

The Marshall Court (1801–1835)

John Marshall was appointed Chief Justice by President John Adams in 1801, three years after he declined to accept a nomination as associate justice. (See "People of the Past: John Marshall," p. 356.) An ardent Federalist who also earlier had declined Washington's offer to become Attorney General, Marshall later came to be considered the most important justice ever to serve on the high court. Part of his reputation is the result of the duration of his service and the historical significance of this period in our nation's history. Marshall also, however, brought much-needed respect and prestige to the Court through his leadership in a progression of cases and a series of innovations.

One of Marshall's first innovations on the Court was to discontinue the practice of *seriatim* (Latin for "in a series") opinions, which was the custom of the King's Bench in Great Britain. Prior to the Marshall Court, the justices delivered their individual opinions in order. There was no single "opinion of the Court," as we are accustomed to today. For the Court to take its place as an equal branch of government, Marshall strongly believed, the justices needed to speak as a *Court* and not as six individuals. In fact, during Marshall's first four years in office, the Court routinely spoke as one, and the Chief Justice wrote twenty-four of its twenty-six opinions.

Judicial Review

During the Philadelphia Convention, the Framers debated and rejected the idea of judicial veto of legislation or executive acts, and they rejected the Virginia Plan's proposal to give the judiciary explicit authority over Congress. They did, however, approve Article VI, which contains the supremacy clause (see Chapter 3).

---

[5] 2 Dall. 419 (1793).
[6] 3 Dall. 171 (1796).

PEOPLE OF THE PAST

John Marshall

John Marshall (1755–1835) was born in a log cabin in Germantown, Virginia, the first of fifteen children of Welsh immigrants. Although tutored at home by two clergymen, Marshall's inspiration was his father, who introduced him to English literature and Sir William Blackstone's influential *Commentaries on the Laws of England*. After serving in the Continental Army and acquiring the rank of captain, Marshall taught himself the law. He attended only one formal course at the College of William and Mary before being admitted to the bar. Marshall practiced law in Virginia, where he and his wife lived and raised a family. Of their ten children, only six survived childhood.

Marshall served as a delegate to the Virginia legislature from 1782 to 1785, 1787 to 1790, and 1795 to 1796, and played an instrumental role in Virginia's ratification of the U.S. Constitution in 1787. As the leading Federalist in Virginia, Marshall was offered several positions in the Federalist administrations of George Washington and John Adams—including Attorney General and associate justice to the Supreme Court—but he refused them all. Finally, Washington persuaded him to run for the House of Representatives in 1799. Marshall was elected, but his career in the House was brief, for he became Secretary of State in 1800 under John Adams. When Oliver Ellsworth resigned as Chief Justice of the U.S. Supreme Court in 1800, Adams nominated Marshall.

Marshall was well suited to the leisurely pace of the Supreme Court in its early days. He enjoyed the outdoors and socializing in the clubs and saloons around Richmond, and he excelled at quoits (similar to horseshoes).

Marshall dominated the Court during his thirty-four years as Chief Justice. As one commentator noted, "Marshall found the Constitution paper; and he made it power. He found a skeleton, and he clothed it with flesh and blood."* In essence, Marshall transformed the Court into a co-equal branch of government through a series of key decisions that established:

- The practice by which the view of the Court is expressed in a single opinion instead of a series of opinions, as had previously been the case. Marshall insisted on unanimity, and discouraged dissenting and concurring opinions, thereby winning for the Court the prestige it needed to resolve many of the conflicts and controversies that came before it.
- The Court as the final arbiter of constitutional questions, with the right to declare congressional acts void (*Marbury* v. *Madison* [1803]).
- The authority of the Supreme Court over the judiciaries of the various states, including the Court's power to declare state laws invalid (*Fletcher* v. *Peck* [1810]; *Martin* v. *Hunter's Lessee* [1816]; *Cohens* v. *Virginia* [1821]).
- The supremacy of the federal government and Congress over state governments through a broad interpretation of the "necessary and proper" clause (*McCulloch* v. *Maryland* [1819]).

During the Marshall era, the Court operated like a family firm. The justices came to Washington for only a few months at a time, so they lived together in a boarding house where they often discussed cases at dinner over wine.

Personalities and individual characteristics had a tremendous influence on the Court. Although Marshall had had little experience in the practice of law and none as a judge prior to his appointment to Chief Justice, his personality and leadership capabilities allowed him to shape the Court and the federal judiciary into a branch of the government with authority and respect.

* Schwartz, *The Law in America*, p. 49.

In Federalist No. 78, Alexander Hamilton first publicly endorsed the idea of judicial review, noting, "whenever a particular statute contravenes the Constitution, it will be the duty of the judicial tribunals to adhere to the latter and disregard the former." Nonetheless, because the power of judicial review is not mentioned in the U.S. Constitution, the actual authority of the Supreme Court to review acts of Congress to determine their constitutionality was an unsettled question. During its first decade, the Supreme Court (or justices riding circuit) had often reviewed acts of Congress, but it had not found any unconstitutional. But in **Marbury v. Madison** (1803),[7] John Marshall claimed this sweeping authority for the Court by asserting the right of judicial review.

In the final hours of the Adams administration, William Marbury was appointed a justice of the peace for the District of Columbia. But in the confusion of winding up matters, John Marshall, Adams's Secretary of State, failed to deliver Marbury's commission. Marbury then asked James Madison, Thomas Jefferson's Secretary of State, for the commission. Under direct orders from Jefferson, who was irate over the Adams administration's last-minute appointment of several federal judges (quickly ratified by the Federalist Congress), Madison refused to turn over the commission. Marbury and three other Adams appointees who were in the same situation then filed a writ of *mandamus* (a legal motion) asking the Supreme Court to order Madison to deliver their commissions.

Political tensions ran high as the Court met to hear the case. Jefferson threatened to ignore any order of the Court. Marshall realized that he and the prestige of the Court could be devastated by any refusal of the executive branch to comply with the decision. Responding to this challenge, in a brilliant opinion that in many sections reads more like a lecture to Jefferson than a discussion of the merits of Marbury's claim, Marshall concluded that although Marbury and the others were entitled to their commissions, the Court lacked the power to issue the writ sought by Marbury. Marshall further ruled that the parts of the Judiciary Act of 1789 that had extended the jurisdiction of the Court to allow it to issue writs was inconsistent with the Constitution and therefore unconstitutional.

Although the immediate effect of the decision was to deny power to the Court, its long-term effect was to establish the rule that "it is emphatically the province and duty of the judicial department to say what the law is." Through judicial review, the Supreme Court most dramatically exerts its authority to determine what the Constitution means. And since *Marbury*, the Court has routinely exercised the power of judicial review to determine the constitutionality of acts of Congress, the executive branch, and the states.

The Legal System

The judicial system in the United States can best be characterized as a dual system consisting of the federal court system and the judicial systems of the fifty states. Both are basically three-tiered. As depicted in Figure 9-1, at the bottom are district trial courts, where litigation begins. In the middle are appellate courts in the state systems and the Courts of Appeals in the federal system. And a supreme court sits at the top of

---

[7] 5 U.S. 137 (1803).

358 ❖ Chapter 9 The Judiciary

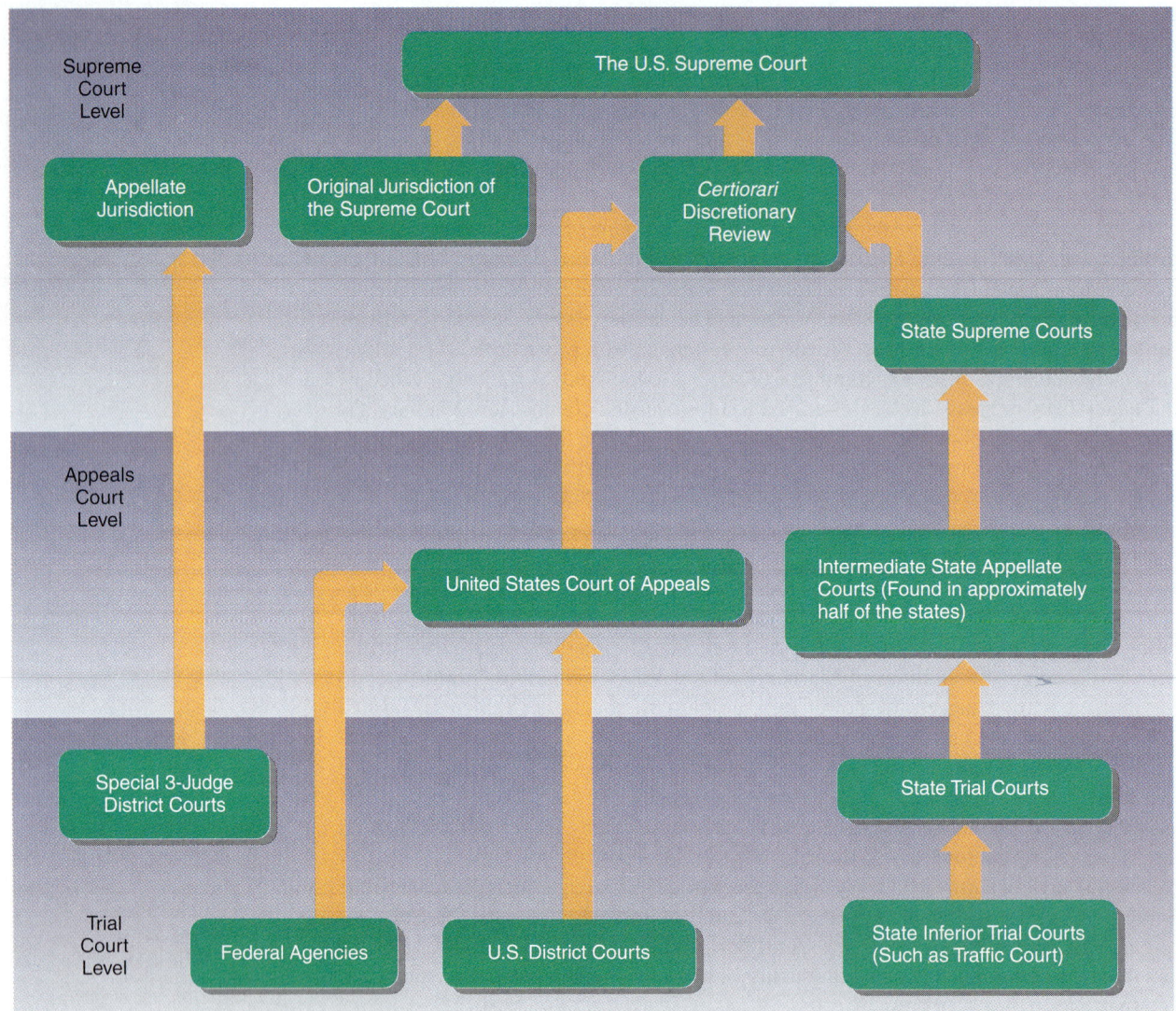

FIGURE 9-1
The American Court System

the pyramid as the final word in each system (except New York, which calls its Supreme Court the Court of Appeals). The courts of appeal and supreme courts are **appellate courts** that, with few exceptions, review on appeal only cases that already have been decided in lower courts.

Jurisdiction

There are two kinds of jurisdiction; that is, authority of a court to decide a certain question: original and appellate. *Original jurisdiction* refers to a court's authority to hear disputes as a trial court. (The Menendez brothers' and O. J. Simpson's cases, for example, were heard in Los Angeles County, California, state trial courts.) The facts of a case are established at the trial court level. More than 90 percent of all cases end at this stage.

Appellate jurisdiction refers to a court's ability to review cases already decided by a trial court. Appellate courts do not review the factual record; instead, they review legal procedures to make certain that the law was applied properly to the issues presented in the case. *To appeal* means to take a case to a higher court.

Criminal and Civil Law

The body of law that grades, describes, and sets punishments for crimes is known as **criminal law**. A crime is an action considered to be an offense against authority, or a violation of a duty owed to the public. Crimes are graded as felonies, misdemeanors, or offenses, according to their severity. Some acts—for example, murder, rape, and robbery—are considered crimes in all states. Others—such as sodomy, and some forms of gambling, such as lotteries or bingo—are illegal only in some states. Moreover, although all states outlaw murder, their penal, or criminal, codes treat the crime quite differently; the penalty for murder differs considerably from state to state.

In contrast to civil law, criminal law assumes that society itself is the victim of the illegal act; therefore, the government prosecutes, or brings an action, on behalf of an injured party (acting as a plaintiff) in criminal but not civil cases. Criminal trials are often depicted on television programs like "Perry Mason" and "L.A. Law."

In criminal cases, a defendant is charged with violating a specific law. A state (or federal) prosecutor or district attorney then generally takes the case before a **grand jury** to see if there are sufficient reasons to issue an **indictment**—a formal accusation—and proceed to trial. If an indictment is issued, the defendant can often negotiate or plea-bargain with the prosecutor for reduced charges in exchange for a guilty plea. (See Chapter 4, "The Bill of Rights and the Procedural Protections Guaranteed throughout the Criminal Justice Process," p. 130.)

Civil law is the body of law dealing with noncriminal matters, such as the laws of property, commercial law, and family law. It is used to regulate relationships between private individuals or companies. Because the actions at issue do not constitute a threat to society at large, persons who believe they have been injured by another party must take action on their own to seek judicial relief. Civil cases, then, involve lawsuits filed to recover something of value, whether it is the right to vote, fair treatment, or monetary compensation for an item or service that cannot be recovered. Most cases seen on the television program "The People's Court" are civil cases. Divorce and child-custody proceedings, employment discrimination claims, and disputes arising from contracts or accidents are all examples of civil law. Divorce and child-custody cases generally involve only issues of state law and so are not heard, except in rare cases, in the federal court system. Allegations of employment discrimination based on gender or race, however, are generally filed in federal court because such discrimination violates the Civil Rights Act of 1964, a federal statute.

Civil and criminal cases can involve state and federal offenses. Take the case of Rodney King, for example. At first, the Los Angeles police officers who beat King were tried in a state court on state criminal charges. When the officers were found not guilty by the jury, the U.S. federal government then brought different federal charges against them for basically the same actions, but this time they were charged with violating federal law. The officers were found guilty by the federal jury.[8]

---

[8] The constitutional prohibition against double jeopardy does not apply in this case, because in the two trials King's assailants were charged with different crimes arising out of the same incident. In state court the officers were charged with using excessive criminal force; in federal court, they were charged with violating King's civil rights.

Before a criminal or civil case gets to court, much has to happen. In fact, most legal disputes that arise in the United States never get to court. Individuals and companies involved in civil disputes routinely settle their disagreements out of court. Often these settlements are not reached until minutes before the case is to be tried. And many civil cases that go to trial are settled during the course of the trial—before the case can be handed over to the jury or submitted to a judge for a decision or determination of guilt. In 1993, silicon breast implant manufacturers, including Dow Chemical Company, agreed to create a $4.75 billion dollar fund to resolve all legal claims involving 800,000 American women, in effect settling the 8,000 lawsuits already filed in U.S. district courts.

Each civil and criminal case has a plaintiff who brings charges against a defendant. Sometimes the government is the plaintiff. The government may bring criminal or civil charges against a person or corporation for violating the law on behalf of the citizens of the state or the national government. Cases are known by the name of the plaintiff first, and of the defendant second. So in *Marbury* v. *Madison*, William Marbury was the plaintiff, suing the defendants, the U.S. government and James Madison as its Secretary of State, for not delivering his judicial commission.

During trials, judges must often interpret the intent of laws enacted by Congress and state legislatures as they bear on the issues at hand. To do so, they read reports, testimony, and debates on the relevant legislation and study the results of other similar legal cases. They also rely on the presentations made by lawyers in their briefs and at trial. If it is a jury trial, the jury ultimately is the finder of fact, while the judge is the interpreter of the law.

The Federal Court System

The federal district courts, circuit courts of appeal, and the Supreme Court are called **constitutional** (or Article III) **courts** because Article III of the Constitution authorizes Congress to establish them. Judges who preside over these courts are selected by the president (with the advice and consent of the Senate), and they serve lifetime terms, as long as they engage in "good behavior."

In addition to constitutional courts, **legislative courts** are set up by Congress, generally for special purposes. The U.S. Court of Military Affairs (which hears appeals of cases involving the military), the Court of Customs and Appeals (which hears appeals from decisions of customs courts and the Patent Office), and bankruptcy courts are examples of legislative courts. The judges who preside over these courts are appointed by the president (subject to Senate confirmation) and serve fixed, limited terms.

District Courts

As we saw earlier, Congress recognized the need for federal trial courts soon after ratification of the Constitution. The district courts were created by the Judiciary Act of 1789. By 1992 there were ninety-four federal district courts. Because of one of the compromises of the Judiciary Act of 1789, no district court cuts across state lines. Every state has at least one federal district court, and the largest states—California, New York, and Texas—each have four (see Figure 9-2).[9]

---

[9] David W. Neubauer, *Judicial Process: Law, Courts and Politics* (Pacific Grove, CA: Brooks/Cole, 1991), p. 57.

FIGURE 9-2
The Federal Court System

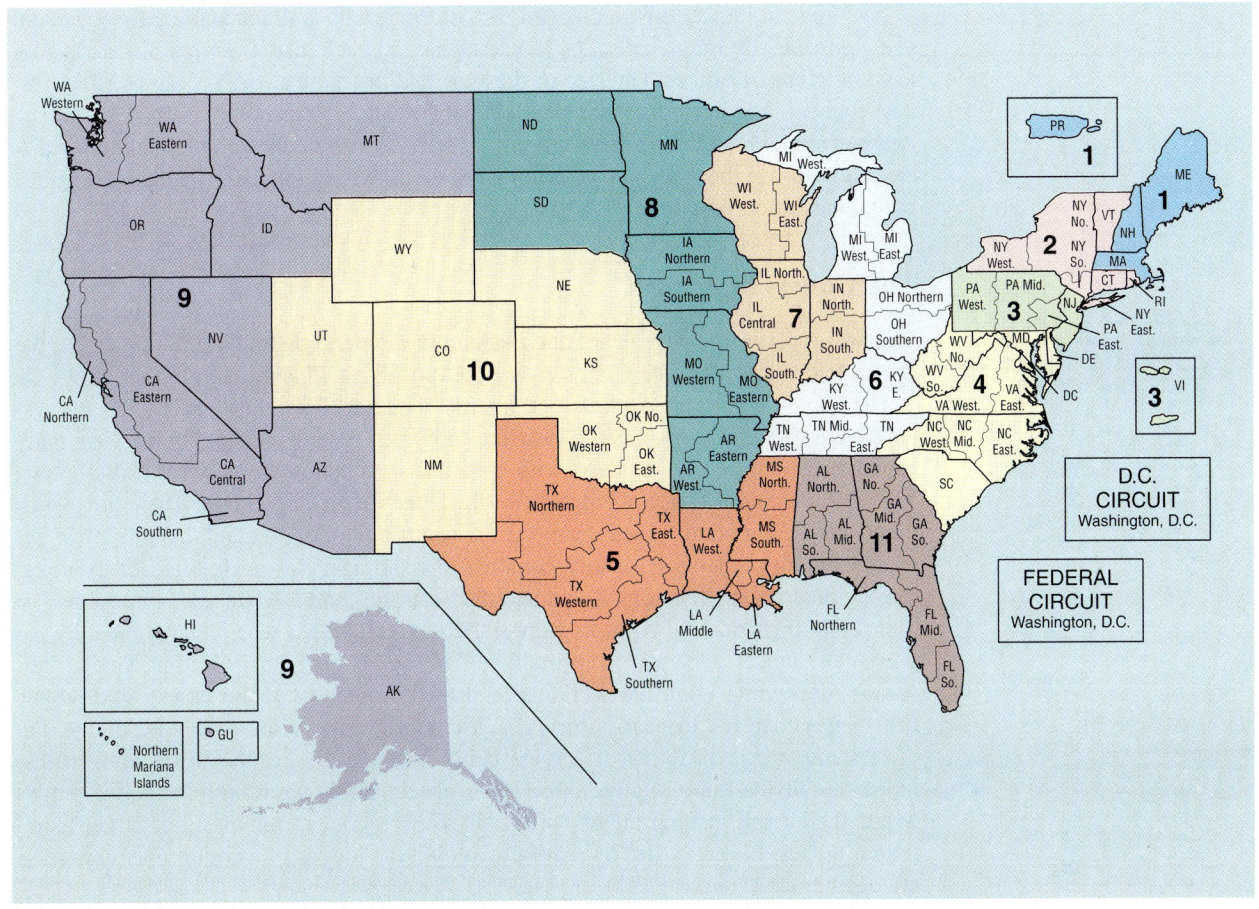

This map shows the locations of the Circuit Courts of Appeal and the boundaries of the Federal District Courts with more than one district.

Federal district courts have the authority, or jurisdiction, to hear only specific types of cases. (Cases involving other kinds of issues generally must be heard in state court.) Although the rules governing district court jurisdiction can be complex, cases heard there generally fall into one of three categories:

1. They present a federal question based on a claim under the U.S. Constitution, a treaty with another nation, or a federal statute. Federal question jurisdiction can involve criminal or civil law.
2. They involve the federal government as a party.[10]

---

[10] The most commonly filed cases in the federal district courts involve challenges to determinations made by the Social Security Administration concerning disability payments. In fact, more than 50 percent of the civil cases heard by some federal district courts involve these kinds of issues.

3. They involve cases in which citizens are from different states, and the amount of money at issue is more than $50,000.[11]

Each federal judicial district has a U.S. Attorney, who is nominated by the president and confirmed by the Senate. The U.S. Attorney in each district is that district's chief law enforcement officer. The size of the staff and the number of Assistant U.S. Attorneys who work in each district depend on the amount of litigation in each district. U.S. Attorneys, like district attorneys within the states, have a considerable amount of discretion as to whether they pursue criminal or civil investigations or file charges against individuals or corporations.

The Courts of Appeal

The losing party in a case heard and decided in a federal district court can appeal the decision to the appropriate Circuit Court of Appeals, as illustrated in Figure 9-1.

The Circuit Courts of Appeals, the intermediate appellate courts in the federal system, were established in 1789 to hear appeals from federal district courts. Originally called circuit courts, these courts with appellate jurisdiction are now officially known as the United States Court of Appeals for the [First–Eleventh] Circuit. There are eleven numbered circuit courts (see Figure 9-2.) A twelfth, the D.C. Circuit, handles most appeals involving federal regulatory commissions and agencies, including, for example, the National Labor Relations Board and the Securities and Exchange Commission.

In 1994, the Courts of Appeals were staffed by 156 judges who are appointed by the president, subject to Senate confirmation. The number of judges within each circuit varies—depending upon the workload and the complexity of the cases—and ranges from fewer than ten to nearly thirty. Each circuit is supervised by a chief judge, the most senior judge in terms of service below the age of seventy. In deciding cases, judges are divided into rotating three-judge panels, made up of both the active judges within the circuit, visiting judges (primarily district judges from the same circuit), and retired judges. In rare cases, by majority vote all the judges in a circuit may choose to sit together (*en banc*) to decide a case.

The Courts of Appeals have no original jurisdiction. Rather, Congress has granted these courts appellate jurisdiction over two general categories of cases: appeals from criminal and civil cases from the district courts, and appeals from administrative agencies. Criminal and civil case appeals constitute about 90 percent of the workload of the Courts of Appeals. In contrast, appeals from administrative agencies make up only about 10 percent of their workload. And because so many agencies are located in Washington, D.C., the D.C. Circuit Court of Appeals hears an inordinate number of such cases. The D.C. Circuit Court of Appeals, then, is considered the second most important court in the nation because its decisions govern the regulatory agencies.

Once a decision is made by a federal Court of Appeals, a litigant no longer has an automatic right to an appeal. The losing party may submit a petition to the Supreme Court to hear the case, but the Court grants few of these requests, as illustrated in Figure 9-3. The Courts of Appeals, then, are the courts of last resort for almost all federal litigation. Keep in mind, however, that most cases, if they actually go to trial, go no further than the district court level.

---

[11] Cases involving citizens from different states can generally be filed in either state or federal court.

The Federal Court System ❖ 363

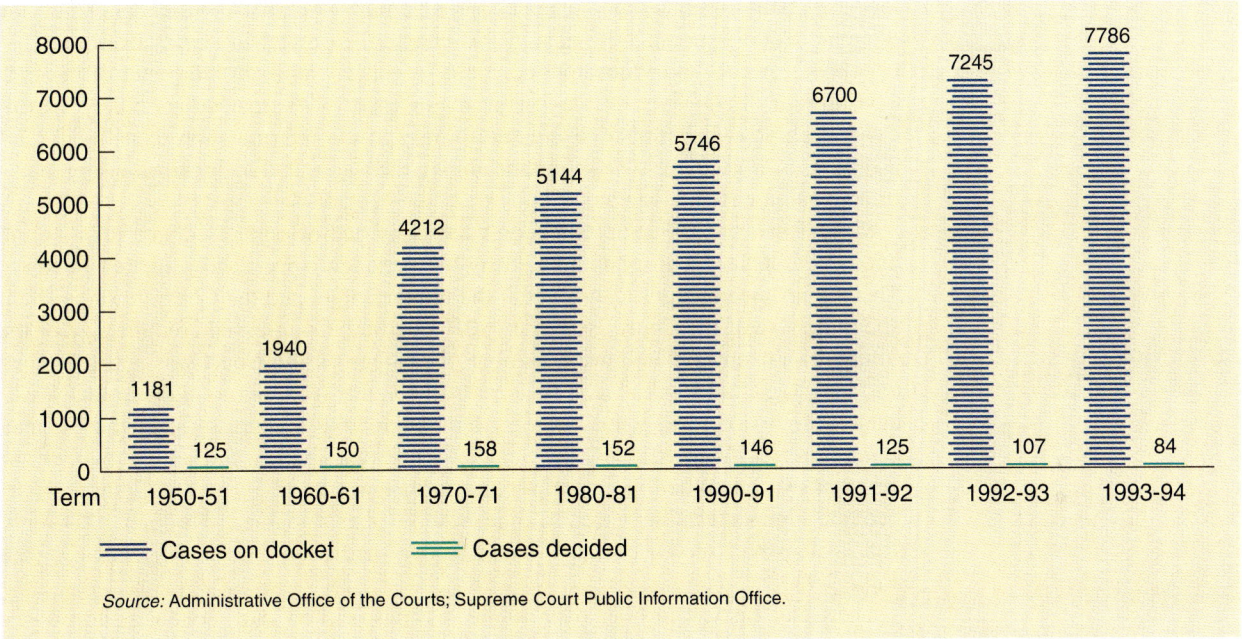

FIGURE 9-3
Supreme Court Caseload, 1950-1994

Source: Administrative Office of the Courts; Supreme Court Public Information Office.

The figure shows the upward trend of case filings at the U.S. Supreme Court since 1950. Also shown is the fairly constant number of cases that the justices have actually accepted for full review and for which they have issued opinions. The Court usually decides only one or two cases a term under its original jurisdiction. Almost all the rest of its workload consists of petitions from lower federal or state courts.

In general, Courts of Appeals try to correct errors of law and procedure that have occurred in the lower court or administrative agency. Courts of Appeals hear no new testimony; instead, lawyers submit written arguments, called **briefs** (also submitted in trial courts), and then appear to argue the case and orally present their arguments to the court. In deciding these cases, the judges rely on the briefs, oral argument, and **precedents** (past decisions) in making their decisions.

Although decisions of any Court of Appeals are binding on only the district courts within the geographic confines of the circuit, decisions of the U.S. Supreme Court are binding throughout the nation and establish precedents. This reliance on past decisions or precedents to formulate decisions in new cases is called *stare decisis* (a Latin phrase meaning "let the decision stand"). The principle of *stare decisis* allows for continuity and predictability in our judicial system. If a party goes to court, it is incumbent on the lawyer to know how a court has acted in similar cases. Although *stare decisis* can be helpful in predicting decisions, at times judges carve out new ground and ignore, decline to follow, or even overrule precedents in order to reach a different conclusion in a case involving similar circumstances. In one sense, that is why there is so much litigation in America today. Parties know that one cannot always predict the outcome of a case; if such prediction were possible, there would be little reason to go to court.

The Supreme Court

At the top of the judicial pyramid is the U.S. Supreme Court, which, as discussed below, has both original and appellate jurisdiction. (We discuss the details of the Supreme Court's jurisdiction later in this chapter.) In reviewing cases from the U.S. Courts of Appeals and state supreme courts, it acts as the final interpreter of the U.S. Constitution. It not only decides many major cases with tremendous policy significance each year, but it also ensures uniformity in the interpretation of national laws and the Constitution, resolves conflicts among the states, and maintains the supremacy of national law in the federal system.

Since 1869, the U.S. Supreme Court has consisted of eight associate justices and one Chief Justice, who is nominated by the president specifically for that position. There is no special significance about the number nine, and the Constitution is silent about the size of the Court. Between 1801 and 1869, Congress altered the size of the Court several times. The lowest number of justices on the Court was six; the most, ten. In 1866, Congress reduced the size of the Court from ten to eight so that President Andrew Johnson, who was very unpopular with Congress (and who escaped being removed from office by the Senate by just one vote), could not fill two vacancies that existed. When the more popular former war hero Ulysses S. Grant took office, the number was increased to nine, where it has remained. Through 1994, only 108 justices had served on the Court and there had been fifteen chief justices (see Table 9-1).

The Chief Justice presides over public sessions of the Court, conducts the Court's conferences, assigns the writing of opinions (if he is in the majority; otherwise the most senior justice in the majority makes the assignment), and by custom administers the oath of office to the president and the vice president on Inauguration Day (any federal judge can administer the oath, as has happened when presidents have died in of-

A *Washington Post* cartoon pokes fun at FDR's court packing plan and the changes that have occurred over the years in the Court's size.

From Herblock: A Cartoonist's Life (Lisa Drew Books/Macmillan Publishers, 1993).

Table 9.1 ♦ Chief Justices of the Supreme Court

CHIEF JUSTICE	NOMINATING PRESIDENT	YEARS OF SERVICE
John Jay	Washington	1789–1795
John Rutledge*	Washington	1795
Oliver Ellsworth	Washington	1796–1800
John Marshall	Adams	1801–1835
Roger B. Taney	Jackson	1836–1864
Salmon P. Chase	Lincoln	1864–1873
Morrison R. Waite	Grant	1874–1888
Melville W. White	Cleveland	1888–1910
Edward D. White	Taft	1910–1921
William Howard Taft	Harding	1921–1930
Charles Evans Hughes	Hoover	1930–1941
Harlan Fiske Stone	F. Roosevelt	1941–1946
Fred M. Vinson	Truman	1946–1953
Earl Warren	Eisenhower	1953–1969
Warren E. Burger	Nixon	1969–1986
William H. Rehnquist	Reagan	1986–present

*Not confirmed by the Senate.

fice). By law, the Chief Justice, like the rest of the justices, is authorized to hire four clerks. Chief Justice William H. Rehnquist, however, has a tradition of hiring only three. He also has several secretaries and a messenger to help him with his duties. In 1972, Congress authorized the position of administrative assistant to serve at the pleasure of the Chief Justice. Chief Justice Warren E. Burger (1969–1986) used his assistant to help him in his nonlegal judicial duties by conducting research, monitoring judicial administration, supervising Court operations, and educating the public about the role of the Supreme Court.

In addition to their law clerks, justices are assisted in their duties by personal secretaries and other members of the Court's support staff, including

- The Clerk of the Court: In 1790, the justices authorized the appointment of the Clerk as the Court's official business manager. The Clerk accepts all filings, administers the Court's docket (all the cases it is asked to hear) receives all appeals, petitions, and motions, and prepares the Court's formal judgments; advises attorneys about Court rules, schedule, etc.
- The Marshal of the Court: In 1867, Congress authorized this position of the Court's chief security officer. Today, the duties of the Marshal and his staff include supervising physical facilities and grounds, and fiscal affairs including salaries, etc.
- The Reporter of Decisions: Originally this was an informal position. For several years, private individuals called "Reporters" published opinions of the Court and were com-

pensated by sales. In 1817, Congress created the official position. The Reporter edits opinions and supervises their printing in the Court's official reporter, *The United States Reports*.

- The Public Information Officer: answers questions from the press and the public about the Court and the justices.
- The Legal Office: Created by the Court in 1973, it has two attorneys who serve four-year terms. They serve as in-house counsel on questions regarding the Court and also assist with screening petitions when necessary.

It is not uncommon to hear a disgruntled party emerge from a local courthouse and angrily vow to take his or her appeal "all the way to the Supreme Court." In reality, this seldom happens. Although the Court received a record 7,786 petitions for review

Then and Now

Law Clerks

As early as 1850, the justices of the Supreme Court had beseeched Congress to approve the hiring of an "investigating clerk" to assist each justice, particularly in copying opinions. Congress denied the request, so when Justice Horace Gray hired the first law clerk in 1882, he paid the clerk himself. Justice Gray's clerk was a top graduate of Harvard Law School whose duties included cutting Justice Gray's hair and running personal errands. Finally, in 1886, Congress authorized each justice to hire a "stenographer clerk" for $1,600 a year.

Today, clerks generally serve for periods of one to two years. In the past, however, some justices employed their clerks for longer periods. Pierce Butler's clerk, for example, served sixteen years.

Over time, the number of clerks employed by the justices has increased. Through the 1946 to 1969 terms, most justices employed two clerks. By 1970, most had three; and by 1980 all but three had four. In 1994, there were thirty-nine clerks serving the nine justices, whereas twenty years ago there were half as many. This growth in clerks has had many interesting ramifications on the Court. As noted by Richard A. Posner, "between 1969 and 1972—the period during which the justices each became entitled to a third law clerk— . . . the number of opinions increased by about 50 percent and the number of words tripled."* After the justices were authorized to hire a fourth clerk in 1980, a substantial growth in the number of citations and footnotes in each case occurred again.** And until recently, the number of cases decided annually increased as more help was available to the justices.

The justices have complete discretion over whom they hire and the nature and amount of the work they assign. Clerks are typically selected from candidates at the top of the graduating classes of prestigious law schools (see the accompanying figure). They perform a variety of tasks, ranging from searching every page of *United States Reports* for some particular information to playing tennis or taking walks with the justices. Clerks spend most of their time researching material relevant to particular cases, reading and summarizing cases, and helping justices write opinions. Just how much help they provide in the writing of opinions is not known. Although it is occasionally alleged that a particular clerk wrote a particular opinion delivered by a justice, no such allegation has ever been proved. The relationship between clerks and the justices for whom they work is close and confidential, and many aspects

* Richard A. Posner, *The Federal Courts: Crisis and Reform* (Cambridge, MA: Harvard University Press, 1985), p. 114.

** Ibid., p. 114.

in its 1993–1994 term, it handed down full opinions in only 184 cases for plenary (full) review—down from 146 in 1989 and 170 in 1988, as revealed in Figure 9-3. Furthermore, the appellate process (the process of appealing decisions of one court to a higher court) is costly and lengthy. A case could take at least five years to get to the Supreme Court, and litigation of more than twenty years' duration is not out of the question, as cases get bounced back and forth on different issues between courts of different levels. For example, many inmates have been on death row for ten or more years as they await the appeals of their cases on various grounds (although, as noted in Chapter 4, the Court is trying to limit these appeals and to expedite the process). Criminal cases, including death penalty cases, come before the Court through its appellate jurisdiction. A much less common way for a case to reach the Court is through its original jurisdiction (described later in this chapter).

---

of the relationship are kept secret. Clerks may sometimes talk among themselves about the views and personalities of their justices, but rarely has a clerk leaked such information to the press.

Some former clerks try to exploit their connection to their justice, but at times this tactic can backfire. When North Dakota Attorney General Nicholas Spaeth, a former clerk to Justice Byron White, appeared before the Court, he did so sporting a necktie covered with buffaloes that White had given him years earlier. He jokingly referred to the tie, saying he had worn it because he particularly needed the vote of White, the only justice in the majority of an earlier, similar case still on the Court. White looked annoyed, the other justices did not laugh, and Justice Kennedy's later questioning revealed his obvious displeasure with Spaeth's theatrics.[†]

[†]Tony Mauro, "The Highs and Lows of the 1992 Court," *Legal Times* (December 28, 1992): 12.

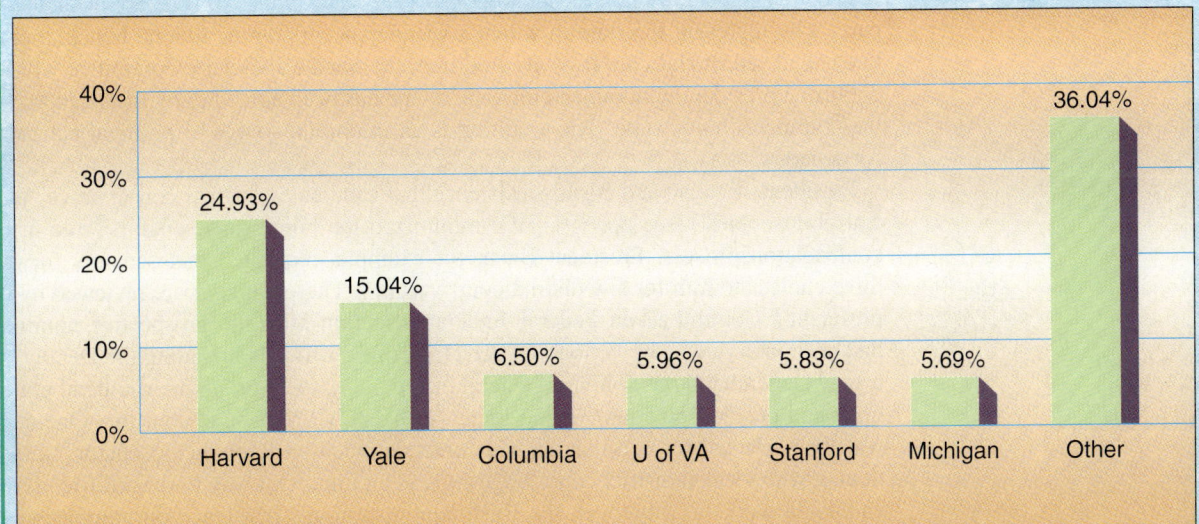

Where Do Law Clerks Come From? Law Schools of 738 Supreme Court Clerks Between 1958 and 1985.

- Harvard: 24.93%
- Yale: 15.04%
- Columbia: 6.50%
- U of VA: 5.96%
- Stanford: 5.83%
- Michigan: 5.69%
- Other: 36.04%

Source: Karen O'Connor and John R. Hermann, "The Clerk Connection: A History and Analysis of Clerk Participation Before the U.S. Supreme Court," paper prepared for delivery at the 1993 annual meeting of the Midwest Political Science Association.

How Federal Court Judges Are Selected

Although specific, detailed provisions in Articles I and II specify the qualifications for president, senator, and member of the House of Representatives, the Constitution is curiously silent on the qualifications for federal judge. This may have been because of an assumption that all federal judges would be lawyers, but to make such a requirement explicit might have marked the judicial branch as too elite for the tastes of common men and women. Also, it would have been impractical to require formal legal training, given that there were so few law schools in the nation, and the fact that most lawyers became licensed after clerking or apprenticing with another attorney.[12]

The selection of federal judges is often a very political process with important political ramifications, since they are nominated by the president and must be confirmed by the U.S. Senate. During the Reagan/Bush years, for example, 553 basically conservative Republican judges were appointed to the federal bench (see Figure 9-4). The cumulative impact of this conservative block of judges led many liberal groups to abandon their efforts to expand rights through the federal courts. (See "The American Civil Liberties Union," p. 126.)

Typically, federal district court judges have held other political offices, such as those of state court judge or prosecutor, as illustrated in Table 9.2. Most have been involved in politics, which is what usually brings them into consideration for a position on the federal bench. Griffin Bell, Attorney General in the Carter administration and former federal circuit court judge, once remarked, "For me, becoming a federal judge wasn't very difficult. I managed John F. Kennedy's presidential campaign in Georgia. And I was campaign manager and special counsel for the governor [Carter]."[13]

Each year, a large number of federal district court judgeships become available through death and retirement, and other openings occur as Congress continually adds new positions in an effort to meet the increasing demands on the federal court system. Presidents Jimmy Carter and Ronald Reagan, for example, each appointed more than 200 judges to the federal district courts.

Presidents generally defer selection of district court judges to senators of their own party who represent the state in which a vacancy occurs on the federal bench, a practice called **senatorial courtesy**. By tradition, the Senate Judiciary Committee will not confirm a presidential nominee unless he or she has been agreed to by the senator(s) of the nominee's home state. This tradition is an important source of political patronage for senators.

Presidents Reagan and Bush's insistence that candidates possess conservative "judicial philosophies" (see pp. 391–392) minimized the home-state senators' role in the confirmation process. President Bush, for example, requested that senators forward three choices to him for any district court vacancy. These names were reviewed by the president's Committee on Federal Judicial Selection after the prospective nominees had been interviewed by various Justice Department officials including the Deputy Attorney General and the Solicitor General (see p. 384), to ascertain their judicial philosophy and position on controversial issues such as civil rights and abortion. One name was then selected for nomination. This practice incensed Republican senators, in particular, who viewed district court judgeships as an important way to reward friends and campaign workers. Moreover, the Bush administration's insistence on nominees who

---

[12] John R. Vile and Mario Perez-Reilly, "The U.S. Constitution and Judicial Qualifications: A Curious Omission," *Judicature* (December/January 1991): 198–202.

[13] Quoted in Nina Totenberg, "Will Judges Be Chosen Rationally?" *Judicature* (August/September 1976): 93.

FIGURE 9-4
How a President Affects the Federal Judiciary

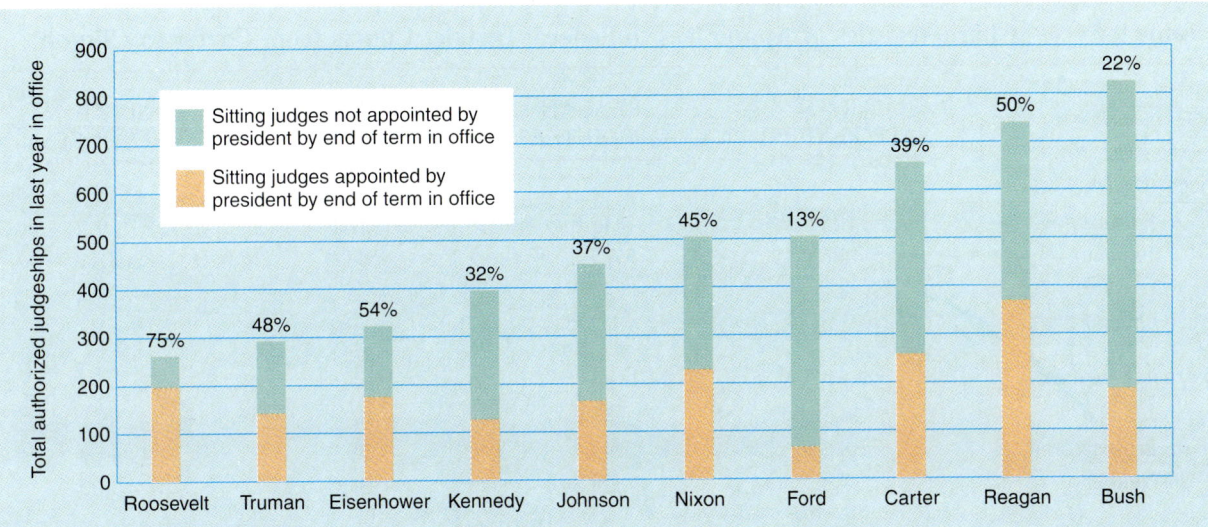

President	Appointed to Supreme Court	Appointed to Court of Appeals (a)	Appointed to District Courts (b)	Total Appointed	Total Number of Judgeships (c)	Percentage of Judgeships Filled by President
Roosevelt (1933-45)	9	52	136	197	262	75%
Truman (1945-53)	4	26	115	141	292	48
Eisenhower (1953-61)	5	45	125	175	322	54
Kennedy (1961-63)	2	21	103	126	395	32
Johnson (1963-69)	2	40	122	164	449	37
Nixon (1969-74)	4	45	179	228	504	45
Ford (1974-77)	1	12	52	65	504	13
Carter (1977-81)	0	56	202	258	657	39
Reagan (1981-89)	3	78	290	368	740	50
Bush (1989-93)	2	37	148	185	825	22
Clinton (d) (1993-94)	2	13	71	100	837	12

(a) Does not include the appeals court for the Federal Circuit
(b) Includes district courts in the territories
(c) Total judgeships authorized in president's last year in office
(d) Data for Clinton is through August 1994.

Source: "Imprints on the Bench," *CQ Weekly Report*, January 19, 1991, p. 173. Reprinted by permission. Data on Clinton and Bush provided by the Senate Judiciary Committee.

This figure shows the number of authorized federal judgeships in the last year of a president's term and the percent of those judgeships filled by appointees of the president. The table below the figure breaks down the president's appointments for each level of the judiciary.

369

Table 9.2 ♦ Characteristics of Appointees to Federal District Courts from Carter to Clinton

	CARTER APPOINTEES	REAGAN APPOINTEES	BUSH APPOINTEES	CLINTON NOMINEES*
Occupation (percent)				
Politics/gov't	4.4	12.8	10.8	9.1
Judiciary	44.6	37.2	44.9	51.1
Lawyer	57.7	47.3	45.2	38.7
Other	3.5	2.8	2.1	1.1
Experience (percent)				
Judicial	54.5	46.6	46.6	55.7
Prosecutorial	38.6	44.1	39.2	44.3
Neither	28.2	28.3	31.8	23.9
Political Affiliation (percent)				
Democrat	92.6	4.8	5.4	87.5
Republican	4.4	93.1	88.5	3.4
Independent	2.9	2.1	6.1	6.8
Religion (percent)				
Protestant	60.4	60.3	64.2	N/A
Catholic	27.7	30.0	28.4	N/A
Jewish	11.9	9.3	7.4	N/A
Race/ethnicity (percent)				
White	78.7	92.4	89.2	60.2
Black	13.9	2.1	6.8	27.3
Asian-American	0.5	0.7	—	1.1
Hispanic	6.9	4.8	4.0	10.2
Sex				
Percent Female	14.4	8.3	19.6	32.9
Net Worth (percent)				
Under $200,000	35.8**	17.6	10.1	15.9
200-499,999	41.2**	37.6	31.1	21.6
500-999,999	18.9**	21.7	26.4	33.0
1,000,000+	4.0**	23.1	32.4	29.5
Total number of appointees	202	290	148	88
Average age at nomination (years)	49.7	48.7	48.1	49.4

* Appointees through June 7, 1994.

** These figures are for appointees confirmed by the 96th Congress. Professor Elliot Slotnick of Ohio State University provided the net worth figures for all but six Carter district court appointees, for whom no data were available.

Source: Sheldon Goldman, "The Bush Imprint on the Judiciary: Carrying on a Tradition," *Judicature* 74 (April–May 1991). Clinton data was compiled by Professor Goldman. The Clinton data is for all *nominees* to *all* lower federal courts, not just the federal district courts.

were "philosophically conservative"[14] resulted in a considerable number of vacancies on the federal bench. When President Bush left office, there were over 100 vacancies on the federal courts for President Clinton to fill.

Senatorial courtesy does not operate to the same degree in the selection of the more prestigious Courts of Appeals judgeships, largely because the jurisdiction of each circuit includes at least three states. When vacancies on the Courts of Appeals occur, presidents frequently consult senators of the various states in the circuit, but ultimately the Justice Department plays the key role in the selection process.

To ensure diverse representation of African-Americans, women, and other groups traditionally underrepresented on the federal bench, President Jimmy Carter established judicial nominating commissions (consisting of lawyers and laypersons selected by the president) in each circuit. Each commission was charged with submitting three to five names to the president for his consideration when vacancies occurred. According to political scientist Elliot E. Slotnick, in spite of President Carter's efforts to depoliticize the process, the judges selected in this manner were no different from those chosen more traditionally. Like those chosen in the past, they were overwhelmingly from the president's party and were likely to have been involved in party politics.[15] But Carter's efforts to open up the process did produce more women and minority judges than even before.

The commissions were abandoned by President Reagan, whose Justice Department (and increasingly, the White House counsel) played a key role in selecting Court of Appeals judges. George Bush's administration followed in this tradition, as it searched for ideological conservatives who could further both administrations' political agendas through rulings from the bench. Bill Clinton created a three-member committee in the White House to help him fill federal court vacancies. He was criticized for taking so long to fill vacancies—by August 1993, only 14 nominations were forwarded to the Senate to fill the 136 existing vacancies. White House officials insisted that the delay occurred because it took Democratic senators so long to get their nominating commissions in place after 12 years of Republican rule. By June 1994, Clinton had appointed 100 federal judges. Nearly one-third were women, thirty-eight percent were members of minority groups and two of those minorities were Native Americans.

Appointments to the U.S. Supreme Court

The Constitution is silent on the qualifications for appointment to the Supreme Court (as well as to other constitutional courts), although Justice Oliver Wendell Holmes once remarked that a justice should be a "combination of Justinian, Jesus Christ and John Marshall."[16] In Great Britain, where the Lord Chancellor is the highest court official (formally appointed by the Crown but actually chosen by the prime minister), ideology is often not a concern in court appointments; experience as a trial judge is. In the United States, until recently Supreme Court justices generally have had little previous judicial experience on any level. Of the 108 justices who have served or are serving on the Court, only twenty-four had had ten or more years of experience on any bench, and forty-two had had no judicial experience at all.

According to insurance company statistics, only conductors of symphony orchestras enjoy longer life spans than Supreme Court justices.

---

[14] Sheldon Goldman, "The Bush Imprint on the Federal Judiciary: Carrying on a Tradition," *Judicature* (April/May 1991): 297.

[15] Elliot E. Slotnick, "Federal Appellate Judge Selection During the Carter Administration: Recruitment Changes and Unanswered Questions," *Justice System Journal* 6 (Fall 1981): 293–304.

[16] Quoted in Judge Irving R. Kaufman, "Charting a Judicial Pedigree," *The New York Times* (January 24, 1981): 23.

372 ❖ Chapter 9 The Judiciary

The justices of the Court gather before the 1994–1995 term begins upon the occasion of the investiture of its newest member, Justice Stephen Breyer, the sixth new Justice since 1986. Left to right are Justices Clarence Thomas, Antonin Scalia, Sandra Day O'Connor, Anthony Kennedy, David Souter, Stephen Breyer, John Paul Stevens, Chief Justice William H. Rehnquist, and Ruth Bader Ginsburg.

Like other federal court judges, the justices of the Supreme Court are nominated by the president and must be confirmed by the Senate. Historically, however, because of the special place the Supreme Court enjoys in our constitutional system, its nominees have encountered more opposition than district or Court of Appeals judges. As the role of the Court has increased over time, so too has the amount of attention given to nominees. And with the increased attention has come greater opposition, especially to nominees with controversial views.

Nomination Criteria

Justice Sandra Day O'Connor once remarked that "You have to be lucky" to be appointed to the Court.[17] Although luck is certainly important, over the years nominations to the bench have been made for a variety of reasons. Depending on the timing of a vacancy, a president may or may not have a list of possible candidates or even a specific individual in mind. Until recently, presidents often have looked within their circle of friends or their administration to fill a vacancy. Nevertheless, whether the nominee is a friend or someone known to the president only by reputation, at least six criteria are especially important:

1. *Competence and ethical standards.* Most prospective nominees are expected to have had at least some judicial or governmental experience. John Jay, the first Chief Justice, was one of the authors of *The Federalist Papers* and was active in New York politics. John Marshall was a former Secretary of State. (See People of the Past, "John Marshall," p. 356.) As Table 9.3 shows, unlike justices of the past, most recent appointees to the Court have had some prior judicial experience. Moreover, Justices John Paul Stevens, Anthony Kennedy, Antonin Scalia, David Souter, Clarence Thomas, and Ruth Bader Ginsburg all served on the U.S. Court of Appeals.

---

[17] Quoted in Lawrence Baum, *The Supreme Court*, 3rd. ed. (Washington: CQ Press, 1989), p. 108.

Table 9.3 ◆ The Supreme Court, 1994

NAME	YEAR OF BIRTH	YEAR OF APPOINTMENT	POLITICAL PARTY	LAW SCHOOL	APPOINTING PRESIDENT	RELIGION	PRIOR JUDICIAL EXPERIENCE	PRIOR GOVERNMENT EXPERIENCE
William H. Rehnquist	1924	1971 1986*	R	Stanford	Nixon	Lutheran	—	Assistant U.S. Attorney General
John Paul Stevens	1920	1975	R	Chicago	Ford	Non-denominational Protestant	U.S. Court of Appeals	—
Sandra Day O'Connor	1930	1981	R	Stanford	Reagan	Episcopalian	Arizona Court of Appeals	State Legislator
Antonin Scalia	1936	1986	R	Harvard	Reagan	Catholic	U.S. Court of Appeals	—
Anthony M. Kennedy	1936	1988	R	Harvard	Reagan	Catholic	U.S. Court of Appeals	—
David H. Souter	1939	1990	R	Harvard	Bush	Episcopalian	U.S. Court of Appeals	New Hampshire Attorney General
Clarence Thomas	1948	1991	R	Yale	Bush	Catholic	U.S. Court of Appeals	Chair, Equal Employment Opportunity Commission
Ruth Bader Ginsburg	1933	1993	D	Columbia	Clinton	Jewish	U.S. Court of Appeals	—
Stephen Breyer	1938	1994	D	Harvard	Clinton	Jewish	U.S. Court of Appeals	Chief Counsel, Senate Judiciary Committee

*Promoted to Chief by Reagan in 1986.

Anita Hill testifies before the then all-male Senate Judiciary Committee as it considered the appointment of Clarence Thomas to the Supreme Court.

Recently, some have begun to question the advisability of having so many former judges on the Court. In the past, many great Supreme Court justices, including John Marshall, Earl Warren (Governor and Attorney General of California), Hugo Black (U.S. Senate), and William O. Douglas (Chair of the Securities and Exchange Commission) had more extensive *governmental* and policy experience. In 1994, the Court had but one member with any prior experience as an elected governmental official: Sandra Day O'Connor, who had served in the Arizona State Senate for ten years, and as her party's Majority Leader. Some argue that it is important for a Court that makes major policy to have members with a broader range of practical *political* experience.

It is rare for the ethical standards or personal lives of prospective members of the Court to be challenged. In 1968, upon Lyndon B. Johnson's nomination of Associate Justice Abe Fortas to the position of Chief Justice, enough questions were raised about the propriety of Fortas's business dealings that his nomination was withdrawn. More recently, in 1991 the nation sat riveted to their television sets as they watched Clarence Thomas being questioned about charges of sexual harassment levied against him by a former employee, Anita Hill. Although these charges were not enough to stand in the way of his confirmation, they did result in one of the closest confirmation votes ever for a Supreme Court justice: fifty-two to forty-eight.

2. *Ideological or policy preferences.* Most presidents seek to appoint to the Court individuals who share their policy preferences, and almost all have political goals in mind when they appoint a justice. Upon the death of staunch Federalist Justice William Cushing, for example, Thomas Jefferson wrote to one of his allies,

> I observe old Cushing is dead. At length, then, we have a chance of getting a Republican majority in the Supreme Judiciary. For ten years has that branch braved the spirit and will of the nation. . . . The event is a fortunate one, and so timed as to be a godsend to me.[18]

Presidents Franklin D. Roosevelt, Richard M. Nixon, and Ronald Reagan were very successful in molding the Court to their own political beliefs. Roosevelt was quickly able to appoint eight justices from 1937 to his death in 1945, solidifying support for his liberal New Deal programs. In contrast, Nixon and Reagan publicly proclaimed that they would nominate only individuals who favored a **strict constructionist** approach to constitutional decision making—that is, an approach emphasizing the initial intentions of the Framers (see p. 392). Justices William Rehnquist and Antonin Scalia, in particular, have been very vocal in support of this view, believing that it is inappropriate for the judiciary to make policy through broad or expansive interpretations of the Constitution.[19] Instead, they argue, the Court should construe the Constitution narrowly.

While Bush's predecessors forwarded some fairly controversial nominees to the Senate Judiciary Committee for its approval, President Bush, in contrast, looked to a nominee with virtually no public record when his first vacancy occurred. Many believe that it was the absence of any controversial pronouncements in David Souter's background that prompted his nomination. Upon Souter's nomination, Bush said that

---

[18] Quoted in William H. Rehnquist, *The Supreme Court: How It Was, How It Is* (New York: Morrow, 1987), p. 237.

[19] But see Sue Davis, *Justice Rehnquist and the Conservative Judicial Philosophy* (Princeton, NJ: Princeton University Press, 1989).

Supreme Court justices should be beyond the "flames of political passion" and urged the Senate to avoid allowing abortion or any other issue to become a "litmus test."[20] Some viewed Bush's self-stated goal of de-politicizing the selection of Supreme Court justices with skepticism that appeared warranted when Bush nominated Clarence Thomas to the high court in 1991. Thomas was well regarded in conservative circles and known for his writings and strong opinions on affirmative action and the role of the states in the federal system.

3. *Rewards.* Historically, many of those appointed to the Supreme Court have been personal friends of presidents. Abraham Lincoln, for example, appointed one of his key political advisers to the Court. More recently, Lyndon B. Johnson appointed his longtime friend Abe Fortas to the bench. In addition, most presidents select justices of their own party affiliation. Chief Justice Rehnquist was long active in Arizona Republican Party politics, as was Justice O'Connor before her appointment to the bench; both were appointed by Republican presidents. Party activism can also be used by presidents as an indication of a nominee's commitment to certain ideological principles.

4. *Pursuit of political support.* During Ronald Reagan's successful campaign for the presidency in 1980, some of his advisers feared that the "gender gap" would hurt him. Polls repeatedly showed that he was far less popular with female voters than with men. Particularly troublesome was his vocal opposition to the pending Equal Rights Amendment. To gain support from women, Reagan announced during his campaign that should he win, he would appoint a woman to fill the first vacancy on the Court. When Justice Potter Stewart, a moderate, announced his early retirement from the bench, President Reagan nominated Sandra Day O'Connor of the Arizona State Court of Appeals to fill the vacancy. It probably will not hurt President Clinton that his first appointment was a woman *and* Jewish (at a time when no Jews served on the Court).

5. *Religion.* Ironically, religion, which historically has been an important issue, was hardly mentioned during the most recent Supreme Court vacancies. Some did, however, hail Clinton's appointment of Ginsburg, noting that the traditionally "Jewish" seat on the Court had been vacant for over two decades, since Abe Fortas's resignation in 1969.

Through 1994, of the 108 justices who have served on the Court, almost all have been members of traditional Protestant faiths. Only nine have been Catholic and only seven have been Jewish.[21] Twice during the Rehnquist Court, more Catholics—Brennan, Scalia, and Kennedy and then Scalia, Kennedy, and Thomas—have served on the Court at one time than at any other period in history. Today, however, it is clear that religion cannot be taken as a sign of a justice's conservative or liberal ideology: When William Brennan was on the Court, he and Antonin Scalia were at ideological extremes.

6. *Race and gender.* Only two African-Americans and two women have served on the Court. Race was undoubtedly a critical issue in the appointment of Clarence Thomas to replace Thurgood Marshall, the first African-American justice. But President Bush refused to acknowledge his wish to retain a "black seat" on the Court. In-

---

[20] Laurene McQuillan, "Bush Urges Senate to Avoid Abortion Litmus Test on Souter," *Reuters*, July 24, 1990, NEXIS.

[21] Clarence Thomas is considered Catholic here, although he currently attends an Episcopalian church, having been barred from Catholic sacraments because of his remarriage.

stead, he announced that he was "picking the best man for the job on the merits," a claim that was met with considerable skepticism by many observers.

In contrast, O'Connor was pointedly picked because of her gender. Ginsburg's appointment was more matter-of-fact, and her selection surprised many after the Clinton administration appeared to consider seriously several men for the appointment first. (See "Lobbying for a Top Spot?," below.)

The Supreme Court Confirmation Process

Before 1900, about one-fourth of all presidential nominees to the Supreme Court were rejected by the Senate. In 1844, for example, President John Tyler sent six nominations to the Senate, and all but one were defeated. In 1866, Andrew Johnson nominated his brilliant Attorney General, Henry Stanberry, but the Senate's hostility to Johnson led it to *abolish* the seat to prevent Johnson's filling it.

As noted earlier, the Constitution gives the Senate the authority to approve all nominees to the federal bench, and the Senate takes this duty, given to it in the Advice and Consent clause, very seriously when considering nominees to the Supreme Court. Ordinarily, nominations are referred to the Senate Committee on the Judiciary. In the 103rd Congress, all but one member of the committee were lawyers. As detailed later, this committee investigates the nominees, holds hearings, and votes on its recommendation for Senate action. The full Senate then deliberates on the nominee before voting. A simple majority vote is required for confirmation.

Lobbying for a Top Spot?

In their book on the Supreme Court, *The Brethren*, Bob Woodward and Scott Armstrong wrote critically of Court of Appeals Judge Warren Burger's apparent lobbying of Richard Nixon for the position of Chief Justice.* How times have changed. In 1993, Martin Ginsburg, the husband of Court of Appeals Judge Ruth Bader Ginsburg, unabashedly orchestrated a letter-writing campaign on behalf of his wife's nomination to the Supreme Court. Martin Ginsburg, a prominent tax attorney and Georgetown University law professor, contacted his wife's former students, the presidents of Stanford and Columbia, academics, legal scholars, and even Texas Governor Ann Richards to call or write the White House urging his wife's nomination. Said the nominee's husband of his campaign on his wife's behalf after her nomination, "If there was something I could have done to be helpful, I would have done it, because I think my wife is super, and the president couldn't have made a better appointment than the one he just made."**

Unconventional? Yes. Effective? You decide.

*Bob Woodward and Scott Armstrong, *The Brethren* (New York: Simon and Schuster, 1979).

**Eleanor Randolph, "Ginsburg's spouse says he arranged letter campaign," *Washington Post* (June 17, 1993): A-17.

Lobbying on Ginsburg's behalf paid off when she became the second woman on the nation's highest court joining Sandra Day O'Connor.

Investigation.   Once a president settles on a nominee to the Supreme Court, the nominee's name is sent to the Federal Bureau of Investigation. Some "investigation" actually occurs before the formal nomination process. When Ronald Reagan, for example, announced he was *planning* to nominate Douglas Ginsburg of the Washington, D.C. U.S. Court of Appeals, enough "information" about Ginsburg's use of drugs with students while a law professor at Harvard led Reagan *not* to nominate him formally. Similarly, in 1993, President Clinton at first appeared to be leaning toward the appointment of Judge Stephen Breyer of the U.S. Court of Appeals until it was revealed that he had failed to pay social security taxes for a domestic worker. Breyer left his hospital bed to meet with the president and even wrote his acceptance speech at Clinton's insistence. However, Breyer's tax problem caused the president to abandon his apparent first choice for the Court. Breyer later became Clinton's second nominee.

While the FBI conducts an extensive background check of the formal nominee, the Senate Judiciary Committee also begins to investigate his or her background. (The same process is used for nominees of the lower federal courts, although such investigations generally are not nearly as extensive as for Supreme Court nominees.)

To begin its task, the Senate Judiciary Committee asks each nominee to complete a lengthy questionnaire detailing previous work (dating as far back as high-school summer jobs), judicial opinions written, judicial philosophy, speeches, and even all interviews ever given to members of the press. Committee staffers also contact potential witnesses who might offer testimony concerning the nominee's fitness for office.

At the same time, the president also forwards the name of the nominee to the American Bar Association (ABA), the politically powerful organization that represents the interests of the legal profession. After its own investigation, the ABA rates the nominee, based on his or her qualifications, as Highly Qualified (now called "Well-Qualified"), Qualified, or Not Qualified. (The same system is used for lower federal court nominees.)[22]

David Souter, Bush's first nominee to the Court, received a unanimous rating of Highly Qualified from the ABA, as did both of Clinton's nominees, Ruth Bader Ginsburg and Stephen Breyer. In contrast, another Bush nominee, Clarence Thomas, was given only a Qualified rating (well before the charges of sexual harassment became public), with two members voting Not Qualified. Of the twenty-two previous nominees rated by the ABA, he was the first to receive less than at least a unanimous Qualified rating.

Lobbying by Interest Groups.   The ABA is an organization that is asked formally to rate nominees, but other groups are also keenly interested in the nomination process.

Until recently, interest groups have played a minor and backstage role in most appointments to the U.S. Supreme Court. Although interest groups generally have not lobbied on behalf of any one individual, in 1981, women's rights groups successfully urged President Reagan to honor his campaign commitment to appoint a woman to the high court.

It is more common for interest groups to lobby *against* a prospective nominee. Even this, however, is a relatively recent phenomenon. In 1937, the National Association for the Advancement of Colored People (NAACP) lobbied unsuccessfully against the appointment of Hugo Black to the Supreme Court. Although the Alabama native was a former member of the Ku Klux Klan, the NAACP was unable to mobilize sufficient

---

[22] Over the years, the exact labels have varied.

opposition to block his confirmation. More successful was the American Federation of Labor (AFL), which in 1930 was able to block the nomination of John J. Parker, chief judge of the U.S. Fourth Circuit Court of Appeals. The AFL opposed Parker's nomination because he supported agreements allowing employers to prohibit their employees from joining or assisting a labor union. Moreover, Parker's hostile racial sentiments caused the NAACP to join the chorus against his nomination. Most observers see this alliance of interests as key to the success of the effort to block the Parker nomination. After a sixteen-week fight, he became the first nominee rejected in the twentieth century, on a close vote of forty-one to thirty-nine.

In 1987, the nomination of Robert H. Bork to the Supreme Court produced an unprecedented amount of interest-group lobbying on both sides of the nomination. The Democratic-controlled Judiciary Committee delayed the hearings, thus allowing liberal interest groups time to mobilize the most extensive radio, television, and print media campaign ever launched against a nominee to the U.S. Supreme Court. This opposition was in spite of the fact that Bork sat with distinction on the D.C. Court of Appeals, and was a former U.S. Solicitor General, a top-ranked law school graduate, and a Yale Law School professor. (His actions as Solicitor General, especially his firing of the Watergate Special Prosecutor—see "Watergate and Its Effect on the Presidency," pp. 264–265—however, made him a special target for traditional liberals.)

In the national elections of 1986, Democrats recaptured the majority in the U.S. Senate after six years as the minority party. Many new Democratic senators were elected from the South, and all could attribute their victories to the power of the black vote. When President Reagan nominated Judge Bork, long an outspoken opponent of affirmative action and any kind of judicial activism, civil rights groups contacted key Democratic senators to remind them of their narrow victories and who was responsible for them. Interest groups also banded together and carefully planned the testimony they would give before the Judiciary Committee in opposition to Bork.

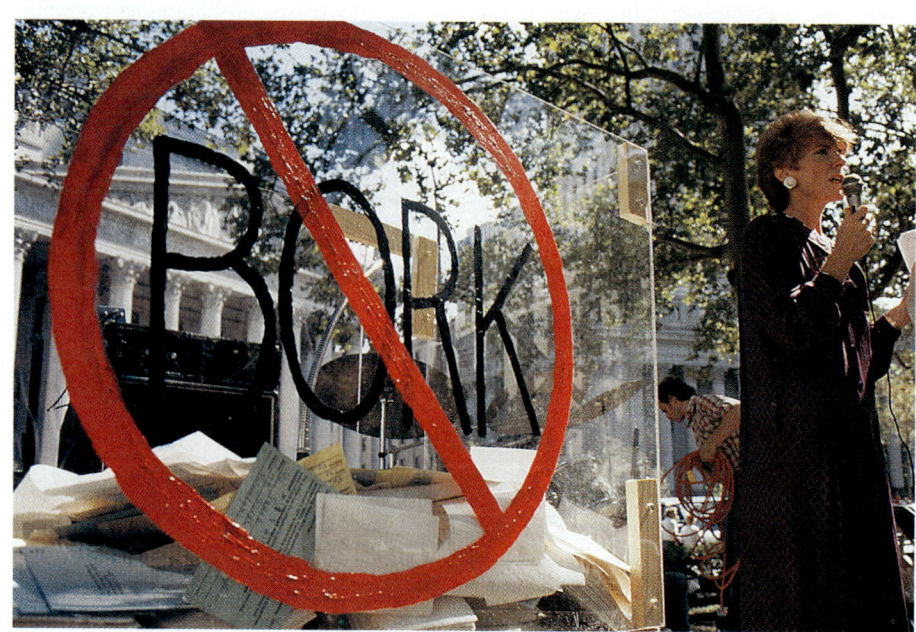

The scrutiny by the public and press of President Reagan's Supreme Court nominee Robert H. Bork set a new standard of inquiry into the values—both political and personal—of future nominees. Bork's nomination was rejected by the Senate in 1987.

These interest groups and the media also used the time between the nomination and the confirmation hearings to garner unprecedented amounts of information on the nominee—even Judge Bork's personal video-rental preferences were brought to public attention. In the end, Bork's nomination was defeated by a vote of fifty-eight to forty-two.

The Senate Committee Hearings. As the uneventful Ginsburg hearings attest (she was confirmed by a Senate vote of ninety-seven to three), not all nominees inspire the kind of intense reaction that kept Bork from the Court and, more recently, almost blocked the confirmation of Clarence Thomas. Until 1929, all but one Senate Judiciary Committee hearing on a Supreme Court nominee was conducted in executive session—that is, closed to the public. The 1916 hearings on Louis Brandeis, the first Jewish justice, were conducted in public and lasted nineteen days, although Brandeis himself was never called to testify. In 1939, Felix Frankfurter became the first nominee to testify in any detail before the committee. Subsequent revelations about Brandeis's payment to Frankfurter for his participation in cases (while Brandeis was on the Court) raise questions about the fitness of both Frankfurter and Brandeis for the bench. Still, no information about Frankfurter's legal arrangements with Brandeis was unearthed during the committee's investigations or Frankfurter's testimony.[23]

Until recently, modern nomination hearings were no more thorough in terms of the attention given to nominees' backgrounds. In 1969, for example, Chief Justice Warren E. Burger was confirmed by the Senate on a vote of ninety-four to three, just nineteen days after he was nominated!

---

[23] See Bruce Allen Murphy, *The Brandeis/Frankfurter Connection* (New York: Oxford University Press, 1982).

The Hearings that Rocked the Nation

♦ ♦ ♦

The Clarence Thomas hearings originally proceeded true to the form of previous hearings. Democratic senators tried not only to pin Judge Thomas down on his views on a variety of controversial issues, but also to question him about the numerous speeches he had delivered and conservative articles he had written. Like most nominees before him, Thomas steadfastly refused to answer these questions. At one point, he even responded to a series of questions on abortion by saying that he had never even discussed it, a response that many found difficult to believe.

After Thomas's initial hearings and a seven-to-seven committee vote, Nina Totenberg, a reporter for National Public Radio, reported on the eve of the vote of the full Senate that a complaint of sexual misconduct had been made to Senate staffers and was contained in the FBI report, but had not been mentioned during the hearings. Reacting to public pressure and to Thomas's own request to clear his name, the Senate committee then held an unprecedented additional several days of hearings. As the nation sat transfixed before its television sets, Anita Hill, a law professor, recounted in graphic detail her allegations of Clarence Thomas's on-the-job sexual harassment of her while he headed the Equal Employment Opportunity Commission (ironically, the federal agency charged with investigating such complaints). Thomas angrily denounced her charges, characterizing the whole Senate hearing process as a "high-tech lynching." In spite of this controversy, Thomas was confirmed as the Court's 106th justice.

Since the 1980s, it has become standard for Senators to ask the nominees probing questions, but most nominees (with the notable exception of Robert Bork) have declined to answer most of them on the grounds that these issues might ultimately come before the Court.

The Vote in the Senate. After hearings are concluded, the Senate Judiciary Committee usually makes a recommendation to the full Senate. Any rejections of presidential nominees to the Supreme Court generally occur only after the Senate Judiciary Committee has recommended against a nominee's appointment. Few recent confirmations have been close; prior to Clarence Thomas's fifty-two to forty-eight vote, Rehnquist's nominations as associate justice (sixty-eight to twenty-six) and as Chief Justice (sixty-nine to thirty-three) were the closest in recent history.

The Supreme Court Today

Given the judicial system's vast size and substantial power (at least indirect) over so many aspects of our lives, it is surprising that so many Americans know next to nothing about the judicial system in general and the Supreme Court in particular. Until very recently, Senate Judiciary Committee hearings concerning nominees were conducted with little or no publicity, and little attention has been paid to the personnel of the Court. Even today, at a time when the Court is enjoying unprecedented media attention, few Americans can correctly name the Chief Justice, let alone the other eight justices. A *Washington Post* poll found that while more than 50 percent of Americans knew of Judge Joseph Wapner of the TV show "The People's Court," fewer than 10 percent knew of Chief Justice Rehnquist.[24] Another poll conducted in 1990 for the Court's 200th anniversary revealed that only 23 percent of Americans queried knew how many justices sit on the Court, and nearly two-thirds could not name a single member of the Court.[25]

Although much of this ignorance can be blamed on the American public's lack of interest, part of the problem stems from the Court itself. Its rites and rituals contribute to the Court's mystique and encourage a "cult of the robe." Consider, for example, the way judicial proceedings are conducted. Oral arguments are not televised, and deliberations concerning the outcome of cases are conducted in utmost secrecy. In contrast, C-SPAN brings us daily coverage of various congressional hearings and floor debate on bills and important national issues, and Court TV (and sometimes other networks) provides gavel-to-gavel coverage of many important state court trials.

Deciding to Hear a Case

Although more than 7,000 cases a year are now filed at the Supreme Court, this was not always the case. From 1790 to 1801, the Court heard only eighty-seven cases under its appellate jurisdiction.[26] In the Court's early years, the bulk of the justices'

---

[24] Phil Rosenthal, "Why Not Wapner?," *The San Diego Union-Tribune* (March 25, 1993): F-5.
[25] Marcia Coyle, "How Americans View High Court," *The National Law Journal* (February 26, 1990): 1.
[26] Stephen L. Wasby, *The Supreme Court in the Federal Judicial System,* 4th ed. (Chicago: Nelson-Hall, 1988), p. 194.

workload involved their circuit-riding duties. From 1862 to 1866, only 240 cases were decided. Creation of the Courts of Appeals in 1891 resulted in an immediate reduction in Supreme Court filings—from 600 in 1890 to 275 in 1892.[27] As recently as the 1940s, fewer than 1,000 cases were filed annually. Since that time, filings have increased at a dramatic rate as revealed in Figure 9-3.

Jurisdiction

The Constitution specifically sets out the scope of the Supreme Court's original jurisdiction; that is, cases for which the Court functions as a trial court having the first, or original, hearing in the case. The Court has original jurisdiction "over all Cases affecting Ambassadors, other public Ministers and Consuls, and those in which a State shall be a party." Most cases arising under the Court's original jurisdiction involve disputes between two states, usually over issues such as ownership of offshore oil deposits, territorial disputes caused by shifting river boundaries, or controversies caused by conflicting claims over water rights, such as when a river flows through two or more states.[28] In earlier days, the Court would actually sit as a trial court and hear evidence and argument. Today, the Court usually appoints a Special Master—often a retired judge or an expert on the matter at hand—to hear the case in a district court on behalf of the Supreme Court and then report his or her findings and recommendations to the Court. It is rare for more than two or three of these cases to come to the Court in a year.

Most cases arrive at the Court under its appellate jurisdiction; that is, its authority to hear appeals from other courts in the state or federal systems (see Figure 9-1). The appellate jurisdiction of the Court can be changed by the Congress at any time, a power that has been a potent threat to the authority of the Court. The Judiciary Act of 1925 gave the Court discretion over its own jurisdiction, meaning that it does not have to accept all appeals that come to it. This so-called "Judge's Bill" was largely written by the Court itself under the direction of Chief Justice William Howard Taft (incidentally, the only member of the Court who also served as president of the United States). The idea behind the bill was that the intermediate Courts of Appeal should be the final word for almost all federal litigants, thus freeing the Supreme Court to concentrate on constitutional issues, unless the Court decided that it wanted to address other matters. The Court, then, is not expected to exercise its appellate jurisdiction simply to correct errors of other courts. Instead, appeal to the Supreme Court should be taken only if the case presents important issues of law, or what is termed "a substantial federal question." Since 1988, as illustrated in Figure 9-1, all appellate cases that come to the Supreme Court arrive there on a petition for a **writ of *certiorari*** (from the Latin "to be informed"), which are requests for the Supreme Court—at its discretion—to order up the records of the lower courts for purposes of review.

About one-third of all Supreme Court filings involve criminal law issues.[29] Many of these, in fact more than one-half of all petitions to the Court, are filed ***in forma pauperis*** (IFP) (literally from the Latin, "as a pauper"). About 80 percent of these are filed

---

[27] Ibid.
[28] Neubauer, *Judicial Process,* p. 370. (See n. 9.)
[29] William P. McLauchan, "The Business of the United States Supreme Court, 1971–1983: An Analysis of Supply and Demand," paper presented at the 1986 annual meeting of the Midwest Political Science Association.

by indigent prison inmates seeking review of their sentences. Permission to proceed *in forma pauperis* allows the petitioner to avoid filing and printing costs. Any criminal defendant who has had a court-appointed lawyer in a lower court proceeding is automatically entitled to proceed in this fashion.

In recent years, the Court has tended more and more to deny requests to file *in forma pauperis*. In *In re Sindram* (1991), for example, the Rehnquist Court chastised Michael Sindram for filing his petition *in forma pauperis* to require the Maryland courts to expedite his request to expunge a $35 speeding ticket from his record. Sindram was no stranger to the Supreme Court: During the previous three years, he had filed forty-two separate motions on various legal matters, twenty-four of them in the 1990 term. In denying Sindram's request to file as an indigent, the majority noted that "[t]he goal of fairly dispensing justice . . . is compromised when the Court is forced to devote its limited resources to the processing of repetitious and frivolous requests." Along with the order denying the petition, the Court issued new rules to provide for denial of "frivolous" or "malicious" IFP motions.[30]

The Rule of Four

Unlike other courts, the Supreme Court controls its own case load through the *certiorari* process and decides which cases it wants to hear, rejecting most cases that come to it. All petitions for *certiorari* must meet two criteria:

1. They must come from the U.S. Court of Appeals, special three-judge district courts, or a state court of last resort. Generally, this means that the case has already been decided by the state supreme court.
2. The case must involve a federal question. This means that the case must present questions of interpretation of federal constitutional law or involve a federal statute or treaty. The reasons why the Court should accept the case for review and legal argument supporting that position are set out in the petition (also called a brief).

The Clerk of the Court's office transmits petitions for writs of *certiorari* to the Chief Justice's office, where his clerks first review the petitions, and then to the individual justices' offices. All the justices on the Rehnquist Court except Justice John Paul Stevens participate in what is called the "cert pool."[31] As part of the pool, they review their assigned fraction of petitions and share their notes with each other. Those cases that the justices deem noteworthy are then placed on what is called the "discuss list"—a list of cases to be discussed—prepared by the Chief Justice's clerks and circulated to the chambers of the justices. Only about 30 percent of submitted petitions make it to this list. What helps a case make it onto the discuss list? Political scientists have interviewed justices and clerks, has conducted statistical analyses, and has concluded there are certain factors that increase the chances: (1) the U.S. government is a petitioning party; (2) conflict exists in the lower courts on an important point of law; and/or

---

[30] 111 S. Ct. 596 (1991).

[31] Justice Stevens chooses not to join this pool. According to one former clerk, "He wanted an independent review," but Stevens himself examines only about 20 percent of the petitions, leaving the rest to his clerks. Tony Mauro, "Ginsburg Plunges into the Cert Pool," *Legal Times* (September 6, 1993): 8.

(3) the filing by an interest group of an *amicus curiae* brief urging the justices to accept the case for review.[32]

During one of the justices' weekly conference meetings, the cases on the discuss list are reviewed. The Chief Justice speaks first, then the rest of the justices, according to seniority. The decision process ends when the justices vote, and by custom, *certiorari* is granted according to the **Rule of Four**—when at least four justices vote to hear a case. Justice Stevens has suggested that this be changed to a "rule of five" to reduce the Court's caseload. According to Stevens, between 23 and 30 percent of the cases in the 1979, 1980, and 1981 terms had the support of only four justices.[33]

If *certiorari* is granted, the case is slated for oral argument and decision. Even under the Rule of Four, very few cases make it this far. Although the number of cases filed has increased, the number the Court accepts for oral argument and then decides has actually declined (see Figure 9-3).

The content of the Court's docket is every bit as significant as its size. Prior to the 1930s, the Court generally heard cases of interest only to the immediate parties. In the 1930s, cases requiring the interpretation of constitutional law began to take a growing portion of its workload, leading the Court to take a more important role in the policy-making process. At that time, only 5 percent of the Court's cases involved questions concerning the Bill of Rights. By the late 1950s, one-third of filed cases involved such questions, and by the 1960s, half did.[34] In 1990, only 30 percent of the Court's caseload dealt with constitutional questions.

Characteristics of a Supreme Court Case

The reasons the Court decides to hear cases are many and diverse. The Court does not offer reasons, and "the standards by which the justices decide to grant or deny review are highly personalized and necessarily discretionary," noted former Chief Justice Earl Warren. Moreover, he continued, "those standards cannot be captured in rules or guidelines that would be meaningful."[35] Political scientists have nonetheless attempted to determine the characteristics of the cases the Court accepts; not surprisingly, they are similar to those that help a case get on the discuss list. Among the cues are the following:

- The federal government is the party asking for review.
- The case involves conflict among the circuit courts.
- The case presents a civil rights or civil liberties question.
- The case involves ideological and/or policy preferences of the justices.
- The case has significant social or political interest as evidenced by the presence of interest group *amicus curiae* briefs.

---

[32] See Gregory A. Caldeira and John R. Wright, "The Discuss List: Agenda Setting in the Supreme Court," *Law Society Review* 24 (1990), pp. 809-813; H.W. Perry, Jr., *Deciding to Decide: Agenda Setting in the United States Supreme Court* (Cambridge, MA: Harvard University Press, 1991), and Doris Marie Provine *Case Selection in the United States Supreme Court* (Chicago: University of Chicago Press, 1980).

[33] Wasby, *The Supreme Court*, p. 206.

[34] Ibid., p. 199. Much of this change occurred as the result of an increase in state criminal cases, of which nearly 100 percent concerned constitutional questions.

[35] "Retired Chief Justice Warren Attacks . . . Freund Study Group's Composition and Proposal," *American Bar Association Journal* 59 (July, 1973): 728.

384 ❖ Chapter 9   The Judiciary

As Solicitor General of the United States, Drew Day III is responsible for handling litigation on behalf of the United States government before the U.S. Supreme Court.

One of the most important cues for predicting whether the Court will hear a case is the position the U.S. **Solicitor General** takes on it. The Solicitor General, appointed by the president, is the fourth-ranking member of the Justice Department and is responsible for handling all appeals on behalf of the U.S. government to the Supreme Court. The Solicitor's staff is like a small, specialized law firm within the Justice Department. But because this office has such a special relationship with the Supreme Court, even having a suite of offices within the Supreme Court, the Solicitor General is often referred to as the Court's "ninth and a half member."[36] Moreover, the Solicitor General appears as a party or as an *amicus curiae* in more than 50 percent of the cases heard by the Court each term.

This special relationship with the Court helps explain the overwhelming success the Solicitor General's office enjoys before the Supreme Court. The Court generally accepts 70 to 80 percent of the cases where the U.S. government is the petitioning party, compared to about 5 percent of all others.[37] But, because of this special relationship, the Solicitor General often finds himself playing two conflicting roles: representing both the president's policy interests and the broader interests of the United States in Court. At times, solicitors find these two roles difficult to reconcile. Former Solicitor General Rex E. Lee (1981–1985), for example, noted that on more than one occasion he refused to make in Court arguments that had been advanced by the Reagan administration (a stand that ultimately forced him to resign his position). Said Lee, "I'm not the pamphleteer general; I'm the solicitor general. My audience is not 100 million people; my audience is nine people. . . . Credibility is the most important asset that any solicitor general has."[38]

The credibility of the Solicitor General became an even bigger issue during the tenure of Lee's replacement, Charles Fried, appointed by Reagan in 1985. On behalf of the administration, Fried regularly urged the Court (unsuccessfully) to reverse its prior decisions on abortion and affirmative action, causing him to lose credibility with the Court.[39]

Conflict among the lower courts is apparently another reason why the justices take cases. When interpretations of constitutional or federal law are involved, the justices seem to want consistency throughout the federal court system.

Often, these conflicts occur when important civil rights or civil liberties questions arise. Then, the political ideology of the justices often is key. As revealed in Table 9.3, all but one of the justices through 1994 were appointed by (conservative) Republican presidents. The more conservative Burger and Rehnquist Courts were more likely to take cases when lower courts had ruled in favor of civil rights or civil liberties claims—generally to overrule those liberal decisions. As political scientist Lawrence Baum has commented, "justices' evaluations of lower court decisions are based largely on their ideological position."[40]

Interest group participation is another "quick" way for the justices to gauge the ideological ramifications of a particular case. Richard C. Cortner has noted that "cases do

---

[36] Kathleen Werdegar, "The Solicitor General and Administrative Due Process," *George Washington Law Review* (1967–1968): 482.

[37] Rebecca Mae Salokar, *The Solicitor General: The Politics of Law* (Philadelphia: Temple University Press, 1992), p. 3.

[38] Quoted in Elder Witt, *A Different Justice: Reagan and the Supreme Court* (Washington, DC: CQ Press, 1986), p. 133.

[39] Lincoln Caplan, *The Tenth Justice: The Solicitor General and the Rule of Law* (New York: Knopf, 1987).

[40] Lawrence Baum, *The Supreme Court*, 4th ed. (Washington, DC: CQ Press, 1992), p. 106.

not arrive on the doorstep of the Supreme Court like orphans in the night."[41] Most cases heard by the Supreme Court involve either the government or an interest group—either as the sponsoring party or as an *amicus curiae*. Liberal groups such as the ACLU (see p. 126), People for the American Way, the NAACP Legal Defense Fund, and conservative groups including the Washington Legal Foundation, Concerned Women for America, or Americans United for Life Legal Defense Fund routinely sponsor cases or file *amicus* briefs either urging the Court to hear a case or asking it to deny *certiorari*. Research by political scientists has found that "not only does [an *amicus*] brief in favor of *certiorari* significantly improve the chances of a case being accepted, but two, three and four briefs improve the chances even more."[42] Clearly, it's more the merrier, whether or not the briefs are filed for or against granting review. Interest group participation may highlight lower court and ideological conflicts for the justices by alerting them to the amount of public interest in the issues presented in any particular case.

Starting the Case

Once the Court decides to hear a case, a flurry of activity begins. If a criminal defendant is proceeding *in forma pauperis*, the Court appoints an expert lawyer to prepare and argue the case. Unlike the situation in many state courts, where appointed lawyers are often novices, it is considered an honor to be asked to represent an indigent before the Supreme Court in spite of the fact that such representation is on a *pro bono*, or no fee, basis.

Whether or not they are being paid, lawyers on both sides of the case begin to prepare their written arguments for submission to the Court. In these briefs, lawyers cite prior case law and make arguments as to why the Court should find in favor of their client.

More often than not, these arguments are echoed or expanded in *amicus curiae* briefs filed by interested parties, especially interest groups. Often, lawyers will seek the support of sympathetic interest groups to buttress their claims before the Court, although most *amicus* briefs are filed independently, without requests from one of the two major parties in the case. In the 1987 term, 80 percent of the cases decided by the Court had at least one *amicus curiae* brief.

Since the 1970s, interest groups have increasingly used the *amicus* brief as a way to lobby the Court. Because litigation is so expensive, few individuals have the money (or time or interest) to pursue a perceived wrong all the way to the U.S. Supreme Court. All sorts of interest groups, then, find that joining ongoing cases through *amicus* briefs is a useful way of advancing their policy preferences. Major cases such as *Brown* v. *Board of Education* (1954), *Bowers* v. *Hardwick* (1986), and *Harris* v. *Forklift Systems* (1993), which involved the degree of psychological damage a victim of sexual harassment must show, all attracted large numbers of *amicus* briefs as part of interest groups' efforts to lobby the judiciary and bring about desired political objectives.[43] (See "*Amicus* Briefs in Support of *Harris*," p. 386.)

---

[41] Richard C. Cortner, *The Supreme Court and Civil Liberties* (Palo Alto, CA: Mayfield, 1975), p. vi.

[42] Gregory A. Caldeira and John R. Wright, "*Amicus Curiae* before the Supreme Court: Who Participates, When and How Much?" *Journal of Politics* 52 (August 1990): 803.

[43] 114 S. Ct. 367 (1993).

Amicus Briefs in Support of *Harris*

In *Harris* v. *Forklift Systems* (1993), the U.S. Supreme Court unanimously ruled that the federal civil rights laws created a "broad rule of workplace equality." In *Harris*, the Court found that Title VII of the Civil Rights Act was violated when Teresa Harris was subjected to "intimidation, ridicule, and insults" of a sexually harassing nature by her supervisor. The following groups or governments filed *amicus* briefs:

In support of *Harris*

1. United States
    Equal Employment Opportunity Commission
2. National Conference of Women's Bar Associations
    Women's Bar Association of District of Columbia
3. National Organization for Women Legal Defense and Education Fund
    Catherine MacKinnon
    American Jewish Committee
    American Medical Women Association
    Asian-American Legal Defense and Education Fund
    Association for Union Democracy
    Center for Women's Policy Studies
    Chicago Women in Trades
    Illinois Coalition Against Sexual Harassment
    National Organization for Women
    Northern Tradeswomen's Network
    Northern New England Tradeswomen Institute
    Puerto Rican Legal Defense and Education Fund
    Women's Law Project
4. NAACP Legal Defense and Education Fund
    National Conference of Jewish Women
5. Women's Legal Defense Fund
    National Women's Law Center
    AFL-CIO
    Ayuda, Inc.
    Bar Association of San Francisco
    California Women Lawyers
    Center for Women Policy Studies
    Coalition of Labor Union Women
    Committee for Justice for Women of North Carolina
    Federally Employed Women, Inc.
    Federation of Organizations for Professional Women
    Institute for Women's Policy Research
    Mexican American Women's National Association
    National Association of Female Executives
    National Association of Social Workers, Inc.
    National Center for Lesbian Rights
    National Council of Negro Women, Inc.
    9to5
    National Association of Working Women
    Older Women's League
    Trial Lawyers for Public Justice
    Wider Opportunities for Women
    Women Employed
    Women's Action Alliance
    Women's Bar Association of the District of Columbia
    Women's Law Center of Maryland
    YWCA of the U.S.A.
6. Employment Law Center
    California Women Lawyer's Committee
    Equal Rights Advocates
7. National Employment Lawyers Association
8. American Civil Liberties Union
    American Jewish Congress
9. Feminists for Free Expression
10. Southern States Police Benevolent Association
    North Carolina Police Benevolent Association
11. National Conference of Women's Bar Associations
    Women's Bar Association of the District of Columbia

In Support of *Forklift Systems*

Equal Employment Advisory Council

For Neither Party

American Psychological Association

Teresa Harris celebrates her victory after the Supreme Court ruled that her employer's conduct was illegal sexual harassment.

Interest groups also provide the Court with information not necessarily contained in the major-party briefs, help write briefs, and assist in practice moot-court sessions. In these sessions, the lawyer who will argue the case before the nine justices goes through a complete rehearsal, with prominent lawyers and law professors playing the roles of the various justices.

Oral Arguments by Attorneys

Once a case is accepted by the Court for full review and after briefs and *amicus* briefs are submitted on each side, oral argument takes place. The Supreme Court's annual term begins the first Monday in October, as it has since the late 1800s, and runs through early July. In the early nineteenth century, sessions of the Court lasted only a few weeks twice a year. Today, justices hear oral argument from the beginning of the term until early April. Special cases, such as *U.S.* v. *Nixon* (1974), have been heard even later in the year. During the term, "sittings," periods of about two weeks in which cases are heard, alternate with "recesses," also about two weeks long. Oral arguments are usually heard Monday through Wednesday during two-week sitting sessions.

Oral argument is generally limited to the immediate parties to the case, although it is not uncommon for the U.S. Solicitor General to appear to argue orally as an *amicus curiae*. Oral argument at the Court is fraught with time-honored tradition and ceremony. At precisely 10:00 every morning when the Court is in session, the Court Marshal (dressed in a cutaway) emerges to intone "Oyez! Oyez! Oyez!" as the nine justices emerge from behind a reddish-purple velvet curtain to take their places on the raised and slightly angled bench. (From 1790 to 1972, the justices sat on a straight bench. Chief Justice Burger modified it so that justices at either end could see and hear better.) There, the Chief Justice sits in the middle with the justices to his right and left, alternating in seniority.

Almost all attorneys are allotted one-half hour to present their cases, and this allotment includes the time taken by questions from the bench. Justice John Marshall Harlan once noted that there was "no substitute for this method in getting at the heart of an issue and in finding out where the truth lies."[44] As the lawyer for the appellee approaches the mahogany lectern, a green light goes on, indicating that the attorney's time has begun. A white light flashes when five minutes remain. When a red light goes on, Court practice mandates that counsel stop immediately. One famous piece of Court lore told to all attorneys concerns a counsel who continued talking and reading from his prepared argument after the red light went on. When he looked up, he found an empty bench—the justices had quietly risen and departed while he continued to talk. On another occasion, Chief Justice Charles Evans Hughes stopped a leader of the New York bar in the middle of the word "if."

Questions asked at oral argument can be very important. Lawyers are routinely interrupted as justices pepper them with questions and comments. Lawyers are now prohibited by formal rules from reading from prepared texts, but they may use notes. Other kinds of aids are usually barred, but the Court allowed the deaf lawyer in *Rowley Board of Education* v. *U.S.* (1982), a case involving the amount of assistance a public school district had to provide a deaf student, to use a video display screen from which he could read questions from the justices that were typed into it by a stenotypist.[45]

---

[44] Quoted in Wasby, *The Supreme Court*, p. 229. (See n. 26.)
[45] 458 U.S. 176 (1982).

> ## Oral Arguments
> ♦ ♦ ♦
>
> Oral arguments are a holdover from the nineteenth century, when the Court relied much more heavily on them than on written briefs. In those days, oral arguments could last for days. In *McCulloch* v. *Maryland*, for example, the Court permitted the lawyers to argue for nine days, because the issues at stake were considered so significant. Daniel Webster, the finest oral advocate of his time, argued the case for McCulloch.
>
> The strain of oral argument can take its toll on even the most seasoned lawyers. Solicitor General Stanley Reid once fainted. On another occasion, one lawyer got so caught up in his argument that his false teeth popped out of his mouth. Undaunted, he caught them in mid-air and flipped them back into place, hardly missing a beat of his argument. Not a single justice even smiled until after leaving the bench for the day.
>
> In 1993, a controversy arose when Professor Peter Irons made audiotape copies of twenty-three oral arguments of major Supreme Court cases he obtained from the National Archives, and packaged and sold them in a tape-and-book set. These tapes have long been available to researchers, who must sign an agreement to use the tapes for their private use, but not to the general public. When news of Irons's tapings for profit reached the Court, the public information officer reported that the justices were considering "legal remedies." A few months later, the Court's Marshal notified the National Archives that any future requests by Irons would be considered a request for "commercial use or broadcast," that must be forwarded to the Court for *its* approval. After Irons suggested that he might take the Court to court, the Court backed down and made the tapes available to all for broadcast and commercial use.*
>
> *Joan Biskupic, "Supreme Court Limits Access by Seller of Tapes," *The Washington Post* (Sept. 24, 1993): A-3.

Questioning from the bench can become quite active, especially if the case is controversial. Until Justice Ginsburg joined the Court, Justice Scalia was considered the most loquacious jurist on the bench. Several justices have, in fact, privately expressed irritation over Scalia's "bull doggedness" from the bench. In one series of eight cases, Justice William J. Brennan did not ask a single question, whereas Justice Scalia asked 126. The Court also will often ask one side more questions than another. In the companion case to *Brown* v. *Board of Education*, for example, the lawyer defending segregation was interrupted only eleven times, whereas Thurgood Marshall, as counsel for the NAACP, was interrupted 127 times.[46] Continual interruptions can fluster even the most experienced lawyers. During the 1960 term, Justice Felix Frankfurter repeatedly questioned an obviously nervous lawyer, only to hear Justice William O. Douglas an-

---

[46] Milton Dickens and Ruth E. Schwartz, "Oral Argument Before the Supreme Court: Marshall v. Davis in the School Segregation Cases," *Quarterly Journal of Speech* 57 (February 1971): 39.

swer the questions. "I thought you were arguing the case," Frankfurter yelled to the lawyer, who answered, "I am, but I can use all the help I can get."[47]

Although many Court watchers have tried to figure out how a particular justice will vote based on the questioning at oral argument, most find that the nature and number of questions asked does not help much in predicting the outcome of a case. Nevertheless, many believe that oral argument has several important functions. Oral argument is the only opportunity for even a small portion of the public (who may attend the hearings) and the press to observe the workings of the Court. It assures lawyers that the justices have heard their case, and it forces lawyers to focus on arguments believed important by the justices.

Oral argument also provides the Court with additional information, especially concerning the Court's broader political role, an issue not usually addressed in written briefs. For example, the justices can ask how many people might be affected by its decision or where the Court (and country) would be heading if a case were decided in a particular way.

The Conference and Vote

The justices meet in closed conference on Wednesday afternoons and Fridays when the Court is hearing oral argument. The Wednesday conferences deal with cases heard on Mondays; the Friday conferences with cases heard on Tuesdays and Wednesdays and with *certiorari* petitions and appeals.

Since the ascendancy of Chief Justice Roger B. Taney to the Court in 1836, the justices have begun each session with a round of handshaking. Once the door to the Conference Room closes, no others are allowed to enter. The justice with the least seniority acts as the doorkeeper for the other eight, communicating with those waiting outside to fill requests for documents, water, and so on.

Conferences highlight the importance and power of the Chief Justice, who presides over them and makes the initial presentation of each case. Each individual justice then discusses the case in order of seniority on the Court, the most senior justice first. Most accounts of the decision-making process reveal that at this point some justices try to change the minds of others, but that most enter the conference room with a clear idea of how they feel. Although other Courts have followed different procedures, on the Rehnquist Court the justices generally vote at the same time they discuss the case. Initial conference votes are not final, allowing justices to change their minds before final votes are taken later.

Writing the Opinions of the Court

The Chief Justice, if he is in the majority, has the job of assigning the writing of the opinion, in which the reasons behind a decision are set forth. This privilege enables him to wield tremendous power. (If he is in the minority, the assignment falls to the most senior justice in the majority.) During the Burger Court years (1969–1986), the Chief Justice was heavily criticized for his tendency to wait to announce his vote at conference so that he could be in the majority (even when his initial comments indicated a different opinion) and thus assign the opinion. Burger could then, in essence,

---

[47] Reported in Anthony Lewis, "The Justices' Supreme Job," *The New York Times Magazine* (June 11, 1961): 31.

water down the force of the opinion and possibly weaken its overall impact. Today, however, the Chief Justice is regularly in the majority, so tactics like Burger's are no longer considered necessary.

The justice assigned to write the majority opinion circulates drafts of the opinion to all members of the Court. The Court must provide legal reasons for its positions. The reasoning behind any decision is often as important as the outcome, because, under our system of *stare decisis*, both are likely to be relied on later by lower courts confronted with cases involving similar issues. And the justice who drafts the opinion can have an important impact on how any issues are framed. Informal caucusing and negotiation then often take place as justices may "hold out" for word changes or other modifications as a condition of their continued support of the majority opinion. At the same time, **dissenting opinions**, disagreeing with the outcome, and/or **concurring opinions**, agreeing with the outcome but not the legal rationale for the opinion (or further clarifying support) also circulate through the various chambers. The justices are often assisted in their writing of opinions by their clerks, who also can serve as intermediaries between the justices as they talk among themselves.

A good example of how politics can be involved at the opinion-writing stage is evident in *Bowers* v. *Hardwick* (1986),[48] the Georgia sodomy case discussed in Chapters 4 and 5. Justices White and Burger voted for *certiorari* to state that the Constitution doesn't protect homosexual acts. The liberal Marshall and Brennan thought they had enough votes to overturn the law, but when Brennan perceived he would lose, he withdrew his vote for *certiorari*. Then, according to papers kept by Justice Thurgood Marshall, the opinion quickly became one of shifting coalitions. Justice Lewis Powell originally indicated at Conference that he would vote with the majority to find the law unconstitutional. After drafts of the majority and minority opinions were circulated, however, he changed his mind, thus changing a five-to-four majority to strike down the law into a five-to-four majority to uphold it.[49]

This kind of communal work can result in poorly written opinions, as was the case with *U.S.* v. *Nixon* (1974).[50] Although the court order for Nixon to turn over tape recordings of his conversations (see "Watergate and Its Effect on the Presidency," pp. 264–265) was issued under Chief Justice Burger's name, many believe that it was a combination of several justices' contributions and additions. Sensing the need for the Court to speak unanimously on such an important decision—one that pitted two branches of government against each other—Justice Burger apparently made concessions to get support.[51] This process led to sometimes confused prose.

Recently, tensions have grown on the Court concerning some issues, and dissents or concurring opinions have become quite pointed. The protocol of the Court has always been characterized by politeness, but this has not stopped some justices from openly ridiculing their brethren from the bench. Justice Scalia, for example, publicly criticized Justice O'Connor's opinion in *Webster* v. *Reproductive Health Services* (1989), saying that her "assertion that a fundamental rule of judicial restraint requires [the Court] to avoid reconsidering *Roe* [v. *Wade*] cannot be taken seriously."[52]

---

[48] 478 U.S. 186 (1986).

[49] "Justices' Files Show Struggle Over Georgia Sodomy Case," *The Atlanta Journal and Constitution* (May 25, 1993): A-9. The Marshall papers also reveal politics at the *certiorari* stage.

[50] 418 U.S. 683 (1974).

[51] Bob Woodward and Scott Armstrong, *The Brethren* (New York: Simon and Schuster, 1979), pp. 65, 288–347.

[52] 492 U.S. 490 (1989).

How the Justices Vote

Justices are human beings who do not make decisions in a vacuum. Principles of *stare decisis* dictate that the justices follow the law of previous cases in deciding cases at hand. But more factors are usually operating. A variety of legal and extra-legal factors have been shown to affect Supreme Court decision-making. For example, a number of scholars have tried to predict voting patterns by examining individual justices' social background characteristics (such as their education or party identification).[53] Others have attempted to predict voting based on the factual patterns in a case,[54] and others have relied on their perceptions of the justices' roles.[55] All of this research indicates to one degree or another that justices do not make decisions in a vacuum. Each is influenced by a variety of factors, and many in fact were appointed to the Court with the expectation that they would further a particular ideology or approach to interpreting the Constitution.

Legal Factors

Judicial Philosophy and Original Intent. One of the primary issues of judicial power focuses on what is called the activism/restraint debate. Advocates of judicial restraint argue that courts should allow the decisions of other branches to stand, even when they offend judges' own sense of principles.[56] Restraintists defend their position by asserting that the federal courts are composed of unelected judges, which makes the judicial branch the least democratic branch of government. Consequently, the courts should defer policy making to other branches of government as much as possible.

Restraintists refer to *Roe* v. *Wade* (1973), the case that liberalized abortion laws, as a classic example of judicial activism run amok. They maintain that the Court should have deferred policy making on this sensitive issue to the states or to the other branches of the federal government—the legislature and executive—because their officials are elected and therefore are more receptive to the majority's will.

Advocates of judicial activism contend that judges should use their power broadly to further justice, especially in the areas of equality and personal liberty. Activists argue that it is the courts' appropriate role to correct injustices committed by the other branches of government. Explicit in this argument is the notion that courts need to protect oppressed minorities.[57]

---

[53] C. Neal Tate, "Personal Attribute Model of the Voting Behavior of U.S. Supreme Court Justices: Liberalism in Civil Liberties and Economic Decisions, 1946–1978," *American Political Science Review* 75 (June 1981): 355–367.

[54] See, for example, Jeffrey A. Segal, "Predicting Supreme Court Cases Probabilistically: The Search and Seizure Cases, 1962–1981," *American Political Science Review* 78 (September 1978): 891–900, where he argues that the facts of the case are a critical determinant in Supreme Court voting.

[55] According to role theory, which posits that individual justices act differently in different cases primarily due to differing expectations about what is proper, helps explain how the justices vote. James L. Gibson, "Discriminant Functions, Role Orientations and Judicial Behavior: Theoretical and Methodological Linkages," *Journal of Politics* 39 (November 1977): 984–1007.

[56] Stanley C. Brubaker, "Reconsidering Dworkin's Case for Judicial Activism," *The Journal of Politics* 46 (1984): 504.

[57] Donald L. Horowitz, *The Courts and Social Policy* (Washington, DC: Brookings Institution, 1977), p. 538.

Activists point to *Brown* v. *Board of Education* (1954) as an excellent example of the importance of judicial activism. In *Brown*, the Supreme Court ruled that racial segregation in public schools violated the equal protection clause of the Fourteenth Amendment. Segregation was nonetheless practiced after passage of the Fourteenth Amendment, and an activist would point out that if the Court had not reinterpreted its provisions, many states probably would still have laws or policies mandating segregation in public schools.

The debate over activism versus restraint often focuses on how the Court should translate the meaning of the Constitution. Advocates of judicial restraint generally agree that judges should be strict constructionists; that is, they should interpret the Constitution as it was written and intended by the Framers. They argue that in determining the constitutionality of a statute or policy, the Court should rely on the explicit meanings of the clauses in the document, which can be found by looking at the intent of the Framers.

Edwin Meese III, the U.S. Attorney General in the Reagan administration, is a leading "interpretivist," who believes that judges should look to the Framers' original intent when interpreting the Constitution. As a "strict constructionist," Meese argues that judges should "resist any political effort to depart from the literal provisions of the Constitution."[58]

In contrast, "non-interpretivists" generally argue that the Framers intended the Constitution to be a flexible document whose provisions should be read in light of changing historical circumstances and needs. They believe that judges must move beyond the text of the Constitution and impart to it values that are not explicitly in the document, all the while explaining what the Constitution means for a developing and dynamic system.

Former Supreme Court Justice William J. Brennan Jr. is a leading "non-interpretivist." He believes the "Constitution was not intended to preserve a preexisting society but to make a new one, to put in place new principles that the prior political community had not sufficiently recognized."[59]

Of late, most non-interpretivist judges, such as Justice Brennan have tended to be liberal activists. There is, however, no necessary connection between activism and liberalism. Some believe, for example, that the conservative Rehnquist Court could adopt an activist approach as it puts its conservative stamp on its construction and interpretation of statutes and the Constitution.

Precedent. Most Supreme Court decisions are laced with numerous references to previous Court decisions. *Stare decisis* holds that once the Supreme Court has interpreted the Constitution or a statute in a certain way, that interpretation should be used to decide the case at hand. Adherence to *stare decisis* allows for stability and consistency in the law as justices look to past cases for guidance.

Some justices, however, believe that *stare decisis* and adherence to precedent is no longer as critical as it once was. Chief Justice Rehnquist, for example, has noted that while "*stare decisis* is a cornerstone of our legal system . . . it has less power in constitutional cases."[60] In contrast, Justices O'Connor, Kennedy and Souter explained their

---

[58] Edwin Meese III, in *The Great Debate: Interpreting Our Written Constitution* (Washington, DC: The Federalist Society, 1986), p. 2.

[59] William J. Brennan Jr., in *The Great Debate: Interpreting Our Written Constitution* (Washington, DC: The Federalist Society, 1986), p. 18.

[60] *Webster* v. *Reproductive Health Services*, 492 U.S. at 518 (1989).

reluctance to overrule *Roe* v. *Wade* (1973) in *Planned Parenthood of Southeastern Pennsylvania v. Casey* (1992): "to overrule under fire in the absence of the most compelling reason to reexamine a watershed decision would subject this Court's legitimacy beyond any serious question."[61]

Interestingly, a 1990 study of the American public's knowledge and perceptions of the Court indicated that only 44 percent believed that the Court decides cases primarily on the basis of facts and law. Nearly 50 percent believe that the Court decides based on other factors, including political pressures (28 percent), political/personal beliefs (18 percent), and religious beliefs (1 percent). Although *theoretically* the Framers envisioned the Court to be above these pressures, the American public does not appear to be particularly upset about the role of politics and personal beliefs in the decision-making process. In fact, those polled want the Court to take a more active role in the areas of discrimination against women and minorities.

Extra-Legal Factors

Public Opinion. According to Chief Justice Rehnquist,

> Judges, so long as they are relatively normal human beings, can no more escape being influenced by public opinion in the long run than can people working at other jobs. And if a judge on coming to the bench were to decide to hermetically seal himself off from all manifestations of public opinion, he would accomplish very little; he would not be influenced by current public opinion, but instead would be influenced by the state of public opinion at the time he came to the bench.[62]

Public opinion can act as a check on the power of the courts as well as an energizing factor. Activist periods on the Supreme Court have generally corresponded to periods of social or economic crisis. For example, the Marshall Court supported a strong national government, much to the chagrin of a series of pro-states' rights Democratic-Republican presidents in the early crisis-ridden years of the republic. Similarly, the Court capitulated to political pressures and public opinion when, after 1936, it reversed many of its earlier decisions that had blocked President Roosevelt's New Deal legislation.

The courts also can be the direct target of public opinion. During the spring of 1989, when the case of *Webster* v. *Reproductive Health Services* was about to come before the Supreme Court, the Court was subjected to unprecedented lobbying as groups and individuals on both sides of the abortion issue marched and sent appeals to the Court. Earlier, in the fall of 1988, Justice Harry Blackmun, author of *Roe* v. *Wade*, had warned a law school audience in a public address that he feared that the decision was in jeopardy. This in itself was a highly unusual move; until recently, it was the practice of the justices never to comment on cases or the Court.

Speeches like Blackmun's put pro-choice advocates on guard, and many took advantage of the momentum that had built around their successful campaign against the nomination of Robert H. Bork. In 1989, their forces mounted one of the largest demonstrations in the history of the United States when more than 300,000 people marched from the White House to the Supreme Court. In addition, full-page advertise-

---

[61] 112 S. Ct. 2791 (1992).
[62] William H. Rehnquist, "Constitutional Law and Public Opinion," paper presented at Suffolk University School of Law, Boston, April 10, 1986, pp. 40–41.

The 1989 pro-choice rally in Washington, D.C., was part of an intense lobbying effort to influence the Court's decision in the *Webster* case. Justice Sandra Day O'Connor, viewed as a swing vote on the case, was a particular target of the lobbying.

ments appeared in prominent newspapers, and supporters of *Roe* v. *Wade* were urged to contact members of the Court to voice their support. Justice Sandra Day O'Connor, at the time the Court's lone woman, was targeted by many who viewed her as the crucial swing justice on the issue. Mail at the Court, which usually averages about 1,000 pieces a day, rose to an astronomical 46,000 pieces when *Webster* reached the Court, virtually paralyzing normal lines of communication. Several justices spoke out against this kind of "extra-judicial" communication and voiced their belief in its ineffectiveness. In *Webster* v. *Reproductive Health Services* (1989) Justice Scalia lamented

> We can now look forward to at least another Term with carts full of mail from the public, and streets full of demonstrators, urging us—their unelected and life tenured judges who have been awarded those extraordinary, undemocratic characteristics precisely in order that we might follow the law despite the popular will—to follow the popular will.

But the fact remains that the Court *is* very dependent on the public for its prestige as well as for compliance with its decisions. In times of war and other emergencies, for example, the Court frequently has decided cases in ways that commentators have attributed to the sway of public opinion and political exigencies. In *Korematsu* v. *The United States* (1944),[63] for example, the high court upheld the obviously unconstitutional internment of Japanese-American citizens during World War II. Moreover, Chief Justice Rehnquist himself has suggested that the Court's restriction on presidential authority in *Youngstown Sheet & Tube* (1952),[64] which invalidated President Harry S Truman's seizure of the nation's steel mills, was largely attributable to Truman's un-

---

[63] 323 U.S. 214 (1944).
[64] 343 U.S. 579 (1952).

Table 9.4 ♦ The Court versus the American Public

In recent years, the Court has agreed and disagreed with the public on various issues, such as:

ISSUE	COURT	PUBLIC
Should TV and other recording devices be permitted in the Supreme Court?	No	Yes (59%)
Should a parent be forced to reveal the whereabouts of a child even though it could violate Fifth Amendment rights?	Yes	Yes (50%) No (39%) Don't know (11%)
Should a family be allowed to decide to end life-support systems?	Yes	Yes (88%)
Before getting an abortion, whose consent should a teenager be required to gain?	One parent	Both parents (38%) One parent (37%) Neither parent (22%)
Is the death penalty constitutional?	Yes	Yes (72% favor)

Source: Table compiled from general social surveys and Gallup Poll data.

popularity and that of the Korean War.[65] And, as Table 9.4 reveals, the public and the Court often are in agreement on many controversial issues.

Behavioral Characteristics. Many political scientists have concluded that a variety of behavioral characteristics motivate judicial decision making. Most notable of these are background characteristics and attitudes.

Some, for example, argue that social background differences, including childhood experiences, religious values, education, earlier political and legal careers, and political party loyalties are likely to influence how a judge evaluates the facts and legal issues presented in any given case. Harry Blackmun's service at the Mayo Clinic is often pointed to as a reason why his opinion for the Court in *Roe* v. *Wade* was so soundly grounded in medical evidence. Similarly, Justice Potter Stewart, who was generally considered a moderate on most civil liberties issues, usually took a more liberal position on cases dealing with freedom of the press. Why? It may be that Stewart's early job as a newspaper reporter made him more sensitive to these claims. Similarly, Justices Scalia and Thomas's Roman Catholic backgrounds often appear to affect their decisions dealing with abortion and First Amendment religion issues.

Ideology. Critics of the social background approach argue that attitudes or ideologies can better explain the justices' voting patterns. Since the 1940s, the two most prevailing ideologies in the United States have been conservative and liberal. On the Supreme Court, justices with "conservative" views generally vote against affirmative action, abortion rights, expanded rights for criminal defendants, and increased power

---

[65] In *Youngstown Sheet and Tube Co.* v. *Sawyer,* 343 U.S. 579 (1952), the Supreme Court had ruled that President Truman's seizure and operation of U.S. steel mills in the face of a strike threat were unconstitutional, because the Constitution implied no such broad executive power. See Alan Westin, *Anatomy of a Constitutional Law Case* (New York: Macmillan, 1958).

for the national government. In contrast, "liberals" tend to support the parties advancing these positions.

Over time, however, scholars have generally agreed that identifiable ideological voting blocs have occurred on the Court. During the New Deal period, for example, five justices, a critical conservative bloc, routinely voted to strike down the constitutionality of New Deal legislation. Traditionally, such voting blocs or coalitions have centered on liberal/conservative splits on issues such as states' rights (conservatives supporting and liberals opposing), economic issues (conservatives being pro-business; liberals, pro-labor), and civil liberties and civil rights (conservatives being less supportive than liberals). On death-penalty cases, for example, Justices William Brennan Jr. and Thurgood Marshall (sometimes joined by John Paul Stevens) consistently voted against the imposition of the death penalty. The current Rehnquist Court, however, has fewer of these blocs, because its members are ideologically more homogeneous then most courts in the past. All but John Paul Stevens, Ruth Bader Ginsburg, and Stephen Breyer usually take what could be termed conservative positions on most issues.

Judicial Policy Making and Implementation

When the Court decides to hear (or not to hear) a case, it takes its first step in policy making. Thus, it is through interpreting statutes or the Constitution that federal courts, and the Supreme Court in particular, make policy in several ways. Judges can interpret a provision of a law to cover matters not previously understood to be covered by the law or can "discover" new rights, such as that of privacy, from their reading of the Constitution.

This power of the courts to make policy presents difficult questions for democratic theory, as noted by Justice Scalia in *Webster*, because democratic theorists believe that the power to make law resides only in the people or their elected representatives. Yet court rulings, especially Supreme Court decisions, routinely affect policy far beyond the interests of the immediate parties.

One measure of the power of the courts is that more than one hundred federal laws have been declared unconstitutional. Although many of these laws have not been particularly significant, others have. For example, in *Immigration and Naturalization Service* v. *Chadha* (1983)—discussed in Chapter 6—the Court found that legislative vetoes were unconstitutional.[66]

Another measure of the power of the Supreme Court is its ability to overrule itself. Although the Court generally abides by the informal rule of *stare decisis*, by one count it has overruled itself in more than 140 cases since 1810. *Brown* v. *Board of Education* (1954), for example, overruled *Plessy* v. *Ferguson* (1896), thereby reversing years of constitutional interpretation concluding that racial segregation was not a violation of the Constitution. Moreover, in the past few years, the Court has repeatedly reversed earlier decisions in the areas of criminal defendants' rights, affirmative action, and the establishment of religion, thus revealing its powerful role in determining national policy.

A measure of the growing power of the federal courts is the degree to which they now handle issues that, after *Marbury* v. *Madison* (1803), had been considered to be

---

[66] 462 U.S. 919 (1983).

political questions more appropriately left to the other branches of government to decide. Prior to 1962, for example, the Court refused to hear cases questioning the size (and populations) of congressional districts, no matter how unequal they were.[67] The boundary of a congressional district was considered to be a political question. Then, in 1962, writing for the Court, Justice William Brennan concluded that simply because a case involved a political issue did not mean that it involved a political question, thus opening up the floodgates to cases involving a variety of issues that the Court formerly had declined to address.[68]

Not all acts of Congress are easily challenged, and not everyone can challenge a law. Litigants (those who bring a case to court) must have what is called *standing to sue*. Over the years, this has come to mean that a person bringing a lawsuit must have a strong interest and personal stake in the outcome of the case. Generally, these individuals must show the court that they have sustained or are in immediate danger of sustaining a direct and substantial injury from another party or some action of the government.

Recently, the courts have been more willing to allow people to sue under a tactic called a class-action lawsuit, which allows a small number of individuals to sue on behalf of themselves *and* the class of all other citizens similarly situated. Class-action lawsuits are frequently used in the areas of civil rights, prisoners' rights, product liability, and toxic torts (cases that involve personal harm from hazardous substances such as asbestos or waste products) when a large group of people may be affected by a practice but do not have the resources to bring individual lawsuits. Such lawsuits have already nearly overwhelmed the capacity of the federal courts. And in the wake of Energy Secretary Hazel O'Leary's startling announcement that thousands of Americans had been subject to secret atomic medical experiments, more toxic torts suits are likely to be brought.

Implementing Court Decisions

President Andrew Jackson, annoyed about a particular decision handed down by the Marshall Court, is alleged to have said "John Marshall has made his decision; now let him enforce it." Jackson's statement raises a question: How do Supreme Court rulings translate into public policy? In fact, although judicial decisions carry legal and even moral authority, all courts must rely on other units of government to carry out their directives. *Judicial implementation* refers to how and whether judicial decisions are translated into actual public policies affecting more than the immediate parties to the lawsuit.

How well a decision is implemented often depends on how well crafted or popular it is. Hostile reaction in the South to *Brown* v. *Board of Education* (1954) and the absence of precise guidelines to implement the decision meant that the ruling went largely unenforced for years. The *Brown* experience also highlights how much the Supreme Court needs the support of both federal and state courts as well as other governmental agencies to carry out its judgments. Many of you, for example, may have graduated from high school since 1992 when the Supreme Court ruled that public middle- and high-school graduations could not include a prayer. Yet, many of your commencement ceremonies probably included one.

---

[67] See *Colegrove* v. *Green*, 328 U.S. 549 (1946), for example.
[68] *Baker* v. *Carr*, 369 U.S. 186 (1962).

Students and government workers around the nation celebrate May 5, 1994 as National Prayer Day. In spite of Supreme Court decisions ordering a wall of separation between church and state, celebrations like this one held in a Georgia public high school are held all over America each May in public buildings or on public grounds.

Charles Johnson and Bradley C. Canon suggest that the implementation of judicial decisions involves what they call an *implementing population* and a *consumer population*.[69] The implementing population consists of those people responsible for carrying out a decision. It varies depending on the policy and issues in question, but can include lawyers, judges, public officials, police officers and police departments, hospital administrators, government agencies, and corporations. In the case of school prayer, the implementing population could include teachers, school administrators, or the school board. The consumer population consists of those people who might be directly affected by a decision.

For effective implementation of a judicial decision, the first requirement is that the members of the implementing population must act to show that they understand the original decision. For example, the Supreme Court ruled in *Reynolds* v. *Sims* (1964)[70] that every person should have an equally weighted vote in electing governmental representatives. This "one person, one vote" decision might seem simple enough at first glance, but in practice it can be very difficult to understand. The implementing population in this case consists chiefly of state legislatures and local governments, which determine voting districts for federal, state, and local offices (see Chapter 6). If a state legislature draws districts in such a way that African-American voters are spread thinly across a number of separate constituencies, the chances are slim that any particular district will elect a representative who is especially sensitive to blacks' concerns. Does that violate "equal representation"? (In practice, the courts and the Justice Department have intervened in many cases to ensure that elected officials will include minority representation.)

---

[69] Charles Johnson and Bradley C. Canon, *Judicial Policies' Implementation and Impact* (Washington, DC: CQ Press, 1984), Chapter 1.
[70] 377 U.S. 533 (1964).

The second requirement is that the implementing population must actually follow Court policy. Thus, when the Court ruled that men could not be denied admission to a state-sponsored nursing school, the implementing population—in this case, university administrators and the Board of Regents of the nursing school—had to enroll qualified male students.

Judicial decisions are most likely to be implemented smoothly if responsibility for implementation is concentrated in the hands of a few highly visible public officials, such as the president or a governor. By the same token, these officials can also thwart or impede judicial intentions. Recall from Chapter 5, for example, the effect of Governor Orval Faubus's initial refusal to allow black children to attend all-white public schools in Little Rock, Arkansas.

The third requirement for implementation is that the consumer population must be aware of the rights that a decision grants or denies them. Teenagers seeking an abortion, for example, are consumers of the Supreme Court's decisions on abortion. They need to know that most states require them to inform their parents of their intention to have an abortion or get parental permission to do so. Similarly, criminal defendants and their lawyers are consumers of Court decisions and need to know, for example, the implications of recent Supreme Court decisions for evidence presented at trial.

Toward Reform

Clearly, the American public regards the Supreme Court as a powerful policy maker. In a 1990 poll, most respondents said they believed that the Court was more powerful than the president (31 percent versus 21 percent) and that the Court was close to being as powerful as Congress (38 percent).

Considering how poorly informed the American public is about the Court, interest in its activities appears to be growing as more Americans come to understand the importance of the Court in shaping our social and economic agenda and as Court appointments continue to get extensive media coverage.

In the wake of the Clarence Thomas hearings, much was said about the need to reform the judicial selection process. Criticism was directed in particular at Senate confirmation hearings, special-interest groups, and ideological politics. As time has passed, however, little has been done in response to these concerns, and the Ruth Bader Ginsburg and Stephen G. Breyer hearings, which went like clockwork, seem to indicate that the Bork and Thomas hearings were anomalies.

Historically, in fact, there has been little inclination to tinker with the judicial system—even though the courts have grown in power—except when the Supreme Court has stepped on too many toes. Congress and the president have, from time to time, limited, or attempted to limit, the jurisdiction of the Court. When Democratic-Republicans were unable to get rid of Federalist judges by impeachment, they abolished the federal circuit courts. Following the Civil War, Radical Republicans cut the size of the Court and changed its appellate jurisdiction to prevent it from hearing a case involving the constitutionality of some Reconstruction legislation.[71] And in 1936, President Franklin D. Roosevelt tried unsuccessfully to change the size of the Court so that he could pack it with supporters of his New Deal.

---

[71] *Ex parte McCardle*, 74 U.S. 506 (1869).

Table 9.5 ♦ The Future Composition of the Supreme Court

JUSTICE	AGE IN 1994	PHILOSOPHY	PROJECTED YEAR OF RETIREMENT*
Stevens	74	Moderate	2001
Rehnquist	70	Conservative	2005
O'Connor	64	Conservative	2011
Scalia	58	Conservative	2017
Kennedy	58	Conservative	2017
Souter	55	Conservative	2020
Thomas	46	Conservative	2029
Ginsburg	62	Moderate/Liberal	2009
Breyer	56	Moderate	2019

* This is based on the last six Justices (Brennan, Burger, Marshall, Powell, White, and Blackmun) when they retired from 1986–1994—81 years of age.

More recently, proposals have been made to alter the Court's jurisdiction on matters such as abortion, but little has come of them. If the current Court continues its conservative pattern, it may someday find itself in conflict with a more liberal Democratic president and Congress. As revealed in Table 9.5, even with a Democratic Congress and president, if the present members of the Court retire at the same average age as their recent predecessors, it would still take many years for the Court to be re-made in a more liberal model.

The question may more properly be: Are the courts too political? Should their independence be curbed? The courts and the judiciary occupy a peculiar place in our democratic system. Not elected by the people, federal judges serve for life with no direct responsibility or accountability to those who can be affected so profoundly by their decisions. Yet, suggestions such as the one made by FDR to change the Supreme Court have not met with much enthusiasm by Congress or the public.

Summary

The judiciary and the legal process—on both the national and state levels—are complex and play a far more important role in the setting of policy than the Framers ever envisioned. To explain the judicial process and its evolution, we have made the following points:

1. Many of the Framers viewed the judicial branch of government as little more than a minor check on the other two branches, ignoring Anti-Federalist concerns about an unelected judiciary and its potential for tyranny. The Judiciary Act of 1789 established the basic federal court system we have today. It was the Marshall Court (1801–1835), however, that interpreted the Constitution to include the Court's major power, that of judicial review.

2. Ours is a dual judicial system consisting of the federal court system and the separate judicial systems of the fifty states. In each system, there are two basic types of courts: trial courts and appellate courts. Each type deals with cases involving criminal and civil law. Original jurisdiction refers to a court's ability to hear a case as a trial court; appellate jurisdiction to a court's ability to review cases already decided by a trial court.

3. The federal court system is made up of constitutional and legislative courts. Federal district courts, courts of

appeals, and the Supreme Court are constitutional courts.

4. District court and court of appeals judges are nominated by the president and subject to Senate confirmation. Senators often play a key role in "suggesting" district court appointees from their home state. Supreme Court justices are nominated by the president but must also win Senate confirmation. Presidents use different criteria for selection, but important factors include competence and ethical standards, ideology, rewards, pursuit of political support, religion, race, and gender.

5. Several factors go into the Court's decision to hear a case. Not only must the court have jurisdiction, but at least four justices must vote to hear the case, and cases with certain characteristics are most likely to be heard. Once a case is set for review, briefs and *amicus curiae* briefs are filed and oral argument scheduled. The justices meet after oral argument to discuss the case, votes are taken, and opinions written and circulated.

6. Several legal and extra-legal factors affect how the Court arrives at its decision. Legal factors include judicial philosophy, the original intent of the Framers, and precedent. Extra-legal factors include public opinion, and the behavioral characteristics and ideology of the justices.

7. The Supreme Court is an important participant in the policy-making process. The process of judicial interpretation gives the Court powers never envisioned by the Framers.

8. Unlike the other two branches of government, the Supreme Court and the federal judiciary have not been the subjects of many reform efforts, and periodic calls for change have met with little support.

Key Terms

amicus curiae
judicial review
Marbury v. *Madison*
appellate courts
criminal law
grand jury
indictment

civil law
constitutional courts
legislative courts
briefs
precedents
stare decisis
senatorial courtesy

strict constructionist
writ of *certiorari*
in forma pauperis
Rule of Four
Solicitor General
dissenting opinions
concurring opinions

Suggested Readings

Abraham, Henry. *The Judicial Process*, 6th ed. New York: Oxford University Press, 1993.

Baum, Lawrence. *American Courts: Process and Policy*. Boston: Houghton Mifflin, 1989.

———*The Supreme Court,* 4th ed. Washington: CQ Press, 1992.

Epstein, Lee, et. al. *The Supreme Court Compendium: Data, Decisions, and Developments*. Washington, DC: Congressional Quarterly Inc., 1994.

Hickock, Eugene and Gary McDowell. *Justice vs. Law: Courts and Politics in American Society*. New York: Macmillan, 1993.

Hall, Kermit L. ed., *The Oxford Companion to the Supreme Court of the United States*. New York: Oxford University Press, 1992.

Levy, Leonard W., et al., eds. *American Constitutional History*. New York: Macmillan, 1989.

Marshall, Thomas. *Public Opinion and the Supreme Court*. Boston: Unwin and Hyman, 1989.

O'Brien, David M. *Storm Center: The Supreme Court in American Politics*, 2nd ed. New York: Norton, 1990.

O'Connor, Karen. *Women's Organizations' Use of the Courts*. Lexington, MA: Lexington Books, 1980.

Provine, Doris Marie. *Case Selection in the United States Supreme Court*. Chicago: University of Chicago Press, 1980.

Salokar, Rebecca Mae. *The Solicitor General: The Politics of Law*. Philadelphia: Temple University Press, 1992.

Wasby, Stephen. *The Supreme Court in the Federal Judicial System*, 4th ed. Chicago: Nelson-Hall, 1993.

Woodward, Bob, and Scott Armstrong. *The Brethren: Inside the Supreme Court*. New York: Simon and Schuster, 1979.

Political Behavior

I have often taken notice that Providence has been pleased to give this one connected country to one united people—a people descended from the same ancestors, speaking the same language, professing the same religion, attached to the same principles of government, very similar in manners and customs....

John Jay
Federalist No. 2

The Framers may have wished for all Americans to share a common culture. At no time, however, has the American public resembled Jay's description. Because public opinion is crucial to democracy and the formation of the policies and laws that govern our lives, it is extremely important to understand the makeup of the American people—what they think, what they believe, and what they say, in all their many voices.

CHAPTER 10

Public Opinion

WHAT IS PUBLIC OPINION?
EARLY EFFORTS TO INFLUENCE PUBLIC OPINION
EARLY ATTEMPTS TO GAUGE PUBLIC OPINION
POLITICAL SOCIALIZATION: THE FIRST STEP TOWARD FORMING OPINIONS
POLITICAL IDEOLOGY
HOW WE FORM POLITICAL OPINIONS
HOW WE MEASURE PUBLIC OPINION
HOW POLLING AND PUBLIC OPINION AFFECT POLITICIANS, POLITICS, AND POLICY
TOWARD REFORM

When John Jay wrote so glowingly of the sameness of the American people in 1787, he and other writers of *The Federalist Papers* believed that Americans had more in common than not. Many of those who could vote were of English heritage; almost all were Christian. Moreover, most believed that certain rights such as freedom of speech, association, and religion were unalienable rights. This was part of the shared political culture that Jay celebrated in *Federalist No. 2*. There, he also spoke of shared public opinion and of the need for a national government reflecting American ideals. But Jay overstated the universality of the public's support for a strong national government. Moreover, even though Americans at the time generally shared one language, religion, and a common ancestry, existing class and philosophical differences were already producing the kind of factions that the Federalists feared.

The Federalist Papers were themselves one of the first major attempts to change public opinion—in this case, to gain public support for the newly drafted U.S. Constitution. Even prior to publication of *The Federalist Papers,* Thomas Paine's *Common Sense* and later his *Crisis* papers were widely distributed throughout the colonies in an effort to stimulate patriotic feelings and increase public support for the Revolutionary War. From the very early days of the republic, political leaders recognized the impor-

405

Like President Ronald Reagan, Bill Clinton has been a master manipulator of the media and public opinion. He regularly uses televised town hall meetings as a way to move public opinion.

tance of public opinion and used all the means at their disposal to manipulate it for their purposes.

In his first year in office, President Clinton revealed his understanding of the importance of public support. His major legislative victories—the budget bill, the North American Free Trade Agreement (NAFTA), and the Brady gun-control bill—were won with the support of very different groups of people. His efforts to mobilize public opinion included town hall meeting appearances and having his vice president, Al Gore Jr., debate Ross Perot on "Larry King Live" in order to bring the case for NAFTA directly to the American public.

The proper role of public opinion in the making of policy is just one question we explore in this chapter. Other areas of concern are how political attitudes and public opinion have been manipulated and measured over time, how opinions are formed, and what enduring issues have been important to politicians and the public.

What Is Public Opinion?

At first blush, **public opinion** seems to be a very straightforward term: It is what the public thinks about a particular issue or set of issues at a particular time. Since the 1930s, governmental decision makers have relied heavily on **public opinion polls**—interviews with a sample of citizens that are used to estimate public opinion of the entire population—to determine what the public is thinking. According to the founder of modern-day polling, George Gallup (see "People of the Past: George Gallup," p. 414), polls have played a key role in defining issues of concern to the public, shaping administrative decisions, and helping "speed up the process of democracy" in the United

States.[1] But as we discuss later in this chapter, what the public thinks about various issues is difficult to know with certainty simply because public opinion can change so quickly. For example, two weeks before the United States bombed Iraq in January 1991, public opinion polls revealed that only 61 percent of the American public believed that the United States should engage in combat in Iraq. One week after the invasion, however, 86 percent reported that they approved of President Bush's handling of the situation.

Similarly, as revealed in Figure 10-1, public support for NAFTA soared from 34 percent to 57 percent after the vice president debated former presidential candidate Ross Perot. Not only did support for NAFTA go up 23 percent, but so did the public's favorable view of Al Gore Jr!

Throughout our nation's history, political thinkers have argued that a just government rests on the wishes of the people. In *Federalist No. 10*, for example, James Madison articulated this notion: "The public voice, pronounced by the representatives of the people, will be more consonant to the public good." Madison stressed that government should respond to the will of the people but not to momentary changes in opinion occasioned by dramatic events. Governments, he argued, need respond only to those enduring beliefs shared by the public. As we see throughout this book, many such enduring beliefs are reflected in the Declaration of Independence (see Appendix I) and in the Bill of Rights.

---

[1] Allan M. Winkler, "Public Opinion," in Jack Greene, ed., *The Encyclopedia of American Political History* (New York: Charles Scribner's Sons, 1988), p. 1038.

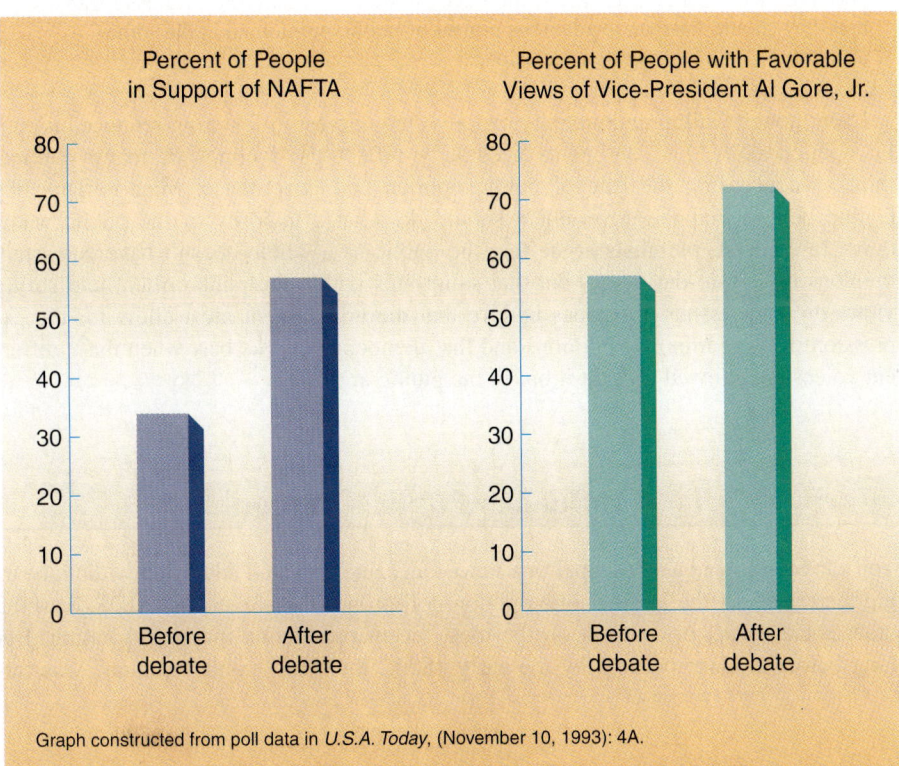

FIGURE 10-1

Public opinion on NAFTA and Al Gore Jr. before and after his televised debate on NAFTA with Ross Perot on "Larry King Live"

By Steve Kelley, The San Diego Union-Tribune, Copley News Service

Not all commentators agree with Madison, however. According to pollster George Gallup, leaders must constantly take public opinion—no matter how short-lived—into account. Like the Jacksonians of a much earlier era, Gallup was distrustful of leaders who were not in tune with the "common man." According to Gallup,

> in a democracy we demand the views of the people be taken into account. This does not mean that leaders must follow the public's view slavishly; it does mean that they should have an available appraisal of public opinion and take some account of it in reaching their decision.[2]

Even though Gallup undoubtedly had a vested interest in fostering reliance on public opinion polls, his sentiments accurately reflect the feelings of many political thinkers concerning the role of public opinion and governance. Majoritarians like Gallup believe that the government should do what a majority of the public wants done. In contrast, pluralists argue that the public as a whole doesn't have consistent opinions on day-to-day issues but that subgroups within the public often hold strong views on some issues. Pluralists believe that the government must allow for the expression of these minority opinions and that democracy works best when these different voices are allowed to fight it out in the public arena.

Early Efforts to Influence Public Opinion

You can hardly read a newspaper or a news magazine or watch television without hearing the results of the latest public opinion poll on health care, crime, AIDS, or some other social issue, or a report on the most recent presidential popularity rating. But long before modern polling, by the early 1800s, the term "public opinion" was fre-

---

[2] *Public Opinion Quarterly* 29 (Winter 1965–66): 547.

quently being used by the educated middle class. As more Americans became educated, they became more vocal about their opinions and were more likely to vote. A more educated, reading public led to increased demand for newspapers, which in turn provided more information about the process of government. And as the United States grew, there were more elections and more opportunities for citizens to express their political opinions through the ballot box. As a result of these trends, political leaders were more frequently forced to try to gauge public opinion in order to remain responsive to the wishes and desires of their constituents.

An example of the power of public opinion is the public's response to the 1851 through 1852 serialization of Harriet Beecher Stowe's *Uncle Tom's Cabin*. This novel was one of the most powerful propaganda statements ever issued about slavery, and by the time the first shots of the Civil War were fired at Fort Sumter in 1861 more than one million copies of the book were in print. Even though Stowe's words alone could not have caused the public outrage over slavery that contributed to Northern support for the war, her book convinced the majority of the American people of the justness of the abolitionist cause and solidified public opinion against slavery in the North.

Decades later, one hallmark of the Progressive era of the late nineteenth and early twentieth centuries was the restructuring of government to be more responsive to the views of the people. Many governmental reforms were enacted to make legislative assemblies more responsive to public opinion. During this period measures such as the **initiative, referendum,** and **recall** (see "Election Reform," right), and the restructuring of primary elections were undertaken to give more citizens an opportunity to voice their views in the electoral process (see also, Chapter 12)..

During the Progressive era there was also a growing belief that the pressure of public opinion would act as a safeguard in the conduct of both domestic and international affairs. In 1909, speaking on behalf of compulsory arbitration of international disagreements to avoid war, President William Howard Taft (1909–13) noted that once a court hearing was held and the dispute decided, "few nations will care to face the condemnation of international public opinion and disobey the judgment [of the international court]."[3] (He obviously hadn't envisioned leaders like Adolf Hitler or Saddam Hussein.)

During World War I, while some people argued that public opinion didn't matter at all, President Woodrow Wilson (1913–1921), like Taft, argued that public opinion would temper the actions of international leaders. Therefore, only eight days after the start of the war, Wilson created a Committee on Public Information. Run by a prominent journalist, the committee immediately undertook to unite U.S. public opinion behind the war effort. It used all of the tools available—pamphlets, posters, and speakers who exhorted the patrons of local movie houses during every intermission—in an effort to garner support and favorable opinion for the war. In the words of the committee's head, it was "the world's greatest adventure in advertising."[4]

In the wake of World War I, Walter Lippmann, a well-known journalist and author who was extensively involved in propaganda activities during the war, openly voiced his concerns about how easily public opinion could be manipulated and his reservations about the weight it should be given. In his seminal work, *Public Opinion* (1922), Lippmann wrote, "Since Public Opinion is supposed to be the prime mover in democracies, one might reasonably expect to find a vast literature. One does not find it."[5] By

Election Reform

Initiative: A method by which state and local voters can propose laws or constitutional amendments. Generally, special-interest groups draft the initiatives and then circulate them on petitions. Usually the initiative must attract the signatures of at least 5 to 10 percent of the registered voters in the state or community in order to be submitted to the electorate for a popular vote.

Referendum: Procedure whereby a legislature submits proposed legislation to the voters for their approval or disapproval.

Recall: A procedure whereby incumbent elected officials can be ousted by a popular vote prior to the end of their terms.

---

[3] Quoted in Winkler, "Public Opinion," p. 1031.
[4] Ibid., p. 1035
[5] Ibid.

the 1920s, although numerous efforts had been made to manipulate public opinion, scientific measurement of the public opinion had yet to occur.

Early Attempts to Gauge Public Opinion

Public opinion polling as we know it today did not begin to develop until the 1930s. Researchers in a variety of disciplines, including political science, heeded Lippmann's call to learn more about public opinion. Some tried to use scientific methods to measure political thought through the use of surveys or polls. As methods for gathering and interpreting data improved, survey data began to play an increasingly important role in all walks of life, from politics to retailing.

Even before the 1930s, many people had tried to forecast the results of political elections. As early as 1824, for example, one Pennsylvania newspaper tried to predict the winner of that year's presidential contest. Later, in 1883, the *Boston Globe* sent reporters to selected election precincts to poll voters as they exited voting booths in an effort to predict the results of key contests. And in 1916, *Literary Digest,* a popular magazine, began mailing survey postcards to potential voters in an effort to predict

"The world's greatest adventure in advertising." During World War I, the Committee on Public Information created a vast gallery of posters designed to shore up public support for the war effort.

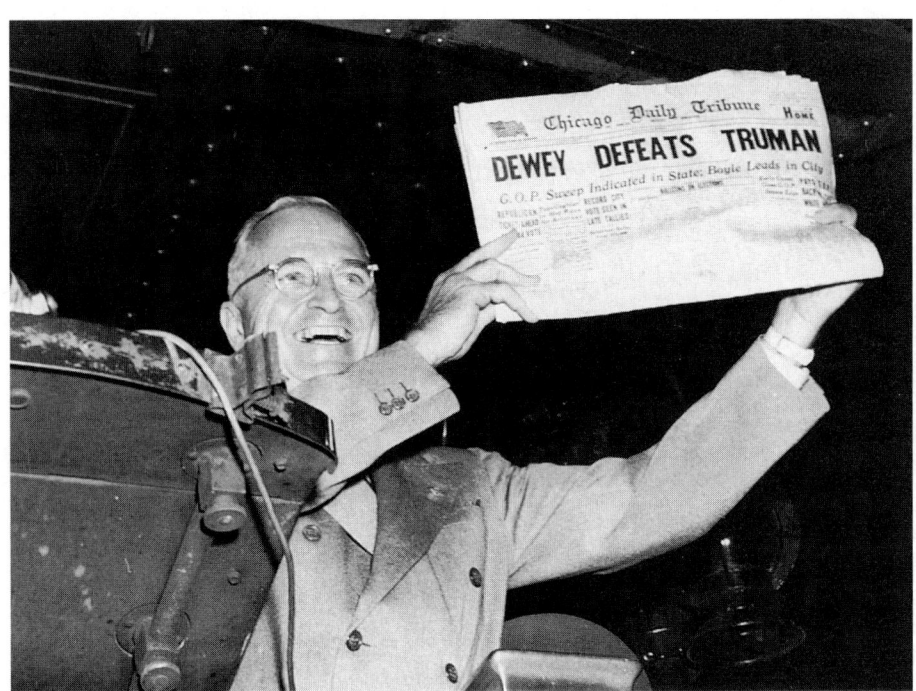

Not only did advance polls in 1948 predict that Republican nominee Thomas E. Dewey would defeat Democratic incumbent Harry S Truman, but based on early and incomplete vote tallies, some newspapers' early editions even on the day *after* the election declared Dewey to have won. Here a triumphant Truman holds aloft the *Chicago Tribune*.

election outcomes. The *Literary Digest* drew its survey sample from "every telephone book in the United States, from the rosters of clubs and associations, from city directories, lists of registered voters [and] classified mail order and occupational data."[6] Using the data it received from the millions of postcard ballots sent out throughout the United States, the *Literary Digest* correctly predicted every presidential election from 1920 to 1932.

The *Literary Digest* used **straw polls** to predict the popular vote in those four presidential elections. Its polling methods were widely hailed as "amazingly right" and "uncannily accurate."[7] In 1936, however, its luck ran out. The *Literary Digest* predicted that Republican Alfred M. Landon (his daughter Nancy Kassebaum was elected to the U.S. Senate in 1984) would beat incumbent President Franklin D. Roosevelt by a margin of 57 percent to 43 percent. Roosevelt, however, won in a landslide election, receiving 62.5 percent of the popular vote and carrying every state except Vermont and Maine. The problems with the *Literary Digest*'s polling methods are discussed in "Then and Now: Straw Polls," p. 412).

Through the late 1940s, the number of polling groups and increasingly sophisticated polling techniques grew by leaps and bounds as new businesses and politicians relied on the information they provided to market products and candidates. In 1948, however, the polling industry suffered a severe, although fleeting, setback. George Gallup and many other pollsters incorrectly predicted that Thomas E. Dewey would defeat President Harry S Truman.

---

[6] *Literary Digest* 122 (22 August 1936): 3.
[7] *Literary Digest* 125 (14 November 1936): 1.

THEN AND NOW

Straw Polls

In the early 1900s, polls like those conducted by the *Literary Digest* reached out to as many potential respondents as possible, with no regard for modern sampling techniques that require respondents be selected or sampled according to strict rules of cross-sectional representation. Respondents, in essence, were like "straws in the wind," hence the term "straw polls."

The *Literary Digest*'s sample had three fatal errors. First, its sample was drawn from telephone directories and lists of automobile owners. This technique oversampled the upper middle class and rich, groups heavily Republican in political orientation. In 1936, this oversampling proved to be particularly problematic because voting polarized along class lines. Thus, the oversampling of wealthy Republicans severely underestimated the Democratic vote. The *Literary Digest*'s second problem was timing: Questionnaires were mailed in early September. Thus, the changes in public sentiment that occurred as the election drew closer were not measured. Its third error occurred because of a problem we now call self-selection: Only highly motivated individuals sent back the cards—only 22 percent of those surveyed responded. Those who respond to mail surveys are quite different from the general electorate; they often are wealthier and better educated and care more fervently about issues. The *Literary Digest*, then, failed to observe one of the now well-known cardinal rules of survey sampling: "One cannot allow the respondents to select themselves into the sample."*

Although these crude techniques are now looked on with disfavor by serious students of public opinion, straw polls are still in use today. Interest groups, for example, frequently poll their members on relevant issues. Perhaps the most common form of straw poll used today are those conducted by local television news programs. Many have nightly features asking viewers to call in their sentiments (with one phone number for pro and another for con). The results of these unscientific polls vary widely because individuals who feel very strongly about the issue often repeatedly call in their votes.

At least one pollster, however, correctly predicted the results of the 1936 election: George Gallup. (See "People of the Past: George Gallup," page 414) Gallup had written his dissertation on how to measure the readership of newspapers and then expanded his methods to study public opinion about politics. He was so sure about his methods that he demonstrated his confidence when he gave all of his newspaper clients this money-back guarantee: If his poll predictions weren't closer to the actual election outcome than those of the highly acclaimed *Literary Digest* (remember that the *Literary Digest* had predicted every election correctly), he would refund their money. The *Digest* predicted Alf Landon; Gallup predicted Roosevelt to win. As a consequence, although he underpredicted Roosevelt's victory by nearly 7 percent, the fact that he got the winner right was what everyone remembered, especially given the *Literary Digest*'s dramatic miscalculations. And, as revealed in Figure 10-2, the Gallup Organization, now run by George Gallup's son, continues to be a successful predictor of elections today.

*Robert S. Erikson, Norman Luttbeg, and Kent Tedin, *American Public Opinion: Its Origin, Content and Impact* (New York: Wiley, 1980), p. 28.

In spite of errors like these, pollsters have been quick to defend their craft. Gallup readily admitted the mistakes that affected his 1948 poll, including the early cutoff date of his sample, noting that he and his organization were learning continually. He consistently argued that the judgment of the masses was basically good and often far better than that of their leaders.

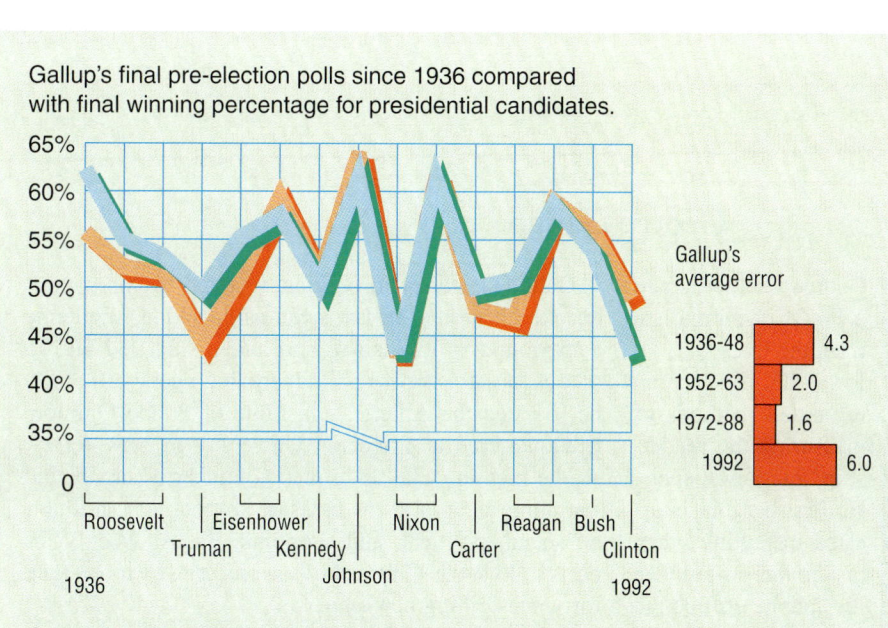

FIGURE 10-2
The Success of the Gallup Poll

Political Socialization: The First Step Toward Forming Opinions

Political scientists believe that many of our attitudes about issues are grounded in political values, which are acquired through a process called **political socialization.** Political socialization "is the process through which an individual acquires his [or her] particular political orientations—his [or her] knowledge, feelings and evaluations regarding his [or her] political world."[8] Through the process of political socialization we become aware of political facts and events and form political values. Family, schools, houses of worship, peers, friends, and the media are often important influences or agents of political socialization. Try to remember your earliest memory of the president of the United States. For many of you it was probably Jimmy Carter or Ronald Reagan (older students probably remember earlier presidents). What did you think of him? Of the Republican or Democratic Party? It's likely that your earliest feelings or attitudes were shaped by what your parents thought about that particular president and his party. Similar processes also apply to your early attitudes about the flag of the United States, or even the police.

Students of political socialization argue that children who grew up during the Vietnam era (1964–1973) or during the Watergate scandal have many more negative feelings about the president than do children who grew up later in households that approved of President Reagan.

---

[8] Richard Dawson et al. *Political Socialization,* 2nd ed. (Boston: Little, Brown, 1977), p. 33.

PEOPLE OF THE PAST

George Gallup

George Gallup

George Gallup earned a Ph.D. in journalism from the University of Iowa; his dissertation examined methods of measuring the readership of newspapers. He first became interested in polling when his mother-in-law ran for public office in 1932. She was running against a popular incumbent, and most observers considered her candidacy a lost cause. Nevertheless, because of the Democratic landslide of 1932, she was swept into office on Franklin D. Roosevelt's coattails.

Gallup's interest in politics, fostered by his experience in his mother-in-law's campaign and his academic background in journalism and advertising, led him to take a job at a New York advertising agency. In 1935 he founded the American Institute of Public Opinion, headquartered at Princeton University in New Jersey. At the Institute, Gallup refined a number of survey and sampling techniques to measure the public's attitudes on social, political, and economic issues. Weekly reports called the Gallup Polls were sent to more than forty subscribing newspapers.

Gallup attracted considerable national attention when he correctly predicted the outcome of the 1936 presidential election. Recognizing many flaws of the *Literary Digest*'s poll, he relied on a sample of a few thousand people who represented the voting population in terms of important demographic variables, such as age, gender, political affiliation, and region.

The Family

The influence of the family can be traced to two factors: communication and receptivity. Children, especially during their preschool years, spend tremendous amounts of time with their parents; early on they learn their parents' political values, even though these concepts may be vague. One study, for example, found that the most important visible public figures for children under the age of ten were police officers and, to a much lesser extent, the president. Children almost uniformly view both as "helpful." But by the age of ten or eleven, children become more selective in their perceptions of the president. By this age, children raised in Democratic households are much more likely to be critical of a Republican president than are those raised in Republican households.

In 1958, 72 percent of the children in Republican households adopted their parents' party identification. By 1988, 58 percent of children in Republican households identified themselves as Republicans, and many developed strong positive feelings toward Ronald Reagan, the Republican president. Support for and the popularity of Ronald Reagan translated into strong support for the Republican Party through the 1988 presidential elections and also contributed to the growing conservative ideological self-identification of first-year college students depicted in Figure 10-3.

Political Socialization: The First Step Toward Forming Opinions ❖ 415

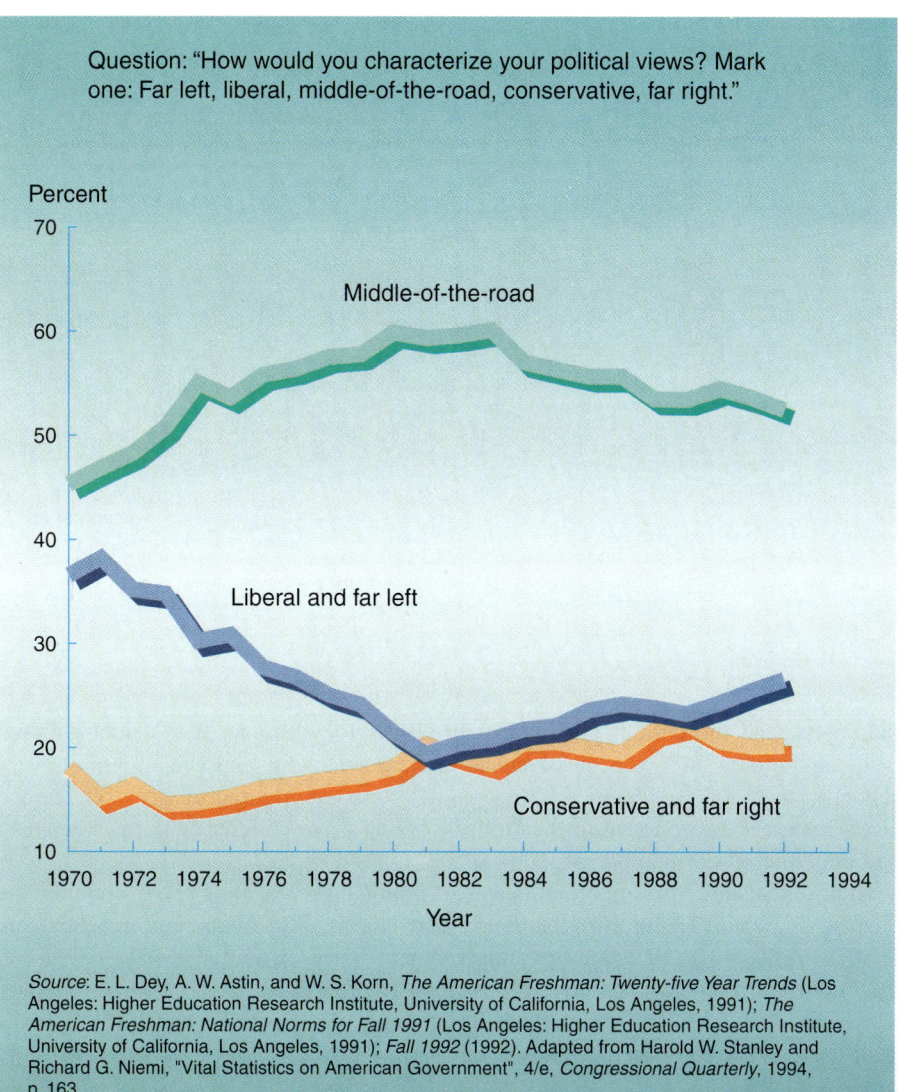

FIGURE 10-3

Ideological Self-Identification of College Students' First Year, 1970–1992

School

Researchers report mixed findings concerning the role of the schools in the political socialization process. There is no question that, in elementary school, children are taught respect for their nation and its symbols. Most school days begin with the Pledge of Allegiance, and patriotism and respect for country are important, although subtle, components of most school curricula. Figure 10-4 illustrates the importance of symbols that evoke our feelings of nationalism in development of our notions of political culture as they are taught at home and school. The terms "flag" and the "United States" evoke very positive feelings from a majority of Americans. Support for these two icons serves the purpose of maintaining national allegiance and underlies the success of the U.S. political system in spite of relatively negative views about Congress,

FIGURE 10-4

Attitudes of American Adolescents about the United States and Its Symbols, Government, and Institutions

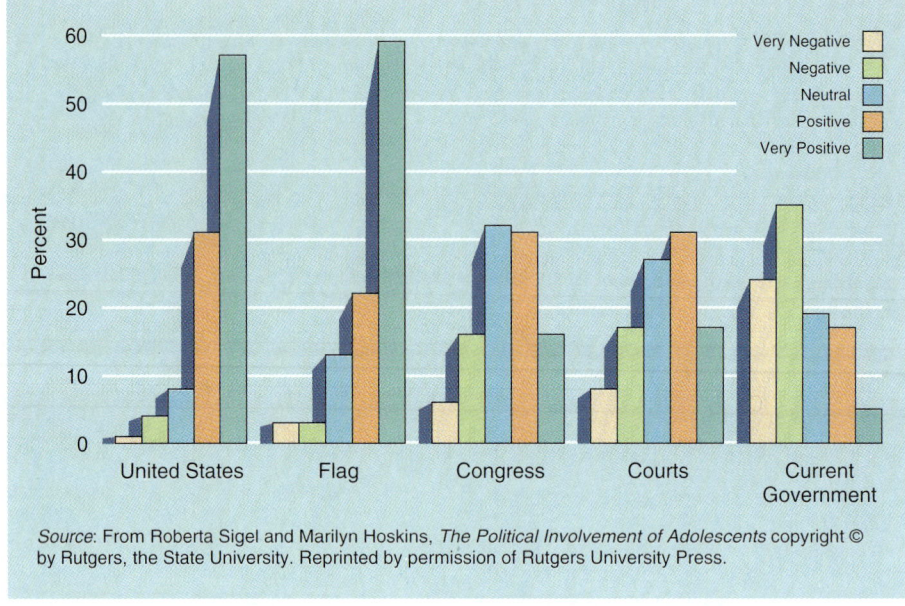

Source: From Roberta Sigel and Marilyn Hoskins, *The Political Involvement of Adolescents* copyright © by Rutgers, the State University. Reprinted by permission of Rutgers University Press.

the courts, and the current government. In 1991, for example, few school children were taught to question U.S. involvement in the Persian Gulf. Instead, at almost every school in the nation, children were encouraged or even required to write servicemen and servicewomen stationed in the Gulf, involving these children with the war effort and implying school support for the war.

High schools are also important agents of political socialization. They continue the elementary school tradition of building good citizens and often reinforce textbook learning with trips to the state or national capital. They also offer courses on current U.S. affairs. Presentation of civic information is especially critical at the secondary school level because the formal education of many people in the United States ends with high school and because research shows that better-informed citizens vote more often as adults.

Learning at the college level is often different from that encountered in grade school or high school. Many college courses and texts like this one are designed in part to provide you with the information necessary to think critically about issues of major political consequence. It is common in college for students to be called on to question the appropriateness of certain political actions or to discuss underlying reasons for certain political or policy decisions. Therefore, most researchers believe that college has a liberalizing effect on students. Since the 1920s, studies have shown, students become more liberal each year they are in college.

Peers

Throughout the United States, most schoolchildren start the day with a "Pledge to the Flag." From a very early age, children are taught respect for national symbols and ideals.

Although the influence of the schools on political socialization is often called into doubt, a child's peers—that is, children about the same age as a young person—do seem to have an important effect on the socialization process. Whereas parental influences are greatest during the tender years from birth to age five, a child's peer group becomes increasingly more important as the child gets older.

The Impact of Events

While there is no doubt that parents—and, to a lesser degree, school and peers—play a role in a person's political socialization, the role of key political events is also very important. You probably do not have a single professor who cannot remember what she or he was doing on the day that President John F. Kennedy was killed—November 22, 1963. This dramatic event is indelibly etched in the minds of virtually all people who can remember it. In 1993, on the thirtieth anniversary of JFK's assassination, in fact, one major network televised a program in which celebrities recounted what they were doing when they learned of the tragedy.

President Richard M. Nixon's fall from grace and forced resignation in 1973 also had a profound impact on the socialization process of all Americans, possibly to the greatest extent on young people, who were forced to realize that their government was not always right or honest.

In fact, one problem in discussing political socialization is that many of the major studies on this topic were conducted in the aftermath of these and other crucial events, including the civil rights movement and the Vietnam War, all of which produced a marked increase in Americans' distrust of government. The findings reported in Figure 10-5 reveal the dramatic dropoff of trust in government that began in the mid-1960s and continued through the election of Ronald Reagan in 1980. In a study of Boston children conducted in the aftermath of the Watergate scandal, for example, one political scientist found that children's perception of the president went from that of a benevolent to a "malevolent" leader.[9] These findings are indicative of the low confidence most Americans had in government in the aftermath of Watergate and President Nixon's ultimate resignation from office to avoid impeachment.

Social Groups

Also affecting the development and continuity of political beliefs and opinions are group effects, that is, certain characteristics that allow persons to be lumped into categories. Among the most important of these groups are religion, educational attainment, income, region, and race. More recently, researchers have learned that gender and age are becoming increasingly important determinants of public opinion, especially on certain issues.

Religion. Religion plays a very important role in the life of Americans. As shown in Figure 10-6, many more Americans attend church regularly than do citizens of European countries. In 1991, 56 percent of Americans identified themselves as Protestant, 25 percent as Catholic, 2 percent as Jewish, and 6 percent as other. Only 11 percent claimed to have no religious affiliation. Over the years, analysts have found continuing opinion differences among these groups, with Protestants being the most conservative on many issues and Jews the most liberal, as shown in Figure 10-7.

Shared religious attitudes tend to affect voting and stances on particular issues. Catholics tend to vote Democratic more than do Protestants, and they tend to vote for other Catholics. For example, Catholics overwhelmingly cast their ballots for John F. Kennedy, who became the first Catholic president, in 1960. Catholics as a group also favor aid to parochial schools, most Jews support aid to Israel, and many fundamentalist Protestants support organized prayer in public schools.

---

[9] F. Christopher Arterton, "The Impact of Watergate on Children's Attitudes Toward Political Authority," *Political Science Quarterly* 89 (June 1974): 273.

418 ❖ Chapter 10   Public Opinion

FIGURE 10-5

Individual Trust in Government, 1952–1992

The percentage difference index is calculated by subtracting the number of those giving a trusting response to the question from the number of those giving a cynical response. A positive number in the index indicates an overall trust in government; a negative number indicates overall distrust.

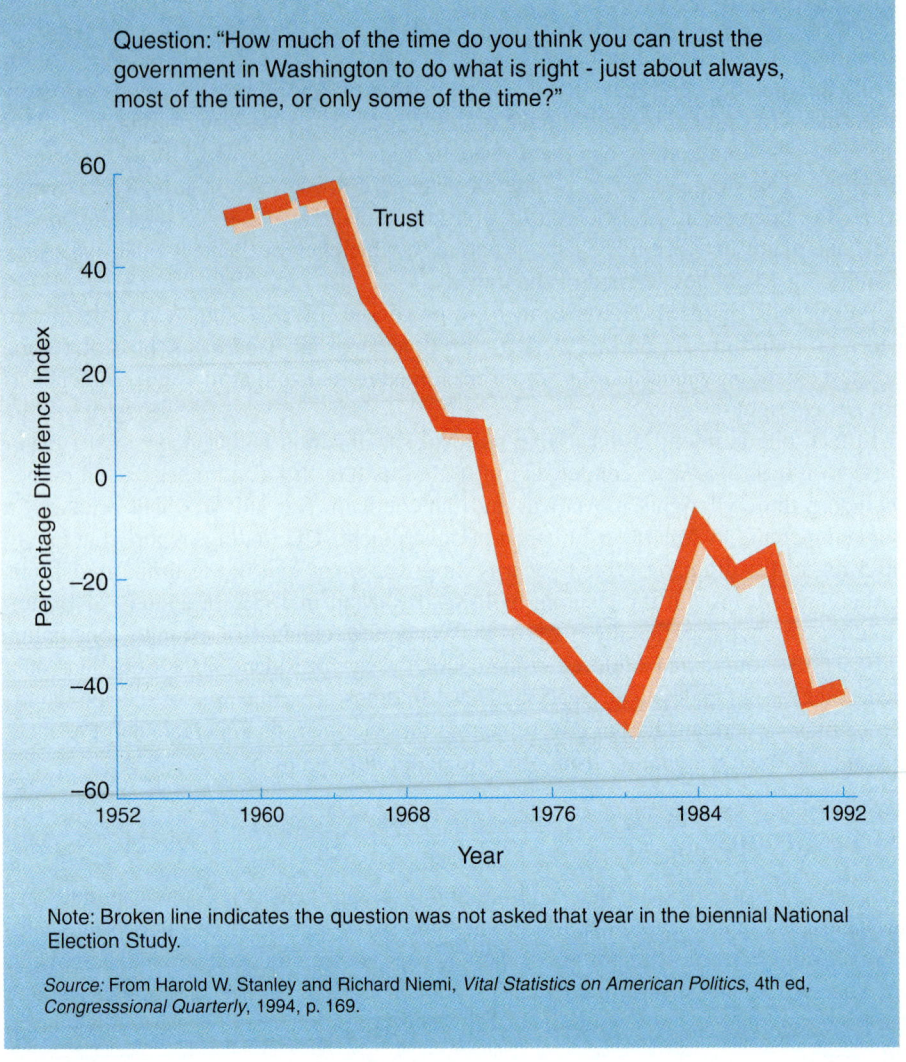

Note: Broken line indicates the question was not asked that year in the biennial National Election Study.

Source: From Harold W. Stanley and Richard Niemi, *Vital Statistics on American Politics*, 4th ed, *Congresssional Quarterly*, 1994, p. 169.

Region. Since colonial times, regional differences have been important to the development and maintenance of public opinion. As the United States grew and developed into a major industrial nation, waves of immigrants, with different religious traditions and customs, entered the United States and often settled in areas they viewed as hospitable to their way of life. For example, thousands of Scandinavians settled in cold, snowy, rural Minnesota, and many Irish settled in the urban centers of the Northeast, as did many Italians, and Jews. All brought with them unique views about many issues as well as about the role of government. Many of these regional differences continue to affect public opinion today, sometimes resulting in conflict at the national level.

Recall, for example, that during the Constitutional Convention most Southerners staunchly advocated a weak national government. The Civil War was fought in part because of basic differences in philosophy toward government (states' rights in the South versus national rights in the North) and the question of the moral and political validity of the institution of slavery.

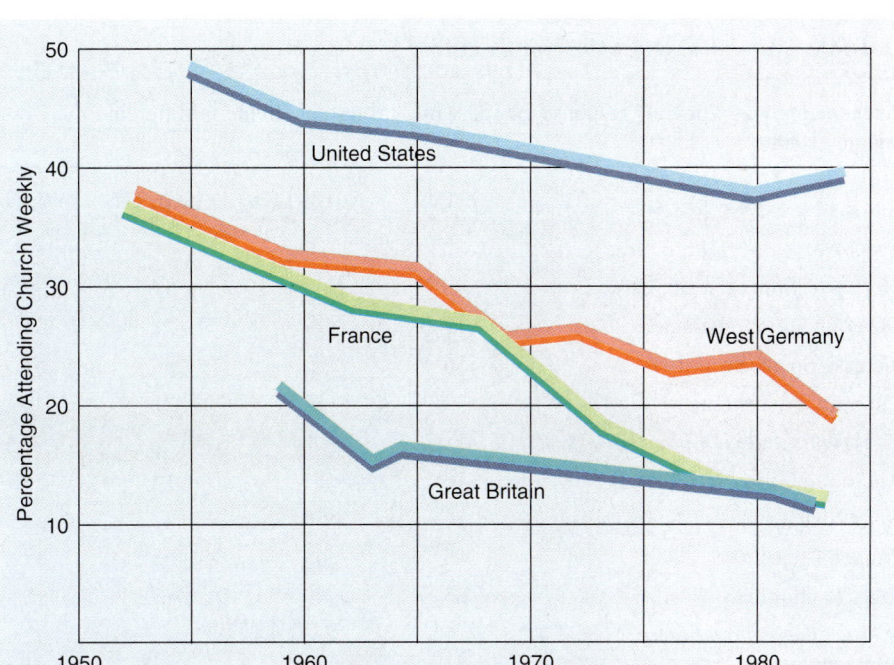

FIGURE 10-6
Weekly Church Attendance

As we know from the results of modern political polling, the South has continued to lag behind the rest of the nation on support for civil rights, while continuing to favor return of power to the states at the expense of the national government, as revealed in Table 10.1.

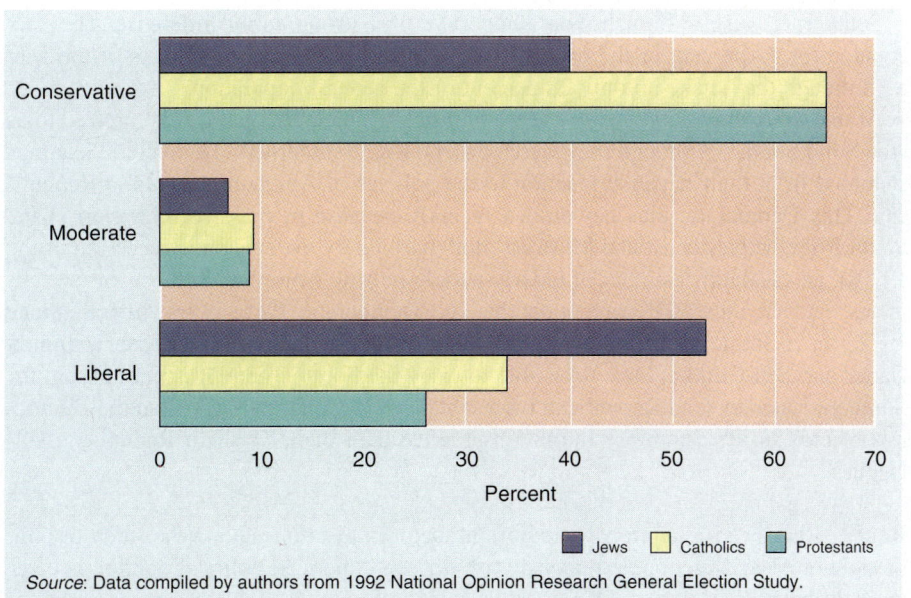

FIGURE 10-7
Liberal/Conservative Self-Identification of Protestants, Catholics, and Jews

Table 10.1 ♦ Does the South Differ?

Percentage giving "liberal" response among white Protestants living in different regions, 1988

ISSUE	EAST	MIDWEST	SOUTH	WEST
Economic and welfare issues:				
More government health care	48%	35%	37%	39%
Government job guarantees	19	19	22	21
Increase Social Security	56	50	59	53
Cut military spending	32	35	21	30
Civil rights and civil liberties issues:				
Aid to minorities	16	14	14	23
Homosexual rights	56	56	47	52
Women's equality	63	65	62	69
Right to abortion	65	49	45	60
Average percentage liberal, all issues	41%	37%	34%	41%

Source: Compiled by Daron Shaw. Reprinted with permission of the Center for Political Studies, University of Michigan.

During the drive to ratify the Equal Rights Amendment (1972–1981), Southern legislators made much about whether the national government should mandate how the states treat "their women." Not surprisingly, it was the Southern states that effectively blocked passage of the ERA.

Southerners also are much more supportive of a strong national defense. They accounted for 41 percent of the troops in the Persian Gulf in the early days of the war, even though they make up only 28 percent of the general population.

At one time, the South was so overwhelmingly Democratic that it was referred to as "the Solid South." Although they were conservative, Southerners' Democratic leanings stemmed from their negative reaction to the policies of Abraham Lincoln, a Republican. This Democratic bias has eroded recently because of massive migration to the South from the Northeast and Midwest (both hard hit by the economic recession of the 1970s), an escalating number of elderly people retiring from the North to warmer climates, and an increased perception that the Democratic Party is too liberal. Since 1972, for example, only the Southern Democratic candidates for president, Jimmy Carter and Bill Clinton, have been able to carry the South. Today it is not unusual for Southern states to send Republican representatives to Congress, and often the Democrats elected in the South are more conservative than their Northern Republican colleagues.

Race. Race is an exceptionally important factor in elections and in the study of public opinion. The direction and intensity of African-American political opinion is often quite different from that of whites. As revealed in Figure 10-8, whites oppose affirmative action plans at significantly higher levels than do African Americans. Likewise,

Political Socialization: The First Step Toward Forming Opinions ❖ 421

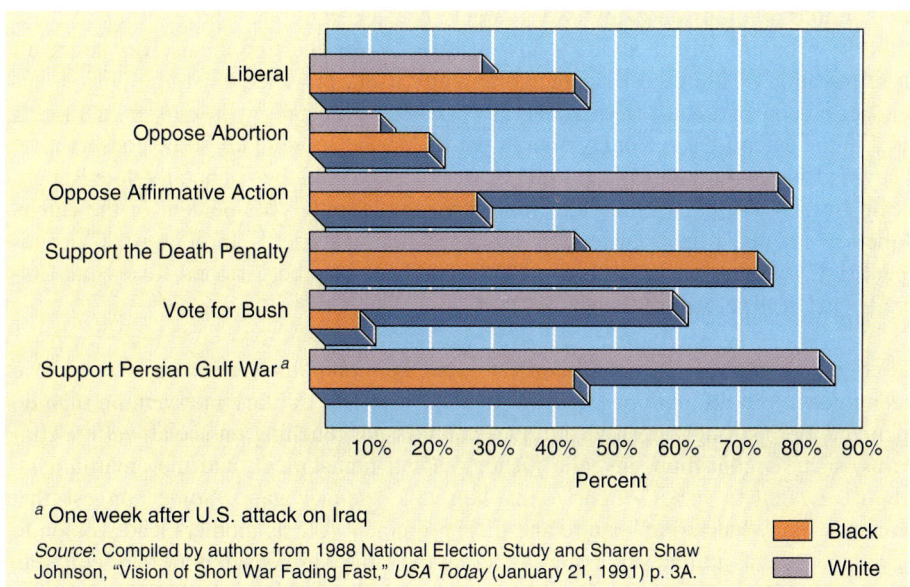

FIGURE 10-8
Black versus White Attitudes

significant differences arose in support for the Persian Gulf War and support for the death penalty.

Native Americans, Hispanics, and Asian or Pacific Islanders are other identifiable ethnic minorities in the United States (see Figure 10-9). According to the last census, in 1991, Native Americans made up 1 percent of the population, Hispanics made up 9 percent, and Asian/Pacific Islanders represented 3 percent. These groups also often respond differently to issues than do whites. Generally, Native Americans and Hispanics

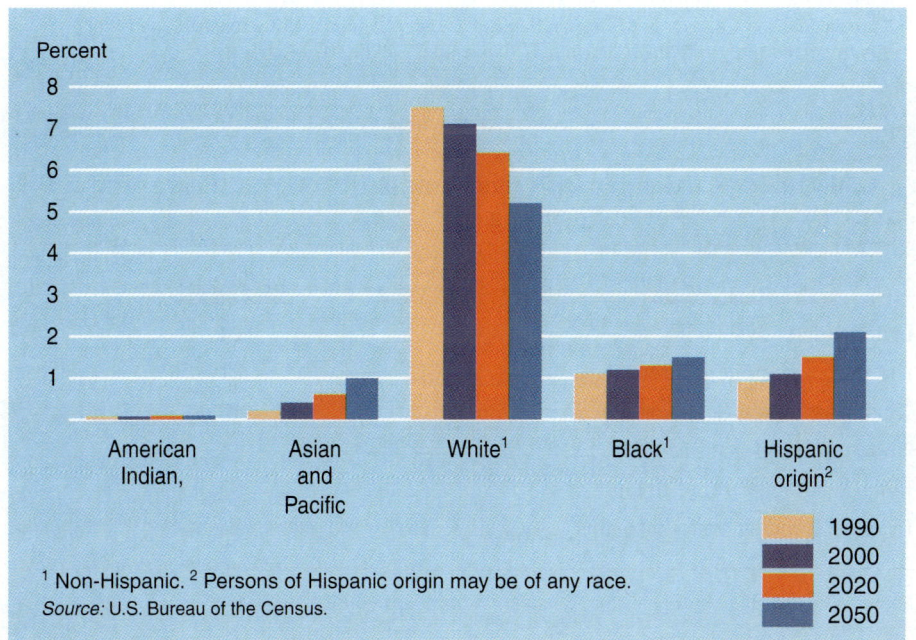

FIGURE 10-9
Percentage Distribution of the Population, by Race and Hispanic Origin: 1990 to 2050

hold similar opinions on many issues largely because significant proportions of these minority-group members belong to low-income groups and find themselves targets of discrimination. Within the Hispanic community itself, however, existing divisions often depend on national origin. Generally, Cuban Americans who cluster in Florida (and in the Miami-Dade County area in particular) are more likely to be conservative. They fled from communism and Fidel Castro in Cuba, and they generally vote Republican. In the 1976 presidential election, for example, only 40.2 percent of the Cuban Americans in the Miami-Dade area voted for Jimmy Carter.[10] In contrast, Chicanos (people of Mexican origin) voting in California, New Mexico, Arizona, Texas and Colorado cast 83.1 percent of their votes for Carter that year.[11]

Gender. From the time that the earliest public opinion polls were taken, women have been known to hold more negative views about war and military intervention than do men and more strongly positive attitudes about issues touching on social welfare concerns, such as education, juvenile justice, capital punishment, and the environment. Many researchers have sought to explain this "gender gap." Some suggest that women's more "nurturing" nature and their prominent role as mothers lead women to have more liberal attitudes on issues affecting the family or the safety of their children. Research by Pamela Johnston Conover and Virginia Sapiro, however, finds no support for a maternal explanation.[12]

Polls taken in the late 1980s reveal that women continue to hold very different opinions from men on a variety of issues, as shown in Table 10.2. Ironically, however, during the debate over the Equal Rights Amendment, men supported the amendment more than did women voters. Men also appear today to support a woman's right to have an abortion to a greater extent than do women.

---

[10] Alejandro Portest and Rafael Mozo, "The Political Adaptation Process of Cubans and Other Ethnic Minorities in the United States: A Preliminary Analysis," in F. Chris Garcia, ed. *Latinos and the Political System,* (Notre Dame, IN: University of Notre Dame Press, 1988), p. 161.

[11] John A. Garcia and Carlos H. Arce, "Political Orientations and Behaviors of Chicanos: Trying to Make Sense Out of Attitudes and Participation," in Ibid., pp. 125–151.

[12] Pamela Johnson Conover and Virginia Sapiro, "Gender, Feminist Consciousness, and War," *American Journal of Political Science* 37 (November 1993): 1079–1099.

Table 10.2 ♦ Gender Differences on Issues of War, Peace, and Social Spending

ISSUES FAVORED	MALES	FEMALES
Increase defense spending	34	24
Aid to foreign military groups	42	21
"Star Wars" (defense) spending	24	10
No return to a peacetime draft	48	61
Initial sending of troops to Gulf	72	53
Increase spending on food stamps	18	24

Source: Data supplied by Center for American Women and Politics.

Democratic primary candidate Bill Clinton campaigned hard in Florida to attract the elderly vote.

Age. As Americans live longer, senior citizens are becoming a potent political force. In states such as Florida, to which many Northern retirees have flocked, seeking relief from cold winters and high taxes, the elderly have voted as a bloc to defeat school tax increases and to pass tax breaks for themselves. As a group, senior citizens are much more likely to favor an increased governmental role in the area of medical insurance while opposing any cuts in Social Security benefits.

In the future, the "graying of America" will have major social and political consequences. As we discuss in Chapter 12, the elderly under age 70 vote in much larger numbers than do their younger counterparts. Moreover, the fastest-growing age group in the United States is that of citizens over the age of sixty-five. Thus, not only are there more persons in this category, but they are also the most active at the ballot box and will undoubtedly continue to have their wishes heard and heeded.

Political Ideology

An individual's coherent set of values and beliefs about the purpose and scope of government is called his or her **political ideology.** As discussed in "The American Voter and Ideology" p. 424, Americans' attachment to, or evidence of, strong ideological positions has varied over time. In sharp contrast to spur-of-the-moment responses, these sets of values, often greatly affected by political socialization, can prompt citizens to favor a certain set of policy programs. "Conservative Versus Liberal" p. 425 notes that conservatives are likely to support smaller, less activist governments. In contrast, liberals favor big governments that play active roles.

The terms "conservative" and "liberal" are difficult to define. Conservative and liberal ideologies focus on the function of liberty and equality in our society and on the

> ## The American Voter and Ideology
> ♦ ♦ ♦
>
> In 1960, Angus Campbell and three colleagues tried to determine the ideological sophistication of the U.S. electorate by assessing their responses to questions about numerous issues and about the 1956 presidential election. Only 12 percent of the electorate responded in ideological terms. Forty-two percent assessed the candidates based on their "benefits to groups," that is, depending on how a candidate would affect the group to which the respondent belonged (laborers, businesspersons, etc.). Others tended to evaluate candidates based on what was termed "the nature of the times." Twenty-two percent (nearly one-quarter of the sample) did not appear to be motivated by any issue or ideological underpinnings. These voters judged candidates on their personalities alone.
>
> Other studies have concluded that the electorate of the 1950s was relatively apathetic and not representative of other eras. For example, in *The Changing American Voter* (1976), the authors argued that from 1956 to 1972 voters were much more interested in politics and more ideologically sophisticated than were voters of the 1950s.* Other studies have found that the more ideological the candidates are—for example, as in the 1964 Barry Goldwater/Lyndon B. Johnson race—the more likely are voters to respond in ideological terms.
>
> *Norman H. Nie, Sidney Verba, and John R. Petrocik, *The Changing American Voter* (Cambridge, MA: Harvard University Press, 1976).

proper role of government. These two terms reflect opposing attitudes on a wide range of economic, social, and political issues. Although many Americans continue to identify themselves as conservatives or liberals, over the years these terms have had very different meanings. During the nineteenth century, for example, conservatives supported governmental power and favored a role for religion in public life; in contrast, liberals supported freedom from undue governmental control. Today, these terms have very different meanings to the general public. **Conservatives** are thought to believe that a government is best that governs least and that big government can only infringe on individual personal and economic rights. Conservatives also believe that domestic problems like homelessness, poverty, and discrimination are better dealt with by the private sector than by the government. In contrast, **liberals** now are considered to favor extensive governmental involvement in the economy and the provision of social services and also to take an activist role in protecting the rights of women, the elderly, minorities, and the environment.

There are indications that college students are becoming more liberal as reflected in Figure 10-3, discussed earlier. The increase in the number of persons identifying themselfes as liberals, as of the fall of 1992, may reflect identification with a younger presidential candidate, Bill Clinton.

While political scientists and politicians often talk in terms of conservative and liberal ideologies, the general public does not appear to be as enamored of this kind of labeling. When asked, most Americans respond that their political beliefs are "middle of the road" or moderate, although a substantial number call themselves conservatives, as revealed in Figure 10-10 on page 426. Less than 30 percent of the American public labels itself "liberal." As the United States became more conservative in recent years, the term "liberal" clearly came to be a label to be avoided in the 1980s. In the 1988 presidential election, George Bush was able to stick the label "liberal" on his opponent, Michael S. Dukakis. In the minds of the public, "liberal" was associated with big government, big spending, and support for affirmative action programs. The more the "liberal" label came to be associated with Dukakis, the more his support eroded.

But even the word "liberal" no longer appears to be the "dirty word" that it was often considered during 1980s. As revealed in Figure 10-11 on page 427, 67 percent of the U.S. public polled in 1993 believed that the national government under Clinton was becoming more liberal. Yet, only 28 percent of those polled thought that this trend was a bad thing.

"Conservative" versus "Liberal"

We often hear the terms "conservative" and "liberal" applied to politicians; but what do these ideological labels mean? The interpretations of both terms have evolved over the years. William Safire describes these changes in his Political Dictionary.

Conservative: A defender of the status quo who, when change becomes necessary in tested institutions or practices, prefers that it come slowly, and in moderation. . . .

The political origin of the word can be traced to the *Senat Conservateur* in the 1795 French Constitution, and . . . it was soon applied in America to the Whigs, amid some derision.

Today the more rigid conservative generally opposes virtually all governmental regulation of the economy. He favors local and state action over federal action, and emphasizes fiscal responsibility, most notably in the form of balanced budgets. . . .

But there exists a less doctrinaire conservative who admits the need for government action in some fields and for steady change in many areas. Instead of fighting a rear-guard action, he seeks to achieve such change within the framework of existing institutions, occasionally changing the institutions when they show need of it.

Liberal: Currently one who believes in more government action to meet individual needs; originally, one who resisted government encroachment on individual liberties.

In the original sense the word described those of the emerging middle classes in France and Great Britain who wanted to throw off the rules the dominant aristocracy had made to cement its own control.

In U.S. politics the word was used by George Washington to indicate a person of generosity or broadmindedness, as he expressed distaste for those who would deprive Catholics and Jews of their rights.

The word became part of the American vocabulary in its earlier meaning during a rump convention of Republicans dissatisfied with the presidency of Ulysses S. Grant, at Cincinnati in 1872. . . . The short-lived party born of the convention was called "The Liberal Republican" party.

In its present usage, the word acquired significance during the presidency of Franklin D. Roosevelt, who defined it this way during the 1932 campaign for his first term: ". . . say that civilization is a tree which, as it grows, continually produces rot and dead wood. The radical says: 'Cut it down.' The conservative says: 'Don't touch it.' The liberal compromises: 'Let's prune, so that we lose neither the old trunk nor the new branches.'"

Adlai Stevenson, the Democrats' presidential candidate in 1952 and 1956, once described a liberal as "one who has both feet firmly planted in the air."

Source: From *Safire's New Political Dictionary* by William Safire. Copyright © 1993 by The Cobbet Corporation. Copyright © 1968, 1972, 1978 by William Safire. Reprinted by permission of Random House, Inc.

FIGURE 10-10

Self-Identification as Liberal, Moderate, or Conservative, 1973–1992

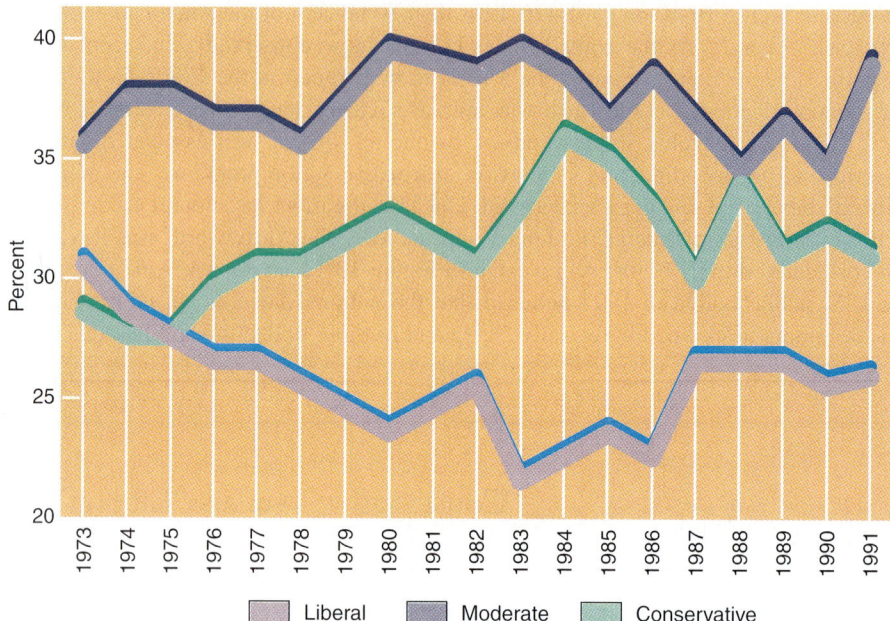

Note: "Liberal" equals the combined percentages of those identifying themselves as extremely liberal, liberal, or slightly liberal; "conservative" equals the combined percentages of those identifying themselves as extremely conservative, conservative, or slightly conservative.

Source: General Society Survey, National Opinion Research Center,

The labels "conservative" and "liberal" can be quite misleading. Studies reveal, for example, that many people who call themselves conservative actually take fairly liberal positions on many policy issues.[13] People who take conservative stances against "big government" often support increased government spending for the elderly, education, or health care. Thus, conservative or liberal ideology does not necessarily allow us to predict political opinions. In a "perfect" world, liberals would be liberal and conservatives would be conservative. Instead, Americans are inconsistent. Studies reveal that anywhere from 20 to 68 percent will take a traditionally "conservative" position on one issue and a traditionally "liberal" position on another.[14] Indeed, today, many people put differing emphases on the role of government in economic, social, and political spheres. It thus is not unusual to encounter a person who could be considered liberal on social issues such as abortion and civil rights and who also holds conservative views on economic or "pocketbook" issues.

Despite their inconsistencies, most Americans believe that they do hold a political ideology, as reflected in Figure 10-11. However, the political culture in the United States places a high premium on individual liberty, equality, and the right of self-government, values which lead people to hold a set of political beliefs that no longer allow them to be placed on a single liberal/conservative continuum.

---

[13] Lloyd Free and Hadley Cantrill, *The Political Belief of Americans* (New York: Simon & Schuster, 1968).

[14] Philip E. Converse, "The Nature of Belief Systems in Mass Publics," in David E. Apter, ed., *Ideology and Discontent* (New York: Free Press, 1964), pp. 206–221.

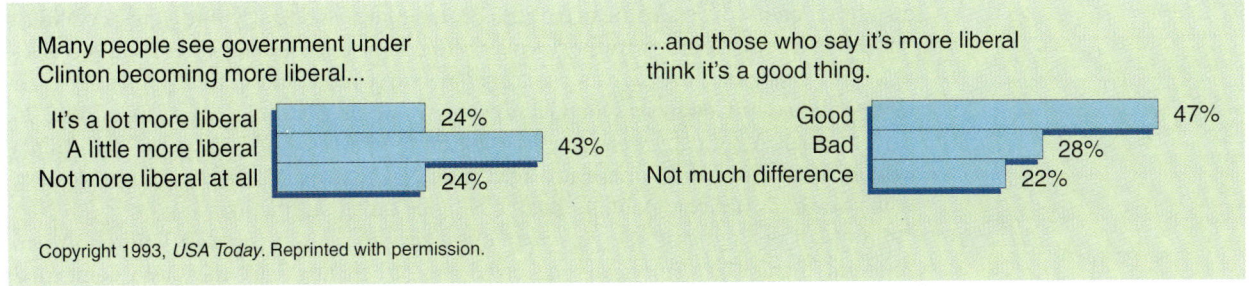

FIGURE 10-11

Washington Becomes More Liberal

How We Form Political Opinions

Many of us hold opinions on a wide range of political issues. In general, many of these ideas can be traced to the wide variety of social groups and different experiences each of us has had. Some individuals (called ideologues) think about politics and vote strictly on the basis of liberal or conservative ideology. Most people don't. In this section we explore how most people—those who are not ideologues—make up their minds on political issues. Chief among the factors that lead people to form political opinions are personal benefits, political knowledge, and cues from various leaders or opinion makers.

Personal Benefits

Most people choose policies that benefit them personally. You've probably heard the adage "People vote with their pocketbooks." Taxpayers generally favor lower taxes; hence, the popularity of candidates pledging "No new taxes." Similarly, the elderly usually support Social Security increases, and African Americans support strong civil rights laws and affirmative action programs.

Some government policies, however, don't really affect us *individually*. Legalized prostitution and the death penalty, for example are often perceived as moral issues that few citizens experience. Individuals often form attitudes toward issues such as these based on underlying values they have acquired through the years.

When individuals are faced with policies that don't affect them personally and don't involve moral issues, they often have difficulty forming an opinion. Foreign policy is an area in which this phenomenon is especially true. Most Americans often know little of the world around them. Unless moral issues such as apartheid in South Africa or human-rights violations in China are involved, American public opinion is likely to be quite volatile in the wake of any new information. For example, George Bush's popularity fell as soon as Americans viewed the results of Saddam Hussein's post-war ravaging of the Kurds.

Political Knowledge

Americans enjoy a relatively high literacy rate, and most Americans graduate from high school. And, unlike Great Britain, most Americans have access to a range of higher education opportunities. In spite of that access to education, however, Americans' level of actual political knowledge is low. As illustrated in Table 10.3, Americans, as a whole, don't know much about politics. In 1992, for example, 92 percent couldn't identify the Chief Justice of the United States and nearly three-quarters didn't know that Thomas Foley was the Speaker of the House. Moreover, after the 1986 elections, for example, only 22 percent of people surveyed could correctly identify their representative in Congress. One Gallup study done in 1988, moreover, found that 75 percent of all Americans were unable to locate the Persian Gulf on a map. Two-thirds couldn't find Vietnam. Americans aged eighteen to twenty-four scored the lowest, with two-thirds not being able to point to France on an outline map.[15]

Professor of English E. D. Hirsch Jr. criticizes the schools for their failure to teach "cultural literacy."[16] Americans, he concludes, frequently lack the basic contextual knowledge—where Africa is, when the Civil War was fought and why, for example—necessary to sort out the rest of the information they receive. So, although millions of Americans read a daily newspaper and watch television news, they still have low levels of knowledge. In fact, one study of citizens' ability to recall the facts of recent major news stories revealed that less than 15 percent of those surveyed could get the facts right, prompting its authors to conclude that "ignorance is widespread, if not rampant."[17] Political scientist Doris Graber echoes that sentiment: "By and large . . . people do not seem to gain much specific information from the media,"[18] or elsewhere, it would seem.

In spite of their low levels of knowledge, Americans are still generally willing to offer opinions on a wide range of issues, from abortion to the budget to the North American Free Trade Agreement to the First Lady. Since her husband's election in 1992 (and even before), Hillary Rodham Clinton has been the object of unprecedented attention of pollsters.

Low levels of knowledge, however, can lead to the rapid opinion shifts on issues. The ebb and flow of popular opinion can be affected dramatically by political leaders.

---

[15] "Geography: A Lost Generation," *Nation* (August 8, 1988): 19.
[16] E. D. Hirsch Jr., *Cultural Literacy* (Boston: Houghton Mifflin, 1986).
[17] Lee Sigelman and Ernest Yanarella, "Public Information on Public Issues," *Social Science Quarterly* 67 (June 1986): 404.
[18] Doris Graber, *Mass Media and American Politics,* 2nd ed. (Washington, DC: CQ Press, 1984), p. 157.

Table 10.3 ◆ American Political Knowledge

PERCENTAGE UNABLE TO IDENTIFY:	
Name of vice president (1992)	12
Name of the Speaker of the House (1992)	74
Party with most members in Senate before election (1984)	70
Chief Justice of United States (1992)	92

Sources: National Opinion Research Center, General Social Surveys and Center for Political Studies, American National Election Studies.

The president, especially, is often in a position to mold public opinion through effective use of the "bully pulpit," as discussed in Chapter 7.

Cues from Leaders

Given the visibility of political leaders and their access to the media, it is easy to see the important role they play in influencing public opinion. Political leaders, members of the news media, and a host of other experts have regular opportunities to influence public opinion, given the lack of deep conviction with which most Americans hold many of their political beliefs.

The president—particularly a popular one—can have an exceptionally powerful effect on public opinion. Political scientist John E. Mueller concludes, in fact, that there is a group of citizens—called followers—who are inclined to rally to the support of the president no matter what he does.[19] According to Mueller, the president's strength, especially in the area of foreign affairs (where public information is lowest), derives from the "majesty" of his office and his singular position as head of state.[20] Recognizing this phenomenon, presidents often take to television in an effort to drum up support for their programs.[21] President Clinton, like Reagan before him, has clearly realized the importance of mobilizing public opinion. He frequently takes his case directly to the public, urging the people to support his programs and to convey that support to their elected officials. He has also used his vice president to mobilize public opinion in order to help him get his programs through Congress.

How We Measure Public Opinion

To guide their policy decisions, public officials use a variety of measures as indicators of public opinion. These measures include election results, the number of telephone calls pro and con on any particular issue, letters to the editor in hometown papers, and the size of demonstrations or marches. But the most commonly relied on measure of public sentiment continues to be the public opinion survey, more popularly called a public opinion poll.

The polling process most often begins when someone says, "Let's find out about X and Y." Xs and Ys can be many things. Answers to questions including how to shape a candidate's campaign, how the public views the First Lady, how to market a new product, or how to package a new health care system can be partially acquired by knowing what the public wants at any given time. Potential candidates for local office may want to know how many people have heard of them (the device used to find out is called a name recognition survey). Better-known candidates contemplating running for higher office might want to know how they might fare against an incumbent. Polls can provide those answers. And news organizations routinely poll potential voters over the course of a campaign (or the duration of a war or presidential term, for example) to measure changes in public opinion and to measure the fluctuations in a candidate's popularity as Election Day nears.

According to the Federal Election Commission, former President George Bush spent $216,000 for public opinion polls in 1989 and 1990. In 1993 alone, President Clinton spent $1,986,410.

---

[19] John E. Mueller, *War, Presidents and Public Opinion* (New York: Wiley, 1973), p. 69.
[20] Ibid.
[21] Roderick P. Hart, *The Sound of Leadership: Presidential Communication in the Modern Age* (Chicago: University of Chicago Press, 1987).

Determining the Content and Phrasing the Questions

Once a candidate, politician, or news organization decides to measure the public's attitudes via a poll, special care has to be taken in constructing the questions to be asked. For example, if your professor asked you, "Do you think my grading procedures are fair?" rather than asking, "In general, how fair do you think the grading is in your American Politics course?" you might give a slightly different answer. The wording of the first question tends to put you on the spot and personalize the grading style; the second question is more neutral. Even more obvious differences appear in the real world of polling, especially when interested groups want a poll to yield particular results. Responses to highly emotional issues such as abortion, busing, and affirmative action are often skewed depending on the wording of the question. As "Poll Wording" (page 432) suggests, answers to questions about abortion appear to differ considerably depending on how the questions are worded. And, as revealed in Table 10.4, support for abortion can range from around 40 to 90 percent, depending on the question asked about abortion. Moreover, respondents often react to emotional cues in the question, which tends to skew survey results.

Selecting the Sample

Once the decision is made to take a poll, pollsters must determine the universe, or entire group whose attitudes they wish to measure. This universe could be all Americans, all voters, all city residents, all women, or all Democrats. Although in a perfect world each individual would be asked to give an opinion, this kind of polling is simply not practical. Consequently, pollsters take a sample of the universe in which they are interested. One way to do obtain this sample is by **random sampling.** This method of selection gives each potential voter or adult the same chance of being selected. In theory, this sounds good, but it is actually impossible to achieve because no one has lists of every person in any group.

Table 10.4 ♦ Public Opinion on Abortion, 1962–1992 (in percentages)
Abortion Should Be Legal Under These Circumstances

YEAR	MOTHER'S HEALTH	RAPE	BIRTH DEFECT	LOW INCOME	SINGLE MOTHER	AS A FORM OF BIRTH CONTROL	ANY REASON
1965	70	56	55	21	17	15	—
1973	91	81	82	52	47	46	—
1982	90	83	81	50	47	46	39
1992	92	87	84	49	45	45	43

Note: "—" indicates figures not available. Question: "Please tell me whether or not you think it should be possible for a pregnant woman to obtain a legal abortion [in the order asked in the survey] if there is a strong chance of serious defect in the baby? If she is married and does not want any more children? If the woman's own health is seriously endangered by the pregnancy? If the family has a very low income and cannot afford any more children? If she became pregnant as a result of rape? If she is not married and does not want to marry the man? The woman wants it for any reason?"

Sources: 1965: National Opinion Research Center surveys; 1973, 1983: General Social Survey. Compiled in Harold W. Stanley and Richard G. Niemi, *Vital Statistics on American Politics,* 4th ed. (Washington, DC: CQ Press, 1994), p. 35. 1992 figures from National Opinion Research Center.

Doonesbury
BY GARRY TRUDEAU

DOONESBURY copyright 1989 G. B. Trudeau. Reprinted with permission of Universal Press Syndicate. All rights reserved.

Most national surveys and commercial polls use samples of from 1,000 to 1,500 individuals and use a variation of the random sampling method called **stratified** or **multistage** area **sampling.** Simple random samples aren't very useful at predicting voting because they may undersample (or oversample) key populations that are not likely to vote. The *Literary Digest* sample discussed earlier was a straw poll (see "Then and Now," page 412) and not a random sample. It suffered from an oversampling of voters whose names were drawn from telephone directories and car registrations; this group was hardly representative of the general electorate in the midst of the Depression.

To avoid these problems, stratified sampling uses census data, which provide the number of residences in an area and their location. Researchers divide the country into four sampling regions. They then randomly select a set of counties and standard metropolitan statistical areas in proportion to the total national population. Generally, about eighty primary sampling units are chosen. Once certain primary sampling units are selected, they are often used for many years because it is cheaper for polling companies to train interviewers to work in a fixed area.

About twenty respondents from each primary sampling unit are selected to be interviewed. Generally four or five city blocks or areas are selected, and then four or five target families from each district are used. Large, sophisticated surveys like the National Election Study and General Social Survey attempt to sample from lists of persons living in each household. The key to the success of this method is not to let people volunteer to be interviewed—volunteers as a group often have different opinions from those who don't volunteer.

Stratified sampling (the most rigorous sampling technique) is generally not used by most survey organizations. Instead, they randomly survey every 10th, 100th, or 1,000th person or household. If those individuals are not at home, they go to the home or apartment next door.

Not all polls are based on probability sampling. A less reliable but frequently used method is known as **nonprobability sampling.** The *Literary Digest* poll is one good example, as are the polls taken by local television stations. Such "straw polls" are not representative samples, because only those individuals who are aware of the poll and are highly motivated about it are included in the sample.

Another kind of nonprobability sample involves "surveys" taken by organized interests. Generally, these groups send "questionnaires" to their members. The tallies of these very biased polls are then sent to the press, members of Congress, and members of the executive branch to indicate support of group goals.

> ## Poll Wording
> ♦ ♦ ♦
>
> Polls, supported by each side in the abortion debate, differ depending on how the question is worded
>
> One poll, partly paid for by the National Right to Life Committee, asked: "The U.S. Supreme Court recently ruled that the federal government is not required to use taxpayer funds for family planning programs to perform, counsel, or refer for abortion as a method of family planning. Do you favor or oppose this ruling?"
>
> | Favor | 48 percent |
> | Oppose | 48 percent |
> | Don't know/refuse | 4 percent |
>
> *Source:* Wirthlin Group poll of 1,000 adults taken on June 17–19; margin of error is 3 percentage points.
>
> Another poll, commissioned by Planned Parenthood, asked: "Do you favor or oppose that Supreme Court decision preventing clinic doctors and medical personnel from discussing abortion in family planning clinics that receive federal funds?"
>
> | Oppose | 65 percent |
> | Favor | 33 percent |
> | Not sure | 2 percent |
>
> *Source:* Lou Harris and Associates poll of 1,254 adults, May 31–June 5; margin of error: 3 percentage points.
>
> *Source:* "Words Affect Poll Numbers," *USA Today* (June 25, 1991): 7–A.

A more reliable nonprobability sample is a **quota sample,** in which pollsters draw their sample based on known statistics. Assume a citywide survey has been commissioned. If the city is 30 percent black, 15 percent Hispanic, and 55 percent white, interviewers will use those percentages to determine the proportion of particular groups they will sample in that city. These kinds of surveys are often conducted at local malls and shopping centers. Perhaps you've wondered why the man or woman with the clipboard has clearly passed you up to ask questions of other shoppers. Now you know it is likely that you did not fit into one of the categories of individuals that particular pollster was charged with locating. Although this kind of sampling technique can yield fairly impressive findings, the degree of accuracy falls short of that of surveys based on probability samples. Moreover, these polls generally oversample visible populations, such as shoppers. The views of stay-at-homes, who may be glued to CNN, C-SPAN, shopping networks, or soap operas are therefore underrepresented.

Kinds of Polls

Telephone Polls. The most common form of polls are random-digit dialing surveys, in which a computer randomly selects telephone numbers to be dialed. This kind of poll is described in "A Common Poll Description" on page 434. Because it is estimated that as many as 95 percent of the American public have phones in their homes, samples selected in this manner are likely to be fairly representative. George Gallup observed in 1967 that the quickest and cheapest way to poll people is by telephone.

A typical polling instrument

```
                        NATIONAL STUDY

INTERVIEWER_____              STUDY #  5483
TARRANCE & ASSOCIATES                 CODING_____
GREENBERG-LAKE                        COMPUTER_____
PERSONAL/CONFIDENTIAL                 FINANCE_____
                                      INTERVIEWING___

Hello, I'm _____ of Tarrance & Associates, a national
research firm. We're calling from our national telephone center.
We're talking to people in the nation today about public leaders
and issues facing us all.

A.   Are you registered to vote
     in your state and will you be
     able to vote in the election
     for President that will be
     held in 1992?
_____

     IF "NO", ASK: Is there someone
     else at home who is registered
     to vote? (IF "YES", THEN ASK:
     MAY I SPEAK WITH HIM/HER?)
                         Yes  (CONTINUE)

                         No   (THANK AND TERMINATE)
```

But you run into a problem. . . . You're more likely to reach conservatives and more Republicans than Democrats. If you could reach people in theaters or bars or massage parlors, you'd find the Democrats.[22]

In spite of Gallup's obvious biases and stereotyping, he revealed one truth—some telephone polls can be less than accurate. But, today, modern pollsters have worked hard to refine their polling methods to remedy these shortcomings. Thus, today, in spite of some continued problems (such as the fact that many people don't want to be bothered, especially at dinner time), most polls done for newspapers and news magazines are conducted this way.

In-Person Polls. Individual, in-person interviews are conducted by some groups, such as by the University of Michigan for its National Election Studies. Some analysts favor such in-person surveys, but others argue that the unintended influence of the questioner or pollster is very important and can lead to errors. How the pollster dresses, relates to the person being interviewed, and even asks the questions can affect responses. (Some of these factors, such as tone of voice, can also affect the results of telephone surveys.)

Exit Polls. **Exit polls** are polls conducted at selected polling places on Election Day. Generally, large news organizations send pollsters to selected precincts to sample every tenth voter as he or she emerges from the polling place. The results of these polls are used to help the television networks predict the outcome of key races, often

---

[22] Quoted in Eric Pace, "George H. Gallup Is Dead at 82," *The New York Times* (July 28, 1984): A–1.

just a few minutes after the polls close in a particular state and generally before voters in other areas—sometimes in a later time zone—have cast their ballots.

In 1980, his own polling and the results of network exit polls led President Jimmy Carter to concede defeat three hours before the polls closed on the West coast, leading many Democratic Party officials and candidates to criticize Carter and network predictions for harming their chances at victories. (Many Democrats argued that if the presidential election had already been "called," voters were unlikely to go to the polls.) In the aftermath of that controversy, all networks agreed not to predict the results of presidential contests until all polling places were closed.

Governor L. Douglas Wilder of Virginia, whose election in 1989 demonstrated some of the difficulties of polling. Despite advance surveys and exit polls that indicated a comfortable lead, Wilder's actual margin of victory was razor-thin. Apparently, voters, for fear of admitting racism, were unwilling to admit that they had voted against him.

A Common Poll Description

Most major poll reports now include a section containing information on how the poll was conducted. The following is from a poll on President Clinton and foreign policy reported in *The New York Times* on June 29, 1993.

HOW THE POLL WAS TAKEN

The latest New York Times/CBS News Poll on President Clinton and foreign policy is based on telephone interviews conducted both before and after the United States attack on Baghdad over the weekend.

On June 21 to 24, a total of 1,363 adults were interviewed around the United States, excluding Alaska and Hawaii. On Sunday, 1,000 of the same respondents were called back and 622 were successfully re-interviewed to gauge their initial reactions to the attack.

The sample of telephone exchanges called was selected by a computer from a complete list of exchanges in the country. The exchanges were chosen to assure that each region was represented in proportion to its population. For each exchange, the telephone numbers were formed by random digits, thus permitting access to both listed and unlisted numbers. Within each household, one adult was designated by a random procedure to be the respondent for the survey.

The results have been weighted to take account of household size and number of telephone lines into the residence, and to adjust for variations in the sample relating to region, race, sex, age and education.

In theory, in nineteen cases out of twenty, the results based on such samples will differ by no more than 3 percentage points in either direction from what would have been obtained by seeking out all American adults.

For smaller subgroups the potential sampling error is larger. For example, for the group re-interviewed on Sunday, the margin of sampling error was plus or minus 4 percentage points.

In addition to sampling error, the practical difficulties of conducting any survey of public opinion may introduce other sources of error. For instance, the results of the post-attack calls on Sunday are subject to additional potential error because of the limited time available to pursue hard-to-reach people.

Source: From Richard L. Berke, "Raid on Baghdad: Poll Shows Raid on Iraq Buoyed Clinton's Popularity," *The New York Times* (June 29, 1993): A7. Copyright © 1993 by the New York Times Company. Reprinted by permission.

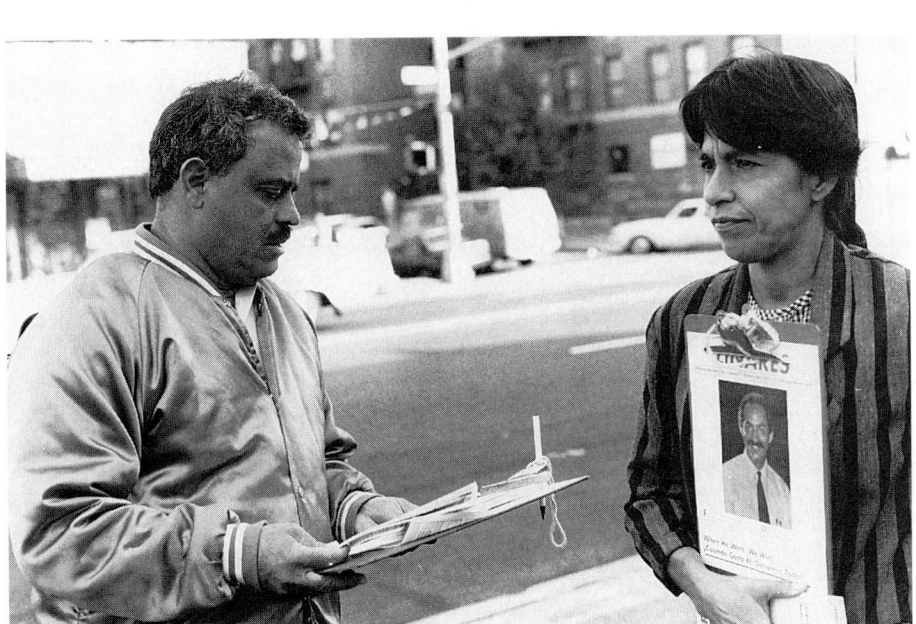

Exit polls can be undertaken by news networks, newspapers, polling organizations, or, as in this case, directly by a candidate's campaign staff.

Exit polls have also been faulted because it appears that not all voters are willing to reply truthfully to pollsters' questions. In 1989, for example, when L. Douglas Wilder ran for the Virginia governorship, the results of exit polls were way off. Surveys done before the race showed the African-American lieutenant governor winning by margins of 4 to 15 percent. A television exit poll showed him winning by 10 percent. Wilder won, but with a razor-thin margin (.0037 percent) of only 6,582 votes out of a record 1.78 million cast. Clearly, pollsters had been lied to or misled by "some Democratic-leaning white Virginians who could not bring themselves to vote for a black candidate . . . and few voters are secure enough in their bigotry to confess such blatant bias."[23] It seems that many white voters were unwilling to say that they had not voted for Wilder; therefore, they told pollsters that they *had* voted for Wilder, the African-American candidate, when they had not.

A similar phenomenon occurred during the Louisiana senatorial primary in 1990. Many whites who voted for David Duke, the former Ku Klux Klansman, apparently lied to pollsters, who underpredicted his support. Duke received a majority of the white vote, although he ultimately was soundly defeated in the general election.

Tracking Polls. During the 1992 presidential elections, "tracking polls," which were taken on daily basis by some news organizations (see Figure 10-12), were introduced to allow candidates to monitor short-term campaign developments and the effects of their campaign strategy.

Tracking polls involve small samples of interviews conducted every twenty-four hours (usually of registered voters contacted at certain times of day) and are usually combined with some kind of a moving statistical average to boost the sample size and

---

[23] Walter Shapiro, "Breakthrough in Virginia," *Time* (November 20, 1989): 54.

436 ❖ Chapter 10 Public Opinion

FIGURE 10-12

A Tracking Poll from *USA Today*'s Coverage of the 1992 Presidential Election

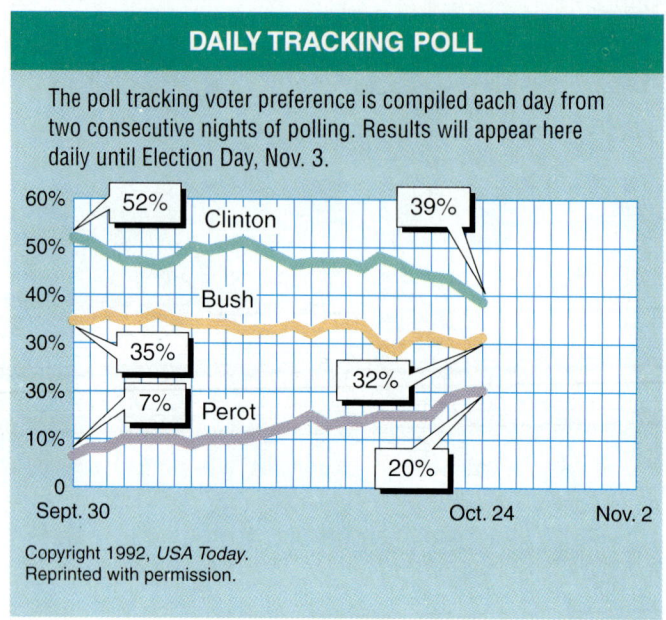

therefore the statistical reliability.[24] Even though such one-day surveys are fraught with reliability problems, most major news organizations used them during the 1992 election campaign, and, as a result, often provided the public with inaccurate views of the campaign.

Shortcomings of Polling

The accuracy of any poll depends on the quality of the sample that was drawn. Small samples, if properly drawn, can be very accurate if each unit in the universe has an equal opportunity to be sampled. If a pollster, for example, fails to sample certain populations, his or her results may reflect that shortcoming. Often, the opinions of the poor and/or homeless are underrepresented because insufficient attention is given to making certain that these groups are representatively sampled. And, in the case of tracking polls, if you choose to sample only on weekends or from 5 P.M. to 9 P.M., you may get more Republicans, who are less likely to have jobs that require them to work in the evening or on weekends.

There comes a point in sampling, however, where increases in the size of the sample have little effect on a reduction of the **sampling error**, the difference between the actual universe and the sample.

All polls contain errors. Standard samples of approximately 1,500 individuals provide fairly good estimates of actual behavior (in the case of voting, for example). Typically, the **margin of error,** or sampling error, in a sample of 1,500 will be about 3 percent. If you ask "Do you like ice cream?" of 1,500 people and 52 percent say "yes" and 48 percent say "no," the results are too close to tell whether more people like ice

[24] Michael W. Traugott, "The Polls in 1992: Views of Two Critics; A General Good Showing, But Much Work Needs to Be Done," *The Public Perspective*, 4 (November/December 1992): 14–16.

cream than not. Why? Because the margin of error implies that somewhere between 55 percent (52 + 3) and 49 percent (52 − 3) of the people like ice cream while between 51 percent (48 + 3) and 45 percent (48 − 3) do not. The margin of error in a close election makes predictions very difficult.

Public opinion polls may also be "off" when they attempt to gauge attitudes about issues that some or even many individuals don't care about or about which the public has little information. For example, few Americans probably care about the elimination of the electoral college. If a representative sample were polled, many would answer pro or con without having given much consideration to the question.

Low levels of knowledge or the inability to understand complex issues also confound pollsters. The Gramm-Rudman-Hollings Act, for example, was passed in late 1986 amidst considerable publicity because it would force limits on federal spending in an effort to balance the budget and forestall the need for the much-feared (at least by many members of Congress) balanced budget constitutional amendment. After President Reagan signed the Gramm-Rudman-Hollings bill into law, a Washington Post/ABC poll asked respondents if they had "read or heard anything about Congress passing the Gramm-Rudman-Hollings bill, which requires the government to balance the federal budget by 1991." Only sixty out of every one hundred respondents had. Among those 60 percent, only three-fifths reported having an opinion about its provisions.

The poll would have received many more responses if the "have you heard" question had not been used as a filter to exclude those who knew nothing about the bill. If the poll had asked only, "Do you favor or oppose the Gramm-Rudman-Hollings Act?" many of the 40 percent who hadn't heard of the bill might nevertheless have responded pro or con.

Most academic public opinion research organizations, such as the National Election Study, for example, use some kind of filter question that first asks respondents whether or not they have thought about the question. These screening procedures generally allow surveyors to exclude as many as 20 percent of their respondents, especially on complex issues like the federal budget. Questions on more personal issues such as moral values, drugs, crime, race, and women's role in society get far fewer "no opinion" or "don't know" responses, as indicated in Table 10.5.

Another shortcoming of polls concerns their inability to measure intensity of feeling about particular issues. Whereas a respondent might answer affirmatively to any question, it is likely that his or her feelings about issues such as abortion, the death penalty, or support for U.S. troops in the Gulf are much more intense than are his or her feelings about the electoral college.

How Polling and Public Opinion Affect Politicians, Politics, and Policy

The authors of *The Federalist Papers* noted that "all government rests on public opinion," and, as a result, public opinion inevitably influences the actions of politicians and public officials. The public's perception of crime as a problem, for example, was the driving force behind the comprehensive crime bill President Clinton submitted to Congress in 1994 and congressional passage of the Brady gun control bill in 1993. As Figure 10-13 shows, the public's concern with crime skyrocketed to an all-time high in 1994, and politicians at all levels were quick to convert that concern into a campaign issue.

Table 10.5 ♦ Public Opinion on Issues of Varying Public Prominence, 1990

"Would you favor or oppose a law which would require a person to obtain a police permit before he or she could buy a gun?"*

Favor: 79%   Oppose: 20%   Don't know: 2%

"The U.S. Supreme Court has ruled that no state or local government may require the reading of the Lord's Prayer or Bible verses in public schools. What are your views on this—do you approve or disapprove of the court ruling?"

Favor: 40%   Oppose: 56%   No opinion: 4%

"A proposed amendment to the Constitution would require Congress to approve a balanced federal budget each year. Government spending would have to be limited to no more than expected revenues, unless a three-fifths majority of the Congress voted to spend more than the expected revenues." Would you favor or oppose this amendment to the Constitution? (1989)

Favor: 59%   Oppose: 24%   No opinion: 17%

"The U.S. Supreme Court has required states to change their legislative districts so that each member of the upper house represents the same number of people. Some people would like to return to the earlier method of electing members of the upper house according to counties or other units regardless of population." Would you favor continuing the present equal districting plan or returning to the earlier plan?

Favor: 52%   Oppose: 23%   No opinion: 25%

* Numbers do not equal 100 percent due to rounding.

Source: Harold W. Stanley and Richard G. Niemi, *Vital Statistics on American Politics*, 4th ed. (Washington, DC: CQ Press, 1994) pp. 20–22.

Politicians and government officials spend millions of dollars each year taking the "pulse" of the public. Even the federal government spends millions annually on polls and surveys designed to evaluate programs and to provide information for shaping policies. But, as political scientist Benjamin Ginsburg noted, "the data reported by opinion polls are actually the product of an interplay between opinion and the survey instrument." They interact with each other and, in essence, often change the "character of the views receiving public expression."[25] Polls can thus help transform public opinion.

We know that politicians rely on polls, but it's difficult to say just how much. Several political scientists have attempted to study whether public policy is responsive to

---

[25] Benjamin Ginsburg, "How Polls Transform Public Opinion," in Michael Margolis and Gary A. Mauser, eds., *Manipulating Public Opinion* (Pacific Grove, CA: Brooks/Cole, 1989), p. 273.

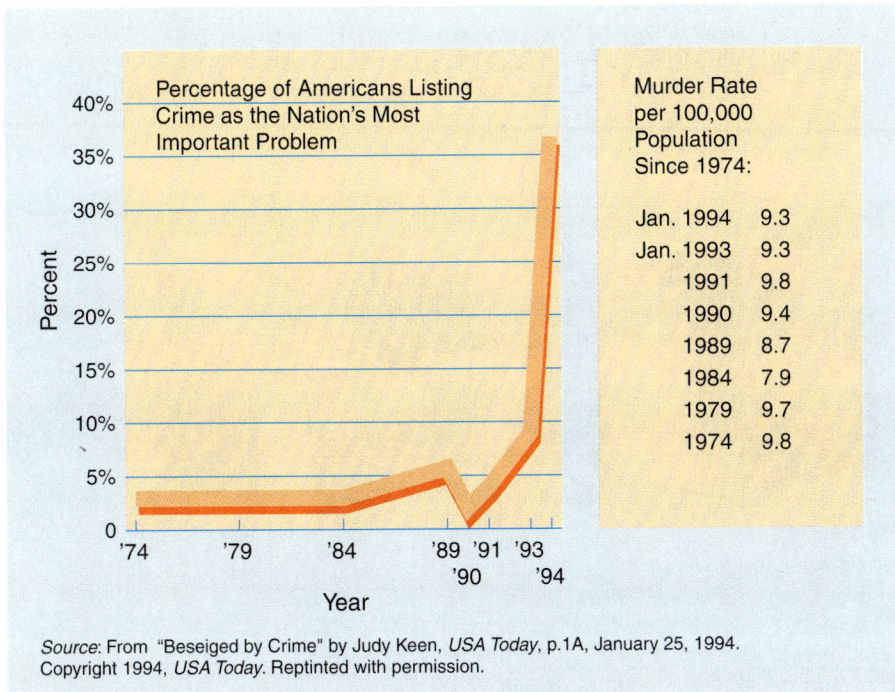

FIGURE 10-13

Percentage of People Who Say Crime Is the Most Important Problem in the United States

public opinion, with mixed results.[26] As we have seen, public opinion can fluctuate, making it difficult for a politician or policy maker to assess. Some critics of polls and their use by politicians argue that polls hurt democracy and make leaders weaker. Some say that politicians are simply driven by the results of polls that do not reflect a serious debate of issues. In response to this argument, George Gallup retorted, "One might as well insist that a thermometer makes the weather."[27]

Polls can clearly distort the election process by creating what are called "bandwagon" and "underdog" effects. In a presidential campaign, an early victory in the Iowa caucuses or the New Hampshire primary, for example, can boost a candidate's standings in the polls as the rest of the nation begins to think of him or her in a more positive light. New supporters jump on the bandwagon. A strong showing in the polls, in turn, can generate more and larger donations, the lifeblood of any campaign. Political scientist Herbert Asher has noted that "bad poll results, as well as poor primary and caucus standings, may deter potential donors from supporting a failing campaign."[28]

Political scientist Benjamin Ginsburg argues that public opinion polls weaken democracy.[29] He claims that these polls allow governments and politicians to say they

---

[26] See, for example, Benjamin Page and Robert Shapiro, "Effects of Public Opinion on Policy" *American Political Science Review* 57 (March 1983): 175–190.

[27] Quoted in Pace, "George Gallup Is Dead at 82," p. A–1. (See n. 22.)

[28] Herbert Asher, *Polling and the Public: What Every Citizen Should Know* (Washington, DC: CQ Press, 1988), p. 109.

[29] Benjamin Ginsburg, *The Captive Public* (New York: Basic Books), 1986, chapter 4.

Don Wright, the *Palm Beach Post*.

have considered public opinion in spite of the fact that polls don't always measure the intensity of feeling on an issue or might overreflect the views of the responders who lack sufficient information to make educated choices. Ginsburg further argues that democracy is better served by politicians' reliance on telephone calls and letters—active signs of interest—than on the passive voice of public opinion.

Toward Reform

When all the major television networks proclaimed that Ronald Reagan was going to easily defeat incumbent President Jimmy Carter, Carter went on television and conceded his defeat several hours before the polls closed on the west coast. Democrats, in particular, were furious, and they pressured the news media not to broadcast any winners in the future until all polls were closed—no matter what their exit polls indicated. This concession or reform was viewed as one that was good for democracy; after all, some voters were likely to stay home if they knew that the election had already been decided.

In the aftermath of the 1992 elections and their unprecedented use of polling—especially tracking polls—the use of those polls came under attack. There was "faulty polling" and "faulty tracking," which make analysis of the election difficult.[30] Some pollsters have called for either the American Association for Public Opinion Research or the National Council of Public Polls to conduct an open inquiry about the use and misuse of these kinds of polls.

[30] Ibid.

Summary

Public opinion is a subject constantly mentioned in the media, especially in presidential election years or when important policies (such as health care, balancing the budget, or gun control) are under consideration. What public opinion is, where it comes from, how it's measured, and how it's used are aspects of a complex subject. To that end, this chapter has made the following points:

1. Public opinion is what the public thinks about an issue or a particular set of issues. Public opinion polls are used to estimate public opinion.
2. Almost since the beginning of the United States, various attempts have been made to influence public opinion about particular issues or to sway elections.
3. Modern-day polling did not begin until the 1930s. Over the years, polling to measure public opinion has become more and more sophisticated and more accurate because pollsters are better able to sample the public in their effort to determine their attitudes and positions on issues. Pollsters recognize that their sample must be reflective of the population whose ideas and beliefs they wish to measure.
4. The first step in forming opinions occurs through a process called political socialization. The family, school, peers, and even the impact of events as well as the social groups of which one is a member—including religion, region, race, gender, and age—all affect how one views political events and issues, as do the major events themselves. Our political ideology—whether we are conservative, liberal, or moderate—also provides a lens by which we filter our political views.
5. All of these factors affect how we form our opinions. So does our level of personal benefit and our political knowledge of issues and events. Even the views of other people affect our ultimate opinions of a variety of issues, including race relations, the death penalty, abortion, and federal taxes.
6. Measuring public opinion can be difficult. The most frequently used measure is the public opinion poll. Determining the content, phrasing the questions, selecting the sample, and choosing the right kind of poll are critical to obtaining accurate and useable data.
7. Knowledge of the public's views on these issues is often used by politicians to tailor campaigns or to drive policy decisions.
8. In the aftermath of problems that have occurred with the media's use of polls, projected winners—based on exit polls—are no longer broadcast before the polls close. And, in the wake of the widespread use of tracking polls in the 1992 elections, calls for better study of their reliability and interpretation have been made.

Key Terms

public opinion
public opinion polls
initiative
referendum
recall
straw polls
political socialization
political ideology
conservatives
liberals
random sampling
stratified sampling
multistage sampling
nonprobability sampling
quota sample
exit polls
sampling error
margin of error

Suggested Readings

Asher, Herbert. *Polling and the Public: What Every Citizen Should Know.* Washington, DC: CQ Press, 1988.

Brace, Paul, and Barbara Hinckley. *Follow the Leader: Opinion Polls and Modern Presidents.* New York: Basic Books, 1992.

Campbell, Angus, et al. *The American Voter.* New York: Wiley, 1960.

Crespi, Irving. *Public Opinion, Polls, and Democracy.* Boulder, CO: Westview Press, 1989.

Ginsburg, Benjamin. *The Captive Public.* New York: Basic Books, 1986.

Graber, Doris. *Processing the News: How People Tame the Information Tide.* New York: Longman, 1984.

Jennings, M. Kent, and Richard Niemi. *Generations and Politics: A Panel Study of Young Adults and Their Parents.* Princeton, NJ: Princeton University Press, 1981.

Key, V. O. Jr. *Public Opinion and American Democracy.* New York: Alfred E. Knopf, 1961.

Niemi, Richard G., John Mueller, and Tom Smith. *Trends in Public Opinion: A Compendium of Survey Data.* New York: Greenwood Press, 1989.

Yeric, Jerry L., and John R. Todd. *Public Opinion: The Visible Politics,* 3rd ed. Itasca, IL: Peacock, 1994.

> There are two methods of curing the mischiefs of faction: The one, by removing its causes; the other, by controlling its effects.
>
> *James Madison*
> *Federalist No. 10*

Of all the phenomena feared by the Framers, political parties have proved to be the most pervasive and lasting. In this famous passage, Madison expresses distrust of factions, by which he meant interest groups and parties—a distrust that arose from the fear that the divisiveness they represented would make it difficult to hold the new and fragile nation together.

CHAPTER 11

Political Parties

WHAT IS A POLITICAL PARTY?
THE EVOLUTION OF AMERICAN PARTY DEMOCRACY
THE ROLES OF THE AMERICAN PARTIES
ONE-PARTYISM AND THIRD-PARTYISM
THE BASIC STRUCTURE OF AMERICAN POLITICAL PARTIES
THE PARTY IN GOVERNMENT
THE MODERN TRANSFORMATION OF PARTY ORGANIZATION
THE PARTY-IN-THE-ELECTORATE
TOWARD REFORM

Ross Perot and his supporters would surely have agreed with the Federalist Papers' stand on the "mischiefs of faction," since they hold the excesses of modern Democrats and Republicans responsible for the massive national debt. Many of the Framers harbored a deep distrust of political parties and other "factions," fearing the divisiveness they might engender at a time when the success of the infant federal Constitution was still far from certain. In this regard we need only remember President George Washington's 1796 farewell address, in which he warned the new nation "in the most solemn manner against the baneful effects of the spirit of party generally." Judging by his arguments in *Federalist No. 10,* James Madison held the same views as far back as the 1780s. Yet Madison was wise enough to understand that the "cure" for factionalism—the absence of a citizen's liberty to join together with others freely—is far worse than the disease. Furthermore, Madison recognized that the formation of factions of various sorts, whether narrow special-interest groups or broad-based parties, was inevitable in any republic.

Madison also correctly foresaw that the mechanisms of the federal system would temper the "mischiefs of faction." The division of governmental powers among several branches; the layers of federal, state, and local governments; the numerous checks and balances in the Constitution; and the vigorous competition among and between the factions themselves all help to counteract or limit the ill effects of faction. In fact, for a variety of reasons that this chapter explains, the United States is the only highly developed democracy with only two parties of consequence.

In the centuries since Madison's and Washington's criticisms of faction, Americans have had a love/hate relationship with the political parties. While usually voting for either Democrats or Republicans, a sizable portion of the electorate has backed a third-party or independent candidate from time to time; Ross Perot in 1992 is the most recent example. Still, political scientists have come to see political parties in a light different from Madison's. Far from viewing parties as an evil to be tempered, political scientists believe that parties have provided our system of government with the stability and choice that preserve it. As this chapter explains, the political scientist E. E. Schattschneider was not exaggerating when he wrote, "modern democracy is unthinkable save in terms of the parties."[1]

In this chapter we first define our terms, then review the evolution of American party democracy, the roles played by the modern parties (including third parties), and the parties' basic structure. We attempt to help you understand political parties by examining them from several vantage points—the party as it operates in government, the party as a campaign organization, and the party as a collection of supportive voters. Finally, we suggest some ways political parties might change to strengthen themselves—and American democracy.

What Is a Political Party?

Any definition of "political party" must be kept general, because there are so many kinds of parties in the United States. In some states and localities, party organizations are strong and well-entrenched, whereas in other places the parties exist more on paper

---

[1] E. E. Schattschneider, *Party Government* (New York: Holt, Rinehart and Winston, 1942), p. 1. This book stands as one of the most eloquent arguments for a strong political party system ever penned.

The major national parties are not always recognized as progressive forces, but in fact many advances in suffrage and voting rights have been spearheaded by the parties as they search for new sources of support. Although still seriously underrepresented, women in recent years have made inroads as delegates, candidates, and officeholders.

than in reality. This diversity would probably please James Madison, validating as it does his vision of a varied federalism. But it also complicates our tasks of explaining and understanding the political parties.[2]

At the most basic level, a **political party** is a group of office holders, candidates, activists, and voters who identify with a group label and seek to elect to public office individuals who run under that label. Notice how pragmatic this concept of party is. The goal is to *win* office, not just compete for it. This objective is in keeping with the practical nature of Americans and the country's historical aversion to most ideologically driven, "purist" politics (as we discuss later in this chapter). Nevertheless, the group label—also called **party identification** for the voters who embrace the party as their own—can carry with it clear messages about ideology and issue positions. Although this is especially true of minor, less broad-based parties that have little chance of electoral success, it also applies to the national, dominant political parties in the United States—the Democrats and the Republicans.

The definition of "party" also identifies the three groups of individuals who make up any political party: (1) the office holders and candidates who run under the party's banner (the **governmental party**), (2) the workers and activists who staff the party's formal organization (the **organizational party**), and (3) the voters who consider themselves to be allied or associated with the party (the **party-in-the-electorate**). We examine each of these groups later in the chapter after first reviewing the history and development of political parties in the United States.

The Evolution of American Party Democracy

It is one of the great ironies of the early republic that George Washington's public farewell, which warned the nation against parties, marked the effective end of the brief era of partyless politics in the United States (see Figure 11–1). Washington's unifying influence ebbed as he stepped off the national stage, and his vice president and successor, President John Adams, occupied a much less exalted position. Adams was allied with Alexander Hamilton, and to win the presidency in 1796 he narrowly defeated Thomas Jefferson, Hamilton's former rival in Washington's Cabinet. Hamilton and Jefferson, before ratification of the Constitution, had been leaders of the Federalists and Anti-Federalists, respectively (see Chapter 2). Over the course of Adams's single term, two competing congressional party groupings (or caucuses) gradually organized around these clashing men and their principles: Hamilton's Federalists supported a strong central government, whereas the Democratic-Republicans of Thomas Jefferson and his ally James Madison inherited the mantle of the Anti-Federalists and preferred a federal system in which the states were relatively more powerful. (Jefferson actually preferred the simpler name "Republicans"—a very different group from today's party of the same name—but Hamilton insisted on calling them "Democratic-Republicans" to link them to the radical democrats of the French Revolution.) In the presidential election of 1800, the Federalists supported Adams's bid for a second term, but this time the Democratic-Republicans prevailed with their nominee, Jefferson, who became the first U.S. president elected as the nominee of a political party.

---

[2] For more information on this topic, see Larry J. Sabato, *The Party's Just Begun: Shaping Political Parties for America's Future* (Glenview, IL: Scott, Foresman/Little, Brown, 1988).

FIGURE 11-1

American Party History at a Glance

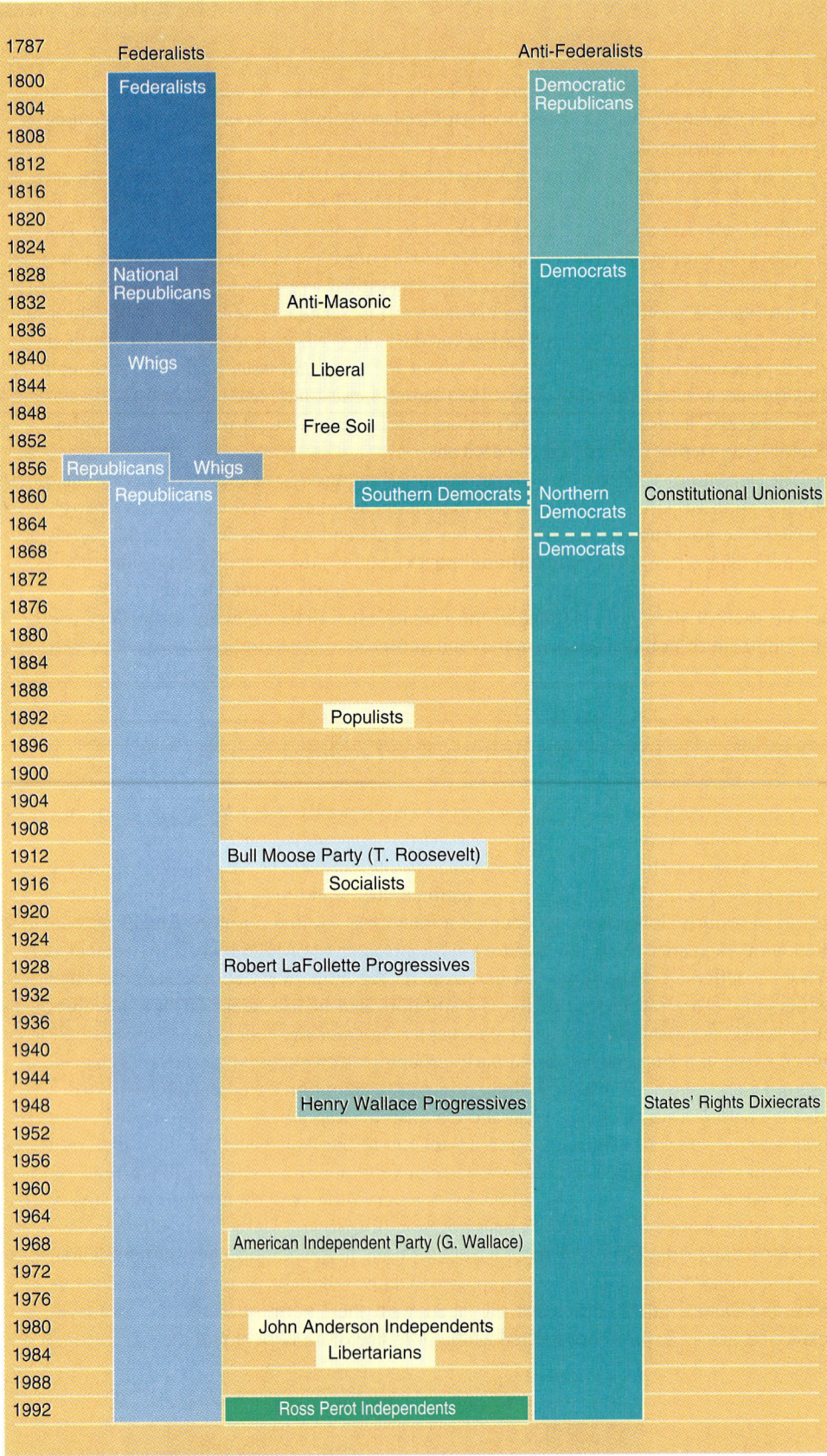

The Evolution of American Party Democracy ❖ 447

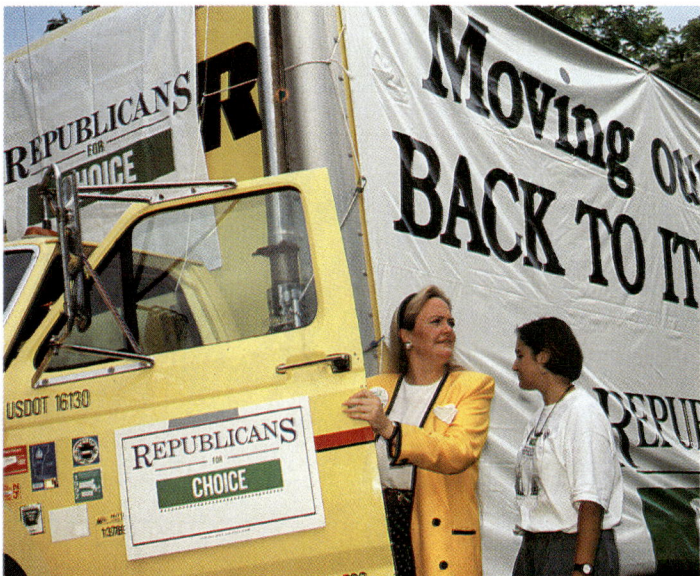

All political parties, whether major national organizations such as the Democrats and Republicans, or small local or issue-oriented parties, consist of the same three constituencies: the *governmental* group is the parties' candidates and officeholders; the *organizational* group is the staff who run campaigns and administer the day-to-day business of the party's office; finally, the *party-in-the-electorate* are those voters who identify with the party and its platforms.

Jefferson was deeply committed to the ideas of his party, but not nearly as devoted to the idea of a party system. He regarded his party as a temporary measure necessary to defeat Adams and Hamilton. Neither Jefferson's party nor Hamilton's enjoyed widespread "party identification" among the citizenry akin to that of today's Democrats and Republicans. Although Southerners were overwhelmingly partial to the Democratic-Republicans and New Englanders to the Federalists, no broad-based party organizations existed on either side to mobilize popular support. Just as the nation was in its infancy, so, too, was the party system, and attachments to both parties were weak at first. The various eras of American political parties are summarized in Landmark Events in the American Party System (p. 448).

Landmark Events in the American Party System		
1796	♦	Federalists v. Democratic-Republicans
1832	♦	Whigs v. Democrats
1860	♦	Republicans v. Democrats I (balance)
1896	♦	Republicans v. Democrats II (Republican dominance)
1932	♦	Republicans v. Democrats III (Democratic dominance)
1968	♦	Republicans v. Democrats IV (intermittent divided government)*

*Exceptions to this generalization occurred in 1977–1981 and 1993–current day.

The Early Parties Fade

After the spirited confrontations of the republic's early years, political parties faded somewhat in importance for a quarter of a century. The Federalists ceased nominating presidential candidates by 1816, having failed to elect one of their own since Adams's victory in 1796, and by 1820 the party had dissolved. James Monroe's presidency from 1817 to 1825 produced the so-called Era of Good Feelings, when party politics was nearly suspended at the national level. Even during Monroe's tenure, though, party organizations continued to develop at the state level. Party growth was fueled in part by the enormous increase in the electorate that took place between 1820 and 1840, as the United States expanded westward and most states abolished property requirements as a condition of white male suffrage. During this twenty-year period, the number of votes cast in presidential contests rose from 300,000 to more than 2 million.

At the same time, U.S. politics was being democratized in other ways. By the 1820s all the states except South Carolina had switched from state legislative selection of presidential electors to popular election of electoral college members. This change helped transform presidential politics. No longer just the concern of society's upper crust, the election of the president became a matter for all qualified voters to decide.

The party base broadened along with the electorate. Small caucuses of congressional party leaders had previously nominated candidates, but after much criticism of the process as elitist and undemocratic, this system gave way to nominations at large party conventions. The country's first major national presidential nominating convention was held in 1832 by the Democratic Party,[3] the successor to the old Jeffersonian Democratic-Republicans. (The shortened name had gradually come into use in the 1820s.) Formed around the charismatic populist President Andrew Jackson, the Democratic party attracted most of the newly enfranchised voters, who were drawn to Jackson's style. His strong personality helped to polarize politics, and opposition to the president coalesced into the Whig Party. The Whig Party was descended from the Fed-

---

[3] The National Republican (one forerunner of the Whig Party) and the Anti-Masonic Parties each had held more limited conventions in 1831.

This banner commemorates the inauguration of President Andrew Jackson in 1829. Jackson's Democratic Party was the successor to the Democratic-Republicans of Thomas Jefferson and James Madison. In the election of 1932, Jackson's Democrats won again, becoming the first party with a truly national base.

eralists; its early leaders included Henry Clay, the Speaker of the House from 1811 to 1820. The incumbent Jackson defeated Clay in the 1832 presidential contest. He became the first chief executive who won the White House as the nominee of a truly national, popularly based political party. (See "People of the Past: Henry Clay," p. 223.)

The Whigs and the Democrats continued to strengthen after 1832, establishing state and local organizations almost everywhere. Their competition was usually fierce and closely matched, and they brought the United States the first broadly supported two-party system in the Western world.[4] Unfortunately for the Whigs, the issue of slavery sharpened the many existing divisive internal party tensions that led to its gradual dissolution and replacement by the new Republican Party. Formed in 1854 by anti-slavery activists, the Republican Party set its sights on the abolition (or at least the containment) of slavery. After a losing presidential effort for John C. Frémont in 1856, the party was able to assemble enough support primarily from the Whigs and anti-slavery Northern Democrats to win the presidency for Abraham Lincoln in a fragmented 1860 vote. In that year, the South voted solidly Democratic, beginning a habit so strong that not a single Southern state voted Republican for president again until 1920.

The British political system, which has been characterized by competition between two main political parties with significant third-party activity, provides an interesting contrast to the American case. In Britain, the massive extension of suffrage in 1867 prompted the emergence of two modern, mass political parties (the Liberals and the Conservatives), which were needed to organize and mobilize the now unwieldy elec-

---

[4] By contrast, Great Britain did not develop truly national, broad-based parties until the 1870s.

torate. In the aftermath of World War I, the Liberals gave way to the Labour Party as the Conservatives' principal contender for power.

Democrats and Republicans: The Golden Age

From the presidential election of 1860 to this day, the same two major parties—the Republicans and the Democrats—have dominated elections in the United States, and control of an electoral majority has seesawed between them. The dominance of the Republicans (now often called the Grand Old Party, or GOP) in the post–Civil War Reconstruction era eventually gave way to a closely competitive system from 1876 to 1896, in part because the Democrats were more successful at integrating new immigrants into U.S. society in port cities like New York, Boston, and Chicago. In the later years of the nineteenth century, however, the Republicans skillfully capitalized on fears of a growing anti-establishment, anti-big business sentiment in the Democratic Party. They fashioned a dominant and enduring majority of voters that essentially lasted until the early 1930s, when the Great Depression created the conditions for a Democratic resurgence.

President Franklin D. Roosevelt's New Deal coalition of 1932 (consisting of the South, racial and ethnic groups, organized labor, farmers, liberals, and big-city "machines"—as well-oiled party organizations are sometimes called) characterized both the Democratic Party and the prevailing national majority until at least the late 1960s. Since 1970, neither party has been clearly dominant, as more and more voters have seemed to be less committed to either of the two parties. In this same period, the Republicans have dominated presidential elections and Democrats have won most congressional contests. (The development of a "divided government" is discussed later in this chapter.)

The Modern Era versus the Golden Age

The modern era seems very distant from the "golden age" of parties that existed from the 1870s to the 1920s. Emigration from Europe (particularly from Ireland, Italy, and Germany) fueled the development of big-city party organizations that ruled their domains with an iron hand. Party and government were virtually interchangeable, and the parties were the providers of much-needed services, entertainment, and employment. These big-city party organizations were a central element of life for millions of people: They sponsored community events, such as parades and picnics, and provided social services, such as helping new immigrants settle in and giving food and temporary housing to those in immediate need—all in exchange for votes.

The parties offered immigrants not just services but also the opportunity for upward social mobility as they rose in the organization. Because they held the possibility of social advancement, the parties engendered among their supporters and office holders intense devotion that helped to produce startlingly high voter turnouts—75 percent or better in all presidential elections from 1876 to 1900, compared with only about 50 to 55 percent today.[5] They also fostered the greatest party-line voting ever achieved in Congress and many state legislatures.[6] (See "People of the Past" on p. 455.)

The Grand Old Party

♦ ♦ ♦

Ever since the 1880s, the term "Grand Old Party" has been used to refer to the Republican Party. The phrase seems to have taken its inspiration from Great Britain, where Prime Minister William Gladstone was dubbed "the Grand Old Man" or "GOM" in 1882. Soon after that, "GOP" made its debut in headlines appearing in the *New York Tribune* and the *Boston Post*.

---

[5] Voter turnout in presidential elections from 1876 to 1900 ranged from 75 to 82 percent of the potential (male) electorate, compared with 50 to 55 percent in contemporary elections. See *Historical Statistics of the United States: Colonial Times to 1970,* Part 2, Series Y–27–28 (Washington, DC: Government Printing Office, 1975), based on unpublished data prepared by Walter Dean Burnham.

[6] Frank J. Sorauf, *Party Politics in America,* 5th ed. (Boston: Little, Brown, 1984), p. 22.

Is the Party Over?

The heyday of the political party—at least this kind of party—has passed. In the twentieth century, many social, political, technological, and governmental changes have contributed to party decline. Historically, the government's gradual assumption of important functions previously performed by the parties—such as printing ballots, conducting elections, and providing social welfare services—had a major impact. Social services began to be seen as a right of citizenship rather than as a privilege extended in exchange for a person's support of a party. Also, as the flow of immigrants slowed dramatically in the 1920s, party organizations gradually withered in most places.

The **direct primary,** whereby party nominees were determined by the ballots of qualified voters rather than at party conventions, was widely adopted by the states in the first two decades of the twentieth century. The primary removed the power of nomination from party leaders and workers and gave it instead to a much broader and more independent electorate, thus loosening the tie between the party nominee and the party organization. **Civil service laws** also removed much of the patronage used by the parties to reward their followers. (Civil service laws require appointment on the basis of merit and competitive examinations, whereas **patronage**—also called the **spoils system**—awards jobs on the basis of party loyalty.) These changes were encouraged by the Progressive Movement (consisting of politically liberal reformers), which flourished in the first two decades of the twentieth century.

In the post–World War II era, extensive social changes led the movement away from strong parties. Broad-based education gave rise to **issue-oriented politics,** politics that focuses on specific issues, such as civil rights, tax cutting, environmentalism, or abortion, rather than on party labels. Issue politics tends to cut across party lines and encourages voters to **ticket-split,** that is, to vote for candidates of different parties for various offices in the same election. Another post–World War II social change that has affected the parties is the shift in the population. Millions of people have moved out of the cities, which are easily organizable because of population density, and into the sprawling suburbs, where a sense of privacy and detachment can deter the most energetic organizers.

Politically, many other trends have contributed to the parties' decline. Television, which has come to dominate U.S. politics, naturally emphasizes candidate personality rather than abstract concepts such as party labels. In addition, the modern parties have many rivals for the affections of their candidates, including **political consultants,** the hired guns who manage campaigns and design television advertisements. Both television and consultants have replaced the party as the intermediary between the candidate and the voter. It is little wonder that many candidates and office holders who have reached their posts without much help from their parties remain as free as possible of party ties.

With a wink, Mayor James M. Curley of Boston files his application to run for a fifth term. In many cities, the parties ruled over vast organizations, offering the growing population of recent immigrants a sense of cohesion, upward mobility, and "patronage"—jobs in exchange for loyalty and service to the party. These party "machines" were the target of liberal reform movements beginning in the 1920s.

The Parties Endure

The parties' decline can easily be exaggerated, however. Viewing parties in the broad sweep of U.S. history, it becomes clear that first, although political parties have evolved considerably and changed form from time to time, they usually have been reliable vehicles for mass participation in a representative democracy. In fact, the gradual but steady expansion of suffrage itself was orchestrated by the parties. As political scientist E. E. Schattschneider concluded, "In the search for new segments of the populace that might be exploited profitably, the parties have kept the movement to liberalize the franchise well ahead of the demand.... The enlargement of the practicing

Although the parties have evolved—and in some ways weakened—over time, they continue to help define and resolve conflict in the national arena and provide consistently strong competition for each other. Here, James Carville and the Clinton-Gore campaign staff in the "war room" in Little Rock, on the eve of Democratic victory in 1992.

electorate has been one of the principal labors of the parties, a truly notable achievement for which the parties have never been properly credited."[7]

Second, the parties' journey through U.S. history has been characterized by the same ability to adapt to prevailing conditions that is often cited as the genius of the Constitution. Flexibility and pragmatism are characteristics of both and help ensure their survival and the success of the society they serve.

Third, despite massive changes in political conditions and frequent dramatic shifts in the electorate's mood, the two major parties have not only achieved remarkable longevity, but they also have almost consistently provided strong competition for each other and the voters at the national level. Of the twenty-eight presidential elections in the century-plus from 1884 to 1992, for instance, the Republicans won fifteen and the Democrats thirteen. Even when calamities have beset the parties—the Great Depression in the 1930s or the Watergate scandal of 1973–74 for the Republicans (see Chapter 7), the Civil War or left-wing McGovernism in 1972 for the Democrats—the two parties have proved tremendously resilient, sometimes bouncing back from landslide defeats to win the next election. After losing badly in 1988, for example, the Democrats managed to win in 1992, demonstrating again that the only constant in politics is change.

Perhaps most of all, history teaches us that the development of parties in the United States (outlined in Figure 11-1) has been inevitable, as James Madison feared. Human nature alone guarantees conflict in any society; in a free state, the question is simply how to contain and channel conflict productively without infringing on individual liberties. The Founders' utopian hopes for the avoidance of partisan faction have given way to an appreciation of the parties' constructive contributions to conflict definition and resolution during the years of the American republic.

[7] E. E. Schattschneider, *Party Government*, p. 48. (See n. 1.)

The Roles of the American Parties

The definition and resolution of conflict are two vital functions performed by the party system in the United States. But the parties play many other roles, too, and accomplish much for politics and society, as the following sampler suggests.

Mobilizing Support and Gathering Power

Party affiliation is enormously helpful to elected leaders. They can count on disproportionate support among their partisans in times of trouble and in close judgment calls. Therefore, the parties thus aid office holders by giving them room to develop their policies and by mobilizing support for them. When the president addresses the nation and requests support for his policies, for example, his party's activists are usually the first to respond to the call, perhaps by flooding Congress with telegrams urging action on the president's agenda.

Because there are only two major parties, pragmatic citizens who are interested in politics or public policy are mainly attracted to one or the other standard, creating natural majorities or near-majorities for party office holders to command. The party creates a community of interest that bonds disparate groups over time into a **coalition.** This continuing mutual interest eliminates the necessity of creating a new coalition for every campaign or every issue. Imagine the constant chaos and mad scrambles for public support that would ensue without the continuity provided by the parties.

A Force for Stability

As mechanisms for organizing and containing political change, the parties are a potent force for stability. They represent continuity in the wake of changing issues and personalities, anchoring the electorate in the midst of the storm of new political policies and people. Because of its unyielding, practical desire to *win* elections (not just to *contest* them), each party in a sense acts to moderate public opinion. The party tames its own extreme elements by pulling them toward an ideological center in order to attract a majority of votes on Election Day.

Another aspect of the stability the parties provide is found in the nature of the coalitions they forge. There are inherent contradictions in these coalitions that, oddly enough, strengthen the nation even as they strain party unity. Franklin D. Roosevelt's Democratic New Deal coalition, for example, included many African-Americans and most Southern whites—opposing elements nonetheless joined in common political purpose. This party union of the two groups, as limited a context as it may have been, provided a framework for acceptance of change and contributed to reconciliation of the races in the civil rights era. Nowhere can this reconciliation be more clearly seen than in the South, where most state Democratic parties remained predominant after the mid-1960s by building on the ingrained Democratic voting habits of both whites and blacks to create new, moderate, generally integrated societies.

Unity, Linkage, Accountability

Parties provide the glue that holds together the disparate elements of the fragmented U.S. governmental and political apparatus. The Founders designed a system that divides and subdivides power, making it possible to preserve individual liberty but difficult to coordinate and produce action in a timely fashion. Parties help compensate for this drawback by linking all the institutions of power one to another. Although rivalry between the executive and legislative branches of U.S. government is inevitable, the partisan affiliations of the leaders of each branch constitute a common basis for cooperation, as any president and his fellow party members in Congress usually demonstrate daily. Each time President Bill Clinton proposed a major new program (such as health care and crime control), for instance, Democratic members of the Congress were the first to speak up in favor of the program and to orchestrate efforts at its passage.

Even within each branch there is intended fragmentation, and the party once again helps narrow the differences between the House of Representatives and the Senate, or between the president and his chiefs in the executive bureaucracy. Similarly, the division of national, state, and local governments, while always an invitation to conflict, is made more workable and easily coordinated by the intersecting party relationships that exist among office holders at all levels. Party affiliation, in other words, is a basis for mediation and negotiation laterally among the branches and vertically among the layers.

The party's linkage function does not end there. Party identification and organization are natural connectors and vehicles for communication between the voter and the candidate as well as between the voter and the office holder. The party connection is one means of increasing accountability in election campaigns and in government. Candidates on the campaign trail and elected party leaders in office are required from time to time to account for their performance at party-sponsored forums, nominating primaries, and conventions.

Political parties, too, can take some credit for unifying the nation by dampening sectionalism. Because parties must form national majorities in order to win the presidency, any single, isolated region is guaranteed minority status unless it establishes ties with other areas. The party label and philosophy build the bridge that enables regions to join forces; and in the process, a national interest, rather than a merely sectional one, is created and served.

The Electioneering Function

The election, proclaimed author H. G. Wells, is "democracy's ceremonial, its feast, its great function," and the political parties assist this ceremony in essential ways. First, the parties funnel eager, interested individuals into politics and government. Thousands of candidates are recruited each year by the two parties, as are many of the candidates' staff members—the people who manage the campaigns and go on to serve in key governmental positions once the election has been won.

This function is even more crucial in the British parliamentary system. In the postwar period, the *only* avenue to national power (i.e., the prime minister's office or a choice seat on the Cabinet) has been through either the Conservative Party or the Labour Party. Ambitious politicians must work their way up through the party hierarchy and build a supporting coalition along the way.

Elections can have meaning in a democracy only if they are competitive, and in the United States they probably could not be competitive without the parties. Even in the South, traditionally the least politically competitive U.S. region, the parties today regularly produce reasonably vigorous contests at the state (and, increasingly, the local) level.

PEOPLE OF THE PAST

Plunkitt of Tammany Hall

Tammany Hall was a powerful New York City political organization during the mid–nineteenth and early twentieth centuries. Originally formed as a social club in 1797, it had been transformed into an influential political machine by 1850, with membership including most of the city's prominent Democrats.

Of all the organization's politicians, one of the most renowned at the turn of the twentieth century was ward boss George Washington Plunkitt. Starting as a teenager, this son of Irish immigrants worked his way up through the ranks of the organization to become the leader of the city's Fifteenth Assembly District. (An assembly district is made up of many smaller units, called election districts.) He is remembered as one of the shrewdest politicians of his time. Plunkitt was born poor but died a millionaire, acquiring most of his wealth through what he called "honest graft," a term best described in his own candid words:

> My party's in power in the city, and its goin' to make a lot of public improvements. Well, I'm tipped off, say, that they're going to lay out a new park at a certain place.
>
> I see my opportunity and I take it. I go to that place and I buy up all the land I can in the neighborhood. Then the board of this or that makes it public, and there is a rush to get my land, which nobody cared particular for before.
>
> Ain't it perfectly honest to charge a good price and make a profit on my investment and foresight? Of course, it is. Well, that's honest graft.

For Plunkitt there was a difference between dishonest and honest graft, "between [dishonest] political looters and [honest] politicians who make a fortune out of politics by keepin' their eyes wide open":

> The looter goes in for himself alone without considerin' his organization or his city. The politician looks after his own interests, the organization's interests, and the city's interests all at the same time.

Plunkitt certainly looked after his constituents' interests. During Tammany's reign, the population of New York City was made up predominantly of poor immigrants, mostly Irish, for whom Plunkitt and his fellow district leaders served as a bridge between the Old and New Worlds and also as a way out of the slums. Besides assimilating these newcomers to life in the United States and acquainting them with the processes of self-government, the ward bosses used the patronage at their disposal to provide tangible benefits. Be it a job, liquor, a pushcart license, or even cash, the ward boss was always happy to help out a needy constituent—in exchange, of course, for loyalty at the ballot box during election time.

In contrast to the issue-oriented or image-appeal politics we know today, Plunkitt's politics were *personal*. As Plunkitt put it, "[I] learned how to reach the hearts of the great mass of voters. I don't bother about reaching their heads." Plunkitt understood the value of this personalized, community-oriented politics to both voters and leaders. His advice to aspiring politicians was simply to know and study the members of their communities and to "study human nature and act accordin'."

Plunkitt's brand of politics had all but disappeared by the mid–twentieth century. First, a drastic decline of emigration during the 1920s strangled the fuel line that fed the fires of city machines. Second, many of the services the parties provided gradually came to be viewed as rights of citizenship rather than as rewards for supporting a particular party; therefore, government replaced party organizations as the dispensers of benefits. Most important, however, and much to the chagrin of Plunkitt himself, were the new civil service laws passed by reformers in the 1920s to combat the alleged corruption of machine politics. These laws, which struck at the heart and soul of machine politics—patronage and the spoils system—induced Plunkitt to deem the civil service laws "the biggest fraud of the age" and the ruin of the nation:

> There can't be no real patriotism while it lasts. How are you goin' to interest our young men in their country if you have no offices to give them when they work for their party? . . . I know more than one man in the past years who worked for the ticket and was just overflowin' with patriotism, but when he was knocked out by the civil service humbug he got to hate his country and became an anarchist.

For better or worse, however, the reformers prevailed, and by the mid–twentieth century, civil service had come to dominate government at every level, consigning Plunkitt's brand of politics to America's past.

Source: William L. Riordon, ed., *Plunkitt of Tammany Hall* (New York: Dutton, 1963), pp. 11, 89.

Sen. Huey Long (D-La.) campaigned for the presidency in 1935 on a populist platform, arguing in fiery speeches that neither of the major parties' policies had the people's best interests at heart.

Party as a Voting and Issue Cue

A voter's party identification acts as an invaluable filter for information, a perceptual screen that affects how he or she digests political news. Therefore, party affiliation provides a useful cue for voters—particularly for the least informed and least interested, who can use the party as a shortcut or substitute for interpreting issues and events they may not fully comprehend. But even better-educated and more involved voters find party identification helpful. After all, no one has the time to study every issue carefully or to become fully knowledgeable about every candidate seeking public office.

Policy Formulation and Promotion

U.S. Senator Huey Long (D.-La.), one of the premier spokesmen for "the people" of this century, was usually able to capture the flavor of the average person's views about politics. Considering an independent bid for president before his assassination in 1935, Long liked to compare the Republican and Democratic parties to the two patent medicines offered by a traveling salesman. Asked the difference between them, the salesman explained that the "High Populorum" tonic was made from the bark of the tree taken from the top down, while "Low Populorum" tonic was made from bark stripped from the root up. The analogous moral, according to Long, was this: "The only difference I've found in Congress between the Republican and Democratic leadership is that one of 'em is skinning us from the ankle up and the other from the ear down!"[8]

---

[8] As quoted in Ken Bode, "Hero or Demagogue?" *The New Republic* 195 (March 3, 1986): 28.

Long would certainly have insisted that his fable applied to the **national party platforms,** the most visible instrument by which parties formulate, convey, and promote public policy. Every four years, each party writes for the presidential nominating conventions a lengthy platform explaining its positions on key issues. Most citizens in our own era undoubtedly still believe that party platforms are relatively undifferentiated, a mixture of pabulum and pussyfooting. Yet political scientist Gerald Pomper's study of party platforms from 1944 through 1976 has demonstrated that each party's pledges were consistently and significantly different, a function in part of the varied groups in their coalitions.[9] Interestingly, about 69 percent of the specific platform positions were taken by one party but not the other. On abortion, for example, the Democrats are strongly for abortion rights while the Republicans are firmly against them in their most recent platforms.

Granted, then, party platforms are quite distinctive. Does this elaborate party exercise in policy formulation mean anything? One could argue that the platform is valuable, if only as a clear presentation of a party's basic philosophy and as a forum for activist opinion and public education. But platforms have much more impact than that. About two-thirds of the promises in the victorious party's presidential platform have been completely or mostly implemented; even more astounding, one-half or more of the pledges of the *losing* party find their way into public policy (with the success rate depending on whether the party controls one, both, or neither house of Congress).[10] The party platform also has great influence on a new presidential administration's legislative program and on the president's State of the Union address. And while party affiliation is normally the single most important determinant of voting in Congress and in state legislatures,[11] the party–vote relationship is even stronger when party platform issues come up on the floor of Congress. Gerald Pomper concludes: "We should therefore take platforms seriously—because politicians appear to take them seriously."[12]

Besides mobilizing Americans on a permanent basis, then, the parties convert the cacophony of hundreds of identifiable social and economic groups into a two-part (semi)harmony that is much more comprehensible, if not always on key and pleasing to the ears. The simplicity of two-party politics may be deceptive given the enormous variety in public policy choices, but a sensible system of representation in the American context might be impossible without it. And the people who would suffer most from its absence would not be the few who are individually or organizationally powerful—their voices would be heard under almost any system. As political scientist Walter Dean Burnham has pointed out, the losers would be the many individually powerless for whom the parties are the only effective devices yet created that can generate collective power on their behalf.[13]

---

[9] Gerald M. Pomper with Susan Lederman, *Elections in America,* 2nd ed. (New York: Longman, 1980), pp. 145–150, 167–173.

[10] See David E. Price, *Bringing Back the Parties* (Washington, DC: CQ Press, 1984), pp. 284–288.

[11] See, for example, Sarah McCally Morehouse, "Legislatures and Political Parties," *State Government* 59:1 (1976): 23.

[12] Pomper with Lederman, *Elections in America,* 2nd ed., p. 150.

[13] Walter Dean Burnham, *Critical Elections and the Mainsprings of American Politics* (New York: Norton, 1970), pp. 132–133.

One-Partyism and Third-Partyism

The two-party system has not gone unchallenged. At the state level, two-party competition was severely limited or nonexistent in much of the country for most of this century.[14] Especially in the one-party Democratic states of the Deep South and the rock-ribbed Republican states of Maine, New Hampshire, and Vermont, the dominant party's primary nomination was often equivalent to election, and the only real contest was an unsatisfying intraparty one in which colorful personalities often dominated and a half-dozen major candidacies in each primary proved confusing to voters.[15] Even in most two-party states many cities and counties had a massive majority of voters aligned with one or the other party and thus were effectively one-party in local elections. In Britain, one-partyism at the subnational level is a relatively common phenomenon; for example, certain regions like the Northeast have voted overwhelmingly for the Labour Party in general election after general election.

Historical, cultural, and sectional forces primarily accounted for the concentration of one party's supporters in certain areas. The Civil War's divisions, for instance, were mirrored for the better part of a century in the Democratic predisposition of the South and the Republican proclivities of the Yankee Northern states. Whatever the combination of factors producing **one-partyism**—a political system in which one party dominates and wins virtually all contests—the condition has certainly declined precipitously in the last quarter century.[16]

The spread of two-party competition, while still uneven in some respects, is one of the most significant political trends of recent times, and virtually no one-party states are left. There are no purely Republican states any more, and the heavily Democratic contingent has been reduced to, at most, Alabama, Louisiana, Mississippi, Arkansas, and Maryland. (Note, though, that in each of these states one or more Republicans have been elected to the governorship or U.S. Senate since 1970, and the Deep South states usually vote Republican in presidential contests as well, unless a Southerner heads the Democratic ticket.)

Ironically, the growth of two-party competition has been spurred less by the developing strength of the main parties than by party weakness, illustrated by the decline in partisan loyalty among the voters. In other words, citizens now are somewhat more inclined to cross party lines in order to support an appealing candidate regardless of party affiliation, thus making a victory for the minority party possible whether or not it has earned the victory through the party's own organizational hard work. It should also be noted that the elimination of pockets of one-party strength adds an element of instability to the system, since at one point, even in lean times of national electoral disaster, each party was assured of a regional base from which a comeback could be staged. Nonetheless, the increase in party competitiveness can be viewed positively, since it eliminates the effects of one-partyism and guarantees a comprehensible and credible partisan choice to a larger segment of the electorate than ever before.

---

[14] See V. O. Key Jr., *American State Politics: An Introduction* (New York: Knopf, 1956).

[15] See V. O. Key Jr., *Southern Politics in State and Nation* (New York: Knopf, 1949).

[16] See Bibby et al., "Parties in State Politics," in Virginia Gray, Herbert Jacob, and Kenneth Vines, eds., *Politics in the American States,* 4th ed. (Boston: Little, Brown, 1983), Table 3.3, p. 66; also see Larry J. Sabato, *Goodbye to Good-Time Charlie: The American Governorship Transformed,* 2nd ed. (Washington, DC: CQ Press, 1983), pp. 116–138.

Minor Parties

Third-partyism has proved more durable than one-partyism, though its nature is sporadic and intermittent, and its effects on the political system are on the whole less weighty. Given all the controversy third parties generate, one could be excused for thinking that they were extraordinarily important on the American scene. But as Frank Sorauf has concluded, third parties in fact "have not assumed the importance that all the [academic] attention lavished on them suggests."[17] No minor party has ever come close to winning the presidency, and only eight minor parties have won so much as a single state's electoral college votes (see Table 11.1). Just five third parties (the farmer-backed Populists in 1892, Theodore Roosevelt's Bull Moose Party in 1912, the reform-minded Progressives in 1924, former Alabama Governor George Wallace's racially-based American Independent Party in 1968, and Ross Perot's independents in 1992) have garnered more than 10 percent of the popular vote for president.[18] (Roosevelt, incidentally, abandoned the Republican Party—under whose banner he had won the presidency in 1904—in order to form the Bull Moose Party, composed mainly of reformist Republicans.)

Third parties find their roots in sectionalism (as did the South's states' rights Dixiecrats, who broke away from the Democrats in 1948); in economic protest (such as the agrarian revolt that fueled the Populists, an 1892 prairie-states party); in specific issues (such as the Prohibition Party's proposed ban on the sale of alcoholic beverages); in ideology (the Socialist, Communist, and Libertarian Parties are examples); and in appealing, charismatic personalities (Theodore Roosevelt is perhaps the best case). Many of the minor parties have drawn strength from a combination of these sources. The American Independent Party enjoyed a measure of success because of a dynamic leader (George Wallace), a firm geographic base (the South), and an emotional issue (civil rights). And in 1992 Ross Perot, the billionaire with a folksy Texas manner, was a charismatic leader whose campaign was fueled by the deficit issue (as well as by his personal fortune).

Above all, third parties make electoral progress in direct proportion to the failure of the two major parties to incorporate new ideas or alienated groups or to nominate attractive candidates as their standard-bearers. Certainly in the media age, this latter qualification has grown in importance. The 1980 independent presidential bid of U.S. Representative John Anderson (R.-Ill.) was spurred not by geography or specific issues or Anderson's persona but by intense dissatisfaction among some voters with the major-party nominees, Jimmy Carter and Ronald Reagan.[19]

Explanations

Third parties in the United States are akin to shooting stars that appear briefly and brilliantly but do not long remain visible in the political constellation. In fact, the United

---

> ### The "Bull Moose" Party
>
> During his hunting expeditions in the Western United States, Theodore Roosevelt was so impressed with the great strength and stamina of the bull moose that "as strong as a bull moose" became one of his favorite expressions.
>
> In 1912, when he refused to support Republican President William Howard Taft (1909–1913) for re-election, the "Bull Moose" became the nickname and symbol of the independent movement he led.

---

[17] Frank Sorauf, *Party Politics in America,* 5th ed., p. 51. (See n. 6.)

[18] Theodore Roosevelt's 1912 effort was the most successful; the Bull Moose Party won 27 percent of the popular vote for president (although only 17 percent of the electoral college votes). Roosevelt's is also the only third party to run ahead of one of the two major parties (the Republicans).

[19] Anderson received only 7 percent of the vote in the end, although at times during the contest, polls had shown him with well above 20 percent.

Table 11.1 ♦ Third Party and Independent Presidential Candidates Receiving 5 Percent or More of Popular Vote

CANDIDATE (PARTY)	YEAR	PERCENTAGE OF POPULAR VOTE	ELECTORAL VOTES
Ross Perot (Independent)	1992	18.9	0
John B. Anderson (Independent)	1980	6.6	0
George C. Wallace (American Independent)	1968	13.5	46
Robert M. LaFollette (Progressive)	1924	16.6	13
Theodore Roosevelt (Bull Moose)	1912	27.4	88
Eugene V. Debs (Socialist)	1912	6.0	0
James B. Weaver (Populist)	1892	8.5	22
John C. Brekinridge (Southern Democrat)	1860	18.1	72
John Bell (Constitutional Union)	1860	12.6	39
Millard Fillmore (Whig-American)	1856	21.5	8
Martin Van Buren (Free Soil)	1848	10.1	0
William Wirt (Anti-Masonic)	1832	7.8	7

Source: Congressional Quarterly Weekly Report, October 18, 1980, p. 3147 (as adapted), and official election returns for 1992.

States is the only major Western nation that does not have at least one significant, enduring national third party; there are a number of explanations for this. Unlike many European countries that use **proportional representation** (awarding legislative seats in proportion to the number of votes received) and that guarantee parliamentary seats to any faction securing as little as 5 percent of the vote, the United States has a "single-member, plurality" electoral system that requires a party to get one more vote than any other party in a legislative district or in a state's presidential election in order to win. To paraphrase the legendary football coach Vince Lombardi, finishing first is not everything, it is the only thing in U.S. politics; placing second, even by a smidgen, doesn't count. This condition encourages the grouping of interests into as few parties as possible (the democratic minimum being two).

A New Third Party

Ross Perot announced on CNN's "Larry King Live" on February 20, 1992, that he would be willing to run for president if the American people placed him on the ballot in all fifty states. At the time few observers thought this would happen, given the effort required to mount such a campaign. But grassroots America, especially middle-class suburbanites, responded to Perot's appeal based on his concern about the national debt and dissatisfaction with the likely major party nominees, George Bush and Bill Clinton. Perot personally funded the operation, and by late summer (despite Perot's temporary withdrawal from the race) the Independent candidate was on the ballot in every state.

After Perot secured a surprising 19 percent of the national vote in November 1992, he announced the formation of "United We Stand America," a citizen's organization with branches in all states. Hundreds of thousands of Americans paid the $15 membership fee. Will the UWSA become a third party? Only Ross Perot can make this decision, but some UWSA branches indicated that they will at least endorse candidates for state and local offices, based on the politicians' support of Perot's platform.

Perot's fortunes took a downswing in late 1993, when he debated Vice President Albert Gore Jr. on the North American Free Trade Agreement (NAFTA), which now links the United States, Canada, and Mexico in a continent-sized trading zone with few restrictions and no tariffs. NAFTA was strongly favored by the Clinton administration *and* most Republican officeholders, but Perot fiercely opposed it and claimed NAFTA would result in millions of lost jobs for the United States.

While Congress was considering whether to approve NAFTA, Perot and Gore squared off on CNN's "Larry King Live" on November 9, 1993, and, by all accounts, Gore won the confrontation hands down. Shortly thereafter, both the House and the Senate passed NAFTA—a major boost for Clinton and Gore and a serious setback for Perot. Nonetheless, Perot remains active and visible, and he may run for president again in 1996.

Other institutional factors also undergird the two-party system:

- The laws in most states make it difficult for third parties to secure a place on the ballot by requiring large numbers of signatures, whereas the Democratic and Republican parties are often granted automatic access.
- Democrats and Republicans in the state legislatures may have little in common, but one shared objective is to make sure that the political pie is cut into only two sizable pieces, not three or more smaller slices.
- The public funding of campaigns (financing from taxpayer dollars), where it exists, is much more generous for the two major parties. At the national level, for instance, third-party presidential candidates receive money only *after* the general election, *if* they have garnered more than 5 percent of the vote, and *only* in proportion to their total vote; the major-party candidates, by contrast, get large, full general-election grants immediately upon their summer nominations. (This funding difference does not affect wealthy politicians like Perot.)
- The news media are biased—legitimately so—against minor parties; these parties are usually given relatively little coverage compared with that given to major-party nominees. The media are only reflecting political reality, of course, and it would be absurd

to expect them to offer equal time to all comers. Still, this is a vicious cycle for minor-party candidates: A lack of broad-based support produces slight coverage, which minimizes their chances of attracting more adherents. Of course, once a third candidate such as Ross Perot becomes prominent, the media flock to his appearances and clamor to schedule him on their news shows.

Beyond the institutional explanations are historical, cultural, and social theories of two-partyism in the United States. The **dualist theory,** frequently criticized as overly simplistic, suggests that there has always been an underlying binary nature to U.S. politics. Whether it was the early conflict between Eastern financial interests and Western frontiersmen, the sectional division of North and South, the more current urban-versus-rural or urban-versus-suburban clashes, or even the natural tensions of democratic institutions (the government against the opposition, for instance), dualists believe that the processes and interests of politics inevitably push the players into two great camps.

Other political scientists emphasize the basic social consensus existing in U.S. life. Despite great diversity in our heritage, the vast majority of Americans accept without serious question the fundamental structures of our system: The Constitution, the governmental set-up, a lightly controlled free enterprise economy, for example. This consensus, when allied with certain American cultural characteristics developed over time (pragmatism, acceptance of the need for compromise, a lack of extreme and divisive social-class consciousness), produces the conditions necessary for relatively non-ideological, centrist politics that can naturally support two moderate alternative parties but has little need for more.

The passion for power and victory that drives both Democrats and Republicans overrides ideology and prevents rigidity. Unless a kind of rigor mortis takes hold in the future in one or both major parties—with, say, the capture of the party organization by unyielding extremists of right or left—it is difficult to imagine any third party becoming a major, permanent force in U.S. politics (although Ross Perot's organization bears watching—see the box on p. 461). The corollary of this axiom, though, is that the major parties must be eternally vigilant if they are to avoid ideologically inspired takeovers; perhaps they can expand their participation in party activities to a group of voters that is as broad-based as possible.

For the foreseeable future, though, third parties likely will continue to play useful supporting roles similar to their historically sanctioned ones: They can popularize ideas that might not receive a hearing otherwise. They can serve as vehicles of popular discontent with the major parties and thereby induce change in major-party behavior and platforms. They may presage and assist party realignments in the future as they have sometimes done in the past. In a few states, third parties will also continue to take a unique part in political life, as the Conservative and Liberal Parties of New York State do.[20] But in a two-party system that is supplemented by generous means of expressing dissent and registering political opposition in other ways (court challenges, interest-group organizing, for example), third parties will probably continue to have a limited future in the United States.

---

[20] New York election law makes the Conservatives and Liberals (and, more recently, the Right to Life [anti-abortion] Party) potential power brokers because as an alternative to placing their own adherents on the ballot they can nominate the candidates of a major party to run under their labels, thus encouraging the major parties and their nominees to court them assiduously.

The Basic Structure of American Political Parties

The structure of the two major parties is not elaborate. Figure 11-2 summarizes the levels of each party, from grassroots base to pinnacle.

National Committees

The first national party committees were skeletal and formed some years after the creation of the presidential nominating conventions in the 1830s. Every four years, each party holds a national convention to nominate its presidential and vice-presidential candidates. First the Democrats in 1848 and then the Republicans in 1856 established

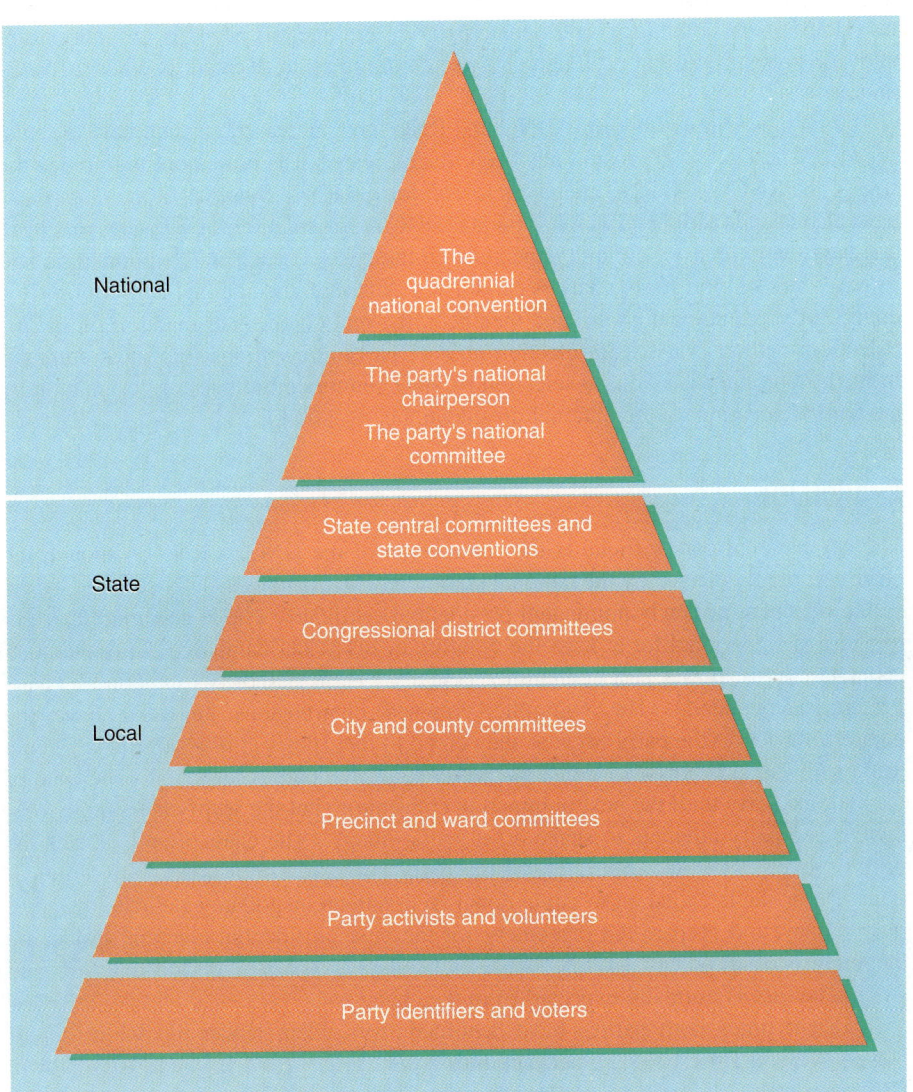

FIGURE 11-2
Political Party Organization in America: From Base to Pinnacle

national governing bodies (the Democratic National Committee, or DNC, and the Republican National Committee, or RNC) to make arrangements for the conventions and to coordinate the subsequent presidential campaigns. The DNC and RNC were each composed of one representative from each state; this was expanded to two in the 1920s after the post of state committeewoman was established. The states had complete control over the selection of their representatives to the national committees. In addition, to serve their interests, the congressional party caucuses in both houses organized their own national committees, loosely allied with the DNC and RNC. The National Republican Congressional Committee (NRCC) was started in 1866 when the Radical Republican congressional delegation was feuding with Abraham Lincoln's moderate successor, President Andrew Johnson, and wanted a counterweight to his control of the RNC. At the same time House and Senate Democrats set up a similar committee.

After the popular election of U.S. senators was initiated in 1913 with the ratification of the Seventeenth Amendment to the Constitution, both parties organized separate Senate campaign committees. This three-part arrangement of national party committee, House party committee, and Senate party committee has persisted in both parties until the present day, and each party's three committees are located together in Washington.

The memberships of both the DNC and RNC have increased considerably over the decades. The DNC's expansion has been much greater; it is now more than twice the size of the RNC—390 DNC members to 165 for the RNC. Since 1972 the Democrats have also abandoned the principle of equal DNC representation for all states and have assigned the number of committeepersons on the basis of each state's population and its past voter support for the party's candidates. Although the national conventions formally ratify all national committee members, the real choices are made in the states. Selection methods vary, from election at state party conventions (the most common means), to primary election, to selection by state central committees or designation by the party delegation, to the national presidential convention.

Leadership

The key national party official is the chairperson of the DNC or RNC. Although the chair is formally elected by the national committee, he or she is usually selected by the sitting president or newly nominated presidential candidate, who is accorded the right to name the individual for at least the duration of his or her campaign. Only the post-campaign out-of-power party committee actually has the authority to appoint a chairperson independently. The committee-crowned chairpersons generally have the greatest impact on the party because they come to their posts at times of crisis when a leadership vacuum exists. (A defeated presidential candidate is technically the head of the national party until the next nominating convention, but the reality is naturally otherwise as a party attempts to shake off a losing image.) The chair often becomes the prime spokesperson and arbitrator for the party during the four years between elections. He or she is called on to damp down factionalism, negotiate candidate disputes, raise money, and prepare the machinery for the next presidential election. Balancing the interests of all potential White House contenders is a particularly difficult job, and strict neutrality is normally expected from the chair.

In recent times both parties have benefited from adept leadership while out of power. William Brock, RNC chairman during the Carter presidency, and Ron Brown, DNC chairman—the first African-American to chair the DNC—during the Bush term, both skillfully used their positions to strengthen their parties organizationally and to polish the party images. Brock and Brown frequently appeared on news shows to give the out-of-power party's viewpoint. By contrast, party chairpersons selected by incumbent presidents and presidential candidates tend to be close allies of the presidents or candidates and often subordinate the good of the party to the needs of the campaign or White House. During the Carter presidency, for example, DNC Chairman Kenneth Curtis and his successor John White were creatures of the White House; they acted as cheerleaders for their chief executive but did little to keep the Democratic Party competitive with the then-strengthening GOP organization.

Because of their command of presidential patronage and influence, a few national-party chairpersons selected by presidents have become powerful and well known, such as Republican Mark Hanna during the McKinley presidency (1897–1901) and Democrat James Farley under President Franklin D. Roosevelt. Most presidentially appointed chairs, however, have been relatively obscure; the chance for a chairperson to make a difference and cut a memorable figure generally comes when there is no competition from a White House nominee or occupant. President Clinton named thirty-six-year-old national campaign manager, David Wilhelm, a veteran of Chicago politics, to head the DNC. Many observers believed that the appointment was also made to appease Chicago Democrats, who were disappointed when a prominent Chicagoan (William Daley, brother of Chicago's Mayor Daley) was passed over for Secretary of Transportation. Wilhelm's newly elected Republican counterpart is Haley Barbour, an ex-aide to Ronald Reagan; he was a Washington, D.C., lawyer and lobbyist at the time of his election by the RNC.

Ron Brown, former chairman of the Democratic National Committee, was an effective organizer and advocate for the party while the Republicans were in the White House.

National Conventions

Much of any party chairperson's work involves planning the presidential nominating convention, or **national convention,** the most publicized and vital event on the party's calendar. Until 1984, gavel-to-gavel coverage was standard practice on all national television networks. Even after the recent cutbacks by some news organizations, a substantial block of time is still devoted to the conventions. (In 1992, for example, all the networks devoted at least a couple of prime-time hours per night to convention coverage.) Although the nomination of the presidential ticket naturally receives the lion's share of attention, the convention also fulfills its role as the ultimate governing body for the party itself. The rules adopted and the platform passed at the quadrennial conclave are durable guidelines that steer the party for years after the final gavel has been brought down.

Most of the recent party chairpersons, in cooperation with the incumbent president or likely nominee, have tried to orchestrate carefully every minute of the conventions in order to project just the right image to voters. By and large, they have succeeded, though at the price of draining some spontaneity and excitement from the convention process.

From 1974 to 1982 the Democratic Party also held a **midterm convention** (also called a mini-convention). Designed to provide party activists a chance to express themselves on policy and presidential performance (whether the chief executive was a Democrat or a Republican), the midterm convention instead mainly generated worry among the party leadership and elected officials about the factional infighting and ideological posturing that might be on display before a national audience. Even though none of the midterm gatherings was a disaster, none was a roaring success, either. By 1986 the Democrats had decided to avoid potential divisiveness and save the $2 million necessary to hold the convention, and they canceled it.

States and Localities

Although national committee activities of all kinds attract most of the media attention, the party is structurally based not in Washington but in the states and localities. Except for the campaign finance arena, virtually all governmental regulation of political parties is left to the states, for example, and most elected officials give their allegiance to the local party divisions they know best. Most important, the vast majority of party leadership positions are filled at subnational levels.

THEN AND NOW

The Political Machines

Political machines played an important role in party politics in the United States, especially in the early-mid-twentieth century. In the 1950s and 1960s, for example, Chicago Mayor Richard J. Daley's legendary political machine dominated Chicago politics, controlling judges, politicians, municipal agencies, and the police and fire departments. The force behind the Daley machine was its control of municipal and county elections, in which supporters were rewarded with patronage and other tangible benefits, and opponents were disciplined accordingly. After more than two decades of command, the Daley machine gradually faded with the mayor's death in 1977, decimated by infighting, reformers, the institution of more civil service appointments, and court rulings that struck at the heart of the patronage system.

That all party organizations have gone the way of Chicago's is a commonly held belief, even among political observers. In fact, the weakening of the party organization is unmistakable in many cities and counties, and most county parties have no paid staff, central party headquarters, or even a telephone listing. But recent studies of the 7,300 county-level party organizations in the United States have revealed that many local parties—Democratic as well as Republican—are surprisingly active and have not really become less so over the decades. Some local parties appear to have a life of their own aided by substantial help from the state and (on the Republican side) national committees. These local organizations seem to endure and sometimes prosper despite party reversals at state or national levels. In the most successful cases, this prosperity is due to one of two sources of strength: either a well-nourished grassroots organization fed by patronage or a technologically advanced party with a solid base of ideologically attuned contributors and supporters.

A present-day example of the former, more traditional local organization is the Republican Party of

To many, Chicago Mayor Richard J. Daley personified old-style machine party politics. While ward politics continues to flourish in many cities, it is being replaced by a more modern (although less personal) style of direct-mail fund raising and issue management

The pyramidal arrangement of party committees provides for a broad base of support. The smallest voting unit, the precinct, usually takes in a few adjacent neighborhoods and is the fundamental building block of the party. Each of the more than 100,000 precincts in the United States potentially has a committeeman or committeewoman to represent it in each party's councils. The precinct committeepersons are the key foot soldiers of any party, and their efforts are supplemented by party committees above them in the wards, cities, counties, towns, villages, and congressional districts.

Nassau County, New York. No doubt Mayor Daley would have found much to like about this rigid and hierarchial machine that controls more than 20,000 jobs and features an elaborate superstructure of ward chairpersons, precinct committee members, and block captains who turn out the vote on Election Day. Originally built on New York City's out-migration of blue-collar Irish and Italian ethnics who wanted to dissociate themselves from the city's liberal politics, the machine now takes great care to recruit young people, in part by distributing plum summer jobs. Many of these youths go on to base their whole careers on service to the party. In the best tradition of machine politics, aspiring office holders are expected to work their way up the ladder slowly, toiling for years in the back rooms and the neighborhoods, delivering votes for the party candidates and dollars for the party war chest.

But the Nassau County machine is not without its problems. Corruption charges against some of its leaders have been proven, and its command of so many patronage positions is under attack. Yet electoral success keeps the organization humming, and it regularly wins a large majority of the area's county, state legislative, and congressional posts. The machine has even produced one of New York's U.S. senators, Alfonse D'Amato. First elected in 1980, D'Amato was a supervisor of Nassau's Hempstead township and a top leader of the party organization prior to his Senate bid. Learning constituency-service politics well in the county machine, he attended assiduously to his state's interests just as he had done for his township, earning a landslide reelection in a 1986 campaign that even included an endorsement from the liberal *New York Times*. In 1992, D'Amato managed to win a narrow reelection that was nonetheless amazing in the face of a Democratic landslide in the state.

If Chicago and Nassau County represent the old-style political machine, then the Waxman-Berman machine in California may suggest the future directions of strong local parties. Named after its founders, liberal California Democratic Congressmen Henry Waxman and Howard L. Berman, this Los Angeles-based machine has built its success on direct mail and new campaign technologies rather than on patronage and ward committee members. In many ways, the Waxman-Berman machine is the polar opposite of the Nassau County organization: informal, candidate (not party) centered, and a creation of California's anti-party environment. Also unlike their Nassau brethren, who virtually ignore national politics and concentrate on local offices, Waxman, Berman, and their allies care little about local politics; most of their energies are devoted to electing congressional candidates and influencing national and international policy.

While the differences between the traditional and modern political machines are substantial, there is one fundamental link between them: they both accumulate power by helping friends gain elective and appointive office. The new technologically advanced model of strong local parties probably has more of a future than the older, ethnically based or patronage-fed machine. Yet the latter should not be dismissed so easily, not only because it has proven hardier in some places than many expected, but also because there is a great deal to be said for such personalized, neighborhood-oriented parties. Indeed, the ideal self-sustaining party might be a carefully crafted combination of modern technology and community service-centered organization.

The state governing body supervising this collection of local party organizations is usually called the state central (or executive) committee. It comprises representatives from all major geographic units, as determined by and selected under state law. Generally, state parties are free to act within the limits set by their state legislatures without interference from the national party, except in the selection and seating of presidential convention delegates. National Democrats have been particularly inclined to regulate this aspect of party life. With the decline of big-city political machines, few local parties have the clout to object to the national party's dictates. (See "Then and Now" box, pp. 466–467).

Informal Groups

The formal structure of party organization is supplemented by numerous official, semi-official, and unaffiliated groups that combine and clash with the parties in countless ways. Both the DNC and RNC have affiliated organizations of state and local party women (The National Federation of Democratic Women and the National Federation of Republican Women). The youth divisions (the Young Democrats of America and the Young Republicans' National Federation) have a generous definition of "young"—up to and including age thirty-five. The state governors in each party have their own party associations, too.

Just outside the party orbit are the supportive interest groups and associations that often provide money, labor, or other forms of assistance to the parties. Labor unions, progressive political action committees (PACs), teachers, African-American and liberal women's groups, and the Americans for Democratic Action are some of the Democratic Party's organizational groups. Business PACs, the Chamber of Commerce of the United States, fundamentalist Christian organizations, and some anti-abortion agencies work closely with the Republicans. Similar party-interest group pairings occur in Britain. Trade unions have aligned themselves with the Labour Party, providing the bulk of the party's contributions, and business has been closely allied with the Conservatives.

Each U.S. party also has several institutionalized sources of policy ideas. Though unconnected to the parties in any official sense, these so-called think tanks (institutional collections of policy-oriented researchers and academics) are quite influential. During the Reagan administration, for instance, the right-wing Heritage Foundation placed many dozens of its conservatives in important governmental positions, and its issue studies on subjects ranging from tax reform to South Africa carried considerable weight with policy makers. The more moderate and bipartisan American Enterprise Institute also supplied the Reagan team with people and ideas. On the Democratic side, liberal think tanks proliferated during the party's Reagan- and Bush-induced exile. More than a half-dozen policy institutes formed after 1980 in an attempt to nurse the Democrats back to political health. The Center for National Policy and the Progressive Policy Institute, to cite two, sponsored conferences and published papers on Democratic policy alternatives.

Finally, there are extraparty organizations that form for a wide variety of purposes, including "reforming" a party or moving it ideologically to the right or left. In New York City, for example, Democratic reform clubs were established in the late 1800s to fight the Tammany Hall machine, the city's dominant Democratic organization at the time. About seventy clubs still prosper by attracting well-educated activists committed to various liberal causes. More recently, both national parties have been favored (or bedeviled) by the formation of new extraparty outfits. The Democrats have been pushed by both halves of the ideological continuum. The Democratic Leadership Council (DLC) was launched in 1985 by moderate-conservative Democrats concerned about what they perceived as the leftward drift of their party and its image as the captive of liberal special-interest groups. It is composed of more than one hundred current and former Democratic office holders (such as Senator Sam Nunn of Georgia and House Majority Leader Richard Gephardt of Missouri). The DLC has not always been popular with the national party leadership, which has sometimes viewed it as a potential rival, but it nurtured and strongly backed Bill Clinton's candidacy in 1992. Several DLC leaders have been appointed to positions in the Clinton administration.

The DLC formed in part to counter a left-leaning force organizing from within the partisan ranks, Jesse Jackson's National Rainbow Coalition. The Coalition is partly a vehicle for Jackson's ambitions. Beyond that, its goals of mass membership, hundreds of state and local charter affiliates, and endorsements of independent candidates when Democratic nominees are found to be "unacceptable" present a challenge to the Democratic Party in the eyes of at least some party officials.

Republicans have their extraparty agents too. The most prominent is North Carolina Senator Jesse Helms's Congressional Club, one of the largest political action committees in the United States. Echoing the philosophy of its founder, the Club is fiercely conservative. And much like Jesse Jackson and the Rainbow Coalition at the opposite end of the political spectrum, Helms and the Club will maneuver within or without the party as circumstances dictate.

The Party in Government

The structure of political parties reviewed so far has been organizational, self-contained, and apart from governing institutions. Another dimension of party exists—and thrives—*within* government as a critical, essential mechanism of all its branches and layers.

The Congressional Party

In no segment of U.S. government is the party more visible or vital than in the Congress. In this century, the political parties have dramatically increased the sophistication and impact of their internal congressional organizations. Prior to the beginning of every session, each party in both houses of Congress gathers (or "caucuses") separately to select party leaders (House Speaker or minority leader, Senate majority and minority leaders, party whips, and so on) and to arrange for the appointment of members of each chamber's committees. In effect, then, the parties organize and operate the Congress. Their management systems have grown quite elaborate; the web of deputy and assistant whips for House Democrats now extends to about one-fourth of the party's entire membership. Although not invulnerable to pressure from the minority, the majority party in each house generally holds sway, even fixing the size of its majority on all committees—a proportion frequently in excess of the percentage of seats it holds in the house as a whole.

Discipline. Congressional party leaders have some substantial tools at their disposal to enforce a degree of discipline in their troops. Even though seniority usually determines most committee assignments, an occasional choice plum may be given to the loyal or withheld from the rebellious. A member's bill can be lovingly caressed through the legislative process, or it can be summarily dismissed without so much as a hearing. Pork barrel—government projects yielding rich patronage benefits that sustain many a legislator's electoral survival—may be included or deleted during the appropriations process. Small favors and perquisites (such as the allocation of desirable office space or the scheduling of floor votes for the convenience of a member) can also be useful levers. Then, too, there are the campaign aids at the command of the leadership: money from party sources, endorsements, appearances in the district or at fund-raising events, and so on. On rare occasions, the leaders and their allies in the party caucus may even impose sanctions of various sorts (such as the stripping of seniority rights or prized committee berths) in order to punish recalcitrant law makers.[21]

In spite of all these weapons in the leadership's arsenal, the congressional parties lack the cohesion that characterizes parliamentary legislatures. This is not surprising, since the costs of bolting the party are much less in the United States than in, say, Great Britain. A disloyal English member of Parliament might be replaced as a party candidate at the next election; in the United States, it is more likely that the independent-minded member of Congress would be electorally rewarded—hailed as a free spirit, an individual of the people who stood up to the party bosses. Moreover, defections from the ruling party in a parliamentary system bring a threat of the government's collapse and with it early elections under possibly unfavorable conditions. Fixed election dates in the United States mean that the consequences of defection are much less dire. Also, a centralized, unicameral parliament (in which executive and legislative branches are effectively fused) permits relatively easy hierarchical control by party leaders.

There are other limits to coordinated, cohesive party action. For example, the separate executive branch, the bicameral power-sharing, and the extraordinary decentralization of Congress's work all constitute institutional obstacles to effective party action. Finally, party discipline is hurt by the individualistic nature of U.S. politics: campaigns that are candidate-centered rather than party-oriented; diverse electoral constituencies to which members of Congress must understandably be responsive; the largely private system of election financing that indebts legislators to wealthy individuals and nonparty interest groups more than to their parties; and the importance to law makers of attracting the news media's attention—often more easily done by showmanship than by quiet, effective labor within the party system.

Results. These are formidable barriers to the operation of responsible, potent legislative parties. Therefore, it is impressive to discover that party labels have consistently been the most powerful predictor of congressional roll-call voting, and in the last few years even more votes have closely followed the partisan divide. While not invariably predictive, as in strong parliamentary systems, a member's party affiliation has proven

---

[21] Such cases are few, but a deterrent nonetheless. Several U.S. senators were expelled from the Republican caucus in 1925 for having supported the Progressive candidate for president the previous year. In 1965, two Southern House Democrats lost all their committee seniority because of their 1964 endorsement of GOP presidential nominee Barry Goldwater, as did another Southerner in 1968 for his backing of George Wallace's third-party candidacy. In early 1983 the House Democratic caucus removed Texas Representative Phil Gramm from his Budget Committee seat because of his "disloyalty" in working more closely with Republican committee members than with his own party leaders. (Gramm resigned his seat in Congress, changed parties, and was reelected as a Republican. He then used the controversy to propel himself into the U.S. Senate in 1984.)

to be the indicator of his or her votes more than 70 percent of the time in recent years; that is, the average representative or senator sides with his or her party on about 70 percent of the votes that divide a majority of Democrats from a majority of Republicans. In most recent years, more than half of the roll-call votes in the House and Senate also found majorities of Democrats and Republicans on opposite sides.

High levels of party cohesion are especially likely when votes are taken in several areas. The votes that organize the legislative chambers (such as the election of a Speaker), set up the election machinery and campaign laws, and determine the results of disputed elections command nearly unanimous support on behalf of the party's basic interests. Votes involving key parts of the president's program also frequently divide along party lines. Finally, certain policy issues (such as Social Security, welfare programs, and union–management relations), as well as party platform issues that directly and manifestly affect the party's image or its key constituencies, produce substantial party voting.[22]

Until the 1980s there had been a substantial decline in party voting in Congress. At the turn of the century almost three-quarters of all the recorded votes saw a majority of one party voting against a majority of the other party, and astoundingly a third or more of a session's roll calls would pit at least 90 percent of one party against 90 percent or more of the other party. At this time two Speakers of the House (Republicans Thomas B. Reed and Joseph G. Cannon, who in succession controlled the Speakership most of the years between 1889 and 1911) possessed almost dictatorial authority and therefore could enforce strict voting discipline. But a rebellious House drastically curtailed the Speaker's powers between 1909 and 1911. This development, combined with internal GOP strains and splits, reduced party harmony and unity in congressional voting.

Two decades later, when the Democrats of the New Deal coalition held sway, they also had their own fractures and contradictions (African Americans versus whites, Northern liberals versus Southern conservatives, urban versus rural areas, and so forth). These tensions and other anti-party trends discussed earlier in this chapter left party majorities voting with each other on about 60 percent of recorded votes through the latter 1960s and the 1970s. This situation is reflected in Figure 11-3. In 1970, for example, neither the Democrats nor the Republicans were particularly unified; a majority of Democrats in Congress voted together on key votes less than 60 percent of the time, and the same was true for the Republicans.

In the past several years, however, party voting has increased noticeably, as reflected in the widening gap between Democrats and Republicans in Figure 11-3. In 1993, for instance, both the average Democratic member and Republican member voted with his or her party (on votes dividing party majorities) about 88 percent of the time. President Clinton's economic programs in his first year in office clearly polarized the Congress, and the proportion of party voting jumped considerably from the already high (79 percent) level recorded in 1992.

There are many reasons for the recent growth of congressional party unity and cohesion. Some are the result of long-term political factors. Both congressional parties, for instance, have gradually become more ideologically homogeneous and internally consistent. Southern Democrats today are more moderate and much closer philosophically to their Northern counterparts than the South's legislative barons of old ever were. Similarly, there are few liberal Republicans left in either chamber of Congress,

---

[22] See Julius Turner with Edward V. Schneier Jr., *Party and Constituency: Pressures on Congress* (Baltimore: John Hopkins University Press, 1970), pp. 33–39.

FIGURE 11-3
Congressional Party Unity Scores, 1959–1993

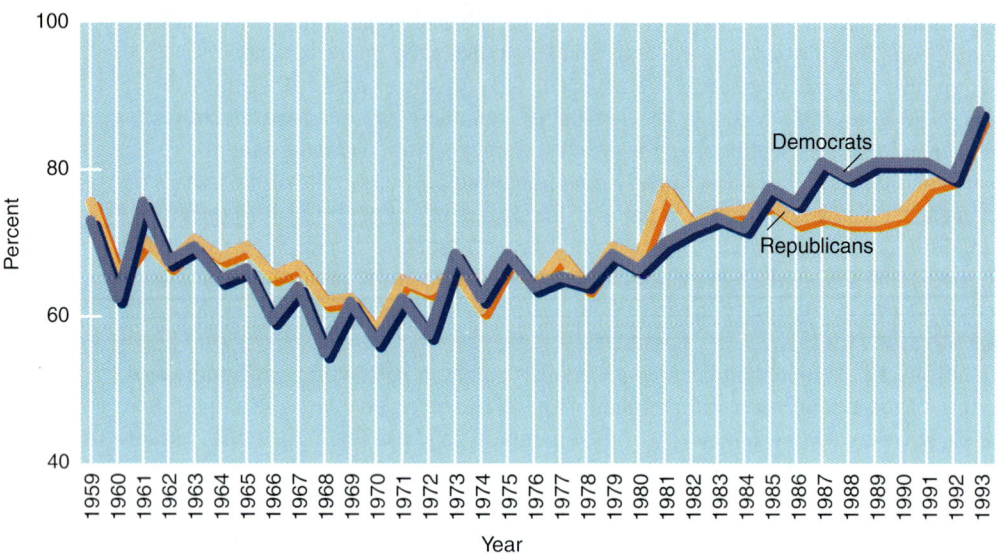

Source: *CongressionalQuarterly Almanacs* (Washington: Congressional Quarterly, Inc.).

A party unity vote is one in which a member of Congress votes with his or her party on issues that divide a majority of Democrats from a majority of Republicans. This graph traces the average percentage of party unity votes for all members of Congress from 1959 to 1993.

In 1991, for example, Democrats in Congress voted together 81 percent of the time and Republicans voted together 78 percent of the time on votes that divided a majority of Democrats from a majority of Republicans. Votes that divide a majority of one party from a majority of the other are instructive because they show us the important differences that exist in the views of the two major parties. Also, when one party is more unified than the other—cases in which the two lines in Figure 11-3 diverge—the unified party has obvious advantages in legislative maneuvering and in projecting a coherent image to the citizenry.

and GOP House members from all regions of the country are—with a few exceptions—moderately to solidly conservative. At the same time, strong two-party competition has come to almost all areas of the nation. The electoral insecurity produced by vigorous competition seems to encourage party unity and cooperation in a legislature (perhaps as a kind of "circling the wagons" effect).[23]

The circumstances of contemporary politics are also producing greater party cohesion. There is renewed satisfaction on the Republican side of the House aisle with that party's return to majority status. The increased militancy of former Minority Whip and now Speaker of the House Newt Gingrich of Georgia has raised the partisan hackles of many Democrats, polarizing the House a bit more

---
[23] Joseph A. Schlesinger, "The New American Political Party," *American Political Science Review* 79 (1985): 1168.

along party lines. On the other side of the Capitol, the continuing, close partisan struggle since 1980 over control of the Senate has appeared to increase the party consciousness of both groups of senators.

One of the least recognized but most enduring effects of the Watergate scandal was to stimulate the strengthening of the congressional parties long after Richard M. Nixon had departed the White House. The Watergate-spawned election of seventy-five reform-minded freshman Democrats in 1974 led to a revolt against the seniority system in early 1975. Three unresponsive senior chairmen were deposed, and the power of the committee system was diminished; a crucial barrier to the influence of party thus fell. When a rigid seniority system protected independent-minded members, committee chairs not surprisingly often voted against their party's wishes. After the 1975 display of caucus muscle, however, chairpersons dramatically increased their solidarity with the party majority, scoring even higher than backbenchers (junior members) on party unity scales.[24]

The political party campaign committees have also played a role in the renewed cohesiveness observed within Congress. Each national party committee has been recruiting and training House and Senate candidates as never before, and devising common themes for all nominees in election seasons—work that may help to produce a consensual legislative agenda for each party. The carrot and stick of party money and campaign services, such as media advertising production and polling, are also being used to convert candidates into party team players. Clearly, the more important the party organization can be to a legislator's election and reelection, the more attention a legislator is likely to pay to his or her party.

The Presidential Party

Political parties may be more central to the operation of the legislative branch than the executive branch, but it is the presidential party that captures the public imagination and shapes the electorate's opinion of the two parties. In our very personalized politics, voters' perceptions of the incumbent president and the presidential candidates determine to a large extent how citizens perceive the parties.

A chief executive's successes are his party's successes; the president's failures are borne by the party as much as by the individual. The image projected by a losing presidential candidate is incorporated into the party's contemporary portrait, whether wanted or not. As the highest elected candidate of the national party, the president naturally assumes the role of party leader, as does the White House nominee of the other party (at least during the campaign).

The juggling of contradictory roles is not always easy for a president. Expected to bring the country together as ceremonial chief of state and also to forge a ruling consensus as head of government, the president must also be an effective commander of a sometimes divided party. Along with the inevitable headaches party leadership brings, though, are clear and compelling advantages that accompany it. Foremost among them is a party's ability to mobilize support among voters for a president's program. Also, the executive's legislative agenda might be derailed more quickly without the common tie of party label between the chief executive and many members of Congress; all pres-

---

[24] Sara Brandes Crook and John R. Hibbing, "Congressional Reform and Party Discipline: The Effects of Change in the Seniority System on Party Loyalty in the U.S. House of Representatives," *British Journal of Political Science* 15 (April 1985): 207–226.

idents appeal for some congressional support on the basis of shared party affiliation, and they generally receive it depending on circumstances and their executive skill.

In recent decades, as Figure 11-4 shows, the average legislator of the president's party has backed the chief executive two-thirds to three-quarters of the time, whereas the average member of the opposition has done so only one-third to one-half the time. In 1992, for example, George Bush had little pull among Democrats in the last year of his term: Senate Democrats backed him on only 32 percent of the votes and House Democrats on only 25 percent of the votes. (In fact, in 1992 Bush won just 43 percent of the congressional votes on his program, the lowest support level in the forty-one years *Congressional Quarterly* had compiled the information.) Ronald Reagan fared better, in part because his support among GOP senators was exceptionally high. By contrast,

FIGURE 11-4

Average Support by Members of Congress on Votes Related to the President's Program, 1953–1993

Source: *Congressional Quarterly Almanacs* (Washington, DC: Congressional Quarterly, Inc.).

This graph shows the percentage of recorded votes on which members were in agreement with the president's announced position. In the last full year of the Bush presidency, for example, Senate Democrats supported President Bush only 32 percent of the time; House Democrats, 25 percent; Senate Republicans, 73 percent; and House Republicans, 71 percent. When a Democrat took office as president in 1993, the parties reversed roles. Senate and House Democrats overwhelmingly supported President Clinton in recorded votes, while Republicans in both houses were solidly in opposition.

Jimmy Carter and Dwight D. Eisenhower (in his second term) had problems because of relatively little support from their House partisans.

In his first year in office, President Bill Clinton demonstrated exceptionally strong support among his fellow Democrats in Congress. House Democrats backed him 77 percent of the time, and Senate Democrats, an impressive 87 percent. Of course, Republicans were much less accommodating: just 39 percent of the House GOP and 29 percent of the Senate Republicans backed Clinton on average. Overall, though, because Democrats controlled both houses of Congress, Clinton was quite successful, winning 86 percent of the 191 votes on which he had declared a position. That was double George Bush's congressional rating of 1992, and it was the highest presidential percentage since Lyndon Johnson's first full year in office (1964).

These party gifts to the president are reciprocated in other ways. In addition to compiling a record for the party and giving substance to its image, presidents appoint many activists to office, recruit candidates, raise money for the party treasury, campaign extensively for party nominees during election seasons, and occasionally provide some "coattail" help to fellow office seekers who are on the ballot in presidential election years.

Pro-Party Presidents. Some presidents take their party responsibilities more seriously than others. In this century Democrats Woodrow Wilson and Franklin D. Roosevelt were exceptionally party-oriented and dedicated to building their party electorally and governmentally. In his first term, Wilson worked closely with Democratic congressional leaders to fashion a progressive and successful party program, and Roosevelt was responsible for constructing the enduring New Deal coalition for his party and breathing life into a previously moribund Democratic National Committee. Republican Gerald R. Ford, during his brief tenure from 1974 to 1977, also achieved a reputation as a party builder. He was willing to undertake campaign and organizational chores for the GOP (especially in fund raising and in barnstorming for nominees) that most other presidents minimized or shunned. Perhaps Ford's previous role as House minority leader made him more sensitive to the needs of his fellow party officeholders.

Managing relations with the legislature is much less problematic in the British parliamentary system. The party in power in the government consists of individuals from the majority in Parliament, who continue to hold their seats in Parliament. Moreover, the life of the Parliament is tied intimately to the life of the government; should the latter fall, the former almost certainly will. This system provides the party in power with a compelling argument to use with recalcitrant partisans in the legislature.

Nonpartisan Presidents. Most U.S. modern chief executives have been cast in an entirely different mold. Dwight D. Eisenhower elevated "nonpartisanship" to a virtual art form, and while this may have preserved his personal popularity, it proved a disaster for his party. Despite a full two-term occupancy of the White House, the Republican Party remained mired in minority status among the electorate, and Eisenhower never really attempted to transfer his high ratings to the party. Lyndon B. Johnson kept the DNC busy with such trivial tasks as answering wedding invitations sent to the First Family. When many of the Democratic senators and representatives elected on his presidential coattails were endangered in the 1966 midterm election, LBJ canceled a major campaign trip on their behalf lest his policies get tied too closely to their possible defeats. Democrats lost forty-seven House seats, three Senate seats, and eight governorships in the 1966 debacle.

In 1972 the late Richard M. Nixon discouraged the GOP from nominating candidates against conservative Southern Democrats in order to improve his own electoral and congressional position, since the grateful unopposed legislators would presumably be less likely to cause Nixon trouble on the campaign trail or in Congress. Nixon also subordinated the party's agenda almost wholly to his own reelection. Shunting aside the Republican National Committee, Nixon formed the Committee to Re-Elect the President, which became known by the acronym, CREEP. So removed were party leaders from the Committee's abuses (see the box on Watergate in Chapter 7) that the Republican Party organization itself escaped blame during the Watergate investigations.

Jimmy Carter also showed little interest in his national party. Elected as an outsider in 1976, Carter and his top aides at first viewed the party as another extension of the Washington establishment they had pledged to ignore. Carter and his DNC chairmen failed to develop the Democratic Party organizationally and financially in order to keep it competitive during a critical period, while the Republicans were undergoing a dramatic revitalization stimulated by their desire to recover from the Watergate scandal. Later, during his fateful 1980 reelection campaign, Carter was properly criticized for diverting DNC personnel and resources to his presidential needs such as travel and Christmas cards rather than permitting them to pursue essential partywide electoral tasks.

Reagan and Bush. Carter's two Republican successors took a very different approach. Ronald Reagan was one of the most party-oriented presidents of recent times.[25] In 1983 and 1984, during his own reelection effort, Reagan made more than two dozen campaign and fund-raising appearances for all branches of the party organization and candidates at every level. More than 300 television endorsements were taped as well, including one for an obscure Honolulu city council contest. Reagan also showed a willingness to get involved in the nitty-gritty of candidate recruitment, frequently calling in strong potential candidates to urge them to run. During the intense and ultimately unsuccessful battle to retain Republican control of the U.S. Senate in 1986, Reagan played the good soldier, visiting twenty-two key states repeatedly and raising $33 million for the party and its candidates. Unlike Eisenhower, Reagan was willing to attempt a popularity transfer to his party and to campaign for Republicans whether or not they were strongly loyal to him personally. Unlike Johnson, Reagan was willing to put his prestige and policies to the test on the campaign trail. Unlike Nixon, Reagan spent time and effort helping underdogs and long-shot candidates, not just likely winners. Unlike Carter, Reagan signed more than seventy fund-raising appeals for party committees and took a personal interest in the further strengthening of the GOP's organizational capacity. George Bush, a former RNC chairman, emulated the Reagan model during his own presidency.

However, neither Reagan nor Bush had long enough coattails to help elect their party's nominees lower down on the ballot. Reagan's initial victory in 1980 was one factor in the election of a Republican Senate, but his landslide reelection in 1984 had,

---

[25] Rhodes Cook, "Reagan Nurtures His Adopted Party to Strength," *Congressional Quarterly Weekly* 43 (September 28, 1985): 1927–1930.

like Nixon's in 1972, almost no impact on his party's congressional representation. And Bush provided no coattails at all to the GOP in 1988. There is little question that the coattail effect—whereby party nominees lower on the ballot can receive additional votes generated by a popular presidential candidate—has diminished sharply compared with a generation ago.[26] Partly, the decreased competitiveness of congressional elections has been produced by artful redistricting and the growing value of incumbency.[27] But voters are also less willing to think and cast ballots in purely partisan terms—a development that limits presidential leadership and hurts party development. (We return to this subject in the next chapter.)

Clinton. Because Bill Clinton won with such a small plurality (43 percent) in 1992, he also produced little coattail for his party's candidates. Like Reagan and Bush, though, he has campaigned vigorously for many Democrats across the country since taking office. Unlike his predecessors, however, Clinton has had little success in transferring popularity. Democrats lost both governor's races in 1993 (Virginia and New Jersey) and a special Senate election in Texas since Clinton won the presidency. Clinton vigorously stumped for New York Mayor David Dinkins as well, but even in that heavily Democratic city, a Republican (Rudolph Guliani) triumphed in November 1993.

---

[26] George C. Edwards III, *Presidential Influence in Congress* (New York: Freeman, 1980); and Herbert M. Kritzer and Robert B. Eubank, "Presidential Coattails Revisited: Partisanship and Incumbency Effects," *American Journal of Political Science* 23 (1979): 615–626.

[27] Lyn Ragsdale, "The Fiction of Congressional Elections as Presidential Events," *American Politics Quarterly* 8 (1980): 375–398; and Thomas E. Mann and Raymond E. Wolfinger, "Candidates and Parties in Congressional Elections," *American Political Science Review* 74 (1980): 617–632.

The "coattail effect"—the ability of a president to generate votes for his party's candidates in state and local elections—has declined sharply over the past generation. For Mayor David Dinkins of New York, not even the combined firepower of Clinton, Governor Mario Cuomo, and U.S. Senator Daniel Patrick Moynihan were enough to keep him in office.

The Parties and the Judiciary

Many Americans view the judiciary as "above politics" and certainly as nonpartisan, and many judges are quick to agree. Yet not only do members of the judiciary sometimes follow the election returns and allow themselves to be influenced by popular opinion, but they are also products of their party identification and possess the same partisan perceptual screens as all other politically aware citizens.

Legislators are much more partisan than judges, but it is wrong to assume that judges reach decisions wholly independent of partisan values. First, judges are creatures of the political process, and their posts are considered patronage plums. Judges who are not elected are appointed by presidents or governors for their abilities but also as members of the executive's party and increasingly as representatives of a certain philosophy of or approach to government. In this century, every president has appointed judges overwhelmingly from his own party; Jimmy Carter and Ronald Reagan, for instance, drew 95 percent or more of their judicial choices from their respective parties. Furthermore, Democratic executives are naturally inclined to select for the bench liberal individuals who may be friendly to the welfare state or critical of some business practices. Republican executives generally lean toward conservatives for judicial posts, hoping they will be tough on criminal defendants, anti-abortion, and restrained in the use of court power.

Research has long indicated that party affiliation is in fact a moderately good predictor of judicial decisions, at least in some areas.[28] In other words, party matters in the judiciary just as it does in the other two branches of government, although it certainly matters less on the bench than in the legislature and in the executive.

Many judges appointed to office have had long careers in politics as loyal party workers or legislators. Supreme Court Justice Sandra Day O'Connor, for example, was an active member of the National Republican Women's Club and is a former Republican state legislator. Some jurists are even more overtly political, since they are elected to office. In a majority of states at least some judicial positions are filled by election, and seventeen states hold outright partisan elections, with both parties nominating opposing candidates and running hard-hitting campaigns. In some rural counties across the United States, local judges are not merely partisanly elected figures; they are the key public officials, controlling many patronage jobs and the party machinery itself.

Obviously, therefore, in many places in the United States, judges by necessity and by tradition are not above politics but are in the thick of it. Although election of the judiciary is a questionable practice in light of its specially sanctioned role as impartial arbiter, partisan influence exerted both by jurists' party loyalties and by the appointment (or election) process is useful in retaining some degree of accountability in a branch often accused of being arrogant and aloof.

---

[28] See Sidney Ulmer, "The Political Party Variable on the Michigan Supreme Court," *Journal of Public Law* 11 (1962): 352–362; Stuart Nagel, "Political Party Affiliation and Judges' Decisions," *American Political Science Review* 55 (1961): 843–850; David W. Adamany, "The Party Variable in Judges' Voting: Conceptual Notes and a Case Study," *American Political Science Review* 63 (1969): 57–73; Sheldon Goldman, "Voting Behavior on the United States Courts of Appeals, 1961–1964," *American Political Science Review* 60 (1966): 374–383; and Robert A. Carp and C. K. Rowland, *Policymaking and Politics in the Federal District Courts* (Knoxville: University of Tennessee Press, 1983).

The Parties and State Governments

Most of the conclusions just discussed about the party's relationship to the legislature, the executive, and the judiciary apply to those branches on the state level as well. The national parties, after all, are organized around state units, and the basic structural arrangement of party and government is much the same in Washington and the state capitals. Remarkably, too, the major national parties are the dominant political forces in all fifty states. This has been true consistently; unlike Great Britain or Canada, the United States has no regional or state parties that displace one or both of the national parties in local contests. Occasionally in U.S. history a third party has proven locally potent, as did Minnesota's Farmer-Labor Party and Wisconsin's Progressives, both of which elected governors and state legislative majorities earlier in this century. But over time, no such party has survived,[29] and every state's two-party system mirrors national party dualism, at least as far as labels are concerned.

Parties and Governors. There are some party-oriented differences at the state level, though. Governors in many states tend to possess even greater influence over their parties' organizations and legislators than do presidents. Many governors have many more patronage positions at their command than does a president, and these material rewards and incentives give governors added clout with activists and office holders. In addition, tradition in some states permits the governor to play a role in selecting the legislature's committee chairs and party floor leaders, and some state executives even attend and help direct the party legislative caucuses—activities no president would ever undertake. Moreover, forty-three governors possess a power denied the national executive—the item veto, which permits the governor to veto single items (such as individual pork barrel projects) in appropriations bills. Whereas a president must often accept objectionable measures as part of a bill too urgent or important to be vetoed, a governor gains enormous leverage with legislators by means of the line-item veto.

Parties and State Legislatures. Just as the party relationship between the executive and the legislature tends to be stronger at the state level than in Washington, so also is the party role in the legislature itself more high-profile and effective. Most state legislatures surpass the U.S. Congress in partisan unity and cohesion. Even though fewer than half of congressional roll calls in the post–World War II era have produced majorities of the two parties on opposite sides, a number of state legislatures (including Massachusetts, New York, Ohio, and Pennsylvania) have achieved party voting levels of 70 percent or better in some years. Not all states display party cohesion of this magnitude, of course. Nebraska has a nonpartisan legislature, elected without party labels on the ballot. In the South, the lack of two-party competition has left essentially one-party legislatures split into factions, regional groupings, or personal cliques. As real interparty competition reaches the legislative level in Southern states, however, party cohesion in the legislatures is likely to increase.

---

[29] The Farmer-Labor Party did survive in a sense; having endured a series of defeats, it merged in 1944 with the Democrats, and Democratic candidates still officially bear the standard of the Democratic-Farmer-Labor (DFL) Party. At about the same time, also having suffered severe electoral reversals, the Progressives stopped nominating candidates in Wisconsin. The party's members either returned to the Republican Party, from which it had split early in the century, or became Democrats.

Republicans and States' Rights

The party names "Democrat" and "Republican" have remained constant since 1860, but the philosophies the names represent have not. The Republican Party first gained power in 1860, determined to preserve the federal Union and to battle those who believed that states had the right to secede. By the New Deal era, though, the GOP had become the advocate of states' rights, and the party's officials often sounded the alarm against federal encroachment on state prerogatives—a policy that continues today. Conversely, the Democratic Party has been transformed from the more conservative and states' rights-oriented party in the 1800s to the more liberal and pro-government party of today.

One other party distinction is notable in many state legislatures. Compared with the Congress, state legislative leaders have much more authority and power; this is one reason party unity is higher in the state capitols.[30] The strict seniority system that usually controls committee assignments in Congress is less absolute in most states, and legislative leaders often have considerable discretion in appointing the committee chairs and members. The party caucuses, too, are usually more active and influential in state legislatures than in their Washington counterparts. In some legislatures, the caucuses meet weekly or even daily to work out strategy and count votes, and nearly one-fourth of the caucuses bind all the party members to support the group's decisions on key issues (such as appropriations measures, tax issues, and procedural questions).

Not just the leaders and caucuses but the party organizations as well have more influence over legislators at the state level. State legislators are much more dependent than their congressional counterparts on their state and local parties for election assistance. Whereas members of Congress have large government-provided staffs and lavish perquisites to assist (directly or indirectly) their reelection efforts, state legislative candidates need party workers and, increasingly, the party's financial support and technological resources at election time.

The Modern Transformation of Party Organization

The parties are not just convenient labels for office holders; they are functioning organizations with bureaucracies in virtually every hamlet in the United States. However, the vitality of the organizations varies widely from place to place and from era to era.

Republican Strengths

Until 1992, the modern Republican Party thoroughly outclassed its Democratic rival in almost every category of campaign service and fund raising. There are a number of explanations for the disparity between the two major parties. Until 1980, the Republicans were almost perennially disappointed underdogs, especially in congressional contests; they therefore felt the need to give extra effort. The GOP had the willingness, and enough electoral frustrations, to experiment with new campaign technologies that might hold the key to elusive victories. Also, since Democrats held most of the congressional offices and thus had most of the benefits of incumbency and staff, Republican nominees were forced to rely more on their party to offset built-in Democratic advantages. The party staff, in other words, compensated for the Democratic congressional staff, and perhaps also for organized labor's divisions of election troops, which were usually at the beck and call of Democratic candidates. Then, too, one can argue that the business and middle-class base of the modern GOP has a natural managerial and entrepreneurial flair demonstrated by the party officers drawn from that talented pool of people.

Whatever the causes, the contemporary national Republican Party has organizational prowess unparalleled in American history. In fundraising the Republicans have

---

[30] *State Government*, p. 19–24. (See n. 11.)

surpassed the Democrats by large margins in recent election cycles—never by less than two to one and usually by a considerably higher ratio (see Figure 11-5). Democrats must struggle to raise enough money to meet the basic needs of most of their candidates, while, in the words of a past chairman of the Democratic Senatorial Campaign Committee, "The single biggest problem the Republicans have is how to legally spend the money they have."[31]

Most of the Republican money is raised through highly successful mail solicitation. This procedure started in the early 1960s and accelerated in the mid-1970s, when postage and production costs were relatively low. From a base of just 24,000 names in 1975, for example, the national Republican Party has expanded its mailing list of proven donors to several million in the 1990s. Mailings produce about three-quarters of total revenue, and they do so with an average contribution of less than $35. In this fashion, the GOP may have broadened its committed base, because contributing money usually strengthens the tie between a voter and any organization. Most of the rest of the GOP's funds come from donors of larger amounts who secure membership in various Republican contributor groups. For instance, the Republican National Committee designates any $10,000 annual giver an "Eagle."

---

[31] Senator George J. Mitchell (D.-Me.), as quoted in the *Washington Post* (February 9, 1986): A–14.

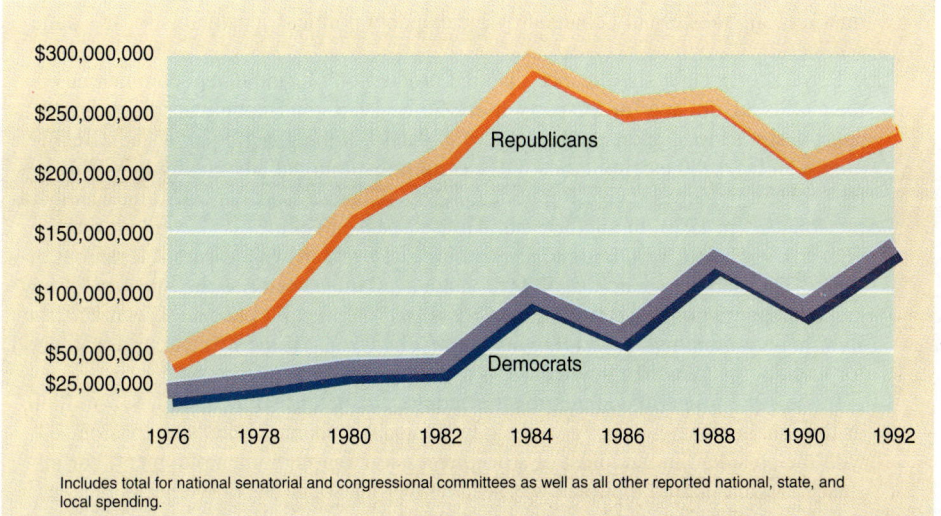

FIGURE 11-5
Political Party Finances, 1976–1992: Total Receipts.

Includes total for national senatorial and congressional committees as well as all other reported national, state, and local spending.

Source: Federal Election Commission.

Both parties raise their money primarily from individuals and interest groups, and both spend it mainly on staff and services to their candidates and officeholders. Republicans consistently raise more money than Democrats do, but notice that the Democrats are doing better.

The Republican cash is used to support a dazzling variety of party activities and campaign services, including the following.

1. **Party Staff.** Several hundred operatives are employed by the national GOP in election years, and even in the off years, many more than one hundred people hold full-time positions. There is great emphasis on field staff—that is, on staff members sent to and stationed in key districts and states who maintain close communication between local and national party offices.

2. **Voter Contact.** The Republicans frequently conduct massive telephone canvassing operations to identify likely Republican voters and to get them to the polls on Election Day. In 1986, for instance, the GOP used paid callers in seventeen phone centers across the country to reach 10.5 million prospective voters in twenty-five states during the general election campaign. Nearly 5.5 million previously identified Republicans were re-called just before Election Day, many of them hearing an automated message from the president: "This is Ronald Reagan and I want to remind you to go out and vote on Tuesday. . . ." In addition, 12 million pieces of "persuasive" (non-fund-raising) mail were sent to households in the last two weeks of the campaign.

3. **Polling.** The national Republican committees have spent millions of dollars for national, state, and local public opinion surveys, and they have accumulated an enormous storehouse of data on American attitudes generally and on marginal districts in particular. Many of the surveys are provided to GOP nominees at a cut-rate cost. In important contests, the party will frequently commission **tracking polls**—continuous surveys that enable a campaign to chart its daily rise or fall. The information provided in such polls is invaluable in the tense concluding days of an election.

4. **Media Advertising.** The national Republican Party operates a sophisticated in-house media division that specializes in the design and production of television advertisements for party nominees at all levels. About seventy to one hundred candidates are helped in an election cycle. They obtain expert and technically superior media commercials, and the party also offers its wares for a minimal fee, often including the actual buying of time—that is, the purchase of specific time slots on television shows for broadcasting the advertising spots. The candidates thus save the substantial commissions and fees usually charged by independent political consultants for the same services.

    Perhaps of greater significance than the production of candidates' commercials is the GOP's advertising for the party itself. Since 1978, the Republicans have aired spots designed to support not specific candidates but the generic party label. Beginning with the 1980 election, the GOP has used institutional advertising to establish basic election themes. "Vote Republican—for a Change" spots attacked the Democratic Congress in 1980. In another spot, House Speaker Thomas P. O'Neill was lampooned by an actor who ignored all warning signs and drove a car until it ran out of fuel. ("The Democrats are out of gas," announced the narrator as the Speaker futilely kicked the automobile's tire.) Another ad starred an unemployed factory worker from Baltimore, a lifelong Democrat, who plaintively asked, "If the Democrats are so good for working people, then how come so many people aren't working?"

    In the 1982 midterm congressional elections, the defensive focus of a $15-million institutional campaign was "give the guy [Reagan] a chance" and "stay the course" with the president in the midst of a deep recession and high unemployment. For instance, a white-haired mailman was seen delivering Social Security checks fattened with a cost-of-living increase, reminding elderly voters that Reagan had kept his promise, and urging, "For gosh sake, let's give the guy a chance." The spot, like the earlier 1980 ads, was highly rated by viewers. Although some moderate Republican candidates resisted being tied to Reagan during one of the most unpopular periods of his presidency, pre- and post-election surveys suggested that the GOP-sponsored media campaign had been, on the whole, helpful to the party and to individual candidates.

5. **Campaign Staff Training and Research.** The party trains many of the political volunteers and paid operatives who manage the candidates' campaigns. Since 1976 the Republicans have held annually about a half-dozen week-long "Campaign Management Colleges" for staffers. In 1986 the party launched an ambitious million-dollar "Congressional Campaign Academy" that offers two-week, all-expenses-paid training courses for prospective campaign managers, finance directors, and press relations staff. Early in each election cycle, the national party staff also prepares voluminous research reports on Democratic opponents, analyzing their public statements, votes, and attendance records. The reports are made available to GOP candidates and their aides.

Results

Despite its financial edge and service sophistication, all is not well in the Republican organization. Success has bred self-satisfaction and complacency, encouraged waste, and led the party to place too much reliance on money and technology, and not enough on the foundation of any party movement—people. As former U.S. Senator Paul Laxalt (R.-Nev.), outgoing general chairman of the national Republican Party, was forced to admit in 1987:

> We've got way too much money, we've got way too many political operatives, we've got far too few volunteers. . . . We are substituting contributions and high technology for volunteers in the field. I've gone the sophisticate route, I've gone the television route, and there is no substitute for the volunteer route.[32]

As Laxalt's comments imply, technology and money can probably only add two or three percentage points to a candidate's margin. The rest is determined by the nominee's quality and positions, the general electoral tide prevailing in any given year, and the energy of party troops in the field. Republicans were to learn this anew in 1992, when George Bush's large warchest could not stave off defeat.

Democratic Party Gains

Parties, like people, change their habits slowly. The Democrats were reluctant to alter a formula that had been a winning combination for decades of New Deal dominance. The prevailing philosophy was, "Let a thousand flowers bloom"; candidates were encouraged to go their own way, to rely on organized labor and other interest groups allied with the Democrats, and to raise their own money, while the national party was kept subservient and weak.

The massive Democratic defeats suffered in 1980 forced a fundamental reevaluation of the party's structure and activities. Democrats, diverse by nature, came to an unaccustomed consensus that the party must change to survive, that it must dampen internal ideological disputes and begin to revitalize its organization. Thus was born the commitment to technological and fund-raising modernization, using the Republican Party's accomplishments as a model, that drives the Democratic Party today.

Comprehension of the task is the first step to realization of the goal, so even after more than a decade, Democrats still trail their competitors by virtually every signifi-

---

[32] As quoted in a speech to the RNC by the Associated Press, January 24, 1987, and in the *Washington Post* (same date): A–3.

484 ❖ Chapter 11 Political Parties

cant measure of party activity. Yet the figures of party finances (receipts), graphed in Figure 11-6, can be read a different way. While the GOP has consistently maintained an enormous edge, the Democrats have considerably increased their total receipts, now raising many times more than just a few years ago. More importantly, Democrats are contributing much more to their candidates and have actually come close to the GOP's larger total recently (see Figure 11-6). Several national party chairs (Paul Kirk, Ronald Brown, and David Wilhelm) have aggressively sought more funds from party supporters and friendly interest groups.

With the 1992 elections, the Democrats reaped the benefits of their substantially increased receipts, winning the presidency for the first time in sixteen years. The Clinton administration also redoubled Democratic Party efforts as the midterm elections of 1994 approached, and their exertions again made the Democrats more competitive with the Republicans.

The decision in 1981 to begin a direct-mail program for the national party was a turning point. From a list of only 25,000 donors before the program began, the DNC's support base has grown to 500,000. The Democrats have imitated the Republicans not just in fund raising but also in the uses to which the money is put. For instance, in 1986 the party opened a $3-million media center that produces television and radio spots at rates much lower than those charged by independent political consultants. The Democratic Party is attempting to do more for its candidates and their campaign staffs,

FIGURE 11-6

Political Party Finances, 1976–1992: Total Party Contributions to and Expenditures for Candidates

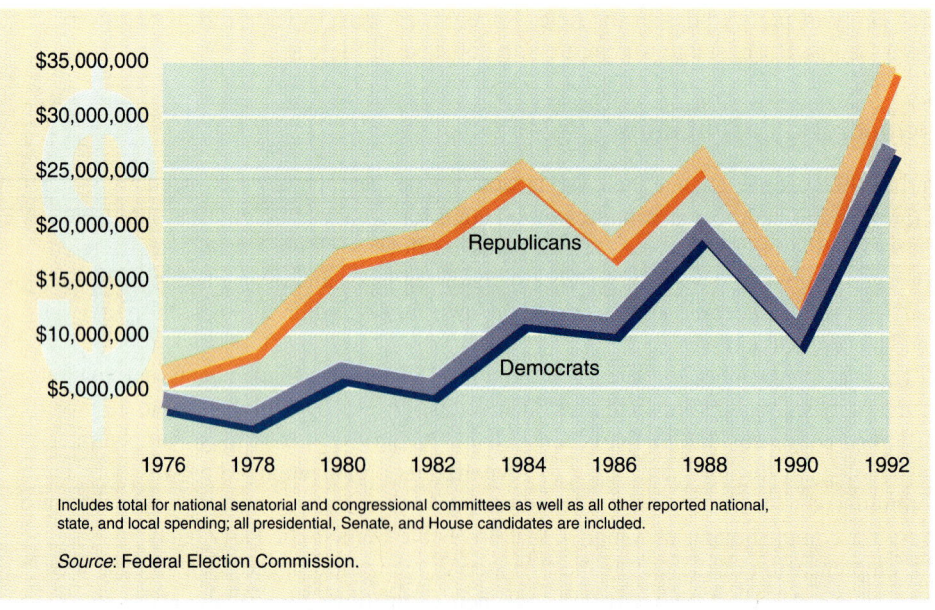

Includes total for national senatorial and congressional committees as well as all other reported national, state, and local spending; all presidential, Senate, and House candidates are included.

Source: Federal Election Commission.

Only a fraction of the total monies raised in each party goes *directly* to the party's candidates. The rest of the war chest is spent to maintain the large staffs and buildings of the national parties in Washington, D.C. Also, notice in this figure that, while the GOP still gives more money to its candidates, the Democrats are clearly closing the gap.

too, creating the Democratic National Training Institute in 1985. The Institute coordinates campaign schools for party workers from around the country. "Smart money" is a term used to describe campaign contributions that flow to the candidates and political party expected to win in an election year. With Bill Clinton leading every public opinion poll taken after mid-July during the 1992 campaign, Democrats were flooded with smart money. As Figures 11-5 and 11-6 show, the Democratic Party dramatically increased both its receipts and expenditures in 1992. The Republicans did equally well, but the GOP's well-oiled fund-raising machinery has regularly produced massive war chests. For the Democrats, being financially well-off was a new and delightful experience.

Thus, both party organizations have grown mightier in recent years—at the time when political parties have seemed to be in decline in some other ways. Most important, many voters appear to have less a sense of partisan identification and loyalty today than in generations past. Why is this so?

The Party-in-the-Electorate

A political party is much more than its organizational shell, however dazzling the technologies at its command, and its reach extends well beyond the relative handful of men and women who are the party-in-government. In any democracy, where power is derived directly from the people, the party's real importance and strength must come from the citizenry it attempts to mobilize. The party-in-the-electorate—the mass of potential voters who identify with the Democratic or Republican labels—is the most significant element of the political party, providing the foundation for the organizational and governmental parties. But in some crucial respects, it is the weakest of the components of U.S. political party system. In recent decades fewer citizens have been willing to pledge their fealty to the major parties (see Figure 11-7), and many of those who have declared their loyalties have done so with less intensity. Also, voters of each partisan stripe are increasingly casting ballots for some candidates of the opposing party, and partisan identification is a less reliable indicator of likely voting choices today than it once was.

Party Identification

Most American voters *identify* with a party but do not *belong* to it. There is no universal enrolled party membership; there are no prescribed dues, no formal rules concerning an individual's activities, and no enforceable obligations to the party assumed by the voter. The party has no real control over or even an accurate accounting of its adherents, and the party's voters subscribe to few or none of the commonly accepted tenets of organizational membership, such as regular participation and some measure of responsibility for the group's welfare. Rather, party identification or affiliation is an informal and impressionistic exercise whereby a citizen acquires a party label and accepts its standard as a summary of his or her political views and preferences.

However, just because the acquisition is informal does not mean that it is unimportant. The party label becomes a voter's central political reference symbol and perceptual screen, a prism or filter through which the world of politics and government flows and is interpreted. For many Americans, party identification is a significant aspect of their political personality and a way of defining and explaining themselves to others.

486 ❖ Chapter 11   Political Parties

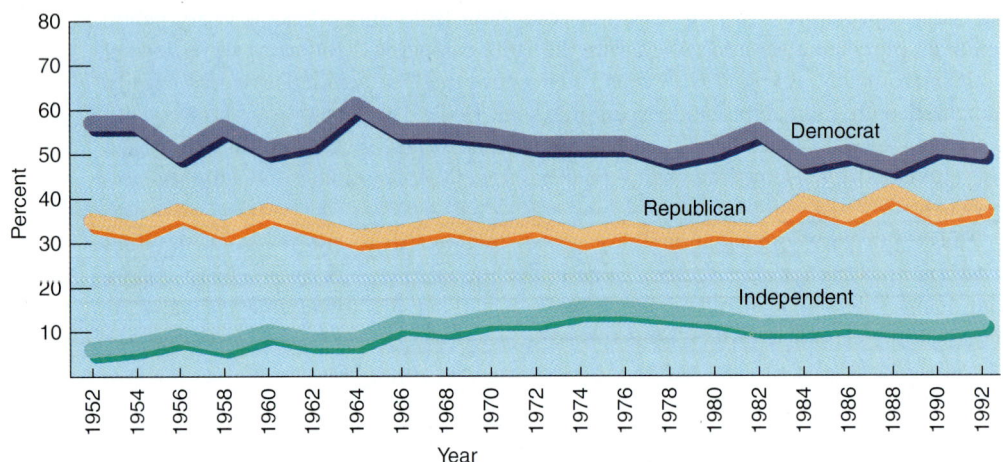

FIGURE 11-7

Party Identification, 1952–1992

Partisan totals do not add to 100% since "apolitical" and "other" responses were deleted. Sample size from poll to poll varied, from a low of 1,130 to a high of 2,850.

Pure independents only. Independent "leaners" have been added to Democratic and Republican totals.

Source: Center for Political Studies/Survey Research Center of the University of Michigan, made available through the Inter-University Consortium for Political and Social Research. Also, Leon D. Epstein, *Political Parties in the American Mold* (Madison: University of Wisconsin Press, 1986), Table 8.1, p. 257.

This graph, based on a biennial poll, shows the percentage of people identifying themselves as either Democrat, Republican, or Independent.

The loyalty generated by the label can be as intense as any enjoyed by sports teams and alma maters; in a few areas of the country, "Democrat" and "Republican" are still fighting words.

On the whole, though, Americans regard their partisan affiliation with lesser degrees of enthusiasm, viewing it as a convenience rather than a necessity. The individual identifications are reinforced by the legal institutionalization of the major parties. Because of restrictive ballot laws, campaign finance rules, the powerful inertia of political tradition, and many other factors, voters for all practical purposes are limited to a choice between a Democrat and a Republican in virtually all elections—a situation that naturally encourages the pragmatic choosing up of sides. The party registration process that exists in about half of the states, requiring a voter to state a party preference (or independent status) when registering to vote and thus restricting voter participation in primaries to party registrants, also is an incentive for voters to affiliate themselves with a party.[33]

---

[33] See Steven E. Finkel and Howard A. Scarrow, "Party Identification and Party Enrollment: The Difference and the Consequence," *Journal of Politics* 47 (May 1985): 620–642.

Sources of Party Identification. So from where do party loyalties come? Whatever the societal and governmental forces undergirding party identification, the explanations of partisan loyalty at the individual's level are understandably more personal. Not surprisingly, parents are the single greatest influence in establishing a person's first party identification. Politically active parents with the same party loyalty raise children who will be strong party identifiers, while parents without party affiliations or with mixed affiliations produce offspring more likely to be independents. (See Chapter 10)

Early socialization is hardly the last step in the acquisition and maintenance of a party identity; marriage and other aspects of adult life can change one's loyalty. So can charismatic political personalities, particularly at the national level (such as Franklin D. Roosevelt and Ronald Reagan), cataclysmic events (the Civil War and the Great Depression are the best examples), and maybe intense social issues (for instance, abortion). Interestingly, social class is not an especially strong indicator of likely partisan choice in the United States, at least in comparison with Western European democracies. Not only are Americans less inclined than Europeans to perceive class distinctions—preferring instead to see themselves and most other people as members of an exceedingly broad middle class—but other factors, including sectionalism and candidate-oriented politics, tend to blur class lines in voting.

Declining Loyalty

Over the past two decades, many political scientists as well as other observers, journalists, and party activists have become increasingly anxious about a perceived decline in partisan identification and loyalty. Many public opinion surveys have shown a significant growth in independents at the expense of the two major parties. The Center for Political Studies/Survey Research Center (CPS/SRC) of the University of Michigan, for instance, has charted the rise of self-described independents from a low of 19 percent in 1958 to a peak of 38 percent twenty years later. Before the 1950s (although the evidence for this research is more circumstantial because of the scarcity of reliable survey research data), there are indications that independents were fewer in number, and party loyalties considerably firmer.

Yet the recent decline of party identification can be exaggerated, and in some ways there has been remarkable stability in the voters' party choices. Over more than thirty years, during vast political, economic, and social upheavals that have changed the face of the nation, the Democratic Party has nearly consistently drawn the support of a small majority and the Republican Party has attracted a share of the electorate in the low to mid-30-percent range. Granted, there have been peaks and valleys for both parties. The Lyndon B. Johnson landslide of 1964 helped Democrats top the 60 percent mark, and the Reagan landslide of 1984 and the post–Persian Gulf war glow of 1991 sent Democratic stock below the majority midpoint. The Barry Goldwater debacle of 1964 and the Watergate disaster of 1974 left the Republicans with less than one-third of the populace; Reagan's reelection brought the GOP to the threshold of 40 percent. Some slight average erosion over time in Democratic Party strength is certainly apparent, as is a small Republican gain during the Reagan and Bush eras. Yet these sorts of gradations are more akin to rolling foothills than towering mountain ranges. The steady nature of modern partisanship goes beyond the fortunes of each party. Identification with the two parties in modern times has never dipped below 83 percent of the U.S. electorate (recorded during the disillusionment spawned by Watergate in 1974) and can usually be found in the mid-to-upper-80-percent range.

When pollsters ask for party identification information, they generally proceed in two stages. First, they inquire whether a respondent considers himself or herself a Democrat, Republican, or independent. Then the party identifiers are asked to categorize themselves as "strong" or "not very strong" supporters, while the independents are pushed to reveal their leanings with a question such as, "Which party do you normally support in elections—the Democrats or the Republicans?" It may be true that some independent respondents are thereby prodded to pick a party under the pressure of the interview situation, regardless of their true feelings. But research has demonstrated that independent "leaners" in fact vote very much like real partisans, in some elections more so than the "not very strong" party identifiers. There is reason to count the independent leaners as closet partisans, though voting behavior is *not* the equivalent of real partisan identification.

In fact, the reluctance of "leaners" to admit their real party identities is in itself worrisome because it reveals a change in attitudes about political parties and their role in our society. Being a socially acceptable, integrated, and contributing member of one's community once almost demanded partisan affiliation; it was a badge of good citizenship, signifying that one was a patriot. Today, the labels are avoided as an offense to a thinking person's individualism, and a vast majority of Americans insist that they vote for "the person, not the party."

The reasons for these anti-party attitudes are not hard to find. The growth of an issue-oriented politics that cuts across party lines for voters who feel intensely about certain policy matters is partly the cause. So, too, is the emphasis on personality politics by the mass media (especially television) and political consultants. Underlying these causes, though, are two much more disturbing and destructive long-term phenomena: the perceived loss of party credibility and the decline of the party's tangible connections to the lives of everyday citizens. Although the underlying partisanship of the American people has not declined significantly since 1952, voter-admitted partisanship has dropped considerably. About three-quarters or more of the electorate volunteered a party choice without prodding from 1952 to 1964, but since 1970 an average of less than two-thirds has been willing to do so. Professed independents (including leaners) have increased from around one-fifth of the electorate in the 1950s to one-third or more in the 1970s and 1980s. Also cause for concern is the marginal decline in strong Democrats and strong Republicans. Strong partisans are a party's backbone, the source of its volunteer force, candidates, and dependable voters. Even a slight shrinkage in these ranks can be troublesome.

Group Affiliations

Just as individuals vary in the *strength* of their partisan choice, so, too, do groups vary in the degree to which they identify with the Democratic Party or the Republican Party. There are enormous variations in party identification from one region or demographic group to another. Consider the following examples:

- Geographic region: While all other geographic regions in the United States are relatively closely contested between the parties, the South still exhibits the Democratic Party affinity cultivated in the last century and hardened in the fires of the Civil War. In all regions, party strengths vary by locality, with central cities almost everywhere heavily Democratic, the swelling suburbs serving as the main source of GOP partisans, and the small town and rural areas split evenly between the two major parties.

> ## The "Gender Gap"
> ♦ ♦ ♦
>
> Some political scientists argue that the difference in the way men and women vote first emerged in 1920, when newly enfranchised women registered overwhelmingly as Republicans. It was not until the 1980 presidential election, however, that a noticeable and possibly significant *gender gap* emerged. This time, the Democratic Party was the apparent beneficiary. While Ronald Reagan trounced incumbent Democratic President Jimmy Carter, he did so with the votes of only 46 percent of the women, compared to 54 percent of the men.
>
> This gender gap continues to persist at all levels of elections. In 1990, exit polls conducted after seventy races revealed a gender gap in 61 percent of the races analyzed. In 1992, as in previous elections, more voters were women (54 percent) than men (46 percent). Again, more women—47 percent—voted for the Democrat (Clinton) than men—41 percent. Among working women the gap was even more pronounced—51 percent voted for Clinton, only 31 percent for Bush.)

- Gender: Women and men differ somewhat in their partisan choice, a phenomenon called the **gender gap,** which has yawned at least since 1980. Women generally favor the Democratic Party by 5 to 10 percent, and men often give the GOP a similar edge. Besides abortion and women's rights issues, female concerns for peace and social compassion may provide much of the gap's distance. For instance, women are usually much less likely than men to favor American military action, and they are less inclined to support cuts in government funding of social welfare programs.
- Race and ethnicity: Blacks are the most dramatically different population subgroup in party terms. The 80-percent-plus advantage they offer the Democrats dwarfs the edge given to either party by any other segments of the electorate, and their proportion of strong Democrats (about 40 percent) is three times that of whites. Blacks account almost entirely for the slight lead in party affiliation that Democrats normally enjoy over Republicans, since the GOP has recently been able to attract a narrow plurality of whites to its standard. Perhaps as a reflection of the massive party chasm separating blacks and whites, the two races differ greatly on many policy issues, with blacks overwhelmingly on the liberal side and whites closer to the conservative pole. An exception, incidentally, is abortion, where religious beliefs may lead blacks to the more conservative stance. The much smaller population group of Hispanics supplements blacks as a Democratic stalwart; by more than three to one, Hispanics prefer the Democratic label. An exception is the Cuban-American population, whose anti–Fidel Castro tilt leads to Republicanism.
- Age: Young people are once again becoming more Democratic. Polls in 1972 indicated that the group of eighteen- to twenty-four-year-olds, and particularly students, was the only age group to support Democratic presidential nominee George McGovern.[34] But

---

[34] Even the eighteen- to twenty-four-year-olds were very closely split between McGovern and Nixon in most polls, but McGovern ran more than a dozen percentage points better among the very young than among the electorate as a whole.

In order to continue to prosper, the parties must continually renew themselves by attracting young people as voters, campaign workers, and even as candidates.

by the 1990s the eighteen-to-thirty-four-year-old age group was the most Republican of all. Much of this margin was derived from strong student affiliation with the Republicans. Perhaps because of the bad economy from 1990 to 1992, which limited job availability for college graduates, young people swung back to the Democrats in 1992. Bill Clinton ran strongly among eighteen- to twenty-four-year-olds, and they were among his best groups in the electorate.

- Social and economic factors: Some traditional strengths and weaknesses persist for each party by occupation, income, and education. The GOP remains predominant among executives, professionals, and white-collar workers, whereas the Democrats lead substantially among blue-collar workers and the unemployed. Labor union members are also Democratic by two-and-a-half to one. The more conservative, retired population leans Republican. Women who do not work outside the home are less liberal and Democratic than those who do. Occupation, income, and education are closely related, of course, so many of the same partisan patterns can be detected in all three classifications. Democratic support usually drops steadily as one climbs the income scale. Similarly, as years of education increase, identification with the Republican Party climbs—until graduate school, when the Democrats rally a bit and only narrowly trail GOP partisans.

- Religion: The party preferences by religion are also traditional, but with modern twists. Protestants—especially Methodists, Presbyterians, and Episcopalians—favor the Republicans by a few percentage points, whereas Catholics and, even more so, Jews are predominantly Democratic in affiliation. Less polarization is apparent all around, though.[35] Democrats have made inroads among many Protestant denomina-

---

[35] The presidential election of 1960 may be an extreme case, but John F. Kennedy's massive support among Catholics and Nixon's less substantial but still impressive backing by Protestants demonstrates the polarization that religion could once produce. See Philip E. Converse, "Religion and Politics: The 1960 Election," in Angus Campbell et al., *Elections and the Political Order* (New York: Wiley, 1966), pp. 96–124.

tions over the past three decades, and Republicans can now sometimes claim up to 25 percent of the Jewish population and nearly 40 percent of the Catholics. The "born again" Christians, who have received much attention in recent years, are somewhat less Republican than commonly believed. The GOP usually has just about a 10 percent edge among them, primarily because so many blacks classify themselves as members of this group.

- Marital status: Even marital status reveals something about partisan affiliation. People who are married, a traditionally more conservative group, and people who have never married, a segment weighted toward the premarriage young who currently lean toward the Republicans, are closely divided in party loyalty. But the widowed are Democratic in nature, probably because there are many more widows than widowers; in this, the gender gap is again expressing itself. The divorced and the separated, who may be experiencing economic hardship and appear to be more liberal than the married population, are a substantially Democratic group.
- Ideology: Ideologically, there are few surprises. Lending credence to the belief that both parties are now relatively distinct philosophically, liberals are overwhelmingly Democratic and conservatives are staunchly Republican in most surveys and opinion studies.

As party identification has weakened, so, too, has the likelihood that voters will cast ballots predictably and regularly for their party's nominees. (Chapter 12 discusses this in some detail.) In the present day—as at the founding of the republic—Americans are simply not wedded to the idea or the reality of political parties.

The strong party system that prevails in Great Britain provides an illuminating contrast. A large majority of Britons strongly identifies with either the Conservatives (Tories) or the Labour Party, and voters rarely switch allegiances on Election Day. Of course, the British parliamentary system is party-based whereas U.S. politics is far more personality-oriented. In Britain, a voter essentially casts a ballot for a party rather than for a person who will serve as prime minister, who is elected by the parliament, not by the people directly; in the United States, many voters pick presidents more by their characters and personalities than on the basis of their party labels. The British parties also polarize the electorate because of the strong ideological cast of the Tories (free enterprise) and the Labour Party (socialist). While there are clear differences between a liberal Democratic Party and a conservative Republican Party, the American contrast is much less sharp than that of Great Britain. Nevertheless, observers of British politics point to recent developments that echo the U.S. experience. Within the past two decades, a general "dealignment" of the electorate has taken place, with stable party allegiances on the decline. Hardest hit has been the Labour Party, which has apparently lost its grip on traditional sources of support among the working class.

Toward Reform

Taking into account all the aspects and roles of parties that we discuss in this chapter, the following are a list of attributes that healthy political parties should possess and also some suggested means for helping them secure and maintain these attributes.

Philosophical Attributes	**Possible Means**
Fairness and legitimacy	Promote an open structure within the parties, which invites participation by *all* interested citizens.
Participation	Get local parties more involved in meeting the needs of the community and neighborhoods.
Accountability	Keep parties in closer touch with their constituents.
Incentives	Increase patronage positions so more party workers can be rewarded.
Operational Attributes	
Autonomy	"Deregulate" the parties; allow them to set their own rules as much as possible instead of having government do it for them.
Conflict control	Grant more power to party leaders so that they can control factional conflict within the party.
Broad electoral appeal	Prevent party takeover by ideological extremists.
Policy capacity	Establish an active policy council in each party to work on position papers year round.
Purposeful Attributes	
Resources	Broaden the financial base of the parties.
Candidate assistance	Provide services such as television advertisement production and placement to the party's candidates.

The effect of all of these measures would be to strengthen the parties. Stronger parties would help bring apathetic voters back into the fold of electoral participation and would also provide a strong, unifying force to overcome regional disputes in Congress.

Before closing, let's look at one specific reform idea (related to the "participation" attribute above) and see how it would work and why it might be a good idea for political parties. A proposal has been made to build modern grassroots parties on an old-style model by designating party "ombudsmen" in key constituencies and establishing mobile party offices.[36]

Compared to European parties or even U.S. parties of a century ago, U.S. political parties today maintain remarkably little personal contact with average voters. Fully 77 percent of the electorate report that they have never "been helped with a problem by a member of a political party." A party representative would also be among the last individuals a voter in need of assistance would call: When asked, "if you had a problem or concern with the government, whom would you most likely contact for help—an elected official, or an official of your political party, or someone else?", only 14 percent of the respondents named the party.

---

[36] This idea is discussed in more detail in Sabato, *The Party's Just Begun*, pp. 179–183, 197–198. The poll results mentioned in this section are taken from the survey conducted for that study of parties. (See n. 2, p. 447.)

This result should be no surprise. Party officials and scholars alike have long noted the atrophy of many local party organizations. Even when the local party committee rosters are at full strength, relatively few of the individual committee members tend to be active or particularly well known in the precinct they are charged with organizing. The rewards (social and political) for energetic service are often nonexistent or too small to encourage any other kind of behavior; committee posts are unpaid, and there are generally no sanctions (save expulsion) to be levied for indolence. The result, of course, is that the party becomes invisible in the community; people fail to see a useful connection between their party and their lives. Precisely this disjunction is cited by some scholars to explain the growing estrangement between voter and party.[37]

Both parties, in different ways, have recognized the problem and made some minor efforts to remedy it. The Republicans established the Working Partners program in 1982, which puts local GOP leaders to work on well-publicized community projects. In several hundred successful outings, party activists cleaned up litter in the Grand Canyon; refurbished a facility for autistic adults in Santa Rosa, California; held job fairs (with the NAACP) in Tulsa, Baltimore, and St. Paul; organized food banks for the needy in a half-dozen cities and towns, and sponsored safety fingerprinting of children in San Diego and La Mesa, California. The national Democratic party has no organizational counterpart, but individual local committees, often spurred by Democratic candidates and officeholders, have orchestrated similar events in scattered locales around the country.

Two questions might reasonably be asked: Do people really want the parties to strike out in the direction of community involvement? and, Would it make much difference to voters' partisan loyalties even if the parties did adopt an activist posture? An historical answer is certainly provided by the big-city machines of old; their devotion to their constituents' daily needs made them a dominant element of urban life and was richly rewarded at election time with votes from grateful beneficiaries. Evidence from modern public opinion also supports party activism. In one survey, respondents were asked this question:

> It has been suggested that there be a basic change in the role played by political parties in America. Some people want political parties to be more active as social and civic organizations to help people deal with government and better their communities. Do you believe that such a change should happen, or should political parties stay the way they are now?

A substantial majority (58 percent) favored a shift in party activity. The proposal was popular among all major segments of the population, and it was viewed especially favorably by groups that have sometimes been excluded from the party mainstream (women, blacks, and young people). Interestingly, Americans who live in the sprawling suburbs—the *least* organizable demographic unit, where parties are currently *least* in evidence—were *most* supportive of change, signaling both their desire for visible party assistance and an opening for the parties to appeal to them. Perhaps most important, the idea of a party role change appealed particularly to segments of the electorate who were more alienated from the parties and the political system: the unregistered and those who admitted becoming "less committed" to their political party over the

---

[37] See, for example, Jack Dennis, "Public Support for the American Party System," in William J. Crotty, ed., *Paths to Political Reform* (Lexington, MA: D. C. Heath, 1980), p. 43.

last five years. This finding suggests at least the possibility that the least involved, most party-neutral citizens might establish or strengthen their partisan loyalties if a party tangibly contributed to their lives.

The abstract concept of greater civic involvement by the parties is certainly attractive to many people, but how could the idea be practically applied? One appealing way would be the designation of certain party precinct or ward committeepersons as **party ombudsmen.** The word literally means "red-tape cutter," and the ombudsman's job would be akin to the ward healer of old: to keep in touch with his or her neighbors, to be alert to their needs, and to act as their advocate when problems arise. From getting potholes filled to organizing "crime watch" neighborhood security programs, ombudsmen could perform valuable services for voters, who surely would be grateful and perhaps more receptive to their benefactor's party as well. Some people may see this as a crass appeal for votes, but others point out there is nothing inherently wrong with the time-honored, pragmatic U.S. tradition of "votes given for favors done." It is, in fact, the operating premise of the constituency service operations run by incumbent members of Congress.

Undoubtedly, volunteer spirit and party fealty alone will not be enough to spur many designated ombudsmen to energetic action, so they should probably receive a stipend commensurate with such part-time work, perhaps several thousand dollars a year. Both parties are in a financial position to do this in at least some states and localities, and the program would inevitably be targeted (at least at first) to marginal, closely contested areas where the political payoff would be greatest.

A less expensive alternative to the ombudsman program—or, more grandiosely, a supplement to it—would be the establishment of **party mobile offices** that would travel from precinct to precinct and locality to locality on a regular schedule. Staffed by both volunteers and paid workers, these mobile offices could raise the party's profile in nonelection seasons, assist residents with governmental problems, and serve as a field base for party operations.

If these units sound suspiciously like the mobile offices many members of Congress send throughout their districts, they are intended to be. In fact, one purpose of these units could be to provide service competition to incumbent members of Congress, and the party's mobile offices could be used heavily in marginal districts controlled congressionally by the opposition party. At present, incumbent legislators are essentially "unopposed" in their delivery of assistance to voters and use several hundred thousand dollars of taxpayer funds each year to do it—a fact that accounts in part for the very high House incumbent reelection rate. Using mobile units may be one way for parties to inject more competition into congressional politics, as well as to help themselves and the voters. The attractiveness of both the ombudsman scheme and the mobile units stems from the opportunities they give to build the parties in the only way likely to prove enduring: person to person, from the bottom up.

Summary

Political parties are an extra-constitutional invention that has proven essential to the successful organization of U.S. government. Despite the Framers' doubts about "factions," it is difficult to imagine our system without parties. In this chapter we have suggested some of the reasons—as well as reviewed the structure and operation of our political parties. Some of the basic points made here include these:

1. Political parties encompass three separate components: the governmental party comprises the office holders and candidates who run under the party's banner; the organizational party comprises the workers and activists who staff the party's formal organization; the party-in-the-electorate refers to the voters who consider themselves to be allied or associated with the party.

2. The evolution of U.S. political parties has been remarkably smooth, and the stability of the Democratic and Republican groupings—despite name changes—is a wonder considering all the social and political tumult in U.S. history.
3. The U.S. party system is uniquely a two-party system. While brief periods of third-party or independent activism (such as the Perot phenomenon) can prevail, the greatest proportion of all federal, state, and local elections are contests between the Republican and Democratic parties only.
4. Despite their lack of staying power, third parties have a vital role to play in our system, not least forcing the two established parties to adapt to changes in society and to tackle new issues and ideas.
5. Parties perform many functions. They create a community of interest that over time bonds disparate groups. They moderate extreme views into more pragmatic, stable, centrist positions. They offer voters a cue for judgment and allow them to hold politicians responsible for large policy questions. They also serve as incubators for new policy positions by creating national platforms every four years.
6. The basic structure of the major parties is simple and pyramidal. The state and local parties are more important than the national ones, though campaign technologies and fundraising concentrated in Washington are invigorating the national party committees.
7. Even though parties are most visible during their quadrennial national conventions, party activity is vital to the operation of Congress, the presidency, and state governments. The influence of party is even visible in the supposedly above-the-fray judiciary.
8. In recent years, the party-in-the-electorate seems to be declining, insofar as more and more voters prefer to call themselves independent. Moreover, voters have frequently chosen to elect Democratic Congresses and Republican presidents, suggesting that the voters' loyalty to neither party is strong. Nevertheless, party identification remains a critical element of most citizens' personal identity.
9. If political parties are to reverse the decline in voters' loyalty to them, they may have to regenerate grassroots activities and services to people, rebuilding party strength neighborhood by neighborhood.

Key Terms

political party
party identification
governmental party
organizational party
party-in-the-electorate
direct primary
civil service laws
patronage
spoils system
issue-oriented politics
ticket-split
political consultants
coalition
national party platforms
one-partyism
third-partyism
proportional representation
dualist theory
national convention
midterm convention
tracking polls
gender gap
party ombudsman
party mobile office

Suggested Readings

Broder, David S. *The Party's Over.* New York: Harper & Row, 1971.

Epstein, Leon. *Political Parties in the American Mold.* Madison: University of Wisconsin Press, 1986.

Kayden, Xandra, and Eddie Mahe. *The Party Goes On.* New York: Basic Books, 1985.

Key, V. O. Jr. *Politics, Parties, and Pressure Groups,* 5th ed. New York: Thomas Y. Crowell, 1964.

Maisel, L. Sandy, ed. *The Parties Respond.* Boulder, CO: Westview Press, 1990.

Polsby, Nelson W. *Consequences of Party Reform.* New York: Oxford University Press, 1983.

Pomper, Gerald M., ed. *Party Organizations in American Politics.* New York: Praeger, 1984.

Price, David E. *Bringing Back the Parties.* Washington, DC: CQ Press, 1984.

Riordan, William L., ed. *Plunkitt of Tammany Hall.* New York: Dutton, 1963. (First published in 1905.)

Sabato, Larry J. *The Party's Just Begun: Shaping Political Parties for America's Future.* Glenview, IL: Scott, Foresman/Little, Brown, 1988.

Schattschneider, E. E. *Party Government.* New York: Holt, Rinehart and Winston, 1942.

Sorauf, Frank J., and Paul Allen Beck. *Party Politics in America,* 6th ed. Glenview, IL: Scott, Foresman/Little, Brown, 1988.

Sundquist, James L. *Dynamics of the Party System,* rev. ed. Washington, DC: The Brookings Institution, 1983.

Wattenberg, Martin P. *The Decline of American Political Parties, 1952–1988.* Cambridge, MA: Harvard University Press, 1988.

The fabric of the American empire ought to rest on the solid basis of THE CONSENT OF THE PEOPLE. The stream of national power ought to flow immediately from that pure, original fountain of legitimate authority.

Alexander Hamilton
Federalist No. 22

Both of the chief authors of The Federalist Papers included passages designed to win over the hearts of the colonists. Here, Hamilton argues eloquently that the consent of the people is the linchpin of democracy. The consent of the people is best reflected in the results of elections at all levels of government.

CHAPTER 12

Voting and Elections

THE PURPOSES SERVED BY ELECTIONS
DIFFERENT KINDS OF ELECTIONS
PRESIDENTIAL ELECTIONS
CONGRESSIONAL ELECTIONS
VOTING BEHAVIOR
TOWARD REFORM

Recall for a moment election night, November 3, 1992. A plurality of the voting electorate, simply by casting ballots peacefully across a continent-sized nation, removed from office the most powerful man on earth, commander-in-chief of the world's mightiest armed forces. We take this process for granted, but it is a marvel and a direct result of the Framers' design for the American system.

Despite the noble sentiments expressed in the quotation that opens this chapter, neither Alexander Hamilton nor James Madison desired a pure democracy, believing as they did that "mob rule" was an excess to be avoided at all costs. Nonetheless, they would surely have agreed with the novelist H. G. Wells, who, as noted in Chapter 11, declared an election to be "democracy's ceremonial, its feast, its great function." For it is through free and competitive elections that the consent of the people is obtained and the government gains its democratic legitimacy.

The United States of America is a democrat's paradise in many respects because it probably conducts more elections for more offices more frequently than any nation on earth. Moreover, in recent times the U.S. **electorate**—those citizens eligible to vote—has been the most universal in the country's history; no longer can one's race or sex or creed prevent participation at the ballot box.

But Hamilton's eloquent words in *Federalist No. 22* have been realized only after two centuries of struggle. In Hamilton's time, and long thereafter, women could not vote; slaves could not vote; members of certain religious groups could not vote in some jurisdictions; and people without property were barred from the ballot box in many places. The history of U.S. elections is in part a study of the contrast between Hamilton's high ideals and the harsh reality of a limited suffrage (as the right to vote is called). Although the denial of a basic right to millions of Americans throughout the country's history is a fact, the gradual but steady broadening of the voting franchise is

497

a triumph for the people whose courage won them a full measure of freedom—and also for the U.S. system, which has repeatedly proven its ability to redeem itself by fulfilling Hamilton's vision.

The challenge of democracy is a challenge not just for the system but for the American people, too. After all the blood spilled and energy expended to expand the suffrage, only a little more than half the potentially eligible voters bother to go to the polls, a statistic we discuss later in the chapter. Also in this chapter we discuss the purposes served by elections, the various kinds of elections held in the United States, and patterns of voting over time. We concentrate in particular on presidential and congressional contests, both of which have rich histories that tell us a great deal about the American people and their changing hopes and needs.

The Purposes Served by Elections

Both the ballot and the bullet are methods of governmental change around the world, and surely the former is preferable to the latter. Although the United States has not escaped the bullet's awful effects, most change has come to this country through the election process. Regular elections guarantee mass political action and enable citizens to influence the actions of their government. Election campaigns may often seem unruly, unending, harsh, and even vicious, but imagine the stark alternatives: violence and social disruption. Societies that cannot vote their leaders out of office are left with little choice other than to force them out by means of strikes, riots, or *coups d'etat.*

Popular election confers on a government the legitimacy that it can achieve no other way. Even many authoritarian and communist systems around the globe recognize this

Democrat Bill Clinton with his running mate Al Gore Jr. (left) and Republican President Bush with Vice President Dan Quayle (right) accept their parties' nominations during the presidential election campaign of 1992.

and, from time to time, hold "referenda" to endorse their regimes or one-party elections even though these so-called elections offer no real choice that would ratify their rule. The *symbolism* of elections as mechanisms to legitimize change, then, is important, but so is their practical value. After all, elections are the means to fill public offices and staff the government. The voters' choice of candidates and parties helps to organize government as well. Because candidates advocate certain policies, elections also involve a choice of platforms and point the society in certain directions on a wide range of issues, from abortion to civil rights to national defense to the environment.

Regular elections also ensure that government is accountable to the people it serves. At fixed intervals the electorate is called on to judge those in power. If the judgment is favorable, and the incumbents are reelected, the office holders may continue their policies with renewed resolve. Should the incumbents be defeated and their challengers elected, however, a change in policies will likely result. Either way, the winners will claim a **mandate** (literally, a command) from the people to carry out their platform.

Sometimes the claim of a mandate is suspect because voters are not so much endorsing one candidate and his or her beliefs as rejecting his or her opponent. Frequently this occurs because the electorate is exercising **retrospective judgment;** that is, voters are rendering judgment on the performance of the party in power. This judgment makes sense because voters can evaluate the record of office holders much better than they can predict the future actions of the out-of-power challengers. Consider for a moment how voters retrospectively judged recent presidential administrations in reaching their ballot decisions:

- *1968:* No one could know what Richard M. Nixon's promised "secret plan to end the Vietnam War" really was, but the electorate knew that President Lyndon B. Johnson had failed to resolve the conflict. Result: Republican Nixon elected over Johnson's Democratic vice president, Hubert H. Humphrey.
- *1972:* The American people were satisfied with Nixon's stewardship of foreign affairs, especially his good relationship with the Soviet Union, the diplomatic opening of China, and the "Vietnamization" of the war. The Watergate scandal (involving Nixon's coverup of his campaign committee's bugging of the Democrats' national headquarters) was only in its infancy, and the president was rewarded with a forty-nine-state sweep over Democrat George McGovern.
- *1976:* Despite confusion about Jimmy Carter's real philosophy and intentions, the relatively unknown Georgia Democrat was elected president as voters held President Gerald Ford responsible for an economic recession and deplored his pardon of Richard M. Nixon for Watergate crimes.
- *1980:* Burdened by difficult economic times and the Iranian hostage crisis (one year before Election Day, Iranian militants had seized fifty-three Americans, whom they held until January 20, 1981, Inauguration Day), Carter became a one-term president as the electorate rejected the Democrat's perceived weak leadership. At age sixty-nine, Ronald Reagan was not viewed as the ideal replacement by many voters, and neither did a majority agree with some of his conservative principles. But the retrospective judgment on Carter was so harsh that an imperfect alternative was considered preferable to another term of the Democrat.
- *1984:* A strong economic recovery from a midterm recession and an image of strength derived from a defense buildup and a successful military venture in Grenada combined to produce a satisfied electorate and a forty-nine-state landslide reelection for Reagan over Jimmy Carter's vice president, Walter Mondale.
- *1988:* Continued satisfaction with Reagan—a product of strong economic expansion and superpower summitry—produced an electoral endorsement of Reagan's vice presi-

dent, George Bush. Bush was seen as Reagan's understudy and natural successor; the Democratic nominee, Michael Dukakis, offered too few convincing reasons to alter the voters' considered retrospective judgment.

- *1992:* A prolonged economic recession and weak growth in jobs plus Ross Perot's candidacy that split the Republican base denied a second term to George Bush, despite his many significant triumphs in foreign policy (the Persian Gulf War victory and arms control agreements, for example). In the end, voters preferred to gamble on a little-known governor, Bill Clinton, than order up more of the same by reelecting Bush.

Whether one agrees or disagrees with these election results, there is a rough justice at work here. When parties and presidents please the electorate, they are rewarded; when they preside over hard times, they are punished. A president is usually not responsible for all the good or bad developments that occur on his watch, but the voters nonetheless hold him accountable—not an unreasonable way for citizens to behave in a democracy.

Different Kinds of Elections

So far we have referred mainly to presidential elections, but in the U.S. system, elections come in many varieties.

Primary Elections

In **primary elections,** voters decide which of the candidates *within* a party will represent the party's ticket in the general elections. The primaries themselves vary in kind. For example, **closed primaries** allow only a party's registered voters to cast a ballot,

By the end of the 1992 primary season Bill Clinton had secured the nomination of the Democratic Party for president, but polls suggested that he was poorly regarded by the electorate-at-large. In June, he appeared on "The Arsenio Hall Show" in what turned out to be the beginning of a campaign to improve his image.

FIGURE 12-1
Open and Closed Primaries for State Offices*

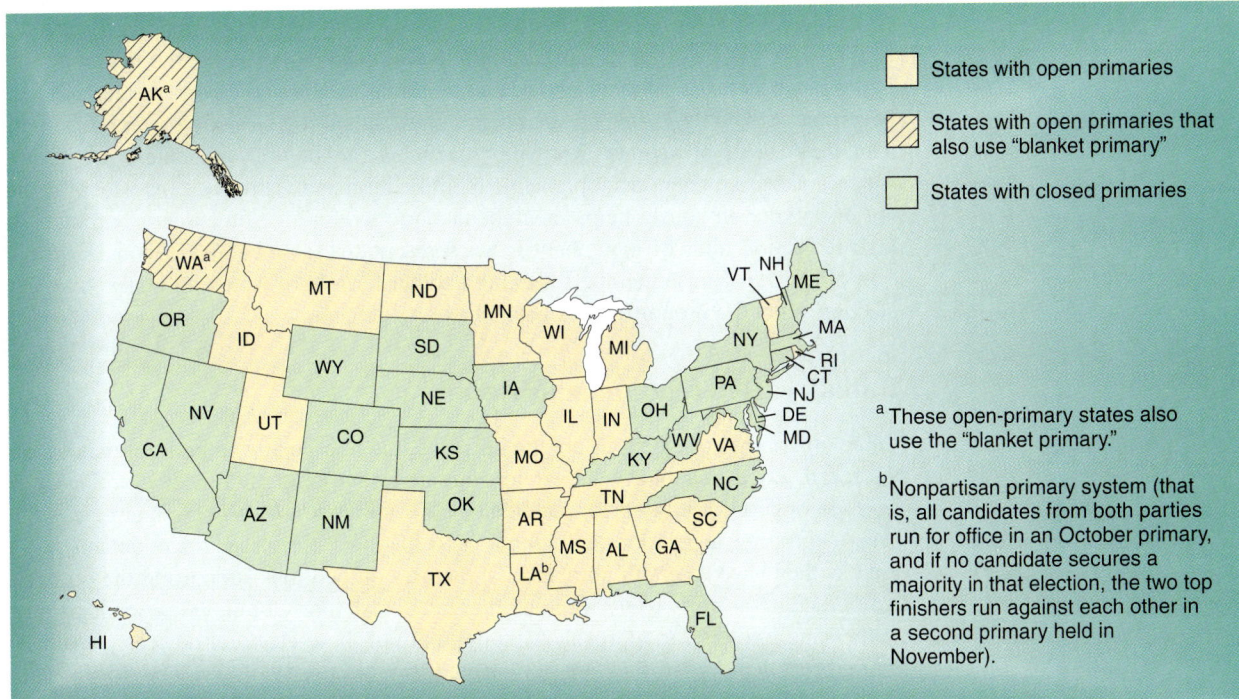

* Many states employ the caucus method of nomination rather than a primary for *presidential delegate* selection. See Table 12–1.

and **open primaries** allow independents and sometimes members of the other party to participate. (Figure 12-1 shows the states with open and closed primaries for state offices. Closed primaries are considered healthier for the party system ballot, because they prevent members of one party from influencing the primaries of the opposition party.) In the **blanket primary,** voters are permitted to vote in either party's primary (but not both) on an office-by-office basis. When none of the candidates in the initial primary secures a majority of the votes, there is a **runoff primary,** a contest between the two candidates with the greatest number of votes. The **white primary,** in which all nonwhite voters were systematically excluded from voting, is no longer in existence. White primaries ended when the Supreme Court ruled in *Smith v. Allwright* 321 U.S. 649 (1944) that they violated the Fifteenth Amendment to the Constitution.

General Elections

Once the party candidates for various offices are chosen, **general elections** are held. In the general election, voters decide which candidates will actually fill the nation's elective public offices. These elections are held at many levels, including municipal, county, state, and national. While primaries are contests between the candidates *within* each party, general elections are contests between the candidates of *opposing* parties.

General elections come in many varieties because Americans perceive the various offices as substantially different from one another. In sizing up presidential candidates, voters look for leadership and character, and they base their judgments partly on foreign policy and defense issues that do not arise in state and local elections. Leadership qualities are vital for gubernatorial and mayoral candidates, as are the nuts-and-bolts issues (such as taxes, schools, and roads) that dominate the concerns of state and local governments. Citizens often choose their congressional representatives very differently than they select presidents. Knowing much less about the candidates, people will sometimes base a vote on simple name identification and visibility. This way of deciding one's vote obviously helps incumbents and therefore to some degree explains the high reelection rates of incumbent U.S. representatives: Since World War II, 92 percent of all U.S. House members seeking another term have won, and in several recent election years the proportion has been above 95 percent.

Initiative, Referendum, and Recall

Three other types of elections are the initiative, the referendum (plural, referenda), and the recall. Used in about twenty states, initiatives and referenda involve voting on *issues* (as opposed to voting for candidates). An initiative is a process that allows citizens to propose legislation and submit it to the state electorate for popular vote, as long as they have a certain number of signatures on petitions supporting the proposal. A referendum is a procedure whereby the state legislature submits proposed legislation to the state's voters for approval. Although both of these electoral devices provide for more direct democracy, they are not problem-free. In the 1990 elections, for instance, California had so many referenda and initiatives on its ballot that the state printed a lengthy two-volume guide in an attempt to explain them all to voters. Despite this, many Californians complained that it was virtually impossible for even a reasonably informed citizen to vote intelligently on so many issues.

The third type of election (or "de-election") found in many states is the recall, whereby an incumbent can be removed from office by popular vote. Recall elections are very rare, and sometimes they are thwarted by the official's resignation or impeachment prior to the vote. For example, Arizona Governor Evan Mecham was impeached and ousted in 1988 by the state legislature for mishandling campaign finances (among other offenses) just a few weeks before a recall election had been scheduled.

British election varieties pale in comparison. In Great Britain, one encounters national elections to the House of Commons, which must be called sometime during the five-year life of a Parliament; local elections, which are held every three years; elections to the European Parliament, which occur at five-year intervals; and three instances of national referenda.

Presidential Elections

Variety aside, no U.S. election can compare to the presidential contest. This spectacle, held every four years, brings together all the elements of politics and attracts the most ambitious and energetic politicians to the national stage. The election itself is a marathon—not a single election but a collection of fifty separate state elections in each party, held over a six-month period, to pick convention delegates. The election of delegates is followed in midsummer by the parties' grand national conventions and then by a final set of fifty separate state elections all held on the Tuesday after the first Monday in November. This lengthy process exhausts candidates and voters alike, but it allows the diversity of the United States to be displayed in ways a shorter, more homogeneous presidential election process could not. Every state has its moment in the sun, every local and regional problem a chance to be aired, every candidate an opportunity to break away from the pack.

The state party organizations use a number of methods to elect national convention delegates. There are six basic systems of delegate selection.

1. *Winner-take-all:* Under this system, the candidate who wins the most votes in a state secures all of that state's delegates. The Democrats moved away from this mode of delegate selection in 1976 and no longer permit its use because of the arguable unfairness to all candidates except the primary winner. Republicans do *not* prohibit winner-take-all contests, thus enabling a GOP candidate to amass a majority of delegates more quickly. This approach can give the GOP candidate a head start in planning for the general election.
2. *Proportional representation:* Under this system, candidates who secure a threshold percentage of votes (usually around 15 percent) are awarded delegates in proportion to the number of popular votes won. This system is now strongly favored by the Democrats and is used in many states' Democratic primaries. Although proportional representation is probably the most fair way of allocating delegates to candidates, its downfall is that it renders majorities of delegates more difficult to accumulate—and thus it can lengthen the contest for the nomination.
3. *Proportional representation with bonus delegates:* This system also awards delegates to candidates in proportion to the popular vote won and then gives one bonus delegate to the winner of each district. The appeal of this system is that it is a compromise between pure proportional representation and the winner-take-all method.
4. *Beauty contest with separate delegate selection:* The results of this type of primary have no bearing on actual delegate selection, which usually takes place in later conventions. The "beauty contest" serves as an indication of popular sentiment for the conventions to consider as they choose the actual delegates.
5. *Delegate selection with no beauty contest:* Under this system the primary election chooses delegates to the national conventions who are not linked on the ballot to specific presidential contenders. Well-known names and party-endorsed delegates are often favored under this system.
6. *The caucus:* The caucus is the oldest, most party-oriented method of choosing delegates to the national conventions. Traditionally, the caucus was a closed meeting of party members in each state that selected the party's choice for presidential candidate. In the late nineteenth and early twentieth centuries, however, these caucuses came to be viewed by many people as elitist and anti-democratic, and reformers succeeded in replacing them with direct primaries in most states. While there are still presidential nominating caucuses today, as in Iowa, they are now more open and attract a wider range of the party's membership.

Senator Tom Harkin (D.-Iowa) campaigning in New Hampshire in February, 1992. New Hampshire's position as the first primary has historically given it unusual influence on presidential elections; candidates spend more time campaigning there (often six weeks or more) than in any other state before a primary vote.

Primaries versus Caucuses

The mix of preconvention contests has changed over the years, with the most pronounced trend being the shift to primaries: Only seventeen states held presidential primaries in 1968, compared with thirty-eight in 1992. The increase in the number of primaries is supported by some people who claim that this type of election is more democratic. The primaries are open not only to party activists, but also to anyone, wealthy or poor, urban or rural, Northern or Southern, who wants to vote. Theoretically, then, representatives of all these groups have a chance of winning the presidency. Related to this idea, advocates argue that presidential primaries are the most representative means by which to nominate presidential candidates. They are a barometer of a candidate's popularity with the party rank and file. Finally, the proponents of presidential primaries claim that they constitute a rigorous test for the candidates, a chance to display under pressure some of the skills needed to be a successful president.

Critics of presidential primaries, however, see the situation somewhat differently. First, they argue, although it may be true that primaries attract more participants than do caucuses, this quantity is more than matched by the quality of caucus participation. Compared with the unenlightening minutes spent at the primary polls, caucus attendees spend several hours learning about politics and the party, listening to speeches by candidates or their representatives, and taking cues from party leaders and elected officials. Moreover, voters may not know very much about any of the field of candidates in a primary, or they may be excessively swayed by popularity polls, television ads, and other media presentations, such as newspaper and magazine coverage.

Critics also argue that the scheduling of primaries unfairly affects their outcomes. For example, the earliest primary is in the small, atypical state of New Hampshire, which is heavily white and conservative, and it receives much more media coverage than warranted simply because it is first. Such excessive coverage undoubtedly skews the picture for more populous states that hold their primaries later. The critics also argue that the qualities tested by the primary system are by no means a complete list of those a president needs to be successful. For instance, skill at playing the media game is by itself no guarantee of an effective presidency. Similarly, the exhausting schedule of the primaries may be a better test of a candidate's stamina than of his or her brain power.

The primary proponents have obviously had the better of the arguments so far, though the debate continues, as do efforts to experiment with the schedule of primaries. From time to time, proposals are made for **regional primaries.** Under this system, the nation would be divided into five or six geographic regions (such as the South or the Midwest). All the states in each region would hold their primary elections on the same day, with perhaps one regional election day per month from February through June of presidential election years. This change would certainly cut down on candidate wear and tear. Moreover, candidates would be inspired to focus more on regional issues. On the other hand, regional primaries would probably cost candidates at least as much as the state-by-state system, and the system might needlessly amplify the differences and create divisive rifts among the nation's regions.

Occasionally a regional plan is adopted. In 1988, for instance, fourteen Southern and border South states joined together to hold simultaneous primaries on "Super Tuesday" (March 8) in order to maximize the South's impact on presidential politics. This was an attempt by conservative Democrats to influence the choice of the party nominee. Their effort failed, however, since the two biggest winners of Super Tuesday were liberals Jesse Jackson (who won six Southern states) and Michael Dukakis, who carried the mega-states of Texas and Florida. This outcome occurred because, in general, the kinds of citizens who vote in Democratic primaries in the South are not greatly different from those who cast ballots in Northern Democratic primaries—most tend toward the liberal side of the ideological spectrum.

The primary schedule has also been altered by a process called frontloading, the tendency of states to choose an early date on the primary calendar. Fully half or more of all the delegates to both party conventions are now chosen before the end of April (see Table 12-1). This trend is hardly surprising given the added press emphasis on the

Table 12.1 ♦ 1992 Presidential Nominating Season at a Glance

STATE	Delegate Count D	R	FORM OF DELEGATE SELECTION	DATE OF MAIN EVENT
Alabama	62	38	Open Primary	June 2
Alaska	18	19	Closed Caucus (D)/Open Caucus (R)[a]	April 2
Arizona	47	37	Closed Caucus	March 7
Arkansas	43	27	Open Primary	May 26
California	382	201	Closed Primary	June 2
Colorado	54	37	Open Primary[a]	March 3
Connecticut	61	35	Closed Primary	March 24
Delaware	19	19	Closed Caucus (D)/Open Caucus (R)	March 3
District of Columbia	29	14	Closed Primary	May 5
Florida	160	97	Closed Primary	March 10
Georgia	88	52	Open Primary	March 10
Hawaii	26	14	Closed Caucus	March 10
Idaho	24	22	Open Caucus (D)/Open Primary (R)	March 3
Illinois	183	85	Open Primary	March 17
Indiana	86	51	Open Primary	May 5
Iowa	57	23	Open Caucus[a]	February 10
Kansas	42	30	Open Primary[a]	April 7
Kentucky	62	35	Closed Primary	May 26
Louisiana	69	38	Closed Primary	March 10
Maine	30	22	Open Caucus[a]	February 23
Maryland	80	42	Closed Primary	March 3
Massachusetts	107	38	Open Primary[a]	March 10
Michigan	148	72	Closed Primary	March 17
Minnesota	87	32	Open Caucus	March 3
Mississippi	45	32	Open Primary	March 10
Missouri	86	47	Open Caucus	March 10
Montana	22	20	Open Primary	June 2
Nebraska	31	24	Closed Primary	May 12
Nevada	23	21	Closed Caucus	March 7
New Hampshire	24	23	Open Primary[a]	February 18
New Jersey	117	60	Closed Primary	June 2
New Mexico	33	25	Closed Primary	June 2
New York	268	100	Closed Primary	April 7
North Carolina	93	57	Closed Primary	May 5
North Dakota	20	17	Open Caucus (D)/Open Primary (R)	June 9
Ohio	167	83	Open Primary	June 2
Oklahoma	52	34	Closed Primary	March 10
Oregon	53	23	Closed Primary	May 19
Pennsylvania	188	90	Closed Primary	April 28
Rhode Island	28	15	Open Primary[a]	March 10
South Carolina	50	36	Open Primary	March 7
South Dakota	20	19	Closed Primary	February 25

Continued

Table 12.1 ♦ Continued

STATE	Delegate Count D	Delegate Count R	FORM OF DELEGATE SELECTION	DATE OF MAIN EVENT
Tennessee	77	45	Open Primary	March 10
Texas	214	121	Open Primary	March 10
Utah	28	27	Open Caucus	April 20
Vermont	19	19	Open Caucus	March 31
Virginia	92	54	Open Caucus	April 11
Washington	80	35	Open Primary	May 19
West Virginia	38	18	Closed Primary (D)/Open Primary (R)[a]	May 12
Wisconsin	91	35	Open Primary	April 7
Wyoming	19	20	Closed Caucus	March 7
Puerto Rico	57	14	Open Primary	March 15
U.S. Territories	12	12		
Democrats Abroad	9			
Unassigned	262			
Totals	**4,282**	**2,206**		

[a]Independents may participate; voters registered by party may participate only in their party's primary or caucus.

Source: Congressional Quarterly Weekly.

first contests and the voters' desire to cast their ballots before the competition is decided. Ever since 1976, when the then-unknown Jimmy Carter scored an upset win in the Iowa caucuses, Iowa's first-in-the-nation delegate selection in February has drawn enormous attention. So has the first primary state, New Hampshire, which holds its election shortly after the Iowa caucuses (see Tables 12-2 and 12-3). In fact, except for 1992, the New Hampshire primary has the distinction of having voted for the eventual winner of the presidency in every election since 1952. Despite this record, the focus on early contests, coupled with frontloading, can result in a party's being saddled with a nominee too quickly, before press scrutiny and voter reflection are given enough time to separate the wheat from the chaff.

The Party Conventions

The seemingly endless nomination battle does have a conclusion: the national party convention held in the summer of presidential election years. The out-of-power party traditionally holds its convention first, in late July, followed by the party holding the White House in mid-August. Preempting some of prime-time television for four nights, these remarkable conclaves are difficult for the public to ignore; indeed, they are pivotal events in shaping the voters' perceptions of the candidates.

Yet the conventions once were much more: They were deliberative bodies that made actual decisions, where party leaders held sway and deals were sometimes cut in "smoke-filled rooms" to deliver nominations to little-known contenders (called "dark horses"—see the "Then and Now," pages 510–511). But this era pre-dated the

Table 12.2 ♦ Recent New Hampshire Primary Results

YEAR	TURNOUT	TOP CANDIDATES	PERCENTAGE
Democrats			
1992	167,815	Paul Tsongas	33
		Bill Clinton	25
		Jerry Brown	8
		Others	34
1988	123,512	Michael Dukakis	36
		Richard Gephardt	20
		Paul Simon	17
		Jesse Jackson	8
		Albert Gore	7
1984	101,131	Gary Hart	37
		Walter Mondale	28
		John Glenn	12
		Jesse Jackson	5
		George McGovern	5
1980	111,930	Jimmy Carter	47
		Edward Kennedy	37
		Jerry Brown	10
1976	82,381	Jimmy Carter	28
		Morris Udall	23
		Birch Bayh	15
		Fred Harris	11
		Sargent Shriver	8
Republicans			
1992	174,165	George Bush	53
		Patrick Buchanan	37
		Others	10
1988	157,644	George Bush	38
		Robert Dole	28
		Jack Kemp	13
		Pete du Pont	10
		Pat Robertson	9
1984	75,570	Ronald Reagan	86
1980	147,157	Ronald Reagan	50
		George Bush	23
		Howard Baker	13
		John Anderson	10
1976	111,674	Gerald Ford	49
		Ronald Reagan	48

Source: Congressional Quarterly Weekly.

Table 12.3 ♦ Recent Iowa Caucus Results

YEAR	TURNOUT	TOP CANDIDATE	PERCENTAGE
Democrats			
1992	30,000	Tom Harkin	76
		Uncommitted	12
		Paul Tsongas	4
		Bill Clinton	3
		Robert Kerrey	2
		Jerry Brown	2
		Others	1
1988	126,000	Richard Gephardt	31
		Paul Simon	27
		Michael Dukakis	22
		Jesse Jackson	9
1984	75,000	Walter Mondale	49
		Gary Hart	16
		George McGovern	10
1980	100,000	Jimmy Carter	59
		Edward M. Kennedy	31
Republicans			
1992[a]	—	—	—
1988	108,838	Robert Dole	37
		Pat Robertson	25
		George Bush	19
		Jack Kemp	11
1984[b]	—	—	—
1980	106,051	George Bush	32
		Ronald Reagan	30
		Howard Baker	15

[a]Republicans did not hold an Iowa caucus in 1992.
[b]In 1984, incumbent president Reagan faced no opposition.
Source: Congressional Quarterly Weekly.

modern emphasis on reform, primaries, and proportional representation, all of which have combined to make conventions mere ratifying agencies for pre-selected nominees.

In the 1830s the national nominating convention replaced the congressional caucus (an organization of all the party's members of Congress) as the means for selecting the presidential ticket. The national convention consists of a delegation from each state. The delegation, whose size is determined by the national party, includes leaders from the state's various localities. Consequently, the nominee of the convention is, in effect, the choice of a congregation of state and local parties. Unlike the congressional caucus system, the convention is compatible with the federal separation of powers and provides for the broad participation of party members. In addition to selecting the party's

In 1836, Martin Van Buren became the first nonincumbent candidate nominated by a major party convention to win the presidency. Previously a loyal vice president to Andrew Jackson (and the last sitting vice president to win the presidency before George Bush in 1988), Van Buren proceeded to solidify the Democrats' party politics through patronage and active leadership. It is interesting that, just as Bush lost his 1992 reelection bid because of a rocky economy, so too did Van Buren fail in his 1840 race for a second term.

presidential ticket, the convention drafts the party's platform (see Chapter 11) and establishes party rules and procedures.

The first national convention was held in 1831 by the Anti-Masonic Party. In 1832 Andrew Jackson's nomination for reelection was ratified by the first Democratic National Convention. Just four years later, in 1836, Martin Van Buren became the first non-incumbent candidate nominated by a major party convention (the Democrats) to win the presidency.

From the 1830s to the mid–twentieth century, the national conventions remained primarily under the control of the important state and local party leaders—the so-called bosses or kingmakers—who would bargain within a splintered, decentralized party. (See the "Then and Now," pages 510–511.) During these years state delegations in the convention consisted mostly of **uncommitted delegates** (that is, delegates who had not pledged to support any particular candidate). These delegates were selected by party leaders, a process that enabled the leaders to broker agreements with prominent national candidates. Under this system a state party leader could exchange delegation support for valuable political plums—for instance, a Cabinet position or even the vice presidency—for an important state political figure.

The convention today, however, is fundamentally different. First, its importance as a party conclave, at which compromises on party leadership and policies can be worked out, has diminished. Second, although the convention still formally selects the presidential ticket, most nominations are settled well in advance. New preconvention political processes have lessened the role of the convention in three areas.

1. *Delegate selection.* The selection of delegates to the conventions is no longer the function of party leaders but of primary elections and grassroots caucuses. Moreover, recent reforms, especially by the Democratic Party, have generally weakened any remaining control by local party leaders over delegates. A prime example of such reform is the Democrats' abolition of the **unit rule,** a traditional party practice under which the majority of a state delegation (say, twenty-six of fifty delegates) could force the minority to vote for its candidate. Another new Democratic Party rule decrees that a state's delegates be chosen in proportion to the votes cast in its primary or caucus (so that, for example, a candidate who receives 30 percent of the vote gains

Then and Now

Dark Horses versus Worn-out Horses

The national party convention of the present day is a different animal from that of the past. No longer is it a deliberative forum for choosing the party presidential nominee; rather, the convention now merely ratifies the choices of the preconvention state caucuses and primaries. A look at the Republican and Democratic Party conventions sixty years apart—in 1920 and 1980—illuminates one key contrast between the old-style and new-style conventions: the absence of dark horses—relatively unknown candidates who emerge at the convention and occasionally win a nomination as a compromise choice in order to break a deadlock.

The 1920 Republican convention featured a rift in the party. On one side was the party's old presidential faction, moderate and internationalist, with Abraham Lincoln and Theodore Roosevelt serving as its models. On the other side stood the more conservative wing of the party, with Senator Henry Cabot Lodge of Massachusetts at the helm and including most if not all of Capitol Hill's GOP leadership.

The "presidential" party during those days usually exerted more influence in presidential nominations than did the congressional party. But this changed in 1920 because Lodge's congressional party had garnered more power and influence during the latter part of Democratic President Woodrow Wilson's White House tenure (1913–21), when Wilson was seriously ill and his policies were under attack. Could the two wings of the party compromise on a presidential candidate for 1920? Any such compromise would undoubtedly be difficult to come by because most potential candidates were aligned firmly with one wing of the party or the other.

Senator Warren G. Harding of Ohio was one possible compromise candidate. A small-town politician and onetime editor of a staunchly Republican Ohio newspaper, Harding had a reputation in the Senate based primarily on his ability to win allies in all factions of the Republican Party. But Harding's chances appeared bleak at the outset of the convention, and after the first ballot, he was considerably behind a number of other Republican hopefuls. Yet, several frontrunners continued to deadlock in ballot after ballot, testing the patience of the delegates, who were baking in the hot Chicago summer.

The weather, combined with the seemingly unresolvable convention impasse, spurred a group of influential Senate leaders to meet at a nearby hotel room to attempt to hammer out a compromise—the classic gathering of party leaders behind the closed doors of a smoke-filled room. At the meeting, Harding's name continued to be floated. Although most of the party leaders questioned the Ohioan's convictions and leadership abilities, he did have some attractive qualities: He was handsome (it was said that Harding "looked like a president"), he hailed from a politically important state, and he could be expected to work with leaders of both party factions. The GOP kingmakers therefore decided to test the waters with Harding but agreed to reconvene later in the more likely event that the delegates rejected him. Harding soon went to work to ensure that no new meeting would be needed, however; he campaigned vigorously for his candidacy throughout the evening, roaming the halls and trying to convince any delegate he could find of his credibility as a candidate.

about 30 percent of the convention delegates). This change has had the effect of requiring delegates to indicate their presidential preference at each stage of the selection process. Consequently, the majority of state delegates now come to the convention already committed to a candidate. Again, this diminishes the discretionary role of the convention and the party leaders' capacity to bargain.

In sum, the many complex changes in the rules of delegate selection have contributed to the loss of decision-making powers by the convention. And even though many of these changes were initiated by the Democratic Party, the Republicans were carried along as many Democrat-controlled state legislatures enacted the reforms as

---

The deadlock at the convention continued for a few more ballots, but the frazzled delegates gradually realized that Harding perhaps was the only candidate with the potential to secure a majority. This realization sent frontrunners scurrying around the convention to build a coalition to stop Harding. They failed, however, and dark-horse candidate Harding—on the tenth ballot—secured enough votes to win the nomination.

The Democrats also needed a candidate to unite the party in 1920, one who could emphasize Wilson's successes yet downplay his failures. After thirty-eight ballots at the Democratic National Convention, no majority candidate had yet emerged, instilling in Wilson a hope that the party might again turn to him as the nominee, despite his deteriorated physical condition. It was one thing for the Democrats to remain loyal to Wilson—which they did by endorsing his policies and paying him homage in the party platform—and another for the party to nominate him for a third term. A return to Wilson was ultimately unnecessary, as Ohio Governor James M. Cox finally secured the nomination on the forty-fourth ballot.

Conditions are very different today. Nominations are no longer decided in smoke-filled back rooms at the conventions; instead, the critical moments occur well beforehand in the highly visible primary-and-caucus obstacle course that creates not dark horses but worn-out horses by convention time. In 1980, for example, many Democrats were dissatisfied with the Carter presidency. The situation was so dismal for the incumbent president that a strong nomination challenge came from a prominent fellow Democrat, Senator Edward M. Kennedy of Massachusetts. At first, the polls were encouraging for Kennedy—he enjoyed a two-to-one margin over Carter in the summer of 1979. But the Iran hostage crisis—the seizing by Iranian militants of more than fifty Americans from the U.S. embassy in Tehran—led to a sharp rise in public support for Carter, ultimately giving him a decisive margin over Kennedy in the vital early contests. Despite the initial strong challenge from Kennedy and the party's dissatisfaction with Carter's presidency, the incumbent's nomination was secured by April 1980, before the primaries had ended and four months before the Democratic convention opened. Even with a deep fissure in the Democratic Party, no dark-horse candidate emerged because most delegates arrived at the convention already bound by the rules of the party to either Carter or Kennedy.

No dark-horse candidate emerged in the Republican field in 1980, either. The most well-known of the Republicans was a former movie actor and California governor, Ronald Reagan, sixty-nine years old and a conservative who appealed to the right wing of the party. Moderate U.S. Senate Minority Leader Howard Baker of Tennessee and Senator Robert Dole of Kansas were both in the running, as were former Texas Governor John Connally, Representative John Anderson of Illinois (who would later declare himself an independent candidate for president), and George Bush, a former member of Congress from Texas and U.S. ambassador to China. Though Bush won the Iowa precinct caucuses (the first major contest in 1980), Reagan won handily in the next big challenge, New Hampshire, securing almost twice Bush's vote. Like the Democratic nomination, the Republican contest was settled four months before the party convention, and only the brokering over Reagan's choice of a vice-presidential running mate was left to generate excitement at the convention.

The 1980 conventions are typical of those in the modern era, where presidential candidates secure victory by appealing directly to the people, not the party leaders. For better or worse, the deliberative conventions at which dark-horse candidates flourished, such as those of 1920, are probably consigned to the American political past.

state laws. There have been new rules to counteract some of these changes, however. For instance, since 1984 the number of delegate slots reserved for elected Democratic Party officials—called **superdelegates**—has been increased, so that all Democratic governors and 80 percent of the congressional Democrats among others are now included as voting delegates at the convention.

2. *National candidates and issues.* The political perceptions and loyalties of voters are now influenced largely by national candidates and issues, a factor that has undoubtedly served to diminish the power of state and local party leaders at the convention. The national candidates have usurped the autonomy of state party leaders with their preconvention ability to garner delegate support. And issues, increasingly national in scope, are significantly more important to the new, issue-oriented party activists than to the party professionals, who, prior to the late 1960s, had a monopoly on the management of party affairs.

3. *The news media.* The mass media have helped to transform the national conventions into political extravaganzas for the television audience's consumption. They have also helped to preempt the convention, by keeping count of the delegates committed to the candidates; as a result, the delegates and even the candidates now have much more information about nomination politics well before the convention. From the strategies of candidates to the commitments of individual delegates, the media cover it all. Even the bargaining within key party committees—formerly done in secret—is now subject to some public scrutiny, thanks to open meetings. The business of the convention has been irrevocably shaped to accommodate television: Important roles are now assigned to attractive speakers, and most crucial party affairs are saved for prime-time viewing hours.

Extensive media coverage of the convention has its pros and cons. On the one hand, such exposure helps the party launch its presidential campaign with fanfare. On the other hand, it can expose rifts within a party, as happened in 1968 at the Democratic convention in Chicago. Dissension was obvious when "hawks," supporting the Vietnam war and President Lyndon B. Johnson, clashed with the antiwar "doves" both on

The Texas delegation to the 1992 Republican convention announces the votes that clinched the nomination of President Bush for a second term.

the convention floor and in street demonstrations around the convention hall. Whatever the case, it is obvious that saturation media coverage of pre-election events has led to the public's loss of anticipation and exhilaration about convention events.

Some reformers have spoken of replacing the conventions with national direct primaries, but it is unlikely that the parties would agree to this. Although its role in nominating the presidential ticket has often been reduced to formality, the convention is still a valuable political institution. After all, it is the only real arena where the national political parties can command a nearly universal audience while they celebrate past achievements and project their hopes for the future.

Who Are the Delegates? In one sense, party conventions are microcosms of the United States: every state, most localities, and all races and creeds find some representation there. Yet delegates are an unusual and unrepresentative collection of people in many other ways. It is not just their exceptionally keen interest in politics that distinguishes delegates. These activists also are ideologically more pure and financially better off than most Americans.

In 1992, for example, both parties drew their delegates from an elite group that had income and educational levels far above the average American's. The distinctiveness of each party was also apparent. Democratic delegates tended to be younger and were more likely to be African American, female, divorced or single, and a member of a labor union. Republicans drew their delegates more heavily from people over forty-five years old, whites, married men, and Protestants. GOP conventioneers were also more likely to be elected or appointed officials and to have attended previous party conventions.

The contrast in the two parties' delegations is no accident; it reflects not only the differences in the party constituencies but also conscious decisions made by party leaders. After the tumultuous 1968 Democratic National Convention (which, as noted, was torn by dissent over the Vietnam War), Democrats formed the McGovern-Fraser Commission (named for Senator George McGovern and Representative Donald Fraser) to examine the condition of the party and to propose changes in its structure. As a direct consequence of the commission's work, the 1972 convention was the most broadly representative ever of women, African Americans, and young people, because the party required these groups to be included in state delegations in rough proportion to their numbers in the population of each state. (State delegations failing this test were not seated.) This new mandate was very controversial, and it has since been watered down considerably. Nonetheless, women and blacks are still more fully represented at Democratic conventions (as Table 12.4 shows) than at Republican conventions. GOP leaders have placed much less emphasis on proportional representation, and instead of procedural reforms, Republicans have concentrated on strengthening their state organizations and fund-raising efforts, a strategy that has clearly paid off at the polls in the elections of 1980, 1984 and 1988, which saw Republicans elected as President.

The delegates in each party also exemplify the philosophical gulf separating the two parties (see Table 12.5). Democratic delegates are well to the left of their own party's voters on most issues, and even further away from the opinions held by the nation's electorate as a whole. Republican delegates are a mirror image of their opponents—considerably to the right of GOP voters and even more so of the entire electorate. Although it is sometimes said that the two major parties do not present U.S. citizens with a "clear choice" of candidates, it is possible to argue the contrary. Our politics are perhaps too polarized, with the great majority of Americans—moderates and pragmatists overwhelmingly—left underrepresented by parties too fond of ideological purity.

Women as Delegates

Since 1980 Democratic Party rules have required that women comprise 50 percent of the delegates to its national convention. The Republican Party has no similar quotas. Nevertheless, both parties have tried to increase the role of women at the convention. Some "firsts" for women at conventions include:

1876	First women to address a national convention
1890	First women delegates to conventions of both parties
1940	First woman to nominate a presidential candidate
1951	First woman asked to chair a national party
1972	First women keynote speaker
1984	First major party woman nominated for vice president (Democrat Geraldine Ferraro)

Source: Center for the Study of American Women in Politics.

Table 12.4 ♦ A Comparison of Delegates to the 1992 Presidential Nominating Conventions[a]

	DEMOCRATIC DELEGATES	REPUBLICAN DELEGATES	ALL VOTERS IN NOV. 1992 PRESIDENTIAL ELECTION
Level of Education			
High school or less	9%	12%	32%
Some college	18	20	29
College graduate	28	35	23
Graduate school	44	33	16
Household Income			
Under $12,000	1%	1%	10
$12,000 to $19,999	3	2	9
$20,000 to $29,999	8	5	19
$30,000 to $49,999	20	16	30
$50,000 or more	68	76	32
Ideology			
Very liberal	12%	0%	} 21
Liberal	40	1	
Moderate	42	28	49
Conservative	3	58	} 30
Very conservative	0	12	
Age			
18–29	4%	3%	21
30–39	19	15	27
40–59	59	54	32
60 and older	18	28	20
Race/Ethnicity			
White	74%	89%	87
Black	17	4	8
Hispanic	6	4	2
Other	3	3	2
Marital Status			
Married	68%	85%	66
Divorced	13	7	9
Widowed	5	4	5
Single	13	4	19
Labor Union			
Member	28%	3%	19
Not a member	72	97	81
Sex			
Male	50%	58%	48
Female	50	42	52

Continued

Table 12.4 ◆ Continued

	DEMOCRATIC DELEGATES	REPUBLICAN DELEGATES	ALL VOTERS IN NOV. 1992 PRESIDENTIAL ELECTION
Past Convention Attendance			
Was a delegate or alternate before	39%	46%	—
Not a delegate or alternate before	61	54	—
Public or Party Position			
Elected public/party official	47%	55%	—
Appointed public/party official	8	15	—
Both elected and appointed	4	6	—
Not an official	41	24	—
Religion			
Protestant	51%	67%	42
Catholic	36	27	27
Other/None	13	6	17

[a]Margin of sampling error is plus or minus 4.5 percentage points when figures do not include those who declined to answer the question; the margin of error is plus or minus 2 percentage points for all others. Other totals may not add up to 100 percent because of rounding.

Source: Figures in the first two columns are from a *Washington Post* telephone poll of 511 Republican delegates from July 29 to August 7, 1992, and 496 Democratic delegates from June 22 to July 8. Figures in the last column are adapted from the Voter Research & Surveys (VRS) poll of 15,232 Americans as they exited from their voting booths on November 3, 1992. VRS is an association of ABC News, CNN, CBS News, and NBC News.

The philosophical divergence is usually reflected in the party platforms, even in years such as 1992, when one party attempts to water down its rhetoric and avoid specifics (see Table 12.6). (The Democrats did so in 1992; the Republicans have done so in earlier years, as in 1968.)

The Electoral College: How Presidents Are Elected

Given the enormous output of energy, money, and time expended to nominate two major-party presidential contenders, it is difficult to believe that the general election could be more arduous than the nominating contests—but it usually is. The actual campaign for the presidency (and other offices) is described in Chapter 13, but the object of the exercise is clear: winning a majority of the electoral college. This uniquely American institution consists of representatives of each state who cast the final ballots that actually elect a president.

Table 12.5 ♦ Comparison of the Views of the Public with Those of Delegates to the 1992 Presidential Nominating Conventions[a]

The views held by delegates to the 1992 Democratic and Republican National Conventions, contrasted those views with the positions taken by average citizens who identify with the Democratic Party or the Republican Party, as well as by all the voters taken as a whole. Notice how liberal the Democratic delegates are and how conservative the Republican delegates are, compared with the other groups of less politically active citizens.

Question: "I am going to read a few statements. After each, please tell me if you agree with the statement or disagree with it, or if, perhaps, you have no opinion about the statement." (Figures show percentage who agreed with the statement.)

	ALL VOTERS	DEMOCRATIC DELEGATES	DEMOCRATS	REPUBLICAN DELEGATES	REPUBLICANS
A. Parents should have the right to send their children to any public school that they want to.	85%	56%	86%	86%	82%
B. Black people in the United States are still a long way from having the same chance in life that white people have.	53	87	57	44	43
C. The government should raise taxes now as one means of dealing with the federal budget deficit.	20	47	21	7	19
D. There is nothing wrong with using the CIA to support governments that are friendly to the United States and to undermine hostile foreign governments.	Not asked	21	Not asked	60	Not asked
E. Large corporations have too much power for the good of the country.	73	66	79	14	76
F. We should stop building nuclear power plants because of safety and waste problems.	Not asked	56	Not asked	11	Not asked
G. Taxes on businesses should be cut to stimulate the economy.	74	74	65	96	82
H. There should be a constitutional amendment outlawing abortion.	25	3	24	28	30
I. The government should institute and operate a national health care program.	79	88	92	12	66
J. The United States can meet its national security obligations with a much smaller military budget than we have today.	60	93	66	44	53

Continued

Table 12.5 ◆ Continued

Question: "I'm going to read you two statements. I'd like you to tell me if you agree more with the first statement or more with the second statement, or if, perhaps, you can't make up your mind."

	ALL VOTERS	DEMOCRATIC DELEGATES	DEMOCRATS	REPUBLICAN DELEGATES	REPUBLICANS
A. The government in Washington should see to it that everyone who wants to work has a job.	45%	62%	55%	7%	30%
B. It is not the role of government to see to it that everyone has a job.	50	29	39	87	65
No opinion.	5	9	6	6	4

Question: "Would you say you favor smaller government with fewer services or large government with many services?"

Smaller government	55%	34%	39%	97%	69%
Large government	38	45	52	2	26
No opinion	7	20	10	1	5

[a]Margins of sampling error are plus or minus 5 percentage points for figures based on delegates (Republicans and Democrats) and 3 points for figures based on all voters.

Source: Figures are from a *Washington Post* telephone poll of 511 Republican delegates from July 29 to August 7, 1992; 496 Democratic delegates from June 22 to July 8; and a *Washington Post*-ABC News telephone poll of 1,506 registered voters from July 1 to 8.

The electoral college was the result of a compromise between Framers like Roger Sherman and Elbridge Gerry, who argued for selection of the president by the Congress, and those such as James Madison, James Wilson, and Gouverneur Morris, who favored selection by direct popular election. The electoral college compromise, while not a perfect solution, had practical benefits. Since there were no mass media in those days, it is unlikely that common citizens, even reasonably informed ones, would know much about a candidate from another state. This situation could have left voters with no choice but to vote for someone from their own state, thus making it improbable that any candidate would secure a national majority. On the other hand, the **electors** (members of the electoral college) would be men of character with a solid knowledge of national politics who were able to identify, agree on, and select prominent national statesmen. There are three essentials to understanding the Founders' design of the electoral college: (1) It was meant to work *without* political parties, (2) it was designed to cover both the nominating *and* electing phases of presidential selection, and (3) it was constructed to produce a nonpartisan president.

The machinery of the electoral college was somewhat complex. Each state designated electors (through appointment or popular vote) equal in number to the sum of its representation in the House and Senate. The electors met in their respective states. Each elector has *two* votes for president, an attempt by the Founders to ensure that at

Table 12.6 ♦ Selected Contrasts in the 1992 Party Platforms

Domestic Policy

	REPUBLICANS	DEMOCRATS
Abortion	"Support human life amendment to the Constitution . . . oppose the use of public revenues for abortion"	"Stand behind the right of every woman to choose . . . regardless of ability to pay"
Gay rights	"Oppose efforts . . . to include sexual preference as a protected minority"	"Provide civil rights protection for gay men and lesbians"
Taxes	"Oppose any attempts to increase taxes"	"Forc[e] the rich to pay their fair share"
Campaign reform	"Oppose arbitrary spending limits for congressional candidates"	"We must limit overall campaign spending [for congressional candidates]"

Foreign and Defense Policy

South Africa	"Condemn all violence . . . and applaud those who seek reconciliation"	"Consider reimposing [U.S. government] sanctions against South Africa"
China	"Maintain the relationship with China so that we can effectively encourage [democratic] reform"	"Condition . . . favorable trade terms for China on respect for human rights"

Sources: 1992 Democratic and Republican Party Platforms.

---

least one candidate would secure a majority of electoral votes needed for victory. The candidate with the most votes, providing he received votes from a majority of the total number of electors, won the presidency; the candidate securing the second greatest number of votes won the vice presidency. If two candidates received the same number of votes and both had a majority of electors, the election was decided in the House of Representatives, with each state delegation acting as a unit and having one vote to cast. In the event that no candidate secured a majority, the election would also be decided in the House, with each state delegation having one vote to cast for any of the top five electoral vote-getters. In both of these scenarios a majority of the total number of states was necessary to secure victory.

But the Framers' idea of nonpartisan presidential elections lasted barely a decade, ending for the most part after George Washington's two terms. In 1796, their arrangement for presidential selection produced a president and vice president with markedly different political philosophies, which, as we noted in Chapter 7, is a circumstance unthinkable in modern times. This occurred when a tie in the electoral college sent the election into the House of Representatives, which selected Federalist John Adams as president and his political opponent, the Democratic-Republican Thomas Jefferson, as vice president.

> **Landmark Events in Voting and Elections**
>
> 1804 ♦ Twelfth amendment ratified (provides for separate election for president and vice president in Electoral College)
>
> 1830s ♦ Nominating conventions replace congressional caucuses as means of selecting presidential ticket
>
> 1850s ♦ Critical elections period: Whig Party dissolves, Republican Party develops
>
> 1890s ♦ Critical elections period: Republicans strengthen majority status and voter attachments that last until the 1930s
>
> 1932 ♦ Electorate decisively rejects Republicans and propels Democrats to power during Great Depression

The Election of 1800. By the election of 1800, both of the two emerging national parties—the Federalists and the Democratic-Republicans—nominated presidential and vice presidential candidates through their respective congressional caucuses before electors had even been chosen in the states. At the same time, the national parties were also gaining influence in the states, and this resulted in the selection of electors committed to their presidential and vice-presidential nominees. In other words, the once-deliberative electors lost their independent judgment and assumed the less important role of instructed party agents. This was, of course, a far cry from the nonpartisan system envisioned by the Founders.

The republic's fourth presidential election also revealed a flaw in the Framers' plan. In 1800, when Thomas Jefferson and Aaron Burr were, respectively, the Democratic-Republican Party's candidates for president and vice president, supporters of the Democratic-Republican Party controlled a majority of the electoral college. Accordingly, each Democratic-Republican elector in the states cast one of his two votes for Jefferson and the other one for Burr, a situation that resulted in a tie for the presidency between Jefferson and Burr, since there was no way under the constitutional arrangements for electors to earmark their votes separately for president and vice president. And even though most understood Jefferson to be the actual choice for president, the Constitution mandated that a tie be decided by the House of Representatives. And so it was, of course, and in Jefferson's favor—but only after much energy was expended to persuade lame-duck Federalists not to give Burr the presidency.

The Twelfth Amendment, ratified in 1804 and still the constitutional foundation for presidential elections, was an attempt to remedy the confusion between the selection of vice presidents and presidents that beset the election of 1800. The amendment provided for separate elections for each office, with each elector having only *one* vote to cast for each. In the event of a tie or when no candidate received a majority of the total number of electors, the election still went to the House of Representatives; now, however, each state delegation would have one vote to cast for one of the *three* candidates who had received the greatest number of electoral votes.

The electoral college modified by the Twelfth Amendment fared better than the college as originally designed, but it has not been problem-free. For example, in the 1824 election between John Quincy Adams and Andrew Jackson, neither presidential candidate secured a majority of electoral votes, once again throwing the election into the House. Despite the fact that Jackson had more electoral and popular votes than Adams, the House voted for the latter as president. On two other occasions in the nineteenth century the presidential candidate with fewer popular votes than his opponent won the presidency. In the 1876 contest between Republican Rutherford B. Hayes and Democrat Samuel J. Tilden, no candidate received a majority of electoral votes; the House decided in Hayes's favor even though he had only one more (disputed) electoral vote and 250,000 fewer popular votes than Tilden (see the "People of the Past" box below). In the election of 1888, President Grover Cleveland secured about 100,000 more popular votes than did Benjamin Harrison, yet Harrison won a majority of the electoral college vote, and with it the presidency.

PEOPLE OF THE PAST

How Rutherford B. Hayes Was Elected President in 1876

The story of Rutherford B. Hayes's ascent to the presidency is a fascinating one. It began with the dismal record of Republican President Ulysses S. Grant's administration, the corruption and incompetence of which was so well established by 1876 that the Republican Party's only hope of winning that year's presidential election was probably in running an obscure candidate. It was under these circumstances that Hayes, a little-known former governor of Ohio, received his party's nomination over James G. Blaine of Maine by only five votes on the seventh ballot at the Republican National Convention in Cincinnati. Conversely, Hayes's Democratic opponent, New York Governor Samuel J. Tilden, easily secured his party's nomination on the second ballot.

National prominence aside, both candidates considered themselves reformers. Having played a crucial role in the breakup of the Democrats' New York City machine run by party boss William M. Tweed, Tilden staked his reputation on reform. And Hayes went so far as to vow that, if elected, he would not seek a second term, ensuring that patronage would not be used to secure his reelection.

Again, however, the Grant administration's record, combined with the nation's depressed economy, made Democrat Tilden the likely victor. Accepting this seemingly inevitable conclusion, Hayes retired to bed early on election evening, and with good reason: Early, unofficial election returns indicated that Tilden had carried New York, New Jersey, Connecticut, Indiana, and most of the South, apparently giving him 203 electoral votes, 18 more than the 185 needed to win. The contest was not yet finished, though. Hayes carried most of the Western United States, and he could still win if he captured the Southern states that had Republican governors. In these states the vote leaned to Tilden but was extremely close. Not ready to concede, Republican Party operative General Daniel E. Sickles telegraphed Republican leaders in Florida, Louisiana, and South Carolina, explaining that "with your state for Hayes, he is elected," and admonishing them to "Hold your state." The Republicans responded with newfound assurance of a Hayes victory, which fueled the ensuing controversy.

In the three Southern states contacted by Sickles, Republican-dominated election boards disputed the legitimacy of many Democratic votes. During the late nineteenth century, voter fraud was rampant, as many states had no registration laws and political parties printed their own ballots. Therefore, each state had an election board charged with counting ballots and discounting fraudulent votes. In South Carolina the five-member board discarded enough allegedly fraudulent votes to give Hayes a narrow 600-vote victory. Florida's election board, too, ultimately pruned enough supposedly fraudulent votes to secure for

The Electoral College in the Twentieth Century. Although generally more stable than the previous two centuries, the twentieth century has also witnessed a number of near crises pertaining to the electoral college. For instance, in the turbulent year of 1968, the possibility that the presidential election would be decided in the House increased considerably with the entrance into the race of third-party candidate George Wallace. And the election of 1976 was almost a repeat of those nineteenth-century contests in which the candidate with fewer popular votes won the presidency: Even though Democrat Jimmy Carter received about 1.7 million more popular votes than Republican Gerald Ford, a switch of some 8,000 popular votes in Ohio and Hawaii would have secured for Ford enough votes to win the electoral college, and hence the presidency. Had Ross Perot stayed in the 1992 presidential contest without his summer hiatus, it is possible that he could have thrown the election into the House of Repre-

---

Hayes a 900-vote victory. Even in Louisiana—where Tilden ostensibly won by 6,300 votes—the election board threw out 15,000 votes, 13,000 of which were Democratic. This allowed Hayes to carry the state by 3,000 votes.

On December 6, 1876, each state's electors formally cast their ballots and sent them to Congress for official tallying. In most states the process occurred without incident. But the exceptions—Florida, Louisiana, Oregon, and South Carolina—each forwarded conflicting electoral votes to Washington. Consequently, the result of the initial Washington count included twenty disputed electoral votes—all, of course, claimed by both the candidates—along with 184 electoral votes for Tilden and 165 for Hayes.

How could this crisis be resolved? The Constitution states only that electoral votes be "directed to the President of the Senate," who "shall, in the presence of the Senate and House of Representatives, open all the certificates and the Votes shall then be counted." The document makes no mention of who decides which votes to include when a state's votes are in dispute. Enjoying a majority in the Senate, the Republicans argued that Michigan Republican Thomas W. Ferry, the president of the Senate, should decide. (Henry Wilson, who as vice president of the United States would have been the Senate's presiding officer, had died in office in 1875.) The Democrats, who controlled the House and commanded a comfortable majority in Congress as a whole, contended that the House and the Senate combined should decide. Neither side was able to persuade the other, so in the end a compromise was forged: A bipartisan commission was set up to decide the fate of the disputed electoral votes, the results of which would be final unless *both* houses of Congress vetoed them.

The parties turned next to the issue of the commission's composition, with the result being another moderate compromise. The commission would include four Supreme Court justices—two Democrats and two Republicans—who would in turn select a fifth judge. Most observers assumed the fifth judge would be Judge David Davis, an independent. Additionally, the commission would include ten members of Congress—five representatives and five senators, of whom half would be Republicans and half Democrats. Unexpectedly, however, Judge Davis refused the invitation to sit on the commission, and Republican Supreme Court Justice Joseph Bradley was chosen instead, giving the Republicans an eight-to-seven majority on the commission.

The commission's partisan colors became obvious as it decided which electoral votes to accept from the four disputed states. In all cases, the Republican majority gave Hayes the disputed electoral votes and, therefore, a 185 to 184 overall electoral college victory. Thus was the presidency awarded to Rutherford B. Hayes in 1876—despite his having received fewer popular votes than Tilden, even after accounting for voter fraud. Despite encouragement from some supporters to march on Washington and seize control of the government, Tilden accepted the results and permitted Hayes to enter the White House. But Hayes was never regarded as a legitimate occupant of 1600 Pennsylvania Avenue by many Tilden backers, and he was frequently referred to as "His Fraudulency" throughout his single term in office from 1877 to 1881.

sentatives. His support had registered from 30–36 percent in the polls for much of the spring and early summer of 1992. When he reentered the race, some of that backing had evaporated, and he finished with 19 percent of the vote and carried no states, as Figure 12.2 shows. However, Perot drained a substantial number of Republican votes from George Bush, thus splitting the GOP base. This enabled Clinton to win many normally GOP-leaning states such as Georgia, Nevada, and Montana—although he carried them with well less than a majority of the votes.

FIGURE 12-2

The States Drawn in Proportion to Their Electoral College Votes

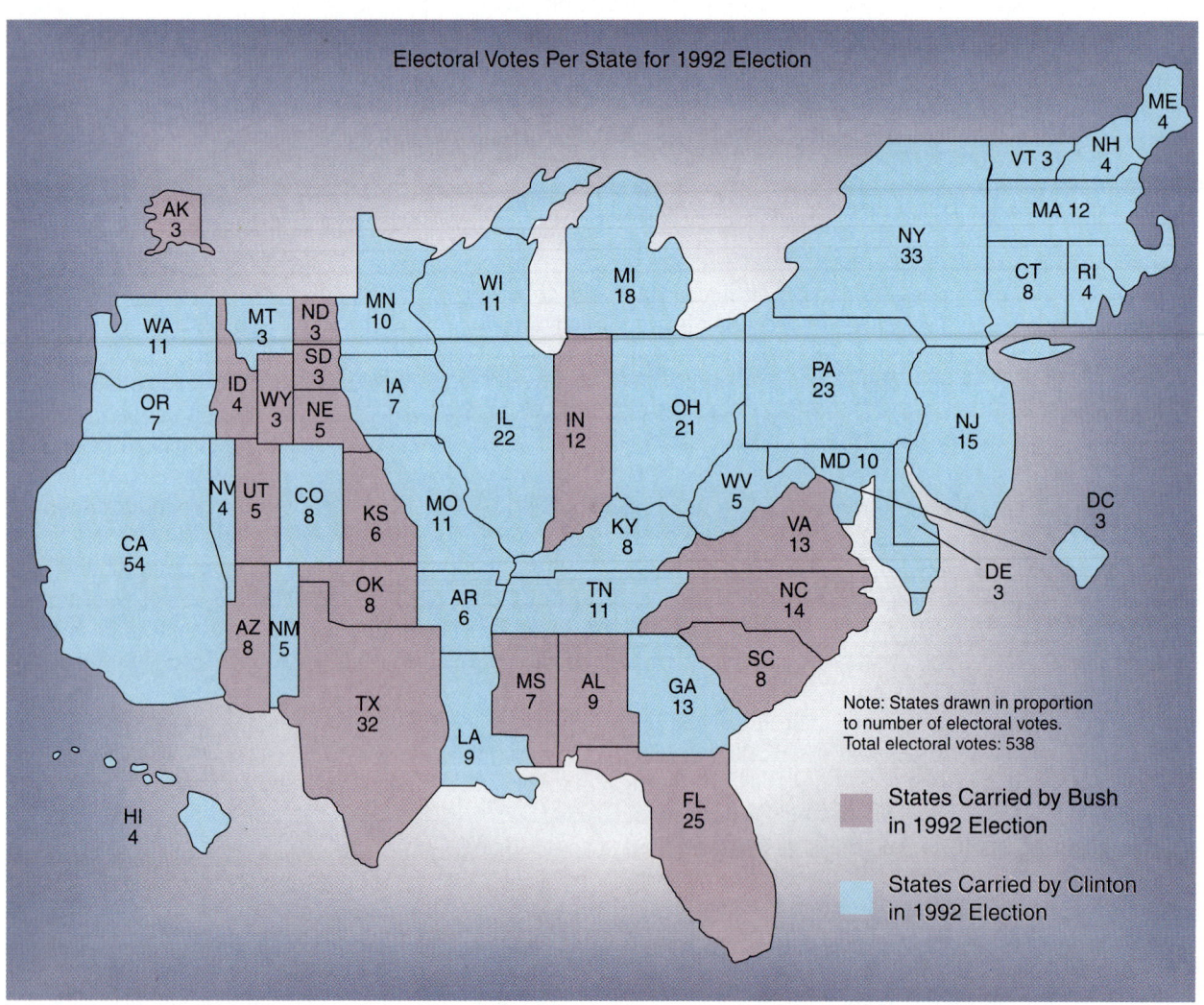

The states are pictured here with the size merited by their number of electoral college votes. Some states (such as New Jersey and California) are much larger than they appear on a regular map, while others (such as Alaska and Nevada) are much smaller.

Before the election of 1876, Cartoonist Nast was quite confident the Republican Party would easily trample Samuel Tilden and Thomas Hendricks, the Democratic nominees for president and vice president.

After the election: Nast's elephant, battered and bandaged, moans with Pyrrhus, "Another such victory and I am undone." Hayes was elected by a margin of a single electoral vote.

Superdelegates

Occasionally, a political party finds a new idea in an old one. Such is the case with the Democrats and "superdelegates." Before 1972 most delegates to a Democratic National Convention were not bound by primary results to support a particular candidate for president. This freedom to maneuver meant that conventions could be exciting and somewhat unpredictable gatherings, where last-minute events and deals could sway wavering delegates. Since 1972, however, all the Democratic conventions have been predetermined by primary elections and the party has been committed to a nominee for weeks or months prior to the convention.

Democrats attempted to add more flexibility to their 1984, 1988, and 1992 conventions and to add the "peer review" of potential nominees that used to take place when party bosses made decisions behind closed doors by allotting several hundred superdelegate slots—positions reserved for the party's high elected and appointed officials. To this point, though, superdelegates have made little practical difference, because they usually support the candidate who has won the primaries. However, if the primary results are ever split and a convention is deadlocked, superdelegates could prove to be critical in the selection of the party's presidential candidate, just as the bosses of old were.

Patterns of Presidential Elections

The electoral college results reveal more over time than simply who won the presidency. They show which party and which region(s) are coming to dominance and how voters may be changing party allegiances in response to new issues and generational changes.

Party Realignments. Usually such movements are gradual, but occasionally the political equivalent of a major earthquake swiftly and dramatically alters the landscape. During these rare events, called **party realignments,**[1] existing party affiliations are subject to upheaval: Many voters may change parties, and the youngest age group of voters may permanently adopt the label of the newly dominant party. Until recent times, at least, party realignments have been spaced about thirty-six years apart in the U.S. experience.

A major realignment is precipitated by one or more **critical elections,** which may polarize voters around new issues and personalities in reaction to crucial developments, such as a war or an economic depression. In Britain, for example, the first postwar election held in 1945 was critical, since it ushered the Labour Party into power for the first time and introduced to Britain a new interventionist agenda in the fields of economic and social welfare policies.

In the entire history of the United States, there have been six party alignments, as indicated by "Landmark Events in Voting and Elections" on page 519. Three tumultuous eras in particular have produced significant critical elections (see Figure 12-3). First, during the period leading up to the Civil War, the Whig Party gradually dissolved and the Republican Party developed and won the presidency. Second, the populist radicalization of the Democratic Party in the 1890s enabled the Republicans to greatly strengthen their majority status and make lasting gains in voter attachments. Third, the Great Depression of the 1930s propelled the Democrats to power, causing large numbers of voters to repudiate the GOP and embrace the Democratic Party. In each of these cases, fundamental and enduring alterations in the party equation resulted.

The last confirmed major realignment, then, happened in the 1928–36 period, as Republican Herbert Hoover's presidency was held to one term because of voter anger about the Depression. In 1932, Democrat Franklin D. Roosevelt swept to power as the electorate decisively rejected Hoover and the Republicans. This dramatic vote of "no confidence" was followed by substantial changes in policy by the new president, who demonstrated in fact or at least in appearance that his policies were effective. The people responded to his success, accepted his vision of society, and ratified their choice of the new president's party in subsequent presidential and congressional elections.

Simultaneously, the former majority party (Republican) reluctantly but inevitably adjusted to its new minority role. So strong was the new partisan attachment for most voters that even when short-term issues and personalities that favored the Republican Party dislodged the Democrats from power, the basic distribution of party loyalties did not shift significantly. In 1952, 1956, 1968, and 1972, then, Republicans won the presidency, but the New Deal Democratic coalition was still visible in the voting patterns, and it survived to emerge again in future elections.

The elections of 1952, 1956, 1968, and 1972 are examples of alignment-*deviating* presidential elections. In these elections, the results (the victories of Republicans Dwight D. Eisenhower and Richard M. Nixon) were at odds with what would be expected, given the underlying Democratic voting majority in the electorate at the time.

---

[1] On the subject of party realignment, see Walter Dean Burnham, *Critical Elections and the Mainsprings of American Politics* (New York: Norton, 1970); Kristi Andersen, *The Creation of a Democratic Majority* (Chicago: University of Chicago Press, 1979); and John R. Petrocik, "Realignment: New Party Coalitions and the Nationalization of the South," *Journal of Politics* 49 (May 1987): 347–375.

Presidential Elections ◆ 525

FIGURE 12-3
Electoral College Results for Three Realigning Presidential Contests

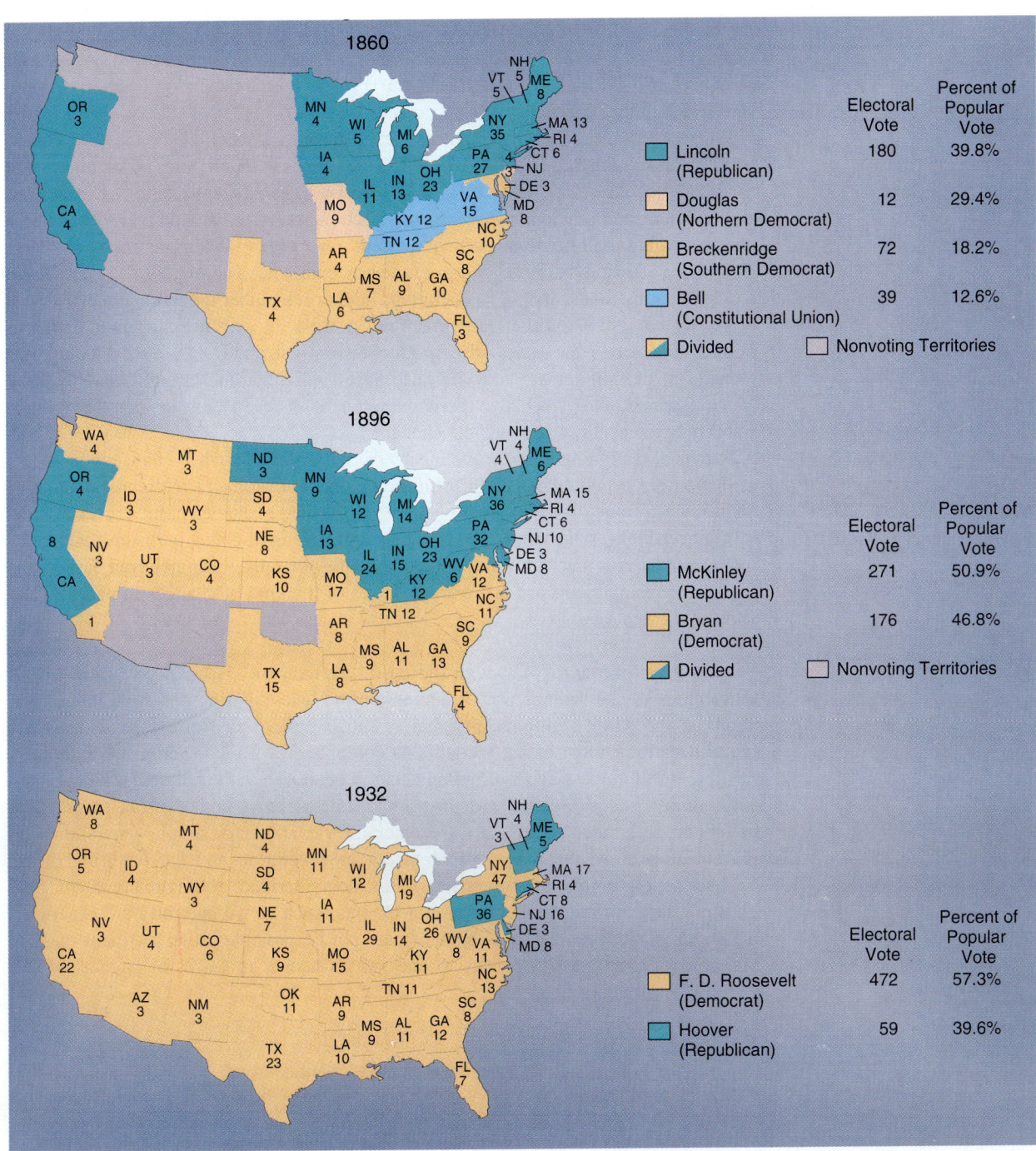

The elections of 1860, 1896, and 1932 changed the way many Americans viewed their politics and partisan alignments. The victories of Abraham Lincoln and William McKinley pushed the country in a Republican direction, while Franklin D. Roosevelt's triumph began a long period of Democratic rule.

(Eisenhower won mainly because of his war record and appealing personality, and Nixon gained the White House thanks to internal splits in the Democratic Party over the Vietnam War and racial issues.) We can contrast these four deviating elections with the alignment-*maintaining* elections of 1940, 1944, 1948, 1960, 1964, and 1976. In these six elections, the New Deal coalition prevailed in the presidential contests, as Democrats Franklin D. Roosevelt, Harry S Truman, John F. Kennedy, Lyndon B. Johnson, and Jimmy Carter won office.

With the aid of timely circumstances, realignments are accomplished in two primary ways.[2] Some voters are simply converted from one party to the other by the issues and candidates of the time. New voters may also be mobilized into action: Immigrants, young voters, and previous nonvoters may become motivated and then absorbed into a new governing majority. However vibrant and potent party coalitions may be at first, as they age, tensions increase and grievances accumulate. The majority's original reason for existing fades, and new generations neither remember the traumatic events that originally brought about the realignment nor possess the stalwart party identifications of their ancestors. New issues arise, producing conflicts that can be resolved only by a breakup of old alignments and a reshuffling of individual and group party loyalties. Viewed in historical perspective, party realignment has been a mechanism that ensures stability by controlling unavoidable change.

A critical realigning era is by no means the only occasion when changes in partisan affiliation are accommodated. In truth, every election produces realignment to some degree, since some individuals are undoubtedly pushed to change parties by events and by their reactions to the candidates. Recent research suggests that partisanship is much more responsive to current issues and personalities than had been believed earlier, and that major realignments are just extreme cases of the kind of changes in party loyalty registered every year.[3]

Secular Realignment. Although the term "realignment" is usually applied only if momentous events such as war or depression produce enduring and substantial alterations in the party coalitions, political scientists have long recognized that a more gradual rearrangement of party coalitions could occur.[4] Called **secular realignment,** this piecemeal process depends not on convulsive shocks to the political system but on slow, almost barely discernable demographic shifts—the shrinking of one party's base of support and the enlargement of the other's, for example, or simple generational replacement (that is, the dying off of the older generation and the maturing of the younger generation). A recent version of this theory, termed "rolling realignment,"[5] argues that in an era of weaker party attachments (such as we currently are experiencing), a dramatic, full-scale realignment may not be possible. Still, a critical mass of voters may be attracted for years to one party's banner in waves or streams, if that

---

[2] Barbara Farah and Helmut Norpoth, "Trends in Partisan Realignment, 1976–1986: A Decade of Waiting," paper prepared for delivery at the annual meeting of the American Political Science Association, Washington, DC, August 27–31, 1986.

[3] Morris P. Fiorina, *Retrospective Voting in American National Elections* (New Haven, CT: Yale University Press, 1981); and Charles H. Franklin and John E. Jackson, "The Dynamics of Party Identification," *American Political Science Review* 77 (1983): 957–973.

[4] See, for example, V. O. Key Jr., "A Theory of Critical Elections," *Journal of Politics* 17 (February 1955): 3–18.

[5] The less dynamic term "creeping realignment" is also sometimes used by scholars and journalists.

party's leadership and performance are consistently exemplary. Something of this nature began in Britain when Margaret Thatcher led the Conservatives to victory in 1979; thereafter, the Labour Party has lost its hold on traditional sources of support, and the party now faces a difficult road to restored political viability.

Some scholars and political observers also contend that the decline of party affiliation has in essence left the electorate *dealigned* and incapable of being realigned as long as party ties remain tenuous for so many voters. Voters shift with greater ease between the parties during de-alignment, but little permanence or intensity exists in identifications made and held so lightly. If nothing else, the obsolescence of realignment theory may be indicated by the calendar; if major realignments occur roughly every thirty-six years, then we are long overdue. The last major realignment took place between 1928 and 1936, and so the next one might have been expected in the late 1960s and early 1970s.

As the trends toward ticket-splitting, partisan independency, and voter volatility suggest, there is little question that we have been moving through an unstable and somewhat "de-aligned" period at least since the 1970s. The foremost political question today is whether de-alignment will continue (and in what form) or whether a major realignment is in the offing. Each previous de-alignment has been a precursor of realignment,[6] but realignment need not succeed dealignment, especially under modern conditions. It may be that the outlines of the Democratic New Deal coalition will continue to be seen and to prevail in U.S. politics, or that the system may be so dealigned that only short-term and transitory majority coalitions are possible. The other alternative—plausible but without hard evidence to support it—is one more to the liking of Republican activists: a full-scale or rolling realignment of the electorate that builds on the electoral successes of the Reagan and Bush years and produces a stable GOP majority.

Of course, Republican analysts attempted to convince the political world of the reality of major realignment after Ronald Reagan's decisive presidential victory in 1980, just as another contingent had tried to do following Richard M. Nixon's successes in 1968 and 1972. As evidence, GOP boosters pointed to increased levels of Republican identification, especially by the young, and to a string of presidential victories that supposedly imply a Republican "lock" on an electoral college majority.

Democrats insisted all along that the Republican claims were nothing more than wishful thinking. Resurrecting a popular advertising slogan used as a 1984 campaign retort, Democrats again asked, "Where's the beef?," noting their overwhelming edge in local offices, continuous firm control of the House of Representatives, and recapture of the Senate in 1986. The 1992 presidential election served as a vindication of sorts for these Democratic arguments—although the 43-percent victory of Bill Clinton really proves nothing except that the Republicans were too optimistic.

Clearly, major changes in the U.S. electorate have been occurring, but these changes may or may not constitute a major critical realignment of party balance. The Democrats are not the dominant party they once were, but the GOP has not obtained majority status, either. The struggle between the parties for dominance continues, and the outcome is as yet uncertain.

---

[6] See Paul Allen Beck, "The Dealignment Era in America," in Russell J. Dalton et al., *Electoral Change in Advanced Industrial Democracies: Realignment or Dealignment?* (Princeton, NJ: Princeton University Press, 1984), p. 264. See also Philip M. Williams, "Party Realignment in the United States and Britain," *British Journal of Political Science* 15 (January 1985): 97–115.

Congressional Elections

Many similar elements are present in different kinds of elections: Candidates, voters, issues, and television advertisements are constants. But there are distinctive aspects of each kind of election as well. Compared with presidential elections, congressional elections are a different animal.

First, most candidates for Congress labor in relative obscurity. While there are some celebrity nominees for Congress—television stars, sports heroes, even local TV news anchors—the vast majority of party nominees are little-known state legislators and local office holders. For them, just getting known, establishing name identification, is the biggest battle. No major-party presidential nominee need worry about this elementary stage because so much media attention is focused on the race for the White House. This is not so for most congressional contests; elections for spots in the House of Representatives receive remarkably little coverage in many states and communities.

The Incumbency Advantage

Under these circumstances, the advantages of **incumbency** (that is, already being in office) are enhanced, and a kind of electoral inertia takes hold: Those people in office tend to remain in office. Every year the average member of the U.S. House of Representatives expends about $750,000 in taxpayer funds to run the office. Much of this money directly or indirectly promotes the legislator by means of mass mailings and constituency services—the term used to describe a wide array of assistance provided by a member of Congress to voters in need (for examples, tracking a lost Social Security check, helping a veteran receive disputed benefits, or finding a summer internship for a college student). In addition to these institutional means of self-promotion, most incumbents are highly visible in their districts. They have easy access to local media, cut ribbons galore, attend important local funerals, and speak frequently at meetings and community events. Nearly a quarter of the people in an average congressional district claim to have met their representative, and about half recognize their legislator's name without prompting.

This spending and visibility pays off: reelection rates for sitting House members range well above 90 percent in most election years.

Frequently the reelection rate for senators is as high, but not always. In a "bad" year for House incumbents, "only" 88 percent will win (as in the Watergate year of 1974), but the senatorial reelection rate can drop much lower on occasion (to 60 percent in the 1980 Reagan landslide, for example). There is a good reason for this lower senatorial reelection rate. A Senate election is often a high-visibility contest; it receives much more publicity than a House race. So while House incumbents remain protected and insulated in part because few voters pay attention to their little-known challengers, a Senate-seat challenger can become well known more easily, and thus be in a better position to defeat an incumbent.

Redistricting, Scandals, and Coattails

For the relatively few incumbent members of Congress who *do* lose their reelection bids, three explanations are paramount: redistricting, scandals, and coattails. Every ten years, after the census, all congressional district lines are redrawn (in states with more than one congressperson) so that every legislator represents about the same number of

Senator Robert Byrd (D.-W.V.) making a speech. Former majority leader of the Senate, Byrd has become a master at promoting himself to his state. His pork-barrel tactics have included legislation that relocates federal offices to West Virginia, bringing lots of jobs with them for the citizens of his state.

citizens. Redistricting inevitably puts some incumbents in the same districts as other incumbents, and weakens the base of other congresspersons by adding territory favorable to the opposition party. In 1992 ten incumbents were paired together—five therefore lost—and about a dozen more incumbents were defeated in part because of unfavorable redistricting.

Scandals come in many varieties in this age of the investigative press. The old standby of financial impropriety (bribery and payoffs, for example) has been supplemented by other forms of career-ending incidents, such as personal improprieties (sexual escapades, for instance). The power of incumbency is so strong, however, that many legislators survive even serious scandal to win reelection. Congressman Barney Frank (D.-Mass.), for instance, an acknowledged homosexual, hired a male prostitute who ran a prostitution service out of Frank's apartment in Washington. This situation became public knowledge in 1989. Though Frank claimed ignorance of the man's activities, he admitted having some of his parking tickets "fixed." Despite the sordid nature of this arrangement, most of Frank's constituents were satisfied with his representation of them and easily reelected him in 1990, and again in 1992.

The defeat of a congressional incumbent can also occur as a result of the presidential coattail effect. As Table 12.7 shows, successful presidential candidates usually carry into office a substantial number of congressional candidates of the same party in the year of their election. Notice the overall decline in the strength of the coattail effect in modern times, however, as party identification has weakened and the powers and perks of incumbency have grown. Whereas Harry S Truman's party gained seventy-six House seats and nine additional Senate seats in 1948, George Bush's party actually

Table 12.7 ♦ Congressional Election Results, 1948–1992

GAIN (+) OR LOSS (–) FOR PRESIDENT'S PARTY

President/Year	Presidential Election Years House	Senate	Year	Off-Year Elections House	Senate
Truman (D): 1948	+76	+9	1950	–29	–6
Eisenhower (R): 1952	+24	+2	1954	–18	–1
Eisenhower (R): 1956	–2	0	1958	–48	–13
Kennedy (D): 1960	–20	–2	1962	–4	+3
Johnson (D): 1964	+38	+2	1966	–47	–4
Nixon (R): 1968	+7	+5	1970	–12	+2
Nixon (R): 1972	+13	–2	Ford: 1974	–48	–5
Carter (D): 1976	+2	0	1978	–15	–3
Reagan (R): 1980	+33	+12	1982	–26	+1
Reagan (R): 1984	+15	–2	1986	–5	–8
Bush (R): 1988	–3	–1	1990	–9	–1
Clinton (D): 1992	–10	0	1994	–52	–9*

*Includes the switch from Democrat to Republican of Alabama U.S. Senator Richard Shelby.

> ## Voting Rights
>
> Both the Civil Rights Act of 1964 and the Voting Rights act of 1965 were intended to guarantee voting rights to African Americans nearly a century after passage of the Fifteenth Amendment. Since 1965, African-American voters have used their strength at the ballot box to elect black officials at all levels. Only seventy African Americans held public office in the eleven Southern states covered by the Act in 1965; by the early 1980s more than 2,500 held elected office in those states.
>
> Today, most Voting Rights Act cases deal not with bars to voting by African Americans but with the drawing of election lines. As amended in 1982, the Voting Rights Act not only prohibits state legislatures from diluting African-American voting strength by distributing black voters among white districts or packing them into one black district, it also *requires* states to create as many African-American districts as possible. But, as discussed in Chapter 6, the constitutionality of this provision is under serious legal question.
>
> The redrawing of election-district lines comes under careful scrutiny after each national census. Most Southern states must have all revisions in their districts "pre-cleared" by the U.S. Justice Department, which is charged with enforcing the Voting Rights Act. After the 1980 and 1990 censuses, the Republican-controlled Justice Department insisted that the maximum number of African-American districts be drawn, recognizing that the more black districts there are, the more likely it will be to gain Republican districts elsewhere in a state (since 90 percent of African Americans are Democrats).
>
> In 1980, not only African Americans but Hispanics, too, closely watched the redistricting process. In 1981, for example, the nation's largest Hispanic organization, League of United Latin American Citizens (LULAC) revived its political action and played an active role along with the Mexican American Legal Defense Fund (MALDEF) (See pp. 191–199) to get additional Hispanic seats, especially in Texas, which experienced a spectacular growth in its Hispanic population.
>
> The results of the 1990 census have given rise to numerous lawsuits. African Americans, however, are no longer at the forefront of this movement. White Republicans are challenging the new "black" districts (see p. 208). And throughout the Southwest, Hispanic voters are increasingly going to court to protect their voting rights, which they frequently see as diluted by unfavorable drawing of legislative district lines by state legislatures.

lost three House seats and one Senate berth in 1988, despite Bush's handsome 54 percent majority. The gains can be minimal even in presidential landslide reelection years such as 1972 (Nixon) and 1984 (Reagan). Occasionally, though, when the issues are emotional and the voters' desire for change is strong enough, as in Reagan's original 1980 victory, the coattail effect can still be substantial.

Off-Year Elections

Elections in the middle of presidential terms—**off-year elections**—present a different threat to incumbents. This time it is the incumbents *of the president's party* who are most in jeopardy. Just as the presidential party usually *gains* seats in presidential election years, it usually *loses* seats in off years. The problems and tribulations of governing normally cost a president some popularity, alienate key groups, or cause the public to want to send the president a message of one sort or another. An economic downturn or a scandal can underline and expand this circumstance, as the Watergate scandal of 1974 and the recession of 1982 demonstrated.

What is most apparent from the off-year statistics of Table 12.7, however, is the frequent tendency of voters to punish the president's party much more severely in the sixth year of an eight-year presidency (1958, 1966, 1974).[7] After only two years voters are still willing to "give the guy a chance," but after six years voters are often restless for change. Finally, notice in the table that Senate elections are less inclined to follow these rules than are House elections. The idiosyncratic nature of Senate contests is due to both their intermittent scheduling (only one-third of the seats come up for election every two years) and the existence of well-funded celebrity candidates who can sometimes swim against whatever political tide is rising. Also worth remembering is that midterm elections in recent history have a much lower voter turnout than presidential elections. As Figure 12-4 shows, a midterm election may draw only 35 to 40 percent of adult Americans to the polls, while a presidential contest attracts 50–55 percent.

---

[7] The Kennedy–Johnson years (1961–1969) and the Nixon–Ford years (1969–1977) are each considered an eight-year unit for our purposes here.

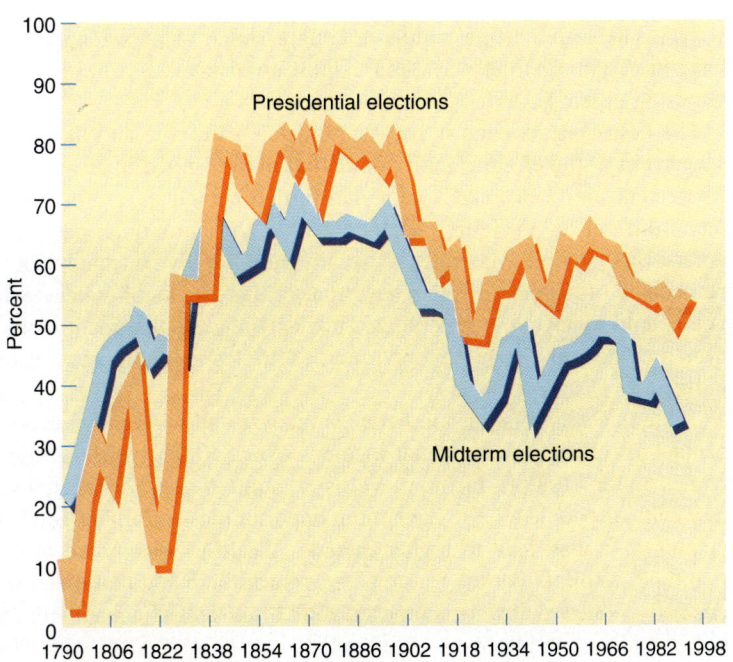

FIGURE 12-4

Voter Turnout in American Presidential and Midterm Congressional Elections

Voter turnouts have varied dramatically in the course of U.S. history, but since the 1830s, presidential elections have always drawn more voters to the polls than midterm congressional elections.

Source: Adapted from Harold W. Stanley and Richard G. Niemi, *Vital Statistics on American Politics*, 3rd ed. (Washington: CQ Press, 1992), Figure 3–1, p. 85.

532 ❖ Chapter 12 Voting and Elections

In November, 1994, Iran-*Contra* scandal figure Oliver North narrowly lost a U.S. Senate seat to Virginia's incumbent Democrat Charles Robb. North received 43 percent of the vote to Robb's 46 percent. An independent Republican candidate, Marshall Coleman, garnered the remaining 11 percent.

Voting Behavior

Whether they are casting ballots in congressional or presidential elections, voters behave in certain distinct ways and exhibit unmistakable patterns to political scientists who study them.

The first clear division is between citizens who vote and those who do not. About 40 percent of the eligible adult population in the United States vote regularly, whereas 25 percent are occasional voters. Thirty-five percent rarely or never vote. There are many differences, including socioeconomic and attitudinal, between voters and nonvoters. First, people who vote are usually more highly educated than nonvoters. A high percentage of registered voters have four or more years of college, whereas many nonvoters tend to have less schooling. This fact suggests that institutions of higher education provide citizens with opportunities to learn about and become interested in politics.

There is also a relationship between income and voting. A considerably higher percentage of citizens with annual incomes over $40,000 vote than do citizens with incomes under $10,000. Income level is, to some degree, connected to education level, as wealthier people tend to have more opportunities for higher education and more education also may lead to higher income. Wealthy citizens are also more likely than poor ones to think that the "system" works for them and that their votes make a difference. By contrast, lower-income citizens often feel alienated from politics, possibly believing that conditions will remain the same no matter for whom they vote.

There is also a correlation between age and voter participation rates. A much higher percentage of citizens age thirty and older vote than do citizens younger than thirty, although voter turnout decreases over the age of seventy, primarily because of physical infirmity, which makes it difficult to get to the polling location. Regrettably, less than half of the eligible eighteen- to twenty-four-year age group is even registered to vote. The most plausible reason for this is that younger people are more mobile; they have not put down roots in a community. Because voter registration is not automatic, people who relocate have to make an effort to register.

Another voter difference is related to race: Whites vote more regularly than do blacks. This is due in part to the relative income and educational levels of the two racial groups. African Americans tend to be poorer and have less formal education than whites, and, as mentioned earlier, both of these are factors in voter turnout. Significantly, though, highly educated and wealthier African Americans tend to participate in elections to a *greater* degree than their white counterparts.

Race also explains why the South has long had a lower turnout than the rest of the country (see Figure 12.5). In the wake of Reconstruction, the Southern states made it extremely difficult for African Americans to register to vote, and only a small percentage of the eligible African-American population was registered throughout the South. The Voting Rights Act of 1965 changed this situation, and gradually the South's voting participation has approached that of the rest of the nation, although the region still lags behind.

Although socioeconomic factors undoubtedly weigh heavily in voter participation rates, an interest in politics must also be included as an important factor. Many citizens who vote have grown up in families interested and active in politics, and they in turn

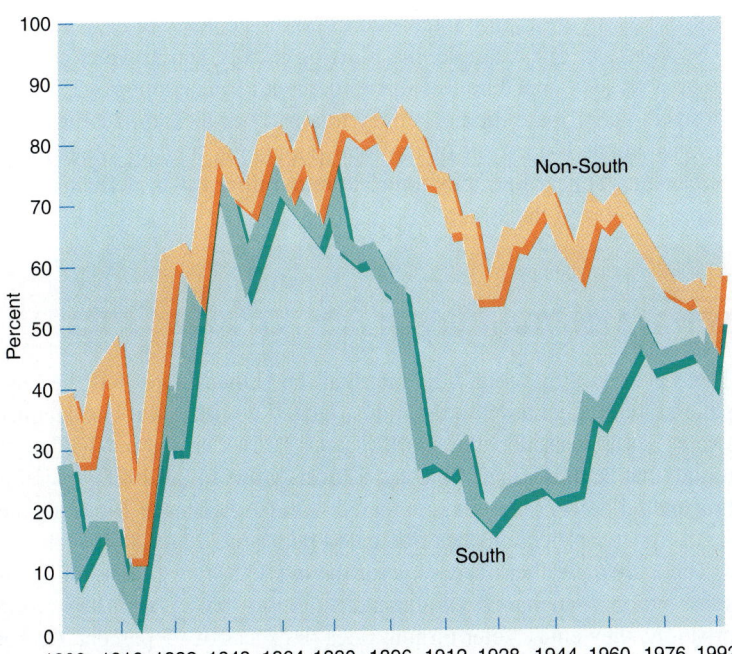

Source: Harold W. Stanley and Richard G. Niemi, *Vital Statistics on American Politics*, 4th ed. (Washington: CQ Press, 1993), Figure 3–2, p. 86.

FIGURE 12-5

The South Versus the Non-South for Presidential Voter Turnout

Mainly because of racially discriminatory registration restrictions, the South had dramatically lower voter turnout than the rest of the nation from the post–Civil War period until the 1960s, when civil rights laws (especially the Voting Rights Act of 1965) eliminated much of the turnout difference. Note that voter participation in the South still remains somewhat below that of the other regions.

In 1992, the "Rock the Vote" campaign (partially funded—and heavily promoted—by MTV) set out to register record numbers of young voters who traditionally are among the lowest demographics of voter turnout.

stimulate their children to take an interest. Conversely, many nonvoters simply do not care about politics or the outcome of elections, never having been taught their importance at a younger age.

People who are highly interested in politics constitute only a small minority of the U.S. populace. For example, the most politically active Americans—party and issue-group activists—make up less than 5 percent of the country's 250 million people. And those who contribute time or money to a party or a candidate during a campaign make up only about 10 percent of the total population. On the other hand, although these percentages appear low, they translate into millions of Americans who contribute more than just votes to the system.

Why Is Voter Turnout So Low?

There is no getting around the fact that the United States has the lowest voter participation rate of any nation in the industrialized world, and it has declined somewhat (see "Voter Turnout around the World," page 535). Only about half of the eligible electorate (that is, those age eighteen and over) voted in the 1988 general presidential election and 55 percent in 1992, compared with 62 percent in 1960. In contrast, turnout for British postwar elections has fluctuated between 72 and 84 percent.

There are a number of reasons for the low U.S. rates. First, unlike the United States, some nations—such as Australia and Belgium—have *compulsory* voting laws; not surprisingly, they enjoy voter turnout rates in excess of 95 percent. (In some nations, citizens pay a tax if they do *not* vote.) Second, many nations automatically register all of their citizens to vote. In the United States, however, citizens must jump the extra hurdle of voter registration. Indeed, it is no coincidence that voter participation rates

> ## Voter Turnout around the World
>
> Almost all democracies around the globe have a higher percentage of voter turnout than the United States, as this table shows. Only Switzerland has a voter turnout lower than that of the United States. One reason for a poor U.S. showing is our requirement that citizens *register* to vote before being able to participate in elections. In all other nations listed in this table (except for France) citizens are *automatically* registered by the government or, in the cases of Australia and New Zealand, are compelled by law both to register and to vote.
>
> ### PERCENT OF AVERAGE TURNOUT IN NATIONAL ELECTIONS, BY COUNTRY[a]
>
> | | |
> |---|---|
> | Italy, 94 | Netherlands, 82 |
> | Austria, 88 | Norway, 81 |
> | Belgium, 88 | France, 77 |
> | Sweden, 88 | Ireland, 77 |
> | Denmark, 87 | United Kingdom, 75 |
> | Australia, 84 | Japan, 73 |
> | West Germany, 84 | Canada, 67 |
> | New Zealand, 84 | United States, 54 |
> | Finland, 82 | Switzerland, 43 |
> | Israel, 82 | |
>
> [a]Either all parliamentary elections or, for France and the United States, presidential elections held from 1970 to 1979.
>
> *Source:* Robert W. Jackman, "Political Institutions and Voter Turnout in the Industrial Democracies," *American Political Science Review* 81 (June 1987): 420.

dropped markedly after reformers pushed through strict voter registration laws in the early part of the twentieth century. Also a factor in the United States' low voter turnout are stringent absentee ballot laws. Many states, for instance, require citizens to apply in person for absentee ballots, a burdensome requirement given that one's inability to be present in his or her home state is often the reason for absentee bailoting in the first place. Another explanation for low voter turnout in this country are the sheer number and frequency of elections, which few if any other democracies can match. Yet an election cornucopia is the inevitable result of federalism and the separation of powers, which result in layers of often separate elections on the local, state, and national levels.

Although some of the reasons for low voter participation are due to the institutional factors we have just reviewed, voter attitudes play an equally important part. As noted previously, alienation afflicts some voters, and others are just plain apathetic—possibly because of a lack of pressing issues in a particular year, satisfaction with the status

In her 1994 California Gubernatorial campaign, Kathleen Brown failed to extend her family's dynasty in that state, losing to incumbent Governor Pete Wilson. Both Brown's father and brother are former Governors of California.

quo, or uncompetitive (even uncontested) elections. Furthermore, many citizens may be turned off by the quality of campaigns in a time when petty issues and personal mudslinging are more prevalent than ever.

Reformers have suggested many ideas to increase voter turnout in the United States. Always on the list is raising the political awareness of young citizens, a reform that inevitably must involve our nation's schools. No less important, and perhaps simpler to achieve, are the institutional reforms, though many of these reforms, if enacted, may result in only a marginal increase in turnout.

To begin, many observers propose making it easier for citizens to register to vote. The typical thirty-days-before-an-election registration deadline could be shortened to a week or ten days. After all, most people become more interested in voting as Election Day nears. Better yet, all U.S. citizens could be registered automatically at the age of eighteen. Absentee ballots could also be made easier to obtain by eliminating the in-person requirement. A more concise and clear ballot might help, too. A short ballot, listing only a few offices up for election, keeps a sharper election focus for easily distracted citizens; the long ballot, on which few offices are appointive and a dozen or more statewide posts are elective, pleases populists but usually results in uninformed voting.

Another worthwhile idea is the proposal to make Election Day a holiday. Besides removing an obstacle to voting (the busy workday), this might focus more voter attention on the contests in the critical final hours. Finally, reformers have long argued that strengthening the political parties would increase voter turnout, because parties have historically been the organizations in the United States best suited for and most successful at mobilizing citizens to vote. During the late 1800s and early 1900s, the country's "Golden Age" of powerful political parties, one of their primary activities was getting out the vote on Election Day. And even today, the parties' Election Day get-out-the-vote drives increase voter turnout by as many as several million in national contests.

Other ideas to increase voter turnout are less practical or feasible. For example, holding fewer elections might sound appealing, but it is difficult to see how this could be accomplished without diluting many of the central tenets of federalism and separation of powers that the Founders believed essential to the protection of liberty.

In 1993 a major advance toward easier registration was achieved with the passage by Congress of the so-called "motor voter" bill, which required states to permit individuals to register by mail, not just in person. The law, strongly backed by President Clinton, also allows citizens to register to vote when they visit any motor vehicles office, public assistance agency, or military recruitment division.

A New Voting Pattern: Ticket-Splitting

Among citizens who do cast their ballots, an important voting trend cannot be ignored. Citizens have been increasingly deserting their party affiliations in the polling booths. The practice of ticket-splitting—voting simultaneously for candidates of both parties for different offices—has soared dramatically.

The evidence of this development abounds. As already reviewed in this chapter, Republican presidential landslides in 1956, 1972, 1980, and 1984 were accompanied by the election of substantial Democratic majorities in the House of Representatives.

Divided government, with the presidency held by one party and one or both houses of Congress held by the other party, has never been as frequent in U.S. history as it has been recently. From 1920 to 1944 about 15 percent of the congressional districts voted for presidential and House candidates of different parties, but from 1960 to 1988, at least 25 percent of the districts cast split tickets in any presidential year, and in 1984 nearly 50 percent of the districts did so. Similarly, at the statewide level only 17 percent of the states electing governors in presidential years between 1880 and 1956 elected state and national executives from different parties. Yet from 1960 to 1992 almost 40 percent of states holding simultaneous presidential and gubernatorial elections recorded split results. (In 1992 the proportion was somewhat lower, just 25 percent.)

These percentages actually understate the degree of ticket-splitting by individual voters. The Gallup Poll has regularly asked its respondents, "For the various political offices, did you vote for all the candidates of one party, that is, a straight ticket, or did you vote for the candidates of different parties [ticket-splitting]?" Since 1968 the proportion of voters who have ticket-split in presidential years has consistently been around 60 percent of the total.[8] Other polls and researchers have found reduced straight-ticket balloting and significant ticket-splitting at all levels of elections, especially since 1952.

Not surprisingly, the intensity of party affiliation is a major determinant of a voter's propensity to split the ticket. Strong party identifiers are the most likely to cast a straight-party ballot; pure independents are the least likely. Somewhat greater proportions of ticket-splitters are found among high-income and better-educated citizens, but there is little difference in the distribution by gender or age. Blacks exhibit the highest straight-party rate of any population subgroup; about three-quarters of all black voters stay in the Democratic Party column from the top to the bottom of the ballot.

There are a number of explanations for the modern increase in ticket-splitting, many of them similar to the perceived causes of the dip in party identification levels (see Chapter 11). The growth of issue-oriented politics, the mushrooming of single-interest groups, the greater emphasis on candidate-centered personality politics, and broader-based education are all often cited. A strong independent presidential candidacy such as Ross Perot's also helps to loosen party ties among many voters. So, too, does the marked gain in the value of incumbency. Thanks in part to the enormous fattening of congressional constituency services, incumbent U.S. representatives and senators have been able to attract a steadily increasing share of the other party's identifiers.[9]

---

[8] Cited in Everett Carll Ladd Jr., "On Mandates, Realignments, and the 1984 Presidential Election," *Political Science Quarterly* 100 (Spring 1985): 23.

[9] Thomas E. Mann and Raymond E. Wolfinger, "Candidates and Parties in Congressional Elections," *American Political Science Review* 74 (September 1980): 617–632; Albert D. Cover, "One Good Term Deserves Another: The Advantage of Incumbency in Congressional Elections," *American Journal of Political Science* 21 (August 1977): 535; and Gary C. Jacobson, *The Politics of Congressional Elections,* 2nd ed. (Boston: Little, Brown, 1987), p. 86.

Toward Reform

Most proposals for electoral reform center on the electoral college, starting with the *faithless elector*—that is, the elector who does not vote for the candidate to whom he or she is committed. In the twentieth century alone, electors have been faithless in seven elections: 1948, 1956, 1960, 1968, 1972, 1976, and 1988. In 1960 Alabama and Mississippi harkened back to the original design of the electoral college by electing a considerable number of "unpledged" electors, rather than supporting either Democrat John F. Kennedy or Republican Richard M. Nixon.

Electors in about half the states are required by law to cast a ballot for the presidential and vice-presidential candidates who win the most votes in the state. While some legal scholars have questioned the constitutionality of these laws, the Supreme Court has upheld them, though the laws are obviously difficult to enforce. Any law to remedy the problem of the faithless elector would therefore have to be in the form of a constitutional amendment, either mandating that electors vote for the candidate who wins a state's popular vote or removing altogether the office of elector and automatically awarding a state's electoral votes to the winner of its popular vote.

Other proposals for reforming the electoral college include getting rid of it altogether—that is, holding a direct national election. Such a change would have three major consequences: (1) The popular vote would be the only determinant for winning the presidency. (2) The slight advantage given to states with small populations under the electoral college would be eliminated. Currently, each state (from lightly populated Wyoming, Vermont, and populous Rhode Island to California) is given the same two additional electoral votes on top of the votes it receives to match the number of representatives it sends to the U.S. House of Representatives. (3) More minor-party candidates would run, since they would no longer be encumbered by the winner-take-all rules of the states and could accumulate votes nationally. In order to preclude a candidate with only a small plurality of the popular vote from winning the election, however, any reasonable plan for a direct national contest would have to stipulate that the winner must receive a certain percentage of the popular vote (perhaps 40 percent), with a runoff election necessary between the top two contenders if no one secures that proportion. A constitutional amendment proposing this reform was passed by a wide margin in the House of Representatives in 1969. However, in a vote ten years later, the Senate failed to come up with the two-thirds majority needed to send the proposal on to the states for ratification.

Defenders of the electoral college concede its problems, but argue that they are not serious enough to warrant change. Moreover, many observers still see value in the electoral college. To begin with, the electoral college helps preserve the contours of federalism by stressing states as the building blocks of presidential victories. Its elimination would hurt less populous states, which enjoy slight overrepresentation. Also, the electoral college magnifies the victory of presidents, helping them claim a mandate to govern. For example, in 1992 Bill Clinton received only a 43 percent plurality of the popular vote, but his landslide 100-vote edge in the electoral college gave him a needed boost as he prepared to take the reins of leadership. Finally, opponents of reform argue against an important component of direct popular elections: the *recount* (another count and tally of all votes cast on election day). In extremely close elections, such as the 1960 contest between John F. Kennedy and Richard M. Nixon, recounts in a few states with sizable blocs of electoral votes are inevitable, but at least under the electoral college system, recounts can be limited to the states in which the numbers are close. With a direct popular election, where only the national vote total matters, a close count would mean the daunting task of recounting every ballot in the nation.

Overall, although individual elections may sometimes be predictable, the electoral system in the United States is anything but static. New generations—and party-changers in older generations—constantly remake the political landscape. At least every other presidential election brings a change of administration and a focus on new issues. Every other year at least a few fresh personalities and perspectives infuse the Congress, as newly elected U.S. senators and representatives claim mandates and seek to shake up the established order. Each election year the same tumult and transformation can be observed in the fifty states and in thousands of localities.

The welter of elections may seem like chaos, but from this chaos come the order and often explosive productivity of a democratic society. For the source of all change in the United States, just as Hamilton and Madison predicted, is the individual citizen who goes to the polls and casts a ballot.

In most societies, there are an insatiable itch for change and a desire to better the conditions of life. In authoritarian countries, repression and violent revolution are the only avenues open to check or provide for change. In democratic nations such as the United States, however, the voters have the opportunity to orchestrate a peaceful revolution every time they visit their polling places.

Elections take the pulse of average people and gauge their hopes and fears; the study of elections permits us to trace the course of the American revolution over 200 years of voting. Much good and some harm have been accomplished by this explosion of balloting—but all of it has been done, as Hamilton insisted, "on the solid basis of THE CONSENT OF THE PEOPLE."

Summary

An old bumper sticker from the cynical 1970s captures one view of voting: "I don't vote—it only encourages 'em." Fortunately, most Americans, though not enough, reject this perspective, and understand why and how elections serve their interests. As we have reviewed, however, the U.S. electoral system is multilayered and often complex. In an effort to explain it, we covered these points in this chapter:

1. Regular elections guarantee mass political action and governmental accountability. They also confer legitimacy on regimes better than any other method of change.

2. When it comes to elections, the United States has an embarrassment of riches. There are various types of primary elections in the country, as well as general elections, initiatives, referenda, and recall elections. In presidential elections, primaries are sometimes replaced by caucuses in which party members choose a candidate in a closed meeting, but recent years have seen fewer caucuses and more primaries.

3. After the primary and caucus season finishes, parties hold their national conventions to choose candidates—who generally have been determined in advance by the nominating elections—for the general election.

4. In the general election that follows, statewide popular votes are used to determine the composition of the electoral college, which ultimately makes the formal choice of a president. The electoral college is a controversial institution, and frequent proposals for reform of it are aired. But it also has its staunch defenders, especially the lightly populated states that benefit from it.

5. Voters tend to vote retrospectively—that is, they judge candidates based on their past performance, or on the past performance of the party in power.

6. There are voting patterns over time that are evident to election scholars. Approximately every thirty-two or thirty-six years, voters have realigned into coalitions that redefine the parties and their candidates. These major realignments are precipitated by one or more

critical elections, which polarize voters around new issues and personalities in reaction to crucial developments, such as wars or depressions. We are long overdue for a critical election, but it may not be possible in an age of lesser party loyalties.

7. Voter participation tends to follow certain patterns: the more educated, affluent, and older the citizens are, the more often they vote; also, whites tend to vote more often than non-whites; Southerners vote less often than non-Southerners.

8. The incumbency advantage in congressional elections is so significant and powerful that relatively few sitting legislators are ever defeated for reelection. Those who do lose usually are victims of redistricting, scandal, or presidential coattail effects.

9. The United States has exceptionally low voter turnout. The reasons include voter registration and absentee ballot barriers, alienation, and voter indifference (due to everything from apathy to satisfaction). Remedies for low turnout are many, ranging from an election day holiday to better civic education in the schools.

10. The practice of ticket-splitting has become commonplace during an era of issue-oriented, candidate-centered politics with weaker partisan loyalties. One consequence is the greater likelihood of split party control of the executive and legislative branches both in Washington and the state capitals.

Key Terms

electorate
mandate
retrospective judgment
primary elections
closed primaries
open primaries
blanket primary
white primary
runoff primary
general elections
regional primaries
uncommitted delegates
unit rule
superdelegates
electors
party realignments
critical elections
secular realignment
incumbency
off-year elections

Suggested Readings

Asher, Herbert B. *Presidential Elections and American Politics,* 4th ed. Chicago: Dorsey Press, 1988.

Bartels, Larry M. *Presidential Primaries and the Dynamics of Public Choice.* Princeton, NJ: Princeton University Press, 1988.

Berelson, Bernard R., Paul F. Lazarsfeld, and William N. McPhee. *Voting: A Study of Opinion Formation in a Presidential Campaign.* Chicago: University of Chicago Press, 1954.

Burnham, Walter Dean. *Critical Elections and the Mainsprings of American Politics.* New York: Norton, 1970.

Campbell, Angus, Philip E. Converse, Warren E. Miller, and Donald E. Stokes. *The American Voter.* New York: Wiley, 1960.

Ceaser, James W. *Presidential Selection: Theory and Development.* Princeton, NJ: Princeton University Press, 1979.

Fiorina, Morris P. *Retrospective Voting in American National Elections.* New Haven, CT: Yale University Press, 1981.

Jacobson, Gary C. *The Politics of Congressional Elections,* 2nd ed. Boston: Little, Brown, 1987.

———. *The Electoral Origins of Divided Government.* Boulder, CO: Westview Press, 1990.

Kelley, Stanley Jr. *Interpreting Elections.* Princeton, NJ: Princeton University Press, 1983.

Key, V. O. Jr., with the assistance of Milton C. Cummings. *The Responsible Electorate.* Cambridge, MA: Harvard University Press, 1966.

Nie, Norman H., Sidney Verba, and John R. Petrocik. *The Changing American Voter.* Cambridge, MA: Belknap Press of Harvard University, 1966.

Polsby, Nelson W., and Aaron Wildavsky. *Presidential Elections: Contemporary Strategies of American Electoral Politics,* 7th ed. New York: Free Press, 1988.

Wayne, Stephen J. *The Road to the White House,* 2nd ed. New York: St. Martin's Press, 1984.

People will enter into the public service under circumstances which cannot fail to produce a temporary affection at least to their constituents. There is in every breast a sensibility to marks of honor, of favor, of esteem, and of confidence, which, apart from all considerations of interest, is some pledge for grateful and benevolent returns.

James Madison
Federalist No. 57

In this passage Madison expresses his belief that public servants will be held in high esteem and honor by the constituents who have elected them—at least for a while—and that those public servants will in return be true to the voters who put them in office.

CHAPTER 13

The Campaign Process

AT THE STARTING BLOCK: AMBITION AND STRATEGY
THE STRUCTURE OF A CAMPAIGN
THE CANDIDATE OR THE CAMPAIGN: WHICH DO WE VOTE FOR?
MODERN CAMPAIGN CHALLENGES
BRINGING IT TOGETHER: THE 1992 PRESIDENTIAL
CAMPAIGN AND ELECTION
TOWARD REFORM

What might James Madison have said about the relentlessly vicious presidential and congressional campaigns of recent years? Of course, even in his day, politics could get down and dirty, with gossip and slander ruling the day. But Madison could not have conceived of television, much less negative attack commercials used to sully the reputations of all contenders in modern campaigns—so we can forgive him for assuming that every winner is awarded the esteem of his or her constituents. Yet in another sense Madison is correct. Each victorious candidate manages to obtain the votes of a plurality of those people going to the polls on Election Day. The candidate accomplishes this personal triumph by means of the campaign, the process of seeking and winning votes in the run-up to an election.

So far we have focused on the election decision itself and have said little about the campaign conducted prior to the balloting. Although modern electioneering is advanced, with dazzling technologies and strategies used to attract voters, its basic purpose is primitive: one person asking another for support, an approach unchanged since the dawn of democracy.

The art of campaigning involves the science of polls, the planning of sophisticated mass mailings, and the coordination of electronic telephone banks to reach voters. More important, it also involves the diplomatic skill of unifying disparate individuals and groups to achieve a fragile but election-winning majority. How candidates perform this exquisitely difficult task is the subject of this chapter. First we examine how campaigns are organized, with a special eye on media—both the press and the separate television advertising that is so dominant today. The money chase—the ways in which candidates raise and spend the enormous sums necessary to win office—is discussed in some detail. Last, an extended look at the ins and outs of the 1992 presidential election attempts to bring together the main lessons of both Chapters 12 and 13.

543

Appealing to various groups: During the first week of March 1992, Governor Bill Clinton campaigned hard in Florida. A densely populated state with a wide range of voters, Florida has been a key early contest for several recent election cycles. On March 4 in Miami, Clinton reiterated a pledge for tax cuts for working people, a position that helped him gain a plurality of both black and white Democratic voters in the statewide contest on March 10.

At the Starting Block: Ambition and Strategy

In Federalist No. 57 James Madison suggests one of the vital motivations that lead candidates to seek public office: the desire for "marks of honor" and "esteem." Fortunately for U.S. democracy, a fair number of people find the often intangible rewards of public service to be sufficient inducement to enter the public arena. They are willing to put up with abuse from citizens, criticism from the press, invasion of their privacy, and frequently a lessening of income in order to win the honor of office. Despite the common notion that "the office seeks the man or woman," it is personal *ambition* that leads most candidates to the starting gate.[1] The ambition is not always selfish. In addition to a desire for power, a candidate may wish to push an issue or cause dear to his or her heart.

Whatever their motivation, candidates quickly recognize the realities of running for office. The candidate's campaign must be geared to appeal to both rank-and-file voters and the leaders of various groups and voting blocs (such as business, labor, and key ethnic populations). The candidate must find issues that motivate voters and must take defensible stands on the controversies of the day. Unavoidably, the candidate must also raise large sums of money in order to compete, as we discuss later.

The Structure of a Campaign

A campaign for high office (such as the presidency, a governorship, or a U.S. Senate seat) is a highly complex effort akin to running a multimillion-dollar business, while campaigns for local offices are usually less complicated mom-and-pop operations. But

---

[1] See Alan Ehrenhalt, *The United States of Ambition* (New York: Random House, 1990).

"Next time, why don't you run? You're a well-known figure, people seem to like you, and you haven't had an original idea in years."

all campaigns, no matter what their size, have certain aspects in common. Indeed, each campaign really consists of several campaigns that are run simultaneously, including the following:

1. The **nomination campaign.** The target is the party elite, the leaders and activists who choose nominees in primaries or conventions. Party leaders are concerned with electability, while activists are often ideologically and issue oriented, so a candidate must appeal to both bases.
2. The **general election campaign.** A far-sighted candidate never forgets the ultimate goal: winning the general election. Therefore, the candidate tries to avoid taking stands that, however pleasing to party activists in the primary, will alienate a majority of the larger general election constituency.
3. The **personal campaign.** This is the public part of the campaign. The candidate and his or her family and supporters make appearances, meet voters, hold press conferences, and give speeches.
4. The **organizational campaign.** Behind the scenes, another campaign is humming. Volunteers telephone voters and distribute literature, staffers organize events, and everyone raises money to support the operation.
5. The **media campaign.** On television and radio the candidate's advertisements (termed **paid media**) air frequently in an effort to convince the public that the candidate is the best person for the job. Meanwhile, campaigners attempt to influence the press coverage of the campaign by the print and electronic news reporters—the **free media.**

British election campaigns are very different from those in the United States. In the first place, candidate selection is controlled by local party organizations, not by any sort of primary system. Second, the national parties control key facets of the campaign, for example, providing the financing, which is regulated by national statute, and executing the campaign strategy. As a result, national party platforms—not candidate personalities—play a dominant role in British campaigns. Finally, the power of the prime minister to call elections at his or her discretion—literally at a moment's notice—produces campaigns of a mere four to five weeks in duration instead of the two years (for a Senate seat) to four-year campaigns (for president) we endure in the United States.

In order to better comprehend the various campaigns, let's examine a few aspects of each, remembering that they must all mesh successfully for the candidate to win.

The Nomination Campaign

A new candidate gets sea legs early on, as he or she adjusts to the pressures of being in the spotlight day in and day out. This is the time for the candidate to learn that a single careless phrase could end the campaign or guarantee a defeat. This is also the time to seek the support of party leaders and interest groups and to test out themes, slogans, and strategies. The press and public take much less notice of shifts in strategy at this time than they will later in the general election campaign.

At this time, there is a danger not widely recognized by candidates: Surrounded by friendly activists and ideological soulmates in the quest to win the party's nomination, a candidate can move too far to the right or the left and become too extreme for the November electorate. Conservative Barry Goldwater, the 1964 Republican nominee for president, and liberal George McGovern, the 1972 Democratic nominee for president, both fell victim to this phenomenon in seeking their party's nomination, and they were handily defeated in the general elections by Presidents Lyndon B. Johnson and Richard M. Nixon, respectively.

The General Election Campaign

Once the choice between the two major-party nominees is clear, both candidates can get to work. Most significant interest groups are courted for money and endorsements, although the results are mainly predictable: liberal, labor, and minority groups usually back Democrats, while conservative and business organizations support Republicans. The most active and intense groups are often coalesced around emotional issues such as abortion and gun control, and these organizations can produce a bumper crop of money and activists for favored candidates.

Virtually all candidates adopt a brief theme, or slogan, to serve as a rallying cry in their quest for office. (The first to do so was William Henry Harrison in 1840 (see "William Henry Harrison and the Media Campaign of 1840," p. 551). Some presidential campaign slogans have entered national lore (see Table 13.1), but most are nondescript and can fit many candidates ("She thinks like us," "He's on our side," "She hears you," "You know where he stands"). Candidates try to avoid controversy in their selection of slogans, and some openly eschew ideology. (An ever-popular one of this genre: "Not left, not right—forward!") The clever candidate also attempts to find a slogan that cannot be lampooned easily. In 1964 Barry Goldwater's handlers may have regretted their choice of "In your heart you know he's right" when Lyndon B. John-

Table 13.1 ♦ Famous Presidential Campaign Slogans

William Henry Harrison (Whig, 1840)	"Tippecanoe and Tyler, Too"[a]
Calvin Coolidge (Republican, 1924)	"Keep Cool with Coolidge"
Herbert Hoover (Republican, 1928)	"A Chicken in Every Pot, a Car in Every Garage."
Dwight D. Eisenhower (Republican, 1952)	"I Like Ike"
Lyndon B. Johnson (Democrat, 1964)	"All the Way with LBJ"
Barry Goldwater (Republican, 1964)	"In Your Heart You Know He's Right"
George Wallace (Independent, 1968)	"Send Them a Message"
Richard M. Nixon (Republican, 1968)	"Nixon's the One!"
Richard M. Nixon (Republican, 1972)	"Now More Than Ever"
Jimmy Carter (Democrat, 1976)	"Why Not the Best?"
Ronald Reagan (Republican, 1984)	"It's Morning in America"
George Bush (Republican, 1992)	"Annoy the Media. Re-elect Bush"
Bill Clinton (Democrat, 1992)	"It's the economy, stupid."[b]

[a]Tippecanoe was a nickname given to Harrison—a reference to his participation in the battle of Tippecanoe—and Tyler was Harrison's vice-presidential candidate, John Tyler of Virginia.

[b]This was a sign posted in Clinton's Little Rock headquarters, and it became the guiding philosophy of his general election campaign.

son's supporters quickly converted it into "In your guts you know he's nuts." (Democrats were trying to portray Goldwater as a warmonger after the Republican indicated a willingness to use nuclear weapons in Vietnam and elsewhere under some conditions.)

The Personal Campaign

In the effort to show voters that they are hard working, thoughtful, and worthy of the office they seek, candidates try to meet personally as many citizens as possible in the course of a campaign. A candidate for high office may deliver up to a dozen speeches a day, and that is only part of the exhausting schedule most contenders maintain. The day may begin at 5:00 A.M. at the entrance gate to an auto plant with an hour or two of handshaking, followed by similar gladhanding at subway stops until 9:00 A.M. Strategy sessions with key advisers and preparation for upcoming presentations and forums may fill the morning. A luncheon talk, afternoon fund raisers, and a series of television and print interviews crowd the afternoon agenda. The light fare of cocktail parties is followed by a dinner speech, perhaps telephone or neighborhood canvassing of voters, and a civic-forum talk or two. More meetings with advisers and planning for the next day's events can easily take a candidate past midnight. Following only a few hours of sleep, the candidate starts all over again. After months of this grueling pace, the candidate may be functioning on automatic pilot and unable to think clearly.

Beyond the strains this fast-lane existence adds to a candidate's family life, the hectic schedule leaves little time for reflection and long-range planning. Is it any wonder

548 ❖ Chapter 13 The Campaign Process

On February 12, 1992, President Bush formally announced his candidacy in Washington and then quickly flew to New Hampshire to begin campaigning with voters at the Bedford, New Hampshire Mall.

that under these conditions many candidates commit gaffes and appear to have foot-in-mouth disease?

Of course considerable rewards are to be had on the campaign trail that balance the personal disadvantages. A candidate can affect the course of the government and community and in so doing become admired and respected by peers. Meeting all kinds of people, solving problems, gaining exposure to every facet of life in one's constituency—these experiences help a public person live life fully and compensate for the hardships of the campaign trail.

Right-wing 1964 Republican candidate Barry Goldwater's famous slogan, "In your heart, you know he's right" was quickly lampooned by incumbent Democratic opponent President Lyndon B. Johnson's campaign as "In your guts you know he's nuts."

Media consultants arrange everything from paid advertising to daily photo opportunities, such as this Oval Office setting for President Clinton.

The Organizational Campaign

If the candidate is the public face of the campaign, the organization behind the candidate is the private face. Depending on the level of the office sought, the organizational staff can consist of a handful of volunteers or hundreds of paid specialists supplementing and directing the work of thousands of volunteers. The most elaborate structure is found in presidential campaigns. Tens of thousands of volunteers distribute literature and visit neighborhoods. They are directed by paid staff that may number three hundred or more, including a couple of dozen lawyers and accountants. At the top of the organizational chart are the campaign manager and the key political consultants, the hired handlers who provide technologies, services, and strategies to the campaign. The best-known consultants for any campaign are usually the **media consultant,** who produces the candidate's television and radio advertisements; the **pollster,** who takes the public opinion surveys that guide the campaign; and the **direct mailer,** who supervises direct-mail fund raising. After the candidate, however, the most important person in the campaign is probably the finance chair, who is responsible for bringing in the large contributions that pay most of the salaries of the consultants and staff.

In addition to raising money, the most vital work of the candidate's organization is to get in touch with voters. Some of this is done in person by volunteers who walk the neighborhoods going door to door to solicit votes. Some is accomplished by telephone as volunteers use computerized telephone banks to call targeted voters with scripted messages. Both contact methods are termed **voter canvass.** Most canvassing takes place in the month before the election, when voters are paying attention. Close to Election Day, the telephone banks begin the vital **get-out-the-vote** (GOTV) effort, reminding supporters to vote and arranging for their transportation to the polls if necessary. (See Figure 13-1 for a summary graph of a campaign's basic organization.)

550 ❖ Chapter 13 The Campaign Process

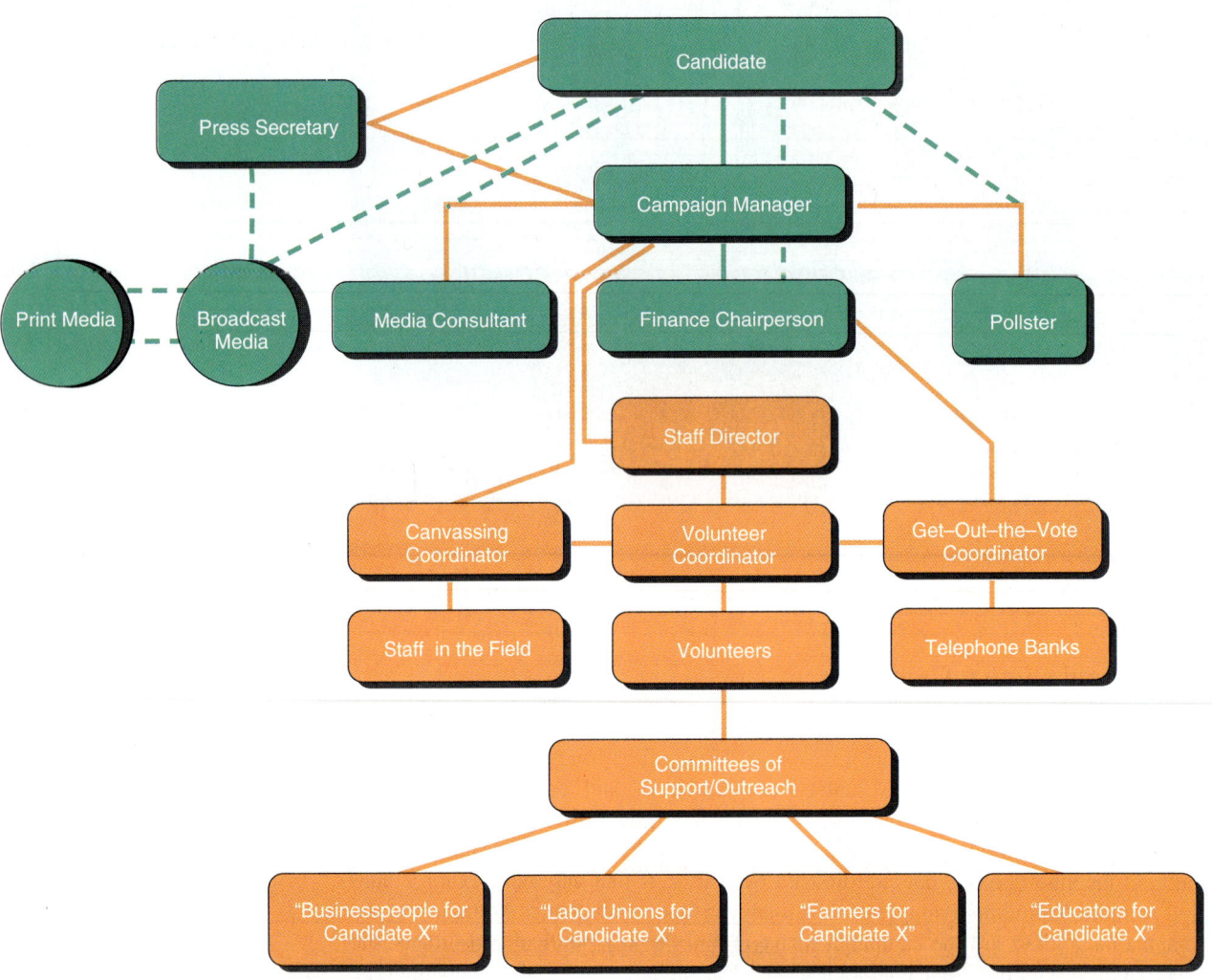

FIGURE 13-1
The Organizational Campaign

Every campaign is organized a bit differently, but most campaigns for office have the common elements listed here. Note that the key personnel (such as the consultants and the finance chair) have direct access to the candidate, even though they technically report to the campaign manager.

The Media Campaign

What voters actually see and hear of the candidate is primarily determined by the paid media (such as television advertising) accompanying the campaign and the free media (newspaper and television coverage). The two kinds of media are fundamentally different: Paid advertising is completely under the control of the campaign, whereas the press is totally independent. Great care is taken in the design of the television advertising, which takes many approaches. **Positive ads** stress the candidate's qualifications, family, and issue positions with no direct reference to the opponent. **Negative ads** attack the opponent's character and platform and (except for a brief legally required identification at the ad's conclusion) may not even mention the candidate who is paying for their airing. **Contrast ads** compare the records and proposals of the candidates—obviously with a bias toward the sponsor. And whether the public likes them or not, all three kinds of ads can inject important (as well as trivial) issues into a campaign.

PEOPLE OF THE PAST

William Henry Harrison and the Media Campaign of 1840

The political historian Keith Melder, among others, has argued that William Henry Harrison's 1840 run for the presidency was the first media campaign, complete with the creation of an image and the means for selling it to the public.

Harrison's campaign began with his pursuit of the Whig Party's nomination, for which Harrison—an accomplished general but a political novice—ran against Henry Clay and Daniel Webster, both experienced politicians. In the first Whig national convention, party leaders unfriendly to Clay and Webster rigged the rules in Harrison's favor, guaranteeing his nomination. For geographic balance, they also added Virginian John Tyler to the ticket as the vice-presidential candidate. (Harrison, although also a native of Virginia, was governor of Indiana.) Moreover, since the party was divided over many issues, the leadership decided early on that waging a colorful and unsubstantial campaign would be the best route to victory in a year when the incumbent Democratic president, Martin Van Buren, was already weakened by a severe economic depression.

Ironically, Harrison's key image was provided not by his own party but by a Democratic newspaper in Baltimore, which caricatured Harrison as a cider-swilling, log cabin-dwelling simpleton. Unfortunately for the Democrats, the Whig Party took hold of this sarcasm and converted it into a powerful campaign theme for the candidate. Harrison, the Whig Party claimed, resided in a log cabin (actually, only the original structure of his home was made from logs) and supposedly possessed all the virtuous qualities of the hard-working frontiersman.

The log cabin issue was pushed vigorously by the Whigs, who used banners, ribbons, songs, and cabin raisings—the construction of log cabins in many communities to serve as the local Whig Party headquarters—to get their message to the public. The Whig Party created a campaign newspaper—named, of course, the *Log Cabin*—that featured speeches by eloquent Whigs and, in a true harbinger of things to come, peddled campaign banners and log cabin souvenirs considered indispensable to the loyal Harrison supporter. In another first, the candidate himself spoke often (a total of twenty-three speeches) on behalf of his candidacy. Before 1840, it had been considered improper for a candidate to participate directly in the electioneering process.

The Harrison campaign of 1840, then, was the first to sell a candidate as a national product, and it became the model for many presidential campaigns to follow. The Democrats complained loudly about Whig showboating, but when Harrison easily defeated Van Buren, the Whig methods seemed vindicated. As for the voters, they clearly preferred the new style of campaigning. Not only did Harrison win handsomely, but nearly 80 percent of those eligible to vote also turned out at the polls—a remarkable proportion at that time, or in ours. (In 1992 only 55 percent of the eligible voters cast a ballot for president.) Tragically for Harrison, his election was the high point of the briefest of all presidencies. After catching cold at his March 1841 inauguration, Harrison died in April, serving as president for only one month.

Bush media consultant Roger Ailes was the mastermind behind one of the most effective negative ad campaigns in history during the 1988 Presidential campaign. The infamous "Willie Horton" ad portrayed Democratic nominee Michael Dukakis as soft on crime by implying that Horton's escape from a Massachusetts prison work-release program and his subsequent terrorizing of a Florida family were a result of Governor Dukakis's liberal policies. Critics charged that this ad, in particular, was both misleading and racist; nevertheless, it seemed to resonate with voters.

Occasionally, advertisements are relatively long (ranging from four-and-one-half-minute ads up to thirty-minute documentaries). Usually, however, the messages are short **spot ads** of sixty-, thirty-, or ten-second durations.

There is little question that negative advertisements have shown the greatest growth in the past two decades. While voters normally need a reason to vote *for* a candidate, they also frequently vote *against* the other candidate—and negative ads can provide the critical justification for such a vote.

Prior to the 1980s, well-known incumbents usually ignored negative attacks from their challengers, believing that the proper stance was to be above the fray. But after some well-publicized defeats of incumbents in the early 1980s in which negative television advertising played a prominent role,[2] incumbents began attacking their challengers with relish. The new rule of politics became "An attack unanswered is an attack agreed to." In a further attempt to stave off brickbats from challengers, incumbents even began anticipating the substance of their opponents' attacks and airing inoculation advertising early in the campaign to protect themselves in advance of the other side's spots. (Inoculation advertising attempts to counteract an *anticipated* attack from the opposition *before* the attack is even launched.) For example, a senator who fears a broadside about her voting record on Social Security issues might air advertisements featuring senior citizens praising her support of Social Security.

The Candidate or the Campaign: Which Do We Vote For?

One important point needs to be made about media and organizational techniques. Much is said and written about them during the campaign, and they are often presented as political magic. Yet although campaign methods have clearly become very sophisticated, the technologies still often fail the candidates and their campaigns. The political consultants who develop and master the technologies of polling, media, and other techniques frequently make serious mistakes in judgment. Despite popular lore and journalistic legend, few candidates are the creations of their clever consultants and dazzling campaign techniques. Partly, this is because politics always has been (and always will be) much more art than science, not subject to precise manipulation or formulaic computation. *In the end—in most cases—the candidate wins or loses the race according to his or her abilities, qualifications, communication skills, issues, and weaknesses.* Although this simple truth is warmly reassuring, it has been remarkably overlooked by election analysts and reporters seemingly mesmerized by the exorbitant claims of consultants and the flashy computer lights of their technologies.[3] Of course, campaign techniques can enhance the candidate's strengths and downplay his or her weaknesses, and in that respect, technique certainly matters.

The voter deserves much of the credit for whatever encouragement we can draw from this candidate-centered view of politics. Granted, citizens are often inattentive to politics and, in effect, force candidates to use empty slogans and glitz to attract their

---

[2] Five liberal Democratic U.S. senators, including George McGovern of South Dakota, were defeated in this fashion in 1980, for example.

[3] See Larry J. Sabato, ed., *Campaigns and Elections: A Reader in Modern American Politics* (Glenview, IL: Scott, Foresman, 1989), pp. 3–4.

attention. But it is also true that most voters want to take the real measure of candidates and retain a healthy skepticism about the techniques of running for office. The political cartoonist Tom Toles suggested as much when he depicted the seven preparatory steps the modern candidate takes: (1) Set out to discover what voters want, (2) Conduct extensive polling, (3) Study demographic trends, (4) Engage in sophisticated interpretation of in-depth voter interviews, (5) Analyze results, (6) Discover that what the voters want is a candidate who doesn't need to do steps one through five, (7) Pretend you didn't. The chastened politician then tells his assembled throng, "I follow my conscience."[4]

Modern Campaign Challenges

The modern candidate faces two major challenges: communicating through the media and raising the money needed to stay in the race. We consider each challenge in turn.

The News Media

The news media present quite a challenge to candidates. Although politicians and their staffs cannot control the press, they nonetheless try to manipulate press coverage. They use three techniques to accomplish this aim. First, the staff often seeks to isolate the candidate from the press, thus reducing the chances that reporters will bait a candidate into saying something that might damage the candidate's cause. Naturally, the media are frustrated by such a tactic and insist on as many open press conferences as possible. Second, the campaign stages media events—activities designed to include brief, clever quotes called "soundbites" and staged with appealing backdrops so that they are all but irresistible, especially to television news. (See box, p. 554.) In this fashion the candidate's staff can successfully fill the news hole reserved for campaign coverage on the evening news programs and in the morning papers. Third, the handlers and consultants have perfected the technique termed "spin"—that is, they put the most favorable possible interpretation for their candidate on any circumstance occurring in the campaign, and they work the press to sell their point of view or at least to ensure that it is included in the reporters' stories. **Candidate debates,** especially the televised presidential variety, are showcases for the consultants' spin patrol, and teams of staffers from each side swarm the press rooms to declare victory even before the candidates finish their closing statements.

In Great Britain, where the House of Commons is structured to provide continuous debate between government and opposition, resorting to such media extravaganza is for the most part superfluous. To be sure, television plays an increasingly important role as a forum for party clashes in British politics, but in no way does it achieve the prominence of television coverage in the United States.

Televised Debates. Candidate debates are media extravaganzas that are a hybrid of free and paid media. As with ads, much of the candidate dialogue (jokes included) is

---

[4] From a 1987 cartoon by Tom Toles, copyrighted by the *Buffalo News*.

> ### Famous Soundbites from Recent Presidential Campaigns
>
> **1992**
>
> "We've got to have the courage to change"
> —Bill Clinton (D)
>
> "Message: I care"
> —George Bush (R), attempting to connect with New Hampshire's economically devastated voters.
>
> "Let's clean out the barn!"
> —Ross Perot (I)
>
> **1988**
>
> "Read my lips; no new taxes."
> —George Bush (R)
>
> "This election isn't about ideology; it's about competence."
> —Michael Dukakis (D)
>
> "Stop lying about my record!"
> —Senator Robert Dole (R.-Kans.), speaking to George Bush during their campaign for the Republican nomination.
>
> "I knew Jack Kennedy; he was a friend of mine. And, Senator, you're no Jack Kennedy."
> —Democratic vice-presidential nominee Lloyd Bentsen (D.-Tex.), responding in an October debate to Republican nominee Dan Quayle's comparison of himself to John F. Kennedy.
>
> "Follow me around . . . [you'll] be very bored."
> —Gary Hart (D.-Colo.) to a reporter shortly before his May 1987 weekend with model Donna Rice.
>
> **1984**
>
> "Where's the beef ?"
> —Walter Mondale to his Democratic rival Gary Hart, who claimed to have "new ideas."
>
> **1980**
>
> "There you go again. . . . "
> —Ronald Reagan (R) to President Jimmy Carter (D), in response to some of Carter's charges against Reagan in a debate.
>
> "Are you better off today than you were four years ago?"
> —Reagan's oft-repeated question to the voters.
>
> "I'll whip his ass."
> —President Carter's pledge to defeat Senator Edward M. Kennedy's (D.-Mass.) challenge to his renomination.

canned and prepackaged. Yet spontaneity cannot be completely eliminated, and gaffes, quips, and slips of the tongue can sometimes be revealing. President Gerald Ford's insistence during an October 1976 debate with Jimmy Carter that Poland was not under Soviet domination may have cost him a close election. Ronald Reagan's refrain, "Are you better off today than you were four years ago?" neatly summed up his case against Carter in 1980. Moreover, Reagan's easygoing performance reassured a skeptical public that wanted Carter out of the White House but was not certain it wanted Reagan in.

Senator John F. Kennedy's visually impressive showing in the first 1960 presidential debate dramatically reduced the utility of two-term Vice President Richard M. Nixon's experience edge. Not only was Nixon ill at the time, but he also was poorly dressed and poorly made up for television. Interestingly, most of those who heard the debate on radio—and therefore could not see the contrast between the pale, anxious, sweating Nixon and the relaxed, tanned Kennedy—thought that Nixon had won.

Modern Campaign Challenges ❖ 555

Democratic candidate Bill Clinton makes a point during the second of three presidential debates in the 1992 election campaign. This debate, held in Richmond, Virginia, had an unusually informal format that allowed the candidates to move about the stage as they responded to questions from an audience of uncommitted voters.

The importance of debates can easily be overrated, however. A weak performance by Reagan in his first debate with Walter Mondale in 1984 had little lasting effect, in part because Reagan did better in the second debate. And most of the debates in 1960, 1976, 1980, and 1988 were unmemorable and electorally inconsequential. Debates usually just firm up the voting predispositions of most Americans and cannot change the fundamentals of an election (the state of the economy, scandal, and presidential popularity, for example). This is what appeared to happen in 1992, when none of the three presidential debates and one vice-presidential debate changed the underlying pro-Clinton trends in the election. Nonetheless, because debates are potentially educational and focus the public's mind on the upcoming election, they are useful. Since they have been held in every presidential campaign from 1976 on, debates are now likely to be an expected and standard part of the presidential election process.[5] They are also an established feature of campaigns for governor, U.S. senator, and many other offices.

Can the Press Be "Handled"? Whether in debates or elsewhere, efforts by candidates to manipulate the news media often fail because the press is wise to their tactics and determined to thwart them. Not even the candidates' paid media are sacrosanct anymore. The press, especially major newspapers throughout the country, has taken to analyzing the accuracy of the television advertisements aired during the campaign—a welcome and useful addition to journalists' scrutiny of politicians.

Less welcome are some other news media practices in campaigns. Many studies have shown that the media are obsessed with the horse race aspect of politics—who's ahead, who's behind, who's gaining—to the detriment of the substance of the candidates' issues and ideas. Public opinion polls, especially tracking polls, many of them

---

[5] Incumbents or frontrunners refused to participate in suggested presidential debates in 1964, 1968, and 1972, but precedent would now probably make such a decision a costly one for any presidential contender, even an incumbent.

> ### The "Outsider" Candidate
>
> Whenever Washington is especially unpopular because of recession, scandal, or policy failures, most presidential candidates adopt the "outsider" label and become crusaders for change. Democrat Jimmy Carter successfully rode the anti-Washington bandwagon in 1976 against longtime insider Gerald Ford. Carter was on the receiving end of this tactic in 1980, when Ronald Reagan rode his white horse from California to take control of the White House. Perhaps because of his constant attacks on the federal government even while in office, Reagan never lost the outsider glow, and he used it again in 1984 in his reelection race against former Vice President Walter Mondale, another Washington insider. The peace and prosperity existing in 1988 enabled classic insider George Bush to take credit for the successes of the Reagan administration, but four years later Democrats jockeyed to win the outsider label as Bush struggled under the weight of a serious recession during his reelection bid.

taken by the news outlets themselves, dominate coverage, especially on network television, where only a few minutes a night are devoted to politics. (Tracking polls were discussed in Chapter 10.)

Related to the proliferation of polls is the media's expectations game in presidential primary contests. With polls as the objective backdrop, journalists set the margins by which contenders are expected to win or lose—so much so that even a clear victory of five percentage points can be judged a setback if the candidate had been projected to win by twelve or fifteen points. Finally, the news media often overemphasize trivial parts of the campaign, such as a politician's minor gaffe, and give too much attention to the private lives of candidates. This superficial coverage and the resources needed to generate it are displacing serious journalism on the issues. These subjects are taken up again in the next chapter, which deals with the news media.

Raising the Money

To run all aspects of a campaign successfully requires a great deal of money. In 1992 alone, more than $675 million was raised and spent in U.S. House and Senate races.[6] This amount was an increase of 40 percent over the 1990 elections, mainly owing to greater competition because of a large number of open seats—one of the effects of redistricting. Because of a vacancy, there were also simultaneous elections in 1992 for two U.S. Senate seats in California, the largest and most expensive state for campaigns. On average, a House incumbent who was seriously challenged and received less than 55 percent of the vote spent nearly $750,000, while his or her opponent spent nearly $400,000. As humorist Will Rogers once remarked early in the twentieth century, "Politics has got so expensive that it takes lots of money even to get beat with."

---

[6] Data provided by the Federal Election Commission.

All this political money is regulated by the federal government under the terms of the Federal Election Campaign Act of 1971, first passed in 1971 and substantially strengthened after Watergate in 1974 and again in 1976. (Still more amendments were passed in 1979.) Table 13.2 summarizes some of the important provisions of this law, which limits what individuals, interest groups, and political parties can give to candidates for president, U.S. senator, and U.S. representative. These limits on contributions are discussed in the passages that follow, but the goal of all limits is the same: to prevent any single group or individual from gaining too much influence over elected officials, who naturally feel indebted to campaign contributors.

Given the cash flow required by a campaign and the legal restrictions on political money, raising the funds necessary to run a modern campaign is a monumental task. Consequently, presidential and congressional campaigns have squads of fund raisers on staff. These professionals rely on several standard sources of campaign money.

Individual Contributions. Individual contributions are donations from individual citizens. The maximum allowable contribution under federal law for congressional and presidential elections is $1,000 per election to each candidate, with primary and general elections considered separately. Individuals are also limited to a total of $25,000

Table 13.2 ♦ Current Contribution Limits for Congressional Candidates (under the Federal Election Campaign Act)

CONTRIBUTIONS FROM	GIVEN TO CANDIDATE (PER ELECTION)[a]	GIVEN TO NATIONAL PARTY (PER CALENDAR YEAR)	TOTAL ALLOWABLE CONTRIBUTIONS (PER CALENDAR YEAR)
Individual	$1,000	$20,000	Limited to $25,000
Political action committee[b]	$5,000	$15,000	No limit
Any political party committee[c]	$5,000	No limit	No limit
All national and state party committees taken together	To House candidates: $30,000 plus "coordinated expenditures"[d] (of $55,240 per candidate in 1992) To Senate candidates: $27,500 plus "coordinated expenditures"[d] (of $110,480 per candidate in smallest states to $2.5 million in California in 1992)		

[a] Each of the following is considered a *separate* election: primary (or convention), run-off, general election.

[b] Multi-candidate PACs only. Multi-candidate committees have received contributions from at least fifty persons and have given to at least five federal candidates.

[c] Multi-candidate party committees only. Multi-candidate committees have received contributions from at least fifty persons and have given to at least five federal candidates.

[d] Coordinated expenditures are party-paid general election campaign expenditures made in consultation and coordination with the candidate.

> ### Women's PACs Continue to Make a Difference
> ❖❖❖
>
> Women's political action committees made a real difference in the 1990 and 1992 elections. In 1990, women's PACs contributed over 2.6 million to candidates and in 1992 nearly triple that.
>
> EMILY's List, which stands for Early Money Is Like Yeast (it makes the dough rise), is the largest contributor to women's campaigns. Founded in 1985, its members contributed nearly 1.5 million to female candidates in 1990. Ann Richards, who ran a hotly contested race for the Texas governorship in 1990, credits EMILY's List with providing crucial funding at a key time. In 1992, EMILY's List provided $6.2 million to 55 pro-choice Democratic women candidates of which 25 won. It spent more than that to support 38 candidates in the 1994 election cycle.
>
> *Source:* Center for the American Woman and Politics, *CAWP News & Notes* (Winter 1991), pp. 10–11; *The Times-Picayune,* "EMILY's List Dough Helps Women Rise," January 26, 1994, p. A1; and, EMILY's List.

in gifts to all candidates combined in each calendar year. Most candidates receive a majority of all funds directly from individuals, and most individual gifts are well below the maximum level.

Political Action Committee (PAC) Contributions. Donations from **political action committees** are those from interest groups (labor unions, corporations, trade associations, and ideological and issue groups). Under federal law these organizations are required to establish officially recognized fund-raising committees, called PACs, in order to participate in federal elections. (Some but not all states have similar requirements for state elections.) Approximately 4,100 PACs are registered with the Federal Election Commission—the governmental agency charged with administering the election laws—and in 1992 all PACs together gave $180 million to Senate and House candidates. (By contrast, individual citizens donated nearly $355 million.) On average, PAC contributions account for 33 percent of the war chests (campaign funds) of House candidates and 20 percent of the treasuries of Senate candidates. (Interest groups are treated in more detail in Chapter 15.)

Political Party Contributions. Candidates also receive donations from the national and state committees of the Democratic and Republican parties. As is mentioned in Chapter 11, political parties can give substantial contributions to their congressional nominees. In 1992 the Democrats funneled $29 million to their standard-bearers, and the Republicans sent nearly $36 million to theirs. In competitive races the parties may provide 15 to 17 percent of their candidates' total war chests.

Candidates' Personal Contributions. Candidates and their families may donate to the campaign. The Supreme Court ruled in 1976 in *Buckley* v. *Valeo* that no limit could be placed on the amount of money candidates can spend from their own families' resources, since such spending is considered a First Amendment right of free speech [424 U.S.1 (1976)]. For wealthy politicians such as U.S. Senators John D. Rockefeller IV (D.-W.Va.) or Herbert H. Kohl (D.-Wisc.), this allowance may mean personal spending in the millions. Most candidates, however, commit much less than $100,000 in family resources to their election bids. Ross Perot, who publicly committed to spend millions, was not the usual candidate. In 1992 the 947 House candidates loaned or contributed almost $55 million to their own campaigns.

Public Funds. **Public funds** are donations from general tax revenues. Only presidential candidates (and a handful of state and local contenders) receive public funds. Under the terms of the Federal Election Campaign Act of 1971 (which first established public funding of presidential campaigns), a candidate for president can become eligible to receive public funds during the nominating contest by raising at least $5,000 in individual contributions of $250 or less in each of twenty states. Once the receipt of this money is certified, the candidate can apply for federal **matching funds,** whereby every dollar raised from individuals in amounts less than $251 is matched by the federal treasury on a dollar-for-dollar basis. This assumes there is enough money in the Presidential Election Campaign Fund to do so. The fund is accumulated by taxpayers who designate $1.00 of their taxes for this purpose each year when they send in their federal tax returns. (Only about 20 percent of taxpayers check off the appropriate box, even though participation does not increase their tax burden.)

For the general election, the two major-party presidential nominees are given a lump-sum payment in the summer before the election ($55 million each in 1992), from which all their general election campaign expenditures must come. A third-party candidate receives a smaller amount proportionate to his or her November vote total *if* that candidate gains a minimum of 5 percent of the vote. Note that in such a case the money goes to third-party campaigns only *after* the election is over; no money is given in advance of the general election. The only third-party candidate to qualify for general election funds so far has been John Anderson, the Independent candidate for president in 1980, who garnered 7 percent of the national vote. Ross Perot chose not to take public funds for his campaign, which was largely self-financed.

Independent Expenditures. Individuals, groups, and PACs also spend money independent of any campaign or candidate. This spending is *not* under the direction or control of the campaign staff and is unlimited because First Amendment free speech is involved. Sometimes the spending is positive and advocates the election of a candidate; on other occasions it is negative, urging the defeat of a targeted candidate. (See

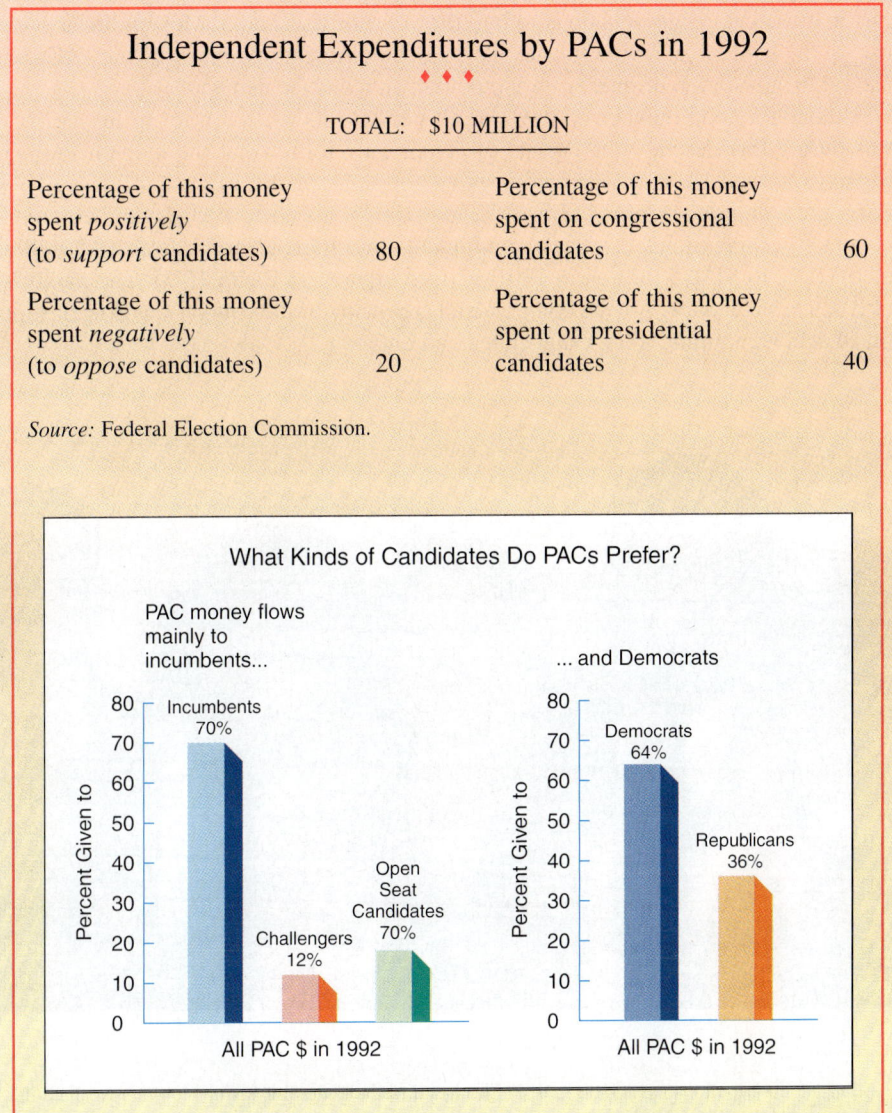

Independent Expenditures by PACs in 1992

TOTAL: $10 MILLION

Percentage of this money spent *positively* (to *support* candidates)	80	Percentage of this money spent on congressional candidates	60
Percentage of this money spent *negatively* (to *oppose* candidates)	20	Percentage of this money spent on presidential candidates	40

Source: Federal Election Commission.

What Kinds of Candidates Do PACs Prefer?

PAC money flows mainly to incumbents...
- Incumbents 70%
- Challengers 12%
- Open Seat Candidates 70%

All PAC $ in 1992

... and Democrats
- Democrats 64%
- Republicans 36%

All PAC $ in 1992

"Independent Expenditures by PACs in 1992," p. 559.) Liberals, conservatives, environmentalists, supporters of Israel, and trade groups representing realtors, doctors, and car dealers are some organizations that have used this supplementary method of campaign spending over the years. In addition, untold millions are spent by labor, corporate, and community groups for grassroots organizing, voter registration, volunteer participation, and internal political communications with their members and employees. Depending on the sponsoring group, all of this activity has a political effect—favoring one candidate or party and hurting others—but that is not always obvious or well publicized. Also, unlike all the other forms of contributions discussed earlier, it is usually not necessary for these indirect gifts to be disclosed to the Federal Election Commission.[7]

Are PACs a Good or Bad Part of the Process?

Of all these forms of spending, probably the most controversial is that involving PAC money. Some observers claim that PACs are the embodiment of corrupt special interests that use campaign donations to buy the votes of legislators. Most political scientists in the field of campaign finance have a quite different opinion, viewing PACs as a natural manifestation of interest-group politics in a diverse democracy.

Although a good number of PACs of all persuasions existed prior to the 1970s, it was during this decade—the decade of campaign reform—that the modern PAC era began. Spawned by the Watergate-inspired revisions of the campaign-finance laws, PACs grew in number from 113 in 1972 to 4,100 by the early 1990s, and their contributions to congressional candidates multiplied almost eighteenfold, from $8.5 million in 1971–72 to $180.5 million in 1991–92 (see Figures 13-2 and 13-3). The rapid rise of PACs has inevitably proved controversial, yet many of the charges made against political action committees are exaggerated and dubious.

It is often alleged that campaign contributions are used illegally. Republican Christine Todd Whitman is shown here with Jesse Jackson and Al Sharpton after her narrow election to the New Jersey governorship as she attempts to counter her campaign manager's contention that the Republicans conspired to lower African-American turnout on election day. Ed Rollins, Whitman's campaign manager, said that the campaign contributed to African-American churches to encourage ministers to refrain from backing Whitman's Democratic opponent, incumbent James Florio, and to encourage others to stay home on election day. An investigation into Rollins' statements found no evidence of wrong-doing.

[7] All *direct* contributions over $100 must be disclosed to the Federal Election Commission, and the report is supposed to include the name, address, and occupation of each donor.

FIGURE 13-2

Growth in Total Number of PACs[a]

[a]As of December 31st of every other year, starting in 1972.
Source: Federal Election Commission.

Some people argue that PACs are newfangled inventions that have flooded the political system with money. Although the widespread use of the PAC structure is new, the fact remains that special-interest money of all types has *always* found its way into politics. Before the 1970s it did so in less traceable and much more disturbing and unsavory ways because, before PACs, little of the money given to candidates was regularly disclosed to public inspection. And although it is true that PACs contribute a massive sum to candidates in absolute terms, it is not clear that there is *proportionately* more interest-group money in the system than before. The proportion of House and Senate campaign funds provided by PACs has certainly increased since the early 1970s, but *individuals,* most of whom are unaffiliated with PACs, together with the political parties still supply more than 60 percent of all the money spent by or on behalf of House

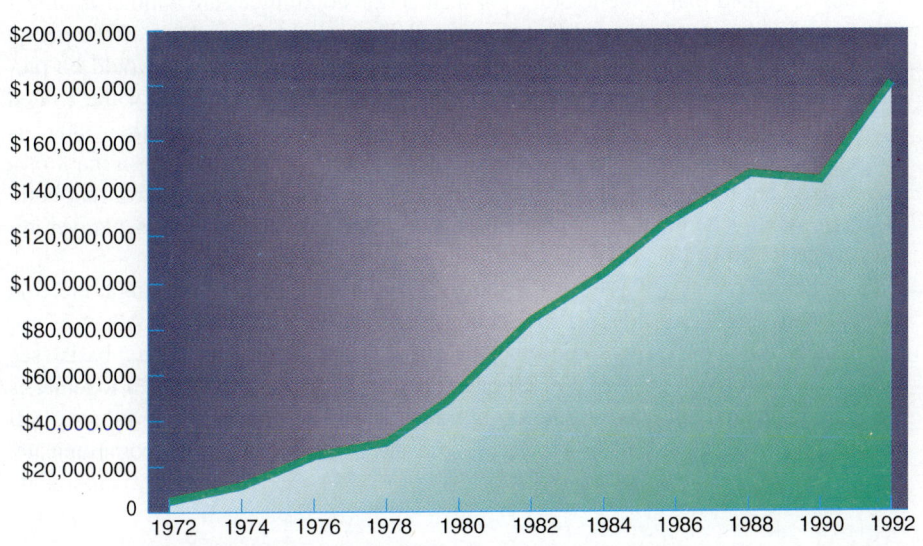

FIGURE 13-3

Growth in Total Contributions by PACs to House and Senate Candidates[a]

For two-year election cycles ending in years shown.
Source: Federal Election Commission.

FIGURE 13-4

Campaign for U.S. Senate, 1992: A "Typical" Candidate's Budget of $2 Million

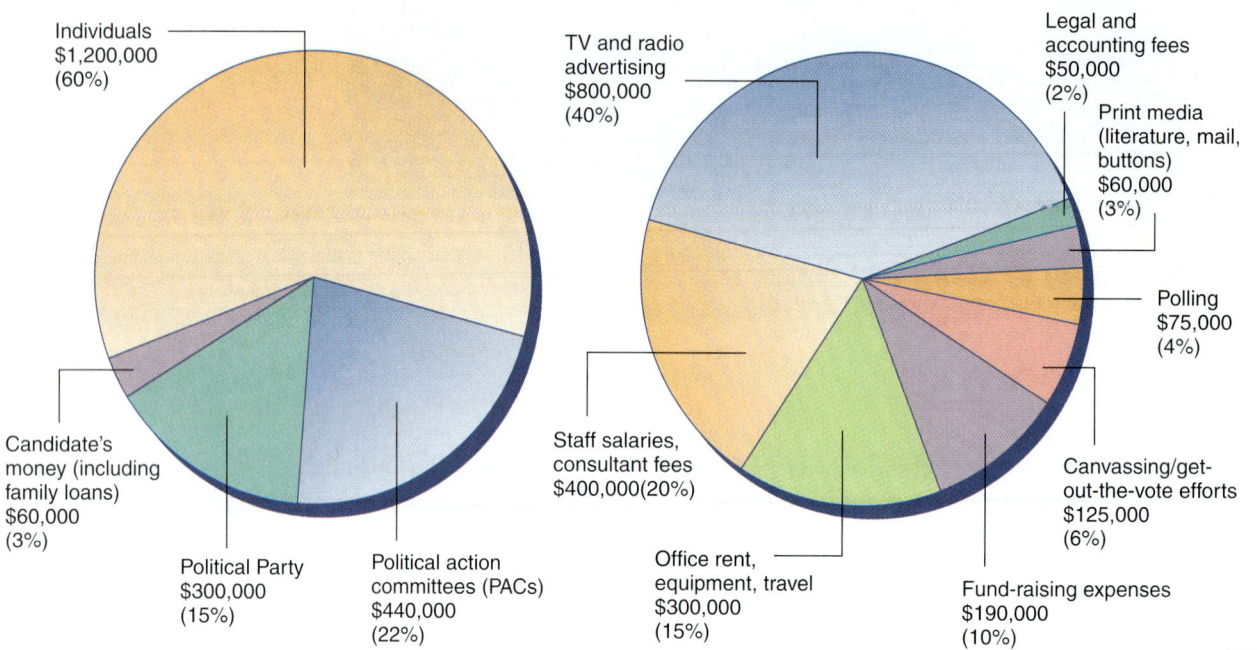

candidates and 75 percent of the campaign expenditures for Senate contenders (see Figure 13-4). So while the importance of PAC spending has grown, PACs clearly remain secondary as a source of election funding and therefore pose no overwhelming threat to the system's legitimacy.

It can be argued that contemporary political action committees are another manifestation of what James Madison called "factions." Through the flourishing of competing interest groups or factions, said Madison in *Federalist No. 10,* liberty would be preserved. In any democracy, and particularly in one as pluralistic as that of the United States, it is essential that groups be relatively unrestricted in advocating their interests and positions. Not only is unrestricted political activity by interest groups a mark of a free society, but it also provides a safety valve for the competitive pressures that build on all fronts in a democracy. It also supplies a means of keeping representatives responsive to legitimate needs.

The election outlays of PACs, like the total amount expended in a single election season, seem huge. But the cost of elections in the United States is less than or approximately the same as in some other nations, measured on a per voter basis (see Table 13.3).[8] Moreover, the cost of all elections in the United States taken together is less than the annual advertising budgets of many individual private corporations to sell cereals, dog food, cars, and toothpaste. These days it is expensive to communicate,

---

[8] See Howard Penniman, "U.S. Elections: Really a Bargain?" *Public Opinion* (June/July 1984): 51.

Table 13.3 ♦ The Costs of Elections Around the Globe

AMOUNT OF MONEY SPENT PER VOTER[a]
IN RECENT NATIONAL ELECTIONS

COUNTRY	(IN DOLLARS)
Venezuela	26.35[c]
Israel	4.34
Ireland	3.93[c]
United States	$3.25[b]
Germany (West only)	3.20[c]
Canada	1.43[c]
Great Britain	0.50[c]

[a] "Voters" include all those who were of age to vote, whether or not they were registered.

[b] Figure does not include free television broadcast time or other government subsidies not available to candidates in the United States.

[c] Includes both presidential and congressional elections.

Source: Adapted from Howard Penniman, "U.S. Elections: Really a Bargain?" *Public Opinion* (June/July 1984): 51.

whether the message is political or commercial. The costs of television time, polling, consultants, and other items have soared over and above the inflation rate.

A Summary of Contributions and Expenses

Figure 13-4 gives an idea of where all the money comes from and goes. A typical U.S. Senate candidate in 1992 received most of his or her war chest (about 60 percent) from relatively small individual donations. PACs supplied about 22 percent, the political party committees 15 percent, and the candidates about 3 percent.

The single greatest outlay (40 percent of the total) was for television advertising; the next-largest item, staff and consultant salaries, was half television's cost (20 percent). The other 40 percent of the budget was spent on everything from polls to travel expenses. Keep in mind that in a large state with a dozen or more media markets (concentrated population centers with many television and radio stations), expenditures often balloon to $5 million, $10 million, and even more.

Some candidates have more difficulty than others in raising the necessary dollar amounts. Those in power—the incumbents—have the least trouble, although challengers who face incumbents weakened by scandal can also find the task of financing the campaign relatively easy. The size of a challenger's war chest is really the key variable. There is a point of diminishing returns for incumbent spending, since most office holders are already well known to the voters. But the challenger's name and platform are likely to be obscure. If the challenger can raise and spend enough to get his or her basic message across, there is a reasonable chance that the election will be at least moderately competitive. As is more common, though, if the challenger is starved for funds, the contest will probably turn into a romp for the well-heeled incumbent.

Bringing It Together: The 1992 Presidential Campaign and Election

A year before the November 1992 presidential election, it looked likely to be a rather boring, predictable affair, much like the 1984 contest that had resulted in a landslide reelection for President Reagan. Most of the strongest potential Democratic candidates, such as New York Governor Mario Cuomo and New Jersey U.S. Senator Bill Bradley, decided not to run for president, and President Bush was still riding a wave of popularity from the Persian Gulf war. In the end, however, 1992 produced one of the most exciting and competitive contests for the White House in modern times (see Figure 13-5).

The Party Nomination Battle

President Bush's hopes for an uncontested renomination were shattered when he was challenged by conservative television commentator Patrick J. Buchanan. Buchanan at-

THEN AND NOW

The Television Advertising Campaigns of 1952 and 1992

Forty years—and a world of difference—separate the presidential campaigns of 1952 and 1992 when viewed through the camera lens of television advertising.

The initial, landmark year for political television was 1952. Television had become truly national, not just regional, and portions of the political parties' national conventions were telecast for the first time. With 45 percent of the nation's households owning television sets, the presidential campaign was forced to take notice. Republican presidential nominee Dwight D. Eisenhower's advisers were particularly intrigued with the device, seeing it as a way to counter Eisenhower's stumbling press-conference performances and to make him appear more knowledgeable.

Eisenhower's advertising campaign was a glimpse of the future. Two associates of the Ted Bates and Company advertising agency of New York designed the spots, targeted them to play in key swing areas of the country, and arranged a television and radio saturation blitz in the last three weeks of the campaign along with the Batten, Barton, Durstine, and Osborn (BBD&O) advertising agency, which actually bought the air time. The three primary themes of the commercials (corruption, high prices, and the Korean War) were chosen after consultation with pollster George Gallup. There was an extraordinarily large number of spots (forty-nine produced for television, twenty-nine for radio). Most spots were twenty seconds in length; the rest, sixty seconds. They played repeatedly in forty-nine selected counties in twelve non-Southern states as well as in a few targeted Southern states. On the day before the election in New York City alone, 130 Eisenhower television ads were shown at station breaks. The GOP's media strategy appeared to have been successful, and the Nielsen ratings showed that Eisenhower's telecasts consistently drew higher ratings than those of his Democratic opponent, Adlai Stevenson.

The commercials themselves were simplistic and technically very primitive in comparison with modern fare. Eisenhower had a peculiarly stilted way of speaking while reading cue cards, and his delivery was amateurish, albeit sincere and appealing. If nothing else, the GOP commercials from 1952 reveal that the issues in U.S. politics never seem to change. Eisenhower's slogan, "It's Time for a Change," is a perennial production, for example. One advertisement was a clever tacked Bush on the economy, on his 1990 abandonment of his 1988 "no new taxes" campaign pledge, and on National Endowment of the Arts funding of such controversial projects as a film about African-American gay males. Buchanan achieved his high watermark on February 19, receiving 37 percent of the vote in the first primary, New Hampshire. (Bush won the primary with 53%.) This state had saved Bush's candidacy in 1988 after his third-place finish in the Iowa caucuses. In 1992, however, many of the state's citizens felt Bush had abandoned them during the recession, which was much more severe in their state than in the country as a whole. Buchanan also won 36 percent of the vote in Georgia on March 3, but he faded thereafter. Although Bush eventually collected nearly all of the delegates to the Republican convention, his overall showing in the primaries was anemic compared to most of his Republican predecessors. Bush won just 73 percent of all the votes cast in GOP contests in 1992, much less than Presidents Eisenhower (86 percent), Nixon (87 percent), and Reagan (99 percent) in their reelection years.

Democrats sponsored one of their standard free-for-alls for the presidential nomination in 1992. The leading announced candidate from the beginning was Governor Bill Clinton of Arkansas, although his status as frontrunner was shaky. He was plagued by

---

adaptation of the "March of Time" newsreel series that preceded the main features in U.S. movie theaters of the period, and various news clips of Eisenhower accompanied the audio.

Narrator: The man from Abilene. Out of the heartland of America, out of this small-frame house in Abilene, Kansas, came a man, Dwight D. Eisenhower. Through the crucial hours of historic D-Day, he brought us to the triumph and peace of VE-Day. Now, another crucial hour in our history. The big question . . .

Man's voice: General, if war comes, is this country really ready?

Eisenhower: It is not. The administration has spent many billions of dollars for national defense. Yet today we haven't enough tanks for the fighting men in Korea. It is time for a change.

Narrator: The nation, haunted by the stalemate in Korea, looks to Eisenhower. Eisenhower knows how to deal with the Russians. He has met with Europe's leaders, has got them working with us. Elect the number-one man for the number-one job of our time. November fourth, vote for peace, vote for Eisenhower.

Yet this spot had an odd ring to it, perhaps because the approach ignored the intimate nature of television, which reaches its viewers in the home's cozy quarters as opposed to the blare of a newsreel in an auditorium. Some other Eisenhower commercials used an even less effective format wherein a film showed Eisenhower mechanically responding to off-camera questions.

By the best estimates this first media blitz cost the Republicans close to $1.5 million. During that campaign the Democrats spent only about $77,000 on television, and the new spots they produced played on New Deal themes and Republican responsibility for the Great Depression: "Sh-h-h-h. Don't mention it to a soul, don't spread it around . . . but the Republican party was in power back in 1932 . . . 13 million people were unemployed . . . bank doors shut in your face. . . ." The Democrats, who had wanted to run an ad blitz but could not raise the money to pay for it, turned instead to broadsides about the GOP's "soap campaign." Stevenson's supporters charged that the Republican ad managers conceived a multimillion-dollar production designed to sell a political party ticket to the American people in precisely the way they sell soap.

The poet Marya Mannes was moved to write "Sales Campaign" in reaction to the Eisenhower advertising effort. Her poem read, in part: "Phillip Morris, Lucky Strike, Alka Seltzer, I Like Ike."

For better or worse, the pattern was set for future campaigns, although 1992's television advertising was far more sophisticated in both presidential camps.

566 ❖ Chapter 13   The Campaign Process

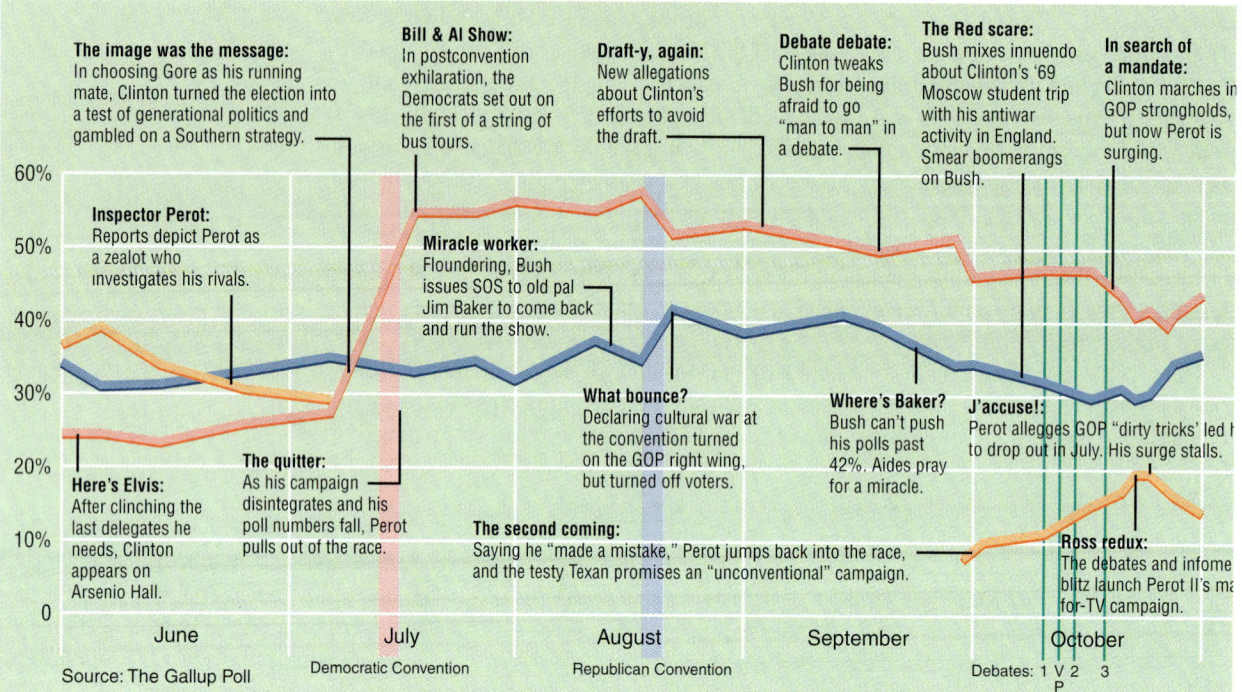

FIGURE 13-5
Landmarks in 1992 Campaign

Percentages indicate percentage of registered voters sampled by the Gallup poll who said they would vote for the candidates.

mini-scandals that threatened to drive him from the race: an alleged affair with an Arkansas woman named Gennifer Flowers, his possible evasion of the draft during the Vietnam War, and his youthful experimentation with marijuana (self-admitted, but with the explanation that he had "never inhaled").

Clinton survived and managed to outflank all his rivals, one by one. The most serious threat was former Massachusetts U.S. Senator Paul Tsongas, whose tough fiscal message—"no more Santa Claus"—attracted white middle- and upper-class Democrats concerned about the budget deficit and the country's deep-seated economic problems. Tsongas won the New Hampshire primary, with Clinton a respectable second. Senator Tom Harkin of Iowa, Senator Robert Kerrey of Nebraska, and former Governor of California Jerry Brown each won other early contests, but starting with Georgia on March 3, Clinton began to generate unstoppable momentum. On "Super Tuesday" (March 10), he swept the Southern contests, but Tsongas did well outside the South. Then, on March 17, Clinton won both Illinois and Michigan decisively. Short of money, Tsongas joined Harkin and Kerrey on the inactive list. Brown persisted, winning a few more contests, but Clinton effectively ended his challenge with a decisive win in New York on April 7. From then on, Clinton scored relatively easy victories everywhere, even in Brown's home state of California on June 2. Voter turnouts were low, however—overall just 12 percent of the voting-age population—and Democrats appeared more resigned than enthusiastic as they looked to a Clinton candidacy. Nonetheless, Clinton's 51.9 percent of the total Democratic primary votes was a solid showing.

In the months before the 1992 election, candidate Clinton was a tireless campaigner. Here he consults with strategist Paul Begala aboard his campaign jet "Longhorn One," while in flight on a 33-hour, cross-country campaign marathon on November 2, the eve of the election.

The Third Force: Ross Perot

On February 20, 1992, Texas billionaire Ross Perot, appearing on CNN's "Larry King Live," announced that if Americans in all fifty states put him on their ballots, he would run for president. Capitalizing on widespread discontent with the two major party nominees, he then launched a most improbable pseudo-candidacy that derived in good part from his intense dislike of fellow Texan Bush.

Although Perot declared a willingness to spend "whatever it takes"—estimates ranged from $100 to $300 million—of his own fortune to be competitive, he actually spent little in the early months of his unannounced candidacy. Instead, he cleverly used the free media, especially the soft-edged talk shows and morning TV ("Larry King Live," "Donahue," "Today"), to advance himself while offering little of detailed substance. With the political press at bay, he could project accessibility with little risk; with party identification on the decline, his independent stand was a magnet for many alienated voters eager for "change" and an end to politics as usual; and with nearly unlimited resources, he was not forced to waste time in a money chase. His folksy image and "can-do" approach to gridlocked government proved popular, and he rocketed to the top of the opinion polls.

Gradually, though, some less flattering facts about Perot began to filter out. The tycoon's autocratic, authoritarian manner unsettled some people, as did his penchant for conspiracy theories and alleged investigations of adversaries' private lives. Still, with a seemingly firm hold on millions of Americans, Perot cast a long shadow over both parties—until he abruptly declined to run on July 16, 1992, the last day of the Democratic National Convention. Unable to work with the feisty Texan, his campaign manager and other key aides had resigned just prior to the withdrawal. Feeling outraged and betrayed, many of Perot's supporters abandoned him, while others urged him to reverse his decision. Stung by the label of "quitter," and claiming disappointment that Bush and Clinton had not adopted his debt-reduction platform, Perot abruptly changed

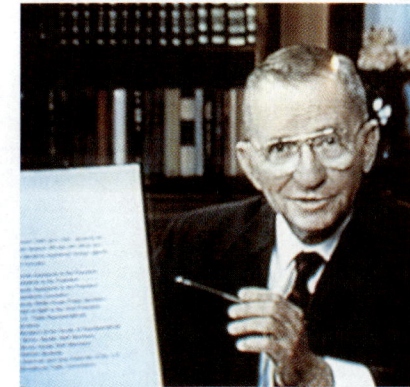

Independent candidate Ross Perot garnered 19% of the popular vote in the 1992 Presidential election. As election day neared, billionaire Perot bought network TV time and staged a series of half-hour infomercials to bring his message directly to voters.

course again on October 1 and announced his independent candidacy. But his luster was clearly gone, and his appeal sharply diminished.

The Party Conventions

Democrats gathered first in convention, in New York City from July 13–17. The week before, Clinton had named Tennessee Senator Al Gore Jr. as his running mate. The privileged son of a senator and unsuccessful candidate for president in 1988, Gore struck many people as similar to Clinton: young (44), Southern, and moderate-liberal. The unusual pairing of two Southerners on the ticket signaled the Democrats' determination to fight for GOP-leaning Dixie's electoral votes, and the match of two post–World War II "baby boom" generation candidates guaranteed a vigorous campaign and an appeal for change (as in so many camapigns in history). Gore's strengths in foreign policy and the environment as well as his Vietnam-era military service balanced several of Clinton's prominent weaknesses.

Democrats were enormously pleased and encouraged by the course of their convention, which they used to showcase a "new" Democratic Party more to the liking of mainstream America. With the exception of Jerry Brown, all of Clinton's former rivals for the nomination warmly embraced him; New York Governor Mario Cuomo gave a stirring nomination speech; the party adopted a platform incorporating important centrist positions on economics and government (for example, that government programs were not the solution to every problem); and the Clinton–Gore ticket was given a rousing sendoff. Following Perot's stunning announcement that he would not run for president, most Perot voters appeared to switch to Clinton as the other "change" candidate, and as the convention concluded, the nominee skyrocketed to a twenty-four point lead over President Bush in a CNN–Gallup survey. Buoyed by this large convention "bounce" and armed with the opportunities provided by a weak economy, Democrats looked forward to the coming campaign and tried not to look back to 1988, when nominee Michael S. Dukakis had squandered a smaller 17-point advantage and lost to George Bush.

Clinton quickly proved that he had learned from Dukakis's mistakes. Setting a pattern he would follow to Election Day, he campaigned vigorously and nearly continuously between the Democratic and Republican conventions, much of the time on a bus tour with his running mate, aggressively countering every attack made by the Bush forces and launching many attacks of his own. Combined with more bad economic news and a listless Bush response, these techniques helped him maintain his lead through the GOP convention and beyond.

Republicans prepared for their party conclave with trepidation. A few conservative activists and columnists called for Bush to step aside and not seek reelection, while other Republicans suggested that Vice President Quayle should step aside. Instead, Bush reaffirmed his ticket, and then delighted his party by moving Secretary of State James Baker— one of the architects of his 1988 victory—out of the State Department and over to the White House to serve as chief of staff and campaign manager.

On that upbeat note, the Republican National Convention opened in Houston, Texas, on August 17. That evening Pat Buchanan enthusiastically endorsed President Bush, but his harsh address, reflecting the influence of the right wing on the tone and substance of the convention, alienated many moderate Americans. Framing the November battle from the Republican perspective, the convention organizers emphasized "family values," foreign policy, and Congress bashing. President Bush gave a generally well regarded closing address on these themes.

1992 Party Primaries

DEMOCRATS

	Number of Primaries Won	Percent of Total Votes
Clinton	32	51.9
Brown	2	19.9
Tsongas	4	18.1
Uncommitted/others	1	10.1

A total of 20,179,973 votes were cast in 39 primaries.

REPUBLICANS

	Number of Primaries Won	Percent of Total Votes
Bush	39	73.0
Buchanan	0	22.4
Uncommitted/others	0	3.6
Duke	0	1.0

A total of 13,025,824 votes were cast in 39 primaries.

Source: Congressional Quarterly Weekly Supplements 50, July 4, 1992, p. 71 and August 8, 1992, p. 67.

In retrospect, many observers concluded that the convention had been poorly organized and, in particular, that giving prominence to the negative messages of Buchanan and others may have been a mistake. Most polls showed Bush achieved some "bounce" from his convention, but much less than Clinton had secured from his. Bush, it became increasingly clear, would be hard pressed to catch up.

The Fall Campaign and General Election Results

As the campaign developed in the months following the Republican convention, each of the more than 275 pre-election public opinion polls showed Bill Clinton ahead. Without question, he ran a technically superb campaign; his strategy, television advertising, use of the media, and energetic stumping (frequently on a bus) were on target and exceptionally clever. Fielding the best Democratic campaign team in a generation, he successfully projected a moderate image that appealed to a wide range of voters. Keeping his message focused on the weak economy, he was able to win back many so-called "Reagan" Democrats—registered Democrats who had voted for Republican presidential candidates since 1980. Appearing on MTV and—with saxophone in hand—on "The Arsenio Hall Show," Clinton also appealed directly and effectively to young voters. Clinton campaigners were quick to respond to Republican attacks, faxing counterstatements and "truth sheets" almost instantaneously to networks and print reporters.

Bush's campaign, in contrast, was slow to organize and even slower to focus on consistent themes. It hopped, skipped, and jumped among topics as diverse as "family values," experience, trust, Clinton's draft evasion and anti-war demonstrating, and the Arkansas record. Even Republicans admit their party had rarely, if ever, mismanaged a presidential campaign so badly. It reminded most observers of the inept effort made by Michael S. Dukakis in 1988—the same year that a finely crafted and executed campaign by George Bush won him the presidency.

Although the differences between the two campaigns was certainly a factor in the outcome of the election, it is also true that any election involving an incumbent president is essentially a referendum on his incumbency, and, in that sense, George Bush lost the election every bit as much as Bill Clinton won it. Here are some of the reasons—beyond his lackluster campaign—that Bush forfeited his second term:

- *The economy.* The U.S. economy, the most basic of all forces in presidential elections, suffered a serious recession in 1990–91 and recovered only fitfully and painfully in the months leading up to the election. In many ways relating to their pocketbooks, voters simply did not believe they were better off than four years earlier, which predisposed them to change the status quo. Clinton and Perot continually hammered away at Bush about the recession and the rising national debt, making the economy the most important issue in the campaign.
- *Presidential domestic inaction and the end of the Cold War.* Known as a "foreign policy president" because of his love of international relations, Bush often seemed disinterested in domestic affairs. His repeated declarations that the economy was improving—designed to increase consumer confidence—made him appear out of touch. Meanwhile, festering problems across the United States (decaying inner cities, infrastructure deterioration, a perceived decline in the quality of health care and education) caused many voters to yearn for a candidate who placed domestic matters at the top of his agenda. The end of the Cold War and the collapse of communism also helped focus the election squarely on domestic policy, leaving foreign affairs on the periphery.

Ideological opposites and determined rivals during the 1992 Presidential campaign, Clinton strategist James Carville and Bush manager Mary Matalin were married in 1993.

- *Vice-presidential candidates.* Bush's vice president, Dan Quayle, was certainly more competent than the news media and the late-night comics portrayed him, but his public image was so negative that he undoubtedly hurt Bush. By contrast, Clinton's vice-presidential pick, Al Gore Jr., was widely viewed as an asset, and the news media gave him extremely positive reviews.
- *The Perot factor.* The billionaire Independent had an intense hatred for his fellow Texan Bush and aimed most of his fire at the President—even charging late in the campaign (with absolutely no evidence) that the GOP planned to disrupt his daughter's wedding. Most of Perot's support was drawn from the white, suburban upper-middle class, a predominantly Republican constituency, and Bush likely suffered disproportionately as a result.
- *Scandals.* Two scandals haunted Bush's reelection effort: Iran Contra and Iraq-gate. The Iran-Contra scandal, which had begun in the Reagan administration, involved the illegal sale of U.S. arms to Iran, with some of the profits improperly diverted to fund the anti-communist *contras* fighting a civil war in the Central American country of Nicaragua. Bush, who was vice president at the time, had repeatedly claimed he was "out of the loop" on this policy, but the release of a memorandum written by Reagan Defense Secretary Casper Weinberger just days before the election suggested that he was very much in the loop. The revelation cost Bush the last-minute campaign momentum he had generated. The Iraq-gate scandal took some of the luster off of Bush's leadership in the Persian Gulf war. It referred to the U.S. policy of arming Iraq's leader, Saddam Hussein, in the years leading up to his invasion of Kuwait in 1990 and the possible postwar coverup of the Bush administration's decisions in this matter. Both scandals hampered efforts by the Bush team to raise questions about Clinton's character (marital infidelity, youthful marijuana use, and draft evasion).
- *News media bias.* Republicans claimed that the national media, particularly the television networks, the *Washington Post,* and the *New York Times,* were tilting heavily to Clinton and putting Bush and the economy in the worst possible light. Although there is some truth to this criticism, it is questionable how much media bias affected the final election outcome. The other factors discussed here weighed more heavily in leading to Bush's defeat.

Election Results. The Reagan–Bush majority coalition that had governed for twelve years simply buckled under the weight of all these burdens. "Reagan" Democrats returned en masse to the Democratic fold. Young people between the ages of eighteen and thirty also moved into Clinton's column after supporting the GOP in 1980, 1984, and 1988. Many women also shifted to Clinton, a result of a bad economy, the Democrat's pro-abortion position, and the Anita Hill–Clarence Thomas hearings of the U.S. Senate when Thomas's nomination to the Supreme Court was under consideration in 1991. Some exit poll findings suggested women comprised as much as 54 percent of the voters on November 3, 1992, so Clinton's edge among women was especially important.

Voter turnout was up in 1992 after a long and worrisome decline. About 55 percent of Americans aged eighteen and over turned up at the polling places in 1992 (and about 80 percent of those *registered* to vote did so). These numbers were a significant increase over 1988, when just 50 percent of those eighteen and older voted. But it is still well below the 62 percent of 1960 and the even higher turnouts regularly recorded in the last century.

Clinton's Electoral College victory (370 for Clinton, 168 for Bush, and 0 for Perot) was much broader than his popular vote plurality (43 percent for Clinton, 38 percent for Bush, and 19 percent for Perot) (see Figure 13-6). He was thus to be a "minority

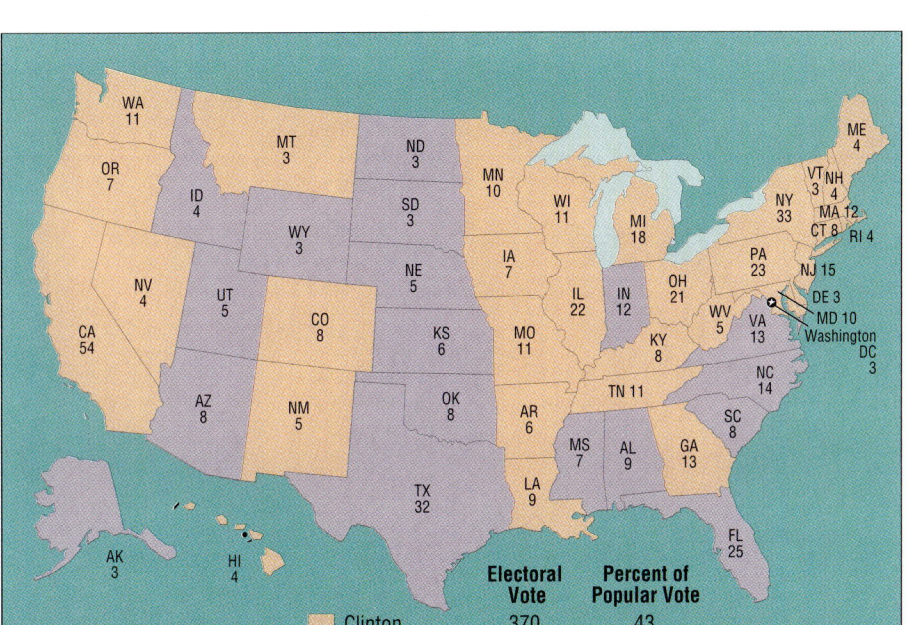

FIGURE 13-6
Results of 1992 Election

president"—elected by less than half the popular vote[9]—but one whose win was nonetheless impressive. After all, since World War II only two other challengers—Jimmy Carter in 1976 and Ronald Reagan in 1980—had ousted incumbents from the White House, and no president had been as popular as Bush was earlier in his term. Bush became the tenth president to lose a bid for reelection.[10]

The Democrats won states in every region of the country. They swept the economically hard-hit Northeast, winning even reliably Republican New Hampshire. Except for Indiana, home of Dan Quayle, the Midwest was solidly Democratic, as was the Pacific Coast. (The Republicans ceded giant California's fifty-four electoral votes to the Democrats months before the election, when polls showed them in a hopeless position there.)

President Bush achieved a respectable showing only in the South. But even in this region, which had long been solidly Republican, Florida and Texas stayed loyal to Bush by only narrow margins, and the Democrats stole Georgia and Louisiana as well as Clinton's Arkansas and Gore's Tennessee. Bush also held onto some Rocky Mountain and Plains states, but significantly, he forfeited four states that had nearly consistently voted Republican in modern times: Colorado, Montana, Nevada, and New Mexico.

---

[9] Fifteen of our forty-two chief executives were elected with less than a majority. The most recent prior to Clinton was Richard Nixon, who (like Clinton) garnered 43 percent of the votes in 1968's three-way race.

[10] The other defeated presidents (and year of defeat) were John Adams (1800), John Quincy Adams (1828), William Howard Taft (1912), Herbert Hoover (1932), Gerald Ford (1976), and Jimmy Carter (1980).

572 ❖ Chapter 13 The Campaign Process

Bill Clinton and Al Gore Jr., with their wives Hillary and Tipper, acknowledge victory in Little Rock, Arkansas on election night.

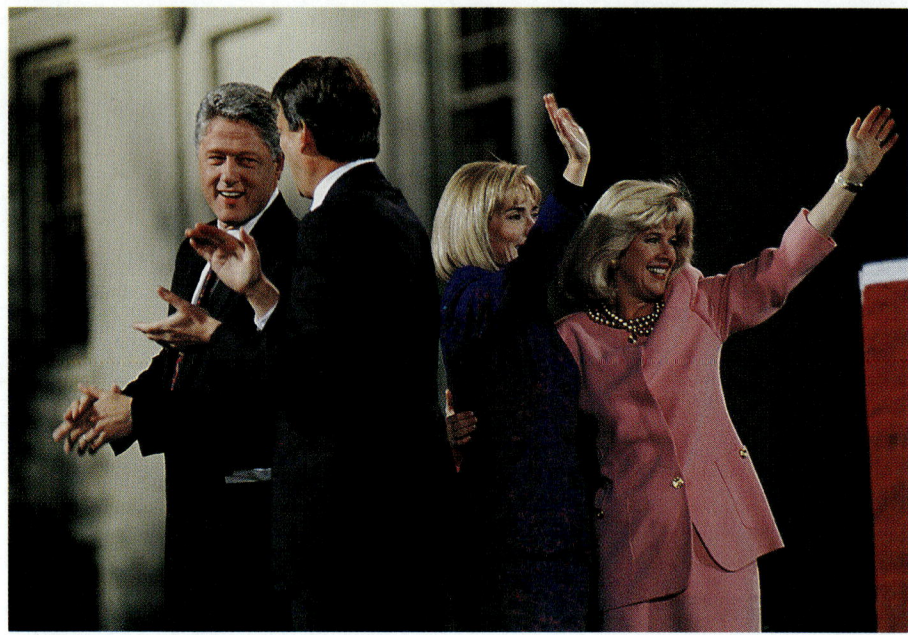

By the standards of recent history, Clinton's Electoral College majority was the most impressive and diverse for a Democrat since Lyndon Johnson's landslide election in 1964. And Bush's collapse from his 427 Electoral College votes in 1988 to 168 in 1992 was stunning. Bush fared far worse than Gerald Ford, who won 240 Electoral College votes in his losing 1976 bid. Still, Jimmy Carter, who captured just forty-nine Electoral College votes in his 1980 reelection bid, holds the post-World War II record for the most decisive defeat of an incumbent.

Toward Reform

In response to the growing concern about the amounts of money spent on federal elections, both Republicans and Democrats have sponsored major campaign-finance reform bills in Congress. But changing the rules of the game can alter the results of elections, and not surprisingly the Democratic proposals favor Democratic candidates and the Republican proposals favor Republican candidates. For many years now, as a consequence, Congress has been at an impasse on campaign reform.

Democrats favor setting a limit on the amount of money any congressional candidate can spend in an effort to win office. (For the House a candidate might be limited to $600,000; the Senate limit would depend on each state's population, with a more heavily populated state having a higher limit.) Republicans are adamantly against these spending caps, arguing that the limits mainly hurt challengers who are not as well known as incumbents are and who need to spend more money to increase their name identification. For example, from 1978 to 1988 only seven of the thirty-two winning Senate challengers remained within the spending limits proposed by the Democrats. Republicans also claim that they must spend more than Democrats do because they do not have access to any volunteer group comparable to organized labor, which aids Democrats overwhelmingly, and hence the GOP candidates normally must pay campaign workers.

Of course, both parties' positions on this issue are rooted in self-interest. The Republicans are more successful than are Democrats at raising money, and the Democrats want to limit that advantage. Moreover, the cost to either party of conceding too much on this issue is the possibility of relinquishing control of Congress for a long time to come. This makes campaign spending an issue that does not easily lend itself to compromise.

Yet many experts inside and outside of Congress argue that there are other ideas concerning campaign finance that would create a more wholesome system without resorting to spending limits. One idea is to limit the influence of political action committees (PACs). Critics charge that PACs reduce political competition by giving overwhelmingly to incumbents—usually about two-thirds to three-quarters of their warchests—while at the same time they corrupt the system by indebting legislators to the special interests that form PACs. Abolishing PACs altogether, however, is probably unconstitutional, since doing so would violate the First Amendment's guarantee of free political association. Restricting their contribution limits too greatly would only divert their money into other forms of political spending that are not easily revealed (such as funneling cash to state and local parties in states that do not require full campaign-finance disclosure). As reformers through the years have discovered, it is nearly impossible to dam the flow of political money in a free and open democratic system in which participation is encouraged.

A better way to control PACs and special-interest groups is to increase the influence and level of spending by political parties. This would limit PACs *indirectly* by augmenting the power of a rival source of campaign funds. As is discussed in Chapter 11, parties can be strengthened in many ways, especially by loosening or eliminating current restrictions on what citizens may give to a party or what a party may donate to its candidates. In addition, parties ought to receive some free broadcast time on all television and radio stations. This air time could then be allocated to the most needy nominees—incumbents who are in trouble, as well as promising challengers. Since candidates spend a major portion of their campaign funds for media advertising time—up to 60 percent in some Senate races—such a reform could conceivably help to cut the burgeoning costs of campaigns. And it would aid challengers and less wealthy candidates in particular, balancing some of the advantages of incumbency. The United States, incidentally, is the only major democratic country that does not provide some free media time to parties or candidates.

Campaign-finance reform is a favorite Washington topic, but for all the good (and bad) ideas that are proposed, little legislation is ever passed. Many incumbents prefer not to alter the system that, whatever its faults, elected them. Democrats and Republicans are also at loggerheads over the partisan effects of various reforms. The American people also remain skeptical of political parties, and little popular support can be found for their cause. The last set of campaign-finance reforms passed in the wake of Watergate, and it may take more scandal to generate enough momentum to pass a successor package of reforms in the Congress.

Summary

As the analysis of the 1992 election suggests, the campaign process in the United States is far from perfect. Campaigns stretch out seemingly interminably, unlike in Great Britain, where the entire parliamentary election process is confined to four or five weeks. Moreover, candidates in the United States are often judged on trivial issues, voters cast many ballots for the lesser of two evils, and some contenders for lower office never raise enough money to get a fair hearing. But those who follow campaigns would also do well to remember the wise words of one of this century's greatest political scientists, V. O. Key Jr. Key's central observation was simple but powerful: "Voters are not fools."* Not every citizen devotes enough time to politics, and many people are woefully uninformed at times. But virtually all voters know their basic interests and cast their ballots accordingly. They are not always right in their judgments, yet over time there is a rough justice to election results. Parties and office holders who produce a measure of prosperity and happiness for the electorate are usually rewarded, and those who do not keep the home folks satisfied may be forced to find another line of work.

In this chapter, we have stressed the following observations:

1. Campaigns, the process of seeking and winning votes in the run-up to an election, consist of five separate components: the nomination campaign, in which party leaders and activists are courted to ensure that the candidate is nominated in primaries or conventions; the general election campaign, in which the goal is to appeal to the nation as a whole; the personal campaign, in which the candidate and his or her family make appearances, meet voters, hold press conferences, and give speeches; the organizational campaign, in which volunteers telephone voters, distribute literature, organize events, and raise money; and the broadcast media campaign waged on television and on the radio.

2. Campaign staffs combine volunteers with a manager at the top and key political consultants—including media consultants, a pollster, and a direct mailer. In recent years, media consultants have assumed greater and greater importance, partly because the cost of advertising has skyrocketed, so that campaign media budgets consume the lion's share of available resources.

3. Despite the dazzle of technology and the celebrity of well-known consultants, the candidate remains the most important component of any campaign. The candidate's strengths, weaknesses, and talents are central to the success or failure of the campaign.

4. Candidates tell their story directly in paid broadcast media advertising. They are much less successful in managing and directing their *press* coverage. (This topic is taken up again in Chapter 14.)

5. Campaigns receive money from several sources. Individual contributions are currently limited to $1,000 per candidate per election; political action committees, which represent interest groups, are limited to $5,000. In addition, candidates can receive large supplements from their party, and they can spend as much of their own money as they like.

6. Campaign finance is regularly a reform issue, because candidates who outspend their opponents tend to win, and raising money is easier for some candidates than for others. Incumbents enjoy a fund-raising edge as well as advantages related to name recognition and some of the perks of office, such as mailing privileges.

---

* See V. O. Key Jr., *The Responsible Electorate* (Cambridge, MA: Harvard University Press, 1966).

Key Terms

nomination campaign
general election campaign
personal campaign
organizational campaign
media campaign
paid media
free media
media consultant
pollster
direct mailer
voter canvass
get-out-the-vote
positive ads
negative ads
contrast ads
spot ads
candidate debates
political action committees
public funds
matching funds

Suggested Readings

Abramson, Paul R., John H. Aldrich, and David W. Rohde. *Change and Continuity in the 1988 Elections.* Washington, DC: CQ Press, 1990.

Alexander, Herbert E., and Monica Bauer. *Financing the 1988 Election.* Boulder, CO: Westview Press, 1991.

Goldenberg, Edie, and Michael W. Traugott. *Campaigning for Congress.* Washington, DC: CQ Press, 1984.

Jackson, Brooks. *Honest Graft: Big Money and the American Political Process.* Washington, DC: Farragut, 1990.

Kern, Montague. *30-Second Politics: Political Advertising in the Eighties.* New York: Praeger, 1989.

Nelson, Michael, ed. *The Elections of 1992.* Washington, DC: CQ Press, 1993.

Orren, Gary R., and Nelson W. Polsby, eds. *Media and Momentum: The New Hampshire Primary and Nomination Politics.* Chatham, NJ: Chatham House, 1987.

Patterson, Thomas E. *The Mass Media Election.* New York: Praeger, 1980.

Pomper, Gerald M., ed. *The Election of 1992: Reports and Interpretations.* Chatham, NJ: Chatham House, 1993.

Sabato, Larry J., ed. *Campaigns and Elections: A Reader in Modern American Politics.* Glenview, IL: Scott, Foresman, 1989.

———. *PAC Power: Inside the World of Political Action Committees.* New York: Norton, 1985.

———. *Paying for Elections: The Campaign Finance Thicket.* New York: Priority Press for the Twentieth Century Fund, 1989.

———. *The Rise of Political Consultants: New Ways of Winning Elections.* New York: Basic Books, 1981.

Salmore, Barbara G., and Stephen Salmore. *Candidates, Parties, and Campaigns,* 2nd ed. Washington, DC: CQ Press, 1989.

Sorauf, Frank J. *Money in American Elections.* Glenview, IL: Scott, Foresman, 1988.

What is the liberty of the press? Who can give it any definition which would not leave the utmost latitude for evasion? . . . [I]ts security, whatever fine declarations may be inserted in any constitution respecting it, must altogether depend on public opinion, and on the general spirit of the people and of the government.

Alexander Hamilton
Federalist No. 84

Hamilton asserted that the rights of a free press, like all other democratic rights, ultimately depend on the support of the public.

CHAPTER 14

The News Media

THE AMERICAN PRESS OF YESTERYEAR
THE CONTEMPORARY MEDIA SCENE
HOW THE MEDIA COVER POLITICIANS AND GOVERNMENT
THE POST-WATERGATE ERA
THE MEDIA'S INFLUENCE ON THE PUBLIC
HOW POLITICIANS USE THE MEDIA
GOVERNMENT REGULATION OF THE ELECTRONIC MEDIA
TOWARD REFORM

The press is now, and has always been, controversial. Whether it is publication of the name of a rape victim or of unsubstantiated rumors about a presidential candidate, or the use of ambush journalism made famous by the television program "60 Minutes," the news media are sure to generate public outcry and criticism with regularity.

The passage by Alexander Hamilton that opens this chapter is a pointed reminder that many of the Framers did not share the belief that guaranteed freedom of the press is fundamental to American democracy. Actually, Federalists such as Hamilton agreed to include freedom of the press and the other amendments in the Bill of Rights only to satisfy states' righters and secure passage of the Constitution. In fact, there is not much evidence that even the staunchest advocates of the Bill of Rights favored *absolute* freedom of the press—that is, a free press unbalanced by other legitimate rights, such as those of personal privacy, fair trial, copyright protection, and national security.[1] The surprising truth is that the Framers devoted little thought and debate to the free press clause because it was not considered a matter of the highest importance. Even its position as the *First* Amendment is deceptive. Originally the rights of free speech and press were included in the third amendment to the proposed Bill of Rights, but the first two amendments were not ratified by the original states. So what we now herald as the all-powerful, preeminent First Amendment was a product of political compromise, relative inattention, and historical accident!

---

[1] See Dom Bonafede, "First Amendment on Trial," *National Journal* 23 (July 20, 1991): 1833.

Nonetheless, the simple words *"Congress shall make no law . . . abridging the freedom of speech, or of the press"* have shaped the American republic as much as or more than any others in the Constitution and its amendments. With the Constitution's sanction, as interpreted by the Supreme Court over two centuries, a vigorous and highly competitive press has emerged. Composed of **print press** (newspapers, magazines, journals) and **electronic media** (television and radio), the news media in the United States arguably have more freedom and are less controlled today than any other press in the world. How this freedom evolved, the ways in which it is manifested, and whether press freedom is used responsibly are subjects we examine in this chapter.[2] We first review the history and development of the press in the colonies and the United States, and then survey the contemporary media scene. We look closely at how journalists cover politicians and government (president, Congress, and the courts), especially the modern emphasis on investigation of private lives. Among other questions addressed are these: Are the news media biased? How much does the press influence the public's voting choice? In what ways do politicians attempt to influence the mass media? Finally, we explain how the government regulates the news business—a delicate matter in a free society.

The American Press of Yesteryear

Journalism—the process and profession of collecting and disseminating the news (that is, new information about subjects of public interest)—has been with us in some form since the dawn of civilization.[3] Yet its practice has often been remarkably uncivilized, and it was much more so at the beginning of the American republic than it is today.

A hint of future directions appeared in the first newspaper published in the North American colonies in 1690, which carried a report that the king of France "used to lie with" his son's wife. George Washington escaped most press scrutiny but detested journalists nonetheless; his battle tactics in the Revolutionary War had been much criticized in print, and an early draft of his "Farewell Address to the Nation" at the end of his presidency (1796) contained a condemnation of the press that has often been described as savage.[4] Thomas Jefferson was treated especially harshly by elements of the early U.S. press. For example, one Richmond newspaper editor, angered by Jefferson's refusal to appoint him as postmaster, concocted a falsehood that survives to this day: that Jefferson kept a slave as his concubine and had several children by her.[5] One can understand why Jefferson, normally a defender of a free press, commented that "even the least informed of the people have learned that nothing in a newspaper is to be believed."

Jefferson probably did not intend that statement literally, since he himself was instrumental in establishing the *National Gazette,* the newspaper of his political faction and viewpoint. The *Gazette* was created to compete with a similar paper (called the

---

[2] For more on this topic, see Larry J. Sabato, *Feeding Frenzy* (New York: The Free Press, 1991).

[3] See Mitchell Stephens, *A History of News: From the Drum to the Satellite* (New York: Viking, 1989).

[4] Charles Press and Kenneth VerBurg, *American Politicians and Journalists* (Glenview, IL: Scott, Foresman, 1988), pp. 8–10.

[5] See Merrill D. Peterson, *Thomas Jefferson and the New Nation* (New York: Oxford University Press, 1970), pp. 185–187.

Landmark Events in the History of the American Media	
1690 ♦	First newspaper published
1789 ♦	First party newspapers circulated
1833 ♦	First penny press
1890 ♦	Yellow journalism spreads
1900 ♦	Muckraking in fashion
1928 ♦	First radio broadcast of an election
1948 ♦	First election results to be covered by television
1952 ♦	First presidential campaign advertisements aired on television
1960 ♦	First televised presidential campaign debates

Gazette of the United States) founded earlier by Alexander Hamilton and his anti-Jefferson Federalists. The era of party newspapers extended from Washington's tenure through Andrew Jackson's presidency. The editor of Jackson's party paper, *The Globe,* was included in the president's influential "kitchen cabinet" (a group of informal advisers), and all of Jackson's appointees with annual salaries greater than $1,000 were required to buy a subscription. (Incidentally, from George Washington through James Buchanan, who left office in 1861, all government printing contracts were awarded to the newspaper associated with the incumbent administration).

A Less Partisan Press

The partisan press eventually gave way to the penny press. In 1833 Benjamin Day founded the *New York Sun,* which cost a penny at the newsstand. It was politically a more independent publication than the party papers, and it was not tied to one party. The *Sun* was the forerunner of the modern press built on mass circulation and commercial advertising to produce profit. By 1861 the penny press had so supplanted partisan papers that President Abraham Lincoln (who succeeded Buchanan) announced that his administration would have no favored or sponsored newspaper.

The press thus became markedly less partisan but not necessarily more respectable. Mass-circulation dailies sought wide readership, and, then as now, readers were clearly attracted by the sensational and the scandalous. The sordid side of politics became the entertainment of the times. One of the best-known examples occurred in the presidential campaign of 1884, when the *Buffalo Evening Telegraph* headlined "A Terrible Tale" about Grover Cleveland, the Democratic nominee.[6] In 1871, while sheriff of

---

[6] For a delightful rendition of this episode, see Shelley Ross, *Fall from Grace* (New York: Ballantine, 1988), Chapter 12.

Buffalo, the bachelor Cleveland had allegedly fathered a child. Even though the woman in question had been seeing other men, Cleveland willingly accepted responsibility since all the other men were married, and he had dutifully paid child support for years. Fortunately for Cleveland, another newspaper, the *Democratic Sentinel,* broke a story that helped to offset this scandal: Republican presidential nominee James G. Blaine and his wife had had their first child just three months after their wedding. There is a lesson for politicians in this double-edged morality tale. Cleveland acknowledged his responsibility forthrightly and took his lumps, whereas Blaine told a fabulously elaborate, completely unbelievable story about having had two marriage ceremonies six months apart. Cleveland won the election (although other factors also played a role in his victory).

The era of the intrusive press was in full flower. First **yellow journalism** and then **muckraking** were in fashion. Pioneered by prominent publishers such as William Randolph Hearst and Joseph Pulitzer, yellow journalism[7] featured pictures, comics, and color designed to capture a share of the burgeoning immigrant population market. These newspapers also oversimplified and sensationalized many news developments. The front-page editorial crusade became common, the motto for which frequently seemed to be "Damn the truth, full speed ahead."

The muckrakers—so named by President Theodore Roosevelt after a special rake designed to collect manure[8]—took charge after the turn of the century in a number of newspapers and nationally circulated magazines. Journalists such as Upton Sinclair and David Graham Phillips searched out and exposed real and apparent misconduct by government, business, and politicians in order to stimulate reform.[9] There was no

---

[7] The name strictly derived from printing the comic strip "Yellow Kid" in color.
[8] Doris A. Graber, *Mass Media and American Politics,* 3rd ed. (Washington, DC: CQ Press, 1989), p. 12.
[9] See Thomas C. Leonard, *The Power of the Press: The Birth of American Political Reporting* (New York: Oxford University Press, 1986), Chapter 7.

"Uncle Sam's Next Campaign—the War Against the Yellow Press." In this 1898 cartoon in the wake of the Spanish American War, yellow journalism is attacked for its threats, insults, filth, grime, blood, death, slander, gore, and blackmail, all of which are "lies." The cartoonist suggests that, after winning the foreign war, the government ought to attack its own yellow journalists at home.

shortage of corruption to reveal, of course, and much good came from these efforts. But an unfortunate side effect of the emphasis on crusades and investigations was the frequent publication of gossip and rumor without sufficient proof.

The modern press corps may also be guilty of this offense, but it has achieved great progress on another front. Throughout the nineteenth century, payoffs to the press were not uncommon. Andrew Jackson, for instance, gave one in ten of his early appointments to loyal reporters,[10] and during the 1872 presidential campaign the Republicans slipped cash to about three hundred newsmen.[11] Wealthy industrialists also sometimes purchased editorial peace or investigative cease-fire for tens of thousands of dollars. Examples of such press corruption are exceedingly rare today, and not even the most extreme of the modern media's critics believe otherwise.

As the news business grew, its focus gradually shifted from passionate opinion to corporate profit. Newspapers, hoping to maximize profit, were more careful to avoid alienating the advertisers and readers who produced their revenues, and the result was less harsh, more objective reporting. Meanwhile, media barons became pillars of the establishment; for the most part, they were no longer the anti-establishment insurgents of yore.

Technological advances obviously had a major impact on this transformation in journalism. High-speed presses and more cheaply produced paper made mass-circulation dailies possible. The telegraph and, later, the telephone made news gathering easier and much faster. And, of course, nothing else could compare to the invention of radio and television. Radio became widely available in the 1920s, and, for the first time, millions of Americans were hearing national politicians instead of merely reading about them. With television—first introduced in the late 1940s and nearly a universal fixture in U.S. homes by the mid-1950s—citizens could see and hear candidates and presidents. The removal of newspapers and magazines as the foremost conduits between politicians and voters had profound effects on the electoral process, as we discuss shortly.

The Contemporary Media Scene

The editors of the first partisan newspapers could scarcely have imagined what their profession would become more than two centuries later. The number and diversity of media outlets existing in the 1990s are stunning: many thousands of daily and weekly newspapers, periodicals (magazines, newsletters, computerized information services), and radio and television stations and networks. In some ways the news business is more competitive than at any time in history, yet, paradoxically, the news media have expanded in some ways and contracted in others, dramatically changing the ways in which they cover politics.

The growth of the political press corps is obvious to anyone familiar with government or campaigns. Since 1983, for example, the number of print (newspaper and magazine) reporters accredited at the U.S. Capitol has jumped from 2,300 to more

Almost from the beginning of his 1992 presidential campaign, Bill Clinton attracted intense media coverage. After placing second in the New Hampshire primary in February, he quickly jumped to front-runner status. Whether this status was real or media-appointed finally mattered little as Clinton made adept use of press scrutiny right up to election day.

---

[10] Richard L. Rubin, *Press, Party, and Presidency* (New York: Norton, 1981), pp. 38–39.
[11] Stephen Bates, *If No News, Send Rumors* (New York: St. Martin's Press, 1989), p. 185.

than 4,100; the gain for broadcast (television and radio) journalists was equally impressive and proportionately larger, from about 1,000 in 1983 to more than 2,400 by 1990.[12] On the campaign trail a similar phenomenon has been occurring. In the 1960s a presidential candidate in the primaries would attract a press entourage of at most a couple of dozen reporters, but in the 1990s a hundred or more print and broadcast journalists can be seen tagging along with a frontrunner. Consequently, a politician's every public utterance is reported and intensively scrutinized and interpreted in the media.

Although there are more journalists, they are not necessarily attracting a larger audience, at least on the print side. Daily newspaper circulation has been stagnant for twenty years at 62 to 63 million papers per day (see Figure 14-1). On a per household basis, circulation has actually fallen 44 percent over these two decades.[13] Barely half of the adult population reads a newspaper every day. Among young people age eighteen to twenty-nine, only one-third are daily readers—a decline of 50 percent in two decades.

[12] Barbara Matusow, "Washington's Journalism Establishment," *The Washingtonian* 23 (February 1989): 94–101, 265–270.

[13] See Eleanor Randolph, "Extra! Extra! Who Cares?" *Washington Post* (April 1, 1990): C1, 4.

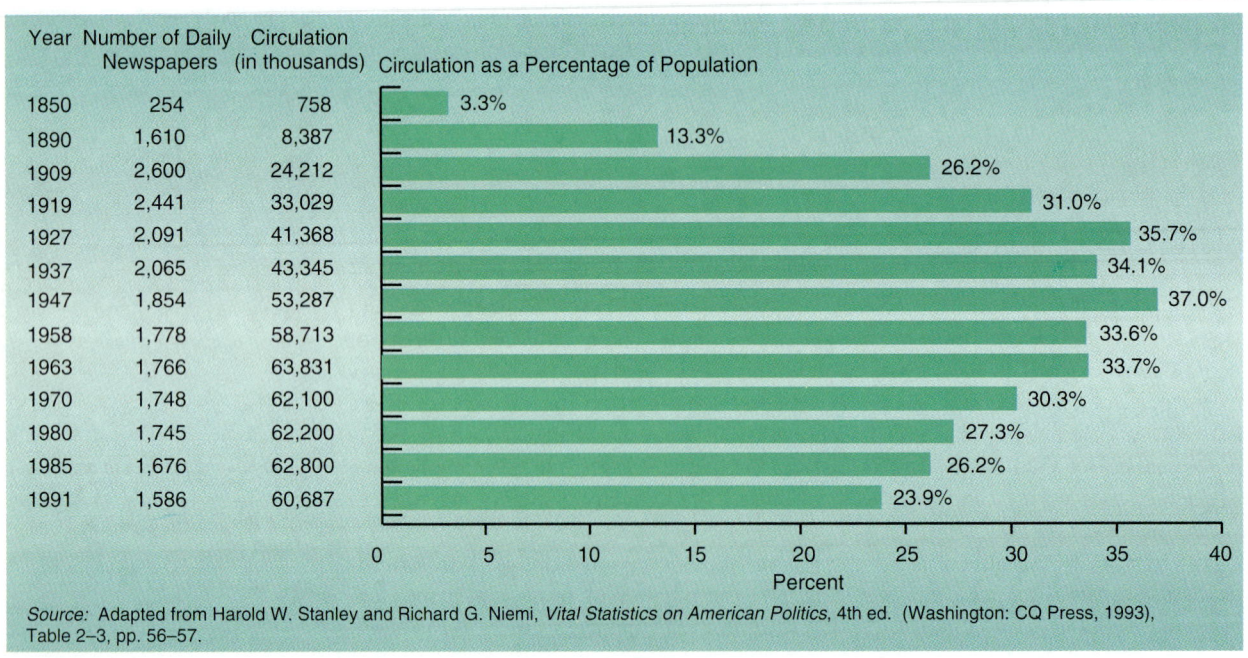

FIGURE 14-1
Circulation of Daily Newspapers, 1850–1991

The number of daily newspapers peaked in 1909, and it has fallen sharply since. The proportion of Americans who subscribe to newspapers has also dropped steadily since 1947, and less than a quarter of the U.S. population subscribes to a daily newspaper today.

Along with the relative decline of readership has come a drop in the overall level of competition. In 1880, 61 percent of U.S. cities had at least two competing dailies, but by 1990 a mere 2 percent of cities did so. Not surprisingly, the number of dailies has declined significantly, from a peak of 2,600 in 1909 to 1,611 today.[14] Most of the remaining dailies are owned by large media conglomerates called chains. In 1940, 83 percent of all daily newspapers were independently owned, but by 1990 just 24 percent remained independent of a chain (such as Gannett, Hearst, Knight-Ridder, and Newhouse). Chain ownership usually reduces the diversity of editorial opinions and can result in the homogenization of the news.

Part of the cause of the newspapers' declining audience has been the increased numbers of television sets and cable subscribers (see Figure 14-2) and the increased popularity of television as a news source. As Table 14.1 shows, at the dawn of the 1960s a substantial majority of Americans reported that they got most of their news from newspapers, but by the latter half of the 1980s television was the people's choice by an almost two-to-one margin.[15] Moreover, by a margin of 55 to 21 percent, Americans now say that they are inclined to believe television over newspapers when conflicting reports about the same story arise. Of course, most individuals still rely on *both* print and broadcast sources,[16] but there can be little question that television news is increasingly important. Despite its many drawbacks (such as simplicity, brevity, and enter-

---

[14] Sunday newspapers are exceptions to the trend. More than one hundred new Sunday papers were created in the decade of the 1980s, and Sunday circulation as a whole has increased 25 percent since 1970.

[15] Harold W. Stanley and Richard G. Niemi, *Vital Statistics on American Politics* (Washington, DC: CQ Press, 1988), Table 2-8, p. 58.

[16] See Evans Witt, "Here, There, and Everywhere: Where Americans Get Their News," *Public Opinion* 6 (August/September 1983): 45–48; June O. Yum and Kathleen E. Kendall, "Sources of Political Information in a Presidential Primary Campaign," *Journalism Quarterly* 65 (Spring 1988): 148–151, 177.

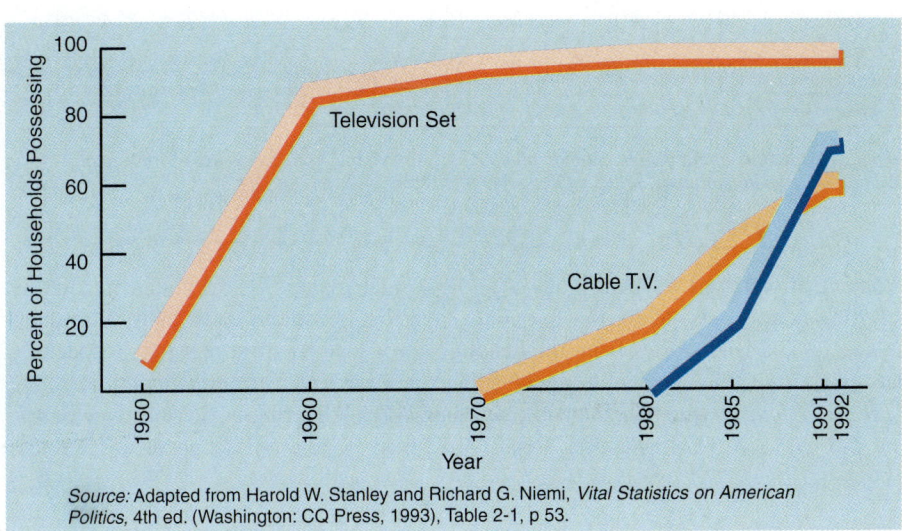

FIGURE 14-2

Television in the American Home

Television sets have been standard equipment in the average American home since the 1960s. Cable television was added only in the 1980s, and this technological innovation has joined U.S. households with phenomenal speed.

Source: Adapted from Harold W. Stanley and Richard G. Niemi, *Vital Statistics on American Politics,* 4th ed. (Washington: CQ Press, 1993), Table 2-1, p 53.

Table 14.1 ♦ Use and Trustworthiness of News Media

In the 1950s, newspapers provided most of the average American's news, and papers were more "believable" than television. By the 1980s, television had triumphed over newspapers in both categories, and TV had also eclipsed the influence of radio and magazines.

Source of most news (by percent)

Question: *"First, I'd like to ask you where you usually get most of your news about what's going on in the world today—from the newspapers or radio or television or magazines or talking to people or where?"* (more than one answer permitted)

	1959	1963	1967	1972	1976	1982	1986	1992
Television	51%	55%	64%	64%	64%	64%	66%	69% (1)
Newspapers	57	53	55	50	49	44	36	43 (2)
Radio	34	29	28	21	19	18	14	16 (3)
Magazines	8	6	7	6	7	6	4	4 (5)
People	4	4	4	4	5	4	4	6 (4)

Most believable (by percent)

Question: *"If you got conflicting or different reports of the same news story from radio, television, the magazines, and the newspapers, which of the versions would you be most inclined to believe—the one on the radio or television or magazines or newspapers?"* (only one answer permitted)

	1959	1963	1967	1972	1976	1982	1986	1992
Television	29%	36%	41%	48%	51%	53%	55%	56% (1)
Newspapers	32	24	24	21	22	22	21	22 (2)
Radio	12	12	7	8	7	6	6	7 (3)
Magazines	10	10	8	10	9	8	7	4 (4)
Don't know/ no answer	17	18	20	13	11	11	12	12 (5)

Source: Adapted from Harold W. Stanley and Richard G. Niemi, *Vital Statistics on American Politics,* 4th ed. (Washington, DC: CQ Press, 1994), Table 2-12, p. 74.

tainment orientation) television news is "news that matters."[17] Although not totally eclipsing newspapers, television frequently overshadows them, even as it often takes its agenda and lead stories from the headlines produced by print reporters (especially those working for the print elite, such as the *New York Times,* the *Washington Post,* the *Wall Street Journal,* the Associated Press, United Press International, *Time, Newsweek,* and *U.S. News & World Report*). Regrettably, busy people today appear to have less

---

[17] This was the fundamental conclusion of Shanto Iyengar and Donald R. Kinder, *News That Matters* (Chicago: University of Chicago Press, 1987).

time to review the printed word, and consequently they rely more on television's brief headline summaries to stay in touch.

The television news industry differs from its print counterpart in a variety of ways. The number of outlets has been increasing, not declining, as with newspapers. The three major networks now receive broadcast competition from Cable Network News (CNN), "Headline News," Cable Satellite Public Affairs Network (C-SPAN), and PBS's "MacNeil/Lehrer NewsHour." Although the audiences of all the alternate shows are relatively small compared with those of the network news shows, they are growing while the networks' audience shares contract. The potential for cable expansion is still large, too; fewer than half of all U.S. households are currently wired for cable. Adding to television's diversity, the national television news corps is often outnumbered on the campaign trail by local television reporters. Satellite technology has provided any of the 1,300 local stations willing to invest in the hardware an opportunity to beam back reports from the field. On a daily basis, local news is watched by more people (67 percent of adults) than is network news (49 percent), so increased local attention to politics has some real significance.

The decline of the major networks' audience shares and the local stations' decreasing reliance on the major networks for news—coupled with stringent belt tightening ordered by the networks' corporate managers—resulted in severe news staff cutbacks at NBC, CBS, and ABC during the 1980s. These economy measures have affected the quality of broadcast journalism. Many senior correspondents bemoan the loss of desk assistants and junior reporters, who did much of the legwork necessary to get less superficial, more in-depth pieces on the air. As a consequence, stories requiring extensive research are often discarded in favor of simplistic, eye-catching, "sexy" items that increasingly seem to dominate campaign and government coverage.

The 51-day seige of the Branch Davidian compound in Waco, Texas, was covered intensely by the four television networks, all major newspapers, the wire services, independent producers, tabloid entertainment programs, and the international press. Even the reaction of cult leader David Koresh's family was covered by the media: the family watched the compound burn to the ground—on television.

Media That Matter

Every newspaper, radio station, and television station is influential in its own area, but only a handful of media outlets really are influential in a national sense. The United States has no nationwide daily newspapers to match the influence of Great Britain's *The Times,* the *Guardian,* and the *Daily Telegraph,* all of which are avidly read in virtually every corner of the United Kingdom. The national orientation of the British print media can be traced to the smaller size of the country and also to London's role as both the national capital and the largest cultural metropolis. The vastness of the United States and the existence of many large cities, such as New York, Los Angeles, and Chicago, effectively preclude a nationally united print medium in this country.

However, national distribution of the *New York Times,* the *Wall Street Journal, USA Today,* and the *Christian Science Monitor* does exist, and other newspapers, such as the *Washington Post* and the *Los Angeles Times,* have substantial influence from coast to coast. These six newspapers also have a pronounced effect on what the four national **networks** (ABC, CBS, NBC, and CNN) broadcast on their evening news programs—or, in the case of CNN, air on cable around the clock. A major story that breaks in one of these papers is nearly guaranteed to be featured on one or more of the network news shows. These news shows are carried by hundreds of local stations—

PEOPLE OF THE PAST

Pioneers of the Broadcasting Industry

One of the first and most prominent broadcast journalists in the United States was the CBS radio anchor Edward R. Murrow. Trained in language and public speaking through childhood Bible readings and endowed with a richly textured voice, Murrow was a superb radio reporter who later adapted his skills to the new medium of television.

Murrow joined CBS in 1935 as director of "talks and education," a position that entailed setting up radio speeches by prominent public officials. In 1937 he became European director of "talks," stationed in London, a move that would prove to be the catalyst for his career as a radio newscaster. When Germany invaded Austria on March 11, 1938, Murrow was on assignment in Poland, but he was soon directed to go to Vienna. Once he was in Austria, which he reached only with great difficulty, Murrow's dramatic eyewitness accounts of Adolf Hitler's takeover mesmerized both Europe and the United States.

Murrow's finest moment, however, came in the 1940 Battle of Britain—the German bombing campaign that

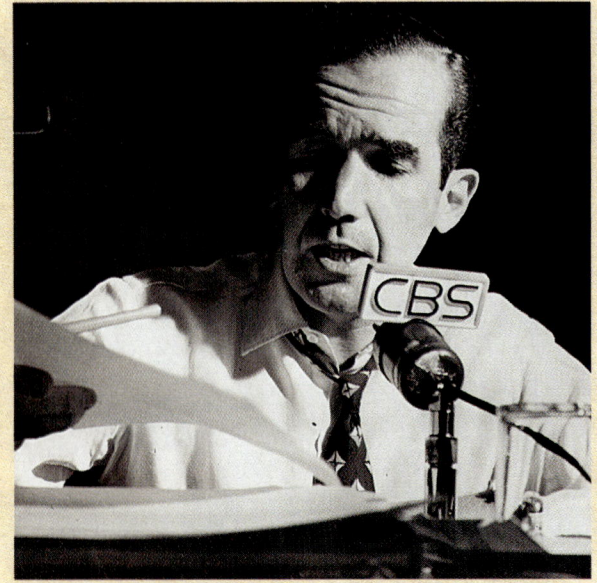

Edward R. Murrow

called **affiliates**—that are associated with the national networks and may choose to carry their programming. A **wire service,** the Associated Press (AP), also nationalizes the news. Most newspapers subscribe to the service, which not only produces its own news stories but also puts on the wire major stories produced by other media outlets. The AP was established in 1848.

The national newspapers, wire service, and broadcast networks are supplemented by a number of national news magazines, whose subscribers number in the millions. *Time, Newsweek,* and *U.S. News & World Report* bring the week's news into focus and headline one event or trend for special treatment. Other news magazines stress commentary from an ideological viewpoint, including *The Nation* (left-wing), *The New Republic* (moderate-liberal), and *The National Review* (conservative). These last three publications have much smaller circulations, but their readerships are composed of activists and opinion leaders, and therefore they have disproportionate influence.

Circumstances can conspire to make a less important publication into a relative giant. For example, the *Manchester Union-Leader* in New Hampshire and the *Des Moines Register* in Iowa are closely read by a national political audience in the months leading up to the early presidential contests in these states. (In presidential election years, New Hampshire holds the nation's first scheduled primary, and Iowa has the first caucus.)

---

flattened much of London. Probably more than any other broadcast journalist, Murrow brought the air battle to the forefront of U.S. public attention. Murrow was so respected by British authorities that only he and two other reporters—NBC's Fred Bates and John Mac-Vane—were permitted to broadcast without first clearing their information with British censors. Murrow, Bates, and MacVane all did rooftop broadcasts during Germany's bombing raids, but CBS's were the most listened to because of Murrow's special talents.

After the war, in 1946, Murrow became vice president of news and public affairs at CBS. His task was to set the course of that network's radio newscasting, and one of his achievements was the development of CBS's first documentary unit. Yet Murrow did not really enjoy administration, and a few years later he returned to the field as a journalist, this time on television. Among his many accomplishments were hard-hitting CBS programs on the right-wing extremism of U.S. Senator Joseph R. McCarthy (R.-Wis.) and on the poverty and exploitation of migrant workers. In 1961 Murrow was appointed director of the United States Information Agency by President John F. Kennedy. He died of cancer in 1965.

Meanwhile, NBC television was establishing the first broadcast news anchor team for its evening news show. Chet Huntley and David Brinkley hosted "The Huntley-Brinkley Report" each night for fifteen minutes. The two had first been paired to cover the 1956 Democratic and Republican presidential conventions, and it was obvious from the start that they were compatible and appealing. Huntley, a North Carolina native who got his start with United Press International, had a solemn, serious style of reporting. Brinkley, a Montanan who began his media career working for KPCB-AM in Seattle while a senior at the University of Washington (he was at once a disc jockey, a writer, a salesman, and a janitor), had a sharp, witty tone that complemented Huntley nicely. Americans quickly became accustomed to their style and their signature signoff at program's end: "Goodnight, David." "Goodnight, Chet." "And goodnight for NBC News."

"The Huntley-Brinkley Report" ran for fourteen years, from 1956 to 1970. In 1963 its time slot was increased to a half hour, mostly in response to competition from CBS, which had initiated the first half-hour news show on network television, anchored by another rising star, Walter Cronkite. In 1970 the team broke up when Chet Huntley decided to retire. Chet Huntley has since died; David Brinkley still broadcasts a Sunday talk show, "This Week with David Brinkley," although he has changed networks, working now for ABC News.

How the Media Cover Politicians and Government

Covering the Presidency

The three branches of the U.S. government—the executive, the legislative, and the judicial—are roughly equal in power and authority, but in the world of media coverage, the president is first among equals. All television cables lead to the White House, and a president can address the nation on all networks almost at will. On television, Congress and the courts appear to be divided and confused institutions—different segments contradicting others—whereas the commander-in-chief is in clear focus as chief of state and head of government. The situation is scarcely different in other democracies. In Great Britain, all media eyes are on No. 10 Downing Street, the office and residence of the prime minister.

Since Franklin D. Roosevelt's time, chief executives have used the presidential press conference to shape public opinion and explain their actions (see Figure 14-3). The presence of the press in the White House enables a president to appear even on very short notice and to televise live, interrupting regular programming. The White House's press-briefing room is a familiar sight on the evening news, not just because presidents use it so often but also because the presidential press secretary has almost daily question-and-answer sessions there.

The press secretary's post has existed only since Herbert Hoover's administration (1929–33), and the individual holding it is the president's main conduit of information to the press. For this vital position, a number of presidents have chosen close aides

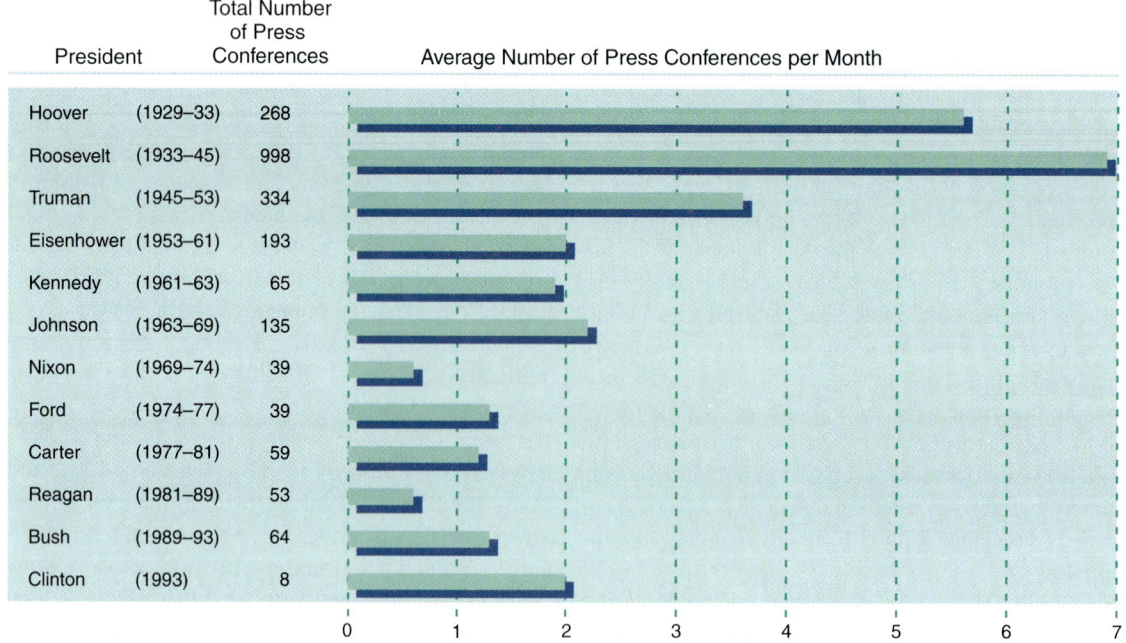

FIGURE 14-3

Presidential News Conferences, 1929–1993

[a] As of May 15, 1993.

Source: Adapted from Harold W. Stanley and Richard G. Niemi, *Vital Statistics on American Politics*, 4th ed. (Washington: CQ Press, 1993) Table 2–4, p. 59.

> ## The White House Press Corps
> ♦ ♦ ♦
>
> Perhaps the most visible part of the national press corps is the group of correspondents who work at the White House. Every network, many large television stations, and virtually all big-city daily newspapers have at least one representative who works in the White House to cover the president and his chief advisers. Other media outlets representing foreign countries are also given access to the White House and are included in the presidential press corps.
>
> White House reporters do not have the run of the place, of course. They are usually restricted to the press room, where the president makes announcements and holds informal question-and-answer sessions. Small cubicles adjoining the press room are also provided for many news outlets. Although presidential appearances in the press room rarely occur more than once or twice a week, the president's news secretary appears daily to brief reporters on the chief executive's current schedule and activities. Frequently the press secretary also makes announcements on behalf of the president (perhaps the chief executive's comments on just-released economic statistics, for example).
>
> Formal presidential news conferences, often held in the East Room of the White House, are an elaborate production, especially if held during prime-time hours. All the networks carry them live and in full, and correspondents jockey to attract the president's attention. The best-known reporters are nearly guaranteed to be selected to ask a question, and these are prime opportunities for them and for the news organizations they represent. Over the years, many of the networks' most prominent professionals have served on the White House beat, including CBS's Dan Rather and Lesley Stahl, NBC's Tom Brokaw, and ABC's Sam Donaldson. Many print journalists, such as United Press International's Helen Thomas, also become well known while on the White House beat. In fact, these reporters become celebrities, and they are often asked to appear on the late-night David Letterman and Jay Leno shows. On occasion, they have played themselves in movies (such as *Dave*).
>
> It is not always easy for the president to have reporters literally underfoot. But the instantaneous access to the American people they give the president is essential to his work, and the scrutiny of the chief executive they offer the American people is vital to the voters as well.

who were very familiar with their thinking. For example, John F. Kennedy had Pierre Salinger (now an ABC News foreign correspondent), Lyndon B. Johnson had Bill Moyers (who now hosts many PBS documentaries), and Jimmy Carter chose his longtime Georgia associate Jody Powell. Probably the most famous recent presidential press secretary is James Brady, who was wounded and disabled in the March 1981 assassination attempt on President Ronald Reagan. President Bill Clinton's press secretary Dee Dee Myers, has also become an instantly recognizable figure. (See the box on page 590.)

Covering Congress

Press coverage of Congress is very different from media coverage of the president. The size of the institution alone (535 members) and its decentralized nature (bicameralism, the committee system, and so on) make it difficult for the media to survey. Nevertheless, the congressional press corps has more than 3,000 members (Figure 14-4). Most news organizations solve the size and decentralization problems by concentrating coverage on three groups of individuals. First, the leaders of both parties in both houses receive the lion's share of attention because only they can speak for a majority of their party's members. Usually the majority and minority leaders in each house and

FIGURE 14-4

Growth of Congressional Press Corps, 1964–1991

Steady growth in the number of reporters covering Congress has occurred from the time of the Civil War to the present day. But only in the 1980s did TV and radio newspeople begin to outnumber newspaper journalists. Press corps members are correspondents entitled to admission to the Senate and House press galleries and to radio and television galleries.

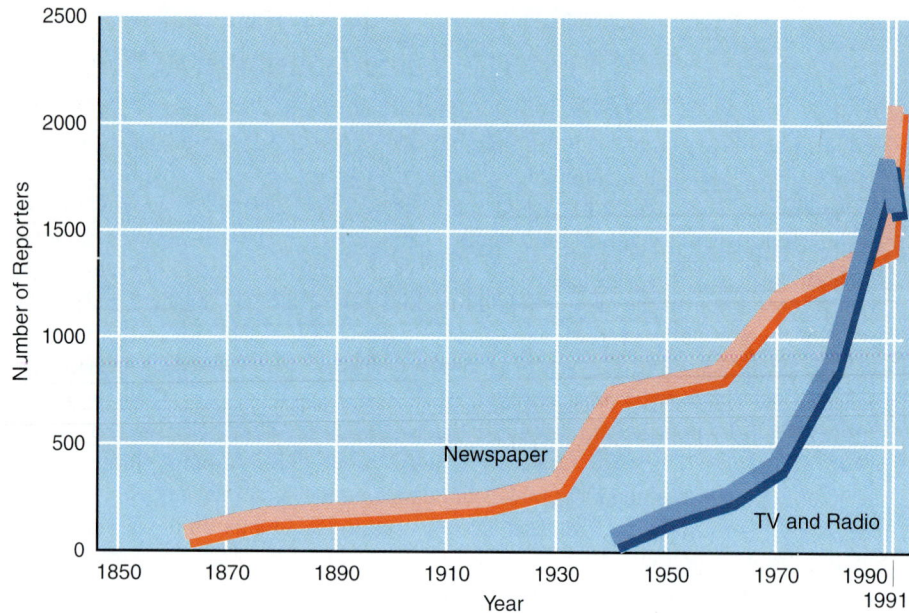

Source: Adapted from Harold W. Stanley and Richard G. Niemi, *Vital Statistics on American Politics*, 4th ed. (Washington: CQ Press, 1993), Figure 2–1, p. 58.

the Speaker of the House are the preferred spokespersons, but the whips also receive a substantial share of air time and column inches. Second, key committee chairs command center stage when subjects in their domain are newsworthy. Heads of the most prominent committees (such as Ways and Means or Armed Services) are guaranteed frequent coverage, but even the chairs and members of minor committees or subcommittees can achieve fame when the time and issue are right. For example, the U.S.

Press Secretary Dee Dee Myers

Dee Dee Myers

President Clinton's press secretary, Dee Dee Myers, has two special distinctions. She is the first woman ever to be presidential press secretary, and, when she was appointed at the age of thirty-one, she became one of the youngest presidential press secretaries in history.

Like many of her male predecessors, Myers first gained visibility as a staffer in her boss's campaign for president. Because she frequently traveled with then-Governor Clinton during his intensely covered 1992 campaign, fielding reporters' questions on the road and in Little Rock, her face became familiar to most Americans. She managed a campaign press staff that eventually numbered forty persons.

A political science graduate of the University of Santa Clara, Myers was promoted to assistant to the president in a 1994 staff reshuffling. Her duties and access to the president were expanded at that time.

Instead of formal press conferences, President Clinton has favored small meetings with the press in the Oval office.

Senate Subcommittee on Surface Transportation is not normally a hotbed of media interest, but in 1989 when the subjects before it were drug dealing and prostitution at highway truck stops, reporters and cameras packed the hearing room, showering attention on an obscure Nebraska senator, James Exon (the subcommittee chairman). Third, local newspapers and broadcast stations will normally devote some resources to covering their local senators and representatives, even when these legislators are junior and relatively lacking in influence. Most office holders, in turn, are mainly concerned with meeting the needs of their local media contingents, since these reporters are the ones who directly and regularly reach the voters in their home constituencies.

One other kind of congressional news coverage is worth noting: investigative-committee hearings. Occasionally, a sensational scandal leads to televised congressional committee hearings that transfix and electrify the nation. In the early 1950s Senator Joseph R. McCarthy (R.-Wis.) held a series of hearings to expose and root out what he claimed were communists in the State Department and other U.S. government agencies, as well as Hollywood's film industry. The senator's style of investigation, which involved many wild charges made without proof and the smearing and labeling of some innocent opponents as communists, gave rise to the term *McCarthyism.*

The Watergate hearings of 1973 and 1974 made heroes out of two committee chairs, Senator Sam Ervin (D.-N.C.) and U.S. Representative Peter Rodino (D.-N.J.). They uncovered many facts behind the Watergate scandal and then pursued the impeachment of President Richard M. Nixon. (Nixon resigned in August 1974 before the full House could vote on his impeachment.)

In 1987 the Iran-Contra hearings—set up to investigate a complicated Reagan administration scheme in which arms were sold to Iran and the profits were then diverted to the Nicaraguan anti-communist *contras*—also created a popular hero. This time, however, the hero was not the committee chair but a witness, Lieutenant Colonel Oliver North, a White House aide deeply involved in the plot. North's boyish appeal and patriotic demeanor projected well on television, on which all the hearings were carried live (as were the McCarthy and Watergate hearings). North capitalized on his fame and in 1994 launched a campaign for a U.S. Senate seat from Virginia. More recently, in October 1991, the nation viewed another televised committee spectacle when Supreme Court nominee Clarence Thomas was accused of sexual harassment (see "The Clarence Thomas Hearings," p. 593).

Covering the Courts

The branch of government that is the most different, in press coverage as in many other respects, is the judicial branch. Cloaked in secrecy—because judicial deliberations and decision making are conducted in private—the courts receive scant coverage under most circumstances. However, a volatile or controversial issue, such as abortion, can change usual type of coverage, especially when the Supreme Court is rendering the decision. Each network and major newspaper has one or more Supreme Court reporters, who are usually well schooled in the law and whose instant analysis of court opinions interprets the decisions for the millions of people without legal training. Gradually, the admission of cameras into state and local courtrooms across the United States is offering people a more in-depth look at the operation of the judicial system. As yet, though, the Supreme Court does not permit televised proceedings.

Even more than the Court's decisions, presidential appointments to the high court are the focus of intense media attention. As the judiciary has assumed a more important role in modern times, the men and women considered for the post are being subjected to withering scrutiny of their records and even of their private lives. The media's disclosure that Douglas Ginsberg had smoked marijuana extensively as an adult forced President Reagan to withdraw his Supreme Court nomination in 1987, for example.

Watergate and the Era of Investigative Journalism

The Watergate scandal of the Nixon administration—which stemmed from White House efforts to eavesdrop on officials of the Democratic National Committee and then to cover up presidential involvement in the scheme—had the most profound impact of any modern event on the manner and substance of the press's conduct. In many respects Watergate began a chain reaction that today allows for intense scrutiny of public officials' private lives. Moreover, coupled with the civil rights movement and the Vietnam War, Watergate shifted the orientation of journalism away from mere description (providing an account of happenings) and toward prescription—helping to set the campaign's (and society's) agenda by focusing attention on the candidates' shortcomings as well as on certain social problems.

A new breed and a new generation of reporters were attracted to journalism, particularly to its investigative role. As a group they were idealistic, although aggressively mistrustful of authority, and they shared a contempt for "politics as usual." The Vietnam and Watergate generation dominates journalism today. They and their younger colleagues hold sway over most newsrooms, with two-thirds of all reporters now under the age of thirty-six and an ever-increasing number of editors and executives who had their start in journalism in the Watergate era.[18]

---

[18] American Society of Newspaper Editors, *The Changing Face of the Newsroom* (Washington: ASNE, May 1989), p. 29.

The Clarence Thomas Hearings

As with Watergate and the Iran-Contra scandal, Clarence Thomas's nomination to the Supreme Court in 1991 gave rise to a television extravaganza that mesmerized the American people. The U.S. Senate Judiciary Committee hearings on allegations of sexual harassment that were lodged against Thomas drew a large audience for three full days in early October 1991.

A few months earlier, President George Bush had nominated Thomas, a black conservative, to succeed retiring Justice Thurgood Marshall, a pillar of the civil rights movement. Thomas appeared to be heading for an easy Senate confirmation when National Public Radio's correspondent Nina Totenberg reported the harassment charges just days before Thomas's scheduled confirmation vote. The all-male Senate Judiciary Committee had earlier disregarded the charges, in part because the chief accuser, University of Oklahoma Law School Professor Anita Hill, was reluctant to come forward publicly. But after the information was leaked to National Public Radio and other news outlets, the Senate was forced to postpone its confirmation vote and hold an additional Judiciary Committee hearing to investigate the allegations, which dated back to Thomas's chairmanship of the Equal Employment Opportunity Commission (EEOC) during the Reagan administration. (Hill had also been an EEOC employee and one of Thomas's subordinates.)

The hearings became a national obsession—a real-life soap opera made for television. Hill's graphic accusations of Thomas's advances and vivid sexual allusions shocked many Americans, who were equally riveted by Thomas's angry denial of the charges and denouncement of the Judiciary Committee inquiry as "a high-tech lynching." Convincing and sincere character witnesses for both sides were produced, leaving most viewers puzzled about the truth. In the absence of hard evidence, a substantial majority of people (as measured by public opinion polls) eventually sided with Thomas, and he managed to win confirmation in the full Senate by a vote of fifty-two to forty-eight — the narrowest affirmative vote for a Supreme Court justice in this century.

The most damaging political consequences of the hearings were visited on the senators themselves. Both sides agreed that the Senate handled the matter poorly—first, by not treating Hill's accusations seriously, then by conducting a public spectacle. The Watergate hearings made heroes of many of the participating legislators (such as U.S. Senator Sam Ervin [D.-N.C.], the folksy chairman of the Senate Watergate panel). But the Thomas hearings only diminished the reputations of most senators who had the misfortune to be in the spotlight. Democrats not known to have a spotless private life, such as Senator Edward M. Kennedy (D.-Mass.), were derided for hypocrisy, while Republicans such as Arlen Specter (R.-Pa.) and Alan Simpson (R.-Wyo.) were criticized for their often harsh questioning of Anita Hill.

The contrast between the Watergate and Thomas hearings demonstrates that intense media coverage is a double-edged sword: When the television cameras are trained on elected officials, these officials can easily emerge as national heroes—or as national objects of scorn.

The intense media attention focused on the Senate Judiciary Committee's confirmation hearings of Judge Clarence Thomas created a three-way spectacle: the senators, the testifiers (pictured at right is Thomas), and the media themselves.

Of course, many people who found journalism newly attractive in the wake of Watergate were not completely altruistic. Young and ambitious journalists saw the happy fate of the *Washington Post*'s youthful Watergate sleuths Bob Woodward and Carl Bernstein, who gained fame, fortune, and big-screen portrayals by Robert Redford and Dustin Hoffman in the movie *All the President's Men*. The young were attracted not just to journalism but to a particular *kind* of journalism. Their role models were not respected, established reporters but two unknowns who succeeded by refusing to play by the rules their seniors had accepted. Whatever their motives, though, journalism's new breed has been determined to get to the bottom of each new scandal.

In the post-Watergate press a volatile mix of guilt and fear is at work. The guilt stems from regret that experienced Washington reporters failed to detect the telltale signs of the Watergate scandal early on; that even after the story broke, most journalists underplayed the unfolding disaster until forced to take it more seriously by the two young *Post* reporters; that over the years journalism's leading lights had become too close to the politicians they were supposed to check and therefore for too long failed to tell the public about dangerous excesses in the government. The press's ongoing fear is deep-seated and complements the guilt. Every political journalist is apprehensive about missing the next big story, of being left on the platform when the next scandal train leaves Union Station.

The Post-Watergate Era

In the post-Watergate era, the sizable financial and personnel investments many major news organizations have made in investigative units almost guarantee that greater attention will be given to scandals and that probably more of them—some real and some manufactured—will be uncovered.

The Character Issue in Media Coverage of Politicians

Another clear consequence of Watergate has been the increasing emphasis by the press on the character of candidates. The issue of character has always been present in U.S. politics—George Washington was not made the nation's first president for his policy positions—but rarely if ever has character been such an issue as it has in elections from 1976 onward. Jimmy Carter's 1976 presidential campaign was characterized by moral posturing in the wake of Watergate. Edward M. Kennedy's 1980 presidential candidacy was destroyed in part by lingering character questions. The 1988 race witnessed an explosion of character concerns so forceful that several candidates (including Gary Hart) were badly scarred by it. And the 1992 contest for the White House became a tawdry debate about the alleged mistresses of Bill Clinton and George Bush. (The evidence in both of the 1992 cases was less than convincing, but that did not stop the media.)

The character issue may in part have been an outgrowth of the "new journalism" popularized by author Tom Wolfe in the 1970s.[19] Contending that conventional journalism was sterile and stripped of color, Wolfe and others argued for a reporting style that expanded the definition of news and, novel-like, highlighted all the personal details of the newsmaker. Then, too, reporters had witnessed the success of such books

---

[19] See Tom Wolfe, *The New Journalism* (New York: Harper & Row, 1973), especially pp. 9–32.

as Theodore H. White's "Making of the President" series and Joe McGinniss's *The Selling of the President 1968,* which offered revealing, behind-the-scenes vignettes of the previous election's candidates.[20] Why not give readers and viewers this information before the election? the press reasoned. There was encouragement from academic quarters as well. "Look to character first" when evaluating and choosing among presidential candidates, wrote Duke University political science professor James David Barber in an acclaimed and widely circulated 1972 volume, *The Presidential Character* (see Chapter 7).[21]

Whatever the precise historical origins of the character trend in reporting, it is undergirded by certain assumptions. First, the press sees that it has mainly replaced the political parties as the screening committee that winnows the field of candidates and filters out the weaker or more unlucky contenders. (This fact may be another reason to support the strengthening of the political parties. Politicians are in a much better position than the press to provide professional peer review of colleagues who are seeking the presidency.) Second, many journalists believe it necessary to tell people about any of a candidate's foibles that might affect his or her public performance. The press's third supposition is that it is giving the public what it wants and expects, more or less. Perhaps television has conditioned voters to think about the private lives of the rich and famous. The rules of television prominence now seem to apply to all celebrities equally, whether they reside in Hollywood or Washington. And, perhaps more important, scandal sells papers and attracts television viewers.

Loosening of the Libel Law. Another factor permits the modern press to undertake character investigations. In the old days, a reporter would think twice about filing a story critical of a politician's character, and the editors probably would have killed the story had the reporter been foolish enough to do so. The reason? Fear of a libel suit. (Recall from Chapter 4 that libel is published defamation of character that unjustly injures a person's reputation.) The first question editors would ask about even an ambiguous or suggestive phrase about a public official was, "If we're sued, can you prove beyond a doubt what you've written?"

Such inhibitions were ostensibly lifted in 1964, when the Supreme Court ruled in ***New York Times Co. v. Sullivan***[22] that simply publishing a defamatory falsehood is not enough to justify a libel judgment. Henceforth a public official would have to prove "actual malice," a requirement extended three years later to all public figures, such as Hollywood stars and prominent athletes.[23] The Supreme Court declared that the First Amendment requires elected officials and candidates to prove that the publisher either believed the challenged statement was false or at least entertained serious doubts about its truth and acted recklessly in publishing it in the face of those doubts. The actual malice rule has made it very difficult for public figures to win libel cases.

Despite *Sullivan,* the threat of libel litigation (and its deterrent effect on the press) persists for at least two reasons. First, the *Sullivan* protections do little to reduce the

---

[20] The first and best in White's series was *The Making of the President 1960* (New York: Atheneum, 1961). See also Joe McGinniss, *The Selling of the President 1968* (New York: Trident, 1969).

[21] See James David Barber, *The Presidential Character* (Englewood Cliffs, NJ: Prentice Hall, 1972), p. 445.

[22] 376 U.S. 254 (1964). See also Steven Pressman, "Libel Law: Finding the Right Balance," *Editorial Research Reports* 2 (August 18, 1989): 462–471.

[23] *Curtis Publishing Co.* v. *Butts,* 388 U.S. 130 (1967); *Associated Press* v. *Walker,* 388 U.S. 130 (1967).

THEN AND NOW

The Character Issue from Grover Cleveland to Bill Clinton

The character issue—which focuses press attention on the private-life activities and personalities of candidates—has been with us throughout U.S. history, as this text's reference to President Grover Cleveland's out-of-wedlock child suggests. Yet the intensity and the reach of the character issue have grown over the centuries, and particularly in recent years, as Democratic presidential candidate Gary Hart discovered to his chagrin in 1987. The press corps had long heard stories about Hart's alleged extramarital affairs, but no usable evidence had come to light. The situation changed dramatically in May 1987, shortly after Hart declared his candidacy for a second run at the White House.

The *Miami Herald* received an anonymous tip that Hart would be meeting an attractive model for a weekend tryst in Washington, D.C. This tip closely followed Hart's public insistence that the womanizing rumors about him were false and that his once-rocky marriage was again on firm ground. Hart had said to one reporter, E. J. Dionne of the *New York Times,* "Follow me around. . . . [You'll] be very bored."

Bored the *Miami Herald* was not when it decided to stake out Hart's Washington townhouse. The paper's reporters apparently observed Hart and Donna Rice, the model, inhabiting the townhouse, although the journalists' surveillance was not continuous and both house entrances were not always covered. Despite the flaws in the investigation, the circumstances were suspicious enough to generate a major scandal that dominated Hart's campaign.

When other indiscretions surfaced in an overwhelming media maelstrom, Hart withdrew from the race on May 8, 1987, with a bitter blast at the "intrusive" press that had brought him down. He briefly reentered the presidential contest in December, but by then Hart was a spent force and received only a handful of votes in the early 1988 primaries.

Probably no event from the 1988 presidential campaign has proved to be as memorable as the undoing of Gary Hart. The Hart episode also marked a milestone for the news media. They had helped eliminate the Democratic Party's frontrunner before a single ballot had been cast in the primaries, and they had done it by ag-

gressively investigating the private life of the unlucky candidate.

Four years later Bill Clinton learned from Gary Hart's mistakes. Before formally announcing his presidential candidacy, he admitted unspecified extramarital indiscretions, but—with the support of his spouse, Hillary Rodham Clinton—Clinton stressed that his marriage had weathered its storms. When lounge singer Gennifer Flowers claimed a past relationship with Clinton in January 1992, the candidate was able to point to his previous revelation (while denying Flowers's specific charge). With a well-timed visit to CBS's "60 Minutes" right after the Super Bowl, the Clintons were able to demonstrate marital solidarity at a moment of crisis. And the mainstream press itself was embarrassed to follow the lead of a supermarket tabloid, *The Star,* which had first carried—and hyped—Flowers's allegations.

With a strong organization behind him, Clinton managed a second-place finish in the New Hampshire primary and dubbed himself "the comeback kid." Clinton earned the title, overcoming an obstacle that had unhorsed frontrunner Hart earlier. Unfortunately for Clinton, various allegations about his involvement with women continued to be made during his presidency, but none threatened seriously to cut short his term—just as Flowers failed to derail his candidacy.

expense of defending defamation claims. The monetary costs have increased enormously, as have the required commitments of reporters' and editors' time and energy. Small news organizations without the financial resources of a national network or the *New York Times* are sometimes reluctant to publish material that might invite a lawsuit because the litigation costs could threaten their existence. The second reason for the continuing libel threat is a cultural phenomenon of heightened sensitivity to the harm that words can do to an individual's emotional tranquility. As a result, politicians are often more inclined to sue their press adversaries, even when success is unlikely.

But high costs and the politicians' propensity to sue cut both ways. The overall number of libel suits filed in recent years has dropped because plaintiffs also incur hefty legal expenses, and—perhaps more important—they have despaired of winning. Some news outlets have added another disincentive by filing countersuits charging their antagonists with bringing frivolous or nuisance actions against them.

In practice, then, the loosening of libel law has provided journalists with a safer harbor from liability in their reporting on elected officials and candidates. Whether it has truly diminished press self-censorship, especially for financially less well-endowed media outlets, is a more difficult question to answer. However, at least for the wealthy newspapers and networks, the libel laws are no longer as severe a restraint on the press as they once were.

The Question of Bias

Whenever the media break an unfavorable story about a politician, the politician usually counters with a cry of "biased reporting"—a claim that the press has told an untruth, has told only part of the truth, or has reported facts out of the complete context of the event. Who is right? Are the news media biased? The answer is simple and unavoidable: Of course they are. Journalists are fallible human beings who inevitably have values, preferences, and attitudes galore—some conscious, others subconscious, but all reflected at one time or another in the subjects selected for coverage or the slant of that coverage. Given that the press is biased, it is important to know in what ways it is biased and when and how the biases are shown.

Truth be told, most journalists lean to the left. First of all, those in the relatively small group of professional journalists (not many more than 100,000, compared with more than 4 million teachers in the United States) are drawn heavily from the ranks of highly educated social and political liberals, as a number of studies, some conducted by the media themselves, have shown.[24] Journalists are substantially Democratic in party affiliation and voting habits, progressive and anti-establishment in political orientation, and well to the left of the general public on most economic, foreign policy, and social issues (such as abortion, affirmative action, gay rights, and gun control). Second, dozens of the most influential reporters and executives entered (or reentered) journalism after stints of partisan involvement in campaigns or government, and a substantial majority worked for Democrats.[25]

---

[24] American Society of Newspaper Editors, "The Changing Face," p. 33; William Schneider and I. A. Lewis, "Views on the News," *Public Opinion* 8 (August/September 1985): 6–11, 58–59; and S. Robert Lichter, Stanley Rothman, and Linda S. Lichter, *The Media Elite* (Bethesda, MD: Adler & Adler, 1986).

[25] See Dom Bonafede, "Crossing Over," *National Journal* 21 (January 14, 1989): 102; Richard Harwood, "Tainted Journalists," *Washington Post* (December 4, 1988): L6; Charles Trueheart, "Trading Places: The Insiders Debate," *Washington Post* (January 4, 1989): D1, 19; and Kirk Victor, "Slanted Views," *National Journal* 20 (June 4, 1988): 1512.

Third, this liberal press bias does indeed show up frequently on screen and in print. A study of reporting on the abortion issue, for example, revealed a clear slant to the pro side on network television news, matching in many ways the reporters' own abortion-rights views.[26] Additionally, the media list to the left on the agenda of topics they choose to cover.[27] In the latter half of the 1980s, for instance, television gave enormous attention to the homelessness issue; in the process, some experts in the field believe, the broadcasters both exaggerated the problem and grossly overstated the role of unemployment in creating the condition of homelessness.[28]

The public, incidentally, senses that most members of the press have somewhat different beliefs from those of the population at large. The Times Mirror Center for the People and the Press, which has commissioned an enlightening series of Gallup surveys on public attitudes toward journalism, found in 1989 that 76 percent of a random sample of the U.S. adult population saw "a great deal" or "a fair amount" of political bias in news coverage.[29] And 68 percent believed that news organizations tend to favor one side rather than to deal fairly with all sides on political and social issues. (Just four years earlier, the proportion citing one-sidedness was only 53 percent.) By decisive margins, respondents who chose to classify press bias saw it as leaning toward the liberal rather than toward the conservative or moderate.

Conservative politicians do not need a Gallup survey to convince them that the press is biased against them. For decades, right-of-center Republican leaders have railed against the "liberal media." When former President Dwight D. Eisenhower attacked the "sensation-seeking" press at the 1964 GOP convention, which nominated Barry Goldwater for president, delegates raged against the media assemblage, cursing and shaking their fists at them. No one has ever launched a more vigorous assault against the U.S. media than did Vice President Spiro T. Agnew, who in November 1969 derided the "small band of network commentators and self-appointed analysts . . . who not only enjoy a right of instant rebuttal to every presidential address but more importantly wield a free hand in selecting, presenting, and interpreting the great issues in our nation."

The events of many national election years underscore conservative complaints. Richard M. Nixon's claim of a Democratic tilt during his 1968 presidential race was supported in a much-circulated—and greatly criticized—1971 book by *TV Guide*'s Edith Efron, *The News Twisters*,[30] in which the author claimed that network news

---

[26] "*Roe v. Webster*," *Media Monitor* 3 (October 1989): 1–6. See also David Shaw, "Abortion and the Media" (four-part series), *Los Angeles Times* (July 1, 1990): A1, 50–51; (July 2, 1990): A1, 20; (July 3, 1990): A1, 22–23; (July 4, 1990): A1, 28–29.

[27] The importance of the agenda-setting function is discussed throughout Shanto Iyengar and Donald R. Kinder, *News That Matters*. See especially pp. 4, 33.

[28] David Whitman, "Who's Who Among the Homeless," *The New Republic* 199 (June 6, 1988): 18–20.

[29] Times-Mirror Center for the People and the Press, "The People and the Press, Part 5: Public Attitudes Toward News Organizations," based on an in-person random sample survey of 1,507 adult Americans, conducted by the Gallup organization between August 9 and 28, 1989 (margin of error: plus or minus 3 percent).

[30] Edith Efron, *The News Twisters* (Los Angeles: Nash, 1971). See the criticisms of Efron's study in Paul Weaver, "Is Television News Biased?" *Public Interest* (Winter 1972): 57–74; and also in Robert L. Stevenson, Richard A. Eisinger, Barry M. Feinberg, and Alan B. Kotok, "Untwisting the News Twisters: A Replication of Efron's Study," *Journalism Quarterly* 50 (Summer 1973): 211–219.

shows had emphasized pro-Democratic and anti-Republican statements throughout the general election campaign. More recently, the 1984, 1988, and 1992 campaigns have stoked conservative fires. Regarding the first, the ticket of Walter Mondale and Geraldine Ferraro received much kinder, more positive coverage than did the Reagan–Bush team, according to a study by political scientists Michael J. Robinson and Maura Clancey.[31] Four years later George Bush still received a highly negative press, although Michael S. Dukakis fared no better.[32] Most rankling to conservatives, though, was this pair of findings: The most liberal candidate for president in 1988, Jesse Jackson, garnered the best press,[33] and the most conservative of the four national party nominees, Dan Quayle, received the worst. And in 1992 Bill Clinton received the most positive general election coverage of the three major presidential candidates, while George Bush registered by far the most critical coverage.

The right wing is not alone in its disgruntlement with the news media. For very different reasons, the left wing joins in the condemnation. Liberals, while acknowledging the press's early tough line on Quayle, have taken the media to task for not keeping the pressure on him throughout the 1988 campaign. The failure of the media to analyze and criticize the sometimes exaggerated claims made in George Bush's anti-Dukakis advertisements is also cited. To the left, the perceived press kindness toward Bush was merely a continuation of its genuflection to Ronald Reagan during his presidency. "Because of the government manipulation and voluntary self-censorship the major American news organizations too often abdicated their responsibility . . . during the

---

[31] Michael J. Robinson and Maura Clancey, "General Election Coverage: Part 1," *Public Opinion* 7 (December/January 1985): 49–54, 59.
[32] See Robert S. Lichter, Daniel Amundson, and Richard E. Noyes, "Election '88 Media Coverage," *Public Opinion* 11 (January/February 1989): 18–19, 52.
[33] See Robert S. Lichter, Daniel Amundson, and Richard E. Noyes, *The Video Campaign: Network Coverage of the 1988 Primaries* (Washington, DC: American Enterprise Institute, 1988).

Early media pressure on Dan Quayle. Immediately after George Bush's 1988 surprise choice of Senator Dan Quayle to be his running mate, the media swarmed over Quayle's political track record, National Guard service record, and even his academic record. Here, reporters surround Quayle in his home state of Indiana.

Reagan years," wrote the left-wing media critic Mark Hertsgaard.[34] Like others of his persuasion over the years, Hertsgaard points to the conservative status-quo interests of the corporate elites who run most media organizations to explain why a Ronald Reagan would be pampered by the press.

There are many conservatives well placed in the U.S. television and print commentary arenas to do the pampering, whether prompted by the media moguls or not. Right-of-center television hosts (Rush Limbaugh, John McLaughlin, William F. Buckley Jr., Patrick J. Buchanan—who became a Republican presidential candidate for 1992—for example) dominate the public broadcasting agenda, and conservative columnists (especially James J. Kilpatrick, George F. Will, William Safire, and Rowland Evans and Robert Novak) have much larger circulations than do most of their liberal counterparts (such as Carl Rowan and Ellen Goodman). Conservative Paul Harvey is the premier radio commentator too. Even the mainstream news shows rely disproportionately on white, male, moderate-to-conservative voices, as a recent study of guests on "Nightline" and the "MacNeil/Lehrer NewsHour" has shown.[35] This generous measure of conservative commentary is supplemented by the heavily Republican tilt of newspaper editorial pages that reflect the views of wealthy publishers. In the sixteen presidential elections from 1932 to 1992 inclusive, a majority of the nation's dailies editorially supported the Republican nominee on fourteen of those occasions.[36] (The only exceptions were 1964 and 1992.)

The question of media bias surfaces frequently in Great Britain, too. Many of the national newspapers sport openly acknowledged editorial lines. For example, the *Daily Telegraph* generally supports the position of the Conservative Party, the *Daily Mirror* sides with Labour, and the *Manchester Guardian* tends to adopt a Social Democratic position. Precisely because of these open political loyalties, the appearance in 1987 of *The Independent* as a self-declared nonpartisan newspaper created quite a splash. The broadcast media are by law required to maintain political impartiality, although they have been a frequent target of conservative criticism for their supposedly leftist leanings.

Other Sources of Bias. From left to right, all of these criticisms have some validity in different times and circumstances, in one media forum or another. But these critiques ignore some non-ideological factors probably more essential to an understanding of press bias. Owing to competition and the reward structure of journalism, the deepest bias most political journalists have is the desire to get to the bottom of a good campaign story—which is usually negative news about a candidate. The fear of missing a good story, more than bias, leads all media outlets to the same developing headlines and encourages them to adopt the same slant. One newspaper that broke

---

[34] See Mark Hertsgaard, *On Bended Knee: The Press and the Reagan Presidency* (New York: Farrar, Straus & Giroux, 1988).

[35] Fairness and Accuracy in Reporting (FAIR), "All the Usual Suspects: MacNeil-Lehrer and Nightline" (New York: FAIR, May 1990).

[36] See Nick Thimmesch, "The Editorial Endorsement Game," *Public Opinion* 7 (October/November 1984): 10–13. However, there has been an accelerating trend toward neutrality on the editorial pages. In 1964, 1968, and 1972 only 23 percent of the pages made no endorsement in the presidential contest. In 1984 the figure was 33 percent; in 1988, 55 percent; and in 1992, 64 percent. See Martin P. Wattenberg, *The Decline of American Political Parties* (Cambridge, MA: Harvard University Press, 1990), Chapter 9.

Campaigning provides candidates with a host of carefully arranged photo opportunities that sometimes don't turn out quite as planned. Is the capturing and replaying of such gaffes a form of non-ideological media bias or just an unintended, but natural, consequence of candidates' reliance on media coverage?

important negative information about Dan Quayle in 1988 was the Quayle family-owned paper, the *Indianapolis News*. (The story concerned Quayle's service in the National Guard rather than in the military during the Vietnam War.)

A related non-ideological bias is the effort to create a horse race where none exists. Newspeople, whose lives revolve around the current political scene, naturally want to add spice and drama, minimize their boredom, and increase their audience. Other human, not just partisan, biases are also at work. Whether the press likes or dislikes a candidate personally is often vital. Former Governor Bruce Babbitt and U.S. Representative Morris K. Udall, both wisecracking, straight-talking Arizona Democrats, were press favorites in their presidential bids (in 1988 and 1976, respectively), and both enjoyed favorable coverage. Richard M. Nixon, Jimmy Carter, and Gary Hart—all aloof politicians—were disliked by many reporters who covered them, and they suffered from a harsh and critical press.

Finally, in their quest to avoid bias, reporters frequently seize on non-ideological offenses such as gaffes, ethical violations, and campaign-finance problems. These objective items are intrinsically free of partisan taint and can be pursued without guilt.

For all the emphasis here on bias, it is undeniably true that the modern U.S. news media are much fairer than their predecessors ever were. News blackouts of the editors' enemies, under which all positive information about the targeted politicians was banned from print, were once shockingly common but are now exceedingly rare and universally condemned. No longer do organized groups of reporters take out advertisements to support or oppose candidates or send telegrams to the president and members of Congress advocating certain public policies—events that occurred as recently as the 1970s.

In sum, then, press bias of all kinds—partisan, agenda-setting, and non-ideological—can and does influence the day-to-day coverage of politicians. But bias is not the be-all and end-all that critics on both the right and left often insist it is. Press tilt has a marginal to moderate effect, and it is but one piece in the media's news mosaic.

The Media's Influence on the Public

Some bias in media coverage clearly exists, as we have just discussed. But how does this bias affect the public that reads or views or listens to biased reporting?

In most cases the press has surprisingly little effect. To put it bluntly, people tend to see what they want to see; that is, human beings will focus on parts of a report that reinforce their own attitudes and ignore parts that challenge their core beliefs. Most of us also selectively tune out and ignore reports that contradict our preferences in politics and other fields. Therefore, a committed Democrat will remember certain portions of a televised news program about a current campaign—primarily the parts that reinforce his or her own choice—and an equally committed Republican will recall very different sections of the report or remember the material in a way that supports the GOP position. In other words, most voters are not empty vessels into which the media can pour their own beliefs. This fact dramatically limits the ability of news organizations to sway public opinion.

And yet the news media *do* have some influence (called **media effects**) on public opinion. Let's examine how this is so.

- First, reporting can sway people who are uncommitted and have no strong opinion in the first place. On the other hand, this sort of politically unmotivated individual is probably unlikely to vote in a given election, and therefore the media influence is of no particular consequence.
- Second, the press has a much greater impact on topics far removed from the lives and experiences of its readers and viewers. News reports can probably shape public opinion about events in foreign countries fairly easily. Yet what the media say about rising prices, neighborhood crime, or child rearing may have relatively little effect because most citizens have personal experience of and well-formed ideas about these subjects.
- Third, news organizations can help tell us what to think *about,* even if they cannot determine *what* we think. As mentioned earlier, the press often sets the agenda for government or a campaign by focusing on certain issues or concerns. For example, in the week following the *Exxon Valdez*'s massive oil spill off the Alaska coast in 1989, every national network devoted extensive coverage to the accident. And sure enough, concern about the environment quickly began to top the list of national problems considered most pressing by the public, as measured by opinion polls. Without the dramatic pictures and lavish media attention that accompanied the spill, it is doubtful that the environment would have risen so quickly to the forefront of the country's political agenda.

How Politicians Use the Media

The Clinton administration has set the pace for shrewd political use of the television media. President Clinton, First Lady Hilary Rodham Clinton, and Vice President Albert Gore Jr. have all appeared on CNN's "Larry King Live." The president has gone on MTV to speak directly to young voters, and the vice president has been a featured guest on David Letterman's late-night CBS show. Journalists, individually and in groups, are wined and dined at numerous White House receptions and intimate gatherings.

Our emphasis so far has been mainly on the ways and means of press coverage of politicians. But, as suggested by the Clinton example, the other side of the story is every bit as interesting: how politicians use the media to achieve their own ends. In Chapter 13, we discuss media events (press conferences at picturesque locations, for example) that are staged to attract coverage. Other manipulations of the press can be more subtle, however. Frequently, elected officials pass along tips to reporters, seeking to curry favor or produce stories favorable to their interests. (Reporters and editors usually decide whether to publish a tip based on its newsworthiness rather than on the motivations of their sources.)

On other occasions, candidates and their aides will go on background to give trusted newspersons juicy morsels of negative information about rivals. **On background**—meaning that none of the news can be attributed to the source—is one of several journalistic devices used to solicit and elicit information that might otherwise never come to light. **Deep background** is another such device; whereas background talks can be attributed to unnamed senior officials, deep background news must be completely unsourced, with the reporter giving the reader no hint about the origin of the information. An even more drastic form of obtaining information is the **off-the-record** discussion, in which nothing the official says may be printed. (If a reporter can obtain the same information elsewhere, however, he or she is free to publish it.) By contrast, in an **on-the-record** session, such as a formal press conference, every word an official utters can be printed—and used against that official. It is no wonder that office holders often prefer the nonpublishable alternatives!

Clearly, these rules are necessary for reporters to do their basic job—informing the public—but ironically, the same rules keep the press from fully informing their readers and viewers. Every public official knows that journalists are pledged to protect the confidentiality of their sources, and therefore the rules can sometimes be used to an official's own benefit—by, say, giving reporters derogatory information to print about a rival without having to be identified as the source. However regrettable the manipulation, it is an unavoidable part of the process.

Some politicians do not manipulate the press so much as they use it well when their talents match the needs of their day's dominant news medium. Franklin D. Roosevelt's folksy manner and mellifluous voice, for example, were tailor-made for radio, and his fireside chats in the 1930s reassured a nation shaken by the Great Depression. John F. Kennedy was the country's first television-wise president; handsome, witty, and vibrant, Kennedy perfected the art of televised press conferences to win public support for his actions. Twenty years later Ronald Reagan, an actor by training, also made masterful use of television in going around Congress to appeal directly to the citizenry, as he did in 1981 in winning congressional approval for his tax cuts and economic policies. Bill Clinton has proved himself to be a superb off-the-cuff speaker and a natural television talk-show guest, and he excels in those forums.

Other presidents with lesser media talent also adapt to the media realities of their time. George Bush could not have been more unlike his charismatic predecessor, Ronald Reagan, and his awkward gestures, high-pitched and nasal voice, poor speech delivery, and choppy sentence structure were widely lampooned. Nonetheless, Bush and his aides recognized that he was at his best in informal, less staged settings, where his hands-on experience and detailed knowledge of government were apparent. Conse-

Left: President Franklin D. Roosevelt during a fireside chat in 1941. Roosevelt's skillful use of radio boosted his popularity throughout his tenure in the White House. **Right:** Today, President Bill Clinton (shown with Bryant Gumbel on the "Today" show) typifies the pro-active stance many politicians take toward controlling their media coverage.

quently, Bush rarely used the Oval Office speech to the nation or the prime-time news conferences that were Reagan's favorite forms of address to the nation. Instead, Bush held mid-morning White House press room briefings and many one-on-one press interviews.

Government Regulation of the Electronic Media

Not only do politicians manipulate the media, but the U.S. government also *regulates* the electronic component of the media. Unlike radio or television, the print media are exempt from most forms of government regulation, although even print media must not violate community standards for obscenity, for instance. There are two reasons for this unequal treatment. First, the airwaves used by the electronic media are considered public property; they are leased by the federal government to private broadcasters. Second, those airwaves are in limited supply, and without some regulation, the nation's many radio and television stations would interfere with one another's frequency signals. It was not, in fact, the federal government but rather private broadcasters, frustrated by the numerous instances in which signal jamming occurred, that initiated the call for government regulation in the early days of the electronic media. Newspapers, of course, are not subject to these technical considerations.

The first government regulation of the electronic media came in 1927, when Congress enacted the Federal Radio Act, which established the Federal Radio Commission (FRC) and declared the airwaves to be public property. In addition, the act required that all broadcasters be licensed by the FRC. In 1934 the Federal Communications

Commission (FCC) replaced the FRC as the electronic media regulatory body. The FCC is composed of five members, of whom not more than three can be from the same political party. These members are selected by the president for five-year terms on an overlapping basis. Because the FCC is shielded from direct, daily control by the president or Congress—although both have influence over the FCC commissioners—it is an independent regulatory agency (see Chapter 8). In addition to regulating public and commercial radio and television, the FCC oversees telephone, telegraph, satellite, and foreign communications in the United States.

Under the FCC's rules, television stations must apply for license renewal every five years; radio stations, every seven years. Until the 1980s, the FCC's criteria for license renewal were how well a station served its community, how judiciously it used the public airwaves, and how much time it devoted to public affairs. In fact, though, few licenses were ever withdrawn, and the tests for license renewal were never truly rigorous. Regulation of the broadcast industry became even looser—nearly non-existent, in fact—during the Reagan administration. For example, license renewal became something of a formality, with most stations able to complete the process simply by dropping a postcard in the mail. The FCC holds a formal hearing only if the license is challenged by a competing group of individuals who want to operate a station at the assigned frequency.

The FCC also regulates private ownership of broadcast stations. For instance, in the 1940s it said that a single person or corporation could own only one radio and one television station in any one community or media market. In the 1950s it enacted the 7-7-7 rule, limiting to seven each the number of AM, FM, and television stations a single company could own throughout the nation. In addition, the FCC forbids ownership of a daily newspaper and a television station in the same media market. Yet deregulation has recently prevailed in the area of ownership rules, too. During the Reagan years, the FCC expanded the limits on ownership of AM, FM, and television stations from 7 to 12, thereby making the 7-7-7 rule the 12-12-12 rule. In 1992, the FCC further expanded the limits of ownership of AM and FM stations, such that the 12-12-12 rule became a new 12-30-30 rule.

Content Regulation

The government also subjects the electronic media to substantial **content regulation** that, again, does not apply to the print media. Charged with ensuring that the airwaves "serve the public interest, convenience, and necessity," the FCC has attempted to promote equity in broadcasting. For example, the **equal time rule** requires that broadcast stations sell campaign air time equally to all candidates *if* they choose to sell it to any, which they are under no obligation to do. An exception to this rule is a political debate: Stations may exclude from this event less well-known and minor-party candidates.

Another noteworthy FCC regulation is the **right-of-rebuttal rule,** which requires that a person who is attacked on a radio or television station be offered the opportunity to respond. This rule was sanctioned judicially in the 1969 Supreme Court case *Red Lion Broadcasting Company* v. *FCC,* 395 U.S. 367 (1969), in which the Court ruled that Fred Cook, the author of a book on U.S. Senator Barry Goldwater (R.-Ariz.) (the 1964 Republican nominee for president), must be afforded the chance to answer an attack on him aired by a Pennsylvania radio station.

Perhaps the most controversial FCC regulation was the **fairness doctrine.** Implemented in 1949 and in effect until 1985, the fairness doctrine required broadcasters to

Extreme left- or right-wing candidates such as Republican David Duke often battle for equal time on the major networks. In reality, however, air time is so expensive and fringe candidates have such a hard time raising large sums of money, that the networks can offer equal time without the candidates' being able to take advantage of it.

be "fair" in their coverage of news events—that is, they had to cover the events adequately and present contrasting views on important public issues. Many broadcasters disliked this rule, however, claiming that fairness is simply too difficult to define and that the rule abridged their First Amendment freedoms. They also argued that it ultimately forced broadcasters to decrease coverage of controversial issues out of fear of a deluge of requests for air time from interest groups involved in each matter.

In a hotly debated 1985 decision, the FCC, without congressional consent, abolished the fairness doctrine, arguing that the growth of the electronic media in the United States during the preceding forty years had created enough diversity among the stations to render unnecessary the ordering of diversity within them. In 1986 a federal circuit court of appeals vindicated the FCC decision, holding that the FCC did not need congressional approval to abolish the rule. Seeking to counter the FCC's decision, Congress attempted to write the fairness doctrine into law, which, if successful, would have forced the FCC to implement it. Although both the House and the Senate passed the bill, President Reagan ended the controversy for the moment by vetoing it, citing his First Amendment concerns about government regulation of the news media.

The abolition of the fairness doctrine has by no means ended debate over its merit, however. Proponents, still trying to reinstate the doctrine, argue that its elimination results in a reduction of quality programming on public issues. In their view, deregulation means more advertisements, soap operas, and situation comedies wasting air time and leaving less room for public discourse on important matters. Opponents of the fairness doctrine, on the other hand, continue to call for decreased regulation, arguing that the electronic media should be as free as the print media—especially because the electronic media are now probably more competitive than are the print media.

Confidentiality of Sources

Another vital aspect of news media practice, both print and electronic, has been influenced by legal statutes and court decisions: the confidentiality of sources. How much a reporter can learn from a source often depends on the journalist's guarantees of confidentiality to that source, that is, a pledge not to reveal the origin of information the journalist may print or air.

Only a small number of states have laws protecting the confidentiality of reporters' sources, and no federal law provides such protection. Therefore, the courts have decided the degree to which confidentiality is protected, largely on a case-by-case basis. For example, in *Branzburg* v. *Hayes* (1972), the Supreme Court ruled that the First Amendment does not protect reporters from having to testify and possibly divulge sources before state or federal grand juries. "The investigation of crime by grand juries," the Court held, "implements a fundamental governmental role of securing the safety of the person and property of the [citizen]."[37] Compared with this overriding governmental interest, the protection of sources is an insufficient reason to treat reporters subpoenaed by grand juries differently from other citizens—or so the high court held.

Journalists have maintained that rulings such as that in *Branzburg* hinder the press's efforts at gathering the news—that without a guarantee of confidentiality, sources will be reluctant to provide crucial information. In response, the Court has noted that although confidentiality of sources does not outweigh the government's interest in prosecuting criminals, a journalist's confidentiality pledge is protected in most cases.

---

[37] 408 U.S. 665 (1972).

Censorship

While not free of government regulation, the media in the United States enjoy considerably more liberty than do their counterparts in Great Britain. One of the world's oldest democracies, Great Britain nonetheless owns that nation's main electronic medium, the British Broadcasting Company (BBC). And the BBC, along with the privately owned media, is subjected to unusually strict regulation on the publication of governmental secrets. For example, the sweeping Official Secrets Acts of 1911 makes it a criminal offense for a Briton to publish any facts, material, or news collected in that person's capacity as a public minister or civil servant. The act was invoked recently when the British government banned the publication of a 1987 novel, *Spy Catcher*, written by Peter Wright, a former British intelligence officer, who undoubtedly collected much of the book's information while on the job.

In the United States, only government officials can be prosecuted for divulging classified information; no such law applies to journalists. Nor can the government, except under extremely rare and confined circumstances, impose prior restraints on the press—that is, the government cannot censor the press. This principle was clearly established in *New York Times* v. *United States* (1971).[38] In this case the Supreme Court ruled that the government could not prevent publication by the *New York Times* of the "Pentagon Papers," classified government documents about the Vietnam War that had been stolen, photocopied, and sent to the *Times* and the *Washington Post* by Daniel Ellsberg, an anti-war activist. "Only a free and unrestrained press can effectively expose deception in the government," Justice Hugo Black wrote in a concurring opinion for the Court. "To find that the President has "inherent power' to halt the publication of news by resort to the courts would wipe out the First Amendment."

[38] 403 U.S. 713 (1971).

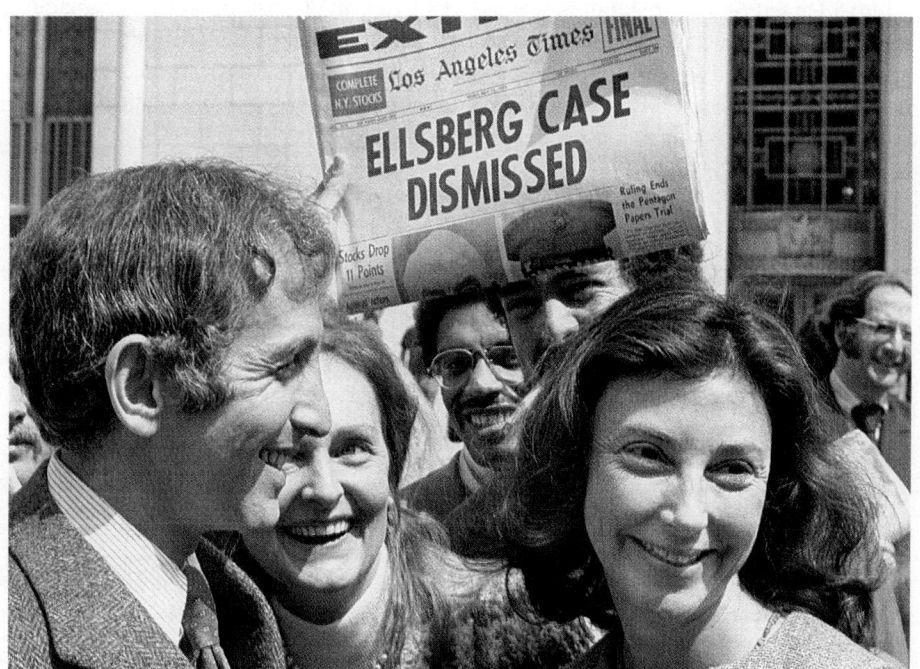

In 1971, the Supreme Court ruled in *New York Times* v. *United States* that the government could not prevent publication of the "Pentagon Papers." Here Daniel Ellsberg, who had stolen and copied the classified "Pentagon Papers," is greeted by well-wishers after the Court's decision.

To assist the media in determining what is and is not publishable, Great Britain provides a system called D-notice, which allows journalists to submit questionable material to a review committee before its publication. But D-notice has not quelled argument over media freedom in the United Kingdom. Indeed, the debate came to the fore during the 1982 Falkland Islands war between Great Britain and Argentina, when it centered on questions of how much information the public had a right to know and whether the media should remain neutral in covering a war in which the nation is involved. Once again, however, the British government prevailed in arguing for continued strict control of the media, declaring, "There can be sound military reasons for withholding the whole truth from the public domain, [or] for using the media to put out 'misinformation.' "[39]

Similar questions and arguments arose in the United States during the 1991 Persian Gulf war. Reporters were upset that the military was not forthcoming about events on and off the battlefield, while some Pentagon officials and many persons in the general public accused the press of telling the enemy too much in their dispatches. Unlike the case in Great Britain, however, the U.S. government had little recourse but to attempt to isolate offending reporters by keeping them away from the battlefield. Even this maneuver was highly controversial and very unpopular with news correspondents because it directly interfered with their job of reporting the news.

Such arguments are an inevitable part of the landscape in a free society. Whatever their specific quarrels with the press, most Americans would probably prefer that the media tell them too much rather than not enough. Totalitarian societies have a tame journalism, after all, so press excesses may be the price of unbridled freedom. Without question, a free press is of incalculable value to a nation, as the recent revolution in the Soviet Union (now the Commonwealth of Independent States) has shown. The 1991 coup against then-Soviet President Mikhail Gorbachev failed in part because the coup leaders could not smother the public's continued desire for freedom, stoked by the relatively uncensored television and print journalism that existed in the final years of Gorbachev's rule.

In the United States, freedom is secured mainly by the Constitution's basic guarantees and institutions. But freedom is also ensured by the thousands of independently owned and operated newspapers, magazines, and broadcast stations. The cacophony of media voices may often be off-key and harsh, but its very lack of orchestration enables us all to continue to sing the sweet song of freedom.

Toward Reform

The phenomenal growth of cable television during the past two decades has given new competition to the three major commercial television networks (ABC, CBS, and NBC). With half of all U.S. households now wired for cable television, the networks' share of the national television audience has declined steadily. Today fewer than six in

---

[39] House of Commons, Defense Committee, *The Handling of the Press and Public Information during the Falklands Conflict* (London: Her Majesty's Stationery Office, 1982), p. x.

every ten viewers are watching the three networks during many prime-time hours, compared with the networks' near-monopoly twenty years ago.

Some aspects of cable television's recent growth have been undesirable, at least in the eyes of critics. A case in point is the trend toward cross ownership—the possession of commercial and cable stations by the same people and corporations. As cable has become more popular and therefore more threatening to the commercial networks, these networks have been buying some cable franchises, and other media giants, such as Time Warner Communications and Times-Mirror, have done the same. The concentration of commercial and cable television ownership in relatively few hands can be troubling, not least because this arrangement can reduce the diversity of programming that was originally cable's great promise.

So far, though, any fair observer would conclude that cable television has greatly increased consumer choice and made available many new options for the U.S. public. The large number of cable channels and information services suggests as much. In March 1988, for instance, 77 percent of all homes that subscribed to cable had access to thirty or more channels, and 90 percent had access to twenty or more channels.

One vital difference between cable and commercial television is the emergence of interactive systems—cable systems that allow interaction between the sender and the consumer. These interactive systems permit viewers to respond instantly to televised polls by using hand-held devices, for example. Potentially, such an arrangement could lead to televised town meetings on issues of general interest. (Both Ross Perot and Bill Clinton have talked about holding electronic "town halls" in the future.) Of course, such developments must be viewed with caution as well as enthusiasm: Instant polls are unscientific and imprecise, since participants are not randomly selected, and those who respond to such public affairs programming constitute only a minute and usually unrepresentative proportion of the population.

The rise of cable television is also having a significant effect on political campaigns. For example, cable systems carry a large number of debates by local candidates. Although debates for state and national offices are televised frequently by the commercial stations, campaigns for local offices have often been neglected, largely because they are of interest to only a relatively small audience. Cable channels are so numerous that access for local candidates is much less of a problem. Cable channels also permit candidates to target paid political advertisements at small, select audiences. Such narrowcasting to targeted groups—as opposed to broadcasting to a large, diversified audience—enables candidates to tailor a message to Hispanics watching a Spanish-language channel, sports fans who watch ESPN, or younger voters who watch MTV, for example.

In general, then, cable means more choice in media and less influence for the commercial networks. These changes can prove to be beneficial, a frequent result of diversity and decentralization, or cable could turn out to be just more wasted fluff in programming that is distinct only because it is packaged a bit differently. Consumers of television—all of us who make up the audience—will help to determine cable television's quality.[40]

---

[40] For further reading, see Jeffrey B. Abramson, F. Christopher Arterton, and Gary R. Orren, *The Electronic Commonwealth: The Impact of Media Technologies on Democratic Politics* (New York: Basic Books, 1988).

Summary

The U.S. press is constantly evolving, including in its relationship with the public. Television talk shows, such as CNN's "Larry King Live," came to prominence in 1992 in part because both the voters and the candidates wanted to communicate directly, without the news media's filter. Yet there will always be a prominent role for a vigorous press to play. As we have reviewed, only the media have the credibility and the resources to inform the public about the government and elected officials. At the same time the press can do its job better, and journalists must constantly strive to minimize bias and reduce the investigative and competitive excesses that have cost them some respect in recent years.

In surveying the news media, we have made a number of general observations about press operations and practices in American life:

1. The modern media consist of print press (newspapers, magazines, journals) and electronic media (television and radio). In the United States the media are relatively uncontrolled and free to express many views, although that has not always been the case. Until the mid- to late-1800s, when independent papers first appeared, newspapers were partisan; that is, they openly supported a particular party.

2. In this century, first radio in the late 1920s and then television in the late 1940s revolutionized the transmission of political information, leading to more candidate-centered, entrepreneurial politics in the age of television.

3. The media have shifted focus in recent years, first toward investigative journalism in the Watergate era and then toward character issues. While these are useful aspects of both kinds of coverage, excesses have been noted, especially unnecessary invasions of privacy and the publication and broadcast of unsubstantiated rumor.

4. Studies have shown that by framing issues for debate and discussion, the media have clear and recognizable effects on voters. For example, people who are relatively uninformed about a topic can be more easily swayed by press coverage about that topic. However, in most cases the press has surprisingly little effect on people's views.

5. Politicians constantly try to manipulate and influence press coverage. One method many officials use is passing along tips (information) on an off-the-record basis.

6. The press is a business—big business, in the case of the networks and large newspapers—and as such it is regulated to some extent by the government. The government has gradually loosened its restrictions on the media. Officially, the Federal Communications Commission (FCC) licenses and regulates broadcasting stations, although in practice it has been quite willing to grant and renew licenses, and recently it has reduced its regulation of licensees. Additionally, cable transmission was first allowed on a widespread basis in the late 1970s, from whence it has grown into a large supplier of information. Finally, content regulations have loosened, with the courts using a narrow interpretation of libel.

Key Terms

print press
electronic media
yellow journalism
muckraking
networks
affiliates

wire service
New York Times Co. v. *Sullivan*
media effects
on background
deep background
off the record

on the record
content regulation
equal time rule
right-of-rebuttal rule
fairness doctrine

Suggested Readings

Arterton, F. Christopher. *Media Politics: The News Strategies of Presidential Campaigns.* Lexington, MA: Lexington Books, 1984.

Berkman, Ronald, and Laura W. Kitch. *Politics in the Media Age.* New York: McGraw-Hill, 1986.

Broder, David S. *Behind the Front Page.* New York: Simon & Schuster, 1987.

Cook, Timothy E. *Making Laws and Making News: Media Strategies in the U.S. House of Representatives.* Washington, DC: The Brookings Institution, 1989.

Crouse, Timothy. *The Boys on the Bus.* New York: Ballantine, 1973.

Entman, Robert M. *Democracy Without Citizens: Media and the Decay of American Politics.* New York: Oxford University Press, 1989.

Epstein, Edward Jay. *News from Nowhere: Television and the News.* New York: Random House, 1973.

Graber, Doris A. *Mass Media and American Politics,* 3rd ed. Washington, DC: CQ Press, 1989.

Iyengar, Shanto, and Donald R. Kinder. *News That Matters.* Chicago: University of Chicago Press, 1987.

Lichter, S. Robert, Stanley Rothman, and Linda S. Lichter. *The Media Elite.* Bethesda, MD: Adler & Adler, 1986.

Press, Charles, and Kenneth VerBurg. *American Politicians and Journalists.* Glenview, IL: Scott, Foresman, 1988.

Ranney, Austin. *Channels of Power: The Impact of Television on American Politics.* New York: Basic Books, 1983.

Sabato, Larry J. *Feeding Frenzy: How Attack Journalism Has Transformed American Politics,* updated ed. New York: Macmillan/The Free Press, 1993.

Stephens, Mitchell. *A History of News: From the Drum to the Satellite.* New York: Viking, 1989.

> *A zeal for different opinions concerning religion, concerning government, and many other points . . . have, in turn, divided mankind . . . inflamed them with mutual animosity, and rendered them more disposed to vex and oppress each other than to cooperate for the common good.*
>
> *James Madison*
> *Federalist No. 10*

Madison believed that one principal purpose of government is to control the possibly divisive effects of groups of people, each of which wants to advance its own special interests and each of which competes with the others for the attentions and resources of the government. The Framers hoped to avoid the formation of official political parties; at the private level, however, they realized that the formation of interest groups was inevitable.

CHAPTER 15

Interest Groups

WHAT ARE INTEREST GROUPS?
THE ROOTS OF AMERICAN INTEREST GROUPS
WHAT DO INTEREST GROUPS DO?
WHAT MAKES AN INTEREST GROUP SUCCESSFUL?
TOWARD REFORM

From his days in the Virginia Assembly, James Madison knew that factions occurred in all political systems and that the struggle for influence and power among such groups was inevitable in the political process. This knowledge led him and the other Framers to tailor a governmental system of multiple pressure points to check and balance these factions, or what today we call interest groups, in the natural course of the political process. As we discuss in Chapter 2, Madison and many of the other Framers were intent on creating a government of many levels—local, state, and national—the national government consisting of three branches. It was their belief that this division of power would prohibit any one individual or group of individuals from becoming too powerful. Decentralizing power also would neutralize the effect of special interests, who would not be able to spread their efforts throughout so many different levels of government. Thus, the "mischief of faction" could be lessened.

Ironically, *The Federalist Papers* were a key component of one of the most skillful and successful examples of interest-group activity in the history of this nation. As discussed in Chapter 2, if "the Federalists [themselves an interest group] had not been as shrewd in manipulation as they were sound in theory, their arguments could not have prevailed."[1]

The Federalists were only one of many interest groups that existed in the era following the Revolutionary War. And, as we discuss in the following sections, interest groups have proliferated over the years. In 1831–1832, Alexis de Tocqueville, a French aristocrat and philosopher, toured the United States extensively. A keen observer of American politics, he was very much impressed by the tendency of Ameri-

---

[1] Samuel Eliot Morrison and Henry Steel Commager, *The Growth of the American Republic* (New York: Oxford University Press, 1930), p. 163.

cans to join groups in order to participate in the policy-making process. "Whenever at the head of some new undertaking you see government in France, or a man of rank in England, in the United States you will be sure to find an association,"[2] wrote de Tocqueville. He was especially impressed by the ability of groups to influence the formal institutions of government, noting:

> It is true that they [representatives of these associations] have not the right, like the others, of making the laws; but they have the power of attacking those which are in force and of drawing up beforehand those which ought to be enacted.[3]

The United States is still a nation of joiners, and many interest groups play important roles as laws or policies are being negotiated. Think of the number of interest groups or voluntary associations to which you belong. It's likely that you belong to some kind of organized religion; a political party; a town, college, or university social, civic, athletic, or academic group; a more general special-interest group, such as Greenpeace, the National Rifle Association, the National Right-to-Life Committee, or Amnesty International. Even if you don't belong to one of these groups, you undoubtedly have heard of their activities or know someone who is a member of one of these groups.

Not all groups are political, but they may become politically active when their members feel that a government policy threatens or affects group goals. Most politically active groups use a technique called **lobbying** to make their interests heard and understood by those who are in a position to influence or cause change in governmental policies. Depending on the type of group and on the role it is looking to play, lobbying can take many forms. You probably have never thought of the Boy Scouts or Girl Scouts of America as "political." Yet, when Congress began debating the passage of legislation dealing with discrimination in private clubs, representatives of both organizations testified in an attempt to persuade Congress to allow each one to remain a single-sex organization. Similarly, you probably don't often think of garden clubs as political. Yet, when issues of highway beautification come before a legislature, representatives from numerous garden clubs are likely to be there to lobby, or to advance, their interests.

In this chapter, we examine what interest groups are, their development since the days of the Founders, and what they do. We also look to see why people join groups, why groups flourish, and the kinds of tactics they use as they attempt to pressure government to achieve their policy objectives.

What Are Interest Groups?

Interest groups go by a variety of names: special interests, pressure groups, organized interests, political groups, lobby groups, and public interest groups are among the common ones. These various terms have produced a diverse collection of operational definitions. Originally, most political scientists talked about "pressure groups";

---

[2] Alexis de Tocqueville, *Democracy in America,* Vol. 1, trans. Phillips Bradley (New York: Knopf, Vintage Books, 1945; orig. published 1835), p. 191.
[3] Ibid.

today, most political scientists use the more neutral terms "interest group" or "organized interest."[4]

Definitions of interest groups vary as much as groups do themselves:

- "any association of individuals, whether formally organized or not, that attempts to influence public policy";[5]
- "an organization which seeks or claims to represent people or organizations which share one or more common interests or ideals";[6]
- "any group that, on the basis of one or more shared attitudes, makes certain claims upon other groups in society for the establishment, maintenance, or enhancement of forms of behavior that are implied by the shared attitudes."[7]

Some definitions stress what a group does. This definition is offered by political scientist Robert H. Salisbury:

- "an interest group is an organized association which engages in activity relative to governmental decisions."[8]

And, distinguished political scientist V. O. Key Jr. tries to differentiate political parties from interest groups by arguing that

- [interest groups] "promote their interests by attempting to influence government rather than by nominating candidates and seeking responsibility for the management of government."[9]

In this book we use **interest group** as a generic term to describe the numerous political activities of organized groups as they try to influence government policy.

Types of Interest Groups

Interest groups generally can be characterized by the kinds of interests they represent or the number of issues in which they are involved.

Economic Interests. Most groups have some sort of "economic" agenda, even if it only involves acquiring enough money in donations to pay the telephone bill or send out the next mailing. **Economic-interest groups** are, however, a special type of interest group: Their primary purpose is to promote the economic interests of their members. Historically, business groups (including trade and professional groups), labor organizations (unions), and organizations representing the interests of farmers have been considered the "big three" of economic interest groups.

As discussed below, however, unions and agricultural organizations no longer have the large memberships or the political clout they once held in governmental circles. In

---

[4] Mark P. Petracca, "The Rediscovery of Interest Group Politics," in Mark Petracca, ed. *The Politics of Interests* (Boulder, CO: Westview Press, 1992), p. 5.
[5] Clive Thomas and Ronald J. Hrebenar, "Changing Patterns of Interest Group Activity: A Regional Perspective," in Ibid., p. 4.
[6] Graham Wilson, *Interest Groups in the United States* (New York: Oxford University Press, 1981), p. 4.
[7] David B. Truman, *The Governmental Process: Political Interests and Public Opinion* (New York: Knopf, 1951), p. 33.
[8] Robert H. Salisbury, "Interest Groups," in Fred I. Greenstein and Nelson W. Polsby, eds. *Handbook of Political Science*, Vol. 4 (Reading, MA: Addison-Wesley, 1975), p. 175.
[9] V. O. Key Jr. *Politics, Parties, and Pressure Groups* (New York: T. J. Crowell, 1942), p. 23.

TOLES copyright 1993 *The Buffalo News*. Reprinted with permission of UNIVERSAL PRESS SYNDICATE. All rights reserved.

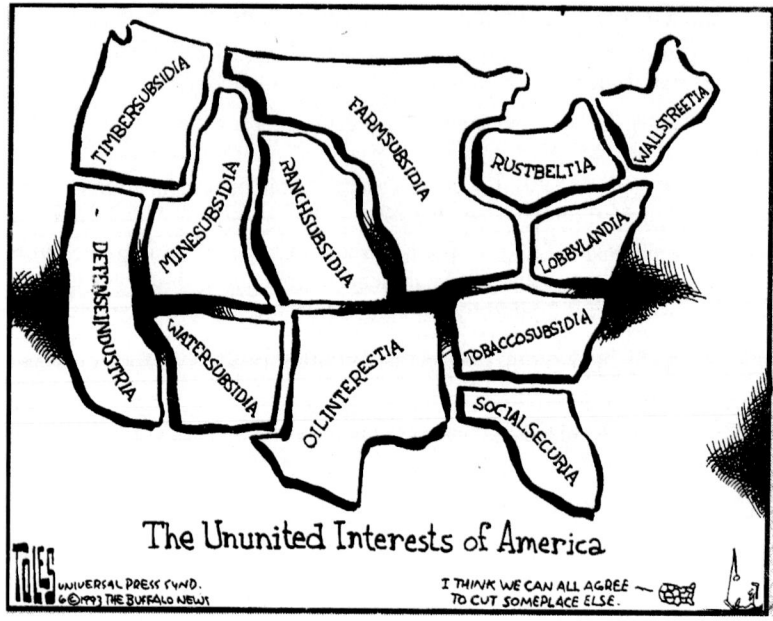

contrast, trade and professional associations such as the Chamber of Commerce or the American Medical Association are usually more powerful and find few doors closed to them in Washington.

Groups that mobilize to protect particular economic interests generally are the most fully and effectively organized of all the types of interest groups.[10] They exist to make profits and to obtain economic benefits for their members. To achieve these goals, however, they often find that they must resort to political means rather than trust the operation of economic markets to produce outcomes favorable to their members.

Public Interest Groups. Political scientist Jeffrey Berry defines **public-interest groups** as groups "that seek a collective good, the achievement of which will not selectively and materially benefit the membership or activists of the organization."[11] Unlike economic-interest groups, public-interest groups do not tend to be particularly motivated by the desire to achieve goals that would benefit their members. As Berry notes, the public interest has many faces. In the past, for example, many Progressive Era groups, perhaps as best personified by the settlement house movement (see p. 624) that began to sweep the United States in the late 1800s, were created to solve the varied problems (such as poor quality housing) of new immigrants and the poor. Today, civil and constitutional rights groups, environmental groups, good-government groups such as Common Cause, peace groups, church groups, and groups that speak out for those who cannot (such as children, the mentally ill, or animals) are examples of public-interest groups. The American Civil Liberties Union (ACLU) (see "The American

---

[10] Robert H. Salisbury, "An Exchange Theory of Interest Groups," *Midwest Journal of Political Science,* 13 (1969): 1–32.

[11] Jeffrey Berry, *Lobbying for the People: The Political Behavior of Public Interest Groups* (Princeton, NJ: Princeton University Press, 1977), p. 7.

Civil Liberties Union," p. 126), for example, is a public-interest organization that fights against, among other things, government entanglement with religion. Group members realize no financial gain when ACLU lawyers argue that the government should not allow nativity scenes to be erected on public lands. Similarly, its members derive no direct economic benefits when the ACLU challenges the constitutionality of New York State's practice of awarding college scholarships to students based on their SAT scores. (The ACLU successfully argued that the SATs discriminate against women.)[12]

Multi-Issue *versus* Single-Issue Groups. Many of the economic- and public-interest groups discussed above are **multi-issue groups,** that is, they are concerned with more than just a single issue. For example, the AFL-CIO, the largest labor union in the United States, which was formed to represent the interests of organized labor, is also concerned with health care, Social Security, and civil rights, among other issues. In 1993, it lobbied hard against passage of the North American Free Trade Agreement (NAFTA), arguing that jobs of union workers would be lost to Mexico. Similarly, the NAACP is interested primarily in race relations, but it is also involved in other areas, including education, the criminal justice system, housing, and welfare rights—all areas of potential concern to its members.

In the 1800s various abolitionist groups opposed to slavery could be classified as single-issue groups. The 1980s witnessed a substantial growth of **single-issue groups,** those organized to influence policy in only one area. Single-issue groups differ from

---

[12] "Will Ruling on S.A.T. Affect College Admissions?" *New York Times* (February 8, 1989): B–10.

The AFL-CIO, the largest and among the oldest labor unions in the country, rallied its members to campaign against NAFTA. It lost with the passage of NAFTA in late 1993.

multi-issue groups both in the range and intensity of their interests. Concentration on one area generally leads to greater zeal in a group's lobbying efforts. Probably the most visible single-issue groups today are those organized on each side of the abortion and gun control debates. Anti-abortion groups like Operation Rescue and pro-choice groups like the National Abortion and Reproductive Rights Action League (NARAL) are good examples of single-issue groups, as are the National Rifle Association (NRA) and Handgun Control, Inc. Today, people single-mindedly pursue all kinds of interests. Drug- or AIDS-awareness groups, environmental groups, and anti-nuclear power groups, for example, can each be classified as a single-issue group. Table 15.1 describes several prominent interest groups active today.

The Roots of American Interest Groups

Political scientists have long debated how and why interest groups arise. Robert H. Salisbury, for example, argues that resource scarcity leads to group formation.[13] Jack L. Walker contends that without what he terms "patrons" (those who often finance a group) few organizations could begin.[14] And, one of the first political scientists to study interest groups, David B. Truman, posed what he termed **disturbance theory** to explain why interest groups form.[15] He hypothesizes that groups form in part to counteract the activities of other groups or of organized special interests. According to Truman, the government's role is to provide a forum in which the competing demands of groups and the majority of the U.S. population can be heard and balanced. He argues that the government's role in managing competing groups is to balance their conflicting demands. Nevertheless, when examining the evolution and growth of interest groups in the United States, we are not always looking at clashes of one group against another, but of one group against the majority of the American public. As with the many different definitions of interest groups, a variety of sound reasons have been offered to explain why interest groups form.

Generally, however, interest groups tend to arise in response to changes. They can be political or economic changes, changes in the population, technological changes, or even changes in society itself. During the 1770s, for example, many groups (such as the Sons of Liberty) arose to fight for political and economic independence from Great Britain. From the 1820s, in a period called the Second Great Awakening, prominent preachers stressed the moral need to end sinful practices. Large revival meetings focused on the sinfulness and evils of slavery, providing a major impetus to the founding of several anti-slavery societies. After the Civil War, trade unions flourished, and the Grange was founded to help farmers. Business associations proliferated in the 1880s and 1890s as revealed in "Landmark Events in the History of Early National Interest Groups" (p. 620). In the early 1900s, other groups were created in reaction to big business and other social and economic forces. And, the 1960s saw the rapid growth of public-interest groups.

---

[13] Salisbury, "An Exchange Theory of Interest Groups," pp. 1–32.

[14] Jack L. Walker, "The Origins and Maintenance of Interest Groups in America," 77 *American Political Science Review* (June 1983): 390–406.

[15] Truman, *The Governmental Process,* chap. 16.

Table 15.1 ♦ Profiles of Selected Interest Groups

NAME (FOUNDED)	SINGLE- OR MULTI-ISSUE	1993 BUDGET (MILLIONS)	MEMBERS	PAC
Economic Groups				
AFL-CIO	M	62	14.1 million	AFL-CIO PAC
American Medical Association (AMA)	M	205	300,000	AMA PAC
Association of Trial Lawyers of America	M	19	60,000	Association of Trial Lawyers of America PAC
National Association of Manufacturers (NAM) (1895)	M	16	12,500	no
Tobacco Institute	S	38	13 (cigarette companies)	no
U.S. Chamber of Commerce (1912)	M	70	180,000 companies	National Chamber Alliance for Politics
Public Interest Groups				
American Association of Retired Persons (AARP) (1958)	M	305	33,000,000	no
Amnesty International U.S.A. (1961)	S	22.3	386,000	no
Handgun Control, Inc. (1974)	S	8	360,000	Handgun Control Voter Education Fund
League of United Latin American Citizens (LULAC) (1929)	M	N/A	110,000	no
National Abortion and Reproductive Rights Action League (NARAL) (1969)	S	9.3	450,000	NARAL PAC
National Association for the Advancement of Colored People (NAACP) (1909)	M	16	345,000	no
National Gay and Lesbian Task Force (1973)	S	1.4	17,000	no
National Rifle Association (NRA) (1871)	S	86.9 (1990)	2,650,000	Political Victory Fund
National Right to Life Committee (1973)	S	13.5	400,000	National Right to Life PAC
Environmental Groups				
Environmental Defense Fund (EDF) (1967)	S	16	150,000	no
Greenpeace USA (1971)	S	35 (1990)	2,100,000	no
Sierra Club (1892)	S	39	650,000	Sierra Club Political Committee
Good Government Groups				
Common Cause (1970)	S	11.3	270,000	no
Public Citizen, Inc. (1971)	M	6.2	100,000	no

Source: Public Interest Profiles, 1993–1994 (Washington, D.C.: Congressional Quarterly, 1993), "Profiles of Interest Groups," *Health Line,* October 13, 1993, "Legal Times: Profiles of Interest Groups Part II," *Health Line,* October 14, 1993, NEXIS.

Landmark Events in the History of Early National Interest Groups		
1830s	♦	Early trade associations formed
1833	♦	American Anti-Slavery Society founded
1848	♦	Seneca Falls Convention for Women's Rights
1851	♦	Young Men's Christian Association (YMCA) founded
1869	♦	National Woman Suffrage Association (NWSA) formed Grange founded
1874	♦	Women's Christian Temperance Union (WCTU) founded
1886	♦	American Federation of Labor (AFL) formed
1896	♦	National Association of Manufacturers begins operation
1897	♦	AFL and other union membership increases 360 percent (pro-labor)
1904	♦	NAM budget increases to fight unions

The Early Years: The Colonial Period to 1830

Many of the first colonists who came to America in the early seventeenth century were escaping religious persecution. They organized themselves into colonies based on their own religious preference. Catholics founded Maryland, the Puritans founded Massachusetts, and the Quakers founded Pennsylvania, for example. In essence, these colonies became some of the first special-interest groups in the New World: They were governmental units organized along religious lines and designed to further certain religious, moral, and policy preferences.

Soon thereafter, skilled laborers such as bricklayers and blacksmiths banded together in craft guilds and trade associations. They viewed their creation of guilds as critical to their ability to restrict competition in the wake of an influx of new settlers who wanted their jobs. Later, as we discussed in Chapter 2, groups of colonists who were dissatisfied with the economic restrictions placed on them by the crown formed the Sons of Liberty and participated in the Boston Tea Party in political protest.

Once the new nation was formed, its highly agricultural nature was reflected in some of its earliest regional societies. In 1785 the Philadelphia Society for Promoting Agriculture was created. Its the goal was to advance "products of the land within the American states." Benjamin Franklin was an active member, and George Washington was an honorary member. The Society for Promoting and Improving Agriculture and Other Rural Concerns was founded around the same time in Charleston, South Carolina. A lack of communications networks prevented any of these associations from becoming national in scope, and none was particularly political in nature. Yet, all worked for the economic benefit of their members.

National Groups Emerge (1830–1880)

In the 1830s, as the nation began to industrialize, communications networks improved, and the first groups national in scope began to emerge. It is interesting to note that an identical flowering of associational activity occurred in Britain at the same time.

Many of these early national organizations were single-issue in scope. Often they were deeply rooted in the Christian religious revivalism that was sweeping the nation. Concern with humanitarian issues such as temperance (total abstinence from alcoholic beverages), peace, capital punishment, education, and, most important, slavery led to the founding of numerous associations dedicated to solving social problems. Among the first of these groups was the American Anti-Slavery Society, founded in 1833 by William Lloyd Garrison. The only woman allowed to speak at its first meeting, Lucretia Mott, went on to organize the first large gathering of women's rights activists in Seneca Falls, New York, in 1848. But no national women's groups were formed until after the Civil War.

In the wake of continued immigration and growing poverty in large, increasingly industrialized cities, concern for the fate of the poor led to the founding of the Young Men's Christian Association (YMCA) in Boston in 1851. Although today many people associate the YMCA with sports and recreation, its founders initially viewed these kinds of activities only as a means of reaching out to the children of immigrants and the poor in urban centers to help integrate them into U.S. society and a Christian lifestyle.

The Civil War (1861–1865) fostered the creation of a national communications network of telegraph lines and railroads. It also brought people together in a variety of new groups, such as sanitary commissions, the Red Cross and, later, veteran's associations. After the war, for the first time in history, railroads, radio, and telegraphs brought people, manufactured goods, agricultural products, and information to the far corners of the nation. And, better methods of communication allowed more people to stay in touch. Right after the Civil War, for example, the National Woman Suffrage Association was founded. Many of its early members and leaders had met while volunteers in the war effort.

Other women founded the Women's Christian Temperance Union (WCTU) in 1874, with the goal of outlawing the sale of liquor. Its members, many of them quite religious, believed that the consumption of alcohol was an evil that was injurious to family life because many men drank away their paychecks, leaving no money to feed or clothe their families. Many women who believed that the national suffrage associations (whose aims were to get women the right to vote) were too radical joined the WCTU to do good for others. Churches and Southerners, in particular, supported the WCTU's goal of prohibiting the manufacture and sale of all alcoholic beverages. The WCTU's activities included conventional and nonconventional forms of activity: organizing prayer groups, lobbying for prohibition legislation, conducting peaceful marches, and engaging in more violent protests that included the destruction of saloons. By the 1890s, the WCTU had more than 200,000 female members at a time when the total U.S. population was 63 million. (In contrast, in 1993, the membership of the National Organization for Women was 280,000 when the total population was more than 250 million.)

While the WCTU and the YMCA were clearly public-interest groups, the Grange, which was also formed during the period following the Civil War, was more concerned with the economic interests of its members. In fact, it was created by six government employees as an educational society for farmers in order to teach them about the latest agricultural developments. Although its charter formally stated that the Grange was not to become involved in "politics," in 1876 it formulated a detailed plan to pressure

622 ❖ Chapter 15 Interest Groups

At the turn of the century, Carry Nation was one of the fiercest advocates of the temperance movement. Unlike some of her fellow prohibitionists, Nation favored direct action over peaceful demonstrations. More than once she was arrested and jailed for breaking up a saloon with an axe.

Congress to enact legislation favorable to farmers. In response to the growth of large businesses and monopolies that affected the prices of livestock and harvests, the Grange's members banded together to influence the traditional political parties to deal more effectively with big-business interests. In essence, government became the mediator between the interests of farmers who belonged to the Grange and big business.

The Grange used posters to convince the public how critical to the economy were the services of farmers.

Here a cartoon shows a U.S. Senator receiving a paycheck from "two masters"—Uncle Sam *and* a railroad representative.

After the Civil War, the demand grew for more railroads to meet the needs of an expanding and united country. In fact, the railroad industry was perhaps the most effective interest group of the day. In a move that couldn't take place today because of its illegality, the Central Pacific Railroad sent its own lobbyist to Washington, DC as early as 1861, before the Civil War ended. There, he eventually became the administrator of both committees of Congress charged with overseeing regulation of the railroad industry. Subsequently, the Central Pacific Railroad received vast grants of land from Congress along its route and large subsidized loans from the national government. The railroad became so important that it later went on to have nearly total political control of the California state legislature.

Business interests soon began to play even larger roles in both state and national politics. A popular saying of the day noted that the Standard Oil Company did everything to the Pennsylvania legislature except refine it. Increasingly, large trusts, monopolies, business combinations, and corporate conglomerations in the oil, steel, and sugar industries became sufficiently powerful to control many representatives in the state and national legislatures.

National Groups Increase (1890–1920)

By the 1890s, a profound change had occurred in the nation's political and social outlook. Rapid industrialization and an influx of immigrants had contributed to a host of problems, including crime, poverty, squalid and unsafe working conditions, widespread political corruption, and high prices and low wages caused by monopolistic business practices. Many Americans began to believe that new measures would be necessary to impose order on this growing chaos and to curb some of the more glaring problems. The political and social movement that grew out of these concerns was called progressivism.

The Progressive Movement and Public Interest Groups. Not even the progressives themselves could agree on what the term "progressive" actually meant. To some

Jane Addams founded Hull House in 1889 in Chicago and helped launch the Progressive Movement. She is pictured here in 1914.

it was a broad societal vision. Others believed that it encompassed a set of moral and humanitarian goals. And to others it was a set of particular good-government reforms. Desire for reform led to an explosion of all types of interest groups. Politically, the movement took the form of the Progressive Party, which sought on the electoral front to run and elect candidates pledged to limit or end the power of the industrialists' near-total control of the steel, oil, railroad, and other key industries.

During its formative stages, the Progressive Movement was epitomized by the rapid growth of settlement houses across the United States. Settlement houses were welfare centers that provided community services such as child care, reading and English language lessons, and job training for the less fortunate. Jane Addams, a young social worker, established one of the first settlement houses, Hull House, in Chicago in 1889. By 1900, there were more than 400 such houses across the nation.

In addition to providing many services to the poor, settlement houses provided room and board for innumerable progressive activists. Here, prominent thinkers met and exchanged ideas; settlement house residents, in essence, were the Progressive Movement. They were active in women's suffrage, in reform of the treatment of juvenile offenders, in education systems (including implementation of a system of kindergartens), and in the reform of corrupt city governments. Many settlement house residents went on to found groups that would later form the core of the civil rights and public-interest movements of the 1960s.

Living at one time or another at Hull House, for example, were Julia Lathrop, the future head of the Federal Children's Bureau and director of the Immigrants' Protective League; members of the future Boards of Directors of the National Association for the Advancement of Colored People (NAACP) (established in 1909) and the American Civil Liberties Union (ACLU) (established in 1919); John Dewey, an educational reformer and inventor of the Dewey decimal library cataloging system; Eugene V. Debs, president of the American Railway Union; Margaret Dreier Robins, the president of the Women's Trade Union League; and the executive directors of the National Child Labor Committee and the National Consumers' League.

Progressive groups relied heavily on the support of the public for various appeals to legislators for reform. For example, the National Consumers' League (NCL) was founded in 1899 by wealthy women to work for improved working conditions for women and children. At that time, many women and children worked for long hours at low wages in substandard buildings lacking proper ventilation or safety features. In addition to extensive lobbying (at the state and national levels) for maximum hour and minimum wage laws for women and children, the NCL's local organizations published a list of approved retailers who treated their employees well by providing them fair wages for reasonable hours in a safe environment. It also allowed companies complying with their conditions to use the NCL label. The NCL also started the "shop early" movement at Christmas time to encourage consumers to do their holiday shopping before the Christmas rush. The League believed that such a campaign would prompt consumers to shop early, thereby reducing the burden placed on shop girls.

Many members of the NCL were also members of the National American Woman Suffrage Association, which was the key organization pushing for a constitutional amendment to give women the right to vote. During the Progressive era, women's organizations were second only to trade organizations in number and influence on Capitol Hill.

In response to the pressure applied by progressive groups, the national government began to regulate business. Because businesses had a vested interest in keeping wages low and costs down, more business groups organized to consolidate their strength and to counter progressive organizations. Not only did governments have to mediate progressive and business demands, but they also had to accommodate the role of organized labor, which often allied itself with progressive groups against big business.

Organized Labor. While wealthy industrialists and large corporations had no problems getting the ear of most politicians, employees generally had little clout. Several early attempts to maximize their bargaining power by organizing local labor groups into national unions were unsuccessful. Not until the creation of the American Federation of Labor (AFL) in 1886 was there any real national union activity. The AFL brought together skilled workers from several trades into one stronger national organization. By 1902, its membership exceeded one million workers. However, its effectiveness in mobilizing for higher wages for workers triggered more and better business organization. As business interests pushed states for "open shop" laws (which allowed employees not to join unions in unionized factories), the AFL became increasingly political. It was also forced to react to the success of big businesses' use of legal injunctions to prohibit union organization.

In Britain, labor organized at the national level much earlier: The Trades Union Congress (TUC), a federation of individual unions, formed in 1868. Conversely, organized business appeared somewhat later in Britain than in the United States: The Federation of British Industry (FBI) opened its doors in 1916, some twenty-one years after its U.S. counterpart, the National Association of Manufacturers (NAM), began operations.

In 1914, massive lobbying by the AFL and its members led to passage of the Clayton Act, which labor leader Samuel Gompers hailed as the "Magna Carta" of the labor movement. This law allowed unions to organize free from prosecution and also guaranteed their right to strike, a powerful weapon against employers.

Samuel Gompers soon ran into trouble when he tried to control American Federation of Labor members who wanted to strike to protest unfair wages and conditions.

Business Groups and Trade Associations. The National Association of Manufacturers (NAM) was founded in 1895 by manufacturers who had suffered business reverses in the economic panic of 1893 and who believed that they were being affected adversely by the growth of organized labor. NAM first became politically active in 1913, when a major tariff bill was under congressional consideration. NAM's tactics were "so insistent and abrasive" and its expenditures of monies so lavish that President Woodrow Wilson was forced to denounce its lobbying tactics as creating an "unbearable situation."[16] Congress immediately called for an investigation of NAM's activities but found no member of Congress willing to testify that he had ever even encountered a member of NAM (probably because many of them had been "bought" with illegal contributions and gifts).

The second major business organization came into being in 1912, when the National Chamber of Commerce was created with the assistance of the Secretary of Commerce and Labor. Like the Grange several years before, government workers served as patrons for the new organization. (This was before that Cabinet post was split into the

---

[16] Quoted in Grant McConnell, "Lobbies and Pressure Groups," in Jack Greene, ed. *Encyclopedia of American Political History,* Vol. 2 (New York: Macmillan, 1984), p. 768.

PEOPLE OF THE PAST

Florence Kelley

Florence Kelley (1859–1932) was the third of eight children born to William Darrah Kelley, a self-educated lawyer who later enjoyed a long career in Congress. Kelley's five sisters died in infancy, and since she was ill quite often herself, her early schooling took place at home. She read her father's entire library and developed strong interests in social reform at an early age. She was particularly influenced by her aunt Sarah, a Quaker reformer and abolitionist, who refused to use cotton or sugar in personal protest against slave labor. Kelley's father, a strong believer in women's suffrage, encouraged her to enter Cornell University. There, Kelley earned a bachelor's degree in 1876 and applied to the University of Pennsylvania to study law, but she was refused admittance because of her sex.

While traveling in Europe, Kelley met M. Carey Thomas, the first American woman to earn a Ph.D., who urged Kelley to attend her alma mater, the University of Zurich. There, Kelley translated several major

The National Consumers' League used this "White Label" in the early 1900s to certify that goods were produced under working conditions that were acceptable as stipulated by the NCL.

works by Karl Marx and Friedrich Engels, and she met and married a Polish medical student and socialist. They had three children before returning to New York City. Kelley's husband abused her, however, and finally in 1891, she took her children and fled to Chicago, where she obtained a divorce and went back to using her maiden name.

Department of Commerce and the Department of Labor.) The administration of President William Howard Taft believed that the government should have one body to consult with concerning the interests of business. Also, regional chambers of commerce saw the need to operate on the national level. They had been distressed by the progressive, seemingly anti-business, anti-monopoly policies of President Theodore Roosevelt (who left office in 1909) and were alarmed by the increased political activity of organized labor.

NAM, the Chamber of Commerce, and **trade associations,** groups that represent specific industries, were effective spokespersons for their member companies. They were unable to defeat passage of the Clayton Act, but groups such as the Cotton Manufacturers planned successful elaborate court campaigns to overturn key provisions of the act in the courts.[17] And, the Clayton Act aside, innumerable pieces of pro-business legislation were passed by Congress, whose members continued to insist that they had never been contacted by business groups.

In 1928 the bubble burst for some business interests. At the Senate's request, the Federal Trade Commission (FTC) undertook a massive investigation of the lobbying

---

[17] Lee Epstein, *Conservatives in Court* (Knoxville: University of Tennessee Press, 1985).

In Chicago, Kelley joined Jane Addams and other women reformers at Hull House, one of the nation's first social settlements. Concerned with child labor, she published a pamphlet in 1892, *Our Toiling Children*. Three years later she published *Hull House Maps and Papers* based on her investigations of the "sweatshops" in garment factories and a survey of the condition of city slums. Described as a "guerilla warrior" in the "wilderness of industrial wrongs" by the local press, Kelley pushed to get legislation limiting the number of hours a woman could work, prohibiting child labor, and controlling tenement sweatshops. Frustrated by her inability to get cases prosecuted, Kelley took night classes in 1894 and earned a law degree from Northwestern University.

To attack child labor from another angle, Kelley eagerly accepted the position of general secretary of the newly established National Consumers' League (NCL), a position she held from 1899 until her death in 1932. The NCL used consumer pressure to ensure that goods were manufactured under acceptable working conditions. Kelley spoke to groups all over the country on behalf of her cause. She established sixty Consumers' Leagues in twenty states and organized two international conferences. She helped set up the New York Child Labor Committee in 1902 and the National Child Labor Committee in 1904.

Kelley pursued a number of other interests as well. She was a founding member of the National Association for the Advancement of Colored People and the Women's International League for Peace and Freedom. She was also active from 1911 onward in the Intercollegiate Socialist Society, serving as its president from 1918 to 1920. In 1912 she joined Eugene V. Debs's Socialist Party of America. She also served as vice president of the National Woman Suffrage Association for several years and lobbied for women's legislation as an active member of the Women's Joint Congressional Committee that was founded in the early 1920s after passage of the Nineteenth Amendment.

Under Kelley's leadership, the NCL launched a successful defense of protective legislation in the courts. Kelley's efforts were also key to congressional passage of the Sheppard-Towner Maternity and Infancy Act in 1921, which provided federal funds to the states that offered pre- and postnatal care for women and for their babies (see "Then and Now," p. 27).

tactics of the business community. The FTC's examination of Congress revealed extensive illegal lobbying by another group, the National Electric Light Association (NELA). Not only did the NELA lavishly entertain members of Congress, but it also went to great expense to educate the public on the virtues of electric lighting. Books and pamphlets were produced and donated to schools and public libraries to sway public opinion. Needy teachers and ministers who were willing to advocate electricity were "helped" with financial grants. These tactics were considered unethical by many people, and business was held in public disfavor. It was these kinds of activities that led the public to view lobbyists in a negative light.

Though issues changed and the Progressive Movement gave way under the weight of the Depression and World War II, the general balance of groups maintained itself until well past the mid-twentieth century.

The Modern Era of Interest-Group Activity (1960 to the present)

After the Depression, the New Deal, and the country's entry into World War II, many progressive groups fell into disarray. Others remained active, but with less vitality. Many business, labor, and professional groups, however, continued to flourish. According to a study conducted by Kay Lehman Schlozman and John Tierney, nearly 70 percent of today's Washington, D.C.-based political organizations established their offices after 1960.[18] Nearly half opened their offices after 1970. Not surprisingly, given the social and economic thrust of President Lyndon B. Johnson's "Great Society" programs, most of the new groups were formed to take advantage of the money and opportunities those programs offered.

From 1960 to 1992, the number of interest-group representatives registered (as required by law) in Washington increased from fewer than 500 to 6,083. The federal government had clearly become the primary target of policy change, and it was natural for groups to concentrate their resources in the nation's capital. As revealed in Figure 15-1, numerous interest groups and law firms that are hired as lobbyists are clumped together in a small section of Washington, D.C.

Public-Interest Groups. During the 1960s and 1970s, the progressive spirit found renewed vigor in the rise of public-interest groups. Generally, these groups devoted themselves to representing the interests of African Americans, women, the elderly, the poor, and consumers or to working on behalf of the environment. Many of their leaders and members had been active in the civil rights and anti-Vietnam War movement efforts of the 1960s. Other groups, like the ACLU and NAACP, which had survived for nearly a century, gained renewed vigor. Many of them had as their patron the liberal Ford Foundation, which helped to bankroll numerous groups, including the Mexican-American Legal Defense and Education Fund, the Puerto Rican Legal Defense and Education Fund, and the Native American Rights Fund. Another group that came to prominence in this era was the American Association of Retired Persons (AARP). The elderly are the fastest growing group in the United States, and AARP is the largest single interest group in the country, with thirty-three million members in 1994.

---

[18] Kay Lehman Schlozman and John T. Tierney, *Organized Interests and American Democracy* (New York: Harper and Row, 1986).

The Roots of American Interest Groups ❖ 629

FIGURE 15-1
Where Washington Lobbyists Work and Lunch

Source: Atlanta Journal & Constitution, November 22, 1992, p. A-8.

Common Cause and the Nader Network. The civil rights and anti-war movements of the 1960s and 1970s left many Americans feeling cynical about a government that they believed failed to respond to the will of the majority. They also believed that if citizens banded together, they could make a difference. Thus, two major new public interest groups—Common Cause and Ralph Nader's Public Citizen, Inc.—were founded during this period. Common Cause, a "good government" group similar to

Then and Now

Lobbying

The exact origin of the term "lobbying" is disputed. In the mid-seventeenth century there was a room located near the floor of the English House of Commons where members of Parliament would congregate and could be approached by their constituents and other people who wanted to plead a particular cause. Similarly, in the United States, people often waited outside the chambers of the House and Senate to speak to members of Congress as they emerged. Because they waited in the lobbies to argue their cases, by the nineteenth century they were commonly referred to as "lobbyists." Another piece of folklore explains that when Ulysses S. Grant was president he would frequently walk from the White House to the Willard Hotel on Pennsylvania Avenue just to relax in its comfortable and attractive lobby. Interest-group representatives and people seeking favors from Grant would crowd into that lobby and try to press their claims. Soon they were nicknamed "lobbyists."

Lobbying reached an infamous peak in the late 1800s, when railroads and other big businesses openly bribed state and federal legislators to obtain the passage of favorable legislation. Congress finally began regulating some aspects of lobbying in 1946 with the Regulation of Lobbying Act. The Act required paid lobbyists to register with the House and Senate and to file quarterly financial reports, including an account of all contributions and expenditures as well as the names and addresses of individuals to whom they gave $500 or more. Organizations also were required to submit financial reports, although they did not have to register officially. The purpose of the Act was to publicize the activities of lobbyists, thus removing some uncertainty surrounding the influence of lobbying on legislation.

In 1954, however, a lower court ruled the Act unconstitutional. Although the Supreme Court reversed the decision, the Court's narrow interpretation undermined the effectiveness of the Act. The Court ruled that the Act was applicable only to persons or organizations who solicited, collected, or received money for the principal purpose of influencing legislation by directly lobbying members of Congress. Consequently, many lobbyists do not register at all. The National Association of Manufacturers, for example, was formed in 1895 but did not register as a lobbying group until 1975. Of the organizations that do register, more than 90 percent do not file complete financial reports.

Congress continually considers legislation creating a unified lobbying disclosure law in an effort to reduce many loopholes in the current regulations. While lobbyists are currently required to disclose all meetings with House and Senate members, time spent with personal or committee staff is not counted. And while the expenses incurred during those meetings with members of Congress must be reported, the total spending of lobbyists remains unknown. Stricter regulations on lobbying will reveal a more accurate picture of who is trying to influence legislation and with how much money.

some of the early progressive good-government groups, has effectively challenged aspects of the congressional seniority system, successfully urged the passage of sweeping campaign-financing reforms, and played a major role in the enactment of legislation authorizing federal financing of presidential campaigns. It continues to lobby for accountability in government and for more efficient and responsive governmental structures and practices.

Perhaps more well known than Common Cause is the collection of groups headed by Ralph Nader under the name Public Citizen, Inc. In 1965 Nader, a young lawyer, was thrust into the limelight with the publication of his book *Unsafe at Any Speed*. In it he charged that the Corvair, a General Motors (GM) car, was unsafe to drive; he produced voluminous evidence of how the car could flip over at average speeds on curved roads. In 1966 he testified about auto safety in front of Congress and then learned that General Motors had spied on him in an effort to discredit his work. The $250,000 that GM subsequently paid to Nader in an out-of-court settlement allowed him to establish the Center for the Study of Responsive Law in 1969. The Center analyzed the activities of regulatory agencies and concluded that few of them enforced anti-trust regulations or cracked down on deceptive advertising practices. Nader then turned again to lobbying Congress, which led him to create Public Citizen, Inc., which would act as an umbrella organization for what was to be called the "Nader Network" of groups.

These good-government groups have had a significant impact on governmental policy making, as have other public interest groups, including those concerned with the environment and women's issues. Good-government groups and other public-interest groups have enjoyed considerable success in the legislative forum.

Conservative Backlash: Religious and Ideological Groups. The growth and successes that various public-interest groups had in the 1960s and 1970s ultimately led to a conservative backlash. Many of these liberal groups' advances were made through litigation, that is, by challenging existing laws and practices through the courts. As discussed in detail in Chapter 9, since the days of the progressive National Consumers' League, liberal groups had targeted the courts, especially the Supreme Court, in an effort to secure their goals. Women and African Americans won many rights through expanded readings of the equal protection clause of the Fourteenth Amendment and judicial interpretation of the requirements of the Civil Rights Act of 1964 (such as the end of segregated public schools and the right to a job free from discrimination), and the Nader groups and environmentalists secured many governmental regulations that adversely affected business interests. Conservative groups quickly took notice of these successes and began responding to them.

By the mid- to late 1970s, conservatives became very concerned about the successes of liberal groups in shaping and defining the public agenda, and religious and ideological conservatives became a potent force in U.S. politics. The largest new religious conservative group was the Reverend Jerry Falwell's Moral Majority, founded in 1978. At one time, the Moral Majority had an extensive television ministry and in its peak year, 1984, raised $11 million for political lobbying. It was widely credited with assisting Ronald Reagan's 1980 presidential victory as well as the defeats of several liberal Democratic senators that same year. Falwell claimed to have sent from three to four million newly registered voters to the polls.[19] In June 1989, Falwell announced

---

[19] Peter Stienfels, "Moral Majority to Dissolve; Says Mission Accomplished," *New York Times* (June 12, 1989): A–14.

that he was terminating the Moral Majority after the group suffered from a series of financial and sexual scandals involving television evangelists. To some extent, the end of the Reagan era seemed to trigger an end to the effectiveness of the religious right in national politics. Other conservatives, however, were not so daunted.

In 1973, friends of Ronald Reagan, who was then the governor of California, were dismayed by the repeated successes in the courts of liberal public-interest groups. Liberal groups were continually victorious in challenging the "reforms" of the Reagan administration—particularly those concerning welfare and the environment. Reaganites were incensed that these liberal groups continually went to court claiming to represent the "public interest." Therefore, Reagan supporters in California founded the Pacific Legal Foundation, the chief aim of which was to present the conservative side of the public interest in court. In the late 1970s, the Pacific Legal Foundation was sufficiently successful to justify the creation of several regional law centers throughout the United States.[20] The conservative law centers' goal was to bring to court cases that would secure the reversal of liberal decisions involving the environment, affirmative action, and other issues of concern to conservatives. As the Supreme Court took a more conservative turn, these conservative public-interest firms renewed their efforts to bring to the Court test cases on issues involving civil rights, affirmative action, the environment, and prayer in schools.

Impressed by the successes of these groups in court, other conservatives moved to fill the void left by the demise of the Moral Majority. In 1990, the televangelist Pat Robertson, host of the popular "The 700 Club," formed a new group, the Christian Coalition (see "Conservatives Reorganize," p. 633), which again is giving conservatives new clout at the ballot box.

Business Groups. Conservative public-interest groups were not the only ones organized to advance conservative views beginning in the 1970s. Many members of the business community believed that both the Chamber of Commerce and the National Association of Manufacturers were too reactionary and shrill in their condemnation of governmental policies and practices. In addition, some members of the business community believed that both were too slow to act and therefore were ineffective representatives of big business. To fill this perceived void and to counter the effects of the Nader Network, the Business Roundtable was created in 1972. Largely made up of the chief executive officers of major businesses, the Roundtable uses its members for direct lobbying and policy formation. It is "a fraternity of powerful and prestigious business leaders that tells 'business's side of the story' to legislators, bureaucrats, White House personnel, and other interested public officials."[21] One of its first battles led to the defeat of legislation backed by the Carter administration that would have created a federal consumer protection agency, a pet project of Ralph Nader's.

Unlike public-interest groups, organizations like the Chamber of Commerce and the Business Roundtable enjoy many of the benefits other businesses do as lobbyists: They already have extensive organization, expertise, large numbers, a strong financial base, and a longstanding relationship with key actors in government. Such natural ad-

---

[20] Karen O'Connor and Bryant Scott McFall, "Conservative Interest Group Litigation in the Reagan Era and Beyond," in Mark P. Petracca, ed. *The Politics of Interests* (Boulder, CO: Westview Press, 1992), pp. 263–281.

[21] David Mahood, *Interest Groups Participation in America: A New Intensity* (Englewood Cliffs, NJ: Prentice-Hall, 1990), p. 23.

> ### Conservatives Reorganize
> ♦ ♦ ♦
>
> The Christian Coalition which aims to have 450,000 dues-paying members and another 300,000 volunteers says it is gaining 10,000 members a month. This growth is translating into political victories as Christian Coalition candidates win local races such as school and library boards, state legislatures, and city and county Republican organizations all over the country. Success has been possible largely through a complex grass-roots organizing and loyal church-based workers.
>
> "Clinton may control the White House; we control the grass roots," says coalition president Ralph Reed, Jr. "By the end of the decade we'll be the mainstream."
>
> Soon the Coalition will begin to target blacks and Hispanics through their churches to join the mainly white Protestants. In California, the coalition will use a "school choice" initiative to win the support of these groups. It will spend at least $100,000 on radio ads and literature. Referring to a new coalition poll, Reed says, "(Blacks') greatest concerns, besides the economy, are crime, drugs and education."
>
> *Source:* Richard Benedetto, "Religious Right to Flex Muscles," *USA Today* (September 10, 1993): 6A. Copyright 1993, USA TODAY. Reprinted by permission.

vantages have led to a huge number of business groups. One observer describes their proliferation this way:

> If you want to understand government, don't begin by reading the Constitution. It conveys precious little of today's statecraft. Instead, read selected portions of the Washington Telephone Directory, such as pages 354–58, which contain listings for all of the organizations with titles beginning with the word "National." . . . There are, of course, the big ones, like the National Association of Manufacturers, and the National Association of Broadcasters. But the pages teem with others, National Cigar Leaf Tobacco Association, National Association of Mirror Manufacturers, National Association of Miscellaneous Ornamental and Architectural Product Contractors, National Association of Margarine Manufacturers.[22]

Many of these national groups devote tremendous resources to fighting government regulation. And quite often, they find themselves on the opposite side of organized labor on any issue.

Organized Labor. Labor became a stronger force in U.S. politics when the American Federation of Labor and the Congress of Industrial Organizations merged in 1955. The new AFL-CIO immediately turned its energies to pressuring the government to protect concessions won from employers at the bargaining table. Concentrating its ef-

---

[22] Quoted in Ronald J. Hrebenar and Ruth K. Scott, *Interest Group Politics in America,* 2nd ed. (Englewood Cliffs, NJ: Prentice-Hall, 1990), p. 263.

forts largely on the national level, the AFL-CIO and other unions have been active in a wide range of issues, including minimum wage laws, the environment, civil rights, medical insurance, and consumer and education issues.

But the once-fabled political clout of organized labor has been on the wane. By the late 1970s it was clear that even during a Democratic administration (Carter's), organized labor lacked the impact it had had during earlier decades. During the Reagan administration, organized labor's influence fell to an all-time modern-day low. In spite of the tremendous resources behind the AFL-CIO and other unions, membership has dropped and continues to do so, as revealed in Figure 15-2. In 1983, 20.1 percent of workers were unionized; in 1992 only 15.8 percent were. President Clinton backs legislation banning companies from permanently replacing striking employees. Labor leaders hope that its passage will reverse the decline in union membership.

Professional Associations. In contrast to the labor union situation, the political influence of professional societies continues to expand. The American Medical Association (AMA), for example, waged an all-out battle to fend off President Clinton's proposed system of national guaranteed health care. In the early 1960s, the AMA spent millions of dollars in an unsuccessful effort to fight Medicare. Once some sort of medical assistance for the elderly was inevitable, the AMA turned its efforts toward the drafting and implementation of legislation and regulations, an effort that produced considerable financial rewards for physicians. It will probably try to play a similar role in a national health care system.

The National Education Association (NEA), which represents the interests of teachers, professors, and administrators, is another influential professional association. It was instrumental in the establishment of the Department of Education during the

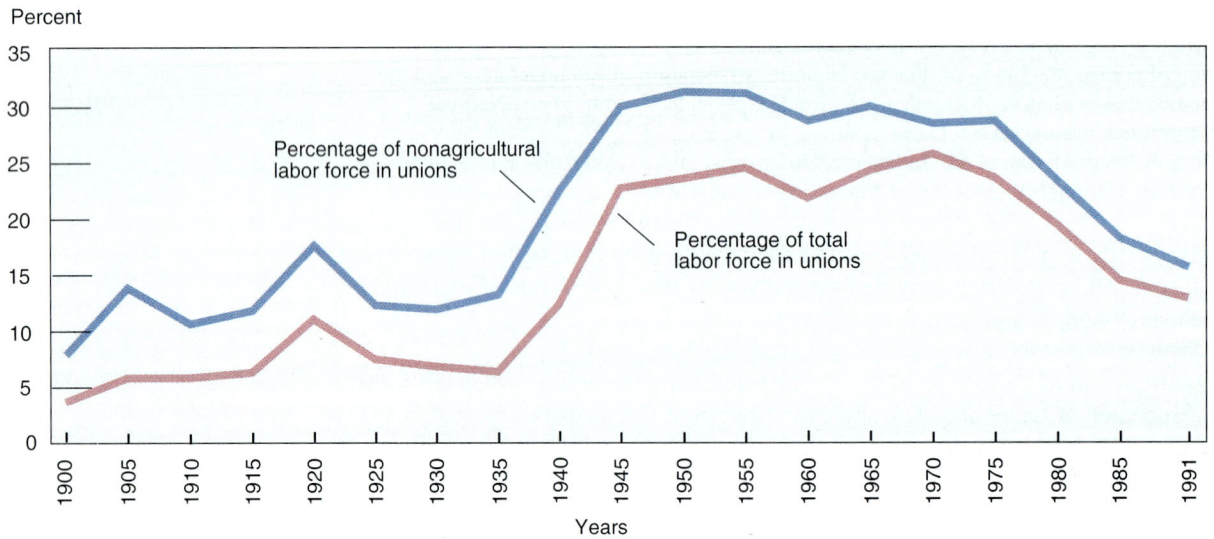

FIGURE 15-2

Labor Union Membership, 1900 to 1993

Source: Adapted from Harold W. Stanley and Richard G. Niemi, *Vital Statistics on American Politics*, 4th ed. (Washington, DC: CQ Press, 1994) Table 6-11, p. 190.

Carter administration. Also influential is the American Bar Association (ABA), which represents many of the nation's lawyers. As discussed in Chapter 9, the ABA plays a key role in nominations to the federal bench via its rating of judicial nominees.

What Do Interest Groups Do?

Americans have long debated the nature of interest groups and their role in a democratic society. Do interest groups contribute to the betterment of society, or are they an evil best controlled by government?

Interest groups often fill voids left by the traditional political parties and give Americans another opportunity to take their claims directly to the government. Interest groups give the unrepresented or underrepresented an opportunity to have their voices heard, thereby making the government and its policy-making process more representative of diverse populations and perspectives.

Interest groups also enhance political participation by motivating like-minded individuals to work toward a common goal. Legislators are often much more likely to listen to or be concerned about the interests of a group as opposed to the interests of any one individual. The congressional testimony of Kimberly Bergalis, the first known individual who claimed to have contracted HIV from a dentist, was given heavy media coverage. Yet the likelihood is slim that Congress will approve mandatory HIV testing of all health care workers without the backing of one or more organized groups to support Bergalis's requests for mandatory testing.

Just as members of Congress are assumed to represent the interests of their constituents in Washington, D.C., interest groups are assumed to represent the interests of their members to policy makers at all levels of government. In the 1950s, for example, the National Association for the Advancement of Colored People (NAACP) was able to articulate and present the interests of African Americans to national decision makers even though as a group they had little or no electoral clout, especially in the South. Without the efforts of the civil rights groups discussed in Chapter 5, it is unlikely that either the courts or Congress would have acted as quickly to make discrimination illegal. All sorts of individuals, from railroad workers to women to physical therapists to campers to homosexuals to mushroom growers, have found that banding together with others who have similar interests and hiring a person to advocate those interests in Washington, D.C., or a state capital increase the likelihood that issues of concern to them will be addressed and acted on favorably.

There is also a downside to interest groups. Because groups make claims on society, they can increase the cost of public policies. The elderly can push for more costly health care and Social Security programs, people with disabilities for improved access to public buildings, industry for tax loopholes, and veterans for improved benefits. Many Americans believe that interest groups exist simply to advance their own selfish interests, with little regard for the rights of other groups or, more important, of people not represented by any organized group.

Whether good or bad, interest groups play an important role in U.S. politics. In addition to *enhancing* the democratic process by providing increased representation and participation, they increase public awareness about important issues, help frame the public agenda, and often monitor programs to guarantee effective implementation. Most often they accomplish these things through some sort of lobbying or informational campaign.

Table 15.2 ♦ Percentage of Groups Using Each Lobbying Technique to Exercise Influence

LOBBYING TECHNIQUE USED	PERCENTAGE
Testifying at hearings	99%
Contacting government officials directly to present your point of view	98
Engaging in informal contact with officials—at conventions, over lunch, etc.	95
Presenting research results or technical information	92
Sending letters to members of your organization to inform them about your activities	92
Entering into coalitions with other organizations	90
Attempting to shape the implementation of policies	89
Talking with people from the press and the media	86
Consulting with government officials to plan legislative strategy	85
Helping to draft legislation	85
Inspiring letter-writing or telegram campaigns	84
Shaping the government's agenda by raising new issues and calling attention to previously ignored problems	84
Mounting grassroots lobbying efforts	80
Having influential constituents contact their member of Congress	80
Helping to draft regulations, rules, or guidelines	78
Serving on advisory commissions and boards	76
Alerting members of Congress to the effects of a bill on their districts	75
Filing suit or otherwise engaging in litigation	72
Making financial contributions to electoral campaigns	58
Doing favors for officials who need assistance	56
Attempting to influence appointments to public office	53
Publicizing candidates' voting records	44
Engaging in direct-mail fund raising for your organization	44
Running advertisements in the media about your position on issues	31
Contributing work or personnel to electoral campaigns	24
Making public endorsements of candidates for office	22
Engaging in protests or demonstrations	20

Source: Adapted from Kay Lehman Schlozman and John T. Tierney, "More of the Same: Washington Pressure Group Activity in a Decade of Change," *Journal of Politics* 45 (1988): 351–375.

"Lobbying" is generally at the top of the agendas of most interest groups. Lobbying is the process by which interest groups attempt to assert their influence on the policy process. The term **lobbyist** refers to any representative of a group who attempts to influence a policy maker by one or more of the tactics illustrated in Table 15.2. It is important to note that not only do large, organized interests have their own lobbyists, but other groups, including colleges, trade associations, cities and even foreign nations, also hire lobbying firms (some law firms have lobbying specialists) to represent them in the halls of Congress or to get through the bureaucratic maze.

As Table 15.2 indicates, there are at least twenty-seven ways to lobby. Lobbying allows interest groups to try to convince key governmental decision makers *and* the public of the correctness of their positions. Almost all interest groups lobby by testifying at hearings and contacting legislators. Other groups also provide information that decision makers might not have the time, opportunity, and/or interest to gather on their own. Of course, information these groups provide is designed to present the group's position in a favorable light, although a good lobbyist for an interest group will also note the downside to proposed legislation. Interest groups also file lawsuits to lobby the courts, and some even engage in protests or demonstrations as a form of "lobbying" public opinion or decision makers.

As journalist Hedrick Smith has noted, "... lobbying kindles an image of wickedness only barely less disreputable than the skullduggery of the Mafia."[23] While this may be the case, it appears to be a necessary evil in our governmental system. Said an official at the University of Alabama, a school that opted to retain a D.C. lobbying firm to represent its interests (a nice name for lobbying) along with several other schools also in low-income states, "So many different agencies are involved, so many programs are competing with one another through subcommittees—there's so much of it, we could never do it without some sort of central organization. It's just enormously helpful to have someone who knows about the Washington process."[24] Within four years, these institutions won almost $68 million in grants from the National Science Foundation and six other federal agencies, a figure that could rise to $84 million in 1994.[25]

Lobbying Congress. Members of Congress are the targets of a wide variety of lobbying activities: individual letters from interested constituents, campaign contributions, or the outright payment of money for votes. Of course, the last item is illegal, but there are numerous documented instances of money changing hands for votes.

Lobbying Congress is a skill that many people have developed over the years. In 1869, for example, women meeting in Washington, D.C., for the second annual meeting of the National Woman Suffrage Association marched to Capitol Hill to hear one of their members (unsuccessfully) ask Congress to pass legislation to enfranchise women under the terms of the Fourteenth Amendment.

Practices such as these floor speeches are no longer permitted. Some interest groups do, however, still try mass marches to Congress. For example, after the Supreme Court ruled in 1976 that discrimination against a pregnant woman was not prohibited by the Civil Rights Act of 1964, hordes of lobbyists from various women's rights groups descended on Congress at one time. In response, Congress quickly enacted the Pregnancy Discrimination Act of 1978.

Today, lobbyists try to develop close relationships with senators and representatives in an effort to enhance their access to the policy-making process. A symbiotic relationship between members and interest-group representatives often develops. Repre-

---

[23] Hedrick Smith, *The Power Game* (New York: Random House, 1988), p. 231.
[24] Michael Wines, "For New Lobbyists, It's Now What They Know," *New York Times* (November 3, 1993): B–14.
[25] Ibid.

sentatives and their staff members, who face an exhausting workload and legislation they know little about, frequently look to lobbyists for information. "Information is the currency on Capitol Hill, not dollars," said one lobbyist.[26] According to one aide:

> My boss demands a speech and a statement for the *Congressional Record* for every bill we introduce or co-sponsor—and we have a lot of bills. I just can't do it all myself. The better lobbyists, when they have a proposal they are pushing, bring it to me along with a couple of speeches, a *Record* insert, and a fact sheet.[27]

Not surprisingly, lobbyists work most closely with representatives who share their interests. A lobbyist from the National Rifle Association (NRA), for example, would be unlikely to try to influence a liberal representative who was on record as strongly in favor of gun control. Instead, it is much more effective for a group like the NRA to provide useful information for its supporters and to those who are undecided. Good lobbyists can also encourage members to file amendments to bills favorable to their interests. They can also urge their supporters in Congress to make speeches (often written by the group) and to pressure their colleagues in the chamber.

A lobbyist's effectiveness depends largely on his or her reputation for fair play and provision of accurate information. No member of Congress wants to look uninformed. As one member noted:

> It doesn't take very long to figure out which lobbyists are straightforward, and which ones are trying to snow you. The good ones will give you the weak points as well as the strong points of their case. If anyone ever gives me false or misleading information, that's it—I'll never see him again.[28]

Successful lobbyists are essentially "on call" when a member of Congress might need them. In 1977 when the Senate was being threatened by a filibuster over gas deregulation, during the all-night session

> the Natural Gas Committee, organized with a $600,000 annual budget to work solely for deregulation, set up a post just outside the Senate Chamber by commandeering a corridor bench and stacking it with manila envelopes full of position papers on pending amendments. . . .
> "We keep a person sitting at a window seat with the files," said one lobbyist for the committee, which represents more than one hundred companies. "Everybody knows where he is. We also have a group of runners because there isn't even a phone there. . . ."
> To cope with the staggering pile of 508 inhibiting amendments . . . the gas industry put a computer to work cranking out "instant economic replay" to a terminal in the National Gas Committee's Connecticut Avenue headquarters, with the results quickly taxied to Capitol Hill.[29]

Even though these kinds of tactics are still used, lobbyists have been dramatically affected by the decentralization of congressional power that has occurred over the

---

[26] Ibid.
[27] Quoted in Schlozman and Tierney, *Organized Interests,* p. 85.
[28] Quoted in Norman J. Ornstein and Shirley Elder, *Interest Groups, Lobbying and Policy Making* (Washington, DC: CQ Press, 1978), p. 77.
[29] Ibid., pp. 85–86.

By permission of Mike Luckovich and Creators Syndicate.

years. The weakening of the power of committee chairs, the diffusion of power to junior House members, and the proliferation of subcommittees have required interest groups to expand the scope and intensity of their lobbying efforts. More and more frequently they are resorting to media campaigns that go directly to the voters to urge them to pressure their representatives, as discussed below.

Because lobbying plays such an important role in Congress, many effective lobbyists often are former members of that body, former staff aides, former White House officials or Cabinet officers, or Washington insiders. This type of lobbyist frequently drops in to visit members of Congress or their staff members and often takes them to lunch, golf, or parties.

Every year hundreds of White House aides or key executive branch staffers take lucrative jobs in the private sector as lobbyists. By December 1993, forty-eight of the 121 lawmakers who left Congress after the 1992 election had become lobbyists. So had at least 50 of their top assistants and more than 30 senior members of the Bush administration.[30] Even some Clinton administration staffers—whom Clinton required to sign a pledge saying they wouldn't use their influence to lobby government agencies for five years after leaving office—weren't stopped from taking lucrative jobs. White House Deputy Chief of Staff Roy Neel left to run a telecommunications lobbying group, and Clinton's first year chief legislative strategist, Howard Paster, left to head a public relations firm that specializes in lobbying.[31]

While much of that activity may be ethically questionable, most is not illegal (see "Ethics in Government Act," p. 641). There are well-publicized exceptions, however. Michael K. Deaver, once a top aide to President Ronald Reagan, was convicted of perjury in connection with a grand jury investigation of his use of his former government contacts to help clients in his public relations firm.

---

[30] Wines, "For New Lobbyists, It's Not What They Know," p. B–14.

[31] Carol Jovzaitis, "Clinton's Bumpy First Year; Failed Promises Shadow Successes," *Chicago Tribune* (December 26, 1993): C–1.

Lobbying the Executive Branch and Executive Agencies. As the scope of the federal government has expanded, lobbying the executive branch has increased in importance and frequency. Groups often target one or more levels of the executive branch because there are so many potential access points—the president and White House staff, the numerous levels of the bureaucracy, and the independent regulatory commissions. Groups try to work closely with the administration in an effort to influence policy decisions at their formulation and implementation stages. And, like the situation with congressional lobbying, the effectiveness of a group often lies in its ability to provide decision makers with important information and a sense of where the public stands on the issue.

Historically, group representatives have met with presidents or their staff members to urge policy directions. In 1992, representatives of the auto industry even accompanied President Bush to lobby the Japanese for more favorable trade regulations. Most presidents also specifically set up staff positions "explicitly to serve as brokerages or clearinghouses to provide greater access to presidential attention for professional, demographic or specialized organizations."[32] Political scientist Thomas Cronin has suggested that "presidents have appointed either an aide or an office for every American dilemma."[33] Among these are offices of domestic policy, economic policy, science and technology, consumer affairs, the environment, and minority affairs. At various times, special liaison offices have been created to deal with women, Jews, African Americans, and bankers, among others.

An especially strong link exists between interest groups and the regulatory agencies (see Chapter 8). Because of the highly technical aspects of much regulatory work, many groups employ Washington attorneys to deal directly with the agencies. So great is interest-group influence in the decision-making process of these agencies that many people charge that the agencies have been captured by the interest groups. The Interstate Commerce Commission (ICC), for example, was created in 1887 at the urgings of progressive groups to protect the public from the rampant price fixing and other corrupt practices commonplace in the railroad industry. Yet the ICC—heavily influenced by the railroads themselves—frequently set trucking and railroad freight shipping fees at high levels. At one point, early in the 1900s, the ICC and the trucking association even shared offices in the same federal building!

Even after the extensive deregulation that took place during the Carter and Reagan administrations, some groups still complained that certain agencies were unduly influenced by some groups. The National Coal Association (NCA), for example, has argued that the ICC has granted excessive increases in rail freight rates that adversely affect the coal industry. The head of the NCA once remarked: "I used to say that the ICC is a wholly owned subsidiary of the Association of American Railroads. But now I'm older and wiser and as a consequence of these outrageous decisions I now contend that the ICC is a wholly owned subsidiary of the coal-carrying railroads."[34]

With or without former government officials on their staffs, interest groups strive to form stable and cozy relationships with Congress and the bureaucracy to achieve their goals. The term "iron triangle" is commonly used to describe the informal yet semipermanent relationship of these three actors in the policy process (see Chapter 8).

---

[32] Thomas Cronin, *The State of the Presidency* (Boston: Little, Brown, 1975), p. 123.
[33] Ibid.
[34] Quoted in Hrebenar and Scott, *Interest Group Politics,* p. 216.

Ethics in Government Act
♦ ♦ ♦

In 1978, in the wake of Watergate, Congress passed the Ethics in Government Act. Its key provisions dealt with financial disclosure and employment after government service:

Financial disclosure: The president, vice president, and top-ranking executive employees must file annual public financial disclosure reports that list:

- The source and amount of all earned income; all income from stocks, bonds, and property; any investments or large debts; and the source of a spouse's income, if any.
- Any position or offices held in any business, labor, or nonprofit organizations.

Employment after government services: Former executive branch employees may not:

- Represent anyone before any agency for two years after leaving government service on matters that came within the former employees' sphere of responsibility (even if they were not personally involved in the matter).
- Represent anyone on *any* matter before their former agency for one year after leaving it, even if the former employees had no connection with the matter while in the government.

Sources: National Journal (November 19, 1977): 1796–1803; and *Congressional Quarterly Weekly Report* (October 28, 1978): 3121–3127. Reprinted by permission.

Being part of an iron triangle has significant advantages for interest groups. They cement their access to key legislators and bureaucrats by building loyalties, thereby maintaining these triangles. Each corner of the triangle has something to offer the other two, and these relationships tend to become ironclad. As described in Chapter 8, interest-group ties to congressional subcommittees, staffers, and bureaucrats are an invaluable source of influence.

Similar group behavior can be observed in Britain. Because interest groups tend to concentrate their lobbying efforts where it will do them the most good, this practice leads to perceptibly different patterns of interaction. In the British case, however, since Parliament lacks the institutional power of the U.S. Congress, interest groups tend to cluster around the bureaucracy and the occasional government minister who is known to be open to influence. As a result, one rarely observes classic iron triangles in the British system.

Lobbying the Courts. Finally, the courts have proved a useful target for interest groups.[35] Although you might think that the courts decide cases that affect only the

---
[35] Some political scientists speak of iron rectangles, reflecting the growing importance of a fourth party, the courts, in the lobbying process.

The American Association of Retired Persons
◆ ◆ ◆

The American Association of Retired Persons (AARP) was founded in 1958 and today counts more than thirty-three million members over the age of fifty-five. It is not only the fastest-growing interest group in the United States, but it is also the second largest not-for-profit organization in the world. Like other minority groups, it frequently resorts to traditional lobbying as well as litigation to achieve its objectives. In conjunction with the National Senior Citizens' Law Center, founded in 1972, AARP often participates in litigation involving the concerns of senior citizens, including pension and retirement issues, Medicaid benefits, Social Security disability benefits, and mandatory retirement.

Members of the American Association of Retired Persons (AARP) meet with President Clinton in 1993.

parties involved or that they should be immune from political pressures, interest groups have for years recognized the value of lobbying the courts, especially the Supreme Court. As shown in Table 15-2, 72 percent of the Washington-based groups surveyed participated in litigation as a lobbying tool. Richard C. Cortner has noted that "Cases do not arrive on the doorstep of the Supreme Court like orphans in the night."[36] Most major cases noted in this book have either been sponsored by an interest group or one or both of the parties in the case have been supported by a friend of the court brief.

Generally, interest group lobbying of the courts can take two forms: direct sponsorship and *amicus curiae* (friend of the court) briefs. Groups such as the liberal Native American Rights Fund or the Natural Resources Defense Council routinely represent clients to advance the interests of their groups.

When cases come to the Supreme Court that raise issues a particular organization is interested in but not actually sponsoring, often the organization will file an *amicus* brief—either alone or with other like-minded groups — to inform the Justices of their policy preference, generally offered in the guise of legal arguments. (See "Amicus Briefs in Support of Harris," p. 388). Over the years, as the number of groups viewing litigation as a useful tactic has increased, so has the number of briefs submitted to the Court, as revealed in Figure 15-3.

In addition to litigating, interest groups try to influence who is nominated to the federal courts. They also have played an important role of late in Senate confirmation

---

[36] Richard C. Cortner, "Strategies and Tactics of Litigation in Constitutional Cases," *Journal of Public Law* 17 (1968): 287.

FIGURE 15-3

Interest Group Participation in Supreme Court Litigation

*1987 term
Source: Figures compiled by the authors. See also, Karen O'Connor and Lee Epstein, "Amicus Curiae Participation in U.S. Supreme Court Litigation: An Appraisal of Hakman's 'Folklore,'" Law & Society Review 16(1981-82): pp. 318-319.

hearings, as discussed in Chapter 9. As highlighted in Table 15.3, in 1991 numerous groups lined up in favor of the nomination of Clarence Thomas to the U.S. Supreme Court—and many other groups lined up against his nomination.

Table 15.3 ♦ Interest Groups Taking Sides on the Nomination of Clarence Thomas to the U.S. Supreme Court

FOR THOMAS	AGAINST THOMAS
U.S. Chamber of Commerce	NAACP
Coalition for Self-Reliance	AFL-CIO
Coalitions for America	National Organization for Women
American Conservative Union	National Abortion Rights Action League
Concerned Women for America	United Church of Christ
Eagle Forum	League of United Latin American Citizens
Family Research Council	Congressional Black Caucus
The Council of 100	National Women's Political Caucus
Simon Wiesenthal Center	National Education Association
Women For Judge Thomas*	Americans for Democratic Action
	The Women's Legal Defense Fund
	People for the American Way
	Service Employees International Union
	Alliance for Justice

*Group created expressly to support Thomas.

Source: "The Opposition Mounts," *USA Today,* August 8, 1991: A–1.

Grassroots Lobbying. As this term implies, "grassroots lobbying" is a form of pressure-group activity that attempts to involve those people at the bottom level of the political system. It often involves door-to-door informational or petition drives—a tried and true method of lobbying. As early as the 1840s, for example, women (who could not vote) used petition campaigns to persuade state legislators to enact Married Women's Property Acts that gave women control of their earnings and a greater legal say in the custody of their children. Today, environmentalists frequently go door-to-door to alert their friends and neighbors about pending legislation, the creating or locating of hazardous waste materials, or other perceived threats.

When these forms of pressure-group activity are unsuccessful or appear to be too slow to achieve results, some groups resort to more forceful measures to attract attention to their cause. In April 1992, for example, women's rights activists concerned about reproductive freedom held one of the largest mass marches to date in Washington, D.C. During the civil rights movement, as discussed in Chapter 5, Martin Luther King Jr. and his followers frequently resorted to nonviolent marches to draw attention to the plight of African Americans in the South. These forms of organized group activity were legal. Proper parade permits were obtained, and government officials notified. The protesters who tried to stop the freedom marchers, however, were engaging in illegal protest activity, another form of activity sometimes resorted to by interest groups.

Today, interest groups regularly try to stir up their members, hoping that lawmakers will respond to those pressures and the attendant publicity. For example, in 1987, when President Ronald Reagan nominated Judge Robert H. Bork of the Washington, D.C., Court of Appeals to the U.S. Supreme Court, an unprecedented coalition of liberal interest groups banded together to stop his nomination. They took out a series of full-page advertisements in leading newspapers to inform the public about Judge Bork's likely effect on the Court and on its handling of such issues as abortion and civil rights, and they even produced a series of television ads to urge constituents to contact their senators and ask them to vote against his nomination. Similarly, when Congress was debating the "Brady Bill" (to limit the sale of handguns) in the early 1990s, groups on both sides of the debate used mass mailings and print ads to educate the public. In essence, the goal of many organizations is to persuade ordinary voters to serve as their advocates. In the world of lobbying, there are few things more useful than a list of committed supporters.

Lobbyists now use electronic technologies to quickly reach and recruit thousands of Americans at the grassroots level, causing "Congress to govern more by fear and an intense desire for simple, easy answers,"[37] said Representative Steve Gunderson (R-Wis.). Today, the simple grassroots campaigns of just a few years ago (fill-in-the-blank post cards and forms torn out of the newspaper) have grown much more sophisticated and become more effective.

To mobilize their members, many interest groups and trade groups have installed banks of computerized fax machines to send faxes automatically around the country overnight, instructing each member to ask his or her employees, customers, or other people to write, call, or fax their members of Congress. Other lobbyists now run carefully targeted and costly television advertisements pitching one side of an argument. Their opponents must generally respond or lose. Many of these advertisements end

---

[37] Joel Brinkley, "Cultivating the Grass Roots to Reap Legislative Benefits," *New York Times* (November 1, 1993): A–1.

with a toll-free phone number that viewers can call if they find the pitch convincing. New telemarketing companies answer these calls and transfer the callers directly to the offices of the appropriate members of Congress.[38]

Lobbying 1990s Style. The interactions that took place between interest groups, congressional committees, and the White House as Congress was deliberating the energy tax in 1993 is illustrative of how special interests can get what they want through a combination of most of the forms of lobbying discussed in this chapter. As revealed in Table 15.5, interest groups representing grain growers, farmers, the Northeastern states, and other factions were able to get all kinds of concessions for their special interests as Congress deliberated taxing energy output of all levels measured in British Thermal Units (BTU). The administration, said the president of the National Association of Manufacturers (NAM), "allowed their proposal to move from a relatively fair tax, across the board, to one that was riddled with loopholes."[39] The Corn Growers Association went to the Secretaries of the Treasury and Agriculture, the Budget Director, and senators from corn-producing states to argue for exceptions to the gas tax. Joining them was the Renewable Fuels Association, whose members would also be adversely affected by the tax.

Other organized interests soon joined their cause. Soon, too, anti-tax coalitions, fueled by money from NAM and the Chamber of Commerce, signed up 1,400 other member groups. They hired a direct marketing company to launch a mail campaign and a public relations firm to help them attack the proposed tax. They orchestrated as many as ten television interviews an hour with local television stations in key states via satellite communications networks.

They didn't stop there. In states where Democratic senators were still undecided, this coalition of groups spent $100,000 on street rallies and newspaper ads. They also publicized toll-free telephone numbers for voters to use to call their representatives to complain about the tax. Said their chief strategist, we "ignited a real brush fire." And, as Table 15.4 illustrates, their efforts were largely successful; many concessions were won after their intensive efforts on all levels.[40]

The American Trucking Association uses a satellite network to advise its affiliates and members when and how to lobby legislators.

Election Activities

When interest groups are unable to achieve their goals through conventional forms of lobbying, they may decide to become involved more directly in the electoral process. Many groups claim to be nonpartisan, that is, nonpolitical. Usually they try to have friends in both political parties to whom they can look for assistance and access. Some organizations, however, routinely endorse candidates for public office, pledging money, group support, and often even campaign volunteers. Endorsements from some groups may be used by a candidate's opponent to attack the candidate. When several labor unions endorsed Walter Mondale in his 1984 campaign against President Ronald Reagan, he was labeled a "tool of the labor unions" by Republicans.

---

[38] Ibid.
[39] Michael Wines, "Tax's Demise Illustrates First Rule of Lobbying: Work, Work, Work," *New York Times* (June 14, 1993): B–6.
[40] Ibid.

Table 15.4 ♦ The Energy Tax: How It Was Changed Through Lobbying

A partial listing of tax relief measures granted industries and interests by the White House and the House Ways and Means Committee during consideration of the Clinton administration's B.T.U. tax:

INTEREST GROUP	BENEFIT	HOW ACHIEVED
Grain growers and grain companies	Tax break for ethanol	White House **granted** break at request of industry and Congress; Ways and Means Committee **then revoked** tax break.
Farmers	Tax break for farm diesel fuel	Ways and Means panel **granted** break to compensate for loss of ethanol exemption.
Northeastern states	Tax break for home heating oil	**Granted** at request of Senate, including majority leader, George J. Mitchell of Maine and Finance Committee chairman, Daniel Patrick Moynihan of New York.
Coal states	Tax break for coal; moved tax collection point to consumer	White House altered tax break and **granted** industry and Senate request.
Chemicals, glass, other heavy energy users	Tax on competing imports	Ways and Means Committee **granted** industry request.
Aluminum	Tax break on electricity	Ways and Means panel **granted** request of Speaker Thomas S. Foley and 12 House members.
Barges	Lowered tax on fuel	Ways and Means panel **granted** industry request.
Natural gas industry	Moved tax collection point to consumer	Ways and Means panel **granted** industry request.
	Methanol exempted from taxation	White House **granted** industry request.

Sources: Ways and Means Committee report; interviews; *National Journal.* Michael Wines, "Tax's Demise Illustrates First Rule of Lobbying: Work, Work, Work," *The New York Times,* June 14, 1993: A–1.

Some liberal or conservative ideological groups rate candidates in order to help their members (and the general public) evaluate the voting records of members of Congress. The American Conservative Union (conservative) and the Americans for Democratic Action (liberal)—two groups at ideological polar extremes—routinely rate candidates and members of Congress based on their votes on key issues of importance to the group, as illustrated in Table 15.5.

Other groups target certain individuals and campaign against them to show their clout and to scare other elected officials into paying more attention to them. Beginning in 1970, for example, Environmental Action (EA) labeled twelve members of the House of Representatives "the dirty dozen" because of their votes against bills that the group believed were necessary to protect the environment. Over the years, the designation of more than thirty members of Congress with a similar label was widely publicized by the media and through direct-mail campaigns to voters interested in the environment. To date, only seven members to earn EA's anti-environmental nickname have stayed in office.

Similarly, in 1980, the Moral Majority targeted several liberal Democratic senators who were up for reelection and saw all of them defeated. Its clout, although short-lived, clearly made many vulnerable senators think twice about risking the wrath of

Table 15.5 ♦ 1992 Interest Group Ratings of Select Members of Congress*

MEMBER	AMERICAN CONSERVATIVE UNION	AMERICANS FOR DEMOCRATIC ACTION	AFL-CIO	CHAMBER OF COMMERCE
Senate				
Sen. Jesse Helms (R.-N.C.)	100	5	13	100
Sen. Nancy Kassebaum (R.-Kans.)	67	25	25	100
Sen. Edward M. Kennedy (D.-Mass.)	0	100	92	20
Sen. Robert Kerrey (D.-Nebr.)	0	100	83	10
House				
Rep. Vic Fazio (D.-Calif.)	8	90	75	50
Rep. E. (Kika) de la Garza (D.-Tex.)	19	70	75	43
Rep. Newt Gingrich (R.-Ga.)	100	10	58	50
Rep. Olympia Snowe (R.-Maine)	60	50	58	50

*Members are rated on a scale from 1 to 100, with 1 being the lowest and 100 being the highest support of a particular group's policies.

what seemed to be a very powerful group able to produce results at the polls. More recently, the Conservative Coalition has made substantial inroads by taking over local party organizations and running its own candidates (often in "non-partisan" elections) for local school boards and town councils in order to get its views about school prayer, homosexuality, sex education, and other items on its agenda implemented at the local level.

Another interest-group strategy is to form a political party in order to publicize a cause and even possibly win a few public offices. In 1848, the Free Soil Party was formed to publicize the crusade against slavery; twenty years later, the Prohibition Party was formed to try to ban the sale of alcoholic beverages. Similarly, in 1976, the National Right-to-Life Party was formed to publicize the anti-abortion position.

The effectiveness of an interest group in the election arena has often been overrated by members of the news media. In general, it is very difficult to assess the effect of a particular group's impact on any one election because of the number of other factors present in any election or campaign. However, the one area in which interest groups do seem able to affect the outcome of elections directly is through a relatively new device called the political action committee.

Interest Groups and Political Action Committees. Throughout most of history, powerful interests and individuals have often used their money to "buy" politicians or their votes. Even if outright bribery was not involved, huge corporate or other interest-group donations certainly made some politicians look as if they were in the "pocket" of certain special interests. Congressional passage of the Federal Election Campaign

By permission of Mike Luckovich and Creators Syndicate.

Act began to change most of that. The 1971 Act required candidates to disclose all campaign contributions and limited the amount of money that they could spend on media advertising. In 1974, in the wake of the Watergate scandal (see Chapter 7), amendments to the Act made it more far-reaching. They sharply limited the amount of money any interest group could give to a candidate for federal office. However, they also made it legal for corporations, labor unions, and interest groups to form political action committees, often referred to as PACs, that could make contributions to candidates for national elections. (See Chapter 13 for more on this subject.)

Technically, a "PAC" is a political arm of a business, labor, trade, professional, or other interest group legally authorized to raise funds on a voluntary basis from employees or members in order to contribute to a political candidate or party. These monies have changed the face of U.S. elections. Unlike some contributions to interest groups, however, contributions to PACs are not tax deductible, and PACs generally don't have members who call legislators; instead, PACs have contributors who write checks specifically for the purpose of campaign donations. For many congressional incumbents, for example, PAC money plays a significant role in their campaigns—averaging 35 percent of a House candidate's total campaign spending. PACs generally contribute to those who have helped them before and who serve on committees or subcommittees that routinely consider legislation of concern to that group.

The number of PACs is increasing rapidly. Roughly 3,000 PACs contributed in the 1992 congressional elections, making about 214,000 contributions in that election cycle (see Table 15.6).[41] In light of the 1992 campaign's focus on health care reform, it is not surprising that health care industry PACs increased their giving to congressional candidates by 32 percent over 1990. The American Trial Lawyers of America PAC gave 2.3 million dollars to candidates, hoping to head off tort reform legislation that

---

[41] Glenn R. Simpson, "Study: PAC Spending Jumps 18% in 1992," *Roll Call* (June 3, 1993).

Table 15.6 ◆ Doling out PAC Dollars

Whle organized labor's political action committees contributed the most money to 1992 congressional races, health-care industry PACs showed the sharpest increase in activity since 1990.

SECTOR	TOTAL	CHANGE FROM '90	PAC MONEY SPLIT DEM.	REP.
Agriculture	$15,027,605	10%	51%	49%
Communications/electronics	$9,334,146	14%	56%	44%
Construction	$4,575,364	–5%	38%	62%
Defense	$7,228,724	–2%	55%	45%
Energy/natural resources	$13,113,938	8%	48%	52%
Finance/insurance/real estate	$28,792,287	13%	56%	44%
Health	$14,406,370	32%	61%	39%
Labor	$42,557,697	17%	94%	6%
Lawyers/lobbyists	$5,590,745	22%	80%	20%
Transportation	$11,992,988	22%	52%	48%

Source: Center for Responsive Politics. Reprinted in Richard Benedetto, "Health PACs' Giving Rises," *USA Today,* March 12, 1993: 4A.

would affect lawyers by limiting the amounts of money awarded by juries (and therefore lawyers' fees) in negligence cases. One of the biggest increases in PAC contributions came from women's groups, which experienced a 314 percent increase over 1990. Especially important was EMILY's List, which stands for "Early Money Is Like Yeast—it makes the dough rise"; this group was the largest single contributor to Democratic women congressional candidates in 1992 and 1994. Its early successes even spawned a Republican counterpart—WISH (Women in the Senate and House).

Protest Activity. When other forms of lobbying activity don't seem to be getting an interest group very far quickly enough, some groups resort to protest activity. Over the years, organized interests have engaged in both legal (sit-ins, for example) and illegal forms of mass protest. Since the Revolutionary War, violent, illegal protest has been one tactic of organized interests. The Boston Tea Party, for example, involved breaking all sorts of laws although no one was hurt physically. Other forms of protest such as the Shays's Rebellion (p. 39) ended in tragedy for some participants.

Groups on both ends of the political spectrum historically have resorted to violence. Abolitionists, anti-nuclear activists, anti-war activists, animal-rights advocates, and other groups on the "left" have broken laws, damaged property, and even injured or killed innocent bystanders. On the "right," groups such as Operation Rescue and the Ku Klux Klan have broken the laws and even hurt or killed people in the furtherance of their objectives. From the early 1900s until the 1960s, African Americans were routinely lynched by KKK members. Today, Operation Rescue members regularly block

> ## How Events Can Affect Interest Groups
> ◆ ◆ ◆
>
> In the wake of the Clarence Thomas hearings in 1991, liberal women's interest groups attempted to capitalize on women's anger through a variety of well-written pleas for funds to prevent any other women from being treated as Anita Hill was treated by the all-male Senate Judiciary Committee. The results:
>
> | ORGANIZATION | RESULT |
> |---|---|
> | EMILY's List | $300,000 raised in a direct-mail solicitation sent out two weeks after the hearings |
> | Fund for the Feminist Majority | 30% increase in direct-mail contributions |
> | National Organization for Women (NOW) | Direct-mail contributions up 25%–30%; threefold increase in paid memberships |
> | National Women's Political Caucus | $85,000 raised from one newspaper ad |
> | Women's Campaign Fund | 50% increase in direct-mail contributions |
>
> *Source:* Jill Abramson, "Women's Anger About Hill–Thomas Hearings Has Brought Cash into Female Political Causes," *Wall Street Journal* (January 6, 1992): A–16. Reprinted by permission of the *Wall Street Journal* © copyright 1992 Dow Jones & Company, Inc. All rights reserved worldwide.

the entrances to abortion clinics; others active in the anti-abortion movement have taken credit for clinic bombings.

Most groups, however, have few members so devoted as to put everything on the line for their cause. It is much more usual for a group's members to opt for more conventional forms of lobbying or to influence policy through the electoral process.

What Makes an Interest Group Successful?

Throughout our nation's history, all kinds of interests in society have organized to pressure the government for policy change. Some have been successful, and some have not. E. E. Schattschneider once wrote, "Pressure politics is essentially the politics of small groups.... Pressure tactics are not remarkably successful in mobilizing general interests."[42] He was correct; historically, corporate interests often prevail over the concerns of public interest groups such as environmentalists.

---

[42] E. E. Schattschneider, *The Semi-Sovereign People* (New York: Holt, Rinehart and Winston, 1960), p. 35.

Table 15.7 ◆ Potential versus Actual Interest Groups

The goal of most groups is to mobilize all potential members. Often that task is impossible. As Mancur Olson Jr. points out, the larger the group, the more difficult it is to mobilize. To illustrate the potential versus actual membership phenomenon, here are several examples of groups and their potential memberships.

POPULATION	GROUP	NUMBER OF POTENTIAL MEMBERS	NUMBER OF ACTUAL MEMBERS
Governors	National Governor's Association	55	55 (includes territories)
Political Science Faculty	American Political Science Association	17,000	8,250
Doctors	American Medical Association (AMA)	548,000	288,000
Women	National Organization for Women (NOW)	127,000,000	250,000
African Americans	National Association for the Advancement of Colored People (NAACP)	30,600,000	345,000

To understand this point better, it's important to distinguish between an actual and a potential group and to understand that most groups seek only members who agree with them on most (if not all issues) (see Table 15.7). Theoretically, all women could be members of a women's rights group, all campers members of a conservation group, or all gun owners members of the National Rifle Association. Potential groups include *all* people who might be group members because they share a common trait or interest.[43] An actual group consists of only those people who actually join, and it is almost *always* smaller than the potential group. No group can ever attract all potential members; no one group is so monolithic that it could appeal to all people in the potential group. All farmers won't want to belong to the Grange, and all pro-life activists don't want to join Operation Rescue.

Groups vary tremendously in their ability to enroll potential members, as revealed in Table 15.7. Economist Mancur Olson Jr. notes that all groups, whether economic or non-economic, provide some **collective good**—that is, something of value, such as money, a tax write-off, a good feeling, or a better environment—that can't be withheld from a non-group member.[44] If one union member at a factory gets a raise, for example, all other workers at that factory will, too. Therefore, those who don't join or work for the benefit of the group still reap the rewards of the group's activity. This phenom-

---

[43] Truman, *The Governmental Process*, p. 511.
[44] Mancur Olson, Jr. *The Logic of Collective Action: Public Goods and the Theory of Groups* (Cambridge, MA: Harvard University Press, 1965).

enon is called the **free rider problem.** Consequently, Olson asserts, potential members are unlikely to join a group because they realize that they will receive many of the benefits the group achieves regardless of their participation. Not only is it irrational for free riders to join any group, but the bigger the group, the greater the free rider problem. Small groups like the AMA or the American Political Science Association have an organizational advantage because in a small group, any individual's share of the collective good may be great enough to make it rational to join. The "patrons" deemed important by political scientist Jack L. Walker often eliminate the free rider problem for public interest groups by making the "costs" of joining minimal.[45]

The Role of Leaders

Interest-group theorists frequently acknowledge the key role that leaders play in the formation and viability of groups. The role of an interest-group leader is similar to that of an entrepreneur in the business world. As in the marketing of a new product, an interest-group leader must have something attractive to offer in order to persuade members to join. Potential members of the group must be convinced that the benefits of joining outweigh the costs. Union members, for example, must be persuaded that the cost of their union dues will be offset by the union's winning higher wages for them. The leader of the group must convince potential members that the group can effectively lobby the government and achieve particular goals.

Without the powerful pen of William Lloyd Garrison in the 1830s, would the abolitionist movement have been as successful? Similarly, Frances Willard was the prime mover behind the Women's Christian Temperance Union (WCTU), as were Marian Wright Edelman of the Children's Defense Fund in 1968, and the Reverend Jerry Falwell of the Moral Majority in the 1980s. Most successful groups, especially public-interest groups, are led by charismatic individuals who devote most of their energies to "the cause."

Leaders often differ from the rank and file of the group in that they are usually more future oriented, better educated, and affluent. Accounts of the early efforts of a former elementary school teacher, Susan B. Anthony, to secure the vote for women indicate that she did not expect that suffrage would be forthcoming quickly. Her belief in a future victory led her to continue where more faint-hearted individuals might not have bothered. Similarly, without Ralph Nader, a Yale-educated lawyer, there might not be a Public Citizen, Inc.

Group Structure

The success of any group can be affected by its leader's choice of organizational structure, which is often based on the activities and goals of the group. There are two basic group structures: federated and unitary. A federated association is basically one made up of other groups. Key functions (such as lobbying or education), authority, and activities are divided between the national office and the state or local affiliates. The National Organization for Women (NOW), for example, is a federated association; it has a national office in New York City, and affiliates in all fifty states. The National Association for the Advancement of Colored People (NAACP) also uses a federated structure and often relies on its 1,700 adult and 450 college affiliates in most states to alert it to discriminatory practices or policies.

---

[45] Walker, "The Origins and Maintenance of Interest Groups," pp. 390–406.

Unitary associations have only one level of decision making and organization. The Business Roundtable, for example, is a unitary association. So, too, is the American Political Science Association, although numerous independent regional and state political science associations exist.

It is especially important for large national associations to convince their members that their "support" helps. Thus, members are likely to be the target of frequent mailings telling them how crucial their contributions are and informing them of how their support has enabled the organization to accomplish specific goals.

Funding

Funding is crucial to all interest groups. In a 1983 study, Jack L. Walker found that patrons—those who fund groups—were key to many interest-group successes.[46] Government, foundations, and wealthy individuals all serve as patrons providing crucial start-up funds for groups, especially public-interest groups.

Groups also rely heavily on membership contributions, dues, and other fund-raising activities. During the 1980s, conservative groups, for example, relied on the direct mail skills of marketing wizard Richard Viguerie to raise monies for a variety of conservative causes. In the 1990s, pro-choice groups have successfully appealed to supporters by requesting funds to campaign for legislation in anticipation of the Supreme Court's reversal of *Roe* v. *Wade*. When the Supreme Court's decision in *Casey* v. *Planned Parenthood of Southeastern Pennsylvania* (1992)[47] did not overrule *Roe* v. *Wade* (1973) and then when Ruth Bader Ginsburg was appointed to the Supreme Court, contributions to pro-choice groups such as NARAL and Planned Parenthood dropped precipitously.

Suffrage leader Susan B. Anthony in later life. Although she died before passage of the Nineteenth Amendment, her efforts on its behalf were critical.

Membership

Organizations are usually composed of three kinds of members. At the top are a relatively small number of leaders who devote most of their energies to the single group. The second tier of members are generally involved psychologically as well as organizationally. They are the workers of the group—they attend meetings, pay dues, and chair committees to see that things get done. In the bottom tier are the rank and file, members who don't actively participate. They pay their dues and call themselves group members, but they do little more. Most group members fall into this last category.

E. E. Schattschneider has noted that the interest-group system in the United States has a decidedly "upper class bias," and he concluded that 90 percent of the population does not participate in an interest-group, or what he called the pressure-group, system.[48] Since the 1960s, survey data have revealed that group membership is drawn primarily from people with higher income and education levels. Individuals who are wealthier can afford to belong to more organizations because they have more money and, often, more leisure time. Money and education are also associated with greater confidence that one's actions will bring results, a further incentive to devote time to organizing or supporting interest groups.

People who do belong to groups often belong to more than one. This overlapping membership can often affect the cohesiveness of a group. Imagine, for example, that

---

[46] Ibid.
[47] 112 S. Ct. 2791 (1992).
[48] Schattschneider, *The Semi-Sovereign People,* p. 35.

Handgun Control, Inc. (HCI) is a national, non-profit lobbying organization that is working to enact a national gun control policy. HCI has worked to pass the Brady Bill as well as a ban on semi-automatic assault weapons. In addition, HCI has introduced comprehensive legislation, the Gun Violence Prevention Act of 1994 or Brady II, that looks to overhaul the way we buy and sell guns in this country.

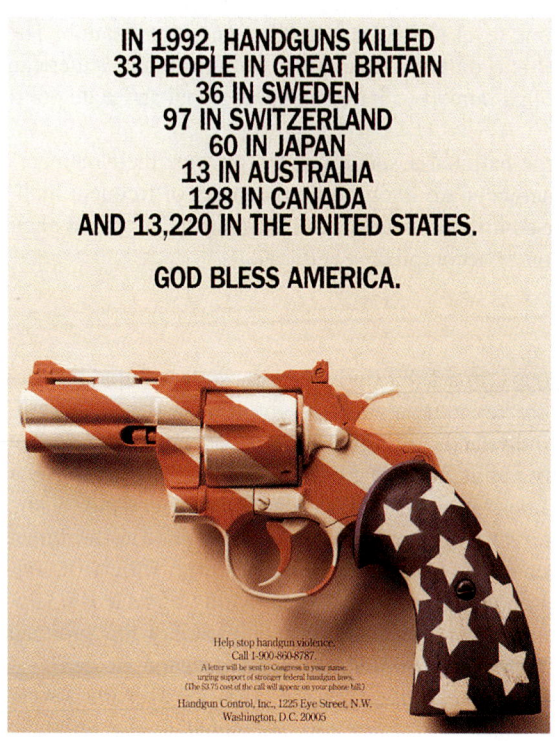

you are an officer in the college Young Republicans. If you call a meeting, people may not attend because they have academic, athletic, or social obligations. Divided loyalties and multiple group memberships can often affect the success of a group, especially if it has too many members who simply fall into the dues-paying category.

Getting Ideas on the Public Agenda. Throughout this chapter, we discuss a variety of groups. Most of them have been the "successful" ones—the ones that were lucky enough to have committed leaders, adequate financing or patrons, and ideas that appealed to enough people to make those ideas viable in the political process.

A successful group usually can use its resources to put its ideas on the government's policy agenda. As groups mobilize to push their policy goals, they often bring into the public forum issues that might not have otherwise surfaced at that time. The Humane Society, for example, has been in existence since the turn of the century, but it was not until more aggressive groups such as People for the Ethical Treatment of Animals (PETA) made the public aware of the widespread testing of many products on animals did the pressure of the general public effectively forced many manufacturers to alter their testing programs. For many groups, simply getting their issues on the public agenda equals success. Government responses may not be forthcoming, but their activities can mean that the public is made sufficiently aware of a certain practice or policy to work for changes to be made (or, at the very least, to make the changes themselves).

Program Monitoring. Successful groups, to stay successful, must often monitor how the laws or policies they advocated are implemented. Thus, successful interest groups often find it useful, once a law is passed or a regulation written that affects them, to monitor how that law or regulation is implemented. The National Organization for Women (NOW), for example, created the Project on Educational Equity Review (PEER) to monitor the enforcement of Title IX, the purpose of which is to ban sex discrimination in schools receiving federal funding. Its newsletter, *PEER Perspective,* provides detailed analyses of Title IX legislative and administrative activity. Moreover, PEER staffers are in regular contact with government officials to discuss enforcement and to lobby against regulations that would hinder the enforcement of Title IX.

Toward Reform

Since the turn of the century, when good-government groups formed in response to blatant political corruption and the conflicts of interest between big business and government, the public has been uniform in its support of reforming and reducing the influence of "special interests." But, as James Madison pointed out two centuries earlier in *Federalist No. 10,* it may be dangerous for governments to regulate factions too strictly, for such actions could limit liberty itself. Madison optimistically believed that competition among factions could be balanced by governments; but as we have seen in this chapter, all groups are not created equal. Generally, wealthy and powerful people, and the groups that represent them, have more political sway than do the poor and disenfranchised.

In 1946, in an effort to limit the power of lobbyists, Congress passed the Federal Regulation of Lobbying Act, which required anyone hired to lobby any member of Congress to register and file quarterly financial reports. Few lobbyists actually file these reports, and the Justice Department has not even opted to try to enforce the provisions of the Act, believing its vagueness makes it virtually unenforceable. While some good-government groups argue that the laws should be strengthened, civil liberties groups such as the American Civil Liberties Union (ACLU) (see page 126) argue that registration provisions violate the First Amendment's freedom of speech and the right of citizens to petition the government.

In 1992, in the wake of the Savings and Loan scandal and the 1991 recession, Congress passed fairly sweeping reform legislation aimed at limiting interest groups, but it was vetoed by President George Bush.

Summary

The United States has always been a nation of joiners. National groups first emerged in the country in the 1830s. Since that time, the type, nature, sophistication, and tactics of groups have changed dramatically. To that end, we have made the following points:

1. Those who study interest groups have offered a variety of definitions to explain what they are. Most definitions revolve around notions of "associations or groups of individuals" who "share" some sort of "common" "interest" or "attitude" and who try to "influence" or "engage in activity" to effect "governmental policies" or the people in "government." In general, interest groups represent economic or the public interest and are single- or multi-issue.

2. The history of interest groups in this country is longer than that of the nation itself. Groups national in scope, however, did not begin until around the 1830s as communications networks improved to facilitate their development. After the Civil War, the number of groups increased as groups that had never organized before, including African Americans and women, began to form associations. Industrialization also brought about fledgling attempts by employees to form labor unions.

3. The dawn of the Progressive era (1890–1920) brought with it more new groups. Settlement houses were often a gathering spot for people active in all kinds of public interest groups. During this period organized labor began to gain political clout, and the National Association of Manufacturers (NAM) and the Chamber of Commerce became some of its biggest enemies.

4. After the Progressive era, some groups faltered while others continued to flourish. Beginning in the 1960s, however, hundreds of new interest groups were formed; many of them were Washington, D.C.–based in order to better advance their interests in the nation's capitol. Many of these groups are similar, but larger, versions of the socially concerned or good-government groups that were the hallmark of the Progressive era. This time, however, a new, more effective breed of conservative groups arose to counter their claims before legislatures, as well as in the courts. Professional associations, too, became an active presence in Washington, D.C.

5. Interest groups often fill voids left by the major political parties and give Americans opportunities to make claims, as a group, on government. The most common activity of interest groups is lobbying, which takes many forms. Groups routinely pressure members of Congress and their staffs, the president and the bureaucracy, and the courts; they use a variety of techniques to educate and stimulate the public also to pressure key governmental decision makers. Interest groups also attempt to influence the outcome of elections; some even run their own candidates for office. Others "rate" elected officials to inform their members how particular legislators stand on issues of importance to them. Political action committees (PACs), a way for some groups to contribute money to candidates for office, are another method of gaining support from elected officials and ensuring that their "friends" stay in office.

6. Just as groups are diverse, so are the ways in which they become successful and measure their success. Strong leaders or patrons are critical to the success of most interest groups, as are adequate resources, whether in the form of a dedicated membership or a reliable source of funds. Leaders and funds allow groups to engage in a variety of lobbying activities and, once they get the programs or laws they seek, to monitor their implementation.

7. Adverse reaction to the potential power of interest groups and the possibility of inappropriate influence have led Congress periodically to draft legislation to regulate lobbying. PACs, in particular, have come under an increasing amount of criticism.

Key Terms

lobbying

interest group

economic-interest groups

public-interest groups

multi-issue groups

single-issue groups

disturbance theory

trade associations

lobbyist

political action committee (PAC)

collective good

free rider problem

Suggested Readings

Berry, Jeffrey M. *The Interest Group Society,* 2nd ed. Glenview, IL: Scott, Foresman/Little, Brown, 1989.

———. *Lobbying for the People: The Political Behavior of Public Interest Groups.* Princeton, NJ: Princeton University Press, 1977.

Cigler, Allan J., and Burdett A. Loomis, eds. *Interest Group Politics,* 4th ed. Washington, DC: CQ Press, 1991.

Hrebenar, Ronald J., and Ruth K. Scott. *Interest Group Politics in America,* 2nd ed. Englewood Cliffs, NJ: Prentice-Hall, 1990.

McGlen, Nancy E., and Karen O'Connor. *Women, Politics and American Society.* Englewood Cliffs, NJ: Prentice-Hall, 1995.

Olson, Mancur Jr. *The Logic of Collective Action: Public Good and the Theory of Groups.* Cambridge, MA: Harvard University Press, 1965.

Sabato, Larry J. *PAC Power: Inside the World of Political Action Committees.* New York: Norton, 1984.

Schlozman, Kay Lehman, and John T. Tierney. *Organized Interests and American Democracy.* New York: Harper & Row, 1986.

Truman, David B. *The Governmental Process: Political Interests and Public Opinion.* (New York: Knopf, 1951).

Public Policy

> Congress shall have the "power to make all laws which shall be necessary and proper for carrying into execution the foregoing powers, and all other powers vested by this Constitution...."
> Few parts of the Constitution have been assailed with more intemperance than this....
>
> *James Madison*
> *Federalist No. 44*

The necessary and proper clause, quoted in this passage, has served to expand greatly congressional power under the Constitution and thus to enable the government to respond to the problems of a modern society.

CHAPTER 16

Social Welfare Policy

THE POLICY-MAKING PROCESS
SOCIAL WELFARE POLICIES
PUBLIC EDUCATION
INCOME SECURITY
MEDICAL CARE
TOWARD REFORM

As James Madison indicated in *Federalist No. 44,* the Framers heatedly debated how strictly to limit the federal government. The necessary and proper, or elastic clause, discussed in Chapters 2 and 6, was viewed with particular distrust by many Anti-Federalists because it allowed Congress broad and undefined authority to pass what were termed "necessary" laws. Madison and the Federalists prevailed, however, and the elastic clause was made part of Article I.

The necessary and proper clause, along with the commerce clause, and the Supreme Court's interpretation of these clauses and others, ultimately gave the national government—as well as the states—sweeping powers to regulate, influence and, some would say, interfere in the lives and well-being of the country's inhabitants through a variety of social welfare policies.

Social welfare policies is a term that designates a broad and varied range of government policies designed to provide people with protection against want and deprivation, to improve their health and physical well-being, to provide educational and employment training opportunities, and otherwise to enable them to lead more satisfactory, meaningful, and productive lives. In a nutshell, social welfare policies are intended to enhance the quality of life. They benefit all segments of society, but they are especially helpful for the less fortunate members, who often find it more difficult to provide for themselves and their families. More specifically, social welfare policies focus on such matters as public education, income security, medical care, sanitation and disease prevention, public housing, employment training, children's protective services, and improvements in human nutrition.

State and local governments in the United States have long operated public schools and provided assistance to the needy members of society, though often in a tight-fisted and mean-spirited fashion. The twentieth century, however, has witnessed a great ex-

659

660 ❖ Chapter 16 Social Welfare Policy

The formation and implementation of social welfare policy is both highly visible and contentious. It is visible because, as this cartoon penned before the Pure Food and Drug Act of 1906 illustrates, it is often meant to have a direct effect on the public good. It is contentious because other interests, often economic ones, come into opposition. This conflict falls along the lines political theorists characterize as pluralist vs. elitist.

pansion in social welfare policies and spending for their support at all levels of government—local, state, and national—although the United States has tended to act more cautiously then most other democracies in this arena (see Figure 16-1). Universal, compulsory public education became firmly established in the early decades of the century. Public health, income security, and other social welfare programs multiplied and expanded. And, since the 1930s (as discussed in Chapter 3), the national government has become a major, and sometimes dominating, participant in this policy area, which was once largely the domain of the state and local governments.

Before we discuss social welfare policies, however, we consider the nature of the policy-making process. Public policies do not just happen; rather, they are typically the products of a predictable pattern of events. Models for analyzing the policy-making process (see Figure 16-2, "The Public Policy Cycle") do not always explain why public policies take the specific forms that they do, however. That depends on the political struggles over particular policies. Nor do models necessarily tell us who dominates or controls the formation of public policy.

However, this model does provide a manageable way of dissecting the policy-making process and examining its components. Moreover, policy making frequently does follow the sequence of stages in the model. Sometimes, though, some of the stages merge, such as the formulation and adoption stages. Another instance of stages merging occurs when administrative agencies are forming policy through rule-making at the same time that they are implementing it, as in the case of the Occupational Safety and Health Administration (OSHA). Finally, it must be mentioned that what happens at one stage of the policy-making process affects action at later stages in the process, and sometimes such action is done deliberately in anticipation of these effects. Thus, particular provisions may be included in a law either to help or hinder its implementation, depending on the interests of the provisions' proponents.

FIGURE 16-1

Enactment of National Social Programs in Ten Nations

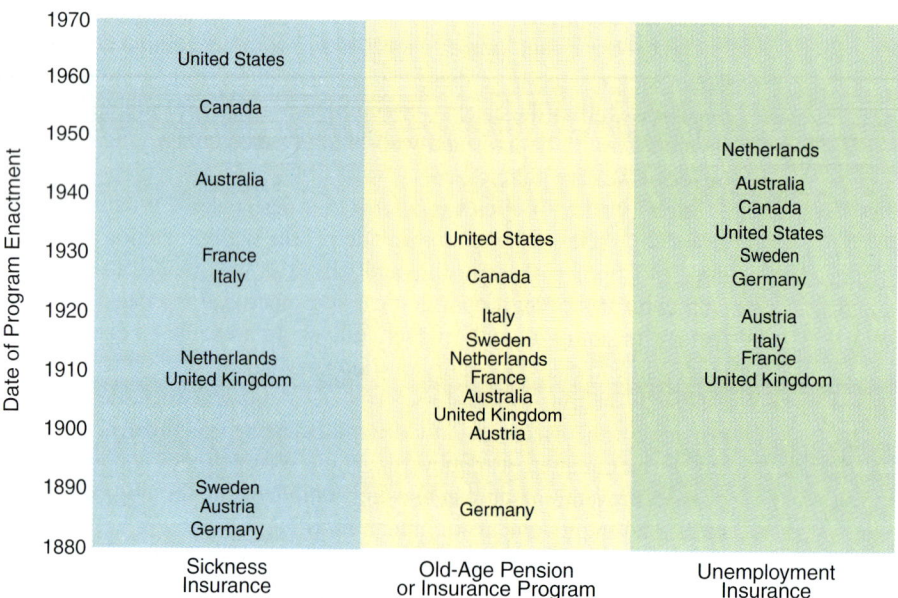

Source: D. B. Robertson and D. R. Judd, *The Development of American Public Policy* (Glenview, IL: Scott Foresman, 1989), p. 59.

FIGURE 16-2
The Public Policy Process

1. Problem Recognition and Definition
Public officials and environmental groups identify acid rain as a problem.

2. Agenda Setting
Action by the president, members of Congress, and interest groups put acid rain on the national policy agenda.

7. Evaluation
In time there will be evaluation of the emissions trading system to determine its effectiveness in reducing acid rain. A finding that it is ineffective, for example, will likely restart the policy process.

6. Implementation
An emissions trading system was created, and in 1993 the first sales of allowances for the discharge of sulfur dioxide (a prime component of acid rain) were held.

3. Policy Formulation
The White House, executive agencies, and interest groups develop proposed courses of action for controlling acid rain.

4. Policy Adoption
Provisions providing for an emissions trading system to reduce acid rain are included in the Clean Air Act of 1990.

5. Budgeting
Funds are appropriated so that the Environmental Protection Agency can put the acid rain control system into effect.

The Policy-Making Process

A good workable definition of a **public policy** states that it is a purposive course of action followed by government in dealing with some problem or matter of concern.[1] Public policies are thus governmental policies; based on law, they are authoritative and binding on people. Individuals, groups, and even government agencies that do not comply with policies can be penalized through fines, loss of benefits, or even jail terms. As the phrase "course of action" implies, policies develop or unfold over time. They involve more than a legislative decision to enact a law or a presidential decision to issue an executive order. Also important is how the law or executive order is carried out. Whether a policy is vigorously enforced, enforced only in some instances, or not enforced at all helps determine its meaning and impact on people. Although their intentions are important, it is what governments actually do that constitutes public policy and that really counts in shaping or influencing people's behavior.

Political scientists and other social scientists have developed many theories and models of the formation of public policies. Some theories, such as elite theory and plu-

---

[1] James E. Anderson, *Public Policymaking: An Introduction,* 2nd ed. (Boston, Houghton Mifflin, 1994), p. 5. This discussion draws on Anderson's study.

ralist theory, focus on who dominates or controls the making of policy. As discussed in Chapter 1, elite theorists contend that policy reflects the interests of a small, well-to-do segment of society. Pluralists, in contrast, argue that policy is the product of interaction and struggle among many groups and powerholders in society. Needless to say, these are markedly divergent theories that have caused much intellectual conflict among political and social scientists.

Who dominates or controls the formation of public policy is an important question, but we do not wrestle with it here. Rather, we present a widely used model of the policy-making process that views it as a sequence of stages or functional activities. Collectively, the sequence constitutes a policy cycle. A brief synopsis of the model follows.

A *problem* that disturbs or distresses people gives rise to demands for relief, often through governmental action. Individual or group efforts are then made to get the problem placed on a governmental *agenda*. If successful, this step is followed by the *formulation* of alternatives for dealing with the problem. *Policy adoption* involves the formal enactment or approval of an alternative. *Budgeting* provides financial resources to carry out the approved alternative, which can now be called a "policy." *Policy implementation*, the actual administration or application of the policy to its targets, may then be followed by *policy evaluation* to determine the policy's actual accomplishments or consequences. Evaluation may restart the policy cycle by touching off an attempt to modify or terminate the policy. With this overview in mind, let's now look in more detail at the various stages of the policy process or cycle.

Problem Definition

A problem involves some condition or situation in society that causes distress or dissatisfaction or generates needs for which some kind of relief or corrective action is sought—often from the government (national, state, or local). At any given time there are many conditions that disturb or distress people—polluted air, unsafe workplaces, earthquakes and hurricanes, too much or too little rain, the rising cost of medical care, the poor academic performance of high school students, too many handguns, too few "dedicated" public officials, or no prayers in the public schools, for example. All disturbing conditions do not automatically become problems; some of them may be accepted as trivial, appropriate, inevitable, or beyond the control of government.

For a condition to become a problem, there must be some criterion—a standard or value—that leads people to believe that the condition does not have to be accepted or acquiesced to and, further, that it is something with which government can effectively and appropriately deal. Earthquakes, for example, are unlikely to become a policy problem because there is nothing that government can do directly about them. The consequences of earthquakes, the human distress and property destruction that they bring, are another matter. Their relief can be a focus of government action, as in the instance of the January 1994 Los Angeles earthquake, for which Congress appropriated several billion dollars for recovery activities.

Conditions that at one time are accepted as appropriate and beyond government responsibility may at a later time be perceived as problems because of changes in public attitudes. Child abuse is illustrative.[2] Until the 1870s, reports Barbara J. Nelson, the

---

[2] Barbara J. Nelson, *Making an Issue of Child Abuse* (Chicago: University of Chicago Press, 1984), pp. 1–17.

In 1993 President Clinton signed the National Child Protection Act. The Act, which establishes a national database to track child abusers, is the latest of several pieces of legislation passed over many years, as the problem of child abuse has waxed and waned on the public agenda.

maltreatment of children was of minimal concern to society. The disciplining of children, even when harsh, was usually viewed as a parental prerogative, except perhaps in instances of extreme brutality. Newspaper accounts of a gruesome instance of child beating in New York City in 1874 put the matter on the public agenda. In fact, some of the first efforts to protect children occurred under laws barring cruelty to animals! In the late 1800s, many large cities created units of the Society for the Prevention of Cruelty to Children modeled after Humane Societies for animals. In time, however, the problem receded from public view, although some protective activity for children continued.

Child abuse was rediscovered as a problem in the 1960s, a time of social activism and concern about people's rights. According to Professor Nelson, an article entitled "The Battered Child Syndrome," written by a physician and published in a leading medical journal, was the catalyst. Newspapers and popular magazines picked up the issue, and child abuse was again viewed as an urgent public problem.[3] Between 1963 and 1967, all fifty state legislatures enacted laws requiring the reporting of child abuse. In 1974 Congress manifested its concern by passing the Child Abuse Prevention and Treatment Act, which requires the states to have child protection agencies. Since that time, the problem of child abuse has continued to concern policy makers. In 1993, President Clinton signed the National Child Abuse Protection Act. This Act establishes a national database to track child abusers in an effort to prevent their employment in child-care centers.

Usually there is not a single agreed-on definition of a problem. Indeed, political struggle often occurs over defining the problem because how the problem is defined

---

[3] C. Henry Kempe et al., "The Battered-Child Syndrome," *The Journal of the American Medical Association*, Vol. 181 (July 7, 1962): 17–24.

helps determine what sort of action is appropriate. If access to transportation for people with disabilities is defined as a transportation problem, then an acceptable solution is to provide the people with transportation by adapting the regular transportation system or by establishing other means of transport, such as a special van service. If access to transportation is defined as a civil rights problem, however, then people with disabilities are entitled to equal access to the regular transportation system. The solution to the problem defined as a civil rights problem might require extensive and expensive alterations to make *all* public transport accessible to people with disabilities. After some wavering between these definitions in the 1980s the national government appeared to be moving toward the transportation view of the problem. But congressional passage of the Americans with Disabilities Act forced local governments to take a civil rights perspective when they were compelled to provide accessible transportation to the elderly and to all people with disabilities.

Problems differ not only in terms of how they are defined but also in terms of their tractability, that is, in terms of how easy they are to ameliorate or resolve. For instance, problems that affect large numbers of people or require widespread behavioral changes are more difficult to resolve. The Voting Rights Act of 1965, intended to ensure equal voting rights for African Americans, was easier to implement than was policy requiring desegregation of public schools. Only a small number of voting registrars were directly affected in the first instance; vast numbers of school officials, students, and parents were affected by school desegregation. Tangible problems, such as low incomes or potholes in streets often are more amenable too solutions than are more intangible problems, such as racism or sexism.

One additional point needs to be made. Public policies themselves are frequently viewed as problems or the causes of problems. Thus, for some people, gun control legislation is a solution to the handgun problem. To the National Rifle Association (NRA), however, any laws that restrict gun ownership are a problem because of the NRA's view that such laws inappropriately restrict an individual's right to keep and bear arms. To conservatives, overly generous welfare programs are a problem, whereas for many liberals laws restricting the right to abortion fall into the problem category.

Agenda Setting

Once a problem is recognized and defined, it must be brought to the attention of public officials and it must secure a place on an agenda.

An **agenda** is a set of problems to which policy-makers believe they should be attentive. Professors Roger W. Cobb and Charles D. Elder have identified two basic agenda types: the **systemic agenda** and the governmental or institutional agenda.[4] The systemic agenda is essentially a discussion agenda; it comprises "all issues that are commonly perceived by the members of the political community as meriting public attention and as involving matters within the legitimate jurisdiction" of governments.[5] Every political community—national, state, and local—has a systemic agenda.

A **governmental** or **institutional agenda** includes only problems to which legislators or other public officials feel obliged to devote active and serious attention. Not all the problems that attract the attention of officials are likely to have been widely dis-

---

[4] Roger W. Cobb and Charles D. Elder, *Participation in American Politics: The Dynamics of Agenda-Building,* 2nd ed. (Baltimore: Johns Hopkins University Press, 1983), Chapter 5.

[5] Ibid., p. 85.

Every so often an event occurs that galvanizes public awareness of a problem, forcing it higher on the policy agenda. The 1989 grounding off the coast of Alaska of the tanker *Exxon Valdez* focused media and public attention on the grave environmental dangers of oil spills, and resulted in new legislation the following year.

cussed by the general public, or even the "attentive" public—those who follow certain issues closely. Acid rain was a widely discussed public problem in the 1980s that was addressed by the Clean Air Act of 1990, but there was little public awareness of the Pollution Prevention Act, also adopted in 1990. This Act set priorities for pollution control programs in an attempt to improve their effectiveness.

Problems or issues (an issue emerges when disagreement exists over what should be done about a problem) may move onto an institutional agenda, whether from the systemic agenda or elsewhere, in several ways. The congressional agenda is the focus of the discussion here.

Getting on the Congressional Agenda. As discussed in Chapter 7, the president is an important agenda-setter for Congress. In his State of the Union address, his budget, and in special messages, the president presents Congress with a legislative program for its consideration. Much of Congress's time is spent deliberating presidential recommendations, although by no means does Congress always respond as the president might wish. Congress can be balky even when the president and congressional majorities come from the same party, as President Bill Clinton quickly discovered in his first year in the White House on such issues as homosexuals in the armed forces and tax increases.

Interest groups are major actors and initiators in the policy process. Interest groups and their lobbyists frequently request Congress to legislate on problems of special concern to them. Environmentalists, for instance, call for government action on such issues as global warming, the protection of wetlands, and the reduction of air pollution. Business groups may seek protection against foreign competitors or larger competitors, restrictions on product liability lawsuits, and unfriendly corporate takeovers.

Problems may secure agenda status because of some crisis, natural disaster, or other extraordinary event. Coal mine explosions in the past put mining safety on the congressional agenda. An Amtrak railway accident in 1993 that caused the deaths of

> ## The Presidents and Programs
>
> Some U.S. presidents have had a vision of the country that has included a place for the needy. Traditionally, Democratic presidents have been more concerned than Republican presidents with the plight of the less fortunate. As part of his "Great Society" program, Lyndon B. Johnson declared a "War on Poverty." Naming the program was at times as difficult as carrying it through. Lyndon B. Johnson, for example, tried out several names including "Better Deal" and a "Glorious Kind of Society" before settling on "Great Society" to characterize his programs. Below are some presidents and their programs:
>
> Franklin D. Roosevelt: "I pledge to you, I pledge to myself, to a 'New Deal' for the American people. Let us all here assembled constitute ourselves prophets of a new order of competence and courage." (acceptance speech at the 1932 Democratic National Convention)
>
> John F. Kennedy: "We stand today on the edge of a 'New Frontier'—the frontier of the 1960s, a frontier of unknown opportunities and paths, a frontier of unfulfilled hopes and threats...." (acceptance speech at the Democratic National Convention, 1960)
>
> Lyndon B. Johnson: "The 'Great Society' demands an end to poverty and racial injustice.... It is a place where every child can find knowledge to enrich his mind...." (speech at Ann Arbor, Michigan, May 22, 1964)

forty-three passengers gave railroad safety agenda status. Some four years earlier the major oil spill in Prince William Sound in Alaska, caused when the supertanker *Exxon Valdez* ran aground, focused attention on ocean oil spills and led to enactment of the Oil Pollution Act of 1990. Such events trigger the interest of policy makers and the public.

Some problems and issues draw the attention of the news media and consequently gain agenda status, more salience, or both. Poignant television coverage was instrumental in putting hunger and starvation in Somalia in the early 1990s on both congressional and presidential agendas. The news media probably are more important in developing and sustaining interest in problems than in initially identifying them.

Individual private citizens, members of Congress, and other officials, acting in the role of policy entrepreneurs, may push issues onto the congressional agenda. In the 1960s Ralph Nader's book *Unsafe at Any Speed* and Rachel Carson's *Silent Spring* (see "People of the Past," p. 667) brought motor vehicle safety and the misuse of pesticides, respectively, to the attention of Congress and many citizens. Representative Leonor Sullivan (D.-Mo.) worked for a decade to secure the adoption in 1964 of a permanent food stamp program to help the needy. Senator Edmund Muskie (D.-Maine) for many years was a leader in securing and shaping governmental action to protect the environment, as has Vice President Al Gore Jr. His book, *Earth in the Balance,* written while he was a U.S. Senator, was a wake-up call to many people about possible environmental disaster.

Finally, political changes may contribute to agenda setting. The landslide election of Democratic President Lyndon B. Johnson in 1964, along with strong, favorable Demo-

PEOPLE OF THE PAST

Rachel Carson

Rachel Carson

Rachel Carson was a solitary child who spent most of her spare time in the woods learning about flowers, insects, and nature. From an early age she aspired to be a writer; at age ten she had an article published in a children's magazine.

In college, a biology class proved to be a turning point in her life. She changed her major from English to that field. " 'I have always wanted to write,' she told a college friend, 'but I know I don't have much imagination. Biology has given me something to write about. I will try in my writing to make animals in the woods and waters where they live as alive and as meaningful to others as they are to me.' "*

After her college graduation, Carson entered Johns Hopkins University, where she received a Master's degree in Zoology in 1932. After teaching at the University of Maryland and working a stint at the Marine Biological laboratory in Woods Hole, Massachusetts, she accepted a position at the U.S. Bureau of Fisheries. While there she wrote several feature articles for newspapers and magazines on the sea. These features revealed her unique ability to write about science in a way that appealed to the public.

Her first book, *Under the Sea Wind* (1941) was well received by critics. *The Sea Around Us* (1951), her second book, was a huge commercial success. *The Sea Around Us,* moreover, won the National Book Award and was named the outstanding book of the year in a *New York Times* public opinion poll.

These successes allowed her to leave her job in order to devote full time to her writing. Her most widely known book, *Silent Spring,* was more difficult to write and publish than those that came before it. In the aftermath of World War II, the potentially disastrous consequences of the widespread use of the insecticide DDT began to cause Carson concern, but she was unable to interest—at least initially—any magazine in this issue. When the bird sanctuary of a close friend of Carson's was sprayed with DDT under a compulsory state mosquito eradication program, many birds and harmless insects also were killed. Carson then resolved to write a book to alert the public to the dangers of DDT and other harmful synthetic toxic chemicals that were poisoning the air, water, and earth.

Silent Spring (1962) proved to be the catalyst that sparked creation of the environmental movement. As is so often the case, the actions of one person led to a new issue being put on the public agenda. Carson's book, which details her belief that chemical companies were destroying the earth, put the discussion of pollutants on the public agenda and pressure on politicians to do something about them. President John F. Kennedy, in fact, was prompted to create the President's Science Advisory Committee to study the effect of pesticides on the environment. And, in spite of repeated attacks on Carson and her works and of intensive lobbying by the chemical industry, the Committee's report supported Carson's findings and led the way for governmental involvement in environmental issues.

Carson, who fell ill as she was finishing *Silent Spring,* testified before Congress to urge passage of laws to outlaw chemical dumping and the use of some pesticides. Her continued efforts on behalf of the environment took their toll; she died at age fifty-six in 1964. Her legacy continues today.

*Quoted in Paul Brooks, "Rachel Carson," in Barbara Sicherman and Carol Hurd Green, eds, *Notable American Women: The Modern Period* (Cambridge, MA: The Belknap Press of Harvard University Press, 1980), p. 138.

cratic majorities in Congress, made possible the enactment of a flood of Great Society legislation intended to mitigate social welfare problems such as poverty and inadequate medical care for the elderly and needy and to provide education for disadvantaged children. Similarly, the 1980 election of conservative Republican Ronald Reagan, who in his inaugural address asserted that "Government is not the solution; government is the problem," eased the movement of issues concerning the size and activities of government onto national policy agendas. Only limited success in cutting back the size of the government was realized by his administration, however.[6]

It is useful to think of **agenda setting** as a competitive process. Congress, for instance, does not have the time or resources to take on all the problems and issues it is called on to handle. Whether because of their influence, skill in developing political support, or presentation of more attractive issues, some players are more successful than others in steering items onto the agenda. Chance plays a small role in agenda setting, except in cases of accidents or natural disasters.

Policy Formulation

Policy formulation involves the crafting of appropriate and acceptable proposed courses of action to ameliorate or resolve public problems. It has both political and technical components. The political aspect of policy formulation encompasses determining generally what should be done to reduce acid rain, for example—whether standard setting and enforcement or emissions testing should be used. The technical facet involves correctly stating in specific language what one wants to authorize or accomplish, so as to adequately guide those who implement policy and to prevent distortion of legislative intent. Political scientist Charles O. Jones suggests that formulation may take different forms:[7]

1. *Routine formulation* is "a repetitive and essentially changeless process of reformulating similar proposals within an issue area that is well established on the government agenda." For instance, the formulation of policy on agricultural price and income supports does not change much from one farm bill to another.
2. In *analogous formulation* a new problem is handled by drawing on the experience of developing proposals for similar problems in the past. What has been done in the past to cope with the activities of terrorists? What has been done in other states to deal with child abuse or divorce law reform?
3. *Creative formulation* involves attempts to develop new or unprecedented proposals that represent a departure from existing practices and that will better resolve a problem. The people seeking to reform the welfare system, for example, have sought to develop innovative proposals that will provide care for the needy while preserving the incentive to work. This is a daunting task. Nowhere can this be seen as clearly as in the Clinton administration's efforts to reform the health care system.

Policy formulation may be undertaken by various players in the policy process—the president and his aides, agency officials, specially appointed task forces and commissions, interest groups, private research organizations (or "think tanks"), and legislators

---

[6] Charles O. Jones ed., *The Reagan Legacy: Promise and Performance* (Chatham, N.J.: Chatham House, 1988). The essays in this volume examine several aspects of the Reagan administration.
[7] Charles O. Jones, *An Introduction to the Study of Public Policy,* 3rd ed. (Monterey, CA: Brooks/Cole, 1984), pp. 87–89.

and their staffs. The Bush administration's version of the Clean Air Act of 1990 was drafted by White House aides working with officials in the Environmental Protection Agency (as discussed in Chapter 6). In Congress, professional aides played a major role in drafting the detailed provisions of the law. Several competing alternatives may be formulated for a problem, such as the reform of health care (discussed later in this chapter).

The people engaged in formulation are usually looking down the road toward policy adoption. Particular provisions may be included or excluded from a proposal in an attempt to enhance its likelihood of adoption. To the extent that formulators think in this strategic manner, the formulation and adoption stages of the policy process often become muddled. Political feasibility is always on the mind of the wise policy formulators; they are more interested in getting action on a problem than in creating political issues.

Policy Adoption

Policy adoption involves the approval of a policy proposal by the people with requisite authority, such as a legislature or chief executive. This approval gives the policy legal force. Because most public policies in the United States are based on legislation, policy adoption frequently requires the building of majority coalitions necessary to secure the enactment of legislation.

In Chapter 6, we discuss how power is diffused in Congress and how the legislative process comprises a number of roadblocks or obstacles—House subcommittee, House Committee, House Rules Committee, and so on—that a bill must successfully navigate before it becomes law. A majority is needed to clear a bill through each of these obstacles; hence, not one majority, but a series of majorities are needed for congressional policy adoption. To secure the needed votes, a bill may be watered down or modified at each of these decision points. Or, the bill may fail to win a majority at one of them and die, at least for the time being.

Much negotiation, bargaining, and compromise are entailed in the adoption of major legislation, such as the Tax Reform Act of 1986 or the Brady Bill. In some instances, years or even decades may be needed to secure the enactment of legislation on a controversial matter. Federal aid to public education was considered by Congress off and on over several decades before finally winning approval in 1965. At other times, the approval process may move quickly. The Flag Protection Act, for example, was passed quickly by Congress after the Supreme Court ruled that a Texas statute banning flag burning was constitutional.[8] The Supreme Court, however, quickly found that new federal law was also an unconstitutional violation of the First Amendment.[9]

The tortuous nature of Congressional policy adoption has some important consequences. First, substantial periods of time may be required in order to pass complex legislation. Second, the legislation passed is often incremental, making only limited or marginal changes in existing policy. Third, legislation is frequently written in general or ambiguous language, as in the Clean Air Act. Necessary to reduce conflict over a law's adoption, such language may both provide considerable discretion to the people who implement the law and also leave them in doubt as to its intended purposes.

---

[8] *Texas v. Johnson,* 492 U.S. 397 (1989).
[9] *U.S. v. Eichman,* 496 U.S. 310 (1990).

Not all policy adoption necessitates the forming of majority coalitions. Presidential decision making on foreign affairs, military actions, and other matters is often a one-man affair. Although the president has many aides and advisers and is bombarded with much information and advice, the power of final decision rests with him. Ultimately, too, it is the president who decides whether to veto a bill passed by Congress. President Clinton's decision not to intervene militarily in 1993 in Bosnia, for example, was ultimately his responsibility.

Budgeting

Most policies require money in order to be carried out; some policies, such as those involving income security (discussed later in this chapter), essentially involve the transfer of money from taxpayers to the government and back to individual beneficiaries. Funding for most policies and agencies is provided through the budgetary process (discussed in Chapter 17). Whether a policy is well funded or poorly funded has a significant effect on its scope, impact, and effectiveness.

A policy can be nullified by an absence of funding or refusal to fund, which was the fate of the Noise Control Act. In 1981, the Reagan administration decided not to seek funds for the Office of Noise Abatement and Control, the unit within EPA that enforced the Act. Because Congress followed the president's lead, this decision ended implementation of noise control policy.

Other policies or programs often suffer from inadequate funding. Thus, the Occupational Safety and Health Administration (OSHA) can afford to inspect only a small fraction of the workplaces within its jurisdiction annually. Similarly, the Department of Housing and Urban Development has funds sufficient to provide rent subsidies only to approximately 20 percent of the eligible low-income families.

The budgetary process also gives the president and the Congress an opportunity to review the government's many policies and programs, to inquire into their administration, to appraise their value and effectiveness, and to exercise some influence on their conduct. All of the government's hundreds of programs are not fully examined every year. But, over a period of several years, most programs come under scrutiny. Some agencies, moreover, may come under sharp attack and experience cutbacks and restraints. In recent years, for example, conservatives in Congress have used the budget as a venue for attacking the activities of the National Endowment for the Arts (NEA). Charging that some of the art projects funded by the Endowment are obscene or pornographic, they have sought to reduce funding for the NEA. Their actions have apparently made NEA officials more cautious and circumspect in the funding of art projects.

In a given year, most agencies experience only limited or marginal changes in their funding. Still, budgeting is a vital part of the policy process that helps determine the impact and effectiveness of public policies.

Policy Implementation

Most public policies are carried out or implemented primarily by administrative agencies (see Chapter 8). Some, however, are enforced in other ways. Product liability and product dating are two examples. Product liability laws are usually enforced by lawsuits initiated in the courts by injured consumers or their survivors. In contrast, state product-dating laws are implemented more by voluntary compliance when grocers take out-of-date products off their shelves or by consumers when they choose not to buy food products after the use dates stamped on them. The courts also get involved in implementation when they are called on to interpret the meaning of legislation, review the legality of agency rules and actions, and determine whether the administration of institutions such as prisons and mental hospitals conforms to legal and constitutional standards.

Administrative agencies may be authorized to use a number of different techniques to implement the public policies within their jurisdictions. These techniques can be categorized as authority, incentive, capacity, and hortatory techniques, depending on the behavioral assumptions on which they are based.[10]

Authoritative techniques for policy implementation rest on the notion that people's actions must be directed or restrained by government in order to prevent or eliminate activities or products that are unsafe, unfair, evil, or immoral. Thus, people who drive while intoxicated can, by law, have their licenses revoked. On the federal level, consumer products must meet certain safety regulations and radio stations can have their licenses revoked if they broadcast obscenities.

Many governmental agencies have authority to issue rules and set standards to regulate such matters as meat and food processing, the discharge of pollutants into the environment, the healthfulness and safety of workplaces, and the safe operation of commercial airplanes. Compliance with these standards is determined by inspection and monitoring, and penalties may be imposed on people and/or companies that violate the rules and standards set forth in a particular policy. For example, under Title IX, the federal government can terminate funds to colleges or universities that discriminate against female students. This pattern of action is sometimes stigmatized as "command and control regulation" by its detractors, although in practice it often involves much education, bargaining, and persuasion in addition to the exercise of authority. In the case of Title IX, for instance, the Department of Education will try to negotiate with a school to bring it into compliance before funding is terminated.

Incentive techniques for policy implementation are based on the assumption that people are utility maximizers who act in their own best interest and must be provided with payoffs or financial inducements to get them to comply with public policies. Tax deductions may be given to encourage charitable giving, or grants awarded to companies for the installation of pollution control equipment. Subsidies are given to farmers to make their production (or nonproduction) of wheat, cotton, and other commodities more profitable. Conversely, sanctions such as high taxes may be adopted to discourage the purchase and use of such products as tobacco or liquor, and pollution fees may be levied to reduce the discharge of pollutants by making this action more costly to businesses.

Capacity techniques provide persons with information, education, training, or resources that will enable them to undertake desired activities. The assumption underlying the provision of these techniques is that people have the incentive or desire to do what is right but lack the capacity to act accordingly. Job-training may enable able-bodied people to find employment, and accurate information on interest rates will enable people to protect themselves against interest-rate gouging. Financial assistance can help the needy acquire better housing and warmer winter coats and perhaps lead more comfortable lives.

---

[10] This discussion draws on Anne Schneider and Helen Ingram, "Behavioral Assumptions of Policy Tools," *Journal of Politics,* 52 (May 1990): 510–529.

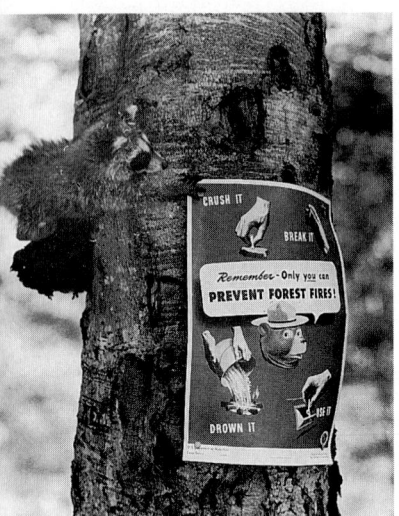

The U.S. Forest Service's famous Smokey the Bear campaign employs a hortatory technique of policy implementation, imploring campers and hikers to take responsibility for their own actions. "Only You can prevent forest fires!"

Hortatory techniques encourage people to comply with policy by appealing to peoples' "better instincts" in an effort to get them to act in desired ways. In this instance, the policy implementors assume that people decide how to act on the basis of their personal values and beliefs on matters such as right and wrong, equality, and justice. In the mid-1960s and late 1970s, the Johnson and Carter administrations, respectively, instituted voluntary (i.e., there were no "punishments" for noncompliance) wage and price control programs to control inflation. Presidential appeals were made to individuals, labor unions, and businesses to avoid inflation-causing behavior. Hortatory techniques also include the use of highway signs tell us "Don't Be a Litterbug" and "Don't Mess with Texas" to discourage littering. And slogans such as "Only You Can Prevent Forest Fires" are meant to encourage compliance with fire and safety regulations in national parks and forests.

The capacity of agencies to administer public policies effectively depends partly on whether the agencies are authorized to use appropriate implementation techniques. Many other factors also come into play, including the clarity and consistency of the policies' statutory mandates, adequacy of funding, political support, and the will and skill of agency personnel. There is no easy formula that will guarantee successful policy implementation; in actuality, many policies only partially achieve their goals.

Policy Evaluation

Essentially, practitioners of **policy evaluation** are concerned with determining whether a policy is accomplishing its goals or, perhaps, anything at all. They may also try to determine whether a policy is being fairly or efficiently administered. In the case of welfare programs, for instance, uncovering evidence of "waste, fraud, or abuse" in their administration has often been of more interest to official evaluators than whether the programs are meeting the needs of the poor.

Policy makers frequently make judgments on the effectiveness and necessity of particular policies and programs. These evaluations are often based mostly on anecdotal and fragmentary evidence rather than on solid facts and thorough analyses. Sometimes a program has been adjudged to be a good program simply because it is politically popular. In recent decades, however, policy evaluation has often taken a more rigorous, systematic, and objective form. Carefully designed studies or inquiries by social scientists and qualified investigators are undertaken to measure the societal impact of programs and to determine whether these programs are achieving their specified goals or objectives. The national executive departments and agencies often contain officials and units with responsibility for policy evaluation; so do state governments.

Policy evaluation may be engaged in by a variety of players: congressional committees, through investigations and other oversight activities; presidential commissions; administrative agencies themselves; university researchers; private research organizations such as the Brookings Institution and the American Enterprise Institute; and the General Accounting Office (GAO). The GAO, for example, originally created in 1921, is an important evaluator of public policies. Every year the GAO undertakes hundreds of studies of government agencies and programs either at the request of members of Congress or on its own initiative. The titles of three of its 1993 evaluations convey a notion of its work: *Pesticides: Pesticide Reregistration May Not Be Completed Until 2006; Energy Conservation: Appliance Standards and Labeling Programs Can Be Improved;* and *Federal Research: Super Collider Is Over Budget and Behind Schedule.* Subsequent congressional and agency actions may be guided by these studies.

Evaluation research and studies can stimulate attempts to modify or terminate policies and thus restart the policy process. Legislators and administrators may formulate and advocate amendments designed to correct revealed problems or shortcomings in a policy. In 1988, for example, legislation was adopted to correct weaknesses in the enforcement of the Fair Housing Act of 1968, which banned discrimination in the sale or rental of most housing. Or, some people may decide that the best alternative is simply to eliminate the policy. On occasion, policies are terminated; for example, by the Airline Deregulation Act of 1978, Congress eliminated the Civil Aeronautics Board and its program of economic regulation of commercial airlines. This action was taken on the assumption that competition in the marketplace would better protect the interests of airline users. More likely, however, a troubled program either will be modified or will be allowed to continue to limp along because it is doing something that some people strongly want done, even if the program is not doing it well.

This model provides a manageable way of dissecting the policy process and examining its components. In reality, policy making frequently does follow the sequence of stages laid out in this model. Keep in mind, however, that what is done at one stage of the policy process often affects action at later stages in the process, and that actions are often undertaken at one stage in anticipation of what *might* happen at another.

Social Welfare Policies

The remainder of this chapter focuses on three areas of social welfare policy—public education, income security, and health care. Each area encompasses many complex policies and programs. While all levels of government (national, state, and local) are involved with the development and implementation of social welfare policies, we highlight the national government's role. The discussion in each of the three areas illustrates the expansion of national action as a consequence of dissatisfaction with what the state and local governments were doing.

Public education was almost the exclusive province of the state and local governments until well into the twentieth century. Even though some commentators and critics argue that education was one area the Framers intended to be reserved to the states by the Tenth Amendment, the national government has been involved in education since passage of the Northwest Ordinance in 1785. Moreover, constitutional justification for the national government's action on public education rests on a broad view of its delegated powers, such as taxing and spending for the general welfare. National financial aid for the public schools has been an agenda item from time to time during the twentieth century and has now become a permanent aspect of public school funding. This topic draws most of our attention here.

Most income security programs in the United States are largely a product of the twentieth century, although their origins can be traced far into the nation's past. As U.S. society became more urban and industrial, self-sufficiency declined and people became more interdependent and reliant on a vast system of production, distribution, and exchange. The Great Depression of the 1930s revealed both that hard work alone would not provide economic security for everyone and that the state governments and private charities did not possess adequate resources to alleviate economic want and distress. Beginning with the Social Security Act of 1935, a variety of national pro-

Landmark Events in Social Welfare Policy	
1867 ♦	U.S. Office of Education established
1935 ♦	The Social Security Act
1964 ♦	Food Stamp program made permanent Medicare and Medicaid programs established
1965 ♦	Elementary and Secondary Education Act
1975 ♦	Individuals with Disabilities Education Act
1988 ♦	The Family Child and Support Act

grams aimed to provide economic security have emerged. We survey some of them in the section in the chapter on income security policies.

Federal concern with national health is much more recent. The federal health program was a result of the Sheppard Towner Maternity Act of 1923, which provided money to the states to fund prenatal programs for pregnant women. Over the years, the national government's role in health care has grown tremendously. Congressional passage of the Medicaid program in 1965 was an attempt to bring health care to the nation's poor. The federal government is extensively involved not only in the provision of health care, through Medicaid and the U.S. Public Health Service, but also in the improvement of the health of all Americans. The Centers for Disease Control and Prevention (CDC), in particular, works to prevent disease.

Public health policies, for example, have been highly effective in reducing the incidence of infectious disease such as measles, infantile paralysis (poliomyelitis), and small pox. Most Americans accept and support extensive government spending on medical research. Congress, in fact, often appropriates more money for medical research than the president recommends.

Public Education

Historically, public education was the province of the state and local governments. From the founding of the United States through the nineteenth century, local governments bore most of the responsibility for public education. In the twentieth century the state governments have continually expanded their involvement until, at present, they are the largest source of funding for the public schools. The states have also created an extensive legal framework for local school systems; they have exerted control over such aspects of school administration as curricula, textbook selection, graduation requirements, eligibility for extracurricular activity, and teacher certification and competence. Nonetheless, local independent school districts, governed by appointed or elected boards, continue to exercise much control over the daily operation of the public schools. The school districts are responsible, for example, for constructing and maintaining school buildings, hiring teachers, transporting students, operating school lunch programs, and designing educational programs.

The primary mission of the public schools in the United States once was to educate students, to provide them with reading, writing, and cognitive skills so that they could live more satisfactory and productive lives and become better citizens. This is still the primary mission of public schools, but they have also had many additional tasks loaded on them as parents and society increasingly view schools as a place to learn values and norms. As political scientist Thomas Dye portrays the situation:

> Today, schools are expected to do many things: resolve racial conflict and build an integrated society; inspire patriotism and good citizenship; provide values, aspirations, and a sense of identity to disadvantaged children; offer various forms of recreation and mass entertainment (football games, bands, choruses, majorettes, and the like); teach children to get along with others and adjust to group living; reduce the highway accident toll by teaching students to be good drivers; fight disease and ill health through physical education, health training, and even medical treatment; eliminate unemployment and poverty by teaching job skills; end malnutrition and hunger though school lunch and milk programs; produce scientists and other technicians to continue America's progress in science and technology; fight drug abuse and educate children about sex; and act as custodians for teenagers who have no interest in education but who are not permitted to work or roam the streets unsupervised.[11]

If there is some hyperbole in Dye's statement, quite a bit of it still rings true. Much is expected of the public schools, perhaps more than they can fairly be expected to deliver.

Many political issues are generated by the tasks that Dye lists, but we lack space here to examine them. Rather, we focus our attention on another matter of fundamental importance—financing the public schools—especially as this involves federal financial aid to the public schools. This has been a contentious political issue for many years.

In 1990, national, state, and local governments in the United States spent nearly $273 billion on public (elementary and secondary) education (see Figure 16-3). Of this amount, 51.5 percent came from the state governments, 37.5 percent from local school districts, and 11.4 percent from the national government. Private citizens and parochial and private schools spent another $103 billion. There is much variation among states, and among school districts within states, on educational expenditures, as measured by spending on a per-student basis. Some states spend two or three times as much as other states according to this measure.

Although federal dollars are the smallest share of public school funding, these dollars are still vital to school systems that are usually financially strapped and sometimes in dire need of additional revenue.

Federal Aid to Education

The roots of the national government's participation in public education extend into the country's history. The Northwest Ordinance of 1785 provided that one section of land in each township in the Northwest Territory (now the states of Ohio, Michigan,

FIGURE 16-3
Sources of Public School Spending, 1990

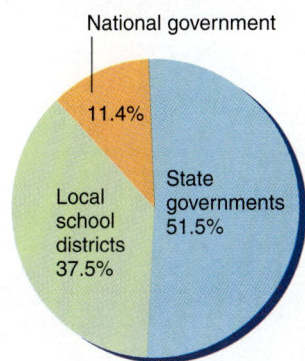

Source: *Statistical Abstract of the United States, 1993.* (Washington, DC: U.S. Government Printing Office, 1993), p. 150.

---

[11] Thomas R. Dye, *Politics in States and Communities,* 7th ed. (Englewood Cliffs, NJ: Prentice-Hall, 1991), p. 411.

Indiana, Illinois, and Wisconsin) be set aside for the support of education. The U.S. Office of Education was established in 1867 to collect and disseminate statistical and other information on education. In 1917 the Smith-Hughes Act created a federal grant-in-aid program to support vocational education in agriculture, home economics, and industrial arts in the public schools. In all, however, the national government was a minor participant in public education. Until after World War II, local control of the schools dominated.

In the two decades following World War II, the school-age population doubled. Classroom shortages were widespread, and many urban schools operated on two shifts. At the same time technological knowledge was expanding rapidly, further challenging the adequacy of public education. Many people came to view federal financial assistance (more simply, federal aid) as a necessary part of the solution to the inadequacies of public education. Consequently, federal aid to education has been an item on the national policy agenda almost continually from the early 1950s.

Efforts in Congress to enact federal aid to education legislation initially foundered on a number of issues, however. One issue was aid to parochial schools, favored by Roman Catholic groups but stoutly opposed by various Protestant, Jewish, and educational organizations, which opposed the use of government money to finance schools run by a religious organization. A second issue, of much interest in the South, was the fear that federal aid would be used as a lever to bring about school desegregation. Two other troublesome issues were how funds would be allocated among the various states and whether with federal aid would come "federal control" of the schools. The divisiveness of these issues made it impossible to put together the needed majority coalitions to enact federal aid legislation.

This situation ended following the landslide election of Lyndon B. Johnson in 1964, which was accompanied by the election of large Democratic majorities in both houses of Congress. In the early months of 1965 the president and his congressional supporters acted quickly to secure passage of the Elementary and Secondary Education Act (ESEA). Section One (it is now called Chapter 1) provided funding to improve schooling for the educationally and culturally disadvantaged. Federal dollars went to 95 percent of the nation's school districts, allocated among schools on the basis of the number of low-income students they enrolled. This provision took care of the allocation issue referred to. Section Two made federal grants available to the states for the purchase of textbooks and other instructional materials for students in both private and public schools. In all cases ownership of these materials rested with public school authorities. This strategem finessed the issue of aid to parochial schools and won support for the legislation from the Catholic hierarchy.

Other provisions of ESEA supported learning centers for disadvantaged students and educational research. The issue of aid to segregated schools had been resolved by Title VI of the Civil Rights Act of 1964, which prohibited racial discrimination in programs receiving federal funds. In the 1970s several billions of dollars were annually provided for public education under ESEA. The Education Consolidation and Improvement Act of 1981, enacted with strong support from the Reagan administration, consolidated ESEA and some related programs into a single block-grant program that gave the states and school districts more discretion in the use of federal money.

In 1988, President George Bush and the nation's governors agreed to a program called Goals 2000 to improve the nation's schools. In 1994, Congress enacted the Goals 2000: Educate America Act to help all children achieve higher educational standards. For the first time, national standards were established (see "What High School Graduates Should Know," p. 677). Compliance with these standards by the states is voluntary.

> ## What High School Graduates Should Know
>
> Among some of the items high school graduates must know are:
>
> ### ARTS
> - Know dances and dancers prior to the 20th century
> - Identify historical sources of American musical theater
> - Identify famous musicians
>
> ### MATH
> - Know how to use a calculator
> - Interpret tables, charts, graphs
>
> ### CIVICS AND GOVERNMENT
> - Identify the Bill of Rights, Magna Carta, Declaration of Independence
> - Explain the difference between a citizen and an alien
> - Know the function of the U.N., NATO, Amnesty International
>
> ### GEOGRAPHY
> - Know how to use an atlas, a map, a globe
> - Explain how war, famine, and disease play significant roles in human migration
>
> ### SCIENCE
> - Know what matter is
> - Understand reproduction and heredity
> - Define a cell
>
> ### ENGLISH
> - Write clearly
> - Know how to use a thesaurus
>
> ### HISTORY
> - Develop a position as to whether the Civil War was avoidable
>
> *Source:* "The Multitudinous Rs" *Time,* (April 4, 1994): p. 14.

National legislation also sometimes imposes requirements on the public schools that are mandatory but not fully funded by the national government. An example is education for children with disabilities. Several million school-age children currently have disabilities that can range from mild physical disability to severe mental retardation. In the past many of these children were excluded from the regular public school systems; some were enrolled in special state institutions, such as schools for the "deaf and dumb," as they were once called.

Beginning in the 1960s, the education of children with learning disabilities moved from the state to the national policy agenda. In 1975 Congress passed what is now called the Individuals with Diabilities Education Act to mandate that the states provide education for children with disabilities.[12] This law transformed the education of children with disabilities by providing that every such child is legally entitled to a "free

---

[12] Erwin L. Levine and Elizabeth M. Wexler, *PL94–142: An Act of Congress* (New York: Macmillan, 1981.)

appropriate public education" provided through the regular public school system. For children with severe disabilities, this can be a quite costly task. Because national funding covers only about one-fifth of the costs of educating children with disabilities, the states and local school districts bear the major costs of this national policy.

Inequality in Spending Among School Districts

The revenues raised by most local school districts come almost entirely from property taxes. Because of substantial differences among districts in the value of the taxable property within their boundaries, some communities are able to generate much more revenue than others, even with lower tax rates. This variation is then reflected in spending disparities among schools when measured on a per-pupil basis. Within a given state some districts may spend more than twice as much per pupil as others. Many parents, educators, and public officials believe that such unequal spending results in significant disparities in the quality of the education that students receive.

A challenge to inequality in education spending that arose out of the Texas public school system was decided in 1973 by the U.S. Supreme Court.[13] The five-justice majority ruled that the right to an education was not of such fundamental character that differences in per-pupil spending among districts would constitute a violation of the Fourteenth Amendment's equal protection of the laws clause. Although expressing concern about the inequalities in school funding, the Court held that this was a problem for the state governments to resolve.

Most conflicts concerning the quality of education that a state must provide have been solved through state administrative procedures. In some situations, however, disputes have ended up in the U.S. Supreme Court. In 1993, for example, the Court ruled that a school district must provide a sign language interpreter for a deaf child attending a Roman Catholic school.[14] In 1994, however, the U.S. Supreme Court ruled that a New York school district had gone too far to accommodate religious needs. The creation of a new school district to educate the special-needs children of the Satmar Hasidim, a strict Jewish sect, was declared to be a violation of the First Amendment's establishment clause.[15]

Since the early 1970s, school finance has been a priority item on the policy agendas in many states. In some states, inequality in expenditures among districts has been held to violate the state constitution. In New Jersey, for instance, the state court practically forced the state legislature to adopt an income tax to finance the schools.[16] School finance has been a volatile and vexing issue in many other states. Most people want good schools; paying for good schools, particularly if this requires raising taxes, stirs up much opposition in a time when "no new taxes" is a mantra with wide popular appeal.

---

[13] *San Antonio Independent School District* v. *Rodriguez,* 411 U.S. 1 (1973).

[14] *Zobrest* v. *Catalina Foothills School District,* 113 S. Ct. 2462 (1993).

[15] *Board of Education of Kiryas Joel Village School District* v. *Grumet,* 114 S. Ct. 2481 (1994).

[16] John J. Harrigan, *Policy and Politics in States and Communities,* 3rd ed. (Glenview, IL: Scott, Foresman, 1988), pp. 300–301.

Income Security

Income security programs protect people against loss of income because of retirement, disability, unemployment, or death or absence of the family breadwinner. Although cases of total deprivation are now rare, many people are unable to provide a minimally decent standard of living for themselves and their families. They are poor in a relative if not an absolute sense. In 1993 an urban family of four earning $14,350 or less per year was officially below the poverty line. Millions of family units do not fare that well.

Income security programs fall into two general categories. *Social insurance* programs are non-means-based programs that provide cash assistance to qualified beneficiaries. **Means-tested programs** require that people must have incomes below specified levels in order to be eligible for benefits (see Table 16.1). Benefits of means-tested programs may take the form either of cash assistance or in-kind benefits, such as food stamps.

Table 16.1 ♦ Recipients of Social Insurance Programs, 1990

PROGRAM	NUMBER OF RECIPIENTS (THOUSANDS)	PERCENTAGE OF U.S. POPULATION
Non-means-tested		
Social Security (OASDI)	39,832	16.0
Medicare (hospital insurance)	33,407	13.4
Veterans programs	3,572	1.4
Railroad programs	913	0.4
State unemployment insurance	2,596	1.0
Means-tested		
Medicaid	25,255	10.2
Supplementary Security Income	4,888	2.0
Aid to Families with Dependent Children	11,695	4.7
Food stamps	20,038	8.1
General assistance	1,220	0.5

Note: "Means-tested" refers to the requirement of demonstration of financial need based on income and assets. People may receive benefits from more than one program. For example, in 1985, 16 percent of U.S. households received one or more means-tested benefits; in addition to the programs listed above, these include free or reduced-price school lunches and publicly owned or subsidized housing. OASDI beneficiaries as of December 31. Medicare enrollees as of July 1. Veterans programs beneficiaries as of December 31. Railroad programs beneficiaries as of December 31 (except for unemployment). State unemployment insurance is the average weekly number in December. Medicaid is the number of recipients during the year. SSI is the number of recipients in December. AFDC is the average number of monthly recipients. Food stamp number is the average during the year. General assistance is the average monthly number.

Source: Harold W. Stanley and Richard G. Niemi, *Vital Statistics on American Politics,* 4th ed. Washington, DC: CQ Press, 1994, p. 392.

In his book *Losing Ground,* policy analyst Charles Murray argues that rather than helping the poor get on their feet, welfare programs encourage dependency.[17] He calls for the abolition of such programs. While not going this far, many conservatives believe that the poor should do more to help themselves. Liberals, on the other hand, are generally supportive of income security programs; they believe that dependency and want result more from social causes than from personal shortcomings, such as laziness. But even liberals sometimes question the effectiveness of some income security programs and call for reforms that will help the poor help themselves.

Roots of Income Security Programs

Until well into the twentieth century, programs to assist the needy and dependent were mostly the responsibility of state and local governments and private charitable organizations. When assistance was available, and often it was not, it was grudgingly provided in small amounts.

Social welfare efforts by the national government were limited to groups for which it had particular responsibility or political obligation, namely veterans, Native Americans, and merchant seamen. Interestingly, in the late decades of the nineteenth century and in the early twentieth century, the national government provided pensions for most of the veterans who had fought for the North during the Civil War. (a substantial portion of the elderly white male population at the time).[18]

The Great Depression of the 1930s completely overwhelmed the attempts of the state and local governments and private charities to assist the needy, although in 1934 twenty-eight states had laws authorizing old-age assistance programs. In some states the programs were inoperative because of the lack of funding; in only ten states were the programs fully statewide in coverage. Most states paid pensions of less than $10 monthly. In Indiana the average monthly pension was $4.50; in North Dakota, it was 69 cents.[19]

Only quite limited assistance had been made available by the national government to the needy during the Hoover administration (1929–1933), which was in accord with the individualistic philosophy of President Herbert Hoover. The response of Franklin D. Roosevelt's New Deal (begun in 1933) took a very different tack. Initially, programs for direct cash assistance and work relief, such as the Works Progress Administration (WPA), were created to help the needy. Although frequently derided as a "make work" program that paid people for such activities as leaf raking, the WPA helped many people weather the Great Depression.

The Roosevelt administration then turned its attention to a search for permanent programs that would address the problems of income insecurity and economic dependency. Roosevelt appointed the Committee on Economic Security to investigate the economic situation and make policy recommendations. Most of its proposals were subsequently endorsed by the president and enacted into law by Congress in 1935 as the **Social Security Act.**

---

[17] Charles Murray, *Losing Ground: American Social Policy, 1950–1980* (New York: Basic Books, 1984).

[18] Theda Skocpol, *Protecting Soldiers and Mothers: The Political Origins of Social Policy in the United States* (Cambridge, MA: Harvard University Press, 1992), Chapter 2.

[19] Merle Fainsod, Lincoln Gordon, and Joseph C. Palamountain Jr., *Government and the American Economy,* 3rd ed. (New York: Norton, 1959), p. 776.

The Great Depression, beginning in late 1929 and continuing throughout the 1930s, dramatically pointed out to average Americans the need for a broad social safety net, and gave rise to a host of income, health, and finance legislation.

The Social Security Act constituted a transformation in public social welfare policy. The national government now became the major contributor on a permanent and extensive basis in the income security area. Three major programs were put in place by the Act: old age insurance (what we now call Social Security); public assistance for the needy aged, blind, and families with dependent children (later, people with disabilities were added); and unemployment insurance (or compensation). Even though the programs instituted as part of the Social Security Act have been modified and other income security programs have been added, these three programs formed the foundation of today's income security policies.

Social Insurance

Social insurance programs operate in a manner somewhat similar to private automobile or life insurance. Contributions are made to the programs by or on behalf of the prospective beneficiaries, their employers, or both. When a person becomes eligible for benefits, the monies are paid as a matter of right, regardless of how much wealth or unearned income (for example, from dividends and interest payments) the recipient has. (For Social Security, a limit is imposed on earned income. There is no means test.)

Old Age, Survivors, and Disability Insurance. This program began as old-age insurance, providing benefits only to retired workers. Its coverage was extended to survivors of covered workers in 1939 and to the permanently disabled in 1956. This is the program customarily called "Social Security." It is not, as many people believe, a pension program that collects contributions from workers, invests them, and then returns them with interest to beneficiaries. In essence, as the program actually operates, the current generation of workers pays taxes to provide benefits for the previous generation. Presently, a payroll tax of 7.5 percent on the first $60,600 of wages or salaries is

I've Got Your Number

When the Social Security System was established in 1936, the sole reason for having Social Security numbers was for the Social Security Administration to maintain accurate records of individuals' earnings so that when they later sought benefits, they could be properly credited with their contributions to the program. This simple, original purpose, was soon altered. A 1943 executive order authorized use of Social Security numbers by any federal agency establishing their own identifying system. Later, in 1961, the Internal Revenue Service (IRS) adopted the nine-digit Social Security number (which has a capacity of almost one billion registrants) as its way to identify taxpayers. By the 1970s, Social Security Numbers were also being used by some school districts to track high school students. They also were used to identify some welfare recipients, military personnel, patients at Veteran's hospitals, and Native Americans receiving public health benefits. Moreover, universities routinely used Social Security numbers in lieu of students ID numbers, and many even posted grades by Social Security number.

Concerned with the increasing use of Social Security numbers for identification purposes and also with possible abuses, Congress enacted the Privacy Act of 1974. Federal government agencies were barred from requiring anyone to disclose his or her Social Security number—unless the requirement was in place before 1975 or use was *specifically* authorized in a new statute. Despite this statute, some states soon began to use Social Security numbers as a condition of some welfare programs, including food stamps, driver's licenses, and vehicle registrations.

And, because use of Social Security numbers is an effective way of preventing tax fraud, the IRS, convinced that taxpayers were inventing children by declaring non-existent dependents on their taxes, persuaded Congress to require all children over the age of five to have Social Security numbers. Prior to this time, only people who were employed or who sought benefits were required to have numbers. This requirement proved so successful (saving the IRS nearly $3 billion) that by 1991 all children over age one were required to have Social Security numbers.

Concern over abuse of the widespread use and possible abuse of private information that can be generated by use of Social Security numbers has led some people to go to court to challenge their use for non-Social Security purposes. Marc Greidinger, a staff lawyer for the U.S. Circuit Court of Appeals, for example, sued the Commonwealth of Virginia in 1993 when the state refused to register him to vote unless he provided his Social Security number. He lost his challenge in the District Court, but the Appeals Court (where he works) agreed with his contention that the Privacy Act was violated because Virginia sells voter registration lists to political parties and campaign organizations and permits access to registration applications.*

Privacy experts say that they hope that this decision will halt the growing use of Social Security numbers for general identification.

*Michael decourcy Hinds, "Privacy Fights on Social Security Numbers," *New York Times* (March 25, 1993): A18.

paid by the employee and another 7.5 percent is paid by the employer into the Social Security trust fund. Nearly all employees and most of the self-employed (who pay a 12.8 percent tax) are now covered by the Social Security program. People earning less money pay a greater share of their income into the Social Security program than do workers earning more.

People are eligible to receive retirement benefits at age sixty-five. Individuals who opt to retire earlier, at age sixty-two, receive a reduced benefit. In the early 1990s the average retired worker received $674 a month. The maximum benefit in 1994 for a retired workers was $1,147 per month. An additional 50 percent was paid if the worker had a spouse. For many retired people, Social Security payments are their primary source of income; were it not for Social Security they would likely be living in poverty. However, eligible people are entitled to Social Security benefits regardless of how much *unearned* income (e.g., dividends and interest payments) they also receive. Until they reach the age of seventy, there is a limit of $11,160 on the annual *earned* income they can receive without a reduction in their benefits. A dollar of benefits is lost for every three dollars by which one exceeds that limit.

Expenditures for Social Security have greatly increased during the last couple of decades because the number of beneficiaries is growing, they are living longer, and benefit levels are rising. More than forty million people, including some three million workers with disabilities, currently receive Social Security benefits. Total program expenditures were $304 billion in 1993, making Social Security by far the national government's largest entitlement program (see Figure 16-4).

In the early 1980s, because of unstable economic conditions and a major increase in benefit levels, the Social Security program was in severe economic trouble. Benefits paid out were exceeding revenues, and the program's reserve fund was emptying, leading to fears that the programs would go broke. To solve this problem Democrats in Congress favored increasing Social Security taxes, while Republicans called for reduced benefits. Neither alternative drew much public support.

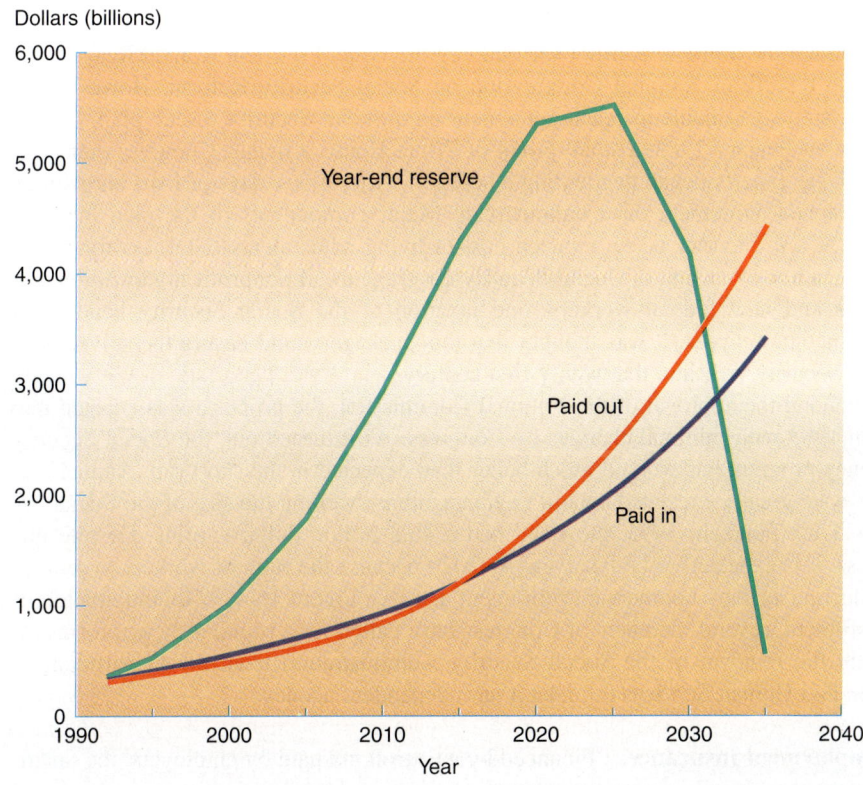

FIGURE 16-4
Social Security Receipts, Spending, and Reserve Estimates, 1992–2035

Note: The combined OASI and DI Trust Funds (Social Security) are estimated to become exhausted during 2035 under alternative II projections. For details see source.

Source: U.S. Congress, House, House Committee on Ways and Means, "1992 Report of The Board of Trustees of the Federal Old-Age and Survivors Insurance and Disability Insurance Trust Funds," 102d Cong., 2d sess., April 2, 1992, 182.

684 ❖ Chapter 16 Social Welfare Policy

TOLES copyright 1993 *The Buffalo News.* Reprinted with permission of UNIVERSAL PRESS SYNDICATE. All rights reserved.

To lessen the political conflict surrounding the issue, President Ronald Reagan created the bipartisan National Commission on Social Security Reform. However, the commission was unable to reach agreement on a Social Security rescue plan. Consequently, in January 1983, a small group of White House officials, Congress members, and private experts began negotiating a solution. After a few days of hard bargaining, they reached agreement on a bailout plan. Major components of the plan included higher Social Security taxes, reduced cost-of-living adjustments (COLAs) for retirement benefits, extension of Social Security coverage to all nonprofit organization employees and new federal workers, and taxation of the Social Security benefits of upper-income retirees. It was thought that this package would ensure the solvency of Social Security well into the twenty-first century.

Receiving the approval of the National Commission, the proposal was enacted into law in 1983 with minimal changes by Congress. As it turned out, the Social Security solvency program has worked much better than expected in the short run. Annual revenues have greatly exceeded benefit payments, thus swelling the size of the Social Security Trust Fund. In 1993, the Fund had a 46.8 billion dollar surplus. Despite this success, it is expected to be insolvent by 2029 because the ratio of workers to retirees will decline as baby boomers hit retirement age (see Figure 16-4).[20] In anticipation of this problem, several members of Congress have called for a round of new reforms including the removal of the Social Security Administration from the Department of Health and Human Services to make it an independent agency.

Unemployment Insurance. Financed by a payroll tax paid by employers, the unemployment insurance program pays benefits to covered workers who are unemployed through no fault of their own; for example, by being laid off during a recession. The

[20] *Bondweek* (April 25, 1994), NEXIS.

Social Security Act provided that if a state set up a comparable program and levied a payroll tax for its support, most of the federal tax would be forgiven (not collected). The states were thus accorded a choice—either they could set up and administer an acceptable unemployment program, or they could let the national government handle the matter. Within a short period of time all of the states had established their own programs.

Unemployment insurance covers employers of four or more persons, but not part-time or occasional workers. Benefits are paid to unemployed workers who have neither been fired nor quit their jobs and who are willing and able to accept suitable employment. The fifty state unemployment programs differ considerably in levels of benefits, length of benefit payment, and eligibility for benefits. Average weekly benefit payments, for example, range from $222 in Massachusetts and $212 in Michigan to $116 in Mississippi and $111 in Louisiana. The most generous programs exist in the northern industrial states, where labor unions are more powerful and influence the nature of these programs. Nationwide, only about half of the people counted as unemployed at any given time will be receiving benefits. (Figure 16-5 illustrates the variation among the states in unemployment rates.)

In recent years Congress has passed legislation providing emergency unemployment benefits for long-term unemployed workers who have exhausted their regular state-paid benefits. These emergency benefits are paid entirely by the national government and have extended the payment period from twenty to seven weeks, depending on the level of unemployment in each state.[21]

[21] *Congressional Quarterly Weekly Report,* 51 (November 27, 1993): 3276.

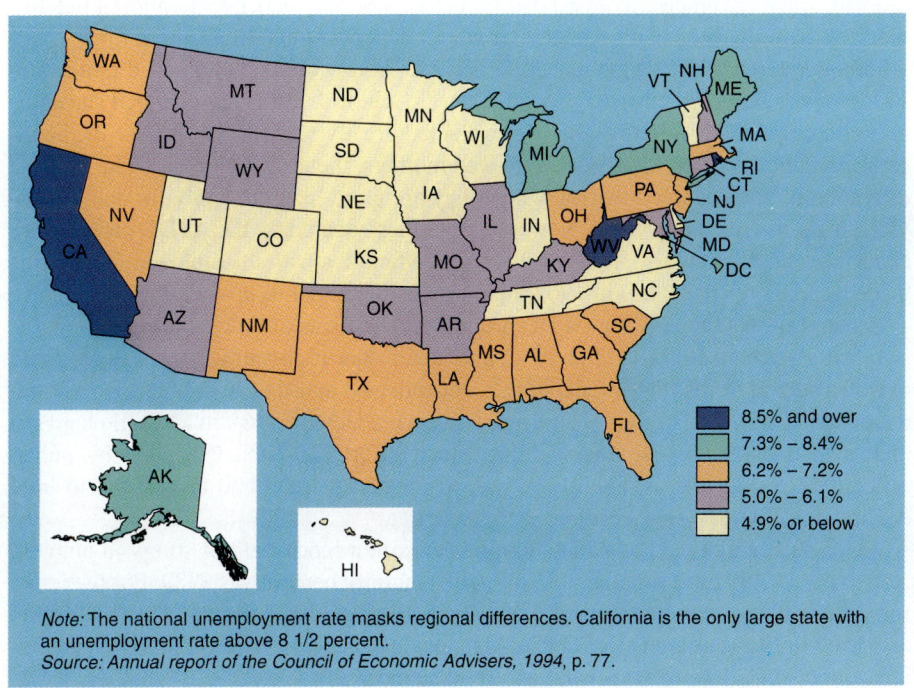

FIGURE 16-5

Unemployment Rate by States, December 1993

8.5% and over
7.3% – 8.4%
6.2% – 7.2%
5.0% – 6.1%
4.9% or below

Note: The national unemployment rate masks regional differences. California is the only large state with an unemployment rate above 8 1/2 percent.
Source: Annual report of the Council of Economic Advisers, 1994, p. 77.

Means-Tested Programs

Means-tested income security programs are intended to help the needy, that is, persons or families whose incomes fall below specified levels, such as a percentage of the official poverty line. Included in this category are the Supplementary Security Income (SSI), Aid to Families with Dependent Children (AFDC), and Food Stamp programs (See Table 16.1).

Supplementary Security Income. This program began under the Social Security Act as a categorical grant-in-aid program to aid the needy aged or blind. Financed jointly by the national and state governments from general revenues, the states played a major role in determining standards of eligibility and benefit levels. In 1950 Congress adopted legislation extending coverage to people who were permanently and totally disabled and could demonstrate a need for assistance.

With the support of the Nixon administration, Congress converted these programs into the Supplementary Security Income (SSI) programs in 1974. Primary funding for SSI is provided by the national government, which prescribes benefit levels that are uniform throughout the nation. To be eligible, beneficiaries can own only a limited amount of possessions. Maximum monthly payments for 1994 were $446 for an individual and $669 for a couple. The states may choose to supplement the federal benefits, and forty-six states do. This program generates little controversy as the modest benefits go to people who obviously cannot provide for themselves.

Aid to Families with Dependent Children (AFDC). In the early 1930s nearly all of the states had programs of cash assistance for mothers (mostly widows) with dependent children under the Social Security Act. A federal grant-in-aid program called Aid to Dependent Children was initiated to supplement the assistance provided by the states. The program was renamed Aid to Families with Dependent Children (AFDC) in 1950, when coverage was expanded to include not only dependent children but also mothers themselves or other adults with whom dependent children were living.

Initially, AFDC was a small program because there were few unmarried mothers in 1935. Most mothers of covered dependents were widows. Much has changed since this program began. The AFDC rolls have expanded greatly since 1960 because of the increasing numbers of children born to unwed mothers, the growing divorce rate, and the migration of poor people to cities, where they are more likely to apply for and be provided benefits (see Table 16.2). Now, most families covered by the AFDC program are headed by single mothers. Assistance for needy families with unemployed fathers was made optional for the states in 1962; many states opted not to provide this coverage.

Because of its clientele, the AFDC program is the focus of much controversy and is frequently stigmatized as "welfare." Critics claim that it encourages promiscuity and out-of-wedlock births, that it encourages dependency, and that it is creating a permanent class of welfare families. There are, however, a lack of research and little hard evidence to document these claims fully. Much effort has been expended by public officials to restrict the availability of aid, to ferret out fraud and abuse, and to hold down the AFDC program's cost.

The cash benefits paid to AFDC families are often modest if not stingy in amount. Nationally, in 1992 the average monthly AFDC family benefit was $380. For the lower forty-eight states, maximum monthly family payments ranged from $642 in California and $507 in Massachusetts to $121 in Alabama and $124 in Mississippi. AFDC recipients are also eligible for Medicaid and food stamps.

Table 16.2 ♦ Aid to Families with Dependent Children, 1970–1993

FISCAL YEAR	FAMILIES	RECIPIENTS (IN THOUSANDS)	CHILDREN	MONTHLY FAMILY BENEFITS	BENEFITS- 1992 DOLLARS	TOTAL BENEFITS (IN MILLIONS)
1970	1,909	7,429	5,494	$178	$644	$4,082
1971	2,532	9,556	6,963	180		5,405
1972	2,918	10,632	7,698	187		6,394
1973	3,123	11,038	7,965	187		6,873
1974	3,170	10,845	7,824	194		7,205
1975	3,342	11,067	7,928	210	548	8,153
1976	3,561	11,339	8,156	226		9,350
1977	3,575	11,108	7,818	242		10,037
1978	3,528	10,663	7,475	250		10,189
1979	3,493	10,311	7,193	257		10,387
1980	3,642	10,597	7,320	274	467	11,540
1981	3,871	11,160	7,615	277		12,844
1982	3,569	10,431	6,975	300		12,857
1983	3,651	10,659	7,051	311		13,607
1984	3,725	10,866	7,153	322		14,371
1985	3,692	10,813	7,165	339	442	14,580
1986	3,747	10,995	7,294	352	451	15,235
1987	3,784	11,065	7,381	359	443	16,323
1988	3,748	10,920	7,326	370	439	16,663
1989	3,771	10,935	7,370	381	431	17,239
1990	3,974	11,460	7,755	389	418	18,539
1991	4,375	12,596	8,515	388	400	20,356
1992	4,857	13,816	9,369	380	380	21,893
1993	4,974	14,128	9,640	377	366	22,486

*1993 numbers are estimates.

Source: *Congressional Quarterly Weekly Report,* 52 (January 22, 1994), p. 121.

In 1988, with strong support from the National Governors Association and the American Public Welfare Association, Congress passed legislation to reform the AFDC system. Titled the Family and Child Support Act, the law's basic goal is to move people off the welfare rolls and into productive jobs. Each state is required to set up and operate a Job Opportunities and Basic Skills (JOBS) program to provide education, training, and job experience for members of welfare families. Most welfare recipients are to be enrolled, with the states providing child care and other services necessary to permit participation. The JOBS program is jointly funded by the national and state governments.

All states are also required by the Family and Child Support Act to participate in the AFDC-UP program. The program provides benefits for two-parent families in which the principal wage-earner is unemployed. A workfare provision included at the insistence of the Reagan administration requires one parent in a UP family to spend at least sixteen hours weekly in a work activity. Other provisions of the Act call for stronger enforcement of court orders for child support payments and greater efforts to establish paternity for children born out of wedlock.

The Family and Child Support Act has been called the most significant reform of the welfare system in half a century. Because its provisions were phased in, it was not fully implemented until in the early 1990s. In 1991, only seven states used their funding allocations for the program, and less than 60 percent of federal monies dedicated to the program were claimed.[22] By early 1992, however, some 500,000 persons were participating in the Act's education and training programs, a number that exceeded the required level of participation.[23] On the other hand, some states have experienced difficulty providing welfare recipients with sufficient job and training opportunities.[24]

In spite of the apparent success of the 1988 Act, both liberals and conservatives are urging reform of the welfare system including AFDC, and some states are moving to cap benefits in an effort to penalize women who bear children while receiving benefits. President Clinton, moreover, has proposed a two-year limit on welfare for young recipients and more job training and child-care programs.

Earned Income Tax Credit Program (EITC). Designed to help the working poor, this program was created in 1975 at the insistence of Senator Russell Long (D.-La.). It helps the working poor by subsidizing their wages, and it also provides an incentive for people to go to work. Drawing extensive support from both Democrats and Republicans in Congress, the Earned Income Tax Credit (EITC) is frequently described as being "pro-work and pro-family." The EITC program has been expanded several times, most recently in 1993 at the request of the Clinton administration.

When the latest version of EITC is fully phased in, working-poor families with two or more children will received a $4 tax credit for every $10 of the first $8,425 that they earn. The maximum EITC is $3,370. When a family's income reaches $11,000, the credit will begin to be reduced and will be totally eliminated at an income level of $27,000. Lesser tax credits are available to one-child families and single workers. It is expected that in 1996 around nineteen million families will qualify for the tax credit at a total cost of $25 billion. The EITC program is administered by the Internal Revenue Service through the income tax system.

Food Stamp Program. The initial food stamp program (1939–1943) was primarily an effort to expand domestic markets for farm commodities. Attempts to re-establish the program during the Eisenhower administration failed, but in 1961 a new pilot program was began under the Kennedy administration. It was made permanent in 1964. Although strongly opposed by the Republicans in Congress, the Democrats were able to put together a majority coalition when urban Democrats agreed to support a wheat and cotton price support program wanted by rural and Southern Democrats in return for their support of the food stamp program.

---

[22] *BNA Daily Labor Report* (March 16, 1994).

[23] *Congressional Quarterly Weekly Report,* 50 (March 28, 1992): 809–810.

[24] *New York Times* (May 5, 1993): C23.

Initially, recipients of food stamps had to make a cash payment for them, but this practice was halted by the Carter Administration in 1977. Subsequently, the program gradually was extended to all counties in each state in the nation. Benefiting poor and low-income families, the program has helped to combat hunger and reduce malnutrition. Spending for the program was reduced somewhat in the early years of the Reagan administration, but its growth has since resumed. Food stamps were provided to more than thirteen million beneficiaries in 1994 at a cost of $24 billion, and they are expected to increase by three billion people over the next five years.

Several other food programs targeted at the needy are also operated by the national government. These programs include a state child nutrition program; a special nutritional program for women, infants, and children (WIC); a school breakfast and lunch program; and an emergency food assistance program. These programs cost the national government several billions of dollars a year.

General Assistance.   Some states and local governments, especially in the Northeast and Midwest, administer general assistance programs that assist poor people who are ineligible for AFDC or SSI. Persons who are physically able but not working may receive assistance, for instance. General assistance programs receive no support from the national government. Budgetary pressures have caused several states to cut back on their programs in recent years.

The Effectiveness of Income Security Programs

Many of the income security programs, including Social Security, Social Security Insurance, and food stamps, are **entitlement programs.** That is, Congress sets eligibility criteria—such as age, income level, or unemployment—and all persons who meet the criteria are legally "entitled" to receive benefits. Moreover, unlike such programs as public housing, military construction, and space exploration, spending for entitlement programs is mandatory. Year after year funds *must* be provided for them unless the laws creating the programs are changed. This feature of entitlement programs has made it quite difficult to control spending for them.

Although poverty and economic dependency have not been eliminated by income security programs, such programs have improved the lives of large numbers of people. Millions of elderly people in the United States would be living below the poverty line were it not for Social Security. Income security programs are basically alleviative rather than curative or remedial in their consequences. Poverty and economic dependency will not be eradicated so long as the conditions that give rise to them persist. And there will probably always be people who are unable to provide adequately for themselves, whether because of old age, mental or physical disability, adverse economic conditions, or youth. A panoply of income security programs is a characteristic of all democratic industrial societies.

Medical Care

Governments in the United States have long been active in the health field. Local governments began to establish public health departments in the first half of the nineteenth century and were followed by state health departments in the second half. As knowledge of the bacteriological causes of diseases and human ailments and of the adverse health effects of urbanization and industrialization expanded in the late nineteenth and early twentieth centuries, significant advances were made in improving public health. Public sanitation and clean water programs, pasteurization of milk, immunization programs, and other health activities reduced greatly the incidence of infectious and communicable diseases. The increase in life expectancy at birth in the United States from forty-seven years in 1900 to seventy-five years in 1990 is mostly due to public health programs.

Beginning in 1798 with the establishment of the National Marine Service (NMS) for "the relief of sick and disabled seamen," which was the forerunner of the Public Health Service, the national government has directly provided health care for some segments of the population. Currently many millions of people receive medical care through the medical branches of the armed forces, the hospitals and medical programs of the Department of Veterans Affairs, and the Indian Health Service. Many billions of dollars are expended for the construction and operation of facilities and for the salaries of the doctors and other medical personnel who staff these facilities. The government's medical business is truly big business.

Most medical research currently is financed by the national government, primarily through the National Institutes of Health (NIH). The National Cancer Institute, the National Heart, Lung, and Blood Institute, The National Institute of Allergy and Infectious Diseases, and the other NIH institutes and centers expend more than $10 billion annually on biomedical research. The research is conducted both by NIH scientists and by scientists at universities, medical schools, and other research centers receiving NIH research grants.

In recent years national government spending for AIDS research has expanded greatly, exceeding a billion-and-a-half dollars in 1993. In the early 1980s, however, many public officials were disinclined to do much on the AIDS problem, regarding it as a condition afflicting a narrow segment of the population. In part, at least, the decision to hold back on funding AIDS research reflected moralistic, anti-homosexual sentiments.[25] Research scientists and advocates for the gay community, however, were able to convince policy makers that AIDS constituted a dire public health problem and that a major governmental response was required. Some critics now assert that too large a share (around one-sixth) of medical research dollars is being channeled into AIDS research, while others still believe that not enough is being done.

A different situation exists in government programs that assist individuals in paying the costs of their own medical care. In helping people defray their medical costs, the United States continues to provide less assistance than other western industrial democracies as shown in Figure 16-6, "Rising Medicare and Medicaid Costs" (see Table 16.3); all of them have long had some sort of national health insurance program.

The Roots of National Health Insurance

National health insurance was considered by the Committee on Economic Security when it was planning Social Security legislation. Because of the strong opposition of the American Medical Association (AMA), which was the dominant force in American medicine, health insurance was omitted for fear that its inclusion would jeopardize adoption of the other Social Security programs. Health insurance remained on the policy back burner for several years.

---

[25] See Randy Shilts, *And the Band Played On* (New York: St. Martin's Press, 1987).

Medical Care ♦ 691

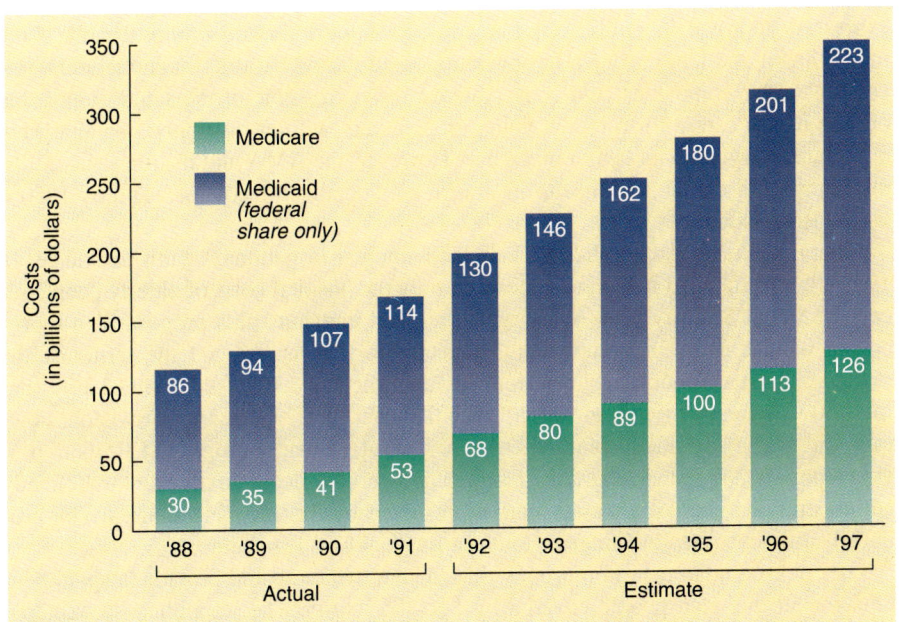

FIGURE 16-6
Rising Medicare and Medicaid Costs

Note: Medicare and Medicaid are the governments's fastest growing entitlements. Congress has slowed the growth rate for Medicare but Medicaid costs have doubled since 1988.
Source: Congressional Quarterly Weekly Report, Vol. 51 (January 2, 1993), p.29.

In late 1945 President Harry S Truman put the issue on the national policy agenda by calling for the enactment of compulsory national health insurance. Truman's advocacy touched off a titanic political struggle. The initial public reaction to compulsory health insurance was favorable: Of persons who had heard of the proposal, 58 percent

Table 16.3	♦	Government Expenditures as a Percent of Total Health Expenditures, 1991, by Country

United States	43.9%	Italy	81.1%
Australia	62.9%	Japan	70.8%
Austria	68.8%	Luxembourg	92.8%
Belgium	83.4%	Netherlands	74.7%
Canada	74.7%	New Zealand	83.6%
Denmark	85.2%	Norway	98.4%
Finland	79.0%	Portugal	72.4%
France	78.8%	Spain	79.9%
Germany (West)	75.0%	Sweden	92.5%
Greece	82.2%	Switzerland	67.5%
Iceland	88.2%	Turkey	27.3%
Ireland	82.2%	United Kingdom	89.6%

Source: Statistical Abstract of the United States 1993 (Washington, D.C.: Government Printing Office, 1993), p. 849.

expressed approval in public opinion polls.[26] Support for the proposal came from many liberal and labor groups. In opposition were the AMA, drug manufacturers, private insurance companies, and conservatives; these are some of the same groups that oppose health care reform today. Some groups were willing to support voluntary but not compulsory national health insurance. However, the AMA and its allies succeeded in stigmatizing compulsory health insurance as "socialized medicine," and by 1950 it was a dead issue.

Liberal political leaders did not lose their interest in national health insurance. In 1958 a bill introduced in Congress covered only the hospital costs of elderly people receiving Social Security. The AMA again weighed in against this proposal; but by focusing on the aged, the proponents of health insurance changed the terms of the struggle. Strong support developed for providing medical assistance to the elderly, and in 1960 Congress passed legislation benefiting the *needy* aged. This provision, however, did not satisfy liberals and other supporters of a broader program. Efforts to provide a non-means-tested program continued but were unsuccessful during the Kennedy administration. The issue was essentially resolved by the 1964 elections, which produced sufficient votes in Congress to enact medical care legislation.

The Johnson administration proposed Medicare, which would provide hospital benefits for all the aged people covered by Social Security. The Republicans countered with a plan for subsidized voluntary insurance that would cover major medical risks and physicians' services. The AMA sponsored a similar proposal. Representative Wilbur Mills (D.-Ark.), chair of the House Ways and Means Committee (which had jurisdiction over the legislation), took hold of the policy process at this point. Wanting to put his own stamp on the legislation, he proposed combining the administration and Republican proposals and also adding an expanded program for the poor. This expanded proposal was enacted into law as **Medicare** and **Medicaid**.

Medicare. Medicare, which covers persons receiving Social Security benefits, is administered by the Health Care Financing Administration in the Department of Health and Human Services. Medicare coverage is divided into two parts, called Parts A and B. Benefits under Part A come to all Americans automatically at age sixty-five, when they qualify for Social Security. Part A covers hospitalization, some skilled nursing care, and home health services. In 1994 individuals had to pay $696 in medical bills before they are eligible for Part A benefits. Medicare is financed by a payroll tax of 1.45 percent paid each by both employees and employers on the total amount of one's wages or salary.

Part B, which is optional, covers payment of physicians' services, outpatient and diagnostic services, x-rays, and some other items not covered by Part A. Excluded from coverage are prescription drugs, eyeglasses, hearing aids, and dentures. This portion of the Medicare program is financed partly by monthly payments from beneficiaries and partly by general tax revenues. Almost all of the eligible people have opted for Part B coverage, which in 1994 cost $41.10 a month.

Medicare has become a costly program both because elderly people need more hospital and physicians' services and because of the rapidly rising costs of medical care. Attempts to limit or cap expenditures for the program have had only marginal effects. One attempt occurred in 1983, when Congress authorized use of the diagnosis related

---

[26] Paul Starr, *The Social Transformation of American Medicine* (New York: Basic Books, 1982), p. 282.

group (DRG) system, which pays a prescribed amount to a hospital for a given medical procedure or operation, regardless of what the actual cost is to the hospital. Previously, Medicare had compensated hospitals for "all reasonable costs." Hospitals have responded by reducing the length of patient stays and otherwise economizing on medical care costs. They have also shifted the unreimbursed costs of Medicare patients that result from the application of the DRG system to privately insured patients, which increases the share of total medical costs paid by private insurance companies. Figure 16-7 shows the various sources of payment for all medical costs in the United States.

In 1989, the Congress turned its attention to the costs of physicians' services for Medicare patients. The Physician Payment Review Commission, which advises Congress on Medicare's physician reimbursement policies, recommended that payments to physicians be determined on the basis of the work involved in a given treatment plus geographical factors (whether service is provided in a large city or rural area, for instance) and other considerations.[27] Enacted into law by Congress, these physician-cost-control practices were being placed into effect in the mid-1990s.

Medicare does not cover long-term or catastrophic health care costs. Congress sought to remedy this situation in 1988 when, with the support of the Reagan administration, it passed the Catastrophic Health Care Act. This Act provided elderly people with expanded hospital and physicians' benefits and limited nursing home and prescription drug coverage. These expenses were to be financed by a small monthly fee levied on all Medicare recipients and also by a tax paid by the more well-to-do among Medicare recipients. President Reagan had insisted that the elderly themselves had to pay for the program.

Many better-off elderly people quickly mobilized to protest the new law. The members of Congress were bombarded with letters, petitions, and telephone calls and were accosted by outraged elderly constituents at town meetings. Overwhelmed by this stampede of opposition from the wealthier elderly, both houses of Congress voted by wide margins in 1989 to repeal the Catastrophic Health Care Act. Although many of the wealthier elderly had private health insurance providing protection for themselves similar to that in the Act, the poorer elderly were left with no protection.[28] Many people did not view this action as one of Congress's finer moments.

Medicaid. Enacted into law at the same time as Medicare, the Medicaid program provides comprehensive health care, including hospitalization, physicians service, prescription drugs, and long-term nursing home care (unlike Medicare). This care is provided for all persons who qualify as needy under AFDC and SSI.

In 1986 Congress acted to provide Medicaid coverage for pregnant women and for children under age six in families with incomes of less than 133 percent of the official poverty level. The states were also accorded the option of extending coverage to all pregnant women and to all children under one year of age in families with incomes below 185 percent of the poverty level. By 1993, twenty-nine of the states had chosen to provide this coverage.

Medicaid covered 32.6 million people in 1992. Most of the benefits paid out under the program went to elderly people. Approximately one-seventh of the benefits went to children under the AFDC program.

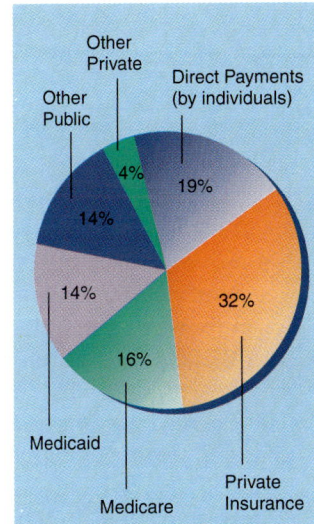

FIGURE 16-7

Who Pays Medical Costs?

* Other public includes public health, medical research, veterans care, and other programs.
Source: Statistical Abstract of the United States, 1993 (Washington, DC: Government Printing Office, 1993), p. 108.

---

[27] *Congressional Quarterly Weekly Report,* 47 (February 25, 1989): 588–589.

[28] David Wilsford, *Doctors and the State: The Politics of Health Care in France and the United States* (Durham, NC: Duke University Press, 1991), pp. 189–193.

THEN AND NOW

From the '60s to Now: Medicaid's Legal Activists

During the 1970s, a group of young lawyers and researchers operating out of a ramshackle office near the campus of the University of California at Los Angeles set out to advance the cause of better health care for the poor. Activists with the National Health Law Program (NHeLP), one of the offshoots of President Lyndon B. Johnson's war on poverty, they harried federal and state officials who were not abiding by the Medicaid law, filed lawsuits against hospitals not serving the indigent, hung out together and often married each other.

First through their energy and acumen on the front lines and later in behind-the-scenes positions on Capitol Hill and in the offices of powerful interest groups, they helped, often anonymously, to bring about the Medicaid changes of the 1980s, and they have played an influential role in formulating President Clinton's health reform proposals.

Among them are:

- Andreas G. Schneider, the health care specialist for Democratic Rep. Henry A. Waxman of California since 1979. He has helped formulate most of the Medicaid provisions that emerged for the House Energy and Commerce subcommittee on health, which Waxman chairs. Along with subcommittee staff director Karen Nelson, who was not in NHeLP, Schneider is widely considered the person to see on Medicaid matters in the House.

- Sara Rosenbaum, the Children's Defense Fund's top health expert and operative on Capitol Hill throughout the 1980s. Rosenbaum battled for the expansion of Medicaid benefits to children and women, lobbying and frequently testifying in front of Waxman's subcommittee. She is now at the George Washington University Center for Health Policy Research and has advised Clinton health care reformers. She and her husband, David Chavkin, were both NHeLP lawyers in Los Angeles in the 1970s. Chavkin, who became director of NHeLP's Washington office, now teaches health law at the University of Maryland.

- Diane Rowland, who worked on Medicaid issues part time for Waxman in the 1980s. Now executive directory of the Kaiser Commission on the Future of Medicaid, she served on Hillary Rodham Clinton's health reform task force.

- Judy Waxman joining NHeLP's Washington office in 1979 and is now director of government affairs for Families USA, which has lobbied for Medicaid changes effecting the elderly. No relation to Rep. Waxman, she is married to James Weill, a former member of the NHeLP national board and now general counsel of the Children's Defense Fund.

"They're people who picked up a certain idea in the '60s about the transforming power of the law," says Gordon Bonnyman, a Nashville Legal Services lawyer who knows Schneider and other NHeLP graduates. "It's a kind of a priesthood."

NHeLP was organized in the 1960s, as one of the backup legal groups under the Office of Economic Opportunity, headquarters of the Great Society's war on poverty. Eventually, it was brought under the quasi-independent Legal Services Corp. and provided legal research and backup for public interest lawyers.

"It was a very exciting time because it was uncharted water," says Sylvia Drew Ivey, a Howard Law School graduate who directed NHeLP in the 1970s. "We were asking 'What is Medicaid and what is it not doing?' We were making health law a substantive force. That wasn't being done in may law schools."

Although many from NHeLP have moved into jobs that have a national impact on health care policy, Ivey chose to stay on the front lines. Today, she directs a health clinic in south-central Los Angeles that was in the middle of the 1992 riot area.

Source: Dan Morgan, *The Washington Post Weekly Edition,* February 7–13, 1994.

Jointly financed by the national and state governments, the national government pays 50 to 79 percent of Medicaid costs on the basis of a formula based on average per capita income, which awards more financial support to poor than to wealthy states. Each state is responsible for the administration of its own program and sets specific standards of eligibility and benefit levels within the boundaries set by national guidelines. Nearly all of the needy people are covered by Medicaid in some states; in others only one-third or so of the needy are protected. Some states also award coverage to the "medically indigent," that is, to persons who do not qualify for welfare but for whom large medical expenses would constitute a severe financial burden.

The Cost of Health Care

Vastly exceeding early estimates, the costs of Medicare and Medicaid have been major contributors to the ballooning costs of health care. In 1993 national expenditures for Medicare were $143 billion and for Medicaid, $76 billion as indicated in Table 16.4. The states collectively spent another $50 on Medicaid. Barring any changes, costs of these two programs are expected to rise sharply over the next decade (see Figure 16-6).

Total health care expenditures in the United States have also soared in recent decades, growing from $27.1 billion in 1960 to $250.1 billion in 1980, to $838.5 billion in 1992.[29] In 1992 health care costs comprised 14 percent of the gross domestic product. The national government's health spending for Medicare, Medicaid, medical research, and other purposes amounted to 40 percent of total health spending.

[29] *Statistical Abstract of the United States,* 1993, p. 92; and *New York Times* (January 5, 1993): 1.

Table 16.4 ♦ Entitlements and Projections

THE BIGGEST ENTITLEMENTS IN 1993 (IN BILLIONS)		PROJECTIONS FOR 1999 (IN BILLIONS)	
1. Social Security	$302	1. Social Security	$408
2. Medicare	$143	2. Medicare	$264
3. Medicaid	$76	3. Medicaid	$151
4. Federal civilian retirement	$39	4. Federal civilian retirement	$51
5. Unemployment compensation	$35	5. Supplemental Security Income	$35
6. Military retirement	$26	6. Military retirement	$35
7. Food stamps	$25	7. Food stamps	$30
8. Supplemental Security Income	$21	8. Unemployment compensation	$26
9. Veterans' benefits	$17	9. Earned Income Tax Credit	$22
10. Farm price supports	$16	10. Family support	$20

Source: Congressional Budget Office and *The Atlanta Journal Constitution,* February 7, 1994, p. A7.

696 ❖ Chapter 16 Social Welfare Policy

Passage of a universal health care bill has been the first priority of the Clinton Administration. But, hope for massive reform died in the 103rd Congress when Democrats and Republicans were unable to agree on coverage and cost issues.

A number of factors have contributed to the high and rising costs of health care. First, more people are living longer and are requiring costly and extensive care in their declining years. Second, the range and sophistication of diagnostic practices and therapeutic treatments, which are often quite expensive, have increased. Third, the expansion of private health insurance, along with Medicare and Medicaid, has reduced the direct costs of health care to most people and increased the demand for services. More people, in short, can afford needed care. They may also be less aware of the costs of care. Fourth, the costs of health care have also increased because of its higher quality and because labor costs have outpaced productivity in the provision of hospital care.[30] Fifth, U.S. medicine focuses less on preventing illnesses and more on curing them, which is more costly.

Public opinion polls indicate that the major cause of Americans' dissatisfaction with the health care system is its cost. While most people indicate that they are satisfied with the quality of health care services provided by physicians and hospitals, a substantial majority express dissatisfaction over the costs of health care.[31] There is, as a consequence, a strong belief in the need to improve the nation's health care system, and this task is viewed as appropriate for the government to handle.

Toward Reform

Endemic in Americans is an urge to reform government—to tinker with and modify governmental structures, processes, and policies in an attempt to render them more efficient and effective. Nowhere is the reform urge more prevalent than in the area of social welfare policies. Because of their variety, complexity, uncertain effects, and sometimes lack of strong political support, social welfare policies present good targets for proponents of change. Probably nothing angers people in the United States more than welfare; as many see it, the welfare system transfers their hard-earned dollars to the unambitious and undeserving. And when was there not some sort of "crisis" in public education?

In this section we have focused on health care reform, which the Clinton administration has made its major domestic policy initiative and for which U.S. public support has been increasing. Although President Clinton pledged to "end welfare as we know it" and also to make various changes in national education programs, health care reform became (in the view of many commentators) the "defining issue" of his administration.

The cost of health care has been a nagging political problem in the United States for many years. In the late 1970s, for instance, the Carter administration sought unsuccessfully to impose mandatory cost controls. His proposal was rejected by Congress, in part because the hospitals said they would act voluntarily to control costs. Their actions proved ineffectual.

---

[30] Henry J. Aaron, *Serious and Unstable Condition: Financing America's Health Care* (Washington, DC: Brookings Institution, 1991), Chapter 2.

[31] Lawrence R. Jacobs, Robert Y. Shapiro, and Eli C. Schulman, "Medical Care in the United States: An Update," *Public Opinion Quarterly,* 57 (Fall 1993): 394–427. This article contains data from a large number of opinion polls.

The control of health care costs gained salience in 1991 because of the U.S. Senate race in Pennsylvania. Democrat Harris Wofford, a distant underdog, used the health care reform issue to come from behind and defeat Republican candidate Richard Thornburgh, former governor of Pennsylvania and Attorney General of the United States. Then, in 1992, both George Bush and Bill Clinton talked to voters about the need to control medical care costs. Opinion polls indicated that voters perceived Clinton as more able than Bush to deal with the issue.

Early in 1993 the Clinton administration set up a Task Force on National Health Care Reform to craft its health care reform proposal. Chaired by Hilary Rodham Clinton, the task force comprised a half dozen Cabinet secretaries, several White House aides, and the director of the Office of Management and Budget. Staffed by more than 500 health-care specialists drawn from government agencies and the private sector, over a period of several months, the Task Force gathered and analyzed large quantities of information, engaged in extensive deliberations, and finally agreed on a detailed proposal. Clinton outlined the plan in a speech to Congress in late September 1993. Some changes were subsequently made to reduce opposition to the plan, and it was formally introduced in Congress near the end of October. Highly detailed and complex, the proposal was more than 1,300 pages in length.[31] The basic purposes of the plan are twofold: (1) to provide universal health care coverage (from thirty-seven to forty million people, or about 14.9 percent of the population, were not covered by health insurance in 1994) (see Figure 16-8); and (2) to hold down the costs of health care.

The gist of the Clinton proposal can be sketched here, although no one seemed to understand fully how this complex, wordy plan would operate in practice.

- All citizens and legal residents of the United States were to be continually covered by health care insurance by 1998. Employers would pay 80 percent of health care insurance premiums for their employees, who would pay the remainder. Small employers would receive government subsidies to help them meet the cost of insurance. For employees retiring early (between the ages of fifty-five and sixty-five), the government would pay insurance costs.
- Most people would acquire their insurance from large state-run or nonprofit purchasing cooperatives called "health alliances." There would be one or more health alliances in each state. They could bargain with insurance companies and the providers of medical care to hold down rates.
- Limits would be placed on consumer expenses.
- Funding for the plan would come from cuts in Medicare and Medicaid spending and also from a major increase in the cigarette tax.
- A seven-member National Health Board would have authority to oversee the health alliances, to help make national health policies, and to control health-care spending.

A smorgasbord of other health-care plans were also introduced in Congress. These plans ranged from a "single payer" plan sponsored by about ninety liberal Democrats to a plan making only modest changes in the existing health care system and supported by some conservative Republicans. Many of the plans falling between these poles embodied some features of the Clinton proposal.

[31] *New York Times* (October 28, 1993): 1, A–10.

FIGURE 16-8

Health Insurance Coverage

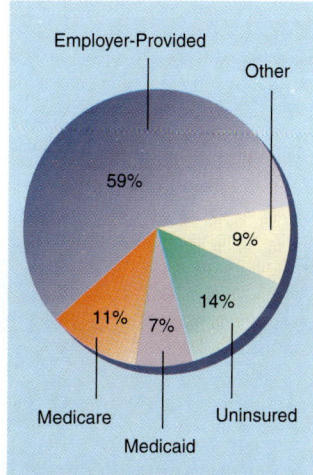

Note: Most Americans receive health insurance through their employers. Other includes, for example, privately purchased health insurance and the Department of Veterans Affairs.
Source: *Annual Report of the Council of Economic Advisors*, 1993, (Washington, DC: Government Printing Office, 1993), p. 126.

> ### The Canadian System
>
> Since 1971, all Canadians have been covered by public health insurance plans administered by the Provinces. In Canada, it is illegal to sell private insurance for services provided by the public plans and participating physicians and hospitals may not accept direct payment from patients for those services. While the Provinces differ in the methods they use to finance health care, most funding comes from general tax revenues.
>
> Physicians are paid by the provincial governments on a fee-for-service basis according to a fee schedule negotiated by the provincial governments and physician associations. There have been very substantial increases in the utilization of physician services since the introduction of public health insurance. Attempts to cut total costs by limiting physicians' fees have been partially thwarted by these continuing increases in utilization.
>
> Hospitals receive annual lump sum, or global, budgets that are not tied directly to hospital expenditures. Hospitals cannot purchase new equipment without governmental approval and many types of high-technology equipment are less common in Canadian than in U.S. hospitals. The global budget reimbursement system and restrictions on the purchase of equipment have led to waiting lists for some nonemergency hospital services.
>
> *Source: Annual Report of the Council of Economic Advisers, 1993, p. 122.*

The single-payer plan provided that all citizens and legal residents of the United States would be enrolled automatically in a health insurance program established by the national government and administered by the states. Private health insurance companies would be eliminated by the single-payer plan, whose costs would be met by a combination of payroll taxes paid by employers, income tax hikes, and other taxes. Patients would be free to choose their own doctors. Simple in design, the single-payer plan would create a health care system similar to the one in Canada, as depicted in the box above.

In contrast, the Republican plan—the Comprehensive Family Health Access and Savings Act—would leave most health care financing decisions to individuals. Employers would not be required to offer health insurance to their employees. If an employer did provide coverage, employees would have to be given a choice from among a regular insurance plan, coverage in a health maintenance organization (HMO), or a medical savings account program. Under the medical savings program, some of the money used for employee health insurance would go to purchase a low-cost catastrophic health policy; the remainder would be put into a tax-deferred medical savings account that could be used for ordinary medical expenses. Under this plan, consumers would likely pay a larger share of medical costs.[31]

---

[31] *Congressional Quarterly Weekly Report* 51 (October 30, 1993): 2968–2977.

Strong opposition to the Clinton proposal quickly emerged from small business groups who were distressed by the employer mandate. Although many large corporations provide health insurance for their employees, most big business groups, such as the U.S. Chamber of Commerce, the Business Roundtable, and the Health Insurance Association of America also opposed the Clinton proposal, as did the American Medical Association. The Health Insurance Association of America sponsored a series of television ads featuring a yuppie couple, "Harry and Louise," who found various alleged faults in the Clinton proposal. These were credited with creating public doubt about the desirability of health care reform.

In Congress, the Senate Finance and Labor and Human Resources committees and the House Ways and Means, Education and Labor, and Energy and Commerce committees shared jurisdiction over health care reform. All except the House Energy and Commerce Committee eventually reported out some sort of health care bill. Only that produced by the Senate Finance Committee had real bipartisan support. Although the committee bills all differed in significant ways from the administration's proposal, they appealed mostly to liberal Democrats. In the Senate, a bipartisan group of about twenty moderate Democrats and Republicans calling itself the "Mainstream Coalition" also put together a bill.

Debate on health care did not get underway on the floor of the Senate until August, 1994. By then, strong opposition from the Republicans and divisions within the ranks of the Democrats made the enactment of legislation appear a long shot. A few weeks later, following unsuccessful attempts by Senate Majority Leader George Mitchell (D., Me.) to work out a compromise with the Mainstream Coalition, health care reform was declared dead for the year.

A number of factors contributed to the demise of health care reform. First, the complexity of the Clinton proposal made it difficult to explain to the public and subject to attack by special interests feeling adversely affected by its various provisions. Second, a slow-down in the rise in health care prices caused a lessening of concern about cost control. Consequently, the various health care proposals were especially concerned with the scope of coverage. Third, there was no consensus on what the extent of coverage should be or how the cost of extended coverage should be handled. Fourth, there was minimal bipartisan support, especially in the House, for health care reform. The Democrats never made much effort to seek a compromise with the Republicans. On the other hand, quite a few Republicans seemed most interested in killing health care reform legislation, perhaps to gain a partisan advantage in the 1994 congressional elections. Fifth, the strong opposition to the Clinton proposal that emanated from the business community caused many people to fear that major health care reform might lead to higher taxes, job losses, or the rationing of health care. Public opinion polls consequently showed a weakening of public support for reform.

It was unclear whether the defeat of health care reform in 1994 was simply the opening battle in a continuing struggle or a more lasting defeat. It is the case that it often requires several years to build sufficient support for the enactment of major policy changes. Moreover, President Clinton and Democratic and Republican congressional leaders all indicated that health care reform would again be on the policy agenda in 1995. If legislation is passed, it will be the consequence of significant compromise between the Clinton administration and the Democrats and Republicans in Congress. That is a customary feature of major policymaking in this American system.

Summary

This chapter examined the policy-making process and social welfare policies. To that end, we made the following points:

1. The policy-making process can be viewed as a sequence of functional activities beginning with the identification and definition of public problems. Once identified, problems must get on the governmental agenda. Other stages of the process include policy formulation, policy adoption, budgeting for policies, policy implementation, and the evaluation of policy.
2. Governments at all levels are involved in the policy process. The social welfare policies highlighted here are education, income security, and national health.
3. Public education was the province of state and local governments through the nineteenth century. In the twentieth century the national government has become more deeply involved. Through a variety of federal laws, Congress has attempted to improve educational standards, especially for disadvantaged students and also for people with disabilities. Today, the national government provides a modest but vital share of the financing for public schools.
4. Income security programs to relieve economic dependency and poverty were mostly handled by state and local governments, albeit in minimal fashion, through the nineteenth century. With the adoption of the Social Security Act in 1935 the national government moved to become the dominant player in the economic security policy area. Most income security programs generally take two forms: non-means-based programs and means-tested programs, which means that all people who meet eligibility criteria automatically are entitled to receive benefits.
5. Governments in the United States have a long history of involvement in the health of Americans. Most state and local governments have health departments, and the U.S. government has several public health and medical research divisions. Since Harry S Truman's presidency, there has been a push for national health insurance. Medicare and Medicaid are the two most prominent national programs. As the cost of health care has risen, however, new demands have been made for a national plan.
6. Since the election of Bill Clinton in 1992, reform of the public welfare and health care systems have been major policy issues on the public agenda. His Task Force on National Health Care Reform's suggestions for change, in particular, have been a lightning rod for discussion of major health-care reform.

Key Terms

social welfare policies
public policy
agenda
systemic agenda
governmental agenda
institutional agenda
agenda setting
policy formulation
policy adoption
policy implementation
policy evaluation
means-tested programs
Social Security Act
entitlement programs
Medicare
Medicaid

Suggested Readings

Chubb, John and Terry Moe, *Politics, Markets and America's Schools.* Washington, DC: Brookings Institution, 1990.

Coleman, James S. *Public and Private High Schools: The Impact of Community.* New York: Basic Books, 1987.

Derthick, Martha. *Agency Under Stress: The Social Security Administration in American Government.* Washington, DC: Brookings Institution, 1990.

Gutmann, Amy. *Democratic Education.* Princeton, NJ: Princeton University Press, 1987.

Katz, Michael B. *In the Shadow of the Poorhouse.* New York: Basic Books, 1986.

Lindblom, Charles E., and Edward J. Woodhouse. *The Policy-Making Process,* 3rd ed. Englewood Cliffs, NJ: Prentice-Hall, 1993.

Marmor, Theodore R. *The Politics of Medicare.* Chicago: Aldine, 1973.

Ripley, Randall B., and Grace A. Franklin. *Congress, the Bureaucracy, and Public Policy,* 5th ed. Pacific Grove, CA: Brooks/Cole, 1991.

Shilts, Randy, *And the Band Played On.* New York: St. Martin's Press, 1987.

Smith, David G. *Paying for Medicare: The Politics of Reform.* Chicago: Aldine, 1992.

Starr, Paul. *The Social Transformation of American Medicine.* New York: Basic Books, 1982.

Van Horn, Carl E., Donald C. Baumer, and William T. Gormley Jr. *Politics and Public Policy,* 2nd ed. Washington, DC: CQ Press, 1992.

Wilsford, David. *Doctors and the State: The Politics of Health Care in France and in the United States.* Durham, NC: Duke University Press, 1991.

Wirt, Frederick, and Michael Kirst. *Schools in Conflict: The Politics of Education.* Berkeley, CA: McCutchan, 1982.

The general government is charged with the care of providing for the payment of the debt of the United States; supporting the general government, and providing for the defence of the union. To obtain these ends, they should be furnished with the means. But does it thence follow, that they should command all the revenues of the United States! Most certainly it does!

Brutus
No. VI

The Anti-Federalists feared that a powerful national government would eventually rely on Article I, Section 8's necessary and proper clause to allow it tax to regulate the economy. Anti-Federalists accurately foresaw that Congress would have to tax to meet its growing financial obligations.

CHAPTER 17

Economic Policy

ROOTS OF GOVERNMENT INTERVENTION IN THE ECONOMY
STABILIZING THE ECONOMY
THE ECONOMICS OF REGULATING ENVIRONMENTAL POLLUTION
TOWARD REFORM

To many people politics and economics seem to be separate and distinct spheres of activity. Economics is concerned with the production, distribution, and exchange of goods and services. Economic decisions, which are made primarily through markets governed by prices, involve action by private consumers, workers, and firms pursuing their self-interest. Politics, in comparison, centers on government and the development of policies by which a people are governed. Political decisions in a democracy are made by majorities in elections and legislatures, and by bureaucrats who service power legislatively delegated to them. Although politics is by no means devoid of self-interested behavior, its basic concern is promotion of the broader public interest.

In actuality, government and the economy in the United States have always been closely intertwined. The U.S. economic system would be unable to survive and thrive in the absence of such government activities as the definition and protection of property rights, the maintenance of law and order, the enforcement of contracts, the provision of a common monetary system, and granting of corporate charters, the issuance of patents and copyrights, and the adoption of legislation to handle bankruptcy. This core of government activities, many of which are the responsibility of the state governments, provide the foundation for the U.S. capitalist (or free enterprise) economy. Many other governmental policies intended to influence and control economic activity have also always been a part of the political landscape. In the twentieth century such policies have become much more numerous and important.

In this chapter we deal somewhat selectively with public economic policies. First, we take a historical look at some of the major developments in government intervention in the economy—the kinds of interventions feared by Anti-Federalists. Second, we examine the government's role in stabilizing the economy; this is sometimes called macroeconomic regulation. Third, we look at regulation to control environmental pollution; this is an important area of microeconomic regulation. In total, this chapter highlights the growth and impact of government intervention in the economy. Put a different way, this chapter demonstrates the accuracy of James Madison's contention in *Federalist No. 10* that the regulation of "various and interfering interests [including economic] forms the principal task of modern legislation."

Roots of Government Intervention in the Economy

The Nineteenth Century

Although the U.S. economic system is a capitalist system, characterized by the private ownership of property, private enterprise, and marketplace competition, governments in the United States have always been deeply involved in the economy. The national government has long played an important role in fostering economic development through its tax, tariff, public lands disposal, and public works policies, and also through the creation of a national bank (see Chapter 3). For much of the nineteenth century, however, national regulatory programs were few and were restricted to such topics as steamboat inspection and the regulation of trade with the Indian tribes.

The state governments, in comparison, were quite active in both promoting and regulating private economic activity. They constructed such public works as the Erie Canal, built roads, and subsidized railroads to encourage trade within and among the states; they also carried on many licensing, inspection, and regulatory programs.

The experience of Pennsylvania is a case in point. Pennsylvania regulated such matters as creditor-debtor relations, labor relations, liquor traffic, and banks and insurance companies. Inspection programs to guarantee the quality of products covered "such articles as flour, fish, beef, pork, hogslard, flaxseed, butter, biscuits, harness and leather, tobacco, shingles, potash and pearlash, staves, heading and lumber, ground black-oak bark, pickled fish, spirituous liquors, and gunpowder." Licenses were required for "innkeepers, peddlers, retailers of foreign goods, liquor merchants, brokers of various kinds, wharfage pilots, and auctioneers."[1] On the whole, the state governments were

---

[1] Louis Hartz, *Economic Policy and Democratic Thought: Pennsylvania 1776–1860* (Cambridge, MA: Harvard University Press, 1948).

Public works projects such as the building of the Erie Canal spurred settlement and building throughout New York state.

Landmark Events in Economic Policy

Year	Event
1887	The Interstate Commerce Act
1890	The Sherman Act (anti-trust)
1913	The Federal Reserve Act; Sixteenth Amendment (established federal income tax)
1914	The Federal Trade Commission established
1921	The Budget and Accounting Act
1929	Stock market crashes on Oct. 27; Great Depression sets in
1932	FDR elected; New Deal policies establish national government as major player in economy
1946	The Full Employment Act
1985	The Balanced Budget and Emergency Deficit Reduction Act

capable of dealing adequately with the small scale and mostly agrarian economy of early nineteenth century United States.

Following the Civil War, however, the United States entered a period of rapid economic growth. The rise of industrial capitalism brought extensive industrialization and the creation of large-scale manufacturing enterprises. Many people began working in factories for wages and crowded into large cities. New problems resulted from industrialization—industrial accidents and disease, labor/management conflict, unemployment, and the emergence of huge businesses that could exploit workers and consumers. Another problem was the loss of income by people because of **business cycles,** which became more severe in the new industrial society. Business cycles involve fluctuations between growth and recession, or periods of "boom and bust," and seem an inherent part of modern capitalist economies. During recessions many people lose their jobs, and a low or even negative growth rate afflicts the economy.

Many people were disturbed by the problems resulting from industrialization and turned to government for help. Because the states with their limited jurisdictions appeared inadequate to cope with industrial problems, the national government was called on to control these new forces. Businesses and conservatives, who had welcomed national action to aid economic development in the early decades of the nineteenth century, now proclaimed their faith in *laissez faire*. Based on Adam Smith's *The Wealth of Nations* (published in 1776), the doctrine of *laissez faire* holds that governmental regulation of the economy is wrong and that the role of government should be limited to the maintenance of order and justice, the conduct of foreign affairs, and the provision of necessary public works such as roads or lighthouses, which are not profitable for private persons to provide. Beyond that, individuals should be left free to pursue their self-interest. In so doing, Smith held, people would be guided by an "unseen hand" to promote the public welfare, that is, to provide consumers with a sufficient quantity of goods at reasonable prices. Competition and the laws of supply and demand would control their behavior and ensure that self-interest did not get out of hand.

Although opposed to regulation of their activities, businesses did not shun other forms of governmental intervention in the economy. They strongly supported tariffs that provided protection from foreign competitors. Other favored policies included the giveaway of public lands, subsidies for railroad construction, and the use of armed force to put down strikes. Essentially, what businesses and their supporters wanted, and what they thought of as *laissez faire,* was an economic system and a set of governmental policies that would be congenial to the amassing of business profits.[2]

In time, because of pressures from the Grangers (see Chapter 15) and other powerful agrarian protest groups in the Midwest, small businesses, and reformers in the cities, the national government was impelled to action. In 1887, following nearly two decades of agitation, Congress adopted the Interstate Commerce Act to regulate the railroads. To be enforced by the new Interstate Commerce Commission (ICC), the act required that railroad rates should be "just and reasonable." The Act also prohibited such practices as pooling (rate agreements), rate discrimination, and charging more for a short haul than for a long haul of goods. Three years later, Congress dealt with the problem of "trusts," the name given to large-scale, monopolistic business that dominated many areas of production, including oil, sugar, whiskey, salt, cordage, and meatpacking. The Sherman AntiTrust Act of 1890 is simple in its terms. Section 1 prohibits all restraints of trade, and Section 2 prohibits all monopolization or attempts to monopolize. (Restraint of trade include price-fixing, bid-rigging, and market allocation agreements; monopolization involves domination of a market by one company or a few companies.) The Act was to be enforced by the AntiTrust Division of the Department of Justice, which was empowered to sue violators in the federal courts. The Interstate Commerce Act and the Sherman AntiTrust Act comprise the nineteenth- and early twentieth-century response of the national government to the new industrialization.

Changes in agriculture, the largest sector of the economy throughout the nineteenth century, also involved a shift from subsistence farming to production for the market. Farmers became more dependent on a vast system of distribution and exchange for their livelihoods. As this change occurred, and notwithstanding their storied individualism, farmers turned successfully to the national government for aid to improve their economic situation. The year 1862 was notably good for agriculture; it saw the establishment of the Department of Agriculture, which gained cabinet status in 1889; the adoption of the Homestead Act, which gave 160 acres of public land in the west free to people willing to live on the land and improve it; and passage of the Morrill Land Grant act, which subsidized the establishment of state colleges ("land grant schools") that offered instruction in the "agricultural and mechanical arts" (see Chapter 3). Further intervention occurred in 1887, when the Hatch Act funded agriculture experiment stations in the various states to do basic and applied research. Other legislation provided regulatory programs to deal with such farm problems as pesticides, commodity standards, plant and insect pests, and the rail shipment of livestock. The expansion of farm programs continued in the early decades of the twentieth century. By the beginning of World War I, the Department of Agriculture had became a major regulatory agency.

---

[2] Howard R. Smith, *Government and Business* (New York: Ronald Press, 1958), p. 99.

Here, a political cartoonist depicts how U.S. government is perceived by some as being built by and of various trusts.

The Progressive Era (1901–1917)

The Progressive movement drew much of its support from the middle class and sought to reform the political, economic, and social systems of U.S. society. Economically, there was a desire to bring corporate power fully under the control of government and make it more responsive to democratic ends. Under the progressive leadership of Presidents Theodore Roosevelt and Woodrow Wilson, regulatory programs to control railroads, business, and banking and to protect consumers were strengthened. Several laws intended to make railroad regulation move effective were passed. Notable among these laws was the Hepburn Act (1906), which gave the Interstate Commerce Commission authority to set maximum reasonable rates for railroads. Strongly opposed by most of the railroads, the Hepburn Act helped make the ICC a more effective regulator.

Consumer protection legislation came in the form of the Pure Food and Drug Act and the Meat Inspection Act, both enacted in 1906. These statutes mark the beginning of consumer protection as a major task of the national government. The Meat Inspection Act was passed partly in response to publication of Upton Sinclair's novel *The Jungle,* which graphically portrayed the unsavory and unsanitary conditions in the Chicago meat-packing plants. The food and drug law prohibited the adulteration and mislabeling of foods and drugs, which were common practices at this time.

The year 1913 saw passage of the Federal Reserve Act. The Act created the Federal Reserve System to exercise control over the national banking system and to provide for flexibility in the money supply in order to better meet commercial needs and to combat financial panics.

In addition, antitrust policy was enhanced by passage of the Federal Trade Commission (FTC) Act and Clayton Act of 1914. The FTC Act created the Federal Trade Commission and authorized it to prevent "unfair methods of competition." The commission also shared jurisdiction with the Department of Justice to enforce the Clayton Act, which prohibited a number of unfair business practices, such as price discrimination, exclusive dealing contracts, and corporate mergers that lessened competition. The basic notion underlying these two statutes was that they would prevent businessmen from forming monopolies or trusts.

Throughout the nineteenth century, the revenue needs of the national government were adequately met by protective tariffs and a few excise taxes, such as those on alcoholic beverages. Indeed, in the late decades of the nineteenth century, the government was sometimes hard pressed to spend all of the funds generated by protective tariffs. Generous government pensions for members of the Grand Army of the Republic and ample spending on internal infrastructure improvements helped absorb the available revenues.

As the national government's functions began to expand in the early twentieth century, however, the government began to experience shortages of revenue. New sources of revenues became necessary and, in time, the attention of public officials focused on the income tax as a way to raise money. In 1895, however, the Supreme Court had held that the income tax was a direct tax, which, according to the U.S. Constitution, had to be allocated among the states in proportion to their population.[3] This ruling made the income tax a political and administrative impossibility. Consequently, the Sixteenth Amendment was added to the Constitution in 1913 to undo that decision. The Sixteenth Amendment authorized the national government "to lay and collect taxes on incomes, from whatever source derived" without being apportioned among the states. Personal and corporate income taxes have since become the national government's major sources of general revenues. They have also been a source of political controversy.

The Great Depression and the New Deal

The outbreak of World War I brought the Progressive era to an end. During the 1920s, under the conservative aegis of the administrations of Warren G. Harding, Calvin Coolidge, and Herbert Hoover, the expansion of national intervention in the economy was slowed almost to a halt.[4] Only a few new regulatory programs were adopted; the Railway Labor Act and the Packers and Stockyards Act stand out. The economy grew at a rapid pace, and many Americans thought that the resulting prosperity would last forever. However, "forever" came to an end on Thursday, October 27, 1929, when the stock market collapsed and the catastrophic worldwide economic decline known as the Great Depression set in. The initial response of the Hoover administration was to de-

---

[3] *Pollock v. Farmers' Loan and Trust Co.* 158 U.S. 429 (1895).

[4] This discussion of the New Deal draws on Louis M. Hacker and Helene S. Zahler, *The United States in the 20th Century* (New York: Appleton-Century-Crofts, 1952); and William E. Leuchtenburg, *Franklin D. Roosevelt and the New Deal* (New York: Harper & Row, 1963).

After the stock market crashed, during the Great Depression, "Hoovervilles" sprang up all over the United States as temporary shelters for the homeless and unemployed.

clare that the economy was fundamentally sound, but few people believed this assertion. Investors, business people, and other lost confidence in the economy. Prices dropped, production declined, and unemployment rose. In the winter of 1932–1933 it was estimated that a quarter of the labor force was unemployed. Many other people worked only part-time or at jobs below their skill levels. The economic distress produced by the Great Depression, which lasted for a decade, was unparalleled before or since.

There had been numerous financial panics and recessions before 1929, but none on the scale of the Great Depression had ever occurred. Although the Depression was worldwide in scope, the United States was especially hard hit. All sectors of the economy suffered—business, finance, labor, agriculture, and manufacturing. No economic groups or social class was spared, although some fared better than others. Fully industrialized, the United States could no longer rely on subsistence agriculture as a refuge in times of economic decline.

Many intellectuals, economic experts, and disgruntled citizens viewed the Depression as a massive institutional failure of the capitalist system. Whatever its shortcomings, such as substantial inequality in the distribution of wealth and income and the exploitation of some workers and farmers, no one had seriously questioned capitalism's productive capabilities. When economic declines had occurred, it was accurately assumed that they would be of short duration. Moreover, before the Depression few people thought there was much that the government could do to prevent recessions or to stabilize the economy. These assumptions were now called into question.

Calling for a New Deal for the American people, Franklin D. Roosevelt overwhelmed Herbert Hoover and the Republican Party in the 1932 presidential election. Although Roosevelt's campaign speeches and declarations were often general and am-

The WPA

The largest and most famous of the New Deal's job-creation programs was the WPA—the Works Progress Administration. Enacted in the midst of the Great Depression, the program had the purpose of not simply providing jobs for the unemployed—it was also intended to build public works, and this it did on a massive scale. variety and magnitude of what the WPA accomplished is staggering. From 1935 to 1941 more than 600,000 miles of roads and streets were built or repaired, enough to encircle the world twenty-four times! Bridges were constructed or rebuilt, 116,000 of them; and nearly 600 airplane landing fields were constructed. More than 100,000 public libraries, schools, and other public buildings were erected. If only the *new* buildings were distributed evenly among the 3,000 counties in the United States, each county would have had about 10. WPA projects included draining swamps and repairing library books; teaching illiterate adults and serving school lunches; building stadiums and painting murals; planting trees and harvesting oysters. The projects ranged from modest ones costing a few hundred dollars to the building of major municipal airports and bridges, each of which cost tens of millions of dollars.

The WPA was not free of controversy and criticism. Some people objected in principle to the government's provision of jobs to so many people, and others complained that too much of the money was wasted on "make work" and used by politicians to reward their friends.

A construction project of the Works Progress Administration (WPA). This New Deal government program was created to provide jobs building roads, bridges, parks, and other public facilities.

Source: Donald S. Howard, *The WPA and Federal Relief Policy* (New York: Russell Sage Foundation, 1943).

biguous, it was clear that he favored strong government action to relieve economic distress and to reform the capitalist economic system, while preserving its basic features, through the processes of democratic government. In some nations, like Germany, the Depression helped put dictatorial regimes in power. In others, like Great Britain and France, the governments bumbled along until the 1930s, when spending on rearmament policies to combat Nazi Germany's expansionist actions began to revive their economies.

The Depression and the New Deal marked a major turning point in U.S. history in general and in U.S. economic history in particular. During the 1930s, the *laissez-faire* state was replaced with the **interventionist state,** in which the government plays an active and extensive role in guiding and regulating the private economy. Up to the 1930s, the national government's role in the economy was consistent with a broad interpretation of *laissez-faire* doctrine in that the government mostly provided a framework of rules within which the economy was left alone to operate. After the 1930s, that was no longer true. The New Deal established the national government as a *major* regulator of private businesses, as a provider of social security (see Chapter 16), and as ultimately responsible for maintaining a stable economy (see "The WPA" on p. 710).

Although the New Deal was not (and is not) without critics, most people today accept the notion that these areas of responsibility are properly within the scope of national governmental power. Specifically, *how* matters of social security and economic stability should be handled rather than *whether* they should be the province of the national government is now the basis for political conflict. Only the most diehard opponents of governmental action think that the government should not be involved at all in security and stability issues.

The major reforms brought about during the New Deal are discussed here.

Financial Reforms. The first actions of the New Deal were directed at reviving and reforming the nation's financial system (see "Then and Now: Regulation of Financial Markets," p. 712). Because of bad investments and poor management, many banks failed in the early 1930s. To restore confidence in the banks, the day after he was inaugurated, Roosevelt declared a bank holiday, closing all of the nation's banks. Then, on the basis of emergency legislation passed by Congress, only financially sound banks were permitted to reopen. Many unsound banks were closed for good and their depositors paid off.

The major New Deal banking laws were the Glass-Steagall Act (1933) and the Banking Act (1935). The Glass-Steagall Act required the separation of commercial and investment banking and set up the Federal Deposit Insurance Corporation (FDIC) to insure bank deposits, originally for $5,000 per account. Although it had long been opposed by conservatives, bank deposit insurance has now become an accepted feature of the U.S. banking system. The Banking Act reorganized the Federal Reserve System, removed the Secretary of the Treasury as an ex-officio member, and formally established the Open Market Committee (discussed later in this chapter).

Legislation was also passed to control other abuses in the stock markets. The Securities Act (1933) required that prospective investors be given full and accurate information about the stocks or securities being offered to them. And, the Securities Exchange Act (1934) created the Securities and Exchange Commission (SEC), an independent regulatory commission. The SEC was authorized to regulate the stock exchanges, to enforce the Securities Act, and to reduce the number of stocks bought on margin (that is, with borrowed money).

Then and Now

Regulation of Financial Markets and the Fed

Throughout the eighteenth and nineteenth centuries, the U.S. economy was plagued periodically by financial panics. Downturns in the business cycles were accompanied by runs on banks, widespread defaults on loans, bankruptcies of large enterprises, and sharp declines in stock prices. Panics, often proceeded by speculative booms in real estate or securities, usually resulted when a spectacular failure cause a sudden, drastic reappraisal of business prospects. From 1790 to 1907, there were twenty-one panics or about one every six years. In 1914, Congress passed the Federal Reserve Act to regulate the currency and credit operations of banks in the United States, which had been manipulating financial markets. The law was designed to improve cooperation among the nation's banks and to decentralized financial control. As illustrated in Figure 17-1 on page 722, it divided the United States into twelve districts with a Federal Reserve Bank in each.

In spite of these precautions, the stock market crash in October, 1929, set off a succession of banking panics, with more than 9,000 bank failures between 1930 and 1933. The Federal Reserve Banks had no authority to prevent these disasters, to keep them from spreading, or to ease their effects.

Thus in 1933, Congress passed the Banking Act of 1933. It changed some of the ways in which Federal Reserve Banks worked and created the Federal Deposit Insurance Corporation. The objective of the Act was to stabilize banking in the United States.

Today, the Federal Reserve System is empowered to create money to meet the seasonal needs of business and to counteract panics. In addition, the Federal Reserve imposed controls over bank reserves, accounting procedures, and management; produced a uniform currency; cleared checks and collections; and handled government finance. The Federal Reserve injects money into the financial system by purchasing government bonds. So when "the Fed" decides that the economy needs more money, it prints new money and promptly spends some (on bonds).

The Federal Reserve plays a critical role in stabilizing the financial system. For instance, without the Fed in operation, the 1987 stock market crash could have had a more devastating impact than it did. When the stock market crashed, the Federal Reserve immediately flooded the financial markets with money in order to prevent further panic.

For all of its power and importance, the Federal Reserve System is a mysterious entity to most Americans. One observer has likened it to a religious institution, a characterization that, at first, seems bizarre, but that on closer examination reveals a bit of truth about the Fed. Housed in a dignified marble "temple" on Constitution Avenue in Washington, D.C., the "high priests" of monetary policy direct the economy in ways that are hidden from, and incomprehensible to, the average citizen. Their deliberations take place in secret. Their debates are conducted in the technical language of economics. Their powers to create money and to make it disappear inspire awe and fear. Such powers cannot be entrusted to ordinary "mortals" but must be exercised only by "priests" undefiled by "political considerations."

The Fed's mystique has not been lost on the Fed itself, which has often portrayed itself as the master of an arcane science. A former officer of the Fed described the induction of economists into the fraternity of the Fed staff as "taking the veil," similar to nuns entering a convent. One member of Congress described the senior economists at the Fed as "the monks." Richard Syron, a vice president of the Boston Fed, compared the institution to the Catholic church:

> The System is just like the Church. That's probably why I feel so comfortable with it. It's got a pope, the chairman; and a college of cardinals, the governors and bank presidents; and a curia, the senior staff. The equivalent of the laity is the commercial banks . . . We even have different orders of religious thought like Jesuits and Franciscans and Dominicans only we call them pragmatists and monetarists and neoKeynesians.

Source: Quotation and paraphrasing from William Greider, *Secrets of the Temple: How the Federal Reserve Runs the Country* (New York: Simon & Schuster, 1987), Chapter 2.

Agriculture. The economic condition of U.S. agriculture, which had been weak even during the prosperous 1920s, became much worse with the Depression. The Agriculture Adjustment Act (AAA) of 1933 sought to boost farm income by restricting agriculture production in order to bring it into better balance with demand. Farmers who reduced their crop production in line with the program were eligible to receive cash payments and other benefits. In 1936, however, the Supreme Court held the AAA unconstitutional on the grounds that the national government lacked authority through any of its powers set out in Article I, Section 8.[5] Congress quickly replaced the AAA with Soil Conservation and Domestic Allotment Act, which paid farmers for taking land out of crop production and devoting it to soil-conservation purposes. The crops taken out of production generally were those whose prices the AAA had been designed to increase. This ploy did not work very well to increase farm income.

In 1938, Congress adopted the second Agricultural Adjustment Act. The second AAA provided for subsidies to farmers raising crops such as corn, cotton, and wheat who grew no more than their allotted acreage. If two-thirds of the growers of a commodity voting in a referendum approved, then the allotments became mandatory, and farmers exceeding them were penalized. Direct payments and commodity loans were also available to participating farmers. In 1941, the Supreme Court upheld the constitutionality of the second AAA as an appropriate exercise of Congress's power to regulate interstate commerce.[6] The Act remains the foundation of the current agricultural price support programs.

Labor. Organized labor had long been handicapped in its relationships with management by unfriendly public officials and hostile public policies. The fortunes of labor unions, which were strong supporters of the New Deal, took a market turn for the better in 1935 when Congress passed the National Labor Relations Act. Better known as the Wagner Act after Senator Robert Wagner (D.-NY), its sponsor, this statute guaranteed workers' right to organize and bargain collectively through unions of their own choosing. A series of "unfair labor practices," such as discriminating against employees because of their union activities, was prohibited. The National Labor Relations Board (NLRB) was created to carry out the Act and to conduct elections to determine which union, if any, employees wanted to represent them. Unions prospered under the protection provided by the Wagner Act.

The last major piece of New Deal economic legislation was the Fair Labor Standards Act (FLSA) of 1938. Intended to protect the interests of low-paid workers, the law set twenty-five cents an hour and forty-four hours per week as initial minimum standards. Within a few years, wages were to rise to forty cents per hour and hours to decline to forty per week. Not all employees were covered by the FLSA, however; farm workers, domestic workers, and fishermen, for example, were exempted. The Act also banned child labor.

In 1994 the minimum wage stood at $4.25 an hour. Controversy continues over whether minimum wage legislation creates employment by pricing some workers out of the labor market. It is argued by economists that these workers would have jobs if they could be paid a lower wage. Also, illegal alien workers are often paid substantially less than the minimum wage.

---

[5] *U.S.* v. *Butler,* 297 U.S. 1 (1936).
[6] *Wickard* v. *Filburn,* 317 U.S. 111 (1942).

714   ❖   Chapter 17   Economic Policy

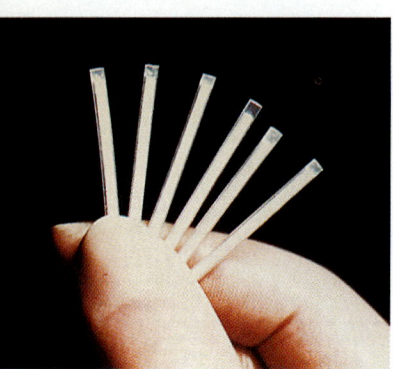

In 1992, the FDA approved the first new major method of birth control for women in three decades. Norplant is a long-acting contraceptive that is implanted in a woman's body. Some charge that not enough testing was done on its safe removal to gain FDA approval.

Industry Regulations. Several industries were the subjects of new or expanded regulatory programs. The Federal Communications Commission (FCC) was created in 1934 to replace the old Federal Radio Commission and was given extensive jurisdiction over the radio, telephone, and telegraph industries. The Civil Aeronautics Board (CAB) was put in place in 1938 to regulate the commercial aviation industry. And the Motor Carrier Act of 1935 put the trucking industry under the jurisdiction of the Interstate Commerce Commission (ICC). Regulation of industries such as trucking and commercial aviation, like railroad regulation, extended to such matters as entry into the business, routes of service, and rates. To a substantial extent, government regulation, as a protector of the public interest, replaced competition in these industries. Supporters of these programs frequently spoke of a need to prevent destructive or excessive competition, as among large numbers of trucking companies.

Consumer Protection. Even though consumers as a group were poorly organized in the 1930s, a few laws were passed to help protect their interests. The Wheeler-Lea Act (1938) expanded the jurisdiction of the Federal Trade Commission (FTC) to include deceptive practices and false and misleading advertising. The Act gave the FTC a clear mandate to engage in consumer protection.

The Pure Food, Drug, and Cosmetic Act (1938) represented an effort to plug some of the loopholes and remedy the shortcomings of the Pure Food and Drug Act of 1906. Cosmetic and therapeutic devices were added to foods and drugs as matters subject to government regulation. All traffic in foods that were injurious to health was banned. Also, factories producing foods, drugs, and cosmetics were brought under inspection by the Food and Drug Administration (FDA). Drugs and cosmetics had to bear informative labels relating to their use. Moreover, the marketing of any drug was prohibited until it had been tested and found safe when properly used. Most responsibility for enforcing the 1938 law was given to the Food and Drug Administration, which today is part of the Department of Health and Human Services.

Just as World War I brought down the curtain on the Progressive Era, the war clouds gathering in Western Europe in the late 1930s diverted Americans' attention from domestic reform to international affairs and brought an end to the New Deal era. Many of the New Deal programs, however, became permanent parts of our public policy landscape. Moreover, the New Deal established the legitimacy and viability of national governmental intervention in the economy. Passive government was replaced with activist government, and the government in Washington became the people's primary source of solutions for economic problems (see Landmark Events in Federal Intervention in the National Economy, p. 705).

The Post-World War II Era

In the two decades following the end of World War II, many areas of economic policy were fairly well settled and produced few major policy struggles. Transportation, finance and banking, agriculture, and consumer protection, for example, experienced little change. There were, however, some important policy developments in other areas. Here, we look at two of the most significant developments: the Employment Act and the Taft-Hartley Act.

The Employment Act. As World War II neared its conclusion, policy planners and public officials began to worry that the conversion from a wartime to a peacetime economy would bring with it a new depression, as had happened after World War I.

Officials in the administration of President Harry S Truman and liberal and labor groups wanted to commit the national government to the use of **fiscal policy** (the government's taxing and spending policies) to create conditions providing full employment.[7] They backed a bill introduced in Congress by Senator James Murray (D.-Mont.) to guarantee a "right to employment" to anyone willing and able to work. To accomplish this goal, Murray proposed that the president submit a "National Production and Employment Budget" to estimate the size of the labor force, the total national production needed to provide jobs for all, and the total investment required to provide that level of production. If the anticipated level of private investment was insufficient to achieve this level of production, then the national government would provide the additional investment and spending needed to reach the goal of full employment.

The Murray proposal ran into strong opposition from a conservative coalition of Republicans and Southern Democrats, egged on by many business groups. They feared that this bill would result in excessive government spending and control of the economy. Conservatives stressed the capacity of the private economy to provide jobs. What finally emerged from Congress as the Employment Act of 1946 was a substantially weakened version of the Murray bill. The declaration of policy in Section 2 of the Employment Act states that "It is the continuing policy and responsibility of the federal government to use all practicable means consistent with its needs and obligations . . . to promote maximum employment, production and purchasing power."

Some policy machinery was established to carry out this policy. A Council of Economic Advisers (CEA), consisting of three professional economists and a small support staff, was created to advise the president on economic issues. The CEA later became quite influential in the Kennedy, Johnson, and Carter administrations. The president was directed to present an annual Economic Report to Congress. In this report, the president analyzed current economic conditions and recommended a program for meeting the Act's goals. Within Congress the Employment Act set up a Joint Economic Committee composed of ten Senators and ten Representatives to consider the president's economic report and to advise the two Houses on its content and recommendations. The Committee also holds hearings and commissions studies on economic policy. In all, the Joint Economic Committee has helped increase the "economic literacy" of Congress.

It is incorrect to dismiss the Employment Act as merely symbolic and without real impact. Its enactment reflected a high level of agreement among the members of Congress and provided a general direction for public policy makers. As economist Herbert Stein states, "It helped put an end to futile, tiresome, and meaningless debate between extremists and cleared the way for practical work to evolve a program" for stabilizing the economy and putting more people to work.[8] Since 1946 the national government has performed the role of overall manager of the economy.

The Taft-Hartley Act. Business and conservative groups, which had stoutly opposed the Wagner Act in 1935, continued to be highly critical of it. When the Republican Party gained control of Congress following the 1946 elections, it got the opportunity to do something about its dissatisfaction with the Wagner Act and labor

---

[7] Stephen A. Bailey, *Congress Makes a Law: The Story Behind the Employment Act of 1946* (New York: Columbia University Press, 1951).

[8] Herbert Stein, *The Fiscal Revolution in America* (Chicago: University of Chicago Press, 1969), p. 204.

union power. Major strikes in the automobile, steel, meat packing, railroad, and other industries in the months following the end of World War II had created negative public feelings toward unions. If organized labor and the Truman administration had been able to agree on moderate labor reform proposals, they might have been able to fend off the drastic changes in labor law contained in the Taft-Hartley Act. They were not, however, and the conservative coalition favoring the Act was strong enough to enact it into law in 1947 over Democratic President Harry S Truman's veto.

Essentially, the Taft-Hartley Act sought to increase the power of management in collective bargaining by imposing a variety of restraints on labor unions while also strengthening management prerogatives. The Act prohibited as unfair a number of union activities, such as featherbedding (requiring that extra employees be assigned to a job), jurisdictional strikes, and coercing employees to join a union. Unions were directed to file detailed reports on their finances and procedures with the Department of Labor. Employees of the national government were absolutely barred from striking. A procedure involving an eighty-day injunction against striking was authorized to help settle strikes that affected the "national health or safety." The closed shop arrangement, under which an employer agreed to hire only union members, was prohibited. A union shop, under which workers had to join the union (or at least pay union dues) within a designated time to retain their jobs, was permitted, except in states that had "right-to-work" laws. These laws, which now exist in about twenty states, provide that union membership or nonmembership cannot be a condition of employment. The result is an open shop. Labor union officials often called the Taft-Hartley Act a "slave labor" law.

Now, decades later, when labor unions have declined in membership and lost some of their political and economic strength (see Figure 15-2, p. 634), it is difficult to imagine the bitterness and intensity of the conflict that for years swirled around the Taft-Hartley Act. It injected government much more deeply into labor-management relations than did the Wagner Act. Conservatives who feared that the Full Employment Act would result in too much government control of the economy shed that concern when the control of labor unions was at stake. Sooner or later, everyone finds government programs of which he or she approves; this is one major reason for the growth and persistence of big government.

The Social Regulation Era

Economists and political scientists frequently distinguish between economic regulation and social regulation. **Economic regulation** focuses on such matters as control of entry into a business, prices or rates of charge, and service routes or areas, and regulation is usually tailored to the conditions of particular industries, such as railroads or stock exchanges. "Simply put, economic regulation places government in the driver's seat with respect to the economic direction and performance of the regulated industry."[9] In contrast, **social regulation** is concerned with such areas as the quality and safety of products and the conditions under which goods are produced and services rendered. Put another way, social regulation strives to protect and enhance the quality of life. Regulation of product safety by the Consumer Product Safety Commission is an example of social regulation. Professor Michael Reagan helps make the distinction between the two kinds of regulation: "Social regulation can generally be differentiated

---

[9] Larry N. Gerston, Cynthia Fraleigh, and Robert Schwab, *The Deregulated Society* (Pacific Grove, CA: Brooks/Cole, 1988). p. 27.

from economic regulation by the former's concern with harm to our physical (and sometimes moral and aesthetic) well-being, rather than harm to our wallets."[10]

Most of the regulatory programs established through the 1950s fell into the category of economic regulation. From the mid-1960s to the mid-1970s, however, a huge wave of social regulatory legislation emanated from the national government on such topics as consumer protection, health and safety, and environmental protection. This legislation generally passed under Congress' authority under the commerce clause.

Several major new regulatory agencies were set up to implement these new social regulations. These agencies include the Consumer Product Safety Commission, the Occupational Safety and Health Administration (OSHA), the Environmental Protection Agency (EPA), the Office of Surface Mining Reclamation and Enforcement, the Mining Enforcement and Safety Administration, and the National Transportation Safety Administration (see Chapter 8). Most of these agencies have jurisdictions that cut across industry lines, in contrast to the industry-focused agencies born during the New Deal.

The social regulatory statutes took various forms. Some had specific targets and goals, such as the Egg Product Inspection Act and the Lead-Based Paint Poison Prevention Act. Others were quite lengthy and detailed, loaded with specific standards, deadlines, and instructions for the administering agency. Illustrative are the Clean Air Act of 1970 and Employee Retirement Income Security Act (intended to protect workers' pensions provided by private employers). Other statutes conferred broad substantive discretion on the implementing agency. Thus, the Occupational Safety and Health Act guarantees workers a safe and healthful workplace, but it contains no health and safety standards with which workplaces must comply. These standards are set through rulemaking proceedings conducted by the Occupational Safety and Health Administration, which also has responsibility for their enforcement. (See Chapter 8.)

As a consequence of this flood of social regulation, many industries that previously had had limited dealings with government now found government regulation to be of major importance in the conduct of their operations. A good example is the automobile industry, which previously had been lightly touched by the antitrust, labor relations, and other general statutes. By the early 1970s, however, the quality of its products were heavily regulated by EPA motor vehicle emissions standards and federally mandated safety standards. The automobile companies found this experience both galling and expensive. The chemical industry found itself in much the same situation.

Four factors contributed to the surge of social regulation.[11] First, the late 1960s and early 1970s were a time of social activism; the consumer and environmental movements were at the peak of their influence. Public interest groups such as the Consumers Union, Common Cause, the Environmental Defense Fund, the Sierra Club, and Ralph Nader's organizations were effective voices for consumer, environmental, and other programs (see Chapter 15). Strong support also came from organized labor.

Second, the public had become much more aware of the dangers to health, safety, and the environment associated with various modern products. Unsafe products had always existed, but their numbers had been multiplied by modern technology. Products widely viewed as unsafe included the chemical DDT, cigarettes, leaded gasoline, poisonous household cleaners, the Chevrolet Corvair, spray cans, phosphates, vinyl chlo-

---

[10] Michael Reagan, *Regulation: The Politics of Policy* (Boston: Little, Brown, 1987), p. 86.
[11] Gerston, Fraleigh, and Schwab, *The Deregulated Society,* pp. 32–34.

ride, lead-based paint, cyclamates, and some forms of intrauterine birth control devices such as the Dalkon Shield. And add to this list the large quantities of toxic substances spewed into the air, dumped in streams and lakes, and buried in the ground. There was, noted one observer, "a level of public consciousness about environmental, consumer, and occupational hazards that appears to be of a different order of magnitude from public outrage over such issues during both the Progressive Era and the New Deal."[12]

Third, members of Congress, aided and abetted by their professional staffs, saw the advocacy of social regulation as a way to gain visibility and national prominence and thus to enhance their election prospects. Some members became policy entrepreneurs. Senator Edmund Muskie (D.-Maine), for example, took the lead on environmental issues, and Senator Warren Magnuson (D.-Wash.) successfully pushed for a number of consumer protection laws.

Fourth, the presidents in office during most of this period—Lyndon B. Johnson and Richard M. Nixon, one a liberal, the other a pragmatic conservative—each gave his support to the social regulation movement. For them, too, it was good politics to be in favor of health, safety, and environmental legislation. Also, in most instances the direct costs to the government of this legislation were minimal.

Deregulation

Even before the wave of social regulation began to wane, deregulation emerged as an attractive political issue. Although this situation may seem paradoxical, there is a fairly simple explanation for what happened. The focus of the deregulation movement was on the economic regulatory programs for such industries as railroads, motor carriers, and commercial air transportation; most social regulatory programs continued to enjoy strong public support and were left largely alone by the deregulation movement.

Beginning in the 1950s and 1960s, economists, political scientists, and journalists began to point out defects in some of the economic regulatory programs.[13] They contended that regulation sometimes produced monopoly profits, discrimination in services, and inefficiency in the operation of regulated industries. Moreover, regulation often made it difficult for industries to compete on the basis of prices and for new competitors to enter the market. For instance, no new major commercial airline was permitted to enter the industry after the Civil Aeronautics Board (CAB) began to regulate the industry in 1938. Consequently, consumers paid higher prices for airfares and had fewer choices than they would in a more competitive market. Regulated firms like the commercial airlines, on the other hand, were comfortable with the higher profits and less competitive rigors of their regulated markets. Critics contended that regulatory commissions like the CAB and the Interstate Commerce Commission were more responsive to the interests of the regulated firms than to the public interest.

For some time nothing changed in the regulatory arena, despite these criticisms. In the mid-1970s, however, President Gerald R. Ford decided to make deregulation a focal point of his administration. He saw regulation as one cause of the inflation that was then besetting the economy. Also, as a conservative Republican he found deregulation consistent with his beliefs in less government and a free market. Along about this time

---

[12] David Vogel, "The 'New' Social Regulation in Historical and Comparative Perspective," in Thomas K. McCraw, ed., *Regulation in Perspective* (Cambridge, MA: Harvard University Press, 1981), p. 160.

[13] A leading study is Martha Derthick and Paul J. Quirk, *The Politics of Deregulation* (Washington, DC: Brookings Institution, 1985).

Senator Edward M. Kennedy (D.-Mass.) became chair of a subcommittee of the Senate Judiciary Committee. Wanting to use his new position and acting on the advice of his staff, he decided to hold hearings on airline deregulation. The combined action of Ford and Kennedy put deregulation on the national policy agenda and got the deregulatory movement underway. Democrats and Republicans, liberals and conservatives, all found deregulation to be an appealing political issue.

Some of the many economists who favored deregulation were appointed to the regulatory commissions. Once on the commissions, they used the discretionary authority available to them to reduce the impact of regulation. This was done, for example, by economist Alfred Kahn, who was appointed chair of the CAB. Commission action of this sort both pressured and made it easier for Congress to act on deregulation. Economists also mustered a substantial body of empirical research showing that efficiency gains would flow from deregulation and, further, that deregulation would not have disruptive effects on the economy, as some opponents argued. Competition was depicted as a beneficent and effective regulator of the economy.[14]

One deregulation act was passed during the Ford administration. Deregulation picked up momentum after Jimmy Carter became president in 1977 and made deregulation a high priority for his administration. Legislation that deregulated aspects of commercial airlines, railroads, motor carriers, and financial institutions was enacted during his term. Two additional deregulation laws were adopted in the early years of the first Reagan administration.

Deregulation usually involved a reduction in the entry, rate, and other controls imposed on an industry. The exception was the Airline Deregulation Act, which completely eliminated economic regulation of commercial airlines over several years. Although many new passenger carriers flocked into the industry when barriers to entry were first removed, they were unable to compete successfully with the existing major airlines. All of these new entrants have now disappeared. Indeed, so have some of the major airlines that were operating at the time of deregulation; consequently there are now fewer major carriers than under the regulatory regime. Competition has lowered some passenger rates, but the extent to which passengers have benefited from deregulation is in dispute because many routes have been abandoned.

The deregulation of the savings and loan business, coupled with the failure of the Reagan administration adequately to enforce the remaining controls on savings and loans, led in time to a costly instance of deregulatory failure. Previously restricted to financing individual homes, deregulation took the lid off of what savings and loans could invest in. As a consequence of poor management, bad commercial investments, and corruption, hundreds of savings and loans, especially in southwestern states, went bankrupt, sometimes to the tune of hundreds of millions of dollars or more.[15] After years of delay, during which the problem got worse, the Bush administration and Congress finally took action. The Financial Institutions Reform, Recovery, and Enforcement Act (1989) revamped the regulatory system for savings and loans, provided for the liquidation of insolvent associations, and bailed out their depositors. Expectations are that the total direct cost to taxpayers of the bailout will be $150 billion to $200 billion. With interest, the cost may increase to $500 billion.[16] Much of the cost of the

---

[14] Ibid., Chapters 1, 2; Dorothy Robyn, *Braking the Special Interests: Trucking Deregulation and the Politics of Policy Reform* (Chicago: University of Chicago Press, 1987), Chapter 4.

[15] Martin Mayer, *The Greatest-Ever Bank Robbery: The Collapse of the Savings and Loan Industry* (New York: Scribner's, 1990).

[16] L. William Seidman, *Full Faith and Credit: The Great S&L Debacle and Other Washington Sagas* (New York: Times Books, 1993). Seidman was in charge of the Resolution Trust Corporation during the early years of the S&L bailout.

bailout could have been avoided by more timely and effective action. What is surprising is that the public has accepted this financial debacle with minimal complaint or criticism.

The pendulum has now completed its deregulatory swing. The broad consensus that made possible "pro-competitive" or economic deregulation does not exist for the field of social regulation. Strong support continues for regulation to protect consumers, workers, and the environment. In some areas in which deregulation occurred, there have been calls to "re-regulate." This has occurred in the airline industry because of concern about its domination by a small number of companies. And in 1992, because of dissatisfaction with the rates charged for service, Congress overrode President Bush's veto and enacted legislation reregulating the cable television business.[17]

In the following sections of this chapter, we take a detailed look at two areas of government regulation of economic activity, both of which are of much interest to most Americans. The first is macroeconomic regulation to influence the overall performance of the economy. The second is regulation to control environmental pollution.

Stabilizing the Economy

Until the early 1930s the prevailing view in the United States was that the country's economy was controlled by natural economic laws that could be disrupted but not improved on by the government. Fluctuations in the economy were accepted with a sense of inevitability. At a Conference on Unemployment sponsored by the national government in 1921, President Warren G. Harding stated the position of the government in his opening remarks: "There has been vast unemployment before and there will be again. There will be depression and inflation just as the tides ebb and flow. I would have little enthusiasm for any proposed remedy that seeks palliation or tonic from the Public Treasury."[18] At the time, it was thought that the best things the government could do if a depression struck would be to increase taxes, cut spending, and balance the budget, or the situation might be made worse by a lack of public confidence in the government's financial condition. This was the tack taken by Herbert Hoover and, for a time, by Franklin D. Roosevelt during the early years of the Great Depression.

The policy change represented by the Employment Act of 1946, which committed the government to maintaining "maximum employment, production and purchasing power," stemmed from a confluence of several factors.[19] First, the massive scale and persistence of the Great Depression refuted the notion that depressions were "self-correcting." Second, new techniques of economic measurement and analysis enabled people to better understand the operation of the economy.

Third, the ideas of the famed English economist, John Maynard Keynes, had gained acceptance and influence. In his *General Theory of Employment, Interests, and Money* (1936) Keynes argued that deficit spending by a government could supplement the total or aggregate demand for goods and services. Government spending would offset a

---

[17] *Congressional Quarterly Weekly Report,* 50 (October 31, 1992): 3518–3521.

[18] Quoted in Robert A. Gordon, *Economic Instability and Growth: The American Record* (New York: Harper & Row, 1974), p. 22.

[19] The following discussion draws on James E. Anderson, David W. Brady, Charles S. Bullock III, and Joseph Stewart Jr., *Public Policy and Politics in America,* 2nd ed. (Monterey, CA: Brooks/Cole, 1984), Chapter 2.

decline in private spending and thus help maintain high levels of spending, production, and employment. During the New Deal the national government engaged in limited deficit spending, which was sometimes referred to as "pump-priming," but it was not sufficient to bring economic recovery. Fourth, World War II brought with it a tremendous increase in government spending and large budget deficits. The economy expanded, production rose, and unemployment fell below 2 percent. The interaction of these factors contributed to the national government's assuming responsibility for maintaining economic stability.

Economic stability can be defined as a situation in which there is economic growth and a rising national income along with high employment and steadiness in the general level of prices. Conversely, economic instability may involve inflation or recession. **Inflation** occurs when there is too much demand for the available supply of goods and services, with the consequence that general price levels rise as buyers compete for the available supply. Prices may also rise if large corporations and unions have sufficient economic power to push prices and wages above competitive levels. A **recession** involves a decline in the economy. Investment sags, production falls off, and unemployment increases.

John Maynard Keynes (1883–1946)

The primary means available to government to maintain economic stability or, if one prefers, to combat instability, are monetary and fiscal policy. Our attention now turns to a discussion of these concepts.

Monetary Policy

Monetary policy, which is a form of macroeconomic regulation, involves regulating a nation's money supply and interest rates. A modern industrial economy operates on the basis of money, which is the medium through which nearly all income and all buying and selling transactions take place. When money is mentioned, most of think of currency and coins, items we can feel, count, and carry in our pockets. But currency and coins are only a small portion of the nation's money supply. The term "money" also includes bank deposits and other financial assets. The Federal Reserve Board has three definitions of **money** based on this broader conception. *M1* (the first definition) includes currency, checking accounts, travelers checks, NOW accounts, and other checkable deposits. *M2* includes all of *M1* plus savings and small time deposits and money market account balances. *M3* includes *M2* plus large time deposits and institutional money market fund balances. The *M2* definition is of the most concern to the Federal Reserve Board.

The Federal Reserve Board has responsibility for the formation and implementation of monetary policy because of its ability to control the credit-creating and lending activities of the nation's banks. When individuals and corporations deposit their money in financial institutions such as commercial banks (which accept deposits and make loans) and savings and loan associations, these deposits serve as the basis for loans to borrowers. In effect, the loaning of money creates new deposits or financial liabilities—new money that did not previously exist. But, we are getting ahead of our story. A look at the Federal Reserve System and its authority is needed at this point.

The Federal Reserve System. Created in 1913 to adjust the money supply to the needs of agriculture, commerce, and industry, the Federal Reserve System comprises the Federal Reserve Board (FRB) (formally, the Board of Governors of the Federal Reserve System; informally, the "Fed"), the Federal Open Market Committee, and the twelve Federal Reserve Banks in regions throughout the country (see Figure 17-1). The Fed represents a mixture of private interests and governmental authority.

722 ❖ Chapter 17 Economic Policy

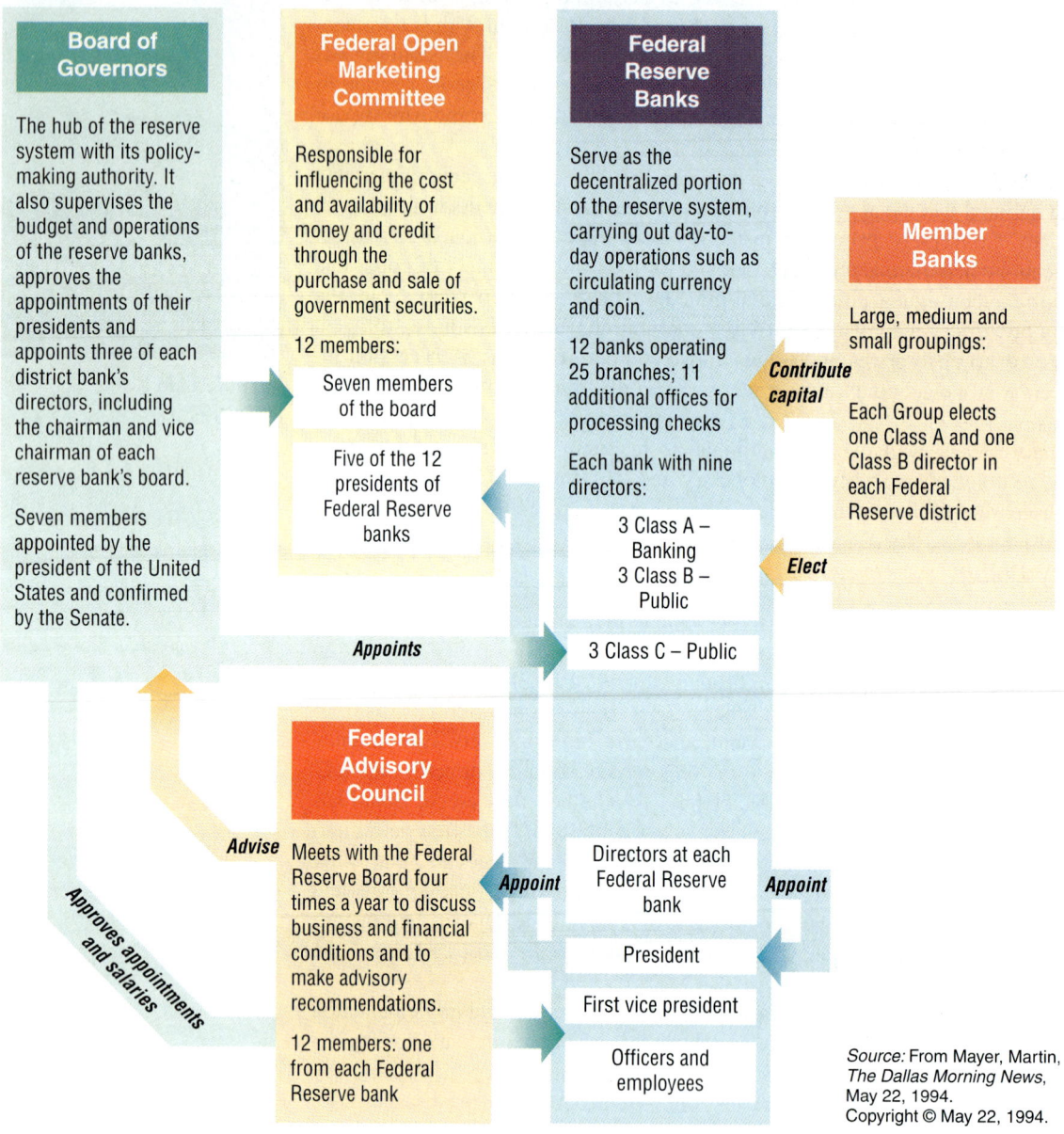

FIGURE 17-1
Inside the Federal Reserve System

Source: From Mayer, Martin, *The Dallas Morning News*, May 22, 1994. Copyright © May 22, 1994.

The Federal Reserve system is the central banking system of the United States. It consists of 12 privately owned regional reserve banks subject to close control by the board of governors in Washington, an agency of the U.S. government. The Federal Reserve banks are not profit-seeking institutions, and they do not deal directly with the general public. They perform services for the U.S. treasury and for deposit institutions—commercial banks, savings banks, savings and loan associations, and credit unions—the operations of which they also regulate. The banks issue the country's paper currency. Through their influence on reserve positions, they control the supply of money and credit.

The seven members of the Federal Reserve Board, who direct the system, are appointed by the president for fourteen-year, overlapping terms with the approval of the Senate. A member can be removed from office by the president for stated causes, but this has never occurred. One board member is designated by the president to serve as chair for a four-year term, which runs from the midpoint of one presidential term to the midpoint of the next to ensure economic stability during a change of administrations. Formally, the FRB has much independence from the executive branch, ostensibly so that monetary policy will not be influenced by political considerations. Defenders of the FRB's independent position assert that monetary policy is too important, complex, and technical to be under the day-to-day control of elected public officials, who might be inclined to make monetary decisions to advance their own short-term political interests (such as being reelected).

At the base of the Federal Reserve System are the twelve Federal Reserve Banks. These are "bankers' banks"; they are formally owned by the Federal Reserve System member banks in each region and they do not do business with the public. A majority of the board of directors of each Federal Reserve Bank is elected by the commercial member banks in its region. The president of a Federal Reserve Bank is selected by its board of directors, not by the president of the United States.

The middle of the Federal Reserve System is occupied by the Federal Open Market Committee (FOMC). This committee consists of twelve members—all seven FRB members, plus five presidents from the Federal Reserve Banks. The representatives from the reserve banks rotate among the twelve regions, except for the New York Federal Reserve Bank. Because of its importance in the financial world, the New York Federal Reserve Bank is always represented on the FOMC.

Alan Greenspan, chairman of the Federal Reserve, testifying before Congress. Because of the enormous power of the "Fed," public statements by its leader are always closely watched. Often, when the chairman testifies to Congress, his statements are examined closely for signals of future changes in monetary policy, and hundreds of private investors react accordingly.

The primary monetary policy tools are the setting of reserve requirements for members banks, control of the discount, and open market operations. Formally, authority to use these tools is allocated to the FRB, the Federal Reserve Bank boards of directors, and the FOMC, respectively. In actuality, however, all three are dominated by the FRB, which, in turn, in recent decades has been under the sway of its chair. Arthur Burns and Paul Volcker (past chairs) and Alan Greenspan, the current chair, have been influential and respected policymakers. Much attention is given by public officials and the financial community to the utterances of the Fed's chair for clues to the future course of monetary policy.

Reserve requirements designate the portion of the banks' deposits that must be retained as backing for their loans. Raising the reserve requirement limits the capacity of banks to make new loans; lowering it enables them to expand their loans. Hypothetically, if the reserve requirement is 10 percent, banks can make more loans on a given amount of deposits than they can if the requirement is raised to 15 percent. When the FRB wants to increase the money supply in circulation it can lower the reserve requirements; to reduce the money supply, it can raise the reserve requirement.

The **discount rate** is the rate of interest at which member banks can borrow money from their regional Federal Reserve Bank when they need additional reserves to support their loans. Raising the discount rate should discourage borrowing by banks to make loans and, in turn, will make loans more costly to persons wanting to borrow money. Conversely, lowering the discount rate should expand the money supply and encourage borrowing both by member banks and by people wanting money to expand business and for other purposes. The assumption here is that what people do will be directly affected by whether interest rates are higher or lower.

Open market operations involve the buying and selling of government securities by the FRB in the market, that is, wherever government securities are bought and sold.

Government securities are interest-bearing bonds that are regularly bought and sold by investors in their quest for profits. When the FRB buys securities in the market, it ultimately pays for them by creating deposits for the sellers in the federal reserve banks. These deposits serve as additional reserves for commercial banks and enable them to expand their loans to borrowers. On the other hand, when the FRB sells government securities in the market, the buyers' payments for them are deducted from commercial banks reserve accounts, reducing these reserves and thus the capacity of banks to lend money to their customers. As a rule of thumb, when the FRB buys securities, it expands the money supply; when the FRB sells securities, it restricts, or "tightens," the money supply. Open market operations are the tools the FRB uses most frequently because of their flexibility and direct impact.

Moral suasion refers to the capacity of the FRB to influence the actions of banks and other members of the financial community by suggestion, exhortation, and informal agreement. Because of its commanding position as a monetary policy maker, much attention and respect are given by the media, economists and market observers to verbal signals about economic trends and conditions emitted by the FRB and its chair.

How the FRB uses these policy tools depends in part on how they perceive the state of the economy. (Here we should note that much more is known about the condition of the economy six months ago than about its current state because of lags in the availability of needed data). If inflation appears to be the problem, than the Fed would likely restrict or tighten the money supply. The Fed could raise the reserve requirement and the discount rate and could sell government securities in the market. If a recession with rising unemployment appears to threaten the economy, then the FRB would probably act to loosen or expand the money supply in order to stimulate the economy. The Fed could lower the reserve and discount rates and could buy government securities in the market. In the early 1990s the Fed continually lowered interest rates to counteract a recession. Then, in early 1994, as the economy gained momentum, the FRB began to worry about inflation and acted several times to nudge up interest rates, somewhat to the consternation of Clinton administration officials.[20] Such short-term actions are often characterized as "leaning against the wind."[21]

The President and the FRB. Although the public generally holds the president responsible for maintaining a healthy economy, he does not really possess adequate constitutional or legal authority to meet this obligation. Responsibility for fiscal policy is shared with Congress, and the FRB is authorized by Congress to make monetary policy. In the area of monetary policy presidential power is truly "the power to persuade." There are many informal contacts between the White House and the FRB, however, such as during periodic luncheon meetings, at which monetary policy is discussed. More formal meetings also take place. A group called the Quadriad, which consists of the Secretary of the Treasury, the Director of the Office of Management and Budget, the Chair of the Council of Economic Advisers, and the Chair of the Federal Reserve Board, has met with varying frequency with the president since the time of the Kennedy administration. These meetings allow the president to express his views on monetary policy to the FRB. In turn, the FRB chair can convey some of his views on

---

[20] *Time* (March 7, 1994): 42.

[21] William Greider, *Secrets of the Temple: How the Federal Reserve Runs the Country* (New York: Simon & Schuster, 1987), Chapter 10.

the economy to the administration. In all, there is quite a bit of contact and cooperation between the White House and the FRB. The result of this activity is that the monetary policy made by the FRB is customarily acceptable to the president, even if it is not precisely what he would prefer.[22]

Fiscal Policy

Fiscal policy involves the deliberate use of the national government's taxing and spending policies to influence the overall operation of the economy and maintain economic stability. Fiscal policy is formulated by the president and Congress and is conducted through the federal budget process. The powerful instruments of fiscal policy are budget surpluses and deficits. These are achieved by manipulating the overall or "aggregate" levels of revenue and expenditures.

According to standard fiscal policy theory, at some level of total or aggregate spending, the economy will operate at a full employment level. Total spending is the sum of consumer spending, private investment spending, and government spending. If consumer and business spending does not create demand sufficient to cause the economy to operate at full employment, then the government should make up the shortfall by increasing spending in excess of revenues. This was essentially what Keynes recommended that the national government should do during the Great Depression. If inflation is the problem confronting policy makers, then government can reduce demand for goods and services by reducing its expenditures and running a budget surplus.[23]

Discretionary fiscal policy involves deliberate decisions by the president and Congress to run budget surpluses or deficits. This can be done by increasing or decreasing spending while holding taxes constant; by increasing or cutting taxes while holding spending stable; or by some combination of changes in tax and expenditure.

The first significant application of fiscal policy theory occurred in 1964. When John F. Kennedy, an activist president committed to getting the country "moving again," took office in 1961, he brought Keynesian economists to Washington as his economic advisers. (See "People of the Past: Walter Heller," p. 726). These advisers believed that government action was needed to stimulate the economy in order to achieve full employment, and they were able to convince President Kennedy of this. The need, as they saw it, was for a budget deficit to add to aggregate demand. The problem was, however, that budget deficits were strongly opposed by many conservatives as bad public policy and perhaps even as immoral. Thinking strategically, President Kennedy's advisors decided that many conservatives and members of the business community would find deficits more palatable, or less objectionable, if they were achieved by cutting taxes rather than by increasing government spending. (Businesses had been complaining about high taxes.) Furthermore, a tax cut would increase private sector spending on goods and services. Higher government spending, on the other hand, would mean more spending on public goods and services and bigger government.

The result was the adoption of the Revenue Act of 1964, which reduced personal and corporate income tax rates. This variant of fiscal policy, which was more acceptable to the business community, has been labeled "commercial Keynesianism." The

---

[22] This is the conclusion reached by John T. Woolley, *Monetary Politics: The Federal Reserve and the Politics of Monetary Policy* (New York: Cambridge University Press, 1984).

[23] Anderson et al., pp. 38–40.

PEOPLE OF THE PAST

Walter Heller

Walter Heller with President John F. Kennedy

Walter Heller was the most influential economist in Washington through much of the 1960s. He is given a great deal of credit for the adoption of modern Keynesian techniques of economic management in the United States. For Heller, policy makers spent the Eisenhower years foolishly clinging to balanced budgets. As chairman of President John F. Kennedy's Council of Economic Advisers, Heller was a tireless advocate of the aggressive use of fiscal policy to stimulate economic growth. His policy prescription went beyond the notion of using a fiscal stimulus to get out of recessions; he proposed that it be used to eliminate slack in the economy altogether, even when the economy was not in recession. As CEA chairman, Heller kept up a steady flow of information to Kennedy on the state of the economy and the benefits that would accrue from a tax cut. Heller served, in effect, as the president's tutor—educating him in the "new economics" and persuading him to push Congress to adopt a tax cut. His persistence bore fruit with the passage of the Tax Reduction Act of 1965.

Heller received his undergraduate degree from Oberlin College and his Ph.D. from the University of Wisconsin in 1941. His career was split between academia and government service. After working in the Treasury Department, he taught for many years at the University of Minnesota. He then held several posts as an economic adviser in the federal government until he was named chairman of the CEA. Heller was described in *Current Biography* in 1961 as a "practical economist interested in public service" and as one who "brings to 'the dismal science' a light and lucid touch." He died in 1987 at the age of seventy-six.

tax-cut stimulus contributed to expansion of the economy through the remainder of the 1960s and reduced the unemployment rate to less than 4 percent, its lowest peacetime rate and what many people then considered to be full employment.[24]

In 1968 Congress enacted a tax increase at the urging of the Johnson administration in order to restrain inflation, which was stimulated by increased spending for Great Society programs and the Vietnam War. The tax increase contributed to a balanced budget in fiscal year 1969, the last year in which the national budget has been balanced. Tax changes were also used during the 1970s to stabilize the economy. Since the early 1980s, however, the government has incurred large annual budget deficits. These deficits can be viewed either as "neutralizing" fiscal policy, because they have politically foreclosed most major alterations in taxing and spending rates, or as a source of continuing stimulation to the economy.[25] Consequently, much of the burden of economic stabilization has been placed on FRB and monetary policy.

---

[24] James D. Savage, *Balanced Budgets and American Politics* (Ithaca, NY: Cornell University Press, 1988), pp. 176–179.

[25] Herbert Stein, *Presidential Economics: The Making of Economic Policy from Roosevelt to Reagan and Beyond* (New York: Simon & Schuster, 1984), pp. 290–291.

What we have discussed thus far is discretionary fiscal policy, so called because public officials must make overt decisions concerning its use. There are also some automatic stabilizers that have been built into the economy, whether intentionally or unintentionally, that operate without decisions by policy makers. These automatic stabilizers "act as buffers when the economy weakens by automatically reducing taxes and increasing government spending."[26] When the economy declines, for example, mandatory spending for such programs as unemployment insurance, food stamps, and Medicaid increases because eligibility for benefits depends on people's income or employment status. The tax system also acts as an automatic stabilizer. When the economy slows down and personal income and corporate profits decline, tax payments fall and help reduce the decline in after-tax incomes that would otherwise occur.[27] Conversely, when the economy revives, taxes begin to take a bigger bite out of incomes and thus help hold down spending. Although the automatic stabilizers are helpful in mitigating economic fluctuations, they are by themselves inadequate to stabilize the economy.

The Budgetary Process

The Budget and Accounting Act of 1921 gave the president authority to prepare an annual budget and submit it to Congress for approval. A staff agency now called the Office of Management and Budget (OMB) was created to assist the president and handle the details of budget preparation (see also Chapter 7). The budget runs for a single fiscal year, now beginning on October 1 of one calendar year and running through September 30 of the following calendar year. The fiscal year takes its name from the calendar year in which it ends; thus, the time period from October 1, 1995, through September 30, 1996, is designated fiscal year (FY) 1996. An overview of where the federal government gets its money and how the money gets spent is presented in Figure 17-2.

The president sends his budget to Congress in January or February of each year. Work on the budget within the executive branch will have begun nine or ten months earlier, however. (Table 17.1 indicates the timing of budget actions.) Acting in accordance with presidential decision on the general structure of the budget, the OMB provides the various departments and agencies with instructions and guidance on presidential priorities to help them in preparing their budget requests. The departments and agencies then proceed to develop their detailed funding requests. Each agency believes in the value and necessity of its set of programs and seeks to expand or at least maintain its budget. The OMB's role, on the other hand, is to put together a budget that reflects the president's preferences and priorities. Consequently, agency budget requests are frequently modified and revised downward by the OMB. Agencies that are aggrieved by OMB reductions may try to appeal these decisions to president. If this happens, the president usually agrees with the OMB. During the early years of the Reagan administration this traditional "bottom-up" process of preparing the budget, in which the agencies' requests shape the budget, was replaced by a "top-down" process. In "top-down" budgeting, directives from the president and the OMB dominate the budgetary process.[28]

---

[26] *Annual Report of the Council of Economic Advisers, 1993* (Washington, DC: Government Printing Office, 1993), p. 108.

[27] Ibid., p. 109.

[28] This discussion of budgeting draws on James E. Anderson, *Public Policymaking: An Introduction*, 2nd ed. (Boston: Houghton Mifflin, 1994), Chapter 5.

728 ❖ Chapter 17 Economic Policy

FIGURE 17-2

The Federal Government Dollar: Fiscal Year 1995 Estimates

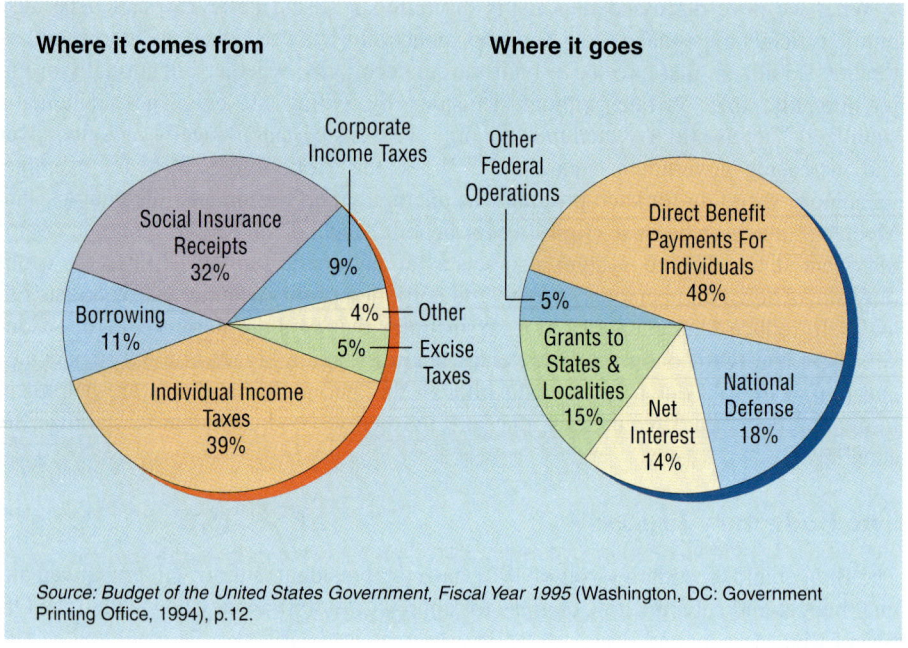

Source: *Budget of the United States Government, Fiscal Year 1995* (Washington, DC: Government Printing Office, 1994), p.12.

Article I of the Constitution provides that "no money shall be drawn from the Treasury, but in consequence of appropriations made by law." Congress and its legislative committees (such as the committees on natural resources, education and labor, and the armed services) may authorize that money be spend on programs, but it is Congress *and* the appropriations committees that actually provide the funding needed to carry out these programs. The appropriations committees often deny some, and once in a while all, of the funding authorized by the legislative committees. Consequently, the legislative committees sometimes have resorted to backdoor spending—authorizing agencies to borrow money from the Treasury or creating entitlement programs that make funding mandatory in order to circumvent the appropriations committees.[29]

Conflicts often develop between Congress and the president over both the details of the budget and its overall dimensions, such as the size of the deficit or the balance between military and domestic spending. Throughout the 1980s there was conflict between the Democrats in Congress, who favored more domestic spending and less military spending, and President Ronald Reagan and his administration, whose spending preferences leaned in the opposite direction. In 1993 the Clinton administration touched off a titanic partisan political struggle in Congress with its budget deficit-reduction plan involving a combination of spending cuts and tax increases. Drawing almost unanimous opposition from the Republicans in Congress also from some conservative Democrats, the Clinton proposal was passed by Vice President Albert Gore Jr.'s tie-breaking vote in the Senate and by a margin of two votes in the House.[30] The Clinton administration, moreover, had to make many deals with members of Congress in order to secure the votes needed to adopt its budget proposal.

[29] Donald F. Kettl, *Deficit Politics: Public Budgeting in Its Institutional and Historical Context* (New York: Macmillan, 1992), pp. 140–141.
[30] *Congressional Quarterly Weekly Report* (August 7, 1993): 2122–2129.

Table 17.1 ♦ The Federal Budget Process

First Monday in February	Congress receives the President's budget
February 15	Congressional Budget Office (CBO) reports to the Budget Committees on fiscal policy and budget priorities, including an analysis of the President's budget
February 25	Congressional committees submit views and estimates on spending to the Budget Committee.
April 1	Budget committees report concurrent resolution on the budget, which sets a total for budget outlays, an estimate of expenditures for major budget categories, and the recommended level of revenues. This resolution acts as an agenda for the remainder of the budgetary process.
April 15	Congress completes action on concurrent resolution on the budget.
May 15	Annual appropriations bills may be considered in the House.
June 10	House Appropriations Committee completes action on regular appropriations bills.
June 15	Congress completes action on reconciliation legislation, bringing budget totals into conformity with established ceilings.
June 30	House completes action on all appropriations bills.
October 1	The new fiscal year begins.

Source: Adapted from Howard E. Shuman, *Politics and the Budget,* 3rd edition (Englewood Cliffs, NJ: Prentice Hall, 1992) p. 67.

As with other legislation, appropriations bills passed by Congress need the president's approval to become law. Conventional wisdom once held that appropriations bills were "veto proof" because they provided the funds necessary to keep the government in operation. However, Presidents Richard M. Nixon and Gerald R. Ford both vetoed appropriations bills that they called "budget-busting" and inflationary because more funds were appropriated for some programs than the presidents wanted. These bills were later enacted into law after appropriations were reduced in an effort to meet presidential preferences.

The use of the budget as a part of fiscal policy to counteract fluctuations in the economy is handicapped by the fact that planning begins roughly a year-and-a-half before the beginning of the fiscal year in which it is to take effect. Once a budget is adopted, it takes time to implement its provisions. Add to this the difficulty of predicting the future state of the economy and one discovers that the budget—which embodies changes in taxing and spending rates—is a rather blunt instrument for manipulating the economy.

For many years the budgetary process was a fragmented and disjointed operation. Appropriations and revenue decisions were considered separately by different committees. For purposes of congressional consideration and enactment, the president's budget was (and still is) divided into 13 appropriations bills, each of which was handled by a different subcommittee of the House Appropriations Committee, where the most intensive examinations was accorded budget requests. Each of the bills was also considered separately in the Senate Appropriations Committee. The 13 appropriations bills were eventually enacted into law one by one. This disjointed process created two problems. First, it was difficult to establish spending priorities between domestic and military programs or among the many domestic programs. Second, the determination of total revenues and expenditures, and, consequently, the size of the budget surplus or deficit was accidental, something that simply happened rather than being planned.

This disjointed system differed markedly from the centralized process that prevails in Great Britain. Although there are complaints about interminable budget wrangles, departmental egoism, and runaway expenditures, the British executive has a much firmer grasp on the budgetary process than does the U.S. president. The weaknesses of the House of Commons as a legislative body, when combined with the strong control exercised by Her Majesty's Treasury over all of the critical components of the budgetary process, provides the prime minister with a much more manageable arena in which to operate and dominate.

To provide itself with more control over the budget process, Congress initiated and enacted the Budget and Impoundment Control Act of 1974. The Act establishes a budget process that includes setting overall levels of revenues and expenditures, the size of the budget surplus or deficit, and priorities among different "functional" areas (e.g., national defense, transportation, agriculture, foreign aid, and health). New budget committees were established in the House and Senate to perform these tasks. The Congressional Budget Office (CBO), a professional staff of technical experts, was created to assist the budget committees and to provide members of Congress with their own source of budgetary information so they would be more independent of OMB.

The budget committees hold hearings on the president's proposed budget, soliciting advice from the OMB and CBO, executive agencies, and other members of Congress. The committees then formulate a concurrent budget resolution that set targets for overall levels of revenues and spending, and ceilings for each functional area in the budget. The budget resolution is supposed to be completed by April 15, although this deadline is often missed. Once the concurrent budget resolution is adopted (it does not require the president's approval), the House and Senate appropriations committees and their subcommittees are expected to act within its limits when making their decisions on the details of appropriations requests by various agencies. In most years, reconciliation legislation is necessary to ensure that the revenue and spending targets in the budget resolution are actually met. The reconciliation process requires the taxation and legislative committees to propose changes in existing tax laws and entitlement programs, such as Medicare and food stamps. Typically, these changes involve cutting spending and increasing taxes by specified amounts. The budget committees then consolidate these proposed changes into a single reconciliation bill, which must be passed by both houses. Unlike the budget resolution, which is an internal congressional matter, the reconciliation bill requires presidential approval. Reconciliation legislation makes permanent changes in the laws involving the affected policies and program. For instance, taxes may be increased or the benefits available under an entitlement program may be lowered.[31] Overall growth in both entitlements and discretionary spending are shown in Figure 17-3.

Legislative action on all appropriations bills is supposed to be completed by October 1, the start of the fiscal year. More often than not, however, some appropriations bills have not emerged from Congress by this date. When this happens the Congress

---

[31] John Cranford, *Budgeting for America,* 2nd ed. (Washington, DC: CQ Press, 1989), pp. 197–198.

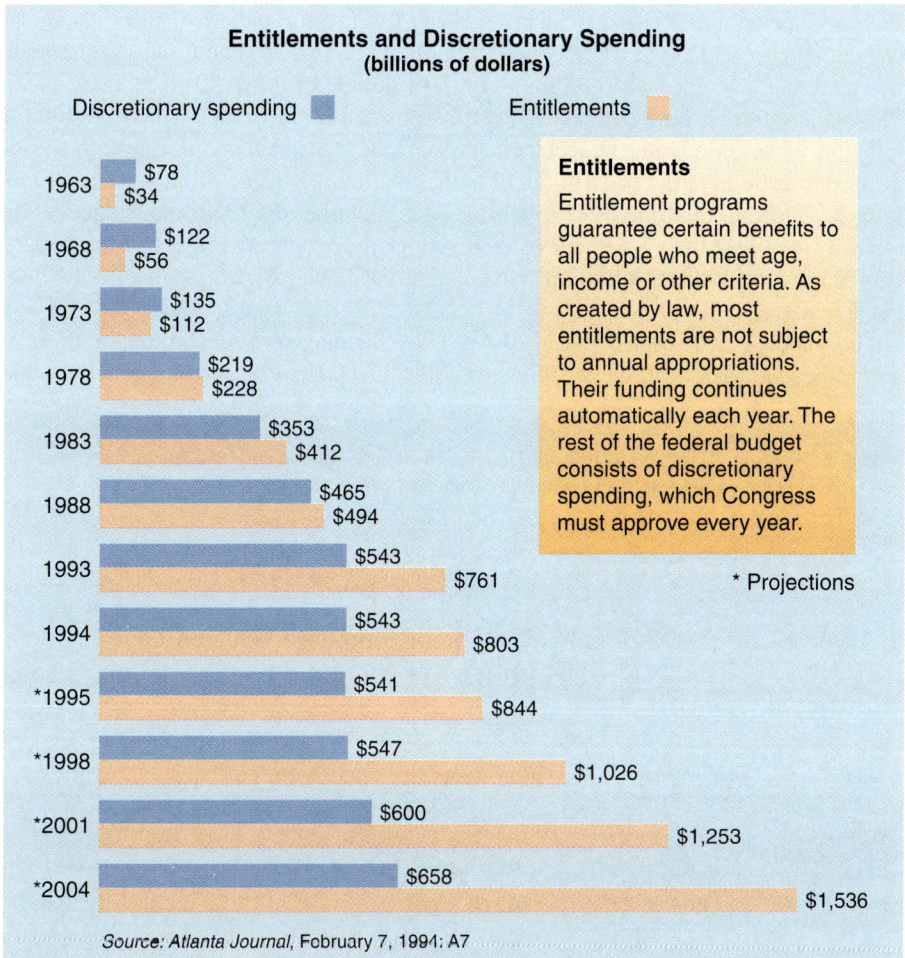

FIGURE 17-3

Entitlements and Discretionary Spending

must pass a continuing resolution, which authorizes agencies to continue operating on the basis of last year's appropriation until their new appropriation is enacted. This procedure can cause some uncertainty in agency operations.

The budget process put in place in 1974 was intended to make the national budgetary process more rational, comprehensive, and coherent. To some extent it has done that. It has also compelled members of Congress to consider the overall dimensions of the budget and to directly confront the deficit. It has not done much to help Congress balance the budget, however.

The Deficit and the Debt

Large annual budget deficits and a rapidly growing national debt (which is the cumulation of the annual budget deficits) have characterized government finance during the past decade and a half. Several factors have contributed to this situation: a severe recession in the early 1980s; the large tax cut enacted in 1981; sharply increased spending for national defense during the 1980s; and continuously expanding spending on such entitlement programs as Social Security, Medicare, and Medicaid.[32] National budget deficits, which rarely exceeded $60 billion before 1980 and usually were much less than that, averaged $150 billion during the decade of the 1980s (see Table 17.2). These dollar figures have increased in part because of inflation. One way to control for inflation when comparing budget deficits is to view the deficits as a percentage of **gross domestic product** (GDP). (GDP is the total market value of all goods and services produced in the United States during a year.) During the 1960s the budget deficit typically was less than 1 percent of GDP, compared with between 3 to 5 percent of GDP during the 1980s. This comparison also reveals a major increase in absolute budget deficit levels.

The national debt tripled during the 1980s. Standing at $908 billion in 1980, it soared beyond $2.87 trillion in 1989 (see Table 17.1). (In 1994 the national debt was

---

[32] Paul E. Peterson, "The New Politics of Deficits," in John E. Chubb and Paul E. Peterson, eds., *The New Direction in American Politics* (Washington, DC: Brookings Institution, 1985), Chapter 13.

Table 17.2 ♦ National Government Finances, Selected Years, 1940–1994 (billions of current dollars)

YEAR	RECEIPTS	OUTLAYS	SURPLUS OR DEFICIT	NATIONAL DEBT
1940	6.5	9.5	–2.9	50.7
1945	45.2	92.7	–47.6	260.1
1950	39.4	42.6	–3.1	256.9
1955	65.5	68.4	–3.0	274.4
1960	92.5	92.2	0.3	290.5
1965	116.8	118.2	–1.4	322.3
1970	192.8	195.6	–2.8	380.9
1975	279.1	332.3	–53.2	541.9
1980	517.1	590.9	–72.7	908.5
1985	734.1	946.4	–212.3	1817.0
1988	909.0	1064.1	–155.2	2600.8
1989	990.7	1143.2	–152.5	2867.5
1990	1031.3	1252.7	–221.4	3206.2
1991	1054.3	1323.8	–269.5	3598.3
1992	1090.5	1380.9	–290.4	4001.9
1993	1153.5	1408.2	–254.7	4351.2
1994*	1249.1	1483.8	–234.8	4676.0

*Estimates

Source: Annual Report of the Council of Economic Advisers, 1994 (Washington, DC: Government Printing Office, 1994), p. 359.

nearly $4.7 trillion.) Measured against GDP, the national debt increased from 34 to 55 percent of GDP during the 1980s (Figure 17-4). Interest payments on the national debt now account for about 15 percent of the national budget. It may make the reader feel better to know that, while the national debt has grown, so has the value of the national government's assets—including land, buildings, military installations, and equipment. According to one calculation, the government's assets approximately equaled its liabilities in 1960; by 1980 assets exceeded liabilities by $279 billion.[33] But a massive selloff of assets is highly unlikely.

Strong partisan conflict and policy differences between the Democrats in Congress and the Reagan administration over the size and composition of the budget made reduction of the budget deficit impossible through conventional budgetary procedures. The alarming size of the deficits and public concern over them pushed Congress into taking extraordinary action in 1985. Called "a bad idea whose time had come," the Balanced Budget and Emergency Deficit Reduction Act created a procedure for auto-

[33] Robert Eisner and Paul J. Peiper, "A New View of the Federal Debt and Budget Deficits," *American Economic Review,* 74 (March 1994): 23.

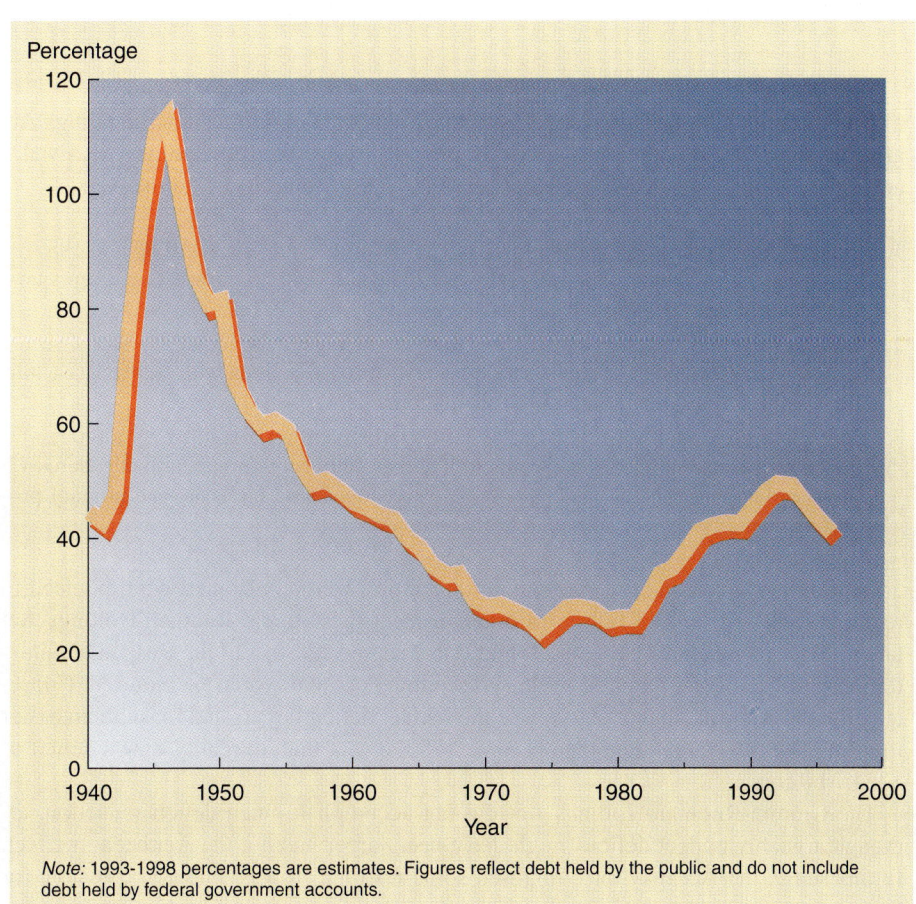

FIGURE 17-4

The National Debt as a Percentage of GDP, 1940–1998

Note: 1993-1998 percentages are estimates. Figures reflect debt held by the public and do not include debt held by federal government accounts.

Sources: 1940–1992: Office of Management and Budget, *Budget Baselines, Historical Data, and Alternatives for the Future* (Washington, DC: U.S. Government Printing Office, 1993), p. 1346. 1993–1998: Office of Management and Budget, *Budget of the U.S. Government Fiscal Year 1994* (Washington, DC: U.S. Government Printing Office, 1993), p. 32.

Senators (left to right) Warren B. Rudman (R.-N.H.), Phil Gramm (R.-Tex.), and Ernest F. Hollings (D.-S.C.), who cosponsored a 1985 law that attempted to control spiraling deficits. The budget process has proven very difficult to control, however, and their original statute was revised and superseded by the budget agreement of 1990.

matic deficit reduction. This Act is better known as the Gramm-Rudman-Hollings Act after its three Senate sponsors—Phil Gramm (R.-Tex.), Warren Rudman, (R.-N.H.), and Ernest Hollings, (D.-S.C.). There were three basic components to the Act:

1. Budget deficit goals of $171.9 billion and $144 billion were set for 1986 and 1987. After that, the deficit goal would be lowered annually by $36 million decrements until it reached zero in 1991.
2. Several programs were exempted from automatic budget cuts, including Social Security, Medicaid, veterans' benefits, food stamps, Aid to Families with Dependent Children, child nutrition, and interest on the national debt.
3. If at the *beginning* of a fiscal year the deficit target was not met, then, by a process called sequestration (Congress seems to like these clumsy terms), automatic, across-the-board budget cuts, divided equally between nonexempt domestic and military programs, would be levied, sufficient to meet the deficit target.

In 1987 Congress and the Reagan administration were confronted with the need to reduce the deficit by $45 billion in order to meet the Gramm-Rudman-Hollings Act target. Most members of Congress found this disagreeable, as did the Reagan administration because of the required military spending cuts that would be required. Consequently, the Act was amended to revise the budget deficit targets and make them easier to meet. The zero target date then became 1993, a year that, in reality, saw a deficit of $254.7 billion.

The Gramm-Rudman-Hollings Act did not accomplish much deficit reduction, although arguably budget deficits might have been larger had not the Act been in effect. In this sense, the Act may have imposed some restraint. It was, however, possible for Congress to avoid the requirements of the Act. Deficit targets set by Congress can be altered by Congress, as they were in 1987. Budget gimmickry, or "blue smoke and mirrors," was also resorted to, as in the following instance:

In 1989, for example, budget makers agreed to change the Pentagon's payday from the first day of the month to the last day of the month. Checks that would have been distributed on fiscal 1990 New Year's Day, Oct 1, 1989 (and counted against the fiscal 1990 deficit), were distributed instead on the last day of fiscal 1989, September 30. The government thus *reduced* the fiscal 1990 deficit by billions of dollars and made the job of hitting the Gramm-Rudman targets for the year that much easier. The deficit for fiscal 1989, of course, was *increased* by the exact same amount, but for Gramm-Rudman purposes, this did not matter. The "snapshot" for the fiscal 1989 deficit [whether it met the budget deficit target] had been taken a year before, and changes made after that snapshot did not matter. The result: absolutely no real effect on the government's financial condition, but apparent progress in reducing the budget deficit.[34]

Also used were optimistic forecasts ("rosy scenarios") of future economic conditions (on which estimated spending and revenue levels are based) that deceptively underestimated the size of the budget deficit that would actually result.

The Gramm-Rudman-Hollings Act was extensively revised and extended by the Budget Enforcement Act of 1990, which was negotiated by Bush administration officials and congressional leaders. As amended in 1993, the Budget Enforcement Act (BEA) runs through fiscal year 1998.[35] It seeks to lower deficits by imposing controls on spending. The BEA distinguishes between discretionary spending, which is controlled through annual appropriations, and direct spending, which is also called mandatory spending. Approximately two-thirds of national spending falls into the direct or mandatory category, with monies going mostly for entitlement programs and interest on the national debt.

The Act sets annual spending limits for discretionary spending, which can be adjusted for inflation and emergencies. If it is estimated that discretionary spending during a year will exceed the specified limit, then most programs will be reduced by an across-the-board cut, or sequester, sufficient to bring spending programs and the revenues for them into balance. Direct or mandatory spending is constrained by "pay-as-you-go" rules. The cumulative effects of legislation changing direct spending or receipts must not increase the budget deficit. For instance, a legislative increase in benefit payments under an entitlement program would have to be offset by either revenue increases or payment reductions in other entitlement programs. Under the Budget Enforcement Act and because of the efforts of the Clinton administration, there has been modest progress in reducing the budget deficit.

Most likely, however, the BEA, or any similar effort, will not eliminate the budget deficit. Such approaches essentially involve an attempt to contrive a procedural solution for a substantive problem. The deficit exists because people in the United States like receiving the benefits and services of government programs more than they like paying taxes to finance them. Government officials reflect this ambivalence in their behavior. There is no easy, painless way to balance the budget, although the alternatives can be quickly stated: increase taxes, cut spending, or use a combination of the two. All the decision makers have to determine is which taxes to raise or which spending programs to cut. The difficulties in doing that account for the existing budget situation and continue to handicap the quest for a solution.

---

[34] Kettl, *Deficit Politics*, p. 100.

[35] This discussion is based on *Budget of the United States, Fiscal Year 1995: Analytical Perspectives* (Washington, DC: Government Printing Office, 1994), pp. 423–424.

The Economics of Regulating Environmental Pollution

A large number and variety of the national government's economic policies entail some sort of direct control of or restriction on private economic activity. These economic regulatory policies are variously intended to prevent or mitigate actions and conditions regarded as unfair, undesirable, unhealthy, and/or immoral. Collectively, they comprise an extensive framework of rules governing the conduct of private (and occasionally public) economic activity. Here, we focus on one important segment of this web of regulatory policies—regulation of environmental activity to protect the public health and the national environment.

Until the late 1960s the national government was only minimally involved in the control of environmental pollution. The national government had long been concerned with the conservation of natural resources and the management of public lands—national forests, national parks, and grazing lands in the western states. However, air and water pollution were seen as matters for the state and local governments to handle, if they so chose. But few states opted to do this—indeed, many states did little or nothing to control pollution in the pre-World War II decades of the twentieth century. Pollution was not perceived as a problem, partly because the environment had considerable capacity to absorb wastes without great harm to people. Also, the volume of pollution was lower than it would become in later years.

Population growth, increased urbanization, industrialization, and the extensive production and use of chemicals after World War II changed this situation. Environmentalist J. Clarence Davies provided an explanation:

> The massive growth in production and in the availability of resources which have characterized the American economy . . . affect the problem of pollution in several ways. The increase in production has contributed to an intensification of the degree of actual pollution; the increase in the standard of living has permitted people the comparative luxury of being able to be concerned about this; and the availability of ample public and private resources has given the society sufficient funds and skilled manpower to provide the potential for dealing with the problem.[36]

In the course of the 1960s the problem of environmental pollution became a prominent item on the national political agenda. Because of strong public concern it continues to have that status.

Pollution involves the discharge into the environment of harmful and noxious substances—chemicals, human and animal waste, and other contaminants—that prevent or interfere with desired human uses of the air, water, and soil. Chemicals discharged into streams, for example, make them unsafe as sources of drinking water or for recreational purposes. (The fish often don't fare too well, either.) Because this definition of pollution hinges on *human* use (which is not limited to consumption of environmental resources), it implies that desirable levels of environmental quality will depend on preferred uses. Thus, the quality of water that should be maintained in a given river depends on whether it is to be used as a source of drinking water or for fishing and swimming, transportation, or waste disposal. Much cleaner water is required for the

---

[36] J. Clarence Davies, *The Politics of Pollution,* 2nd ed. (Indianapolis: Bobbs-Merrill, 1975), p. 7.

river if it is used as a source of drinking water than primarily as a medium of transportation. The levels of water quality required for particular uses can be scientifically determined (although in practice scientists often disagree); whether a particular level of quality *should* be sought is a political issue over which various prospective users of our hypothetical river disagree.

Pollution interferes with human uses of the environment in various ways. Pollution may make the air unsafe to breathe, especially for people with respiratory ailments, or water unsafe to drink. Bodies of water may become unsafe or uninhabitable for fish populations for human consumption. Lake Erie, for example, became nearly a "dead" body of water in the 1970s because of industrial pollution. Damage to forest, crops, and property may occur from pollution. Natural curiosities may be damaged, and scenic vistas may be obscured. In the 1980s air pollution often made it impossible to see across the Grand Canyon. Because Americans seem health conscious, the effects of pollution on human health often attract the greatest attention from policy makers.

Environmental Policy Making

Pollution control is the responsibility of government operating through the policy process. The market, which works through competition and the price system, is unable to deal satisfactorily with the problem of pollution. As economists tell us, pollution is an *externality*, or a *social cost* of industrial activity. This is so because, in the nature of things, air and water are "free" or public goods. Industries can dispose of wastes (pollutants) at low or no cost by emitting them into the air or dumping them into nearby bodies of water. Consequently, the costs of waste disposal are borne by the people adversely affected by the wastes, for example, by people who breathe the air or use the water. Because the costs of waste disposal do not need to be considered in determining the prices of products, industries can sell—and consumers can buy—products at lower prices. A business has no incentive to clean up its pollutants because this action would drive up its expenses and thus the prices it charges. Moreover, if a business did clean

In western states, strip mining operations have been the subject of protests since the 1960s. In this type of mining, whole layers of soil are stripped away in order to leach out minerals. Strip mines have been blamed for a host of environmental problems, from soil erosion, to pollution of the water table.

up its pollutants, this would put it at an economic disadvantage with competitors who chose not to stand the costs of pollution reduction. Consequently, in the absence of government action, control of pollution is unlikely to occur.

The organized groups supporting environmental protection have greatly increased in number, membership size, technical skill, and political sophistication since the early 1970s. Such well-known groups as the Wilderness Society, the Sierra Club, the National Wildlife Federation, the Environmental Defense Fund, and the Natural Resources Defense Council constitute the core of the environmental movement. They are flanked on the left by more radical groups like Earth First! and Greenpeace, who take direct action to protect the environment.[37] On the right, the Nature Conservancy works through the marketplace, buying land valuable for natural resources protection and thus removing it from business use. These and other environmental groups have been major forces pushing Congress to enact new environmental legislation and to strengthen existing laws. During the years of the Reagan administration, which was skeptical toward environmental and pollution control programs, environmental groups thrived. Professors Norman J. Vig and Michael E. Kraft explain:

> Paradoxically, Reagan actually strengthened environmental forces in the nation. Through his lax enforcement of pollution laws and pro-development policies, he created political issues around which national and grass-roots environmental groups could organize. They appealed successfully to a public that was increasingly disturbed by the health and environmental risks of industrial society and by threats to ecological stability. As a result, membership in environmental organizations soared and a new grass-roots activism developed, creating further political incentives for environmental activism at all levels of government.[38]

Environmental groups have also benefited from strong public opinion in support of pollution control.

Conflicts over pollution control legislation typically become a struggle between liberal environmental groups and their supporters (organized labor usually takes a pro-pollution-control stance) and business groups and conservatives favoring fewer or less costly pollution controls. Pollution controls are often quite costly and, on the basis of the principle that "the polluter pays," most of the financial and other costs of complying with them fall initially on the business community. Thus, Bush administration officials estimated that the costs of complying with the Clean Air Act of 1990 would run more then $20 billion annually.[39] Pollution controls, by increasing the costs of doing business, may also discourage economic growth and job creation, or so it is frequently argued. Environmental groups want the strongest legislation possible. Business and economic development groups usually do not oppose all controls; rather, they favor controls that will be less stringent, intrusive, and costly to business. This is a politically more viable policy position than total opposition. As one would expect, resulting legislation usually reflects compromise between the environmental and business perspectives. An exception was the Clean Air Act of 1970, which called for a 90 percent reduction in automobile emissions and strong controls on industrial pollution. Driven by exceptionally strong public support for environmental protection, which was high-

---

[37] Rick Scarce, *Eco-Warriors: Understanding the Radical Environmental Movement* (Chicago: Noble Press, 1990).

[38] Norman J. Vig and Michael E. Kraft, eds., *Environmental Policy in the 1990s,* 2nd ed. (Washington, DC: CQ Press, 1994), p. 15.

[39] Richard E. Cohen, *Washington at Work: Back Rooms and Clean Air* (New York: Macmillan, 1992).

lighted by the first Earth Day (April 22, 1970), this legislation became stronger as it moved through Congress.[40]

Since 1970 Congress has enacted a large volume of pollution control legislation intended to help clean up the nation's air and water and to regulate the disposal of hazardous and toxic wastes. A brief summary of the major laws is presented here[41] and an excerpt from one law (The Clean Air Act of 1990) appears on page 740.

- *Clean Air Act.* This statute directs the Environmental Protection Agency to set standards for motor vehicle emissions, ambient air quality, hazardous air pollutants and new sources of pollution; to prevent significant deterioration of air quality in clean air areas; to reduce stratospheric ozone; and to control acid rain through an emissions trading system.
- *Clean Water Act.* This law creates a federal grant program to help finance sewage treatment plant construction, authorizes technological standards to reduce water pollution, and establishes programs to control non-point source pollution, such as runoff from parking lots and livestock feedlots.
- *Safe Drinking Water Act.* This act provides for drinking water standards to protect public health, the regulation of underground waste injection, and control of water contaminants.
- *Toxic Substances Control Act.* Testing of chemicals and regulation of their use is authorized by the act in order to protect health and the environment.
- *Resource Conservation and Recovery Act.* A cradle-to-grave system of regulation for hazardous substances and waste is provided by this statute, as well as a control program for underground storage tanks, such as those at gasoline stations.
- *Comprehensive Environmental Response, Compensation, and Liability Act.* Commonly referred to as Superfund, this statute creates a fund from taxes on polluters to pay the costs of cleaning up abandoned hazardous waste sites.
- *Federal Insecticide, Fungicide, and Rodenticide Act.* This statute calls for EPA registration and regulation of the use of pesticides.
- *National Environmental Policy Act.* Agencies taking actions that will have a major impact on the environment are required to prepare environmental impact statements (EISs), which are subject to review by EPA.
- *Pollution Prevention Act.* This Act stipulates that the prevention of pollution shall be an EPA priority and authorizes actions for reducing the sources of pollution.

Responsibility for the implementation of these laws rests primarily with the Environmental Protection Agency, to which we now turn.

The Environmental Protection Agency

The Environmental Protection Agency (EPA) was created in 1970 by Congress at the urging of President Richard M. Nixon. A number of environmental programs previously located in five executive departments were vested in EPA, which is an independent agency (that is, the agency is located outside of the executive departments) that reports directly to the president. The EPA administrator is appointed by the president with the approval of the Senate. Efforts to make the EPA an executive department, which would enhance its clout both within the government and in its dealings with other countries, have been ongoing for several years and seem destined to succeed.

---

[40] Charles O. Jones, *Clean Air: The Policies and Politics of Pollution Control* (Pittsburgh: University of Pittsburgh Press, 1975).

[41] This listing relies partly on Walter A. Rosenbaum, "The Clenched Fist and the Open Hand: Into the 1990s at EPA," in Vig and Kraft, eds., *Environmental Policy in the 1990s,* pp. 126–127.

A Page from the Clean Air Act Amendments of 1990

Note: This excerpt illustrates the detail often found in environmental legislation. It is taken from Title IV, "Acid Deposition Control," of the Clean Air Act Amendment of 1990.

Regulations.

"(d) PROCESS SOURCES.—Not later than 18 months after enactment of the Clean Air Amendments of 1990, the Administrator shall establish a program under which the owner or operator of a process source that emits sulfur dioxide may elect to designate that source as an affected unit for the purpose of receiving allowances under this title. The Administrator shall, by regulation, define the sources that may be designated; specify the emissions limitation; specify the operating, emission baseline, and other data requirements; prescribe CEMS or other monitoring requirements; and promulgate permit, reporting, and any other requirements necessary to implement such a program.

"(e) ALLOWANCES AND PERMITS.—The Administrator shall issue allowances to an affected unit under this section in an amount equal to the emissions limitation calculated under subsection (c) or (d), in accordance with section 403. Such allowance may be used in accordance with, and shall be subject to, the provisions of section 403. Affected sources under this section shall be subject to the requirements of sections 403, 408, 411, 412, 413, and 414.

"(f) LIMITATION.—Any unit designated under this section shall not transfer or bank allowances produced as a result of reduced utilization or shutdown, except that, such allowances may be transferred or carried forward for use in subsequent years to the extent that the reduced utilization or shutdown results from the replacement of thermal energy from the unit designated under this section, with thermal energy generated by any other unit or units subject to the requirements of this title and the designated unit's allowances are transferred or carried forward for use at such other placement unit or units. In no case may the Administrator allocate to a source designated under this section allowances in an amount greater than the emissions resulting from operation of the source in full compliance with the requirements of this Act. No such allowances shall authorize operation of a unit in violation of any other requirements of this Act.

Regulations.

"(g) IMPLEMENTATION.—The Administrator shall issue regulations to implement this section not later than eighteen moths after enactment of the Clean Air Act Amendments of 1990.

"(h) SMALL DIESEL REFINERIES.—The Administrator shall issue allowances to owners or operators of small diesel refineries who produce diesel fuel after October 1, 1993, meeting the requirements of subsection 211(i) of this Act.

"(1) ALLOWANCE PERIOD.—Allowances may be allocated under this subjection only for the period from October 1, 1993, through December 31, 1999.

"(2) ALLOWANCE DETERMINATION.—The number of allowances allocated pursuant to this paragraph shall equal the annual number of pounds of sulfur dioxide reduction attributable to desulfurization by a small refinery divided by 2,000. For the purposes of this calculation, the concentration of sulfur removed from diesel fuel shall be the difference between 0.274 percent (by weight) and 0.050 percent (by weight).

"(3) REFINERY ELIGIBILITY.—As used in this subsection, the term 'small refinery' shall mean a refinery or portion of a refinery—

"(A) which, as of the date of enactment of the Clean Air Act Amendments of 1990, has bona fide crude oil throughput of less than 18,250,000 barrels per year, as reported to the Department of Energy . . .

Source: U.S. Statutes at Large. Volume 104, p. 2622.

The EPA is the nation's largest regulatory agency. In 1994 it had approximately 18,000 employees located in Washington and in ten regional offices throughout the country. Its budget for operations was around $2.6 billion dollars. Although this may seem like a lot of money and employees, it really is not given the extensive research, rulemaking, and implementation duties assigned to EPA under the statutes listed above, plus many other lesser statutes, such as some relating to ocean dumping of medical and other wastes. In fact, EPA's budget has not grown proportionately as the duties assigned to it have multiplied in recent years. Consequently, it lacks the resources necessary to enforce adequately all of the legislation over which it has jurisdiction.

The activities of EPA can be conveniently grouped under the headings of research, rulemaking, and enforcement. The agency has to perform much research on the effects of various pollutants on human health and the natural environment in order to provide an evidentiary basis for its rulemaking. The expectation is that EPA rules will be supported by substantial evidence; hunches and fragments of evidence will not do. Rules are necessary to convert the goals and requirements of pollution control legislation into standards and specifications that can be implemented. For example, the Clean Air Act directs the EPA to set ambient air standards (ambient air is air that circulates around us) for such pollutants as carbon dioxide, ozone, and lead that will provide an "adequate margin of safety" to protect public health. The standards, stated in terms of parts per million, are enforced against potential polluters.

State pollution control agencies, with the cooperation and supervision of EPA regional offices, do much of the actual enforcement work. Pollution control enforcement is thus basically a two-step process. The EPA must induce state agencies to act in appropriate ways, and the state agencies must then secure compliance from the companies and individuals to whom the pollution standards apply. There is often considerable slippage in both steps of the process.

There have been three major eras in the political life of the EPA.[42] The first era, which extended through the 1970s, was characterized by growth in the EPA's budget, increase in the number of employees, expansion of its legislative authority, and substantial efforts to gain compliance with pollution control standards, both through legal enforcement and voluntary compliance. The second era began with the inception of the Reagan administration in 1981 and lasted through 1983. Opposed to strong pollution control programs, the Reagan administration appointed people to top-level EPA positions who were hostile or indifferent to its goals. Substantial cuts were made in the agency's budget and personnel, and it became demoralized. The third era began in late 1983 and continues to the present. The EPA's budget and personnel levels have been restored. Enforcement activity has been strengthened, but it features "explicit efforts to balance environmental protection against its economic costs."

Two environmental problems of concern in recent years are the disposal of hazardous and toxic wastes and the control of acid rain. An examination of each problem can highlight both the difficulties and politics of protecting the environment.

Hazardous and Toxic Wastes. Hazardous substances are toxic, corrosive, ignitable, or chemically reactive materials that present threats to human beings or the environ-

---

[42] Kent E. Portney, *Controversial Issues in Environmental Policy: Science vs. Economics vs. Politics* (Newbury Park, CA: Sage Publications, 1992), pp. 47–49. The quotation is on p. 49.

ment. Toxic substances, which are a smaller category, produce "detrimental effects in living organisms."[43] Most chemical substances are not considered harmful either to people or to the environment, but more than a few are. People are most concerned about carcinogenic substances. The increase in the production and use of chemicals in the twentieth century has contributed importantly to a higher standard of living in the United States, but not without social costs. How to dispose of waste chemicals safely has become a major problem. Whether emitted into the air, injected into the ground, dumped into bodies of water, or incinerated, chemicals still pose risks to human health and to the environment; many people find these risks intolerable.

National policy to control hazardous wastes takes three approaches. The Toxic Substances Control Act (1976) takes the preventive approach. The Act is designed to regulate the manufacture and distribution of toxic substances in order to identify hazardous chemicals and keep them out of the environment. The EPA is authorized to suspend production of a chemical permanently when it has "a reasonable basis to conclude that the chemical will present an unreasonable risk of injury to the health of the environment."

The Resource Conservation and Recovery Act (1976) is focused on ensuring the safe disposal of hazardous wastes currently being produced. The EPA is directed to develop criteria for environmentally safe hazardous-waste disposal sites and for identifying hazardous wastes. The EPA is also authorized to create a "manifest system" (receipts) that would permit tracking hazardous wastes from their points of origin to their final, safe disposal. This "cradle-to-grave" regulation was intended to eliminate "midnight dumping" and other unsafe forms of waste disposal. In 1984 amendments to the Act provided for the elimination of leaking underground storage tanks, such as might be found at gasoline stations. If their enforcement programs meet national standards, state agencies can implement these regulations.

In 1980 Congress enacted the Comprehensive Environmental Response, Compensation, and Liability Act, commonly referred to as Superfund, to provide for the clean up of abandoned hazardous waste sites, of which there are tens of thousands in the United States. One such site was Love Canal, near Niagara Falls in upstate New York. In the 1940s and 1950s, the Hooker Chemical Company used the dry canal bed as a disposal site for hazardous chemical wastes. The canal was then covered with a layer of earth and later donated as a site for a public school and homes. In the 1970s chemicals began to ooze to the surface, and noxious fumes entered people's homes. Adults and children suffered from a variety of medical ailments. These occurrences led to a major controversy and to the eventual evacuation of people from the area. In time the site was cleaned up at a cost of more than $300 million. In the 1980s people began moving back into the area.

The Love Canal disaster contributed to Congress's hurried enactment of the Superfund legislation in late 1980. The EPA was directed to compile a National Priority List (NPL) of hazardous waste sites urgently in need of cleanup. If the responsible parties could not be located or failed to clean up a site, EPA would do so. A Hazardous Substance Response Fund, financed mostly by a tax on oil, chemical, and other industries, was set up to pay the costs of cleaning up hazardous waste sites. Subsequent amendments have increased the size of the Superfund to more than $15 billion.

---

[43] Walter A. Rosenbaum, *Environmental Politics and Policy,* 2nd ed. (Washington, DC: CQ Press, 1991), p. 214.

This is an actual page from the *U.S. Statutes at Large*. It deals with gaining compliance with Clean Air Act requirements.

---

104 STAT. 2616 PUBLIC LAW 101-549—NOV. 15, 1990

42 USC 7651g.

"SEC. 408. PERMITS AND COMPLIANCE PLANS.

"(a) PERMIT PROGRAM.—The provisions of this title shall be implemented, subject to section 403, by permits issued to units subject to this title (and enforced) in accordance with the provisions of title V, as modified by this title. Any such permit issued by the Administrator, or by a State with an approved permit program, shall prohibit—

"(1) annual emissions of sulfur dioxide in excess of the number of allowances to emit sulfur dioxide the owner or operator, or the designated representative of the owners or operators, of the unit hold for the unit,

"(2) exceedances of applicable emissions rates,

"(3) the use of any allowance prior to the year for which it was allocated, and

"(4) contravention of any other provision of the permit.

Permits issued to implement this title shall be issued for a period of 5 years, notwithstanding title V. No permit shall be issued that is inconsistent with the requirements of this title, and title V as applicable.

"(b) COMPLIANCE PLAN.—Each initial permit application shall be accompanied by a compliance plan for the source to comply with its requirements under this title. Where an affected source consists of more than one affected unit, such plan shall cover all such units, and for purposes of section 502(c), such source shall be considered a 'facility'. Nothing in this section regarding compliance plans or in title V shall be construed as affecting allowances. Except as provided under subsection (c)(1)(B), submission of a statement by the owner or operator, or the designated representative of the owners and operators, of a unit subject to the emissions limitation requirements of sections 404, 405, and 407, that the unit will meet the applicable emissions limitation requirements of such sections in a timely manner or that, in the case of the emissions limitation requirements of sections 404 and 405, the owners and operators will hold allowances to emit not less than the total annual emissions of the unit, shall be deemed to meet the proposed and approved compliance planning requirements of this section and title V, except that, for any unit that will meet the requirements of this title by means of an alternative method of compliance authorized under section 404 (b), (c), (d), or (f) section 407 (d) or (e), section 409 and section 410, the proposed and approved compliance plan, permit application and permit shall include, pursuant to regulations promulgated by the Administrator, for each alternative method of compliance a comprehensive description of the schedule and means by which the unit will rely on one or more alternative methods of compliance in the manner and time authorized under this title. Recordation by the Administrator of transfers of allowances shall amend automatically all applicable proposed or approved permit applications, compliance plans and permits. The Administrator may also require—

"(1) for a source, a demonstration of attainment of national ambient air quality standards, and

"(2) from the owner or operator of two or more affected sources, an integrated compliance plan providing an overall plan for achieving compliance at the affected sources.

"(c) FIRST PHASE PERMITS.—The Administrator shall issue permits to affected sources under sections 404 and 407.

Action under Superfund has been a slow, tedious process because of problems in determining financial liability for cleaning up waste sites (which often entails much litigation), in deciding how clean each site must be, and in designing and carrying out remedial work. In early 1994, out of the 1,345 sites placed on the NPL, only 56 had been fully cleaned up; another 168 sites were nearly cleaned up.[44] Given the complexity of this task, EPA's record is better than the numbers indicate because on only a few of the NPL sites have no action been taken.

Acid rain. Acid rain is a by-product of the consumption of fossil fuels, especially high-sulfur coal.[45] Acid rain (or acid deposition, which is the more descriptive term) occurs when sulphur and nitrogen oxides combine with water vapor in the atmosphere and later fall to earth as rain, snow, or mist, or as particulate matter. The acidity of the precipitation can harm both fish and plant populations. Fish, for instance, cannot live in highly acidic lakes.

Acid rain did not become a major environmental issue until the early 1980s. It was not recognized as a problem in 1970, when the Clean Air Act was adopted. Indeed, tall smokestacks (200 to 800 feet in height) built at coal-burning electric utility plants in the Midwest and elsewhere contributed to the problem. These smokestacks spewed sulphur and nitrogen oxides higher into the atmosphere, which improved the quality of ambient air in their vicinity and helped localities comply with air quality standards under the Clean Air Act. These smokestacks also increased the likelihood that these pollutants would fall to earth somewhere downwind.[46] The sulphur and nitrogen oxides emitted by electric utility plants particularly in the midwest fall to earth as acid rain in the Northeastern states and in Eastern Canada.

The Reagan administration delayed taking regulatory action on acid rain on the grounds that more research was needed to better understand its causes and consequences. Electric utility companies, high-sulphur coal producers, and other businesses endorsed this point of view. As research findings accumulated, however, it became increasingly clear that action on the acid rain problem was necessary. Action of some kind became a near certainty in early 1989, when President George Bush, who said he wanted to be the "environmental president," called for major amendments to the Clean Air Act, including action on acid rain.

The Clean Air Act Amendments of 1990 provided for a major reduction in the emission of sulphur dioxide, the prime component of acid raid, by electric utility plants (see Chapter 6). As part of the strategy to control acid rain, the act authorized an emissions trading system. Each of the 110 electric utility plants named in the act, most of which are located in the Midwest, was allocated a specified number of "allowables." An allowable authorizes a utility plant to legally discharge one ton of sulphur dioxide effective in 1995, or in the year 2000, when more stringent limitations on sulphur dioxide emissions are phased in. If a company reduces its emissions below its specified level by burning low-sulphur coal, installing smokestack scrubbers, or other pollution control methods, it can "bank" its excess allowables or sell them to other utility companies. A company that exceeds its specified limit and does not buy allowables to cover its excess emissions is subject to heavy fines. The Chicago Board of Trade, a large commodity exchange, has been authorized by EPA to establish a market for the purchase and sale of sulphur dioxide allowables.

Economists have argued that the use of economic incentives, as in an emissions trading system, would be more effective in controlling pollution than is the traditional

---

[44] *Congressional Quarterly Weekly Report,* (February 5, 1994): 239–240.

[45] Gary C. Bryner, *Blue Skies, Green Politics: The Clean Air Act of 1990* (Washington, DC: CQ Press, 1993), p. 68.

[46] James L. Regens and Robert W. Rycroft, *The Acid Rain Controversy* (Pittsburgh: University of Pittsburgh Press, 1988), pp. 45–47.

standard setting and enforcement pattern of regulation.[47] Economic incentives, runs the argument, will provide companies with positive motivation—the pursuit of their self-interest—to reduce the discharge of pollutants. Whether the emissions trading system for acid rain reduction will be successful remains to be seen. If it is, its success will encourage wider use of economic incentives as a regulatory device, whether to control pollution or for other purposes.

Toward Reform

In the area of economic policy, the national budget deficit has been the nation's primary problem, drawing the most attention from reformers in recent years. Although budget deficits have long been a nagging concern, their huge size since the early 1980s has stimulated intensified efforts to cope with them. Public opinion polls reveal that a substantial majority of people in the United States favor a balanced national budget.

The reform proposals that have gained the most consideration are those to give the president a line-item veto on appropriations legislation and to add a balanced budget amendment to the U.S. Constitution. President Ronald Reagan sometimes stated that if Congress would give him the line-item veto, which would allow him to veto specific portions of a bill without rejecting the bill in its entirety, he would balance the budget. Four-fifths of the state governors do possess line-item veto authority. This power makes it difficult for state legislators to slip favored projects or programs past the governor by tucking them into general appropriations bills.

President Reagan's statement was based on the assumption that appropriations bills include much unnecessary or wasteful spending, often in the form of pork-barrel projects. These projects include funding for river and harbor improvement projects, highway demonstration projects, recreation facilities, research programs and facilities, and other programs that benefit particular states or localities but that do little to promote national interests. Pork-barrel projects are popular with most members of Congress and large numbers of their constituents. Although the complete elimination of pork-barrel spending might reduce the budget by a few billion dollars, this would have little overall impact on the budget deficit. Moreover, it should be kept in mind that what one person views as wasteful or unnecessary projects may be seen as important by another party.

Congress has not shown much inclination to equip the president with the line-item veto, at least partly because this ability would enhance presidential power at Congress's expense. There has, however, been strong support among the members of Congress for a **balanced budget amendment** to the Constitution. Essentially, such an amendment would provide that in a given fiscal year, the national government's expenditures could not exceed the revenue it took in.

Several versions of a balanced budget amendment have been considered in Congress. One that has gained strong support has the following components. The president and Congress would annually have to adopt a balanced budget (one in which revenues at least equaled expenditures) unless three-fifth of the total membership of each house decided otherwise. An exception would be made for wartime emergencies. Three-fifths majorities would also be needed to enact legislation increasing the limit on the

---

[47] See Charles L. Schultze, *The Public Use of Private Interest* (Washington, DC: Brookings Institution, 1977).

national debt, and majorities of the total House and Senate would be required to increase taxes. A proposed amendment along these lines came with twelve votes of getting the necessary two-thirds approval for constitutional amendments in the House in March 1994.

Proponents of a balanced budget amendment argue that only by this means can the members of Congress be compelled to tackle eliminating the budget deficit. In support of their position they note that Vermont is the only state that does *not* have either a constitutional or statutory requirement for a balanced budget. Thus, they say, they are only asking the national government to live by the same rules as most of the states. In reality, however, many states balance only their operating budgets, which go for day-to-day expenses. Borrowing and indebtedness are reflected in their capital budgets, which are used for long-term expenditures on buildings, highway construction, and other capital activities. All of the national government's expenditures, whether for operations or long-term improvements, are lumped together in a single budget.

The opponents of a balanced budget amendment argue that it is no substitute for political will and that it involves inappropriate tinkering with the Constitution. Further, they say, a balanced budget amendment would prevent use of the budget as an antirecessionary instrument of fiscal policy. Various opponents of the amendment further contend that the balanced budget requirement would result in either large tax increases or major cuts in entitlement program spending.

Support in Congress for the balanced budget amendment comes from a coalition of Republicans and conservative Democrats. Opposition stems from Northern or liberal Democrats. Early in 1994, the proponents of the amendment fell only twelve votes short of the needed two-thirds majority. The Senate came equally close, failing by a four-vote margin. The Democratic leadership in Congress had to wage an all-out campaign to defeat the amendment. All that one can be sure of is that the proponents of the balanced budget amendment, spurred by their near success, will continue to work for its approval. Should the amendment win congressional approval, it likely would be quickly ratified by three-fourths of the states. Then a real struggle over the budget deficit would ensue. The only ways to balance the budget, as mentioned, are to cut spending or to increase taxes or to use some combination of the two methods. A constitutional amendment would not make this task any less difficult and painful. Predictably, Congress would find some ways to dodge the full consequences of balancing the budget.

Summary

The nature and role of the government, especially the national government, in the economy have changed significantly since colonists first came to America in the 1600s. In analyzing these developments, this chapter has made the following points:

1. Although the national government played an important role in fostering national economic development through its tax, tariff, and public works policies, it played little role in regulating the economy; it left regulation to the states. As rapid growth occurred in the nation and in its economy, discernible business cycles—fluctuations between growth and recession—occurred, and more national intervention in the form of anti-monopoly policies resulted. The dawn of the progressive era also resulted in more business and consumer protection regulation.

   The Depression, which affected all economic and social groups, facilitated the election of a Democratic president, Franklin D. Roosevelt, who pledged to end the nation's economic woes through his New Deal. The Depression also signaled an end to the *laissez-faire* state, which was replaced with the interventionist state.

   After World War II, many areas of economic policy were well settled. Full employment, employee/employer relations, and social regulation became new concerns of government. Even before social regulation began to ebb, economic deregulation, which involves the reduction in the entry, rate, and other controls, emerged as an attractive political issue.

2. In the wake of the Depression, the national government intervened in the economy to maintain economic stability. It continues to regulate monetary policy by regulating the nation's money supply and interest rates. Monetary policy is controlled by the Federal Reserve Board. Fiscal policy, which involves the deliberate use of the national government's taxing and spending policies, is another tool the national government uses to maintain economic stability.

   Setting the national budget is a process involving the president and Congress. The budgetary policy frequently involves conflicts between the two branches of government. Although the budget is initially suggested by the president, Congress has attempted to reassert itself in the process. Despite efforts to control the national budget, annual deficits have led to a growing national debt and thus to calls for major budgetary reform.

3. The environment is one area in which the national government has used is economic regulatory powers to alter business practices. Conflicts over environmental regulation frequently pit the business community against environmental groups. The Environmental Protection Agency (EPA), which was created as an independent agency, is the nation's largest regulatory agency.

4. The huge national debt has led many people to suggest reforms in economic policy. Chief among these have been calls for a line-item veto and a constitutional amendment to require a balanced budget.

Key Terms

business cycles
interventionist state
fiscal policy
economic regulation
social regulation
economic stability

inflation
recession
monetary policy
money
reserve requirements

discount rate
open market operations
gross domestic product
pollution
balanced budget amendment

Suggested Readings

Bailey, Stephen. *Congress Makes a Law: The Story Behind the Employment Act of 1946.* New York: Columbia University Press, 1946.

Bryner, Gary C. *Blue Skies, Green Politics: The Clean Air Act of 1990.* Washington, DC: CQ Press, 1993.

Conlan, Timothy J., Margaret T. Wrightson, and David R. Beam. *Taxing Choices: The Politics of Tax Reform.* Washington, DC: CQ Press, 1990.

Derthick, Martha, and Paul J. Quirk. *The Politics of Deregulation.* Washington, DC: Brookings Institution, 1985.

Eisner, Marc Allen. *Regulatory Politics in Transition.* Baltimore: Johns Hopkins University Press, 1993.

Hughes, Jonathan R. T. *The Governmental Habit,* 2nd ed. Princeton, NJ: Princeton University Press, 1991.

Kettl, Donald F. *Deficit Politics: Public Budgeting in Its Institutional and Historical Context.* New York: Macmillan, 1992.

Pfiffner, James P., ed. *The President and Economic Policy.* Philadelphia: Institute for the Study of Human Issues, 1986.

Rosenbaum, Walter A. *Environmental Politics and Policy,* 2nd ed. Washington, DC: CQ Press, 1991.

Switzer, Jacqueline Vaughn. *Environmental Politics: Domestic and Global Dimension.* New York: St. Martin's, 1994.

Wilson, James Q., ed. *The Politics of Regulation.* New York: Basic Books, 1980.

Woolley, John T. *Monetary Politics: The Federal Reserve and the Politics of Monetary Policy.* London: Cambridge University Press, 1984.

Young, James Harvey. *Pure Food: Securing the Federal Food and Drugs Act of 1906.* Princeton, NJ: Princeton University Press, 1990.

If they see that our national government is efficient and well administered, our trade prudently regulated, our militia properly organized and disciplined, our resources and finance discreetly managed, our credit re-established, our people free, contented, and united, they will be much more disposed to cultivate our friendship than provoke our resentment.

Publius (John Jay)
Federalist No. 4

In this passage, John Jay argues that American security depends on a strong, unified government. Without it, Jay predicted that the British, French, and Spanish would divide the states against one another and make the United States more susceptible to foreign intervention.

CHAPTER 18

Foreign and Military Policy

THE ROOTS OF U.S. FOREIGN AND MILITARY POLICY
THE EARLY HISTORY OF FOREIGN AND MILITARY POLICY
THE GREAT SHIFT
THE MACHINERY OF MODERN FOREIGN POLICY MAKING
CHALLENGES TO PRESIDENTIAL POWER
TOWARD REFORM

The Treaty of Paris of 1784, which marked the end of the Revolutionary War, made trouble for the new American nation from the very beginning. Most important, British troops did not leave their forts along the Northwest frontier of the United States and assisted the Native American tribes in their efforts to stop American migration west. Under the Articles of Confederation, the national government was given so little power that it could do nothing to evict the British. With war among Great Britain, France, and the other great powers apparently inevitable, the United States was likely to be a battleground in their global conflict.

John Jay and other Federalists argued that the United States could avoid being a pawn in European struggles only if it were united. With authority in foreign affairs and defense issues centralized in a strong national government and not distributed among the states, the European powers could not play one state or region against another. A new capacity of the national government to raise an army and provide for a navy would help deter Great Britain or other European powers from ventures against the United States.

The Federalist views on the importance of national unity derive from the emergence of the **nation-state,** (ideally, a country where almost all of the people of one nationality govern themselves) as the most powerful political organization. With its roots in the Reformation and the political system of Europe in the 1600s, the nation-state was and is the dominant form of political organization in international politics. This form of political organization is based on the idea that one government should have sole authority over a well-defined territory. By appeals to nationalism, the government could support large military forces to defend its interests. These national interests include preserving its territorial boundaries, maintaining a relatively sovereign (independent) form of government, and promoting economic prosperity.

Nation-states range in size and resources from micro-states, such as Grenada, Monaco, and Tuvalu, to superpowers like the United States and the former Soviet Union. International power—that is, the power of any one nation-state relative to another—depends not only on the power of other nation-states but also on the issue involved. International power also varies over time. Even though the collapse of the Soviet Union increased the relative military power of the United States in the 1990s, many scholars argue that the overall power of the United States has been in decline since the early 1970s, similar to the rise and fall of other great powers over the last four centuries. As noted historian Paul Kennedy contends, the United States

> cannot avoid confronting the two great tests which challenge the *longevity* of every major power that occupies the "number one" position in world affairs: whether . . . it can preserve a reasonable balance between the nation's perceived defense requirements and the means it possesses to maintain those commitments; and whether . . . it can preserve the technological and economic bases of its power from relative erosion in the face of ever-shifting patterns of global production.[1]

Recent debates about military intervention in Bosnia, Haiti, Somalia, and elsewhere are really about building a consensus on the most appropriate role for the United States in the world. This debate takes place in every era, particularly when key political, technological, or economic changes have taken place either at home or abroad.

In this chapter, we expand on these themes as we look at the roots of U.S. foreign and military policy and of the current status of the United States on the international front. In particular, we focus on the machinery of foreign policy and the president's key role in that process.

The Roots of U.S. Foreign and Military Policy

In its early years, the United States was a weak country on the margins of international affairs, and, historically, weak states often depend on more powerful countries for security. The Atlantic Ocean and other physical barriers to the projection of European power in the Americas and abundant natural and human resources meant that the United States had another option: It could choose not to be involved in European affairs. To understand the origins of U.S. foreign policy, we must examine both the pre-constitutional era and the Constitution itself.

The Pre-Constitutional Era

As indicated in "Landmark Events Leading up to the Great Shift in U.S. Foreign Policy," John Adams, under the direction of the Continental Congress, developed a Plan

---

[1] Paul Kennedy, *The Rise and Fall of the Great Powers: Economic Change and Military Conflict form 1500 to 2000* (New York: Vintage Books, 1989), p. 514.

Landmark Events Leading up to the Great Shift in American Foreign Policy

Year	Event
1776	Plan of Treaties / Declaration of Independence
1778	Franco-American Treaty
1787	The Constitution
1792	Militia Act of 1792
1795	Jay Treaty
1796	Washington's Farewell Address
1801–1805	Barbary Wars
1812–1815	War of 1812
1823	Monroe Doctrine
1846–1848	War with Mexico
1852–1854	Matthew C. Perry opens Japan to Western interests
1861–1865	Civil War
1898	Spanish-American War
1914–1917	World War I
1941–1945	World War II

of Treaties in 1776 that outlined many of the primary themes of early U.S. foreign policy.[2] Adams called for greater freedom of trade between nations without political or military ties. This echoed the views of Thomas Paine, who argued in *Common Sense* that independence was the only way to avoid entanglements (see pages 33–34).

The struggle for independence made foreign aid and military assistance an unavoidable requirement. The French gave substantial military and economic assistance to the newborn United States after U.S. forces won their first major military victory over British forces at the battle of Saratoga in 1777. The aid came only because the French

---

[2] Howard Jones, *The Course of American Democracy,* Vol. I, 2nd ed. (Chicago: The Dorsey Press), pp. 6–8.

were locked in a conflict with the British for global power at that time. This conflict between the British and the French prompted the Franco-American Treaty of 1778, which created a military alliance between France and the United States. The United States sought similar alliances with other European powers, but from this point until World War II, the United States entered no other military alliance with any of them.

In its early days, the United States had only a rudimentary military establishment. At the close of the Revolutionary War, the Continental Congress ordered the discharge of all but 80 men from the Continental Army. The Articles of Confederation authorized a standing army, but, at the Constitutional Convention, Elbridge Gerry wanted a Constitutional provision that limited the size of an army to 2,000 or 3,000 regular soldiers. Gerry's proposal prompted George Washington to suggest, in a stage whisper, an amendment to the Constitution limiting foreign armies that might attack the United States to the same size. Nevertheless, Gerry's proposal was in keeping with the general desire for a limited army. When the first Congress of the new United States eventually met in 1789, it authorized an army, but only at a maximum strength of 840.

The Constitution

The Framers generally agreed that the republic's foreign policy was important but limited—its tasks were to keep the United States out of European affairs and to keep European countries out of U.S. affairs. The institutional framework for foreign and defense policy is laid out in the Constitution. Making and implementing foreign policy is clearly given to the federal government rather than to the states, although the states had an important function in creating state militias.

Scholars agree that the Constitution intended a division of responsibility between Congress and the president in foreign affairs. Although the office of the president combined the powers of head of state (with the authority to appoint and receive ambassadors, sign treaties, and otherwise represent the United States in dealings with other countries) and head of government (with the responsibility for overseeing the daily affairs of making and executing public policy), the power of the president was not to be comparable to the power of a monarch. Congress provides funds for the army and navy and declares war; as commander-in-chief—that is, having constitutional power over all combined U.S armed forces—the president leads the nation's military forces. Congress has the power to regulate commerce with foreign nations; the president has authority to negotiate and sign the treaties that govern such commerce (although for such treaties to become valid, two-thirds of the Senate are constitutionally required to ratify them). The president appoints ambassadors and other key foreign and military officials; the Senate grants advice and consent on these appointments.

Additionally, many powers not enumerated in the Constitution (such as the capacity to acquire territory by treaty) generally are accorded to the national government. Moreover, through the doctrines of implied and inherent powers, the president and Congress have often gone beyond the powers outlined in the Constitution.

The Early History of Foreign and Military Policy

The pre-constitutional desire for a limited foreign and defense policy carried over to the new republic. In keeping with this approach, the standing army remained small, with most of the nation's military strength decentralized in the form of state militias.

Theoretically, the Militia Act of 1792 created a universal obligation of able-bodied males to participate in the state militias. When the young republic needed a modest force to put down rebels in western Pennsylvania who refused to pay taxes during the Whiskey Rebellion, it had difficulty recruiting enough men.

This distrust of armies conflicted with another tendency, the country's desire to push its frontiers into territory technically owned by the British, French, or Spanish and inhabited mostly by the Native American population. Often the Native American population of the frontiers received both diplomatic and material support from European powers. Resistance to U.S. expansion, frontier raids, and armed conflict were common. The British even proposed creating another country in the Northwest Territories to be governed by British allies among the Native American tribes. In spite of the desire to expand, Congress was reluctant to authorize a large military establishment, and most Americans were reluctant to participate in one.

The first important treaty entered into by the new United States regularized relations with Great Britain. The treaty, generally referred to as the **Jay Treaty** after its chief negotiator, John Jay (see "People of the Past: John Jay," p. 754), helped settle disputes between Great Britain and the United States over the boundaries of the new nation, debts incurred during the war, and commerce between the two nations. Bitterness in the aftermath of the Revolutionary War led some members of Congress to oppose the treaty. But these diehards were in the House, not the Senate, and, according to the Constitution, only the Senate had the power to ratify treaties.

Members of the House tried another tack to undermine the treaty. Because the House would have to appropriate funds to carry it out, members asked President George Washington to submit all papers relating to the treaty. Washington refused on the constitutional grounds that the Senate alone had the power to approve treaties and on the practical grounds that successful diplomacy depended on secrecy. By approving the funds despite Washington's refusal to submit papers, the House gave in, helping to establish the precedent of executive privilege—the right of the president to withhold from Congress information about the inner workings of the executive branch. The doctrine would have a long history. Richard M. Nixon invoked it to avoid inquiry on Watergate, as did Ronald Reagan to avoid inquiry on secret assistance to Iran.

The French Revolution of 1789 and the subsequent rise of Napoleon Bonaparte to power drove Europe into virtually constant warfare for the next quarter of a century. In 1796, George Washington, in his last public statement as president, discussed the dangers of divisive party politics and warned strongly against foreign entanglements. In his *Farewell Address* (coauthored with Alexander Hamilton), Washington suggested that it be "our true policy to steer clear of permanent alliances with any portion of the foreign world." Washington believed that U.S. democracy and economic prosperity, two key national interests, depended not on complete isolation, but on keeping free of European politics.

Domestic politics and the large European colonies in the Americas made this a difficult proposition. A policy of neutrality allowed U.S. ships and U.S. exports to do business with all sides in the conflict. U.S. trade grew at an unprecedented rate. At the same time, this meant that U.S. carriers were often in contested waters.

The French believed U.S. neutrality violated the Franco-American Treaty of 1778. War with France seemed likely in 1798, and Federalist legislation in Congress began to limit political freedom in the name of national security. In two years, the U.S. Navy captured nearly one hundred armed ships, but the conflict was settled diplomatically, and the Franco-American Treaty of 1778 was discarded. In 1801, again without the protection of any European power, U.S. shipping was threatened when the Pasha of

People of the Past

John Jay

A member of the Continental Congress, diplomat, and first Chief Justice of the U.S. Supreme Court, John Jay is perhaps best known for the treaty that bears his name. He began his distinguished political career with election to the First Continental Congress in 1774. Although Jay initially favored reconciliation with Great Britain, he later became a strong supporter of ratification of the Constitution and would have contributed far more than the five essays he wrote for *The Federalist* had it not been for ill health.

After holding positions as minister to Spain during the Revolutionary War and secretary of foreign affairs under the Artcticles of Confederation, Jay was nominated by President George Washington to be the first Chief Justice of the Supreme Court in 1789.

His experience in European diplomacy led Alexander Hamilton and some other Federalists to urge Washington to appoint John Jay, while he was Chief Justice, as a special emissary to England to resolve problems that continued to exist between the two nations. Tensions ran high in the wake of British seizures of American ships and restrictions on trade with the British West Indies. Even Jay himself recognized the nearly impossible task ahead of him: "[No] man could frame a treaty with Great Britain without making himself unpopular and odious."* Though many had anticipated that Jay might become President of the United States, his association with the treaty ruined his chances. Although the treaty that Jay negotiated (known as the Jay Treaty) settled many unresolved British-American disputes, those who opposed Washington's foreign policy felt that it failed to secure adequate British recognition of American rights of neutrality.

After returning to America, Jay resigned from the Supreme Court and served two terms as governor of New York. Scholars now recognize the dispute settlement procedures in the Jay Treaty as establishing the modern concepts used in international arbitration.

* Howard Jones, *The Course of American Diplomacy: Volume I to 1913*, 2nd ed. (Chicago, IL: The Dorsey Press, 1988), p. 37.

Source: Eric Foner and John Garraty, eds., *The Reader's Companion to American History* (Boston: Houghton Mifflin Company, 1991), pp. 589–590.

Tripoli had the flagpole of the U.S. consulate chopped down as his way of declaring war on the United States. And, reversing his views on the importance of Congress in the foreign policy process, President Thomas Jefferson fought the Barbary Wars (battles to protect U.S. merchant ships from harassment and robbery by Barbary pirates) without a congressional declaration of war through his powers as commander-in-chief.

After a brief lull in the European conflict, the war intensified in 1804. Great Britain began to adopt rules of the sea that worsened Anglo-American relations, eventually demanding that all ships going to France, its colonies, or its allies first dock in England, obtain a license, and pay a tax on their cargo. Great Britain's vigorous pursuit of the policy of impressment added to worsening conditions. The British Navy applied its practice of impressment, that is, taking British subjects by force to serve on ships under cruel conditions. Because many sailors deserted, the British Navy stopped and searched U.S. ships for deserters. Since Great Britain viewed all its subjects as citizens for life and the United States allowed immigrants to become citizens, many U.S. sailors were at risk.

In June 1807, a British Navy ship in U.S. waters, the *Leopard,* fired on a U.S. Navy ship, the *Chesapeake,* after the captain of the *Chesapeake* refused to allow British sailors to search his ship for deserters. After suffering many casualties, the *Chesapeake* surrendered and was searched. Four men, three of whom were born in the United States, were taken by the British. The *Chesapeake* managed to return to port in Norfolk, Virginia. Upon hearing news of the attack, mobs gathered and demanded that President Thomas Jefferson assemble a special session of Congress to declare war on Great Britain.

Instead of assembling Congress to obtain a declaration of war, Jefferson tried peaceful measures. Even the British saw the need to discipline their officers, return three U.S. sailors (one had been hanged), and offer monetary compensation to the victims and their families. The British would not, however, renounce their right to search ships for deserting sailors.

President Jefferson and Secretary of State James Madison still tried to avoid war. In December 1807, the United States passed the Embargo Act, stopping U.S. ships from leaving the country for any port in another country. Jefferson and Madison believed that the European powers relied so much on U.S. shipping and raw materials that the Embargo Act would force the Europeans to change their policies and respect the rights of Americans at sea. The Act (and complementary laws) required government approval before goods could be loaded onto a ship, allowed the federal government to confiscate ships and cargo suspected of illicit destinations, and required traders shipping between U.S. ports to post bonds of twice the value of their cargos.

The Embargo Act proved very costly. Not only did European policies fail to change, but U.S. exports also fell by 80 percent, harming economic interests in virtually every region except those bordering Canada (since overland trade was not prohibited). With as many as 100,000 people having lost their jobs and inflation climbing in the depression created by the Embargo Act, dissatisfaction with the Act allowed the Federalist Party to make noticeable gains in the election of 1808. Although the Republicans retained control of the presidency and the Congress, the Embargo Act was replaced by milder measures.

In April 1809, in an exchange of diplomatic notes between U.S. Secretary of State Robert Smith and David Erskine, the British Minister in Washington, many of the disputes appeared settled. The Erskine agreement, as this was called, was the first important **executive agreement,** a government-to-government accord entered into by the United States and binding only on the current administration. Unfortunately, Minister Erskine was soon replaced by a more hostile representative of the British government, and the agreement lasted only a few months. Relations with Great Britain continued to deteriorate.

President Jefferson was more fortunate in his dealings with France. Napoleon's plans to expand French influence in the Americas had dimmed by the spring of 1803, and Napoleon feared that either the British or the Americans would take the Louisiana territory with a new round of war in Europe. Napoleon offered to sell the Louisiana territory to the United States; after negotiations, he settled on a price of $15 million. Although President Jefferson questioned his own authority under the Constitution to accept the territory, he signed the treaty and the Senate consented. The Supreme Court upheld the purchase under the treaty-making power of the federal government in 1828.

This expansion of territory brought the United States into even greater conflict with Great Britain. Many of the Congressional advocates of peace were defeated in the election of 1810. Nonetheless, many people in the Northeast supported a peace candi-

The burning of Washington by the British in 1814.

date against President James Madison in the election of 1812, because the young republic was not prepared for war. The continued deterioration of Anglo-American relations, however, led Great Britain and the United States to fight each other in the War of 1812.

In general, U.S. forces did not do well during the war, and financing the war proved extremely difficult. Prominent opponents of the war in Congress, such as Representative Daniel Webster (D.-N.H.), helped defeat some war proposals, including a draft. While peace talks began even before the first battles, the war ended only when the British decided to concentrate on defeating Napoleon. The British agreed to abide by the borders, treaty obligations, and other conditions in existence before the war, signing the Treaty of Ghent in December 1814 (the Battle of New Orleans was fought after the signing of the peace treaty). With the defeat of Napoleon in the summer of 1815, the British ceased the practice of impressment, and Anglo-American tensions eased. From this point on, disputes between U.S. and British interests were increasingly settled by consultation, negotiation, and specially designated panels, commissions, or courts to arbitrate conflicts.

The unpopularity of the war spawned the development of peace societies in Massachusetts and New York in 1815, largely supported by the Federalists. Americans participated in a series of peace congresses in Europe during the 1840s and 1850s, and by the Civil War there were around fifty peace groups in the United States calling for pro-

Barbary pirates' harassing American ships on the east coast prompted President Jefferson to take action without a congressional declaration of war.

hibition of the sale of war materials, a reduction in arms, increased use of arbitration as a means of settling disputes, and a congress of nations to address world problems. The United States fought Algiers and the Barbary pirates again in 1815, but actions by the U.S., British, and Dutch navies over a two-year period effectively ended that threat. The United States then turned its focus away from military power and European disputes. In the three decades of relative peace among the European powers that followed Napoleon's defeat, the United States focused on continental expansion and economic growth. After the War of 1812, the United States had established itself in world affairs as a minor military power with substantial private economic resources but with interests that led it away from Europe.

Early Trade and Aid Policy

Clearly, shipping and trade played important roles in the foreign relations of the early American republic. In the 1780s and 1790s, the United States entered into trade treaties with the Netherlands, Sweden, Prussia, and Great Britain. After the War of 1812, the United States returned to this practice and made numerous treaties to standardize trade practices with other countries. For U.S. industries, however, global peace meant increased competition at home and abroad. In 1816, the United States took the crucial step of adopting **tariffs,** taxes on imports, to protect some domestic industries from foreign competition, instead of simply using tariffs to raise money for the federal government. Tariffs were the primary source of federal revenue every year from 1789 to 1863, when receipts from special Civil War taxes increased. Overall, Congress and the president proved very receptive to demands for economic protection; and high tariffs, usually from 20 to 30 percent of the value of the import but with some individual tariffs as high as 100 percent, became the norm well into the next decade.

High tariffs discouraged U.S. trade, since other countries kept their tariffs on U.S. goods high in retaliation for most of this period. For most of the years before the Civil War, the United States imported more than it exported, and the volume of trade declined steadily through 1830. Although trade increased after 1830, international trade grew at a rate slower than that of trade within the United States.

The slave trade was another area of foreign trade with which the United States had to deal in its early years. The Constitution prohibited the importation of slaves after 1808, but illicit trade continued for another half century. When Great Britain outlawed all slave trade in its own empire in the 1820s, British and U.S. interests clashed on this issue on several occasions but were settled peaceably.

On the investment side of foreign economic policy, the industrialization of the United States attracted many European investors. In fact, in the nineteenth century foreign investment in the United States usually exceeded U.S. investment abroad. This influx of wealth helped create the intricate economic infrastructure—the railroads, canals, and ports—that supported American economic expansion.

By world standards, private charity and assistance have always played unusually important roles in American life. The colonists set up funds to start colleges and hospitals and to provide aid for the poor within their own colonies. Government assistance for these undertakings, either at home or abroad, was something else. The United States simply offered little or no foreign aid throughout the nineteenth century. The federal government was relatively small well into the 1850s, employing fewer than 30,000 civilians including postal workers, and it had limited funds. Indeed, Congress sometimes lowered tariffs because the government was thought to have more money than necessary.

The Monroe Doctrine

The limited capacity of the U.S. government to provide military or foreign economic assistance helps explain its response to the revolutions in the 1820s that helped most Latin American countries gain their independence. President James Monroe threatened action if European powers attempted to recolonize the region and if the Russians extended their presence on the western coast of North America. In an annual message to Congress in December 1823, Monroe declared that it would be dangerous to American peace and safety for European states to attempt to extend "their system" to the Western Hemisphere. This approach to hemispheric relations became known as the **Monroe Doctrine.**

Although tough sounding, the Monroe Doctrine was more preference than policy, and it was hardly mentioned in foreign affairs until 1842, when it was used to justify U.S. expansion in the Oregon territories. Americans have often spoken of the Monroe Doctrine as if it were a form of divine revelation. American politicians accuse other countries of violating the Monroe Doctrine. President Ronald Reagan's first Secretary of Defense, Caspar Weinberger, stated that the United States would give aid to support guerrillas seeking to overthrow the government of Afghanistan but would not tolerate

Soviet arms supplies to guerrillas seeking to overthrow the government of El Salvador because "such aid would violate the Monroe Doctrine."[3]

In fact, the Monroe Doctrine was respected largely because it was also Great Britain's aim to keep other European powers out of the Western Hemisphere in order to preserve British commercial interests. The difference between British and U.S. policy was that the incomparable British Navy could enforce the policy. In fact, the British expanded their limited colonial presence in Latin America several times after 1823 without U.S. policymakers invoking the Doctrine.

The United States as an Emerging Power

Despite a preference for remaining uninvolved in world affairs, the nineteenth-century U.S. republic was active in international relations. U.S. foreign policy at this time was concerned mainly with events in the Western Hemisphere or with trade policy. Military activity was mainly within or on the borders of the United States—hostile relations with Canada during and following the War of 1812, hostile relations with Spain over Florida, war with Mexico in 1846, war with the seceding confederate states between 1861 and 1865, and wars in the South and West with Chief "The Shooting Star" Tecumseh's confederacy and other Native American nations (Creeks, Seminoles, Sioux, Comanche, Apache) that resisted expansion into their territory.

The result of these wars was a country that stretched from one ocean to another. In particular, the defeat of Mexico in 1848 brought California under U.S. control. U.S. expansion was not seen as foreign policy or military conquest but as **manifest destiny,** a divinely mandated obligation to expand across North America to the Pacific Ocean and "overspread the continent allotted by Providence for the free development of our yearly multiplying millions."[4]

Nor did the Pacific stop the westward expansion of the United States. Soon after the British forced the Chinese to open their markets to British goods, U.S. officials negotiated a commercial treaty with China and sought to keep any single European power from restricting U.S. trade with China. In 1852 and 1854, Commodore Matthew C. Perry took the East India Squadron of the U.S. Navy into Japanese waters and opened Japan to Western interests.

During the Civil War (1861–65), the Confederacy tried to bring the European powers into the war. The lack of a substantial confederate victory on Northern soil, the growing industrial and military might of the Union forces, and anti-slavery sentiment in Great Britain all thwarted Southern efforts to involve the Europeans in the conflict.

For the decades after the Civil War, there was little consensus on the appropriate role for the United States in global affairs. Most often, divided government existed as the same party failed to control the presidency and both houses of Congress. Both major political parties were generally against acquiring colonies but were divided on such issues as free trade and military intervention. The United States did move to control Midway, the Hawaiian islands, and the Samoan islands to protect its interests in the Pacific, but these actions heightened the debate about how to use U.S. power.

---

[3] Caspar Weinberger quoted in Howell Raines, "Reagan Hinting at Arms for Afgan Rebels," *The New York Times,* March 10, 1983: A3.

[4] John L. O'Sullivan, writing in 1845, cited by Julius W. Pratt, "The Ideology of American Expansion," in Avery Craven, ed., *Essays in Honor of William E. Dodd* (Chicago: University of Chicago Press, 1935).

President Theodore Roosevelt supported building the Panama Canal to strengthen the U.S. naval presence in the world.

In the 1890s, the Republican Party gained control of Congress and the presidency on a platform of protection for U.S. goods from foreign imports and an expansionist foreign and military policy. At the time, the major foreign policy issue was the revolt against Spain by Cuban rebels, which harmed U.S. economic interests in the island. The Spaniards used harsh tactics against the rebels. With a brand of journalism known as the yellow press, U.S. newspapers competed to describe these atrocities, whether true or invented, in lurid detail. By the late 1890s, in a show of national unity unprecedented since the Civil War, many Americans believed that the United States had to fight Spain for civilization, commerce, and Cuban independence.

Sparked by the sinking of the battleship *S.S. Maine* in Havana's harbor, the United States and Spain went to war in April 1898. Within months the United States defeated Spanish forces around the world. Cuba was freed, and the United States acquired as its first colonies the Philippines, Guam, and Puerto Rico, among others. Later, in a series of U.S. Supreme Court cases, collectively called the *Insular Cases,* the Justices affirmed the right of the national government to take new territories and to create new forms of government for those territories.[5]

The Spanish-American War, as it was called, propelled the United States from a regional to a world power, as illustrated in Figure 18-1. Under the expansionist vision of President Theodore Roosevelt in particular, the U.S. fleet went on to become a global navy, with military bases all over the world. As president, Roosevelt supported the construction of the Panama Canal to make it easier for the U.S. Navy to operate in two oceans, and he received the newly created Nobel Peace Prize for his efforts to end the Russo-Japanese War of 1904–05 and the Franco-German crisis over Morocco in 1905.

The belief in manifest destiny did not prepare the U.S. public for the revolution in the Philippines against U.S. rule in 1899. (The Philippines had been ceded to the United States by Spain in the Treaty of Paris [1898], which ended the Spanish-American War.) The United States sent nearly 200,000 troops to the islands over the next three years. When the fighting ceased in 1902, tens of thousands of Filipinos had died along with five thousand Americans. The atrocities committed on both sides dampened U.S. enthusiasm for foreign adventures.

Foreign Trade and Aid Policy at the Turn of the Century

During the Civil War, the United States had increased its average duties on imports to almost 50 percent of their value. Debate between Democrats and Republicans grew as the high tariff rates occasionally created surpluses in government revenue (and few wanted the government to have too much money) and as the European countries began to adopt lower tariffs and other free trade policies. President Chester A. Arthur appointed a commission to study the tariff issue in 1881, but the tariff was reduced very little. The Democrats and Republicans made the tariff a major election issue throughout the 1880s, but the Republican victory in 1888 ensured the continuation of high tariffs. The 57 percent average rate of the Dingley Tariff Act of 1897 raised tariffs to a new high. They would remain high until Democratic electoral victories in 1912.

From the Civil War on, the United States became increasingly self-sufficient. Self-sufficiency, coupled with high tariffs, reduced the relative demand for imported goods. At the same time, U.S. agriculture became more mechanized and U.S. industry more productive as many European states, particularly England, had greatly reduced their tariffs. This meant that U.S. goods became relatively cheaper to other countries and

---

[5] See, for example, *DeLima* v. *Bidwell,* 182 U.S. 1 (1901) and *Dooley* v. *United States,* 182 U.S. 222 (1901).

FIGURE 18-1
The United States Emerges as a World Power

Source: James A. Henretta, *America's History; Volume 2: Since 1865*, Worth Publishers.

In 1890 Alfred T. Mahan wrote that the United States should regard the oceans as "a great highway" across which the United States would carry on world trade. That was precisely what resulted from the empire the United States acquired in the wake of the Spanish-American War. The Caribbean possessions, strategically located Pacific islands, and, in 1903, the Panama Canal Zone gave the United States commercial and naval access to a wider world.

thus much more competitive on the world market. After 1895 the United States exported more than it imported for all but a few of the next seventy-five years.

The late nineteenth century witnessed the rise of thousands of extremely wealthy business tycoons, some so ruthless that they were known as robber barons. Some tycoons, such as John D. Rockefeller and Andrew Carnegie, believed their fortunes brought responsibility as well as power, and they created charitable foundations to aid society, mainly in the United States but also overseas. Some new private institutions were founded to assist the international community, such as the Carnegie Endowment for International Peace and the World Peace Foundation.

World War I

When World War I broke out in Europe in 1914, many Americans were happy to stay neutral. In words that echoed the thoughts of many, "We never appreciated so keenly

Woodrow Wilson campaigned for reelection pledging to keep Americans out of war. His campaign promises were broken when the United States reluctantly entered World War I.

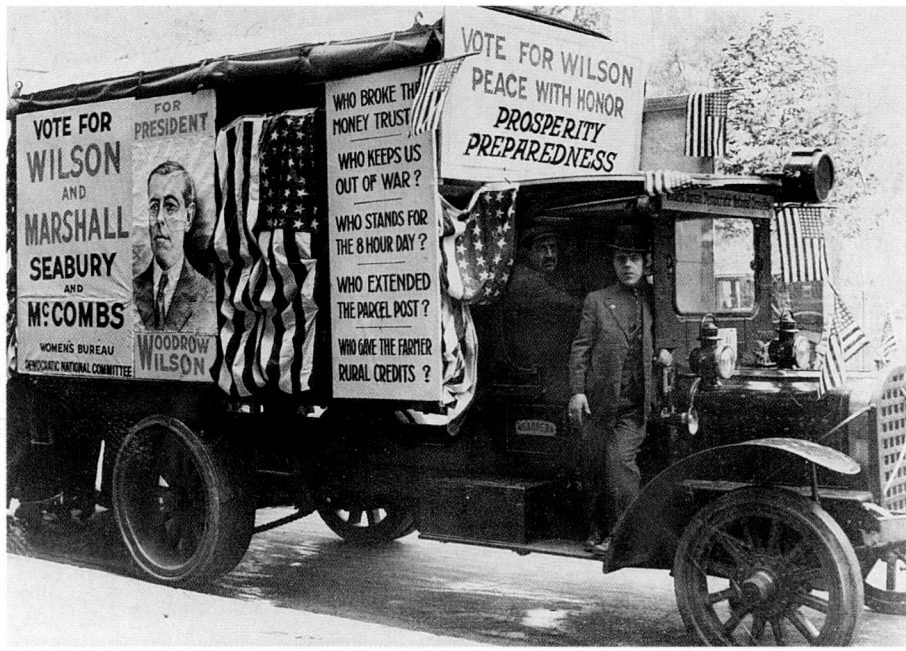

as now the foresight of our fathers in emigrating from Europe."[6] For a nation of immigrants, it was also politically expedient to stay out of the war, because choosing sides would inevitably anger one group or another. Many Americans of British descent favored the British, many of German descent favored the Germans, and many Irish favored any side that did not include the British.

President Woodrow Wilson ran for a second term in 1916 on the slogan "He kept us out of war," yet world events soon forced him to enter the conflict. Especially disturbing was the German policy of "unrestricted submarine warfare," which meant that U.S. ships carrying cargo to Great Britain would be sunk even though the United States had declared itself neutral.

Talking of a "war to end all wars," Wilson took the United States into its first great European conflict. Troops and aid from the United States began to arrive just when the human and material resources of the British and French were nearly exhausted. Almost five million Americans served in the armed forces during the war. The newly created Food Administration, under Herbert Hoover (who had run a successful campaign to provide relief to Belgium early in the war), dramatically increased food production to supply the United States and its allies. The United States also provided the allies with $11 billion in loans during and shortly after the war. Even though it had entered the war late, the United States, by intervening militarily and economically, helped make possible the defeat of the German and Austro-Hungarian empires.

Wilson put great faith in an international organization that would be formed after the war to keep the peace. He was instrumental in writing the document that set up the **League of Nations**—the first global organization of states dedicated to preserving peace—and in getting it incorporated into the Versailles Peace Treaty ending World

---

[6] Wabash (Indiana) *Plain Dealer* (August 1914).

War I. Wilson's central role was symbolized by the provision that stated that the initial meeting of the League would be convened by the president of the United States.

Wilson had been so absorbed in foreign policy that he neglected to build support at home. He was a Democratic president facing a Senate controlled by Republicans, and he had not courted them by such devices as including a senator among the U.S. delegates to the Versailles Peace Conference. Many senators found membership in the new world body incompatible with the principles of U.S. independence. Progressive western senators indicated that the treaty brought the United States too close to European politics. Indeed, U.S. troops landed in the Soviet Union in 1918 and for the next two years fought against the communists; this became a lasting source of mistrust between the two countries. Even the senators not totally opposed to the treaty added amendments or "reservations," giving to Congress the power to ratify certain League actions in regard to territory and trade, as well as declaring that the subject of the Monroe Doctrine was entirely outside the jurisdiction of the League.

When Wilson realized that the treaty was in trouble, he tried to win public opinion at home by going on a nationwide tour making speeches; but his efforts came too late. The Senate refused to give the necessary two-thirds vote to approve the ratification of the treaty.

The destruction of Europe during the war benefited the U.S. economy. As a source of credit and goods, the United States became the leading country of the world, and new technologies and cheap energy sustained this boom.

Although Congress stopped a major presidential initiative on foreign affairs and defense when it voted against the League of Nations, Congress was responsible for an initiative with major international consequences. During the Wilson administration, Congress had reduced tariffs. In the 1920s a Republican-controlled Congress began raising tariffs to protect U.S. industry, especially manufacturers that had prospered during the war from reduced European competition. In 1930, in response to demands by U.S. industry for protection from foreign competition, Congress passed a very high tariff, called the Smoot-Hawley Tariff Act after its congressional sponsors. As many people had predicted, other countries responded by raising their tariffs. World trade declined rapidly. By 1932, the middle of the Great Depression, trade was at only about one-third of its former level.

The refusal of the United States to participate in the League of Nations and attempts to erect a high wall of tariffs around the U.S. economy reflected the post-World War I attitudes of **isolationism** and **unilateralism,** the beliefs that the United States should stay completely out of European affairs and could, if necessary, take action without consulting other foreign powers. Many Americans thought that U.S. national interests were best served by keeping out of foreign political or economic affairs and by acting alone, if action had to be taken. The Great Depression began to change this view. Not only did it create a better understanding of the links between the U.S. and foreign economies, but leaders later attributed the rise of Adolf Hitler and other rulers bent on world domination to the economic turmoil of the times. The failure to participate in the League of Nations also meant that the world community had little chance of preserving the peace. Germans saw the League as part of an unreasonably harsh peace treaty, while the Russians, Japanese, and Italians viewed the League as opposing their national interests. Without U.S. power behind it, the League had only Great Britain and France to rely on, neither of which had recovered fully from World War I.

The desire to stay out of European affairs persisted throughout the 1930s in many quarters in the United States, particularly Congress. There, American isolationists, mostly Republicans, passed a series of Neutrality Acts to keep President Franklin D.

Roosevelt, other officials, or private citizens from involving the country in foreign conflicts. Through its immigration policy, the United States also prevented many refugees from persecution in Europe and Asia from entering the country, although many scientists fleeing European oppression did arrive in the 1930s and later played an important role in developing U.S. military and nuclear power.

In *United States* v. *Curtiss-Wright Export Corporation* (1936), the U.S. Supreme Court upheld the right of the Congress to grant broad authority to the president to act in foreign affairs and specifically to him to prohibit arms shipments to participants in foreign wars.[7] While referring to an isolationist policy, in this ruling the U.S. Supreme Court recognized the primary importance of the president in foreign policy and affirmed that the national government did not share power over foreign relations with the states. This marked the first time that the Supreme Court formally recognized the concept of inherent powers of the national government in foreign affairs.

The Great Shift

In part because of the failure of the United States to play a responsible role in world affairs, the world found itself at war again in 1939. The resistance of American isolationists finally crumbled in December 1941, when the Japanese attacked U.S. territory by bombing Pearl Harbor in Hawaii and Germany declared war on the United States.

President Franklin D. Roosevelt quickly mobilized the U.S. economy for war. Increased spending for war materials helped boost U.S. industry out of its slow recovery from the Great Depression. Through its lend-lease program, by which Congress gave the president the authority to lend or lease any equipment to any country whose defense he believed necessary to the defense of the United States, the country provided its allies with the weapons, equipment, and supplies necessary to wage war against the Axis powers (Germany, Italy, and Japan). As the tide of World War II began to favor the United States and its allies, they began to plan for a more peaceful and prosperous world.

Before the end of World War II, the United States and fifty-one of its allies created a new international governmental organization, the **United Nations.** Its purposes were to guarantee the security of member nations when attacked and to promote economic, physical, and social well-being around the world. This guarantee depended on the cooperation of the five great powers that had worked together to defeat the Axis powers—China, France, Great Britain, the Soviet Union, and the United States; these nations made up the United Nations Security Council. The search for peace had become even more important with the development of a weapon of immense destructive power, the atomic bomb, which the United States had dropped on Hiroshima and Nagasaki in August 1945 to help end the war with Japan.

After the war, the allies also created new international economic organizations to encourage trade, which many people believed would lead to both greater prosperity and peace. To stabilize exchange rates among various currencies, the allies established the **International Monetary Fund** (IMF). To provide funds for large-scale projects in an effort to help heal the war-torn economies of Europe and Japan, the allies started the International Bank for Reconstruction and Development, better known as the

Political scientist Jeane Kirkpatrick was the U.S. ambassador to the United Nations during the Reagan administration.

[7] 299 U.S. 304 (1936).

During much of the Cold War, both the United States and the Soviet Union carried on testing of nuclear weapons. The rapid expansion of nuclear arsenals resulted in a stalemate position known as Mutually Assured Destruction (MAD), whereby a first strike by either superpower would result in a devastating counterstrike.

World Bank. Finally, to lower trade barriers, the allies hoped to create an International Trade Organization, but fears that the organization would threaten control over the national economy led the U.S. Congress to reject these efforts. In its place, the allies began work on the **General Agreement on Tariffs and Trade** (GATT), a set of agreements which brought about a substantial reduction in tariff levels and which continues to guide international trade today.

U.S. participation in these institutions indicated a shift from unilateralism to **multilateralism,** that is, a belief that foreign policy actions should be taken in cooperation with other states after extensive consultation. With promises of peace and cooperation in the air, the U.S. Army's size dropped from more than eight million at the close of World War II to less than one million by 1947. The peace and cooperation were not to last, however.

The Origins of the Cold War

Cooperation between the United States and the Soviet Union, critical to peace after the war, quickly eroded. The leader of the Soviet Union, Joseph Stalin, seemed willing to do anything to make the countries of Central Europe communist. In the eastern Mediterranean, particularly Greece and Turkey, the British had maintained a sphere of influence (an area dominated although not directly controlled by a country) before World War II. Because they had been weakened financially by the war, the British did not think they could continue this influence. They asked the United States to assume support for countries in the region now threatened by communist forces. In a flurry of activity, the State Department in a period of fifteen weeks devised a set of policies that turned the United States into a global power.

The Republican chair of the Senate Foreign Relations Committee, Arthur Vandenberg of Michigan, was sympathetic to this policy shift but remembered how Republicans—Vandenberg himself among them—had resisted President Roosevelt's attempts to end isolationism before World War II. He counseled President Harry S Truman to "scare hell out of the country" in order to win support for global policies. Truman did, in a 1947 speech to both houses of Congress that laid out the policy known as the **Truman Doctrine,** that is, a policy of containment of Soviet expansion. In a key passage, Truman stated "it must be the policy of the United States to support free peoples who are resisting attempted subjugation by armed minorities or by outside pressures."[8]

The speech created an ideological consensus that cut across all parties and justified participation in world events—the consensus of anti-communism. It also created the belief that national security was something Americans needed to worry about even when the world was at peace and even when there were no apparent direct military threats to the United States.

Truman's speech also created the belief that public support for foreign and military policy required "scaring hell" out of the American people. President Truman's successors have tried to make external dangers as frightening as possible: the Soviets can attack us with long-range rockets (John F. Kennedy on "the missile gap"), a communist victory in Vietnam would endanger the Hawaiian islands (Lyndon B. Johnson on Vietnam), the military buildup in the U.S.S.R. ("the Evil Empire") has created a "window of vulnerability" (Ronald Reagan on military spending), and, even as late as 1990, nothing that has happened in the former Soviet Union should "lull us into a sense of complacency" (George Bush).

These presidents were intuitive historians who saw the appeasement of Hitler in the 1930s as leading to World War II. They all wanted to avoid another Munich Pact, in which the British and French agreed to allow Nazi Germany to occupy part of Czechoslovakia without a fight in the mistaken belief that Hitler would stop there. To the post-World War II presidents, allowing Soviet-style communists to take over a country without resistance would simply encourage Soviet expansionism.

Truman's innovative words were followed by innovative actions. U.S. military forces were stationed permanently overseas for the first time. The U.S. naval presence in the Mediterranean, which it had planned to end, now became a permanent fixture called the Sixth Fleet. In 1948, for the first time since World War II, long-range American bombers were sent to Great Britain. Conscription of young men into the military service, something Americans had previously been subject to only in wartime, now continued into peacetime (until the creation of the all-volunteer army in 1971). And for the first time in its history the United States entered into military and political alliances in peacetime.

The Marshall Plan, NATO, and Containment

Through much of his time in office, President Harry S Truman was unpopular. He had not been elected to the office but had inherited it on the death of Roosevelt in 1945. His support in the public opinion polls, high at first, dwindled. Yet he accomplished remarkable things in foreign policy and won reelection in 1948. He proposed and got Congress to approve the European Recovery Program, often called the **Marshall Plan** after his Secretary of State, George C. Marshall. In a break with tradition, the Marshall Plan provided a massive transfer of aid from the United States mainly to Western Eu-

---

[8] Quoted in Henry Steel Commager, *Documents of American History,* 7th ed. (New York: Appleton-Century-Crofts, 1963), p. 525.

FIGURE 18-2

The Cold War in Europe

In 1949 the United States sponsored the creation of the North Atlantic Treaty Organization (NATO), an alliance of ten European nations, the United States, and Canada. West Germany was formally admitted to NATO membership in May 1955. A few days later the Soviet Union and seven other Communist nations established a rival alliance, the Warsaw Pact.

Source: James A. Henretta, *America's History; Volume 2: Since 1865*, Worth Publishers.

rope. In its first year alone, 1948–49, the Marshall Plan sent the West Europeans more than $6 billion. At that time, that amounted to 10 percent of the entire federal budget, 4.1 percent of the gross domestic product, and 2.8 percent of the gross national product. A program of equal magnitude forty years later would have cost the United States about $100 billion. The Plan succeeded in rebuilding the basis for strong economies in Western Europe, which, in turn, helped prevent communist parties from winning elections there.

Another indication of Truman's authority in foreign affairs is that the United States for the first time joined a political and military alliance in peacetime. The North Atlantic Treaty, signed in 1949, provided that a military attack against any of the signatories (Belgium, Canada, Denmark, France, Great Britain, Iceland, Italy, Luxembourg, the Netherlands, Norway, Portugal, and the United States) would be considered an attack against all of them. The **North Atlantic Treaty Organization** (NATO), which created a mutual defense organization, was set up the following year to implement the treaty (see Figure 18-2). Even though the United States was not at war and was not directly threatened by any hostile state, hundreds of thousands of U.S. troops were moved to Europe (more, in fact, than were moved to Asia during the same years to fight the Korean War) in an effort to stop the spread of communism.

Two crises—one in Europe, the other in Asia—quickly set the stage for U.S. policy in the postwar era. In 1947 the communists seized power in Czechoslovakia and the allies failed to intervene. The following year, the Soviet Union blockaded access by highway, rail, and waterway to the Western sectors of the former German capital city,

Berlin (similar to the occupation of the rest of Germany, the allies had agreed to control different zones of Berlin). Even though the Germans had recently been the enemies of the United States, Truman decided to supply Berlin's population with food and other essentials by air. Despite doubts raised by his military advisers (in the middle of an election year), Truman acted decisively and persisted until the Soviets lifted the blockade a year later.

Two years after winning the 1948 election, Truman was confronted with a crisis in Asia. After World War II, Korea had been partitioned into two zones, the one in the North occupied by Soviet troops, the one in the South by U.S. troops. Disagreements between the United States and the Soviet Union prevented reunification and led instead to the creation of separate states. Then, in 1950, North Korea invaded South Korea. The United States was taken by surprise, but after brief consideration Truman decided to commit U.S. forces to help South Korea resist. The United States was able to get support for its action from the United Nations only because the Soviets were not attending Security Council meetings in protest of the recent decision not to replace the nationalist Chinese delegation to the Security Council with that of the communist government in Beijing. (Security Council resolutions require unanimous approval of all permanent members present.)[9] U.S. troops did not stop the North Koreans in the first weeks, but the tide of the war was reversed by a dramatic amphibious landing staged by the U.S. commander General Douglas MacArthur at the port city of Inchon. The tide of war reversed again when Chinese troops intervened in force on North Korea's behalf in November 1950.

The Marshall Plan, NATO, and U.S. actions in Berlin and Korea are examples of what became known as **containment.** Based on the observations of a U.S. diplomat, George Kennan, the United States sought to contain Soviet communism. Kennan argued that if the allies could stop the spread of communism, especially in Europe, the nature of the Soviet leadership and its political system would collapse. In practice this meant surrounding the Soviet Union with U.S. or allied military forces in an effort to deter the Red Army and deny or delay access to many Western goods and technologies through restrictions on trade and investment. This policy was criticized by the left as too hostile (because the military deployments would provoke the Soviets) and by the right as too soft (because the United States did not roll back communism in Eastern Europe and China). Much of the policy was clarified in a complete review of U.S. foreign and defense policy conducted by the President's National Security Council (see pp. 774–775). NSC Study number 68 (NSC-68), completed in 1950, maintained that the security of the United States was the same as the security of the Western, democratic world. With some modifications, containment was the framework of U.S. foreign and military policy until the 1990s.

The Cold War Era

Looking back, containment limited communist expansion in Europe until the Soviet Union collapsed, as Kennan had theorized. The political and military stability provided by the policy of containment and the economic stability promoted by international economic institutions, such as the IMF, the World Bank, and the GATT, allowed the Western allies (particularly the NATO members and Japan) to focus on economic

---

[9] Permanent members of the Security Council are the United States, the Soviet Union (now Russia), France, Great Britain, and China.

development. The rapid recovery of Western Europe resulted in a spectacular round of global economic prosperity. Between 1950 and 1973, world trade grew every year but one and did so at unprecedented rates. Private U.S. investment overseas, mainly in Western Europe, and foreign investment in the United States increased dramatically after 1950. Finally, the Gross National Product of the United States in constant dollar terms expanded in all but seven years between 1948 and 1990; this was an exceptional amount of sustained economic growth.

Most important, containment did not lead to another world war. In 1940, the last year before the United States entered World War II, federal expenditures on defense were equal to 17.5 percent of the total federal budget and only 1.7 percent of the U.S. Gross Domestic Product (GDP). In contrast, between 1947 and 1987, U.S. defense expenditures averaged 39.9 percent of the budget and 7.7 percent of GDP. Also, in contrast to efforts to curb arms sales before World War II, after the war the United States became the major supplier of arms to the rest of the Western world. As President Eisenhower later noted, by the 1950s the U.S. government had created a "military-industrial complex" that made the military and defense industries a dominant factor in U.S. politics.

After the Soviet Union exploded its own atomic bomb in 1949, both sides began to build nuclear arsenals. Although the United States maintained a significant advantage in the early years, both sides eventually had enough nuclear weapons to absorb an attack by the other and launch a devastating nuclear strike in retaliation. This situation, known as Mutually Assured Destruction (MAD), deterred each side from attacking the other. As the dangers of nuclear war became clearer after the Cuban Missile Crisis (the United States–U.S.S.R. confrontation in 1962 over the installation of Soviet ballistic missiles in Cuba), both sides began efforts to agree on limits to the size of their own nuclear forces and to attempt to stop the spread of nuclear weapons to other countries.

During the Cuban Missile Crisis in 1962, President Kennedy watches U.S. aircraft taking off for Cuba.

Containment was less clear on defining the appropriate role for the United States in wars of "national liberation," such as Vietnam. With little information on the nature of the Vietnam conflict, such as the relative independence of the Vietnamese communist movement from Soviet or Chinese control or the history of U.S. involvement in the region, Congress and the public were easily deceived on the extent and consequences of U.S. involvement by more than one administration. Perhaps the worst instance was the degree to which the Johnson administration misled Congress in order to pass the Gulf of Tonkin Resolution, which originally authorized a massive commitment of U.S. forces to support a series of an anti-communist—though not democratic—governments in South Vietnam. As the war expanded, U.S. casualties escalated, and repeated promises of victory were never fulfilled. More and more Americans questioned the wisdom of U.S. involvement.

U.S. forces left South Vietnam in 1973, but the 57,000 dead and 300,000 other casualties, the unpopularity of the war at home (see Figure 18-3), and the failure to build a truly democratic government in Vietnam created a much longer legacy. Much like the lesson of appeasement for the World War II generation of leaders, many current leaders see Vietnam as a lesson on the limits of U.S. military power. In fact, in the

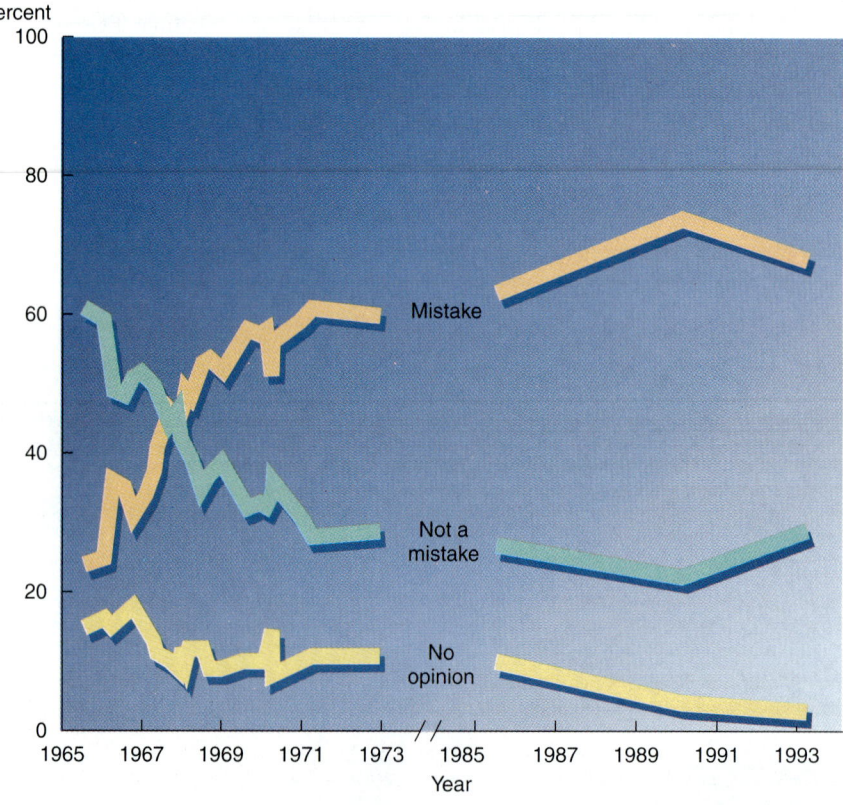

FIGURE 18-3
Public Opinion on the Vietnam War, 1965–1993

Note: Question: "In view of the developments since we entered the fighting in Vietnam, do you think the United States made a mistake sending troops to fight in Vietnam?" In 1985, 1990, and 1993, the question was, "Looking back, do you think...?" The question was not asked between 1974 and 1984.
Sources: Gallup polls cited in John Mueller, *War, Presidents and Public Opinion* (New York: Wiley, 1973), 54-55 (reprinted in 1985 by University Press of America, Lanham, Md.); *The Gallup Poll, 1972-1975*, vol. I (Wilmington, Del: Scholarly Resources, 1977), 87; *The Gallup Poll Monthly,* January 1993, 37.
"Foreign and Military Policy", p.356 in: *Vital Statistics on American Politics*, 4th ed. Harold Stanley and Richard Niemi, eds. 1994 Congressional Quarterly, Inc. Reprinted by permission.

Presidents and Unpopular Wars

On Memorial Day 1993, President Bill Clinton went to the Vietnam Memorial, where he faced the jeers of Vietnam veterans who were angered by Clinton's anti-war activities during the Vietnam War. Clinton is not the only president to have opposed the United States' participation in a war. President Ulysses S. Grant, who actually served with distinction in the Mexican War (1846–48) said of it, "I do not think there was ever a more wicked war than that waged by the United States in Mexico. I thought so at the time, when I was a youngster, only I had not the moral courage enough to resign." Likewise, President Warren G. Harding said of World War I, "It's a lie from beginning to end that we are in the war for democracy's sake."*

*"Questions in the News," *Atlanta Journal-Constitution* (June 2, 1993): A2.

Vietnam veterans protest President Clinton's anti-Vietnam War activities.

days following the death of several U.S. soldiers in Somalia in 1993, many members of Congress echoed the sentiment of Representative Jim Ramstad (R.-Minn.), who warned, "The president better get his foreign policy act together before Somalia becomes another Vietnam."[10]

Containment also said little about an appropriate foreign economic policy for the United States once Europe and Japan recovered from World War II. Encouraged by U.S. success in rebuilding Europe in the 1950s, President John F. Kennedy saw U.S. foreign aid and assistance programs and international economic institutions as means

---

[10] "U.S. Boosts Forces in Somalia," *Star Tribune* (October 5, 1993): 1A.

of transforming poor countries in Africa, Asia, and Latin America into prosperous, anti-communist nations. The United States, together with other wealthy countries, did not offer programs as large as the Marshall Plan for problems that turned out to be much more difficult to solve.

Foreign assistance programs take many forms, including low-interest loans, free food or weapons, and outright grants-in-aid. Often, direct U.S. aid to another country is tied to that country's promises to purchase U.S. goods. One reason for the success of multilateral lending institutions, such as the World Bank, is the demand for aid without such strings attached.

Most U.S. loans and grants are made by the U.S. Agency for International Development. Although for most of the last four decades the United States has made the largest foreign aid contributions (in dollar amounts) of any country, the total aid is typically around one-half of one percent of the federal budget (around $8 billion in 1993), much less than the amounts given by many other rich countries. Of the roughly $78 billion dollars distributed by the U.S. Agency for International Development or its predecessors between 1962 and 1989, most went to governments threatened by communist forces, as in El Salvador, Korea, Pakistan, the Philippines, South Vietnam, and Turkey. The two countries receiving the most aid were Israel and Egypt, because of their role in the Middle East conflict. Diplomatic and military policies, however, are not the only determinant of U.S. aid. Substantial sums of money and supplies have gone for humanitarian purposes to countries in the Third World.

By the 1970s, global economic conditions had changed dramatically from the 1940s. Japan and some of the countries of the European Community (an economic and political association consisting mainly of the allies of the United States in Western Europe) had dramatically improved their economic strength and technological ability and their products were challenging those of the United States in the global marketplace. In the early 1970s, the global economy also suffered its first major depression since the end of World War II. Many people in the United States began to complain that non-tariff barriers to trade used by other governments were hurting U.S. exports, while the U.S. market was relatively open. As a result, support for U.S. free trade policies began to decline.

One key element of postwar economic recovery was the stability of the U.S. dollar, with the values of most currencies fixed to the value of gold and the dollar (called the fixed exchange-rate system). Through the IMF, the dollar had become the global currency, with large deposits of U.S. dollars overseas. This meant that the U.S. government had less capacity to influence inflation and interest rates through its control over the money supply. In 1971, President Richard M. Nixon abandoned this system, which eventually led to the current system, in which the value of the U.S. dollar and other major currencies depends on what people are willing to pay for them (called a floating exchange-rate system).

Finally, many Third World countries now viewed the United States and other rich, industrialized countries as economic adversaries and called for the creation of a new world economic order. In 1960 some of these countries joined together in a cartel known as the Organization of Petroleum Exporting Countries (OPEC). They gained influence in the global economy by raising the price of oil during much of the 1970s. Although the success of OPEC proved to be an exception compared with other efforts by Third World countries to control the supply or price of raw commodities, it symbolized Third World dissatisfaction with the global economy.

The United States and the other key industrial powers have tried to coordinate their trade, investment, and monetary policies more closely since the 1970s. The leaders of

> ## The Third World
>
> In 1952, Alfred Sauvy, a French sociologist, coined the term *tiers monde* or Third World to describe the countries that were neither aligned with the United States (the First or Free World) or the Soviet Union (the Second or Communist World). The term is patterned after the phrase *Third Estate* used to describe the less powerful commoners of France when it was ruled by a king and the Catholic clergy. Although widely used in the U.S. in the 1960s to refer to most Asian, African, and Arab countries, the term is now in disrepute. By grouping so many countries together, many policy makers and analysts underestimated crucial social, economic, and political variations in the Third World. In the last two decades, oil- and export-induced economic growth made some Third World countries much richer than others, causing some to suggest that there was now a Fourth World comprised of the poorest of the poor countries. Coupled with the collapse of Soviet communism, the phrase *Third World* seems to have little meaning for international relations in the 1990s.
>
> *Source:* William Safire, *Safire's New Political Dictionary* (New York: Random House, 1993), p. 795.

the Group of seven countries—Canada, France, Germany, Great Britain, Italy, Japan, and the United States—now hold annual economic summits to discuss political and economic issues of mutual concern. Substantial disagreements remain, however, and many people fear that the world is dividing into three competing economic blocs—East Asia, Europe, and North America. Taken together, these problems have diminished the consensus in the United States in support of freer trade and an open economy.

The Machinery of Modern Foreign Policy Making

In *Federalist No. 8,* John Jay noted that "it is the nature of war to increase the executive at the expense of the legislative authority." One consequence of World War II and the Cold War was the creation of a foreign policy-making process in the United States in which the president plays the major role. Congress supported a larger role for the United States in global military affairs with the **National Security Acts of 1947 and 1949.** These Acts consolidated the army, the navy, and the new air force into one department under civilian leadership, with the name the Department of Defense. (Previously the military office in the Cabinet had been named the War Department.) The legislation also set up two agencies: (1) the Central Intelligence Agency (CIA), which would collect and analyze the information deemed necessary to meet national security threats, and (2) the National Security Council (NSC), made up of the president, the vice president, the Secretaries of State and Defense, the chair of the Joint Chiefs of Staff, and the Director of Central Intelligence. The NSC, along with the newly created post of Assistant to the President for National Security Affairs (the National Security Advisor), would advise the president on foreign and military affairs.

This policy-making process differed sharply from the process the United States had followed in the past. The president now commanded a vast military-industrial complex supported by a large foreign policy and intelligence network. The NSC, set up to institutionalize the system by which the U.S. government had conducted World War II, was used in later years to coordinate foreign policy issues, such as dealing with the fall of the shah of Iran or negotiating a new canal treaty with Panama.

In most critical military and foreign policy matters, direction is provided by the president with advice from the members of the NSC, the National Security Advisor, and the NSC staff with input from other executive departments and agencies as the president desires. For foreign economic policy, President Bill Clinton created a National Economic Council (NEC) with a role parallel to the NSC's influence on security policy. The inner core of the NEC includes a presidential advisor who chairs the council, the Secretaries of Labor, Treasury, and Commerce, the Director of the Office of Management and Budget, the U.S. Trade Representative, and the head of the Council of Economic Advisors. The NSC and the NEC work together, even share staff, on a number of issues, including trade. They also work with the Domestic Policy Council on some non-economic issues.

Compared with domestic policy, Congress and interest groups generally have a relatively smaller role in making foreign and military policy. Their role in foreign economic and military funding policies is somewhat larger, but not as large as their role in purely domestic policies.

President Harry S Truman and his successors have been able to win support for their foreign and military policies so often that we must conclude that success flows *not* from the person in office but the *office itself.* The U.S. political system bestows tremendous formal and informal powers on the president in the area of relations with foreign countries and in the policy areas of foreign relations and defense. The question then is, how and why has this happened?

Most important, the nature of foreign and military policy often differs from the nature of domestic policy in ways that reinforce the power of the president. Alexander Hamilton, in *Federalist No. 75,* recognized that foreign policy was different from domestic policy because it required

1. Accurate and comprehensive knowledge of foreign politics
2. A steady and systematic adherence to the same views
3. A nice and uniform sensibility to national character
4. Decision, secrecy, and despatch [sic].

On each point, the office of the president has an advantage over Congress. The advantage is captured neatly by the story of the Cuban Missile Crisis, which brought the United States and the Soviet Union very close to nuclear war. In foreign affairs, crises often arise in which the country faces a great threat with little time for decision making. In late summer of 1962, the Soviet Union secretly began placing nuclear missiles in Cuba. President John F. Kennedy knew, through the resources of the executive branch, what the Soviets were doing—although the Soviets did not know that he knew. (Without secrecy, the Soviets might have sped up their construction of missile bases, thus increasing the likelihood of war.) At most, Kennedy had a few weeks before Soviet preparations in Cuba were complete. After three days of deliberation, Kennedy and his advisers decided on a blockade to force the missiles out. Soviet vessels

> ## How Did JFK Handle Crises?
> ## Clinton Seeks Help in History
>
> In the midst of handling an endless series of crises—from Haiti and Somalia to NAFTA and health care—President Clinton took two hours off this week to try to learn how John F. Kennedy dealt with adversity.
>
> You know the parallels: Young, bright president, inexperienced in foreign policy, sandbagged by poor staffing, staggering from one foreign policy debacle to another: the Bay of Pigs, the disastrous summit with Nikita Khrushchev in Vienna, Austria.
>
> So the Clintons met with Richard Reeves, author of the acclaimed new biography of Kennedy that has become must reading at the White House. The brief Oval Office drop-by became lunch with an impromptu invitation from Hillary Rodham Clinton. Reeves; his wife, columnist Catherine O'Neill; and Washington lobbyist Liz Robbins, a mutual friend who arranged the visit, ate at a small table on a patio off the president's private office.
>
> The group held a wide-ranging discussion, comparing the Washington of the early 1960s with Washington today.
>
> One difference, Clinton observed, is that in matters of foreign policy, Kennedy had the benefit of being able to explain crises comparable to Haiti and Somalia within a Cold War context. He was always able to say the country had to act this way or that because the Russians were coming.
>
> Kennedy detested the military, Reeves noted, saying that he did not trust them and thought they were, with some exceptions, stupid. "Clinton rejected this," at the lunch, Reeves said, with the president saying that the military is much better educated and much more sophisticated than the fighters of World War II and that today's military better understands the political element involved in any equation.
>
> Another aspect of Kennedy that intrigues Clinton was JFK's ability to delay his decisions until his team had fully finished all deliberations. "How Kennedy kept situations open so long without making a decision," Reeves recalled.
>
> "The answer, of course, is you stay out of sight, don't be on television every day," Reeves noted. Naturally, that was much easier for Kennedy than Clinton, because the press was much less pervasive in the early 1960s.
>
> *Source:* From: "For Lunch, a Course on JFK," by Al Kamen, *Washington Post,* October 22, 1993. Reprinted with permission of The Washington Post.

stopped short of U.S. naval forces surrounding Cuba, and the Soviet leader, Nikita Khrushchev, agreed to remove the missiles.

By confining his decision making to a small group of trusted advisers, Kennedy gained time. It is unlikely that within a larger body the secret could have been kept. Kennedy was also able to decide quickly, while Congress would have had many opportunities for delay. As the only federal official elected by the nation as a whole, President Kennedy could more easily consider the national interest than could members of Congress, who were responsible to a particular district or state. Finally, Kennedy had all of the executive branch at his command while Congress had few resources directly under its control.

The Information Gap

A president's command of the executive branch is an important reason the president dominates foreign policy making: The president has great access to and control over information. This situation is quite unlike that of domestic politics, in which many

THEN AND NOW

Communication Technology and Foreign Policy

Traditionally the slowness of communications and the vast oceans separating the United States from the rest of the world permitted a slow and orderly reaction to world events. The war between the British and the United States that began in 1812 illustrates how slowly news traveled.

A traditional American banjo tune known as "The 8th of January" celebrates the 1815 date of the Battle of New Orleans, when General Andrew Jackson held off the British, suffering 350 casualties to the British's 2,450. But officially the War of 1812 had already been ended by a treaty signed in Belgium on December 24, 1814. The British ratified the treaty and then Americans and Britons boarded a ship in London on January 2, 1815, to bring the treaty and the British ratification to the United States. Because of bad weather, the ship did not arrive in New York until February 11. News did not reach the nation's capital until February 15.

By contrast, when U.S. aircraft and cruise missiles began their opening strike against Iraq on January 17, 1991, the event was covered live on U.S. television. Several cable network reporters in a hotel room were able to broadcast the battle of Baghdad as it happened. It became the first prime-time war. Later, television recorded Iraqi Scud missiles landing in Israel, a practice criticized as providing important targeting information to the Iraqis. During the war in the Persian Gulf, cable subscriptions increased dramatically, and cable audiences increased 350 percent in February 1993.

Since then, many world leaders, including President Bill Clinton, have come to rely on cable television news as a source of information for current events. Television crews bring starvation in Somalia, shelling in Bosnia, and former President Carter's diplomatic mission to Haiti into our homes and into the White House.

people, including those in the Congress, the media, and interest groups, often have important information that bears on policy decisions. Such information is a source of power.

When dealing with foreign affairs, the president has exclusive sources of information—diplomats working for the State Department, military attachés working for the Defense Department, agents controlled by the CIA, and technical devices (such as satellites) controlled by the National Security Agency (the NSA, which is in charge of electronic intelligence gathering). Private citizens, companies, interest groups, even Congress cannot balance the president's information with their own on issues such as the number of Soviet missiles in Cuba or the extent of Iraq's nuclear weapons program. Even the one source of information available to the president's critics, the news media, is dominated by the president (see Chapter 14).

The president's authority is enhanced by the aura of secret information available to him: diplomatic cables, CIA reports, NSA intercepts. Sometimes, to win points in debates against rivals, the president will declassify secret information. Virtually any other citizen could be prosecuted for revealing classified material, but the president may do so freely. In 1962 the presence of Soviet missiles in Cuba was a tightly held secret until President John F. Kennedy chose to reveal it in a dramatic nationwide broadcast. In the 1980 election campaign, President Jimmy Carter, under attack from Republican opponents for neglecting U.S. defenses, authorized his Secretary of De-

U.S. Marine headquarters after the bombing by Lebanese terrorists in which 241 American soldiers and marines were killed.

fense to reveal that the United States had been developing a plane that would be invisible to radar, the Stealth bomber.

Challenges to Presidential Power

The president is powerful in the field of foreign policy but not omnipotent. International factors place limits on the power of the president. The foreign and military policy of the United States is often criticized as simply a reaction to the policies of other countries. In addition, all presidents face domestic constraints on their power from Congress, the bureaucracy, the media, and the public as well.

Congress

The most consistent restraint on presidential power in foreign affairs comes from Congress. The Constitution gives a lesser role to Congress in foreign affairs than in domestic affairs, but much of the modern-day power of the president comes from broad authority granted the executive through legislation, not through the Constitution. Congress also exercises its oversight powers on the foreign policy and military activities of the president and the executive branch.

Congressional Leadership. Normally the president proposes a foreign policy and Congress accepts, modifies, or rejects it. Congress also has the power to develop and implement policy. When the Soviet Union launched *Sputnik,* the first artificial Earth satellite, in 1957, President Dwight D. Eisenhower, unlike many prominent Americans, did not treat it as a serious threat to U.S. security. With no proposal of action from the president, under the guidance of Senate Majority Leader Lyndon B. Johnson, the Preparedness Subcommittee of the Senate Armed Services Committee held hear-

Presidential power in matters of foreign policy, while broader than that of the Legislative branch, is not absolute. President Clinton seeks public support for his foreign policy initiatives, just as he does for his domestic policies.

ings on the threat posed by Soviet space potential. Determining that there was indeed a threat, Congress set up the National Aeronautics and Space Administration (NASA) to run a U.S. space program and the National Defense Education Act to provide funding for science and foreign language education. Although technically civilian programs, these were seen at the time as very much a part of U.S. defense policy.

Congressional Oversight. Congressional oversight is a relatively new check on the president's power to set foreign and military policy. During and after World War II, weapons became more and more complex, and Congress was willing to defer to presidential recommendations and military advice on what weapons the country needed. But in 1969, Congress for the first time challenged a president on a major defense expenditure. President Richard M. Nixon proposed a nationwide system of radar and interceptor missiles to defend against incoming missiles, known at the time as Anti-Ballistic Missiles (ABMs). The Senate, relying on expert testimony by Defense Department officials who had actually tried to develop such systems and believed they would not work, came within a single vote of turning down Nixon's request. Since 1969 the U.S. public has become accustomed to congressional scrutiny of weapon development and deployment.

Treaties and Executive Agreements. The Constitution gives the Senate explicit power to approve treaties; the defeat of the Versailles Peace Treaty and the League of Nations in 1919 reminded everyone that this power was real. Even though in U.S. history treaties have been rejected outright only sixteen times, the power is effective because presidents try to avoid direct defeats. For example, President Jimmy Carter withdrew the SALT II treaty, which put limits on U.S. strategic nuclear forces, rather than let the Senate vote it down.

As noted in Chapter 7, presidents can avoid the treaty process altogether by using executive agreements and have done so more and more frequently since World War II,

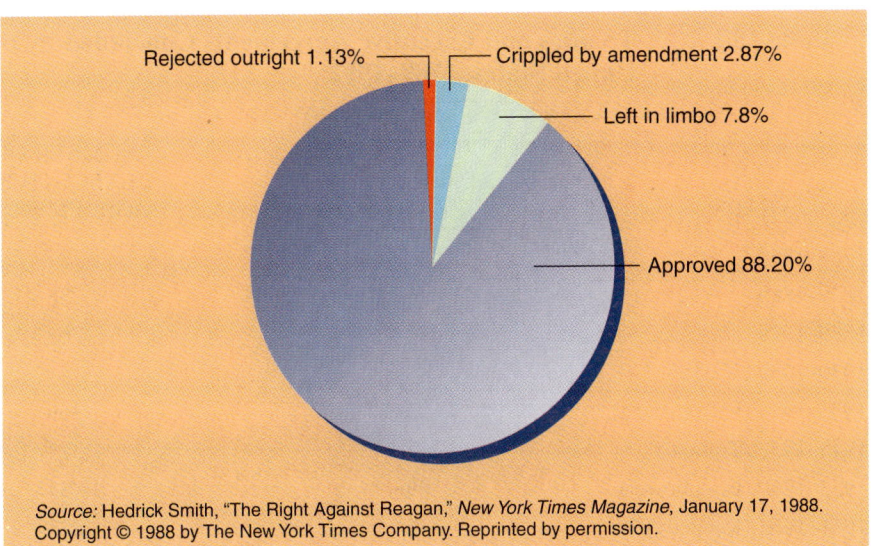

FIGURE 18-4

Fate of Treaties Submitted to the Senate, 1788–1988

as illustrated in Table 18-1. An executive agreement is a government-to-government agreement that does not bind future administrations, and Senate ratification is not required. Normally executive agreements are used for routine business matters, such as purchasing and running embassies. But sometimes executive agreements, such as the Erskine Agreement, have important policy implications. Several executive agreements that established U.S. military bases overseas in such countries as Spain and the Philippines had the effect of allying the United States with these countries without debate or approval by the Senate. Prior to the Case Act of 1972, the president did not even have to inform Congress of the texts of these accords.

Appointments. As head of state and government, the president appoints ambassadors and other persons involved in the formation and implementation of foreign and defense policy. The Constitution gives the Senate the right to provide advice and consent. As in the domestic arena, important political appointees for foreign and defense policy frequently have close connections to Congress. A key link in President Ronald Reagan's foreign policy was the appointment of Richard Perle as Assistant Secretary of Defense. A proponent of a strong anti-Soviet policy, Perle had worked for many years as a staff advisor to conservative Senator Henry "Scoop" Jackson (D.-Wash.), and his knowledge of the issue area, Reagan's policy aims, and the Congress made Perle a powerful figure.

Senators can put a hold on the confirmation process of some foreign policy positions to express concern about an issue as well as about the appointee (see Chapter 6). Sometimes the reasons for withholding consent can be very minor. Senator Jesse Helms (R.-N.C.) stalled President George Bush's nomination of George Fleming Jones as ambassador to Guyana for a record seventeen months in 1991. Helms was upset because he had not been shown State Department memos by Jones, a career diplomat, on a 1986 visit to the U.S. embassy in Chile, where Jones worked at the time. Senator Helms finally removed his hold at the personal request of Deputy Secretary of State Lawrence S. Eagleburger. He used the hold privilege again in 1994 to delay the appointment of political scientist Robert Pastor as ambassador to Panama. Helms dis-

Table 18.1 ♦ Treaties and Executive Agreements Concluded by the United States, 1789–1992

YEARS	NUMBER OF TREATIES	NUMBER OF EXECUTIVE AGREEMENTS
1789–1839	60	27
1839–1889	215	238
1889–1929	382	763
1930–1932	49	41
1933–1944 (F. Roosevelt)	131	369
1945–1952 (Truman)	132	1,324
1953–1960 (Eisenhower)	89	1,834
1961–1963 (Kennedy)	36	813
1964–1968 (L. Johnson)	67	1,083
1969–1974 (Nixon)	93	1,317
1975–1976 (Ford)	26	666
1977–1980 (Carter)	79	1,476
1981–1988 (Reagan)	125	2,840
1989–1992 (Bush)	67	1,371
1993–1994 (Clinton)	17	256

Note: Number of treaties includes those concluded during the indicated span of years. Some of these treaties did not receive the consent of the U.S. Senate. Varying definitions of what comprises an executive agreement and their entry-into-force date make the above numbers approximate.

Sources: 1789–1980: *Congressional Quarterly's Guide to Congress,* 291; 1981–1982: Office of the Assistant Legal Adviser for Treaty Affairs, U.S. Department of State; 1993–1994: Harold Stanley and Richard Niemi, eds., *Vital Statistics on American Politics,* 4th ed. (Washington, DC: Congressional Quarterly, Inc., 1994), p. 280. Reprinted by permission. Clinton data provided by Treaties Office, Department of State.

trusted Pastor's role in the Carter administration's relations with Nicaragua's formerly Marxist government.

Appropriations. Congress can also try to control foreign policy through its power to appropriate funds. The power to go to war is shared between the executive and legislative branches of government, but the power to appropriate funds belongs to the legislature alone. Congress has been cautious about applying this power. In the case of Vietnam, it concentrated its efforts on keeping the war from widening into the neighboring country of Cambodia.

Congress also used its appropriation power to limit U.S. involvement in Nicaragua. In 1979, an insurrection led by guerrillas named after an earlier Nicaraguan hero, Augusto Sandino, allowed the Sandinistas to come to power. But the policies of the Sandinistas provoked opposition from some of the U.S. public. Because the Sandinistas received aid from Cuba and the Soviet Union, those opposing them, known as counterrevolutionaries, or *contras,* found that the Reagan administration was willing to aid them. At first such aid was provided secretly and then in what were called secret or covert operations but in fact were publically known.

However, many people in the United States opposed funding the *contras,* and after much debate, Congress in December 1982 decided to cut the appropriations. The *contras* continued to receive supplies of weapons, however. In 1986 it was revealed that the supplies had been paid for with funds solicited from foreign states and from private individuals and with proceeds from arms deals with the Khomeini regime in Iran (associated with the trading of arms for U.S. hostages in Lebanon, in which members of the Reagan administration participated).

The War Powers Act. Frustrated with their failure to influence policy on Vietnam, members of Congress tried in 1973 to prevent intervention overseas without congressional approval by passing the **War Powers Act** (see "The War Powers Act," below). Under the Act, the president was limited in his deployment of troops overseas to a sixty-day period in peacetime (which could be extended for an extra thirty days to permit withdrawal) unless Congress explicitly gave its approval for a longer period. Under the Act, the president could respond to an emergency, such as rescue of endangered Americans abroad, but not engage in a prolonged struggle without congressional approval.

The War Powers Act has been an issue in the struggle for control of foreign policy between the president and Congress ever since. When first passed, it was vetoed by President Richard M. Nixon. Congress overrode the veto in March 1973, but Nixon called the Act unconstitutional and said he was not bound by it. No issue arose to test the competing claims before Nixon was forced to resign in 1974, but such issues did arise under his successors. President Gerald R. Ford dispatched troops to rescue the crew of the merchant ship *Mayaguez,* captured as it sailed near Cambodia in 1975; in

---

The War Powers Act

❖❖❖

Key provisions of the twenty-year-old law:

- The president must consult Congress "in every possible instance" before committing military forces to imminent or probable combat overseas and must report any such mission to Congress within forty-eight hours.
- Military forces must be brought home within sixty days unless Congress either declares war, otherwise approves of the mission, or extends the withdrawal deadline.

Proposals made in 1988 and 1993 by Senator Sam Nunn (D.-Ga.):

- Sets up a "permanent consultative body" of House and Senate leaders and key committee chairs to meet regularly with the president on foreign policy issues.
- Once military forces are committed overseas, Congress can force their withdrawal only by passing specific legislation. Congress can also pass legislation approving of the mission.
- Spending of federal funds contrary to congressional legislation, such as an order to withdraw troops, would be prohibited.

1980 President Carter dispatched troops in an abortive attempt to rescue U.S. diplomats held hostage in Iran. In neither case did the action last sixty days, but the presidents provided notice to Congress, as the Act required, although in both instances after some delay.

The first serious test of the War Powers Act came under President Ronald Reagan. In 1982 Reagan ordered Marines into Lebanon as part of a peacekeeping mission. Because the troops were not in combat, Congress did not object. But after a year, the Marines came under increasing fire from various factions in Lebanon's civil war. Although Marines were being killed, Congress was slow to invoke the War Powers Act. In the midst of a drawn out debate over U.S. involvement in Lebanon, a Lebanese terrorist drove an explosive-filled truck into the Marine barracks in Beirut, killing 241 servicemen. Shortly thereafter, all Marines were withdrawn on the president's initiative. In this and subsequent actions, presidents have usually complied with parts of the War Powers Act, especially the requirements for notifying key members of Congress. More important, President George Bush solicited congressional approval for the use of force in the Persian Gulf War, recognizing the importance of bringing Congress into the decision-making process. In January 1994 President Bill Clinton, for example, told NATO leaders that he would seek Congressional approval before agreeing to the use of U.S. air strikes or ground troops in Bosnia.

The Bureaucracy

One major check on the foreign policy and military powers of the president comes from inside the executive branch. The president is recognized as the ultimate executive authority, but, as noted in Chapter 8, the federal bureaucracy must implement those decisions. Without full support of career bureaucrats, who usually have expert knowledge of the issues and procedures, policy decisions and actions can be ignored or delayed, and information can be leaked to Congress or the media to raise issues on the political agenda or to embarrass the president. Since many bureaucrats have strong ties to Congress or interest groups such as the defense industries, their loyalties may be divided. Former Secretary of State and National Security Advisor Henry Kissinger even tapped the telephones of some of his subordinates based on his suspicion that someone was leaking damaging information about the Vietnam War to the media. This old and unsubstantiated allegation resurfaced to undermine the nomination of Morton Halperin as an Assistant Secretary of Defense in 1994 when the charges were exploited by opponents of the Clinton administration.

Information. The president can access a broader range of information than any other public official or private individual in the United States, but rarely is this information received in the form of raw data. Even presidents who are "policy wonks" (people who immerse themselves in the numerous details of policy) such as Presidents Carter and Clinton cannot filter the huge amount of information that comes in every minute. By the time the president gets information from the CIA, the State Department, and other sources, it has usually gone through a few levels of bureaucratic screening. During the early years of the Cold War, for example, air force intelligence sources consistently argued that the Soviet Union had more long-range bombers than the CIA estimated. Not surprisingly, the more Soviet long-range bombers there were, the more funding the air force could demand to meet the increased Soviet threat from the air.

Implementation. Once the president makes a foreign or military policy decision, the bureaucracy must act. Decisions to integrate blacks and women into the U.S. military were resisted by many career military personnel, and incidents of racial and gender discrimination persisted long after the original orders. More recently, President Bill Clinton's interest in ending discrimination against homosexuals into the military was opposed by so many career military personnel (as well as many members of Congress and the public) that he compromised to develop a "don't ask, don't tell" policy.

The News Media

Along with Congress and the bureaucracy, the press provides some check on presidential power in foreign and military affairs. During World War II and the early Cold War years, the press tended to support the president. As a rule, editors assumed that government statements were true and printed them as unquestioned fact. In the mid-1960s, however, the press's role as a prop for foreign policy began to change.

Investigation. Fidel Castro had taken over Cuba in 1959 and installed a regime that he himself called Marxist-Leninist. The Democrats made much in the 1960 election of the fact that a communist regime had been set up "only ninety miles" from Florida. When an insurrection broke out in the neighboring Dominican Republic in 1965, President Lyndon B. Johnson came under pressure to act to prevent "another Cuba." The U.S. government provided transportation to the Dominican Republic to reporters, and the U.S. embassy provided a briefing, complete with stories of atrocities committed by the rebels. The reporters quickly discovered, however, that the stories were not true. Relations between press and government swiftly became adversarial as reporters challenged statements at press conferences.

Critical reporting spread distrust of the president within the United States. In September 1965, six months after the U.S. Marines had landed, the respected chair of the Senate Foreign Relations committee, Senator William Fulbright (D.-Ark.), gave a major speech on the floor of the Senate in which he denounced the administration for what he called "the arrogance of power." Part of his critique was based on the negative press reports.

What was unusual in the invasion of the Dominican Republic became commonplace in the Vietnam War. The press routinely challenged government officials at briefings. The daily military briefing in Vietnam became known among the media as "the Five O'Clock Follies." Stories critical of the war ran on television. The press examined in great detail the differences between what the president was claiming and the reality. Beginning with the live coverage of parts of the Foreign Relations Committee hearings on the Vietnam War in February 1966, dissent became a regular feature of television coverage. From 1966 on, about 20 percent of all Vietnam coverage (on CBS television, for which data are available) concerned various forms of domestic controversy.[11]

In the years since, the news media have not been uniformly hostile to the president. During the Persian Gulf War in 1991, some press critics suggested that the press too willingly accepted the government's version of events. Yet the fact that the media discussed their own shortcomings suggests that the country has not returned to the inno-

---

[11] Daniel Hallin, *The "Uncensored War"* (Berkeley: University of California Press, 1989), p. 192.

cent days of the past. The mass media have been very critical of the Clinton administration's foreign policy regarding Bosnia, Haiti, Somalia, and Cuba. President Clinton's first Secretary of Defense, Les Aspin, resigned as a result of the criticism. President Clinton complained that the press ignored the administration's foreign policy successes with the former Soviet Union on proliferation, the European Union with the General Agreements on Tariffs and Trade, and in the Middle East. In President Clinton's whirlwind visit to Europe in January 1994, much of the press coverage of the tour was on presidential reaction to a domestic question, the Whitewater real-estate deal, instead of on the substantive issues of the trip, including defining a new role for NATO, clarifying the fate of nuclear weapons and foreign aid to the former Soviet Union, and improving the prospects for Syrian-Israeli peace talks.

Agenda setting. The media can put issues on the foreign policy agenda. The problem of famine in the 1980s in East Africa, especially in Ethiopia, was well known to aid agencies such as CARE and OXFAM, as well as to government officials. It did not become a major issue in U.S. politics until television crews broadcast stories on the subject, complete with pictures of the dead and dying, into American living rooms. Countless reports about atrocities in Bosnia raised calls for action by the president, although long, brutal civil wars in many other parts of the world, such as the Sudan, remain virtually unknown to most of the United States. Such complex issues as increasing international trade or reducing Third World debt that take time to explain and offer little opportunity for startling footage, receive less attention than do stories about war and disaster, even though their ultimate impact may be much more economically significant to the average American.

The Public

How U.S. public opinion is divided on general dimensions of foreign policy also constrains the president. Many scholars argue that public opinion has two dimensions, militarism/nonmilitarism and isolationism/internationalism, creating four basic opinion groups. Others argue that a third dimension, unilateralism/multilateralism (essentially the difference between acting alone and acting in concert with other countries), is also important. Although the public is not equally divided among different opinion groups, U.S. foreign policies usually have to appeal across these dimensions to two or more groups in order to achieve widespread popular support. At the same time, the existence of these various dimensions mean that almost every U.S. foreign policy will have a core group of opponents who are likely to try to limit the impact of the policy.

A crisis in foreign policy generally leads to a rise in a president's popularity, although the increase is often temporary, as noted in Chapter 7. Table 7.2 on page 293 indicates that although surges caused by major international events do occur, they generally don't last long. As revealed in Table 7.2, each of the last ten presidents experienced at least one rallying point based on a foreign event. Rallies lasted an average of ten weeks, with the longest being seven months.[12]

Support for leaders in other democracies follows this pattern too. The Falkland Islands war in 1982 between Great Britain and Argentina greatly increased the popularity of Prime Minister Margaret Thatcher, whose popularity had slipped because of a

---

[12] Michael R. Kagay, "History Suggests Bush's Popularity Will Ebb," *The New York Times* (May 22, 1991): A10.

slumping domestic economy. The British victory in the Falklands provided her with a theme that she used to gain a victory in the general election the following year. But British prime ministers can (within limits) call for elections when they think they will win. U.S. President George Bush, by contrast, could not take advantage of his exceptionally high popularity in the wake of the Persian Gulf War to win reelection. Instead he had to wait until his constitutionally ordained four-year cycle was completed, by which time the country was in a recession that contributed to Bush's defeat.

Elections. Harry S Truman completed President Franklin D. Roosevelt's unexpired term and then won election in 1948 in his own right. He was eligible to run again in 1952, but his popularity was so low that he stood no chance. Sensing sure defeat, he withdrew from the race. The issue that made Truman so unpopular was one of foreign and military policy, the Korean War. Truman had committed the United States to fight on behalf of South Korea in 1950, and by 1952 the stalemated war was still dragging on, with about 250,000 U.S. troops committed to combat on the Korean peninsula and deaths approaching what would be their final total of 34,000. Popular dissatisfaction with the no-win war was very high, and it was a major issue in the 1952 election. The voters chose as president a popular military leader and hero from World War II, General Dwight D. Eisenhower. During the campaign, Eisenhower never made clear what he would do about Korea, beyond a vague pledge to "go there" to see for himself what was going on. The vote Eisenhower received seems to have been based mostly on the widespread belief that a general would know how to bring a war to an end. President Eisenhower helped bring an end to the fighting by agreeing to a truce with North Korea in 1953.

In 1968 Lyndon B. Johnson decided not to run for a second term, in large part because of the unpopularity of his policy of escalating the war in Vietnam. A surprisingly strong showing for a peace candidate, Senator Eugene McCarthy (D.-Minn.), in the New Hampshire primary suggested to Johnson that although he would probably win his party's nomination, he might not win the election.

The elections in 1948 and 1968 provide evidence that the voters can check the president's power in foreign affairs. But the electorate can control the president only at set intervals—every fourth year when an election is held. Even then, this control is exercised in only the crudest of ways. The voters can approve or disapprove of an existing policy, but they can send no clear message for an alternative policy. In 1952 Eisenhower was elected to end the war in Korea, but he was as free to end it by introducing nuclear weapons (which he did not) as by negotiating an end (which he did). Richard M. Nixon was elected to succeed Lyndon B. Johnson without having made clear what he would do to end the war in Vietnam. The most that most voters knew was that some newspapers attributed to him the vague statement that "I have a plan."

Since the time of George Washington, successful military leaders have used their popularity to launch a bid for national office. Speculation abounds concerning the political ambitions of retired General Colin Powell, especially after he played a key role in negotiations to return a democratically elected government to Haiti, avoiding an American invasion of that nation.

Public Opinion. As revealed in Figure 18-5, the U.S. public is much more interested in what goes on at home. Since the 1960s Americans have considered domestic problems to be much more important than foreign ones. Yet even when it is not an election year, or Congress is not exerting pressure, or foreign policy is not the subject of media attention, public opinion is likely to be on the president's mind when examining foreign policy. President Ronald Reagan's standing in the Gallup public opinion polls in the later years of his administration was higher than that of any of his predecessors in the past decades. (See Figure 7-3: "Presidential Approval Since 1938," p. 291.) His own themes while campaigning were military strength and the restoration of American confidence. If any president had a mandate to be tough, he did. Yet Reagan and his ad-

786 ❖ Chapter 18 Foreign and Military Policy

FIGURE 18-5

The Most Important Problem: Domestic or Foreign, 1947–1993

Note: Typical Question: "What do you think is the most important problem facing this country today?"
Source: Reprinted by permission of The Gallup Organization.
"Foreign and Military Policy", p.356 in: *Vital Statistics on American Politics*, 4th ed. Harold Stanley and Richard Niemi, eds. 1994 Congressional Quarterly, Inc. Reprinted by permission.

visers found themselves restrained by their perceptions of what the public would tolerate. Shortly after taking office in 1981, Reagan emphasized the need to help the right-wing Central American government of El Salvador fight leftist insurgents trying to overthrow it. The White House saw El Salvador as an issue that would generate even more support for Reagan, playing as it did on themes of anti-communism and national security. Yet to the White House's surprise, Reagan's standing in the public opinion polls began to go down.

The president's advisers determined that their problem was that the conflict in El Salvador was being portrayed as another Vietnam. Advisers quickly stopped mentioning El Salvador. The war there went on, but since the president was apparently paying no attention, it ceased to be a major news item. Reagan's ratings in the polls went back up. As other presidents had learned, the president could influence what went on the public's agenda but not the opinions the public would form.

Public Action. Foreign and military policies do not consist only of government action. Without the public taking action that supports these policies, they are not likely to be effective. Despite federal restrictions on commerce with British colonies during the War of 1812, for example, many businesses continued to trade with Canada. Widespread resistance to the draft during the Vietnam War made it much more difficult to reach the personnel levels desired by the military and helped move the U.S. military toward an all-volunteer force. More recently, the Bush and Clinton administrations have tried to increase U.S. private investment in Russia with little impact because many Americans are simply reluctant to invest there, given Russia's highly uncertain political and economic environment.

Even though foreign and defense powers are concentrated in the national government, state and local governments do play some role in foreign and military policy. Border states make compacts with local governments in Canada and Mexico on a variety of issues, particularly in the area of transportation. State and local governments court overseas investors by offering tax breaks and other incentives. State governments promote home-grown products in the global market, most maintaining at least one office in Europe or Asia. Local activists join or work with international nongovernmental organizations that may oppose the president on issues ranging from the environment (Greenpeace, for example) or sports (such as the International Olympic Committee). Even in military affairs, the president faces potential opposition from state and local government officials. In the 1980s some state governors argued that their national guard units could not be used overseas without their approval, in order to keep the units from being used to support Reagan administration initiatives in Central America.

The authority of the president in foreign and military policy is challenged by Congress, the federal bureaucracy, the media, and citizens expressing their will. Yet each of these restraints on presidential authority is imperfect.

In part this imperfection comes from certain advantages bestowed on the president by the Constitution. One restraint is that the president combines the roles of head of government and head of state. Unlike the British system, where the monarch serves as head of state and the prime minister serves as head of government, the United States Constitution puts both these functions in the hands of the president. This union has the effect of making the president not just a political actor but also the symbol of the nation.

Another advantage is that the president (along with a hand-picked vice president) is the only official elected by the nation as a whole. It is not surprising, then, that Congress, the media, and the American people look to the president as a leader. The prevailing view was summarized by one senator after a foreign policy vote: "In foreign policy initiatives, there should be a presumption in favor of supporting the President of the United States."[13]

Toward Reform

The anti-communist consensus that dominated U.S. foreign and military policy for four decades from World War II to the late 1980s had some desirable results even for people who did not always share in its approach. Without that consensus, for example, it is unlikely the Congress would ever have appropriated money for foreign aid in the quantities that it did. The large burden of the Marshall Plan was justified primarily in the name of strengthening Europe against communism.

With the fading of the threat that provoked the consensus, old programs need new justification. Some people still advocate providing foreign aid for humanitarian reasons. But they must prevail against many others who want to use the money for domestic purposes—sheltering the homeless, rescuing savings institutions, or just reducing the deficit.

---

[13] Senator Slade Gorton (R.-Wash.) quoted in Steven V. Roberts, "Senate, 52–48, Supports Reagan on AWACs Sale to Saudis," *The New York Times,* (October 29, 1981): A4.

The Lack of Consensus

In the absence of a consensus on the role of the United States, foreign policy issues have become partisan issues, provoking debates between Republicans and Democrats, liberals and conservatives. Some partisanship in foreign policy has always been present, of course, but there has been a perceptible increase as the Cold War has waned. Although controversial and costly, the objective of anti-communism gave U.S. foreign policy a consistent direction for more than forty years. Without anti-communism as a guide, debate on the direction of U.S. foreign policy has become more partisan.

In June 1989, for example, Americans watched in horror as the Chinese government used tanks to crush pro-democracy demonstrators in Tienanmen Square. Some members of Congress indicated their outrage at the Chinese government by calling for Chinese already in the United States on student visas to be able to extend their stays. President George Bush, who was the U.S. envoy to China during the Ford administration, thought this action would anger the Chinese government. The resulting debate in Congress, the votes in Congress to allow the students to stay, the veto by the president, and finally the failed attempt to override the veto went almost completely along party lines.

Without the guidance of the anti-communist consensus, debates on the procedure of U.S. foreign policy making increased as well. Presidents have dispatched U.S. forces on more than 200 occasions when combat was very likely or did occur, including Korea, Vietnam, and, more recently, Somalia. When these deployments became unpopular, Congress tried to stop them, using legislative devices such as the War Powers Act or bill amendments that curtail specific foreign policy activities. Presidents at the time called these efforts an unconstitutional meddling in their authority.

President Jimmy Carter tried to build a new foreign policy consensus based on support for human rights, much as the United States had formed a domestic consensus in support of civil rights. Supporters argued that this would align U.S. policy against both communists, such as the Soviets, and non-communist dictators, such as the shah of Iran. Opponents argued that U.S. policy should not be based on ideal principles and that the battle against communism sometimes required helping non-democratic leaders. President Ronald Reagan tried to rebuild the anti-communist consensus by identifying the Soviet Union as an "evil empire" and supporting less-than-democratic forces in struggles against communists in Angola, Nicaragua, and elsewhere.

The Gulf War. The invasion of Kuwait by Iraq on August 2, 1990 required President George Bush to try to build on the role of the United States both at home and abroad. Iraq had long been supported by the Soviet Union. Since communism was on the decline, the invasion posed a unique opportunity for the United States and the Soviet Union to act together in the United Nations to oppose Iraq. At home, congressional attempts to restrain the president could be circumvented in the short run, but a lengthy war would require substantial funds. Iraq was potentially a more formidable opponent than either Panama or Nicaragua was, and the United States would require several months of preparation before any serious military campaign could be undertaken. During the preparatory period, Congress tried to force the issue, with the Senate holding hearings on the war.

President Bush initially denied that congressional authorization was necessary, arguing that he was acting to carry out mandates of the United Nations Security Council, but he also recognized political realities. A long and costly war conducted without congressional approval would quickly become "Bush's war," just as Korea had become "Truman's war" and Vietnam had become "Johnson's war."

Bush was reluctant to ask for a resolution of support until he was certain it would pass, and Congress was reluctant to act until asked. But as the January 15, 1991, deadline for Iraq to leave Kuwait—agreed to by the United Nations—approached, members of Congress took the initiative in pressing for a debate. As the debate approached, the Bush administration began to focus discussion on Iraqi efforts to obtain nuclear, chemical, and biological weapons (and the missiles to deliver them) as well as on the aggression in Kuwait and the atrocious human rights record of the Hussein regime.

Congress avoided a direct declaration of war by debating instead a resolution authorizing the use of U.S. armed forces to carry out a U.N. resolution (which had itself only suggested that armed force could be used but had not called for it). Congress sidestepped the issue of war powers by stating that the resolution was "consistent with" (as opposed to "pursuant to") the War Powers Act, which would mean the president accepted the Act.

After several days of serious debate, legislators voted for the resolution by a substantial margin (250 to 183) in the House and a narrow margin (52 to 47) in the Senate. Members of Congress closed ranks once the vote was taken: The Democrats who had opposed the resolution declared that they too would support the president. Some Middle East experts suggested that Saddam Hussein, the ruler of Iraq, had misread the U.S. constitutional process and assumed the debate meant that he faced a divided and therefore irresolute opponent.[14] Though military operations were concluded swiftly and with great success, Saddam Hussein remained in power.

Finding the United States' Place in the World

Despite the apparent success of the Persian Gulf War, the United States faces many challenges that require a coherent foreign policy. Poverty, food shortages, and economic collapse in many parts of the world are so severe that they may threaten U.S. security. Similarly, civil wars and political oppression in one country often disrupt life in other countries through the spread of terrorism or the influx of refugees. Rising economic tensions among the United States, the European Union, Japan, and the other emerging industrial nations of the Pacific Rim, however, suggest that economic policy issues, more than global or regional war, will dominate the agenda of international politics into the next century.

On trade issues, all recent U.S. presidents have declared their support for free trade. In finalizing the Uruguay Round trade talks in 1993, President Bill Clinton concluded negotiations begun under President Ronald Reagan and continued by President George Bush with the other members of the GATT to decrease tariffs generally and liberalize non-tariff barriers to trade in agriculture and the service industries, among others. But as foreign imports put pressure on U.S. business, Congress has been slowly recapturing trade policy from the president. A major milestone was the 1988 Omnibus Trade and Competitiveness Act, which limited presidential discretion in making trade policy. It imposed mandatory requirements for retaliation under Section 301 of the Act, for example, against countries that maintained substantial barriers to trade and whose exports greatly exceeded their imports from the United States. Through the mandatory provisions of Section 301, Congress attempted to gain more control over U.S. trade policy. Because Congress responds readily to economic interests (such as automobile

---

[14] This was the view of Hosni Mubarak, president of Egypt. See Elaine Sciolino, "Hussein's Errors: Complex Impulses," *The New York Times* (February 28, 1991): A10.

producers), the president finds it difficult to develop a coherent national policy on trade. The debate on the passage of the **North American Free Trade Agreement** (NAFTA) (discussed in "The Politics of NAFTA," p. 791), has brought the role of economic interest groups more clearly into focus.

Presidents would also like to see military spending fit into a coherent foreign policy strategy. In 1993, then-Secretary of Defense Les Aspin identified four major threats to U.S. national security:

- The proliferation of weapons of mass destruction, such as nuclear bombs, and the means to deliver those weapons
- Regional conflicts in the Middle East, Korea, and elsewhere
- The emergence of anti-democratic forces in Russia
- The erosion of U.S. economic strength

With the decline of the perception of Soviet or other military threats, the nation now faces the problem of how to cut defense spending. The president and Secretary of Defense try to justify a military spending program according to national security needs. When faced with an impending cut in the military budget, members of Congress look first at the effect on their districts—and just about every congressional district benefits from defense spending. Even members of Congress conspicuous for their vocal opposition to the vague concept of military spending fight to retain military bases that provide jobs for their constituents. The resulting defense budget reflects not a coherent strategy but a patchwork quilt of local interests. Senator Sam Nunn (D.-Ga.), for example, heads the Senate Armed Services Committee. Not surprisingly, Georgia has more than half a dozen large military bases, and Nunn's home state's economy could be disastrously affected by military cuts and base closings.

Finally, wholly new international issues have emerged in foreign affairs. The dramatic international impact of the Russian nuclear accident at Chernobyl and the discovery of a large hole in the ozone layer of the earth's atmosphere that appears to be related to the use of chlorofluorocarbons (CFCs) and other gases are two incidents in a growing understanding of the importance of international environmental threats to the security of the United States. U.S. Vice President Al Gore Jr., in particular, stresses the importance of this issue.

The end of the Cold War, as the end of World War II, is an opportunity for the United States to define its role in the world. Congress is likely to take more responsibility in foreign affairs. In 1988 and again in 1993, Senator Sam Nunn (D.-Ga.) attempted to rewrite the War Powers Act (see "The War Powers Act," p. 781) and to restructure U.S. security institutions. Said Catherine Kelleher, a National Security Council staff member under President Jimmy Carter and now a senior fellow at the Brookings Institution, "Until you dismantle a lot of that, the Congress is just never going to get it. . . . We built the national security state, this whole apparatus around the threat of the Cold War, surrounding and almost enobling the president to make all of these tough decisions that were going to have to be taken because the missile threat was twenty-four minutes away."[15]

With the immense powers of the office, the president, however, is primarily responsible for defining the role of the United States in the world and building a political coalition to support the appropriate policies. President Clinton and his advisors suggest that U.S. policy in the 1990s should be based on two principles, **engagement** and

---

[15] Quoted in Mike Christensen, "Nunn Aims to Give Congress More Clout in Post-Soviet World," *Atlanta Journal and Constitution* (October 30, 1993).

The Politics of NAFTA

Prior to 1930, Congress was the dominant player in making tariff policy. The disastrous impact of the Smoot-Hawley Tariff Act of 1930 helped push Congress to give more authority to the president in tariff and trade policy. Since World War II, presidents have been able to set U.S. tariffs through international negotiations. Congress still has to authorize negotiations and pass legislation to implement changes in U.S. laws as a result of the negotiations, but it usually must deal with a large, single package of changes that should have more positive than negative effects in most Congressional districts.

With many districts only slowly recovering from a prolonged economic recession, special economic interests put pressure on members of Congress to vote against the North American Free Trade Agreement (NAFTA), which would reduce trade barriers among Canada, Mexico, and the United States. To ease passage of the necessary legislation, President Bill Clinton negotiated side agreements with Canada and Mexico on labor and environmental policy. Nonetheless, Congressional opponents of NAFTA, led by many prominent Democrats, appeared to have enough votes to defeat NAFTA. With time for approval running out, President Clinton began to offer members of Congress a variety of incentives to support the bill. These included cutting the cost of the use of federal lands, protecting the sugar industry, and even agreeing to host a conference in one member's district. The administration also sought to demonstrate the value of NAFTA to the general public through public endorsements from industry leaders and government officials. Most unusual of all was a well-publicized debate on CNN's "Larry King Live" between Vice President Albert Gore Jr. and administration critic and former presidential candidate Ross Perot. Many people criticized the president for making too many compromises, but the tide turned in favor of NAFTA. NAFTA passed its final test in the House in November 1993 with a slim bipartisan majority.

Vice President Al Gore Jr. and Texas billionaire Ross Perot agree to disagree about the North American Free Trade Agreement (NAFTA) on "Larry King Live."

enlargement. Engagement means that the United States will not retreat into isolationism but will continue to take the lead in international political and economic affairs. Enlargement means that the United States will promote democracy, open markets, and other Western political, economic, and social values around the world. Other than assistance to Israel, Egypt, and the post-communist countries, most foreign aid to support specific countries would be stopped. Instead, aid would be used to promote democracy, stimulate free trade, resist terrorism, and combat the proliferation of weapons of mass destruction (nuclear, chemical, and biological) and their delivery systems. The foreign aid programs would all emphasize population control and raising the status of women, closely coordinated between the U.S. Agency for International Development and the recipients.

Will these two principles be the basis for a new consensus on the role of the United States? Under the leadership of a strong president who understands the nation's capabilities, the United States can meet these challenges proactively with a coherent foreign policy. Although now only the United States appears to have the military and economic power to influence almost any issue in virtually any place in the world, U.S. power remains limited. Into the next century, Russia, China, the European Union, and Japan are likely to remain great powers, for either military or economic reasons or both. Some other countries, such as the oil-rich states of the Middle East or the increasingly industrialized countries in Asia and Latin America, are likely to increase their influence on global affairs. Finally, rogue nations, such as North Korea and Iraq, with their interest in weapons of mass destruction, may challenge any emerging world order not to their liking. Unlike the bipolar conflict between the United States and the Soviet Union, the multipolar world of the 1990s creates new opportunities for cooperation and conflict.

The policy of containment helped give shape and purpose to the Cold War world order. Unless the president and Congress develop a new framework to guide U.S. actions in the post-Cold War era, not only will U.S. foreign and military policy in the late 1990s drift from one problem to another, but the U.S. government also will influence the shape of the next world order only by accident, not design. For two decades, the United States been divided on involvement in the global arena. The end of the Cold War will bring new military and economic challenges for U.S. policymakers.

Summary

Foreign and military policies differ in significant ways from other components of U.S. government. Their history has not been one of continuous development. To demonstrate that development, this chapter has made the following points:

1. Federalists and the Framers believed that a strong national government was the key to assuring a strong nation. To this end, after winning a war of national liberation, with crucial support from France, Americans withdrew behind their two-ocean moat.

2. For more than a century, foreign and military policy played—with occasional exceptions—only a minor part in American life. George Washington's warnings against foreign entanglements were heeded.

3. As U.S. economic interests grew, it became more difficult for the United States to stay out of wars without risking its sovereignty and security. Despite prolonged attempts to regain its relative isolation after intervening in World War I, the United States was unable to avoid participating in World War II.

4. During World War II and the years of the Cold War, foreign and military policy began to dominate the political agenda. Defense spending went from a small fraction of the federal budget to one of its biggest components, even during peacetime. Global affairs went from a peripheral issue of concern only to specialists to the focus of presidential attention and public debate.

5. The complex balances found in many other parts of the U.S. system are absent in the machinery of foreign and military policies. One branch of government, the executive (and one individual in that branch, the president), predominates. The countervailing forces in the

Congress, the media, and the public are weak. Other components of U.S. government, such as the judicial branch and the state and local levels, play almost no role at all. The predominance of the president has given rise to criticism of an imperial presidency, but debate about both the content and the process of foreign and military policy has been inhibited by fears of endangering national security.

6. With the ending of the Cold War and the disintegration of the Soviet Union, the sense of military threat has diminished. The nation can expect a more robust debate on both the content and decision-making process in foreign and military policy. As foreign affairs increasingly concern economic issues, the country can expect the president's authority to diminish, both because the Constitution allocates appropriation powers to Congress and because economic issues affect the pocketbooks of citizens in immediate and tangible ways.

Key Terms

nation-state
Jay Treaty
executive agreement
tariffs
Monroe Doctrine
manifest destiny
League of Nations
isolationism
unilateralism

United Nations
International Monetary Fund
World Bank
General Agreements on Tariffs and Trade
multilateralism
Truman Doctrine
Marshall Plan

North Atlantic Treaty Organization
containment
National Security Acts of 1947 and 1949
War Powers Act
North American Free Trade Agreement
engagement
enlargement

Suggested Readings

Ambrose, Stephen. *Rise to Globalism,* 6th ed. New York: Penguin, 1991.

Barnet, Richard J. *The Rockets' Red Glare: When America Goes to War: The Presidents and the People.* New York: Simon and Schuster, 1990.

Bundy, McGeorge. *Danger and Survival: Choices about the Bomb in the First Fifty Years.* New York: Random House, 1988.

Halberstam, David. *The Best and the Brightest.* New York: Random House, 1972.

Hallin, Daniel. *The "Uncensored War."* Berkeley: University of California Press, 1989.

Karnes, Margaret P., and Karen A. Mingst. *The United States and Multilateral Institutions.* New York: Routledge, 1992.

Kennan, George. *American Diplomacy 1900–1950.* Chicago: University of Chicago Press, 1951.

Kissinger, Henry. *White House Years.* Boston: Little, Brown, 1979.

McGlen, Nancy E., and Meredith Reid Sarkees. *Women in Foreign Policy.* New York: Routledge, 1993.

Mueller, John E. *War, Presidents and Public Opinion.* New York: Wiley, 1973.

Perret, Geoffrey. *A Country Made by War.* New York: Random House, 1989.

Schlesinger, Arthur. *The Imperial Presidency.* Boston: Houghton Mifflin, 1973, 1989.

APPENDIX I

The Declaration of Independence

In Congress, July 4, 1776

The Unanimous Declaration of the Thirteen United States of America

When in the Course of human events it becomes necessary for one people to dissolve the political bands which have connected them with another, and to assume, among the powers of the earth, the separate and equal station to which the Laws of Nature and of Nature's God entitle them, a decent respect to the opinions of mankind requires that they should declare the causes which impel them to the separation.

We hold these truths to be self-evident, that all men are created equal, that they are endowed by their Creator with certain unalienable Rights, that among these are Life, Liberty and the pursuit of Happiness. That to secure these rights, Governments are instituted among Men, deriving their just powers from the consent of the governed. That whenever any Form of Government becomes destructive of these ends, it is the Right of the People to alter or to abolish it, and to institute new Government, laying its foundation on such principles and organizing its powers in such form, as to them shall seem most likely to effect their Safety and Happiness. Prudence, indeed, will dictate that Governments long established should not be changed for light and transient causes; and accordingly all experience hath shewn that mankind are more disposed to suffer, while evils are sufferable, than to right themselves by abolishing the forms to which they are accustomed. But when a long train of abuses and usurpations, pursuing invariably the same Object evinces a design to reduce them under absolute Despotism, it is their right, it is their duty, to throw off such Government, and to provide new Guards for their future security.—Such has been the patient sufferance of these Colonies; and such is now the necessity which constrains them to alter their former Systems of Government. The history of the present King of Great Britain is a history of repeated injuries and usurpations, all having in direct object the establishment of an absolute Tyranny over these States. To prove this, let Facts be submitted to a candid world.

He has refused his Assent to Laws, the most wholesome and necessary for the public good.

He has forbidden his Governors to pass Laws of immediate and pressing importance, unless suspended in their operation till his Assent should be obtained; and when so suspended, he has utterly neglected to attend to them.

He has refused to pass other Laws for the accommodation of large districts of people, unless those people would relinquish the right of Representation in the Legislature, a right inestimable to them and formidable to tyrants only.

He has called together legislative bodies at places unusual, uncomfortable, and distant from the depository of their Public Records, for the sole purpose of fatiguing them into compliance with his measures.

He has dissolved Representative Houses repeatedly, for opposing with manly firmness his invasions on the rights of the people.

He has refused for a long time, after such dissolutions, to cause others to be elected; whereby the Legislative Powers, incapable of Annihilation, have returned to the People at large for their exercise, the State remaining in the mean time exposed to all the dangers of invasion from without, and convulsions within.

He has endeavored to prevent the population of these States; for that purpose obstructing the Laws of Naturalization of Foreigners; refusing to pass others to encourage their migration hither, and raising the conditions of new Appropriations of Lands.

He has obstructed the Administration of Justice, by refusing his Assent to Laws for establishing Judiciary powers.

He has made Judges dependent on his Will alone, for the tenure of their offices, and the amount and payment of their salaries.

He has erected a multitude of New Offices, and sent hither swarms of Officers to harass our people, and eat out their substance.

He has kept among us, in times of peace, Standing Armies without the Consent of our legislatures.

He has affected to render the Military independent of and superior to the Civil power.

He has combined with others to subject us to a jurisdiction foreign to our constitution, and unacknowledged by our laws, giving his Assent to their Acts of pretended Legislation:

For quartering large bodies of armed troops among us:

For protecting them, by a mock Trial, from punishment for any Murders which they should commit on the Inhabitants of these States:

For cutting off our Trade with all parts of the world:

For imposing Taxes on us without our Consent:

For depriving us in many cases, of the benefits of Trial by Jury:

For transporting us beyond Seas to be tried for pretended offences:

For abolishing the free System of English Laws in a neighboring Province, establishing therein an Arbitrary government, and enlarging its Boundaries so as to render it at once an example and fit instrument for introducing the same absolute rule into these Colonies:

For taking away our Charters, abolishing our most valuable Laws, and altering fundamentally the Forms of our Governments:

For suspending our own Legislatures, and declaring themselves invested with power to legislate for us in all cases whatsoever.

He has abdicated Government here, by declaring us out of his Protection and waging War against us.

He has plundered our seas, ravaged our Coasts, burnt out towns, and destroyed the lives of our people.

He is at this time transporting large Armies of foreign Mercenaries to compleat the works of death, desolation and tyranny, already begun with circumstances of Cruelty and perfidy scarcely paralleled in the most barbarous ages, and totally unworthy the Head of a civilized nation.

He has constrained our fellow Citizens taken Captive on the high Seas to bear Arms against their Country, to become the executioners of their friends and Brethren, or to fall themselves by their Hands.

He has excited domestic insurrections amongst us, and has endeavored to bring on the inhabitants of our frontiers, the merciless Indian Savages, whose known rule of warfare, is an undistinguished destruction of all ages, sexes and conditions.

In every stage of these Oppressions We have Petitioned for Redress in the most humble terms: Our repeated Petitions have been answered only by repeated injury: A Prince, whose character is thus marked by every act which may define a Tyrant, is unfit to be the ruler of a free people.

Nor have We been wanting in attention to our British brethren. We have warned them from time to time of attempts by their legislature to extend an unwarrantable jurisdiction over us. We have reminded them of the circumstances of our emigration and settlement here. We have appealed to their native justice and magnanimity; and we have conjured them by the ties of our common kindred to disavow these usurpations, which would inevitably interrupt our connections and correspondence. They too have been deaf to the voice of justice and consanguinity. We must, therefore, acquiesce in the necessity, which denounces our Separation, and hold them, as we hold the rest of mankind, Enemies in War, in Peace Friends.

We, therefore, the Representatives of the United States of America, in General Congress, Assembled, appealing to the Supreme Judge of the world for the rectitude of our intentions, do, in the Name, and by Authority of the good People of these Colonies, solemnly publish and declare, That these

United Colonies are, and of Right ought to be Free and Independent States; that they are Absolved from all Allegiance to the British Crown, and that all political connection between them and the State of Great Britain, is and ought to be totally dissolved: and that as Free and Independent States, they have full power to levy War, conclude Peace, contract Alliances, establish Commerce, and to do all other Acts and Things which Independent States may of right do. And for the support of this Declaration, with a firm reliance on the protection of divine Providence, we mutually pledge to each other our Lives, our Fortunes and our sacred Honor.

JOHN HANCOCK

NEW HAMPSHIRE
Josiah Bartlett,
Wm. Whipple,
Matthew Thornton.

MASSACHUSETTS BAY
Saml. Adams,
John Adams,
Robt. Treat Paine,
Elbridge Gerry.

RHODE ISLAND
Step. Hopkins,
William Ellery.

CONNECTICUT
Roger Sherman,
Samuel Huntington,
Wm. Williams,
Oliver Wolcott.

NEW YORK
Wm. Floyd,
Phil. Livingston,
Frans. Lewis,
Lewis Morris.

NEW JERSEY
Richd. Stockton,
In. Witherspoon,
Fras. Hopkinson,
John Hart,
Abra. Clark.

PENNSYLVANIA
Robt. Morris,
Benjamin Rush,
Benjamin Franklin,
John Morton,
Geo. Clymer,
Jas. Smith,
Geo. Taylor,
James Wilson,
Geo. Ross.

DELAWARE
Caesar Rodney,
Geo. Read,
Tho. M'kean.

MARYLAND
Samuel Chase,
Wm. Paca,
Thos. Stone,
Charles Caroll of Carollton.

VIRGINIA
George Wythe,
Richard Henry Lee,
Th. Jefferson,
Benjamin Harrison,
Thos. Nelson, jr.,
Francis Lightfoot Lee,
Carter Braxton.

NORTH CAROLINA
Wm. Hooper,
Joseph Hewes,
John Penn.

SOUTH CAROLINA
Edward Rutledge,
Thos. Heyward, Junr.,
Thomas Lynch, jnr.,
Arthur Middleton.

GEORGIA
Button Guinnett,
Lyman Hall,
Geo. Walton.

APPENDIX II

The Constitution of the United States of America

*W*e the People of the United States, in Order to form a more perfect Union, establish Justice, insure domestic Tranquility, provide for the common defence, promote the general Welfare, and secure the Blessings of Liberty to ourselves and our Posterity, do ordain and establish this Constitution for the United States of America.

ARTICLE I

SECTION 1. All legislative Powers herein granted shall be vested in a Congress of the United States, which shall consist of a Senate and House of Representatives.

SECTION 2. The House of Representatives shall be composed of Members chosen every second Year by the People of the several States, and the Electors in each State shall have the Qualifications requisite for Electors of the most numerous Branch of the State Legislature.

No person shall be a Representative who shall not have attained to the Age of twenty five Years, and been seven Years a Citizen of the United States, and who shall not, when elected, be an Inhabitant of that State in which he shall be chosen.

Representatives and direct Taxes shall be apportioned among the several States which may be included within this Union, according to their respective Numbers which shall be determined by adding to the whole Number of free Persons, including those bound to Service for a Term of Years, and excluding Indians not taxed, three fifths of all other Persons. The actual Enumeration shall be made within three Years after the first Meeting of the Congress of the United States, and within every subsequent Term ten Years, in such Manner as they shall by Law direct. The Number of Representatives shall not exceed one for every thirty Thousand, but each State shall have at Least one Representative; and until such enumeration shall be made, the State of New Hampshire shall be entitled to chuse three, Massachusetts eight, Rhode-Island and Providence Plantations one, Connecticut five, New-York six, New Jersey four, Pennsylvania eight, Delaware one, Maryland six, Virginia ten, North Carolina five, South Carolina five, and Georgia three.

When vacancies happen in the Representation from any State, the Executive Authority thereof shall issue Writs of Election to fill such Vacancies.

The House of Representatives shall chuse their speaker and other Officers; and shall have the sole Power of Impeachment.

SECTION 3. The Senate of the United States shall be composed of two Senators from each State chosen by the Legislature thereof, for six Years; and each Senator shall have one Vote.

Immediately after they shall be assembled in Consequence of the first Election, they shall be divided as equally as may be into three Classes. The Seats of the Senators of the first Class shall be vacated at the Expiration of the second year, of the second Class at the Expiration of the fourth Year, and of the third Class at the Expiration of the sixth Year, so that one third may be chosen every second Year and if Vacancies happen by Resignation, or otherwise, during the Recess of the Legislature of any State, the Executive thereof may make temporary Appointments until the next Meeting of the Legislature, which shall then fill such Vacancies.

No Person shall be a Senator who shall not have attained to the Age of thirty Years, and been nine Years a Citizen of the United States, and who shall not, when elected, be an Inhabitant of that State for which he shall be chosen.

The Vice President of the United States shall be President of the Senate, but shall have no Vote, unless they be equally divided.

The Senate shall chuse their other Officers, and also a President pro tempore, in the Absence of the Vice President, or when he shall exercise the Office of President of the United States.

The Senate shall have the sole Power to try all Impeachments. When sitting for that Purpose, they shall be on Oath or Affirmation. When the President of the United States is tried, the Chief Justice shall preside: And no Person shall be convicted without the Concurrence of two thirds of the Members present.

Judgment in Cases of Impeachment shall not extend further than to removal from Office, and disqualification to hold and enjoy any Office of honor, Trust or Profit under the United States; but the Party convicted shall nevertheless be liable and subject to Indictment, Trial, Judgment and Punishment, according to Law.

Section 4. The Times, Places and Manner of holding Elections for Senators and Representatives, shall be prescribed in each State by the Legislature thereof; but the Congress may at any time by law make or alter such Regulations, except as to the Places of chusing Senators.

The Congress shall assemble at least once in every Year, and such Meeting shall be on the first Monday in December, unless they shall by Law appoint a different Day.

Section 5. Each House shall be the Judge of the Elections, Returns and Qualifications of its own Members, and a Majority of each shall constitute a Quorum to do Business; but a smaller Number may adjourn from day to day, and may be authorized to compel the Attendance of absent Members, in such Manner, and under such Penalties as each House may provide.

Each House may determine the Rules of its Proceedings, punish its Members for disorderly Behaviour, and with the Concurrence of two thirds, expel a Member.

Each House shall keep a journal of its Proceedings, and from time to time publish the same, excepting such Parts as may in their judgment require Secrecy; and the Yeas and Nays of the Members of either House on any question shall, at the Desire of one fifth of those present, be entered on the Journal.

Neither House, during the Session of Congress, shall, without the Consent of the other, adjourn for more than three days, nor to any other Place than that in which the two Houses shall be sitting.

Section 6. The Senators and Representatives shall receive a Compensation for their Services, to be ascertained by Law, and paid out of the Treasury of the United States. They shall in all Cases, except Treason, Felony and Breach of the Peace, be privileged from Arrest during their Attendance at the Session of their respective Houses, and in going to and returning from the same; and for any Speech or Debate in either House, they shall not be questioned in any other Place.

No Senator or Representative shall, during the Time for which he was elected, be appointed to any civil Office under the Authority of the United States, which shall have been created, or the Emoluments whereof shall have been encreased during such time; and no Person holding any Office under the United States, shall be a Member of either House during his Continuance in Office.

Section 7. All Bills for raising Revenue shall originate in the House of Representatives; but the Senate may propose or concur with Amendments as on other Bills.

Every Bill which shall have passed the House of Representatives and the Senate, shall, before it become a Law, be presented to the President of the United States; If he approves he shall sign it, but if not he shall return it, with his Objections to that House in which it shall have originated, who shall enter the Objections at large on their journal, and proceed to reconsider it. If after such Reconsideration two thirds of that House shall agree to pass the Bill, it shall be sent, together with the Objections, to the other House, by which it shall likewise be reconsidered, and if approved by two thirds of that House, it shall become a Law. But in all such Cases the Votes of both Houses shall be determined by Yeas and Nays, and the Names of the Persons voting for and against the Bill shall be entered on the Journal of each House respectively. If any Bill shall not be returned by the President within ten Days (Sundays excepted) after it shall have been presented to him, the Same shall be a Law, in like Manner as if he had signed it, unless the Congress by their Adjournment prevent its Return, in which Case it shall not be a Law.

Every Order, Resolution, or Vote to which the Concurrence of the Senate and House of Representatives may be necessary (except on a question of Adjournment) shall be presented to the President of the United States; and before the Same shall take Effect, shall be approved by him, or being disapproved by him, shall be repassed by two thirds of the Senate and House of Representatives, according to the Rules and Limitations prescribed in the Case of a Bill.

Section 8. The Congress shall have Power To lay and collect Taxes, Duties, Imposts and Excises, to pay the Debts and provide for the common Defence and general Welfare of the United States; but all Duties, Imposts and Excises shall be uniform throughout the United States;

To borrow Money on the credit of the United States;

To regulate Commerce with foreign Nations, and among the several States, and with the Indian Tribes;

To establish a uniform Rule of Naturalization, and uniform Laws on the subject of Bankruptcies throughout the United States;

To coin Money, regulate the Value thereof, and of foreign Coin, and fix the Standard of Weights and Measures;

To provide for the Punishment of counterfeiting the Securities and current Coin of the United States;

To establish Post Offices and post Roads;

To promote the Progress of Science and useful Arts, by securing for limited Times to Authors and Inventors the exclusive Right to their respective Writings and Discoveries;

To constitute Tribunals inferior to the supreme Court;

To define and punish Piracies and Felonies committed on the high Seas, and Offences against the Law of Nations;

To declare War, grant Letters of Marque and Reprisal, and make Rules concerning Captures on Land and Water;

To raise and support Armies, but no Appropriation of Money to that Use shall be for a longer Term than two Years;

To provide and maintain a Navy;

To make Rules for the Government and Regulation of the land and naval Forces;

To provide for calling forth the Militia to execute the Laws of the Union, suppress Insurrections and repel Invasions;

To provide for organizing, arming, and disciplining, the Militia, and for governing such Part of them as may be employed in the Service of the United States, reserving to the States respectively, the Appointment of the Officers, and the Authority of training the Militia according to the discipline prescribed by Congress;

To exercise exclusive Legislation in all Cases whatsoever, over such District (not exceeding ten Miles square) as may, by Cession of particular States, and the Acceptance of Congress, become the Seat of the Government of the United States, and to exercise like Authority over all Places purchased by the Consent of the Legislature of the State in which the Same shall be for the Erection of Forts, Magazines, Arsenals, dock-Yards, and other needful Buildings;—And

To make all Laws which shall be necessary and proper for carrying into Execution the foregoing Powers, and all other Powers vested by this Constitution in the Government of the United States, or in any Department or Officer thereof.

SECTION 9. The Migration or Importation of such Persons as any of the States now existing shall think proper to admit, shall not be prohibited by the Congress prior to the Year one thousand eight hundred and eight, but a Tax or duty may be imposed on such Importation, not exceeding ten dollars for each Person.

The Privilege of the Writ of Habeas Corpus shall not be suspended, unless when in Cases of Rebellion or Invasion the public Safety may require it.

No Bill of Attainder or ex post facto Law shall be passed.

No Capitation, or other direct, Tax shall be laid, unless in Proportion to the Census or Enumeration herein before directed to be taken.

No Tax or Duty shall be laid on Articles exported from any State.

No Preference shall be given by any Regulation of Commerce or Revenue to the Ports of one State over those of another; nor shall Vessels bound to, or from, one State, be obliged to enter, clear, or pay Duties in another.

No Money shall be drawn from the Treasury, but in Consequence of Appropriations made by Law; and a regular Statement and Account of the Receipts and Expenditures of all public Money shall be published from time to time.

No Title of Nobility shall be granted by the United States: And no Person holding any Office of Profit or Trust under them, shall, without the Consent of the Congress, accept of any present, Emolument, Office, or Title, of any kind whatever, from any King, Prince, or foreign State.

SECTION 10. No state shall enter into any Treaty, Alliance, or Confederation; grant Letters of Marque and Reprisal; coin Money; emit Bills of Credit; make any Thing but gold and silver Coin a Tender in Payment of Debts; pass any Bill of Attainder, ex post facto Law, or Law impairing the Obligation of Contracts, or grant any Title of Nobility.

No State shall, without the Consent of the Congress, lay any Imposts or Duties on Imports or Exports, except what may be absolutely necessary for executing its inspection Laws: and the net Produce of all Duties and Imposts, laid by any State on Imports or Exports, shall be for the Use of the Treasury of the United States, and all such Laws shall be subject to the Revision and Controul of the Congress.

No State shall, without the Consent of Congress, lay any Duty of Tonnage, keep Troops, or Ships of War in time of Peace, enter into any Agreement or Compact with another State, or with a foreign Power, or engage in War, unless actually invaded, or in such imminent Danger as will not admit of delay.

ARTICLE II

SECTION 1. The executive Power shall be vested in a President of the United States of America. He shall hold his Office during the Term of four Years, and, together with the Vice President, chosen for the same Term, be elected as follows.

Each State shall appoint, in such Manner as the Legislature thereof may direct, a Number of Electors, equal to the whole Number of Senators and Representatives to which the State may be entitled in the Congress; but no Senator or Representative, or Person holding an Office of Trust of Profit under the United States, shall be appointed an Elector.

The Electors shall meet in their respective States, and vote by Ballot for two Persons, of whom one at least shall not be an Inhabitant of the same State with themselves. And they shall make a List of all the Persons voted for, and, of the Number of Votes for each; which List they shall sign and certify, and transmit sealed to the Seat of the Government of the United States, directed to the President of the Senate. The

President of the Senate shall, in the Presence of the Senate and House of Representatives, open all the Certificates, and the Votes shall then be counted. The Person having the greatest Number of Votes shall be the President, if such Number be a Majority of the whole Number of Electors appointed; and if there be more than one who have such Majority, and have an equal Number of Votes, then the House of Representatives shall immediately chuse by Ballot one of them for President; and if no Person have a Majority, then from the five highest on the List the said House shall in like Manner chuse the President. But in chusing the President, the Votes shall be taken by States, the Representation from each State having one Vote; A quorum for this Purpose shall consist of a Member or Members from two thirds of the States, and a Majority of all the States shall be necessary to a Choice. In every Case, after the Choice of the President, the Person having the greatest Number of Votes of the Electors shall be the Vice President. But if there should remain two or more who have equal Votes, the Senate shall chuse from them by Ballot the Vice President.

The Congress may determine the Time of chusing the Electors, and the Day on which they shall give their Votes; which Day shall be the same throughout the United States.

No Person except a natural born Citizen, or a Citizen of the United States, at the time of the Adoption of this Constitution, shall be eligible to the Office of President; neither shall any Person be eligible to that Office who shall not have attained to the Age of thirty five Years, and been fourteen Years a Resident within the United States.

In Case of the Removal of the President from Office, or of his Death, Resignation, or Inability to discharge the Powers and Duties of the said Office, the Same shall devolve on the Vice President, and the Congress may by Law provide for the Case of Removal, Death, Resignation or Inability, both of the President and Vice President, declaring what Officer shall then act as President, and such Officer shall act accordingly, until the Disability be removed, or a President shall be elected.

The President shall, at stated Times, receive for his Services, a Compensation, which shall neither be encreased nor diminished during the Period for which he shall have been elected, and he shall not receive within that Period any other Emolument from the United States, or any of them.

Before he enter on the Execution of his Office, he shall take the following Oath or Affirmation—"I do solemnly swear (or affirm) that I will faithfully execute the Office of President of the United States, and will to the best of my Ability, preserve, protect and defend the Constitution of the United States."

Section 2. The President shall be Commander in Chief of the Army, and Navy of the United States, and of the Militia of the several States, when called into the actual Service of the United States; he may require the Opinion, in writing, of the principal Officer in each of the executive Departments, upon any Subject relating to the Duties of their respective Offices, and he shall have Power to grant Reprieves and Pardons for Offences against the United States, except in Cases of Impeachment.

He shall have Power, by and with the Advice and Consent of the Senate, to make Treaties, provided two thirds of the Senators present concur; and he shall nominate, and by and with the Advice and Consent of the Senate, shall appoint Ambassadors, other public Ministers and Consuls, Judges of the supreme Court, and all other Officers of the United States, whose Appointments are not herein otherwise provided for, and which shall be established by Law: but the Congress may by Law vest the Appointment of such inferior Officers, as they think proper, in the President alone, in the Courts of Law, or in the Heads of Departments.

The President shall have Power to fill up all Vacancies that may happen during the Recess of the Senate, by granting Commissions which shall expire at the end of their next Session.

Section 3. He shall from time to time give to the Congress Information of the State of the Union, and recommend to their Consideration such Measures as he shall judge necessary and expedient; he may, on extraordinary Occasions, convene both Houses, or either of them, and in Case of Disagreement between them, with Respect to the Time of Adjournment, he may adjourn them to such Time as he shall think proper; he shall receive Ambassadors and other public Ministers; he shall take Care that the Laws be faithfully executed, and shall Commission all the Officers of the United States.

Section 4. The President, Vice President and all civil Officers of the United States, shall be removed from Office on Impeachment for, and Conviction of, Treason, Bribery, or other high Crimes and Misdemeanors.

ARTICLE III

Section 1. The judicial Power of the United States, shall be vested in one supreme Court, and in such inferior Courts as the Congress may from time to time ordain and establish. The Judges, both of the supreme and inferior Courts, shall hold their Offices during good Behaviour, and shall, at stated Times, receive for their Services, a Compensation, which shall not be diminished during their Continuance in Office.

Section 2. The judicial Power shall extend to all Cases, in Law and Equity, arising under this Constitution, the Laws of the United States, and Treaties made, or which shall be made, under their Authority;—to all Cases affecting Ambassadors, other public Ministers and Consuls;—to all Cases of admiralty and maritime Jurisdiction;—to Controversies to which the United States shall be a Party;—to Controversies between two or more States;—between a State and Citizens of another State;—between Citizens of different States,—between Citizens of the same State claiming Lands under Grants of different States,—and between a State, or the Citizens thereof, and foreign States, Citizens of Subjects.

In all Cases affecting Ambassadors, other public Ministers and Consuls, and those in which a State shall be Party, the supreme Court shall have original Jurisdiction. In all the other Cases before mentioned, the supreme Court shall have appellate Jurisdiction, both as to Law and Fact, with such Exceptions, and under such Regulations as the Congress shall make.

The Trial of all Crimes, except in Cases of Impeachment, shall be by Jury; and such Trial shall be held in the State where the said Crimes shall have been committed; but when not committed within any State, the Trial shall be at such Place or Places as the Congress may by Law have directed.

Section 3. Treason against the United States, shall consist only in levying War against them, or in adhering to their Enemies, giving them Aid and Comfort. No Person shall be convicted of Treason unless on the Testimony of two Witnesses to the same overt Act, or on Confession in open Court.

The Congress shall have Power to declare the Punishment of Treason, but no Attainder of Treason shall work Corruption of Blood, or Forfeiture except during the Life of the Person attainted.

ARTICLE IV

Section 1. Full Faith and Credit shall be given in each State to the public Acts, Records, and judicial Proceedings of every other State. And the Congress may by general Laws prescribe the Manner in which such Acts, Records and Proceedings shall be proved, and the Effect thereof.

Section 2. The Citizens of each State shall be entitled to all Privileges and Immunities of Citizens in the several States.

A Person charged in any State with Treason, Felony, or other Crime, who shall flee from Justice, and be found in another State, shall on Demand of the executive Authority of the State from which he fled, be delivered up, to be removed to the State having Jurisdiction of the Crime.

No Person held to Service or Labour in one State under the Laws thereof, escaping into another, shall, in Consequence of any Law or Regulation therein, be discharged from such Service or Labour, but shall be delivered up on Claim of the Party to whom such Service or Labour may be due.

Section 3. New States may be admitted by the Congress into this Union; but no new State shall be formed or erected within the Jurisdiction of any other State; nor any State be formed by the Junction of two or more States, or Parts of States, without the Consent of the Legislatures of the States concerned as well as of the Congress.

The Congress shall have Power to dispose of and make all needful Rules and Regulations respecting the Territory or other Property belonging to the United States; and nothing in this Constitution shall be so construed as to Prejudice any Claims of the United States, or of any particular State.

Section 4. The United States shall guarantee to every State in this Union a Republican Form of Government, and shall protect each of them against Invasion, and on Application of the Legislature, or of the Executive (when the Legislature cannot be convened) against domestic Violence.

ARTICLE V

The Congress, whenever two thirds of both Houses shall deem it necessary, shall propose Amendments to this Constitution, or, on the Application of the Legislatures of two thirds of the several States, shall call a Convention for proposing Amendments, which, in either Case, shall be valid to all Intents and Purposes, as Part of this Constitution, when ratified by the Legislatures of three fourths of the several States, or by Conventions in three fourths thereof, as the one or the other Mode of Ratification may be proposed by the Congress; Provided that no Amendment which may be made prior to the Year One thousand eight hundred and eight shall in any Manner affect the first and fourth Clauses in the Ninth Section of the first Article; and that no State, without its Consent, shall be deprived of its equal Suffrage in the Senate.

ARTICLE VI

All Debts contracted and Engagements entered into, before the Adoption of this Constitution, shall be as valid against the United States under this Constitution, as under the Confederation.

This Constitution, and the laws of the United States which shall be made in Pursuance thereof; and all Treaties made, or which shall be made, under the Authority of the United States, shall be the supreme Law of the Land; and the Judges in every State shall be bound thereby, any Thing in the Constitution or Laws of any State to the Contrary notwithstanding.

The Senators and Representatives before mentioned, and the Members of the several State Legislatures, and all executive and judicial Officers, both of the United States and of the several States, shall be bound by Oath or Affirmation, to support this Constitution; but no religious Test shall ever be required as a Qualification to any Office or public Trust under the United States.

ARTICLE VII

The Ratification of the Conventions of nine States, shall be sufficient for the Establishment of this Constitution between the States so ratifying the Same.

Done in Convention by the Unanimous Consent of the States present the Seventeenth Day of September in the Year of our Lord one thousand seven hundred and Eighty seven and of the Independence of the United States of America the Twelfth. IN WITNESS whereof we have hereunto subscribed our Names,

Go. WASHINGTON
Presid't. and deputy from Virginia

Attest
WILLIAM JACKSON
Secretary

DELAWARE
Geo. Read
Gunning Bedford jun
John Dickinson
Richard Basset
Jaco. Broom

MASSACHUSETTS
Nathaniel Gorham
Rufus King

CONNECTICUT
Wm. Saml. Johnson
Roger Sherman

NEW YORK
Alexander Hamilton

NEW JERSEY
Wh. Livingston
David Brearley
Wm. Paterson
Jona. Dayton

PENNSYLVANIA
B. Franklin
Thomas Mifflin
Robt. Morris
Geo. Clymer
Thos. FitzSimons
Jared Ingersoll
James Wilson
Gouv. Morris

NEW HAMPSHIRE
John Langdon
Nicholas Gilman

MARYLAND
James McHenry
Dan of St. Thos. Jenifer
Danl. Carroll

VIRGINIA
John Blair
James Madison, Jr.

NORTH CAROLINA
Wm. Blount
Richd. Dobbs Spaight
Hu. Williamson

SOUTH CAROLINA
J. Rutledge
Charles Cotesworth Pinckney
Charles Pinckney
Pierce Butler

GEORGIA
William Few
Abr. Baldwin

Articles in addition to, and amendment of the Constitution of the United States of America, proposed by Congress and ratified by the Legislatures of the several states, pursuant to the Fifth Article of the original Constitution.

(The first ten amendments were passed by Congress on September 25, 1789, and were ratified on December 15, 1791.)

Amendment I

Congress shall make no law respecting an establishment of religion, or prohibiting the free exercise thereof; or abridging the freedom of speech, or of the press; or the right of the people peaceably to assemble, and to petition the Government for a redress of grievances.

Amendment II

A well regulated Militia, being necessary to the security of a free State, the right of the people to keep and bear Arms, shall not be infringed.

Amendment III

No Soldier shall, in time of peace be quartered in any house, without the consent of the Owner, nor in time of war, but in a manner to be prescribed by law.

Amendment IV

The right of the people to be secure in their persons, houses, papers, and effects, against unreasonable searches and seizures, shall not be violated, and no warrants shall issue, but upon probable cause, supported by Oath or affirmation, and particularly describing the place to be searched, and the persons or things to be seized.

Amendment V

No person shall be held to answer for a capital, or otherwise infamous crime, unless on a presentment or indictment of a Grand Jury, except in cases arising in the land or naval forces, or in the Militia, when in actual service in time of War or public danger; nor shall any person be subject for the same offence to be twice put in jeopardy of life or limb; nor shall be compelled in any criminal case to be a witness against himself, nor be deprived of life, liberty, or property, without due process of law; nor shall private property be taken for public use, without just compensation.

Amendment VI

In all criminal prosecutions, the accused shall enjoy the right to a speedy and public trial, by an impartial jury of the State and district wherein the crime shall have been committed, which district shall have been previously ascertained by law, and to be informed of the nature and cause of the accusation; to be confronted with the witnesses against him; to have compulsory process for obtaining witnesses in his favor, and to have the assistance of counsel for his defence.

Amendment VII

In Suits at common law, where the value in controversy shall exceed twenty dollars, the right of trial by jury shall be preserved, and no fact tried by a jury, shall be otherwise re-examined in any Court of the United States, than according to the rules of the common law.

Amendment VIII

Excessive bail shall not be required, nor excessive fines imposed, nor cruel and unusual punishments inflicted.

Amendment IX

The enumeration in the Constitution, of certain rights, shall not be construed to deny or disparage others retained by the people.

Amendment X

The powers not delegated to the United States by the Constitution, nor prohibited by it to the States, are reserved to the States respectively, or to the people.

Amendment XI *(Ratified on February 7, 1795)*

The Judicial power of the United States shall not be construed to extend to any suit in law or equity, commenced or prosecuted against one of the United States by Citizens of another State, or by Citizens or Subjects of any Foreign State.

Amendment XII *(Ratified on June 15, 1804)*

The Electors shall meet in their respective states, and vote by ballot for President and Vice-President, one of whom, at least, shall not be an inhabitant of the same state with themselves; they shall name in their ballots the person voted for as President, and in distinct ballots the person voted for as Vice-President, and they shall make distinct lists of all persons voted for as President, and of all persons voted for as Vice-President, and of the number of votes for each, which lists they shall sign and certify, and transmit sealed to the seat of the government of the United States, directed to the President of the Senate;—The President of the Senate shall, in the presence of the Senate and House of Representatives, open all the certificates and the votes shall then be counted;—The person having the greatest number of votes for President, shall be the President, if such number be a majority of the whole number of Electors appointed; and if no person have such majority; then from the persons having the highest numbers not exceeding three on the list of those voted for as President, the House of Representatives shall choose immediately, by ballot, the President. But in choosing the President, the votes shall be taken by states, the representation from each state having one vote; a quorum for this purpose shall consist of a member or members from two-thirds of the states, and a majority of all the states shall be necessary to a choice. And if the House of Representatives shall not choose a President whenever the right of choice shall devolve upon them, before the fourth day of March next following, then the Vice-President shall act as President, as in the case of the death or other constitutional disability of the President.—The person having the greatest number of votes as Vice-President, shall be the Vice-President, if such number be a majority of the whole number of Electors appointed, and if no person have a majority, then from the two highest numbers on the list, the Senate shall choose the Vice-President; a quorum for the purpose shall consist of two-thirds of the whole number of Senators, and a majority of the whole number shall be necessary to a choice. But no person constitutionally ineligible to the office of President shall be eligible to that of Vice-President of the United States.

Amendment XIII *(Ratified on December 6, 1865)*

SECTION 1. Neither slavery nor involuntary servitude, except as a punishment for crime whereof the party shall have been duly convicted, shall exist within the United States, or any place subject to their jurisdiction.

SECTION 2. Congress shall have power to enforce this article by appropriate legislation.

Amendment XIV *(Ratified on July 9, 1868)*

SECTION 1. All persons born or naturalized in the United States, and subject to the jurisdiction thereof, are citizens of the United States and of the State wherein they reside. No State shall make or enforce any law which shall abridge the privileges or immunities of citizens of the United States; nor shall any State deprive any person of life, liberty, or property, without due process of law; nor deny to any person within its jurisdiction the equal protection of the laws.

Section 2. Representatives shall be apportioned among the several States according to their respective numbers, counting the whole number of persons in each State, excluding Indians not taxed. But when the right to vote at any election for the choice of electors for President and Vice President of the United States, Representatives in Congress, the Executive and Judicial officers of a State, or the members of the Legislature thereof, is denied to any of the male inhabitants of such State, being twenty-one years of age, and citizens of the United States, or in any way abridged, except for participation in rebellion, or other crime, the basis of representation therein shall be reduced in the proportion which the number of such male citizens shall bear to the whole number of male citizens twenty-one years of age in such State.

Section 3. No person shall be a Senator or Representative in Congress, or elector of President and Vice President, or hold any office, civil or military, under the United States, or under any State, who, having previously taken an oath, as a member of Congress, or as an officer of the United States, or as a member of any State legislature, or as an executive or judicial officer of any State, to support the Constitution of the United States, shall have engaged in insurrection or rebellion against the same, or given aid or comfort to the enemies thereof. But Congress may by a vote of two-thirds of each House, remove such disability.

Section 4. The validity of the public debt of the United States, authorized by law, including debts incurred for payment of pensions and bounties for services in suppressing insurrection or rebellion, shall not be questioned. But neither the United States nor any State shall assume or pay any debt or obligation incurred in aid of insurrection or rebellion against the United States, or any claim for the loss or emancipation of any slave, but all such debts, obligations and claims shall be held illegal and void.

Section 5. The Congress shall have power to enforce, by appropriate legislation, the provisions of this article.

Amendment xv   *(Ratified on February 3, 1870)*

Section 1. The right of citizens of the United States to vote shall not be denied or abridged by the United States or by any State on account of race, color, or previous condition of servitude.

Section 2. The Congress shall have power to enforce this article by appropriate legislation.

Amendment xvi   *(Ratified on February 3, 1913)*

The Congress shall have power to lay and collect taxes on incomes, from whatever source derived, without apportionment among the several States, and without regard to any census or enumeration.

Amendment xvii   *(Ratified on April 8, 1913)*

The Senate of the United States shall be composed of two Senators from each State, elected by the people thereof, for six years; and each Senator shall have one vote. The electors in each State shall have the qualifications requisite for electors of the most numerous branch of the State legislatures.

When vacancies happen in the representation of any State in the Senate, the executive authority of such State shall issue writs of election to fill such vacancies: Provided, That the legislature of any State may empower the executive thereof to make temporary appointments until the people fill the vacancies by election as the legislature may direct.

This amendment shall not be so construed as to affect the election or term of any Senator chosen before it becomes valid as part of the Constitution.

Amendment xviii   *(Ratified on January 16, 1919)*

Section 1. After one year from the ratification of this article the manufacture, sale, or transportation of intoxicating liquors within, the importation thereof into, or the exportation thereof from the United States and all territory subject to the jurisdiction thereof for beverage purposes is hereby prohibited.

Section 2. The Congress and the several States shall have concurrent power to enforce this article by appropriate legislation.

Section 3. This article shall be inoperative unless it shall have been ratified as an amendment to the Constitution by the legislatures of the several States, as provided in the Constitution, within seven years from the date of the submission hereof to the States by the Congress.

Amendment xix   *(Ratified on August 18, 1920)*

The right of citizens of the United States to vote shall not be denied or abridged by the United States or by any State on account of sex.

Congress shall have power to enforce this article by appropriate legislation.

Amendment xx   *(Ratified on February 6, 1933)*

Section 1. The terms of the President and Vice President shall end at noon on the 20th day of January, and the terms of Senators and Representatives at noon on the 3d day of January, of the years in which such terms would have ended if this article had not been ratified; and the terms of their successors shall then begin.

Section 2. The Congress shall assemble at least once in every year, and such meeting shall begin at noon on the 3d day of January, unless they shall by law appoint a different day.

SECTION 3. If, at the time fixed for the beginning of the term of the President, the President elect shall have died, the Vice President elect shall become President. If a President shall not have been chosen before the time fixed for the beginning of his term, or if the President elect shall have failed to qualify, then the Vice President elect shall act as President until a President shall have qualified; and the Congress may by law provide for the case wherein neither a President elect nor a Vice President elect shall have qualified, declaring who shall then act as President, or the manner in which one who is to act shall be selected, and such person shall act accordingly until a President or Vice President shall have qualified.

SECTION 4. The Congress may by law provide for the case of the death of any of the persons from whom the House of Representatives may choose a President whenever the rights of choice shall have devolved upon them, and for the case of the death of any of the persons from whom the Senate may choose a Vice President whenever the right of choice shall have devolved upon them.

SECTION 5. Sections 1 and 2 shall take effect on the 15th day of October following the ratification of this article.

SECTION 6. This article shall be inoperative unless it shall have been ratified as an amendment to the Constitution by the legislatures of three-fourths of the several States within seven years from the date of its submission.

Amendment XXI *(Ratified on December 5, 1933)*

SECTION 1. The eighteenth article of amendment to the Constitution of the United States is hereby repealed.

SECTION 2. The transportation or importation into any State, Territory, or possession of the United States for delivery or use therein of intoxicating liquors, in violation of the laws thereof, is hereby prohibited.

SECTION 3. This article shall be inoperative unless it shall have been ratified as an amendment to the Constitution by conventions in the several States, as provided in the Constitution, within seven years from the date of the submission hereof to the States by the Congress.

Amendment XXII *(Ratified on February 27, 1951)*

No person shall be elected to the office of the President more than twice, and no person who has held the office of President, or acted as President, for more than two years of a term to which some other person was elected President shall be elected to the office of the President more than once. But this Article shall not apply to any person holding the office of President when this Article was proposed by the Congress, and shall not prevent any person who may be holding the office of President, or acting as President, during the term within which this Article becomes operative from holding the office of President or acting as President during the remainder of such term.

Amendment XXIII *(Ratified on March 29, 1961)*

SECTION 1. The District constituting the seat of Government of the United States shall appoint in such manner as the Congress may direct:

A number of electors of President and Vice President equal to the whole number of Senators and Representatives in Congress to which the District would be entitled if it were a State, but in no event more than the least populous State; they shall be in addition to those appointed by the States, but they shall be considered, for the purposes of the election of President and Vice President, to be electors appointed by a State; and they shall meet in the District and perform such duties as provided by the twelfth article of amendment.

SECTION 2. The Congress shall have power to enforce this article by appropriate legislation.

Amendment XXIV *(Ratified on January 23, 1964)*

SECTION 1. The right of citizens of the United States to vote in any primary or other election for President or Vice President, for electors for President or Vice President, or for Senator or Representative in Congress, shall not be denied or abridged by the United States or any State by reason of failure to pay any poll tax or other tax.

SECTION 2. The Congress shall have power to enforce this article by appropriate legislation.

Amendment XXV *(Ratified on February 10, 1967)*

SECTION 1. In case of the removal of the President from office or of his death or resignation, the Vice President shall become President.

SECTION 2. Whenever there is a vacancy in the office of the Vice President, the President shall nominate a Vice President who shall take office upon confirmation by a majority vote of both Houses of Congress.

SECTION 3. Whenever the President transmits to the President pro tempore of the Senate and the Speaker of the House of Representatives his written declaration that he is unable to discharge the powers and duties of his office, and until he transmits to them a written declaration to the contrary, such powers and duties shall be discharged by the Vice President as Acting President.

SECTION 4. Whenever the Vice President and a majority of either the principal officers of the executive departments or of such other body as Congress may by law provide, transmit to the President pro tempore of the Senate and the Speaker of the House of Representatives their written declaration that the President is unable to discharge the powers and duties of his office, the Vice President shall immediately assume the powers and duties of the office as Acting President.

Thereafter, when the President transmits to the President pro tempore of the Senate and the Speaker of the House of Representatives his written declaration that no inability exists, he shall resume the powers and duties of his office unless the Vice President and a majority of either the principal officers of the executive department or of such other body as Congress may by law provide, transmit within four days to the President pro tempore of the Senate and the Speaker of the House of Representatives their written declaration that the President is unable to discharge the powers and duties of his office. Thereupon Congress shall decide the issue, assembling within forty-eight hours for that purpose if not in session. If the Congress, within twenty-one days after receipt of the latter written declaration, or, if Congress is not in session, within twenty-one days after Congress is required to assemble, determines by two-thirds vote of both Houses that the President is unable to discharge the powers and duties of his office, the Vice President shall continue to discharge the same as Acting President; otherwise, the President shall resume the powers and duties of his office.

Amendment XXVI *(Ratified on July 1, 1971)*

SECTION 1. The right of citizens of the United States, who are eighteen years of age or older, to vote shall not be denied or abridged by the United States or by any State on account of age.

SECTION 2. The Congress shall have power to enforce this article by appropriate legislation.

Amendment XXVII *(Ratified on May 7, 1992)*

No law varying the compensation for the services of Senators and Representatives shall take effect until an election of Representatives shall have intervened.

APPENDIX III

Presidents, Congresses and Chief Justices: 1789–1992

TERM	PRESIDENT AND VICE PRESIDENT	PARTY OF PRESIDENT	CONGRESS	Majority Party HOUSE	Majority Party SENATE	CHIEF JUSTICE OF THE UNITED STATES
1789–1797	**George Washington** John Adams	None	1st 2d 3d 4th	(N/A) (N/A) (N/A) (N/A)	(N/A) (N/A) (N/A) (N/A)	John Jay (1789–1795) John Rutledge (1795) Oliver Ellsworth (1796–1800)
1797–1801	**John Adams** Thomas Jefferson	Federalist	5th 6th	(N/A) Fed	(N/A) Fed	Oliver Ellsworth (1796–1800) John Marshall (1801–1835)
1801–1809	**Thomas Jefferson** Aaron Burr (1801–1805) George Clinton (1805–1809)	Democratic-Republican	7th 8th 9th 10th	Dem-Rep Dem-Rep Dem-Rep Dem-Rep	Dem-Rep Dem-Rep Dem-Rep Dem-Rep	John Marshall (1801–1835)
1809–1817	**James Madison** George Clinton (1809–1812)[a] Elbridge Gerry (1813–1814)[a]	Democratic-Republican	11th 12th 13th 14th	Dem-Rep Dem-Rep Dem-Rep Dem-Rep	Dem-Rep Dem-Rep Dem-Rep Dem-Rep	John Marshall (1801–1835)
1817–1825	**James Monroe** Daniel D. Tompkins	Democratic-Republican	15th 16th 17th 18th	Dem-Rep Dem-Rep Dem-Rep Dem-Rep	Dem-Rep Dem-Rep Dem-Rep Dem-Rep	John Marshall (1801–1835)
1825–1829	**John Quincy Adams** John C. Calhoun	National-Republican	19th 20th	Nat'l Rep Dem	Nat'l Rep Dem	John Marshall (1801–1835)
1829–1837	**Andrew Jackson** John C. Calhoun (1829–1832)[b] Martin Van Buren (1833–1837)	Democrat	21st 22d 23d 24th	Dem Dem Dem Dem	Dem Dem Dem Dem	John Marshall (1801–1835) Roger B. Taney (1836–1864)
1837–1841	**Martin Van Buren** Richard M. Johnson	Democrat	25th 26th	Dem Dem	Dem Dem	Roger B. Taney (1836–1864)
1841	**William H. Harrison**[a] John Tyler (1841)	Whig				Roger B. Taney (1836–1864)
1841–1845	**John Tyler** (VP vacant)	Whig	27th 28th	Whig Dem	Whig Whig	Roger B. Taney (1836–1864)
1845–1849	**James K. Polk** George M. Dallas	Democrat	29th 30th	Dem Whig	Dem Dem	Roger B. Taney (1836–1864)
1849–1850	**Zachary Taylor**[a] Millard Fillmore	Whig	31st	Dem	Dem	Roger B. Taney (1836–1864)

Appendix III   Presidents, Congresses, and Chief Justices: 1789–1995   ❖   **A15**

TERM	PRESIDENT AND VICE PRESIDENT	PARTY OF PRESIDENT	CONGRESS	Majority Party HOUSE	Majority Party SENATE	CHIEF JUSTICE OF THE UNITED STATES
1850–1853	**Millard Fillmore** (VP vacant)	Whig	32d	Dem	Dem	Roger B. Taney (1836–1864)
1853–1857	**Franklin Pierce** William R.D. King (1853)[a]	Democrat	33d 34th	Dem Rep	Dem Dem	Roger B. Taney (1836–1864)
1857–1861	**James Buchanan** John C. Breckinridge	Democrat	35th 36th	Dem Rep	Dem Dem	Roger B. Taney (1836–1864)
1861–1865	**Abraham Lincoln**[a] Hannibal Hamlin (1861–1865) Andrew Johnson (1865)	Republican	37th 38th 38th	Rep Rep Rep	Rep Rep Rep	Roger B. Taney (1836–1864) Salmon P. Chase (1864–1873)
1865–1869	**Andrew Johnson** (VP vacant)	Republican	39th 40th	Union Rep	Union Rep	Salmon P. Chase (1864–1873)
1869–1877	**Ulysses S. Grant** Schuyler Colfax (1869–1873) Henry Wilson (1873–1875)[a]	Republican	41st 42d 43d 44th	Rep Rep Rep Dem	Rep Rep Rep Rep	Salmon P. Chase (1864–1873) Morrison R. Waite (1874–1888)
1877–1881	**Rutherford B. Hayes** William A. Wheeler	Republican	45th 46th	Dem Dem	Rep Dem	Morrison R. Waite (1874–1888)
1881	**James A. Garfield**[a] Chester A. Arthur	Republican	47th	Rep	Rep	Morrison R. Waite (1874–1888)
1881–1885	**Chester A. Arthur** (VP vacant)	Republican	48th	Dem	Rep	Morrison R. Waite (1874–1888)
1885–1889	**Grover Cleveland** Thomas A. Hendricks (1885)[a]	Democrat	49th 50th	Dem Dem	Rep Rep	Morrison R. Waite (1874–1888) Melville W. Fuller (1888–1910)
1889–1893	**Benjamin Harrison** Levi P. Morton	Republican	51st 52d	Rep Dem	Rep Rep	Melville W. Fuller (1888–1910)
1893–1897	**Grover Cleveland** Adlai E. Stevenson	Democrat	53d 54th	Dem Rep	Dem Rep	Melville W. Fuller (1888–1910)
1897–1901	**William McKinley**[a] Garret A. Hobart (1897–1899)[a] Theodore Roosevelt (1901)	Republican	55th 56th	Rep Rep	Rep Rep	Melville W. Fuller (1888–1910)
1901–1909	**Theodore Roosevelt** (VP vacant, 1901–1905) Charles W. Fairbanks (1905–1909)	Republican	57th 58th 59th 60th	Rep Rep Rep Rep	Rep Rep Rep Rep	Melville W. Fuller (1888–1910)
1909–1913	**William Howard Taft** James S. Sherman (1909–1912)[a]	Republican	61st 62d	Rep Dem	Rep Rep	Melville W. Fuller (1888–1910) Edward D. White (1910–1921)
1913–1921	**Woodrow Wilson** Thomas R. Marshall	Democrat	63d 64th 65th 66th	Dem Dem Dem Rep	Dem Dem Dem Rep	Edward D. White (1910–1921)
1921–1923	**Warren G. Harding**[a] Calvin Coolidge	Republican	67th	Rep	Rep	William Howard Taft (1921–1930)

Appendix III Presidents, Congresses, and Chief Justices: 1789–1995

TERM	PRESIDENT AND VICE PRESIDENT	PARTY OF PRESIDENT	CONGRESS	Majority Party HOUSE	Majority Party SENATE	CHIEF JUSTICE OF THE UNITED STATES
1923–1929	**Calvin Coolidge** (VP vacant, 1923–1925) Charles G. Dawes (1925–1929)	Republican	68th 69th 70th	Rep Rep Rep	Rep Rep Rep	William Howard Taft (1921–1930)
1929–1933	**Herbert Hoover** Charles Curtis	Republican	71st 72d	Rep Dem	Rep Rep	William Howard Taft (1921–1930) Charles Evans Hughes (1930–1941)
1933–1945	**Franklin D. Roosevelt**[a] John N. Garner (1933–1941) Henry A. Wallace (1941–1945) Harry S Truman (1945)	Democrat	73d 74th 75th 76th 77th 78th	Dem Dem Dem Dem Dem Dem	Dem Dem Dem Dem Dem Dem	Charles Evans Hughes (1930–1941) Harlan F. Stone (1941–1946)
1945–1953	**Harry S Truman** (VP vacant, 1945–1949) Alben W. Barkley (1949–1953)	Democrat	79th 80th 81st 82d	Dem Rep Dem Dem	Dem Rep Dem Dem	Harlan F. Stone (1941–1946) Frederick M. Vinson (1946–1953)
1953–1961	**Dwight D. Eisenhower** Richard M. Nixon	Republican	83d 84th 85th 86th	Rep Dem Dem Dem	Rep Dem Dem Dem	Frederick M. Vinson (1945–1953) Earl Warren (1953–1969)
1961–1963	**John F. Kennedy**[a] Lyndon B. Johnson (1961–1963)	Democrat	87th	Dem	Dem	Earl Warren (1953–1969)
1963–1969	**Lyndon B. Johnson** (VP vacant, 1963–1965) Hubert H. Humphrey (1965–1969)	Democrat	88th 89th 90th	Dem Dem Dem	Dem Dem Dem	Earl Warren (1953–1969)
1969–1974	**Richard M. Nixon**[c] Spiro T. Agnew (1969–1973)[b] Gerald R. Ford (1973–1974)[d]	Republican	91st 92d	Dem Dem	Dem Dem	Earl Warren (1953–1969) Warren E. Burger (1969–1986)
1974–1977	**Gerald R. Ford** Nelson A. Rockefeller[d]	Republican	93d 94th	Dem Dem	Dem Dem	Warren E. Burger (1969–1986)
1977–1981	**Jimmy Carter** Walter Mondale	Democrat	95th 96th	Dem Dem	Dem Dem	Warren E. Burger (1969–1986)
1981–1989	**Ronald Reagan** George Bush	Republican	97th 98th 99th 100th	Dem Dem Dem Dem	Rep Rep Rep Dem	Warren E. Burger (1969–1986) William H. Rehnquist (1986–)
1989–1993	**George Bush** J. Danforth Quayle	Republican	101st 102nd	Dem Dem	Dem Dem	William H. Rehnquist (1986–)
1993–	**William J. Clinton** Albert Gore Jr.	Democrat	103d 104th	Dem Rep	Dem Rep	William H. Rehnquist (1986–)

[a]Died in office.
[b]Resigned from the vice presidency.
[c]Resigned from the presidency.
[d]Appointed vice president.

CASE GLOSSARY

Abrams v. *United States,* 250 U.S. 616 (1919): Federal Espionage Act, which banned distribution of leaflets critical of the government, did not violate the First Amendment. (Chapter 4)

Baker v. *Carr,* 369 U.S. 186 (1962): Equitable apportionment of voters among legislative districts is not a political question; instead it is a constitutional question involving the Fourteenth Amendments equal protection clause. (Chapter 6)

Barron v. *Baltimore,* 7 Pet. (32 U.S.) 243 (1833): The federal Bill of Rights limits only the action of the national government and not those of the states. (Chapter 4)

Batson v. *Kentucky,* 476 U.S. 79 (1986): The equal protection clause prohibits prosecutors from using peremptory challenges to remove African-Americans from juries. (Chapter 5)

Board of Education v. *Mergens,* 110 S. Ct. 2356, (1990): A school boards refusal to allow a high-school religious group to meet during a weekly activity period violates the Equal Access Act of 1984. (Chapter 4)

Board of Education of Hendrick Hudson School District v. *Rowley,* 458 U.S. 176 (1982): Public schools must provide assistance to deaf school children. (Chapter 9)

Bolling v. *Sharpe,* 347 U.S. 497 (1954): The due process clause of the Fourteenth Amendment forbids discrimination in public schools by the federal government. (Chapter 5)

Bowers v. *Hardwick,* 478 U.S. 186 (1986): Georgias anti-sodomy law does not violate a gay mans privacy rights. (Chapters 4, 5, 9)

Bradenburg v. *Ohio,* 385 U.S. 444 (1969): Advocacy of illegal action can be punished only if "such advocacy is directed at inciting or producing imminent lawless action and is likely to incite or produce such actions." (Chapter 4)

Bradwell v. *Illinois,* 16 Wall. (83 U.S.) 130 (1873): A womans right to practice law was not a privilege of citizenship protected by the Fourteenth Amendment. (Chapter 5)

Branzburg v. *Hayes,* 408 U.S. 665 (1972): The press is not protected by the First Amendment from divulging sources necessary for government investigation. (Chapters 4, 14)

Briggs v. *Elliott,* (1952): See *Brown* v. *Board of Education of Topeka.* (Chapter 5)

Brown v. *Board of Education of Topeka,* 347 U.S. 483 (1954): The Court reversed its approval of the separate but equal doctrine first enunciated in *Plessy* and ruled that separate but equal in education violates the equal protection clause of the Fourteenth Amendment. (Chapters 3, 4, 5, 9)

Brown v. *Board of Education of Topeka* II, 349 U.S. 294 (1955): The decision in *Brown I* was to be carried out with all deliberate speed and oversight of implementation was placed in the hands of local federal district court judges. (Chapter 5)

Buckley v. *Valeo,* 424 U.S. 1 (1976): The First Amendment prohibits congressional legislation limiting the amount of money candidates can spend from their families personal resources. (Chapter 13)

Cantwell v. *Connecticut,* 310 U.S. 296 (1940): The First Amendment allows for an absolute freedom to believe and a more restricted freedom to act. (Chapter 4)

Chaplinsky v. *New Hampshire,* 315 U.S. 568 (1942): "Fighting words" are not protected by the First Amendment because "such expressions are no essential part of any exposition of ideas . . ." (Chapter 4)

Chisholm v. *Georgia,* 2 U.S. 419 (1793): The Supreme Court has jurisdiction to review disputes involving citizens of one state against another state. (Chapter 9)

Civil Rights Cases, 109 U.S. 3 (1883): Congress could prohibit only governmental but not private acts of discrimination. (Chapter 5)

Cooper v. *Aaron,* 358 U.S. 1 (1958): Delay in the implementation of integration plans in the interest of avoiding unrest violates the rights of African-American students. (Chapter 5)

Craig v. *Boren,* 429 U.S. 190 (1976): The Court fashioned a new intermediate standard of review by which to evaluate claims of sex discrimination. The challenged law did not serve an important governmental purpose nor was it substantially related to achievement of those objectives. Therefore it violated the Fourteenth Amendments equal protection clause. (Chapter 5)

Cumming v. *County Board of Education,* 175 U.S. 528 (1899): Taxpaying African-American parents challenged the practice of using their tax dollars to support a "whites only" high school. The Court upheld this disparate treatment. (Chapter 5)

Davis v. Prince Edward County, (1954): See *Brown v. Board of Education of Topeka.* (Chapter 5)

Debs v. United States, 249 U.S. 211 (1919): The conviction of socialist and anti-war activist Debs was upheld because his speech had the natural tendency of obstructing war recruitment. (Chapter 4)

Dred Scott v. Sandford, 19 How. 393 (1857): The Court ruled that slaves were not citizens of the United States, therefore they had no standing to sue in federal court. The 1820 Missouri Compromise was also ruled invalid because Congress did not have the authority to outlaw slavery in states or territories because slaves were property protected by the Constitution. (Chapters 3, 5)

Edwards v. Aguillard, 482 U.S. 578 (1987): A Louisiana statute requiring that creationism be taught as balance to evolution violated the establishment clause of the First Amendment. (Chapter 4)

Engle v. Vitale, 370 U.S. 241 (1962): Recitation of nondenominational prayers in public schools violates the establishment clause. (Chapter 4)

Everson v. Board of Education of Ewing Township, 330 U.S. 1 (1947): Reimbursing parents for the transportation costs for students of Catholic schools did not violate the establishment clause because it was not furtherance of religion but instead a subsidy to parents. (Chapter 4)

Ex Parte McCardle, 74 U.S. 506 (1869): McCardle, a civilian newspaper editor, was jailed by a military court during Reconstruction. He argued that he was being held unlawfully. Congress removed the Courts jurisdiction over these kinds of cases forcing the Court to concede that it had no authority to hear McCardles appeal. (Chapter 8)

Furman v. Georgia, 408 U.S. 238 (1972): The arbitrary nature of the death penalty violates Eighth and Fourteenth Amendment provisions against cruel and unusual punishment. (Chapter 4)

Garcia v. San Antonio Metropolitan Transport Authority, 469 U.S. 528 (1985): Reversed *National League of Cities* and held that Congress had authority under the commerce clause to set minimum wage and maximum hour laws for state workers. (Chapter 3)

Gebhart v. Belton: See *Brown v. Board of Education of Topeka.* (Chapter 5)

Gibbons v. Ogden, 22 U.S. 1 (1824): Marshall Court broadly interpreted Congresss authority under the commerce clause to include the right to regulate navigation. (Chapter 3)

Gideon v. Wainwright, 372 U.S. 335 (1963): Counsel must be provided to indigents in all felony cases. (Chapter 4)

Gitlow v. New York, 268 U.S. 652 (1925): Although Gitlows conviction was upheld, the Court found that speech is one of the fundamental rights applied to the states through the due process clause of the First Amendment. (Chapter 4)

Gregg v. Georgia, 428 U.S. 153 (1976): Georgias rewritten death penalty sentence guidelines upheld as constitutional. (Chapter 4)

Griggs v. Duke Power Company, 401 U.S. 424 (1971): The use of non-job related tests that excluded African-American workers from certain positions violates the Civil Rights Act of 1964. (Chapter 5)

Griswold v. Connecticut, 381 U.S. 479 (1965): A Connecticut statute making it illegal to disseminate contraceptive devices or information was found to violate a married couples right to privacy as guaranteed by the First, Third, Fourth, Fifth, and Fourteenth Amendments. (Chapter 4)

Grove City College v. Bell, 465 U.S. 555 (1984): Title IX of the Education Amendments of 1972 prohibits gender discrimination on the part of colleges and universities receiving federal funds. However, only those programs directly receiving the funds needed to be nondiscriminatory. (Chapter 5)

Harris v. Forklift Systems, 114 S.Ct 367 (1982): Plaintiffs need not show proof of severe psychological damage to prove that illegal sexual harassment occurred. (Chapter 9)

Heart of Atlanta Motel v. United States, 379 U.S. 619 (1964): The Civil Rights Act of 1964, barring discrimination in public accommodations, was held constitutional when the Court found that Congress was within its right to regulate interstate commerce. (Chapter 5)

Hoyt v. Florida, 368 U.S. 57 (1961): The exclusion of women from juries did not violate the equal protection clause of the Fourteenth Amendment. (Chapter 5)

Hylton v. United States, 3 Dall. (3 U.S.) 171 (1796): Excise tax on carriages not a direct tax; therefore constitutional. (Chapter 9)

Immigration and Naturalization Service v. Chadha, 462 U.S. 919 (1983): Legislative veto ruled unconstitutional. (Chapters 6, 9)

J.E.B. v. Alabama, 1994 U.S. LEXIS 3421 (1994): Aiabama's use of peremptory challenges to exclude men from the jury for a paternity case was unconstitutional. (Chapter 4)

Johnson v. Santa Clara Transportation Agency, 480 U.S. 616 (1987): For the first time, the Court ruled that a public employer could use a voluntary plan to promote women even if there was no judicial finding of prior discrimination. (Chapter 5)

Keyes v. School District No. 1, Denver, Colorado, 413 U.S. 189 (1973): School districts maintenance of segregated schools through racially gerrymandered school attendance zones was ruled unconstitutional. (Chapter 5)

Korematsu v. United States, 323 U.S. 649 (1944): Internment of Japanese-American citizens held constitutional during World War II. (Chapter 9)

Lee v. Weisman, 112 S. Ct. 2649 (1992): A public middle-schools practice of prayer at graduation was ruled unconstitutional as a violation of the establishment clause. (Chapter 4)

Lemon v. Kurtzman, 403 U.S. 602 (1971): The Court devised "the Lemon test" to measure the constitutionality of state laws that appear to further a religion. Such practices are constitutional if they have a secular purpose; neither advance nor inhibit religion; and dont foster excessive governmental entanglement with religion. (Chapter 4)

Lynch v. Donnelly, 465 U.S. 668 (1984): A citys inclusion of a creche as part of its holiday display in a private park does not violate the establishment clause. (Chapter 4)

Mapp v. Ohio, 367 U.S. 643 (1961): Evidence obtained in violation of the Fourth Amendments prohibition of unreasonable searches and seizures cannot be used as evidence at trial. The exclusionary rule applies to the states through the Fourteenth Amendment. (Chapter 4)

Marbury v. Madison, 1 Cranch (5 U.S.) 137 (1803): The Court first asserted the power of judicial review in finding that the congressional statute extending the Courts original jurisdiction was unconstitutional. (Chapters 2, 9)

McCleskey v. Kemp, 481 U.S. 279 (1987): Even if the death penalty was imposed in a racially discriminatory manner, it did not violate the equal protection clause of the Fourteenth Amendment. (Chapter 4)

McCleskey v. Zant, 111 S.Ct. 1454 (1991) Although the use of conversations with another prisoner as evidence violated McCleskeys right to counsel, the Court ruled that this challenge should have been made earlier in proceedings. Thus, McCleskeys conviction was upheld. (Chapter 4)

McCulloch v. Maryland, 4 Wheat. 316 (1819) Congresss authority under the commerce clause gives it the power to create a bank. (Chapters 3, 6, 9)

McLaurin v. Oklahoma State Regents for Higher Education, 339 U.S. 637 (1950): Segregation in graduate education was a violation of the Fourteen Amendments equal protection clause. (Chapter 5)

Miller v. California, 413 U.S. 15 (1973): The Court set out a new test for obscenity. It must first ask "whether the work depicts or describes in a patently offensive way, sexual conduct specifically defined by law." It then must ask "whether the work, as a whole, lacks serious literary, artistic, political or scientific value." (Chapter 4)

Minor v. Happersett, 88 U.S. 162 (1875): Women were not enfranchised by the privileges and immunities clause of the Fourteenth Amendment. Voting is not a privilege of citizenship. (Chapter 5)

Miranda v. Arizona, 384 U.S. 436 (1966): The Fifth Amendment requires that persons arrested for a crime must be advised of their right to remain silent and to have counsel present. (Chapter 4)

Missouri v. Holland, 252 U.S. 416 (1920): National law and treaties are supreme over state law. (Chapter 3)

Muller v. Oregon, 208 U.S. 412 (1908): Oregons ten-hour-a-day maximum hour law for women upheld as constitutional. (Chapter 5)

National League of Cities v. Usury, 426 U.S. 833 (1976): Congress overstepped its authority under the commerce clause when it included state workers under the Fair Labor Standards Act. (Chapter 3)

Near v. Minnesota, 283 U.S. 697 (1931): The first case in which the Court overturned a conviction ruling that the state had violated freedom of the press under the First Amendment. (Chapter 4)

Nebraska Press Association v. Stuart, 427 U.S. 539 (1976): Any attempts by the government to prevent expressions carry a heavy presumption against their constitutionality. Thus, a trial courts "gag order" barring the press from reporting the details of a crime was unconstitutional. The presss right to cover the trial outweighed the defendants right to a fair trial. (Chapter 4)

New York Times Co. v. Sullivan, 376 U.S. 254 (1964) "Actual malice" must be proved to support a finding of libel against a public figure. (Chapters 4, 14)

New York Times Co. v. United States, 403 U.S. 713 (1971): *The New York Times* printed classified documents known as "The Pentagon Papers" regarding the war in Vietnam. After the first installment in the series, the government moved to restrain publication. The Court found that this kind of prior restraint was in violation of the First Amendment. (Chapters 4, 14)

Oregon v. Smith, 294 U.S. 872 (1990): An Oregon law banning the use of peyote was challenged by Native Americans who used the drug as part of a religious observance. The Court ruled that the law does not violate the free exercise clause because peyote is a dangerous drug. (Chapter 4)

Palko v. Connecticut, 302 U.S. 319 (1937): Established the principle that only rights fundamental to our notions of ordered liberty were to be applied to the states via the Fourteenth Amendments due process clause. (See *selective incorporation* in Glossary.) (Chapter 4)

Planned Parenthood of Southeastern Pennsylvania v. Casey, 112 S. Ct. 931 (1992): Pennsylvanias wide array of abortion restrictions including a 24-hour waiting period and parental consent notifications were held constitutional so long as they do not place an undue burden on women seeking abortions. (Chapters 3, 4, 9, 15)

Plessy v. Ferguson, 163 U.S. 537 (1986): Plessy challenged a Louisiana statute requiring that railroads provide separate accommodations for blacks and whites. The Court found that separate but equal accommodations did not violate the equal protection clause of the Fourteenth Amendment. (Chapters 2, 3, 5, 9)

Red Lion Broadcasting Company, Inc. v. FCC, 395 U.S. 367 (1969): The fairness doctrine allows the government to regulate use of the public air waves. Federal Communication Commission regulations, therefore, do not violate the First Amendment. (Chapter 14)

Reed v. Reed, 404 U.S. 71 (1971): For the first time, the Court found that unreasonable gender discrimination violated the equal protection clause of the Fourteenth Amendment. (Chapter 5)

Regents of the University of California v. Bakke, 438 U.S. 265 (1978): The Court found quotas unconstitutional but noted, however, that race may be taken into account along with other admission factors. (Chapter 5)

Regina v. Hicklin, L.R. 2 Q.B. 360 (1868): English tradition holding that, in order to be obscene, material must be shown to deprave and corrupt those into whose hands it might fall. (Chapter 4)

Reynolds v. Sims, 377 U.S. 533 (1964): Congressional and state legislative districts must have "substantially equal" populations, in essence guaranteeing "one man, one vote." (Chapters 6, 9)

Roe v. Wade, 410 U.S. 113 (1973): The Court found that a womans right to an abortion in consultation with her physician was protected by the right to privacy found in the penumbras of several amendments. (Chapters 3, 4, 5, 9, 15)

Roth v. United States, 354 U.S. 476 (1957): To be considered obscene, material must be utterly without redeeming social importance. The *Roth* test asks "whether to the average person, applying contemporary community standards, the dominant theme of the material taken as a whole appeals to the prurient interests." (Chapter 4)

Rust v. Sullivan, 111 S.Ct. 1759 (1991) Prohibiting medical personnel from dispensing abortion information at health clinics receiving federal funding upheld as constitutional. (Chapter 4)

Schenck v. United States, 249 U.S. 47 (1919): Schenck, a Socialist, was convicted of mailing anti-war leaflets encouraging eligible men to avoid the draft. The Court upheld Schencks conviction finding that Schencks speech presented a "clear and present" danger to the United States ability to carry on the war effort successfully. (Chapter 4)

The Slaughterhouse Cases, 83 U.S. 36 (1873): A butchers association charged Louisianas granting of a monopoly for the running of slaughterhouses deprived their members of their livelihood in violation of the Fourteenth Amendment. The Court found that the Fourteenth Amendments privileges and immunities clause applied only to national and not state citizenship. Thus, the states had the right to create a monopoly. (Chapters 3, 5)

Smith v. Allright, 321 U.S. 649 (1944): White primaries violate the Fifteenth Amendment. (Chapter 12)

Stromberg v. California, 283 U.S. 359 (1931): For the fist time, the Court ruled that symbolic speech was entitled to protection under the First Amendment. (Chapter 4)

Swann v. Charlotte-Mecklenburg School District, 402 U.S. 1 (1971): Federal courts could order busing as an appropriate remedy to end segregated education. (Chapter 5)

Sweatt v. Painter, 339 U.S. 629 (1950): Creation of a separate law school for African Americans did not meet the mandates of the Fourteenth Amendments equal protection clause because the facilities were not equal. (Chapter 5)

Texas v. Johnson, 491 U.S. 397 (1989): Burning the U.S. flag during the Republican National Convention was symbolic political speech protected by the First Amendment. (Chapter 4)

Tinker v. Des Moines Independent Community School District, 393 U.S. 503 (1969): Students symbolic speechwearing black arm bands to protest the Vietnam Warwas entitled to First Amendment protection. (Chapter 4)

United States v. Curtiss-Wright Export Corporation, 299 U.S. 304 (1936): Congressional delegation of broad powers to the president in the area of foreign affairs upheld as constitutional. (Chapter 18)

United States v. Nixon, 418 U.S. 683 (1974): There is no constitutional absolute executive privilege that would allow a president to refuse to comply with a court order to produce information needed in a criminal trial. (Chapters 7, 9)

U.S. v. Seeger, 380 U.S. 163 (1965): The Court invalidated the denial of conscientious objector deferments to members of "nontraditional" religions, finding that the mens belief in a supreme being put their religion on a par with others, thus deserving the same constitutional protections. (Chapter 4)

Wallace v. Jaffree, 472 U.S. 38 (1985): An Alabama law requiring a minute of silence for meditation or voluntary prayer was found to not serve a secular purpose and therefore violated the Constitutionally required separation of church and state. (Chapter 4)

Webster v. Reproductive Health Services, 492 U.S. 490 (1989): The Court upheld state-required fetal viability tests in the second trimester and upheld portions of the state law prohibiting abortions to be performed in state hospitals or by state-funded doctors or nurses. (Chapters 3, 4, 9)

Weeks v. United States, 232 U.S. 383 (1914): The Court first articulated the exclusionary rule, which bars the use of illegally obtained evidence in trial. (Chapter 4)

Wisconsin v. Yoder, 406 U.S. 205 (1972): A Wisconsin law requiring school attendance until the age of eighteen violated the free exercise clause because it interfered with the Amishs practice of their religion. (Chapter 4)

Youngstown Steel & Tube Company v. Sawyer, 343 U.S. 579 (1952): President Truman lacked executive power to seize the nation's steel mills. (Chapter 9)

GLOSSARY

absolutist approach: The belief that the First Amendments wording "Congress shall make no law" must be construed to bar any government regulation of First Amendment freedoms. (Chapter 4)

accomodationist approach: A belief that holds that in recognition of religious diversity in the United States, some accommodation for religious differences should be allowed by the government. (Chapter 4)

actual representation: A system by which legislators represent only those voters who elect them. (Chapter 6)

administrative adjudication: A quasi-judicial process in which a bureaucratic agency settles disputes between two parties in a manner similar to the way courts resolve disputes. (Chapter 8)

administrative discretion: The ability of the bureaucracy to make choices concerning the best way to implement congressional intentions. (Chapter 8)

affiliates: Local television stations that carry the programming of a national network. (Chapter 14)

affirmative action: Policies designed to give special attention or compensatory treatment to members of a previously disadvantaged group. (Chapter 5)

agenda: A set of problems to which policy makers believe they should be attentive. (Chapter 16)

agenda setting: The constant process of forming the list of issues to be addressed by government. (Chapter 16)

Americans with Disabilities Act: 1990 law making it illegal for employers to discriminate against persons with physical or mental disabilities. It also guarantees access to all public facilities and requires modifications to make existing facilities available. (Chapters 5, 17)

amicus curiae: "Friend of the court"; a third party to a lawsuit who files a legal brief for the purpose of raising additional points of view in an attempt to influence a courts decision. (Chapters 9, 15)

anti-communism: A campaign in the United States to oppose communism at home and abroad during the Cold War to safeguard national security. This included exposing and punishing suspected communists as subversives. (Chapter 18)

Anti-Federalists: Those who favored strong state governments and a weak national government; opposed the ratification of the U.S. Constitution. (Chapters 2, 4, 7)

appellate courts: Name given to courts of appeal and supreme courts that hear and review cases that already have been decided in lower courts. (Chapter 9)

appellate jurisdiction: A courts authority to hear appeals from other courts in the state or federal system. (Chapter 9)

apportionment: The determination and assignment of representation in a legislature. (Chapters 5, 6)

appropriations: The earmarking of funds by Congress in particular pieces of legislation for particular programs, agencies and so forth. (Chapters 6, 16)

aristocracy: A system of government in which control is based on rule of the highest. (Chapter 1)

Articles of Confederation: The basic framework of the new U.S. government approved by the Second Continental Congress in 1777. Used to govern the United States during the Revolutionary War, the Articles provided for a Congress with very limited authority. (Chapters 2, 6, 18)

articles of impeachment: Precise charges against a president, vice president, or other "civil officers" that are approved by the House of Representatives as a first step to that individuals removal from office. (Chapter 7)

bad tendency test: Engaging in speech that has a tendency to induce illegal behavior or to create a danger; speech that is not protected by the First Amendment. (Chapter 4)

Balanced Budget Amendment: A proposal to require that Congress annually adopt a budget in which revenues at least equal expenditures. (Chapter 17)

bicameral legislature: A legislature divided into two houses; the U.S. Congress and every U.S. state legislature are bicameral (except Nebraskas, which is unicameral). (Chapters 2, 6)

bill: A proposed law. (Chapter 6)

bill of attainder: A law declaring an act illegal without a judicial trial. (Chapter 3)

Bill of Rights: The first ten amendments to the U.S. Constitution guaranteeing specific rights and liberties; ratified in 1791. (Chapters 2, 4)

Black Codes: Laws passed by Southern states following the Civil War to deny most legal rights to newly freed slaves. (Chapter 5)

blanket primary: A primary in which voters may cast ballots in either partys primary (but not both) on an office-by-office basis. (Chapter 12)

block grants: Broad grants with few strings given to states by the federal government for specified activities, such as secondary education or health services. (Chapter 3)

Brady Bill: Law passed in 1993 requiring a national five-day waiting period for purchase of handguns. (Chapters 1, 3, 4)

Brandeis brief: A legal brief that relies heavily on sociological and other forms of nonlegal data, such as statistics, instead of legal precedent. (Chapter 5)

brief: The collected legal written arguments in a case filed with a court by a party prior to a hearing or trial. (Chapter 9)

bureaucracy: A set of complex hierarchical departments, agencies, commissions, and their staffs, that exist to help the president carry out his constitutionally mandated charge to enforce the laws of the nation. (Chapter 8)

bureaucratic theory: The belief that all governmental and all nongovernmental institutions are, in effect, controlled by an all-powerful bureaucracy. (Chapter 1)

bureaucrats: Career government employees who work for federal, state, or local governments. (Chapter 8)

business cycles: Fluctuations between expansion and recession which are a part of modern capitalist economies. (Chapter 17)

Cabinet: The secretaries of major departments of the federal government, the Attorney General, the vice president, and the U.S. Ambassador to the United Nations. All Cabinet members are appointed by the president and confirmed by the Senate. (Chapters 7, 8)

calendar: Congressional schedule. (Chapter 6)

candidate debates: Forums in which political candidates face each other to discuss their platforms, records, and character. (Chapter 13)

capitalism: The economic system that favors private control of business and minimal governmental regulation of private industry. (Chapters 1, 17, 18)

categorical grants: Grants for which Congress appropriates funds for a specific purpose. (Chapter 3)

caucus: Formal or informal groupings of members of Congress by political party, interest, region, or class, and/or other distinctions. (Chapter 6)

Central Intelligence Agency (CIA): Created by the National Security Acts of 1947 and 1949, this agency collects and analyzes information deemed necessary to meet national security threats. (Chapter 18)

checks and balances: A governmental structure that gives each of the three branches of government some degree of oversight and control over the actions of the others. (Chapter 2)

circuit court of appeals (court of appeals): The intermediate appellate courts in the federal system; were established in 1789 to hear appeals from federal district courts. (Chapter 9)

civil law: Noncriminal law, such as the law of property, commercial law, or family law. (Chapter 9)

civil liberties: The personal rights and freedoms that the federal government cannot abridge by law, constitution, or judicial interpretation. (Chapter 4)

civil rights: The political and social right to be free from arbitrary infringement by the government or any individual. (Chapters 4, 5)

Civil Rights Act of 1964: Legislation passed by Congress to outlaw segregation of public facilities and racial discrimination in employment, education, and voting; created the Equal Employment Opportunity Commission. (Chapter 5)

civil service: A federal bureaucracy with appointments made on the basis of competitive examinations rather than political influence. (Chapter 11)

civil service laws: These acts removed the staffing of the bureaucracy from political parties and created a professional bureaucracy filled through competition. (Chapters 11, 12)

Civil Service Reform Act of 1883: See *Pendleton Act*. (Chapter 8)

civil service system: The system created by civil service laws by which appointments to the federal bureaucracy are made. (Chapter 8)

Civil War Amendments: Name given to the Thirteenth, Fourteenth, and Fifteenth amendments to the Constitution, which were concerned with the rights of newly freed slaves. (Chapter 5)

class-action lawsuit: A legal action in which a small number of individuals can sue on behalf of themselves *and* the class of all other citizens who are similarly situated. (Chapter 9)

clear and present danger test: Used by the Supreme Court in an attempt to draw a line between protected and unprotected speech. As the test is applied, the Court looks to see if there is an imminent danger that illegal action would occur in response to the contested speech. (Chapter 4)

clientele agencies: Executive departments that are directed by law to foster and promote the interests of a specific segment or group in the U.S. population (such as the Department of Education). (Chapter 8)

closed primary: A primary election in which only a partys registered voters are eligible to vote. (Chapter 12)

closed shop: Arrangements under which an employer agrees only to hire only union members. (Chapter 17)

cloture: Senate rule that allows the vote of sixty Senators to cut off a filibuster. (Chapter 6)

coalition: A group of interests or organizations that join forces for the purpose of electing public officials. (Chapter 11)

Coercive (or Intolerable) Acts: A series of five acts passed by Parliament in 1774 to punish the American colonists for the Boston Tea Party. (Chapter 2)

collective good: Something of value that cannot be withheld from a non-interest group member.e.g., a tax write-off, a good feeling, etc. (Chapter 15)

commander-in-chief: The constitutional power of the president over all combined U.S. armed forces. (Chapter 7, 18)

commerce clause: Article I, Section 8 of the Constitution allows Congress to "regulate Commerce with foreign Nations, and among the several States, and with the Indian Tribes." (Chapters 2, 3)

Committees of Correspondence: Organizations originated by Samuel Adams in each of the American colonies to keep colonists abreast of developments with the British; served as powerful molders of public opinion against the British. (Chapter 2)

common law: Judge-made law based on adherence to precedents; law common to the realm in the British empire. (Chapter 2)

Common Sense: Pamphlet written by Thomas Paine calling for independence from Great Britain. (Chapters 2, 18)

communism: A political philosophy posited by Karl Marx in which he argued that government was simply a manifestation of underlying economic forces and could be understood according to types of economic production. (Chapters 1, 4, 18)

concurrent powers: Powers shared by the national and state governments. (Chapter 3)

concurring opinions: Opinions written by judges who agree with the outcome of the case but do not agree with the legal rationale for the opinion. (Chapter 9)

confederacy: Type of government in which the national government derives its powers from the states; a league of independent states. (Chapter 2)

confederation: See *confederacy*. (Chapter 2)

conference committee: Joint committee created to iron out differences between Senate and House versions of a specific piece of legislation. (Chapter 6)

Connecticut Compromise: Proposal for a bicameral legislature made by Connecticut during the Philadelphia Convention at which the U.S. Constitution was drafted. (Chapter 2)

conservatives: Those thought to believe that a government is best that governs least and that big government can only infringe on individual, personal, and economic rights. (Chapters 1, 5, 10)

constituency: The individuals who reside in an area from which a representative is elected. (Chapter 6)

constituency service: Assistance that congressional staffs provide to constituents to help cut through the maze of bureaucratic red tape to get government assistance. (Chapter 6)

constitution: Set of written laws and principles that set out a framework for governing. (Chapter 2)

constitutional courts: Courts established by Article III of the Constitution or by congressional action authorized by the Constitution. (Chapter 9)

containment: The argument espoused during the Cold War that if the allies could stop the spread of communism, especially in Europe, that the nature of the Soviet leadership and its political system would collapse. (Chapter 18)

contemporary community standards: In obscenity cases, the Supreme Court allows local communities to determine what they consider to be obscene. (Chapter 4)

content regulation: Governmental attempts to regulate the electronic media. (Chapter 14)

contrast ads: Political campaign advertisements that compare the records of the candidates, favoring the ads sponsor. (Chapter 13)

cooperative federalism: A term used to characterize the relationship between the national and state governments that began with the New Deal. (Chapter 3)

Council of Economic Advisors (CEA): An agency created in 1946 as part of the Executive Office of the President; consists of three economic experts appointed by the president subject to Senate confirmation plus a small staff evenly divided between support personnel and professional economists. (Chapters 7, 17)

covenant: In biblical terms, an agreement, or bargain, between God and his people. In a governmental sense, a formal agreement sworn to a new government to abide by its terms. The Mayflower Compact was a covenant. (Chapter 1)

criminal law: The branch of law dealing with crimes and their punishments. (Chapter 9)

critical elections: An election that signals a party realignment through voter polarization around new issues. (Chapter 12)

Cuban Missile Crisis: U.S.-U.S.S.R. confrontation in 1962 over Soviet ballistic missiles in Cuba. (Chapter 18)

Declaration of Independence: Document drafted by Thomas Jefferson in 1776 that proclaimed the right of the American colonies to separate from Great Britain. (Chapter 2)

Declaration of Rights and Resolves: Call issued by the First Continental Congress for colonial rights of petition and assembly, trial by peers, freedom from a standing army, and the selection of representative assemblies to levy taxes. (Chapter 2)

Declaration of Sentiments: 1848 statement that described widespread discrimination against women in society. (Chapter 5)

deep background: Information gathered for news stories that must be completely unsourced. (Chapter 14)

***de facto* discrimination:** Racial discrimination that results from practice (such as housing patterns or other social factors) rather than law. (Chapter 5)

deficit: The amount spent by the government that exceeds what is taken in. (Chapter 7)

***de jure* discrimination:** Racial discrimination that is a direct result of law or official policy. (Chapter 5)

democracy: A system of government that gives power to the people, whether directly or through their elected representatives. (Chapter 1)

deregulation: The move to end government regulation of various aspects of several industries, including railroads, trucking, airlines, and banking. (Chapter 17)

direct democracy: A system of government in which members of the group meet to discuss all policy decisions and then abide by majority rule. (Chapter 1)

direct incitement test: The advocacy of illegal action is protected by the First Amendment unless imminent action is intended and likely to occur. (Chapter 4)

direct mailer: A professional who supervises a political campaigns direct-mail fund-raising strategies. (Chapter 13)

direct primary: The selection of party candidates through the ballots of qualified voters rather than at party nomination conventions. (Chapter 11)

discharge petitions: Petitions that give a majority of the House of Representatives the authority to bring an issue to the floor in the face of committee inaction. (Chapter 6)

discount rate: The rate of interest at which member banks can borrow money from their regional Federal Reserve Bank. (Chapter 17)

"discuss list": A list of cases taken from the U.S. Supreme Court "cert. pool" that are to be discussed by the Justices; only about 30 percent of submitted petitions make it to this list. (Chapter 9)

dissenting opinions: Opinions written by judges who disagree with the opinion of the majority. (Chapter 9)

district courts: The federal court of original jurisdiction, where most federal cases begin. (Chapter 9)

disturbance theory: The theory offered by political scientist David Truman posits that interest groups form in part to counteract the efforts of other groups. (Chapter 15)

divided government: The situation that exists when the Congress and president come from different political parties. This often makes enactment of policies difficult and had been blamed for gridlock in Washington, DC. (Chapters 2, 6, 7)

divine right of kings: The belief that monarchs were given the right to govern directly from God. (Chapters 1, 2)

double jeopardy: Trying an individual in court more than once for the same crime; prohibited by the U.S. Constitution. (Chapter 4)

dual federalism: The belief that having separate and equally powerful levels of government is the best arrangement. (Chapter 3)

dualist theory: The theory claiming that there has always been an underlying binary party nature to U.S. politics. (Chapter 11)

due process clause: Clause contained in the Fifth and Fourteenth Amendments. Over the years, it has been construed to guarantee to individuals a variety of rights ranging from economic liberty to criminal procedural rights to protection from arbitrary government action. (Chapter 4)

economic interest groups: Groups with the primary purpose of promoting the economic interests of their members. (Chapter 15)

economic regulation: Governmental regulation of business practices, industry rates, routes, or areas serviced by particular industries. (Chapter 17)

elastic clause: A name given to the "necessary and proper clause" found in the final paragraph of Article I, Section 8 of the U.S. Constitution. It gives Congress the authority to pass all laws "necessary and proper" to carry out the enumerated powers specified in the Constitution. (Chapters 1, 2, 3, 16)

electoral college: The body of presidential electors from each state who cast their ballots in their respective state capitals for the president and vice president of the United States. (Chapters 2, 11)

electorate: Those citizens eligible to vote. (Chapter 12)

electors: Members of the electoral college chosen by methods determined in each state. (Chapters 2, 12)

electronic media: The newest form of broadcast media including television, radio, and cable. (Chapter 14)

elite theory: The view that a small group of people actually makes most of the important decisions. C. Wright Mills argued that important policies were set by three loose coalitions of groups—the military, corporate leaders, and a small set of government officials—that he termed the "power elite." (Chapters 1, 16)

Emancipation Proclamation: Proclamation issued by President Abraham Lincoln that provided that all slaves in states still in active rebellion against the United States would automatically be freed on January 1, 1863. (Chapter 5)

engagement: A term meaning that the United States will not retreat into isolationism after the Cold War but will remain involved in global affairs. (Chapter 18)

enlargement: A term meaning that the United States will promote democracy, open markets, and other Western political, economic, and social values around the world. (Chapter 18)

Enlightenment: A movement that occurred in Western Europe in the 1700s that espoused human reason, science, and religious toleration. (Chapter 1)

entitlement programs: Government benefits to which those meeting the specified requirements have a legal right. (Chapters 16, 17)

enumerated powers: Seventeen specific powers granted to Congress under Article I, Section 8 of the U.S. Constitution; these powers include taxation, coinage of money, regulation of commerce, and the authority to provide for a national defense. (Chapters 2, 3)

Equal Employment Opportunity Commission: Federal agency created to enforce provisions of the Civil Rights Act of 1964. (Chapters 5, 9)

equal protection clause: Section of the Fourteenth Amendment that guarantees that all citizens receive "equal protection under the laws"; has been used to bar discrimination against African Americans, women, and other groups. (Chapter 5)

equal time rule: The rule that requires broadcast stations to sell campaign air time equally to all candidates if they choose to sell it to any. (Chapter 14)

establishment clause: The first clause in the First Amendment that prohibits the national government from establishing a national religion. (Chapter 4)

exclusionary rule: Judicially created rule that prohibits police from using illegally seized evidence at trial. (Chapter 4)

executive agreements: Secret and highly sensitive arrangements with foreign nations entered into by the president that do not require the "advise and consent" of Congress. (Chapters 7, 18)

Executive Office of the President: Establishment created in 1939 to help the president oversee the bureaucracy. (Chapters 7, 8, 18)

executive orders: Presidential directives to an agency that provide the basis for carrying out laws or for establishing new policies. (Chapter 8)

executive power: The authority to execute or carry out the laws of the nation; a power vested in the chief executive by Article II of the Constitution. (Chapters 2, 7)

executive privilege: The belief that, at the presidents discretion, communications between him and his aides can be kept confidential from Congress and the courts. (Chapter 7)

exit polls: Polls conducted at selected polling places on election day. (Chapter 10)

ex post facto **law:** Law passed after the fact, thereby making previously legal activity illegal and subject to current penalty; prohibited they the U.S. Constitution. (Chapters 3, 4)

extradite: To return criminals to states where they have been convicted or are to stand trial. (Chapter 3)

faction: Group of individuals with shared traits or common interests. (Chapters 2, 15)

fairness doctrine: Rule in effect from 1949 to 1985 requiring broadcasters to cover events adequately and to present contrasting views on important public issues. (Chapter 14)

Farewell Address: George Washingtons last public statement as president, in which he discussed the dangers of divisive party politics and warned strongly against foreign entanglements. (Chapters 7, 18)

Federal Employees Political Activities Act: 1993 liberalization of Hatch Act. Federal employees are now allowed to run for office in nonpartisan elections and to contribute money to campaigns in partisan elections. (Chapter 8)

federalism: The philosophy that describes the governmental system created by the Framers. See also *federal system.* (Chapter 3)

The Federalist Papers: A series of eighty-five political papers written by John Jay, Alexander Hamilton, and James Madison in support of ratification of the U.S. Constitution. (Chapter 2)

Federalists: Those who favored a stronger national government and supported the proposed U.S. Constitution; later became the first U.S. political party. (Chapters 2, 3, 4, 7)

Federal Register: A daily publication of the federal government that contains all proposed and final regulations of all federal agencies. (Chapter 8)

federal system: Plan of government created in the U.S. Constitution in which power is divided between the national government and the state governments and in which independent states are bound together under one national government. (Chapters 2, 3)

Fifteenth Amendment: Last of the three Civil War Amendments; prohibited states from discriminating against potential voters because of race or previous condition of servitude. (Chapter 5)

fighting words: Words intended to incite or cause injury to those at whom they are addressed; not protected by the First Amendment. (Chapter 4)

filibusters: A formal way of halting action on a bill by means of long speeches or unlimited debate in the Senate. (Chapter 6)

First Continental Congress: Meeting held in Philadelphia from September 5 to October 26, 1774, in which fifty-six delegates (from every colony except Georgia) adopted a resolution that opposed the Coercive Acts. (Chapter 2)

fiscal policy: The deliberate use of the national governments taxing and spending policies to influence the overall economy and maintain economic stability. (Chapter 17)

food stamp program: An in-kind payment to poor families who receive vouchers for the purchase of food. (Chapter 16)

Fourteenth Amendment: Second of the three Civil War Amendments; guaranteed equal protection and due process of laws to all U.S. citizens. (Chapter 5)

franchise: The right to vote. (Chapter 5)

free exercise clause: The second clause of the First Amendment. It prohibits the U.S. government from interfering with a citizens right to practice his or her religion. (Chapter 4)

free market economy: The production and exchange of goods and services without interference from the government. (Chapter 1)

free media: Coverage of a candidates campaign by the news media. (Chapter 13)

free-rider problem: A problem that occurs when those who dont join or work for the benefit of the group still reap the rewards of the groups activity. (Chapter 15)

"freedom of choice" plans: Plans enacted by Southern states in the aftermath of *Brown* v. *Board of Education* to allow parents to send their children to the school of their choice and not to the school closest to their home (especially if it had black children enrolled). (Chapter 5)

freedom rides: Bands of college students and other civil rights activists traveled throughout the South by bus in an effort to force bus stations and other public facilities to desegregate. (Chapter 5)

freedmen: Name given to slaves who obtained freedom either individually (before the Emancipation Proclamation) or collectively (upon the Emancipation Proclamation and the end of the Civil War). (Chapter 5)

full faith and credit clause: Clause in the U.S. Constitution that requires that judicial decrees and contracts made in one state will be binding and enforceable in another. (Chapter 3)

gender gap: The difference between the partisan choices of women and men in the aggregate. (Chapter 11)

General Agreement on Tariffs and Trade (GATT): International agreements to lower trade barriers. (Chapter 18)

general election campaign: That part of a political campaign following a primary election, aimed at winning a general election. (Chapter 13)

general elections: Elections in which voters decide which candidates will actually fill elective public offices. (Chapter 12)

gerrymandering: The legislative process through which the majority party in each statehouse tries to assure that the maximum number of representatives from its political party can be elected to Congress through the redrawing of legislative districts. (Chapter 6)

get-out-the-vote: A push at the end of a political campaign to encourage supporters to go to the polls. (Chapter 13)

government: The institutions and procedures by which a given nation or other territory and its people are ruled. (Chapter 1)

governmental agenda: The changing list of issues to which governments believe they should address themselves. (Chapter 16)

governmental party: The office holders and candidates who run under a political partys banner. (Chapter 11)

government corporations: Businesses set up and created by Congress that perform functions that could be provided by private businesses (such as the U.S. Postal Service). (Chapter 8)

Gramm-Rudman-Hollings Act: The Balanced Budget and Emergency Deficit Control Act of 1985 that was designed to reduce the budget deficit by 1991. (Chapters 6, 7, 17)

grandfather clauses: Statutes that allowed only those whose grandfathers had voted before Reconstruction to vote unless they passed a wealth or literacy test. (Chapter 5)

grand jury: The body of persons selected to serve as an investigatory body of court; they decide whether or not to indict individuals whose cases are brought before them. (Chapter 9)

grants-in-aid: Programs funded by Congress that provide money to state and local governments to accomplish goals desired by the national government. (Chapter 3)

Great Compromise: A decision made during the Philadelphia Convention to give each state the same number of representatives in the Senate regardless of size; representation in the House was determined by population. (Chapter 2)

Great Depression: The severe recessionary period following the stock market crash of 1929. (Chapters 1, 3, 7, 17)

"Great Society": President Lyndon B. Johnsons plan to end poverty and discrimination in the United States through a variety of innovative programs. (Chapters 5, 7)

gross domestic product: The total market value of all goods and services produced in a country during a year. (Chapter 17)

Group of 7: Created in the 1970s, this group of key industrial powers (Canada, France, Germany, Great Britain, Italy, Japan and the United States) work to coordinate their trade, investment, and monetary policies. (Chapter 18)

Gulf of Tonkin Resolution: An agreement that originally authorized a massive commitment of U.S. forces to support a series of anti-communist, although not democratic, governments in South Vietnam. (Chapters 7, 18)

habeas corpus: A court order demanding that individuals in official custody (usually jail or prison) be brought to court and shown the reasons for their detention. According to the U.S. Constitution, *habeas corpus* can be suspended only in times of rebellion or invasion. (Chapters 4, 7)

Hatch Act: Enacted by Congress in 1939 to prohibit civil servants from taking activist roles in partisan campaigns. This act prohibited federal employees from making political contributions, working for a particular party, or campaigning for a particular candidate. (Chapter 8)

holds: A tactic by which a senator asks to be informed before a particular bill is brought to the floor. (Chapter 6)

ideology: The combined doctrines, assertions, and intentions of a social or political group that justify its behavior; a consistent pattern of opinion on political issues that stems from basic underlying beliefs or a set of beliefs. (Chapters 1, 9, 11, 15)

impeachment: The power delegated to the House of Representatives in the Constitution to charge the president, vice president, or other "civil officers," including federal judges, with "Treason, Bribery, or other high Crimes and Misdemeanors." This is the first step in the constitutional process of removing such government officials from office. (Chapters 1, 2, 6, 7)

implementation: The process by which a law or policy is put into operation by the bureaucracy. (Chapters 8, 16)

implied power: A power derived from an enumerated power and the necessary and proper clause. These powers are not stated specifically but are considered to be reasonably implied through the exercise of delegated powers. (Chapter 3)

impoundment: Refusal of the president to spend funds for programs that have been appropriated (authorized) by Congress. (Chapter 6)

incorporation doctrine: Principle in which the Supreme Court has held that most, but not all of the specific guarantees in the Bill of Rights limit states and local governments by incorporating those guarantees through the due process clause of the Fourteenth Amendment. (Chapter 4)

incumbency: The condition of already holding elected office. (Chapter 12)

incumbency factor: The fact that being in office helps a person stay in office because of a variety of benefits from free publicity to, in the case of Congress, free mailing, which go with the position. (Chapter 6)

independent agencies: Governmental units that closely resemble Cabinet departments but have narrower areas of responsibility (such as the Central Intelligence Agency). (Chapter 8)

indictment: A formal accusation decided upon by a grand jury. (Chapter 9)

indirect (representative) democracy: A system of government that gives citizens the opportunity to vote for representatives who will work on their behalf. (Chapter 1)

inflation: A rise in the general price levels of an economy. (Chapter 17)

in forma pauperis: Literally, "in the form of a pauper"; a way for an indigent or poor person to appeal a case to the U.S. Supreme Court. (Chapter 9)

inherent powers: Powers of the president that can be derived from inferences in the Constitution. (Chapter 7)

initiative: A method by which state and local voters can propose laws or constitutional amendments. Generally, special interest groups draft the initiatives and then circulate them on petitions. (Chapter 10)

institutional agenda: The problems to which legislators or other public officials feel obliged to devote active and serious attention. (Chapter 16)

interest group liberalism: All organized interests get something from government, thereby having an impact on how political decisions are made. (Chapter 1)

interest groups: Organized groups that try to influence public policy. (Chapters 14, 15)

interest group theory: The belief posited by David Truman that interest groups not elites, sets of elites, or bureaucrats control the governmental process. (Chapters 1, 15)

intergovernmental lobby: The pressure group or groups that are created when state and local governments hire lobbyists to lobby the national government. (Chapter 3)

International Monetary Fund (IMF): Established by the Allies after World War II to stabilize exchange rates among various currencies. (Chapter 18)

interventionist state: Replaced the *laissez-faire* state as the government took an active role in guiding and regulating the private economy. (Chapter 17)

iron triangles: The relatively stable relationships and patterns of interaction that occur among an agency, interest groups, and congressional committees or subcommittees. (Chapter 8)

isolationism: A form of foreign policy in which a country ignores activity beyond its borders. (Chapter 18)

issue networks: A term used to describe the fuzzy set of relationships that exist among a large number of actors who work in broad policy areas. (Chapter 8)

issue-oriented politics: Politics that focus on specific issues rather than on party, candidate, or other loyalties. (Chapter 11)

Jay Treaty: Negotiated by John Jay, this treaty helped settle disputes between Britain and the United States over the boundaries of the new nation, debts incurred during the Revolutionary War, and commerce between the two nations. (Chapters 7, 18)

Jim Crow laws: Laws enacted by Southern states that discriminated against blacks by requiring segregation in public schools and public facilities, including railroads, restaurants, and theaters. (Chapter 5)

joint committees: Committees formed with members from both houses of Congress, generally to coordinate investigations or special studies. (Chapter 6)

judicial review: The authority of a court to review the acts of the legislature, the executive, or states to determine their constitutionality; enunciated by Chief Justice John Marshall in *Marbury* v. *Madison* (1803). (Chapters 1, 2, 3, 9)

Judiciary Act of 1789: Established the basic three-tiered structure of the federal court system. (Chapter 9)

laissez-faire: A French term literally meaning "to allow to do, to leave alone." It is a hands-off governmental policy that is based on the belief that governmental regulation of the economy is wrong. (Chapters 1, 3, 8, 17)

League of Nations: Created after World War I at the insistence of President Woodrow Wilson, this precursor of the United Nations was the first global organization of nation-states dedicated to preserving peace. (Chapters 6, 7, 18)

legislative courts: Courts established by Congress for specialized purposes, such as the Court of Military Appeals. (Chapter 9)

legislative powers: The authority of Congress to make laws as enumerated in the Constitution. (Chapter 6)

legislative veto: A procedure by which one or both houses of Congress can disallow an act of an executive agency by a simple majority vote. (Chapter 6)

lend-lease program: Program by which Congress gave the president the authority to lend or lease any equipment to any country whose defense he believed necessary to the security of the United States. (Chapter 18)

libel: False statements or statements tending to call someones reputation into disrepute. (Chapter 4)

liberals: Those considered to favor extensive governmental involvement in the economy and the provision of social services and to take an activist role in protecting the rights of women, the elderly, minorities, and the environment. (Chapters 1, 5, 10)

libertarians: Those who stress that government should not involve itself in the plight of the people or attempt to remedy any social ills. (Chapter 1)

line item veto: The power to veto specific provisions of a bill without vetoing the bill in its entirety. (Chapters 7, 17)

lobbying: The activities of groups and organizations that seek to influence legislation and persuade political leaders to support the groups position. (Chapter 15)

lobbyist: Interest group representative who seeks to influence legislation that will benefit his or her organization through political persuasion. (Chapters 14, 15)

logrolling: Congressional vote trading on bills. (Chapter 6)

Magna Carta: A charter of government signed by King John in 1215, guaranteeing the British people certain liberties, including landowner and tenant rights, the right to a trial by jury, and some measure of religious freedom. (Chapter 2)

majority leader: The elected leader of the party controlling the most seats in the U.S. House of Representatives or the Senate; is second in authority to the Speaker of the House and in the Senate is regarded as its most powerful member. (Chapter 6)

majority party: The political party in each house of Congress with the most members. (Chapter 6)

majority rule: The central premise of direct democracy in which only policies that collectively garner the support of a majority of voters will be made into law. (Chapter 1)

mandate: A command, indicated by an electorates votes, for the elected officials to carry out their platforms. (Chapter 12)

mandates: National laws that direct states or local governments to comply with federal rules or regulations (such as clean air or water standards) under threat of civil or criminal penalties or as a condition of receipt of any federal grants. (Chapter 3)

manifest destiny: A popular theory during the U.S. expansion westward that it was a divinely mandated obligation to expand across North America to the Pacific Ocean. (Chapter 18)

margin of error: See *sampling error.* (Chapter 10)

Marshall Plan: Created in 1948, the European Recovery Program named for Secretary of State George Marshall in which the United States funnelled massive amounts of money into the countries of Western Europe to rebuild their economies and help prevent communist parties from winning elections. (Chapter 18)

matching funds: Donations to presidential campaigns from the federal government that are determined by the amount of private funds a qualifying candidate raises. (Chapter 13)

Mayflower Compact: A covenant signed by the Pilgrims aboard the *Mayflower* on November 21, 1620, to ensure an orderly form of government upon their landing in the New World. (Chapter 1)

means-tested programs: Programs intended to assist those whose income falls below a designated level. (Chapter 16)

media campaign: That part of a political campaign waged in the broadcast and print media. (Chapter 13)

media consultant: A professional who produces political candidates television, radio, and print advertisements. (Chapter 13)

media effects: The influence of news sources on public opinion. (Chapter 14)

Medicaid: An expansion of Medicare, this program subsidizes medical care for the poor. (Chapters 3, 16)

Medicare: The federal program, established in the Johnson administration, that provides medical care to elderly Social Security recipients. (Chapter 16)

Mercantilism: An economic theory popular from the sixteenth through the eighteenth centuries premised on the belief that a nations wealth was measured by the amount of gold and silver in its treasury. This belief justified maintenance of strict import/export controls, with exports being favored over imports. (Chapters 2, 18)

merit system: The system by which federal civil service jobs are classified into grades or levels to which appointments are made on the basis of performance on competitive examinations. (Chapter 8)

midterm convention: A national party convention held in nonpresidential congressional election years, for the purposes of rallying the party and adopting new policies. (Chapter 11)

militia: Colonial practice whereby white, male residents were deputized to keep law and order in lieu of a police force or army (Chapters 2, 4, 18)

minority leader: The elected leader of the party with the second highest number of elected representatives in either the House or the Senate. (Chapter 6)

minority party: Party with the second most members in either house of Congress. (Chapter 6)

Miranda rights: Statements that must be made by the police informing a suspect of his or her constitutional rights protected by the Fifth Amendment, including the right to an attorney provided by the court if the suspect cannot afford one. (Chapter 4)

miscegenation laws: Laws passed by most Southern states in the pre-Civil War period prohibiting blacks and whites from marrying each other. (Chapter 5)

Missouri Compromise of 1820: A compromise that attempted to maintain a balance in the Senate between slave and free states; Missouri was admitted as a slave state and Maine as a free state. (Chapter 5)

monarchy: A form of government in which power is vested in hereditary monarchs. (Chapter 1)

monetary policy: A form of government regulation in which the nations money supply and interest rates are controlled. (Chapter 17)

money: A system of exchange for goods and services that includes currency, coins, and bank deposits. (Chapter 17)

monopoly: The control by a single corporation or company of a particular field or enterprise; the absence of competition in a particular market. (Chapter 3)

Monroe Doctrine: Issued by President James Monroe in 1823, this foreign policy statement proclaimed that the United States would not tolerate recolonization or extension of European influence in the Western Hemisphere. (Chapter 18)

Montgomery bus boycott: The first wide-scale nonviolent protest against discrimination in the South; blacks refused to take buses as a protest of the segregation that existed in Montgomerys public accommodations. (Chapter 5)

moral suasion: The capacity of the Federal Reserve Bank to influence the actions of other members of the financial community by suggestion, exhortation, and formal agreement. (Chapter 17)

muckraking: A form of newspaper publishing, in vogue in the early twentieth century, concerned with reforming government and business conduct. (Chapter 14)

multi-issue groups: Groups that are concerned with more than just a single issue (e.g., the AFL-CIO). (Chapters 14, 15)

multilateralism: In foreign policy, action taken in cooperation with other states after extensive consultation. (Chapter 18)

multistage sampling: See *stratified sampling*. (Chapter 10)

Munich Pact: An agreement in which the British and French agreed to allow Nazi Germany to occupy part of Czechoslovakia without a fight in the mistaken belief that Hitler would stop there. (Chapter 18)

Mutually Assured Destruction (MAD): The situation where both the Soviet Union and the United States would each absorb a nuclear strike by the other and still retaliate with its own nuclear weapons. (Chapter 18)

national convention: A party conclave (meeting) held in the presidential election year for the purposes of nominating a presidential and vice-presidential ticket and adopting a platform. (Chapter 11)

national debt: The total remaining of all annual federal budget deficits plus interest. (Chapter 17)

national party platforms: A statement of the general and specific philosophy and policy goals of a political party, usually promulgated at the national convention. (Chapter 11)

National Security Acts of 1947 and 1949: These acts consolidated the army, the navy, and the new air force into one department under civilian leadership. (Chapter 18)

National Security Council: Created by the National Security Acts of 1947 and 1949, this council advises the president on foreign and military affairs. (Chapters 7, 18)

nation-state: Nation-states are based on the idea that one government should have sole authority over a well-defined territory. (Chapter 18)

natural law: A doctrine that human society should be governed by certain ethical principles that are part of nature and, as such, can be understood by reason. (Chapter 1)

necessary and proper clause: See *elastic clause*. (Chapter 3)

negative ads: Advertising on behalf of a candidate that attacks the opponents platform or character. (Chapter 13)

network: An association of broadcast stations (radio or television) that shares programming through a financial arrangement. (Chapter 14)

Neutrality Acts: Acts passed by isolationists in Congress in the 1930s to keep the United States out of foreign conflicts. (Chapter 18)

New Deal: The name given to the program of "Relief, Recovery, Reform" begun by President Franklin D. Roosevelt in 1933 designed to bring the United States out of the Great Depression. (Chapters 3, 17)

New Federalism: Term first coined by President Ronald Reagan to describe his administrations emphasis on the return of power to the states; later characterized by the significant reduction in federal aid to the states. (Chapter 3)

New Jersey Plan: A framework for the Constitution proposed by a group of small states whose key features included a one-house legislature with one vote for each state, a multi-person "executive," the establishment of the acts of Congress as the "supreme law" of the land, and supreme judiciary with limited power. (Chapter 2)

nomination campaign: That part of a political campaign aimed at winning a primary election. (Chapter 13)

nonprobability sampling: Unrepresentative sampling for surveys such as straw polls; they generally are unreliable. (Chapter 10)

North American Free Trade Agreement (NAFTA): A treaty between Canada, Mexico, and the United States to reduce tariff and other mutual trade barriers. (Chapters 7, 18)

North Atlantic Treaty: An agreement entered into in 1949 by Belgium, Canada, Denmark, France, Great Britain, Iceland, Italy, Luxembourg, the Netherlands, Norway, Portugal, and the United States in which a military attack against any of the signatories would be considered an attack against all of them. (Chapter 18)

North Atlantic Treaty Organization (NATO): A mutual defense organization created to implement the North Atlantic Treaty. (Chapter 18)

nullification doctrine: The claimed right of a state to nullify, or reject, a federal law. (Chapters 3, 7)

off-the-record: Information gathered for a news story that cannot be used at all. (Chapter 14)

off-year elections: Elections that take place in the middle of a presidential term. (Chapter 12)

oligarchy: A form of government in which the right to participate is always conditioned on the possession of wealth or property. (Chapter 1)

on background: A term for when sources are not included in a news story. (Chapter 14)

one-partyism: A political system in which one party dominates and wins virtually all contests. (Chapter 11)

on-the-record: Information gathered for a news story that can be used and cited. (Chapter 14)

open market operations: The buying and selling of government securities by the Federal Reserve Bank in the securities market. (Chapter 17)

open primary: A primary in which party members, independents, and sometimes members of the other party are allowed to vote. (Chapter 12)

organizational campaign: That part of a political campaign involved in fund raising, literature distribution, and all other activities not directly involving the candidate. (Chapter 13)

organizational party: The workers and activists who staff the partys formal organization. (Chapter 11)

Organization of Petroleum Exporting Countries (OPEC): A cartel formed in 1960 to establish common oil production and pricing policies; members include Algeria, Ecuador, Gabon, Indonesia, Iran, Iraq, Kuwait, Libya, Nigeria, Qatar, Saudi Arabia, United Arab Emirates, and Venezuela. (Chapter 18)

original jurisdiction: The jurisdiction of courts that hear a case first, usually in trial. Courts determine the facts of a case under their original jurisdiction. (Chapter 9)

oversight: Congresss ability to question members of the executive agencies to see if they are enforcing and interpreting the laws passed by Congress as the members intended. (Chapters 6, 8)

paid media: Political advertisements purchased for a candidates campaign. (Chapter 13)

pardoning power: The constitutional authority of the president to restore all rights and privileges of citizenship, usually given to specific individuals for crimes for which they have been convicted. (Chapter 7)

party caucus: A formal gathering of all party members. (Chapter 6)

party conference: Name given to the Republican and Democratic congressional party meetings at which party leaders and committee assignments are named; held at the beginning of each session in each chamber. (Chapter 6)

party identification: A citizens personal affinity for a political party, usually expressed by his or her tendency to vote for the candidates of that party. (Chapter 11)

party-in-the-electorate: The voters who consider themselves to be allied or associated with the party. (Chapter 11)

party mobile office: Units that travel around the country in order to publicize the party, assist residents with governmental problems, and serve as a party field base. (Chapter 11)

party ombudsman: A party representative in the community who attempts to help citizens with their problems. (Chapter 11)

party realignments: A shifting of party coalition groupings in the electorate that remains in place for several elections. (Chapter 12)

party unity vote: A vote in the legislature in which a member votes with his or her party on issues that divide a majority of Democrats from a majority of Republicans. (Chapter 11)

party vote: A vote in the legislature in which a majority of Democrats and Republicans vote on opposite sides. (Chapters 6, 11)

patronage: Jobs, grants, or other special favors that are given as rewards to friends and political allies for their support. (Chapters 7, 8)

patrons: Individuals who often finance interest groups. (Chapter 15)

Pendleton Act: Reform measure that created the Civil Service Commission to administer a partial merit system in the federal service classified the federal service by grades to which appointments were made based on the results of a competitive examination and made it illegal for political appointees to be required to contribute to a particular political party. (Chapter 8)

personal campaign: That part of a political campaign concerned with presenting the candidates public image. (Chapter 13)

personal liberty: A key characteristic of U.S. democracy. Initially meaning freedom from governmental interference, today it includes demands for freedom to engage in a variety of practices free from governmental discrimination. (Chapter 1)

plaintiff: The individual or organization that originally brings a lawsuit to court. (Chapter 9)

pluralist theory: Theory of government in which resources are scattered so widely in our diverse democracy that no single elite group can ever have a monopoly over any substantial area of policy. (Chapter 1)

pocket veto: If Congress adjourns during the ten days the president has to consider a bill passed by both Houses of Congress, the bill figuratively dies in the presidents pocket. (Chapter 6)

policy adoption: The approval of a policy proposal by the people with requisite authority, such as a legislature. (Chapter 16)

policy evaluation: The process of determining whether a course of action is achieving its intended goals. (Chapter 16)

policy formulation: The crafting of appropriate and acceptable proposed courses of action to ameliorate or resolve public problems. (Chapter 16)

policy implementation: The process of carrying out public policy through governmental agencies and the courts. (Chapter 16)

political action committees: Federally mandated, officially registered fund-raising committees that represent interest groups in the political process. (Chapters 13, 15)

political consultants: Professionals who manage campaigns and political advertisements for political candidates. (Chapter 11)

political equality: Government practice in which all individuals have the opportunity to participate equally in governmental affairs. (Chapter 1)

political ideology: An individuals coherent set of values and beliefs about the purpose and scope of government. (Chapter 10)

"politically correct speech" movement: Movement that developed in the late 1980s to limit free speech by banning language thought to be inappropriate or harmful. (Chapter 4)

political machine: An organization affiliated with a political party that often controlled a majority of the votes in a locality, and thus won most public offices. (Chapter 11)

political party: A group of office holders, candidates, activists, and voters who identify with a group label and seek to elect to pubic office individuals who run under that label. (Chapters 6, 11)

political socialization: The process through which an individual acquires particular political orientations; the learning process by which people acquire their political beliefs and values. (Chapter 10)

politics: The process by which policy decisions are made. (Chapters 1, 3)

polls: voting booth; See also *public opinion polls* (Chapter 10)

pollster: A professional who takes public opinion surveys that guide political campaigns. (Chapter 13)

poll tax: Method used by Southern states after the Civil War to exclude blacks from voting by imposing taxes or the payment of fees before a citizen could vote; outlawed in national elections by the Twenty-fourth Amendment in 1964 and in state elections by the Supreme Court in 1966. (Chapter 5)

popular consent: The idea that governments must draw their powers from the consent of the governed. (Chapter 1)

popular sovereignty: The right of the majority to govern themselves. (Chapter 1)

pork barrel: Legislation that allows representatives to "bring home the bacon" to their districts in the form of public works programs, military bases, or other programs designed to benefit their districts directly. (Chapters 6, 17)

positive ads: Advertising on behalf of a candidate that stresses the candidates qualifications, family and issue positions without reference to the opponent. (Chapter 13)

precedent: A judicial decision that serves as a rule for settling subsequent cases of a similar nature. (Chapter 9)

preemption: A concept derived from the Constitutions supremacy clause that allows the national government to override or preempt state or local actions in certain areas. (Chapter 3)

presidential character: According to political scientist David Barber, the patterns of behavior exhibited by presidents based on their energy level and the degree of enjoyment they find in their job. (Chapter 7)

presidential style: A presidents ability to get things done; determined by factors such as his character and approach to office, the perception of others of his ability to lead, and his ability to mobilize public opinion to support his actions. (Chapter 7)

Presidential Succession Act of 1947: Clarifies who replaces the president in case of a vacancy in the vice presidency (or in case of his inability to serve); by law, first the Speaker of the House of Representatives, then the president pro tempore of the Senate, and then the Secretaries of State, Treasury, Defense, and the other Cabinet heads in order of their departments creation. (Chapter 7)

primary elections: Elections in which voters decide which of the candidates within a party will represent the party in the general election. (Chapter 12)

print press: The traditional form of mass media, comprising newspapers, magazines, and journals. (Chapter 14)

prior restraint: Judicial doctrine stating that the government cannot prohibit speech or publication before the fact. (Chapter 4)

privacy: The right to be let alone; a judicially created doctrine encompassing an individuals decision to use birth control or secure an abortion. (Chapters 3, 4)

pro bono: Legal work done for no charge. (Chapter 9)

Progressive Era: Period between 1889 and 1920 that was characterized by concern with reform of political, economic, and social systems in the United States. (Chapters 5, 16, 17)

proportional representation: The practice of awarding legislative seats in proportion to the number of votes received. (Chapter 11)

protectionism: The erection of barriers, such as tariffs, against foreign competitors. (Chapters 16, 17, 18)

public assistance programs: Government-administered programs for needy individuals. (Chapter 16)

public funds: Donations from general tax revenues to the campaigns of qualifying presidential candidates. (Chapter 13)

public-interest group: A group that seeks a collective good that will not selectively and materially benefit the members of the organization. (Chapter 15)

public opinion: What the public thinks about a particular issue or set of issues at any point in time. (Chapter 10)

public opinion polls: Interviews or surveys with a sample of citizens that are used to estimate public opinion of the entire population. (Chapter 10)

public policy: A purposive course of action followed by government in dealing with some problem or matter of concern. (Chapter 16)

quasi-judicial process: Process in which a bureaucratic agency settles disputes between two parties in a manner similar to the way courts resolve disputes. (Chapter 8)

quasi-legislative process: Bureaucratic rule making. The process allows bureaucratics to act as lawmakers when they make rules or draft regulations to implement various congressional statutes. (Chapter 8)

quorum: The minimum number of members of any deliberative body that must be present before official business can be conducted. (Chapter 6)

quota sample: A type of nonprobability sample in which pollsters draw their sample based on known statistics. (Chapter 10)

Radical Republicans: Division of the Republican Party who were critical of Abraham Lincoln for his handling of the Civil War, tried to impeach Andrew Johnson for his conciliatory approach to the South after the war, and used Reconstruction to punish Southern states. (Chapter 5)

random sampling: Using a method of selection that gives each potential voter or adult the same chance of being selected. (Chapter 10)

recall: A procedure for demanding the ouster of elected public officials prior to the end of their term. (Chapter 10)

recession: A short-term decline in the economy that occurs as investment sags, production falls off, and unemployment increases. (Chapter 17)

redistricting: The redrawing of congressional districts to reflect increases or decreases in seats allotted to the states as well as population shifts within a state. (Chapters 6, 12)

red tape: The nickname given to the confusing web of federal rules and regulations that often cause delays in the execution of policy. (Chapter 8)

referendum: The practice of putting pieces of legislation proposed by the state legislature before the voters for their approval or disapproval. (Chapter 10)

Reformation: A movement in the sixteenth century in which various doctrines and practices of the Roman Catholic Church were rejected. It led to the establishment of Protestantism. (Chapter 1)

regional primaries: A proposed system in which the country would be divided into five or six geographic areas and all states in each region would hold their presidential primary elections on the same day. (Chapter 12)

regulations: Rules that govern the operation of all government programs and have the force of law. (Chapter 8)

regulatory commission: An agency of the executive branch that generally is concerned with one aspect of the economy. (Chapter 8)

representative democracy: See *indirect (representative) democracy.* (Chapter 1)

republic: A government rooted in the consent of the governed. A representative or indirect democracy. (Chapter 1)

reserve requirements: Governmental requirement that a portion of member banks deposits must be retained to back loans made. (Chapter 17)

retrospective judgment: A voters evaluation of the performance of the party in power. (Chapter 12)

revenue sharing: Method of redistributing federal monies back to the states with "no strings attached"; favored by President Richard M. Nixon. (Chapters 3, 17)

right-of-rebuttal rule: A Federal Communications Commission regulation that people attacked on a radio or television broadcast be offered the opportunity to respond. (Chapter 6)

right-to-work laws: Regulations providing that union membership or non-union membership cannot be a condition of employment in that state. (Chapter 17)

rule: Given by the House Rules Committee to legislation being reported to the floor for consideration; it contains the date the bill will come up for debate, the time that will be allotted for discussion, and often even specifications concerning what kinds of amendments can be offered. (Chapter 6)

rule making: The administrative process that results in rules and regulations. (Chapter 8)

Rule of Four: At least four justices of the Supreme Court must vote to consider a case before it can be heard. (Chapter 9)

runoff primary: A second primary election between the two candidates receiving the greatest number of votes in the first primary. (Chapter 12)

sample: A relatively small number of individuals chosen in a survey who are interviewed for the purpose of estimating the opinions of the entire population. (Chapter 10)

sampling error: A measure of the accuracy of a pubic opinion poll. (Chapter 10)

Second Continental Congress: Meeting that convened in Philadelphia on May 10, 1775, in which it was decided that an army should be raised and George Washington of Virginia was named commander-in-chief. (Chapter 2)

secular realignment: The gradual rearrangement of party coalitions, based more on demographic shifts than on shocks to the political system. (Chapter 12)

seditious (speech): Speech that advocates the violent overthrow of the government; not protected by the First Amendment. (Chapter 4)

select committees: Temporary committees appointed for specific purposes with fairly limited mandates, generally to conduct special investigations or studies and to report back to the chamber that established them. (Chapter 6)

selective incorporation: A judicial doctrine whereby most but not all of the protections found in the Bill of Rights are made applicable to the states via the Fourteenth Amendment. (Chapter 4)

senatorial courtesy: A practice by which senators can have near veto power over laws or appointments that affect their state in a specific way. (Chapters 6, 9)

seniority: The method by which the person of the majority party with the longest continuous service on a particular committee was automatically made chair. (Chapter 6)

separation of powers: A way of dividing power among the three branches of government in which members of the House of Representatives, members of the Senate, the president, and the federal courts are selected by and responsible to different constituencies; developed by French political philosopher Montesquieu. (Chapter 2)

sequestration: Automatic across-the-board budget cuts mandated by the Gramm-Rudman-Hollings Act. (Chapter 17)

Shays's Rebellion: A rebellion led by Daniel Shays, an army veteran, during the summer of 1786 in which an army of 1,500 disgruntled and angry farmers marched to Springfield, Massachusetts and forcibly restrained the state court from foreclosing on their farms. (Chapter 2)

single-issue groups: Groups that are concerned with only one issue (e.g., National Abortion Rights Action League). (Chapter 15)

slander: Untrue spoken statements that defame the character of a person. (Chapter 4)

"smart money": Campaign contributions to the candidate or political party expected to win in an election year. (Chapter 11)

social contract theory: The belief that people are free and equal by God-given right and that this in turn requires that all men give their consent to be governed, espoused by John Locke and influential in the writing of the Declaration of Independence. (Chapters 1, 2)

socialism: A political system in which the working class owns and controls all means of production and distribution. (Chapters 1, 4)

social regulation: Governmental regulation of the quality and safety of products as well as the conditions under which goods and services are produced. (Chapter 17)

Social Security: A federal social insurance program that provides minimum levels of income maintenance. (Chapter 16)

Social Security Act: A 1935 law that established old age insurance (Social Security), assistance for the needy, children, and others; and unemployment insurance. (Chapter 16)

social welfare policies: Governmental policies designed to enhance an individuals quality of life. (Chapter 16)

Solicitor General: The fourth-ranking member of the Justice Department; responsible for handling all appeals on behalf of the U.S. government to the Supreme Court. (Chapter 9)

Sons of Liberty: A radical organization of colonists created in 1765 to express opposition to the Stamp Act. (Chapter 2)

sovereign: Independent or self-governing. (Chapter 3)

Spanish-American War: A war fought between the United States and Spain in 1898 that began as an intervention by the United States on behalf of Cuba; sparked by the belief that the Spanish sunk the U.S. battleship *Maine* in the Havana harbor. (Chapter 18)

Speaker of the House: The only officer of the House of Representatives specifically mentioned in the Constitution; elected at the beginning of each new Congress by the entire House; traditionally a member of the majority party. (Chapter 6)

special-interest caucuses: Groups that allow congressional members from either party to cross party lines to band together with their colleagues who have a common interest. (Chapter 6)

sphere of influence: An area dominated although not directly controlled by another country. (Chapter 18)

split-ticket voting: The practice of voting for the candidate of one party for president and another for Congress. (Chapters 1, 2, 12)

spoils system: The firing of public-office holders of a defeated political party and their replacement with loyalists of the newly elected party. (Chapters 8, 11)

spot ads: Television advertising on behalf of a candidate that is broadcast in sixty-, thirty-, or ten-second durations. (Chapter 13)

Stamp Act Congress: Meeting of representatives of nine of the thirteen colonies held in New York City in 1765 during which representatives drafted a document to send to the king listing how their rights had been violated. (Chapter 2)

Stamp Act of 1765: A direct tax requiring the purchase of stamps as a tax to be affixed to all documents, including newspapers, magazines, and commercial papers. (Chapter 2)

standing: Over the years this has come to mean that a person bringing a lawsuit must have a strong interest and personal stake in the outcome of the case. (Chapter 9)

standing committees: The committees to which proposed bills are referred for consideration. (Chapter 6)

stare decisis: In court rulings, a reliance on past decisions or precedents to formulate decisions in new cases. (Chapter 9)

statute: A law. (Chapter 6)

stratified sampling: The process by which census data providing the number of residences in an area and their location are used to divide the country into four sampling regions and then sets of counties and standard metropolitan statistical areas are randomly selected in proportion to the total national population. (Chapter 10)

straw polls: Unscientific surveys used to gauge public opinion on a variety of issues and policies. (Chapter 10)

strict constructionist: An approach that emphasizes the Constitutions initial intentions by the Framers. (Chapter 9)

strict scrutiny: A heightened standard of review used by the Supreme Court to determine the constitutional validity of a challenged practice. (Chapter 5)

suffrage: The right to vote. (Chapters 1, 2, 5)

suffrage movement: Term used to refer to the drive for womens right to vote that took place in the United States from 1880 to 1920. (Chapters 1, 5)

Sugar Act of 1764: Act passed by Britains Parliament to help raise revenues to pay for the French and Indian War; taxes were placed on sugar, wine, coffee, and other products commonly exported to the colonies. (Chapter 2)

sunset laws: Laws that provide that agencies or programs are automatically abolished after a fixed period of years unless Congress extends their life. (Chapter 8)

sunshine laws: After passage of the Sunshine Law by Congress in 1976; sunshine laws require that about 50 multi-headed federal agencies hold their meetings in sessions open to the public. (Chapters 6, 8)

superdelegates: Delegate slots to the Democratic Partys national convention that are reserved for elected party officials. (Chapter 12)

supremacy clause: Portion of Article IV of the U.S. Constitution that mandates that national law is supreme to (i.e., supersedes) all other laws passed by the states or by any other subdivision of government. (Chapters 2, 3)

suspect classifications: Categories of classes that trigger the highest standard of scrutiny from the Supreme Court. (Chapter 5)

symbolic speech: Symbols, signs, and other methods of expression generally also considered to be protected by the First Amendment. (Chapter 4)

systemic agenda: All public issues that are viewed as requiring governmental attention; a discussion agenda. (Chapter 16)

tariffs: Taxes on goods imported to or exported from a country. (Chapters 16, 17, 18)

Tecumsehs Confederacy: An effort by Shawnee political leader Tecumseh in the early 1800s to form a confederacy of Native American tribes in the Southwest that would prevent further takings of their lands by colonists. (Chapter 18)

term limits: Legislation designating that state and/or federal elected legislators can serve only a specified number of years. (Chapter 6)

test cases: Cases brought by interest groups as a part of a planned strategy eventually to win their point before the U.S. Supreme Court. (Chapter 5)

third-partyism: The tendency of third parties to arise with some regularity in a nominally two-party system. (Chapter 11)

Thirteenth Amendment: First of the three Civil War Amendments; specifically banned slavery in the United States. (Chapter 5)

Three-Fifths Compromise: Agreement reached at the Constitutional Convention stipulating that each slave was to be counted as three-fifths of a person for purposes of determining population for representation in the U.S. House of Representatives. (Chapter 2)

ticket splitting: Voting for candidates of different parties for various offices in the same election. (Chapter 11)

Title IX: Federal statute prohibiting sex discrimination in educational institutions receiving federal funds. (Chapters 5, 8)

Title VII: Section of the Civil Rights Act of 1964 that prohibits employers from discriminating against employees for a variety of reasons, including race, sex, age, or national origin. (In 1978 the Act was amended to prohibit discrimination based on pregnancy.) (Chapter 5)

totalitarianism: A system of government in which unlimited powers are retained by elite rulers. (Chapter 1)

Townshend Acts: Acts passed by Britains Parliament in 1767 imposing duties on a wide variety of goods imported by the colonists, at least in part to demonstrate to the colonists Britains continued right to tax them. (Chapter 2)

tracking polls: Continuous surveys that enable a campaign to chart its daily rise or fall. (Chapter 11)

trade associations: Groups that represent specific industries. (Chapter 15)

trade deficit: The condition created when the value of imports exceeds the value of exports. (Chapters 17, 18)

treaty: A formal agreement between nations setting forth rights and responsibilities of each. All U.S. treaties must be approved by a two-thirds vote of the Senate. (Chapters 7, 18)

Treaty of Versailles: See *Versailles Peace Treaty*. (Chapters 6, 7, 18)

Truman Doctrine: This policy of containment enunciated by President Harry S Truman in a 1947 speech before Congress began a new U.S. response to Soviet expansion. (Chapter 18)

trusts: Business combinations that lead to monopolistic practices. (Chapters 3, 17)

"two presidencies": A theory postulated by Aaron Wildavsky that there are two presidencies; in one, a president is a strong leader in foreign affairs, and in the other he is a weak one in the realm of domestic affairs. (Chapter 7)

uncommitted delegates: Delegates to a party convention whose support prior to the convention is not pledged to a particular candidate. (Chapter 12)

unemployment insurance: A program begun with the Social Security Act of 1935 that provides funds to workers losing their jobs due to reasons beyond their control. (Chapter 16)

unicameral: One-house legislature, as in the state of Nebraska. (Chapter 6)

unilateralism: The belief that the United States was better off estranged from European affairs and able to take international action without consulting other foreign powers. (Chapter 18)

union shop: Agreement between employers and employees that all employees must contribute to the union through dues whether or not they belong to the union. (Chapter 17)

unitary: Term applied to systems in which all power resides in the central or national government as opposed to regional (subnational) governments. (Chapter 3)

United Nations: Before the end of World War II, this international government organization was formed with the purpose of guaranteeing the security of member nations when attacked and to promote economic and social well-being around the world. (Chapter 18)

unit rule: A traditional party practice under which the majority of a state delegation can force the minority to vote for its candidate. (Chapter 12)

Versailles Peace Treaty: Treaty ending World War I and establishing the League of Nations. (Chapters 6, 7, 18)

veto: A constitutional power of the president to send a bill back to Congress with reasons for rejecting it. A two-thirds vote in each house can override a presidential veto. (Chapters 2, 7)

Virginia Plan: The first general plan for the Constitution, proposed by James Madison, whose key points were a bicameral legislature, an executive chosen by the legislature, and a judiciary also named by the legislature. (Chapter 2)

virtual representation: System of government in which elected representatives are considered to represent the entire nation and not only their home district. (Chapter 6)

voter canvass: The process by which a campaign gets in touch with individual voters, either by door-to-door solicitation or by telephone. (Chapter 13)

Voting Rights Act of 1965: Suspended the use of literacy tests and authorized the federal government to monitor all elections in areas where discrimination was found to be practiced or where less than 50 percent of the voting age population was registered to vote in the 1964 election. (Chapters 5, 12)

War of 1812: Fought from 1812 to 1815, this war between the United States and Great Britain began over British violations of U.S. shipping rights and other disputes. (Chapter 18)

War Powers Act: Under this Act, passed by Congress in 1973, the president was limited in his deployment of troops overseas to a sixty-day period in peacetime (which could be extended for an extra thirty days to permit withdrawal) unless Congress explicitly gave its approval for a longer period. (Chapters 6, 7, 18)

Watergate: Term used to describe the events and scandal resulting from a break-in at the Democratic National Committee headquarters in 1972 (at the Watergate office complex in Washington, DC) and the subsequent cover-up of White House involvement, leading to the eventual resignation of President Richard M. Nixon under the threat of impeachment. (Chapters 1, 7)

whistle blowers: Federal employees who publicly disclose waste or mismanagement in their agencies. (Chapter 8)

white primary: A primary in which nonwhite voters are systematically denied participation (no longer practiced). (Chapter 12)

wire services: An electronic delivery of news gathered by the services correspondents and sent to all member news media organizations. (Chapter 14)

World Bank (also known as the International Bank for Reconstruction and Development): Established by the Allies after World War II to provide funds for large-scale projects to help heal the war-torn economies of Europe. (Chapter 18)

writ of *certiorari*: A formal document issued from the Supreme Court to a lower federal or state court that calls up a case. Four of the Courts nine justices must agree to accept the case before it is granted *certiorari*. (Chapter 9)

"Year of the Woman": Name given to denote the extraordinary number of women who ran for and won elected positions at all governmental levels in the 1992 elections. (Chapter 6)

yellow journalism: A form of newspaper publishing in vogue in the late nineteenth century that featured pictures, comics, color, and sensationalized, oversimplified news coverage. (Chapter 14)

INDEX

Abolitionist movement, 155–57, 409, 621, 652
Abortion, 21, 399
  anti-abortion movement, 144
  cases related to, 143–45, 182
  gag rule, 145
  NARAL, 21, 618, 619
  Operation Rescue, 143, 147, 618, 649–50, 651
  party delegates opinion on, 516
  party platforms and, 518
  privacy issue, 142–45
  pro-choice fund raising, 653
  public opinion concerning, 430, 432
  restrictions state-by-state (1993), 98, 100
  Supreme Court and, 391, 393–94
Abrams v. *United States*, 119
Absentee ballot laws, 535, 536
Abzug, Bella, 220, 243
Accountability of bureaucracy, 332–38, 340–44
  congressional control, 333, 336–38
  executive control, 334–36
  judicial control, 333, 338
  size problems and, 341–42
  system problems and, 342–44
Acid rain, 744–45
Actenberg, Roberta, 268
Activism
  activism/restraint debate, 391–93
  political party, 493–94
  social, 717–18
Actual malice, 127
Actual representation, 217
Adams, Abigail, 60, 151, 263, 294
Adams, John, 34, 40, 262–63, 274, 277, 354, 356, 445, 447, 450, 518, 750–51
Adams, John Quincy, 223, 521
Adams, Samuel, 30, 31, 32
Addams, Jane, 165, 624, 627
Ad hoc (select) committees, 228, 229, 231
Administration for Children and Families, 323
Administrative adjudication, 328, 331–32
Administrative agencies, techniques for policy implementation, 671–72
Administrative discretion, 327
Administrative Procedure Act, 328
Affiliates, 586–87
Affirmative action, 195–96
African Americans
  in Congress, 217, 218, 220, 243
  poll tax and, 97

  public opinion of, 420–21
  redistricting and, 530
  on Supreme Court, 375–76
  See also Civil rights; Race
Age
  party identification and, 489–90
  political socialization and, 423
  voter participation and, 532–33
Age Discrimination Act, 97
Agenda setting, 662, 664–68
  news media and, 784
  types of agenda, 664–65
Agnew, Spiro, 262, 598
Agricultural Adjustment Act, 82, 84, 314, 713
Agricultural Adjustment Administration, 82, 84
AIDS, 194, 323
  AIDS testing, 65
    search and seizure issue, 133–34
  governmental involvement in, 20
  research, 690
Aid to Families with Dependent Children (AFDC), 89, 92, 323, 679, 686–88, 693
  AFDC-UP program, 688
  maximum benefit per month by state, 92
Ailes, Roger, 552
Airline Deregulation Act of 1978, 673, 719
Alien and Sedition Acts, 79, 354
  nature of, 116
Amendments, 57–65
  Bill of Rights, 58, 59, 63, 109
  categories of, 62–64
  to change existing policy, 63
  to change mechanics of government, 62
  to change structure of government, 62, 63
  for expansion of rights, 62–63
  failed amendments, examples of, 62
  judicial interpretation of Constitution and, 64
  to overrule Supreme Court decisions, 63
  proposal of, 58–59
  ratification of, 60
  See also individual amendments
American Anti-Slavery Society, 155–56, 621
American Association for Public Opinion Research, 440
American Association of Retired Persons (AARP), 338, 619, 628, 642
American Bar Association, 635
  rating of Supreme Court nominees, 377

American Civil Liberties Union (ACLU), 125, 126, 146, 624, 628, 655
  functions of, 126, 616–17
  participation in cases, 126
  Women's Rights Project, 183, 184
American College of Surgeons, 699
American Conservative Union, 646
American Enterprise Institute, 468
American Federation of Labor (AFL), 378, 625
American Federation of Labor-Congress of Industrial Organizations (AFL-CIO), 617, 619
  merger, 633–34
American government
  economic system and, 16–20
  national, devising, 11–16
  theories influencing Framers, 7–11
    democratic theory, 12
    natural law, 7
    social contract theories, 8–11
  See also Democracy
American Independent Party, 459
American Indian Movement, 188
American Institute of Public Opinion, 414
American Legion, 338
American Medical Association (AMA), 616, 619, 634, 651, 652, 690, 692, 699
American Political Science Association, 651, 652, 653
American Public Welfare Association, 687
American Railway Union, 118, 624
Americans for Democratic Action, 646
Americans with Disabilities Act, 151, 194, 664
American Trial Lawyers of America, 648–49
American Women, 181
Amicus curiae, 169, 170, 350, 383, 384, 385–87, 642
Amish religion, Old Order, 113
Amnesty International U.S.A., 619
Amtrak, 665
Analogous policy formulation, 668
Anderson, John, 459, 460, 511, 559
Anglican church, 7
Annual Report of the Council of Economic Advisers, 297
Anthony, Susan B., 159, 161, 165, 167, 652, 653
Anti-Ballistic Missiles, 778
Anti-communism, consensus of, 766, 787, 788

I1

Anti-Federalists, 227, 351, 354–55, 445
  fears of, 56
  Federalists vs., 54–57
  as Federal Republicans, 54
  insistence on bill of rights, 108
  position of, 53, 54, 55, 105
Anti-Federalists, The (Main), 53
Anti-Masonic Party, 509
Anti-Trust Division, Justice Department, 706
Appellate courts, 357, 358, 359
Appellate jurisdiction, 359, 362
  Supreme Court, 367, 381
Appointments, presidential, 267–69, 333
  power to make, 267–69
  Senate confirmation of, 251–52, 269, 779–80
  Supreme Court, 350, 371–72
Apportionment, 206–9
Appropriations, congressional, and foreign policy, 780–81
Aquinas, St. Thomas, 7
Aristocracy
  example of, 12
  nature of, 11
Aristotle, 7, 11, 46
Arms, right to keep and bear, 123
  gun control issue and, 70, 123, 147, 406, 437
Arms Control Caucus, 242
Armstrong, Scott, 376
Arthur, Chester A., 760
Articles of Confederation, 28, 36–39, 52, 69, 205, 257, 752
  confederacy and, 36–37
  limitations of, 37–39
  provisions of, 36–37
Articles of impeachment, 261
Asher, Herbert, 439
Asian/Pacific Islanders, 421
Aspin, Les, 224–25, 297, 784, 790
Assimilation of Native Americans, 188
Assistant U.S. Attorneys, 362
Associated Press, 584, 587
Association of Trial Lawyers of America, 619
Attorney General, 295, 308, 321
Authoritative techniques for policy implementation, 671
Authorization for Use of Military Force Against Iraq Resolution, 251
Automatic stabilizers in economy, 727

Babbitt, Bruce, 601
Backdoor spending, 728
Bad tendency test, 117
Baker, Howard, 511
Baker, James, 296, 298, 568
Baker v. *Carr*, 207
Bakke, Allen, 195
Balanced budget amendment, 745–46
Balanced Budget and Emergency Deficit Reduction Act, 59, 284, 733–35
Balance of power, 248–49
Banking Acts
  of 1933, 712
  of 1935, 711
Barbary pirates, 757
Barbary Wars, 754
Barber, James David, 286–87, 595

Barbour, Haley, 465
Barkley, Alben W., 266
Barnes v. *Glen Theater*, 129
Barron v. *Baltimore*, 119, 123
Barry, Marion, 175
Bates, Fred, 587
Batson, James, 138
Baum, Lawrence, 384
Beard, Charles, 19, 53
Beauty contest delegate selection, 503
Becker, Theodore, 13
Bell, Griffin, 368
Bell, John, 460
Bentson, Lloyd, 245
Bergalis, Kimberly, 133, 635
Berger, Karen, 346
Berlin Wall, 768
Berman, Howard, 467
Bernstein, Carl, 594
Berry, Jeffrey, 616
Bias, in reporting by news media, 597–602
Bicameral legislature, 205
  Article I of Constitution, 49–51
  Framers and, 41
Bill
  discharge petition, 230
  hold system, 236
  stages in lawmaking process, 236–41
Bill of attainder, nature of, 73
Bill of Rights, 58, 59, 65, 99, 105–47, 577
  advances in technology and new interpretations of, 65
  amendments of, 58, 59, 63, 109
  civil liberties and, 105–8
  criminal defendants, rights of, 129–41
  First Amendment guarantees, 109–29
  incorporation doctrine and, 119–22
  Madison and, 107–8
  opposition to, 107
  privacy rights, 141–46
  See also individual amendments
Birth control, privacy issue and, 142
Black, Hugo, 109, 111, 136, 377–78, 607
Black Caucus, 242
Black Codes, 158, 160
Blackmun, Harry A., 128, 143, 146, 393, 395
Blacks. *See* African Americans; Race
Blackstone, Sir William, 356
Blaine, James G., 520, 580
Blanket primary, 501
Block grants, 89, 102
Blow, Henry, 79
Board of Education v. *Mergens*, 112
Board of Governors, Federal Reserve System, 721, 723, 724–25
Bolling v. *Sharpe*, 171
"Boll weevils," 242
Bolshevik Party, 3
Bolshevik Revolution, 3
Bond, Julian, 260
Bonior, David, 225, 285
Bonnyman, Gordon, 694
Bork, Robert H., 264, 378–79, 393, 399, 644
Bosnia-Herzogovenia, 3, 6, 669, 782, 784
Boston Globe, presidential election polls of, 410
Boston Massacre, 31, 32
Boston Tea Party, 31–32, 620, 649
Bourgeoisie, 19

Bowen, Catherine Drinker, 46
Bowers v. *Hardwick*, 126, 146, 184, 192, 385, 390
Bowman, James, Sr., 138
Boxer, Barbara, 219
Boycotts of British goods by colonists, 31
Bradley, Bill, 564
Bradley, Joseph, 521
Bradwell v. *Illinois*, 160
Brady, James, 123, 589
Brady, Sarah, 123
Brady Bill (1993), 70, 123, 147, 406, 437, 644, 648, 669
Branch Davidian cult, 65, 342
Brandeis, Louis, 142, 166, 379
"Brandeis Brief," 166
Brandenburg v. *Ohio*, 119
Branzburg v. *Hayes*, 606
Breckinridge, John C., 460
Brennan, William, Jr., 124, 142, 375, 388, 390, 392, 396
Brethren, The (Woodward and Armstrong), 376
Breyer, Stephen G., 377, 396, 399
Briefs, 363
Briggs v. *Elliot*, 171
Brinkley, David, 587
British Broadcasting Company (BBC), 607
British Navy, impressment by, 754–55
British system of parliamentary democracy, 48, 49
British Thermal Units (BTU), 645
Brock, William, 464–65
Brokaw, Tom, 589
Brooks, Preston, 226
Brotherhood of Locomotive Firemen, 118
Brown, Jerry, 565, 568
Brown, John, 155
Brown, Linda, 171
Brown, Oliver, 171
Brown, Ronald, 464–65, 486
Brown II, 172
Brown v. *Board of Education*, 96–97, 162, 170–72, 184, 385, 388, 392, 396, 397
  post-*Brown* activities, 172–73, 178–79
Bryan, Samuel, 104, 105
Bryan, William Jennings, 270
Bryce, James, 66
Buchanan, James, 79
Buchanan, Patrick, 565, 568, 600
Buckley, William F., Jr., 600
Buckley v. *Valeo*, 558
Budget. *See* Federal budget
Budget and Accounting Act of 1921, 727
Budget and Impoundment Control Act, 249–50, 730
Budget Deficit Reduction Act (1993), 225, 284
Budget deficits, 726, 728, 731–35
Budget Enforcement Act of 1990, 735
Buffalo Evening Telegraph, 579
Bull Moose Party, 459
Bumpers, Dale, 248
Bureaucracy, 305–45
  accountability of, 332–38, 340–44
    congressional control, 333, 336–38

executive control, 334–36
judicial control, 333, 338
size problems and, 341–42
system problems and, 342–44
in Britain, 332
bureaucrats, profile of, 317–21
defined, 305
development of, 308–16
civil service system, 311
Civil War era, 309–10
early years, 308–9
Hatch Act, 315
landmark events in, 309
New Deal era, 314–15
regulation of economy and, 312–16
regulatory agencies, 312–13
from spoils system to merit system, 310–12
World War II era, 317
firing of bureaucrat, 319–20, 321
functions of, 306
modern, 316–27, 338–44
accountability of, 340–44
iron triangles (subgovernments), 338–39, 640–41
issue networks, 339–40
nature of, 306
negative opinion of, 306–8
organization of
departments, 321–24
government corporations, 324, 325
independent agencies, 324–26
regulatory boards or commissions, 325, 326–27
policy-making process, 327–32
administrative adjudication, 328, 331–32
rule making, 328–31
toward reform of, 344–46
whistle-blowers and, 320–21
Bureaucratic theory, nature of, 16
Bureaucrats, 305, 317–21
Bureau of Alcohol, Tobacco and Firearms, 342
Bureau of Indian Affairs, 187, 188, 323
Bureau of the Budget, 284, 298
Burger, Warren E., 128, 135, 192, 365, 376, 379, 387, 389–90
Burke, Edmund, 218
Burnham, Walter Dean, 457
Burns, Arthur, 723
Burr, Aaron, 27, 519
Bury My Heart at Wounded Knee (Brown), 188–89
Bush, George, 6, 13, 147, 238, 240, 241, 257–58, 263, 266, 267, 268, 269, 271, 273–74, 286, 293, 307, 321, 334–35, 337, 371, 407, 425, 461, 498, 500, 511, 512, 522, 529, 548, 556, 639, 655, 676, 720, 744, 782
civil rights and, 194, 196, 197
district court nominations and, 368–71
judges appointed by, 369, 370
Supreme Court, 374–75
news media and, 594, 599
1992 presidential campaign and election, 564–72
Persian Gulf War and, 251, 785, 788–89
popularity of, 291–92, 427

as pro-party president, 474, 476, 477
reform of bureaucracy by, 344, 345
style of, 286, 287–88, 292, 603–4
veto of bills, 298, 299, 300
Business cycles, 705, 712
Business groups, 632–33
origins of, 626–27
Business Roundtable, 632, 653, 699
Busing, school desegregation and, 178–79
Butler, Pierce, 366
Buxton, C. Lee, 142
Byrd, Harry, 248
Byrd, Robert C., 225, 233, 302

Cabinet, 294–97
British, 295
origins of, 277, 294–95, 308
secretaries, 321–23
Cable News Network (CNN), 280, 461, 585
Cable Satellite Public Affairs Network (C-SPAN), 585
Cable television, 583, 585, 608–9
Calhoun, John C., 79–80
Califano, Joseph, 250
Campaign process, 543–75
ambition and strategy in, 544
campaign structure, 544–52
general election campaign, 545, 546–47
media campaign, 545, 550–52
nomination campaign, 545, 546
organizational campaign, 545, 549–50
personal campaign, 545, 547–48
candidate vs. campaign, voting for, 552–53
challenges of, 553–63
fund raising, 556–60, 563
news media, 553–56
PACs, 558, 559, 560–63
1992 presidential campaign and election, 564–70
Fall campaign and general election results, 569–72
party conventions, 568–69
party nomination battle, 564–66
Ross Perot, 567–68
toward reform of, 518, 572–73
See also Elections
Campbell, Angus, 424
Campbell, Ben Nighthorse, 189–90, 217, 220
Canadian system of medical care, 698
Candidate debates, 553–55. *See also* Campaign process; Elections
Cannon, Joseph G., 233, 471
Cantwell v. Connecticut, 110
Capacity techniques for policy implementation, 671
Capitalism
Great Depression and, 709
nature of, 17
rise of, 705–6
Cardozo, Benjamin, 120–22
Carmichael, Stokely, 181
Carnal Knowledge, 129
Carnegie, Andrew, 761
Carpetbaggers, 159
Carson, Rachel, 666, 667
Carter, Jimmy, 89, 194, 250, 251, 265, 266, 270–71, 274, 286, 290, 293, 297, 298, 302, 318, 319, 326, 337, 344,

345, 368, 371, 420, 422, 434, 440, 475, 476, 478, 489, 499, 506, 521, 526, 554, 556, 571, 572, 594, 601, 719, 776–77, 778, 788
and Haiti, 776
Iran hostage crisis, 511, 782
judges appointed by, 369, 370
Carter, Rosalyn, 294
Carville, James, 452, 569
Case Act of 1972, 779
Casey, William, 269
Casey v. Planned Parenthood of Southeastern Pennsylvania, 653
Castro, Fidel, 422, 783
Catastrophic Health Care Act, 693
Categorical grants, 87, 88, 89, 91
Catholics, 620
Caucuses
congressional, 223, 225, 227, 242–44
delegate selection, 503
special-interest, 242–44
CBS, 13
Celler, Emanuel, 230
Censorship, news media, 607–8
Census, 206
1990, 209, 530
Center for National Policy, 468
Center for the Study of Responsive Law, 631
Centers for Disease Control (CDC), 134, 319, 323, 674
Central Intelligence Agency (CIA), 325, 782
creation of, 773
Central Pacific Railroad, 623
Certiorari, writ of, 381, 382–83, 385
Cert pool, 382
Chafee, John, 240
Chains, media, 583
Chairpersons, of national committees, 464–65
Challenge Grants, 102
Chamber of Commerce, 616, 619, 626, 627, 632
Changing American Voter, The (Nie, Verba and Petrocik), 424
Chaplinsky v. New Hampshire, 127
Character issue in media coverage of politicians, 594–97
Charles, King, 9
Chase, Salmon, 80
Chavkin, David, 694
Checks and balances, 66
checks on congressional powers, 49, 50
checks on executive powers, 49, 50
checks on judicial powers, 49, 50, 352
nature of, 49
Chernobyl, nuclear accident at, 790
Chicago Board of Trade, 744
Chicanos, 422
Chief Justice, Supreme Court, 45, 364–65, 389–90
Child abuse, 662–63
Child Abuse Prevention and Treatment Act, 663
Child labor, 627
Children, political socialization of, 413–23
Children's Defense Fund, 340, 652, 694
China
commercial treaty with, 759
Tienanmen Square (1989), 3, 7, 788
Chisholm, Shirley, 233

Chisholm v. *Georgia*, 353, 355
Christian Coalition, 632, 633
Christian religious revivalism, 621
Christian Science Monitor, 586
Church of God, 112
Church-state relationship
  colonies and, 109
  Lemon test, 111
  wall of separation concept, 110–12
  See also Religion
Circuit Court of Appeals, 361, 362
Cisneros, Henry, 297
City of Burbank v. *Lockheed*, 70n
Civil Aeronautics Board (CAB), 673, 714, 718
Civilian Conservation Corps, 82, 84
Civil law, nature of, 359–60
Civil liberties, 105–49
  Bill of Rights and, 105–8
  constitutional standards of review and, 183–87
  defined, 106
  privacy rights, 141–46
  toward reform of, 146–47
  See also Criminal defendants, rights of; First Amendment
Civil rights, 106, 151–99
  abolitionist movement, 155–57
  Black Codes and, 158, 160
  Civil Rights Movement, 172–86, 644
    black rights, new move for, 174–75
    Civil Rights Act of 1964, 175, 176–83, 194, 306, 307, 359, 530, 637
    equal protection clause and constitutional standards of review, 183–86
    international effects of, 197
    school desegregation after *Brown*, 172–73
  during Civil War and its aftermath, 157–60
  defined, 151
  disabled Americans and, 193–94
  Fifteenth Amendment, 21, 60, 63, 80, 160, 162–63, 189, 501, 530
  Fourteenth Amendment, 14, 21, 60, 63, 80, 119, 120, 130, 135, 138, 140, 152, 158, 160–61, 162, 163, 181
  Framers' view of, 151
  Hispanic Americans and, 190–92
  homosexuals and, 192–93
  Jim Crow laws and, 158, 161–64, 174
  landmark events in quest for, 154, 173
  miscegenation laws and, 164
  Native Americans and, 187–90
  Niagara Movement, 165
  politics of, 194–97
    affirmative action, 195–96
    legislative response, 196–97
  push for equality (1889–1954), 163–72
    founding of NAACP, 164–65
    litigation, 167–72
    Plessy v. *Ferguson*, 80, 162, 163–64, 396
    women's groups and, 165–67
  Reagan administration and, 194–95
  toward reform of, 197–98
  relationship to women's rights movement, 156, 159–60, 165–67, 180–83
  separate but equal doctrine, 162, 163–64
  slavery and Congress, 153–55

Supreme Court and, 160–63
  challenges to separate but equal doctrine, 167–74
  first cases, 160–63
Thirteenth Amendment, 21, 63, 80, 157–58, 162
violence and, 175, 177–78
voting rights, 60, 159–60, 162–63, 167, 189
Civil Rights Acts
  of 1866, 158, 196
  of 1875, 161
  of 1964, 175, 176–83, 194, 306, 307, 359, 530, 637
    discrimination of public accommodations and, 177
    employment discrimination and, 180
    provisions of, 176–77
    school desegregation and, 178–79
    Title VI, 178–79, 676
    Title VII, 180, 181, 186, 386
  of 1991, 196–97
Civil Rights Cases, 161–62
Civil Rights Movement. *See under* Civil rights
Civil Rights Restoration Act, 195
Civil Service Commission, 311, 319
Civil service laws, 451, 455
Civil Service Reform Act of 1883, 311–12
Civil service system, 311
  merit system, 312, 318
  reform measures, 312–13
  salaries, 318
  Senior Executive Service, 318
  See also Bureaucracy
Civil War, 74, 418, 680, 759
  big government and, 309–10
  causes of, 157
  dual federalism concept and, 78, 80
  effects of, 21
  federal bureaucracy and, 309–10
  freedom of speech and press and, 116–17
  powers of Congress and, 248–49
  Reconstruction, 158, 159, 162
  rise of interest groups and, 621–23
Civil War Amendments, 152, 157–60
Claiborne, Harry R., 210
Clancey, Maura, 599
Clark, Kenneth, 170
Class-action lawsuit, 397
Clay, Henry, 222–23, 226, 449, 551
Clayton Act, 625, 627, 707
Clean Air Act of 1970, 717, 738–39, 744
  Clear Air Act Amendments of 1990, 91, 248, 327, 330–31, 665, 669, 738, 739, 740, 744
  steps in passage of, 238–41
Clean Water Act, 92, 739
Clear and present danger test, 117–19
Clerk of the Court, 365
Cleveland, Grover, 286, 521, 579–80, 596
Clientele agencies, 323
Clinton, Bill, 6–7, 14, 51, 96, 147, 197, 210, 216, 241, 258, 271, 273, 275, 297, 302, 315–16, 326, 327, 331, 341, 343, 406, 420, 424, 437, 454, 461, 465, 469, 471, 475, 485, 490, 498, 500, 538, 544, 555, 556, 634, 669, 782, 783
  on abortion, 145
  appointments of, 268, 269, 336

judges, 369, 370, 371
  Supreme Court justices, 375, 377
budgetary process and, 284
budget deficit-reduction plan, 728
coattail effect of, 477
Congress and, 248, 283–84, 665
foreign policy, 774, 775, 789, 790–92
Gore and, 267
health care reform and, 334, 696–99
homosexuals in the military and, 192–93
New Federalism of, 93
news media and, 581, 594, 596, 599, 602–3, 604, 784
1992 presidential campaign and election, 522, 564–65
personalized presidency of, 281–82
public opinion of, 292
reform of bureaucracy by, 344, 345
reform of federal system and, 101–2
rewards system used by, 285
social welfare and, 688
style of, 287, 291
White House staff, 298, 299–300
Clinton, Hillary Rodham, 15, 294, 299, 334, 340, 428, 596, 602, 694, 697, 775
Closed primary, 500–501
Closed shop, 716
Cloture, 237
"Club movement," 165
Coalition, formation of, 453
Coalition building, 669–70
Coattail effect, 477, 529–30
Cobb, Roger W., 664
Coercive Acts of 1774, 32, 33, 205
Cohens v. *Virginia*, 356
Cold War, 765–73, 782, 788
  end of, 569, 790
  origins of, 765–66
Collective good, interest groups and, 651
Colonies, 28–36
  British rule
    British mercantilism, 29–30
    British rule by decree, 28
    elected assemblies, 28
    French and Indian War, 29
    official churches, 109
    royal governor, 258–59
    taxation by British, 29–30
  roots of legislative branch in assemblies of, 204–5
  steps toward independence
    Articles of Confederation, 28, 36–39, 52, 69, 205, 257, 752
    Boston Tea Party, 31–32, 620, 649
    Committees of Correspondence, 31, 32
    Constitution. *See* Constitution
    Constitutional Convention, 39–45, 205
    Declaration of Independence, 34–36, 151–52, 205, 795–97
    First Continental Congress, 32–33, 37, 109, 205
    Great Compromise, 42–43, 205
    interest group formation, 620
    New Jersey Plan, 42
    Revolutionary War, 33–34, 36, 37, 752
    Second Continental Congress, 33–34, 36, 52–53, 54, 205
    Shays's Rebellion, 39, 44, 649
    Stamp Act Congress, 31
    Virginia Plan, 40–42, 253, 259, 355

Colonists, reasons for coming to New World, 28
Commander-in-chief, president as, 273, 752
Commentaries on the Laws of England (Blackstone), 356
Commerce, regulation of, 80–81
  interstate, 77–78
Commerce clause, 64, 717
Commission on the Status of Women, 294
Committee on Economic Security, 680
Committee on Federal Judicial Selection, 368
Committee on Public Information, 409, 410
Committee on the Constitutional System (CCS), 66, 252
Committees of Correspondence, 31, 32
Committee system, Congressional, 228–35
  committee chairs, power of, 233–34
  membership in, 232–33
  subcommittees, 228, 230, 231, 234–35, 236
  types of committees, 229–32
Committee to Re-Elect the President (CREEP), 478
Common Cause, 616, 619, 629–31
Common law, 26, 115
Common Sense (Paine), 33–34, 405, 751
Communication technology, foreign and military policy and, 776
Communism, 19
  anti-communist consensus, 766, 787, 788
  Cold War era, 569, 765–66, 768–73, 782, 788, 790
  containment policy toward, 768–71, 792
  Marshall Plan and prevention of, 767
  revolutionary discontent against, 3
Comprehensive Environmental Response, Compensation, and Liability Act (Superfund), 739, 742–44
Comprehensive Family Health Access and Savings Act, 698
Concurrent powers, 72–73, 78
  national supremacy and, 75
  types of, 72
Concurring opinions in Supreme Court cases, 390
Confederacy, nature of, 36–37
Conference committee, 228, 230, 238
Confidentiality of sources, news media and, 606
Confirmation of appointments, 251–52
  Supreme Court nominees, 376–80
Congregationalist Church of Massachusetts, 109
Congress, 203–55
  agenda of, 665–68
  beginning of
    Article I of Constitution on, 49–51, 205, 209
    checks on powers of, 49, 50
    elastic clause, 51
    enumerated powers, 51, 71
    implied powers, 72
  bureaucracy and, 333, 336–38
  caucuses, 223, 225, 227, 242–44
  committees. *See* Congressional committees
  Constitution and, 205–12
    apportionment and redistricting, 206–9, 530
    powers of Congress under, 209–12
  decision-making process of, 241–48
    colleagues and caucuses and, 242–44
    constituents and, 247–48
    interest groups and, 246–47
    political parties and, 242
    staff and, 244–46
  federal budget and, 727–31
  judiciary and, checks on power of, 352
  lawmaking process, 235–41, 337
    bill, stages of, 236–41
    example of, 238–41
    filibusters, 236–37, 238
    presidential involvement in, 282–85
    veto, 238
  lobbying of, 628, 630, 637–39
  majority party of, 220
  members of. *See* Congressional members
  news media coverage of, 589–92
  organizational structure of, 220–35. *See also* House of Representatives; Senate
  political parties and, 227–28, 242, 469–73
  powers of, 50, 51, 71, 72
    legislative powers, 209–12
  president and, 248–52
    agenda setting, 665
    balance of power, 248–49
    from 1804–1933, 278–79
    foreign affairs and, 250–51, 777–82, 788–89
    impeachment power, 210–12
    legislative vetoes, 250
    override function, 271
    oversight of executive branch, 249–51, 778
    senatorial consent and appointments, 251–52, 269, 779–80
  president's power to convene, 269
  public's confidence in, 203–4
  toward reform of, 252–54
  roots of, 204–5
  size of, 207
  slavery and, 153–55
  special interest caucuses, 242–44
  support agencies, 246
  term-limit proposals, 253–54
Congressional Budget Office (CBO), 246, 250, 338, 730
Congressional Caucus for Women's Issues, 242, 243
Congressional Club, 469
Congressional committees
  ad hoc committees, 228, 229, 231
  conference committees, 228, 230, 238
  House-Senate compared, 233
  joint committees, 230, 231, 261
Congressional elections, 528–31
  incumbency advantage and, 528
  off-year elections, 529, 530–31
  redistricting, scandals, and coattails, 528–30
Congressional members, 212–20
  characteristics of, 216–17
  formal requirements of, 213
  House bank scandal, 214, 215
  informal requirements of, 213–14
  majority leaders, 225, 227, 469
  perks of office, 212
  representational function of, 217–20
  selection of. *See* Congressional elections
  women and minorities, 216–20, 243
Congressional party, 469–73
  discipline and, 469–70
  results and, 470–73
Congressional press corps, 590
Congressional Research Service, 246, 338
Congressional Women's Caucus, 243
Congress of Industrial Organizations, AFL-CIO merger and, 633–34
Connally, John, 511
Connecticut Compromise. *See* Great Compromise
Conner, Eugene, 175
Conover, Pamela Johnston, 422
Conscientious objectors, 113, 114
Conscription into military service, 766
Consensus
  anti-communist, 766, 787, 788
  foreign and military policy and, 788
Conservative backlash of 1970s and 1980s, 631–32
Conservative Coalition, 647
Conservative Democratic Forum, 242
Conservatives, viewpoints of, 423–26, 427
Constituency service, 245, 528
Constituents
  categories of, 247
  and legislators, 247–48
Constitution, 25–67
  amending, 57–65
    informal methods of, 64–65
  Articles of, 49–52
    on amendment process, 57–65
    on executive branch, 51–52
    on judicial branch, 52, 351–52
    on legislative branch, 49–51
    on state and federal relations, 52
  basic principles of, 46–49
    checks and balances, 49, 50, 66
    federalism, 47, 69–75
    separation of powers, 47–49, 50
  Bill of Rights. *See* Bill of Rights
  Congress and, 205–12
    apportionment and redistricting, 206–9, 530
    powers of Congress, 209–12
  "contract clause" in, 17
  evolution over time
    amendment process, 57–65
    judicial interpretation, 64
    social and cultural change, 64–65
    technological change, 65
  flexibility of, 64
  on foreign and defense policy, 752
  formulation of, *See* Colonies, steps toward independence
  Framers' motives and, 53
  goals of, 46
  historical environment of, 28–39
    Articles of Confederation and, 36–39
    Declaration of Independence and, 34–36
    origins of new nation, 28–34
  philosophical influences on, 46–47
  powers of president under, 267–74
  Preamble to, 45–46
  ratification of, 52–57
    Federalists vs. Anti-Federalists, 54–57
    by state, 56–57
  toward reform of, 65–66
  text of, 798–807

Constitutional Convention, 39–45, 205
  electoral college, 44–45
  Framers and, 6, 40
  Great Compromise, 42–43, 205
  impeachment process, 45
  New Jersey Plan, 42
  on presidency, 44–45
  task of, 39
  Virginia Plan, 40–42, 253, 259, 355
Constitutional courts, 360
Consultants, political, 451
Consumer population, 398, 399
Consumer Product Safety Commission, 716, 717
Consumer protection legislation, 707
Containment, 768–71, 792
Content regulation of news media, 605–6
Continental Congress, formation of, 205
"Contract clause" in Constitution, 17
"Contract with America", 215
Contrast ads, presidential campaign, 551
Conventions
  midterm convention, 465
  presidential election, 506–15
    delegate selection, 503, 509, 510–12, 513–15
    history of, 506–9
    lessened role of, 510–13
    national convention, 465
    news media and, 512–13
    superdelegates, 512, 523
Conyers, John, Jr., 225
Cook, Fred, 605
Coolidge, Calvin, 344–45, 707
Cooper, Anthony Ashley, 10
Cooperative federalism, 74, 85–86
Cooper v. *Aaron*, 172
Corn Growers Association, 645
Corporations, government, 324, 325
Correspondence Club, 344–45
Cortner, Richard C., 384–85, 642
Cotton Manufacturers, 627
Council of Economic Advisers, 297–98, 341, 726
  creation of, 715
Council on Competitiveness, 267, 331
Counsel, right to, 136–37
Court of Customs and Appeals, 360
Court-packing plan, 83, 314, 399
Courts of Appeals, 361, 362–63
  functions of, 363
  judges, 362
    selection of, 371
Court system, American, 357–58, 360–67. *See also* Judiciary
Coverdell, Paul, 93
Cox, Archibald, 264
Cox, James M., 511
Cracking, congressional districts, 207
Craig v. *Boren*, 184, 185
Creation of the American Republic, The (Wood), 53
Creative federalism, 74
Creative policy formulation, 668
Crime
  defined, 359
  public opinion on, 437, 439
Crime bills, 147
Criminal defendants, rights of, 129–41
  counsel, right to, 136–37
  cruel and unusual punishment, prohibition of, 129, 139–41

exclusionary rule, 135–36
  jury trial, 138
  Miranda rights, 135
  due process rights, 129–31
  searches and seizures, 131–34
  self-incrimination and, 134–35
Criminal justice system, stages of, 130
Criminal law
  grand jury and, 359
  indictment in, 359
  nature of, 359–60
Criminal syndicalism statutes, 117
Crises, reform and role of, 21
Critical elections, presidential, 524
Cronin, Thomas, 284, 640
Cruel and unusual punishment, prohibition of, 129, 139–41
C-SPAN, 226
Cuba, 784
Cuban Americans, 422, 489
Cuban Missile Crisis, 296, 769, 774–75
Cumming v. *County Board of Education*, 164
Cuomo, Mario, 98, 99, 477, 564, 568
Curley, James M., 451
Curtis, Kenneth, 465
Cushing, William, 374

Dahl, Robert, 16
Daily Mirror, 600
Daily Telegraph, 586, 600
Daley, Richard, 466
Daley, William, 465
D'Amato, Alfonse, 467
Dark horses, 506, 510–11
Das Kapital (Marx), 19
Davies, J. Clarence, 736
Davis, David, 521
Davis, Jefferson, 153
Davis v. *Prince Edward County*, 171
Dawes Act (1887), 187–88
Day, Benjamin, 579
Daylight Saving Time, 4
DDT, 667
Dean, John, 264
Death penalty, 129
  Supreme Court decisions on, 136–41
Deaver, Michael K., 298, 639
Debates, televised presidential, 553–55
Debs, Eugene V., 118, 460, 624, 627
Debs v. *United States*, 118
Debt, national, 731–35
Decision making in democracy, 15–17
Decision-making process of Congress. *See under* Congress
Declaration of Independence, 151–52, 205
  adoption of, 34
  events preceding, 35
  social contract theory and, 34–36
  text of, 795–97
Declaration of Rights and Resolves, 33
Deep background, 603
De facto discrimination, 179
Defendants, rights of. *See* Criminal defendants, rights of
Deficits, budget, 726, 728, 731–35
De jure discrimination, 178, 179
De La Garza, E. (Kika), 647
Delegate representative, 218
Delegates
  presidential election convention, 503, 509, 510–12, 513–15
  uncommitted, 509

Democracy, 11
  American
    characteristics of, 12–14
    cycles in evolution of, 20
    evolution of party democracy, 445–52
    public expectations of, 20
    role of reform in, 21
    sources of power in, 13–14
    understanding, 20–21
  British system of parliamentary, 48, 49
  decision making in, 15–17
  direct, 12, 13
  Jacksonian, 278
  promotion of, 792
Democratic-Farmer-Labor (DFL) Party, 479n
Democratic Leadership Council, 101, 469
Democratic National Committee, 464
Democratic National Training Institute, 485
Democratic Party
  committees in Congress, 227
  congressional party unity score (1959–1993), 472
  governing body of, 464
  organizational gains of, 483–85
  origins of, 448–50
  party identification with, 486
  realignments of, 524
  states' rights and, 479
Democratic-Republicans, 76, 116, 227, 399, 445, 447, 448
Democratic Sentinel, 580
Democratic Study Group, 242
Department of Agriculture, 296, 309, 310, 323, 324, 706
  Extension Service of, 324
Department of Commerce, 296, 324, 341
Department of Commerce and Labor, 313
Department of Defense, 296, 320, 326, 773
Department of Education, 296, 319, 324, 634, 671
Department of Energy, 296, 324, 334, 337
Department of Health and Human Services, 296, 306, 323, 341, 692
Department of Housing and Urban Development, 296, 317, 337
Department of Interior, 296, 309, 323, 324, 333
Department of Justice, 296, 310, 321, 332, 350, 707
Department of Labor, 296, 313, 324
Department of State, 296, 308, 782
Department of Transportation, 296, 317
Department of Treasury, 296, 308, 341
Department of Veterans Affairs, 296, 319, 324, 339, 340, 690
Departments, bureaucratic, 321–24
  clientele agencies, 324
Depression. *See* Great Depression
Deregulation, 718–20
  and re-regulation, 720
Desegregation, school, 96–97, 170–73, 178–79, 676
Des Moines Register, 587
Dewey, John, 624
Dewey, Thomas E., 411
Diagnosis related group (DRG) system, 692–93
Dingell, John, 240
Dingley Tariff Act of 1897, 760
Dinkins, David, 477
Dionne, E. J., 596
Direct democracy, 12, 13
Direct incitement test, 119

Direct mailer, 549
Direct primary, 451
Direct spending, 735
Disabled Americans, civil rights and, 193–94
    Americans with Disabilities Act, 151, 194, 664
Discharge petition, bills, 230
Discount rate, 723
Discretion, administrative, 327
Discretionary fiscal policy, 727
Discretionary spending, 735
Discrimination
    affirmative action and, 195–96
    de facto discrimination, 179
    de jure discrimination, 178, 179
    employment, 180, 196–97
    in public accommodations, 177
    racial, 106
    sex, 184–86, 307
    statutory remedies for, 186
    Title IX and, 186, 343
    See also Civil rights
Dissenting opinions in Supreme Court cases, 390
District courts, 360–62
    judges
        characteristics of appointees, 370
        selection of, 368–71
    types of cases for, 361–62
Disturbance theory of interest groups, 618
Divine right of kings, 7, 11, 27
Dixiecrats, 459
Doe v. *Bolton*, 126
Dole, Robert, 224, 227, 240, 511
Domestic Council, 336
Domestic oversight of executive branch, 249–50
Domestic policy. *See* Policy-making process; Social welfare policies
Domestic Policy Council, 774
Dominican Republic, 783
Donaldson, Sam, 589
Douglas, William O., 130, 141, 374, 388–89
Douglass, Frederick, 155, 156, 195
Dred Scott v. *Sanford*, 78, 79, 123, 156
Drinking age, twenty-one-year-old, 92
Drug testing, 65
    search and seizure issue in, 133–34
Dual federalism, 74, 78
    Civil War and, 78, 80
    end of, 82
    republicanism and, 74
    transformation of, 80–81
Dualist theory of political parties, 462
DuBois, W. E. B., 164, 165
Due process clause
    incorporation doctrine and, 119–22
    wording of, 119
Due process rights, 129–31
Dukakis, Michael S., 425, 500, 504, 552, 568, 599
Duke, David, 435
Dye, Thomas, 675

Eagleburger, Lawrence S., 780
Earned Income Tax Credit Program (EITC), 688
Earth First!, 738
Earth in the Balance (Gore), 667
Earthquakes, 662
Eastern Europe, 3
East India Company, 31

Eastland, James, 232
Economic-interest groups, 615–16
    business groups and trade associations, 626–28, 632–33
    organized labor, 625, 633–34
    professional associations, 634–35
Economic Interpretation of the Constitution of the United States (Beard), 53
Economic policies, 720–45
    budgetary process, 727–31
    budget deficits and national debt, 726, 728, 731–35
    fiscal policy, 715, 725–27
    landmark events in, 705
    monetary policy, 712, 721–25
    toward reform of, 745–46
    See also Economy
Economic regulation, social regulation vs., 716–17
Economic Research Service, 323
Economic stability, 721
Economic systems, 16–20
    capitalism, 17–18
    communism, 19
    laissez-faire economy, 17–18, 705–6
    socialism, 18–19
    totalitarianism, 19–20
Economy, 703–45
    business cycles, 705, 712
    government intervention in, roots of, 704–20
        deregulation, 718–20
        Great Depression and New Deal and, 708–14
        in nineteenth century, 704–6
        in post-World War II era, 714–16
        in Progressive era (1901–1917), 707–8
        in social regulation era, 716–18
    gross domestic product, 732, 733
    macroeconomic regulation of, 720–35
        budgetary process, 727–31
        budget deficits and national debt, 726, 728, 731–35
        fiscal policy, 715, 725–27
        monetary policy, 712, 721–25
    national efforts to regulate, 312–16
    1992 presidential elections and, 569
    regulation to control pollution, 736–45
        acid rain, 744–45
        environmental policy making, 737–39
        EPA and, 739–45
        hazardous and toxic wastes, 741–44
Edelman, Marian Wright, 175, 652
Education
    Brown v. *Topeka Board of Education*, 96–97, 162, 170–72, 184, 385, 388, 392, 396, 397
    land-grant colleges, 86
    public, 660, 673, 674–78
    school desegregation, 96–97, 170–73, 178–79, 676
Education Amendments of 1972, Title IX, 186, 343, 655, 671
Edwards v. *Aguillard*, 112
Efron, Edith, 598–99
Egg Product Inspection Act, 717
Eighteenth Amendment, 60–61, 62, 63, 65
Eighth Amendment, 59, 108, 121, 129, 130, 139–41
    prohibition of cruel and unusual punishment, 139–41

Eisenhower, Dwight D., 172, 268, 274, 275, 293, 302, 475, 524, 526, 564–65, 598, 769, 777–78, 785
    judges appointed by, 369
Eisenstadt, Stuart, 250
Elastic clause, 51
Elder, Charles D., 664
Elders, Joycelyn, 268
Electioneering, 454
Elections, 497–541
    British, 502, 524, 527
    congressional, 528–31
        incumbency advantage and, 528
        off-year elections, 529, 530–31
        redistricting, scandals, and coattails, 528–30
    costs of, around globe, 563
    critical, 524
    interest group activities in, 645–50
        political action committees and, 558, 559, 560–63, 647–49
        protest activities, 644, 649–50
    landmark events in voting and, 519
    lobbying activities, 645–50
    presidential. *See* Presidential elections
    purposes of, 498–500
    toward reform of, 538–39
    retrospective judgment of voters and, 499–500
    types of, 500–502
        general elections, 501–2
        initiative, referendum, recall, 502
        primary elections, 500–501
    voting behavior, 532–37
        comparisons with other countries, 534, 535
        ticket-splitting, 536–37
        voter turnout, 531, 533, 534–36
    See also Campaign process
Electoral college, 515–21, 538–39, 570, 572
    beginning of, 44–45
    electors, 517
    Framers' conception of, 517–18
    limitations of, 519–22
    reform proposals for, 538–39
    states drawn in proportion to votes in, 522
    Twelfth Amendment revision of, 519–20
    in twentieth century, 521–22
Electoral system, 66
    Supreme Court on, 97
Electorate, meaning of, 497
Electronic media, 578
    lobbying using, 644–45
Electronic voting, 14
Elementary and Secondary Education Act (ESEA), 676
Eleventh Amendment, 63
Elite theory, 15, 661, 662
Ellsberg, Daniel, 607
Ellsworth, Oliver, 352–53, 356
El Salvador, 786
Emancipation Proclamation, 157
Embargo Act, 755
Emerson, Ralph Waldo, 33
EMILY'S List, 649, 650
Employee Retirement Income Security Act, 717
Employment Act of 1946, 714–15, 720
Employment discrimination
    business necessity concept, 180
    Civil Rights Act of 1964 and, 180
    Civil Rights Bill of 1991 and, 196–97

Energy tax, lobbying and changes in, 645, 646
Engagement, foreign policy based on, 790, 792
Engels, Friedrich, 626
Engel v. *Vitale*, 111
English Civil War, 10
English government
  common law, 26
  divine right of kings, 27
  governing bodies, 26
  Magna Carta, 27
  parliamentary democracy, 48, 49
  See also Parliament
Enlargement, foreign policy based on, 792
Enlightenment, 7
Entitlement programs, 689
  costs and projections for, 695
  Social Security, 681–84
  See also Social welfare policies
Enumerated powers of Congress, 51, 71
Environmental Action, 646
Environmental Defense Fund (EDF), 619, 738
Environmental movement, 667, 738
Environmental pollution. *See* Pollution
Environmental Protection Agency (EPA), 5, 326, 327, 330–31, 337, 669, 717, 739–45
  acid rain and, 744–45
  eras in the political life of, 741
  hazardous and toxic wastes and, 741–44
Environmental threats, 790
Equal Access Act, 112
Equal Employment Opportunity Commission (EEOC), 177, 180, 219, 306, 307, 317
Equality, political, 13
Equal protection clause, 138, 141, 152, 183–86, 392, 678
  narrow interpretation of, 152
  standards of review and, 183–86
Equal Rights Amendment (ERA), 62, 65, 182–83, 220, 230, 375, 420
  defeat of, 183
  provisions of, 182
Equal time rule, 605
Era of Good Feelings, 448
Erlichman, John, 345
Erskine, David, 755
Erskine Agreement, 755, 779
Ervin, Sam, 591, 593
Espionage Act, 117, 118, 119
Essay Concerning Human Understanding (Locke), 10–11
Establishment clause, 109–12
  cases related to, 111–12
Ethics in government, 639
Ethics in Government Act, 641
Ethnicity, party identification and, 489
European Community, 772
European Recovery Program, 766–67
Evaluation
  of bureaucratic system, 342
  policy, 662, 672–73
Evans, Rowland, 600
Everson v. *Board of Education of Ewing Township*, 111
Evolution, teaching of, 112
Exchange-rate system, floating, 772
Exclusionary rule, 135–36

Executive agreements, 271, 755, 779, 780
Executive branch. *See* Presidency
Executive control of bureaucracy, 334–36
Executive Office of the President (EOP), 297–98, 336
Executive orders, 335–36
Executive power of president, 51–52, 267–74
  checks on, 49, 50
Executive privilege, 264, 753
Exit polls, 433–35, 440
Exon, James, 591
Ex Parte McCardle, 116
Expectations, changes in public, 20
Ex post facto laws, 73
Externalities, 737–38. *See also* Pollution
Extradition clause, 74
Extradition of criminals, 74
Exxon Valdez, 602, 665, 666
Eyes on the Prize (Williams), 164

Factions, 562
  criticisms of, 443
Fair Housing Act of 1968, 673
Fair Labor Standards Act (FLSA), 83–84, 97, 314, 713
Fairness doctrine, 605–6
Falkland Islands war (1982), 608, 784–85
Falwell, Jerry, 631–32, 652
Families USA, 694
Family, political socialization and, 414
Family and Child Support Act, 687–88
Family and Medical Leave Act, 243
Famine in East Africa, 784
Farley, James, 465
Farm Credit Administration, 84
Farmer-Labor Party, 479
Faubus, Orval, 172, 399
Fazio, Vic, 647
Feder, Judith, 334
Federal, meanings of, 54*n*, 69
Federal aid to public education, 675–78
Federal budget, 727–31
  backdoor spending, 728
  balanced budget amendment and, 745–46
  British budgetary process, 730
  Budget and Impoundment Control Act, 249–50, 730
  budget deficit, 726, 728, 731–35
  Congress and, 727–31
  Office of Management and Budget, 250, 284, 298, 336, 341, 727
  policy making and budgeting, 662, 670
  presidential involvement in, 284
Federal Bureau of Investigation, 377
Federal Children's Bureau, 624
Federal Communications Act, 84
Federal Communications Commission (FCC), 84, 714
  functions of, 604–5
Federal Deposit Insurance Corporation, 314
  creation of, 711, 712
Federal Election Campaign Act, 557, 558, 647–48
Federal Emergency Relief Act, 84
Federal Employees Political Activities Act, 315–16
Federal Farm Mortgage Corporation, 84
Federal Flag Protection Act, 124
Federal Housing Administration, 82, 84

Federal Insecticide, Fungicide, and Rodenticide Act, 739
Federalism, 69–103
  changing nature of, 85–96
    controlling states through mandates and preemptions, 90–92
    federal grants and, 86–89
    intergovernmental lobby, 93–96
  Constitution and, 47, 69–75
    arguments for federalism, 71
    concurrent powers, 72–73, 78
    guarantees/restrictions on states, 73
    relations among states, 73–74
  cooperative, 74, 85–86
  creative, 74
  daily life of Americans and, 69–70
  dual, 74, 78, 80–81, 82
  evolution and development of, 75–81
  Great Depression and, 82–84, 708–9, 711
  nature of, 47
  New Deal period and, 82–84
  New Federalism, 74, 89–90, 93, 95–96, 97
  nullification doctrine and, 79–80
  power of government in, 71–75
  toward reform of, 101–2
  regulatory, 91–92
  rethinking, 93
  roots of federal system, 71–75
  shift in power
    grants-in-aid, 86–89
    intergovernmental lobby, 93–96
    Reagan's New Federalism, 89–90
    revenue sharing, 89
  slavery and, 78–80
  Supreme Court decisions and, 75–80, 96–101
Federalist No. 2, 404, 405
Federalist No. 4, 748
Federalist No. 8, 773
Federalist No. 10, 16, 55, 56, 407, 442, 443, 562, 612, 655, 703
Federalist No. 17, 90
Federalist No. 22, 496, 497
Federalist No. 23, 24, 25
Federalist No. 42, 150
Federalist No. 44, 658, 659
Federalist No. 47, 2
Federalist No. 51, 56, 68, 69, 71, 202, 203
Federalist No. 57, 542, 544
Federalist No. 70, 256, 257
Federalist No. 75, 774
Federalist No. 76, 304
Federalist No. 77, 269
Federalist No. 78, 348, 351–52, 357
Federalist No. 84, 576
Federalist Papers, The, 54–56, 64, 69, 405, 437, 613
  authors of, 54
  purpose of, 26–27, 56
Federalists, 445, 447, 448
  Anti-Federalists vs., 54–57
  position of, 54, 55, 56, 71
Federal Mandate Relief Act, 93
Federal Open Market Committee, 721, 723
Federal Radio Act, 604
Federal Radio Commission, 604
Federal Register, 328, 331
Federal Regulation of Lobbying Act, 655
Federal Reserve Act, 707, 712
Federal Reserve Banks, 721, 722, 723

Federal Reserve Board, 326, 341, 721
Federal Reserve System, 711, 721–25
    Board of Governors, 721, 723, 724–25
    creation of, 707–8
    discount rate, 723
    Federal Open Market Committee, 721, 723
    money supply and, 723–24
    open-market operations, 723–24
    power of, 712
    reserve requirements, 723
Federal Securities Act, 314
Federal system, 42, 69
Federal Trade Commission (FTC), 314, 326–27, 627–28, 708, 714
    creation of, 313
Federal Trade Commission (FTC) Act, 707
Federation of British Industry, 625
Feinstein, Diane, 220
Feminine Mystique, The (Friedan), 181
Fenno, Richard F., Jr., 247
Ferraro, Geraldine, 599
Ferry, Thomas, 521
Fifteenth Amendment, 21, 60, 63, 80, 162–63, 501, 530
    voting rights for blacks, 160, 162–63, 189
Fifth Amendment, 59, 108, 120, 121, 130, 134–35
    guarantee against self-incrimination, 134–35
Fighting words, 115
Filibusters, 236–37, 238, 252, 638
Fillmore, Millard, 460
Financial Institutions Reform, Recovery, and Enforcement Act (1989), 719
Fireside chats, 281
First Amendment, 58, 59, 63, 65, 108, 109–29, 558, 573, 577, 595, 606
    applied to states, 119–22
    freedom of religion, 109–14
        establishment clause, 109–12
        free exercise clause, 110, 112–14
        prayer in school, 112
    freedom of speech and press, 114–29
    privacy rights and, 141
First Continental Congress, 32–33, 37, 109, 205
First Ladies, contributions of, 294
Fiscal policy, 715, 725–27
    discretionary, 727
Fisher, Mary, 20
Flag burning issue, 124
Flag Protection Act, 669
Fletcher v. *Peck*, 356
Floating exchange-rate system, 772
Florio, James, 95, 96, 560
Flowers, Gennifer, 566, 596
Foley, Thomas, 223–25, 240, 252, 428
Food Administration, 762
Food and Drug Administration (FDA), 4, 346, 714
Food Stamps program, 344, 679, 688–89
"For cause" challenges, 138*n*
Ford, Gerald R., 194, 251, 262, 265, 266, 273, 293, 302, 346, 475, 499, 521, 554, 556, 572, 718, 729, 781
    judges appointed by, 369
Ford Foundation, 187, 628
Foreign and military policy, 749–93
    communication technology and, 776
    consensus and, 788

    finding U.S.'s place in world, 789–92
    globalism, 765
    history of, 752–64
        Cold War, 569, 765–73, 782, 788, 790
        constitutional provisions, 752
        containment, 768–71, 792
        Jay Treaty, 277, 295, 354, 753, 754
        manifest destiny concept, 759–60
        Marshall Plan, 766–67, 768
        Monroe Doctrine, 758–59
        NATO, 767–68
        pre-constitutional era, 750–52
        shift from unilateralism to multilateralism, 764–65
        trade and aid policy, 757–58, 760–61
        at turn of century, 760–61
        U.S. as emerging power, 759–60
        World War I and, 761–64
    isolationism, 763–64
    landmark events in, 751
    modern policy-making process, 773–77
    president's power in, 273, 752, 764, 773–87
        bureaucracy and, 782–83
        challenges to, 777–87
        Congress and, 250–51, 777–82, 788–89
        elections and, 785
        information gap and, 775–77
        news media and, 783–84
        the public and, 784–87
    toward reform of, 787–92
Foreign assistance programs, 771–72
Foreign investment in U.S., 758
Formula grants, 89
Fortas, Abe, 136, 374, 375
Foster, Vincent, 298
Fourteenth Amendment, 14, 21, 60, 63, 80, 119, 120, 130, 135, 138, 140, 152, 158, 160–61, 162, 163, 181
    equal protection clause, 138, 141, 152, 183–86, 392, 678
    provisions of, 158–60
    violations of, 185
Fourth Amendment, 59, 65, 108, 121, 130, 131, 135, 136
    privacy right and, 141–42
    unreasonable search and seizure, 131–34
Framers
    concept of judiciary, 349, 350, 351
    Constitutional Convention and, 40
    motives of, 53
    original intent of, 392, 393
    theories influencing, 7–11
France, revolution of 1789 in, 3, 753
Franco-American Treaty of 1778, 752, 753
Frank, Barney, 529
Frankfurter, Felix, 128, 379, 388–89
Franklin, Benjamin, 33, 34, 40, 42–43, 46, 56, 260–61, 271, 620
Fraser, Donald, 513
Freedmen, 161
Freedom of Choice Act, 21, 25, 145
Freedom rides, 175
Free exercise clause, 110, 112–14
    cases related to, 110, 113–14
Free market economy, 17
Free media, 545
Free rider problem, 652
Free Soil Party, 79, 647
Frémont, John C., 449
French and Indian War, 29

French Revolution of 1789, 3, 753
Fried, Charles, 384
Friedan, Betty, 181
Frontloading, presidential primaries, 504–6
Frothingham v. *Mellon*, 87
Fugitive Slave Law, 74
Fulbright, William, 783
Fulton, Robert, 77
Fund for the Feminist Majority, 650
Fund raising, 556–60, 563
    campaign-finance reform and, 573
Furman v. *Georgia*, 140

G.I. Bill, 317
Gaines, Lloyd, 168
Gallup, George, 405, 408, 411–12, 414, 432, 439, 564
Gallup Poll, 411–12, 537
Garcia v. *San Antonio Metropolitan Authority*, 97–98
Garfield, James A., 263, 271, 311
Garner, John Nance, 263, 265
Garrison, William Lloyd, 155–56, 164, 621, 652
Gates, Robert, 269
Gay and Lesbian Advocates and Defenders, 192
Gay rights, 1992 party platforms on, 518. *See also* Homosexuality
Gazette of the United States, 579
Gearan, Mark, 589
Gebhart v. *Belton*, 171
Gender
    party identification and, 489
    political socialization and, 422
    Supreme Court appointees and, 375–76
    See also Women
Gender gap, 489
General Accounting Office (GAO), 246, 337–38, 672
General Agreement on Tariffs and Trade (GATT), 765, 789
General assistance programs, 689
General elections, 501–2
    presidential campaign, 545, 546–47
General Motors, 631
General Services Administration, 325
General Social Survey, 431
General Theory of Employment, Interests, and Money (Keynes), 720
George II, king of England, 6, 11, 32, 33
George Washington University Center for Health Policy Research, 694
Gephardt, Richard, 225, 241, 251, 469
Gergen, David, 299
Gerry, Elbridge, 207, 517, 752
Gerrymandering, 206–9
Get-out-the-vote effort, 549
Ghent, Treaty of (1814), 756
Gibbons v. *Ogden*, 64, 77–78
Gideon, Clarence Earl, 136, 137
Gideon's Trumpet (Lewis), 136
Gideon v. *Wainwright*, 136, 137
Gillespie, Ed, 334
Gingrich, Newt, 212, 213, 225, 226, 472, 647
Ginsburg, Benjamin, 438, 439–40
Ginsburg, Douglas, 377, 592
Ginsburg, Martin, 376

Ginsburg, Ruth Bader, 112, 126, 145, 184, 197, 372, 373, 376, 377, 379, 388, 396, 399, 653
Ginzburg, Ralph, 128
Gitlow, Benjamin, 119
Gitlow v. *New York*, 119–20
Gladstone, William, 450
Glass-Steagall Act, 711
Globe, The, 579
Glossary, 815–30
Goals 2000: Education America Act, 676
Gold Rush, 156
Goldwater, Barry, 470n, 487, 546, 547, 548, 598
Gompers, Samuel, 625
Goodman, Ellen, 600
Gorbachev, Mikhail, 608
Gore, Albert, Jr., 93, 225, 266, 267, 284, 335, 341, 344, 345, 406, 407, 461, 568, 570, 602, 666, 728, 790, 791
Government
  Articles of Confederation's limitations concerning, 38
  forms of
    aristocracy, 11, 12
    democracy, 11
    monarchy, 11, 12, 27
    oligarchy, 11, 12
    republic, 12
  function of, 9
  separation of powers in, 47–49, 50
  unitary, 47
  See also American government
Governmental party, 445, 447
Governmental Process, The (Truman), 16
Government corporations, 324, 325
Government intervention. *See* Regulation(s)
Governors
  partisanship of, 479
  public's blaming of, 95–96
  royal, 258–59
Graber, Doris, 428
Grady, Robert, 239
Gramm, Phil, 470n, 734
Gramm-Rudman-Hollings Act, 59, 284, 431, 733–35
Grandfather clauses, function of, 163
Grand jury, 359
Grand Old Party (GOP), 450. *See also* Republican Party
Grange, 618, 621–22, 651
Grant, Ulysses S., 260, 269, 302, 425, 520, 630
Grants-in-aid, 86–89, 93
  beginning of, 86
  block grants, 89, 102
  categorical grants, 87, 88, 89, 91
  formula grants, 89
  history of, 86–89
  project grants, 89
  shift in power and, 88
Grassroots lobbying, 644–45
Gray, C. Boyden, 239
Gray, Horace, 366
Great Awakening, 618
Great Britain, War of 1812 with, 756. *See also* English government
Great Compromise, 42–43, 205
Great Depression, 21, 64, 82–84, 524, 673, 708–14, 720, 763

  economic decline in, 82, 708–9
  income security programs rising from, 680, 681
  New Deal and. *See* New Deal
  reshaping of federalism and, 82–84, 708–9, 711
Great Society, 342–43, 628, 666–68, 694, 726
Greenpeace USA, 619, 738
Greenspan, Alan, 723
Gregg v. *Georgia*, 140–41
Greidinger, Marc, 682
Griffiths, Martha, 220
Griggs v. *Duke Power Company*, 180
Griswold v. *Connecticut*, 142
Gross Domestic Product (GDP), 732, 769
  national debt as percentage of, 733
Gross National Product (GNP), 769
Group of Seven, 773
Grove City College v. *Bell*, 194–95
Guinier, Lani, 14, 197
Gulf of Tonkin Resolution, 273, 770
Guliani, Rudolph, 477
Gun control, 70, 123, 147, 406, 437
Gunderson, Steve, 644
Gun Violence Prevention Act (Brady II), 648

Habeas corpus, 140, 279
Haiti, 776, 784, 785
Haldeman, H. R., 298
Hall, Arsenio, 569
Halperin, Morton, 782
Hamilton, Alexander, 26, 27, 38, 54, 55, 56, 71, 90, 105, 107, 202, 203, 227, 256, 257, 260, 269, 277, 295, 298, 304, 308, 348, 349, 351–52, 357, 445, 447, 496, 497, 539, 576, 577, 579, 753, 754, 774
Hancock, John, 277
Handgun Control, Inc., 618, 619, 648, 654
Hanna, Mark, 465
Hanson, John, 37
Harding, Warren G., 118, 210–11, 269, 289, 707, 720
Hardwick, Michael, 146
Harkin, Tom, 503, 565
Harlan, John Marshall, 122, 163, 181, 387
Harpers Ferry, 155
Harris, Teresa, 386
Harrison, Benjamin, 520
Harrison, William Henry, 261, 312, 546–47, 551
Harris v. *Forklift Systems*, 385, 386
Hart, Gary, 594, 596, 601
Harvey, Paul, 600
Hastings, Alcee, 210–12
Hatch Act, 315, 706
  liberalization of, 315–16
Hayes, Rutherford B., 159, 311, 520–21, 523
Hazardous and Solid Waste Amendments of 1984, 91
Hazardous and toxic wastes, 741–44
Hazardous Substance Response Fund, 742
Head Start, 323, 342–43, 344
Health care. *See* Medical care
Health Care Financing Administration, 692
Health Insurance Association of America, 699
Health Security Act, 334

Hearst, William Randolph, 580
Heart of Atlanta Motel v. *United States*, 178
Heclo, Hugh, 338
Heller, Walter, 726
Helms, Jesse, 219, 233, 469, 647, 779–80
Hendricks, Thomas, 523
Henry, Patrick, 30, 40
Hepburn Act, 707
Heritage Foundation, 468
Hershey, Marjorie Randon, 214
Hertsgaard, Mark, 600
Hill, Anita, 186, 219, 374, 379, 570, 593, 650
Hinkley, John, 123
Hirsch, E. D., Jr., 428
Hispanic Americans, 421–22
  civil rights and, 190–92
  in Congress, 217, 218
  party identification of, 489
  redistricting and, 530
History, American democracy and, 20–21
Hitler, Adolf, 19, 763, 766
HIV, testing for, 133, 134, 635
Hobbes, Thomas, 8–11
Hold system in Congress, 236
Hollings, Ernest, 734
Holmes, Oliver Wendell, 117–18, 371
Homestead Act, 706
Homosexuality
  AIDS and, 20
  civil rights and, 192–93
  homosexuals in military, 192–93, 783
  1992 party platforms on gay rights, 518
  privacy issue, 145–46, 192–93
Hooker Chemical Company, 742
Hoover, Herbert, 281, 524, 707, 720, 762
Hortatory techniques for policy implementation, 671
Horton, Willie, campaign ad, 552
House Appropriations Committee, 337
House bank scandal, 214, 215
House of Commons, 26, 218, 225, 227, 242
House of Lords, 26
House of Representatives, 43, 49, 57, 222–25
  committees
    compared to Senate, 233
    standing committees, 230, 231
  differences from Senate, 205–6, 211
  impeachment process and, 45, 261
  lawmaking process, 236, 238
  majority and minority leaders, 225
  organization of, 222–25
  Speaker of the House, 222–25, 471
House Senate Affairs Committee, 340
House Subcommittee on Aging, 338
Howe, William, 36
Hoyt, Gwendolyn, 181
Hoyt v. *Florida*, 181
Hughes, Charles Evans, 387
Hull House, 165, 624, 627
Hull House Maps and Papers (Kelley), 627
Human immunodeficiency virus (HIV), testing for, 133, 134, 635
Humphrey, Hubert, 266, 499
Huntley, Chet, 587
Hussein, Saddam, 4, 20, 427, 570, 789
Hyde, Henry, 144, 243
Hyde Amendment, 149, 243
Hylton v. *United States*, 355

Ideas, changes in, 20
Ideological-interest groups, 631–32
Ideology
  party identification and, 491
  political, 423–26
  of Supreme Court justices, voting behavior and, 394–95
Immigrants, 418
Immigrants' Protective League, 624
Immigration and Naturalization Service v. *Chadha*, 250, 396
Impeachment, 248, 261–62
  articles of, 261
  Congress and, 210–12
  Framers and, 45
  Watergate and, 264–65
Implementation, 327
  judicial, 397–98
  policy, 327, 662, 670–72
Implementing population, 398, 399
Implied powers of Congress, 72
Impressment by British Navy, 754–55
Incentive techniques for policy implementation, 671
Income security programs, 660, 673–74, 679–89
  effectiveness of, 689
  means-tested programs, 679, 686–89
  roots of, 680–81
  social insurance, 679, 681–85
Income taxes, 707
Incorporation doctrine, 119–22
  selective incorporation, 120–22
Incumbency, 213–15
  advantages of, 528
  off-year elections and, 530–31
Independence of colonies. *See under* Colonies
Independent, The, 600
Independent agencies, 324–26
Independents, growth of, 488
Indian Health Service, 690
Indian Service Unit, 190
Indictment, 359
Indirect (representative) democracy, 12
Individuals with Disabilities Education Act, 677–78
Industrialization, 705
Inflation, 721, 724, 725
In forma pauperis, 381–82
Information, bureaucratic screening of, 782
Information gap in foreign affairs, 775–77
Inherent powers, of president, 277, 279
Initiatives, 502
  election reform, 409
In-person polls, 433
In re Sindram, 382
Institutional agenda, 664–65
Insular cases, 760
Insurance
  national health, 690–95
  social, 679, 681–85
Interactive Network, Inc., 13
Intercollegiate Socialist Society, 627
Interest group liberalism, 16
Interest groups, 613–56
  British, 641
  Common Cause, 616, 619, 629–31
  congressional decision making and, 246–47
  defining, 614–15
  disturbance theory of, 618
  economic-interest groups, 615–16
    business groups and trade associations, 626–28, 632–33
    organized labor, 625, 633–34
    professional associations, 634–35
  election activities, 645–50
    political action committees and, 558, 559, 560–63, 647–49
    protest activities, 644, 649–50
  free rider effect, 652
  funding of, 653
  history of American, 618–35
    from colonial period to 1830, 620
    modern era (1960 to present), 628–35
    national groups from 1830–1920, 621–28
  ideological-interest groups, 631–32
  leaders, role of, 652
  legislators and, 246–47
  lobbying by, 614, 629, 635–45
    of Congress, 628, 630, 637–39
    of courts, 385–87, 641–43
    defined, 636
    of executive branch and executive agencies, 640–41
    grassroots, 644–45
    origins of, 630
    race and, 644, 649
    style of 1990s, 645, 646
    for Supreme Court nominees, 377–79
    techniques for, 636–37
  membership of, 653–55
  multi-issue vs. single-issue groups, 617–18, 619, 621
  policy making and, 665
  potential vs. actual, 651
  Public Citizen Inc., 619, 629–31, 652
  public-interest groups, 616–17, 619, 717
    conservative backlash to, 631–32
    in modern era, 628–31
    Progressive movement and, 616, 623–25
  toward reform of, 655
  religious-interest groups, 631–32
  structure of, 652–53
  successful, factors for, 650–55
  types of, 615–18, 619
Interest group theory, nature of, 16
Intergovernmental lobby, 93–96
Internal Revenue Service (IRS), 682
International Anti-Slavery Society, 156
International Bank for Reconstruction and Development (World Bank), 764–65, 772
International Monetary Fund (IMF), 764, 772
Interstate commerce, regulation of, 77–78
Interstate Commerce Act, 81, 706
Interstate Commerce Commission, 326, 707, 714
  creation of, 312, 313, 640, 706
Interventionist state, 711
Intolerable Acts, 32
Investigative journalism, 592–94
Iowa caucuses, 506, 508
Iran, hostages in, 782
Iran-*Contra* scandal, 269, 273, 291, 570, 591–95, 781

Iran hostage crisis, 511
Iraq, invasion of Kuwait. *See* Persian Gulf War
Iraq-gate scandal, 570
Irons, Peter, 388
Iron triangles, policy making and, 338–39, 640–41
Isolationism, 763–64
Issue networks, policy making and, 339–40
Issue-oriented politics, 451, 488
Ivey, Sylvia Drew, 694

J.E.B. v. *Alabama* ex rel *T.B.*, 138
Jackson, Andrew, 79, 295–96, 298, 308, 310, 311, 397, 448, 449, 509, 520, 579, 581
  presidential power of, 278–79
Jackson, Henry "Scoop," 779
Jackson, Jesse, 469, 504, 560, 599
Jackson, William, 52–53
Jacksonian democracy, 278
Jacobowitz, Eden, 125
James I, King, 28
James II, King, 11
Jay, John, 26, 27, 54, 55, 354, 372, 404, 405, 748, 749, 753, 754, 773
Jay Court, 353–55
Jay Treaty, 277, 295, 354, 753, 754
Jefferson, Thomas, 11, 12, 34, 36, 40, 41, 107, 110, 116, 227, 277, 298, 308, 344, 353, 357, 374, 445, 447, 518, 519, 578, 754, 755
Jenkins v. *Georgia*, 129
Jim Crow laws, 158, 161–64, 174
  NAACP challenges to, 167–74
Job Opportunities and Basic Skills (JOBS) program, 687
John, King of England, 27
Johnson, Andrew, 45, 158, 159, 210, 248, 261, 273, 274, 364, 376, 464
Johnson, Lyndon B., 62, 176, 194, 248, 249, 251, 266, 273, 282, 283, 287, 288, 293, 306, 335–36, 374, 375, 475, 487, 499, 513, 526, 546–47, 548, 572, 676, 718, 777, 783, 785
  Great Society, 342–43, 628, 666–68, 694, 726
  judges appointed by, 369
  reform of bureaucracy by, 344, 345
  War on Poverty, 87–88, 275, 317, 666, 694
Johnson v. *Santa Clara Transportation Agency*, 196
Johnston, Bennett, 236
Joint Committee on the Organization of Congress, 252
Joint committees, 230, 231, 261
Joint Economic Committee, 715
Jones, Charles O., 668
Jones, George Fleming, 779
Journalism. *See* News media
Judges
  of Court of Appeals, 362
  selection of federal court, 368–80
    Courts of Appeals judges, 371
    district court judges, 368–71
  See also Supreme Court justices
Judge's Bill, 391
Judicial implementation, 397–98
Judicial interpretation of Constitution, 64
Judicial nominating commission, 371

Judicial philosophy, 391–93
Judicial policy making, 396–97
Judicial review
  nature of, 52
  origins of, 351, 355–57
Judicial system
  appellate courts, 357, 358, 359
  under Articles of Confederation, 37
  constitutional courts, 360
  Courts of Appeals, 361, 362–63
  criminal and civil law and, 359–60
  district courts, 360–62
  federal court system, 360–67
  jurisdiction, types of, 358–59, 362
  legislative courts, 360
  See also Supreme Court
Judiciary, 349–402
  checks on power of, 49, 50, 352
  control of bureaucracy, 338
  creation of, 350–57
    Article III of Constitution and, 52, 351–52
    Jay Court, 353–55
    judicial review and, 351, 355–57
    Judiciary Act of 1789 and, 352–55, 357, 360
    Marshall Court (1801–1835), 355, 356, 357, 393, 397
  federal court judges, selection of, 368–80
  Framers' concept of, 349, 350
  legal system and, 357–60
    criminal and civil law, 359–60
    jurisdiction, 358–59
  lobbying of courts, 385–87, 641–43
  oversight of bureaucracy by, 333, 338
  political parties and, 478
  powers of, 50
  president's effect on federal, 368–71
  See also Supreme Court
Judiciary Act
  of 1789, 352–55, 357, 360
  of 1925, 391
Jungle, The (Sinclair), 707
Jurisdiction, 358–59
  appellate, 359, 362
  of Courts of Appeals, 362
  original, 358
  Supreme Court, 367, 381–82
Jury trial, right to, 138

Kahn, Alfred, 719
Kaiser Commission on the Future of Medicaid, 694
Kassebaum, Nancy, 232, 268, 411, 647
Kelleher, Catherine, 790
Kelley, Florence, 626–27
Kennan, George, 768–71
Kennedy, Anthony, 98, 140, 144, 367, 372, 373, 375, 392–93
Kennedy, Edward M., 196, 219, 511, 593, 594, 647, 719
Kennedy, Jacqueline, 286
Kennedy, John F., 62, 175, 176, 181, 274, 275, 283, 286, 287, 288, 290, 293, 294, 296–97, 334, 368, 417, 492*n*, 526, 538, 587, 603, 666, 667, 725, 726, 771, 774–75, 776
  debate with Nixon, 554
  judges appointed by, 369
Kennedy, Paul, 750
Kennedy, Robert, 296
Kentucky v. *Dennison*, 74
Kernell, Sam, 290–91
Kerrey, Robert, 232, 244, 565, 647
Keyes v. *School District No. 1, Denver, Colorado*, 179
Keynes, John Maynard, 720–21, 725
Keynesianism, 725
  commercial type of, 725
Khomeini, Ayatollah Ruhollah, 19, 781
Khrushchev, Nikita, 775
Kilpatrick, James J., 600
Kim, Jay, 217
King, Larry, 281, 282
King, Martin Luther, Jr., 174, 175, 176, 177, 275, 644
King, Rodney, 359
Kingdon, John W., 248
Kirk, Paul, 486
Kirkpatrick, Jeane, 764
Kissinger, Henry, 782
Kleindienst, Richard, 264
Koch, Edward I., 88
Kohl, Herbert H., 558
Koop, C. Everett, 20
Koppel, Ted, 281–82
Koramatsu v. *United States*, 394
Korean War, 768, 785
Koresh, David, 342
Kraft, Michael E., 738
Ku Klux Klan, 106–7, 119, 649
Kuwait, invasion of. *See* Persian Gulf War

Labor-management relations
  National Labor Relations Act and, 82, 84, 314, 713
  Taft-Hartley Act and, 715–16
  See also Organized labor
Labour Party, Great Britain, 491
LaFollette, Robert M., 460
Lago, Willis, 74
LaGuardia, Fiorella, 85
Laissez-faire, 78, 96
  governmental policy, 313–14
  libertarians and, 18*n*
  nature of, 17–18, 705–6
Lake, Anthony, 299
Lambda Legal Defense and Education Fund, 192
Land-grant colleges, 86
Landon, Alfred M., 411, 412
Land rights of Native Americans, 190
Lasswell, Harold D., 305
Lathrop, Julia, 624
Law
  civil, 359–60
  criminal, 359–60
  See also Congress; Judiciary
Law clerks, job of, 366–67
Lawmaking process, 235–41, 337
  bill, stages of, 236–41
  example of, 238–41
  filibusters, 236–37, 238, 252, 638
  in Parliament, 235
  presidential involvement in, 282–85
  veto, 238
Laxalt, Paul, 483
Lead-Based Paint Poison Prevention Act, 717

Leaders
  influence on public opinion, 429
  interest-group, role of, 652
  political party, 464–65
League of Nations, 211–12, 270, 289, 290, 762–63, 778
League of United Latin American Citizens (LULAC), 191, 530, 619
League of Women Voters, 253
Learning disabilities, education of children with, 677–78
Lebanon, Marines in, 782
Lee, Rex E., 384
Lee, Richard Henry, 34
Lee v. *Weisman*, 112
Legal Office (Supreme Court), 366
Legal Services Corp., 694
Legal system. *See* Judiciary
Legislation, lawmaking process, 235–41, 337
Legislative branch. *See* Congress
Legislative courts, 360
Legislative veto, 250
Lemon test, 111
Lemon v. *Kurtzman*, 111
Lesbian Rights Project, 192
Letterman, David, 266, 603
Leviathan (Hobbes), 8–9, 10
Lewis, Anthony, 136
Lewis, John, 175, 213
Lexington and Concord, battle of, 33
Libel, 127
  major case on, 127
  meaning of, 127
  news media and, 595–97
Libelous speech, 115
Liberalism, interest group, 16
Liberals, viewpoints of, 423–26, 427
Liberia, 155
Libertarians, 18*n*
Liberty, personal, 14
Library of Congress, 250
Limbaugh, Rush, 600
Lincoln, Abraham, 80, 116, 155, 156, 159, 248, 262, 274, 287, 288, 289, 300, 309, 375, 420, 449, 464, 510, 525, 579
  presidential power of, 279, 280, 281
Line-item veto, 302, 745
Lippman, Walter, 409–10
Literacy tests, 162, 163
Literary Digest, presidential election polls, 410–11, 412, 431
Livingston, Robert, 34
Lobbying, 614, 629, 635–45
  of Congress, 628, 630, 637–39
  of courts, 385–87, 641–43
    Supreme Court decisions and, 393–95, 641–43
  defined, 636
  of executive branch and executive agencies, 640–41
  forms of, 614
  grassroots, 644–45
  origins of, 630
  regulation of, 630, 655
  style of 1990s, 645, 646
  for Supreme Court nominees, 377–79
  techniques for, 636–37
Lobbyist, 246–47, 636–37
Locke, John, 8–11, 34–36, 46

Lodge, Henry Cabot, 510
Logrolling, 244
Lombardi, Vince, 462
Long, Huey, 456
Long, Russell, 688
Los Angeles Times, 586
Losing Ground (Murray), 680
Lott, Trent, 226
Louis XVI, King, 3
Love Canal, 742
Lowi, Theodore J., 16
Low-Level Radioactive Waste Policy Amendments Act of 1985, 98
Lynch v. *Donnelly*, 110, 126

M1, M2, and M3, 721
MacArthur, Douglas, 768
McCardle, William, 116
McCarthy, Eugene, 785
McCarthy, Joseph R., 587, 591
McCarthyism, 591
McCleskey v. *Kemp*, 141
McCleskey v. *Zant*, 141
McCord, James W., Jr., 264
McCovey, Norma, 143
McCulloch, James, 76
McCulloch v. *Maryland*, 75, 76–77, 356, 388
McCurdy, Dave, 224–25
McGinniss, Joe, 594–95
McGovern, George, 489, 499, 513, 546
McGovern-Fraser Commission, 513
McKinley, William, 525
McKinney, Cynthia, 243
McLarty, Thomas "Mack," 298, 299
McLaughlin, John, 600
McLaurin, George W., 169
McLaurin v. *Oklahoma State Regents for Higher Education*, 169
McNamara, Robert, 248
MacNeil/Lehrer News Hour, 585, 600
MacVane, John, 587
Madison, James, 27, 47, 64, 105, 227, 286, 445, 452, 497, 517, 539, 543, 613, 655, 755, 756
　Bill of Rights and, 107–8
　The *Federalist Papers* and, 16, 24, 25, 26, 46, 54, 55, 56, 69, 71, 150, 151, 407, 442, 443, 542, 544, 562, 612, 658, 659, 703
　Marbury v. *Madison*, 52, 79, 351, 356, 357, 360, 396–97
　on presidential powers, 271, 273, 274, 295
　Twenty-Seventh Amendment and, 61
　Virginia Plan and, 40–41, 42
Magna Carta, provisions of, 27
Magnuson, Warren, 718
Mahan, Alfred T., 761
Main, Jackson Turner, 53
Maine, S.S., 760
Majority leader, 469
　House of Representatives, 225
　Senate, 227
Majority party Congress, 227
Majority rule, definition of, 14
Making of the President (White), 594
Malcolm X, 177, 178
Malice, actual, 127
Manchester Guardian, 600

Manchester Union-Leader, 587
Mandamus, writ of, 357
Mandates, 91–92, 499
Mandatory spending, 735
Manifest destiny concept, 759–60
Mapp v. *Ohio*, 126, 132
Marbury, William, 357, 360
Marbury v. *Madison*, 52, 79, 351, 356, 357, 360, 396–97
Marcy, William Learned, 310
Margin of error, sampling, 436–37
Margolies-Mezvinsky, Marjorie, 204, 285
Marital status, party identification and, 491
Married Women's Property Acts, 644
Marshall, George C., 766
Marshall, John, 52, 64, 75, 76–78, 372, 374
　Marshall Court, 355, 356, 357, 393, 397
Marshall, Thomas R., 263
Marshall, Thurgood, 169, 170, 197, 375, 388, 390, 396, 593
Marshall Plan, 766–67, 768
Marshal of the Court, 365
Martin, Luther, 76
Martin v. *Hunter's Lessee*, 356
Marx, Karl, 19, 626
Mason, George, 107
Massachusetts
　Shays's Rebellion in, 39, 44, 649
　state constitution of, 38
Massachusetts Bay Colony, 28
Mass circulation press, 579–80
Matalin, Mary, 569
Matching funds, in presidential campaign, 558
Matthews, Donald, 244
Mayaguez, 781
Mayflower Compact, 8, 27–28
Means-tested income security, 679, 686–89
Meat Inspection Act, 707
Mecham, Evan, 502
Media. *See* News media
Media campaign, 545, 550–52
Media conglomerates, 583
Media consultant, 549
Media effects, 602
Medicaid, 89, 92, 674, 679, 693–95
Medical care, 16, 674, 689–96
　Canadian system of, 698
　cost of, 691, 695–97
　by country, 691
　health care reform, 334, 696–99
　national health insurance, roots of, 690–95
Medical research, 690
Medicare, 679, 692–93
Meese, Edwin III, 298, 392
Melder, Keith, 551
Menendez brothers, 358
Mercantilism, British-colonial relations and, 29–30
Merit system, civil service, 312, 318
Merit Systems Protection Board, 319, 321
Mexican-American Legal Defense and Education Fund (MALDEF), 187, 191, 192, 530, 628
Miami Herald, 596
Michel, Robert, 226
Midterm convention, 465
Migratory Bird Treaty Act of 1918, 75
Military, commander-in-chief of, 273, 752

Military, homosexuals in, 192–93, 783
Military-industrial complex, 769
Military policy. *See* Foreign and military policy
Military Selective Service Act, 185
Militia Act of 1792, 753
Miller, James III, 326
Miller v. *California*, 128
Mills, C. Wright, 15
Mills, Wilbur, 692
Minimum wage, 713
Mining Enforcement and Safety Administration, 717
Minor, Virginia, 161
Minority party, 233
Minority rights, American democracy and, 14
Minor v. *Happersett*, 160–61
Miracle at Philadelphia, The (Bowen), 46
Miranda, Ernesto, 134–35
Miranda rights, 135
Miranda v. *Arizona*, 126, 134–35
Miscegenation laws, 164
Missouri Compromise, 79
　and slavery, 153–57
Missouri ex rel. Gaines v. *Canada*, 168
Missouri v. *Holland*, 75
Mitchell, George, 227, 240, 244
Mitchell, John, 264
Monarchy
　divine right of kings and, 27
　example of, 12
　nature of, 11
Mondale, Walter, 266, 499, 555–56, 599, 645
Monetary policy, 712, 721–25
　defined, 721
　Federal Reserve System and, 721–25
Money
　Articles of Confederation's lack of provision for, 37, 38
　definitions of, 721
　as informal requirement for membership in Congress, 213
Money supply, 723–24
Monopolies, 81, 707
Monroe, James, 107, 227, 448, 758
Monroe Doctrine, 758–59
Montesquieu, Baron de la Brède et de, 46–47
Montgomery Bus Boycott, 174
Moral Majority, 631, 646–47, 652
Morrill Land Grant Act, 86, 96, 706
Morris, Gouverneur, 45, 46, 517
Moseley-Braun, Carol, 217, 219, 220
Motor Carrier Act of 1935, 714
Mott, Lucretia, 156, 621
Mountain States Legal Foundation, 333
Moyers, Bill, 589
Moynihan, Daniel Patrick, 244, 477
Muckraking, 580–81
Mueller, John E., 429
Muller v. *Oregon*, 166, 167, 182
Multi-issue interest groups, 617–18, 619, 621
Multi-lateralism, 765
Multistage area sampling, 431
Munich Pact, 766
Murray, Charles, 680
Murray, James, 715
Murrow, Edward R., 586–87
Mushroom Caucus, 243

Muskie, Edmund, 666, 718
Mutiny (Quartering) Act (1765), 30, 32
Mutually Assured Destruction (MAD), 769
Myers, Dee Dee, 590

NAACP. *See* National Association for the Advancement of Colored People (NAACP)
Nader, Ralph, 629–31, 632, 652, 666
NAFTA, 204, 228, 285, 406, 407, 461, 617, 790, 791
Napoleon Bonaparte, 753, 755, 756
Narrative of the Life of Frederick Douglass (Douglass), 155
Nast, Thomas, 81, 523
Nation, Carry, 622
Nation, The, 587
National Abortion Rights Action League (NARAL), 21, 618, 619
National Aeronautics and Space Administration (NASA), 319, 326, 778
National American Woman Suffrage Association, 165
National Association for the Advancement of Colored People (NAACP), 617, 619, 624, 627, 628, 635, 651, 652
  challenges to constitution for equality, 167–74
  death penalty position, 139–40
  founding of, 164–65
  Legal Defense and Educational Fund (LDF), 169–72, 191
  lobbying of Supreme Court nominations, 377–78
  number of members of, 156
National Association of Manufacturers (NAM), 619, 625, 626, 627, 630, 632, 645
National Bank, 295–96
National Cancer Institute, 690
National Child Abuse Protection Act, 663
National Child Labor Committee, 624, 627
National Coal Association, 640
National Commission on Social Security Reform, 684
National Consumers' League, 165, 182, 624, 626, 627
National convention, 465
  delegates, methods to elect, 503
National Council of Public Polls, 440
National debt, 731–35
National Defense Education Act, 778
National Economic Council (NEC), 774
National Education Association, 634–35
National Election Study, 431, 433, 437
National Electric Light Association, 628
National Endowment for the Arts (NEA), 669
National Environmental Policy Act, 739
National Federation of Democratic Women, 468
National Federation of Republican Women, 468
National Gay and Lesbian Task Force, 619
National Gazette, 578–79
National Governors' Association, 651, 687
National Governors' Conference, 97
National Guards, 100
National health insurance, 690–95

National Health Law Program (NHeLP), 694
National Heart, Lung, and Blood Institute, 690
National Housing Act, 84
National Industrial Recovery Act, 84, 314
National Institute of Allergy and Infectious Diseases, 690
National Institutes of Health (NIH), 690
Nationalization, 19
  of federal system, 74, 75
National Labor Relations Act (Wagner Act), 82, 84, 314, 713
National Labor Relations Board (NLRB), 84, 326, 362, 713
National League of Cities, 97
National League of Cities v. Usury, 97–98
National Literacy Act, 92
National Marine Service (NMS), 690
National Organization for Women, 181–82, 307, 650, 651, 652, 655
National party committees, 463–64
National party platforms, 457
National Performance Review, 345
National Prayer Day, 398
National Rainbow Coalition, 469
National Recovery Administration, 82, 84
National Republican Congressional Committee, 464
National Restaurant Association, 247
National Review, The, 587
National Rifle Association (NRA), 618, 619, 628, 651, 664
National Right to Life Committee, 432, 619
National Right-to-Life Party, 647
National Science Foundation, 325
National security, threats to U.S., 790
National Security Act of 1947 and 1949, 773
National Security Agency, 776
National Security Council, 296, 297, 768, 773–74
National Security Crisis Management, 267
National Senior Citizens' Law Center, 642
National Service Education Plan, 283
National Socialist Party, 126
National supremacy, concurrent powers and, 75
National Transportation Safety Administration, 717
National Wildlife Federation, 738
National Woman Suffrage Association, 160, 165, 621, 624, 627, 637
National Women's Political Caucus, 182, 650
Nation-state, emergence of, 749–50
Native American Rights Fund (NARF), 187, 189, 190, 628, 642
Native Americans, 421–22, 753
  civil rights and, 187–90
  in Congress, 220
  land rights of, 190
NATO, 767–68
Natural law, definition of, 7
Natural Resources Defense Council, 642, 738
Natural rights, 10
Nature Conservancy, 738
Near v. Minnesota, 120, 124
Nebraska Press Association v. Stuart, 124
Necessary and proper clause, 51, 71–72, 77, 209, 356
Neel, Roy, 639
Negative ads, presidential campaign, 550–51

Nelson, Barbara J., 662–63
Nelson, Karen, 694
Networks (TV), 586
Neustadt, Richard, 274, 288–90
Neutrality Acts, 763
New Deal, 21, 82–85, 86, 280–81, 314–15, 346, 393, 396, 452, 453, 666, 680, 709–14
  agricultural reforms, 713
  consumer protection reforms, 714
  financial reforms, 711–12
  industry regulations, 714
  labor reforms, 713
  legislation of, 84
  reshaping of federalism and, 82–84
  Supreme Court resistance and, 82–84
    court-packing plan and, 83, 314, 399
New England town meeting, 12, 13
New Federalism, 74, 97
  blaming governors for effects of, 95–96
  block grants, 89
  of Clinton, 93
  effects on the poor, 89
  of Reagan, 89–90
  state-national government relationship and, 96
New Frontier, 666
New Jersey Plan, 42
New judicial federalism, 98, 99
New Republic, The, 587
News media, 577–611
  British, 607, 608
  contemporary media scene, 581–87
    influential media, 586–87
  coverage by, 588–94
    of Congress, 589–92
    of courts, 592
    of presidency, 588–89
    Watergate and investigative journalism, 592–94
  foreign and military policy and, 783–84
  government regulation of electronic, 604–8
    censorship, 607–8
    confidentiality of sources, 606
    content regulation, 605–6
  history of, 578–81
    mass circulation press, 579–80
    muckraking, 580–81
    partisan papers, 578–79
    yellow journalism, 580
  influence on public, 602
  landmarks in American, 579
  libel and, 595–97
  media effects, 602
  newspapers, 578–83, 587
  politicians' use of, 602–4
  post-Watergate era, 594–602
    biased reporting, 597–602
    character issue and, 594–97
  presidential campaign and, 550–56
    contrast ads, 551
    focus of media, 558
    media campaign, 545, 550–52
    media consultant, 549
    positive and negative ads, 550–51
    spot ads, 552
    televised debates, 553–55

presidential elections and, 512–13
    1952 and 1992 compared, 564–65
  toward reform, 608–9
  Supreme Court, coverage of, 592
  television, 581, 583–85, 586
    cable, 583, 585, 608–9
  types of, 578
  use and trustworthiness of, 584
  White House press corps, 589
Newspapers, 578–83, 587
  Great Britain, 586, 600
  new journalism, 594–95
  wire services and, 587
News Twisters, The (Efron), 598–99
Newsweek, 584, 587
Newsworthiness, 603
Newton, Isaac, 7
New York Child Labor Committee, 627
New York Sun, 579
New York Times, 570, 584, 586, 596, 607
New York Times Co. v. Sullivan, 127, 595–97
New York Times Co. v. United States, 124, 607
Niagara Movement, 165
Nicaragua, 780–81
Nicholas II, Czar, 3
Nightline, 600
1984 (Orwell), 19
Nineteenth Amendment, 60, 63, 627
  voting rights for women, 167
Ninth Amendment, 58, 59, 108
Nixon, Richard M., 88, 89, 128, 194, 210, 243, 250, 251, 266, 269, 283, 284, 287, 290, 293, 298, 300, 320, 336, 376, 390, 476, 524, 526, 527, 538, 546–47, 601, 718, 729, 753, 772, 778, 785
  debate with Kennedy, 554
  EPA and, 739
  judges appointed by, 369
  pardoning of, 265, 273
  reform of bureaucracy by, 344, 345
  Supreme Court appointees, 374
  War Powers Act and, 781
  Watergate, 21, 262, 264–65, 417, 473, 487, 499, 591, 592–94, 648
Noise Control Act, 669
Nomination campaign, presidential, 545, 546
Nonprobability sampling, 431–32
North, Oliver, 591–92
North American Free Trade Agreement (NAFTA), 204, 228, 285, 406, 407, 461, 617, 790, 791
North Atlantic Treaty Organization (NATO), 767–68
North Star, The, 155
Northwest Ordinance
  of 1785, 675–76
  of 1787, 187
Novak, Robert, 600
Nuclear weapons, 769
Nullification, doctrine of, 79–80
Nunn, Sam, 192, 244, 469, 781, 790

Oakar, Mary Rose, 220
Obscenity, 127–29
Occupational Safety and Health Act, 327, 328–30, 717
Occupational Safety and Health Administration (OSHA), 326, 327, 329–30, 332, 660, 669, 717

O'Connor, Sandra Day, 98, 144, 209, 372–76, 390, 392–93, 394, 478
Office for Civil Rights, 343
Office of Economic Opportunity, 694
Office of Federal Contract Compliance, 335
Office of Management and Budget, 250, 284, 298, 336, 341, 727
Office of Noise Abatement and Control, 669
Office of Personnel Management, 319
Office of Surface Mining Reclamation and Enforcement, 717
Office of Technology Assessment, 246
Office of the Budget, 337
Official Secrets Acts (British), 607
Off-the-record/on-the-record sessions, 603
Off-year elections for Congress, 529, 530–31
Oil Pollution Act of 1990, 666
Old Age, Survivors, and Disability Insurance, 681–84
Old Order Amish religion, 113
O'Leary, Hazel, 397
Oligarchy, 11, 12
Olive Branch Petition, 33
Olson, Mancur, Jr., 651
Omnibus Budget Reconciliation Act, 244
Omnibus Trade and Competitiveness Act, 789
On background, 603
O'Neill, Catherine, 775
O'Neill, Thomas P. (Tip), 226, 285, 482
One-partyism, 458
Open fields doctrine, 132–33
Open Market Committee, 711
Open-market operations, Federal Reserve System, 723–24
Open primary, 500
  states with, 501
Open shop, 625, 716
Operation Desert Storm, 6
Operation Rescue, 143, 147, 618, 649–50, 651
Oregon v. Smith, 114
Organizational campaign, presidential, 545, 549–50
Organizational party, 445, 447
Organization of Petroleum Exporting Countries (OPEC), 772
Organized labor, 633–34
  AFL-CIO merger, 633–34
  beginning of, 625
  decline of, 634
  New Deal reforms and, 713
  Taft-Hartley Act and, 716
Original intent of Framers, 392, 393
Original jurisdiction, 358
  Supreme Court, 367, 381
Orwell, George, 19
Our Toiling Children (Kelley), 627
Oversight, congressional, 249–52, 778
Ozone layer, 790

Pacific Legal Foundation, 632
Packers and Stockyards Act, 707
Packing, congressional districts, 207
Packwood, Bob, 216
PACs. *See* Political action committees (PACs)
Page, Benjamin, 276, 336
Paid media, 545
Paine, Thomas, 33–34, 39, 405, 751
Palko v. Connecticut, 120

Panama Canal, 760
Panama Canal Treaties, 270–71
Panics, financial, 712
Pardoning power of president, 273–74
Paris, Treaty of, 29, 38, 749
Parker, John, J., 378
Parks, Rosa, 174
Parliament, 31
  British Cabinet ministers, 295
  budgetary process, 730
  doctrine of parliamentary sovereignty, 49
  elections, 502, 524, 527
  legislative process in, 235
  political parties, 449–50, 454, 475, 491
  prime minister
    new, 262
    power relative to legislature, 269
  staffers of, 245–46
  virtual representation, 217
Parochial schools, 111, 676
Party caucus, 223, 225
Party conventions, 1992 presidential election, 568–69
Party identification, 445, 454, 485–87
Party-in-the-electorate, 445, 447, 485–91
Party ombudsmen, 493, 494
Party platforms, 457
  1992, examples of, 515, 518
Party realignment, presidential elections and, 524–26
Party unity vote, 472
Passamaquoddie tribe, 190
Paster, Howard, 639
Pastor, Robert, 779
Paterson, William, 42
Patronage, 285–86, 310–11, 312, 368, 451, 455, 479
Peace societies, 756–57
Pearl Harbor, 764
PEER Perspective, 655
Peers, political socialization and, 416
Pendleton Act, 311
Pennsylvania Packet, 54
Penny press, 579
Penobscot tribe, 190
Pension Office, 309–10
Pentagon Papers, 273, 607
People for the American Way, 197
People for the Ethical Treatment of Animals (PETA), 654
Peremptory challenge, 138
Perle, Richard, 779
Perot, Ross, 285, 406, 407, 444, 459, 461, 462, 500, 521–22, 537, 556–60, 567–68, 570, 791
Perry, Matthew C., 759
Persian Gulf War, 6, 251, 291, 292, 420, 421, 570, 608, 782, 785
  congressional authorization of, 788–89
  media coverage of, 783–84
  public opinion about, 407
Personal campaign, presidential, 545, 547–48
Personal liberty, 14
Persuasion, president and, 288–90
Pertschuk, Michael, 326
Petracca, Mark, 276, 336
Philadelphia Society for Promoting Agriculture, 620
Philippines, revolution in (1899), 760
Phillips, David Graham, 580
Physician Payment Review Commission, 69

Pilgrims, 8
Planned Parenthood, 142, 432
Planned Parenthood of Southeastern Pennsylvania v. *Casey*, 98, 126, 144, 393
Plan of Treaties (1776), 751
Plessy, Homer Adolph, 163
Plessy v. *Ferguson*, 80, 162, 163–64, 396
   NAACP challenges to, 167–72
Plunkitt, George Washington, 455
Pluralist theory, 16, 661–62
Pocket veto, 238
Policy adoption, 662, 669–70
Policy entrepreneurs, 718
Policy evaluation, 662, 672–73
Policy formulation, 662, 668–69
Policy implementation, 327, 662, 670–72
Policy-making process, 661–73
   agenda setting, 662, 664–68
   budgeting, 662, 670
   federal bureaucracy and, 327–32
   iron triangles and, 338–39, 640–41
   issue networks and, 339–40
   modern foreign policy making, 773–77
   policy adoption, 662, 669–70
   policy evaluation, 662, 672–73
   policy formulation, 662, 668–69
   policy implementation, 662, 670–72
   political parties and, 456–57
   problem definition, 662–64
   Supreme Court, 396–97
   See also Social welfare policies
Political action committees (PACs), 468, 469
   contributions to presidential campaign, 558, 559, 560–63, 647–49
   distribution of contributions from, 649
   limiting influence of, 573
   rise of, 560, 561
Political consultants, 451
Political equality, American government, 13
Political ideology, 423–26
Political knowledge, 427–29
Politically correct speech movement, 124–27
Political machines, 466–67, 468
Political opinions, formation of, 426–29
   cues from leaders and, 429
   personal benefits and, 427
   political knowledge and, 427–29
Political parties, 227–28, 443–95
   activism of, 493–94
   attributes of healthy parties, 491–92
   basic structure of, 463–68
      informal groups, 468–69
      leadership, 464–65
      national committees, 463–64
      national conventions, 465
      states and localities, 466–68
   British, 449–50, 454, 475, 491
   Congress and, 227–28, 242, 469–73
   contributions to presidential campaign, 558
   definition of, 444–45
   evolution of American party democracy, 445–52
      decline of parties, 451
      early parties, 445–50
      endurance of parties, 451–52
      golden age, 450
      landmarks in, 450
      modern era, 450
   formation of, as interest-group strategy, 647
   within government, 469–80
      congressional party, 469–73
      judiciary, 478
      presidential party, 473–77
      state governments, 479–80
   groups of individuals making up, 445
   international party platforms, 457
   issue-oriented politics, 451, 488
   one-partyism, 458
   organizing activities, 482–83
   party-in-the-electorate, 445, 447, 485–91
      declining loyalty, 487–88
      group affiliations, 488–91
      party identification, 445, 454, 485–87
   party realignments, 524–26
   political consultants and, 451
   toward reform of, 491–94
   roles of, 453–57
      coalition formation, 453
      electioneering, 454
      as force for stability, 453
      policy formation and promotion, 456–57
      unity, linkage, and accountability, 453–54
      as voting and issue cue, 456
   support for president, 285
   third-partyism, 459–62
   ticket-splitting, 451, 527, 536–37
   transformation of party organization, 480–85
      Democratic gains, 483–85
      Republican strengths, 480–83
      results of, 483
   See also Elections
Political socialization, 413–23
   family and, 414
   impact of events, 417, 418
   peers and, 416
   political opinion, formation of, 426–29
   school influences, 415–16
   social groups and, 417–23
      age, 423
      gender, 422
      race, 420–22
      region, 418–20
      religion, 417, 419
Politicians, media coverage of. *See* News media
Politics
   of civil rights, 194–97
   definition of, 6
   Hispanic American participation in, 191
   See also Congress
Polk, James K., 309
Polls, 429–40
   description of poll, 434
   early attempts at, 410–13
   effect of, 437–40
   Gallup Poll, 411–12, 537
   public opinion, 406, 555–56
   questions in, 430
   sample selection, 430–32
   shortcomings of, 436–37
   types of, 432–36
      exit, 433–35, 440
      in-person, 433
      straw, 411–12, 431
      telephone, 432–33, 434
      tracking, 435–36, 440, 482, 555–56
   wording of, 430, 432
Pollster, 549
Poll tax, 97, 162
Pollution
   defined, 736
   economics of regulating environmental, 736–45
      acid rain, 744–45
      environmental policy making, 737–39
      EPA and, 739–45
      hazardous and toxic wastes, 741–44
Pollution Prevention Act, 665, 739
Pomper, Gerald, 457
Popular consent, 7–11, 14
Popularity, presidential
   and foreign policy crisis, 784
   and public opinion, 290–93
Popular sovereignty, meaning of, 14
Populist Party, 459
Pork barrel, 232–33, 470, 745
Pornography, obscenity issue, 127–29
Port Authority of New York and New Jersey, 73
Porter, Roger, 239
Positive ads, presidential campaign, 550
Posner, Richard A., 366
Powell, Colin, 65, 785
Powell, Jody, 589
Powell, Lewis F., Jr., 128, 145, 146, 390
Power Elite, The (Mills), 15
Power in American democracy
   bureaucratic theory, 15
   elite theory, 15, 661, 662
   interest group theory, 15–16
   pluralist theory, 16, 661–62
Prayer in school, 112
Preamble to the Constitution, 45–46
Precedents, 363, 392–93
Precinct, 467
Preemption, 90–91
Presidency, 259–303
   under Articles of Confederation, 37, 51–52
   best/worst presidents, survey results, 289
   bureaucracy and, 334–36
   checks on powers of, 49, 50
   Congress and. *See under* Congress
   constitutional powers of, 267–74
      appointment power, 267–69
      commander-in-chief, 273, 752
      to convene Congress, 269
      to make treaties, 269–71
      pardoning power, 273–74
      veto power, 48, 238, 271–72
   development of power of, 274–93
      budgetary involvement, 284
      Congress and (1804–1933), 278–79
      early presidencies, 277
      legislative process and, 238, 248, 282–85
      methods of winning support, 284–85
      modern presidency, growth of, 258, 279–82
      presidential style, 285–93
   Federal Reserve Board and, 724–25
   foreign and military policy and, 273, 752, 764, 773–87
      bureaucracy and, 782–83

challenges to, 777–87
Congress and, 250–51, 777–82, 788–89
elections and, 785
information gap and, 775–77
news media and, 783–84
the public and, 784–87
Framers and creation of, 44–45, 259–67
qualifications for office, 260
removal from office, 260–61
succession in office, 261–62
term of office, 260
vice president, 44, 262–67
as head of government and head of state, 787
impeachment of, 260–61
imperial presidency concept, 249
influence on public opinion, 429
lobbying activities and, 640–41
motivation for seeking, 544
news media coverage of, 588–89
presidential establishment, 293–300
Cabinet, 294–97
Executive Office of the President (EOP), 297–98, 336
White House staff, 298–300
presidential political party, 473–77
nonpartisan presidents, 475–76
pro-party presidents, 475
president's effect on federal judiciary, 368–71
toward reform of, 300–302
changing two-term limitation, 302
line-item veto, 302, 745
roots of office, 258–59
steps to achieving successful, 289–90
two presidencies concept, 292
Presidential campaign
candidate preparation in, 553
fund raising for, 556
candidates' contributions, 558
challenger's war chest, effects of, 563
independent expenditures, 559–60
individual contributions, 557–58
political action committee contributions, 558, 559, 560–63, 647–49
political party contributions, 558
public funds, 558–59
regulation of, 557
general election campaign, 545, 546–47
judgments of the public and, 552–53
media campaign, 545, 550–52
news media and, 550–56
nomination campaign, 545, 546
organizational campaign, 545, 549–50
outsider position of candidate, 554, 555, 556
personal campaign, 545, 547–48
reform proposals, 572–73
slogans of, 546–47
staff of, 549–50
Presidential character, 286–88
Presidential Character, The (Barber), 595
Presidential Election Campaign Fund, 558
Presidential elections, 502–27
campaign. *See* Presidential campaign
critical elections, 524
delegate selection, 503
election of 1800, 519–20
electoral college, 515–21, 538–39, 570, 572

foreign policy of candidates and, 785
party conventions for, 506–15
patterns of, 523–27
party realignments, 524–26
secular realignment, 526–27
primaries vs. caucuses, 503–6
reform proposals, 538–39
superdelegates, 512, 523
Presidential party, 473–77
Clinton and, 477
nonpartisan presidents, 475–76
pro-party presidents, 475
Reagan and Bush and, 476–77
Presidential Power (Neustadt), 288–90
Presidential style, 285–93
character, 286–88
power to persuade, 288–90
public opinion and, 290–92
Wildavsky's "two presidencies" concept, 292–93
Presidential Succession Act, 262
President's Science Advisory Committee, 667
Press, freedom of. *See* Speech and press, freedom of
Press secretary, 588–89
Price, Melvin, 234
Primary
blanket, 501
closed, 500–501
direct, 451
open, 500, 501
presidential elections, 503–6
frontloading, 504–6
New Hampshire, importance of, 504, 506, 507
of 1992, 568
regional primaries, 504
state-by-state events, 505–6
Super Tuesday, 504, 566
runoff, 501
white, 501
Primary elections, 500–501
Print press, 578
Prior restraint, 115–16, 124
Privacy, right to, 141–46
abortion issue, 142–45
birth control issue, 142
homosexuality issue, 145–46, 192–93
Privacy Act of 1974, 682
Privacy rights, 141–46, 192–93
Product-dating laws, 670–71
Product liability laws, 669
Professional associations, 634–35
Progressive Movement, 163, 167
economic regulation in, 707–8
interest groups, 616, 623–25
public opinion in, 409
Progressive Party, 459, 624
Progressive Policy Institute, 101–2, 468
Progressives, 479
"Prohibition Era," 60
Prohibition Party, 459, 647
Project grants, 89
Project on Educational Equity Review (PEER), 655
Pro-Life Action Network, 147
Property rights, 35
Property taxes, 678
Proportional representation, 460
delegate selection, 503

Protest activity, as lobbying, 644, 649–50
Protestant Reformation, 7
Public Citizen Inc., 619, 629–31, 652
Public education, 660, 673, 674–78
federal aid to, 675–78
inequality in spending among school districts, 678
primary mission of public schools, 675
See also School(s)
Public expectations, changes in, 20
Public funds, contributions to presidential campaign, 558–59
Public goods, 737
Public health policies, 674
Public Health Service, 323, 674, 690
Public Information Officer (Supreme Court), 366
Public-interest groups, 616–17, 619, 717
conservative backlash to, 631–32
in modern era, 628–31
Progressive movement and, 616, 623–25
Public opinion, 405–41
defined, 406
dimensions of, 784
effects on politics and policy, 437–40
foreign and military policy and, 784, 785–86
influencing, early attempts at, 408–10
nature of, 406–8
news media and, 602
political ideology, 423–26
political opinions, formation of, 426–29
cues from leaders and, 429
personal benefits and, 427
political knowledge and, 427–29
political socialization and, 413–23
age and, 423
family influence, 414
gender and, 422
impact of events, 417, 418
peer influence, 416
race and, 420–22
region and, 418–20
religion and, 417, 419
schooling influence, 415–16
social groups and, 417–23
polls for measuring, 429–40
early attempts at, 410–13
effect of, 437–40
Gallup Poll, 411–12, 537
questions in, 430
selecting sample for, 430–32
shortcomings of, 436–37
straw polls, 411–12, 431
types of, 432–36
presidential popularity and, 290–93
toward reform of, 440
Supreme Court justices and, influence on, 350–51, 393–94
Public Opinion (Lippmann), 409–10
Public opinion polls, 406, 555–56
Public policy
defined, 661
environmental, 737–39
theories of formation of, 661–62
See also Policy-making process
Public Works Administration, 84
Puerto Rican Legal Defense and Education Fund, 628
Pulitzer, Joseph, 580
Pure Food, Drug, and Cosmetic Act, 714

Pure Food and Drug Act, 660, 707
Puritans, 620

Quadriad, 724
Quakers, 620
Quartering Act of 1765, 30, 32
Quayle, J. Danforth, 266, 267, 331, 498, 568, 571, 599, 601
Quilici v. *Village of Morton Grove*, 123
Quotas, racial, 195
Quota sample, 432

Race
 abolitionist movement, 155–57, 409, 652
 affirmative action and, 195–96
 African Americans on the Supreme Court, 375–76
 American Anti-Slavery Society, 155–56, 621
 Black Caucus, 242
 blacks and the Constitution, 43
 civil rights and the American independent Party, 459
 civil rights bill filibuster, 238
 civil rights lobbying, 637
 Civil Rights Movement, 172–86, 644
 Civil War Amendments, 152, 157–60
 Congress's sensitivity to black concerns, 219
 impact on exit polls, 435
 interest group lobbying and, 644, 649
 Jim Crow laws, 158, 161–64, 174
  litigation against, 167–74
 NAACP. *See* National Association for the Advancement of Colored People (NAACP)
 New Deal coalition and, 453
 party convention delegates and, 513
 party delegate opinion and, 514
 party identification and, 489
 political socialization and, 420–22
 racial discrimination, 106
 racial divisions in public opinion, 416, 420–22
 redistricting and, 530
 school desegregation and, 676
 slavery. *See* Slavery
 voter participation and, 533, 537
 white primaries, 501
Racial quotas, 195
Radical Republicans, 159, 399
Radio, 581
Railroad industry, 623
Railroad programs, 679
Railway Labor Act, 707
Rainbow Coalition, 469
Ramstad, Jim, 771
Randolph, Edmund, 40
Randolph, John, 226
Random sampling, 430
Rather, Dan, 589
Reagan, Michael, 716–17
Reagan, Nancy, 286
Reagan, Ronald, 20, 92, 96, 98, 123, 133, 241, 242, 251, 263, 267, 269, 281, 282, 285, 290–91, 293, 298, 299, 302, 319, 326, 368, 371, 375, 384, 437, 440, 478, 487, 489, 499–500, 511, 527, 554, 555, 556, 571, 603, 631–32, 644, 668, 684, 745, 753, 779, 782, 788

appointments by, 333
 bureaucratic reform by, 344, 345
 civil rights, 194–95, 196, 197
 deregulation, 89–90
 economic policy, 719
 judges appointed by, 369, 370
  Supreme Court, 374, 377
 New Federalism, 89–90
 news media and, 599–600
 as pro-party president, 474, 476–77
 public opinion of, 414, 785–86
Realignment, party, 524–26
Recall, 502
 election reform, 409
Recession, 721, 724
Reconstruction, 158, 159, 162
Recount in elections, 538–39
Red Cross, 621
Redistricting, 206–9, 530
 congressional elections and, 528–29
Red Lion Broadcasting Company v. *FCC*, 605
Red tape, 341
Reed, Ralph, Jr., 633
Reed, Thomas B., 471
Reed v. *Reed*, 185
Reedy, George, 287–88
Reeves, Richard, 775
Referendum, 502
 election reform, 409
Reform
 effect on American democratic system, 20–21
 role of crises in, 21
Reformation, 7
Regents of the University of California v. *Bakke*, 195
Regina v. *Hicklin*, 128
Region
 party identification and, 488
 political socialization and, 418–20
Regional primaries, 504
Registration, voter, 534, 535, 536
Regulation(s)
 defined, 328
 deregulation and, 718–20
 economic, 312–16, 716–17
  Federal Employees Political Activities Act, 315–16
  Hatch Act, 315, 706
  laissez-faire attitudes, 313–14
  New Deal and, 314–15, 708–14
 of electronic media, 604–8
 of environmental pollution, economics of, 736–45
  acid rain, 744–45
  environmental policy making, 737–39
  EPA and, 739–45
  hazardous and toxic wastes, 741–44
 Keynesianism, 726
 of lobbying, 630, 655
 making of, 330
 of Progressive era, 707–8
 social, 716–18
 waivers of federal, 102
Regulation of Lobbying Act, 630
Regulatory board or commissions
 creation of, 312–13, 326, 707–8
 examples of, 325
 influence of president on, 326–27
 regulations, making of, 330

Regulatory federalism, 91–92
Rehnquist, William, 98, 128, 129, 132, 196, 365, 373, 374, 375, 380, 392, 393, 394
Reid, Stanley, 388
Reilly, William, 239
Religion
 in colonial America, 28
 freedom of, 109–14
  establishment clause, 109–12
  free exercise clause, 110, 112–14
  prayer in school, 112
 party identification and, 490–91
 political socialization and, 417, 419
 Supreme Court appointees and, 375
Religious Freedom Restoration Act (1993), 114
Religious-interest groups, 631–32
Renewable Fuels Association, 645
Reno, Janet, 336, 342
Reporter of Decisions (Supreme Court), 365–66
Representation
 by members of Congress, 217–20
 proportional, 462
 theories of, 217–20
Representative (indirect) democracy, 12
Republic, nature of, 12
Republicanism, dual federalism and, 74
Republican National Committee, 464
Republican Party, 459
 campaign staff training and research, 483
 committees in Congress, 227
 congressional party unity score (1959–1993), 472
 contact with voters, 482
 fund raising methods, 480–81
 governing body of, 464
 media advertising activities, 482
 organizational power of, 480–83
 origins of, 449–50
 party identification with, 486
 polling activities, 482
 realignments of, 524
 shortcomings of, 483
 staff of, 482
 states' rights and, 479
 Working Partners program, 493
Re-regulation, 720
Reservations, Indian, 187–88
Reserve requirements, 723
Resource Conservation and Recovery Act, 739, 742
Retrospective judgment, 499–500
Revenue Act of 1964, 725–26
Revenue sharing, 88–89
Revere, Paul, 32
Revolutionary War, 33–34, 36, 37, 752
Reynolds v. *Sims*, 207–8, 398
Rice, Donna, 596
Rice, Thomas Dartmouth, 162
Richards, Ann, 376
Right-of-rebuttal rule, 605
Rights
 new judicial federalism and, 99
 property, 35
 voting, 60, 159–60, 162–63, 167, 189
 See also Bill of Rights; Civil rights
Robbins, Liz, 775
Robertson, Pat, 632
Robins, Margaret Dreier, 624

Robinson, Michael, 599
Rockefeller, John D., IV, 558, 761
Rockefeller, Nelson, 262
Rodino, Peter, 591
Roe, Robert, 232–33
Roe v. *Wade*, 25, 100, 143–44, 182, 390, 391, 393, 394, 395, 653
Rogers, Will, 556
Rolling realignment, 526
Rollins, Ed, 560
Roosevelt, Eleanor, 127, 294
Roosevelt, Franklin D., 64, 248, 249, 253, 258, 260, 261, 263, 265, 293, 297, 298, 302, 411, 412, 414, 425, 475, 524, 525, 526, 720, 763–64
   judges appointed by, 369, 374
   court-packing attempts, 83, 314, 399
   New Deal, 82–86, 280–81, 314, 346, 393, 452, 453, 666, 680, 709–14
   presidency of, 279, 280–81, 282, 284
   style of, 287, 288, 290, 292, 603, 604
Roosevelt, Theodore, 249, 251, 274, 290, 313, 459, 460, 510, 580, 627, 707, 760
Rosenbaum, Sara, 694
Roth v. *United States*, 128
Rousseau, Jean-Jacques, 11
Routine policy formulation, 668
Rowan, Carl, 600
Rowland, Diane, 694
Rowley Board of Education v. *U.S.*, 387
Royal governors, 258–59
RU-486, 145
Rudman, Warren, 734
Rule making by federal bureaucracy, 328–31
Rule of Four, 382–83
Runoff primary, 501
Rural Electrification Administration, 84
Russia, Bolshevik Revolution in, 3
Rust v. *Sullivan*, 145

Safe Drinking Water Act, 91, 92, 739
Safire, William, 425, 600
Salinger, Pierre, 589
Salisbury, Robert H., 615, 618
SALT II, 778
Sampling, 430–32
   nonprobability, 431–32
   quota, 432
   random, 430
   sampling error, 436–37
   stratified, 431
Sanders, Bernard, 232
Sandino, Augusto, 780
Santería Church, 114
Sapiro, Virginia, 422
Satmar Hasidim, 678
Sauvy, Alfred, 773
Savings and loans, deregulation of, 719–20
Scalawags, 159
Scalia, Antonin, 98, 129, 144, 372, 373, 374, 375, 388, 395, 396
Scandals
   congressional elections and, 529
   House Bank scandal, 214, 215
Schattschneider, E.E., 444, 451, 650, 653
Schenck v. *United States*, 117, 118
Schlesinger, Arthur M., Jr., 265
Schneider, Andreas G., 694
Scholzman, Kay Lehman, 628

School(s)
   desegregation of, 96–97, 170–73, 676
     Brown v. *Board of Education*, 96–97, 162, 170–72, 184, 385, 388, 392, 396, 397
     busing, conditions for, 178–79
     Civil Rights Act of 1964 and, 178–79
     post-*Brown* activities, 172–73, 178–79
   political socialization and, 415–16
   prayer in, 112
   public, 660, 673, 674–78
School districts, 674–75
   inequality in spending among, 678
Schroeder, Patricia, 243
Schuster, Bud, 233
Scopes Case, 126
Scott, Dred, 79
Scowcroft, Brent, 299
Sea Around Us, The (Carson), 667
Searches and seizures, 131–34
   AIDS testing issue, 133–34
   allowable searches, 131–32
   drug testing issue, 133–34
   frisking, 132
   open fields doctrine and, 132–33
   search incident to arrest, 132
   unallowable searches, 131–33
Second Amendment, 58, 59, 108, 121, 123
Second Bank of the United States, 76
Second Continental Congress, 33–34, 36, 52, 54, 205
   the Constitution and, 52–53
Second Treatise on Civil Government (Locke), 10, 11
Secular realignment, presidential elections and, 526–27
Securities Act (1933), 711
Securities and Exchange Commission, 84, 326, 362, 711
Securities Exchange Act (1934), 84, 711
Sedition
   Alien and Sedition Acts, 79, 116, 354
   seditious speech, 115
Segregation
   Jim Crow laws, 158, 161–64, 174
   NAACP challenges to, 167–74
   of public facilities, 174–75, 177
   Rosa Parks case, 174
   school desegregation, 96–97, 170–73, 178–79
   separate but equal doctrine, 80, 162, 163–64
Select (ad hoc) committees, 228, 229, 231
Selective incorporation, 120–22
Self-incrimination, 134–35
Self-interest, political opinion and, 427
Selling of the President 1968, The (McGinniss), 594–95
Senate, 43, 49
   committees
     compared to House, 233
     standing committees, 230, 231
   House of Representatives compared to, 205–6, 211
   impeachment process and, 45, 261
   lawmaking process, 236–38
   majority leader, 227
   organization of, 225–27
   oversight function, 251–52

   presidential appointments and, 251–52, 269, 779–80
   president of, 225
   ratification of treaties, 250–51, 270–71, 778, 779
   Supreme Court confirmation process and, 376, 380
Senate Judiciary Committee, Supreme Court nominees and, 377, 380
Senatorial courtesy, 252, 269, 368–71
Seneca Falls Convention, 155, 156, 621
Senior Executive Service, 318
Seniority system, 233–34, 473
Separate but equal doctrine, 80, 162, 163–64
   NAACP challenges to, 168–74
   Plessy v. *Ferguson*, 80, 162, 163–64, 396
Separation of powers, 47–49, 50
   checks and balances, 49, 50, 66, 352
Separatists in England, 7–8
Seriatim opinions, 355
Settlement house movement, 165, 616, 624
Seventeenth Amendment, 63, 205, 464
Seventh Amendment, 59, 108, 121
Seven Years' War, 29
Sex discrimination, 184–86, 307
Sexual harassment, 307, 374, 379, 385, 386, 592, 593
Sharpton, Al, 560
Shays, Daniel, 38–39, 41
Shays's Rebellion, 39, 44, 649
Shelly, Richard, 248
Sheppard-Towner Maternity and Infancy Act, 87, 627, 674
Shepsle, Kenneth A., 232
Sherman, Roger, 34, 517
Sherman Anti-Trust Act, 81, 706
Sickles, Daniel, 520
Sierra Club, 619, 738
Silent Spring (Carson), 666, 667
Simon, Paul, 232
Simpson, Alan, 593
Simpson, O.J., 358
Sinclair, Upton, 580, 707
Sindram, Michael, 382
Single-issue interest groups, 617–18, 619, 621
Sirica, John J., 262
Sixteenth Amendment, 63, 313, 707
Sixth Amendment, 59, 108, 121, 130, 136–38, 151
   right to counsel, 136–37
   right to jury trial, 138
Skinner, Samuel, 298
Slander, 115, 127
Slaughterhouse Cases, The, 80, 160
Slavery, 116, 152–57
   abolitionist movement, 155–57, 409, 621, 652
   anti-slavery writings, 156
   Civil War Amendments, 152, 157–60
   Congress and, 153–55
   Emancipation Proclamation, 157
   Federalism and, 78–80
   Missouri Compromise and, 153–57
   representation of slaves in Constitution, 43
   slave versus free states, 153–55
   Three-Fifths Compromise, 43, 64, 152
   See also Civil rights
Slave trade, 758
Slotnick, Elliot, 371

Smith, Adam, 17, 705–6
Smith, Hedrick, 213, 637
Smith, Robert, 755
Smith, William French, 298
Smith-Hughes Act, 676
Smith v. *Allwright*, 501
Smoot-Hawley Tariff Act, 763, 791
Snowe, Olympia, 647
Social activism, 717–18
Social contract theories, 8–11
   Declaration of Independence and, 34–36
   Hobbes on, 8–10
   Locke on, 10, 11
Social Democratic Party of America, 118
Social insurance, 679, 681–85
   Old Age, Survivors, and Disability Insurance, 681–84
   recipients (1990), 679
   unemployment insurance, 679, 684–85
Socialism, nature of, 18–19
Socialist Party of America, 118, 627
Socialization, political. *See* Political socialization
Social regulation, 716–18
Social Security, 6, 65, 89, 679, 681–84, 689
Social Security Act, 84, 673, 680–81, 685
Social Security Administration (SSA), 84, 306, 319, 323, 338, 361*n*, 682
Social Security numbers, use of, 682
Social Security Trust Fund, 684
Social welfare policies, 673–701
   defined, 659
   income security programs, 660, 673–74, 678–89
     effectiveness of, 689
     means-tested programs, 679, 686–89
     roots of, 680–81
     social insurance, 679, 681–85
   landmark events in, 674
   medical care, 16, 674, 689–96
     Canadian system of, 698
     cost of, 691, 695–97
     health care reform, 334, 696–99
     Medicaid, 89, 92, 674, 679, 693–95
     Medicare, 679, 692–93
     national health insurance, roots of, 690–95
   public education, 660, 673, 674–78
     federal aid to, 675–78
     inequality in spending among school districts, 678
     primary mission of public schools, 675
   toward reform of, 696–99
Society for Promoting and Improving Agriculture and other Rural Concerns, 620
Society for the Prevention of Cruelty to Children, 663
Socioeconomic status
   party identification and, 490
   voter participation and, 532
Soil Conservation and Domestic Allotment Act, 84, 713
Solicitor General, 350, 368, 387
   Supreme Court cases and, 384
Somalia, 666, 771, 784
Sons of Liberty, 30, 31, 618, 620
Soundbites from recent presidential campaigns, 553, 554
Souter, David, 98, 99, 144, 372, 373, 374–75, 377, 392–93

South, public opinion in the, 418, 420
Southern Christian Leadership Conference, 174–75, 176, 181
Soviet Union, 3
   break-up of, 3, 4, 5
   origins of Cold War and, 765–66
Spaeth, Nicholas, 367
Spanish-American War, 760
Speaker of the House, 222–25, 471
   formal and informal powers of, 224
Special interest caucuses, congressional, 242–44
Special Master, 381
Specter, Arlen, 593
Speech and press, freedom of, 114–29
   Alien and Sedition Acts and, 116
   Civil War and, 116–17
   common-law tradition and, 115
   fighting words, 115
   incorporation doctrine and, 119–22
   libel and slander, 115, 127, 595–97
   obscenity, 127–29
   politically correct speech movement, 124–27
   prior restraint and, 115–16, 124
   restrictions of, 117–19
   seditious speech, 115
   symbolic speech, 122–24
   See also News media
Split ticket voting, 66, 451, 527, 536–37
Spoils system, 310–11, 451, 455
Spot ads, presidential campaign, 552
Sputnik, 777–78
Spy Catcher (Wright), 607
Stability, economic, 721
Stahl, Lesley, 589
Stalin, Joseph, 765
Stamp Act Congress, 31
Stamp Act of 1765, 30, 31
Stanberry, Henry, 376
Standard Oil Company, 623
Standing committees
   House of Representatives, 230, 231
   Senate, 230, 231
Standing to sue, 397
Stanton, Edwin M., 248
Stanton, Elizabeth Cady, 156, 159
Star Chamber, 115
Stare decisis, 363, 390, 391, 392–93, 396
States
   and Constitution
     Articles IV through VII on, 52, 73–75
     guarantees to and restrictions on states, 73
     relations among states, 73–74
   controlling, 90–92
     through mandates, 91–92
     through preemption, 90–91
   federal aid to
     grants-in-aid, 86–89
     Reagan administration and, 89
     revenue sharing, 88–89
   First Amendment guarantees applied to, 119–22
   political parties and, 466–68, 479–80
   powers of, 71–73
   regulation of economy, 704–5
Stearns, Cliff, 334
Steiger, Janet, 327
Stein, Herbert, 715

Stephanopoulos, George, 298, 299
Stevens, John Paul, 372, 373, 382, 383, 396
Stevenson, Adlai, 425, 564
Stewart, Potter, 129, 375, 395
Stimson, James A., 244
Stockman, David, 282
Stock market crash (October, 1929), 712
Storey, Moorfield, 165
Stowe, Harriet Beecher, 156, 409
Stratified sampling, 431
Strauss, Lewis, 268
Straw polls, 411–12, 431
Strict constitutionalist approach, 374
Strict scrutiny, 184, 192
Strikes, labor, 716
Stromberg v. *California*, 122
Student Nonviolent Coordinating Committee, 174–75, 176, 181
Subcommittees, congressional, 228, 230, 231, 234–35, 236
Subgovernments (iron triangles), 338–39, 640–41
Succession, presidential, 261–62
Suffrage, 497–98
   meaning of, 43
Suffrage movement, 21, 156
   Seneca Falls Convention, 155, 156, 621
   voting rights and, 159–60, 167
   women's groups, 165–67
   See also Women's rights
Sugar Act of 1764, 30, 31
Sullivan, Leonore, 666
Sumner, Charles, 226
Sundquist, James L., 66
Sunset laws, 345–46
Sunshine Act, 345
Sunshine laws, 236, 345
Sununu, John, 298
Superdelegates, 512, 523
Superfund, 739, 742–44
Super Tuesday, 504, 566
Supplementary Security Income, 679, 686
Supremacy clause, 75, 355
Supreme Court, 49
   annual term of, 387
   appellate jurisdiction, 367, 381
   cases, 380–90
     characteristics of, 383–85
     concurring opinions, 390
     conference and vote, 389
     decision to hear case, 380–81, 382–83
     dissenting opinions, 390
     glossary of, 811–14
     jurisdiction, 367, 381–82
     oral arguments by attorneys, 387–89
     Rule of Four, 382–83
     starting the case, 385–87
     written opinions of court, 389–90
   on civil liberties
     freedom of religion, 110–14
     freedom of speech and press, 117–19, 122–24, 127–29
     privacy rights, 141–46
     rights of criminal defendants, 129–38, 140–41
   civil rights and, 160–63
     challenges to "separate but equal" doctrine, 167–74
     "separate but equal" doctrine and, 162, 163–64, 169–72

Constitution and, 52, 351–52
  amendments overruling Supreme Court decisions, 63
  judicial interpretation of Constitution, 64
court-packing by F.D. Roosevelt, 83, 314, 399
early
  Jay Court, 353–55
  Marshall Court, 355, 356, 357, 393, 397
federal court system and, 364–67
Federalism and, 75–80, 96–101
federal-state relations and. *See under* Federalism
Framers' concept of, 349, 350, 351
future composition of, 400
on gerrymandering, 208–9
implementation of decisions, 397–98
on independent regulatory commissions, 326
on inequality in education spending, 678
Insular cases, 760
judicial policy making, 396–97
Judiciary Act of 1789 and, 352–55, 357, 360
laissez-faire attitude of, 314
lobbying, effects on, 393–95, 641–43
New Deal and, 82–84
news media coverage of, 592
number of cases heard, 363, 367
original jurisdiction, 367, 381
recognition of inherent power of national government, 764
support staff of, 365–66
on termination of federal employees, 319–20
Supreme Court justices
  Chief Justice, 45, 364–65, 389–90
    first, 353, 354
  confirmation process and, 376–80
    investigation, 377
    lobbying interest groups, 377–79
    Senate committee hearings, 379–80
    vote in Senate on, 380
  how justices vote, 391–95
    behavioral characteristics, 394
    extra-legal factors, 393–95
    ideology, 394–95
    judicial philosophy and original intent, 391–92
    legal factors, 391–93
    precedent, 392–93
    public opinion and, 350–51, 393–94
  partisanship of, 478
  selection of, 369, 371–76
    appointment, 350, 371–72
    nomination criteria, 372–76
    qualifications, 371
  term of, 52
Surface Transportation Act, 92
Surveillance, 133
Surveys, 431
Suspect classification, 183–84, 185, 192
Swann v. *Charlotte-Mecklenburg School District*, 178–79
Sweatt, Herman, 169
Sweatt v. *Painter*, 169–70
Symbolic speech, 122–24
Syron, Richard, 712
Systemic agenda, 664

Taft, Helen, 294
Taft, William Howard, 133, 381, 409, 627
Taft-Hartley Act, 715–16
Tammany Hall, 455, 468
Taney, Roger, 78, 123, 389
Tariff of Abominations, 79
Tariffs, 758, 760, 763
Task Force on National Health Care Reform, 697
Taxes
  Articles of Confederation's lack of provision for, 37
  British, on colonies, 29–30
  fiscal policy and, 725–27
  income, 707
  1992 party platforms on, 518
  property, 678
Tax Reduction Act of 1965, 726
Tax Reform Act of 1986, 669
Tea Act of 1773, 31
Technology, the Constitution and, 65
Telemarketing, lobbying with, 645
Telephone polls, 432–33, 434
Televised debates, 553–55
Television, 581, 583–85, 586
  cable, 583, 585, 608–9
Tennessee Valley Authority, 84, 324
Tenth Amendment, 47, 58, 59, 75, 90, 93, 98, 101, 108, 673
Tenure of Office Act, 248
Term-limit proposals, 253–54
Texas v. *Johnson*, 65
Thatcher, Margaret, 527, 784–95
Third Amendment, 58, 59, 108, 121
Third-partyism, 459–62
Third World, 772, 773, 784
Thirteenth Amendment, 21, 63, 80, 162
  prohibition of slavery, 157–58
Thomas, Clarence, 98, 186, 197, 218, 219, 293, 307, 372, 373, 375, 377, 380, 395, 399, 570, 650
  interest groups taking sides on nomination of, 643
  media coverage of hearings, 592, 593
  sexual harassment issue, 307, 374, 379, 592, 593
Thomas, Helen, 589
Thomas, M. Carey, 626
Thornburgh, Richard, 697
Three-Fifths Compromise, 43, 64, 152
Thurmond, Strom, 176, 238
Ticket-splitting, 66, 451, 527, 536–37
Tienanmen Square (1989), 3, 788
Tierney, John, 628
Tilden, Samuel J., 159, 520–21, 523
Time, 584, 587
Times, The, 586
Times Mirror Center for the People and the Press, 598
Tinker v. *Des Moines Independent Community School District*, 122, 126
Tippecanoe, Battle of, 312
Title IX, 186, 343, 655, 671
Tobacco industry, regulation of, 5–6
Tobacco Institute, 619
Tocqueville, Alex de, 613–14
Toles, Tom, 553
Totalitarianism, nature of, 19–20
Totenberg, Nina, 379, 593
Tower, John G., 268
Town meeting, New England, 12, 13

Townshend Acts, 30, 31
Toxic Substances Control Act, 739, 742
Toxic wastes, 741–44
Tracking polls, 435–36, 440, 482, 555–56
Trade
  in colonial America, 29–30
  after Revolutionary War, 37, 38
Trade and aid policy, 789–90, 791
  early, 757–58
  GATT and, 765, 789
  at turn of century, 760–61
Trade associations, 627–28
Trades Union Congress, 625
Treaties
  executive agreements vs., 271, 778–79, 780
  presidential power to make, 269–71
  ratification by Senate, 250–51, 270–71, 778, 779
Treaty of Paris, 29, 38, 749
Treaty of Versailles, 211, 270, 762–63, 778
Trial of William Prynn, 115
Tribe, Lawrence, 146
Truman, David, 16, 618
Truman, Harry S, 169, 182, 266, 274, 290, 293, 369, 394–95, 411, 526, 529, 691, 715, 716, 766–68, 774, 785
Truman Doctrine, 766
Trustees, representatives as, 218
Trusts, 706, 707
Tsongas, Paul, 565
Tweed, William M., 520
Twelfth Amendment, 63, 519
Twentieth Amendment, 63
Twenty-fifth Amendment, 62, 63, 262, 263
Twenty-first Amendment, 61, 62, 63, 65
Twenty-fourth Amendment, 63
Twenty-second Amendment, 63, 260, 302
Twenty-seventh Amendment, 61, 63
Twenty-sixth Amendment, 60, 63
Twenty-third Amendment, 63
Two Percent Club, 344
Two presidencies concept, 292
Tyler, John, 261–62, 312, 376, 551

Udall, Morris K., 234, 601
Uncle Tom's Cabin (Stowe), 156, 409
Under the Sea Wind (Carson), 667
Unemployment insurance, 679, 684–85
Unemployment of Great Depression, 82
Unemployment rate, 685
Unicameral legislature, 205
Unilateralism, 763
  shift to multilateralism from, 764–65
Union shop, 716
Unitary government, 47
United Daughters of the Confederacy, 219
United Nations, 764
United Press International, 584, 587
U.S. Agency for International Development, 772, 792
U.S. Attorneys, 362
U.S. Census Bureau, 187
U.S. Court of Military Affairs, 360
U.S. Forest Service, 672
U.S. News & World Report, 584, 587
U.S. Office of Education, 676
U.S. Postal Service, 308, 324
U.S. Surgeon General, 5
United States Reports, 366

United States v. *Curtiss-Wright Export Corporation*, 764
United States v. *Miller*, 123
United States v. *Nixon*, 264, 387, 390
U.S. v. *Seeger*, 114
United We Stand America, 461
Unit rule, 510
Unsafe At Any Speed (Nader), 631
Uruguay Round trade talks (1993), 789
USA Today, 586
USA VOTE, 13
US Term Limits, 253

Van Buren, Martin, 460, 509, 551
Vandenberg, Arthur, 765–66
Versailles, Treaty of, 211, 270, 762–63, 778
Veterans' Housing Authority, 317
Veterans of Foreign Wars, 338
Veterans programs, 679, 680
Veto
  of bill, 238
  legislative, 250
  line-item, 302, 745
  pocket, 238
  of president, 48, 238, 271–72
  senatorial courtesy as virtual, 269
Vice president, 45
  Framers' conception of, 44, 262–67
  power/responsibilities of, 263–67
  selection by presidential candidate, 265
  Senate and, 225
  Twenty-fifth Amendment and, 62
Vietnam War, 6, 251, 273, 274, 417, 499, 726, 770–71, 783, 785, 786
Vig, Norman J., 738
Viguerie, Richard, 653
Villard, Oswald Garrison, 164
Violence
  civil rights and, 175, 177–78
  protest activity and, 649–50
Violence Against Women Act, 243
Violent Crime Control and Enforcement Act, 123
Virginia House of Burgesses, 12, 28
Virginia Plan, 40–42, 253, 259, 355
Virtual representation, 217
Volcker, Paul, 723
Volpe, Carl, 334
Von Bulow, Claus, 99
Voter canvass, 549
Voter registration, 534, 535, 536
Voting, 497–98
  electronic, 14
  See also Elections
Voting behavior, 532–37
  comparisons with other countries, 534, 535
  decline in participation, 532, 534–36
  ticket-splitting, 66, 451, 527, 536–37
  voter turnout, 531, 533, 534–36
Voting rights, 60, 159–60
  blacks, 160, 162–63, 189
  women, 159–60, 167
Voting Rights Act of 1965, 189, 209, 530, 533, 664

Wade, Henry, 143

Wage, minimum, 713
Wagner, Robert, 713
Wagner Act, 82, 84, 314, 713
Waivers of federal regulations, 102
Walker, Jack L., 618, 652, 653
Wallace, George, 459, 460, 470n, 521
Wallace v. *Jaffree*, 111–12
Wall Street Journal, 584, 586
Walsh, Lawrence E., 274
War of 1812, 756, 786
War on Poverty, 87–88, 275, 317, 666, 694
War Powers Act, 251, 273, 781–82, 788, 789, 790
Warren, Earl, 128, 135, 137, 170, 374, 383
Warsaw Pact, 767
Washington, George, 33, 38, 40, 41, 53, 56, 257, 258, 260, 267, 271, 274, 293, 298, 354, 355, 356, 425, 443, 445, 518, 578, 620, 752, 753
  presidency of, 276, 277, 281, 295, 308
Washington, Martha, 294
Washington Post, 570, 584, 586, 594, 607
Waste, size of bureaucracy and, 341–42
Watergate scandal, 21, 262, 417, 487, 499, 591, 648
  effect on Presidency, 265
  events of, 264–65, 473
  and investigative journalism, 592–94
Watson, George, 61
Watt, James, 333
Waxman, Henry A., 240, 241, 331, 467, 694
Waxman, Judy, 694
Wealth of Nations, The (Smith), 17, 705–6
Weaver, James B., 460
Weber, Max, 16
Webster, Daniel, 76, 388, 551, 756
Webster v. *Reproductive Health Services*, 98, 101, 149, 390, 393, 394, 396
Weicker, Lowell P., Jr., 489
Weill, James, 694
Weinberger, Caspar, 273, 570, 758–59
Welfare. *See* Social welfare policies
Wells, H.G., 454, 497
Wheeler-Lea Act (1938), 714
Whig Party, 448–49, 524, 551
Whips, party whips, 225, 227, 228, 242
Whiskey Rebellion, 277, 354, 753
Whistle-blowers, 320–21
White, Byron, 192, 367, 390
White, John, 465
White, Theodore, 594
White House
  office space at, 301
  press corps, 589
  staff, 298–300
White primary, 501
Whitewater, 784
Whitman, Christine Todd, 95, 560
Who Governs? (Dahl), 16
Wildavsky, Aaron, 292
Wilder, L. Douglas, 434, 435
Wilderness Society, 738
Wilhelm, David, 465, 486
Will, George F., 600
Willard, Frances, 652
Williams, Juan, 164
Wills, Garry, 288

Wilson, Edith Bolling Galt, 263, 294
Wilson, Henry, 521
Wilson, James, 259–60, 517
Wilson, Woodrow, 64, 118, 119, 211–12, 228, 237, 263, 270, 289, 290, 294, 313, 409, 475, 510, 511, 626, 707
  World War I and, 762–63
Winner-take-all, delegate selection, 503
Wire services, 587
Wirt, William, 460
Wisconsin v. *Yoder*, 113
WISH (Women in the Senate and House), 649
Wofford, Harris, 697
Wolfe, Tom, 594
Women
  in combat, 6
  in Congress, 216–20, 243
  as delegates, 513
  interest groups and, 650
  presidential appointments of, 299
  right to vote, 60
  sex discrimination and, 307
Women's Campaign Fund, 650
Women's Christian Temperance Union (WCTU), 167, 621, 652
Women's Health Equity Act, 243
Women's International League for Peace and Freedom, 627
Women's Joint Congressional Committee, 627
Women's rights
  Equal Rights Amendment, 62, 65, 182–83, 220, 230, 375, 420
  parallel to civil rights movement, 156, 159–60, 165–67, 180–83
  suffrage movement, 21, 155, 156, 159–60, 167, 621
  voting rights, 159–60, 167
  women's movement, 180–83
Women's rights activists, 644
Women's Trade Union League, 624
Wood, Gordon, 53
Woods, Rose Mary, 264
Woodward, Bob, 376, 594
Works Progress Administration (WPA), 84, 680, 710
World Bank, 764–65, 772
World Trade Center, bombing of, 65
World War I, 761–64
  public opinion in, 409, 410
  Wilson's actions, 762–63
World War II, 721, 764
  bureaucracy and, 317
Wright, Peter, 607
Writ of *certiorari*, 381, 382–83, 385

Yellow journalism, 580, 760
Young Democrats of America, 468
Young Men's Christian Association, 621
Young Republicans' National Federation, 468
Youngstown Sheet & Tube v. *Sawyer*, 394–95
"Young Turks," 234
Yugoslavia, former, 3

PHOTO CREDITS

Chapter 1: Roots & Reform

Page 4: Klaus Reisinger/Black Star; 5: Richard Ellis/Reuters/The Bettmann Archive; 6: Andy Clark/Reuters/The Bettmann Archive; 8: Stock Montage, Inc.; 9: The Bettmann Archive; 10 (left): Stock Montage, Inc.; 10 (right): Stock Montage, Inc.; 12: Bob Daemmrich/Stock Boston; 13: Mark Hundley/AP, San Francisco; 14: Bob Laramie/Philadelphia Daily News; 15: Terry Ashe/Gamma-Liaison; 18: The Bettmann Archive; 20: David Longstreath/AP/Wide World Photos.

Chapter 2: Constitutional Law

Page 26: The National Archives; 27 (bottom left): Colonial Williamsburg Foundation; 27 (bottom center): The Metropolitan Museum of Art, Gift of Henry G. Marquand, 1881 (81.11). Copyright © 1987 By The Metropolitan Museum of Art; 27 (bottom right): The Bettmann Archive; 30: Samuel Adams (Detail), by John Singleton Copley. Deposited by the City of Boston. Courtesy, Museum of Fine Arts, Boston; 32: The New York Historical Society; 34: Stock Montage, Inc.; 39: The Bettmann Archive; 45: The Bettmann Archive; 51: Dennis Brack/Black Star; 58: The New York Historical Society; 61: Zigy Kaluzny/PEOPLE Weekly © 1993.

Chapter 3: Federalism

Page 73: Kunio Owaki/The Stock Market; 77: I. N. Phelps Stokes Collection, Miriam and Ira D. Wallach Division of Art, Prints and Photographs. The New York Public Library Astor, Lenox and Tilden Foundations; 78: Drew University Library Archives, Madison, New Jersey; 79: Missouri Historical Society; 81: The Bettmann Archive; 83: Culver Pictures, Inc.; 85: AP/Wide World Photos; 91: Courtesy, Georgia Municipal Association; 95: Mike Derer/AP/Wide World Photos; 96: Greg Gibson/AP/Wide World Photos; 101: Jeffrey Z. Carney/AP/Wide World Photos.

Chapter 4: Civil Liberties

Page 106: Lisa Quinones/Black Star; 110: Charles Bennett/AP/Wide World Photos; 112: AP/Wide World Photos; 113: J. L. Atlan/Sygma; 118: Brown Brothers; 120: AP/Wide World Photos; 123: John Ficara/Sygma; 132: Texas Department of Public Safety; 133: UPI/The Bettmann Archive; 135: AP/Wide World Photos; 137: TheSupreme Court Historical Society; 139: The Bettmann Archive; 142: © Lee Lockwood/Black Star; 143: Rick Maiman/Sygma; 145: Donna Binder/Impact Visuals.

Chapter 5: Civil Rights

Page 153 (top): Old Courthouse Museum, Vicksburg, Miss.; 153 (bottom): Harper's Weekly, Oct. 24, 1874; 155: Libraryof Congress; 156: Library of Congress; 157 (top): The Bettmann Archive; 158: David Fields/New York Times Pictures; 159: The Bettmann Archive; 161: © Elliott Erwitt/Magnum Photos; 164: Schomburg Center for Research in Black Culture/The New York Public Library; 165: Library of Congress; 166: The Supreme Court Historical Society/Courtesy Mrs. Neill Whisnant and Portland, Oregon Chamber of Commerce; 168: AP/Wide World Photos; 171: AP/Wide World Photos; 174: UPI/Bettmann Newsphotos; 175: © Charles Moore/Black Star; 176: © Flip Schulke/Black Star; 178: © Eve Arnold/Magnum Photos; 189: Bill Burke/Impact Visuals; 191: Spencer Grant/Gamma-Liaison; 193: Rick Reinhard/Impact Visuals; 195: UPI/Bettmann Newsphotos.

Chapter 6: Congress

Page 204: © John Ficara/Sygma; 206: The Architect of the Capitol; 212: Susan Greenwood/Gamma-Liaison; 213: Wally McNamee/Woodfin Camp & Associates; 215: AP Photo/John Duricka; 216: Wilkins III/The Register-Guard, Eugene, OR; 218: Paul Hosefros/New York Times Pictures; 219: ABC News/New York Times Pictures; 220: AP/Wide World Photos; 223: Engraving by Robert Whitechurch/Unites States Senate Collection; 224: UPI/The Bettmann Archive; 226: The New York Historical Society; 249: © John Ficara/Sygma.

Chapter 7: The Presidency

Page 258: Reuters/The Bettmann Archive; 260: UPI/Bettmann Newsphotos; 261: Stock Montage, Inc.; 263: Stock Montage, Inc.; 265: AP/Wide World Photos; 266 (top): Alan Singer/CBS; 266 (bottom): AP/Wide World Photos; 267: Les Stone/Sygma; 268: Reuters/The Bettmann Archive; 270: The White House/Sipa Press; 273: The Bettmann Archive; 275 (top left): UPI/The Bettmann Archive; 275 (top center): Wally McNamee/Folio, Inc.; 275 (top right): Brooks Kraft/Sygma; 275 (bottom left): Sygma; 275 (bottom center): UPI/The Bettmann Archive; 275 (bottom right): UPI/The Bettmann Archive; 278: The White House Historical Association; 280: Chicago Historical Society; 286: UPI/The Bettmann Archive; 287: Reuters/The Bettmann Archive; 291: Greg Gibson/AP/Wide World Photos; 297: Keith Jenkins/The Washington Post; 299: Danny Johnston/AP/Wide World Photos.

Chapter 8: The Bureaucracy

Page 309: Richard Hutchings/PhotoEdit; 311: The Bettmann Archive; 312: The Cincinnati Historical Society; 313: Harper's Weekly, April 9, 1887; 314: Richmond Times-Dispatch; 315: The Bettmann Archive; 331: U. S. Government Printing Office; 332: Rick Brady/Uniphoto; 336: Doug Mills/AP/Wide World Photos; 340: Loren Santow/Impact Visuals; 341: J. Scott Applewhite/AP/Wide World Photos; 342: Jacques Chenet/ Woodfin Camp & Associates; 343: Karen O'Connor; 346: Rick Wilking/Reuters/The Bettmann Archive.

Chapter 9: The Judiciary

Page 350: Jose R. Lopez/New York Times Pictures; 352: AP/Wide World Photos; 353 (bottom left): The Bettmann Archive; 353 (bottom right): The Supreme Court Historical Society; 354: Diplomatic Reception Rooms, U.S. Department of State; 356: Boston Athenaeum; 372: Ken Heinen/Associated Press; 374: Rick Wilking/Reuters/The Bettmann Archive; 376: © 1993, Ken Heinen; 378: Frank Fournier/Contact Press Images; 384: David Burnett/Contact Press Images; 386: © Fritz Hofmann/JB Pictures; 394: Jodi Buren/Woodfin Camp & Associates; 398: © Dianne Laakso/Atlanta Journal & Constitution.

Chapter 10: Public Opinion

Page 406: Wally McNamee/Sygma; 409: Chiaki Kawajiri/The Oregonian Staff; 410: The Bettmann Archive; 411: UPI/The Bettmann Archive; 414: UPI/The Bettmann Archive; 41C: Charles Gupton/Stock Boston; 433: Stephen Savoia/AP/Wide World Photos; 434: UPI/The Bettmann Archive; 435: Hilary Marcus/Impact Visuals.

Chapter 11: Political Parties

Page 444: Terry Ashe/Gamma-Liaison; 447 (top left): Rick Maiman/Sygma; 447 (top right): Dennis Brack/Black Star; 447 (bottom right): Lisa Quinones/Black Star; 449: © Smithsonian Institution; 451: UPI/The Bettmann Archive; 452: David Burnett/Contact Press Images; 456: UPI/The Bettmann Archive; 461: Greg Gibson/AP/Wide World Photos; 465: Nola Tully/Sygma; 466: AP/Wide World Photos; 477: Cynthia Johnson/Gamma-Liaison; 490: Ira Wyman/Sygma.

Chapter 12: Voting & Elections

Page 498 (bottom left): AP/Wide World Photos; 498 (bottom right): Allan Tannenbaum/Sygma; 500: Reed Saxon/AP/Wide World Photos; 503: Cynthia Johnson/Gamma-Liaison; 509: Library of Congress; 512: John Swart/AP/Wide World Photos; 523 (top left): The Bettmann Archive; 523 (top right): The Bettmann Archive; 528: Michael Patrick/Folio, Inc.; 532: Paul Aiken/Gamma-Liaison; 534: David Butow/Black Star; 536: Jean-Marc Giboux/Gamma-Liaison.

Chapter 13: The Campaign Process

Page 544: Bob Pearson/Agence France Presse; 548 (top): Greg Gibson/AP/Wide World Photos; 548 (bottom): UPI/Bettmann Newsphotos; 549: Joe Marquette/AP/Wide World Photos; 552: Ira Wyman/Sygma; 555: Wally McNamee/Sygma; 560: Christopher Brown/SABA; 567 (top): Reuters/The Bettmann Archive; 567 (bottom right): Glenn James/Sygma; 569: Jeffrey Markowitz/Sygma; 572: Peter Turnley/Black Star.

Chapter 14: The Mass Media

Page 580: Stock Montage, Inc.; 581: Cynthia Johnson/Gamma-Liaison; 585: Reuters/The Bettmann Archive; 586: UPI/The Bettmann Archive; 590: Diana Walker/Gamma-Liaison; 591: David Burnett/Contact Press Images; 593: Reuters/The Bettmann Archive; 596: AP/Wide World Photos; 599: R. Maiman/Sygma; 601 (top left): Steve Liss/Gamma-Liaison; 601 (top right): UPI/Bettmann Newsphotos; 604 (top left): The Bettmann Archive; 604 (top right): Reuters/The Bettmann Archive; 606: UPI/Bettmann Newsphotos; 607: UPI/The Bettmann Archive.

Chapter 15: Interest Groups

Page 617: Reuters/The Bettmann Archive; 622 (top): UPI/The Bettmann Archive; 622 (bottom): The Bettmann Archive; 623: The Bettmann Archive; 624: Library of Congress; 625: The Bettmann Archive; 626: National Consumers League; 630: The Bettmann Archive; 642: Diana Walker/Gamma-Liaison; 645: Todd McInturf/New York Times Pictures; 653: National Archives; 654: Courtesy of Handgun Control, Inc.

Chapter 16: Social Welfare Policy

Page 660: Colliers; 663: Jeffrey Markowitz/Sygma; 665: Sygma; 667: The Bettmann Archive; 672: The Bettmann Archive; 681: UPI/The Bettmann Archive; 696: Reuters/The Bettmann Archive.

Chapter 17: Economic Policy

Page 704: The Bettmann Archive; 707: The Bettmann Archive; 709: The Bettmann Archive; 710: The Bettmann Archive; 714: AP/Wide World Photos; 721: The Bettmann Archive; 723: UPI/Bettmann Newsphotos; 726: UPI/The Bettmann Archive; 734: UPI/The Bettmann Archive; 737: Zach Singer/AP/Wide World Photos; 743: U.S. Government Printing Office.

Chapter 18: Foreign and Military Policy

Page 756: The Bettmann Archive; 757: The Bettmann Archive; 760: The Bettmann Archive; 762: UPI/The Bettmann Archive; 764: Diana Walker/Gamma-Liaison; 765: Naval Photographic Center, Washington D.C.; 769: © Flip Schulke/Black Star; 771: Win McNamee/Reuters/The Bettmann Archive; 777: © Eli Reed/Magnum Photos; 778: Joey Ivansco/Atlanta Constitution; 785: J. L. Atlan/Sygma; 791: Reuters/The Bettmann Archive.